Psychology

Modules for Active Learning 15e

Dennis Coon

John Mitterer

Brock University

Tanya Martini

Brock University

CENGAGE

Australia • Brazil • Canada • Mexico • Singapore • United Kingdom • United States

CENGAGE

Psychology: Modules for Active Learning,
Fifteenth Edition
Dennis Coon, John Mitterer, Tanya Martini

SVP, Higher Education & Skills Product: Erin Joyner

VP, Higher Education & Skills Product: Thais Alencar

Product Director: Laura Ross

Product Manager: Colin Grover

Product Assistant: Jessica Witczak

Learning Designer: Natasha Allen

Senior Content Manager: Christy Frame

Digital Delivery Lead: Allison Marion

Director, Marketing: Neena Bali

Marketing Manager: Trisha Salata

IP Analyst: Deanna Ettinger

IP Project Manager: Kelli Besse

Production Service: Lori Hazzard, MPS Limited

Designer: Christopher Doughman

Cover Image Source: agsandrew/ShutterStock.com

For product information and technology assistance, contact us at **Cengage Customer & Sales Support, 1-800-354-9706 or support.cengage.com.**

For permission to use material from this text or product, submit all requests online at **www.cengage.com/permissions.**

Library of Congress Control Number: 2020922579

Student Edition:
ISBN: 978-0-357-37159-6

Loose-leaf Edition:
ISBN: 978-0-357-37166-4

Cengage
200 Pier 4 Boulevard
Boston, MA 02210
USA

Cengage is a leading provider of customized learning solutions with employees residing in nearly 40 different countries and sales in more than 125 countries around the world. Find your local representative at **www.cengage.com.**

Cengage is committed to creating inclusive and diverse products, including perspectives that represent the diversity of people across all backgrounds, identities, opinions, and experiences. If you have any feedback related to this, please contact us at **Cengage Customer & Sales Support, 1-800-354-9706 or support.cengage.com.**

To learn more about Cengage platforms and services, register or access your online learning solution, or purchase materials for your course, visit **www.cengage.com.**

Printed in the United States of America
Print Number: 01 Print Year: 2021

Dedication

For Sevren
—DC

For Rue Elizabeth Pante
—JM

For George and Betty Shepherd
and Janis Knifton, because it
takes a village.
—TM

About the Authors

Courtesy of Dennis Coon

Dennis Coon

Dennis Coon is a publishing phenomenon and one of the best-selling authors in the field of psychology. His innovative instructional methods and student-focused style make his works perennial favorites among instructors and students alike. To date, more than two million students have learned psychology with a Coon text as their guide. Dr. Coon graduated with a B.A. in psychology from the University of California, Riverside, and earned his PhD in social psychology from the University of Arizona. He is also coauthor, with John Mitterer and Tanya Martini, of *Introduction to Psychology: Gateways to Mind and Behavior, 16th Edition.*

Courtesy of John Mitterer

John Mitterer

John Mitterer was awarded his PhD in cognitive psychology from McMaster University. He has taught psychology at Brock University to more than 30,000 introductory psychology students. He is an award-winning teacher whose several teaching awards include a National 3M Teaching Fellowship, the Canadian Psychological Association Award for Distinguished Contributions to Education and Training in Psychology, and the Brock University Don Ursino Award for Excellence in the Teaching of Large Classes. He has created textbooks and support materials for both students and instructors, and he has published and lectured on undergraduate instruction throughout Canada and the United States.

Courtesy of Callum Williams

Tanya Martini

Tanya Martini obtained her PhD in developmental psychology from the University of Toronto. In addition to introductory psychology, she also teaches research methods, human learning, and courses aimed at facilitating students' understanding of career-related skills. She has received both the Brock University Distinguished Teaching Award and the Chancellor's Chair for Teaching Excellence. Dr. Martini's research examines how undergraduates think about the skills that are being fostered during university experiences, both inside and outside the classroom. She's also interested in how we can improve students' understanding of career-related skills so that they are in a better position to leverage them when they apply for jobs or post-graduate programs. In addition to her position at the university, Dr. Martini currently sits on the advisory board for the Socio-Emotional Skills Initiative that has been undertaken by the Conference Board of Canada.

Brief Contents

Contents

Preface

To You, the Student—An Invitation to Learn Psychology with Us

Greetings from your authors! We look forward to being your guides as you explore the exciting field of psychology and our ever-evolving understanding of human behavior. In a very real sense, we wrote this book about you, for you, and to you. We sincerely hope you will find, as we do, that what you learn is at once familiar, surprising, and challenging.

Reading *Psychology: Modules for Active Learning*

We have done all we could to make *Psychology: Modules for Active Learning* enjoyable to read and relevant to your everyday life. Each module takes you on a journey into a different realm of psychology, where you will explore areas such as personality, abnormal behavior, memory, consciousness, and human development. Each one is complex and fascinating in its own right, with many pathways, landmarks, and interesting detours for you to discover. Like any journey of discovery, your exploration of psychology will help you better understand yourself, others, and the world around you. It's definitely a trip worth taking.

Studying Effectively with *Psychology: Modules for Active Learning*

As would be the case on any interesting trip, studying psychology will be most rewarding if you adopt a reflective attitude. Psychologists believe that answers to important questions come through engaged and careful thought, observation, and inquiry. Put another way, they often ask "How can we step outside ourselves to look objectively at how we live, think, feel, and act?" As simple as that approach may seem, this type of careful consideration takes practice to develop. *Psychology: Modules for Active Learning*, then, is your passport to an adventure in active, reflective learning, not just passive reading.

We offer at least three different ways to help you develop this type of reflective approach to your studies. First, to help you get off to a good start, we strongly encourage you to read Module 1, our short "manual," *The Psychology of Reflective Studying*. In it, we describe what you can learn by taking this course, including the skills you'll develop that can be helpful in both your personal and professional life. In *The Psychology of Reflective Studying*, you'll also read about a variety of well-established study skills that you can use to get the most out of your psychology course, and your other courses as well.

Second, *MindTap® Psychology* for this text is a digital tool that can help you to learn the material in this book on your own terms. Using MindTap, you can read or listen to the electronic copy of the textbook, highlight key ideas, add notes, and create custom flashcards. MindTap also allows you to reinforce your learning with assignments that revisit topics you have learned about throughout each module. You can track your scores and stay motivated while pursuing your goals. Moreover, you can take advantage of the *MindTap Mobile App* to learn where and when it's convenient for you.

Third and finally, a set of *guided notes* is available for each module. Developed using the well-established Cornell method of note-taking, we have created them to help you distill the most important aspects of each module and develop good study aids to assist you in preparing for tests. Available as MS Word files, you can use the guided notes to help organize your thinking about the material, focus on key ideas and concepts, and practice summarizing important points in your own words.

To You, the Instructor—An Invitation to Teach Psychology with Us

Thank you for choosing *Psychology: Modules for Active Learning* for your students and for your course. Marcel Proust wrote, "The real voyage of discovery consists not in seeing new landscapes but in having new eyes." It is in this spirit that we have written this book—our goal is to promote not just an interest in human behavior but an appreciation for the perspective of the psychological scientist as well.

As the authors of this textbook, we have together accumulated over 80 years of classroom experience, teaching tens of thousands of college and university students. Although we have found most students to be generally well intentioned, our modern world certainly does immerse them in their work, careers, families, intimate relationships, and popular culture. As we compete for ever-more-limited student attention, we need to motivate our students to read and educate them about how to learn effectively—learning, after all, is a life-long endeavor (Matthew & Sternberg, 2009; Paternoster & Pogarsky, 2009).

We have explicitly designed and written the fifteenth edition of *Psychology: Modules for Active Learning* to foster this type of deeper student engagement with the field of psychology. We believe that this will result in better memory for what has been read and studied, and a deeper understanding of how to become more reflective learners and thinkers. To help you and your students reach these goals, we have designed this edition around two key goals: ***integrating support to address instructor learning objectives*** and ***integrating support for active student learning***. In the sections below, we discuss each of these in more detail.

Integrating Support to Address Instructor Learning Objectives

This edition of *Modules* has a structure that we firmly believe will make it easier for instructors to customize their use of the book to address their specific learning outcomes, regardless of whether they are driven by department/state standards or by personal preference. Specifically, each traditional psychology chapter is organized around approximately five modules that represent the "big ideas and issues" in that particular area of psychology. Each of these self-contained modules begins with a set of learning outcomes that are compatible with Bloom's Taxonomy and ends with a short *Reflective Practice* feature that allows students to receive some immediate formative feedback regarding their understanding of the key concepts and ideas from that section. We believe that structuring the book around a smaller number of key topics like this will allow instructors the flexibility to customize their course by having students read only those modules that are central to their unique learning objectives.

In addition, we have worked hard to bring the fifteenth edition of *Modules* in line with the new recommendations put forth by the APA's Introductory Psychology Initiative (APA-IPI), while still maintaining the past edition's compatibility with the broader APA Guidelines for the Undergraduate Major. There are three main themes woven throughout the textbook that are relevant to the APA-IPI. The first is related to *Human Diversity*, including discussions of race, ethnicity, culture, SES, gender, sexual orientation, and age. Too often, such differences needlessly divide people into opposing groups. Our aim throughout this book is to discourage stereotyping, prejudice, discrimination, and intolerance. To that end, all pronouns and examples involving females and males are equally divided by gender. In artwork, photographs, and examples, we have also set out to portray the rich diversity of humanity.

The second APA-IPI theme that is woven throughout this book are sections which highlight psychology as a science. These sections model good critical thinking on topics such as adolescent mental health and the replication crisis, but they're also intended to emphasize how thinking in psychology has evolved with new research, and to highlight areas in which we're still searching for answers (e.g., How should we best conceptualize intelligence? How can we best manage bias in the workplace?).

Finally, you'll see APA-IPI sections woven throughout this book that emphasize how psychological science can be applied to the world around us, including topics such as using laptops to take notes in class, intersex athletes competing at the Olympics, and celebrity endorsements to promote marketing campaigns. Table P.1 underscores the text's compatibility with the APA-IPI and Table P.2 shows how it can help you and your students meet the American Psychological Association's (2013) Guidelines for the Undergraduate Major.

In addition to our compliance with APA initiatives, this edition of *Modules* has a newly revised and expanded Instructor Companion Site that includes an *Instructor's Resource Manual*, which provides a wealth of teaching tips and classroom resources; *Cengage Learning Testing Powered by Cognero* featuring questions correlated to learning objectives, Bloom's taxonomy level, and difficulty; and *PowerPoint slides* providing concept coverage with dynamic animations, photographs, and video. Each of these resources has been designed with your needs in mind and will support you in successfully addressing the learning objectives you've created for your course.

Integrating Support for Active Student Learning

We have built in a number of features into the new edition of *Modules* that we believe will assist students in honing their active learning skills. We'd like to draw your attention to four of them: *assisting with active reading, scaffolding student*

TABLE P.1 | APA-IPI Objectives Addressed by Reading *Psychology: Modules for Active Learning*, 15e

Psychology Content: Identify Basic Concepts and Research Findings	
1.1. Define and explain basic psychological concepts.	All modules, with support provided by *Glossary* and *Guided Notes*
1.2. Interpret research findings related to psychological concepts.	Modules 4–5 (*Research Methods*), Module 6 (*A Psychologist's Skill Set: Information Literacy*), and throughout this book
1.3. Apply psychological principles to personal growth and other aspects of everyday life.	*A Psychologist's Skill Set* modules, and throughout this book
Scientific Thinking: Examples of How to Solve Problems Using Psychology Methods Can Be Found Throughout This Book	
2.1. Draw logical and objective conclusions about behavior and mental processes from empirical evidence.	Module 2 (*Critical Thinking*), Modules 4–5 (*Research Methods*), Module 6 (*A Psychologist's Skill Set: Information Literacy*), and Module 70 (*Statistics Appendix*)
2.2. Describe the advantages and limitations of various research strategies.	Modules 4–5 (*Research Methods*), *A Psychologist's Skill Set* modules, and throughout this book.
2.3. Design, conduct, or evaluate psychological research.	Modules 4–5 (*Research Methods*), *A Psychologist's Skill Set* modules, and throughout this book.
2.4. Evaluate how psychological science can be used to counter unsubstantiated statements, opinions, or beliefs.	Modules 4–5 (*Research Methods*), Module 6 (*A Psychologist's Skill Set: Information Literacy*), and throughout this book
Key Themes: Provide Examples of Psychology's Integrative Themes	
3.A. Psychological science relies on empirical evidence and adapts as new data develop.	All modules throughout this book
3.B. Psychology explains general principles that govern behavior while recognizing individual differences.	All modules throughout this book
3.C. Psychological, biological, social, and cultural factors influence mental processes and behavior.	All modules throughout this book, with specific emphasis on Module 3 (*Biopsychosocial Model*) and Module 49 (*A Psychologist's Skill Set: Diversity and Inclusion*)
3.D. Our perceptions filter our experiences of the world through an imperfect personal lens.	Modules 20–21 (*Attention and Perception*), Module 26 (*A Psychologist's Skill Set: Metacognition*), and throughout this book
3.E. Applying psychological principles can change our lives and communities in positive ways.	Module 77 (*Community Psychology*), *A Psychologist's Skill Set* sections, and throughout this book
3.F. Ethical principles guide psychology research and practice.	Modules 4–5 (*Research Methods*), Module 16 (*Ethical Behavior*)
3.G. Psychologists strive to promote respect for human diversity in its many forms.	All modules, with specific emphasis in Module 49 (*A Psychologist's Skill Set: Diversity and Inclusion*)

note-taking, promoting empirically-supported learning strategies, and *emphasizing practical applications.*

Assisting with Active Reading We have incorporated a number of features into the text itself that are intended to help students to learn actively as they are reading. We'd like to draw your attention to several of them here.

New Bloom's-Oriented Learning Outcomes Act as Advance Organizers to Help Guide Student Reading. Research suggests that, when included at the beginning of each module, learning outcomes help students build cognitive maps of upcoming topics and guide reading in productive ways (Ausubel, 1978; Gurlitt et al., 2012). Each

TABLE P.2 | APA Skills Guidelines 2.0 Addressed by Reading *Psychology: Modules for Active Learning*, 15e

Modules	Topic of Module Cluster	Skills in Action Topic	Chapter Addresses Material from APA Guidelines 2.0:
1	How to Study	N/A	4.1, 5.2, 5.3, 5.5
2–6	Research Methods	Information Literacy	1.1, 1.2, 1.3, 2.1, 2.2, 2.3, 2.4, 2.5, 3.1
7–11	Brain	Self-Regulation	1.1, 1.2, 5.2
12–16	Development	Behaving Ethically	1.1, 1.2, 2.5, 3.2, 5.1
17–22	Sensation and Perception	Communication	1.1, 1.2, 4.1, 4.2, 4.3, 5.4
23–26	Consciousness	Metacognition	1.1, 1.2, 5.2, 5.3
27–31	Learning	Behavioral Self-Management	1.1, 1.2, 5.2
32–36	Memory	Giving Memorable Presentations	1.1, 1.2, 4.2, 5.3
37–41	Cognition and Intelligence	Creativity and Innovation	1.1, 1.2, 1.3, 2.3, 2.5
42–45	Emotion and Motivation	Positivity and Optimism	1.1, 1.2, 1.3, 2.5, 4.3, 5.4
46–49	Sexuality	Diversity and Inclusion	1.1, 1.2, 1.3, 2.5, 3.2, 3.3, 4.3, 5.1, 5.4
50–54	Personality	Leadership	1.1, 1.2, 2.1, 3.3, 5.1, 5.2, 5.4
55–59	Health	Stress Management	1.1, 1.2, 1.3, 3.3, 5.1
60–64	Psychopathology	Perseverance	1.1, 1.2, 3.2, 3.3, 4.3, 5.1, 5.4
65–69	Therapies	Managing Mental Health Problems	1.1, 1.2, 1.3, 3.3
70–74	Social	Teamwork	1.1, 1.2, 3.2, 3.3, 4.3, 5.1, 5.4
75–78	Applied Psychology	Career Preparation	1.1, 1.2, 1.3, 2.3, 5.1, 5.5

module of this book begins with a number of clearly-defined learning outcomes to prime student interest and focus their attention on the key ideas that they will encounter.

Active Questioning Is Emphasized and Modeled. *How can questioning be built into a textbook?* This edition of *Modules* continues our long tradition of using italicized *Dialogue Questions*, such as the previous sentence. They are typically the sorts of questions that students might find themselves thinking as they begin reading a section of text. As such, they model a dialogue in which the questions and the reactions of students are anticipated—that is, *Dialogue Questions* prompt students to look for important ideas as they read, thus promoting active learning while serving as advance organizers. They also clarify difficult points in a lively give-and-take between questions and responses.

Formative Feedback Is Provided to Students as They Read. Each module in this book concludes with a *Reflective Practice* feature that allows students to test their recall and further develop their understanding of the topics presented. Each *Reflective Practice* feature begins with a series of short, noncomprehensive quiz questions to help students actively process information and assess their progress. These questions, which are not as difficult as in-class tests, are meant to offer a sample of what students could be asked about various topics. Students who miss any items are encouraged to backtrack and clarify their understanding before reading further.

Reflective Practice features also include *Think Critically* questions. These stimulating questions challenge students to think critically and analytically about psychology. Each is followed by a brief answer with which students can compare their own thoughts. Many of these answers are based on research and are informative in their own right. Finally, *Reflective Practice* features conclude with *Self-Reflect* questions that encourage students to connect new concepts with personal experiences and prior knowledge.

Built-in Reading Aids Assist Students in Mastering Key Concepts and Ideas. These include:

- Boldface terms, robust illustrations, summaries of information relevant to the learning outcomes at the end of each module.
- In-text links to other material relevant to the reading at hand. For example, a student reading about the Freudian theory of dreams will encounter a link to a relevant discussion of psychoanalysis in a later module.
- *Placeholders*—different colored text and small geometric shapes—are used to draw attention to figure and table references in the text and make it easier for students to return to the section that they were reading after they have paused to view a table or figure.
- The *glossary function* has been made as powerful as possible. The *Main Glossary*, at the end of the book, is integrated with the *Subject Index*, making it easy to link important definitions to where they are discussed in the text. All glossary items are bolded and defined in-text when the term is first encountered. In addition, the parallel *Running Glossary* defines key terms in the margins of the relevant pages, making it easy for students to find, study, and review important terms.

Scaffolding Student Note-Taking We've noticed that many students struggle to take a good set of notes based on their reading of college texts. To address this issue, this new edition of *Modules* comes with guided notes that are designed to scaffold students' ability to address the learning outcomes by extracting the most important information from each module. The notes, which are available in MS Word, were developed using the well-established Cornell method of note-taking.

Each set of notes begins with a single-page multi-level summary of the module called *The Big Picture*, which gives students a bird's eye view of the module as a whole and emphasizes the structure that's created with headers and subheaders. The guided notes themselves focus students' attention on information relevant to the learning outcomes and press them to generate their own examples and summarize important ideas in their own words. Concept maps that are included with the notes are designed to assist students in recognizing the relationships between ideas presented in each section so that they can make important connections.

Promoting Empirically-Supported Learning Strategies One of our goals with *Modules* was to ensure that students begin thinking about skills during your course. Given its far-reaching implications, one that we spend considerable time on relates to effective learning. In the text itself, effective learning is promoted in a few places, beginning with Module 1, *The Psychology of Reflective Studying*, which outlines some of the key features of reflective cognition and underscores its links to deeper understanding and memory. It also introduces students to specific empirically-supported strategies for a variety of different assessments, including multiple choice and short/long answer question formats.

In addition, *MindTap® Psychology* for this text provides a digital learning solution that powers students from memorization to mastery. MindTap gives you complete ownership of your content and learning experience. You have the freedom to customize the interactive syllabi, emphasize the most important topics, and add your own material or notes in the eBook. Assign Mastery Training to encourage students to begin studying early, and reinforce all that they have learned from the eBook with virtual labs, auto-graded writing assignments, and more. Whatever your learning goals may be, MindTap allows you to provide engaging content, and to challenge every single student while building his or her confidence.

Emphasizing Practical Applications To further encourage students' reading, we have emphasized the many ways that psychology relates to practical problems in daily life and addresses issues relevant to the world around us. Another major feature of this book is the *Psychologist's Skill Set* modules that are spaced throughout this book. These high-interest discussions bridge the gap between theory and practical applications by exploring how psychology has contributed to our understanding of the skills that are valuable at work and in our relationships.

We believe that it is fair for students to ask, "Does this mean anything to me? Can I use it? Why should I learn it if I can't?" These two unique sections found throughout the text allow them to see the benefits of adopting new ideas from this text, and they breathe life into psychology's concepts.

Psychology: Modules for Active Learning—What's New in the 15th Edition?

On the content side, the 15th edition of *Psychology: Modules for Active Learning* has been lightly updated and features some of the most recent, reliable, and interesting findings from psychological science, plus updated statistics. The following sections provide some highlights regarding the new topics and features that appear in this edition.

Module 1: The Psychology of Reflective Studying

- What used to be described in previous editions as reflective SQ4R is now described as reflective learning. Aside from no longer exhorting students to survey before reading by thumbing through the textbook pages, all else remains as it was in previous editions.

Modules 2–6: Introducing Psychology

- A new Module 2 opening vignette is followed by a strengthened critique of introspection, which is sustained and echoed throughout the book, stressing the importance of objective evidence. In addition, it is more clearly implied that introspection is still valued as one of many types of evidence.
- The distinction between experimental and nonexperimental (descriptive) research methods is now clearer.
- The final module in this cluster now discusses the popular media in terms of detecting "fake news."
- New material also relates to the pressing need to check sources at a time when it is so easy to create misleading or biased web-based content, as well as quick and practical suggestions related to lateral reading, which is the primary method employed by professional fact checkers.

Modules 7–11: Brain and Behavior

- This cluster of modules contains more recent research concerning mirror neurons, questioning their role in autism (the *broken mirrors hypothesis*).
- Research on self-control in an extended discussion of poverty and the marshmallows addresses recent efforts to replicate Mischel's famous "marshmallow test" and discusses how poverty can impact the results of such self-regulation tasks.

Modules 12–16: Human Development

- *Fetal alcohol syndrome* (FAS) is now referred to as *fetal alcohol spectrum disorder* (FASD). FAS is used to refer to more severe cases of FASD.
- The development of emotions has been reworked for greater clarity and to prefigure the discussion of emotions and emotion schemas in Module 44.
- The section on adulthood has been reorganized.

Modules 17–22: Sensation and Perception

- Material on *attention* has been rewritten and expanded to include new material related to multitasking.

Modules 23–26: States of Consciousness

- With a gentle rewrite, these modules now flow better.
- Drug use statistics are updated throughout.
- The medically correct term *cannabis* is now used instead of the slang term *marijuana*.

Modules 27–31: Conditioning and Learning

- These modules have been significantly modified. Material related to conditioning has been streamlined to allow for a significantly expanded discussion of observational and cognitive learning.
- The first module begins with a new opening vignette and now discusses classical conditioning, with a view to using it to explain some forms of advertising.
- The next module combines and streamlines material on operant conditioning. Material on observational learning is treated next. Material related to observational learning and media-based violence has been updated. Cognitive learning is discussed, and may be of special interest to students pursuing careers in education, as well helping students to better understand their own learning. Newly-written material covers the distinction between school and educational psychologists, Bloom's Taxonomy, and factors that influence cognitive learning (e.g., learner characteristics and learning strategies).

Modules 32–36: Memory

- These modules now more clearly delineate memory systems (that is, types of memory) from memory processes and emphasize the general process of encoding as the means of moving information from working memory into long-term memory.

Modules 37–41: Cognition and Intelligence

- These modules benefited from a light rewrite and now flow more clearly.
- The distinction between experts and novices has been rewritten for greater clarity.
- *G-factor* is now much better described, along with *G-F* and *G-C*, and a good example.
- Material on artificial intelligence has been rewritten to clarify the field of machine learning and its links to psychology.
- A new section on emotional intelligence has been added.

Modules 42–45: Motivation and Emotion

- Self-determination theory is defined and given expanded coverage.
- Material on emotion has been rewritten for greater clarity and to dovetail better with earlier treatments of emotional development and a subsequent more detailed module on emotion.
- Carroll Izard's differential emotions theory and the notion of an emotion schema are introduced.

Modules 46–49: Human Sexuality

- These modules have been lightly revised to better flow.
- Relevant statistics are revised throughout.

Modules 50–54: Personality

- These modules have also been lightly revised.
- The section on the dark triad now suggests that women can also possess these traits.

Modules 55–59: Health Psychology

- These modules have been rewritten for greater clarity.
- Health statistics have been updated where possible.

Modules 60–64: Psychological Disorders

- In all sections, there is a greater emphasis on the biopsychosocial model as a means of understanding psychopathology.
- Prevalence statistics have been updated.
- The distinction between signs and symptoms is introduced in the section on diagnosis.
- A new module on perseverance, or "grit," is now included.

Modules 65–69: Therapies

- The modules concerning therapies have been more thoroughly revised, including a new introduction.
- Sections on the effectiveness of therapy, spontaneous remission, empirically supported therapies, and token economies are now improved.

Modules 70–74: Social Psychology

- A new module opener kicks off coverage of social psychology.
- A discussion of Zimbardo's prison study includes criticisms of the research.
- A new section now reviews the subject of anger management.
- Material on prejudice and managing prejudice has been updated.

Modules 75–78: Applied Psychology

- A new section on performance appraisal and 360-degree feedback is now included.
- The concept of environmental melancholia is introduced.
- Material on the tragedy of the commons has been clarified.
- A new section on community psychology is now included.

Appendix: Behavioral Statistics

- The statistics appendix has been lightly revised.

A Complete Course—Teaching and Learning Supplements

A rich array of supplements accompanies *Psychology: Modules for Active Learning*, including several that make use of the latest technologies. These supplements are designed to make teaching and learning more effective. Many are available free to professors or students. Others can be packaged with this textbook at a discount. Contact your local sales representative for more information on any of the listed resources.

Student Support Materials

Introductory students must learn a multitude of abstract concepts, which can make a first course in psychology difficult. The materials listed here will greatly improve students' chances for success.

MindTap *MindTap®* *Psychology* for Coon/Mitterer/Martini's *Psychology: Modules for Active Learning*, 15th Edition helps you learn on your terms. Begin studying early with Mastery Training, interact with the eBook, and reinforce your learning with assignments that revisit the topics you've learned about and help you prepare for the test. You can also take advantage of the *MindTap Mobile App* to learn on your terms. Read or listen to textbooks and study with the aid of instructor notifications, flashcards, and practice quizzes. No one knows what works for you better than you. Highlight key text, add notes, and create custom flashcards. When it's time to study, everything you've flagged or noted can be gathered into a guide you can organize.

In short, MindTap helps you create your own potential. Track your scores and stay motivated toward your goals. Whether you have more work to do or are ahead of the curve, you'll know where you need to focus your efforts. And the MindTap Green Dot will charge your confidence along the way.

Instructor Resources

Teaching an introductory psychology course is a tremendous amount of work, and the supplements listed here should help make it possible for you to concentrate on the more creative and rewarding facets of teaching. All of these supplements are available online for download. Go to login.cengage.com to create an account and log in.

MindTap *MindTap®* *Psychology* for Coon/Mitterer/Martini's *Psychology: Modules for Active Learning*, 15th Edition is the digital learning solution that powers students from memorization to mastery. It gives you complete control of your course—to provide engaging content, to challenge every single student, and to build his or her confidence. Empower students to accelerate their progress with MindTap. MindTap: Powered by You.

MindTap gives you complete ownership of your content and learning experience. Customize the interactive syllabi, emphasize the most important topics, and add your own material or notes in the eBook. Assign Mastery Training to encourage students to begin studying early, and reinforce all that they have learned from the eBook with virtual labs, auto-graded writing assignments, and more.

The Instructor Companion Site The Instructor Companion Site for this title includes an *Instructor's Resource Manual*, which provides a wealth of teaching tips and classroom resources; *Cengage Learning Testing Powered by Cognero* featuring questions correlated to learning objectives, Bloom's taxonomy level, and difficulty; and *PowerPoint slides* providing concept coverage with dynamic animations, photographs, and video.

Summary

We sincerely hope that both teachers and students will consider this book and its supporting materials a refreshing change from the ordinary. Creating it has been quite an adventurous journey for us; one that we look forward to sharing with you in the modules that follow. We hope that you enjoy the ride.

Acknowledgments

Psychology is a cooperative effort requiring the talents and energies of a large community of scholars, teachers, researchers, and students. Like most endeavors in psychology, this book reflects the efforts of many people. We deeply appreciate the contributions of the following professors, whose sage advice has contributed to *Psychology: Modules for Active Learning*:

We wish to thank Dr. Carol Baldwin, Psychology Department Head at the Salish Kootenai College, for suggesting a way to modify a section of one of our memory modules to become more respectful of our Native American readers.

We also wish to thank Dr. Robin Akawi, Sierra Community College, for her always thoughtful questions, which have led to a number of improvements in this edition, most notably in the discussion of the hindbrain/brain stem distinction.

Dr. Christopher Ferguson, Psychology Department at Stetson University, prompted revisions in our treatment of the Zimbardo prison study, the Kitty Genovese murder, and especially the topic of violence and the media. Thank you, Chris.

We offer a special thank-you to the students at the Nebraska Indian Community College taking Introduction to Psychology in 2015 for triggering a deep conversation with NICC faculty Darla Korol, MSW, Human Services Division Head, and Wynema Morris, Native American Studies Division Head, about the portrayal of American Indians in introductory psychology textbooks.

The following professors also offered invaluable comments on earlier editions of *Psychology: Modules for Active Learning*:

Charlie Aaron, Northwest Mississippi Community College
Jarrod Calloway, Northwest Mississippi Community College
Amanda Dunn, Lincoln Memorial University
Paul Helton, Freed Hardeman University
Scott Keiller, Kent State University at Tuscarawas
Katherine McNellis, Lakeshore Technical College
Sam Olive, Henry Ford Community College
Robert Strausser, Northwest Mississippi Community College
Victoria Wiese, Lakeshore Technical College

Producing *Psychology: Modules for Active Learning* and its supplements was a formidable task. We are especially indebted to the gifted group of professionals at Cengage and elsewhere who have so generously shared their knowledge and talents over the past two years. These are the people who made it happen:

At Cengage, we are especially grateful to our Product Manager, Colin Grover, for his savvy and unconditional support.

We also want to single out Christy Frame. As our Senior Content Manager, Christy patiently kept us on track and offered many deeply appreciated suggestions.

Tricia Salata, Natasha Allen, Kim Buettler, Kelli Besse, and Deanna Ettinger, along with so many others, played key roles.

Thank you also Lori Hazzard from MPS Limited, and Nishabhanu Beegum and Sri Ranjani from Lumina Datamatics.

Up in St. Catharines, Barbara Kushmier, Kayleigh Hagerman, Heather Mitterer, and David and Callum Williams pitched in to lend a hand.

Last of all and, of course, not least, we would like to thank our spouses, Sevren, Heather, and David, for making the journey worthwhile.

MODULE 1

The Psychology of Reflective Studying

Well, Hello There!

As your authors, we are delighted to welcome you to the "manual" for this textbook. No! Don't skip this. Please read on.

Few of us prefer to start a new adventure by reading a manual. We just want to step off the airplane and begin our vacation, get right into that new computer game, or start using our new camera or smartphone. Please be patient. Successfully learning psychology depends on how *reflective* you are as you read your textbook, listen during your classes, study for exams, and then write them.

Students who get good grades tend to work more reflectively, not just longer or harder. They also tend to understand and remember more of what they've learned long after their exams are over. Psychology is for their lives, not just for their exams. In this module, we share a variety of ways to become more reflective learners.

Tyler Olson/Shutterstock.com

~LEARNING OUTCOMES~

After reading this module you should be able to:

1.1 Explain how studying psychology will help you in your personal and professional life

1.2 Describe how you can get the most out of this textbook

1.3 Describe how you can get the most out of class time

1.4 Describe how you can best study and prepare for tests

What's in It for You?—More Than You Might Think

Learning Outcome 1.1 Explain how studying psychology will help you in your personal and professional life

As you begin exploring the field of psychology, you may well be asking yourself what you'll get out of it. In general, most of your courses will offer you opportunities to learn in two important ways. The first has to do with course *content*—in this introductory psychology course, the content is what you'll learn about the field of psychology. This includes what psychological research tells us about memory, social relationships, brain functioning, children's development, and psychopathology (to name just few topics). But taking a psychology course will also promote your learning in a second way—specifically, it will teach you about the *skills* that you'll need to be successful in your personal and professional life.

What do you mean by "skills"? When we talk about skills, we're often talking about things that you can do, such as communicate clearly or work well with others. But in some

TABLE 1.1 | APA Guidelines for the Undergraduate Psychology Major

Goal 1: Knowledge Base of Psychology
Goal 2: Scientific Inquiry and Critical Thinking
Goal 3: Ethical and Social Responsibility in a Diverse World
Goal 4: Communication
Goal 5: Professional Development

Adapted from American Psychological Association, 2013. For complete details, go to: www.apa.org/ed/precollege/about/learning-goals.pdf.

cases, the term *skills* can also refer to personal characteristics; for example, independence, tolerance, and adaptability are often considered to be important skills.

These two broad categories of learning—content and skills—are outlined in the American Psychological Association's (APA) *Guidelines for the Undergraduate Psychology Major (Version 2.0)* (American Psychological Association, 2013). It is well worth having a look at the full document (which is available online), but you can start by having a look at ■ **Table 1.1**.

Do you assume that your only goal is to memorize "the facts," or knowledge base, of psychology? If so, as you can see in Table 1.1, you are thinking in terms of Goal 1. But what about the other goals listed there? Suppose you are given an assignment that involves working in small groups to evaluate some published research articles. Would you wonder why you have to work with other students? Or wish your professor would just get to the point and tell you what the articles are about? Understanding that your education is also about acquiring skills—like being able to think critically (Goal 2), communicate clearly (Goal 4), and work as part of a team (Goal 5)—makes it easier for you to appreciate that professors set up assignments like this to build skills, as well as furthering what you know about psychology.

One of the things that you might notice as you look through Table 1.1 is that many of the skills listed aren't really specific to psychology—they're likely to be just as relevant to someone majoring in history or business or biology. After all, people in all disciplines need to understand how to communicate well, work well with others, and behave ethically.

Some of the most important advice we can give you, then, is to remember to focus on the skills that you are learning throughout your studies at university, whether in psychology or other subjects. They may not always seem obvious when you're reading a textbook or when you're completing your assignments, but when it comes time for you to hit the job market, you'll be happy that you did.

A StockStudio/Shutterstock.com

Working on developing your skills may seem like a waste of your time compared with putting that time into learning course content. But don't sell it short; your skill set will be at least as important as your content expertise whether you go on to postgraduate education or a career.

Psychology and Your Skill Set

To understand why your skill set is important, have a look at ■ **Table 1.2**, which lists a few of the career opportunities open to psychology majors.

TABLE 1.2 | A Skills-Based List of Some Potential Careers for Psychology Majors

Addictions counselor	Manager
Administration	Market research analyst
Advertising	Marketing
Career/employment counselor	Mental health worker
Case worker	Motivational researcher
Child care worker	Personnel
Child welfare worker	Population studies researcher
Community worker	Probation or parole officer
Correctional officer	Professional consultant
Counselor	Program coordinator
Cultural diversity consultant	Psychiatric assistant or aide
Customs or immigration agent	Public health statistician
Day care worker, supervisor	Public opinion interviewer
Educational counselor	Public relations

TABLE 1.2 | (Continued)

Entrepreneur	Recreation specialist
Fundraiser or development officer	Research assistant
Gerontology	Sales representative
Government researcher	Social services
Health services	Social worker
Hospice coordinator	Teaching
Human resources	Technical writer
Immigration officer	Travel agent
Labor relations specialist	Youth worker

Adapted from Canadian Psychological Association (2020).

Travel agent? Think about it for a moment. A travel agent may not need psychology content expertise, such as being able to list Freud's stages of psychosexual development or explain what psychological functions are controlled by the different parts of the brain. But it *would* help to be able to work independently, do your own research, be able to make presentations to individuals or groups, have some sensitivity to cross-cultural issues, write well, and, in general, work well with people. While these sorts of skills also can be learned in other ways, studying psychology provides a "golden opportunity" for you to develop an impressive set of skills that are valued by many employers.

How This Book Will Help You with Skill Development

You probably won't be surprised to learn that *Psychology: Modules for Active Learning* has been written with the APA *Guidelines* in mind, in an effort to help you further develop your career-related skill set. Here are some skill highlights:

- ***A Psychologist's Skill Set* modules:** Every few modules, you will encounter a *A Psychologist's Skill Set* module. Each of these modules connects the field of psychology to a skill that is likely to be useful across a broad range of career paths. These modules, combined with the digital resources for this book, will allow you to measure your skill level and give you practical ideas you can use to improve your skill set.
- **Study skills:** In this module, we discuss a full set of study skills, from how to read and listen for understanding to how to take tests and overcome procrastination. We also introduce the importance of reflective processing, and we carry this idea throughout the book. All of those skills are very helpful in many different jobs.
- **Research skills:** We will introduce you to science and psychological research, from the research methods in Modules 2–6 to the Statistics Appendix. This will help you be a more educated and literate consumer of research in your chosen career, especially if it involves applying psychological research in any way.
- **Critical thinking skills:** From the discussion of critical thinking in Modules 2 and 6 to the *Think Critically* questions at the end of the modules, we stress critical thinking skills. The term *critical thinking* actually encompasses a wide array of related skills, including defining problems, searching for and evaluating information to address those problems, and synthesizing and applying information that you gather. You can see why such skills are in high demand among employers.
- **Cultural awareness skills:** OK, so we couldn't take you on a field trip to Japan, but throughout the book, we will invite you to reflect on the differences among people of different ethnicities, sexual orientations, ages, and genders. This kind of information will be particularly important when you find yourself having to work with others whose background or belief system is not the same as your own.

Not to put too fine a point on it, but that's a lot of career-relevant skills, no?

Of course, we understand that the classroom isn't the only place to learn skills that can help you in your personal life and career. Many college and university students will also have part-time jobs, or they will participate in other learning experiences such as community-based volunteering, or campus activities such as student government or clubs, or study abroad. Often, the skills that you develop through these extra-curricular experiences will support or complement the skills that you can learn through the assignments that you'll complete for your courses.

For example, common part-time student jobs involving interaction with the public (e.g., waiting tables, customer service, or retail jobs) often help to build *verbal* communication skills such as the ability to speak to others, and to listen effectively to what others are saying. In contrast, class assignments often build *writing* skills and the ability to *read and understand* complex material. When you are attempting to persuade an employer that you have a broad range of communication skills, then you should make sure that you discuss what you have learned from a variety of experiences both inside and outside of the classroom to demonstrate the full range of your abilities.

Reflective Learning: The Most Important Ingredient

Simply deciding that you want to learn some content or skills isn't going to actually make it happen. To understand why, think about the last time you spent the evening relaxing in front of the television. It probably was fun, but you may have noticed that you didn't think too much about what you were watching and that your subsequent memories are not detailed. You were engaging in **experiential processing**, more or less passively soaking up the experience (Kahneman, 2011; Norman, 1994).

Now contrast that with your experience in a recent job interview. It is highly unlikely that you got through the interview by relying on experiential processing alone (and even less likely that you landed the job if you did). Instead, you probably actively and carefully listened to the questions and put some serious effort into thinking through the implications of answering in different ways before responding. No drifting off here; you were focused and controlled until you left the interview, when you likely breathed a much-deserved sigh of relief. By reacting mindfully (Siegel, 2007), you engaged in **reflective processing** (Kahneman, 2011; Norman, 1994). Rather than just having the experience, you *actively thought* about it. Similarly, **reflective learning** occurs when you engage in deliberately reflective and active self-regulated study (Anthony, Clayton, & Zusho, 2013; Mega, Ronconi, & De Beni, 2014). Here, in general, is how you can promote reflective learning of both content and skills:

"I'm too busy going to college to study."

William Haefeli/Conde Nast/Cartoon bank

1. **Set specific, objective learning goals.** Begin each learning session with specific goals in mind. What knowledge or skills are you trying to master? What do you hope to accomplish (Pychyl, 2013)?
2. **Plan a learning strategy.** How will you accomplish your goals? Make daily, weekly, and monthly plans for learning. Then put them into action.
3. **Be your own teacher.** Effective learners silently give themselves guidance and ask themselves questions. For example, as you are learning, you might ask yourself, "What are the important ideas here? What do I remember? What don't I understand? What do I need to review? What should I do next?"
4. **Monitor your progress and correct your strategy when necessary.** Reflective learning depends on self-monitoring. Exceptional learners keep records of their progress toward learning goals (pages read, hours of studying, assignments completed, and so forth). They quiz themselves, use study guides, and find other ways to check their understanding while learning. Consider asking yourself these questions regularly as you work toward mastering both course content and skills: Do any specific areas of your work need improvement? If you are not making good progress toward long-range goals, do you need to revise your short-term targets? If you fall short of your goals, you may need to adjust how you budget your time. You may also need to change your learning environment to deal with distractions such as browsing the web, daydreaming, talking to friends, or testing the limits of your hearing with your new ear buds.
5. **Reward yourself.** When you meet your daily, weekly, or monthly goals, reward your efforts in some way, such as going to a movie or downloading some new music. Be aware that self-praise also rewards learning. Being able to say "Hey, I did it!" can be rewarding. In the long run, success, self-improvement, and personal satisfaction are the real payoffs for learning.

If you discover that you lack certain knowledge or skills, ask for help, take advantage of tutoring programs, or look for information beyond your courses and textbooks. Knowing how to reflectively enhance learning can be a key to lifelong enrichment and personal empowerment (Van Blerkom, 2012).

Reflective Reading—How to Tame a Textbook

Learning Outcome 1.2 Describe how you can get the most out of this textbook

One powerful way to get the most out of this textbook is be more reflective is through **self-reference**. As you read, relate new facts, terms, and concepts to your own experiences and information that you already know well. Doing this will make new ideas more personally meaningful and easier to remember. **Critical thinking** is another powerful way to be more reflective. Remember, critical thinkers pause to evaluate, compare, analyze, critique, and synthesize what they are reading (Chaffee, 2019). You should, too. In Module 2, we will learn how to think critically about psychological science.

Does this really work? You bet! Using a reflective reading strategy improves learning and course grades (Taraban, Rynearson, & Kerr, 2000). It also results in enhanced long-term understanding. Simply reading straight through a textbook can give you intellectual indigestion. That's why it's better to stop often to reflect, review, and digest information as you read.

Going Digital

Digital media can also offer several ways to learn more reflectively from this textbook. You can get a good start by exploring MindTap.

MindTap *What is MindTap?* MindTap is a highly personalized, fully online learning platform that integrates in one site all of the authoritative content, assignments, and services that accompany your textbook, *Psychology: Modules for Active Learning.*

What can I expect to get out of MindTap? Many of the more active elements of reflective learning are better presented digitally. There is room, for example, to include only a few practice quizzes in a print textbook (and you, the reader has to self-score them). In contrast, digital media make it feasible to present more extensive practice materials, as well as to provide immediate feedback.

MindTap has been designed to make it easier for you to engage in reflective learning. You will be able to complete reading assignments, annotate your readings, complete homework, and interact with quizzes and assessments. MindTap includes a variety of apps known as "MindApps," allowing functionality such as having the text read aloud to you, as well as synchronizing your notes with your personal Evernote account. MindApps are woven into the MindTap platform and enhance your learning experience with this textbook.

Psychology Websites As you read (reflectively, of course) through this textbook, you may, from time to time, find yourself wanting to read more about a particular topic. Consider following up by looking up some of the references included in this text. Suppose that you were just reading about procrastination and wanted to learn more about the reference *Pychyl* (2013). You can look up all in-module references in the "References" section at the back of this text. There, you will find that *Pychyl* (2013) is a book about overcoming procrastination.

Sometimes, though, the reference that you are interested in will be a psychology journal article. To locate journal articles, you can use *PsycINFO,* a specialized online database offered by the American Psychological Association (APA). **PsycINFO** provides summaries of the scientific and scholarly literature in psychology. Each record in PsycINFO consists of an abstract (short summary), plus notes about the author, title, source, and other details. Entering the author's name(s) and article title will bring you to the article in question. Also, all PsycINFO entries are indexed using key terms. Thus, you can search for various topics by entering words such as *procrastination, postpartum depression,* or *creativity* and find research papers on any topic in psychology that might interest you.

Most colleges and universities subscribe to PsycINFO. You can usually search PsycINFO from a terminal in your college library or computer center—for free. PsycINFO can also be directly accessed (for a fee) through the Internet via APA's PsycINFO Direct service. For more information on how to gain access to PsycINFO, check out www.apa.org/pubs/databases/psycinfo/index.aspx. Beware, though: Many

Experiential processing Thought that is passive, effortless, and automatic.

Reflective processing Thought that is active, effortful, and controlled.

Reflective learning Deliberately reflective and active self-guided study.

Self-reference The practice of relating new information to prior life experience.

Critical thinking An ability to evaluate, compare, analyze, critique, and synthesize information.

PsycINFO A searchable, online database that provides brief summaries of the scientific and scholarly literature in psychology.

of the primary research papers available through PsycINFO are highly technical. Don't be put off by this; read and digest what you can. You'll pick up some interesting information and become a better psychology student in the process.

Aside from PsycINFO, there are a number of good websites that you can consult for reliable information about psychology. For example, the American Psychological Association (APA) and the Association for Psychological Science (APS) maintain online libraries of general-interest articles on many topics. They are well worth consulting when you have questions about psychological issues. You'll find them at www.apa.org and www.psychologicalscience.org. For links to recent articles in newspapers and magazines, check the APA's PsycPORT page at www.apa.org/news/psycport/index.aspx. Other high-quality websites include those maintained by other professional organizations, such as the Alzheimer's Association (www.alz.org), and government agencies, such as the National Institute of Mental Health (www.nimh.nih.gov). (See Module 6 for more on the important skill of information literacy.)

Reflective Note Taking—LISAN Up!

Learning Outcome 1.3 Describe how you can get the most out of class time

Just as studying a textbook is best done reflectively, so, too, is learning in class (Norman, 1994). Like effective reading, good notes come from actively seeking information. A **reflective listener** avoids distractions and skillfully gathers ideas. Here's a listening/note-taking plan that works for many students. The letters LISAN, pronounced like the word *listen,* will help you remember the steps:

L = *Lead. Don't follow.* Read assigned materials before coming to class. Try to anticipate what your teacher will say by asking yourself questions. If your teacher provides course notes or Microsoft PowerPoint® overheads before lectures, survey them before coming to class. Reflective questions can come from those materials or from study guides, reading assignments, or your own curiosity.

I = *Ideas.* Every lecture is based on a core of ideas. Usually, an idea is followed by examples or explanations. Ask yourself often, "What is the main idea now? What ideas support it?"

S = *Signal words.* Listen for words that tell you what direction the instructor is taking. For instance, here are some signal words:

There are three reasons …	Here come ideas
Most important is …	Main idea
On the contrary …	Opposite idea
As an example …	Support for main idea
Therefore …	Conclusion

A = *Actively listen.* Sit where you can get involved and ask questions. Bring questions that you want answered from the last lecture or from your text. Raise your hand at the beginning of class or approach your professor before the lecture. Do anything that helps you stay active, alert, and engaged.

N = *Note taking.* Students who take accurate lecture notes tend to do well on tests (Williams & Eggert, 2002). However, don't try to be a tape recorder. Listen to everything, but be selective and write down only key points. If you are too busy writing, you may not grasp what your professor is saying. When you're taking notes, it might help to think of yourself as a reporter who is trying to get a good story (Ryan, 2001; Wong, 2015).

Most students take reasonably good notes—and then don't use them! Many students wait until just before exams to review. By then, their notes have lost much of their meaning. If you don't want your notes to seem like chicken scratches, it pays to review them periodically (Ellis, 2019).

Using and Reviewing Your Notes

When you review, you will learn more if you take these extra steps (Ellis, 2019; Pychyl, 2013):

- As soon as you can, reflect on your notes to fill in gaps, complete thoughts, and look for connections among ideas.
- Remember to link new ideas to what you already know.
- Summarize your notes. Boil them down and organize them.
- After each class session, write down several major ideas, definitions, or details that are likely to become test questions. Then, make up questions from your notes and be sure that you can answer them.

Summary The letters LISAN are a guide to active listening, but listening and good note taking are not enough. You must also review, organize, reflect, extend, and think about new ideas. Use active listening to get involved in your classes and you will undoubtedly learn more (Van Blerkom, 2012).

Reflective Study Strategies—Making a Habit of Success

Learning Outcome 1.4 Describe how you can best study and prepare for tests

Grades depend as much on effort as they do on intelligence. But good students work more efficiently, not just harder, and that's true when they study as well as when they write exams. In this section, we provide some tips for improving your studying and test-taking skills.

Strategies for Studying

In an interesting paper, researchers reviewed more than 700 research articles on 10 of the most commonly used learning strategies to determine which ones were the most effective (Dunlosky et al., 2013). One of the study strategies most commonly used by students—highlighting or underlining material in the text or lecture notes—was found to be a particularly *ineffective* way to master the material, largely because it doesn't usually promote active or reflective learning. If you cannot imagine your textbook without the pretty neon colors, make sure that you combine your highlighting with one (or more!) of the effective strategies that we discuss below.

Test Yourself A great way to improve grades is to take practice tests before the real one (Karpicke & Blunt, 2011; Sutterer & Awh, 2016), and this strategy came out as a clear winner in the review of learning strategies. In other words, reflective studying should include **self-testing**, in which you pose questions to yourself. You can use flashcards, online quizzes, a study guide, or any other means that you might find helpful. You'll also find *Reflective Practice* self-tests at the end of each major section of this textbook. As you study, try to anticipate potential test questions and be sure you can answer them. Studying without self-testing is like practicing for a basketball game without shooting any baskets.

Use Spaced Study Sessions Another clear winner in the review of learning strategies was the use of spaced study sessions. It is reasonable to review intensely before an exam. However, you're taking a big risk if you are only cramming (learning new information at the last minute). Spaced practice is much more efficient (Dunlosky et al., 2013; Sternberg, 2017). **Spaced practice** consists of a large number of relatively short study sessions. Long, uninterrupted study sessions are called **massed practice**. (If you "massed up" your studying, you probably messed it up, too.) Cramming places a big burden on memory. Generally, you shouldn't try to learn anything new about a subject during the last day before a test. It is far better to learn small amounts every day and review frequently.

Other Suggestions for Studying Ideally, you should study in a quiet, well-lit area free of distractions. If possible, you should also have one place only for studying. Do nothing else there: keep magazines, social media sites, friends, cell phones, pets, video games, puzzles, food, lovers, sports cars, elephants, pianos, televisions, and other distractions out of the area (Przepiorka, Błachnio, & Díaz-Morales, 2016). In this way, the habit of studying will become strongly linked with one specific place.

Also, many students *underprepare* for exams, and most *overestimate* how well they will do. A solution to both problems is **overlearning**, in which you continue studying beyond your initial mastery of a topic. In other words, plan to do extra study and review *after* you think you are prepared for a test. One way to overlearn is to approach all tests as if they will be essays. That way, you will learn more completely, so you really "know your stuff."

Strategies for Taking Tests

OK, but what about actually taking the tests? Are there any strategies for that? You bet! You'll do better on all types of tests if you observe the following guidelines (Van Blerkom, 2012; Wong, 2015):

1. Read all directions and questions carefully. They may give you good advice or clues about what to include in your answer and how to format it.
2. Survey the test quickly before you begin.
3. Answer easy questions before spending time on more difficult ones.
4. Be sure to answer all questions.
5. Use your time wisely.
6. Ask for clarification when necessary.

Reflective listener A person who knows how to maintain attention, avoid distractions, and actively gather information from lectures.

Self-testing Evaluating learning by posing questions to yourself.

Spaced practice Practice spread over many relatively short study sessions.

Massed practice Practice done in a long, uninterrupted study session.

Overlearning Continuing to study and learn after you think that you've mastered a topic.

Objective Tests Several additional strategies can help you do better on objective tests. Such tests (multiple-choice and true–false items) require you to recognize a correct answer among wrong ones or a true statement versus a false one. Here are some strategies for taking objective tests:

1. Relate the question to what you know about the topic. Then, read the alternatives. Does one match the answer that you expected to find? If none match, reexamine the choices and look for a partial match.
2. Read all the choices for each question before you make a decision. Here's why: if you immediately think that *a* is correct and stop reading, you might miss seeing a better answer like both *a* and *d*.
3. Read rapidly and skip items that you are unsure about. You may find free information in later questions that will help you answer difficult items.
4. Eliminate certain alternatives. With a four-choice multiple-choice test, you have one chance in four of guessing right. If you can eliminate two alternatives, your guessing odds improve to 50–50.
5. Be sure to answer any skipped items, unless there is a penalty for guessing. Even if you are not sure of the answer, you may be right. If you leave a question blank, it is automatically wrong. When you are forced to guess, don't choose the longest answer or the letter that you've used the least. Both strategies lower scores more than random guessing does.
6. Following this bit of folk wisdom is a mistake: "Don't change your answers on a multiple-choice test. Your first choice is usually right." This is wrong. If you change answers, you are more likely to *gain* points than to lose them. This is especially true if you are uncertain of your first choice, or it was a hunch and your second choice is more reflective (Higham & Gerrard, 2005).
7. Search for the one best answer to each question. Some answers may be partly true, yet flawed in some way. If you are uncertain, try rating each multiple-choice alternative on a 1 to 10 scale. The answer with the highest rating is the one you are looking for.
8. Remember that few circumstances are always or never present. Answers that include superlatives such as *most, least, best, worst, largest,* or *smallest* are often false.

Essay Tests Essay questions are a weak spot for students who lack organization, don't support their ideas, or don't directly answer the question (Van Blerkom, 2012). When you take an essay exam, try the following:

1. Read the question carefully. Be sure to note key words, such as *compare, contrast, discuss, evaluate, analyze,* and *describe.* These words all demand a certain emphasis in your answer.
2. Answer the question. If the question asks for a definition and an example, make sure that you provide both. Providing just a definition or just an example will get you half marks.
3. Reflect on your answer for a few minutes and list the main points that you want to make. Just write them as they come to mind. Then rearrange the ideas in a logical order and begin writing. Elaborate plans or outlines are not necessary.
4. Don't beat around the bush or pad your answer. Be direct. Make a point and support it. Get your list of ideas into words.
5. Look over your essay for errors in spelling and grammar. Save this for last. Your ideas are more important. You can work on spelling and grammar separately if they affect your grade.

Short-Answer Tests Tests that ask you to fill in a blank, define a term, or list specific items can be difficult. Usually, the questions themselves contain little information. If you don't know the answer, you won't get much help from the questions.

The best way to prepare for short-answer tests is to overlearn the details of the course. As you study, pay special attention to lists of related terms.

Again, it is best to start with the questions whose answers you're sure you know. Follow that by completing the questions whose answers you think you probably know. Questions whose answers you have no idea about can be left blank.

See ➤ **Figure 1.1** for a summary of study skills.

Procrastination: Don't Be Late!

All these techniques are fine. But what can I do about procrastination? **Procrastination**, the tendency to put off working on unpleasant tasks, is almost universal. (When campus workshops on procrastination are offered, many students never get around to signing up!) Even when procrastination doesn't lead to failure, it can cause much suffering (Hensley, 2016; Sirois & Tosti, 2012; Wohl, Pychyl, & Bennett, 2010). Procrastinators work only under pressure, skip classes, give false reasons for late work, and feel ashamed of their last-minute efforts. They also tend to feel frustrated, bored, and guilty more often (Pychyl, 2013).

Time Management

- Make formal schedule
- Set specific goals

Study Habits

- Study in specific area
- Pace study and review
- Create memory aids
- Test yourself
- Overlearn

Reading

- Use reflective SQ4R method
- Study while reading
- Review frequently

Note Taking

- Listen actively
- Use LISAN method
- Review notes frequently

Figure 1.1
Study skills checklist.

Why do so many students procrastinate? Many students equate grades with their personal worth—that is, they act as if grades tell whether they are good, smart people who will succeed in life. By procrastinating, they can blame their poor work on a late start rather than a lack of ability (Haghbin, McCaffrey, & Pychyl, 2012). After all, it wasn't their best effort, was it? Perfectionism is a related problem. If you expect the impossible, it's hard to start an assignment. Students with high standards often end up with all-or-nothing work habits (Rice, Richardson, & Clark, 2012).

While procrastination can be a real problem for students, most can improve by learning to manage time effectively, setting realistic goals, and considering their attitude toward learning. We have already discussed general study skills, so let's consider these other strategies in a little more detail.

Time Management A **weekly time schedule** is a written plan that allocates time for study, work, and leisure activities. To prepare your schedule, make a chart showing all the hours in each day of the week. Then fill in times that are already committed: sleep, meals, classes, work, team practices, lessons, appointments, and so forth. Next, fill in times when you will study for various classes. Finally, label the remaining hours as open or free times. Each day, you can use your schedule as a checklist. That way, you'll know at a glance which tasks are done and which still need attention (Pychyl, 2013).

You may also find it valuable to make a **term schedule** that lists the dates of all quizzes, tests, reports, papers, and other major assignments for each class. The beauty of sticking to a schedule is that you know you are making an honest effort. It will also help you avoid feeling bored while you are working or guilty when you play.

Be sure to treat your study times as serious commitments, but respect your free time, too. And remember, students who study hard and practice time management *do* get better grades (Nandagopal & Ericsson, 2011).

Goal Setting As mentioned earlier, students who are reflective, active learners set **specific goals** for studying. Such goals should be clear-cut and measurable (Pychyl, 2013). If you find it hard to stay motivated, try setting goals for the semester, the week, the day, and even for single study sessions. Also, be aware that more effort early in a course can greatly reduce the stress that you might experience later. If your professors don't give frequent assignments, set your own day-by-day goals. That way, you can turn big assignments into a series of smaller tasks that you can complete. An example would be reading, studying, and reviewing eight pages a day to complete a forty-page chapter in five days. For this textbook, reading one module every day or two might be a good pace. Remember, many small steps can add up to an impressive journey.

Developing a Positive Attitude A final point to remember is that you are most likely to procrastinate if you think that a task will be unpleasant. Learning can be hard work. Nevertheless, reflective students find ways to make schoolwork interesting and enjoyable (Mega, Ronconi, & De Beni, 2014). Try to approach your schoolwork as if it were a game, a sport, an adventure, or simply a way to become a better person. The best educational experiences are challenging, yet fun.

Virtually every topic is interesting to someone, somewhere. You may not be particularly interested in the sex life of South American tree frogs. However, a biologist might be fascinated. (Another tree frog might be, too.) If you wait for teachers to make their courses interesting, you are missing the point. Interest is a matter of *your attitude* (Sirois & Tosti, 2012).

Procrastination The tendency to put off working on unpleasant tasks.

Weekly time schedule A written plan that allocates time for study, work, and leisure activities during a one-week period.

Term schedule A written plan that lists the dates of all major assignments for each of your classes for an entire term.

Specific goals Goals with clearly defined and measurable outcomes.

The Whole Human: Psychology and You

There is a distinction in Zen between *live* words and *dead* words. Live words come from personal experience; dead words are about a subject. This book will be only a collection of dead words unless you accept the challenge of taking an intellectual journey. You will find many helpful, useful, and exciting ideas in the pages that follow. To make them yours, you must set out to actively and reflectively learn as much as you can. The ideas presented here should get you off to a good start. Good luck!

For more information, consult any of the following books:

Chaffee, J. (2019). *Thinking critically* (11th ed.). Boston, MA: Cengage Learning.

Ellis, D. (2019). *The essential guide to becoming a master student* (4th ed.). Boston, MA: Cengage Learning.

Pychyl, T. A. (2013). *Solving the procrastination puzzle: A concise guide to strategies for change*. New York: Tarcher/Penguin.

Van Blerkom, D. L. (2012). *College study skills: Becoming a strategic learner* (7th ed.). Boston, MA: Cengage Learning.

Wong, W. (2015). *Essential study skills* (8th ed.). Boston, MA: Cengage Learning.

MODULE 1 The Psychology of Reflective Studying—Learning Outcomes Revisited

1.1 Explain how studying psychology can help you in your personal and professional life

Two broad categories of learning are learning content and learning skills. Psychology students learn a variety of study skills, research skills, critical thinking skills, cultural awareness skills, and personal skills during their studies—all of which can be useful at work or in your personal life. The study of psychology will also prepare you for many potentially rewarding careers. Some of those exist within the field of psychology, but the skills learned in a psychology degree can also be applied to a wide range of other career paths.

1.2 Describe how you can get the most out of this textbook

Reflective reading, which involves actively thinking about what is being read, is better than passive reading. Using digital media offers another way to be more reflective.

1.3 Describe how you can get the most out of class time

Effective learning in class involves reflective listening. One way to be a more reflective listener in class is to follow the five steps of the LISAN method: lead, don't follow; ideas; signal words; actively listen; note taking.

1.4 Describe how you can best study and prepare for tests

More reflective studying involves studying in a specific place, using spaced study sessions, trying mnemonics, testing yourself, and overlearning. Remember that more specialized strategies may be needed for objective tests, essay tests, and short-answer tests. Avoid procrastination through time management, setting goals, and making learning an adventure.

Reflective Practice

Content Check

1. The facts you pick up during your academic studies are the most important aspect of your education. T or F?
2. Setting learning goals and monitoring your progress are important parts of ____________________ learning.
3. When using the LISAN method, students try to write down as much of a lecture as possible so that their notes are complete. T or F?
4. Spaced study sessions are usually superior to massed practice. T or F?
5. According to research, you should almost always stick with your first answer on multiple-choice tests. T or F?
6. To use the technique known as overlearning, you should continue to study after you feel you have mastered a topic. T or F?
7. Procrastination is related to seeking perfection and equating self-worth with grades. T or F?

Skill Check

Think Critically

8. How is the LISAN method reflective?

Self-Reflect

Do you already use any of the reflective learning techniques discussed in the module? What career paths are you considering? What skills do you think would be valuable in a career like that? Do you already possess these skills? If so, how might you strengthen them? If not, what kinds of experiences can you undertake during your degree to develop these skills? One of the best ways to begin answering these questions is to sit down and undertake an inventory of the skills you have learned from your psychology studies and elsewhere.

ANSWERS

1. F 2. reflective 3. F 4. T 5. F 6. T 7. T 8. LISAN encourages people to be reflective and to actively seek information as a way of learning more effectively.

MODULE 2

Introducing Psychology

Psychology, Critical Thinking, and Science

Living in a Tree House

When Nate Madsen was 25 years old, he learned that loggers were cutting down giant redwoods in a grove that had become his refuge—a restful spot where he could leave behind the stressors of student life. Determined not to simply watch as the trees were destroyed, Nate climbed 160 feet into the branches of a giant redwood and stayed there for more than two years. During that time, he endured heavy rain and winds from above and harassment from people below.

What could Nate possibly have been thinking, you might wonder. But you might equally wonder why people get married, go skydiving, grow roses, become suicide bombers, go to college, or live out their lives in monasteries. You might even wonder why *you* do some of the things you do. In other words, the odds are that you are curious about human behavior (just like your authors). That may even be a part of the reason that you are taking a course in psychology and reading this book.

How, in general, do psychologists set out answer questions about human behavior, such as, "Why, Nate, why?" Let's find out.

Guardian/eyevine/Redux

~LEARNING OUTCOMES~

After reading this module you should be able to:

2.1 Explain why introspection is inadequate for the scientific study of psychology

2.2 Explain the role of critical thinking in psychological science

2.3 Outline the six steps of the scientific method as applied in psychology

Psychology—Behave!

Learning Outcome 2.1 Explain why introspection is inadequate for the scientific study of psychology

We humans have always been curious about humankind. Even the word *psychology* is thousands of years old, coming from the ancient Greek roots *psyche*, meaning mind, and *logos*, meaning knowledge or study. Today, psychology is both a science and a profession. As scientists, some psychologists do research to discover new knowledge. Others apply psychology to solve problems in fields such as mental health, business, education, sports, law, medicine, and the design of machines (Bayne & Jinks, 2013). Still others are teachers who share their knowledge with students. Later, we will return to the profession of psychology. For now, let's focus on how psychologists answer questions in psychology.

Answering Questions in Psychology

If psychology is the study of the mind, then how can a psychologist tell me anything about what is in my own mind? The earliest psychologists would have agreed. After all, you are the only person who can directly observe the inner workings of your own mind, right? To answer questions about you, they would have relied upon **introspection**, the personal observation of your own thoughts, feelings, and behavior. Stop reading, close your eyes, and carefully describe aloud your inner thoughts, feelings, and sensations. You are *introspecting*. (Introspect, Nate, introspect!)

The Failings of Introspection You may be surprised to learn that introspection was abandoned years ago when psychologists realized that it was too flawed to serve as a truly scientific method (see Module 3). To begin to understand the problem, imagine that you are one of the shoppers that psychologists Timothy Wilson and Richard Nesbitt invited to examine four pairs of silk stockings hanging on a rack. The shoppers were asked a deceptively simple question: "Which pair is the highest quality, and why?" (Wilson & Nisbett, 1978). The results can be found in ➤ **Figure 2.1**. As you can see, the order in which the stockings were displayed strongly influenced which pair was chosen.

The shoppers were not told that all the stockings were objectively identical. Also, each pair appeared equally often in each of the four serial positions. This was achieved by changing the order of the four pairs before each shopper made a choice. This made it virtually impossible that the pair in position D was actually consistently of better quality.

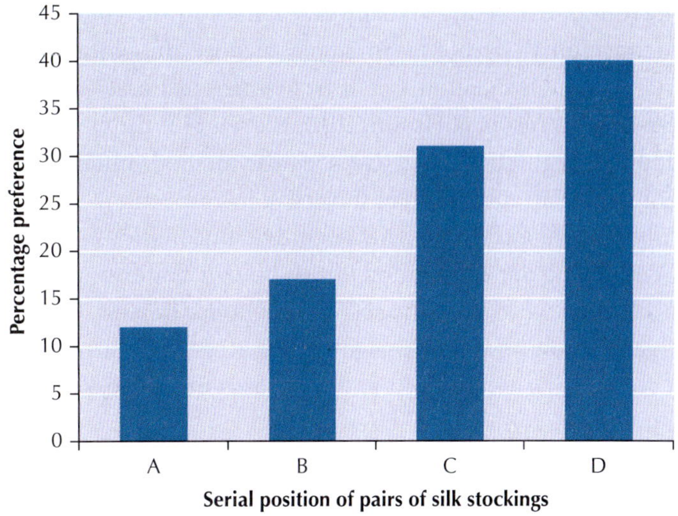

➤ **Figure 2.1**

The effects of serial position on preference. The four pairs of silk stockings in this experiment were labeled A, B, C, and D, from left to right. The results clearly show that the serial position of the individual pairs of stockings; that is, where each pair appeared in the "lineup" influenced shoppers' preferences. (Adapted from Wilson and Nisbett, 1978.)

If the shoppers were introspectively aware of the underlying psychological processes that resulted in their choices, they surely would have identified serial position as a relevant factor. Amazingly, while serial position *objectively* influenced the shopper's choice, no shopper gave serial position as a *subjective* reason for his or her choice. Apparently, you are not always the best judge of why you behave the way you do (Wilson, 2004). That is, even when introspection does yield information, there is no guarantee that the information is accurate.

What reasons did the shoppers give? If you think about it, it *would* be odd to hear someone say, "The pair in position D are the best because they are on the far right." Apparently, not knowing exactly why they made their choice, the shoppers gave the sorts of reasons that you (and they) might expect a thoughtful shopper to give: smoothness, visual appearance, color, weave, and so on. They gave plausible but incorrect answers such as, "I chose the pair in position D because they were the sheerest and most elastic."

Wilson and Nisbett's finding is only one of hundreds of similar reports. Taken together, they confirm that

Freeograph/Shutterstock.com

Psychologists are highly trained professionals who have specialized skills in counseling and therapy, measurement and testing, research and experimentation, statistics, diagnosis, treatment, and many other areas. Here, a psychologist tests a person's intellectual capacity.

Introspection Personal observation of your own thoughts, feelings, and behavior.

much of our thinking actually takes place in the **cognitive unconscious**, a part of the mind of which we are subjectively unaware and is therefore not open to introspection (see, e.g., Bar-Anan, Wilson, & Hassin, 2010; Nisbett & Wilson, 1977). Oddly enough, then, objective scientific methods often yield more accurate answers than subjective introspection.

We will encounter the cognitive unconscious many times during our exploration of psychology. For example, in Module 33, we explore the accuracy of police lineups. Given what you now know, just imagine being arrested on suspicion of committing a murder ... and being assigned to position D in a four-person lineup.

Objectivity in Psychology Because introspection is not the best way to answer many psychological questions, psychologists accept that the mind can't be fully understood from a subjective viewpoint. Accordingly, **psychology** is now defined as the scientific study of behavior and mental processes (i.e., covert behavior). It is this reliance on objective scientific observation to systematically answer questions about all sorts of behaviors that distinguishes psychology from many other fields, such as history, law, art, and business (Stanovich, 2019).

To what does behavior refer in the definition of psychology? Any directly observable action or response—eating, hanging out, sleeping, talking, or sneezing—is an *overt behavior*. So are studying, gambling, watching television, tying your shoes, giving someone a gift, reading this book, and, yes, extreme marathoning. But psychologists haven't left out the mind; they also objectively study *covert behaviors*. These are mental events, such as dreaming, thinking, remembering, understanding what you read, choosing stockings (or murder suspects), and other mental processes (Jackson, 2016).

But how can you study covert behaviors without relying on introspection? Progress in psychology often depends on developing suitable objective **research methods**—systematic scientific approaches to answering particular questions. For example, at one time we had no choice but to rely upon the introspective reports of people who say they never dream. Then the electroencephalograph (EEG) was invented to measure brainwaves. Certain brainwave patterns, as well as the presence of eye movements, can objectively reveal whether a person is dreaming. People who report never dreaming, it turns out, dream frequently. Rather, they forget their dreams upon awakening. If they are awakened when the EEG and eye movement patterns indicate they are dreaming, they vividly remember the dream. Thus, the EEG helped make the study of dreaming more scientific.

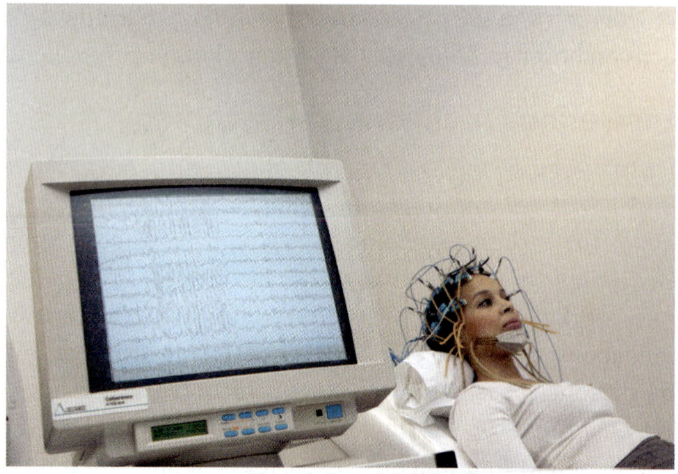

AJPhoto/Science Source

The scientific study of dreaming was made possible by use of the EEG, a device that records the tiny electrical signals the brain generates as a person sleeps. The EEG converts these electrical signals to a written record of brain activity. Certain shifts in brain activity, coupled with the presence of rapid eye movements, are strongly related to dreaming. (See Module 24 for more details.)

Scientific Observation *People have been observing other people for centuries. Isn't psychology, by now, mostly common sense?* You may be surprised to learn how many common-sense beliefs about human behavior are false. For example, have you ever heard that some people are left-brained and some are right-brained? Or that subliminal advertising really works? Or that people prefer to receive thoughtful gifts rather than an impersonal gift, like money? It turns out that these widely held beliefs, and many others, are simply wrong (Lilienfeld et al., 2010).

But how could common sense be wrong so often? One problem with common sense is that it often depends on casual or haphazard observations. For example, has someone ever told you that people in New York City (or Paris, or wherever) are rude? This often means no more than that someone is relying on hearsay or had a bad encounter on one visit. It may well say nothing about New Yorkers or Parisians in general.

Unlike casual observation, psychologists rely on **scientific observation**. Although both are based on gathering *empirical evidence* (information gained from direct observation), scientific observation is *systematic*, or carefully planned. Scientific observations also are *intersubjective*, which means that more than one observer can confirm them. Basically, the scientific approach says, "Let's take a more objective look" (Stanovich, 2019).

Psychologists, then, study behavior directly by systematically collecting data (observed facts) so that they can draw valid conclusions. Would you say it's true, for instance, that "the clothes make the man"? Or do you believe that "you can't judge a book by its cover"? Why argue about it? As psychologists,

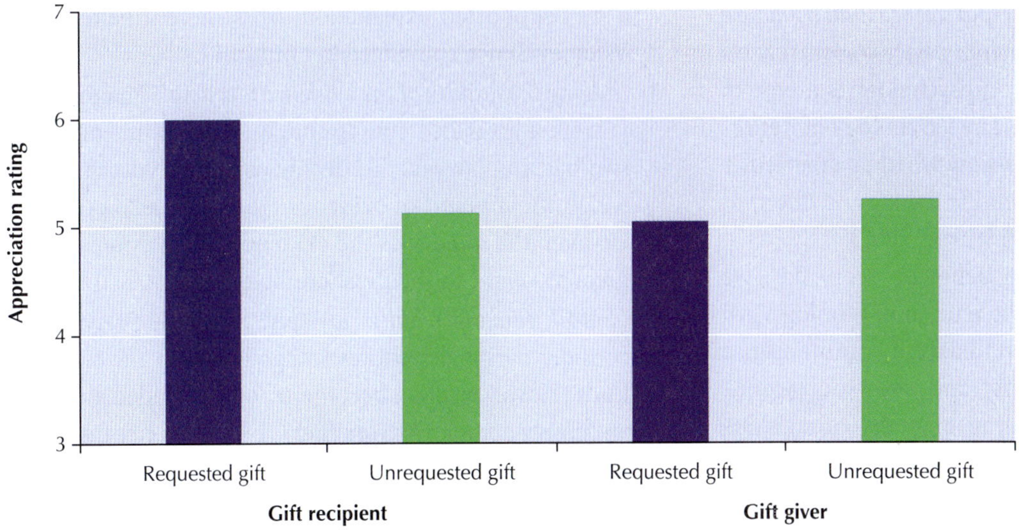

➤ **Figure 2.2**

Results of an empirical study. The graph shows that the recipients of gifts appreciate gifts that they have requested more than gifts that the giver chooses. Gift givers were slightly more likely to believe that recipients would prefer receiving an unrequested gift (although the difference was not statistically significant). (Data adapted from Gino & Flynn, 2011.)

we simply look at some people who are well dressed and some who are not and, through scientific observation, find out who makes out better in a variety of situations.

Here's an example of gathering empirical evidence: Have you ever wondered if, when it comes to giving gifts, it really is "the thought that counts"? Francesca Gino and Francis Flynn (2011) decided to find out. They asked gift recipients to rate how much they would appreciate getting a gift that they requested, as opposed to one chosen by the gift giver. It turns out people prefer gifts that they specifically request over gifts that the giver *thinks* might be appreciated. In contrast, gift givers believed that recipients would be just as appreciative of a gift that they chose for them (see ➤ Figure 2.2).

Isn't the outcome of this study obvious? It isn't if you started out believing otherwise. Sometimes the results of studies match our personal observations or commonsense beliefs, and other times they come as a surprise. In this instance, you may have guessed the outcome. Your suspicions were confirmed by scientific observation. However, it could easily have turned out differently.

How about getting money for a gift—does that make a difference? Gino and Flynn (2011) checked that out as well. They found that gift recipients preferred getting money even more than getting a gift that they requested, even though gift givers thought exactly the opposite. Apparently, we struggle more with the idea of thoughtful gifts when we are the givers than when we are the recipients.

One way to summarize the foregoing is to say that it would be impossible to accurately answer most questions about human behavior without the aid of objective, scientific observation.

Critical Thinking—Take It with a Grain of Salt

Learning Outcome 2.2 Explain the role of critical thinking in psychological science

We humans have always been curious about humankind. Even the word *psychology* is thousands of years old, coming from the ancient Greek roots *psyche*, meaning mind, and *logos*, meaning knowledge or study. Today, psychology is both a science and a profession. As scientists, some psychologists do research to discover new knowledge. Others apply psychology to solve problems in fields such as mental health, business, education, sports, law, medicine, and the design of machines (Bayne & Jinks, 2013). Still others are teachers who share their knowledge with students. Later, we will return to the profession of psychology. For now, let's focus on how psychologists answer questions in psychology.

Cognitive unconscious The part of the mind of which we are subjectively unaware and that is not open to introspection.

Psychology The scientific study of behavior and mental processes.

Research methods Systematic approaches to answering scientific questions.

Scientific observation An empirical investigation structured to answer questions about the world in a systematic and intersubjective fashion (i.e., observations can be reliably confirmed by multiple observers).

But isn't there more to psychology and science than a reliance on scientific observation? Yes. In general, psychologists rely on critical thinking. **Critical thinking** in psychology is a type of reflection (you *did* read Module 1, "The Psychology of Reflective Studying," right?) that involves asking whether a particular belief can be supported by both scientific theory and observation (Vaughn, 2016; Yanchar, Slife, & Warne, 2008).

Because we deal with human behavior every day, we think that we already know what is true in psychology. All too often, however, we are tempted to accept commonsense beliefs, false news, urban legends, and even outrageous claims about the powers of healing crystals, miraculous herbal remedies, astrology describing people's personalities, psychics predicting the future, and so forth. However, critical thinkers are willing to challenge both conventional and unconventional wisdom by asking hard questions (Ruggiero, 2015). For this and many other reasons, learning to think critically is one of the lasting benefits of a college education.

For example, when it comes to achieving our goals, is it better to focus on how far we still have to go before we reach a goal, or should we focus on what we have already accomplished? Critical thinkers might immediately ask: "Is there any theory to support stressing either a goal focus or an accomplishment focus? Is there any empirical evidence either way? What could we do to find out for ourselves?" (Be on the lookout later in this module for some evidence concerning this question.)

Critical Thinking Principles

The heart of critical thinking is a willingness to actively *reflect* on ideas. Critical thinkers evaluate ideas by deliberately probing for weaknesses in their reasoning and analyzing the evidence supporting their beliefs. They question assumptions and look for alternative conclusions. True knowledge, they recognize, comes from constantly revising our understanding of the world. Critical thinking relies on the following basic principles (Jackson & Newberry, 2016; Ruggiero, 2015; Vaughn, 2016):

1. *Few truths transcend the need for logical analysis and empirical testing.* Whereas religious beliefs and personal values are often held as matters of faith, most other ideas can and should be evaluated by applying the rules of logic, evidence, and the scientific method.
2. *Authority or claimed expertise does not automatically make an idea true or false.* Just because a teacher, guru, celebrity, or authority is convincing or sincere doesn't mean that you should automatically believe (or disbelieve) that person. Naively accepting (or denying) the word of an expert is unscientific and self-demeaning unless you ask, "Is this a well-supported explanation, or is there a better one? What evidence convinced her or him?"
3. *Judging the quality of the evidence is crucial.* Imagine that you are a juror in a courtroom, judging claims made by two battling lawyers. To decide correctly, you can't just weigh the *amount* of evidence. You must also critically evaluate the *quality* of the evidence. Then you can give greater weight to the most credible facts.
4. *Critical thinking requires an open mind.* Be prepared to consider daring departures and go wherever the evidence leads. However, don't become so open-minded that you are simply gullible. Astronomer Carl Sagan once noted, "It seems to me that what is called for is an exquisite balance between two conflicting needs: the most skeptical scrutiny of all hypotheses that are served up to us and at the same time a great openness to new ideas" (Kida, 2006, p. 51).
5. *Critical thinkers often wonder what it would take to show that a "truth" is false.* **Falsification** is the deliberate attempt to uncover how a commonsense belief or scientific theory might be false. Critical thinkers adopt an attitude of actively seeking to *falsify* beliefs, including their own. They want to find out when they are wrong, even if it is difficult to accept. As Susan Blackmore (2000, p. 55) said when her studies caused her to abandon some long-held beliefs, "Admitting you are wrong is always hard—even though it's a skill that every psychologist has to learn." On the plus side, finding out what is wrong with a belief often points the way to improving it. Similarly, critical thinkers can be more confident in beliefs that have survived their attempts at falsification.

To put these principles into action, here are some questions to ask as you evaluate new information (Jackson & Newberry, 2016; Ruggiero, 2015; Vaughn, 2016):

1. What is the claim being made? Is it understandable? Does it make logical sense? Does it fit into an existing theory? What are the implications of the claim? Is there another possible explanation? Is it a simpler explanation?
2. What empirical tests of this claim have been made (if any)? How good is the evidence? (In general, scientific observations provide the highest quality evidence.) Can the claim be falsified?
3. Who did the tests? How reliable and trustworthy were the investigators? Do they have conflicts of interest (for example, are they being paid or rewarded in some other way for making these claims)? Do their findings appear to be objective? Has any other independent researcher duplicated the findings?

Uncritical Acceptance and Confirmation Bias *If falsification is a good strategy, then what is the opposite of falsification, and why would people do that?* Good question. We humans are vulnerable to **uncritical acceptance**—the tendency to believe claims because they seem true or it would be nice if they were true. Consider horoscopes, which generally contain mostly flattering traits. Naturally, when your personality and your future are described in *desirable* terms, it is hard to deny that the description has the ring of truth (Rogers & Soule, 2009). On the other hand, how much acceptance would astrology receive if all horoscopes read like this?

> **Virgo:**
> Your nitpicking is unbearable to your friends. You are cold, unemotional, and usually fall asleep while making love. You have no chance of ever finding a person who will love you. Virgos make good doorstops.

Even when a horoscope contains a mixture of good and bad traits, it may seem accurate because we humans are also vulnerable to **confirmation bias**, the tendency to remember or notice things that confirm our expectations and ignore the rest (Lilienfeld, Ammirati, & Landfield, 2009). For example, how well does the following astrological description describe your personality?

> **Your Personality Profile:**
> You have many personality strengths, with some weaknesses to which you can usually adjust. You tend to be accepting of yourself. You are comfortable with some structure in your life but do enjoy diverse experiences from time to time. Although on the inside, you might be a bit unsure of yourself, you appear under control to others. You are sexually well adjusted, although you do have some questions. Your life goals are more or less realistic. Occasionally, you question your decisions and actions because you're unsure that they are correct. You want to be liked and admired by other people. You are not using your potential to its full extent. You like to think for yourself and don't always take other people's word without thinking it through. You are not generally willing to disclose to others because it might lead to problems. You are a natural introvert, cautious, and careful around others, although there are times when you can be an extrovert who is the life of the party.

A psychologist read a similar summary to college students who thought they were taking a personality test. Only a few students felt that the description was inaccurate. Reread the description and you will see that it contains both sides of several personality dimensions ("You are a natural introvert ... although there are times when you can be an extrovert ..."). Its apparent accuracy is an illusion based on confirmation bias.

To summarize, we humans are vulnerable to uncritical acceptance and confirmation bias. The result is the selection of evidence and arguments to support your own beliefs while ignoring contradictory evidence or arguments (Boudry, Blancke, & Pigliucci, 2015). This is a sure-fire way to protect yourself from confronting your mistaken beliefs. It is also a sure-fire way to remain mistaken (Schick & Vaughn, 2014).

Superstition vs. Science Before leaving this topic, we should note that the entire belief system of astrology fails the test of critical thinking. As such, it can be considered a type of **superstition**, an unfounded belief held without objective evidence or in the face of falsifying evidence.

Astrology is based on a zodiac map invented several thousand years ago in the ancient civilization of Babylon. Unlike scientific theories, which are regularly falsified and rejected or revised accordingly, the basic underpinnings of astrology have remained relatively unchanged. Nevertheless, to date, no astrologer has offered a convincing theory of *how* the positions of the planets at a person's birth affect his or her future.

Empirical studies of astrology have also failed to uncover supporting evidence. One classic study of more than 3,000 predictions by famous astrologers found that only a small percentage of them were accurate. These successful predictions tended to be vague ("There will be a tragedy somewhere in the east in the spring") or easily guessed from current events (Culver & Ianna, 1988). Similarly, no connection exists between people's astrological signs and their intelligence or personality traits (Hartmann, Reuter, & Nyborg, 2006). There also is no connection between the compatibility of couples' astrological signs and their marriage and divorce rates or between astrological signs and leadership, physical characteristics, or career choices (Martens & Trachet, 1998).

Many superstitious beliefs such as astrology can seem scientific at first. For example, *graphology*, the study of handwriting, is useful for detecting forgeries. Isn't it plausible that personality traits are also revealed by handwriting? On further examination, though, this turns out to be *pseudoscience* (i.e., *false* science). Graphologists score no better than average on tests of accuracy in rating personality (Dazzi & Pedrabissi, 2009; Furnham, Chamorro-Premuzic, & Callahan, 2003).

Critical thinking In psychology, a type of reflection involving the support of beliefs through scientific explanation and observation.

Falsification The deliberate attempt to uncover how a commonsense belief or scientific theory might be false.

Uncritical acceptance The tendency to believe claims because they seem true or because it would be nice if they were true.

Confirmation bias The tendency to remember or notice information that fits one's expectations, while forgetting or ignoring discrepancies.

Superstition Unfounded belief held without evidence or in spite of falsifying evidence.

In closing, valid psychological principles are based, then, on critical thinking, scientific theory, and objective evidence, not superstitions, pseudoscience, fads, opinions, or wishful thinking.

Scientific Research—How to Think Like a Psychologist

Learning Outcome 2.3 Outline the six steps of the scientific method as applied in psychology

Psychology generally follows the **scientific method**, a form of critical thinking based on the systematic collection of evidence, accurate description and measurements, precise definitions, controlled observations, and repeatable results (Jackson, 2016; Yanchar, Slife, & Warne, 2008). As we noted previously, the first step in the scientific method is the careful recording of observation, the foundation of all science (Stanovich, 2019). To be *scientific*, our observations must be *systematic*, so they reveal something reliable about behavior. To return to an earlier example, if you are interested in whether gift recipients prefer gifts that they requested or gifts that were chosen for them, you will learn little by making haphazard observations of gift-giving at family birthday parties.

The Six Steps of the Scientific Method

In its ideal form, the scientific method has six steps (➤ Figure 2.3). All six steps are found in the following example, from Florida State University psychologist Kyle Conlon and his colleagues (2011). Earlier, we wondered whether goals are more attainable if people maintain a goal focus (stressing how much remains to be done to achieve the goal) or an achievement focus (stressing how much has already been achieved). These researchers decided to find out.

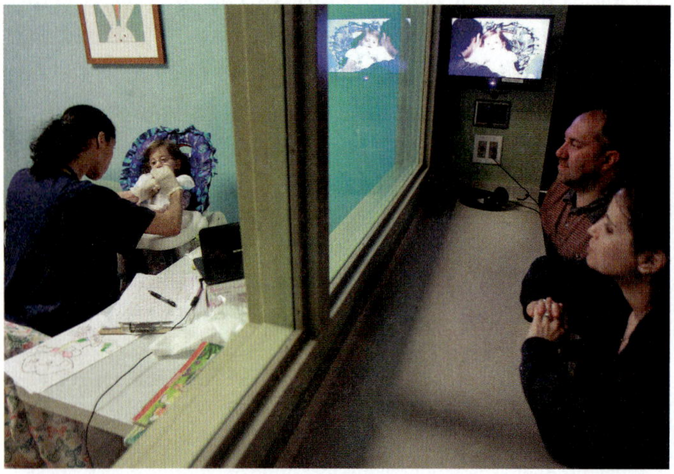

The Star-Ledger/Robert Sciarrino/The Image Works

Applying the scientific method to the study of behavior requires careful observation. Here, two psychologists observe and record a session in which a child's eating behavior is being studied.

Make Observations The researchers reviewed previously published studies, noting that both goal-focused and achievement-focused approaches are popular. If the goal is weight loss, for example, one goal-focused approach is to count down the pounds (only 10 pounds to go!), while one achievement-focused approach is to celebrate milestones (congratulations on losing the first 10 pounds!).

Define the Problem The researchers also noted that maintaining a goal focus seems to inspire more goal-oriented behaviors. Thus, they defined their main problem as "Will people lose more weight if they maintain a goal focus compared to an achievement focus?"

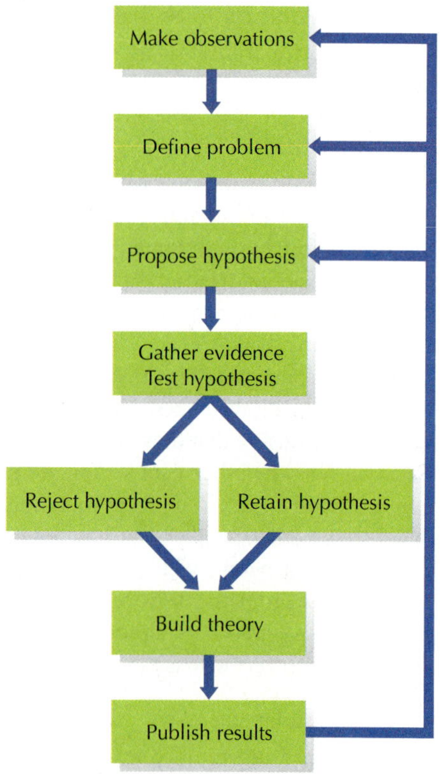

➤ **Figure 2.3**

The scientific method. Psychologists use the logic of science to answer questions about behavior. Specific hypotheses can be tested in a variety of ways, including controlled experiments, naturalistic observation, correlational studies, case studies, and surveys. Psychologists revise their theories to reflect the evidence that they gather. New or revised theories then lead to new observations, problems, and hypotheses.

Propose a Hypothesis *What exactly is a hypothesis?* A theoretical question or statement (like "Will people lose more weight if they maintain a goal focus or if they maintain an achievement focus?") is usually too vague to be assessed directly. In contrast, a **hypothesis** (hi-POTH-eh-sis) is the predicted outcome of an experiment or an educated guess about the relationship between variables. In other words, a hypothesis is a *testable* hunch about behavior.

Theoretical questions are transformed into testable hypotheses through operational definitions. An **operational definition** states the exact procedures used to measure a concept. Conlon and his colleagues began by creating a 12-week exercise program involving weekly group meetings and a companion website. Operationally defining weight loss was straightforward; participants were weighed on a standard digital scale at the beginning of the weight-loss period and once every week until the program ended.

Measuring someone's goal focus or achievement focus was a bit harder since these terms refer to covert behaviors (mental processes). Fortunately, operational definitions also allow covert behaviors that are not directly observable to be tested in real-world terms (see ➤ Figure 2.4). Conlon and his colleagues modified their weight-loss program so that the weekly surveys, feedback, and group discussions revolved around either a goal focus or an achievement focus. They then assigned a third of their participants to one program or the other (the final third was assigned to a group without either focus). For example, every week, goal-focused participants were asked to describe how much more weight they needed to lose to reach their goal, while achievement-focused participants were asked to describe how much weight they had already lost.

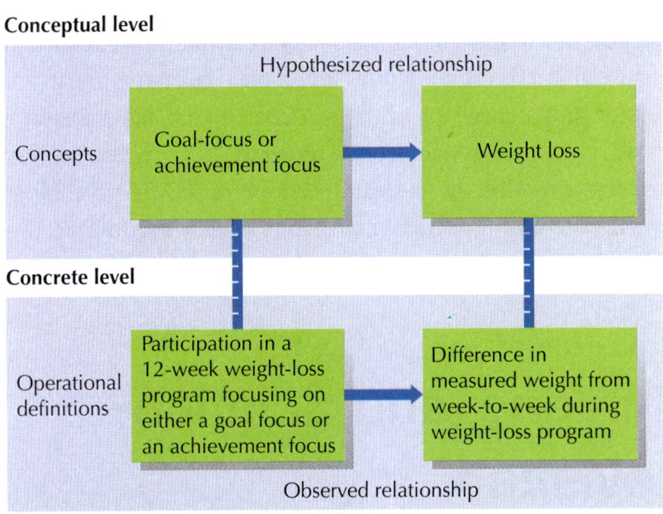

➤ **Figure 2.4**

Operational definition. Operational definitions are used to link concepts with concrete observations. Conlon and his colleagues (2011) define their weight-loss programs in enough detail that other researchers can confirm both the validity of their operational definitions and the accuracy of their results. Operational definitions vary in how well they represent concepts. For this reason, many different experiments may be necessary to draw clear conclusions about hypothesized relationships in psychology.

Gather Evidence/Test Hypothesis Now let's return to the question of whether weight loss is easier when you maintain a goal focus or an achievement focus. As predicted, goal-focused individuals lost more weight than did either achievement-focused or control individuals. They also reported being more committed to reaching their goal weights. Accordingly, the researchers retained the hypothesis rather than rejecting it.

Build Theory *How do theories fit in?* A **theory** is a system of ideas designed to interrelate concepts and facts in a way that summarizes existing data and predicts future observations. Good theories summarize observations, explain them, allow prediction, and guide further research. Without theories of forgetting, personality, stress, mental illness, and the like, psychologists would drown in a sea of disconnected facts (Stanovich, 2019).

Conlon and his colleagues interpreted their results as consistent with theories of motivation that stress the importance of being aware of how much work remains to be done to achieve a goal. The results were also portrayed as extending these theories into the field of health psychology and as being relevant to the design of health-intervention programs.

Publish Results Because scientific information must always be *publicly available*, the results of psychological studies are usually published in professional journals (see ▪ Table 2.1). That way, other researchers can read about the results and make their own observations if they doubt the study's findings (Gravetter & Forzano, 2019). If others are able to *replicate* (repeat) the results of a study, those results become more credible.

In a scholarly article published in the *Journal of Experimental Social Psychology,* Conlon and his colleagues (2011)

Scientific method A form of critical thinking based on careful measurement, controlled observation, and repeatable results.

Hypothesis Predicted outcome of an experiment or an educated guess about the relationship between variables.

Operational definition Defining a scientific concept by stating the specific actions or procedures used to measure it. For example, *hunger* might be defined as the number of hours of food deprivation.

Theory Comprehensive explanation of observable events.

TABLE 2.1 | Outline of a Research Report

- *Abstract.* Research reports begin with a brief summary of the study and its findings. The abstract lets you get an overview of the contents without reading the entire article.
- *Introduction.* The introduction describes the question to be investigated. It also provides background information by reviewing prior studies on the same or related topics.
- *Method.* This section tells how and why observations were made. It also describes the specific procedures used to gather data. That way, other researchers can repeat the study to see if they get the same results.
- *Results.* The outcome of the investigation is presented. Data may be graphed, summarized in tables, or statistically analyzed.
- *Discussion.* The results of the study are discussed in relation to the original question. Implications of the study are explored, and further studies may be proposed.

TABLE 2.2 | Basic Ethical Guidelines for Psychological Researchers

Do no harm.
Describe risks accurately to potential participants.
Ensure that participation is voluntary.
Minimize any discomfort to participants.
Maintain confidentiality.
Do not invade privacy unnecessarily.
Use deception only when absolutely necessary.
Remove any misconceptions caused by deception (i.e., debriefing).
Provide results and interpretations to participants.
Treat participants with dignity and respect.

describe the question they investigated, the methods they used, and the results of their study comparing goal-focused and achievement-focused dieters.

Research Ethics

Aren't there rules about how scientists must treat the people they study? Psychology experiments sometimes raise *ethical* questions. The obedience studies of Stanley Milgram (1963) are a classic example (see Module 71). Participants were ordered to give what they thought were painful electric shocks to another person (no shocks were actually given). Believing that they had hurt someone, many people left the experiment shaken and upset. A few suffered guilt and distress for some time afterward. Such experiments raise serious ethical questions (see also Le Texier, 2019). Did the information gained justify the emotional costs? Was deception really necessary? Currently about 65% of psychologists are women, 16% are members of racial/ethnic minorities, and 5% have a disability

As a reply to such questions, American Psychological Association (APA) guidelines state: "Psychologists must carry out investigations with respect for the people who participate and with concern for their dignity and welfare" (American Psychological Association, 2017b; see ■ **Table 2.2**). Ethical guidelines also apply to animals, where investigators are expected to "ensure the welfare of animals and treat them humanely." To ensure that ethical guidelines are applied properly, most university and college psychology departments have Research Ethics Committees that oversee research. Nevertheless, no easy answers exist for the ethical questions raised by psychology, and debate about specific experiments is likely to continue. (See Module 16 for a more general discussion of ethics.)

MODULE 2 Psychology, Critical Thinking, and Science—Learning Outcomes Revisited

2.1 Explain why introspection is inadequate for the scientific study of psychology

Introspection is of limited use as a research method since there is little consistency between the introspective reports of different people. Also, since the discovery of imageless thought, it has become clear that people are often introspectively unaware of their own mental processes (their cognitive unconscious.)

2.2 Explain the role of critical thinking in psychological science

Critical thinking supports scientific psychology by helping us think more clearly about human behavior.

For example, psychological training makes it easier to avoid uncritical acceptance and confirmation bias and rely on falsification to clarify a commonsense belief, a superstition or a pseudoscientific belief.

2.3 Outline the six steps of the scientific method as applied in psychology

1. Make observations
2. Define the problem
3. Propose a hypothesis
4. Gather evidence/test hypothesis
5. Build theory
6. Publish results

Reflective Practice

Content Check

1. The cognitive unconscious is
   a. better studied objectively
   b. often inaccessible through introspection
   c. often outside subjective awareness
   d. all of the above
2. Psychology is the ____________ study of ____________ behaviors and ____________ mental processes.
3. Horoscopes provided by astrology are stated in positive terms, which have a "ring of truth." This fact is the basis of
   a. uncritical acceptance
   b. confirmation bias
   c. critical thinking
4. A psychologist does a study to see whether exercising increases a sense of well-being. In the study, she will be testing a(n)
   a. theoretical statement
   b. operational definition
   c. empirical definition
   d. anthropomorphic theory
5. ____________ behaviors are operationally defined in terms of ____________ behavior.
   a. Overt, covert
   b. Observable, overt
   c. Covert, overt
   d. Covert, abstract

Skill Check

Think Critically

6. Superstitions like astrology and graphology are harmless. T or F?

Self-Reflect

How stringently do you evaluate your own beliefs and the claims made by others? How might you scientifically test the old saw, "You can't teach an old dog new tricks"? Follow the steps of the scientific method to propose a testable hypothesis and decide how you would gather evidence. (But don't worry—you don't have to publish your results.)

ANSWERS

1. d 2. scientific, overt, covert 3. b 4. a 5. c 6. False. Although superstitions may seem like no more than a quaint nuisance, they can do real harm. For example, people seeking treatment for psychological disorders may become the victims of self-appointed "experts" who offer ineffective, pseudoscientific therapies (Kida, 2006; Lilienfeld, Ruscio, & Lynn, 2008). Or imagine being turned down for a job by a graphologist who was hired by the company to evaluate your suitability by analyzing your handwriting. Even a graphological society recommends that handwriting analysis should not be used to select people for jobs (Simner & Goffin, 2003).

MODULE

3

Introducing Psychology

Psychology Then and Now

From Bumps to Brains

Throughout psychology's history, various viewpoints have helped us understand and interpret human behavior. Early attempts yielded mixed results. One such attempt, *phrenology*, was popularized in the early 1800s by Franz Gall, a German anatomy teacher. Phrenology claimed that the shape of the skull reveals personality traits. Psychological research has long since shown that bumps on the head have nothing to do with talent or ability. The phrenologists were so far off that they listed the part of the brain that controls hearing as a center for combativeness!

Today, little more than 140 years after psychology became a recognized discipline, three complementary perspectives (the biological perspective, the psychological perspective, and the sociocultural perspective) guide research and theorizing in psychology. Also, psychologists around the world are now researching, teaching, and helping people in a wide range of specialties. In this module, we survey the whole of psychology from its beginnings until now.

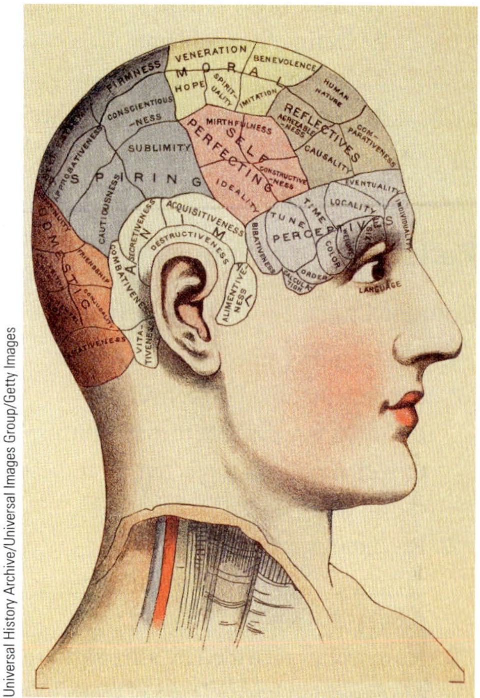

Universal History Archive/Universal Images Group/Getty Images

~LEARNING OUTCOMES~

After reading this module you should be able to:

3.1 Distinguish between the following historical approaches to psychology: Structuralism, functionalism, behaviorism, gestalt psychology, psychoanalytic psychology, humanistic psychology, and cognitive psychology, as well as address the importance of diversity in psychology

3.2 Define the three contemporary perspectives in psychology and explain why they are complementary

3.3 Discuss some of the major specialties in modern psychology, including the distinction between researchers and clinicians

A Brief History of Psychology—Psychology's Family Album

Learning Outcome 3.1 Distinguish between the following historical approaches to psychology: Structuralism, functionalism, behaviorism, gestalt psychology, psychoanalytic psychology, humanistic psychology, and cognitive psychology, as well as address the importance of diversity in psychology

As we noted previously, people have been observing human behavior and philosophizing about it informally for thousands of years. Yet most historians now agree that scientific psychology truly took hold in the late 1800s in Leipzig, Germany (Kardas, 2014). There, in 1879, Wilhelm Wundt

(VILL-helm Voont), the father of psychology, set up a laboratory to study conscious experience.

How, Wundt wondered, do we experience sensations, images, and feelings? To find out, he systematically observed and measured stimuli of various kinds (e.g., lights, sounds, and weights). A **stimulus** is any physical energy that affects a person and evokes a response [stimulus: singular; stimuli (STIM-you-lie): plural]. Wundt then used *introspection*, or looking inward, to probe observers' reactions to various stimuli (Asthana, 2015). Aware that casual introspecting may be unreliable, he sought to train his *introspectionists* to be systematic and scientific. Over the years, Wundt studied vision, hearing, taste, touch, memory, time perception, and many other topics. By insisting on systematic observation and measurement, he asked some interesting questions and got psychology off to a good start (Schultz & Schultz, 2016).

In 1901, one of Wundt's students, Karl Marbe, discovered what he called **imageless thought** (Henley, 2019). He asked trained introspectionists to introspect while they compared two objects of different weights, holding one in each hand. They could clearly describe their experiences of each weight and which one was heavier, but they could not describe the mental process of judging which one was heavier. As Marbe put it, the thought process of comparing the weights did not form a conscious "image."

So does imageless thought take place in the cognitive unconscious? Precisely! Try it for yourself. Close your eyes and extend both hands palms up while a friend gives you two objects of different weights, one in each outstretched palm. You will certainly become aware of the sensations associated with each object and should notice that you *immediately* know which is heavier. It will just "pop into your mind." But *how* did you decide this? Marbe couldn't know it in 1901, but by documenting an example of the *cognitive unconscious* in action (remember the stockings from the previous module?), he set in motion a debate that would soon result in the rejection of introspectionism.

Wilhelm Wundt (1832–1920). Wundt is credited with making psychology an independent science, separate from philosophy. Wundt's original training was in medicine, but he became deeply interested in psychology. In his laboratory, Wundt investigated how sensations, images, and feelings combine to make up personal experience.

Structuralism

Another of Wundt's students, Edward Titchener (TICH-in-er), brought Wundt's ideas to the United States. He developed Wundt's ideas into **structuralism**, the study of sensations and personal experience analyzed as basic elements.

But how could he do that? You can't analyze conscious experience as you do a chemical compound, can you? Although even Wundt didn't think that you could do that, the structuralists tried to explore "mental chemistry," mostly by using introspection. For instance, an observer might hold an apple and decide that she or he had experienced the item's hue (color), roundness, and weight. Another question that a structuralist might have asked is, "What basic tastes mix together to create complex flavors as different as broccoli, lime, bacon, and strawberry cheesecake?"

Once again, introspection proved to be a poor way to answer psychological questions (Benjafield, 2015). No matter how systematic the observations, the structuralists frequently disagreed. Even worse, there was no way to settle intersubjective differences (my trained introspectionists are better than your trained introspectionists?) Marbe and Titchener even quarreled about imageless thought (Henley, 2019). Think about it. If you and a friend both introspect on your perceptions of an apple and end up listing different basic elements, who would be right?

Although introspection is no longer the preferred research method in psychology, it is still used as one source of insight in studies of hypnosis, meditation, problem solving, moods, and many other topics.

Functionalism

American scholar William James broadened psychology to include animal behavior, religious experience, abnormal behavior, and other interesting topics. James's brilliant first book, *Principles of Psychology* (1890), helped establish the field as a separate discipline (Kardas, 2014).

James's interest in how the mind functions to help us adapt to the environment grew into **functionalism**, a school of psychology that considers behaviors in terms of active

Stimulus Any physical energy that an organism senses.

Imageless thought An old term describing the inability of introspectionists to become subjectively aware of some mental processes; an early term describing the cognitive unconscious.

Structuralism Study of sensations and personal experience analyzed as basic elements.

Functionalism School of psychology that considers behaviors in terms of active adaptations.

William James (1842–1910). William James was the son of philosopher Henry James, Sr., and the brother of novelist Henry James. During his long academic career, James taught anatomy, physiology, psychology, and philosophy at Harvard University. He believed strongly that ideas should be judged in terms of their practical consequences for human conduct.

John B. Watson (1878–1958). Watson's intense interest in observable behavior began with his doctoral studies in biology and neurology. Watson became a psychology professor at Johns Hopkins University in 1908 and advanced his theory of behaviorism. He remained at Johns Hopkins until 1920—when he left for a career in the advertising industry.

adaptations. James regarded consciousness as an ever-changing *stream* or *flow* of images and sensations, not a set of lifeless building blocks, as the structuralists claimed.

The functionalists admired Charles Darwin, who deduced that creatures evolve in ways that favor survival. According to Darwin's principle of **natural selection**, physical features that help plants and animals adapt to their environments are retained in evolution. Similarly, the functionalists wanted to find out how the mind, perception, habits, and emotions help us adapt and survive.

What effect did functionalism have on modern psychology? Functionalism brought the study of animals into psychology. It also promoted *educational psychology* (the study of learning, teaching, classroom dynamics, and related topics). Learning makes us more adaptable, so the functionalists tried to find ways to improve education. For similar reasons, functionalism spurred the rise of *industrial/organizational psychology*, the study of people at work (see Module 75).

Behaviorism

Functionalism and structuralism were soon challenged by **behaviorism**, a school of thought in psychology that emphasizes the study of observable actions over study of the mind. Behaviorist John B. Watson objected strongly to the study of the "mind" or conscious experience. He believed that introspection is unscientific precisely because there is no objective way to settle disagreements between observers. Watson realized that he could study the overt behavior of animals even though he couldn't ask animals questions or know what they were thinking (Henley, 2019). He simply observed the relationship between any stimuli (i.e., events in the environment) and an animal's **response** (any muscular action, glandular activity, or other identifiable aspect of behavior). These observations were objective because they did not involve introspecting based on subjective experience. Why not, he asked, apply the same objectivity to study human behavior? For Watson and many other behaviorists, psychology was *not* the study of mind; it was the study of *behavior*.

Watson soon also adopted Russian physiologist Ivan Pavlov's (ee-VAHN PAV-lahv) concept of *conditioning* to explain most behavior. (A *conditioned response* is a learned reaction to a particular stimulus.) Watson claimed, "Give me a dozen healthy infants, well-formed, and my own special world to bring them up in, and I'll guarantee to take any one at random and train him to become any type of specialist I might select—doctor, lawyer, artist, merchant-chief, and yes, beggarman and thief" (Watson, 1913/1994).

Would most psychologists agree with Watson's claim? No. The early behaviorists believed that all responses are determined by stimuli. Today, this is regarded as an overstatement. Just the same, by stressing the study of observable behavior, behaviorism helped make psychology a natural science rather than a branch of philosophy.

Radical Behaviorism The best-known behaviorist, B. F. Skinner (1904–1990), believed that our actions are controlled by rewards and punishments. Many of Skinner's ideas about learning grew out of his work with rats and pigeons. Nevertheless, he believed that the same laws of behavior apply to humans.

As a **radical behaviorist**, Skinner not only rejected introspection, he also rejected the concept of *mind* as an inappropriate subject matter for scientific psychology. Skinner believed that behavior can be explained without reference to mental events, such as *thinking* (Schultz & Schultz, 2016).

Behaviorists deserve the credit for much of what we know about learning, conditioning, and the proper use of rewards and punishments. Skinner was convinced that a designed culture based on positive reinforcement could encourage desirable behavior. He also opposed the use of punishment because it doesn't teach correct responses. Too often, he believed, misguided

B. F. Skinner (1904–1990). Skinner studied simple behaviors under carefully controlled conditions. In addition to advancing psychology, he hoped that his radical brand of behaviorism would improve human lives.

Max Wertheimer (1880–1941). Wertheimer first proposed the Gestalt viewpoint to help explain perceptual illusions. He later promoted Gestalt psychology as a way to understand not only perception, problem solving, thinking, and social behavior, but also art, logic, philosophy, and politics.

rewards and punishments lead to destructive actions that create problems such as overpopulation, pollution, and war.

Behaviorism is also the source of behavior therapy, which uses learning principles to change problem behaviors such as overeating, unrealistic fears, or temper tantrums (see Module 67).

Gestalt Psychology

Imagine playing "Happy Birthday" on a flute and then on a guitar. The guitar duplicates none of the flute's sounds. Yet the melody is still recognizable—so long as the *relationship* between the notes remains the same.

Now imagine what would happen if you played the notes of "Happy Birthday" in the correct order, but at a rate of one per hour. What would you have? Nothing! The separate notes would no longer be a melody. Perceptually, the melody is more than the individual notes that define it.

Observations like these launched the Gestalt school of thought. German psychologist Max Wertheimer (VERT-hi-mer) was the first to advance the Gestalt viewpoint. It is inaccurate, he said, to analyze psychological events into pieces, or elements, as the structuralists did. Accordingly, **Gestalt psychology** studied thinking, learning, and perception as whole units, not by analyzing experiences into parts. Their slogan was, "The whole is greater than the sum of its parts." In fact, the German word *Gestalt* means form, pattern, or whole.

Like a melody, many experiences cannot be broken into smaller units, as the structuralists proposed. For this reason, studies of perception and personality have been especially influenced by the Gestalt viewpoint. Gestalt psychology also inspired a type of psychotherapy (see Module 66).

Psychoanalytic Psychology

As behaviorism's distrust of introspection pushed American psychology to grow more scientific, an Austrian doctor named Sigmund Freud, who also distrusted introspection, was developing radically different ideas that opened new horizons in art, literature, and history, as well as psychology (Barratt, 2013). Freud believed that mental life is like an iceberg: Only a small part is exposed. He called the area of the mind that lies outside personal awareness the *unconscious*.

This design is entirely made up of broken circles. However, as the Gestalt psychologists discovered, our perceptions have a powerful tendency to form meaningful patterns. Because of this tendency, you will probably see a cube in this design, even though it is only an illusion. Your whole perceptual experience exceeds the sum of its parts.

Natural selection Darwin's theory that evolution favors those plants and animals best suited to their living conditions.

Behaviorism School of thought in psychology that emphasizes study of observable actions over study of the mind.

Response Any muscular action, glandular activity, or other identifiable aspect of behavior.

Radical behaviorism A behaviorist approach that rejects both introspection and any study of covert mental events, such as thinking, as inappropriate topics for scientific psychology.

Gestalt psychology Study of thinking, learning, and perception in whole units, not by analysis into parts.

Sigmund Freud (1856–1939). For over 50 years, Freud probed the unconscious mind. In doing so, he altered contemporary views of human nature. His early experimentation with a "talking cure" for hysteria is regarded as the beginning of psychoanalysis. Through psychoanalysis, Freud added psychological treatment methods to psychiatry.

Today, Freud's notion is often referred to as the **dynamic unconscious**, to differentiate it from the concept of the *cognitive unconscious* (Zellner, 2011). According to Freud, our behavior is deeply influenced by unconscious thoughts, impulses, and desires—especially those concerning sex and aggression.

Freud theorized that many unconscious thoughts are *repressed*, or held out of awareness, because they are threatening. But sometimes, he said, they are revealed by dreams, emotions, or slips of the tongue. (Freudian slips are often humorous, as when a student who is late for class says, "I'm sorry I couldn't get here any later.") Because of this, Freud held that you cannot take people's self-reports literally, since much is left out and much of the rest is disguised. To more accurately interpret self-reports, he created **psychoanalysis**, the first fully developed psychotherapy, or "talking cure" to explore unconscious conflicts and emotional problems (see Module 65).

Like the behaviorists, Freud believed that all thoughts, emotions, and actions are *determined.* In other words, nothing is an accident. If we probe deeply enough, we will find the causes of every thought or action. Unlike the behaviorists, he believed that unconscious processes (not external stimuli) were responsible for what people do.

Freud was also among the first to appreciate that childhood affects adult personality (perhaps best expressed in the quote by poet William Wordsworth, "the child is father to the man").

It wasn't long before some of Freud's students modified his ideas. Known as **neo-Freudians** (*neo* means "new" or "recent"), they accepted some of Freud's theory but revised parts of it. Many, for instance, placed less emphasis on sex and aggression and more on social motives and relationships. Some well-known neo-Freudians are Alfred Adler, Anna Freud (Freud's daughter), Karen Horney (HORN-eye), Carl Jung (yoong), Otto Rank (rahnk), and Erik Erikson. Today, Freud's ideas have been altered so much that few strictly psychoanalytic psychologists are left. However, his legacy is still evident in **psychodynamic theory**, which continues to emphasize internal motives, conflicts, and unconscious forces (Moran, F., 2010).

Humanistic Psychology

For a time, radical behaviorism and psychoanalysis combined to offer the unsettling view that we humans don't consciously know much about ourselves. Eventually, *humanists* like Abraham Maslow and Carl Rogers questioned the Freudian idea that we are ruled solely by unconscious forces. They also were uncomfortable with the radical behaviorist emphasis on conditioning and the rejection of mental events, such as thinking, as appropriate topics for scientific psychology (Schultz & Schultz, 2016).

Both views have a strong undercurrent of **determinism**—the idea that behavior is determined by forces beyond our control. Instead, humanists stress **free will**, our ability to make conscious, voluntary choices. Of course, past experiences and the unconscious do affect us. Nevertheless, humanists believe that people can freely *choose* to live more creative, meaningful, and satisfying lives.

Humanistic psychology, then, is the study of people as inherently good and consciously motivated to learn and improve. Humanists believe that everyone has this potential, and they seek ways to help it emerge. Humanists are interested in psychological needs for love, self-esteem, belonging, self-expression, creativity, and spirituality. Such needs, they believe, are as important as our biological urges for food and water. For example, newborn infants deprived of human love may die just as surely as they would if deprived of food. Maslow's concept of self-actualization is a key feature of humanism. **Self-actualization** refers to the process of fully developing personal potential.

How scientific is the humanistic approach? Initially, humanists were less interested in treating psychology as a science. They stressed subjective factors, such as one's self-image, self-evaluation, and frame of reference. (*Self-image* is your perception of your own body, personality, and capabilities. *Self-evaluation* refers to appraising yourself as good or bad. A *frame of reference* is a mental perspective used to interpret events.) Today, humanists still try to understand

Abraham Maslow (1908–1970). As a founder of humanistic psychology, Maslow was interested in studying people of exceptional mental health. Such self-actualized people, he believed, make full use of their talents and abilities. Maslow offered his positive view of human potential as an alternative to the perspectives of behaviorism and psychoanalysis.

TABLE 3.1 | The Early Development of Psychology

Perspective	Date	Notable Events
Experimental psychology	1879	Wilhelm Wundt opens the first psychology laboratory in Germany.
	1883	The first psychology lab in the United States is founded at Johns Hopkins University, in Baltimore, Maryland.
	1886	The first psychology textbook is published in the United States; written by John Dewey.
Structuralism	1898	Edward Titchener advances psychology based on introspection.
Functionalism	1890	William James publishes *Principles of Psychology.*
	1892	American Psychological Association is founded.
Psychodynamic psychology	1895	Sigmund Freud publishes his first studies.
	1900	Freud publishes *The Interpretation of Dreams.*
Behaviorism	1906	Ivan Pavlov reports his research on conditioned reflexes.
	1913	John Watson presents the behaviorist viewpoint.
Gestalt psychology	1912	Max Wertheimer and other researchers advance the Gestalt viewpoint.
Humanistic psychology	1942	Carl Rogers publishes *Counseling and Psychotherapy.*
	1943	Abraham Maslow publishes *A Theory of Human Motivation.*
Cognitive psychology	1956	George Miller publishes *The Magic Number Seven, Plus or Minus Two.*

how we perceive ourselves and experience the world. However, most now do research to test their ideas, just as other psychologists do (Schneider, Bugental, & Pierson, 2001).

Cognitive Behaviorism and Cognitive Psychology

When the radical behaviorists rejected introspection as a legitimate scientific method, they also deliberately ignored the role that thinking plays in our lives. This approach was eventually criticized as "throwing the baby out with the bath water." As a result, behaviorism became less radical, as references to mental processes (thinking) began to be used to explain even the behavior of animals (Zentall, 2002, 2011).

As an example, let's say that a rat frequently visits a particular location in a maze because it offers access to food. A behaviorist would say that the rat visits this location because it is rewarded by the pleasure of eating each time that it goes there. A **cognitive behaviorist** would add that, in addition, the rat *expects* to find food at the location. This is the cognitive part of the rat's behavior.

By the late 1950s, **cognitive psychology** took form as the study of information processing, thinking, reasoning, and problem solving (Goldstein & Brockmole, 2017; Neisser, 1967). Unlike radical behaviorism, cognitive psychology is open to studying the mind and mental events. Like behaviorism (and unlike introspectionism), cognitive psychology relies primarily upon objective observation rather than subjective introspection. ■ **Table 3.1** presents a summary of psychology's early development.

Dynamic unconscious In Freudian theory, the parts of the mind that are beyond awareness, especially conflicts, impulses, and desires not directly known to a person.

Psychoanalysis Freudian approach to psychotherapy emphasizing the exploration of unconscious conflicts.

Neo-Freudians Psychologists who accept the broad features of Freud's theory but have revised the theory to fit their own concepts.

Psychodynamic theory Any theory of behavior that emphasizes internal conflicts, motives, and unconscious forces.

Determinism The idea that all behavior has prior causes that would completely explain one's choices and actions if all such causes were known.

Free will The idea that human beings are capable of making choices or decisions themselves.

Humanistic psychology Study of people as inherently good and motivated to learn and improve.

Self-actualization The process of fully developing personal potentials.

Cognitive behaviorism An approach that combines behavioral principles with cognition (i.e., perception, thinking, and anticipation) to explain behavior.

Cognitive psychology The study of information processing, thinking, reasoning, and problem solving.

The Importance of Diversity in Psychology

Were all the early psychologists Caucasian men? Although women and ethnic minorities were long underrepresented among psychologists, there *were* a few pioneers (Minton, 2000). In 1894, Margaret Washburn became the first woman to be awarded a PhD in psychology. By 1906 in the United States, about one psychologist in 10 was a woman. In 1920, Francis Cecil Sumner became the first African-American man to earn a doctoral degree in psychology. Inez Beverly Prosser, the first African-American female psychologist, was awarded her PhD in 1933.

The predominance of early Caucasian male psychologists is worrisome because it inadvertently introduced a narrowness into psychological theory and research. As one example, Lawrence Kohlberg (1969) proposed a theory about how we develop moral values. His studies suggested that women were morally "immature" because they were not as concerned with justice as men were. However, few women were involved in doing the studies, and Kohlberg merely *assumed* that theories based on men also applied to women. In response, Carol Gilligan (1982) provided evidence that women were more likely to make moral choices based on caring rather than justice. From this point of view, it was men who were morally immature. Today, we recognize that both justice and caring perspectives may be essential to adult wisdom. (See Module 15.)

Margaret Washburn (1871–1939). In 1908, Washburn published *The Animal Mind*, an influential textbook on animal behavior. In 1921 she became the second female to serve as President of the American Psychological Association (Mary Whiton Calkins was the first).

Francis Cecil Sumner (1895–1954). Sumner served as chair of the Psychology Department at Howard University and wrote articles critical of the underrepresentation of African Americans in U.S. colleges and universities.

Inez Beverly Prosser (c. 1895–1934). Prosser was one of the early leaders in the debate about how to best educate African-American children.

Kohlberg's oversight is just one form of **gender bias in research**. This term refers to the tendency for females to be underrepresented as research subjects and female-related topics to be ignored by many investigators. Consequently, investigators assume that conclusions based on men also apply to women. But without directly studying women, it is impossible to know how often this assumption is wrong. A related problem occurs when researchers combine results from men and women. Doing so can hide important male–female differences.

An additional problem is that unequal numbers of men and women may volunteer for some kinds of research. For example, in studies of sexuality, more male college students volunteer to participate than females (Wiederman, 1999). Conversely, more females than males participate in studies of nursing (Polit & Beck, 2013).

The Perils of Ignoring Diversity: Who's WEIRD?

Similar types of bias also arise when it comes to people of different ages, sexual orientations, races, and ethnic groups (Denmark, Rabinowitz, & Sechzer, 2005; Guthrie, 2004). Far too many conclusions have been created by, and based on, small groups of people who do not represent the rich tapestry of humanity. For example, to this day, the vast majority of human participants in psychology experiments are recruited from introductory psychology courses. This fact led psychologist Edward Tolman to note that much of psychology is based on two sets of subjects—rats and college sophomores—and to joke that rats are certainly not people and that some college sophomores may not be, either! Further, most of these participants have, over the years, been Caucasian members of the middle class, and most of the researchers themselves have been Caucasian males (Guthrie, 2004). While none of this automatically invalidates the results of psychology experiments, it may place limitations on their implications.

Perhaps the most general research bias of all becomes clear when you ask about people who live in the oddest societies in the world. The answer is just plain WEIRD (Western, Educated,

Industrialized, Rich, and Democratic). According to Henrich, Heine, and Norenzayan (2010), we have a strongly ingrained tendency to assume that what Western researchers discover studying Western research participants is the norm in human behavior and that the behavior of those in other societies is unusual. However, after a careful review of studies comparing Westerners to people from other societies, Henrich, Heine, and Norenzayan (2010) concluded that exactly the opposite is the case. *We* are WEIRD, so we should be careful to assume that what we learn from studying behavior in our society illuminates the behavior of people in non-Western societies.

The solution to problems of bias is straightforward: We need to encourage a much wider array of people to become researchers and, when possible, researchers need to include a much wider array of people in their studies. In recognition of human diversity, many researchers are doing just that (Henrich, Heine, & Norenzayan, 2010; Lum, 2011).

Fortunately, psychology is coming to better reflect human diversity as the proportion of women and racial/ethnic minorities in the psychology work force continues to increase. Currently about 65% of psychologists are women, 16% are members of racial/ethnic minorities, and 5% have a disability (American Psychological Association, 2017a, 2018).

The Biopsychosocial Model—One Model to Rule Them All

Learning Outcome 3.2 Define the three contemporary perspectives in psychology and explain why they are complementary

Key insights from the early schools of thought continue to influence contemporary psychology. Some early systems, such as structuralism, have disappeared entirely, while new ones have gained prominence. Also, viewpoints such as functionalism and Gestalt psychology have been absorbed into newer, broader perspectives.

Today, one overarching perspective has gained prominence. The **biopsychosocial model** accepts that human behavior and mental processes are strongly influenced by a combination of *biological*, *psychological*, and *social* factors. As all-encompassing as this may at first seem, in practice the biopsychosocial model cannot by itself tell us *which* particular biological, psychological, and social factors influence any particular behavior. Only more detailed research can yield specific answers. Instead, it serves as a constant reminder of the value of taking a biological, psychological, *and* social perspective on that behavior (■ **Table 3.2**).

For example, *anorexia nervosa* is an eating disorder involving a compulsive desire to lose weight (see Module 43). Instead of focusing exclusively on the biological or psychological factors underlying anorexia, the biopsychosocial model suggests we examine social factors as well. Sure enough, research from the social perspective suggests that idealized body images presented in the media play a role in triggering this potentially fatal disorder (Hausenblas et al., 2013).

The Biological Perspective

The **biological perspective** seeks to explain behavior in terms of biological principles such as evolution, genetics, and brain processes. **Evolutionary psychology** is an approach that emphasizes inherited, adaptive aspects of behavior and mental processes. *Biopsychologists* and others who study the brain and nervous system, such as biologists and biochemists, comprise the broader field of **neuroscience**. Using new techniques, *neuroscientists* are producing exciting insights about how the brain relates to thinking, feelings, perception, abnormal behavior, and other topics.

The Psychological Perspective

The **psychological perspective** views behavior as the result of psychological processes within each person. This view continues to emphasize scientific observation, just as the early psychologists did. However, *cognitive psychology* has gained prominence in recent years as researchers have devised suitable operational definitions and research methods to objectively study mental processes, such as thinking, memory, language, perception, problem solving, consciousness, and creativity (Reed, 2013). With a renewed interest in thinking, it can be said that psychology has finally "regained consciousness" (Robins, Gosling, & Craik, 1998).

Gender bias in research A tendency for females and female-related issues to be underrepresented in research, whether psychological or otherwise.

Biological perspective The attempt to explain behavior in terms of underlying biological principles.

Biopsychosocial model Dominant modern perspective which holds that human behavior and mental processes are strongly influenced by a combination of biological, psychological, and social factors.

Evolutionary psychology Approach that emphasizes inherited, adaptive aspects of behavior and mental processes.

Neuroscience The broader field of biopsychologists and others who study the brain and nervous system, such as biologists and biochemists.

Psychological perspective The traditional view that behavior is shaped by psychological processes occurring at the level of the individual.

TABLE 3.2 | Contemporary Ways to Look at Behavior

Biological Perspective
Biopsychological View Key idea: *Human and animal behavior is the result of internal physical, chemical, and biological processes.* Seeks to explain behavior through activity of the brain and nervous system, physiology, genetics, the endocrine system, and biochemistry; a neutral, reductionistic, and mechanistic view of human nature.
Evolutionary View Key idea: *Human and animal behavior is the result of the process of evolution.* Seeks to explain behavior through principles based on natural selection; a neutral, reductionistic, and mechanistic view of human nature.
Psychological Perspective
Behaviorist View Key idea: *Behavior is shaped and controlled by one's environment.* Emphasizes the study of observable behavior and the effects of learning; stresses the influence of external rewards and punishments; a neutral, scientific, and somewhat mechanistic view of human nature.
Cognitive View Key idea: *Much human behavior can be understood in terms of the mental processing of information.* Concerned with thinking, knowing, perception, understanding, memory, decision making, and judgment; explains behavior in terms of information processing; a neutral, somewhat computer-like view of human nature.
Psychodynamic View Key idea: *Behavior is directed by forces within one's personality that are often hidden or unconscious.* Emphasizes internal impulses, desires, and conflicts—especially those that are unconscious; views behavior as the result of clashing forces within personality; a somewhat negative, pessimistic view of human nature.

Freudian psychoanalysis continues to evolve into the broader *psychodynamic view.* Although many of Freud's ideas have been challenged or refuted, psychodynamic psychologists continue to trace our behavior to unconscious mental activity. They also seek to develop therapies to help people lead happier, fuller lives. The same is true of humanistic psychologists, although they stress subjective, conscious experience and the positive side of human nature.

The Sociocultural Perspective

The **sociocultural perspective** stresses the impact that social and cultural contexts have on our behavior. We are rapidly becoming a multicultural society. Over 100 million Americans are now African American, Hispanic, Asian American, Native American, or Pacific Islander (Humes, Jones, & Ramirez, 2011). In some large cities, such as Detroit and Baltimore, minority groups have become the majority.

Cultural Relativity How has this affected psychology? In the past, psychology was based mostly on the cultures of North America and Europe. Now, we must ask, do the principles of Western psychology apply to people in all cultures (WEIRD, remember?)? Are some psychological concepts invalid in other cultures? Are any universal?

As psychologists have probed such questions, one thing has become clear: **Cultural relativity**—the idea that behavior must be judged relative to the values of the culture in which it occurs—can greatly affect our understanding of "other people." Most of what we think, feel, and do is influenced, in one

Rawpixel.com/Shutterstock.com

As illustrated by this photo of office co-workers, America is becoming more diverse. To fully understand human behavior, personal differences based on age, race, culture, ethnicity, gender, and sexual orientation must be taken into account.

way or another, by the social and cultural worlds in which we live (Baumeister & Bushman, 2021; Henrich, Heine, & Norenzayan, 2010). This includes the diagnosis and treatment of mental disorders (Lum, 2011). To be effective, psychologists must be sensitive to people who are ethnically and culturally different from themselves (Lowman, 2013; see Module 65).

A Broader View of Diversity

In addition to cultural differences, the behavior of people is influenced by differences in age, ethnicity, gender, religion, disability, and sexual orientation, which all affect the social norms that guide behavior. **Social norms** are rules that define acceptable and expected behavior for members of various groups. Too often, the unstated standard for determining what is average, normal, or correct has been the behavior of middle-aged, white, heterosexual, middle-class Western males (Henrich, Heine, & Norenzayan, 2010). An appreciation of the fuller spectrum of human diversity can enrich your life as well as your understanding of psychology (Helgeson, 2012).

The Whole Human Today, many psychologists realize that any single perspective is unlikely to fully explain complex human behavior. As a result, they are *eclectic* (ek-LEK-tik) and draw insights from a variety of perspectives. As we will see throughout this book, insights from one perspective often complement insights from the others as we seek to better understand the whole human.

Psychologists—Guaranteed Not to Shrink

Learning Outcome 3.3 Discuss some of the major specialties in modern psychology, including the distinction between researchers and clinicians

Do all psychologists do therapy and treat abnormal behavior? Only about 45 percent of psychologists are directly involved in providing mental health services. Regardless, every **psychologist** is highly trained in the methods, knowledge, and theories of psychology. Psychologists have usually earned a master's degree or a doctorate, typically requiring several years of postgraduate training. About 31 percent are employed full time at colleges or universities (including medical schools), where they teach and do research, consulting, or therapy. The remainder give psychological tests, do research in other settings, or serve as consultants to business, industry, government, or the military (see ➤ **Figure 3.1**).

At present, the American Psychological Association (APA) consists of more than 50 divisions, each reflecting special skills or areas of interest. No matter where they are employed, or what their area of specialization is, many psychologists do research. Some do *basic research*, in which they seek knowledge for its own sake. For example,

Sociocultural perspective The focus on the importance of social and cultural contexts in influencing the behavior of individuals.

Cultural relativity The idea that behavior must be judged relative to the values of the culture in which it occurs.

Social norms Rules that define acceptable and expected behavior for members of a group.

Psychologist A person highly trained in the methods, factual knowledge, and theories of psychology.

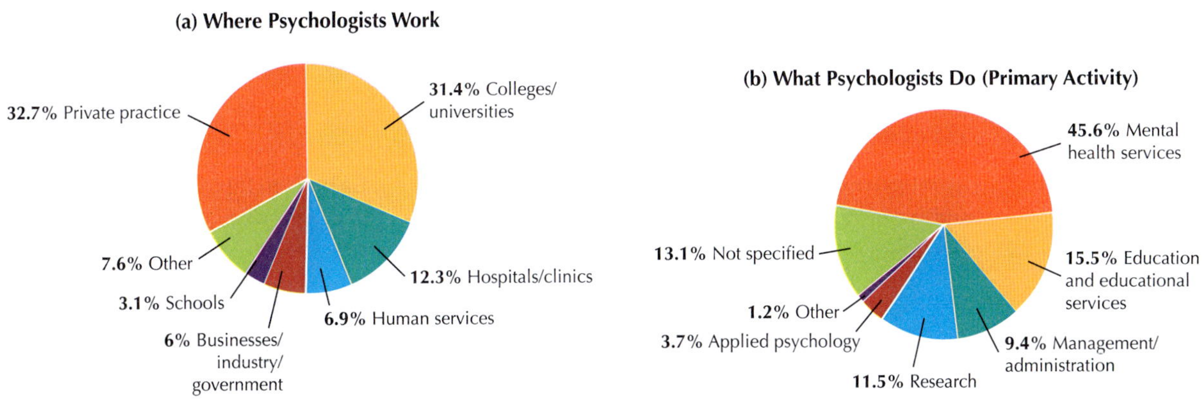

➤ **Figure 3.1**

Where psychologists work and what they do. (*a*) Where psychologists work. (*b*) This chart shows the main activities that psychologists do at work. Any one psychologist might participate in several of these activities during a workweek. As you can see, most psychologists specialize in applied areas and work in applied settings (American Psychological Association, 2017a).

a psychologist might study memory simply to understand how it works. Others do *applied research* to solve immediate practical problems, such as finding ways to improve athletic performance (Davey, 2011). Some do both types of research. Some of the major specialties are listed in ■ **Table 3.3**.

Animals and Psychology *Research involving animals was mentioned in some of the psychology specialties listed in Table 3.3. Why is that?* You may be surprised to learn that psychologists are interested in the behavior of *any* living creature—from flatworms to humans. Indeed, some comparative

TABLE 3.3 | Types of Psychologists and What They Do

Specialty		Typical Activities	Sample Research Topic
Biopsychology	B*	Researches the brain, nervous system, and other physical origins of behavior	"I've been doing some exciting research on how the brain controls hunger."
Clinical	A	Does psychotherapy; investigates clinical problems; develops methods of treatment	"I'm curious about the relationship between early childhood trauma and adult relationships and how it can help adults be more successful in their marriages."
Cognitive	B	Studies human thinking and information-processing abilities	"I want to know how reasoning, problem solving, memory, and other mental processes relate to playing computer games."
Community	A	Promotes community-wide mental health through research, prevention, education, and consultation	"How can we prevent the spread of sexually transmitted diseases more effectively? That's what I want to understand better."
Comparative	B	Studies and compares the behaviors of different species, especially animals	"I'm fascinated by the communication abilities of porpoises."
Consumer	A	Researches packaging, advertising, marketing methods, and characteristics of consumers	"My job is to improve the marketing of products that are environment-friendly."
Counseling	A	Does psychotherapy and personal counseling; researches emotional disturbances and counseling methods	"I am focused on understanding more about why people become hoarders and how to help them stop."
Cultural	B	Studies the ways in which culture, subculture, and ethnic group membership affect behavior	"I am interested in how culture affects human eating behavior, especially the foods that we eat and whether we eat with a spoon, chopsticks, or our fingers."
Developmental	A, B	Conducts research on infant, child, adolescent, and adult development; does clinical work with disturbed children; acts as a consultant to parents and schools	"I'm focusing on transitioning from the teenage years to early adulthood."
Educational	A	Investigates classroom dynamics, teaching styles, and learning; develops educational tests, evaluates educational programs	"My passion is to figure out how to help people with different learning styles be effective learners."
Engineering	A	Does applied research on the design of machinery, computers, airlines, automobiles, and so on for business, industry, and the military	"I'm studying how people use movement-based computer interfaces, like Kinect on the X-box."

TABLE 3.3 | (Continued)

Specialty		Typical Activities	Sample Research Topic
Environmental	A, B	Studies the effects of urban noise, crowding, attitudes toward the environment, and human use of space; acts as a consultant on environmental issues	"I am concerned about global warming and want to understand what impact rising temperatures have on human culture."
Evolutionary	B	Studies how behavior is guided by patterns that evolved during the long history of humankind	"I am studying some interesting trends in male and female mating choices."
Forensic	A	Studies problems of crime and crime prevention, rehabilitation programs, prisons, and courtroom dynamics; selects candidates for police work	"I am interested in improving the reliability of eyewitness testimony during trials."
Gender	B	Researches differences between males and females, the acquisition of gender identity, and the role of gender throughout life	"I want to understand how young boys and girls are influenced by gender stereotypes."
Health	A, B	Studies the relationship between behavior and health; uses psychological principles to promote health and prevent illness	"How to help people overcome drug addictions is my field of study."
Industrial-organizational	A	Selects job applicants; does skills analysis; evaluates on-the-job training; improves work environments and human relations in organizations and work settings	"Which plays a greater role in successful management styles, intelligence or emotion? That is my question."
Learning	B	Studies how and why learning occurs; develops theories of learning	"Right now, I'm investigating how patterns of reinforcement affect learning. I am especially interested in superstitious conditioning."
Medical	A	Applies psychology to manage medical problems, such as the emotional impact of illness, self-screening for cancer, and compliance in taking medicine	"I want to know how to help people take charge of their own health."
Personality	B	Studies personality traits and dynamics; develops theories of personality and tests for assessing personality traits	"I am especially interested in the personality profiles of people who are willing to take extreme risks."
School	A	Does psychological testing, referrals, and emotional and vocational counseling of students; detects and treats learning disabilities; improves classroom learning	"My focus is finding out how to keep students in school instead of having them drop out."
Sensation and perception	B	Studies the sense organs and the process of perception; investigates the mechanisms of sensation; develops theories about how perception occurs	"I am using a perceptual theory to study how we are able to recognize faces in a crowd."
Social	B	Investigates human social behavior, including attitudes, conformity, persuasion, prejudice, friendship, aggression, helping, and so forth	"My interest is interpersonal attraction. I place two strangers in a room and analyze how strongly they are attracted to each other."

*Research in this area is typically applied (A), basic (B), or both (A, B).

C_Gara/Shutterstock.com

This timber wolf is wearing a tracking collar. Through tracking studies and other tests, psychologists are better able to understand how wild wolves think and communicate (Range, Möslinger, & Virányi, 2012). Since wolves are endangered across much of their historical range, this understanding may prove crucial in enhancing efforts to conserve these intriguing creatures.

psychologists spend their entire careers studying rats, cats, dogs, parrots, or chimpanzees.

Although only a small percentage of psychological studies involve animals, they include many different types of research (Baker & Serdikoff, 2013). Some psychologists use an **animal model** to discover principles that apply to humans. For instance, animal studies have helped us understand stress, learning, obesity, aging, sleep, and many other topics. Psychology can also benefit animals. Behavioral studies can help us better care for domestic animals and those in zoos, as well as conserve endangered species in the wild.

Helping People

Although most psychologists help people in one way or another, those interested in emotional problems usually specialize in clinical or counseling psychology (see Table 3.3). A **clinical psychologist** treats psychological problems or does research on therapies and mental disorders. In contrast, a **counseling psychologist** generally treats milder problems, such as troubles at work or school.

To become a clinical psychologist, it is best to have a doctorate (PhD, PsyD, or EdD). Most clinical psychologists have a PhD and follow a *scientist-as-practitioner* model—that is, they are trained to do either research or therapy. Many do both. Other clinicians earn the PsyD (Doctor of Psychology) degree, which emphasizes therapy skills rather than research (Stricker, 2011).

Does a psychologist need a license to offer therapy? Yes. Psychologists must also meet stringent legal requirements. To work as a clinical or counseling psychologist, you must have a license issued by a state examining board. However, the law does not prevent people from calling themselves almost anything else they choose—therapist, rebirther, primal feeling facilitator, cosmic aura balancer, or life skills coach—or from selling "psychological" services to anyone willing to pay. Beware of people with self-proclaimed titles. Even if their intentions are honorable, they may have little actual training. A licensed psychologist who chooses to use a particular type of therapy is not the same as someone trained solely in that technique.

Licensed clinical and counseling psychologists must also follow an ethical code that stresses (1) high levels of competence, integrity, and responsibility; (2) respect for people's rights to privacy, dignity, confidentiality, and personal freedom; and, above all, (3) protection of the client's welfare (American Psychological Association, 2017b; Barnett et al., 2007). (See Module 16 for a more general discussion of ethics.)

Other Mental Health Professionals

Clinical and counseling psychologists often coordinate their efforts with psychiatrists, psychoanalysts, counselors, and other mental health professionals. Each has a specific blend of training and skills.

Psychologists are all shrinks, right? Nope. A *shrink* (a slang term derived from the term *head shrinkers*) is a **psychiatrist**, a medical doctor who treats serious mental disorders, often by prescribing drugs. Today, many psychiatrists also use psychotherapy. Psychologists in New Mexico, Louisiana, and Illinois can also legally prescribe drugs, as can psychologists in the U.S. military. It will be interesting to see whether other states grant similar privileges (McGrath & Moore, 2010).

Animal model In research, an animal whose behavior is studied to derive principles that may apply to human behavior.

Clinical psychologist A psychologist who specializes in the treatment of psychological and behavioral disturbances or who does research on such disturbances.

Counseling psychologist A psychologist who specializes in the treatment of milder emotional and behavioral disturbances.

Psychiatrist A medical doctor with additional training in the diagnosis and treatment of mental and emotional disorders.

Psychoanalyst A mental health professional (usually a medical doctor) trained to practice psychoanalysis.

Counselor A mental health professional who specializes in helping people with problems that do not involve serious mental disorders; examples include marriage counselors, career counselors, and school counselors.

To be a psychoanalyst, you must have a moustache and goatee, spectacles, a German accent, and a well-padded couch—or so the stereotype goes. In reality, to become a **psychoanalyst**, you must have an MD or PhD degree, plus further training in Freudian psychoanalysis. In other words, either a physician or a psychologist may become a psychoanalyst by learning a specific type of psychotherapy.

In many states, counselors also do mental health work. A **counselor** is an adviser who helps solve problems with marriage, career, school, work, or the like. To be a licensed counselor (such as a marriage and family counselor, a child counselor, or a school counselor) typically requires a master's degree (but it doesn't have to be in psychology), plus one or two years of full-time supervised counseling experience. Counselors learn practical helping skills and do not treat serious mental disorders.

MODULE 3 Psychology Then and Now—Learning Outcomes Revisited

3.1 Distinguish between the following approaches to psychology: Structuralism, functionalism, behaviorism, gestalt psychology, psychoanalytic psychology, humanistic psychology, and cognitive psychology, as well as address the importance of diversity in psychology

Wilhelm Wundt used introspection to study conscious experience. His student, Titchener, developed structuralism, a kind of "mental chemistry" based on introspection. William James saw mental events as a continuous stream of events rather than the static building blocks proposed by Titchener's structuralist approach. He developed functionalism in an effort to better understand how behavior helps us to adapt to the environment. His interest in adaptation created a natural bridge with Darwin's views of natural selection and evolution. Behaviorists rejected introspection, choosing instead to study objective behavior. Radical behaviorists rejected the study of mind altogether. Gestalt psychologists such as Wertheimer believed in the value of introspection, but disagreed with structuralists like Titchener about the experience. While structuralists valued the idea of analyzing psychological events in terms of their individual components, Gestalt theorists felt that these events could only be studied as whole units. Sigmund Freud's psychoanalytic psychology is based on a distrust of introspection and the importance of properly interpreting the hidden meaning of conscious thoughts. Humanistic psychology embraced conscious experience, human potential, and personal growth. Cognitive psychology involves studying mental processes, just as Wundt and Titchener did. However, cognitive psychologists approach the study of mental processes more objectively than Wundt and Titchener by operationally defining them in terms of objective measures. Gender bias was inadvertently introduced into psychological research because most early psychologists were Caucasian men, and because the participants in much of the early research were men. Similarly, culture bias stems from an over-reliance on research participants who are from WEIRD (Western, Educated, Industrialized, Rich, and Democratic) societies.

3.2 List the three contemporary perspectives in psychology and explain why they are complementary

The three contemporary perspectives in psychology are the biological, psychological, and social perspectives. They are complementary in that the biopsychosocial model holds that human behavior and mental processes are best understood by combining insights from biology (including biopsychology and evolutionary psychology), psychology (including motivation thinking, personality, perception, and language) and the social world (including culture, access to education, and poverty). Because it considers the three perspectives simultaneously, it is better able to explain complex human behavior (such as eating disorders) and the full range of human diversity.

3.3 Discuss some of the major specialties in modern psychology, including the distinction between researchers and clinicians

The field of psychology now has dozens of specialties, including developmental, forensic, community, environmental, and industrial/organizational psychology. Some psychologists work primarily as researchers, and psychological research can be basic or applied. Researchers may study animals either because they are interested in animal behavior or because animals provide a model of human behavior. Some psychologists work primarily as clinicians, helping other people with mental health issues. They often work alongside other mental health workers (e.g., psychiatrists, psychoanalysts, and psychiatric nurses) whose training and methods differ considerably.

Reflective Practice

Content Check

1. A psychotherapist is working with a person from an ethnic group other than her own. She should be aware of how cultural relativity and ____________ affect behavior.
   a. anthropomorphic error
   b. operational definitions
   c. biased sampling
   d. social norms

Match the following research areas with the topics that they cover.

____ 2. Developmental psychology	A. Attitudes, groups, leadership
____ 3. Learning	B. Behavior as related to the legal system
____ 4. Personality	C. Brain and nervous system
____ 5. Sensation and perception	D. Child psychology
____ 6. Biopsychology	E. Individual differences, motivation
____ 7. Social psychology	F. Processing visual, auditory, and other information
____ 8. Forensic psychology	G. Conditioning, memory

9. A psychologist who specializes in treating human emotional difficulties is called a(n) ________________ psychologist.

Skill Check

Think Critically

10. Modern sciences like psychology are built on intersubjective observations, which can be verified by two or more independent observers. Did structuralism meet this standard? Why or why not?

Self-Reflect

At first, many students think that psychology is primarily about abnormal behavior and psychotherapy. Did you? How would you describe the field now? Which contemporary perspective most closely matches your own view of behavior? Can you explain why so many psychologists are eclectic? Which specialty in psychology is most interesting to you? Why?

ANSWERS

1. d 2. D 3. G 4. E 5. F 6. C 7. A 8. B 9. clinical or counseling 10. No, it did not. Structuralism's downfall was that each observer examined the contents of his or her own mind—which is something that no other person can observe.

Introducing Psychology
The Psychology Experiment

MODULE 4

Getting Causality Right

Would he feel stared at in a pair of those new wearable computer smart glasses? Chan was intrigued that they could display directions while he walked downtown from location to location. It would certainly make his job finding and interviewing people a lot easier. But Chan worried that people would stop to gawk. To see if they would, he borrowed a pair from someone who worked for a company that created them. After wearing them to work for a few days, he realized that people didn't seem to notice them much, compared to his regular glasses. At the same time, the smart glasses seemed to be very helpful; he even wondered if it would be okay to use them while driving his car. Case closed; Chan resolved to get a pair as soon as possible.

Ranta Images/Shutterstock.com

Like Chan, we all conduct little experiments to detect cause-and-effect connections. In a more formal way, that is exactly what psychologists do when *they* want to understand why we act the way we do. Let's see why.

~LEARNING OUTCOMES~

After reading this module you should be able to:

4.1 Explain how an experiment is performed

4.2 Explain what a double-blind experiment is and why it is necessary for the evaluation of causal hypotheses

The Experimental Method—Where Cause Meets Effect

Learning Outcome 4.1 Explain how an experiment is performed

Many different research strategies may be used to investigate human behavior. However, to discover the *causes* of behavior, we must usually conduct an **experiment**—a study in which the investigator manipulates at least one variable while measuring at least one other variable. These are formal trials undertaken to confirm or disconfirm a hypothesis about the causes of behavior (although causes are sometimes revealed by naturalistic observation or correlations). The experimental method allows the careful control of conditions to bring cause-and-effect relationships into sharp focus (Stangor, 2015). Hence, it is generally accepted as the

Experiment A study in which the investigator manipulates at least one variable while measuring at least one other variable.

most powerful scientific research tool. To perform an experiment, you would do the following:

1. Directly vary a condition that you think might affect behavior.
2. Create two or more groups of participants. These groups should be alike in all ways *except* the condition you are varying. Usually, one group serves as a control group with which the other groups are compared.
3. Record whether varying the condition has any effect on behavior.

Suppose that Chan just happened to be a psychologist who wanted to find out if using smart glasses while driving affects the likelihood of having an accident. First, he would form two groups of people. Then he could give the members of one group a test of driving ability while using their smart glasses. The second group would take the same test without using smart glasses. By comparing the average driving ability scores for the two groups, he could tell if the use of smart glasses affects driving ability.

As you can see, the simplest psychological experiment is based on two groups of **experimental subjects**—animals or people whose behavior is investigated. Human subjects are typically called **participants**. One group is the *experimental group*; the other becomes the *control group*. The experimental group and the control group are treated exactly alike except for the condition (or *variable*) that you intentionally vary.

Variables and Groups

What are the different kinds of variables? A **variable** is any factor or characteristic that is manipulated or measured in research. Identifying causes and effects in an experiment involves three types of variables:

1. An **independent variable** is a variable that is manipulated by the researcher in an experiment. The experimenter chooses the values that this variable takes. Independent variables are suspected *causes* for differences in behavior.
2. A **dependent variable** is a variable that measures any effect of manipulating the dependent variable. It measures the extent to which behavior *depends* on the independent variable—that is, dependent variables reveal the *effects* that independent variables have on *behavior.* Such effects are often revealed by measures of performance, such as test scores.
3. An **extraneous variable** is a condition or factor that a researcher wants to prevent from affecting the outcome of the experiment.

We can apply these terms to Chan's smart glasses/driving experiment in this way:

1. The use of smart glasses is the independent variable—he wants to know if using smart glasses affects driving ability.
2. Driving ability (defined by scores achieved on a test of driving ability) is the dependent variable—he wants to know if the ability to drive well depends on whether a person is using smart glasses.
3. All other variables that could affect driving ability are extraneous. Examples of extraneous variables are the number of hours slept the night before the test, driving experience, and familiarity with the vehicle used in the experiment.

As we write this book, your authors are unaware of any published research report testing the hypothesis that using smart glasses interferes with driving. But it would be unsurprising if this turned out to be true, since engaging in almost any extra activity takes the focus away from driving safely. For example, psychologist Davis Strayer and his colleagues have confirmed that almost all drivers talking on cellphones drive no better than people who are legally drunk, and texters perform even worse (Drews et al., 2009; Strayer, Drews, & Crouch, 2006; Watson & Strayer, 2010).

As you can see, the **experimental group** is the group that receives the treatment that the study is designed to test (in the preceding example, this would be the group that wore the glasses). The **control group** includes the subjects in an experimental study who do not receive the treatment being investigated (in the preceding example, this would be the group that didn't wear the glasses).

Is a control group really needed? Can't people just drive a car while navigating wearing smart glasses to see if they do worse? Worse than what? The control group provides a *point of reference* for comparison with the scores in the experimental group. Without a control group, it would be impossible to tell whether using smart glasses had any effect on driving ability. If the average test score of the experimental group is lower than the average of the control group, we can conclude that using smart glasses negatively affects driving ability. If there is no difference, it's clear that the independent variable had no effect on driving ability.

In this experiment, driving ability (indicated by scores on the test) is the dependent variable. We are asking: Does the independent variable *affect* the dependent variable? (Does using smart glasses affect or influence driving ability?)

Random Assignment *How do we know that the people in one group aren't just worse drivers than those in the other group?*

It's true that personal differences in driving ability might affect the experiment. However, an extraneous variable like this one can be controlled by randomly assigning people to groups. **Random assignment** is the use of chance to place subjects in experimental and control groups. In practice, this means that a participant has an equal chance of being in either the experimental group or the control group. Randomization balances personal differences in the two groups. In our driving experiment, this could be done by simply flipping a coin for each participant: heads, and the participant is in the experimental group; tails, it's the control group. This would result in few average differences in the number of people in each group who are better (or worse) drivers, women or men, comfortable navigating with a global positioning system (GPS) or not, hungry, hung over, tall, music lovers, or whatever.

Other extraneous variables—such as the navigation task assigned while driving, the weather on the days that the drivers are tested, the time of day, lighting conditions, and so forth—must also be prevented from affecting the outcome of an experiment. How can we achieve that? Usually, it is done by making all conditions (except the independent variable) *exactly* alike for both groups. When all conditions are the same for both groups—except the presence or absence of the smart glasses—then any decline in driving ability *must* be caused by using the smart glasses (➤ Figure 4.1).

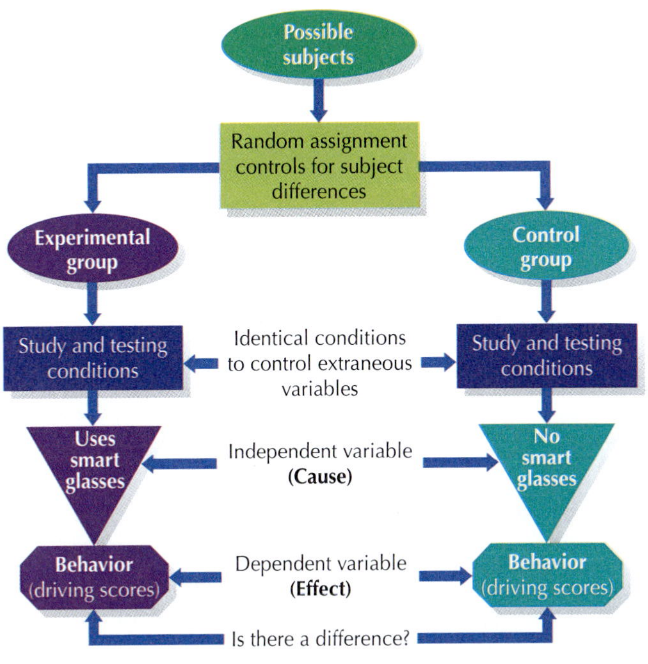

➤ **Figure 4.1**

A simple experiment. Elements of a simple psychological experiment to assess the effects of using smart glasses while driving on test scores of driving ability.

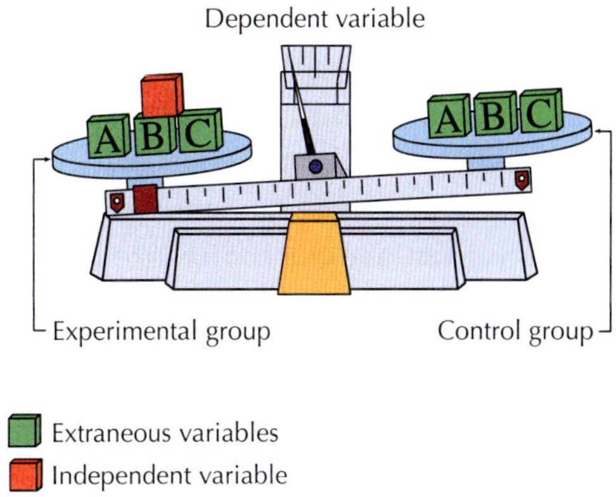

➤ **Figure 4.2**

Controlling extraneous variables. Experimental control is achieved by balancing extraneous variables for the experimental group and the control group. For example, both groups could be formed so that the average age (A), education (B), and intelligence (C) of group members are the same. Then the independent variable can be applied to the experimental group. If their behavior (the dependent variable) changes (in comparison with the control group), the independent variable must be causing the change.

Cause and Effect Now let's summarize. In an experiment, two or more groups of subjects are treated differently with respect to the independent variable. In all other ways, they are treated the same—that is, extraneous variables are equalized for all groups. Then the effect of the independent variable (or variables) on some behavior (the dependent variable) is measured. In a carefully controlled experiment, the independent variable is the only possible cause for any effect noted in the dependent variable. This allows clear cause-and-effect connections to be identified (➤ Figure 4.2).

Experimental subjects Humans (also referred to as *participants*) or animals whose behavior is investigated in an experiment.

Participants Humans whose behavior is investigated in an experiment.

Variable Factor or characteristic manipulated or measured in research.

Independent variable Variable manipulated by the researcher in an experiment.

Dependent variable The element of an experiment that measures any effect of the manipulation.

Extraneous variable A condition or factor that may change and is excluded from influencing the outcome of an experiment.

Experimental group Group that receives the treatment the study is designed to test.

Control group Subjects in an experimental study who do not receive the treatment being investigated.

Random assignment Use of chance to place subjects in experimental and control groups.

Evaluating Results *If the experimental group using the smart glasses performed worse than the control group on the test of driving ability, then we can conclude that the independent variable really made a difference, right?* Almost—but one last issue remains. Suppose the smart glass users scored 40% on the driving test and the control group scored 80%. Scoring half as well as the control group almost certainly means that the smart glass users were driving poorly. But suppose that the difference was 66.3% versus 66.1%? In other words, how big a difference do we have to find before we can conclude that the driving test scores are meaningfully different?

Fortunately, this question can be handled statistically (see the Statistics Appendix for more on inferential statistics). Reports in psychology journals almost always include a statement like this one: "Results were **statistically significant**." This means that the obtained results would occur rarely by chance alone. To be statistically significant, a difference must be large enough that it would occur by chance in fewer than 5 out of 100 experiments. Of course, findings also become more convincing when they can be *replicated* (repeated) by other researchers.

Meta-Analysis As you might guess, numerous studies are done on important topics in psychology. Although each study adds to our understanding, the results of various studies don't always agree. Let's say that we are interested in whether males or females tend to be greater risk-takers. A computer search would reveal that many studies have investigated various types of risk taking (for example, smoking, fast driving, or unprotected sex).

Is there a way to combine the results of the studies? Yes—a statistical technique called **meta-analysis** can be used to combine the results of many studies as if they were all part of one big study (Cooper, 2010). In other words, a meta-analysis is a study of the results of other studies. In recent years, meta-analyses have been used to summarize and synthesize mountains of psychological research. This allows us to see the big picture and draw conclusions that might be missed in a single, small-scale study. Oh, and about that risk-taking: A meta-analysis showed that males do tend to take more risks than females (Byrnes, Miller, & Schafer, 1999). (The most frequent last words uttered by young males just before death are rumored to be, "Hey, watch this!")

Double-Blind—On Placebos and Self-Fulfilling Prophecies

Learning Outcome 4.2 Explain what a double-blind experiment is and why it is necessary for the evaluation of causal hypotheses

Suppose that a researcher hypothesizes that the drug amphetamine (a stimulant) improves learning. She explains her hypothesis to her participants and gives experimental group participants an amphetamine pill before they begin studying. Control group members get nothing. Later, she assesses how much each participant learned. Does this experiment seem valid? Well, it isn't. It is seriously flawed for several reasons.

Why is it flawed? The experimental group took the drug and the control group didn't. Differences in the amount they learned must have been caused by the drug, right? Actually, the drug wasn't the only difference between the groups. Because of what they were told, participants in the experimental group likely *expected* to learn more (as compared to the control group). Any observed differences between groups, then, might reflect differences in expectations, not the actual effect of the drug.

Research Participant Bias

In a well-designed experiment, you must be careful what you tell participants. Small bits of information might create **research participant bias**—changes in participants' behavior caused by the influence of their expectations. Notice also that experimental group participants swallowed a pill, and control participants did not. This is another form of research

sebra/Shutterstock.com

The placebo effect is a major factor in medical treatments. Would you expect the placebo effect to occur in psychotherapy as well? It does, which complicates studies on the effectiveness of new psychotherapies, but likely also enhances the effectiveness of psychotherapy (Justman, 2011).

participant bias. It could be that those who swallowed a pill unconsciously *expected* to do better. After all, pills are medicine, aren't they? This alone might have created a **placebo effect**—a change in symptoms due to a participant's expectation that a drug or treatment will do something.

To control for a placebo effect, the researcher would do better to give the experimental group an amphetamine pill and the control group a **placebo** (plah-SEE-bo), an inactive substance or treatment that is indistinguishable from a real, active substance or treatment. Now, if the experimental group *still* does better than the control group, it cannot be a placebo effect just because a pill was swallowed, since both groups swallowed a pill.

If a placebo has any effect, it must be based on suggestion, not chemistry (White & McBurney, 2013). Even so, placebo effects can be quite powerful and usually account for at least one-third of the apparent effectiveness of the official treatment. For instance, a placebo saline injection is 70 percent as effective as morphine in reducing pain. That's why doctors sometimes prescribe placebos—especially for complaints that seem to have no physical basis. Placebos have been shown to affect pain, anxiety, depression, alertness, tension, sexual arousal, cravings for alcohol, and many other processes (Justman, 2011; Wampold et al., 2005).

How could an inert substance have any effect? Placebos alter our expectations, both conscious and unconscious, about our own emotional and physical reactions (Vance, 2016). Because we associate taking medicine with feeling better, we expect placebos to make us feel better, too (Benedetti, 2009; Czerniak & Davidson, 2012). After a person takes a placebo, brain activity linked with pain is reduced, so the effect is not imaginary (Wager et al., 2004).

Controlling Research Participant Bias *How can you avoid research participant bias?* You could use a **single-blind study**. In this case, participants do not know whether they are in the experimental or the control group or whether they are receiving a real drug or a placebo. All participants are given the same instructions, and everyone gets a pill or injection. People in the experimental group get the real drug, and those in the control group get a placebo. Because all participants are *blind* as to the hypothesis under investigation and whether they received the drug, their expectations (conscious *and* unconscious) tend to be similar. Any difference in their behavior is likely to be caused by the drug itself.

However, even this arrangement is not enough because researchers themselves sometimes unwittingly affect experiments by influencing participants. Let's see how this occurs.

Researcher Bias

How could a researcher unwittingly influence participants? As we noted earlier, when the experimenter explained her hypothesis to the participants, she likely biased the results of the study. But even if a researcher uses a single-blind procedure to avoid deliberately biasing participants, **researcher bias**—changes in behavior caused by the unintended influence of a researcher—remains a problem. Experimenters run the risk of finding what they expect to find because humans are sensitive to hints about what is expected of them (Rosenthal, 1994).

Researcher bias even applies outside the laboratory. Psychologist Robert Rosenthal (1973) reported a classic example of how expectations influence people: At the U.S. Air Force Academy Preparatory School, 100 student pilots were randomly assigned to five different math classes. Their teachers did not know about this random placement. Instead, each teacher was told that his or her students had unusually high or low ability. Students in the classes labeled as "high ability" improved much more in math scores than those in "low-ability" classes. Yet, the initial randomization made it likely that the average ability of all the classes was roughly equal.

Although the teachers were not conscious of any bias, apparently, they subtly communicated their expectations to students. Most likely, they did this through their tone of voice, body language, and encouragement or criticism. Their hints, in turn, created a self-fulfilling prophecy that affected the students. A **self-fulfilling prophecy** is a prediction that prompts people to act in ways that make the prediction come true. For instance, many teachers underestimate the abilities of ethnic minority children, which hurts those

Statistically significant Experimental results that would rarely occur by chance alone.

Meta-analysis A statistical technique for combining the results of many studies on the same subject.

Research participant bias Changes in the behavior of research participants caused by the unintended influence of their own expectations.

Placebo effect A change in symptoms due to a participant's expectation that a drug or treatment will do something.

Placebo Inactive substance or treatment that is distinguishable from a real, active substance or treatment.

Single-blind study An arrangement in which participants remain unaware of whether they are in the experimental group or the control group.

Researcher bias Changes in participants' behavior caused by the unintended influence of a researcher's actions.

Self-fulfilling prophecy A prediction that prompts people to act in ways that make the prediction come true.

students' chances for success (Jussim & Harber, 2005). In short, people sometimes become what we predict for them. It is wise to remember that others tend to live *up* or *down* to our expectations of them (Madon et al., 2011).

The Double-Blind Experiment Because of research participant bias and researcher bias, it is common to keep both participants and researchers *blind*. In a **double-blind experiment**, experiments are conducted so that neither the observer nor the subjects know which subjects received which treatment. This not only controls for research participant bias, but it also keeps researchers from unconsciously influencing participants.

How can the researchers be blind—it's their experiment, isn't it? The researchers who designed the experiment, including preparing the pills or injections, typically hire research assistants to collect data from the participants. The research assistants are blind in that they do not know which pill or injection is a drug or placebo, or whether any particular participant is in the experimental or control group.

Double-blind testing has shown that at least 50 percent of the effectiveness of antidepressant drugs, such as the antidepressant drug Prozac, is due to the placebo effect (Kirsch & Sapirstein, 1998; Rihmer et al., 2012). Much of the popularity of herbal health remedies is also based on the placebo effect (Seidman, 2001).

Double-blind experiment Experiment in which neither the observer nor the subjects know which subjects received which treatment.

MODULE 4 The Psychology Experiment—Learning Outcomes Revisited

4.1 Explain how an experiment is performed

Independent variables are assumed to be the "cause" in a cause-and-effect relationship between variables, and are controlled by the researcher (in the sense that the researcher randomly assigns participants to experience one version, or level, of the independent variable). Dependent variables are assumed to be the "effect" in a cause-and-effect relationship between variables, and are measured by the researcher. Extraneous variables are variables (other than the independent variable) that are believed to influence the dependent variable. They are controlled by the researcher, who attempts to keep them the same for all participants in the study. Experiments involve comparing two or more groups of subjects that differ only regarding the independent variable. Random assignment helps to ensure that the groups are equivalent in all ways except for their experience of the independent variable. Effects on the dependent variable are then measured. All other conditions (extraneous variables) are held constant. Because the independent variable is the only difference between the experimental group and the control group, it is the only possible cause of a change in the dependent variable. To be taken seriously, the results of an experiment must be statistically significant (they would occur very rarely by chance alone). It also strengthens a result if the research can be replicated or if it contributes to the conclusions of a meta-analysis.

4.2 Explain what a double-blind experiment is and why it is necessary for the evaluation of causal hypotheses

A double-blind experiment keeps both the research participants and the researchers blind to the true purpose of the experiment. This simultaneously controls for research participant bias (changes in participant behavior based on their expectations, including the placebo effect) and researcher bias (changes in participant behavior brought about by researcher influence). To control for these problems, neither the research participants nor the researchers collecting data know who was in the experimental group or the control group.

Reflective Practice

Content Check

1. To understand cause and effect, a simple psychological experiment is based on creating two groups: the _______________ group and the __________ group.

2. Three types of variables must be considered in an experiment: ____________ variables (which are manipulated by the experimenter); ____________ variables (which measure the outcome of the experiment); and ____________ variables (factors to be excluded in a particular experiment).
3. A researcher performs an experiment to learn whether room temperature affects the amount of aggression displayed by college students under crowded conditions in a simulated prison environment. In this experiment, the independent variable is which of the following?
   a. room temperature
   b. the amount of aggression
   c. crowding
   d. the simulated prison environment
4. A procedure used to control both research participant bias and researcher bias in psychological experiments is the
   a. single-blind experiment
   b. controlled experiment
   c. double-blind experiment
   d. random assignment of participants

Skill Check

Think Critically

5. The following statement has a loophole: "I've been taking vitamin C tablets, and I haven't had a cold all year. Vitamin C is great!" What is the loophole?

Self-Reflect

We all conduct little experiments to detect cause-and-effect connections. If you enjoy music, for example, you might try listening with different types of headphones. One question might be, "Does the use of earbuds versus sound-cancelling headphones [the independent variable] affect the enjoyment of music [the dependent variable]?" Can you think of an informal experiment that you've run in the last month? What were the variables? What was the outcome?

ANSWERS

1. experimental, control 2. independent, dependent, extraneous 3. *a* 4. *c* 5. The statement implies that vitamin C prevented colds. However, not getting a cold could be a coincidence. A controlled experiment with a group given vitamin C and a control group not taking vitamin C is needed to learn whether vitamin C has any effect on susceptibility to colds.

MODULE 5

Introducing Psychology

Descriptive Research Methods

Get Out the Critter Cam

Because it is not always possible to conduct experiments, psychologists gather evidence and test hypotheses in many other ways (Jackson, 2016). For example, psychologists who want to study behavior as it unfolds in natural settings use *naturalistic observation*. As an example of this technique, New Caledonian crows wearing tiny "crow cams" have been recorded using twigs to forage for food.

Psychologists who are looking for interesting relationships between events often rely on *correlational research*. It also can be difficult or impossible to study rare events or unique individuals with the experimental method. When more detail about, say, mental disorders such as depression or psychosis, is required, a *case study* may be preferred. Likewise, the *survey method* allows questions about the behavior of large groups of people to be answered by conducting polls. Let's see how each of these descriptive methods is used to advance psychological knowledge.

~LEARNING OUTCOMES~

After reading this module you should be able to:

- **5.1** Explain the purpose of carrying out natural observations in psychological research, and two limitations of doing so
- **5.2** Explain the purpose and limitations of correlational research, how the degree of association between two variables is assessed in correlational research, and differentiate between quasi-experiments and real experiments
- **5.3** Explain the purpose of carrying out a case study in psychological research and one limitation of doing so
- **5.4** Explain the purpose of carrying out surveys in psychological research, and two limitations of doing so

Naturalistic Observation

Learning Outcome 5.1 Explain the purpose of carrying out natural observations in psychological research, and two limitations of doing so

Psychologists sometimes rely on **naturalistic observation**, a research method based on careful recording of behavior in normal settings. This often means observing behavior in a *natural setting* (the typical environment in which a person or animal lives). For example, in 1960, Jane Goodall first observed a wild chimpanzee in Tanzania use a grass stem as a tool to remove termites from a termite mound (Van Lawick-Goodall, 1971). Notice that naturalistic observation provides only *descriptions* of behavior. To *explain* observations, we may need information from other research methods. Just the same, Goodall's discovery showed that humans are not the only tool-making animals.

Chimpanzees in zoos use objects as tools. Doesn't that demonstrate the same thing? Not necessarily. Naturalistic observation allows us to study behavior that hasn't been tampered with or altered by outside influences. Only by observing chimps in their natural environment can we tell whether they use tools without human interference.

Limitations

Doesn't the presence of human observers affect the animals' behavior? Yes. The **observer effect**—changes in a subject's behavior caused by an awareness of being observed—is a major problem. Naturalists should be careful to keep their distance and avoid making friends with the animals that they are watching. Likewise, if you are interested in why automobile drivers have traffic accidents, you can't simply get in people's cars and start taking notes. As a stranger, your presence would likely change the drivers' behaviors.

When possible, the observer effect can be minimized by concealing the observer. Another solution is to use hidden recorders. One naturalistic study of traffic accidents was done with video cameras installed in 100 cars (Dingus et al., 2006). It turns out that most accidents are caused by failing to look at the traffic in front of the car (eyes forward!).

As recording devices have become miniaturized, it has become possible to attach "critter cams" directly to many species, allowing observations to be made in a wide range of natural environments. As mentioned previously, zoologist Christian Rutz and his colleagues outfitted shy New Caledonian crows with "crow cams" to better understand their use of tools to forage for food (Rutz & St. Clair, 2012). Not only can these clever crows use twigs to reach food, but they also can use a shorter twig to obtain a longer twig to get food (Wimpenny et al., 2009). Apparently, humans and other primates are not the only tool-using species.

Observer bias is a related problem, in which observers see what they expect to see or record only selected details (Gravetter & Forzano, 2019). For instance, teachers in one classic study were told to watch normal elementary school children who had been labeled (for the study) as learning disabled, mentally challenged, emotionally disturbed, or normal. Sadly, teachers gave the children widely different ratings, depending on the labels used (Foster & Ysseldyke, 1976). In some situations, observer bias can have serious consequences (Page, Taylor, & Blenkin, 2012). For example, a police officer who expects criminal behavior might shoot someone who he assumes is reaching for a gun, even though the person was simply reaching for his wallet or his phone.

A special mistake to avoid when observing animals is the **anthropomorphic error** (AN-thro-po-MORE-fik). This is the error of attributing human thoughts, feelings, or motives to animals, especially as a way to explain their behavior (Waytz, Epley, & Cacioppo, 2010). The temptation to assume that an animal is angry, jealous, bored, or guilty can be strong. If you have pets at home, you probably know how difficult it is to avoid anthropomorphizing, but it can lead to false conclusions. For example, if your dog growls at your date, you might assume that the dog doesn't like your companion. But it's also possible that your date is wearing a cologne or perfume that irritates the dog's nose.

Psychologists doing naturalistic studies make a special effort to minimize bias by keeping a detailed record of data and observations. As suggested by the study of traffic accidents and the use of critter cams, recording video often provides the most objective record of all. Despite its problems, naturalistic observation can supply a wealth of information and raise many interesting questions. In most scientific research, it is an excellent starting point.

Correlational Research

Learning Outcome 5.2 Explain the purpose and limitations of correlational research, how the degree of association between two variables is assessed in correlational research, and differentiate between quasi-experiments and real experiments,

The term **correlational research** refers to any descriptive study that quantifies the degree to which events, measures, or variables are associated (see the Statistics Appendix). Let's say that a psychologist notes an association between the IQs of parents and their children, between beauty and social popularity, or between anxiety and test performance. A **correlation** exists when two observations or events are linked together in an orderly way.

Naturalistic observation Research method based on careful recording of behavior in normal settings.

Observer effect Changes in an organism's behavior brought about by an awareness of being observed.

Observer bias The tendency of an observer to distort observations or perceptions to match his or her expectations.

Anthropomorphic error The error of attributing human thoughts, feelings, or motives to animals, especially as a way to explain their behavior.

Correlational research Descriptive study that quantifies the degree to which events, measures, or variables are associated.

Correlation The existence of a consistent, systematic relationship between two events, measures, or variables.

For example, John Simister and Cary Cooper (2005) decided to find out if there is a correlation between the weather and crime. They obtained data on temperatures and criminal activity in Los Angeles over a four-year period. When they graphed air temperature and the frequency of aggravated assaults, a clear relationship emerged. Assaults and temperatures rise and fall more or less in parallel (so there may be something to the phrase *hot under the collar*). Knowing the temperature in Los Angeles now not only allows us to describe the relationship, it also allows us to predict whether the number of aggravated assaults will increase.

Correlation Coefficients

How is the degree of correlation expressed? The strength and direction of a relationship can be expressed as a **coefficient of correlation**. This can be calculated as a number falling somewhere between +1.00 and −1.00 (see the Statistics Appendix). Drawing graphs of relationships can also help clarify their nature (see ➤ **Figure 5.1**). If the number is zero or close to zero, the association between two measures is weak or nonexistent (see Figure 5.1*c*). For example, the correlation between shoe size and intelligence is zero. (Sorry, size-12 readers.) If the correlation is +1.00, a perfect positive relationship exists (see Figure 5.1*e*); if it is −1.00, a perfect negative relationship has been discovered (see Figure 5.1*a*).

Correlations in psychology are rarely perfect. But the closer the coefficient is to +1.00 or −1.00, the stronger the relationship. For example, identical twins tend to have almost identical IQs. By contrast, the IQs of parents and their children are only generally similar. The correlation between the IQs of parents and children is .35; between identical twins, it's .86 (see Module 40).

What do the terms positive *and* negative *correlation mean?* In a *positive correlation*, higher scores on one measure are matched by higher scores on the other. For example, a moderate positive correlation exists between high school grades and college grades; students who do well in high school tend to do well in college (and vice versa; see Figure 5.1*d*). In a *negative correlation*, higher scores on one measure are associated with lower scores on the other. We might observe, for instance, a moderate negative correlation between the number of hours that students play computer games and their grades—that is, more play is associated with lower grades. (This is the well-known "computer game–zombie" effect; see Figure 5.1*b*.)

Wouldn't that show that playing computer games too much causes lower grades? It might seem so, but as we noted previously, the best way to be confident that a cause-and-effect relationship exists is to perform a controlled experiment.

Correlation and Causation Correlational studies help us discover relationships and make predictions. However,

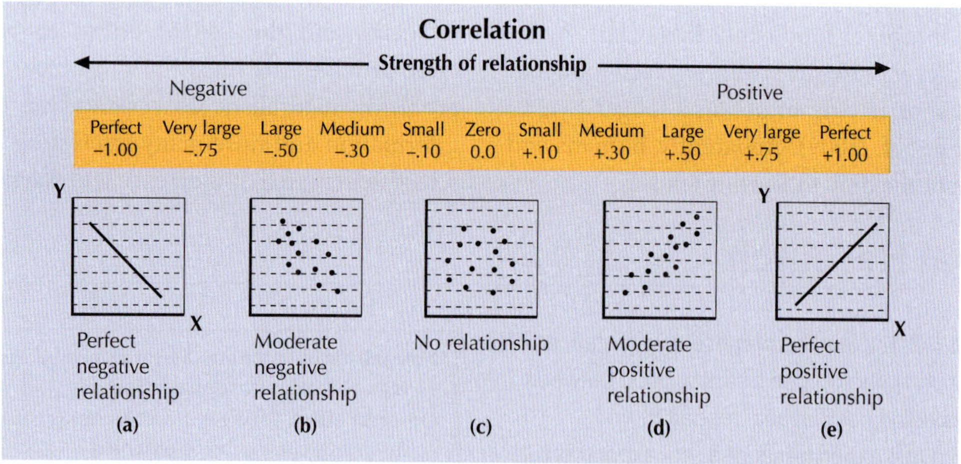

➤ **Figure 5.1**

Correlation coefficients. The correlation coefficient tells how strongly two measures are related. These graphs show a range of relationships between two measures, X and Y. If a correlation is negative (a), increases in one measure are associated with decreases in the other. (As Y gets larger, X gets smaller.) In a positive correlation (e), increases in one measure are associated with increases in the other. (As Y gets larger, X gets larger.) The center-left graph (b; a moderate negative relationship) might result from comparing time spent playing computer games (Y) with grades (X): More time spent playing computer games is associated with lower grades. The center graph (c; no relationship) would result from plotting a person's shoe size (Y) and his or her IQ (X). The center-right graph (d; a moderate positive relationship) could be a plot of grades in high school (Y) and grades in college (X) for a group of students: Higher grades in high school are associated with higher grades in college.

correlation *does not* demonstrate **causation** (Ruggiero, 2015). For instance, it could be that students who aren't interested in their classes have more time for computer games. If so, then their lack of study and lower grades is the result of lack of interest rather than excessive game playing (which would be another result of lack of interest in classes). Just because one thing *appears* to be related directly to another does not mean that a cause-and-effect connection exists.

Here is another example of mistaking correlation for causation: What if a psychologist discovers a correlation between parents who smoke cigarettes and juvenile delinquency in their children? Does this show that parental smoking *causes* juvenile delinquency? Perhaps, but maybe it's that juvenile delinquents drive their parents to take up smoking (to handle the stress of dealing with them). Better yet, maybe both parental smoking and juvenile delinquency are related to some third factor, such as socioeconomic status (SES). Perhaps poorer parents are more likely to be smokers, and poorer juveniles are more likely to become delinquents (➤ Figure 5.2). To reiterate, just because one thing *appears* to cause another does not *confirm* that it does. The best way to be confident that a cause-and-effect relationship exists is to perform a controlled experiment.

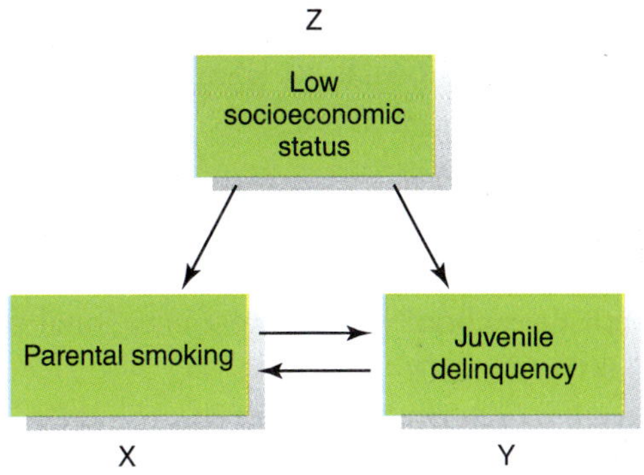

➤ **Figure 5.2**

Correlation and causality. A correlation between two variables might mean that X causes Y, that Y causes X, or that some other, third, variable, Z, causes *both* X and Y.

Quasi-Experiments While it may seem as if the distinction between experimental and correlational research is obvious, nothing could be further from the truth. Imagine, for example, that we're interested in finding out whether getting older causes people to become more conservative in their political beliefs. Here, the independent variable would be age (older or younger), and the dependent variable would be a measure of political beliefs. What is missing from this research design is *random assignment*, the use of chance to place subjects in experimental and control groups.

We saw in Module 4 that when we conduct a true experiment the participants are randomly assigned to a group. This random assignment is critical because it helps to ensure that there are unlikely to be differences between the groups at the outset (that is, it controls for extraneous variables). In fact, *random assignment is the defining feature of a true experiment.*

Try randomly assigning people to be either "old" or "young" in your experiment—there's simply no messing around with people's age (much as some people try!). The same is true for any study in which the independent variable is sex, ethnicity, religion, or any other characteristic that is inherently part of who we are—you can't randomly assign people to different levels of these variables.

When random assignment to the experimental and control groups is not possible—either because it would be unethical or because it's impossible—then we aren't carrying out a true experiment, and consequently *we cannot make cause-and-effect statements about the relationship between the independent and dependent variable.* We can still compare the groups on the dependent variable, but we can't be totally sure that they were equivalent at the outset. As a result, these studies are called **quasi-experimental studies**.

Case Studies

Learning Outcome 5.3 Explain the purpose of carrying out a case study in psychological research and one limitation of doing so

It may be impractical, unethical, or impossible to use the experimental method to study rare events, such as unusual mental disorders, childhood geniuses, or rampage school shootings (Harding, Fox, & Mehta, 2002). In such instances, a **case study (clinical method)**—an in-depth analysis of the

Coefficient of correlation A statistical index ranging from −1.00 to +1.00 that indicates the direction and degree of correlation.

Causation The act of causing some effect.

Quasi-experimental study A descriptive study in which researchers wish to compare groups of people, but cannot randomly assign them to groups.

Case study (clinical method) In-depth analysis of the behavior of one person or a small number of people.

behavior of one person or a small number of people—may be the best source of information. (Because clinical psychologists rely heavily on case studies, this is also referred to as the *clinical method*.) Case studies have been especially useful to investigate mental disorders, such as depression or psychosis. Also, case studies of psychotherapy have provided many useful ideas about how to treat emotional problems (Wedding & Corsini, 2014).

Case studies may also be used to study accidents or other natural events. Gunshot wounds, brain tumors, accidental poisonings, and similar disasters have provided much information about the human brain. One remarkable case was reported by Dr. J. M. Harlow (1868). Phineas Gage, a young foreman on a work crew, had a 13-pound steel rod driven into the front of his brain by a dynamite explosion (➤ Figure 5.3). Amazingly, he survived the accident. Within two months, Gage could walk, talk, and move normally, but the injury forever changed his personality. Instead of the honest and dependable worker he had been before, Gage became a surly, foul-mouthed liar. Dr. Harlow carefully recorded all details of what was perhaps the first in-depth case study of an accidental frontal lobotomy (the destruction of front brain matter).

When a Los Angeles carpenter named Michael Melnick suffered a similar injury in 1981, he recovered completely, with no lasting ill effects. Melnick's different reaction to a similar injury shows why psychologists prefer controlled experiments and often use lab animals for studies of the brain. Since case studies lack formal control groups, the conclusions that can be drawn are limited.

Nevertheless, case studies can provide special opportunities to answer interesting questions. For instance, a classic case study in psychology concerns the Genain sisters, identical quadruplets. In addition to having identical genes, all four women became schizophrenic before age 24 (Duncan, 2013). The chances of identical quadruplets all accidentally becoming schizophrenic are about 1 in 1.5 billion.

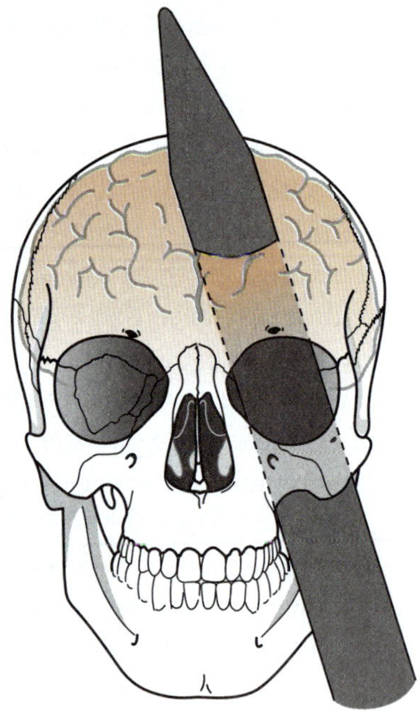

➤ **Figure 5.3**

The case of Phineas Gage. Some of the earliest information on the effects of damage to frontal areas of the brain came from a case study of the accidental injury of Phineas Gage (illustrated here).

The Genains, who have been studied for more than 55 years, were in and out of mental hospitals most of their lives. The fact that they share identical genes suggests that heredity influences mental disorders. The fact that some of the sisters are more disturbed than others suggests that environmental conditions also affect mental illness. Myra, the least ill of the four, was the only sister who was able to avoid her father, an alcoholic who terrorized, spied on, and sexually molested the girls. Thus, cases like theirs provide insights that can't be obtained by any other means (Mirsky et al., 2000). (See Module 61 for more information about the causes of schizophrenia.)

Survey Method

Learning Outcome 5.4 Explain the purpose of carrying out surveys in psychological research, and two limitations of doing so

Sometimes psychologists would like to ask everyone in the world a few well-chosen questions: "What form of discipline did your parents use when you were a child?" "What is the most dishonest thing you've done?" "Why do you think you run extreme marathons?" Honest answers to such questions can reveal much about people's beliefs and behavior. Because it is impossible to question everyone, doing a survey is often more practical.

A **survey** is a descriptive research method in which participants are asked the same questions (Babbie, 2016; Thrift, 2010). Usually, we are interested in surveying entire populations. A **population**—the group of people from which a sample is drawn—might be all the people in a particular category (for example, all college students or all single women). Because surveying entire populations is often not feasible, typically a **sample**—a subset of a population being studied—is asked a series of carefully worded questions.

If a survey is administered to a **representative sample**—a sample that accurately reflects a larger population—we can draw conclusions about the larger population without polling every person. For a sample to be representative, it must include the same proportions of men, women, young, old, professionals, blue-collar workers, Republicans, Democrats, whites, African Americans, Native Americans, Latinos, Asians, and other groups as are found in the population as a whole. Representative samples are often obtained by *randomly* selecting who will be included (➤ **Figure 5.4**). (Notice that this is similar to randomly assigning participants to groups in an experiment.)

How accurate is the survey method? Contemporary surveys like the Gallup and Harris polls can be quite accurate. However, if a survey is based on a biased sample, it could paint a false picture. A **biased sample** does not accurately reflect the population from which it was drawn. Surveys done by magazines, websites, and online information services can be quite biased. Surveys on gun-control laws done by *O: The Oprah Magazine* and *Guns and Ammo* magazine would probably produce different results—neither of which would likely represent the general population. That's why psychologists using the survey method go to great lengths to ensure that their samples are representative. Fortunately, people can often be polled by telephone or the Internet, which makes it easier to obtain large samples. Even if one person out of three refuses to answer survey questions, the results are still likely to be valid (Hutchinson, 2004).

Internet Surveys These days, psychologists often rely on the Internet to do online surveys and experiments. Web-based research can be a cost-effective way to reach large groups of people, especially those who are not easy to survey any other way (Gosling & Mason, 2015). Internet studies have provided interesting information about topics such as anger, decision making, racial prejudice, what disgusts people, religion, sexual attitudes, and much more. Biased samples can limit web-based research (it isn't easy to control who answers your online questionnaire), but psychologists are getting better at gathering valid information online (Weigold, Weigold, & Russell, 2013).

Social Desirability Even well-designed surveys may be limited by another problem. If a psychologist were to ask you detailed questions about your sexual history and current sexual behavior, how accurate would your replies be? Would you exaggerate? Would you be embarrassed? Replies to survey questions are not always accurate or truthful. Many people show a distinct, deliberate *courtesy bias* (a tendency to give polite or socially desirable answers). For example, answers to questions concerning sex, drinking or drug use, income, and church attendance tend to be less than truthful. Likewise, the week after an election, more people will say they voted than actually did—and the ones who did vote may not be honest about who they voted for (Babbie, 2016).

Summary Despite their limitations, surveys frequently produce valuable information. For instance, one survey explored the vulnerability of U.S. retail malls to terrorism,

Survey method Using questionnaires and surveys to poll large groups of people.

Population The entire group of people from which a sample is drawn.

Sample Subset of a population being studied.

Representative sample A small, randomly selected part of a larger population that accurately reflects characteristics of the whole population.

Biased sample A subpart of a larger population that does not accurately reflect characteristics of the whole population.

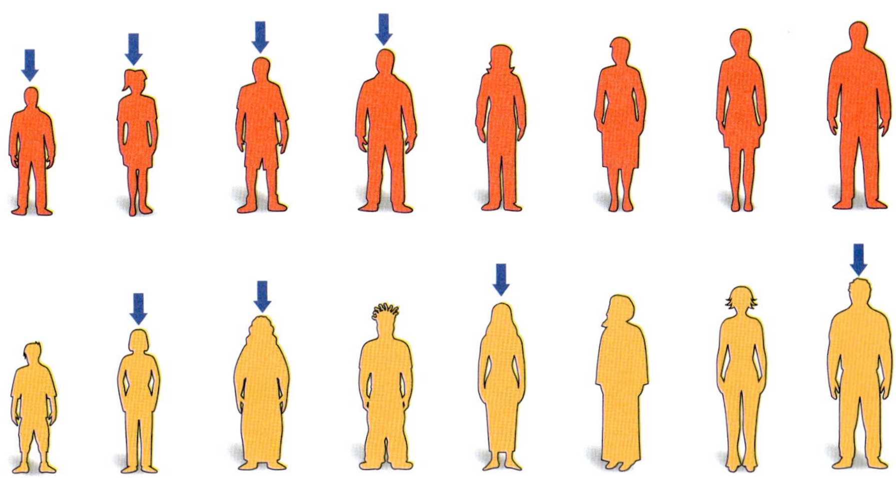

➤ **Figure 5.4**

Random sampling. If you were conducting a survey in which a person's height might be an important variable, the nonrandom sample of shorter people would be very unrepresentative. The random sample, selected using a table of random numbers, better represents the group as a whole.

TABLE 5.1 | Comparison of Psychological Research Methods

	Advantages	Disadvantages
Experimental method	Clear cause-and-effect relationships can be identified; powerful controlled observations can be staged; no need to wait for a natural event	May be somewhat artificial; some natural behaviors are not easily studied in the laboratory (field experiments may address these objections)
Naturalistic observation	Behavior is observed in a natural setting; much information is obtained, and hypotheses and questions for additional research can be formed	Little or no control is possible; observed behavior may be altered by the presence of the observer; observations may be biased; causes cannot be conclusively identified
Correlational research	Demonstrates the existence of relationships; allows prediction; can be used in a lab, clinic, or natural setting	Little or no control is possible; relationships may be coincidental; cause-and-effect relationships cannot be confirmed
Case study	Allows investigation of rare or unusual problems or events	Little or no control is possible; does not provide a control group for comparison; subjective interpretation is often necessary; a single case may be misleading or unrepresentative
Survey method	Allows information about large numbers of people to be gathered; can address questions not answered by other approaches	Obtaining a representative sample is critical and can be difficult to do; answers may be inaccurate; people may not do what they say or say what they actually do

with the goal of improving our capacity to prevent and respond to an attack (Rigakos et al., 2009). To sum up, the survey method can be a powerful research tool. Like other methods, it has limitations, but new techniques and strategies are providing valuable information about our behavior.

Is so much emphasis on science necessary in psychology? In a word, yes. Science is a powerful way of asking questions about the world and getting unbiased, trustworthy answers. (■ **Table 5.1** summarizes many of the important ideas that we have covered so far.)

MODULE 5 Descriptive Research Methods—Learning Outcomes Revisited

5.1 Explain the purpose of carrying out natural observations in psychological research, and two limitations of doing so

Naturalistic observation is a good starting place in many investigations. Two problems with naturalistic observation are the effects of the observer on the observed and observer bias.

5.2 Explain the purpose of correlational research, how the degree of association between two variables is assessed, and a major limitation of correlational research. Additionally, differentiate between quasi-experiments and real experiments

In correlational research, two (or more) traits, responses, or events are measured to gauge the strength of the relationship between those variables. A correlation coefficient ranging between 0 (no relationship) and ±1 (a perfect relationship) can be calculated. The magnitude of the number (ignoring the sign) describes how well you can predict one variable from the other. The sign (– or +) tells you whether the relationship is positive (as the value of one variable increases, the other also increases) or negative (as the value of one variable increases, the other decreases). The major limitation of correlational research is that it cannot assess whether or not a statistical association between two variables is also a causal relationship. Even when researchers wish to compare groups of people, but cannot randomly assign them to groups, the result cannot assess causality. Such studies are referred to as quasi-experiments to distinguish them from true experiments.

5.3 **Explain the purpose of carrying out a case study in psychological research and one limitation of doing so**

By focusing in detail on one individual (or a few individuals), a case study (clinical method) can provide insights into human behavior that can't be gained by other methods. Since case studies lack formal control groups, one important limitation is that the conclusions that can be drawn are limited.

5.4 **Explain the purpose of carrying out surveys in psychological research, and two limitations of doing so**

In the survey method, a sample of people are asked a series of carefully worded questions. Obtaining a representative sample is crucial when the survey method is used to study large populations. Survey data may be compromised if the sample of respondents is not representative (that is, it does not accurately reflect the larger population), or if participants provide answers that are socially desirable rather than truthful.

Reflective Practice

Content Check

1. Two major problems in naturalistic observation are the effects of the observer and observer bias. T or F?
2. The ________________ fallacy involves attributing human feelings and motives to animals.
3. Correlation typically demonstrates causation. T or F?
4. Case studies are frequently used by clinical psychologists. T or F?
5. For the survey method to be valid, a representative sample of people must be polled. T or F?
6. A problem with the survey method is that answers to questions may not always be ________________ or ________________.

Skill Check

Think Critically

7. Attributing mischievous motives to a car that is not working properly is a thinking error similar to anthropomorphizing. T or F?

Self-Reflect

Google "Critter cam" and find one that you can watch. What species did you watch? What behaviors might you observe and record? See if you can identify at least one positive correlation and one negative correlation that involve human behavior. Have you ever known someone who suffered a brain injury or disease? How did his or her behavior change? Have you ever been asked to complete a survey? If you agreed, were you honest about your answers? What would it say about accuracy if many people did not answer honestly?

ANSWERS

1. T 2. anthropomorphic 3. F 4. T 5. T 6. accurate, truthful 7. Yes. It appears to be difficult for humans to resist thinking of other species (and even machines) in human terms.

MODULE 6

A Psychologist's Skill Set

Information Literacy

How Do You Know?

In this *Psychologist's Skill Set* module, we explore *information literacy*, or how to think critically about the information that we see in the popular media. Let's face it: In this era of Internet bots and trolls, and when many people have easy access to software that can realistically alter images and video, you simply can't believe everything you read. Or hear. Or even see! What, for example, should you make of media reports that people can learn to use the power of their minds to protect their feet while they walk on hot coals? Should you be impressed or skeptical? Read on to find out.

TORU YAMANAKA/AFP/Getty Images

~LEARNING OUTCOMES~

After reading this module you should be able to:

6.1 Name and apply six ways that people can critically evaluate information found in the popular press and on social media

Separating Fact from Fiction in the Media—Who Can You Trust?

Learning Outcome 6.1 Name and apply six ways that people can critically evaluate information found in the popular press and on social media

Contemporary media—especially the Internet—functions as a giant echo chamber, awash with rumors, hoaxes, half-truths, and urban legends like the one about giant alligators living in New York sewers (Hughes, 2008). Unfortunately, a great deal of what you will encounter is based on entertainment value rather than critical thinking or science (Ruggiero, 2015). Here are some suggestions for separating high-quality information from misleading fiction (Lawson, Jordan-Fleming, & Bodle, 2015).

Suggestion 1: Consider the Source of Information

The popular media provides an endless stream of information. The Internet, in particular, has transformed our ability to access information in very positive ways: Suddenly, you can find vast amounts of material simply by doing a Google search on your smartphone (but not while driving, right?). But it's becoming clear that there's also a downside to having such easy access. Good information is readily available, but so is unreliable information and provocative content that stirs people up. Nowhere is this more evident than on the various social media platforms (e.g., Facebook, Instagram, Twitter, Snapchat, YouTube) that people gravitate toward on a daily basis.

Lots of people are concerned about "fake news"—online content that is blatantly untrue. So-called "zombie stories" (stories that are repeatedly debunked but refuse to die) abound, and they seem to increase in number every year (as you'd expect from … well … zombies). And of course, people lie outright on the web all the time.

Truthfully, though, obviously fake news is not really the biggest problem we have when it comes to online information. One of the things that's much more challenging now is the ability to critically evaluate material that's biased or poorly informed, but not obviously so. To be very clear, it's not that people are dumb, or easily duped. Rather, website development has evolved to a point where it's sometimes really hard to figure out who or what the source of the website's information is—some websites that are definitely biased or ill-informed (and occasionally genuine purveyors of "fake news") look really slick, and totally trustworthy.

Determining the credibility of a web-based source can be tricky, but there are a few strategies that you can use (Caulfield, 2017). Your go-to strategy should be similar to that of professional fact checkers who work for organizations such as Snopes or Politifact. When these experts want to establish the credibility of an Internet source, their first move—ironically—is to *leave* the webpage they're checking out and search the web to see what other people are saying about the person or group that's behind that site. This strategy is referred to as *reading laterally* and is often helpful in establishing whether the site you're investigating is likely to be providing information that's biased in some particular way (McGrew, Ortega, Breakstone, & Wineburg, 2017).

Here's an example: In many states, politicians have periodically put forward the idea of raising the minimum wage. Such increases are usually pretty controversial. Credible sounding arguments against it (e.g., people will be laid off or fewer people will be hired because employers won't be able to afford the cost; the cost of everything will rise substantially) are often pitted against those in favor of it (it will give lower income people and students more money to spend, thus stimulating the economy).

In the United States, one website that has weighed in on the question of whether it's a good idea to raise the minimum wage is www.minimumwage.com. If you go to the website, you'll see that it's very professional looking and seems like a credible source of information. But try doing a little lateral reading: Type minimumwage.com into a search engine and then move past results that are from the page itself. Looking at other sources on the web, you'll find that the minimumwage.com website is maintained by an organization called the Employment Policies Institute (EPI). You'll also find that this organization is headed by someone who lobbies for the restaurant and hotel industry (and therefore likely has an interest in seeing the minimum wage stay low). Perhaps most important, lateral reading will reveal that a *New York Times* investigative reporter found no evidence that there *was* an EPI office.

Of course, this investigation doesn't mean that everything on the minimumwage.com website is false. Instead, what it reveals is that the information is likely to be biased in favor of a particular position. Knowing this should encourage you to think more critically about what you read on that site and search out information that speaks to the other side of the debate.

Suggestion 2: Beware of Claims Based on Poor—or Carefully Selected—Evidence, and Don't Overgeneralize

For conclusions to be trustworthy, they need to come from research that has been carefully designed. For example, researchers need to ask their questions in such a way that they will not get misleading or biased information from their participants. This means avoiding questions that are vague and unclear, as well as those that are likely to "lead" participants to one particular answer. Statements in the media that are supported by poor data are unlikely to stand the test of time, so it's important to look closely at the quality of the information on which any claim is based.

Of course, even good research can still be used to support claims that are totally misleading. Imagine a website reporting that a new form of therapy has been associated with reduced symptoms of autism in three high-quality research studies. That's quite exciting, right? Maybe not. What the website may have failed to report is that the beneficial effects of the therapy are short term, or that five other studies found that this new form of therapy doesn't seem to work at all. This type of "cherry-picking" is common in the popular media. People are quick to report findings that are in line with the story that they want others to believe but fail to note findings that are contradictory. You should always be looking for disconfirming evidence—even if it means seeking out information that conflicts with something you want to believe. Beware of confirmation bias!

Finally, it's important to distinguish between comments in the media that are based on evidence from a large number of people and those that come from one or two examples, anecdotes, or testimonials. The media is often keen to overgeneralize a finding that is based on one or two cases, suggesting that it should apply to everyone. Unfortunately, such individual cases (or even several) tell us nothing about what is true in general (Stanovich, 2019). For example, good research studies based on large groups of people show that smoking increases the likelihood of lung cancer. It is less relevant if you know a lifelong heavy smoker who is 95 years old. The general finding is the one to remember.

Suggestion 3: Always Consider Alternative Explanations and Remember That Some Things Just Happen by Chance

If you see a person crying, is it correct to assume that she or he is sad? It seems reasonable to make this assumption, but it could easily be wrong. Maybe he or she just peeled some onions or is trying contact lenses for the first time.

Or consider how the Boston Red Sox won the World Series in 2004 after many members of the team began wearing a particular metal-impregnated twisted rope necklace designed to "stabilize the electricity flow through the body." Do you think that the necklaces provided the players with some sort of mystical batting and throwing abilities? While it might be tempting to think that those necklaces brought about something extraordinary, it's always important to stop and consider what else may have caused the events you've observed. The 2004 Red Sox team was a group of dedicated athletes. It's more likely that their success at the World Series was a function of their hard work and talent, and not their choice of jewelry.

But what about your good friend Beth, who tells you that she had a dream about someone that she hadn't seen for months, and then met that very same person at the mall the next day. Do you think that Beth has special powers? What alternative explanation could there possibly be? The truth is not likely to be nearly as exciting as finding out that your friend is psychic: Although such occurrences make for a good story, the reality is that events like meeting a friend at the mall after a long time happen by chance all the time.

Suggestion 4: Ask Yourself If There Was a Control Group

The key importance of a control group in any experiment is frequently overlooked by the unsophisticated—an error to which you are no longer susceptible! The popular media are full of reports of experiments performed without control groups: "Talking to Plants Speeds Growth"; "Special Diet Controls Hyperactivity in Children"; "Graduates of Firewalking Seminar Risk Their Soles."

Consider the last example. Expensive commercial courses have long been promoted to teach people to walk barefoot on hot coals. Firewalkers supposedly protect their feet with a technique called "neurolinguistic programming." Many people have paid good money to learn the technique, and most do manage a quick walk on the coals. But is the technique necessary? And is anything remarkable happening?

To really answer these questions, we need a comparison group that has not learned the technique to see if they, too, can walk on the coals. Fortunately, physicist Bernard Leikind has provided one. Leikind showed with volunteers that anyone (with reasonably callused feet) can walk over a bed of coals without being burned. This is because the coals, which are made of light, fluffy carbon, transmit little heat when touched. The principle involved is similar to briefly putting your hand in a hot oven without touching any of its surfaces. If you touch a pan, you will be burned because metal transfers heat efficiently. But if your hand stays in the heated air, you'll be fine because air transmits little heat (Kida, 2006; Mitchell, 1987). Mystery solved!

Suggestion 5: Look for Errors in Distinguishing Between Correlation and Causation

As you now know, it is dangerous to presume that one thing *caused* another just because they are correlated. In spite of this, you will see many claims based on questionable correlations. Here's an example of mistaking correlation for causation: Jeane Dixon, a well-known astrologer, once answered a group of prominent scientists—who had declared that there is no scientific foundation for astrology—by saying, "They would do well to check the records at their local police stations, where they will learn that the rate of violent crime rises and falls with lunar cycles." Dixon, of course, believed that the moon affects human behavior.

If it is true that violent crime is more frequent at certain times of the month, doesn't that prove her point? Far from it. Increased crime could be due to darker nights, the fact that we expect others to act crazier during a full moon, or any number of similar factors. Besides, direct studies of the alleged lunar effect have shown that it doesn't occur (Dowling, 2005). Moonstruck criminals, influenced by a bad moon rising, are the stuff of fiction (Iosif & Ballon, 2005).

Suggestion 6: Beware of Oversimplifications, Especially Those Motivated by Monetary Gain

You'll find as you read this textbook that most psychological behaviors and phenomena like emotional well-being, healthy relationships, and a good memory typically have multiple causes and often develop over many years. For this reason, you should immediately question any claims that suggest, for example, that *the* cause of aggression has been established. Clearly, people's aggressive behaviors occur for many reasons, including how their parents treated them, the coping strategies that they have learned, and possibly even how their brains are wired.

Likewise, websites that promise to reveal "the secret to unlimited joy, health, money, relationships, love, youth: everything you have ever wanted" should be immediately suspect. According to these sites, all you need to do is send your desires out to the universe and the universe must respond by granting your wishes. And all it will cost you is the price of ordering a video. (It's no secret that the promoters are the real winners in this game.)

Summary

We are all bombarded daily with such a mass of new information that it is difficult to absorb it all. The available knowledge in an area like psychology, biology, or medicine is so vast that no single person can completely know or comprehend it. With this reality in mind, it becomes increasingly important that you become a critical, selective, and informed consumer of information (Lilienfeld et al., 2010).

MODULE 6 Information Literacy—Learning Outcomes Revisited

6.1 Name and apply six ways that people can critically evaluate information found in the popular press and on social media

Consider the source of information. Beware of poor or carefully selected information. Consider alternative explanations and remember things happen by chance. Check to ensure that reported studies had a control group. Distinguish between correlation and causation. Beware of oversimplifications. We hope, that after reading this module, you'll feel more confident evaluating the information that you see and read in a variety of sources!

Reflective Practice

Content Check

1. Popular media reports usually stress objective accuracy. T or F?
2. The finding that people can walk on hot coals after taking a "firewalking" course demonstrates that the course is necessary for people who want to learn this skill. T or F?
3. Blaming the lunar cycle for variations in the rate of violent crime is an example of mistaking correlation for causation. T or F?
4. If a psychology student uses a sleep-learning device to pass a midterm exam, it proves that the device works. T or F?

Skill Check

Think Critically

5. Imagine that you have come across a claim on Twitter reporting on a new study indicating that immunizing children has been conclusively linked to autism in children. How could you evaluate the truth of this claim?

Self-Reflect

How actively do you evaluate and question claims made by an authority or found in the media? Could you be a more critical consumer of information? *Should* you be a more critical consumer of information?

ANSWERS

1. F 2. F 3. T 4. F 5. You could begin by doing a lateral search on the person or organization behind the study, and then do the same for the person or organization responsible for the tweet—you would be looking for any evidence of bias. You should also go directly to the source (that is, the original article) to ensure that the claims are not misrepresenting (or oversimplifying) what was reported in the paper itself.

MODULE

7 Brain and Behavior
The Nervous System

Punch-Drunk

He died of a self-inflicted gunshot wound in February 2011. Not to his head, mind you, but to his chest, because he wanted to leave his brain to science. Two-time Super Bowl winner Dave Duerson blamed his post-football troubles, including memory loss, difficulty spelling words, depression, and moodiness, on the repeated concussions that he suffered on the playing field. Boxers even have a name for it: punch-drunk.

FOTOKITA/Shutterstock.com

Sure enough, autopsies have since revealed the same signs of *chronic traumatic encephalopathy* in the brains of dozens of other deceased National Football League players, as well as in athletes from many other violent sports, such as hockey and boxing. We don't normally notice the key role the nervous system—and especially the brain—plays in all that makes us human. But an injury to this vital system, such as the one Dave Duerson suffered, can dramatically change a person forever. How does it all work? Let's explore this fascinating realm.

~LEARNING OUTCOMES~

After reading this module you should be able to:

- **7.1** Outline the major divisions of the nervous system
- **7.2** Describe how individual neurons function
- **7.3** Describe how neurons communicate with each other
- **7.4** Distinguish between neuroplasticity and neurogenesis

The Nervous System—Wired for Action

Learning Outcome 7.1 Outline the major divisions of the nervous system

Who you are can be traced to electrical impulses flashing through your nervous system. Suppose you suffered a *stroke*, which occurs when an artery carrying blood in the brain bleeds or becomes blocked, causing some brain tissue to die. Almost instantly, you would realize that something is wrong. You might not be able to move, feel parts of your body, see, or speak. However, some nervous system injuries involve less dramatic, but equally disabling, changes in personality, thinking, judgment, or emotions. Some, such as Dave Duerson's chronic traumatic encephalopathy, can take years to become apparent (Montenigro et al., 2015).

Let's begin with an overview of the nervous system by following Mike and Molly, who are out in the park playing catch. A blaze of activity lights up many of the 100 billion or so *neurons* that make up their nervous systems. A **neuron** (NOOR-on) is a cell in the nervous system that transmits information (see ➤ Figure 7.1). All of those neurons are sustained by at least 10 times as many *glia*, cells that support neurons in a variety of ways (Herculano-Houzel, 2012).

The **central nervous system (CNS)** consists of the brain, which contains most of those neurons and does most of the "computing," and the spinal cord (Banich & Compton, 2018). The **spinal cord** is a large column of nerves that transmits information between the brain and the peripheral nervous system. Suppose that Mike's brain, the "command center," gets the bright idea to throw the ball a bit high over Molly's head. His spinal cord then relays the message to his **peripheral nervous system (PNS)**, the parts of the nervous system outside the brain and spinal cord. Directed by messages that flow down many of the 31 pairs of **spinal nerves** carrying sensory and motor messages to and from the spinal cord, Mike's body, right hand, and arm coordinate to throw the ball.

Are nerves the same as neurons? No. Neurons, as we will soon see, are tiny. You usually need a microscope to see one. **Nerves** are large bundles of many neuron fibers (called *axons*). You can easily see nerves without magnification.

Oops. The ball is even higher than Mike anticipated. To catch it, a huge amount of information must quickly be collected by Molly's eyes (Where's that ball going?), muscles (Are my hands in place to catch it?), and other senses (What's that sound behind me? Will I lose my balance if I try to catch it?), and sent to her brain to be interpreted. Information from her muscles flows back to her brain via the spinal nerves while input from her eyes, ears, and sense of balance arrives via some of the 12 pairs of **cranial nerves**, which connect to the brain directly without passing through the spinal cord. Decisions must be made, and messages must then be sent out to direct countless muscle fibers (move my body and hands to catch that ball while avoiding that couple and their dog sitting on the lawn behind me).

The Peripheral Nervous System

The peripheral nervous system can be divided into two major parts. The **somatic nervous system (SNS)** is the network linking the spinal cord with the body and sense organs. In general, it controls voluntary behavior, such as when Molly

Neuron A cell in the nervous system that transmits information.
Central nervous system (CNS) The brain and spinal cord.
Spinal cord A column of nerves that transmits information between the brain and the peripheral nervous system.
Peripheral nervous system (PNS) The parts of the nervous system outside the brain and spinal cord.
Spinal nerves Major nerves that carry sensory and motor messages in and out of the spinal cord.
Nerve A bundle of neuron axons.
Cranial nerves Major nerves that leave the brain without passing through the spinal cord.
Somatic nervous system (SNS) A network linking the spinal cord with the body and sense organs.

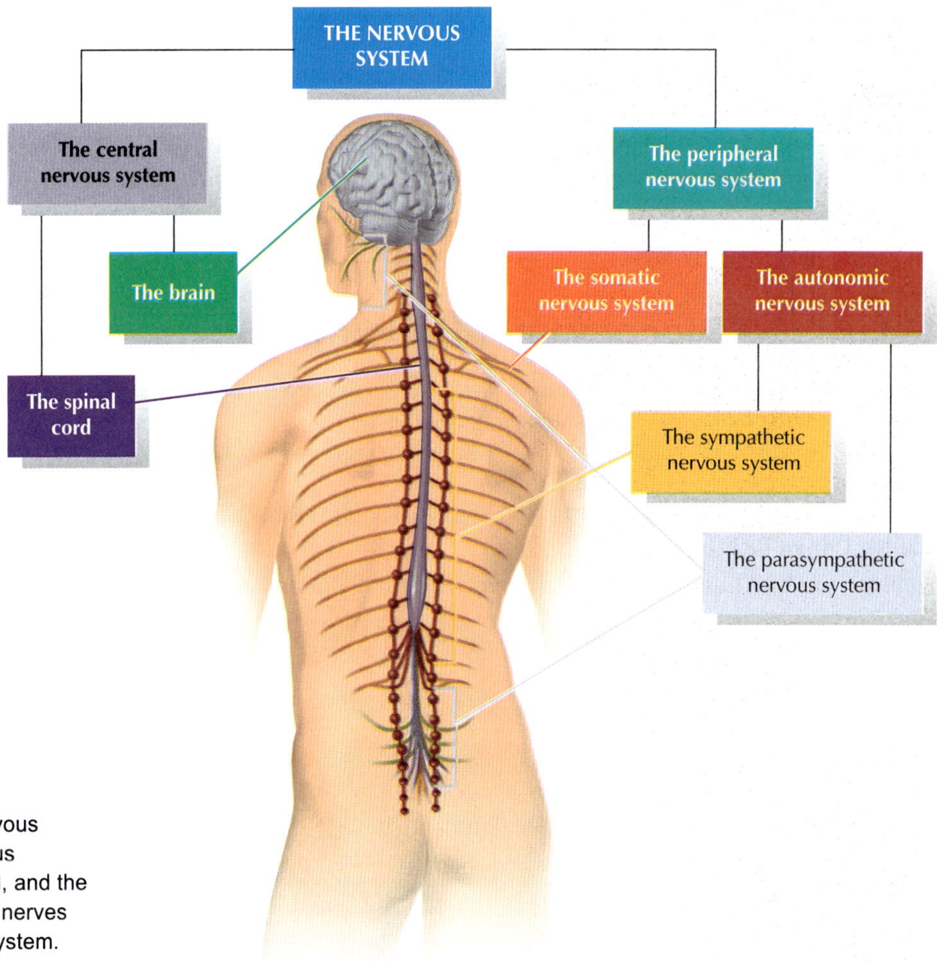

➤ **Figure 7.1**

Divisions of the nervous system. The nervous system can be divided into the central nervous system, made up of the brain and spinal cord, and the peripheral nervous system, composed of the nerves connecting the body to the central nervous system.

lurches backwards to catch the ball. In contrast, the **autonomic nervous system (ANS)** is the collection of axons that carry information to and from internal organs and glands. The word *autonomic* means self-governing. Activities governed by the ANS, such as heart rate, digestion, and perspiration are mostly vegetative or automatic. Thus, messages carried by the SNS can make Molly's hand move, but they cannot make her eyes dilate. Likewise, messages that the ANS carries can stimulate the release of the hormone *adrenaline*, but they cannot help Molly voluntarily dodge that snarling dog. If Molly feels a burst of fear when she almost steps on the dog, or a surge of love for Mike when he shows concern, that activity will be carried by her ANS. The ANS plays a central role in our emotional lives. In fact, without the ANS, a person would feel little emotion. (See Module 44 for more information about the ANS and emotion.)

The SNS and ANS work together to coordinate the body's internal reactions to events in the world outside the body. For example, when the dog lunges at Molly, her SNS controls her leg muscles so that she can jump out of the way. At the same time, her ANS activates her internal organs, raising her blood pressure, quickening her rate of breathing, and causing other automatic reactions. The ANS can be divided into the *sympathetic* and *parasympathetic* branches.

How do the branches of the autonomic system differ? In essence, the **sympathetic nervous system** is the division of the autonomic nervous system that coordinates arousal, while the **parasympathetic nervous system** is the part that quiets the body and conserves energy (➤ Figure 7.2). The sympathetic branch energizes Molly's heightened reaction to the lunging dog. It is responsible for initiating the "fight or flight" reaction during times of danger or high emotion. Right after she escapes the dog, she has to stop and catch her breath for a moment while her parasympathetic branch returns her internal organs to a lower level of arousal. Of course, both branches of the ANS are always active. At any given moment, their combined activity determines the degree to which your body is relaxed or aroused.

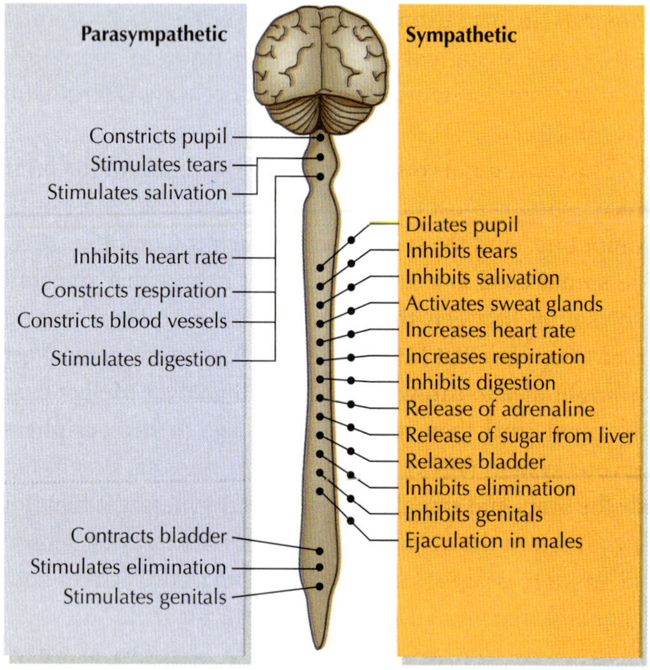

➤ **Figure 7.2**

Branches of the ANS. Both branches control involuntary actions. The sympathetic system generally activates the body. The parasympathetic system generally quiets it. The sympathetic branch relays its messages through clusters of neurons outside the spinal cord.

Neurons—Biocomputer Building Blocks

Learning Outcome 7.2 Describe how individual neurons function

Oddly enough, any single neuron is not very smart—it takes many of them just to make Molly blink. Yet individual neurons are the building blocks of the nervous system. Understanding how they work is a good first step toward better understanding how the nervous system functions.

Parts of a Neuron

While neurons come in very different shapes and sizes, most have four basic parts (➤ Figure 7.3). The **dendrites** (DEN-drytes), which look like tree roots, are neuron fibers that receive incoming messages. The **cell body**, or *soma* (SOH-mah), does the same. In contrast, the **axon** (AK-sahn) is the fiber that carries information away from the cell body of a neuron. Axons branch out into even thinner fibers ending in bulb-shaped **axon terminals**.

Like miniature cables, millions of miles of axons carry messages through the brain and nervous system (Breedlove, Watson, & Rosenzweig, 2013). Although some axons are only 0.1 millimeter long (about the width of a human hair or a pencil line), others stretch for several feet through the nervous system (from the base of your spine to your big toe, for instance). Large bundles of axons comprise most of the spinal cord and the nerves of the peripheral nervous system (PNS). By forming connections with the dendrites and somas of other neurons, axon terminals allow information to pass from neuron to neuron.

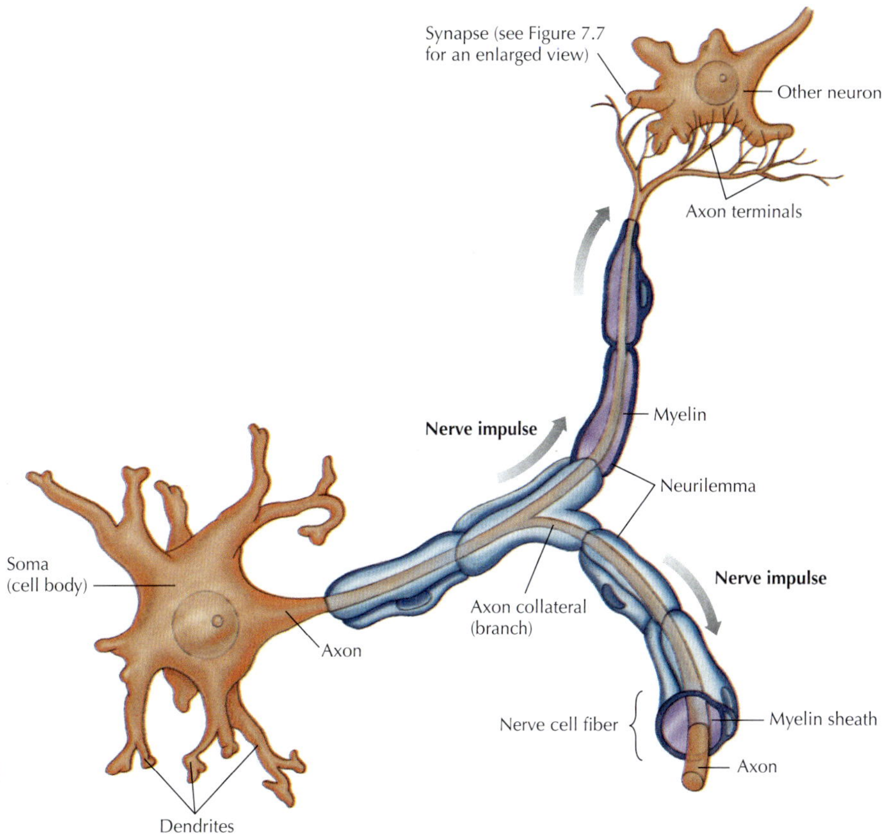

Figure 7.3

A stylized neuron. Action potentials usually travel from the dendrites and cell body to the branching ends of the axon.

Try this metaphor: Imagine that you are standing in a line of people who are holding hands. A person on the left end of the line wants to send a silent message to the person on the right end. She does this by pressing the hand of the person to her right, who presses the hand of the person to his right, and so on. The message arrives at your left hand (your dendrites). You decide whether to pass it on. (You are the soma.) The message goes out through your right arm (the axon). With your right hand (the axon terminals), you squeeze the hand of the person to your right, and the message moves on.

Neural Function

So how does a neuron actually send messages from the dendrites (the left hand in this metaphor) to the axon terminals (the right hand)? Neural function is primarily electrical. That's why electrically stimulating the brain affects behavior. To prove this point, researcher José Delgado once entered a bullring with a cape and a radio transmitter. The bull charged. Delgado retreated. At the last instant, the speeding bull stopped short. Why? Delgado had placed radio-activated electrodes (metal wires) deep within the bull's brain. These, in turn, electrically stimulated control centers that brought the bull to a halt (Blackwell, 2012).

Electrically charged molecules called *ions* (EYE-ons) are found inside each neuron. Other ions lie outside the neuron. Some ions have a positive electrical charge, whereas others have a negative charge. When a neuron is inactive (or resting), more of these plus, or positive, charges exist outside the neuron and more minus, or negative, charges exist inside. As a result, the inside of each resting neuron in your brain has an electrical charge of about –60 to –70 millivolts at the axon. (A millivolt is one-thousandth of a volt.) In this way, every neuron in your brain can be thought of as a tiny biological battery.

Autonomic nervous system (ANS) The collection of axons that carry information to and from internal organs and glands.

Sympathetic nervous system The division of the autonomic nervous system that coordinates arousal.

Parasympathetic nervous system The part of the autonomic nervous system that quiets the body and conserves energy.

Dendrites Neuron fibers that receive incoming messages.

Cell body The part of the neuron or other cell that contains the nucleus of the cell.

Axon A fiber that carries information away from the cell body of a neuron.

Axon terminals Bulb-shaped structures at the ends of axons that form synapses with the dendrites and cell bodies of other neurons.

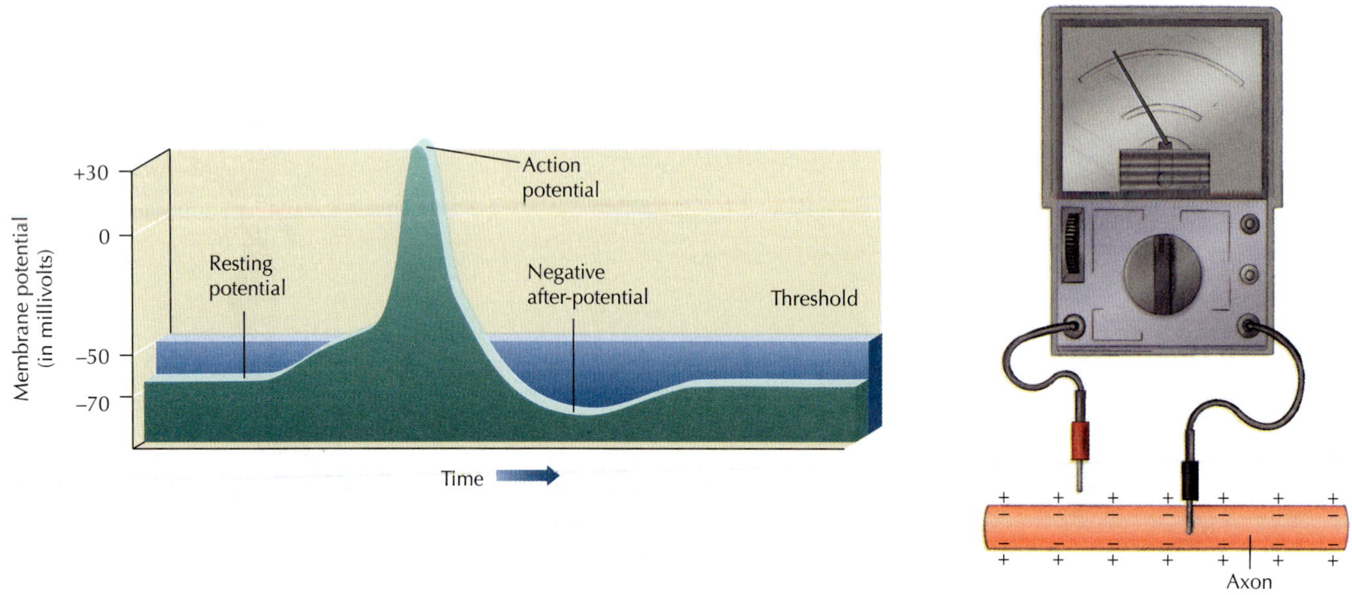

➤ Figure 7.4

Measuring electrical activity in the neuron. Tiny electrical probes called *microelectrodes*, placed inside and outside an axon, measure its activity. The inside of an axon at rest is about –60 to –70 millivolts, compared with the outside. Electrochemical changes in a neuron generate an *action potential*. When sodium ions (Na^+) that have a positive charge rush into the cell, its interior briefly becomes positive. After the action potential, positive potassium ions (K^+) flow out of the axon and restore its negative charge. (See Figure 7.5 for further explanation.)

The electrical charge of an inactive neuron is called its **resting potential**. But neurons seldom get much rest. Messages constantly arrive from other neurons, causing the resting potential to fluctuate. Some inputs excite the neuron, slightly raising the resting potential, while others inhibit the neuron, slightly lowering the resting potential. If enough excitatory inputs arrive within a short span of time, the overall electrical charge will rise quite a bit. At about –50 millivolts, the neuron will reach its *threshold*, or trigger point for firing (see ➤ Figure 7.4). It's as if the neuron says, "Ah-ha! I have had enough combined input to justify an output of my own." When a neuron reaches its threshold, an **action potential**, a brief change in a neuron's electrical charge, sweeps down the axon at up to 200 miles per hour (➤ Figure 7.5). That may seem fast, but it still takes at least a split second to react. That's one reason it is so difficult to return a 130-mile-per-hour professional tennis serve.

What happens during an action potential? Tiny tunnels or holes called **ion channels** in the axon membrane function like tiny gates or doors. Normally, these ion channels are blocked by molecules that prevent sodium ions (Na^+) from entering the axon. During an action potential, the gates pop open. This allows sodium ions (Na^+) to rush into the axon (Freberg, 2021). The channels first open near the soma. Then, gate after gate opens down the length of the axon as the action potential zips along (➤ Figure 7.6).

Each action potential is an *all-or-nothing event* (it occurs completely or not at all). You might find it helpful to picture the axon as a row of dominoes set on end. Tipping over the dominoes is an all-or-nothing act. Once the first domino

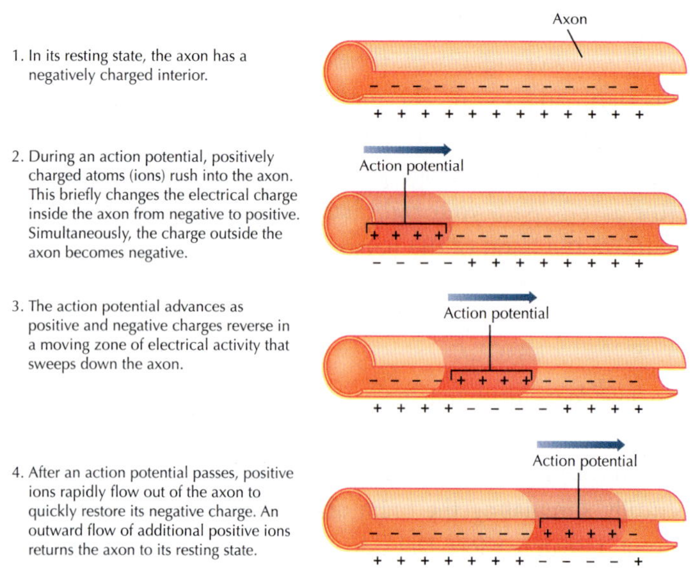

➤ Figure 7.5

The action potential. The inside of an axon normally has a negative electrical charge, and the fluid surrounding an axon is normally positive. As an action potential passes along the axon, these charges reverse, so that the interior of the axon briefly becomes positive. This process is described in more detail in Figure 7.6.

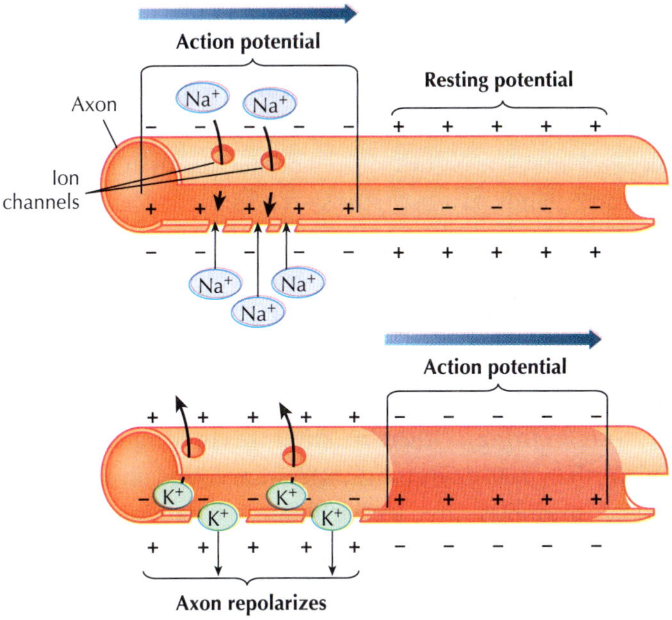

Figure 7.6

The interior of an axon. The right end of the top axon is at rest. Thus, it has a negative charge inside. An action potential begins when ion channels open and sodium ions (Na^+) rush into the axon. In this drawing, the action potential travels from left to right along the axon. In the lower axon, the action potential has moved to the right. After it passes, potassium ions (K^+) flow out of the axon. This quickly renews the negative charge inside the axon, so that it can fire again. Sodium ions that enter the axon during an action potential are pumped out more slowly. Removing them restores the original resting potential.

drops, a wave of falling blocks zips rapidly to the end of the line. Similarly, when an action potential is triggered near the soma, a wave of activity travels down the length of the axon. This is what happens in long chains of neurons as a dancer's brain tells her feet what to do next, beat after beat.

After an action potential, the cell briefly dips below its resting level and becomes less able or ready to fire. This **negative after-potential** occurs because potassium ions (K^+) flow out of the neuron while the membrane gates are open (Figure 7.6). After an action potential, ions flow both into and out of the axon, recharging it for more action. In our model, it takes an instant for the row of dominoes to be set up again. Soon, however, the axon is ready for another wave of activity.

Saltatory Conduction The axons of some neurons (such as the one pictured in Figure 2.3) are coated with an insulating material called the **myelin sheath** (MY-eh-lin). Under a microscope, myelin appears white, while neurons appear gray. Because of this, areas of the brain containing mainly neuron cell bodies are commonly referred to as *gray matter*, while areas containing mainly myelinated axons are labeled *white matter*. Similarly, if you were to cut through the spinal cord, you would see columns of insulating white matter wrapped around a gray-matter core of bundles of axons (look ahead to Figure 7.8).

Small gaps in the myelin help action potentials travel faster. Instead of passing down the entire length of an axon, the action potential leaps from gap to gap, a process called **saltatory conduction**. (The Latin word *saltare* means to jump or leap.) Without the added speed of saltatory action potentials, it would likely be harder to brake in time to avoid many automobile accidents. When the myelin layer is damaged, a person may suffer from numbness, weakness, or paralysis. That is what happens in multiple sclerosis, a disease that occurs when the immune system attacks and destroys the myelin in a person's body (Kipp, 2016).

Synaptic Transmission and Neural Networks—Wiring the Biocomputer

Learning Outcome 7.3 Describe how neurons communicate with each other

Remarkably, individual neurons do not physically touch each other; they are separated by a microscopic gap called the **synapse** (SIN-aps). **Synaptic transmission** occurs when an action potential reaches the tips of the axon terminals, releasing a **neurotransmitter** (NOOR-oh-TRANS-mit-er)—a chemical that moves information from one neuron to another—into the synaptic gap (➤ **Figure 7.7**).

Let's return to our metaphor of people standing in a line. To be more accurate, you and the others shouldn't be holding hands. Instead, each person should have a squirt gun in his or her right hand. To pass along a

Resting potential The electrical charge of an inactive neuron.
Action potential A brief change in a neuron's electrical charge.
Ion channels Tiny openings through the axon membrane.
Negative after-potential A drop in electrical charge below the resting potential.
Myelin sheath Insulating material that covers some axons.
Saltatory conduction The process by which action potentials traveling down the axons of neurons coated with myelin jump from gap to gap in the myelin layer.
Synapse A microscopic space over which messages pass between two neurons.
Synaptic transmission The chemical process that carries information from one neuron to another.
Neurotransmitter A chemical that moves information from one nervous-system cell to another.

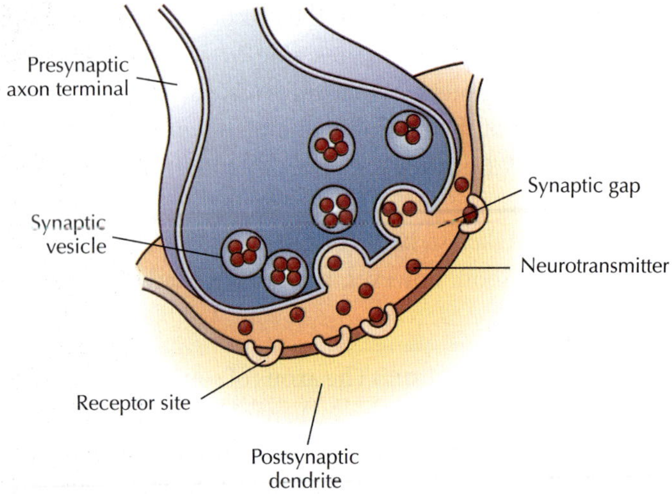

Figure 7.7

The synapse. Neurotransmitters are stored in tiny sacs called *synaptic vesicles* (VES-ih-kels). When an action potential reaches the end of an axon, the vesicles move to the surface and release neurotransmitters. These molecules cross the synaptic gap to affect the next neuron. The size of the gap is exaggerated here; it is actually only about one-millionth of an inch. Some transmitter molecules excite the next neuron and some inhibit its activity.

message, you would squirt the left hand of the person to your right. When that person notices this "message," he or she would squirt the left hand of the person to the right, and so on.

When neurotransmitters cross over a synapse, they temporarily bond to special receiving areas on the next neuron (see Figure 7.7). Each tiny **receptor site** on the cell membrane is sensitive to neurotransmitters. The sites are found in large numbers on neuron cell bodies and dendrites. Muscles and glands have receptor sites, too.

Neurotransmitters

Do neurotransmitters always trigger an action potential? No, but they do change the likelihood of an action potential. Some neurotransmitters *excite* the next neuron (move it closer to firing). Others *inhibit* it (make firing less likely). More than 100 neurotransmitters are found in the brain. Some examples are acetylcholine, dopamine, gamma-aminobutyric acid (GABA), glutamate, norepinephrine, and serotonin (■ **Table 7.1**).

Why are there so many neurotransmitters? Some neurotransmitters are used by specific pathways that interlink regions of the brain. It is as if different pathways "speak" different languages. Perhaps this helps prevent confusing crosstalk or intermixing of messages. For example, the brain has a reward or pleasure system that communicates mainly via dopamine (DOPE-ah-meen) (Mark et al., 2011; Syed et al., 2016).

Slight variations in neurotransmitter function may be related to temperament differences in infancy and

TABLE 7.1 | Major Neurotransmitters

Neurotransmitter	Main Mode of Action	Function in the Brain	Effects of Imbalance
Acetylcholine	Excitatory neurotransmitter	Participates in movement, autonomic function, learning, and memory	Deficiency may play a role in Alzheimer's disease
Dopamine	Excitatory neurotransmitter	Participates in motivation, reward, planning of behavior	Deficiency may lead to Parkinson's disease, reduced feelings of pleasure; excess may lead to schizophrenia
GABA	Inhibitory neurotransmitter	Major inhibitory effect in the CNS; participates in moods	Deficiency may lead to anxiety
Glutamate	Excitatory neurotransmitter	Major excitatory effect in the CNS; participates in learning and memory	Excess may lead to neuron death and autism; deficiency may lead to tiredness
Norepinephrine	Excitatory neurotransmitter	Participates in arousal, vigilance, and mood	Excess may lead to anxiety
Serotonin	Inhibitory neurotransmitter	Participates in mood, appetite, and sleep	Deficiency may lead to depression and/or anxiety

Adapted from Freberg, 2021; Kalat, 2021; Prus, 2017.

personality differences in adulthood (Ashton, 2013). Outright disturbances of any neurotransmitter can have serious consequences. For example, too much dopamine may cause schizophrenia (Howes, McCutcheon, & Stone, 2015), whereas too little serotonin may underlie depression (Torrente, Gelenberg, & Vrana, 2012).

Many drugs mimic, duplicate, or block neurotransmitters. For example, the chemical structure of cocaine is similar to that of dopamine. In the short run, cocaine can trigger an increase in dopamine in the reward system, resulting in a drug high (España et al., 2010). In the long run, the overuse of recreational drugs such as cocaine overstimulates the reward system and disturbs dopamine function, resulting in drug addiction (Taber et al., 2012).

As another example, the drug curare (cue-RAH-ree) causes paralysis. Acetylcholine (ah-SEET-ul-KOH-leen) normally activates muscles. By attaching to receptor sites on muscles, curare blocks acetylcholine, preventing the activation of muscle cells. As a result, a person or animal given curare cannot move—a fact known to the indigenous peoples of South America's Amazon River basin, who use curare as an arrow poison for hunting. Without acetylcholine, a dancer couldn't move a muscle, much less take a step.

Neural Regulators More subtle brain activities are affected by chemicals called **neuropeptides** (NOOR-oh-PEP-tides). Neuropeptides do not carry messages directly. Instead, they *regulate* the activity of other neurons. By doing so, they affect memory, pain, emotion, pleasure, moods, hunger, sexual behavior, and other basic processes. For example, when you touch something hot, you jerk your hand away. The messages for this action are carried by neurotransmitters. At the same time, pain may cause the brain to release neuropeptides called *enkephalins* (en-KEF-ah-lins). These opiate-like neural regulators relieve pain and stress. Yet other neuropeptides called *endorphins* (en-DORF-ins) are released by the pituitary gland. Together, these chemicals reduce the pain so that it is not too disabling (Bruehl et al., 2012).

We now can explain the painkilling effect of placebos (fake pills or injections); they raise endorphin levels (Price, Finniss, & Benedetti, 2008). A release of endorphins also seems to underlie runner's high, masochism, acupuncture, and the euphoria sometimes associated with childbirth, painful initiation rites, and even sport parachuting (Janssen & Arntz, 2001). In each case, pain and stress cause the release of endorphins. In turn, these endorphins induce feelings of pleasure or euphoria similar to being high on morphine. People who say they are "addicted" to running may be closer to the truth than they realize. Ultimately, neural regulators may help explain addiction, depression, schizophrenia, and other puzzling topics.

Neural Networks

While our earlier metaphor for neural functioning and synaptic transmission (people squirting water at each other) is helpful for beginning to understand nervous system function, it is, like all metaphors, an oversimplification. Most importantly, neurons, unlike people, can have thousands of "arms" and "hands." That is, any given neuron may synapse with many thousands of other neurons, especially in your brain. It is this vast overall **neural network** of 100 trillion or more interlinked neurons that allows you to process immense amounts of information, producing intelligence and consciousness (Kalat, 2021; Sporns & Betzel, 2016).

A simple neural network, a **reflex arc**, occurs when a stimulus provokes an automatic response. Such reflexes arise within the spinal cord, without any help from the brain (➤ **Figure 7.8**). Imagine that Molly steps on a thorn. (Yes, she's still playing catch with Mike.) Pain is detected in her foot via a **sensory neuron**, a neuron that carries messages from the senses toward the CNS. Instantly, the sensory neuron fires off a message to Molly's spinal cord.

Inside the spinal cord, the sensory neuron synapses with an *interneuron*, a neuron that links two others. The interneuron in turn activates a **motor neuron**, a neuron that carries commands from the CNS to muscles. The muscle fibers are made up of *effector cells* (cells capable of producing a response). The muscle cells contract and cause Molly's foot to withdraw. Notice that no brain activity is required for a reflex arc to occur. Molly's body reacts automatically to protect itself.

In reality, even a simple reflex usually triggers more complex activity. For example, the muscles of Molly's other leg must contract to support her as she shifts her weight. Even this can be done by the spinal cord, but it involves a bigger network of cells and several spinal nerves. Also, the spinal cord

Receptor site An area on the surface of neurons and other cells that is sensitive to neurotransmitters or hormones.

Neuropeptides Brain chemicals, such as enkephalins and endorphins, that regulate the activity of neurons.

Neural network Interlinked collection of neurons that processes information in the brain.

Reflex arc The simplest behavior, in which a stimulus provokes an automatic response.

Sensory neuron A cell in the nervous system that transmits information from the sense organs to the central nervous system.

Motor neuron A cell in the nervous system that transmits commands from the brain to the muscles.

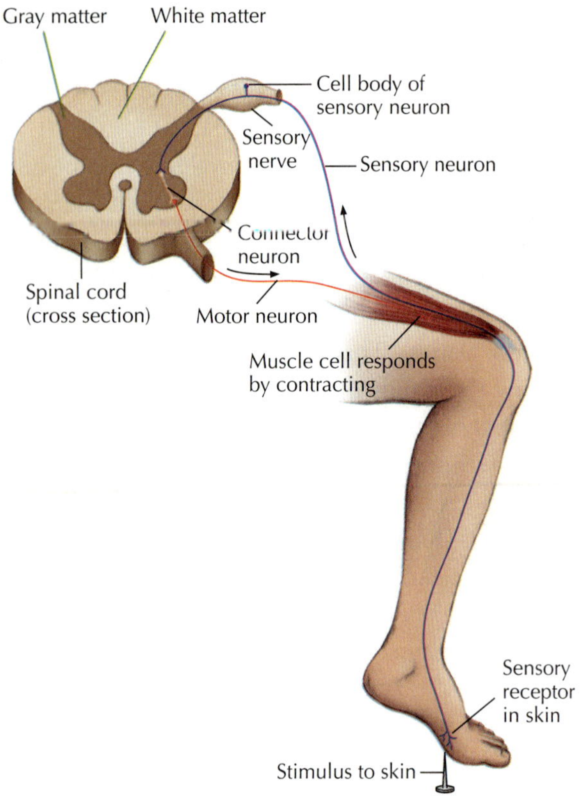

Figure 7.8

A simple reflex. A sensory–motor arc, or reflex, is set in motion by a stimulus to the skin (or other part of the body). The neural message travels to the spinal cord and then back out to a muscle, which contracts. Such reflexes provide "automatic" protective devices for the body.

normally informs the brain of its actions. As her foot pulls away from the thorn, Molly feels the pain and thinks, "Ouch! What was that?"

Perhaps you have realized how adaptive it is to have a spinal cord capable of responding on its own. Such automatic responses free up brain-based neural networks in Mike and Molly to make more complex calculations—such as determining the locations of trees, lampposts, and chatting picnickers—as they take turns deciding how best to make grandstand catches.

How can neural networks make decisions? Simplified greatly, **Figure 7.9** shows a small stylized neural network involved in making a decision. Five neurons synapse with a single neuron that, in turn, connects with three more neurons. At the time depicted in the diagram, the single neuron is receiving one stronger and two weaker excitatory messages (+), as well as two inhibitory ones (–). Does it fire an impulse? It depends: If enough exciting messages arrive close

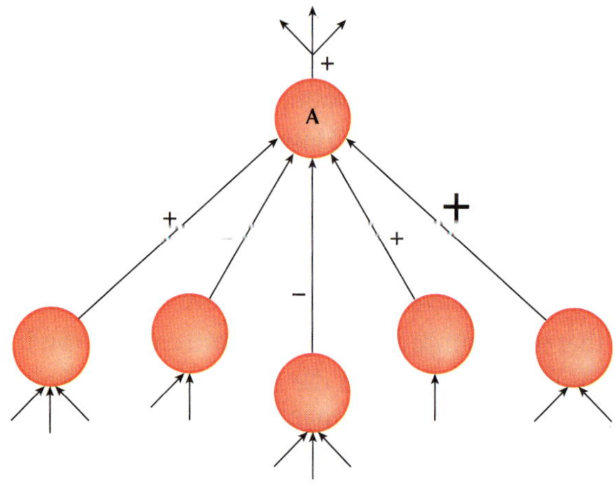

Figure 7.9

A small stylized neural network. In this depiction, neuron A receives inputs from two weaker and one stronger excitatory connections (+) and two inhibitory connections (–) and combines the inputs into a "decision" to launch an action potential, which may, in turn, help trigger further synaptic transmissions in other neurons. Any actual network involved in processing decisions like these would be much more complicated than illustrated here, but the basic idea remains the same.

together in time, the neuron reaches its threshold and fires—but only if it doesn't get too many inhibiting messages that push it *away* from its trigger point. In this way, messages are *combined* before a neuron "decides" to fire its all-or-nothing action potential.

Think of Figure 7.9 in terms of another metaphor. You are out shopping with five friends and find a pair of jeans that you want to buy. Three of them think you should buy the jeans, and your best friend is especially positive (+), while two friends think you shouldn't (–). Because, on balance, the input is positive, you go ahead and buy the jeans. Maybe, in turn, you even tell some other friends that they should buy those jeans. Similarly, any single neuron in a neural network "listens" to the neurons that synapse with it and combines that input into an output. At any instant, a single neuron may weigh hundreds or thousands of inputs to produce an outgoing message. After the neuron recovers from the resulting action potential, it again combines the inputs, which may have changed in the meantime, into another output, and another, and another.

In this way, each neuron in your brain functions as a tiny biocomputer. Compared with the average laptop computer, a neuron is terribly simple and slow. But multiply these events by billions of neurons and trillions of synapses, all operating at the same time, and you have an amazing biocomputer—one that could fit easily inside a shoebox.

Neuroplasticity and Neurogenesis—The Dynamic Nervous System

Learning Outcome 7.4 Distinguish between neuroplasticity and neurogenesis

How is the brain programmed? Although it is appropriate to describe the brain as a *biocomputer*, it is not programmed in the usual sense of the word. Instead, it (and you) learns (Kolb & Whishaw, 2019). This capacity of our nervous systems to change in response to experience is known as **neuroplasticity**.

Consider, for example, taxi drivers from London, England, who must learn the names and locations of tens of thousands of streets in order to earn their licenses. Not only do experienced cabbies have superior memory for street information, but the parts of their brains responsible for processing this learning also are enlarged (Woollett & Maguire, 2011). Similarly, after undergoing cognitive behavior therapy, not only do people with depression become more able to control their negative moods, but images of their brains reveal more normal activity in brain areas related to emotional processing (Ritchey et al., 2011).

Neuroplasticity must be complicated, no? Maybe not. According to *Hebb's rule*, the repeated activation of synapses between two neurons strengthens the connection between them (Hebb, 1949). As a result of repeated experiences, synaptic connections may grow stronger, and new ones may form. (Figure 7.9 shows one particularly strong synapse—the large +.) Conversely, inactive synaptic connections may weaken and even die.

Consequently, every new experience is reflected in synaptic changes in the brain. For example, rats raised in a complex environment have more synapses and longer dendrites in their brains than rats raised in a simpler environment (Kolb, Gibb, & Gorny, 2003). Or consider Nico and Brooke, teenagers who had large portions of their brains removed as infants. Nevertheless, they are functioning well today; over the years, their brains have literally "rewired" themselves (Immordino-Yang, 2008; Kolb et al., 2011).

Are adult human brains also neuroplastic? Could Dave Duerson's brain have healed itself? Although adult brains are much less neuroplastic, they too can be changed with patience and persistence (Livingston-Thomas et al., 2016; Xerri, 2012). Unfortunately for adults like Dave Duerson, who suffer from *chronic traumatic encephalopathy*, the prospects for recovery are not good because the brain damage suffered from head traumas can be extensive and often triggers a subsequent disease process that continues to damage the brain long after the original traumas have ended (Baugh et al., 2012).

Neurogenesis

The nervous system is "plastic" in another way. It has long been known that nerves in the peripheral nervous system (PNS) can *regrow* if they are damaged. Because of this, patients can expect to regain some control over severed limbs once they have been reattached. In contrast, a serious injury to the central nervous system was long thought to be permanent. Recently, however, scientists have begun to make progress repairing damaged neurons in the spinal cord (Rossignol & Frigon, 2011).

Can brain damage also be repaired? Until a few years ago, it was widely believed that we are born with all the brain cells we will ever have (Ben Abdallah et al., 2010). This led to the depressing idea that as we age, we all slowly go downhill because the brain loses thousands of neurons every day. Rather than facing a steady decline, however, we now know that the brain is also capable of **neurogenesis** (noor-oh-JEN-uh-sis), the production of new brain cells (Lee, Clemenson, & Gage, 2012). Each day, thousands of new cells originate deep within the brain, move to the surface, and link up with other neurons to become part of the brain's circuitry. This was stunning news to neuroscientists, who must now figure out what the new cells do. Most likely, they are involved in learning, memory, and our ability to adapt to changing circumstances (Cameron & Glover, 2015).

The discovery of neurogenesis in adult brains is leading to treatment possibilities that offer new hope for people suffering from a variety of other disabilities, such as depression, addiction, and schizophrenia (Chambers, 2012; Fournier & Duman, 2012).

Neuroplasticity The capacity of the brain to change in response to experience.

Neurogenesis The production of new brain cells.

MODULE 7

The Nervous System—Learning Outcomes Revisited

7.1 Outline the major divisions of the nervous system

The nervous system can be divided into the central nervous system (CNS) and the peripheral nervous system (PNS). The CNS is made up of the brain, which carries out most of the "computing" in the nervous system, and the spinal cord, which connects the brain to the PNS. The PNS includes the somatic nervous system (SNS), which carries sensory information to the brain and motor commands to the body, and the autonomic nervous system (ANS), which controls vegetative and automatic bodily processes. The ANS has a sympathetic branch and a parasympathetic branch.

7.2 Describe how individual neurons function

The dendrites and soma of a neuron combine neural input and send it down the axon as an action potential. The action potential travels to the axon terminals. Neural function, including fluctuations of the neuron's resting potential and the firing of the action potential, is basically electrical in nature.

7.3 Describe how neurons communicate with each other

Communication between neurons is chemical. When an action potential reaches the end of the axon terminals, neurotransmitters are released into the synapse and attach to receptor sites on the adjacent neurons, exciting or inhibiting them. Chemicals called *neuropeptides* can also regulate synaptic activity in the brain. All behavior can be traced to networks of neurons.

7.4 Distinguish between neuroplasticity and neurogenesis

Neuroplasticity refers to the brain's ability to change in response to experiences. While neurons and nerves in the PNS often can regenerate, the term neurogenesis refers to the production of new neurons in the brain.

Reflective Practice

Content Check

1. The somatic and autonomic systems are part of the ____________ nervous system.
2. The parasympathetic nervous system is most active during times of high emotion. T or F?
3. The ____________ and ____________ are the receiving areas of a neuron where information from other neurons is accepted.
4. Action potentials are carried down the ____________ to the ____________ ____________.
5. The ____________ potential becomes a(n) ____________ potential when a neuron passes the threshold for firing.
6. The simplest neural network is a(n) ____________ ____________.
7. *Neuroplasticity* refers to the capacity of the nervous system to
   a. grow new neurons
   b. cover some axons with a thin layer of cells
   c. quickly recover from action potentials
   d. form new synaptic connections

Skill Check

Think Critically

8. Where in all the brain's "hardware" do you think the mind is found? What is the relationship between mind and brain?

Self-Reflect

How much of the functioning of your brain can you become aware of through introspection? How does a neural network differ from the central processing unit of a computer?

ANSWERS

1. peripheral 2. F 3. dendrites, cell body 4. axon, axon terminals 5. resting, action 6. reflex arc 7. d 8. These questions, known as the mind–body problem, have challenged thinkers for centuries. We still don't have any definitive answers. One recent view is that mental states are emergent properties of brain activity—that is, brain activity forms complex patterns that are, in a sense, more than the sum of their parts. Or, to use a rough analogy, if the brain were a musical instrument, then mental life would be like music played on that instrument.

MODULE 8

Brain and Behavior

Brain Research

How to Look Under Your Skull

Your 3-pound brain is wrinkled like a walnut, the size of a grapefruit, and the texture of tofu. How could such a squishy little blob of tissue enable us to make music of exquisite beauty? Or design an electric car? Or read a book to a small child? Or become a neuroscientist? *Biopsychology* is the study of how biological processes, especially those occurring in the nervous system, relate to behavior.

Along with other neuroscientists, biopsychologists try to learn which parts of your brain control particular mental or behavioral functions, such as being able to recognize faces or move your hands. That is, they try to learn where functions are localized (located) in the brain. Since it is not possible to settle issues about the brain subjectively, many objective techniques have been developed to help identify brain structures and the functions that they control. For example, the brain in this CT scan was damaged (shown in red) by a stroke, which occurs when an artery carrying blood in the brain bleeds or becomes blocked, causing some brain tissue to die. The location of the stroke determines what mental or behavioral functions are disrupted.

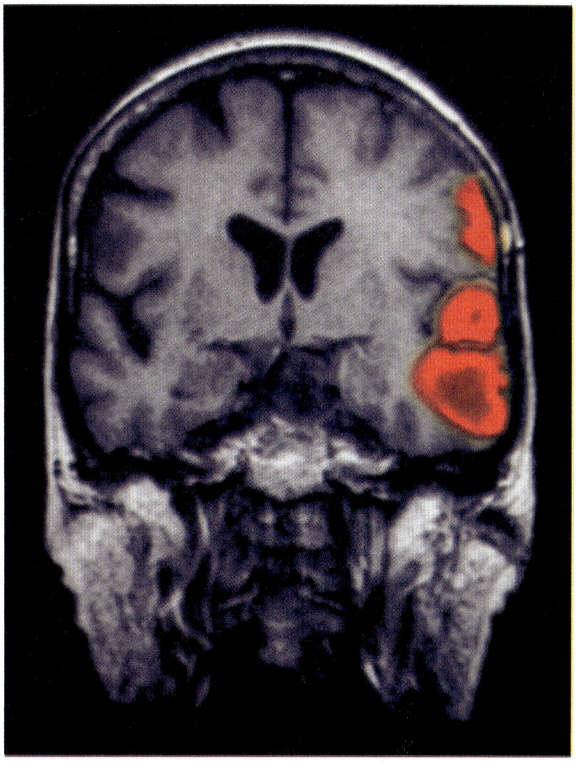
Scott Camazine/Science Source

~LEARNING OUTCOMES~

After reading this module you should be able to:

8.1 Identify three methods that scientists use to map brain structure

8.2 Identify four methods that scientists use to establish the function of brain regions

Mapping Brain Structure—Pieces of the Puzzle

Learning Outcomes 8.1 Identify three methods that scientists use to map brain structure

Anatomists have learned much about the structure of the brain by cutting apart (*dissecting*) autopsied brains. Dissection reveals that the brain is made up of many anatomically distinct areas comprised of *gray matter* (clusters of neuron cell bodies) interspersed with regions of *white matter* (bundles of myelinated axons), or pathways between those clusters. Fortunately, newer, less invasive technologies, such as the *CT scan* and the *MRI scan*, can be used to map brain structures in living brains (Kalat, 2021).

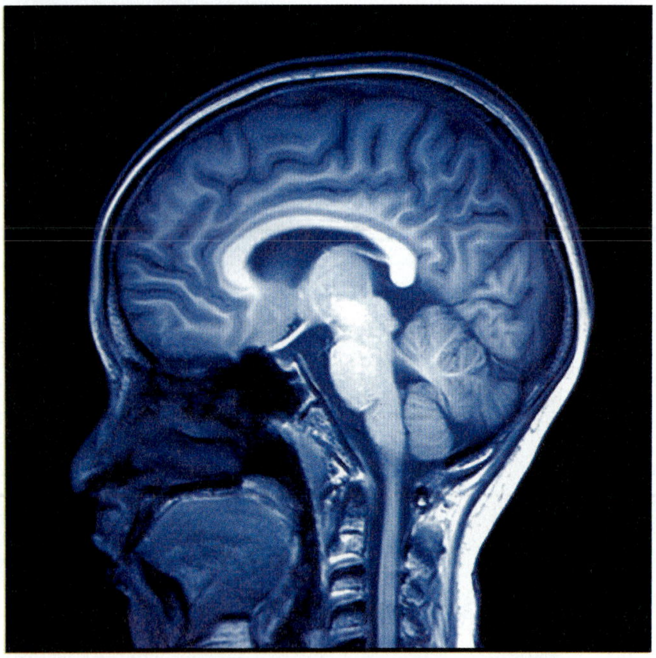

MriMan/Shutterstock.com

A colored MRI scan of the brain reveals many details. Can you identify any brain regions?

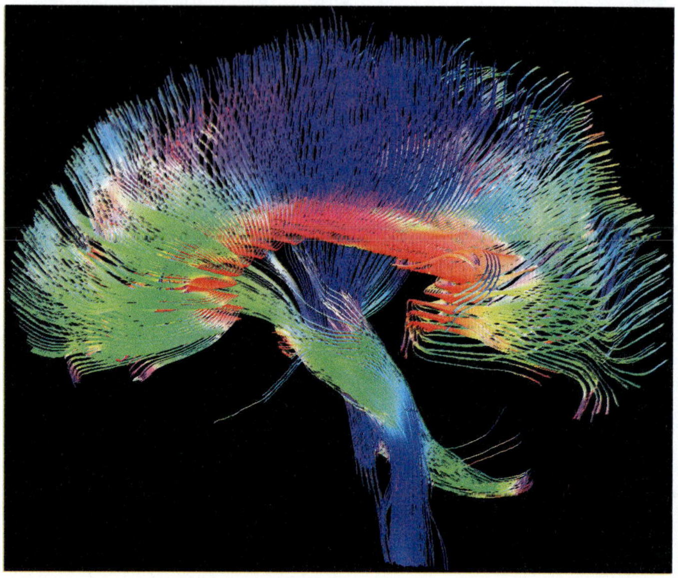

TOM BARRICK, CHRIS CLARK, SGHMS/Science Source

This colored MRI image reveals pathways in the brain of a healthy adult. Each pictured thread is a bundle of hundreds of thousands of axons (Human Connectome Project, 2013).

CT Scans

Computed tomography (CT) scans revolutionized the study of the brain by providing clearer images than those provided by conventional X-ray machines. In a CT scan, a computer collects X-rays of a single location taken from a number of different angles and forms them into an image. This procedure can reveal brain structure, as well as the location of strokes, injuries, tumors, and other brain disorders.

MRI Scans

Since they *are* X-rays, repeated CT scans may expose patients to unhealthy doses of radioactivity. Fortunately a newer technology with no known side effects, **magnetic resonance imaging (MRI) scans**, provide even more detailed images than are possible with CT scans. In an MRI scan, a person's body is placed inside a strong magnetic field. Processing by a computer then creates a three-dimensional model of the brain or body. Any two-dimensional plane, or slice, of the body can be selected and displayed as an image on a computer screen. MRI scans allow us to peer into the living brain, almost as if it were transparent. Recent developments in MRI technology have even made it possible to explore pathways in the brain in great detail (Sporns, 2013).

Exploring Brain Function—What Do the Parts Do?

Learning Outcomes 8.2 Identify four methods that scientists use to establish the function of brain regions

Imagine a mechanic handing you a car part. Even though you can clearly see the *structure* of the thing (it's about an inch long, with a round knob on one end, and a little prong …), you probably won't be able to figure out its *function* (… but is it part of the steering system, the brakes, or what?). Similarly, while it is valuable to be able to examine images of different brain structures and their interconnections, such as those made possible by CT scans and MRIs, it is another matter entirely to understand what role those structures play in normal brain function.

How can we figure out those functions? To answer questions such as this, we must **localize function** by linking psychological or behavioral capacities with particular brain structures. In many instances (the strange case of Phineas Gage reported in Module 5, for example), this has been done through *case studies*. Such case studies examine changes in

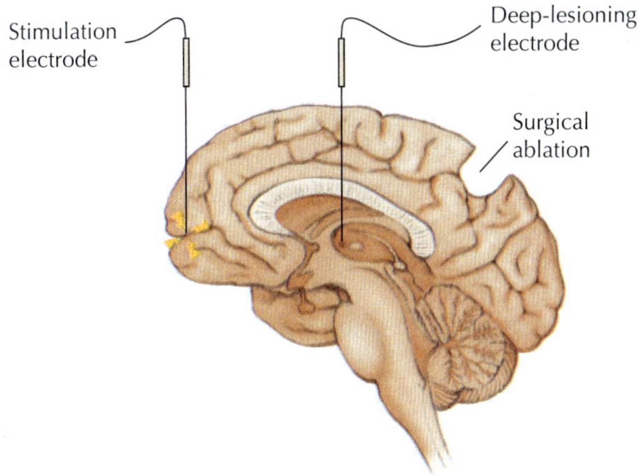

➤ **Figure 8.1**

Activating or removing brain structures. The functions of brain structures are explored by selectively activating or removing them. Brain research is often based on electrical stimulation, but chemical stimulation also is used at times.

personality, behavior, or sensory capacity caused by brain diseases or injuries. If damage to a particular part of the brain consistently leads to a particular loss of function, then we say that the function is localized in that structure. Presumably, that part of the brain controls the same function in all of us.

Although major brain injuries are easy enough to spot, psychologists also look for more subtle behavioral signs that the brain is not working properly. **Neurological soft signs**, as they are called, include clumsiness, an awkward gait, poor eye–hand coordination, and other problems with perception or fine muscle control (Raymond & Noggle, 2013). These telltale signs are "soft" in the sense that they aren't direct tests of the brain, like a CT or MRI scan. Long-term brain damage is usually first diagnosed with soft signs. Likewise, soft signs help psychologists diagnose problems ranging from childhood learning disorders to full-blown psychosis (Banich & Compton, 2018).

In addition to case studies, researchers have learned much from **electrical stimulation of the brain (ESB)** (➤ Figure 8.1). For example, the surface of the brain can be "turned on" by stimulating it with a mild electrical current delivered through a thin insulated wire called an **electrode**. When this is done during brain surgery, the patient can describe the effect of the stimulation. (The brain has no pain receptors, so surgery can be done while a patient is awake. Only local painkillers are needed for the scalp and skull. Any volunteers?) Even structures below the surface of the brain can be activated by lowering a stimulating electrode, insulated except at the tip, into a target area inside the brain. ESB can call forth behavior with astonishing power. Instantly, it can bring about aggression, alertness, eating, drinking, sleeping, movement, euphoria, memories, speech, tears, and more.

An alternative approach is **ablation** (ab-LAY-shun)—the surgical removal of parts of the surface of the brain (see Figure 8.1). When ablation causes changes in behavior or sensory capacity, we also gain insight into the purpose of the missing "part." By using a technique called **deep lesioning** (LEE-zhun-ing), structures below the surface of the brain can also be removed. In this case, an electrode is lowered into a target area inside the brain, and a strong electric current is used to destroy a small amount of brain tissue (see Figure 8.1). Again, any resulting changes in behavior give clues to the function of the affected area.

To find out what individual neurons are doing, we need to do a microelectrode recording. A *microelectrode* is an extremely thin glass tube filled with a salty fluid. The tip of a microelectrode is small enough to detect the electrical activity of a *single* neuron. Watching the action potentials of just one neuron provides a fascinating glimpse into the true origins of behavior. (The action potential shown in Module 7, Figure 7.4, was recorded with a microelectrode.)

Are any less invasive techniques available for studying brain function? Whereas CT scans and MRIs cannot tell us what different parts of the brain *do*, several other techniques allow us to observe the activity of parts of the brain without doing any damage at all. These include the EEG, PET scan, and fMRI (Freberg, 2021), described next.

Computed tomography (CT) scan A computer-enhanced X-ray image of the brain or body.

Magnetic resonance imaging (MRI) scan An imaging technique that results in a three-dimensional image of the brain or body, based on its response to a magnetic field.

Localization of function The research strategy of linking specific structures in the brain to specific psychological or behavioral functions.

Neurological soft signs Behavioral signs of nervous system dysfunction, including clumsiness, an awkward gait, poor hand–eye coordination, and other perceptual and motor problems.

Electrical stimulation of the brain (ESB) Direct electrical stimulation and activation of brain tissue.

Electrode Any device (such as a wire, needle, or metal plate) used to stimulate or destroy nerve tissue electrically or to record its activity.

Ablation In biopsychology, the surgical removal of tissue from the surface of the brain.

Deep lesioning Removal of tissue within the brain by the use of an electrode.

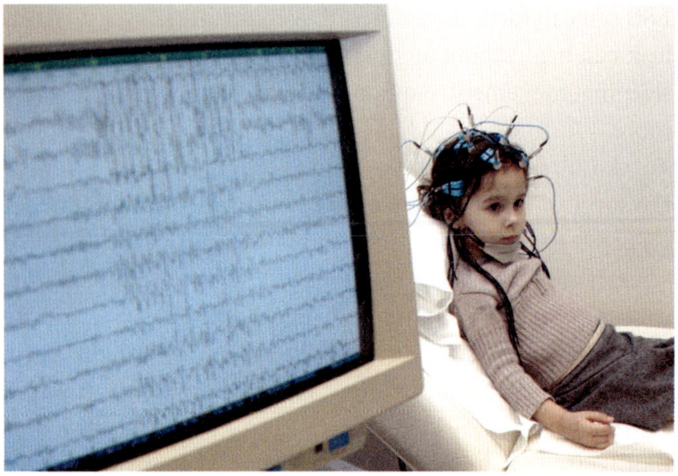

An EEG recording.

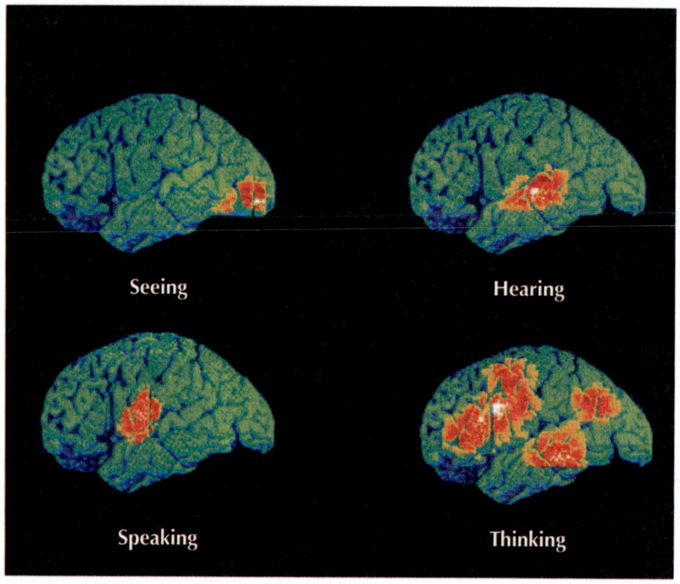

➤ **Figure 8.2**

PET scans. PET scans reveal different patterns of brain activation when we engage in different tasks.

EEG

Electroencephalography (ee-LEK-tro-in-SEF-ah-LOG-ruh-fee) measures the waves of electrical activity produced near the surface of the brain. Small electrodes (disk-shaped metal plates) are placed on a person's scalp. Electrical impulses from the brain are detected and sent to an **electroencephalograph (EEG)**, which amplifies these weak signals (i.e., brain waves) and records them on a moving sheet of paper or a computer screen. Various brain-wave patterns can identify the presence of tumors, epilepsy, and other diseases. The EEG also reveals changes in brain activity during sleep, daydreaming, hypnosis, and other mental states. (Module 24 explains how changes in brain waves help define various stages of sleep.)

PET Scan

Positron emission tomography (PET) is a high-resolution imaging technique that captures brain activity by attaching radioactive particles to glucose molecules. A PET scan detects positrons (i.e., subatomic particles) emitted by weakly radioactive glucose (sugar) as it is consumed by the brain. Because the brain runs on glucose, a PET scan shows which areas are using more energy. Higher energy use corresponds with higher activity. Thus, by placing positron detectors around the head and sending data to a computer, it is possible to create a moving, color video of changes in brain activity (➤ Figure 8.2). PET scans even suggest that different patterns of brain activity accompany major psychological disorders, such as schizophrenia or depression (see Modules 61 and 62).

Is it true that most people use only 10 percent of their brain capacity? This is one of the lasting myths about the brain. Brain scans show that all parts of the brain are active during waking hours. Obviously, some people make better use of their innate brainpower than others. Nevertheless, a normally functioning brain has no great hidden or untapped reserves of mental capacity.

fMRI

A **functional MRI (fMRI)** uses MRI technology to record activity levels in various areas of the brain. For example, if we scanned your brain while you are reading this textbook, areas of your brain involved in understanding what you read would be highlighted in an fMRI image. (In contrast, if we used MRI, rather than fMRI, we would get a beautiful image of your brain structure without any clues as to which parts of your brain were more or less active.)

Psychiatrist Daniel Langleben and his colleagues have even used fMRI images to examine if a person is lying. As ➤ Figure 8.3 shows, the front of the brain is more active when a person is lying rather than telling the truth. This may occur because it takes extra effort to lie, and that extra brain activity is detected with fMRI (Langleben, 2008). Eventually, such findings may validate the use of fMRI evidence in courts of law (Langleben & Moriarty, 2013; Rusconi & Mitchener-Nissen, 2013).

Clearly, it is just a matter of time until even brighter beacons are flashed into the shadowy inner world of thought (Sporns & Betzel, 2016).

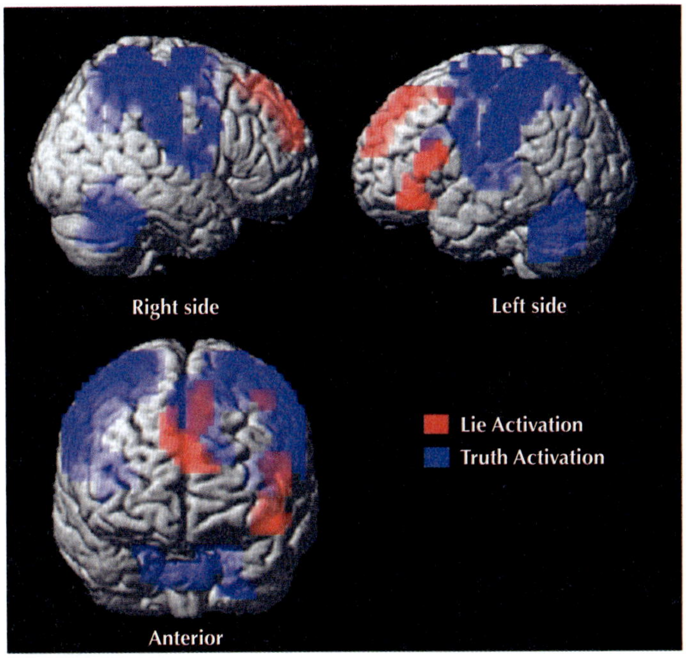

Source: Daniel Langleben, University of Pennsylvania

➤ Figure 8.3

fMRI. Participants were asked to tell the truth or to lie while fMRI images of their brains were taken. When compared with telling the truth (shown in blue), areas toward the front of the brain were active during lying (shown in red). (Adapted from Langleben et al., 2005.)

Electroencephalograph (EEG) A device that records electrical activity in the brain.

Positron emission tomography (PET) scan A high-resolution imaging technique that captures brain activity by attaching radioactive particles to glucose molecules.

Functional MRI (fMRI) An MRI technique that records activity levels in various areas of the brain.

MODULE 8 Brain Research—Learning Outcomes Revisited

8.1 Identify three methods that scientists use to map brain structure

Brain structure is investigated though dissection, as well as less-intrusive CT scans and MRI scans.

8.2 Identify four methods that scientists use to establish the function of brain regions

Brain function is investigated through surgical procedures (electrical stimulation, ablation, deep lesioning), as well as less-intrusive EEG recording, PET scans, and fMRI scans.

Reflective Practice

Content Check

1. Which of the following research techniques has the most in common with case studies of the effects of brain injuries?
   a. EEG recording
   b. deep lesioning
   c. microelectrode recording
   d. PET scan
2. CT scans cannot determine which part of your brain plays a role in speech because they
   a. use X-rays
   b. reveal brain structure, not brain activity
   c. reveal brain activity, not brain structure
   d. use magnetic fields
3. _______________ links brain structures to brain functions.
4. People use only 10 percent of their brain capacity. T or F?

Skill Check

Think Critically

5. Deep lesioning is used to destroy an area in the hypothalamus of a rat. After the operation, the rat loses interest in food and eating. Why would it be a mistake to automatically conclude that the destroyed area is a hunger center?

Self-Reflect

Skill Check

You suspect that a certain part of the brain is related to risk-taking. How could you use case studies, ablation, deep lesioning, and ESB to study the structure? You want to know which areas of the brain's surface are most active when a person sees a face. What methods will you use?

ANSWERS

1. b 2. b 3. Localization of function 4. F 5. Other factors might explain the apparent loss of appetite. For example, the taste or smell of food might be affected, or the rat might have difficulty swallowing. It is also possible that hunger originates elsewhere in the brain, and the ablated area merely relays the messages that cause the rat to eat.

MODULE 9

Brain and Behavior

Hemispheres and Lobes of the Cerebral Cortex

Wrinkle, Wrinkle, Little Star

In many ways, we humans are pretty unimpressive creatures. Other animals surpass us in almost every category of strength, speed, and sensory sensitivity. However, we are the stars when it comes to intelligence; our brains, not our brawn, give us our greatest advantage as a species. Even at first glance, the human brain appears to be composed primarily of the heavily wrinkled tissue called the *cerebral cortex.* We owe our human intelligence not to the overall size of our brains but rather to just how much of our brains are made up of this cortical tissue rather than subcortical tissue.

The cerebral cortex can be divided into two hemispheres, which differ in what abilities they control, and smaller areas known as lobes. Parts of various lobes are responsible for the ability to see, hear, move, think, and speak. Thus, a map of the cerebral cortex is in some ways like a map of human abilities, as we shall see.

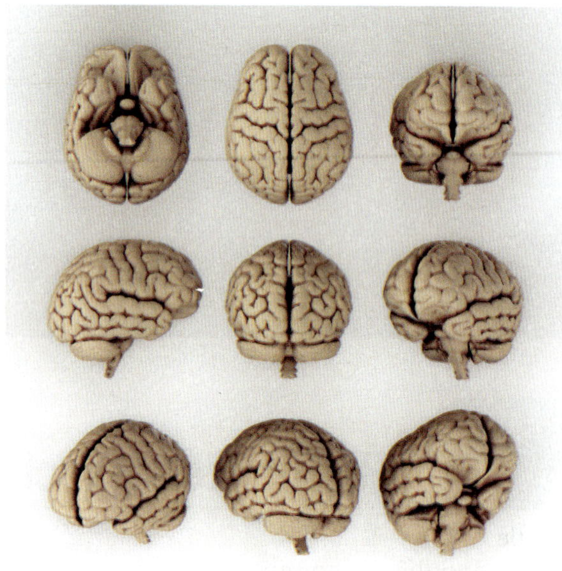

vasabii/Shutterstock.com

~LEARNING OUTCOMES~

After reading this module you should be able to:

9.1 Explain how the left and right hemispheres of the cerebral cortex differ as a result of lateralization, and describe the split-brain operation

9.2 Name the four lobes of the cerebral cortex and describe their function

The Cerebral Cortex—Bigger Is Not Better

Learning Outcome 9.1 Explain how the left and right hemispheres of the cerebral cortex differ as a result of lateralization, and describe the split-brain operation

Do humans have the largest brains? No, that honor goes to whales, whose brains can weigh as much as six times more than the puny 3-pound human brain. However, when we compare brain weight to body weight, we find that a whale's brain makes up as little as 1/10,000 of its total weight. The ratio for humans is 1/60. And yet the ratio for tree shrews (small, squirrel-like, insect-eating mammals) is about 1/30. Our human brains are not noteworthy, then, in terms of either absolute or relative weight (Coolidge & Wynn, 2009; Herculano-Houzel, 2012).

Having a larger brain doesn't necessarily make a person smarter? Although a small positive correlation exists between intelligence and brain size, overall size alone does not determine human intelligence (Kievit et al., 2012; Royle et al., 2013). In fact, many parts of your brain are surprisingly similar to corresponding brain areas in other animals, such as lizards. What is different is your **cerebral cortex**

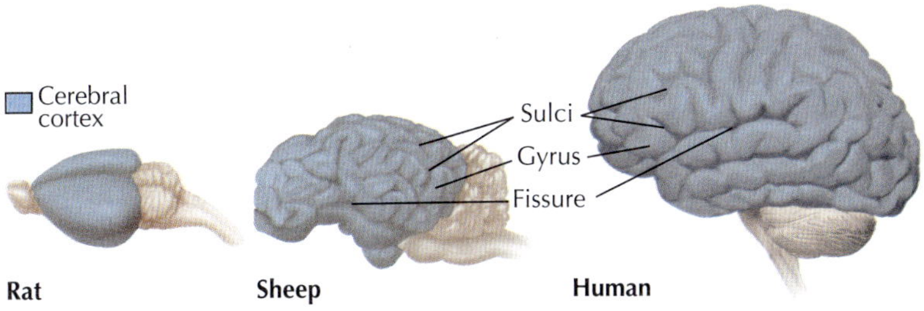

➤ **Figure 9.1**

Corticalization of the human brain. A more wrinkled cortex has greater cognitive capacity. Extensive corticalization is the key to human intelligence.

(seh-REE-brel or ser-EH-brel), the thin, outer covering of the brain in which high-level processes take place.

The cerebral cortex, which looks a little like a giant, wrinkled walnut, consists of the two large hemispheres that cover the upper part of the brain. The two hemispheres are divided into smaller areas known as *lobes*. Parts of various lobes are responsible for the ability to see, hear, move, think, and speak.

The cerebral cortex covers most of the brain with a mantle of *gray matter* (spongy tissue made up mostly of cell bodies). Although the cortex is only 3 millimeters thick (one-tenth of an inch), it contains 70 percent of the neurons in the central nervous system. It is largely responsible for our ability to use language, make tools, acquire complex skills, and live in complex social groups (Coolidge & Wynn, 2009). In humans, the cortex is twisted and folded, and it is the largest brain structure (Striedter, Srinivasan, & Monuki, 2015). In lower animals, it is smooth and small (➤ Figure 9.1). The fact that humans are more intelligent than other animals is related to this **corticalization** (KORE-tih-kal-ih-ZAY-shun), or increase in the size and wrinkling of the cortex. Without the cortex, we humans wouldn't be much smarter than toads.

The Cerebral Hemispheres

The cortex is composed of two sides, or **cerebral hemispheres** (half-globes), connected by a thick band of axon fibers called the *corpus callosum* (KORE-pus kah-LOH-sum) (➤ Figure 9.2). It has long been known that the cerebral cortex displays **lateralization**, a specialization in the abilities of the left and right hemispheres. For example, the left hemisphere mainly controls the right side of the body. Likewise, the right hemisphere controls the left side of the body. If a stroke were to cause you to lose the ability to move your *left* arm, the stroke would have happened in your *right* hemisphere.

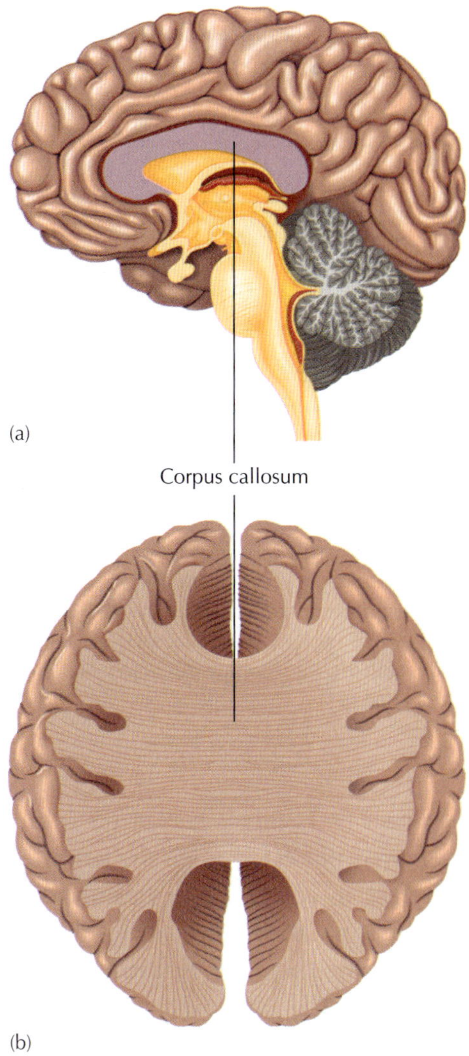

➤ **Figure 9.2**

The corpus callosum. *(a)* The corpus callosum seems unremarkable when seen in cross section. *(b)* Seen from above, with the neurons of the cerebral cortex that normally cover it removed, it is easier to appreciate the full extent of this thick band of axon fibers that richly interconnects the two cerebral hemispheres.

Damage to one hemisphere may also cause a curious problem called *spatial neglect* (Llorens & Noé, 2016). A spatial neglect patient may pay no attention to one side of

Cerebral cortex A thin, wrinkled outer covering of the brain in which high-level processes take place.

Corticalization An increase in the relative size of the cerebral cortex.

Cerebral hemispheres The left and right sides of the cerebral cortex; interconnected by the corpus callosum.

Lateralization Differences between the two sides of the body, especially differences in the abilities of the brain hemispheres.

➤ **Figure 9.3**

Spatial neglect. A patient with right-hemisphere damage asked to copy images will likely neglect the left-hand side when drawing them. Shown images of a human-like stick figure or a playing card, such a patient might produce versions like those shown here. Similar instances of neglect occur in many patients with right-hemisphere damage (Silveri, Ciccarelli, & Cappa, 2011). Of course, a patient with left-hemisphere damage would neglect the right side of these images.

visual space (➤ Figure 9.3). Patients with right hemisphere damage may not eat food on the left side of a plate. Some even refuse to acknowledge a paralyzed left arm as their own (Hirstein, 2005). If you point to the "alien" arm, the patient may well say, "Oh, that's not my arm. It must belong to someone else."

Hemispheric Dominance and Handedness In addition to lateralization, the cerebral hemispheres also display *dominance*. For example, what is your **handedness**—do you prefer to use your right hand or your left hand? If you are right-handed, your **dominant hemisphere** is most likely the left hemisphere (and vice versa for left-handedness). About 90 percent of all humans are right-handed; 10 percent are left-handed (Meguerditchian, Vauclair, & Hopkins, 2013).

If a person is strongly left-handed, does that mean the right hemisphere is dominant? Overall hemispheric dominance is difficult to assess based on handedness alone. For example, about 95 percent of right-handers process speech in the left hemisphere and are left-brain dominant. A good 70 percent of left-handers produce speech from the left hemisphere, just as right-handed people do. However, 19 percent of lefties and 3 percent of righties use their right brain for language. Some left-handers (approximately 12 percent) even use both sides of the brain for language processing. All told, more than 90 percent of the population uses the left brain for language (Szaflarski et al., 2011).

Also, oddly enough, mixed dominance is quite common. Most people (about 75 percent) are strongly right- or left-handed (McManus et al., 2010). The rest show some inconsistency in hand preference. For example, one of your authors plays sports right-handed but writes left-handed. Other people may be *ambidextrous*, preferring either hand (or side) equally. For example, retired professional baseball player Pete Rose, who holds the record for the most hits in a career, was a "switch hitter," batting almost equally well from either the left side or the right side of the plate.

Similarly, you may have mixed preferences for using your left or right feet, eyes, and ears. You even have preferences for which nostril you usually breathe through and which direction you lean your head when kissing (Greenwood et al., 2006; van der Kamp & Cañal-Bruland, 2011). (Do you kiss "right"?)

The Split-Brain In 1981, Roger Sperry (1914–1994) won a Nobel Prize for his remarkable discovery that the right and left brain hemispheres also perform differently on tests of language, perception, music, and other capabilities (Gazzaniga, 2015).

How is it possible to test only one side of the brain? One way is to work with people who've had a **split-brain operation**. In this rare surgery, the corpus callosum is cut to control severe epilepsy. The result is essentially a person with two brains in one body (Schechter, 2012). After the right and left brain are separated, each hemisphere has its own separate perceptions, concepts, and impulses to act. It also becomes possible to send information solely to one hemisphere or the other (➤ Figure 9.4).

How does a split-brain person act after the operation? Having two "brains" in one body can create some interesting dilemmas. One split-brain patient, Karen, has to endure an out-of-control left hand. As Karen put it, "I'd light a cigarette, balance it on an ashtray, and then my left hand would reach forward and stub it out. It would take things out of my handbag and I wouldn't realize so I would walk away. I lost a lot of things before I realized what was going on" (Mosley, 2011). However, such conflicts are actually rare. That's because both halves of the brain normally have about the same experience at the same time. Also, if a conflict arises, one hemisphere usually overrides the other.

Split-brain effects are easiest to see in specialized testing. For example, we could flash a dollar sign to the right brain and a question mark to the left brain of a patient named Tom. (Figure 9.4 shows how this is possible.) Next, Tom is asked to draw what he saw, using his left hand, out of sight. Tom's left hand draws a dollar sign. If Tom is then asked to point with his right hand to a picture of what his hidden left hand drew,

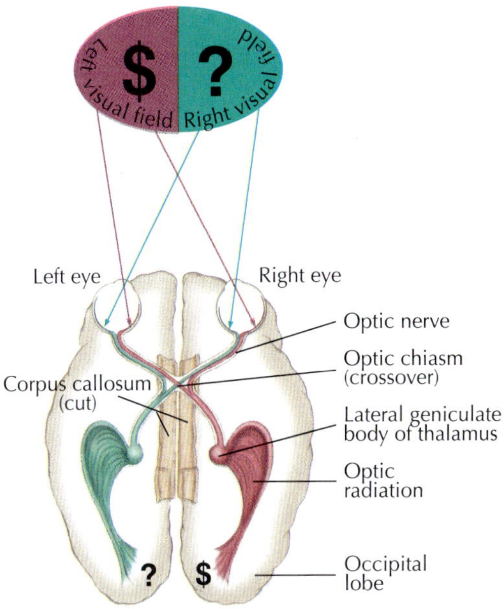

Figure 9.4

Basic pathways of vision. Notice that the left portion of each eye connects to the left half of the brain; likewise, the right portion of each eye connects to the right brain. When the corpus callosum is cut, a split brain results. Then visual information can be sent to just one hemisphere by flashing it in the right or left visual field as the person stares straight ahead.

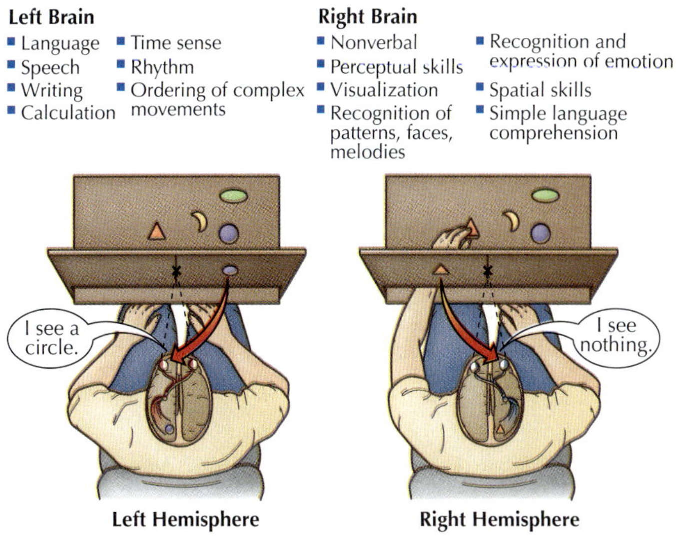

Figure 9.5

The split brain. A circle is flashed to the left brain of a split-brain patient, and he is asked what he saw. He easily replies, "A circle." He can also pick out the circle by merely touching shapes with his right hand, which is out of sight behind a screen. However, his left hand can't identify the circle. If a triangle is flashed to the patient's right brain, he can't say what he saw (speech is controlled by the left hemisphere). He also can't identify the triangle by touch with the right hand. Now, however, the left hand has no difficulty picking out the triangle. In other tests, the hemispheres reveal distinct skills, as listed above the drawing.

he will point to a question mark (Sperry, 1968). In short, for the split-brain person, one hemisphere may not know what is happening in the other. This has to be the ultimate case of the "right hand not knowing what the left hand is doing"! **Figure 9.5** provides another example of split-brain testing.

Hemispheric Lateralization *Earlier, it was stated that the hemispheres differ in abilities. In what ways are they different?* The brain divides its work in interesting ways. As stated previously, roughly 95 percent of us use our left brain for language (speaking, writing, and understanding). In addition, the left hemisphere is superior at math, judging time and rhythm, and coordinating the order of complex movements, such as those needed for speech (Kell et al., 2011; Pinel & Dehaene, 2010).

In contrast, the right hemisphere can produce only the simplest language and numbers. Working with the right brain is like talking to a child who can say only a dozen words or so. To answer questions, the right hemisphere must use nonverbal responses, such as pointing at objects (see Figure 9.5).

Although it is poor at producing language, the right brain is especially good at perceptual skills, such as recognizing patterns, faces, and melodies; putting together a puzzle; or drawing a picture. It also helps you express emotions and detect the emotions that other people are feeling (Castro-Schilo & Kee, 2010).

Even though the right hemisphere is nearly "speechless," it is superior at some aspects of understanding language. If the right side of the brain is damaged, people lose their ability to understand jokes, irony, sarcasm, implications, and other nuances of language. Basically, the right hemisphere helps us see the overall context in which something is said (Dyukova et al., 2010).

In general, the left hemisphere is involved mainly with *analysis* (breaking information into parts). It also processes information *sequentially* (in order, one item after the next). The right hemisphere appears to process information *holistically* (all at once) and *simultaneously*.

To summarize further, you could say that the right hemisphere is better at assembling pieces of the world into a

Handedness A preference for the right or left hand in most activities.

Dominant hemisphere A term usually applied to the side of a person's brain that produces language.

Split-brain operation A surgical procedure that involves cutting the corpus callosum.

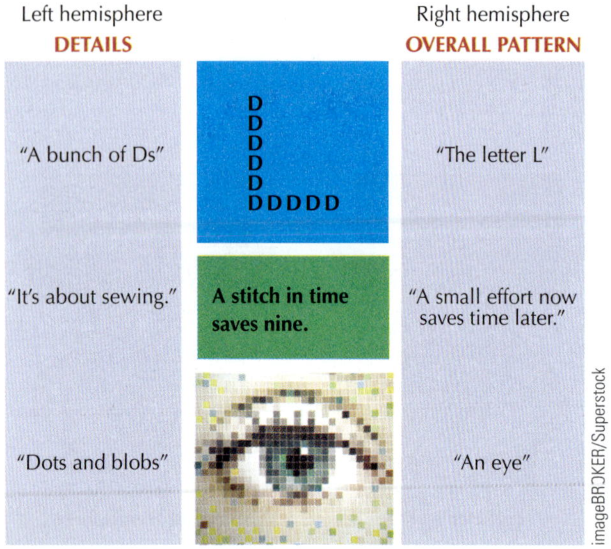

➤ **Figure 9.6**

Local and global processing. The left and right brains have different information processing styles. The right brain gets the big pattern; the left focuses on small details.

coherent picture; it sees overall patterns and general connections. The left brain focuses on small details (➤ **Figure 9.6**). The right brain sees the wide-angle view; the left zooms in on specifics. The focus of the left brain is *local*, the right is *global* (Hübner & Volberg, 2005).

Left Brain/Right Brain *Are there left-brained and right-brained people?* Numerous books and websites have been devoted to how to use the left brain or the right brain to manage, teach, draw, ride horses, learn, and even make love. But this is a drastic oversimplification because people normally use both sides of their brain at all times (Nielsen et al., 2013). It's true that some tasks may make *more* use of one hemisphere or the other. But in most real-world activities, the hemispheres share the work. Each does the parts that it does best and shares information with the other side.

A smart brain is one that grasps both the details and the overall picture at the same time. For instance, during a concert, a guitarist will use her left brain to judge time and rhythm and coordinate the order of her hand movements. At the same time, she will use her right brain to recognize and organize melodies.

Sex Differences: His and Her Brains? *How about men's and women's brains? Are they specialized in different ways?* Yes, they are. Many physical differences between male and female brains have been found, although their implications remain to be better understood (McCarthy et al., 2012). One generalization that may stand the test of time is that the two hemispheres appear to be more interconnected in women than in men (Ingalhalikar et al., 2014; Tomasi & Volkow, 2012). (See ➤ **Figure 9.7**.)

This structural difference may underlie many observed functional differences between men's and women's brains. For example, in one classic series of studies, researchers observed brain activity as people did language tasks. Both men and women showed increased activity in a region called Broca's area, on the left side of the brain, exactly as expected (we will further discuss Boca's area in a few pages). Surprisingly, the *right* side of the brain was also activated in more than half the women tested. Despite this difference, the two sexes performed equally well on a task that involved sounding out words (Shaywitz et al., 1995). Another study, this time focused on intelligence, also found that women are more likely than men to use both sides of their brains (Tang et al., 2010).

It is tempting to conclude that the front-to-back connection pattern of the male hemispheres explains men's readiness to quickly go from perception to action. Similarly, the left-to-right connection pattern in females seems to explain women's greater willingness to combine rational and intuitive judgments. For now, these are just hypotheses that await further research.

Regardless, using both sides of the brain for language and other forms of intelligence may be advantageous

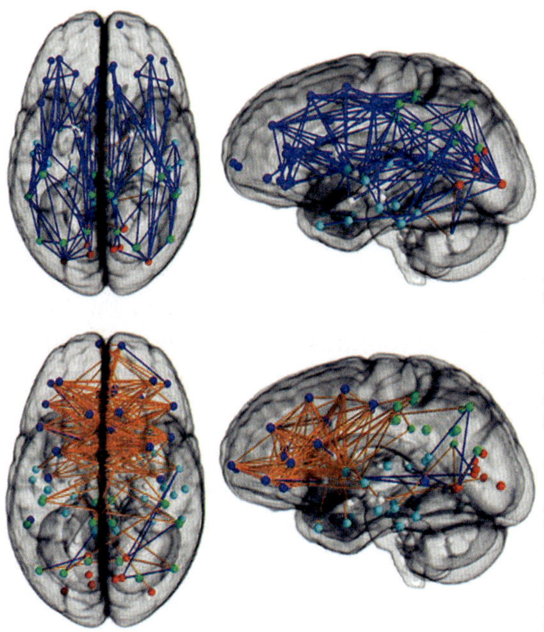

➤ **Figure 9.7**

Male and female brains. (*top*) Male brains have more front-to-back connections in each hemisphere. (*bottom*) Female brains have more left-to-right connections between hemispheres (Ingalhalikar et al., 2014).

(Prichard, Propper, & Christman, 2013). For example, when Broca's area is damaged, some women can use the right side of their brains to compensate for the loss, which allows them to resume speaking (Sommer, 2010). A man with similar damage might be permanently impaired. Thus, when a man says, "I have half a mind to tell you what I think," he may be stating a curious truth.

The Lobes of the Cerebral Cortex—Which Part Does What?

Learning Outcome 9.2 Name the four lobes of the cerebral cortex and describe their function

Each of the two hemispheres of the cerebral cortex can be divided into several smaller lobes. Some of the **lobes of the cerebral cortex** are defined by larger fissures on the surface of the cortex. Others are regarded as separate areas because their functions are quite different (➤ **Figure 9.8**).

The Frontal Lobes

The **frontal lobes** are areas of the cortex associated with movement, sense of self, and higher mental functions. If the frontal lobes are damaged, a patient's personality and emotional life may change dramatically. Remember Phineas Gage, the railroad foreman described in Module 5? He's the person who accidentally destroyed much of his frontal cortex. It's likely that Gage's personality changed after he suffered brain damage because the frontal cortex generates our sense of self, including an awareness of our current emotional state (Jenkins & Mitchell, 2011).

The very front of the frontal lobes is known as the **prefrontal area (prefrontal cortex; ➤ Figure 9.9).** This part of the brain is responsible for the **executive functions**; the higher-level mental processes that allow us to regulate and coordinate our own thought processes (Gruberger et al., 2015). (See Module 11, on *self-regulation,* and Module 26, on *metacognition.*) Damage to the prefrontal cortex will most likely affect reasoning or planning (Roca et al., 2010). Patients with damage to the prefrontal areas often get stuck on mental tasks and repeat the same wrong answers over and over (Stuss & Knight, 2002).

Most of the rest of the frontal lobes are usually referred to as *frontal association areas.* Only a small portion of the cerebral cortex (the primary areas) directly controls the body or receives information from the senses. All the surrounding areas, which are called **association areas (association cortex)**, combine and process information. For example, if you see a rose, association areas help you connect your primary sensory impressions with memories, so that you can recognize the rose and name it.

PET and fMRI scans suggest that much of what we call intelligence is related to increased activity in the prefrontal and frontal association areas of the cortex (Cole et al., 2012; Nestor et al., 2015). Reduced frontal lobe function also leads to greater impulsivity, including increased risk for drug addiction (Crews & Boettiger, 2009). In turn, drug abuse can further damage this important area of the brain (Perry et al., 2011).

Some frontal association areas also contribute to specific higher mental abilities, such as language. For example, a person with damage to association areas in the left hemisphere may suffer **aphasia** (ah-FAZE-yah), an impaired ability to use language.

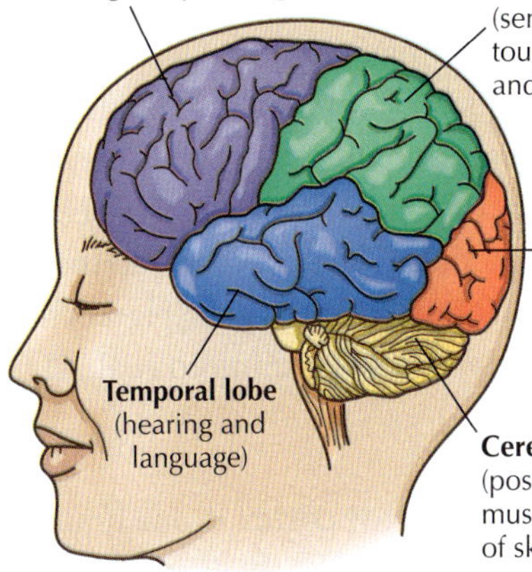

➤ **Figure 9.8**
Functions of the lobes of cerebral cortex.

Lobes of the cerebral cortex Areas on the left and right cortex bordered by major fissures or defined by their functions.

Frontal lobes Areas of the cortex associated with movement, the sense of self, and higher mental functions.

Prefrontal area (prefrontal cortex) The very front of the frontal lobes; involved in the sense of self, executive functions, and planning.

Executive functions The higher level mental processes that allow us to regulate and coordinate our own thought processes.

Association areas (association cortex) All areas of the cerebral cortex that are not primarily sensory or motor in function.

Aphasia A speech disturbance resulting from brain damage.

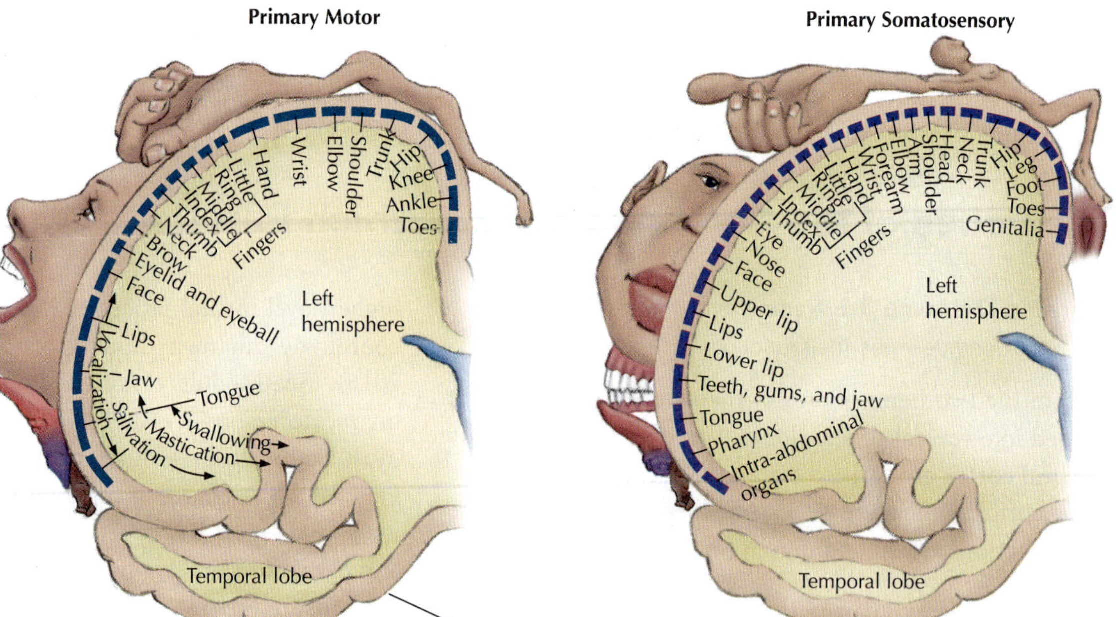

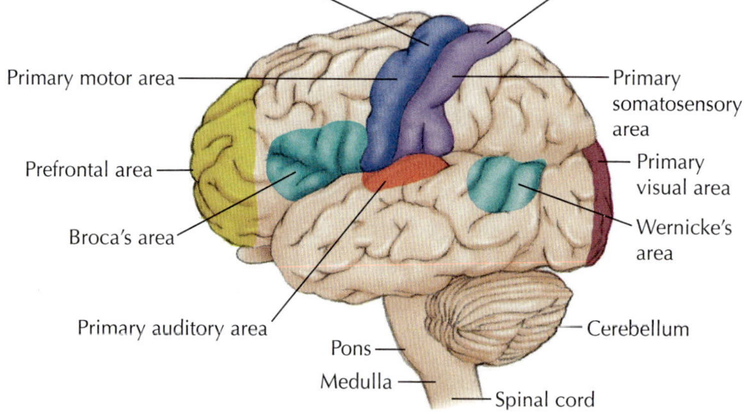

Figure 9.9

Functions of some cortical areas. The lobes of the cerebral cortex and the primary sensory, motor, visual, and auditory areas on each. The top diagrams show (in cross section) the relative amounts of cortex assigned to the sensory and motor control of various parts of the body. (Each cross section, or slice, of the cortex has been turned 90 degrees, so that you see it as it would appear from the back of the brain.)

One type of aphasia is related to **Broca's area** (BRO-cahs), a speech center that is part of the left frontal association area (for 5 percent of all people, the area is part of the right frontal association area). (See Figure 9.9.) Damage to Broca's area causes *motor* (or *expressive*) *aphasia*, a great difficulty in speaking or writing (Flinker et al., 2015). Generally, the person knows what she or he wants to say but can't seem to fluently utter the words (Fridriksson et al., 2012). Typically, a patient's grammar and pronunciation are poor and speech is slow and labored. For example, the person may say "bife" for bike, "seep" for sleep, or "zokaid" for zodiac.

The frontal lobes are also responsible for controlling movement. Specifically, an arch of tissue at the rear of the frontal lobes, called the **primary motor area (primary motor cortex)**, directs the body's muscles. If this area is stimulated with an electrical current, various parts of the body twitch or move. The drawing wrapped around the motor cortex in Figure 9.9 is out of proportion because it reflects the *dexterity* of body areas, not their size. The hands, for example, get more area than the feet. If you've ever wondered why your hands are more skilled or agile than your feet, it's partly because more motor cortex is devoted to the hands. Incidentally, due to neuroplasticity, learning and experience can alter these "motor maps" (Hoenig et al., 2011). For instance, violin, viola, and cello players have larger "hand maps" in motor cortex (Hashimoto et al., 2004).

Mirror Neurons The motor cortex is one brain area that contains **mirror neurons**. These neurons become active when we perform an action *and* when we merely observe someone else carrying out the same action.

Does this chimpanzee imitate researcher Jane Goodall by relying on mirror neurons?

But how could we know that? Italian researchers had just recorded an increase in the activity of a single neuron in the motor cortex of a monkey as it reached for food. A few seconds later, one of the researchers happened to reach for a snack of his own. The same neuron in the monkey's brain obligingly responded as if the monkey had reached for the food itself. Unexpectedly, a neuron involved in controlling a particular motor movement also was activated when the monkey merely observed that same motor movement in someone else. Just like that, the Italians discovered *mirror neurons* (Rizzolatti, Fogassi, & Gallese, 2006).

Their discovery triggered a flood of interest. Researchers were quick to confirm that mirror neurons are found in various areas of the monkey brain and appear to exist in the human brain as well (Molenberghs, Cunnington, & Mattingley, 2012). Psychologists had long assumed that learning new skills by imitating others involved a complicated process (see Module 29 to read more about imitation). But now it seemed possible that newborn humans (and monkeys) easily imitate others because networks of mirror neurons are activated when an infant watches someone perform an action. Then the same mirror network can be used to perform that action (Cook et al., 2014; Meini & Paternoster, 2012). Psychologists and neuroscientists have also speculated that human empathy (the ability to identify with another person's experiences and feelings) may arise from the activation of mirror neurons (Corradini & Antonietti, 2013).

Because imitation and empathy are connected to **autism spectrum disorder** (a condition whose features are impaired communication and social interaction), researchers have wondered whether mirror neurons may play a role in this disorder as well.

To date, results from studies testing these hypotheses have been mixed and some scientists have expressed considerable doubt about the role of mirror neurons in human functioning (Hickok, 2014). Additional research is clearly needed; nevertheless, the possibilities are exciting (Hunter, Hurley, & Taber, 2013; Oberman & Ramachandran, 2015).

The Parietal Lobes

Bodily sensations register in the **parietal lobes** (puh-RYE-ih-tal), located just behind the frontal lobes. Touch, temperature, pressure, and other somatic sensations flow into the **primary somatosensory area (primary somatosensory cortex)** (SO-mat-oh-SEN-so-ree) of the parietal lobes. Again, we find that the map of bodily sensations is distorted. In the case of somatosensory cortex, the drawing in Figure 9.9 reflects the *sensitivity* of body areas, not their size. For example, the lips are large in the drawing because of their great sensitivity, whereas the back and trunk, which are less sensitive, are much smaller. Notice that the hands are also large in the map of body sensitivity—which is obviously an aid to musicians, typists, watchmakers, massage therapists, lovers, and brain surgeons.

The Temporal Lobes

The **temporal lobes** are located on each side of the brain. Auditory information is sent via the auditory nerve directly to the **primary auditory area (primary auditory cortex)**. If we did a PET scan of your brain while you listened to your

Broca's area A language area related to grammar and pronunciation.

Primary motor area (primary motor cortex) A brain area associated with the control of movement.

Mirror neurons Neurons that become active when a motor action is carried out *and* when another organism is observed performing the same action.

Autism spectrum disorder A lifetime disorder whose primary features are impaired communication and social interaction.

Parietal lobes Areas of the cortex in which body sensations register.

Primary somatosensory area (primary somatosensory cortex) A receiving area for body sensations.

Temporal lobes Areas of the cortex that include the sites where hearing registers.

Primary auditory area (primary auditory cortex) The part of the temporal lobe that first receives input from the ears.

favorite song, your primary auditory area would be the first to "light up," followed by association areas in your temporal lobes. Likewise, if we could electrically stimulate the primary auditory area of your temporal lobe, you would "hear" a series of sound sensations.

A left temporal lobe association area called **Wernicke's area** (VER-nick-ees) also functions as a language site (see Figure 9.9; again, for 5 percent of all people, the area is on the right temporal lobe). If it is damaged, the result is a *receptive* (or *fluent*) *aphasia*. Although the person can hear and speak speech normally, he or she has difficulty understanding the meaning of words (Ardila, Bernal, & Rosselli, 2016). Thus, when shown a picture of a chair, someone with Broca's aphasia might say "tssair." In contrast, a Wernicke's patient might *fluently*, but incorrectly, identify the photo as "truck".

The Occipital Lobes

At the back of the brain, we find the **occipital lobes** (awk-SIP-ih-tal), cortical areas that play a role in visual processing. Patients with tumors (cell growths that interfere with brain activity) in the **primary visual area (primary visual cortex)**, the part of the cortex to first receive input from the eyes, experience blind spots in their vision.

Do the primary visual areas of the cortex correspond directly to what is seen? Images are mapped onto the cortex, but the map is greatly stretched and distorted (Freberg, 2021). That's why it's important to avoid thinking of the visual area as a little television screen in the brain. Visual information creates complex patterns of activity in neurons; it does *not* make a television-like image.

One of the most fascinating results of brain injury is **visual agnosia** (ag-KNOW-zyah), an inability to identify seen objects. Visual agnosia is often caused by damage to the association areas on the occipital lobes (Farah, 2004). This condition is sometimes referred to as *mindblindness*. For example, if we show Alice, an agnosia patient, a candle, she can see it and can describe it as "a long narrow object that tapers at the top." Alice can even draw the candle accurately, but she cannot name it. However, if she is allowed to feel the candle, she will name it immediately. In short, Alice can still see color, size, and shape. She just can't form the associations necessary to perceive the meanings of objects.

An especially fascinating form of mindblindness is **facial agnosia**, an inability to perceive familiar faces (Sacks, 2010; Susilo et al., 2015). One patient with facial agnosia couldn't recognize her husband or mother when they visited her in the hospital, and she was unable to identify pictures of her children. However, as soon as visitors spoke, she knew them immediately by their voices.

Areas devoted to recognizing faces and the emotions they convey lie in association areas in the occipital and frontal lobes (Prochnow et al., 2013). These areas appear to be highly specialized. Why would parts of the brain be set aside solely for processing faces? From an evolutionary standpoint, it is not really so surprising. After all, we are social animals for whom facial recognition is very important.

In summary, the bulk of our daily experience and all of our understanding of the world can be traced to the different areas of the cortex. The human brain may be the most advanced and sophisticated of the brain-bearing species on Earth. This, of course, is no guarantee that our marvelous biocomputer will be put to full use. Still, we must stand in awe of the potential it represents.

Wernicke's area A temporal lobe brain area related to language comprehension.

Occipital lobes Cortical areas at the back of the brain that play a role in visual processing.

Primary visual area (primary visual cortex) The part of the occipital lobe that first receives input from the eyes.

Visual agnosia An inability to identify seen objects.

Facial agnosia An inability to perceive familiar faces.

MODULE 9

Hemispheres and Lobes of the Cerebral Cortex—Learning Outcomes Revisited

9.1 Explain how the left and right hemispheres of the cerebral cortex differ as a result of lateralization, and describe the split-brain operation

The cerebral cortex is lateralized, with left and right hemispheres specializing indifferent abilities. The left hemisphere is good at analysis, and it processes small details sequentially. It contains speech or language centers in most people. It also specializes in writing, calculating, judging time and rhythm, and ordering complex movements. The right hemisphere detects overall patterns; it processes information simultaneously and holistically. It is largely nonverbal and excels at spatial and perceptual skills, visualization, and recognition of patterns, faces, and melodies. It is important to note, however, that while the hemispheres appear to specialize in their functions, there is no merit to the idea that people are "left-brained" or "right-brained." Split brains can be created by surgically cutting the corpus callosum. Such an operation allows information to be sent to only one hemisphere or another, thus allowing scientists to see how each hemisphere processes the information in the absence of any input from the other hemisphere.

9.2 Name the four lobes of the cerebral cortex and describe their function

The frontal lobes contain the primary motor area (which includes many mirror neurons) and many association areas that combine and process information. The prefrontal cortex is related to abstract thought and one's sense of self. The parietal lobes contain the primary sensory area, which processes bodily sensations. The temporal lobes contain the primary auditory area and are responsible for hearing and language. The *occipital lobes* contain the primary visual area, which first receives input from the eyes.

Reflective Practice

Content Check

See if you can match the following.

_____ **1.** Corpus callosum	**A.** Visual area
_____ **2.** Occipital lobes	**B.** Language, speech, writing
_____ **3.** Parietal lobes	**C.** Motor cortex and abstract thinking
_____ **4.** Temporal lobes	**D.** Spatial skills, visualization, pattern recognition
_____ **5.** Frontal lobes	**E.** Speech disturbances
_____ **6.** Association cortex	**F.** Hearing
_____ **7.** Aphasias	**G.** Increased ratio of cortex in brain
_____ **8.** Corticalization	**H.** Bodily sensations
_____ **9.** Left hemisphere	**I.** Treatment for severe epilepsy
_____ **10.** Right hemisphere	**J.** Inability to identify seen objects
_____ **11.** Split brain	**K.** Fibers connecting the cerebral hemispheres
_____ **12.** Agnosia	**L.** Cortex that is not sensory or motor in function

Skill Check

Think Critically

13. If your brain were removed, replaced by another, and moved to a new body, which would you consider to be yourself—your old body with the new brain, or your new body with the old brain?

Self-Reflect

Think of learning the functions of the brain lobes as being like learning countries on a map. Try drawing a map of the cortex. Can you label all the different lobes and name their functions? Where is the primary motor area? The primary somatosensory area? Broca's area? Keep redrawing the map until it becomes more detailed and you can do it easily.

ANSWERS

1. K 2. A 3. H 4. F 5. C 6. L 7. E 8. G 9. B 10. D 11. I 12. J 13. Although there is no "correct" answer to this question, your personality, knowledge, personal memories, and self-concept all derive from brain activity—a fact which makes a strong case for your old brain in a new body being more nearly the "real you."

MODULE 10

Brain and Behavior

The Subcortex and Endocrine System

Our Primitive Brain

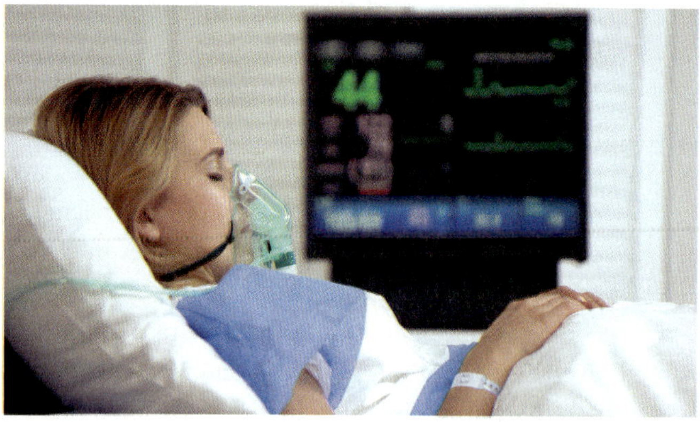
Motortion Films/Shutterstock.com

Although our cerebral cortex makes us uniquely human, it is important to recognize the critical role played by our more primitive subcortex and its links to the endocrine system. For example, the cerebral cortex is surprisingly unnecessary for physical survival. You, or at least your body, would continue to live even if you lost large portions of your cerebral cortex. Not so with the subcortex, the brain structures underneath the cerebral cortex. Hunger, thirst, sleep, attention, sex, breathing, and many other vital functions are controlled by parts of the subcortex. Serious damage to our "lower brain" often leads to coma or even to death. The endocrine glands form a second primitive communication system in the body. Hormones can affect everything from personality and emotions to hunger and reactions to stress. Let's check out our primitive brains.

~LEARNING OUTCOMES~

After reading this module you should be able to:

10.1 Name the three major divisions of the subcortex and describe the main structures that make up each one

10.2 Explain how the endocrine system influences psychological functioning and describe the functions of four glands that are part of the endocrine system

The Subcortex—At the Core of the (Brain) Matter

Learning Outcome 10.1 Name the three major divisions of the subcortex and describe the main structures that make up each one

Like a multilevel parking garage beneath an apartment building, the **subcortex** lies beneath the cerebral hemispheres. In turn, the subcortex can be divided into three layers (➤ **Figure 10.1**):

- The **hindbrain** is the most primitive part of the brain. It comprises the medulla, pons, and cerebellum.
- The **midbrain** is made up of the brain structure that connects the hindbrain with the forebrain.
- The **forebrain** comprises the brain structures, including the limbic system, thalamus, and hypothalamus, that govern higher-order mental processes. (The forebrain also includes the cerebral cortex, which we discuss separately in Module 9 because of its size and importance.)

The Hindbrain

Why are the lower brain areas so important? The *brainstem* is the thickening of the spinal cord where it joins the brain. Virtually all communication between the cerebral cortex and the rest of the body passes through the brainstem, which consists of two major *hindbrain* structures, the *medulla* and the *pons*, along with the *midbrain*. For our purposes, the midbrain can be viewed as a link between the forebrain and the hindbrain. Therefore, let's focus on the rest of the subcortex.

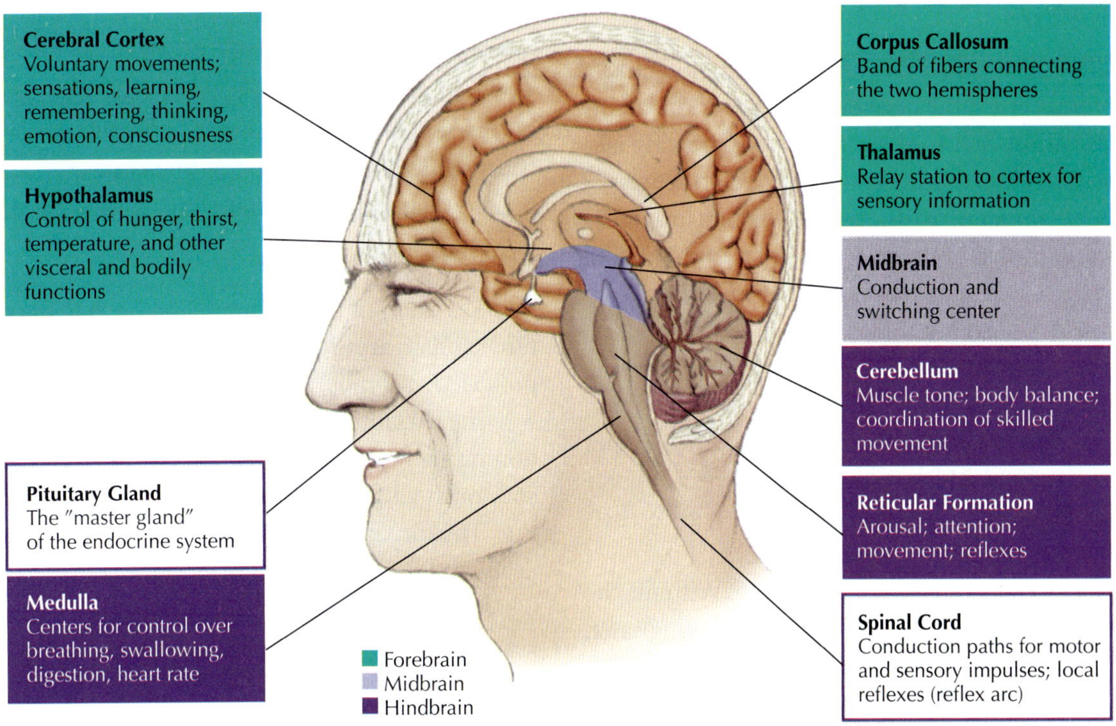

Figure 10.1

Main structures of the human brain. This simplified drawing shows the main structures of the human brain and describes some of their most important features. (You can use the color code in the foreground to identify which areas are part of the forebrain, midbrain, and hindbrain.)

The **medulla** connects the brain with the spinal cord and controls vital life functions. The **pons**, which looks like a small bump on the brainstem, acts as a bridge between the medulla and other brain areas. In addition to connecting with many other locations, including the cerebellum, the pons influences sleep and arousal. Various drugs, diseases, and injuries can disrupt the medulla and end or endanger life.

The Reticular Formation A collection of cells and fibers called the **reticular formation (RF)** (reh-TICK-you-ler) lies inside the medulla and pons. As messages flow into the brain, the RF gives priority to some while turning others aside (Freberg, 2021). By doing so, the RF influences *attention*. The RF doesn't fully mature until adolescence, which may be why children have such short attention spans. The RF also modifies outgoing commands to the body. In this way, the RF affects muscle tone, posture, and movements of the eyes, face, head, body, and limbs. At the same time, the RF controls the reflexes involved in breathing, sneezing, coughing, and vomiting.

The RF also keeps us vigilant, alert, and awake. Incoming messages from the sense organs branch into the RF, which bombards the cortex with stimulation, keeping it active and alert. For instance, let's say that a sleepy driver rounds a bend and encounters a deer standing in the road. The driver snaps to attention and applies the brakes. She can thank her RF for arousing the rest of her brain and averting an accident. If you're getting sleepy while reading this module, try pinching your ear—a little pain will cause the RF to momentarily arouse your cortex.

Subcortex A term referring to all brain structures below the cerebral cortex.

Hindbrain A primitive part of the brain that comprises the medulla, pons, and cerebellum.

Midbrain A structure that connects the hindbrain with the forebrain.

Forebrain A brain structure, including the limbic system, thalamus, hypothalamus, and cortex that governs higher-order mental processes.

Medulla The structure that connects the brain with the spinal cord and controls vital life functions.

Pons An area of the hindbrain that acts as a bridge between the medulla and other structures.

Reticular formation (RF) A collection of cells and fibers in the medulla and pons involved in arousal and attention.

The Cerebellum

The **cerebellum** is also part of the hindbrain. Looking like a miniature cerebral cortex, the cerebellum lies near the brainstem at the base of the brain. Although there is growing evidence that it plays a role in cognition and emotion (Adamaszek et al., 2016; Schmahmann, 2010), the cerebellum primarily regulates posture, muscle tone, and muscular coordination. The cerebellum also stores memories related to "know-how" or skill memories (Alstermark & Ekerot, 2013). "Know-what" memories, such as remembering a person's name or knowing what the cerebellum does, are stored elsewhere in the brain (see Module 34). Once again, we see that experience shapes the brain: Musicians and athletes, who practice special motor skills throughout their lives, have larger than average cerebellums (Hutchinson et al., 2003; Park et al., 2012).

What happens if the cerebellum is injured? Without the cerebellum, tasks such as walking, running, or playing catch become impossible. The first symptoms of a crippling disease called *spinocerebellar degeneration* are tremors, dizziness, and muscular weakness. Eventually, victims have difficulty merely standing, walking, or feeding themselves.

Locked-In Syndrome

At the age of 33, a stroke caused catastrophic damage to Kate Adamson's brainstem. This event cut off communication between her body and her cortex, leaving her with *locked-in syndrome*. Just before the stroke, she was fine, and the next moment, she was totally paralyzed, trapped in her own body and barely able to breathe (Cruse et al., 2011). Unable to move a muscle, but still fully awake and aware, she was unable to communicate her simplest thoughts and feelings to others.

Kate thought that she was going to die. Her doctors, who thought she was *brain dead*, or at best only minimally conscious, did not administer painkillers as they inserted breathing and feeding tubes down her throat. In time, Kate discovered that she could communicate by blinking her eyes. After a recovery that was miraculous by any measure, she went on to appear before the U.S. Congress and even wrote about her experiences (Adamson, 2004).

Not everyone is so lucky. Just think what might have befallen Kate had she not even been able to blink her eyes (Schnakers et al., 2009). In one chilling study, coma researchers used fMRI to reexamine 54 patients previously diagnosed as being practically brain dead. Patients were repeatedly asked to imagine swinging a tennis racket or walking down a familiar street. Five of the patients showed clearly different brain activity for the two tasks, despite being unable to communicate with doctors in any other way (Monti et al., 2010).

What if they could "will" a computer to speak for them? Right on! These results suggest that not all totally locked-in patients are brain dead or minimally conscious. The results also hold out hope that we may eventually be able to develop brain–computer interfaces to help free these patients from their bodily prisons (Laureys & Boly, 2007; Shih & Krusienski, 2012).

The Forebrain

Two key parts of the forebrain are the *thalamus* (THAL-uh-mus) and an area just below it called the *hypothalamus* (HI-po-THAL-uh-mus) (see Figure 10.1).

The **thalamus** acts as a final "relay" for sensory information on its way to the cerebral cortex. Vision, hearing, taste, and touch all pass through this small, football-shaped structure. Thus, injury to even small areas of the thalamus can cause deafness, blindness, or loss of any other sense, except smell.

About the size of a grape, the human **hypothalamus** is a small area of the brain that regulates emotional behaviors and basic biological needs (Kalat, 2021). The hypothalamus affects behaviors as diverse as sex, rage, temperature control, hormone release, eating and drinking, sleep, waking, and emotion. (See, for example, Module 43.)

The hypothalamus is basically a "crossroads" that connects many areas of the brain. It is also the final pathway for many kinds of behavior. That is, the hypothalamus is the last place where many behaviors are organized or "decided on" before messages leave the brain, causing the body to react.

The Limbic System

As a group, the hypothalamus, parts of the thalamus, the amygdala, the hippocampus, and other mainly subcortical structures make up the limbic system (➤ **Figure 10.2**). The **limbic system** plays an important role in controlling emotion and memory (LeDoux, 2012). Rage, fear, sexual response, and intense arousal can be localized to various points in the limbic system. Laughter, a delightful part of human social life, also has its origins in here (Wild et al., 2003).

During evolution, the limbic system was the earliest layer of the forebrain to develop. In lower animals, the limbic system helps organize basic survival responses: feeding, fleeing, fighting, and reproduction. In humans, a clear link to emotion remains. The **amygdala** (ah-MIG-dah-luh), in particular, is associated with emotional processing and is strongly related to fear and the memory of fearful experiences (Bergstrom et al., 2013).

The amygdala provides a primitive, quick pathway to the cortex. Like lower animals, we can be startled and, as such, are able to react to dangerous stimuli before we fully know what is going on (Méndez-Bértolo et al., 2016). In situations

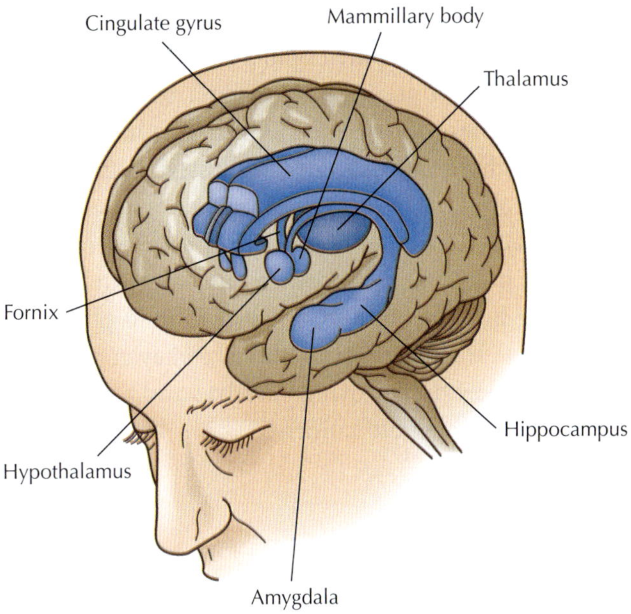

Figure 10.2

Parts of the limbic system. Although only one side is shown here, the hippocampus and the amygdala extend into the temporal lobes at each side of the brain. The limbic system is a sort of primitive core of the brain strongly associated with emotion.

in which true danger exists, such as in military combat, the amygdala's rapid response may aid survival. However, disorders of the brain's fear system can be very disruptive. An example is the war veteran who involuntarily dives into the bushes when he hears a car backfire.

The role of the amygdala in emotion may also explain why people who suffer from phobias and disabling anxiety often feel afraid without knowing why (Lamprecht et al., 2009; Schlund & Cataldo, 2010). For example, people who survive horrible experiences, such as a plane crash, can have debilitating fears years later due to unconscious fear produced by the amygdala. (See the discussion of anxiety disorders in Module 63.)

Some parts of the limbic system have taken on additional, higher-level functions. A part called the **hippocampus** (HIP-oh-CAMP-us) is important for storing memories (Jurd, 2011; Moscovitch et al., 2016). The hippocampus lies inside the temporal lobes, which is why stimulating the temporal lobes can produce memory-like or dream-like experiences. The hippocampus also helps us navigate the space around us. The right side of your hippocampus becomes more active, for instance, if you mentally plan a drive across town (Maguire, Intraub, & Mullally, 2016).

Psychologists have also discovered that animals will learn to press a lever to deliver a dose of electrical stimulation to the limbic system (see Module 28). The animals act like the stimulation is satisfying or pleasurable. Indeed, several areas of the limbic system act as reward, or "pleasure," pathways. Many are found in thc hypothalamus, where they overlap with areas that control thirst, sex, and hunger. As we mentioned in Module 7, commonly abused drugs, such as cocaine, amphetamine, heroin, nicotine, cannabis, and alcohol, activate many of the same pleasure pathways (see also Module 25). This appears to be part of the reason that these drugs feel so rewarding (Niehaus, Cruz-Bermúdez, & Kauer, 2009; Prus, 2017).

You might be interested to know that music you would describe as "thrilling" also activates pleasure systems in your brain. This may explain some of the appeal of music that can send shivers down your spine (Salimpoor et al., 2011). (It also may explain why people pay so much for concert tickets!)

Incidentally, aversive, or "punishment," areas also have been found in the limbic system. When these locations are activated, animals show discomfort and work hard to turn off the stimulation. Because much of our behavior is based on seeking pleasure and avoiding pain, these discoveries continue to fascinate psychologists.

The Whole Human

We have seen that the human brain is an impressive assembly of billions of neurons interconnected by trillions of synapses. The brain regulates vital bodily functions, keeps track of the external world, learns, controls the muscles and glands, responds to current needs, regulates its own behavior, and even creates the mind and the magic of consciousness—*all* at the same time. Three notes of caution are now in order.

First, as impressive as neurons are, they don't act alone. They are sustained by the *glial cells* that surround them, which are charged with providing physical support and insulation, removing waste and providing nutrients. Once thought of as silent servants to neurons, recent research suggests that glia are far more important and sophisticated than scientists had initially believed. For one thing, there are too many of them to ignore: they outnumber neurons by a ratio of about 10 to 1.

Cerebellum The structure in the hindbrain involved in controlling coordination and balance.

Thalamus A brain structure that relays sensory information to the cerebral cortex.

Hypothalamus A small area of the brain that regulates emotional behaviors and basic biological needs.

Limbic system A set of brain structures that play important roles in regulating emotion and memory.

Amygdala A part of the limbic system associated with the rapid processing of emotions; especially fear.

Hippocampus Part of the limbic system associated with storing memories.

For another, they aren't silent—they do indeed communicate with one another, often after "listening in" on the activity of the neurons they surround. Most recently, neuroscientists have suggested that glia should be viewed as partners to neurons, with each making a unique contribution to the smooth functioning of the nervous system (Fields, 2013).

Second, for the sake of simplicity, we have assigned functions to each part of the brain as if it was a computer, but this is only partially true. In reality, incoming information scatters all over the brain and converges again as it goes out through the spinal cord to muscles and glands. The overall system is much more complicated than our discussion of separate parts implies.

Third, try introspecting on how your nervous system allows you to read this paragraph. You are aware of understanding *what* you are reading (right?) but undoubtedly have no awareness of *how* you are reading. Only the use of objective methods such as those discussed in this chapter can clarify how your eyes send information to your primary visual area and how other brain structures cooperate to interpret that information as written language. And yet, understanding how the brain lets you read (and play music, love someone, want to run marathons, and even play catch) may hold the key to improving ourselves and helping those who are experiencing difficulties.

The Endocrine System—My Hormones Made Me Do It

Learning Outcome 10.2 Explain how the endocrine system influences psychological functioning and describe the functions of four glands that are part of the endocrine system

Our behavior is not solely a product of the nervous system. The endocrine (EN-duh-krin) glands form an equally important, parallel communication system in the body (Kalat, 2021). The **endocrine system** is made up of glands that secrete *hormones* directly into the bloodstream or lymphatic system (➤ **Figure 10.3**). Chemically similar to neurotransmitters, **hormones** are carried throughout the body, where they affect both internal activities and visible behaviors such as puberty, personality, dwarfism, jet lag, and much more.

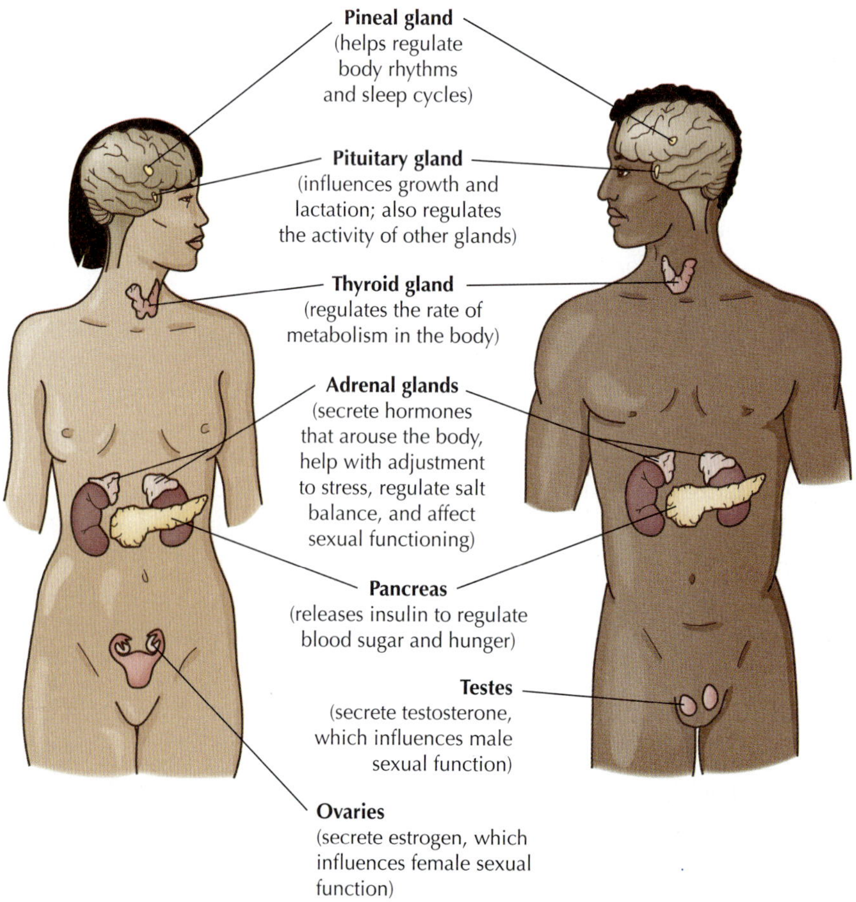

➤ **Figure 10.3**
The endocrine system.

How do hormones affect behavior? Although we are seldom directly aware of them, hormones affect us in many ways (Kalat, 2021). Here is a brief sample: Hormone output from the adrenal glands rises during stressful situations; androgens (meaning "male" hormones) are related to the sex drive in both males and females; hormones secreted during times of high emotion intensify memory formation; at least some of the emotional turmoil of adolescence is due to elevated hormone levels; and different hormones prevail when you are angry rather than fearful. Pregnancy and motherhood cause the release of hormones that lead to the changes involved in maternal behavior (Henry & Sherwin, 2012). Even disturbing personality patterns may be linked to hormonal irregularities (Evardone, Alexander, & Morey, 2007). Because these are just samples, let's consider some additional effects that hormones have on the body and behavior.

Monkey Business Images/Shutterstock.com

Known as the "cuddle" hormone, oxytocin is released by the pituitary gland in a wide variety of intimate situations. For example, a mother's oxytocin levels play an important role in deepening the mother/child bond during the all-important early years (Feldman et al., 2013).

Glands of the Endocrine System

The **pituitary gland** is a pea-sized globe hanging from the base of the brain (see Figure 10.1). The pituitary is often called the "master gland" because it influences the other endocrine glands (especially the thyroid, adrenal glands, and ovaries or testes). These glands in turn regulate such body processes as metabolism, responses to stress, and reproduction. But the master has a master: the pituitary is directed by the hypothalamus, which lies directly above it. In this way, the hypothalamus can affect glands throughout the body. This, then, is the major link between the brain and hormones (Freberg, 2021; Prus, 2017).

One of the pituitary's more important roles is to regulate growth (Beans, 2009). If too little **growth hormone** is released by the pituitary during childhood, a person may remain far smaller than average. If this condition is not treated, a child may be 6 to 12 inches shorter than age-mates. As adults, some will have *hypopituitary* (HI-po-pih-TU-ih-ter-ee) *dwarfism.* Such individuals are perfectly proportioned, but tiny. Regular injections of growth hormone can raise a hypopituitary child's height by several inches, usually to the short side of average.

Too much growth hormone produces *gigantism* (excessive bodily growth). Secretion of too much growth hormone late in the growth period causes *acromegaly* (AK-row-MEG-uh-lee), a condition in which the arms, hands, feet, and facial bones become enlarged. Acromegaly produces prominent facial features, which some people have used as a basis for careers as character actors, wrestlers, and the like.

Oxytocin is another important hormone released by the pituitary. It plays a broad role in regulating many behaviors generally involved in social bonding (Kumsta & Heinrichs, 2013; Stoop, Hegoburu, & van den Burg, 2015). These include pregnancy, parenthood, sexual activity, happiness, trust, and even reducing stress reactions (Gordon et al., 2010; Stallen et al., 2012).

The **pineal gland** (pin-EE-ul) was once considered a useless remnant of evolution. In certain fishes, frogs, and lizards, the gland is associated with a well-developed light-sensitive organ, or so-called *third eye.* In humans, the function of the pineal gland is just now coming to light (so to speak). The pineal gland releases a hormone called **melatonin** (mel-ah-TONE-in) in response to daily variations in light. Melatonin levels in the bloodstream rise at dusk, peak around midnight, and fall again as morning approaches. As far as the brain is concerned, it's bedtime when melatonin levels rise (Norman, 2009). Melatonin can be used to reset the body's "clock" and minimize jet lag for long-distance pilots, aircrews, and travelers (see Module 42).

The **thyroid gland**, located in the neck, regulates *metabolism*, the rate at which energy is produced and expended in

Endocrine system A network of glands that release hormones into the bloodstream.

Hormones A chemical released by the endocrine glands.

Pituitary gland The master gland of the endocrine system that controls the action of all other glands.

Growth hormone A hormone, secreted by the pituitary gland, that promotes body growth.

Oxytocin A hormone, released by the pituitary gland, which plays a broad role in regulating pregnancy, parenthood, sexual activity, social bonding, trust, and even reducing stress reactions.

Pineal gland A gland in the brain that helps regulate body rhythms and sleep cycles.

Melatonin A hormone released by the pineal gland in response to daily cycles of light and dark.

Thyroid gland An endocrine gland that helps regulate the rate of metabolism.

the body. By altering metabolism, the thyroid can have a sizable effect on personality. A person suffering from *hyperthyroidism* (an overactive thyroid) tends to be thin, tense, excitable, and nervous. An underactive thyroid (*hypothyroidism*) in an adult can cause inactivity, sleepiness, slowness, obesity, and depression (Joffe, 2006).

When you are frightened or angry, some important reactions prepare your body for action: your heart rate and blood pressure rise; stored sugar is released into the bloodstream for quick energy; your muscles tense and receive more blood; and your blood is prepared to clot more quickly in case of injury. As we discussed in Module 7, these changes are controlled by the autonomic nervous system (ANS). Specifically, the sympathetic branch of the ANS causes the adrenal glands to release the hormones *epinephrine* and *norepinephrine.* (Epinephrine also is known as adrenaline, a word that may be more familiar to you.) **Epinephrine** (ep-eh-NEF-rin), which is associated with fear, tends to arouse the body. **Norepinephrine**, which also functions as a neurotransmitter in the brain, also tends to arouse the body, but it is linked with anger.

The **adrenal glands** are located just under the back of the rib cage, atop the kidneys. The *adrenal medulla,* or inner core of the adrenal glands, is the source of epinephrine and norepinephrine. The *adrenal cortex,* or outer "bark" of the adrenal glands, produces a set of hormones called corticoids (KOR-tih-coids). One of their jobs is to regulate salt balance in the body. A deficiency of certain corticoids can evoke a powerful craving for the taste of salt in humans. The corticoids also help the body adjust to stress, and they are a secondary source of sex hormones.

An oversecretion of the adrenal sex hormones can cause *virilism* (exaggerated male characteristics). For instance, a woman may grow a beard, or a man's voice may become so low that it is difficult to understand. Oversecretion early in life can cause *premature puberty* (full sexual development during childhood).

In this brief discussion of the endocrine system, we have considered only a few of the more important glands. Nevertheless, this should give you an appreciation of how completely behavior and personality are tied to the ebb and flow of hormones in the body.

Anabolic Steroids While we are on the topic of hormones, there is a related issue worth mentioning. Testosterone, one of the principal androgens, or "male" hormones, is supplied in small amounts by the adrenal glands. (The testes are the main source of testosterone in males.) Perhaps you have heard about the use of anabolic steroids by athletes who want to "bulk up" or promote muscle growth. Most of these drugs are synthetic versions of testosterone.

Although there is some disagreement about whether steroids actually improve athletic performance, it is widely accepted that they may cause serious side effects (Grönbladh, Nylander, & Hallberg, 2016; Kanayama et al., 2013). Problems include voice deepening or baldness in women and shrinkage of the testicles, sexual impotence, or breast enlargement in men (Millman & Ross, 2003). Dangerous increases in hostility and aggression ("roid rage") have also been linked to steroid use (Cunningham, Lumia, & McGinnis, 2013; Hartgens & Kuipers, 2004). Increased risk of heart attack and stroke, liver damage, and stunted growth also are common when younger adolescents use steroids. Understandably, almost all major sports organizations ban the use of anabolic steroids.

Epinephrine An adrenal hormone that tends to arouse the body; epinephrine is associated with fear. (Also known as *adrenaline.*)

Norepinephrine Both a brain neurotransmitter and an adrenal hormone that tends to arouse the body; norepinephrine is associated with anger. (Also known as *noradrenaline.*)

Adrenal glands Endocrine glands that arouse the body, regulate salt balance, adjust the body to stress, and affect sexual functioning.

MODULE 10 The Subcortex and Endocrine System—Learning Outcomes Revisited

10.1 Name the three major divisions of the subcortex and describe the main structures that make up each one

The hindbrain is made up of the medulla (which contains centers essential for reflex control of heart rate, breathing, and other vegetative functions), the reticular formation (which directs sensory and motor messages and acts as an activating system for the cerebral cortex), and the cerebellum (which maintains coordination, posture, and muscle tone). The pons links the medulla with other brain areas. The midbrain connects the hindbrain to the forebrain. The midbrain and two hindbrain structures (pons and medulla) make up the *brainstem,* which is the thickening of the spinal cord where it joins the brain. The forebrain consists of the thalamus (which carries sensory information to the cortex), the hypothalamus (which exerts control over eating, drinking, sleep cycles, body temperature, and other basic motives and behaviors), and the limbic system (which is related to emotion, reward, and punishment, and contains the hippocampus, which is important for forming memories).

10.2 Explain how the endocrine system influences psychological functioning and describe the functions of four glands that are part of the endocrine system

Endocrine glands serve as a chemical communication system within the body. Hormones from the endocrine glands enter the bloodstream, affecting behavior, moods, and personality. Many of the endocrine glands are influenced by the pituitary (the master gland), which is in turn influenced by the hypothalamus. Thus, the brain controls the body through both the fast nervous system and the slower endocrine system. The pituitary gland influences many other glands, including the thyroid and adrenal glands. It is also responsible for growth (through the release of growth hormone), social bonding (through the release of oxytocin). The pineal gland regulates the body's internal clock (through the release of melatonin). The thyroid gland regulates metabolism. The adrenal glands regulate the body's response to stress (through the release of epinephrine and norepinephrine) and sexual development.

Reflective Practice

Content Check

1. Three major divisions of the brain are the ___________, the ___________, and the ___________.
2. Reflex centers for heartbeat and respiration are found in the
   a. cerebellum
   b. thalamus
   c. medulla
   d. RF
3. A portion of the reticular formation serves as an ______________ system in the brain.
   a. activating
   b. alternate
   c. adjustment
   d. aversive
4. The ____________ is a final relay, or switching station, for sensory information on its way to the cortex.
5. Reward and punishment areas are found throughout the ____________ system, which also is related to emotion.
6. The body's ability to resist stress is related to the action of the ____________ glands.

Skill Check

Think Critically

7. Subcortical structures in humans are quite similar to corresponding brain areas in most animals with spinal cords. Why would knowing this allow you to predict, in general terms, what functions the subcortex controls?

Self-Reflect

What are the major subcortical structures, and what functions do they control? Why is it especially important to understand the limbic system and the role that it plays in your emotional life?

ANSWERS

1. hindbrain, midbrain, forebrain 2. c 3. a 4. thalamus 5. limbic 6. adrenal 7. Because the subcortex must be related to basic functions common to all higher animals: motives, emotions, sleep, attention, and vegetative functions such as heartbeat, breathing, and temperature regulation. The subcortex also routes and processes incoming information from the senses and outgoing commands to the muscles.

MODULE

11 A Psychologist's Skill Set

Self-Regulation

One or Two Marshmallows?

Imagine that you are a four-year-old visiting the "Surprise Room" at Stanford University. A woman named Karen lets you choose a treat from a plate of pretzels, cookies, mints, and marshmallows. You eagerly pick the marshmallows. Karen then puts two plates in front of you. With one marshmallow on the first plate and two marshmallows on the second plate, you have a choice to make. Do you want to eat one marshmallow now, or two marshmallows later? Karen explains that if you want the larger reward, you'll have to wait by yourself, with the marshmallows, for about 20 minutes. She also leaves you with a bell so that if you just can't wait any longer, you can ring it and call her back. But she warns that if you do that, you'll only get one marshmallow. What do you do?

doble.d/Moment/Getty Images

You might be surprised to learn that how well you *self-regulate* as an adult is predicted by how many marshmallows you ate in the Surprise Room. What is self-regulation, and what can you do about it as an adult? Let's look into it.

~LEARNING OUTCOMES~

After reading this module you should be able to:

11.1 Explain how self-regulation can help you in your personal and professional life and create a plan to improve your self-regulation skills

Mind Control—Control Yourself!

Learning Outcome 11.1 Explain how self-regulation can help you in your personal and professional life and create a plan to improve your self-regulation skills

Designed by Stanford psychologist Walter Mischel, the "Marshmallow Test" is often used to examine children's ability to resist temptation. Psychologists refer to this as **self-regulation**—the ability to consciously exert self-control. How about you? As a four-year-old, would you have hung in there for two marshmallows, or would you have settled for one? How about you as an adult? In adulthood, for example, youthful self-regulators are likely to enjoy better health ("I should probably skip that extra helping of dessert."), professional success ("I can't party tonight; I have a report to prepare."), and financial situation ("Do I really need to buy a bigger TV?") (Berman et al., 2013).

I was a one marshmallow kid. Does that mean I will always be a poor self-regulator? To some extent, our ability to self-regulate is managed by our brains (Luna et al., 2015). Fortunately, Mischel has found that self-regulation is also a skill—one that anyone can develop with enough practice (Mischel, 2014).

The Frontal Lobes—The Executive Living in Your Brain

For the most part, the roots of self-regulation lie in the brain's frontal lobes (the prefrontal cortex), though some other regions of the brain are also involved. In particular, as mentioned in Module 9, the prefrontal cortex is home to an important set of abilities referred to as *executive functions*, which provide the foundation for higher-level thinking including our ability to demonstrate self-control.

Like an air traffic control system that permits the coordination of incoming and outgoing flights on multiple runways, executive functions coordinate our thinking and behavior so that we can accomplish the things that we need to do. For example, they allow us to pay attention to important things and filter out distractions, prioritize information, make plans, and suppress behaviors that would prevent us from carrying those plans out (Center on the Developing Child at Harvard University, 2011).

Executive functions are at the heart of self-regulation because they allow us to set goals (I'm going to try to wait and get the two marshmallows instead of eating one now), make plans that will help us to achieve those goals (I'm not going to touch the marshmallow), control our attention and emotions in ways that will be helpful as we work toward our goals (I'm going to close my eyes so that I don't have to look at the marshmallow while I'm waiting), and monitor our progress toward the goal so that we know if we need to change our strategy (Only five more minutes before she comes back and I can have two marshmallows. I'm doing great!).

So if self-regulation is based in the brain, is it determined by genetics? Because the ability to control our behavior is so closely connected with the prefrontal cortex, you might imagine that there's little you can do to change how it develops over time. And while it is true that brain development is, in part, controlled by genetics, it's also influenced by our environment and our actions. This is why Walter Mischel believes that self-regulation is a skill that we can all develop.

From Marshmallows to Retirement Funds

If you think about it, there are many times during our adult lives when it becomes important to control the impulse to give in to immediate temptation. Sometime during this semester, for example, you'll probably put aside some time to study for exams rather than going out with friends because you understand that your performance at school can have important implications for your ability to find a job later, after graduation. If you marry and find yourself in a bar with a stranger who is flirting with you, you'll likely want to resist the temptation to cheat on your spouse because you'll recognize that it could one day spell the end of a relationship that is important to you. And when you find yourself with some extra money, you may have to stop yourself from spending it on a new car and instead put it into your retirement savings so that you'll be comfortable many years down the road when you stop working.

There are many more day-to-day examples of how self-regulation can have consequences for later, such as sticking to your diet or your plan to give up cigarettes. Viewed like this, it becomes a bit easier to see how self-regulation has important connections to the quality of our adult lives. Things such as good health and adequate retirement savings often require us to give up immediate rewards for something better later on, even though doing so is really hard work (Baumeister, 2015; Inzlicht & Schmeichel, 2012).

But does the ability to control behavior in childhood really predict what happens so many years later? It may not initially be easy to see how children's behavior in the Marshmallow Task would be connected to the lives that they live as adults, but Mischel's work clearly suggested that it was. Other work from New Zealand has confirmed these findings (Moffitt et al., 2011). Researchers there followed *every child* born in the small town of Dunedin between 1972 and 1973—more than 1,000 of them—until they were in their thirties. They assessed the children's self-regulation in a variety of ways, including the children's own comments about their ability to control themselves, reports from parents and teachers, and observations made by the researchers. Later in life, children who had displayed greater levels of self-regulation were doing better on a variety of measures, including ones that assessed health, substance abuse, finances (saving habits, credit card problems), and antisocial behavior, such as criminal activity.

You may be wondering how a child's behavior could be so important to his or her circumstances as an adult decades later. Though the story behind these relationships is complex and involves brain development, it's also likely that

Self-regulation The ability to consciously exert self-control.

when children grow up having had some success with self-regulation—say, their experiences lead them to realize that waiting generally leads to better results than giving in to impulses—they learn that it pays to control themselves and wait for a larger payoff later. As a result, self-regulation starts to become more natural for them, and they will do it more often. When you think about it this way, it's not too hard to see how a simple task like the Marshmallow Test, done during childhood, might be connected to some of the important outcomes that we see later in life. Kids who are learning that it pays to wait will find themselves in better circumstances as they grow up.

Studying the Science: Self-Regulation and Poverty

More recently, researchers have attempted to replicate Mischel's work with larger and more diverse samples of children. In one particular example, psychologists found that, in keeping with Mischel's studies, children's performance on the Marshmallow Test (that is, early self-regulation) was correlated with their academic performance in high school many years later (recall from Module 5 that correlations tell us about the relationship between two variables; in this case, the relationship between self-regulation and high school grades). The correlation was smaller than in the original study, a finding that likely reflected the larger and more representative sample (Watts, Duncan, & Quan, 2018).

The key difference, however, was that the more recent study also suggested that the correlation between self-regulation and high school achievement may actually be due to a third factor: affluence. Children from wealthier families, on average, did better on the Marshmallow Test *and* had better grades in high school. So perhaps self-regulation isn't important for high school grades at all—maybe it's just whether you come from a wealthy family that matters. So should we consider the Marshmallow Test to be unimportant in predicting what happens later in life? Did Mischel's early studies get it all wrong?

It's worth noting that Mischel had long realized that children from poorer families did not fare as well as more affluent children on the Marshmallow Test. Decades ago, he noted that whether children opt to eat the marshmallow early isn't only a function of their self-regulation abilities—it's also influenced by their life circumstances (Mischel, 1974). Many studies since have demonstrated the same thing: Living in poverty is an experience that prompts people to take a sure thing now rather than waiting for something more later (Evans et al., 2013). If you're a child from a poor family, then, it probably makes a lot of sense to take the marshmallow that's in front of you instead of hoping that someone really will give you a second one later.

This newer research doesn't really contradict Mischel's early work; it simply helps us to better understand the complexity of the relationship between self-regulation and later outcomes like high school grades (Payne & Sheeran, 2018). In effect, a focus on the here-and-now—which makes good sense for people living in poverty—likely compromises their ability to self-regulate in ways that might be beneficial later on. Put another way, it's not *either* affluence *or* self-regulation that influences high school grades; instead, those two factors likely work together to impact future outcomes such as grades, financial stability, and health.

Improving Your Self-Regulation Skills

I can see that self-regulation is important. But if it's really a skill, then how can I get better at it? That's a great question. Imagine, for example, that you are a university student trying to save up for a car so that you don't have to take the bus everywhere. It's hard, though, because there are lots of other ways to spend your money that would give you more immediate pleasure. Maybe you'd like to go out to the pub with your friends or buy some new clothes. Or perhaps you'd like to take a trip during spring break. The tendency to focus on what we want now and ignore the consequences that will come later has been referred to as the *hot emotional system*, and it tends to be associated with the limbic system of the brain. It's the system that will dominate your thinking when you're faced with temptation right now, and it will issue a powerful push to do what you want in that moment. In contrast, the *cool cognitive system* is one that allows you to reflectively consider the potential long-term consequences of your actions (Mischel, 2014). As you might guess, the cool system is associated with the prefrontal cortex, and it's essential for self-regulation.

While it may be difficult to control the hot system when working toward long-term goals like buying a car, researchers such as Walter Mischel have suggested that this is one of the most important ways that people can work toward improving their self-control (Mischel, 2014). There are a number of ways to cool your immediate impulses. For example, work on changing what you pay attention to, a strategy that's called *selective attention*. Employing selective attention means that you focus on things that are removed from the temptation—in other words, you take your attention away from the things that the hot system is focused on. Rather than looking longingly at a friend's brochures for a sun-filled trip during spring break, you might focus your attention on the cars outside and tell yourself that it won't be long before you can have one yourself.

You might also engage in *cognitive reappraisal*, which essentially means that you try to reframe situations in ways that are more likely to help you stay in control (Duckworth, Gendler, & Gross, 2014). For example, your efforts to save money for a car might lead you to think differently about an invitation to go to the pub with your friends. Instead of feeling as though you're missing out if you limit yourself to one drink while you're out, you might think that you won't need an extra trip to the gym to work off the calories that would come with the extra beer!

Mischel also suggests that it's important to find ways to bring the long-term rewards and consequences to the front of your mind, to ensure that the cool system is in control. One way to do this is by stepping outside of the here and now and clearly imagining your future self suffering the consequences of your impulsive actions. If you're saving for a car, then, imagine yourself still standing at the bus stop in two years because you couldn't stop spending your extra money. If you're trying to quit smoking, clearly picture the doctor showing your future self an X-ray and telling you that you have lung cancer.

While strategies aimed at cooling the hot system are very effective, a second way to improve your self-regulation skills is to simply avoid putting yourself in an environment where the temptation will be too great to resist (Duckworth et al., 2014). We can do this by actively *choosing* or *changing the environments* we find ourselves in, so that we are more likely to do what we know is right in the long term. If you were trying to save money for a car, then, you might decide you aren't going to go out for a pricey dinner and drinks with friends (choosing the environment). Alternatively, if you did go out for dinner, you might make sure that you only take a specified amount of money to spend (changing the environment by restricting what you can buy).

Of course, there may be times when you are faced with temptation and find it difficult to change the environment or your thinking. In such cases, you can still rely on the old-fashioned way of showing self-control: Just say no!

MODULE 11 Self-Regulation—Learning Outcomes Revisited

11.1 Explain how self-regulation can help you in your personal and professional life and create a plan to improve your self-regulation skills

Self-regulation is associated with the frontal lobes of the brain, which control our executive functions. Executive functions allow us to set goals, make plans to achieve those goals, control attention and emotions as we work toward our goals, and monitor our progress on the goal so that we know if we need to change our strategy. Because of its close link to goals, self-regulation in childhood predicts many things connected to personal and professional success, including health, antisocial and criminal behavior, and financial security. Self-regulation skills can be improved by changing what we pay attention to, how we think about situations we're in, or the environments we find ourselves in. We hope that after reading this section, you'll be better able to think about how you can use these strategies to help when you need to focus and resist temptation in order to meet your goals!

Reflective Practice

Content Check

1. Executive functions are important to self-regulation because they help us to set goals and work toward them successfully. T or F?
2. The ability to self-regulate in childhood is not related to the ability to self-regulate in adulthood. T or F?
3. Selective attention and cognitive reappraisal are two strategies that can be used to improve self-regulation skills. T or F?

Skill Check

Think Critically

4. If you were setting the goal of losing 10 pounds, how could you improve your chances of resisting the temptation of your favorite foods and sticking to your diet?

Self-Reflect

What types of goals have you currently set for yourself? What kinds of things are likely to get in the way of you achieving those goals? Can you use some of the strategies from this module to help you stay on track with your goals?

ANSWERS

1. T 2. F 3. T 4. You can use strategies like selective attention (when in the kitchen or a restaurant, focus your attention on something other than the foods you are trying to avoid) or cognitive reappraisal (think about those potato chips in terms of how bad they are for your health). You can also try avoiding environments (e.g., fast food restaurants) where you're likely to give in to temptation.

Human Development
Heredity and Environment

MODULE 12

It's a Boy!

With those words, Gloria first glimpsed her amazing newborn baby, Joseph. Like parents everywhere, Gloria and her husband, Jay, wondered: How will Joseph's life unfold? What kind of a person will he be? Will he be a happy teenager, marry, become a father, find an interesting career, live a full and satisfying life?

Research tells a fascinating story about human growth and development, from birth and infancy to maturing, aging, and death. Understanding your development might well help you answer two important questions: "How did I become the person I am today?" and "Who will I become tomorrow?"

Maria Svetlychnaja/Shutterstock.com

Like Joseph, our heredity and our environment will influence every stage of our lives. How does our genetic inheritance combine with our life experiences to shape who we are and who we will become? Let's look at this dance in more detail.

~LEARNING OUTCOMES~

After reading this module you should be able to:

12.1 Explain how heredity (nature) and environment (nurture) interact to shape human development. Be able to give examples from infant motor and sensory development

Nature and Nurture—It Takes Two to Tango

Learning Outcome 12.1 Explain how heredity (nature) and environments (nurture) interact to shape human development. Be able to give examples from infant motor and sensory development

When we think of human development, we naturally think of children growing up into adults. But even as adults, we never really stop growing. **Developmental psychology**, the study of normal changes in behavior that occur across the life span, involves every stage of life from conception to death, or womb to tomb (Kail & Cavanaugh, 2019; Newman & Newman, 2018). Heredity (our "nature") and environment (our "nurture") also affect us throughout our lifetimes.

Which is more important, heredity or environment? Neither. Biopsychologist Donald Hebb once offered a useful analogy: What is more important to define the area of a rectangle, height or width? Of course, both are essential. Without height *and* width, there is no rectangle. Although heredity gives each of us a variety of potentials and limitations, these are, in turn, affected by environmental influences, such as learning, nutrition, culture, and disease. Some events, such as when Joseph reaches sexual maturity, are

Developmental psychology The study of the normal changes in behavior that occur across the life span.

governed more by heredity. Others, such as when Joseph learns to swim, read, or drive a car, are matters primarily of environment.

Ultimately, the person you are today reflects a continuous *interaction,* or interplay, between the forces of nature and nurture (Kalat, 2109). If Joseph grows up to become a prominent civil rights lawyer, his success will be due to both heredity and environment.

Heredity and Maturation

The dance of development begins at conception, when a father's sperm cell fertilizes a mother's egg cell (ovum). The resulting combination of genes from the two parents constitutes the *genome*, the genetic heritage that will determine many of the physical and psychological characteristics of a rapidly developing new life. The term **heredity ("nature")** refers, in part, to this genetic transmission of genes from parents to offspring. If some of the transmitted genes are defective, **genetic disorders** will result. Examples are sickle-cell anemia, hemophilia, cystic fibrosis, muscular dystrophy, albinism, and some types of intellectual disability.

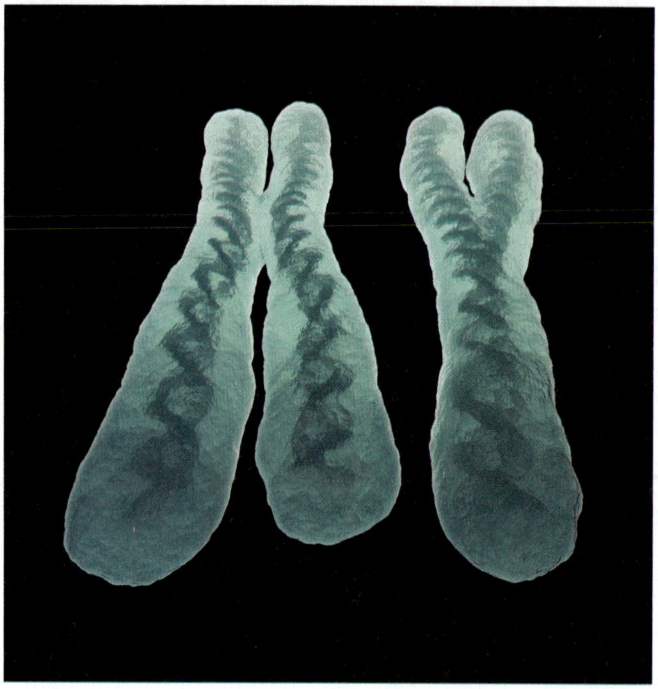

A digital illustration of X and Y human chromosomes (colors are artificial).

The Genome *What, exactly, is the genome?* A major scientific milestone was reached when the Human Genome Project completed sequencing all 3 billion chemical base pairs in human DNA (U.S. Department of Energy Office of Science, 2019). The nucleus of every human cell contains **deoxyribonucleic acid (DNA)** (dee-OX-see-RYE-bo-new-KLEE-ik), a long, ladderlike chain of pairs of chemical molecules (➤ **Figure 12.1**). The order of these molecules, or organic bases, acts as a code for genetic information. The DNA in each cell contains a record of all the instructions needed to make a human—with room left over to spare.

Human DNA is organized into 46 **chromosomes**. (The word *chromosome* means "colored body.") These rod-like structures in the cell nucleus house the genes. Notable exceptions are sperm cells and ova, which contain only 23 chromosomes. Thus, Joseph received 23 chromosomes from Gloria and 23 from Jay. This is his *genome.*

Genes are the coded instructions of heredity—the areas on a strand of DNA that carry hereditary information. Sometimes a single gene is responsible for an inherited feature, such as Joseph's eye color. Genes may be dominant or recessive. When a **dominant gene** controls a feature, that feature will appear every time the gene is present. A **recessive gene** must be paired with a second recessive gene before its effect will be expressed. For example, if Joseph got a blue-eye gene from Jay and a brown-eye gene from Gloria, Joseph will be brown eyed, because brown-eye genes are dominant.

If brown-eye genes are dominant, why do two brown-eyed parents sometimes have a blue-eyed child? If one or both parents have two brown-eye genes, the couple's children can only be brown eyed. But what if each parent has one brown-eye gene and one blue-eye gene? In that case, both parents would have brown eyes. Yet there is one chance in four that their children will get two blue-eye genes and have blue eyes (➤ **Figure 12.2**).

In actuality, single genes control few of our characteristics. Instead, most are **polygenic characteristics** (pol-ih-JEN-ik), controlled by many genes working in combination. So, for example, there is no one gene for height; in fact, about 200 genetic variations have already been shown to play a role in determining height (Allen, Estrada, et al., 2010). Through the expression of genes, heredity determines eye color, height, skin color, and susceptibility to some diseases.

Epigenetics While the genome contains all the instructions needed to make a human, it cannot do so by itself. Like a builder who follows a blueprint to build a house, *epigenetic* processes within cells translate the "genetic blueprint" encoded in the genome, step by step, into an actual organism (the phenome). These processes can intensify or weaken the effects of genes and can even switch genes on or off at certain ages or developmental stages. In this way, heredity continues to exert a powerful influence throughout **maturation**, the physical growth and development of the body, brain, and

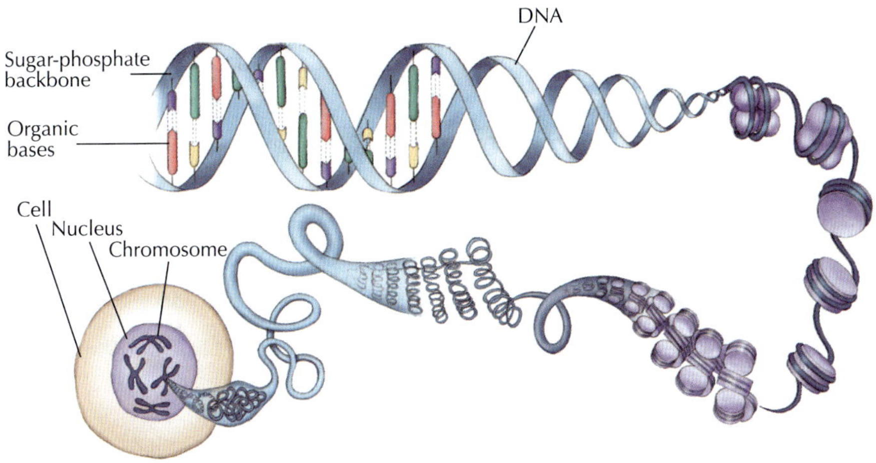

➤ Figure 12.1

DNA. (Top left) Linked molecules (organic bases) make up the rungs on DNA's twisted molecular ladder. The order of these molecules serves as a code for genetic information. The code provides a genetic blueprint that is unique for each individual (except identical twins). The drawing shows only a small section of a DNA strand. An entire strand of DNA is composed of billions of smaller molecules. (Bottom left) The nucleus of each cell in the body contains chromosomes made up of tightly wound coils of DNA.

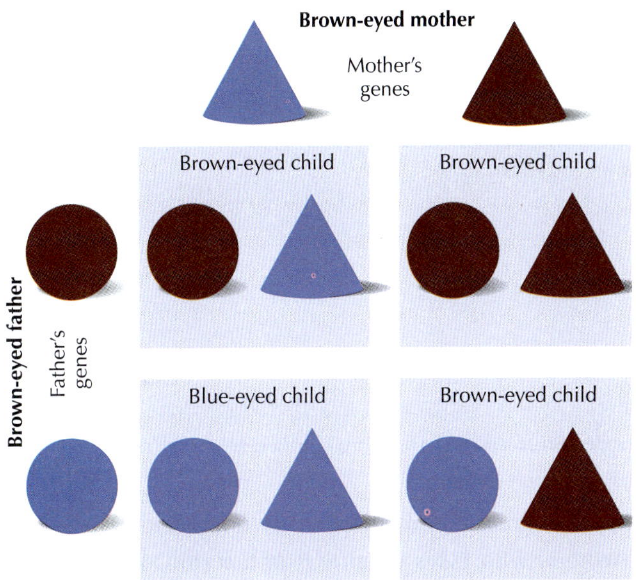

➤ Figure 12.2

Expression of single gene characteristics. Gene patterns for children of brown-eyed parents, where each parent has one brown-eye gene and one blue-eye gene. Because the brown-eye gene is dominant, one child in four will be blue-eyed. Thus, there is a significant chance that two brown-eyed parents will have a blue-eyed child.

Cultura Creative (RF)/Alamy Stock Photo

Twins who share identical genes (identical twins) demonstrate the powerful influence of heredity. Even when they are reared apart, identical twins are strikingly alike in motor skills, physical development, and appearance. At the same time, identical twins are never completely identical and are less alike as adults than they were as children, showing that environmental influences are at work (Freberg, 2021; Larsson, Larsson, & Lichtenstein, 2004).

nervous system (Cummings, 2016). As the *human growth sequence* unfolds over time, genetic instructions continue to influence body size and shape, height, intelligence, athletic potential, personality traits, sexual orientation, and a host of other details (■ **Table 12.1**).

Environment and Maturation

Our environment also exerts a profound influence on our development right from conception onward. **Environment ("nurture")** refers to the sum of all external conditions that affect a person. Although the *intrauterine* (interior of the womb) environment is highly protected, environmental conditions can even affect the developing child. For example,

Heredity ("nature") The transmission of physical and psychological characteristics from parents to offspring through genes.

Genetic disorders Problems caused by defects in the genes or by inherited characteristics.

Deoxyribonucleic acid (DNA) Deoxyribonucleic acid, a molecular structure that contains coded genetic information.

Chromosomes Rodlike structures in the cell nucleus that house an individual's genes.

Genes Areas on a strand of DNA that carry hereditary information.

Dominant gene A gene whose influence will be expressed each time that the gene is present.

Recessive gene A gene whose influence will be expressed only when it is paired with a second recessive gene of the same type.

Polygenic characteristics Personal traits or physical properties that are influenced by many genes working in combination.

Maturation The physical growth and development of the body, brain, and nervous system.

Environment ("nurture") The sum of all external conditions affecting development, including especially the effects of learning.

TABLE 12.1 | Periods of Life*

Period	Approximate Duration	Descriptive Name
Prenatal period	From conception to birth	
Germinal period	Conception to 2 weeks after conception	Zygote
Embryonic period	2 weeks to 8 weeks after conception	Embryo
Fetal period	8 weeks after conception to birth	Fetus
Infancy	From birth to childhood	Infant, baby
Childhood	From infancy to adolescence	Child
Early childhood	18 months to 3 years	Toddler
Preschool period	3 years to about 6 years	Preschooler
Middle childhood	6 years to 12 years	School-age child
Adolescence	From puberty to full social maturity (it's difficult to define the duration of this period)	Adolescent
Adulthood	From adolescence to death	Adult
Young adulthood	20 to 34 years	Emerging adult
Middle age	35 to 64 years	Mature adult
Late adulthood	65 years and older	Old age

*Note: Various periods of life have no exact beginning or ending point. The ages are approximate, and each period may be thought of as blending into the next.

during the last few months of Gloria's pregnancy, Joseph's fetal heart rate changed whenever he heard his mother's voice (Kisilevsky & Hains, 2011).

Many environmental factors can influence epigenesis, and hence maturation. Had Gloria experienced excess stress during her pregnancy, Joseph might have been a smaller, weaker baby at birth (Schetter, 2011). If Gloria's health or nutrition had been poor, or if she had had German measles, syphilis, or Zika, had used alcohol or drugs, or had been exposed to lead or radiation, Joseph's growth sequence might also have been harmed (Lanphear, 2015). In such cases, babies can suffer from **congenital problems**, or birth defects. These environmental problems affect the developing fetus and become apparent at birth.

How is it possible for the embryo or the fetus to be harmed? No direct intermixing of blood takes place between a mother and her unborn child. Yet some substances—especially drugs—can reach the fetus. Any harmful substance that can cause birth defects is called a **teratogen** (teh-RAT-uh-jen). Sometimes women are unknowingly exposed to powerful teratogens, such as radiation, lead, pesticides, or polychlorinated biphenyls (PCBs). But pregnant women do have direct control over many teratogens. For example, a woman who takes cocaine runs a serious risk of injuring her fetus (Minnes et al., 2016). In short, when a pregnant woman takes drugs, her unborn child does, too.

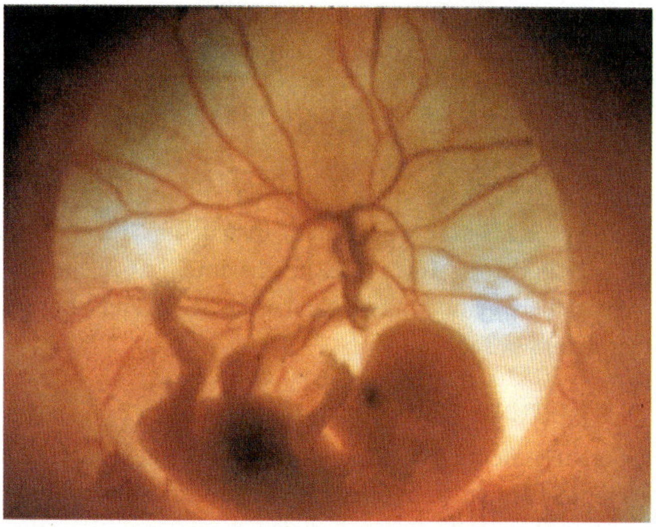
Nestle/Petit Format/Science Source

An 11-week-old fetus. Because of the rapid growth of basic structures, the developing fetus is sensitive to a variety of diseases, drugs, and sources of radiation. This is especially true during the first trimester (three months) of gestation (pregnancy).

Lyn Alweis/The Denver Post/Getty Images

Rick's Photography/Shutterstock.com

Some of the typical features of children with FASD include a small, nonsymmetrical head, a short nose, a flattened area between the eyes, oddly shaped eyes, and a thin upper lip. Many of these features become less noticeable by adolescence. However, intellectual disabilities and other problems commonly follow the FASD child into adulthood. The children shown here represent moderate examples of FASD.

Unfortunately, in the United States, alcohol and drugs are among the greatest risk factors facing unborn children (Keegan et al., 2010). In fact, repeated heavy drinking during pregnancy is the most common cause of birth defects in the United States (Liles & Packman, 2009). Affected infants have **fetal alcohol spectrum disorder (FASD)**; a collection of conditions occurring in children whose mothers consumed alcohol during pregnancy. More severe forms of FASD are commonly referred to as *fetal alcohol syndrome (FAS)*. Children born with FASD often have low birth weight, a small head, bodily defects, and facial malformations. Many also suffer from emotional, behavioral, and mental disabilities (Hepper, Dornan, & Lynch, 2012; Jones & Streissguth, 2010).

If a mother is addicted to morphine, heroin, or methadone, her baby may be born with an addiction. Even tobacco use is harmful. Smoking during pregnancy greatly reduces oxygen to the fetus. Heavy smokers risk miscarrying or having premature, underweight babies who are more likely to die soon after birth. Furthermore, children of smoking mothers score lower on tests of language and mental ability (Clifford, Lang, & Chen, 2012).

Maturation in Infancy

Even though newborn human infants will die if not cared for by adults and cannot lift their heads, turn over, or feed themselves, they are born with physical and mental capacities that continue to surprise researchers and delight parents. The emergence of many of these capacities is closely related to heredity and maturation of the brain, nervous system, and body.

For example, at birth, infants have several adaptive reflexes (Siegler, DeLoache, & Eisenberg, 2014). To elicit the *grasping reflex*, press an object in a newborn's palms, and they will grasp it with surprising strength. Many infants, in fact, can hang from a raised bar, like little trapeze artists. The grasping reflex aids survival by helping infants avoid falling. You can observe the *rooting reflex* (reflexive head turning and nursing) by touching infants' cheeks. Immediately, they will turn toward your finger, as if searching for something. The rooting reflex helps infants find a bottle or a breast. Then, when a nipple touches infants' mouths, the *sucking reflex* (rhythmic nursing) helps them obtain needed food. Like other reflexes, this is a genetically programmed action.

The *Moro reflex* also is interesting. If infants' positions are changed abruptly, or if they are startled by a loud noise, they will make a hugging motion. This reaction has been compared to the movements that baby monkeys use to cling to their mothers. (We leave it to the reader's imagination to decide whether there is any connection.) Human infants mature from helpless babies to independent little people with dazzling speed. At no other time does development proceed as rapidly. By their third year, babies are usually able to stand, walk, talk, and explore.

The Role of Learning Once a baby is born, the environment becomes more important because it provides learning experiences. For example, the brain of a newborn baby has fewer *dendrites* (nerve cell branches) and *synapses* (connections between nerve cells) than an adult brain (➤ Figure 12.3). However, the newborn brain is highly *plastic* (capable of being altered by experience). During the first three years of life, millions of new connections form in the brain every day. At the same time, unused connections disappear. As a result, early learning environments literally shape the developing brain, through the "blooming and pruning" of synapses (Nelson, 1999; Walker et al., 2011).

Although human culture is accelerating the rate at which human DNA is evolving, modern humans are still genetically quite similar to cave dwellers who lived 30,000 years ago (Cochran & Harpending, 2009; Hawks et al., 2007). A Stone Age baby could have become only a hunter or food gatherer. But a bright baby born today could learn to become almost anything—a ballet dancer, an engineer, an extreme marathoner, a boxer, or a biochemist who likes to paint in watercolors.

Congenital problems Defects that originate during prenatal development in the womb.

Teratogen A harmful substance that can cause birth defects.

Fetal alcohol spectrum disorder (FASD) A collection of conditions occurring in children whose mothers consumed alcohol during pregnancy.

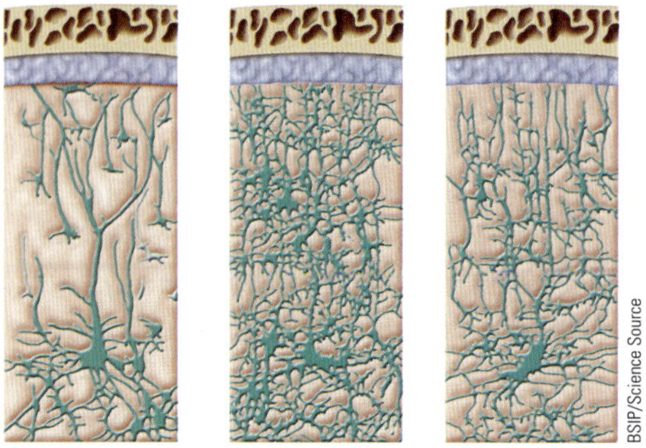

➤ Figure 12.3

Brain development after birth. On the left is an illustration of the neural networks in the brain of a nine-month-old infant. By age two, pictured in the center, the number of synapses and neurons in those networks has dramatically increased. By age four, pictured on the right, the number of synapses and neurons has declined slightly. Nevertheless, at that point, children actually have more brain synapses than adults do. Then, after age 10, the number continues to slowly decline, reaching adult levels at about age 16.

Motor Development in Infancy Infants will rapidly mature past grasping, rooting, sucking, and hugging as they develop more and more motor skills, such as sitting, crawling, standing, and walking. Of course, the *rate* of maturation varies from child to child. Nevertheless, the *order* of maturation is almost universal. For instance, Joseph was able to sit without support from Jay, Gloria, or some other adult before he matured enough to stand. Indeed, infants around the world typically sit before they crawl, crawl before they stand, and stand before they walk (➤ **Figure 12.4**).

Oddly enough, Joseph never crawled. Like Joseph, a few children move directly from sitting to standing to walking. Even so, their motor development is orderly. In general, muscular control spreads in a pattern that is *cephalocaudal* (SEF-eh-lo-KOD-ul), meaning from head to toe, and *proximodistal* (PROK-seh-moe-DIS-tul), meaning from the center of the body to the extremities.

Although maturation has a big impact, motor skills don't simply emerge. Joseph must learn to control his actions. When babies are beginning to crawl or walk, they actively try new movements and select those that work. Joseph's first efforts were flawed—wobbly sitting or some shaky first steps. However, with practice, babies fine-tune their movements to be smoother and more effective. Such learning is evident from the very first months of life (Adolph & Berger, 2011). Motor skills continue to improve throughout childhood, as Joseph learns to run, skate, tie his shoelaces, play the piano, hit a golf ball, and many other motor skills (Kail & Cavanaugh, 2019).

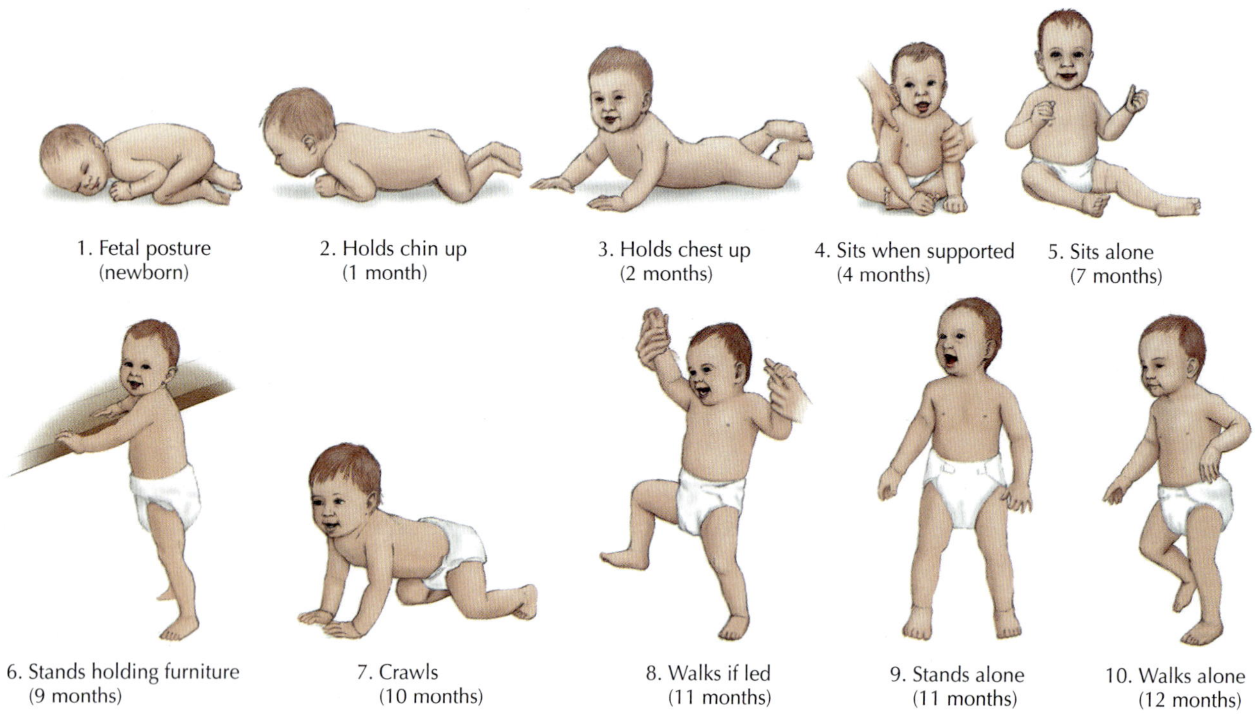

➤ Figure 12.4

Motor development. Most infants follow an orderly pattern of motor development. Although the order in which children progress is similar, there are large individual differences in the ages at which each ability appears. The ages listed are averages for American children. It is not unusual for many of the skills to appear one or two months earlier than average, or several months later (Adolph & Berger, 2011). Parents should not be alarmed if a child's behavior differs some from the average.

Sensory Development in Infancy Babies follow a similar developmental path when it comes to their senses. Contrary to common belief, newborn babies are not oblivious to their surroundings. Newborns can see, hear, smell, taste, and respond to pain and touch. Although their senses are less acute, babies are very responsive. From birth, Joseph could follow a moving object with his eyes and turn in the direction of sounds.

Tests show that newborn vision is not as sharp as that of adults; newborns can most clearly see objects that are about a foot away from them. It is as if they are best prepared to see the people who love and care for them (Leppänen, 2011). Perhaps that's why babies have a special fascination with human faces. Just *hours* after they are born, babies prefer seeing their mother's face rather than a stranger's. When babies are only two to five days old, they will pay more attention to a person who is gazing directly at them rather than one who is looking away (Farroni et al., 2004).

Three-day-old babies also prefer complex patterns, such as checkerboards and bull's-eyes, to simpler colored rectangles. When Joseph was six months old, he was able to recognize categories of objects that differed in shape or color. By nine months of age, he was able to tell the difference between dogs and birds or other groups of animals. By one year of age, he could see as well as his parents (Sigelman & Rider, 2018). So, a person really is inside that little body!

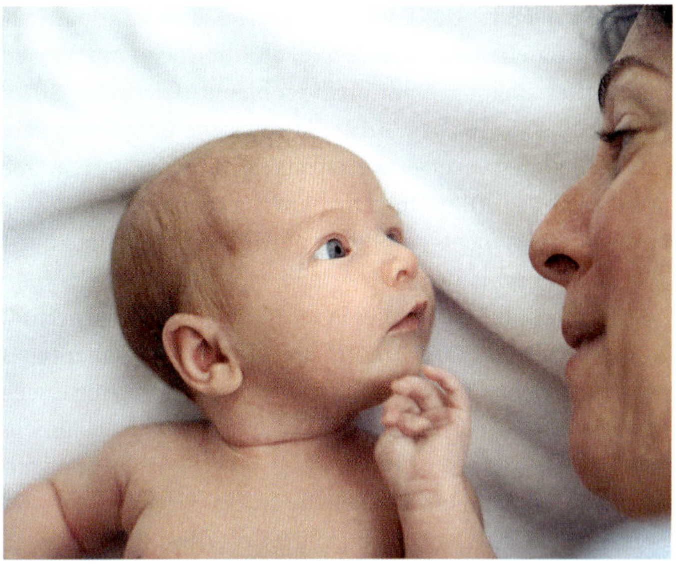

cwa/Alamy Stock Photo

Newborn babies display a special interest in the human face. Infants just days old pay more attention to the faces of people who are gazing directly at them than to people gazing away. A preference for seeing their mother's face develops rapidly and encourages social interactions between mother and baby.

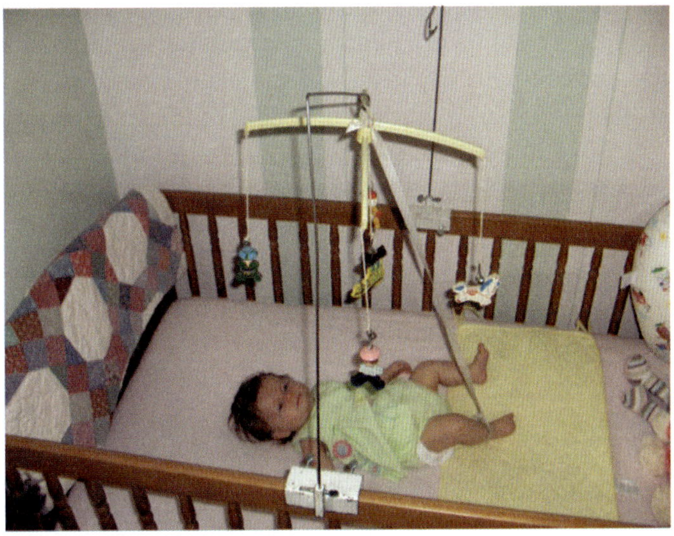

Dr. Carolyn Rovee-Collier

Psychologist Carolyn Rovee-Collier has shown that babies as young as three months old can learn to control their movements. In her experiments, babies lie on their backs under a colorful crib mobile. A ribbon is tied around the baby's ankle and connected to the mobile. Whenever babies spontaneously kick their legs, the mobile jiggles and rattles. Within a few minutes, infants learn to kick faster. Their reward for kicking is a chance to see the mobile move (Hayne & Rovee-Collier, 1995).

Readiness At what ages was Joseph ready to feed himself, to walk alone, or to say goodbye to diapers? Such milestones tend to be governed by a child's **readiness** for rapid learning—that is, a minimum level of maturation must occur before many skills can be learned.

Parents are asking for failure when they try to force a child to learn skills too early (Kiddoo, 2012). It is more difficult, for instance, to teach children to use a toilet before they have matured enough to control their bodies. Current guidelines suggest that toilet training goes most smoothly when it begins between 18 and 24 months of age.

Consider the overeager parents who toilet trained a 14-month-old child in 12 trying weeks of false alarms and accidents. If they had waited until the child was 20 months old, they might have succeeded in just 3 weeks. Parents may control when toilet training starts, but maturation tends to dictate when it will be completed (Au & Stavinoha, 2008).

On the other hand, parents who significantly delay the onset of toilet training may fare no better. The older children are before toilet training begins, the more likely they are to fail to develop full bladder control and become daytime wetters (Joinson et al., 2009). So why fight nature?

Readiness A condition that exists when maturation has advanced enough to allow the rapid acquisition of a particular skill.

Sensitive Periods Early experiences can have particularly lasting effects. For example, children who are abused may suffer lifelong emotional problems (Cicchetti, 2016; Shin, Miller, & Teicher, 2012). At the same time, extra care can sometimes reverse the effects of a poor start in life (Walker et al., 2011). In short, environmental forces guide human development—for better or worse—throughout life.

Why do some experiences have more lasting effects than others? Part of the answer lies in the idea of a **sensitive period**, a time when children are more susceptible to particular types of environmental influences. Events that occur during a sensitive period can permanently alter the course of development (Bedny et al., 2012). For example, forming a loving bond with a caregiver early in life seems to be crucial for optimal development. Likewise, language abilities may become impaired when babies don't hear normal speech during their first year (Gheitury, Sahraee, & Hoseini, 2012).

Deprivation and Enrichment Some environments can be described as *deprived* or *enriched*. **Deprivation** refers to a lack of normal nutrition, stimulation, comfort, or love. **Enrichment** exists when an environment is deliberately made more stimulating, loving, and so forth.

What happens when children suffer severe deprivation? Tragically, a few mistreated children have spent their first years in closets, attics, and other restricted environments. When first discovered, these children are usually mute, intellectually disabled, emotionally damaged, and suffer lifelong consequences (Kennedy et al., 2016; Wilson, 2003). Fortunately, such extreme deprivation is unusual. Nevertheless, milder perceptual, intellectual, or emotional deprivation occurs in many families, especially those that must cope with poverty (Cicchetti, 2016; Matthews & Gallo, 2011). Poverty can affect the development of children in at least two ways (Huston & Bentley, 2010; Sobolewski & Amato, 2005). First, poor parents may not be able to give their children necessities and resources such as nutritious meals, health care, or learning materials. As a result, impoverished children tend to be sick more often, their mental development lags, and they do poorly at school. Second, the stresses of poverty also can be hard on parents, leading to marriage problems, less positive parenting, and poorer parent–child relationships. The resulting emotional turmoil can damage a child's socioemotional development. In the extreme, it may increase the risk of delinquent behavior and mental illness.

Adults who grew up in poverty often remain trapped in a vicious cycle of continued poverty. Because more than 12.3 percent of Americans fell below the poverty line in 2017, this grim reality plays itself out in millions of U.S. homes every day (U.S. Census Bureau, 2018).

Can an improved environment enhance development? To answer this question, psychologists have created *enriched environments* that are especially novel, complex, and stimulating. To illustrate, let's consider the effects of raising rats in a sort of "rat wonderland." The walls of their cages were decorated with colorful patterns, and each cage was filled with platforms, ladders, and cubbyholes. As adults, these rats were superior at learning mazes. In addition, they had larger, heavier brains, with a thicker cortex (Benloucif, Bennett, & Rosenzweig, 1995).

Of course, it's a long leap from rats to people, but if extra stimulation can enhance the intelligence of a lowly rat, it's likely that human infants also benefit from enrichment. Indeed, many studies have shown that enriched environments improve abilities or enhance human development (Phillips & Lowenstein, 2011). It would be wise for Jay and Gloria to make a point of nourishing Joseph's mind as well as his body (Monahan, Beeber, & Harden, 2012).

What can parents do to enrich a child's environment? They can encourage exploration and stimulating play by paying attention to what holds the baby's interest. It is better to childproof a house than to put strict limits on what a child can touch. Actively enriching sensory experiences also are valuable. Infants are not vegetables. It makes perfect sense to take them outside, to hang mobiles over their cribs, to place mirrors nearby, to play music for them, or to rearrange their rooms now and then. Children progress most rapidly when they have responsive parents and stimulating play materials at home (Beeber et al., 2007). In light of this, it is wise to

Oleksiy Rezin/Shutterstock.com

Children who grow up in poverty run a high risk of experiencing many forms of deprivation. There is evidence that lasting damage to social, emotional, and cognitive development occurs when children must cope with severe early deprivation.

view all of childhood as a *relatively sensitive period* (Nelson, 1999; Walker et al., 2011).

The Whole Human Nurture often affects the expression of hereditary tendencies through ongoing reciprocal influences. A good example of such influences is the fact that growing infants influence their parents' behavior at the same time that they are changed by it.

Newborn babies differ noticeably in **temperament**, the general pattern of attention, arousal, and mood that is evident from birth. This is the hereditary, physical core of personality, and it includes sensitivity, irritability, distractibility, and typical mood (Slagt et al., 2016). According to one influential theory, about 40 percent of all newborns are *easy children,* who are relaxed and agreeable. Another 10 percent are *difficult children,* who are moody, intense, and easily angered. *Slow-to-warm-up children* (about 15 percent) are restrained, unexpressive, or shy. The remaining children do not fit neatly into a single category (Chess & Thomas, 1986).

Because of differences in temperament, some babies are more likely than others to smile, cry, vocalize, reach out, or pay attention. As a result, babies rapidly become active participants in their own development. For example, Joseph was an easy baby who smiled frequently and was easily fed. This encouraged Gloria to touch, feed, and sing to Joseph. Gloria's affection rewarded Joseph, in turn causing him to smile more.

In this way, a dynamic relationship blossoms between mother and child. For example, good parenting can reciprocally influence a shy child who, in turn, might become progressively less shy. The reverse also occurs: Difficult children may make parents unhappy and elicit more negative parenting. Alternatively, negative parenting can turn a moderately shy child into a very shy one. This suggests that inherited temperaments are dynamically modified by a child's experiences (Bridgett et al., 2009; Kiff, Lengua, & Bush, 2011).

An individual's **developmental level**, then, is his or her current state of physical, emotional, and intellectual development. To summarize, three factors combine to determine your developmental level at any point in life: *heredity, environment,* and your *own behavior,* and each is tightly interwoven with the others (Easterbrooks et al., 2013).

Sensitive period During development, a period of increased sensitivity to environmental influences. It also is a time during which certain events must take place for normal development to occur.

Deprivation In development, the loss or withholding of normal stimulation, nutrition, comfort, love, and so forth; a condition of absence.

Enrichment In development, deliberately making an environment more stimulating, nutritional, comforting, loving, and so forth.

Temperament The general pattern of attention, arousal, and mood that is evident from birth.

Developmental level An individual's current state of physical, emotional, and intellectual development.

MODULE 12 Heredity and Environment—Learning Outcomes Revisited

12.1 Explain how heredity and environment interact to shape human development. Be able to give examples from infant motor and sensory development

Genes in each cell carry hereditary instructions. Most characteristics are polygenic and reflect the combined effects of dominant and recessive genes. A variety of environmental factors (access to good food and health care, schooling, family members, peer groups, media, and so on) also contribute to the child's development; environments that are deprived will hamper development, while enriched environments will foster it. Physical development tends to look similar across people, as evidenced by common infant reflexes and physical development that proceeds in a cephalocaudal and proximodistal manner. Although such similarities suggest an important role for "nature" or genetic factors, environmental factors (e.g., opportunities to practice motor skills in infancy; maintaining a healthy lifestyle in adulthood) also contribute to physical development. Similarly, infants' vision is not as good as that of older children and adults. However, environmental stimulation combined with maturation of the visual system leads to rapid improvements in visual acuity.

Reflective Practice

Content Check

1. Areas of the DNA molecule called genes are made up of dominant and recessive chromosomes. T or F?
2. Most inherited characteristics can be described as polygenic. T or F?
3. Environmental factors begin to influence a child's development beginning at
   a. infancy
   b. birth
   c. conception
   d. maturity
4. The orderly sequence observed in the unfolding of many basic responses can be attributed to ______________.
5. A sensitive __________ is a time of increased sensitivity to environmental influences.
6. Slow-to-warm-up children can be described as restrained, unexpressive, or shy. T or F?
7. As a child develops, a continuous ________________ takes place between the forces of heredity and environment.

Skill Check

Think Critically

8. What is the most direct way that environmental influences can interact with genetic programming?

Self-Reflect

Can you think of clear examples of some ways in which heredity and environmental forces have combined to affect your development? How would maturation affect the chances of teaching an infant to eat with a spoon? What kind of temperament did you have as an infant? How did it affect your relationship with your parents or caregivers?

ANSWERS

1. F 2. T 3. c 4. maturation 5. period 6. T 7. interaction (or interplay) 8. Environmental conditions sometimes turn specific genes on or off, thus directly affecting the expression of genetic tendencies.

Human Development

Emotional and Social Development in Childhood

MODULE 13

Let's Be Close

Human infants mature from helpless babies to independent little people with dazzling speed. At no other time except infancy does development proceed as rapidly. By their third year, babies are usually able to stand, walk, talk, and explore. During the same period, a baby's early emotional life and relationships with other people also unfold on a timetable that is largely controlled by maturation.

Social development is rooted in emotional attachment and the need for physical contact as infants first form an emotional bond with an adult. One sign of attachment is the storm of crying that sometimes occurs when babies are left alone at bedtime. As many parents know, it is often eased by the presence of security objects, such as a stuffed animal or favorite blanket. While parents are the most important influences in early social development, later development is enhanced when play with other children begins to extend a child's social life beyond the family. Let's trace our early emotional and social development.

Sergei Telegin/Shutterstock.com

~LEARNING OUTCOMES~

After reading this module you should be able to:

13.1 Distinguish between basic and complex emotions

13.2 Describe early attachment relationships between infants and their caregivers

13.3 Outline what is known about parenting styles, including maternal versus paternal styles

Emotional Development in Infancy—Curious, Baby?

Learning Outcome 13.1 Distinguish between basic and complex emotions

As Jay and Gloria can tell you, a baby's emotional life blossoms rapidly and appears to follow a pattern tied to maturation (Music, 2011; Panksepp & Pasqualini, 2005; see ➤ **Figure 13.1**). Experts have determined this by looking carefully at infants' emotional expressions. Beginning with a general expression of excitement, the newborn's emotional life soon differentiates into cries of distress and coos of delight (Bridges, 1932). Although there is still disagreement on the details (see, e.g.,

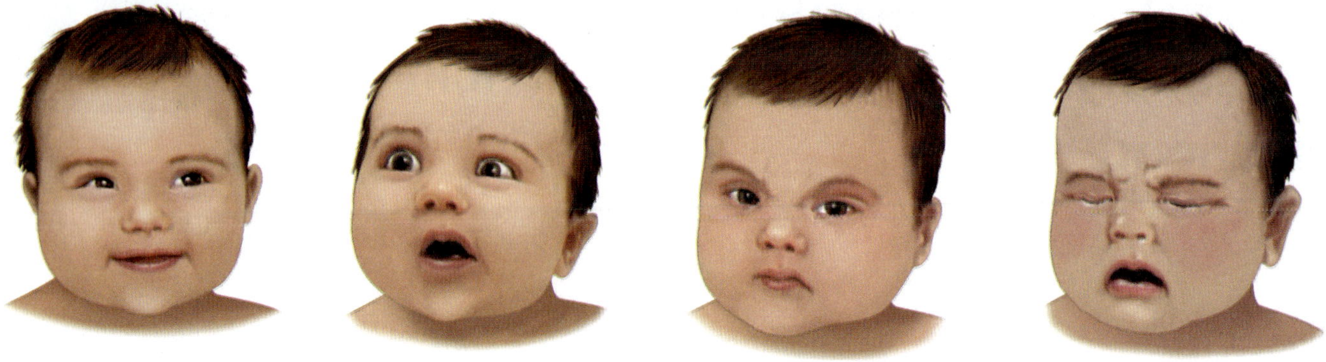

➤ **Figure 13.1**

Emotional expressions in infants. Infants display many of the same emotional expressions as adults do. Carroll Izard believes that such expressions show that many distinct emotions appear within the first months of life. Parents can expect to see a full range of basic emotions by the end of a baby's first year.

Izard, Woodburn, & Finlon, 2010; Shutter & Camras, 2010), by around six months of age further differentiation allows infants to facially express at least six *basic emotions*: happiness, sadness, fear, anger, surprise, and disgust (Kail & Cavanaugh, 2019). Interestingly, it takes further development before infants can read the expression of emotions on other faces; this ability does not appear before 36 to 48 months (Widen & Russell, 2008).

The rapid development of the basic emotions in infants suggests that these emotions are governed by heredity and related to evolution (Izard, 2011; Matsumoto & Hwang, 2019). Perhaps that's why smiling is one of a baby's most common reactions. Smiling may help babies survive by inviting parents to care for them. At first, a baby's smiling is haphazard. By the age of 8 to 12 months, however, infants smile more frequently when another person is nearby (Mcquaid, Bibok, & Carpendale, 2009). This **social smile** is especially rewarding to parents. Infants can even use their social smile to communicate interest in an object, like the time Joseph gazed at his favorite teddy bear and then smiled at his mother (Parlade et al., 2009).

What is an example of a nonbasic emotion? Embarrassment is an example of a *complex emotion*. To feel embarrassed, you first have to be self-aware. Sometime after about 18 months, infants become able to recognize themselves in a mirror. It is not until this age that infants first become able to experience embarrassment (Shaffer & Kipp, 2014). The range of emotional experience continues to expand throughout childhood. (Basic and complex emotions are described in greater detail in Module 42.)

Social Development—Baby, I'm Stuck on You

Learning Outcome 13.2 Describe early attachment relationships between infants and their caregivers

There is, of course, more to emotions than their facial expression. A baby's **affectional needs**—emotional needs for care, love, and positive relationships with others—are every bit as important as more obvious needs for food, water, and physical care. In part to meet their affectional needs, infants rapidly begin to form **attachments**, or close emotional bonds, with their primary caregivers (Music, 2011). As infants form their first emotional bond with an adult, usually a parent, they also begin to develop self-awareness and an awareness of others (Easterbrooks et al., 2013). This early **social development** lays a foundation for subsequent relationships with parents, siblings, friends, and relatives (Shaffer & Kipp, 2014).

To investigate mother–infant relationships, Harry Harlow separated baby rhesus monkeys from their mothers at birth. The real mothers were replaced with **surrogate mothers** (substitutes). Some were made of cold, unyielding wire. Others were covered with soft terry cloth.

When the infants were given a choice between the two mothers, they spent most of their time clinging to the cuddly terry-cloth mother. This was true even when the wire mother held a bottle, making it the source of food. The "love" and attachment displayed toward the cloth replicas was identical to that shown toward natural mothers. For example, when frightened by rubber snakes, wind-up toys, and other "fear stimuli," the infant monkeys ran to their cloth mothers and clung to them for security. These classic studies suggest that attachment begins with **contact comfort**, the

Nina Leen/Time & Life Pictures/Getty Images

An infant monkey clings to a cloth-covered surrogate mother. Baby monkeys become attached to the cloth "contact-comfort" mother but not to a similar wire mother. This is true even when the wire mother provides food and the cloth mother doesn't. Contact comfort may also underlie the tendency of children to become attached to inanimate objects, such as blankets or stuffed toys.

pleasant, reassuring feeling that infants get from touching something soft and warm, especially their mother.

There is a sensitive period (roughly the first year of life) during which attachment must occur for optimal development. Joseph's attachment during this period kept him close to his mother, Gloria, who provided safety, stimulation, and a secure "home base" from which Joseph could go exploring.

Mothers usually begin to feel attached to their babies before birth. For their part, as babies mature, they become more and more capable of bonding with their mothers. For the first few months, babies respond more or less equally to everyone. By 2 or 3 months, most babies prefer their mothers to strangers. By around 7 months, babies generally become truly attached to their mothers, crawling after them if they can. Shortly thereafter, they begin to form attachments to other people as well, such as their father, grandparents, or siblings (Sigelman & Rider, 2018).

A direct sign that an emotional bond has formed appears around 8 to 12 months of age. At that time, Joseph displayed **separation anxiety**—crying and signs of fear—when he was left alone or with a stranger. Mild separation anxiety is normal. When it is more intense, it may reveal a problem. At some point in their lives, about 1 in 20 children suffer from *separation anxiety disorder* (Herren, In-Albon, & Schneider, 2013). These children are miserable when they are separated from their parents, who they cling to or constantly follow. Some fear that they will get lost and never see their parents again. Many refuse to go to school. Children tend to outgrow the disorder (Dick-Niederhauser & Silverman, 2006), but if separation anxiety is intense or lasts for more than a month, parents should seek professional help for their child (Allen, Lavallee et al., 2010).

Sometimes parents are afraid of "spoiling" babies with too much attention, but for the first year or two, this is nearly impossible. All things considered, creating a bond of trust and affection between the infant and at least one other person is a key event during the first year of life. In fact, a later capacity to experience warm and loving relationships may depend on it.

Attachment Style According to psychologist Mary Ainsworth (1913–1999), the quality of attachment is revealed by how babies act when their mothers return after a brief separation (Ainsworth, 1989). Infants who develop **secure attachment** have a stable and positive emotional

Social smile Smiling elicited by a social stimulus, such as seeing a parent's face.

Affectional needs Emotional needs for care, love, and positive relationships with others.

Attachments Emotional bonding between an infant and its parents or caregivers.

Social development The development of self-awareness, attachment to parents or caregivers, and relationships with other children and adults.

Surrogate mother A substitute mother (in animal research, often an inanimate object or a dummy).

Contact comfort A pleasant and reassuring feeling that human and animal infants get from touching or clinging to something soft and warm, usually their mothers.

Separation anxiety Distress displayed by infants when they are separated from their parents or principal caregivers.

Secure attachment A stable and positive emotional bond.

bond. They are upset by the mother's (or caregiver's) absence and seek to be near her when she returns. Infants with an **insecure-avoidant attachment** have an anxious emotional bond. They tend to turn away from the mother (or caregiver) when she returns. **Insecure-ambivalent attachment** also is an anxious emotional bond. In this case, babies have mixed feelings: They both seek to be near the returning mother (or caregiver) and angrily resist contact with her (➤**Figure 13.2**).

Different attachment styles are associated with lasting effects (Morley & Moran, 2011; Moutsiana et al., 2014). Infants who are securely attached during infancy later show resiliency, curiosity, problem-solving ability, and social skills in preschool. By contrast, attachment failures can be quite damaging (Santelices et al., 2011). Consider, for example, the plight of children raised in severely overcrowded orphanages (Rutter et al., 2009). These children get almost no attention from adults for the first year or two of their lives. Once adopted, many are poorly attached to their new parents. Some, for instance, will wander off with strangers, are anxious and remote, and don't like to be touched or to make eye contact with others (O'Conner et al., 2003). In short, for some children, a lack of affectionate care early in life leaves a lasting emotional impact well into adulthood. (Discover your adult attachment pattern in Module 72.)

Promoting Secure Attachment One key to secure attachment is a mother who is accepting and sensitive to her baby's signals and rhythms. Poor attachment occurs when a mother's actions are constantly inappropriate, inadequate, intrusive, overstimulating, or rejecting. Examples include a mother who tries to play with a drowsy infant, or one who ignores a baby who is looking at her and vocalizing. The link between sensitive caregiving and secure attachment appears to apply to all cultures (Santelices et al., 2011).

What about attachment to fathers? Fathers of securely attached infants tend to be outgoing, agreeable, and happy in their marriage. In general, a warm family atmosphere—one that includes sensitive mothering *and* fathering—produces secure children (Gaumon et al., 2016; Mattanah, Lopez, & Govern, 2011).

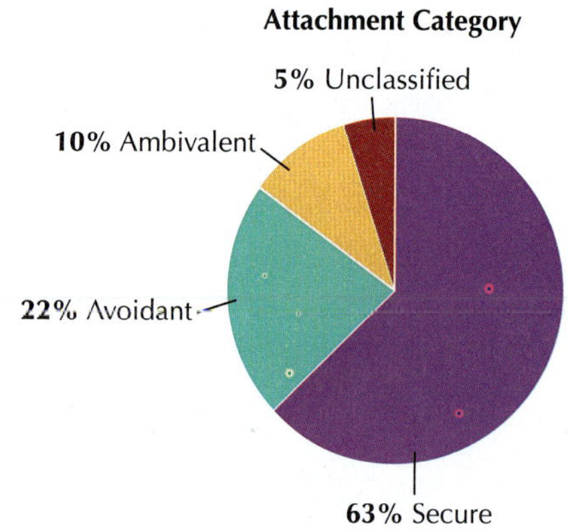

➤ **Figure 13.2**

Distribution of child attachment. In the United States, about two-thirds of all children from middle-class families are securely attached. About one child in three is insecurely attached. [Percentages are approximate. From Kaplan (1998).]

Day Care

Does commercial day care interfere with the quality of attachment? That depends on the quality of day care. Overall, *high-quality* day care does not adversely affect attachment to parents. In fact, high-quality day care can improve children's social and mental skills (National Institute of Child Health and Human Development, 2017). Children in high-quality day care tend to have better relationships with their mothers (or caregivers) and fewer behavior problems. They also have better cognitive skills and language abilities (Li et al., 2013). However, all the positive effects just noted are *reversed* for low-quality day care. Low-quality day care *is* risky and *may* weaken attachment (Phillips & Lowenstein, 2011). Poor-quality day care can even create behavior problems that didn't exist beforehand.

Parents seeking quality day care should look for responsive and sensitive care providers who offer plenty of attention and verbal and cognitive stimulation (Phillips & Lowenstein, 2011). This is more likely to occur in day-care centers with *at least* the following: (1) a small number of children per caregiver, (2) small overall group size, (3) trained care providers, (4) minimal staff turnover, and (5) stable, consistent care.

Parental Influences—Life with Mom and Dad

Learning Outcome 13.3 Outline what is known about parenting styles, including maternal versus paternal styles and parenting styles across cultures

From the first few years of life, when caregivers are the center of a child's world, through to adulthood, the style and quality of mothering and fathering can profoundly influence our psychosocial outcomes (Gopnik, 2016). Let's take a closer look at parenting, beginning with parenting styles.

Parenting Styles

Psychologist Diana Baumrind (1991, 2005) has studied the effects of three major **parental styles**, which are identifiable patterns of parental caretaking and interaction with children. See if you recognize the styles that she describes.

Authoritarian parents enforce rigid rules and demand strict obedience to authority. Typically, they view children as having few rights, but adult-like responsibilities. The child is expected to stay out of trouble and to accept, without question, what parents regard as right or wrong ("Do it because I say so"). Authoritarian parents tend to discipline their children through **power assertion**—physical punishment or a show of force, such as taking away toys or privileges. Power-oriented techniques—particularly harsh or severe physical punishment—are associated with fear, hatred of parents, and a lack of creativity, spontaneity, and warmth (Miller, Lambert, & Neumeister, 2012; Olson & Hergenhahn, 2013).

As an alternative, authoritarian parents may use **withdrawal of love**, or withholding affection, by refusing to speak to a child, threatening to leave, rejecting the child, or otherwise acting as if the child is temporarily unlovable. The children of authoritarian parents are usually obedient and self-controlled; but they also tend to be emotionally stiff, withdrawn, apprehensive, lacking in curiosity, and dependent on adults for approval. In addition, they can develop low *self-esteem*. If you regard yourself as a worthwhile person, you have **self-esteem**. Low self-esteem is related to physical punishment and the withholding of love. And why not? What messages do children absorb if a parent beats them or tells them they are not worthy of love?

Overly permissive parents give little guidance, allow too much freedom, or don't hold children accountable for their actions. Typically, the child has rights similar to an adult's, but few responsibilities. Rules are not enforced, and the child usually gets his or her way ("Do whatever you want"). Permissive parents tend to produce dependent, immature children who misbehave frequently. Such children are aimless and likely to "run wild."

Some overly permissive parents genuinely wish to empower their children by imposing few limits on their behavior, making them feel special, and giving them everything they want. But such good intentions can backfire, leaving parents with children who have developed unrealistically high levels of self-esteem and a sense of entitlement (Mamen, 2004). Overly empowered offspring are often spoiled and self-indulgent and lack self-control (Byrne & O'Brien, 2014).

Baumrind describes **authoritative parents** as those who supply firm and consistent guidance, combined with love and affection. Such parents balance their own rights with those of their children. They control their children's behavior through **management techniques**, which combine praise, recognition, approval, rules, reasoning, and similar means of encouraging desirable behavior. Effective parents are firm and consistent, not harsh or rigid. In general, they encourage the child to act responsibly, to think, and to make good decisions. This style produces children who are *resilient* (good at bouncing back after bad experiences) and who develop the strengths that they need to thrive even in difficult circumstances (Azadyecta, 2011; Masten, 2014). The children of authoritative parents are competent, self-controlled, independent, assertive, and inquiring. They know how to manage their emotions and use positive coping skills (Kudo, Longhofer, & Floersch, 2012).

Insecure-avoidant attachment An anxious emotional bond marked by a tendency to avoid reunion with a parent or caregiver.

Insecure-ambivalent attachment An anxious emotional bond marked by both a desire to be with a parent or caregiver and some resistance to being reunited.

Parental styles Identifiable patterns of parental caretaking and interaction with children.

Authoritarian parents Parents who enforce rigid rules and demand strict obedience to authority.

Power assertion The use of physical punishment or coercion to enforce child discipline.

Withdrawal of love Withholding affection to enforce child discipline.

Self-esteem Regarding oneself as a worthwhile person; a positive evaluation of oneself.

Overly permissive parents Parents who give little guidance, allow too much freedom, or do not require the child to take responsibility.

Authoritative parents Parents who supply firm and consistent guidance combined with love and affection.

Management techniques Approaches that combine praise, recognition, approval, rules, and reasoning to enforce child discipline.

Maternal and Paternal Influences

Don't mothers and fathers parent differently? Yes. Although *maternal influences*—all the effects that a mother has on her child—have a greater impact, fathers also make a unique contribution to parenting (Bjorklund & Hernández Blasi, 2012). Although fathers are spending more time with their children, mothers still do most of the nurturing and caretaking, especially of young children (Craig, 2006).

Studies of *paternal influences*—the sum of all effects that a father has on his child—reveal that fathers are more likely to play with their children and tell them stories. In contrast, mothers are typically responsible for the physical and emotional care of their children (➤ **Figure 13.3**).

It might seem that the father's role as a playmate makes him less important. Not so. Joseph's playtime with Jay is quite valuable. From birth onward, fathers pay more visual attention to children than mothers. Fathers are much more tactile (lifting, tickling, and handling the baby), more physically arousing (engaging in rough-and-tumble play), and more likely to engage in unusual play (imitating the baby, for example) (Fletcher, St George, & Freeman, 2013). In comparison, mothers speak to infants more, play more conventional games (such as peekaboo), and, as noted, spend much more time in caregiving. Young children who spend a lot of time playing with their fathers tend to be more competent in many ways (Fletcher, St George, & Freeman, 2013; Tamis-LeMonda, et al., 2004).

Overall, fathers can be as affectionate, sensitive, and responsive as mothers. Nevertheless, infants and children tend to get very different views of males and females. Females, who offer comfort, nurturance, and verbal stimulation, tend to be close at hand. Males come and go, and when they are present, action, exploration, and risk-taking prevail. It's no wonder, then, that the parental styles of mothers and fathers have a major impact on children's gender role development (Holmes & Huston, 2010; Malmberg & Flouri, 2011).

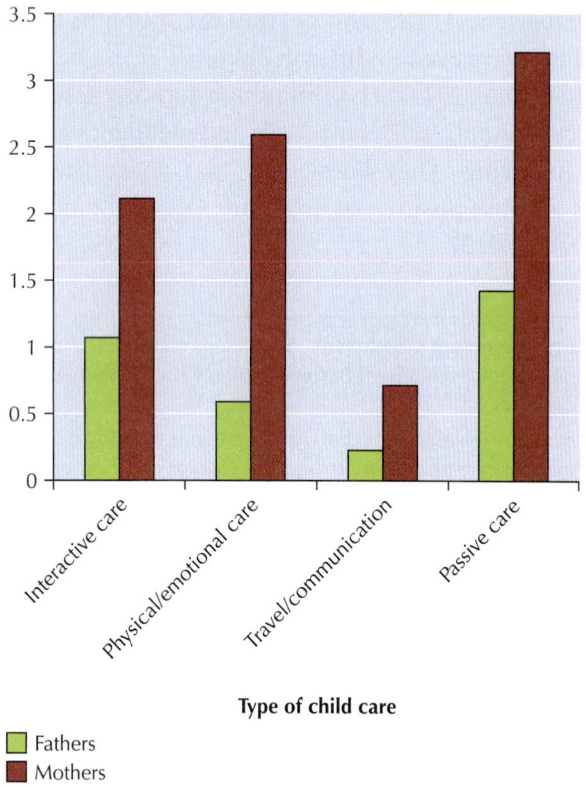

➤ **Figure 13.3**

Mother–child and father–child interactions. This graph shows what occurred on routine days in a sample of over 1,400 Australian homes. Mothers spend about twice as long each day on child care than fathers do. Furthermore, mothers spend more time on physical and emotional care (e.g., feeding, bathing, soothing) than on interactive care (e.g., playing, reading, activities); fathers show the reverse pattern. Finally, mothers spend more time on travel (e.g., driving children to sports or music lessons), communication (e.g., talking to teachers about their children), and passive care (e.g., supervising children while they play). [Adapted from Craig (2006).]

nd3000/Shutterstock.com

Fathering typically makes a contribution to early development that differs in emphasis from mothering.

ZouZou/Shutterstock.com

In other ethnic communities, norms for effective parenting often differ in subtle ways from parenting styles in Euro-American culture. In the final analysis, parenting can be judged only if we know what culture or ethnic community a child is being prepared to enter (Sorkhabi, 2012).

MODULE 13

Emotional and Social Development in Childhood—Learning Outcomes Revisited

13.1 Distinguish between basic and complex emotions

Basic emotions are those that may have an evolutionary basis as they seem to show some level of consistency across cultures. They include happiness, sadness, fear, anger, surprise, and disgust. In contrast some complex emotions, such as embarrassment, shame, guilt, and pride require a sense of the self as separate from others and thus do not develop until later (approximately 18 months).

13.2 Describe early attachment relationships between infants and their caregivers

Research suggests that quality of attachment can be classified as secure, insecure-avoidant, or insecure-ambivalent. Secure relationships are promoted when caregivers are sensitive to their babies' signals.

13.3 Outline what is known about parenting styles, including maternal versus paternal styles and parenting styles across ethnicities

Studies suggest that parental styles have a substantial impact on emotional and intellectual development. Three major parental styles are authoritarian, permissive, and authoritative (effective). Authoritative parenting, relying more on management techniques rather than power assertion or withdrawal of love, appears to benefit children the most, though this conclusion is most likely to hold true in Western countries. Whereas mothers typically emphasize caregiving, fathers tend to function as playmates for infants. Other parenting styles may be more advantageous in other ethnic groups.

Reflective Practice

Content Check

1. Which of the following is not one of the six basic emotions infants express by six months of age?
   a. disgust
   b. fear
   c. sadness
   d. embarrassment
2. Newborns display a social smile as early as 10 days after birth. T or F?
3. The development of separation anxiety in an infant corresponds to the formation of an attachment to parents. T or F?
4. According to Diana Baumrind's research, effective parents are authoritarian in their approach to their children's behavior. T or F?
5. Fathers are more likely to act as playmates for their children, rather than as caregivers. T or F?
6. Overall, fathers are much less affectionate, sensitive, and responsive than mothers. T or F?

Skill Check

Think Critically

7. Can emotional bonding begin before birth?
8. Which parenting style do you think would be most likely to lead to eating disorders in children?

Self-Reflect

Do you think that your experiences as a child, such as your early attachment pattern, affect your life as an adult? Can you think of any examples from your own life? Do you know any parents who have young children and who are authoritarian, permissive, or authoritative? What are their children like? Do you think parenting depends on ethnicity? If so, why? If not, why not?

ANSWERS

1. d 2. F 3. T 4. F 5. T 6. F 7. It certainly can for parents. When a pregnant woman begins to feel fetal movements, she becomes aware that a baby is coming to life inside her. Likewise, prospective parents who hear a fetal heartbeat at the doctor's office or see an ultrasound image of the fetus begin to become emotionally attached to the unborn child (Sigelman & Rider, 2018). 8. Authoritarian parents who are too controlling about what their children eat, as well as permissive parents who are too willing to withdraw from conflicts over eating, can create dietary issues in their children (Haycraft & Blissett, 2010).

MODULE 14

Human Development

Language and Cognitive Development in Childhood

Make It Warmer, Mommy

There's something almost miraculous about a baby's early language and thought, which often leaves parents scratching their heads. For example, when Joseph's older brother, Manny, was 3, he thought his bath was too hot and said to Gloria, "Make it warmer, Mommy." At first, Gloria was confused. The bath was already fairly hot. She grinned as she realized that Manny meant, "Bring the water closer to the temperature we call *warm*." It makes perfect sense if you look at it that way.

As infants, how did we manage to leap into the world of language and thought? Although maturation (nature) provides the foundation for language learning and cognitive development, social development (nurture) plays a critical role, too. For example, parents use a distinctive style, called *motherese* or *parentese*, when speaking to an infant. In what other ways do nature and nurture work together to foster language and cognitive development in young children? Let's find out.

Gary Conner/Photolibrary/Getty Images

~LEARNING OUTCOMES~

After reading this module you should be able to:

14.1 Explain the contributions of nature and nurture to language development

14.2 Distinguish between Piaget's conception of "assimilation" and "accommodation, his four stages of cognitive development, as well as object permanence, egocentrism, and conservation. Outline three criticisms of Piaget's theory of cognitive development, including the central ideas that underlie Vygotsky's theory of cognitive development, including the zone of proximal development

Language Development—Who Talks Baby Talk?

Learning Outcome 14.1 Explain the contributions of nature and nurture to language development

As every parent knows, babies can cry from birth on. By 1 month of age, they use crying to gain attention. Typically, parents can tell whether an infant is hungry, angry, or in pain from the tone of the crying (Nakayama, 2010). Around 6 to 8 weeks of age, babies begin *cooing* (the repetition of vowel sounds such as "oo" and "ah").

Language development is closely tied to maturation (Gleason & Ratner, 2013). By 7 months of age, Joseph's nervous system was mature enough to allow him to grasp objects, smile, laugh, sit up, and *babble*. In the babbling stage, the consonants *b*, *d*, *m*, and *g* are combined with the vowel sounds to produce meaningless language sounds: *dadadadada* or *bababa*. At first, babbling is the same around the world. But soon, the language spoken by parents begins to have an influence (Goldstein et al., 2010)—that is, Japanese babies start to babble in a way that sounds like Japanese, Mexican babies babble in Spanish-like sounds, and so on (Garcia-Sierra et al., 2011).

At about 1 year of age, children respond to real words such as *no* or *hi*. Soon afterward, the first connection between words and object forms, and children may address their parents as "Mama" or "Dada." By age 18 months to 2 years, a child's vocabulary may include 100 words or more. First comes the *single-word stage*, during which children use one word at a time, such as "go," "juice," or "up." Soon after, words are arranged in simple two-word sentences called *telegraphic speech*: "Want-Teddy"; "Mama-gone."

Language and the Terrible Twos

At about the same time that children begin to put two or three words together, they become much more independent. It's true that 1-year-olds can do plenty of things parents don't want them to do. A 1-year-old may assert his independence by saying, "No drink," "Me do it," "My cup, my cup," and the like. It can be worse, of course. During their second year, children become increasingly capable of mischief and temper tantrums. It's usually 2-year-olds who do things *because* you don't want them to (Raphael-Leff, 2012). A 2-year-old may look at you intently, make eye contact, listen as you shout "No, no!" and still pour her juice on the cat.

Thus, calling this time "the terrible twos" is not entirely inappropriate. Perhaps parents can take some comfort in knowing that a stubborn, negative 2-year-old is simply becoming more independent. When children are 2 years old, their parents are wise to remember "This, too, shall pass."

After age 2, the child's comprehension and use of words takes a dramatic leap forward. From this point on, vocabulary and language skills grow at a phenomenal rate (Fernald, Perfors, & Marchman, 2006). By first grade, Joseph will be able to understand around 8,000 words and use about 4,000. He will have truly entered the world of language.

The Roots of Language

What accounts for this explosion of language development? Linguist Noam Chomsky (1986) has long claimed that humans have a **biological predisposition**, or hereditary readiness, to develop language. According to Chomsky, language patterns are inborn, much like a child's ability to coordinate walking. If such inborn language capacity does exist, it may explain why children around the world use a limited number of patterns in their first sentences. Typical patterns include the following (Mussen et al., 1979): identification ("See kitty."), nonexistence ("Allgone milk."), possession ("My doll."), agent-action ("Mama give."), negation ("Not ball."), and question ("Where doggie?").

Does Chomsky's theory explain why language develops so rapidly? It is certainly part of the story (Saxton, 2010). But many psychologists feel that Chomsky underestimates the importance of learning and the social contexts that shape language development (Behne et al., 2012; Hoff, 2014). *Psycholinguists* (specialists in the psychology of language) have shown that imitation of adults and rewards for correctly using words (as when a child asks for a cookie) are an important part of language learning. Also, babies actively participate in language learning by asking questions, such as "What dis?" (Domingo & Goldstein-Alpern, 1999).

When a child makes a language error, parents typically repeat the child's sentence, with needed corrections, or ask a clarifying question to draw the child's attention to the error (Hoff, 2014). More important is the fact that parents and children begin to communicate long before the child can speak. A readiness to interact *socially* with parents may be as important as innate language processing. The next section explains why.

Early Communication *How do parents communicate with infants before they can talk?* Parents go to a great deal of trouble to get babies to smile and vocalize. In doing so, they quickly learn to change their actions to keep the infant's attention, arousal, and activity at optimal levels. A familiar example is the "I'm-Going-to-Get-You" game. In it, the adult says, "I'm gonna getcha ... I'm gonna getcha ... I'm gonna getcha ... Gotcha!" Through such games, adults and babies come to share similar rhythms and expectations (Carroll, 2008). Soon a system of shared **signals** is created, including touching, vocalizing, gazing, and smiling. These help lay a foundation for later language use (De Schuymer et al., 2011; Kraus & Slater, 2016). Specifically, signals establish

Biological predisposition The presumed hereditary readiness of humans to learn certain skills, such as how to use language or a readiness to behave in particular ways.

Signals In early language development, behaviors, such as touching, vocalizing, gazing, or smiling, that allow nonverbal interaction and turn-taking between parent and child.

a pattern of "conversational" *turn-taking* (alternate sending and receiving of messages).

Gloria	*Joseph*
	(smiles)
"Oh what a nice little smile!"	
"Yes, isn't that nice?"	(burps)
"Well, excuse you!"	
"Yes, that's better, yes."	(vocalizes)
"Yes."	(smiles)
"What's so funny?"	

From the outside, such exchanges may look meaningless. In reality, they represent real communication (Behne et al., 2012). One study found that 6-week-old babies change their gaze at an adult's face when the adult's speech changes (Crown et al., 2002). Infants as young as 4 months engage in vocal turn-taking with adults (Jaffe et al., 2001). The more children interact with parents, the faster they learn to talk and the faster they develop thinking abilities (Hoff & Tian, 2005). Unmistakably, social relationships contribute to early language learning (Hoff, 2014; Vernon-Feagans et al., 2012).

Parentese When they talk to infants, parents use an exaggerated pattern of speaking called **motherese (parentese)**. Typically, they raise their tone of voice, use short, simple sentences, repeat themselves, and use frequent gestures (Gogate, Bahrick, & Watson, 2000). They also slow their rate of speaking and use exaggerated voice inflections: "Did Joseph eat it A-L-L UP?"

What is the purpose of such changes? Parents are apparently trying to help their children learn language (Soderstrom, 2007). When a baby is still babbling, parents tend to use long, adult-style sentences. But as soon as the baby says its first word, they switch to parentese. By the time that babies are 4 months old, they prefer parentese over normal speech (Cooper et al., 1997).

In addition to being simpler, parentese has a distinct "musical" quality (Trainor & Desjardins, 2002). No matter what language mothers speak, the melodies, pauses, and inflections they use to comfort, praise, or give warning are universal. Psychologist Anne Fernald has found that mothers of all nations talk to their babies with similar changes in pitch. For instance, we praise babies with a rising, then falling pitch ("BRA-vo!" "GOOD girl!"). Warnings are delivered in a short, sharp rhythm ("Nein! Nein!" "Basta! Basta!" "No! Dude!"). To give comfort, parents use low, smooth, drawn-out tones ("Oooh poor baaa-by." "Oooh pobrecito."). A high-pitched, rising melody is used to call attention to objects ("See the pretty BIRDIE?") (Fernald, 1989).

Parentese helps parents get babies' attention, communicate with them, and teach them language (Newman, Rowe, & Bernstein, 2016). Later, as a child's speaking improves, parents tend to adjust their speech to the child's language ability. Especially from 18 months to 4 years of age, parents seek to clarify what a child says and prompt the child to say more.

In summary, some elements of language are innate. Nevertheless, our inherited tendency to learn language does not determine whether we will speak English or Vietnamese, Spanish or Russian. Environmental forces also influence whether a person develops simple or sophisticated language skills. The first seven years of life are a sensitive period in language learning (Hoff, 2014). Clearly, a full flowering of speech requires careful cultivation.

Cognitive Development—Escaping Egocentrism

Learning Outcome 14.2 Distinguish between Piaget's conception of "assimilation" and "accommodation, his four stages of cognitive development, as well as object permanence, egocentrism, and conservation. Outline three criticisms of Piaget's theory of cognitive development, including the central ideas that underlie Vygotsky's theory of cognitive development, including the zone of proximal development

Now that we have Joseph talking, let's move on to a broader view of intellectual development. Babies are smarter than many people think. From an evolutionary perspective, a baby's mind is designed to soak up information, which it does at an amazing pace (Bjorklund, 2012). Although baby Joseph was a "sponge," soaking up new experiences, by the time he reaches old age, he will find it much harder to learn new skills (such as becoming fluent in a second language) and will rely much more on what he already knows.

From the earliest days of life, babies are learning how the world works. They immediately begin to look, touch, taste, and otherwise explore their surroundings. In the first months of life, babies are increasingly able to think, to learn from what they see, to make predictions, and to search for explanations. For example, Jerome Bruner (1983) observed

Sally and Richard Greenhill/Alamy Stock Photo

When this mother sticks out her tongue, her infant son imitates her. Is this common? To find out, Andrew Meltzoff videotaped mothers and researchers as they made facial gestures at infants and recorded the infant's responses. The resulting videotapes of both adults and of tested infants helped ensure objectivity.

that 3- to 8-week-old babies seem to understand that a person's voice and body should be connected. If a baby hears his mother's voice coming from where she is standing, the baby will remain calm. If her voice comes from a loudspeaker several feet away, though, the baby will become agitated and begin to cry.

As another example, psychologist Andrew Meltzoff has found that babies are born mimics. Videos of babies confirm that they imitate adult facial gestures while they can see them (mirror neurons, anyone?). As early as 9 months of age, infants can remember and imitate actions a day after seeing them (Heimann & Meltzoff, 1996; Meltzoff, 2005). Such mimicry obviously aids rapid learning in infancy.

Swiss psychologist and philosopher Jean Piaget (Jahn pea-ah-ZHAY) (1896–1980) provided some of the first great insights into how children develop thinking abilities when he proposed that children's cognitive skills progress through a series of maturational stages.

Piaget's Theory of Cognitive Development

Piaget's ideas have deeply affected our view of children (Barrouillet, 2015). According to Piaget (1951, 1952), children's thinking is, generally speaking, less abstract than that of adults. They tend to base their understanding on particular examples and objects that they can see or touch. Also, children use fewer generalizations, categories, and principles. Piaget also believed that all children mature through a series of distinct stages in intellectual development.

Mental Structures and Processes

Like any new parent, Piaget immediately recognized that babies are born "blank slates." That is, we come into life equipped with very little learned specific knowledge or skills (also sometimes referred to as *crystallized intelligence*). For example, Lily knew nothing about horses when she was born; she had, of course, never even seen one. But she eventually saw horses on television and was given a stuffed toy horse for her second birthday. She even knew the word "horse." According to Piaget, Lily had formed a **schema**—an organized learned body of knowledge or skills about a particular topic—in this case, for her understanding of the concept of "horse."

Piaget also realized that babies are born with a remarkable capability for rapid learning (*fluid intelligence*). He proposed that intellect grows through mental processes that he called *assimilation* and *accommodation*.

Assimilation refers to the application of an established schema to new objects or problems. Let's say that little Lily is taken for a drive in the country. She sees her first live horse in a field, points, and calls out, "Horse!" She has already seen horses on television and even has a stuffed toy horse. In this case, she adds this new experience to her existing concept of *horse*. Piaget would say that it has been *assimilated* to an existing schema.

In **accommodation (learning)**, existing schemas are modified to fit new objects or problems. For instance,

Jean Piaget (1896–1980). Philosopher, psychologist, and keen observer of children. Many of his ideas came from observing his own children as they solved various thought problems. (It is tempting to imagine that Piaget's illustrious career was launched one day when his wife said to him, "Watch the children for a while, will you, Jean?")

Farrell Grehan/Historical/Corbis

Motherese (parentese) A pattern of speech used when talking to infants, marked by a higher-pitched voice; short, simple sentences; repetition; slower speech; and exaggerated voice inflections.

Schema A mental structure composed of an organized learned body of knowledge or skills about a particular topic, according to Piaget.

Assimilation The application of an established schema to new objects or problems, according to Piaget.

Accommodation (learning) Modification of an established schema to fit a new object or problem, according to Piaget.

suppose that a month later, Lily goes to the zoo, where she sees her first zebra. Proudly, she again exclaims, "Horse!" This time, her father, Cameron, replies, "No dear, that's a zebra." Little Lily has *failed to assimilate* the zebra to her horse schema, so now she must *accommodate* by creating a new schema, *zebra*, and modifying her schema of horse (to *not* include black and white stripes).

Sensorimotor Stage (0–2 Years) Look up from this paragraph until your attention is attracted to another object in the room. Then refocus on this paragraph. Is the object still there? How do you know? As an adult, you can keep a mental image of the object in your "mind's eye." According to Piaget, newborns, who are in the **sensorimotor stage**, cannot create *internal representations* such as mental images. As a result, they lack **object permanence**, a recognition that physical things continue to exist even when they are no longer visible. Concepts and language are other types of internal representation. (See Module 37 for more information.)

For this reason, in the first two years of life, Joseph's intellectual development was largely nonintellectual and nonverbal. His mental activity was concerned mainly with learning to coordinate information from his sensory perception with his motor skills. But sometime during his first year, he, like other babies, began to actively pursue disappearing objects. By age 2, infants can anticipate the movement of an object behind a screen. For example, when watching a toy train, they will look ahead to the end of a tunnel, rather than stare at the spot where the train disappeared.

In general, developments in this stage indicate that the child's conceptions are becoming more *stable*. Objects cease to appear and disappear magically, and a more orderly and predictable world replaces the confusing and disconnected sensations of infancy.

Preoperational Stage (2–7 Years) Close your eyes again. Imagine the room you sleep in. What would it look like if you were perched on the ceiling and your bed was missing? Now you have operated mentally on your image by *transforming* it. According to Piaget, even though children in the **preoperational stage** can form mental images or ideas, they are *pre*operational because they cannot easily use mental *operations*, or **transformations**, to manipulate those images or ideas in their minds.

Difficulty in using transformations is why although children begin to think *symbolically* and use language before the age of 6 or 7, they still engage in concrete, **intuitive thought**—it makes little use of reasoning and logic. (Do you remember as a child thinking that the Sun and the Moon followed you when you took a walk?)

Let's visit Joseph at age 5: If you show him a short, wide glass full of milk and a taller, narrow glass full of milk, most likely he will tell you that the taller glass contains more milk (even if it doesn't). Joseph will tell you this even if he watches you pour milk from the short glass into an empty taller glass. Older children can mentally transform the pouring of the milk by mentally *reversing* it, to see that the shape of the container is irrelevant to the volume of milk that it contains. But Joseph is preoperational: He cannot engage in the mental operation of transforming the tall, narrow glass of milk back into a short, wide glass. Thus, he is not bothered by the fact that the milk appears to be transformed from a smaller to a larger amount. Instead, he responds only to his current understanding that *taller* seems to mean *more*.

After about age 7, children are no longer fooled by this situation. Perhaps that's why age 7 has been called the "age of reason." From age 7 on, we see a definite trend toward more logical, adultlike thought.

According to Piaget, during the preoperational stage, the child displays **egocentrism**, believing that everyone thinks as he or she does. Due to this inability to take the viewpoints of other people, the child's ego seems to stand at the center of his or her world. To illustrate, show a preoperational child a two-sided mirror. Then hold it between you and her, so she can see herself in it. If you ask her what she thinks *you*

Tony Freeman/PhotoEdit

Children under age 7 intuitively assume that a volume of liquid increases when it is poured from a short, wide container into a taller, thinner one. This boy thinks the tall container holds more than the short one. In reality, each holds the same amount of liquid. Children make such judgments based on the height of the liquid, not its volume.

Pavel L Photo and Video/Shutterstock.com

Crossing a busy street can be dangerous for the preoperational child. Because their thinking is still egocentric, younger children cannot understand why the driver of a car can't see them if they can see the car. Children under the age of 7 also cannot judge the speeds and distances of oncoming cars consistently. Likewise, adults can overestimate the "street smarts" of younger children easily. It is advisable to teach children to cross with the light, in a crosswalk, with assistance, or all three.

can see, she imagines that you see *her* face reflected in the mirror, instead of your own. She cannot mentally transform the view that she sees into the view that you must be seeing.

Such egocentrism explains why children can seem exasperatingly selfish or uncooperative at times. If Lily blocks your view by standing in front of the television, she assumes that you can see it if she can. If you ask her to move so you can see better, she may move so that *she* can see better! Lily is not being selfish in the ordinary sense. She just doesn't realize that your view differs from hers.

In addition, the child's use of language is not as sophisticated as it might seem. Children tend to confuse words with the objects that they represent. If Lily calls a toy block a "car" and you use that block to make a "house," she may be upset. To children, the name of an object is as much a part of the object as its size, shape, and color.

Concrete Operational Stage (7–11 Years) The hallmark of a child in the **concrete operational stage** is the ability to carry out mental operations such as *reversing* thoughts. A 4-year-old boy in the preoperational stage might have a conversation like the following (showing how a child's thinking lacks reversibility):

"Do you have a brother?"

"Yes."

"What's his name?"

"Billy."

"Does Billy have a brother?" "No."

Reversibility of thought allows children in the concrete operational stage to recognize that if $4 \times 2 = 8$, then 2×4 does, too. Younger children must memorize each relationship separately. Thus, a preoperational child may know that $4 \times 9 = 36$, without being able to tell you what 9×4 equals.

The development of mental operations allows mastery of **conservation**—Piaget's term for the awareness that physical quantities stay constant despite changes in their shape or appearance. Children have learned conservation when they understand that rolling a ball of clay into a "snake" does not increase the amount of clay. Likewise, pouring liquid from a tall, narrow glass into a shallow dish does not reduce the amount of liquid. In each case, the volume remains the same, no matter what shape the material takes, or how it appears. The original amount of matter is *conserved*.

During the concrete operational stage, children begin to use concepts of time, space, and number. The child can think logically about concrete objects or situations, categories, and principles. Such abilities help explain why children stop believing in Santa Claus when they reach this stage. Because they can *conserve* volume, they realize that Santa's sack couldn't possibly hold enough toys for millions of girls and boys.

Formal Operational Stage (11 Years and Up) According to Piaget's theory, after about the age of 11, children begin to rely less on concrete objects and specific examples. Thinking is based more on abstract principles, such as democracy, honor, or correlation. Children who reach the **formal operational stage** become self-reflective about their

Sensorimotor stage Piaget's initial stage of development, when the infant's mental activity is only sensory perception and motor skills.

Object permanence Recognizing that physical things continue to exist, even when they are no longer visible.

Preoperational stage Piaget's second stage of cognitive development, characterized by the use of symbols and illogical thought.

Transformation (Piagetian) The mental ability to change the shape or form of a substance (such as clay or water) and to perceive that its volume remains the same.

Intuitive thought Thinking that makes little or no use of reasoning and logic.

Egocentrism The belief that everyone thinks as you do.

Concrete operational stage Piaget's third stage of cognitive development, characterized by logical thought.

Conservation Piaget's term for the awareness that physical quantities stay constant despite changes in shape or appearance.

Formal operational stage Piaget's fourth stage of cognitive development, characterized by the ability to engage in thinking that includes abstract, theoretical, and hypothetical ideas.

thoughts, and they become less egocentric. Older children and young adolescents also gradually become able to consider hypothetical possibilities (suppositions, guesses, or projections). For example, if you ask a younger child, "What do you think would happen if it suddenly became possible for people to fly?" the child might respond, "People can't fly." Older children are better able to consider such possibilities.

Full adult intellectual ability is attained during the stage of formal operations. Older adolescents are capable of inductive and deductive reasoning, and they can comprehend mathematics, physics, philosophy, psychology, and other abstract systems. They can learn to test hypotheses in a scientific manner. Of course, not everyone reaches this level of thinking. Also, many adults can think formally about some topics, but their thinking becomes concrete when the topic is unfamiliar. This implies that formal thinking may be more a result of culture and learning than maturation. In any case, after late adolescence, improvements in intellect are based on gaining specific knowledge, experience, and wisdom, rather than on any leaps in basic thinking capacity.

How can parents apply Piaget's ideas? Piaget's theory suggests that the ideal way to guide intellectual development is to provide experiences that are only slightly novel, unusual, or challenging. Remember that a child's intellect develops mainly through accommodation. It is usually best to follow a *one-step-ahead strategy*, in which your teaching efforts are aimed just beyond a child's current level of comprehension (Brainerd, 2003).

Parents should avoid *forced teaching*, or "hothousing," which is like trying to force plants to bloom prematurely. Forcing children to learn reading, math, gymnastics, swimming, or music at an accelerated pace can bore or oppress them. True intellectual enrichment respects the child's interests. It does not make the child feel pressured to perform.

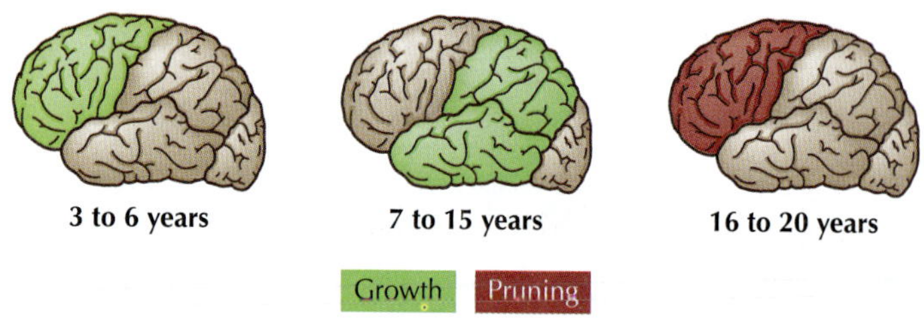

➤ Figure 14.1

Brain maturation and cognition. Between the ages of 3 and 6 years, a tremendous wave of growth occurs in connections among neurons in the frontal areas of the brain. This corresponds to the time when children make rapid progress in their ability to think symbolically. Between the ages of 7 and 15, peak synaptic growth shifts to the temporal and parietal lobes. During this period, children become increasingly adept at using language, a specialty of the temporal lobes. In the late teens, the brain actively destroys unneeded connections, especially in the frontal lobes. This pruning of synapses sharpens the brain's capacity for abstract thinking (Restak, 2001).

"Young man, go to your room and stay there until your cerebral cortex matures."

Barbara Smaller/Conde Nast/Cartoon bank

Piaget Today

Today, Piaget's theory remains a valuable road map for understanding how children think. On a broad scale, many of Piaget's ideas have held up well. However, there has been disagreement about specific details. For example, according to learning theorists, children continuously gain specific knowledge; they do not undergo stage-like leaps in general mental ability (Miller, 2011; Siegler, 2005). On the other hand, the growth in connections between brain cells occurs in waves that parallel some of Piaget's stages (Lefmann & Combs-Orme, 2013). (See ➤ **Figure 14.1**.) Thus, the truth may lie somewhere between Piaget's stage theory and modern learning theory.

In addition, it is now widely accepted that children develop cognitive skills somewhat earlier than Piaget originally thought (Bjorklund & Causey, 2012). For example, Piaget believed that infants under the age of 1 year cannot think (i.e., use internal representations). Such abilities, he believed, emerge only after a long period of sensorimotor development. Babies, he said, have no memory of people and objects that are out of sight. Yet we now know that infants begin forming representations of the world very early in life. For example, babies as young as 3 months of age appear to know that objects are solid and do not disappear when out of view (Baillargeon, 2004).

Why did Piaget fail to detect the thinking skills of infants? Most likely, he mistook babies' limited *physical* skills for *mental* immaturity. Piaget's tests required babies to search for objects or reach out and touch them. Newer, more sensitive methods are uncovering abilities that Piaget missed. One such method takes advantage of the fact that babies, like adults, act surprised when they see something "impossible" or unexpected occur. To use this effect, psychologist Renee Baillargeon (1991, 2004) puts on little "magic shows" for infants. In her "theater," babies watch as possible and impossible events occur with toys or other objects. Some 3-month-old infants act surprised and gaze longer at impossible events, for example, seeing two solid objects appear to pass through each other. By the time that they are 8 months old, babies can remember where objects are (or should be) for at least one minute (➤ Figure 14.2).

Theory of Mind: I'm a *Me*! ... and You're a *You*!

Piaget thought that children remain egocentric during the preoperational stage and become aware of perspectives other than their own only at age 7. Researchers have since begun to refer to this development as **theory of mind,** the understanding that people have mental states, such as thoughts, beliefs, and intentions, and that other people's mental states can be different from one's own. Psychologists currently believe that children as young as age 4 can understand that other people's mental states differ from their own (Apperly, 2012; Baillargeon, Scott, & Bian, 2016).

A sense of self, or self-awareness, develops at about age 18 months. Before children develop self-awareness, they do not recognize their own image in a mirror. Typically, they think they are looking at another child. Some children hug the child in the mirror or go behind the mirror looking for the child they see there (Lewis, 1995).

When you look in a mirror, you recognize the image staring back as your own—except, perhaps, early on Monday mornings. Like many such events, initial self-awareness depends on maturation of the nervous system. In a typical test of self-recognition, infants are shown images of themselves on a television. Most infants are 18 months old before they recognize themselves (Nielsen & Dissanayake, 2004).

But just because a 2-year-old knows that he is a *me* doesn't mean he knows that you are a *you* (Samson & Apperly, 2010). At age 3, Manny once put his hands over his eyes and exclaimed to his cousin Luke, "You can't see me now!" He knew that he had a point of view, but he did not know that his cousin's point of view could be different from his own. Earlier, we saw that Piaget used the term *egocentrism* to refer to this endearing feature of young children and proposed that young children remain egocentric until they enter the concrete operational stage at about age 7. More recent evidence suggests that children become less egocentric beginning at about age 4 (Doherty, 2009).

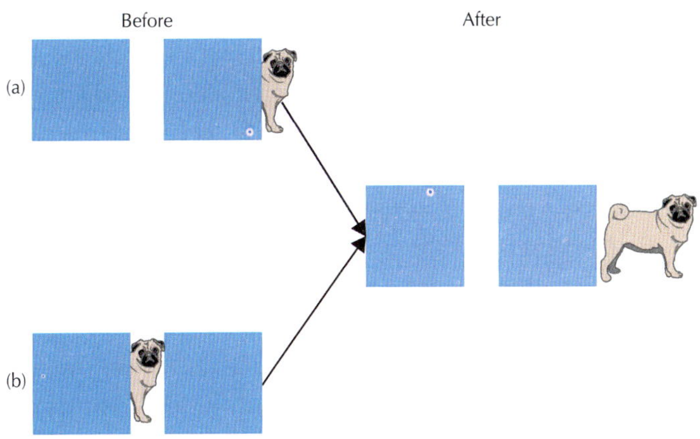

➤ **Figure 14.2**

Testing for object constancy in infancy. An infant watches as a toy is placed behind the right of two screens (*a*). After a delay of 70 seconds, a possible event occurs as the toy is brought back into view from behind the right screen. Then the infant watches as the toy is placed behind the left of two screens (*b*). Now an impossible event occurs, as the toy is again retrieved from behind the right screen. (A duplicate toy was hidden there before testing.) Eight-month-old infants react with surprise when they see the impossible event staged for them. Their reaction implies that they remember where the toy was hidden. Infants appear to have a capacity for memory and thinking that greatly exceeds what Piaget claimed is possible during the sensorimotor period (Baillargeon, Scott, & Bian, 2016). [Adapted from Baillargeon, De Vos, & Graber (1989).]

Theory of mind The understanding that people have mental states, such as thoughts, beliefs, and intentions, and that other people's mental states can be different from one's own.

One way to assess whether a child understands that other people have their own mental states is the false-belief (or Sally-Anne) task. In this test, a child is shown two dolls, Sally and Anne. Sally has a basket and Anne has a box. Sally puts a coin in her basket and goes out to play. In the meantime, Anne takes the coin from Sally's basket and puts it into her box. Sally comes back and looks for the coin. To assess theory of mind, the child is asked where *Sally* will look for her coin. Although the child knows that the coin is in Anne's box, the correct answer is that Sally will look in her basket. To answer correctly, the child must understand that Sally's point of view did not include what the child saw.

Theory of mind develops over time. It takes further growth to appreciate that other people may lie, be sarcastic, make jokes, or use figures of speech (Imuta et al., 2016). The available evidence suggests that children with autism spectrum disorders are particularly poor at this task (Kimhi, 2014).

Vygotsky's Sociocultural Theory

Another criticism of Piaget is that he underestimated the impact of culture on mental development. While Piaget stressed the role of maturation in cognitive development, Russian scholar Lev Vygotsky (1896–1934) focused on the impact of sociocultural factors on development. Many psychologists are convinced that Piaget gave too little credit to the effects of the learning environment. For example, children who grow up in villages where pottery is made can correctly answer questions about the conservation of clay at an earlier age than Piaget would have predicted. Vygotsky's (1962, 1978) key insight is that children's thinking develops through dialogues with more-capable persons.

How does that relate to intellectual growth? So far, no one has published *A Child's Guide to Life on Earth*. Instead, children must learn about life from various "tutors," such as parents, teachers, and older siblings. Even if *A Child's Guide to Life on Earth* did exist, we would need a separate version for every culture. It is not enough for children to learn how to think. They also must learn specific intellectual skills valued by their culture.

Like Piaget, Vygotsky believed that children actively seek to discover new principles. However, Vygotsky emphasized that skillful tutors guide many of a child's most important "discoveries." Psychologists Jay Shaffer and Katherine Kipp (2014) offer the following example:

> Tanya, a 4-year-old, has just received her first jigsaw puzzle as a birthday present. She attempts to solve the puzzle but gets nowhere until her father comes along, sits down beside her, and gives her some tips. He suggests that it would be a good idea to put together the corners first, points to the pink area at the edge of one corner piece, and says, "Let's look for another pink piece." When Tanya seems frustrated, he places two interlocking pieces near each other so that she will notice them, and when Tanya succeeds, he offers words of encouragement. As Tanya gradually gets the hang of it, he steps back and lets her work more and more independently (p. 233).

Interactions like this are most helpful when they take place within a child's **zone of proximal development**.

What did Vygotsky mean by that phrase? The word *proximal* means "close" or "nearby." Vygotsky realized that at any given time, some tasks are just beyond a child's reach. The child is close to having the mental skills needed to do these tasks, but they are a little too complex to be mastered alone. However, children working within this zone can make rapid progress if they receive sensitive guidance from a skilled partner (Gredler, 2012). (Notice that this is similar to the Piagetian one-step-ahead strategy described previously.)

Vygotsky also emphasized a process that he called **scaffolding**. A scaffold is a framework or temporary support. Vygotsky believed that adults help children learn how to think by "scaffolding," or supporting, their attempts to solve problems or discover principles (Daniels, 2005). To be most effective, scaffolding must be responsive to a child's needs. For example, as Tanya's father helped her with the puzzle, he tailored his hints and guidance to match her evolving abilities. The two of them worked together, step by step, so that Tanya could better understand how to assemble a puzzle. In a sense, Tanya's father set up a series of temporary bridges that helped her move into new mental territory. As predicted by Vygotsky's theory, the reading skills of 8- to 10-year-old children are closely related to the amount of verbal scaffolding that their mothers provided at ages 3 and 4 (Dieterich et al., 2006).

During their collaborations with others, children learn important cultural beliefs and values. For example, imagine that a boy wants to know how many baseball cards he has. His mother helps him stack and count the cards, moving each card to a new stack as they count it. She then shows him how to write the number on a slip of paper so that he can remember it. This teaches the child not only about counting, but also that writing is valued in our culture. In other parts of the world, a child learning to count might be shown how to make notches on a stick or tie knots in a cord.

Zone of proximal development A term referring to the range of tasks that a child cannot yet master alone, but that she or he can accomplish with the guidance of a more capable partner.

Scaffolding The process of adjusting instruction so that it is responsive to a beginner's behavior and supports the beginner's efforts to understand a problem or gain a mental skill.

MODULE 14 Language and Cognitive Development in Childhood—Learning Outcomes Revisited

14.1 Explain the contributions of nature and nurture to language development

Language development proceeds from crying to cooing, then babbling, to the use of single words, and then to telegraphic speech. The underlying patterns of telegraphic speech suggest a biological predisposition to acquire language. However, learning augments this innate tendency. In particular, both prelanguage communication between parent and child (which involves shared rhythms, nonverbal signals, and turn-taking) and motherese/parentese (a simplified, musical style of speaking that parents use with very young children) help with language learning.

14.2 Distinguish between Piaget's conception of "assimilation" and "accommodation, his four stages of cognitive development, as well as object permanence, egocentrism, and conservation. Outline three criticisms of Piaget's theory of cognitive development, including the central idea that underlies Vygotsky's theory of cognitive development, including the zone of proximal development

Assimilation refers to a situation in which a child encounters something novel and is able to successfully integrate it with a concept (or schema) that she has already developed. Accommodation refers to a situation in which something novel does not fit into an existing schema and a new schema must be established. Piaget believed that children go through a fixed series of cognitive stages. The stages and their approximate age ranges are sensorimotor (0–2 years), preoperational (2–7 years), concrete operational (7–11 years), and formal operational (11 years–adult). Object permanence refers to children's ability to understand that people and objects continue to exist even when they are no longer visible. Egocentrism refers to children's inability to understand that the world looks different to other people. Egocentrism can relate to the physical world, when children fail to understand that people standing in other locations may not see what they can see from where they are situated. It may also relate to the mental world, when children do not understand that others have thoughts and feelings that differ from their own. When children begin to understand that others have their own unique thoughts and feelings, we say that they have acquired a theory of mind. Conservation refers to the understanding that physical quantities stay the same even if they change their shape or appearance. Contrary to Piaget's ideas, many psychologists now believe that cognitive development proceeds in a more gradual manner rather than in sharply defined stages. More recent research suggests that children acquire cognitive milestones earlier than Piaget believed. Researchers have suggested that Piaget may have underestimated the role of the environment (including culture) in guiding cognitive development. Lev Vygotsky's sociocultural theory places a particular emphasis on the role of culture and the environment in guiding cognitive development. In particular, he stressed that a child's mental abilities are advanced by interactions with more competent partners. Mental growth takes place in a child's zone of proximal development, where a more skillful person may scaffold the child's progress.

Reflective Practice

Content Check

1. Simple two-word sentences are characteristic of ________________ speech.
2. Noam ________________ advanced the idea that language acquisition is built on innate patterns.
3. Prelanguage turn-taking and social interactions are of special interest to a psycholinguist. T or F?

Match each item with one of the following Piagetian stages.

a. Sensorimotor
b. Preoperational
c. Concrete operational
d. Formal operational

4. _____ egocentrism
5. _____ abstract or hypothetical
6. _____ purposeful movement
7. _____ intuitive thought
8. _____ conservation
9. _____ reversibility thought
10. _____ object permanence

11. _____ nonverbal development

12. Vygotsky called the process of providing a temporary framework of supports for learning new mental abilities ___________.

Skill Check

Think Critically

13. In Western cultures, children as young as age 4 can understand that other people have mental states that differ from their own. In other words, they have developed a *theory of mind.* Is this ability uniquely Western, or might children from other cultures also develop a theory of mind?

Self-Reflect

See if you can name and imitate the language abilities that you had as you progressed from birth to age 2 years in order of occurrence. You are going to make cookies with children of various ages. See if you can name each of Piaget's stages and give an example of what a child in that stage might be expected to do. You have been asked to help a child learn to use a calculator to do simple addition. How would you identify the child's zone of proximal development for this task? How would you scaffold the child's learning?

ANSWERS

1. telegraphic 2. Chomsky 3. T 4. B 5. D 6. A 7. B 8. C 9. C 10. B 11. A 12. scaffolding 13. All humans need to be able to base their actions on their understanding of the intentions, desires, and beliefs of others. Thus, children from Micronesia, a group of small islands in the Pacific Ocean, also develop a theory of mind at around 4 years of age (Oberle, 2009).

Human Development
Adolescence and Adulthood

MODULE 15

Never a Grownup

One common misconception of the idea of human development is that it ends with childhood or in adolescence. At that point, you have finished growing; you are a "grownup." While our individual development might be more obvious when we are young, it is, in reality, never really over until the end of our lives. Personality theorist Erik Erikson's psychosocial theory provides a good overview of the major psychological stages of development that occur during a "typical" life.

Nevertheless, adolescence and young adulthood is a time of exuberance and youthful searching. It also can be a time of worry and problems. During adolescence, a person's identity and moral values come into sharper focus even as the transition to adulthood is occurring at ever-later ages. In adulthood, we all face many additional challenges, including physical aging. We must also face our own inevitable death.

Halfpoint/Shutterstock.com

Let's trace Erikson's stages with a focus on adolescence and adulthood.

~LEARNING OUTCOMES~

After reading this module you should be able to:

15.1 Outline the eight psychosocial dilemmas described by Erikson

15.2 Explain some of the challenges associated with adolescence

15.3 Name and describe Kohlberg's three stages of moral development and identify Carol Gilligan's criticism of Kohlberg's theory

15.4 Name some challenges and elements of subjective well-being in adulthood

15.5 Describe how people typically react to death

The Story of a Lifetime—Rocky Road or Garden Path?

Learning Outcome 15.1 Outline the eight psychosocial dilemmas described by Erikson

Every life is marked by a number of *developmental milestones* (Kail & Cavanaugh, 2019). These are notable events, markers, or turning points in personal development. Some examples include being born, learning to speak, going to school, graduating from school, voting for the first time, getting married, watching a child leave home (or move back!), burying a parent, becoming a grandparent, retiring, and, in the end, dying. Thus far, we have traced progress through the first few years of life. What are some of the challenges we must face during adolescence and adulthood?

Erikson's Psychosocial Theory

Perhaps the best way to get a preview of a life is to consider some of the major psychological milestones and challenges that we are likely to encounter. Broad similarities between people can be found in the life stages of infancy, childhood, adolescence, young adulthood, middle adulthood, and late adulthood. Each developmental stage confronts a person with new **developmental tasks**, specific challenges that must be mastered for optimal development. Examples are learning to read in childhood, adjusting to sexual maturity in adolescence, and establishing a vocation as an adult.

In a highly influential book entitled *Childhood and Society*, Erik Erikson (1963) suggests that we face a specific *psychosocial dilemma*, or "crisis," at each stage of life. A **psychosocial dilemma** is a conflict between personal impulses and the social world. Resolving each dilemma creates a new balance between a person and society. A string of "successes" produces healthy development and a satisfying life. Unfavorable outcomes throw us off balance, making it harder to deal with later crises. Life becomes a "rocky road," and personal growth is stunted. ■ **Table 15.1** lists Erikson's dilemmas.

What are the major developmental tasks and life crises? A brief description of each psychosocial dilemma follows.

Stage 1: First Year of Life During the first year of life, infants are completely dependent on others. Erikson believes that a basic attitude of **trust or mistrust** is formed at this time. *Trust* is established when babies are given warmth, touching, love, and physical care. *Mistrust* is caused by inadequate or unpredictable care and by parents who are cold, indifferent, or rejecting. Basic mistrust may lead to insecurity, suspiciousness, or an inability to relate to others later. Notice that trust comes from the same conditions that help babies become securely attached to their parents.

Stage 2: 1–3 Years In stage 2, children develop **autonomy or shame and doubt**, as they express their growing self-control by climbing, touching, exploring, and trying to do things for themselves. Jay and Gloria fostered little Joseph's *autonomy* by encouraging him to try new skills. However, his first efforts were sometimes crude, involving spilling, falling, wetting himself, and other "accidents." If Jay and Gloria had ridiculed or overprotected Joseph, they might have led him to feel *shameful* about his actions, *doubt* his abilities, or both.

TABLE 15.1 | Erikson's Psychosocial Dilemmas

Age	Characteristic Dilemma
Birth to 1 year	Trust versus mistrust
1–3 years	Autonomy versus shame and doubt
3–5 years	Initiative versus guilt
6–12 years	Industry versus inferiority
Adolescence (12–19 years)	Identity versus role confusion
Young adulthood (20–34 years)	Intimacy versus isolation
Middle adulthood (35–64 years)	Generativity versus stagnation
Late adulthood (65 years and older)	Integrity versus despair

Stage 3: 3–5 Years In stage 3, children move beyond simple self-control to develop **initiative or guilt**. Through play, children learn to make plans and carry out tasks. Parents reinforce *initiative* by giving children freedom to play, ask questions, use imagination, and choose activities. Feelings of *guilt* about initiating activities may be formed if parents criticize severely, prevent play, or discourage a child's questions.

Stage 4: 6–12 Years Many events of middle childhood are symbolized by that fateful day when you first entered school. With dizzying speed, your world expanded beyond your family, and you faced a whole series of new challenges. In school, children begin to learn skills valued by society, and success or failure can affect a child's feelings of **industry or inferiority**. Children learn a sense of *industry* if they win praise for productive activities, such as building, painting, cooking, reading, and studying. If a child's efforts are regarded as messy, childish, or inadequate, feelings of *inferiority* result.

Personality theorist Erik Erikson (1903–1994) is best known for his life-stage theory of human development.

Ted Streshinsky/Historical/Corbis

For the first time, teachers, classmates, and adults outside the home become as important as parents in shaping attitudes toward oneself.

Stage 5: Adolescence Adolescence can be a turbulent time as adolescents develop **identity or role confusion**. Erikson considers answering the question "Who am I?" the primary task during this stage of life. As Joseph matures mentally and physically, he will have new feelings, a new body, and new attitudes. Like other adolescents, he will need to build a consistent *identity* out of his talents, values, life history, relationships, and the demands of his culture. His conflicting experiences as a student, friend, athlete, worker, son, lover, and so forth must be integrated into a unified sense of self. Persons who fail to develop a sense of identity suffer from *role confusion*, an uncertainty about who they are and where they are going.

Stage 6: Young Adulthood After establishing a stable identity, the young adult is challenged to share meaningful love or deep friendship with others (Beyers & Seiffge-Krenke, 2010). The result is **intimacy or isolation**. By *intimacy*, Erikson means an ability to care about others and to share experiences with them. And yet marriage or sexual involvement is no guarantee of intimacy: Many adult relationships remain shallow and unfulfilling. Failure to establish intimacy with others leads to a deep sense of *isolation*—feeling alone and uncared for in life. This often points the way to later difficulties.

Stage 7: Middle Adulthood According to Erikson, an interest in guiding the next generation results in **generativity or stagnation**. Erikson called this quality *generativity*. Emotional balance in middle adulthood is expressed by caring about oneself, one's children, and future generations. Joseph may achieve generativity by guiding his own children or by helping other children, as a teacher or coach, for example (Hebblethwaite & Norris, 2011). Productive or creative work also can express generativity. In any case, a person must broaden his or his concerns and energies to include the welfare of others and society as a whole. Failure to do this is marked by a feeling of *stagnation*—concern with one's own needs and comforts. Life loses meaning, and the person feels bitter, dreary, and trapped.

Stage 8: Late Adulthood *What does Erikson see as the conflicts of old age?* Late adulthood is a time of reflection, leading to **integrity or despair** (Hearn et al., 2012). According to Erikson, when Joseph grows old, it would be better if he were able to look back over his life with acceptance and satisfaction. People who have lived richly and responsibly develop a sense of *integrity*, or self-respect. This allows them to face aging and death with dignity. If previous life events are viewed with regret, the elderly person experiences *despair*, or heartache and remorse. In this case, life seems like a series of missed opportunities. The person feels like a failure, knowing that it's too late to reverse what has been done. Aging and the threat of death then become sources of fear and depression.

The Whole Human To squeeze a lifetime into a few pages, we had to leave out countless details. Although

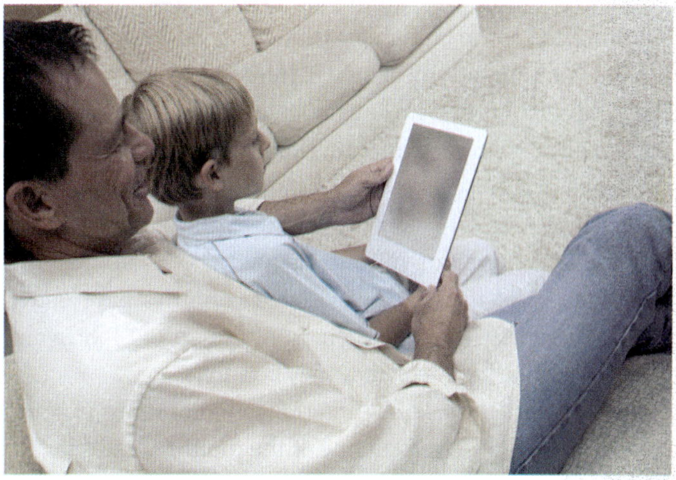

bikeriderlondon/Shutterstock.com

According to Erikson, an interest in future generations characterizes optimal adult development.

Developmental tasks Skills that must be mastered, or personal changes that must take place, for optimal development.

Psychosocial dilemma A conflict between personal impulses and the social world.

Trust or mistrust A conflict early in life about learning to trust others and the world.

Autonomy or shame and doubt A conflict created when growing self-control (autonomy) is pitted against feelings of shame or doubt.

Initiative or guilt A conflict between learning to take initiative and overcoming feelings of guilt about doing so.

Industry or inferiority A conflict in middle childhood centered around lack of support for industrious behavior, which can result in feelings of inferiority.

Identity or role confusion A conflict of adolescence, involving the need to establish a personal identity.

Intimacy or isolation The challenge of overcoming a sense of isolation by establishing intimacy with others.

Generativity or stagnation A conflict of middle adulthood in which self-interest is countered by an interest in guiding the next generation.

Integrity or despair A conflict in late adulthood between feelings of integrity and the despair of viewing previous life events with regret.

much is lost, the result is a clearer picture of an entire life cycle. Is Erikson's description, then, an exact map of anyone's unique past, present, and future? Probably not. Still, psychosocial dilemmas are major events in many lives. Knowing about them may allow you to anticipate typical trouble spots in your own life. You also may be better prepared to understand the problems and feelings of friends and relatives at various points in the life cycle.

Adolescence—The Best of Times, the Worst of Times

Learning Outcome 15.2 Explain some of the challenges associated with adolescence

Adolescence is the culturally defined period between childhood and adulthood (Bjorklund & Hernández Blasi, 2012). Socially, the adolescent is no longer a child, yet not quite an adult. Almost all cultures recognize this transitional status. However, the length of adolescence varies greatly from culture to culture. For example, most 14-year-old girls in North America live at home and go to school. In contrast, many 14-year-old girls in rural villages of many less-developed countries have gotten married and may have children. In our culture, 14-year-olds are adolescents. In others, they may be adults.

Is marriage the primary criterion for adult status in North America? No—it's not even one of the top three criteria. Today, the most widely accepted standards are (1) taking responsibility for oneself, (2) making independent decisions, and (3) becoming financially independent. In practice, this typically means breaking away from parents by getting a job and setting up a separate residence (Arnett, 2016).

Puberty

Many people confuse adolescence with puberty. However, puberty is a *biological* event, not a social status. During **puberty**, hormonal changes promote rapid physical growth and sexual maturity. Biologically, most people reach reproductive maturity in their early teens. Social and intellectual maturity, however, may lie years ahead. Young adolescents often make decisions that affect their entire lives, even though they are immature mentally and socially. The tragically high rates of teenage pregnancy and drug abuse are prime examples. Despite such risks, most people manage to weather adolescence without developing any serious psychological problems (Rathus, 2014).

How much difference does the timing of puberty make? For boys, maturing early is generally beneficial. It typically enhances their self-image and gives them an advantage socially and athletically. Early-maturing boys tend to be more relaxed, dominant, self-assured, and popular. However, early puberty carries some risks because early-maturing boys also are more likely to get into trouble with drugs, sex, alcohol, and antisocial behavior (Steinberg, 2001).

For girls, the advantages of early maturation are less clear-cut. In elementary school, fast-maturing girls are *less* popular and have poorer self-images, perhaps because they are larger and heavier than their classmates (Deardorff et al., 2007). This is a growing problem (no pun intended ...) as more American girls are reaching puberty at earlier ages (Biro et al., 2010). By junior high, however, early development includes sexual features. This leads to a more positive body image, *greater* peer prestige, and adult approval. Early-maturing girls tend to date sooner and are more independent and more active in school. However, like their male counterparts, they also are more often in trouble at school and more likely to engage in early sex (Negriff & Trickett, 2010).

As you can see, early puberty has both costs and benefits. One added cost of early maturation is that it may force premature identity formation. When Joseph is a teenager and he begins to look like an adult, he may be treated like an adult. Ideally, this change can encourage greater maturity and independence. However, if the search for identity ends too soon, it may leave Joseph with a distorted, poorly formed sense of self.

The Search for Identity

Although problems of identity occur at other ages, too, identity formation is a key challenge faced by adolescents (McLean & Pasupathi, 2012). In a very real sense, puberty signals that it's time to begin forming a new, more mature self-image (Rathus, 2014). Many problems stem from unclear standards about the role that adolescents should play within society. Are they adults or children? Should they be autonomous or dependent? Should they work or play? Such ambiguities make it difficult for young people to form clear images of themselves and how they should act.

Answering the question "Who am I?" is also spurred by cognitive development. After adolescents attain the stage of formal operations, they are better able to ask questions about their future place in the world and about morals,

What identity will these teenagers develop as they ask themselves, "Who am I?

values, politics, and social relationships. Being able to think about hypothetical possibilities allows the adolescent to contemplate the future and ask more realistically.

Identity and Ethnic Diversity Ethnic heritage is an important aspect of personal identity (Corenblum, 2013). For adolescents of ethnic descent, the question often is not just "Who am I?" Rather, it is "Who am I at home? Who am I at school? Who am I with friends in my neighborhood?"

As ethnic minorities in the United States continue to grow in status and prominence, adolescents are less and less likely to feel rejected or excluded because of their ethnic heritage as they try to find their place in society. This is fortunate because ethnic adolescents have often faced degrading stereotypes concerning their intelligence, sexuality, social status, manners, and so forth. The result can be lowered self-esteem and confusion about roles, values, and personal identity (Charmaraman & Grossman, 2010). At the same time, the increasingly multicultural nature of contemporary American society raises new questions for adolescents about what it means to be American.

In forming an identity, adolescents of ethnic descent face the question of how they should think of themselves. Is Lily an American, a Vietnamese American, or both? Is Manny a Latino, an American, or a Columbian American? The answer typically depends on how strongly adolescents identify with their family and ethnic community. Teens who take pride in their ethnic heritage have higher self-esteem, a better self-image, and a stronger sense of personal identity (Galliher, Jones, & Dahl, 2011). They also are less likely to engage in drug use or violent behavior (French, Kim, & Pillado, 2006; Williams et al., 2014).

Group pride, positive models, and a more tolerant society could do much to keep a broad range of options open to *all* adolescents. In many ways, adolescence is more emotionally turbulent than adulthood. One important aspect of this period is the struggle with telling right from wrong—the need to develop moral values—which is discussed next.

Moral Development—Growing a Conscience

Learning Outcome 15.3 Name and describe Kohlberg's three stages of moral development and identify Carol Gilligan's criticism of Kohlberg's theory

Consider the following problem:

> A woman was near death from cancer, and there was only one drug that might save her. The druggist who discovered it was charging 10 times what it cost to make the drug. The sick woman's husband, Heinz, could pay only $1,000, but the druggist wanted $2,000. He asked the druggist to sell it cheaper or to let him pay later. The druggist said no. So, Heinz became desperate and broke into the store and stole the drug for his wife. [This scenario is adapted from Kohlberg (1969).]

How do you feel about Heinz's theft? Do you think that the husband should have done what he did? Was it wrong, or right? Why? Finally, what would you do if it was up to you? These are *moral* questions, or questions of *ethics* (Haidt, 2012).

Like *attitudes*, morals have emotional and cognitive, as well as behavioral, dimensions (Shaffer & Kipp, 2014). (For more on attitude formation and change, see Module 70.)

Moral development begins in early childhood and continues into adulthood, as we acquire the specific values that, along with appropriate emotions and cognitions, guide responsible behavior (King, 2009). Moral values are especially likely to come into sharper focus during adolescence and the transition to adulthood as the capacities for reflection and abstract thinking increase (Hart & Carlo, 2005; Krettenauer et al., 2014).

Adolescence The culturally defined period between childhood and adulthood.

Puberty Biologically defined period during which a person matures sexually and becomes capable of reproduction.

Moral development The development of values that, along with appropriate emotions and cognitions, guide responsible behavior.

Moral Emotions

Did you get a "gut feeling" that what Heinz did was right or wrong? According to psychologist Jonathan Haidt (2013), our morals are, first and foremost, immediately and intuitively *felt*. Even infants as young as 15 months of age notice when toys are not being fairly shared, long before they can explain the concept of fairness (Sommerville et al., 2013).

Fundamental moral intuitions about the wrongness of harming others and the rightness of fairness may be, in part, biologically innate, part and parcel of our evolved social nature (Hamlin, 2013). Nevertheless, moral intuitions also develop, in part, through early childhood experiences. For example, the children of authoritative parents who deal calmly with conflicts are likely to resist playing with a prohibited toy at a younger age (by the age of 3) than children of less calm and authoritative parents (Laible & Thompson, 2002).

Moral Thinking

What is moral reasoning? Once we begin to experience moral intuitions, we seek to explain them (Nucci & Gingo, 2011). In an influential account, psychologist Lawrence Kohlberg (1981) held that we clarify our values through thinking and reasoning. To study moral development, Kohlberg posed dilemmas, like the one that Heinz faced, to children of different ages. Each child was asked what action the husband should take. Kohlberg classified the reasons given for each choice and identified three levels of moral development. Each is based not so much on the choices made, but on the reasoning used to arrive at a choice.

Preconventional Moral Reasoning At the lowest, **preconventional moral reasoning** level, moral thinking is guided by the consequences of actions (punishment, reward, or an exchange of favors). For example, a person at this level might reason: "The man shouldn't steal the drug because he could get caught and sent to jail" (avoiding punishment) or "It won't do him any good to steal the drug because his wife will probably die before he gets out of jail" (self-interest). The preconventional level is most characteristic of young children and delinquents (Forney, Forney, & Crutsinger, 2005).

Conventional Moral Reasoning At the second, **conventional moral reasoning** level, thinking is based on a desire to please others or to follow accepted authority, rules, and values. For example, a person at this intermediate level might say, "He shouldn't steal the drug because others will think he is a thief. His wife would not want to be saved by thievery" (avoiding disapproval), or "Although his wife needs the drug, he should not break the law to get it. Everyone has to obey the law. His wife's condition does not justify stealing" (traditional morality of authority). Conventional, group-oriented morals are typical of older children and most adults. Some adults may not reach even the conventional level. For instance, a significant number of men in their first year of college think unwanted sexual aggression is acceptable (Tatum & Foubert, 2009).

Postconventional Moral Reasoning At the highest, **postconventional moral reasoning** level, moral behavior is directed by self-chosen ethical principles that tend to be general, comprehensive, or universal. People at this level place a high value on justice, dignity, and equality. For example, a highly principled person might say, "He should steal the drug and then inform the authorities that he has done so. He will have to face a penalty, but he will have saved a human life" (self-chosen ethical principles).

Does everyone eventually reach the highest level? Kohlberg estimated that only about 20 percent of the adult population achieves the self-direction and higher principles of postconventional morality.

Fairness or Caring? Also, as we mentioned in Module 3, Kohlberg's studies suggested that women were morally "immature" because they were not as concerned with justice as men were. In response, Carol Gilligan (1982) pointed out that Kohlberg's theory is concerned mainly with *fairness*, or *justice*. Based on studies of women who faced real-life dilemmas, Gilligan argued that there is also an ethic of *harm*, or *caring* about others. As one illustration, she presented the following story to 11- to 15-year-old American children:

The Porcupine and the Moles

Seeking refuge from the cold, a porcupine asked to share a cave for the winter with a family of moles. The moles agreed. But because the cave was small, they soon found they were being scratched each time that the porcupine moved. Finally, they asked the porcupine to leave. But the porcupine refused, saying, "If you moles are not satisfied, I suggest that you leave."

Boys who read this story tended to opt for justice in resolving the dilemma: "It's the moles' house. It's a deal. The porcupine leaves." In contrast, girls tended to look for solutions that would keep all parties happy and comfortable, such as "Cover the porcupine with a blanket."

Gilligan's point is that male psychologists have, for the most part, defined moral maturity in terms of fairness and autonomy. From this perspective, a woman's concern with relationships can look like weakness rather than strength. (A woman who is concerned about what helps or harms others would be placed at the conventional level in Kohlberg's system.) But Gilligan believes that caring also is a major element of moral development, and she suggests that males may lag in achieving it (Lambert et al., 2009). Indeed, several studies have found little or no difference in men's and women's overall moral reasoning abilities (Glover, 2001). Both men and women may use caring *and* justice to make moral decisions. The moral yardstick that they use appears to depend on the situation that they face (Wark & Krebs, 1996).

Developing a "moral compass" is an important part of growing up. Many of the choices we make every day involve fundamental questions of right and wrong. The ability to think clearly about such questions is essential to becoming a responsible adult. (For more on the topic of moral reasoning, see Module 16.)

Adulthood—You're an Adult Now!

Learning Outcome 15.4 Name some challenges and elements of subjective well-being in adulthood

Although Erikson's dilemmas extend into adulthood, they are not the only challenges that adults face. Once adulthood has been reached, physical changes due to "nature" become more gradual and subtle. Most adults focus on the challenges provided by "nurture"—specifically their social and cultural environments. A core issue now becomes how to successfully negotiate the many challenges of adulthood in positive ways.

Challenges of Adulthood

Among the many new challenges adulthood brings are emerging adulthood, careers, marriage, children, parents, health, and ageism (Cavanaugh & Blanchard-Fields, 2015; Damman, Henkens, & Kalmijn, 2011).

Emerging Adulthood Nowadays, many young people are deferring adulthood, prolonging identity explorations well into their twenties before they commit to life choices in work and love. Western industrialized societies, such as the United States and Canada, have become increasingly tolerant of **emerging adulthood**, a socially accepted period of extended adolescence (Arnett, 2011, 2016). For many young adults, extended adolescence is an unstable, in-between, self-focused period of time to explore identities and life possibilities.

Are such people still adolescents who are struggling to find their identity? Or are they self-indulgent young adults trapped in a "maturity gap" (Smith, 2011)? Either way, emerging adulthood is an unstable, in-between, self-focused period of time to explore identities and life possibilities.

Careers The work that adults do—as homemakers, volunteers, hourly workers, or in their careers—is critical to subjective well-being (Raymo et al., 2010). While peak earnings commonly occur during these years, growing expenses may continue to create financial pressures, from childcare to tuition fees for children, and paying rent or a mortgage. This is one reason that career difficulties and unemployment can pose such serious challenges to adult well-being. Another reason, of course, is that many adults derive much of their identity from their work (Sigelman & Rider, 2018).

Marriage, Children, and Parents Most adult Americans identify their social relationships—especially with children, spouses, and parents—as another important aspect of adult life (Raymo et al., 2010). Creating and sustaining social relationships can involve finding a life partner, working through the stresses of child-rearing, becoming "empty nesters" when children move away, becoming grandparents, experiencing marital strife or divorce, living as singles or in blended families, and seeing parents grow old, need support, and die, to mention some of the more common social challenges faced by adults.

Health Joseph's father, Jay, just hurt his back while golfing. Jay has encountered the obvious; he is getting older. Although some adults face far more serious health issues, from heart attacks to cancer, every adult faces the routine wear and tear of aging. How an adult deals with the inevitable decline during adulthood strongly influences that person's degree of life satisfaction and can complicate personal development, especially after the late fifties. Fortunately, most of the time, declines happen slowly enough that they can be offset by increased life experience (Sigelman & Rider, 2018).

For example, people do experience a gradual loss of *fluid intelligence* (abilities requiring speed or rapid learning) as they age, but this can often be offset by *crystallized intelligence* (abilities involving already learned knowledge and skills), such as vocabulary and stored-up facts, which may

Preconventional moral reasoning Moral thinking based on the consequences of one's choices or actions (punishment, reward, or an exchange of favors).

Conventional moral reasoning Moral thinking based on a desire to please others or to follow accepted rules and values.

Postconventional moral reasoning Moral thinking based on carefully examined and self-chosen moral principles.

Emerging adulthood A socially accepted period of extended adolescence that is now quite common in Western and Westernized societies.

actually improve—at least into the sixties (Schaie, 2005). (Remember that infants show just the opposite pattern, being high in fluid intelligence but low in crystallized intelligence.) Wisdom and expertise can usually more than compensate for any loss of mental quickness (Agrigoroaei & Lachman, 2011; Cavanaugh & Blanchard-Fields, 2015).

Ageism Discrimination or prejudice based on age, known as **ageism**, can oppress the young as well as the old (Bodner, 2009). For instance, a person applying for a job may just as well hear "You're too young" as "You're too old." In some societies, ageism is expressed as respect for the elderly. In Japan, for instance, aging is seen as positive, and greater age brings more status and respect. In most Western nations, however, ageism tends to have a negative impact on older individuals.

Ageism is often expressed through patronizing language. Older people are frequently spoken to in an overly polite, slow, loud, and simple way, implying that they are infirm, even when they are not (Nelson, 2005). Popular stereotypes of the "dirty old man," "meddling old woman," "senile old fool," and the like also help perpetuate myths about aging. But such stereotypes are clearly wrong: a tremendous diversity exists among the elderly—ranging from the infirm to aerobic-dancing grandmothers.

Successful Aging and Subjective Well-Being

How do people maintain a state of subjective well-being as they run the gauntlet of modern life? According to psychologist Ed Diener and his associates, **subjective well-being** is high when people are generally satisfied with their lives, have frequent positive emotions, and have relatively few negative emotions (Diener, 2013; Tay & Diener, 2011). Psychologist Gloria Ryff believes that subjective well-being throughout adulthood involves six elements (Ryff & Singer, 2009; van Dierendonck et al., 2008): self-acceptance, positive relations with others, autonomy (personal freedom), environmental mastery, a purpose in life, and continued personal growth.

D Dipasupil/FilmMagic/Getty Images

Shown here at the *Saturday Night Live* 40th Anniversary Celebration in 2015, Betty White celebrated her 98th birthday in 2020. Still active after over 80 years as a popular entertainer, Betty is proof that aging does not inevitably bring an end to engaging in challenging activities.

Despite the emphasis on youth in our culture, then, middle age and beyond can be a rich period of life in which people feel secure, happy, and self-confident (Lilgendahl, Helson, & John, 2013). For many adults, age-related physical declines are offset by positive relationships and greater mastery of life's demands. Typically, successful adults have continued to work and remain intellectually and emotionally vital (Hooyman & Kiyak, 2011; Mather, 2016; Wilhelm et al., 2010).

What are older adults doing to help them experience these positive outcomes? One of the most stable findings in the research on aging is the *positivity effect*, or the tendency for older adults to pay attention to, and remember, more positive information than negative information (Carstensen & DeLiema, 2018). In addition, compared to adolescents and young adults, older adults also appear to be more skilled at regulating, or controlling, their emotional responses (Scheibe, Sheppes, & Staudinger, 2015). Some research suggests that they do this through a process of situation selection, or choosing to spend most of their time doing things with people that they care about (Sims, Hogan, & Carstensen, 2015).

Death and Dying—The Final Challenge

Learning Outcome 15.5 Describe how people typically react to death

We have seen throughout this module that it is valuable to understand major trends in the course of development. With this in mind, let's explore emotional responses to death, the biologically inevitable conclusion of every life.

Reactions to Impending Death

A highly influential account of emotional responses to death comes from the work of Elisabeth Kübler-Ross (1926–2004). Over the years, she spent hundreds of hours at the bedsides of the terminally ill, where she observed five basic emotional reactions to impending death (Kübler-Ross, 1975):

1. **Denial and isolation.** A typical first reaction is to deny death's reality and isolate oneself from information confirming that death is really going to occur. Initially, the person may be sure that "it's all a mistake." She or he thinks, "Surely the doctor made an error."
2. **Anger.** Many dying individuals feel anger and ask, "Why me?" As they face the ultimate threat of having life torn away, their anger may spill over into rage toward the living.
3. **Bargaining.** In another common reaction, the terminally ill bargain with themselves or with God. The dying person thinks, "Just let me live a little longer and I'll do anything to earn it."
4. **Depression.** As death draws near and the person begins to recognize that it cannot be prevented, feelings of futility, exhaustion, and deep depression may set in.
5. **Acceptance.** If death is not sudden, many people manage to come to terms with dying and accept it calmly. The person who accepts death is neither happy nor sad, but at peace with the inevitable.

Kübler-Ross's list is best understood as describing typical reactions to impending death. Not all terminally ill persons display all these reactions, nor do they always occur in this order. In general, one's approach to dying will mirror his or her style of living (Yedidia & MacGregor, 2001). Note, as well, that many of the same reactions accompany any major loss, be it divorce, loss of a home due to fire, death of a pet, or loss of a job.

How can I use this information? First, it can help both the dying and the survivors to recognize and cope with periods of depression, anger, denial, and bargaining. Second, it helps to realize that close friends or relatives may feel many of the same emotions before or after a person's death because they, too, are facing a loss (Leming & Dickinson, 2021).

Perhaps the most important thing to recognize is that dying persons need to share their feelings and to discuss death openly (Corr, Nabe, & Corr, 2013). Too often, dying persons feel isolated and separated from others. If someone in your life is dying, be genuine, be ready to listen, be respectful, be aware of feelings and nonverbal cues, be comfortable with silence, and most of all, be there, no matter what (Dyer, 2001).

John Mitterer

Death may be inevitable, but it can be faced with dignity and sometimes even light-heartedly. While she was alive, nobody took Pearl Roberts's health complaints seriously because she always had such a sense of humor.

Ageism Discrimination or prejudice based on a person's age.

Subjective well-being General life satisfaction combined with frequent positive emotions and relatively few negative emotions.

MODULE 15 Adolescence and Adulthood—Learning Outcomes Revisited

15.1 Outline the eight psychosocial dilemmas described by Erikson

Erik Erikson identified a series of specific psychosocial dilemmas that occur as we age. Successful resolution of the dilemmas produces healthy development, whereas unsuccessful outcomes make it harder to deal with later crises. In order, the dilemmas are: trust vs. mistrust, autonomy vs. shame/doubt, initiative vs. doubt, industry vs. inferiority, identity vs. role confusion, intimacy vs. isolation, generativity vs. stagnation, and integrity vs. despair.

15.2 Explain some of the challenges associated with adolescence

The timing of puberty can complicate the task of identity formation, a major task of adolescence. Identity formation is even more challenging for adolescents of ethnic descent. In Western industrialized societies, the transition into adulthood is further complicated because it is increasingly delayed until people reach well into their twenties (emerging adulthood).

15.3 Name and describe Kohlberg's three stages of moral development and identify Carol Gilligan's criticism of Kohlberg's theory

Preconventional: moral thinking is guided by consequences (e.g., reward, punishment); Conventional: moral thinking is guided by a desire to please others or follow rules; Postconventional: moral thinking is guided by self-chosen ethical principles. Most people function at the conventional level of morality, but some never get beyond the preconventional level. Only a minority of people attain the highest, or postconventional, level of moral reasoning. Carol Gilligan distinguished between Kohlberg's fairness (justice) perspective and a harm (caring) perspective. Because Kohlberg's theory placed a high value on justice, she argued that women—who reason more frequently from a caring perspective—wrongly appeared to demonstrate less moral maturity than men. Now, most researchers believe that mature adult morality likely involves reasoning from both perspectives, and cultural research suggests that there may also be other moral foundations that underlie people's values.

15.4 Name some challenges and elements of subjective well-being in adulthood

Challenges in adulthood include managing emerging adulthood, careers, marriage, children, parents, health, and ageism (prejudice, discrimination, and stereotyping on the basis of age) that is based on stereotypes, myths, and misinformation. Subjective well-being during adulthood consists of six elements: self-acceptance, positive relations with others, autonomy, environmental mastery, having a purpose in life, and continued personal growth.

15.5 Describe how people typically react to death

Typical emotional reactions to impending death include denial, anger, bargaining, depression, and acceptance, but not necessarily in that order, nor do all of them appear in every case.

Reflective Practice

Content Check

1. During middle adulthood, the crisis is generativity versus ____________.
2. Identity formation is spurred by ____________ and ____________.
3. According to Jeffrey Arnett, the trend in affluent Westernized cultures toward allowing young people to take longer to settle into their adult roles is best referred to as
   a. emerging adulthood
   b. hurried childhood
   c. a maturity gap
   d. extended adolescence
4. Moral intuitions develop before moral reasoning. T or F?
5. After age 65, a large proportion of older people show significant signs of mental disability and most require special care. T or F?
6. In the reaction that Kübler-Ross describes as bargaining, the dying individual asks, "Why me?" T or F?

Skill Check

Think Critically

7. Do labels like *adolescent* or *young adult* reflect heredity or environment?

Self-Reflect

See if you can think of a person you know who is facing one of Erikson's psychosocial dilemmas. Now see if you can think of specific people who seem to be coping with each of the other dilemmas. To what extent does the concept of identity formation apply to your own experience during adolescence? Do you think emerging adults (are you one?) are adolescents who are taking longer to find their identity or young adults avoiding their need to establish themselves in the world of adults? Describe three instances of ageism you have witnessed.

ANSWERS

1. Stagnation 2. puberty, cognitive development 3. a 4. T 5. F 6. F 7. Environment, rather than heredity, is the better answer. Even better, the meanings of terms such as *adolescence* or *adult* vary considerably from culture to culture, indicating that it is really a matter of definition (Arnett, 2016).

MODULE 16

A Psychologist's Skill Set

Behaving Ethically

To Thine Own Self Be True

If you follow popular media, you don't have to look far to find a scandal. We regularly see stories about athletes who took illegal drugs to win competitions, Hollywood stars who cheated on their partners, business executives who engaged in illegal practices to ensure larger profits, and politicians who misled people so that they could win elections. This type of behavior isn't just confined to the rich and powerful, either: Individuals download illegal copies of music, movies, and software every day. They also file misleading tax returns and fraudulent insurance claims for items that were never stolen. And at school, roughly two-thirds of students admit to cheating in their courses (McCabe, Butterfield, & Trevino, 2012).

tuaindeed/Shutterstock.com

Although a sense of right and wrong begins to emerge in early childhood, the most important growth in this area doesn't occur until adolescence, when we develop the capacity for abstract thought that's so important in guiding our values. This also fits with what we know about self-regulation (see Module 11). The prefrontal cortex—the part of our brain that's important in guiding our ability to resist temptation—is still developing well into the teens and early twenties. So how "grown-up" are your ethics?

~LEARNING OUTCOMES~

After reading this module you should be able to:

16.1 Outline four strategies that you can use to create conditions that will help you behave in ways that align with your values

Thinking About Ethics—Valuing Values

Learning Outcome 16.1 Outline four strategies that you can use to create conditions that will help you behave in ways that align with your values

Check out the following list of behaviors. How much would someone have to pay you to do each of these things *if no one else would ever know*? Would you do any of them for free? How about a thousand dollars? A million dollars? Is there anything on the list that you simply wouldn't do for any amount of money (adapted from Graham, Haidt, & Nosek, 2009)?

1. Kick a dog in the head, hard.
2. Sign a secret-but-binding pledge to hire only people of your race at your company.

3. Burn your country's flag in private.
4. Give a disrespectful hand gesture to your boss or professor.
5. Get a transfusion of disease-free, compatible blood from a convicted child molester.

For years, when psychologists wrote about moral values, they focused on ideas related to *harm* (which makes us care about suffering and cruelty) and *fairness* (which makes us think about justice, and how cheaters should be punished). (See Module 15.) The first two examples on the list above are related to these two values. More recently, psychologists have expanded their thinking about morality, partly because diverse groups often have very different ideas about what it means to behave ethically in our everyday lives (Haidt, 2007, 2012). In particular, current ideas about ethical behavior go beyond focusing on harm and fairness and emphasize the link between our moral values and both the cultural groups we belong to and our religious beliefs (Graham et al., 2011; Haidt, 2013).

For example, research on morality now includes discussions about how core beliefs can also be shaped by our feelings about *loyalty*. This aspect of morality is focused on our connection to groups that are very important to us, and how we respond to a betrayal of that group (such as burning your country's flag). *Power* also appears to be an important idea that shapes our values. For example, we're very sensitive to signs of social status and can react strongly to people who don't act in line with their "position" in life (say, giving the finger to your boss). Finally, psychologists have also found that our morals are related to our ideas about the *purity/sanctity* of our bodies and environment (which is why some of you will have said that you wouldn't want the blood of a child molester running through your veins for any amount of money).

Ethical Behavior—Truth or Consequences

Learning Outcome 16.1 Outline four strategies that you can use to create conditions that will help you behave in ways that align with your values

We're all aware that there can be important consequences for behaving in an unethical way. When the actions are illegal, people can be arrested or fined large sums of money. But even when unethical behavior isn't against the law, it can still result in severe consequences. For example, relationships may end, or people can be fired from their jobs or expelled from college. Perhaps more important, though, is how these behaviors affect the way you think about yourself. Research suggests that people want to behave with integrity, and make an effort to resist temptation because they place a high value on being ethical. People are also prone to seeing themselves as moral, and are highly motivated to preserve that image because an inability to do so has negative implications for their self-concept (Barkan et al., 2012; Mazar, Amir, & Ariely, 2008).

Preparing to Behave Ethically

Ok, so I can see it's important to behave in line with my values, but is there any way that I can increase my chances of doing that? That's a great question, because it focuses attention on an unusual idea suggested by Mary Gentile (2010); namely that behaving ethically ourselves—and promoting ethical behavior in others—is a skill that can be taught. It's important to realize that this doesn't mean you must change your values. Instead, she has outlined several ways in which you can try to create the conditions that will help you speak and behave in ways that are in keeping with your core beliefs, even when the situation is challenging. Her ideas can be summarized as follows:

Recognize Everyday Ethical Challenges If you consider some of the ethical dilemmas that make headlines in the news, it might be tempting to think that challenges to your integrity will only arise if you're working in very senior positions with large companies, or if you were involved in politics or Hollywood romances. In reality, though, each of us faces moral issues with surprising regularity because they're a very normal part of everyday life. They can arise at school, on sports teams, while working, or in our relationships with friends and family.

For example, at school you may be asked to cheat on a test or let a friend copy your homework assignment. At work you may be asked to "upsell," convincing a client that they ought to purchase more from you than they need. Or imagine a friend asking you to cover for him with his girlfriend while he's on a date with someone else. When we accept how frequently ethical challenges can arise, it allows us to consider, in advance, the possible ethical traps we may find ourselves in and—more importantly—how we might manage them.

Anticipate Conditions That Promote or Interfere with Ethical Responses Once you have become more aware of situations that are likely to present challenges to your values, ask, "What conditions will either promote ('enablers') or discourage ('inhibitors') behavior that's in line with my values?" For example, people may feel more comfortable speaking up in ethically challenging situations at work when there are enabling forces present, such as having a like-minded colleague who'd be willing to express support for your position. On the flipside, people may have more trouble being true to their values if they feel that there are disabling forces at work. For example, it may be challenging to express your values and beliefs if you have a boss who is disinterested in the views of people she supervises, or if you work at an organization that does not encourage open communication. Being aware of these enabling and inhibiting forces can help you map out a strategy that will help you to behave with integrity.

Plan How to Manage Them Once you have a handle on the moral dilemmas you might face and the conditions that would enable or inhibit your ability to act in line with your values, you can begin to anticipate how you might manage such situations. But Gentile argues that you should go much further than just thinking about these situations. Instead, she suggests that you should actively imagine possible scenarios in detail, and think about what you would like to say, and how you would say it. She even suggests that it might be valuable to practice what you'd say aloud, or run it by other people so that you can get feedback about your response.

There are at least three reasons why this type of advance planning can be helpful. First, preparation makes it less likely that you will be put in a position where you need to make a quick decision about what to do, without having time to think things through. Instead, formulating your thoughts (and your words!) ahead of time makes it more likely that you'll be able to speak up and behave in keeping with your values when the time comes. We've already seen that doing so has a positive impact on how you perceive yourself, but another consequence is that behaving with integrity early in a relationship helps to set up other people's expectations about you in a positive way. That's important because if the same situation arises again, people will expect you to behave as you have in the past. More importantly, *you'll* expect yourself to behave as you have in the past.

A second benefit of advance planning for ethically challenging situations is that it allows you to consider how you can best explain the reasons that underlie your value-based decision. The planning you do is likely to mean that you will be more confident when you present your views. Presenting your beliefs in a calm, clear way may be helpful in ensuring that you won't engage in highly emotional "shaming and blaming," and that other people will listen and take you seriously.

A third benefit that arises from practicing how you would manage ethically challenging situations in advance is that it gives you the opportunity to think about your audience. For example, is there any way to make the person you're talking to feel more comfortable, or to improve the chances that she will listen to you with an open mind? What questions are other people likely to ask about your position on this ethical issue, and how you might respond to any arguments that are raised in opposition to your way of thinking?

Counteract Others' Support for Nonethical Choices You should also anticipate how people might try to "explain away" their support of nonethical choices and how you can counteract this tendency. Recently, psychologists have offered three suggestions about how you can reduce the likelihood that those around you will behave unethically (Ayal et al., 2015). The first suggestion is based on the finding that people are prone to justifying unethical behavior by taking advantage of ambiguities or "gray areas" ("It's not really the company's responsibility"; "It's not written down anywhere"; "Everyone does it"; "It may not be right, but it's not really important enough to worry about"). To counteract this tendency, you can offer reminders—even subtle ones—that will make others think about their own moral character before they have the opportunity to make an unethical choice. A teacher whose goal is to reduce the likelihood of cheating during an exam might remind students that she views them as honest people, and that she knows that her students want to behave with integrity.

A second suggestion for minimizing others' unethical behavior involves providing cues that restrict any feelings of anonymity ("No one's going to know"), since people are more likely to violate morals when they believe that their behavior is anonymous. During the exam, then, that same teacher would be walking through the aisles and keeping an eye on each of her students, making eye contact if possible when they look up from their exams.

Finally, unethical behavior often results from the fact that while values and morals are somewhat abstract, ethically questionable behaviors are typically concrete. As a result, it can be easy to avoid connecting the two. The third suggestion, then, is to reduce unethical behavior by creating the necessary connections between abstract moral values and more concrete behaviors. To this end, the teacher might have each of her students do something concrete, such as sign an "honor pledge" before the exam indicating that they understand what's meant by cheating on the test (which can be a somewhat abstract idea).

The Last Word *What you're saying makes sense, but what if I find myself in an ethically challenging situation and I have no time to prepare myself?* It's true that you can't always predict when you're going to find yourself in a situation that challenges your values. In those situations, Gentile's best advice is simply to know yourself well, so that if you do find yourself in a difficult situation, you'll be in a stronger position to act with integrity. Consider your strengths and what feels most comfortable for you. Are you most effective in a group or one on one? Orally or in writing? If you have a strong sense of what's most comfortable for you, then when you experience a values conflict, you can try to frame it in such a way as to play to your strengths. Remember, too, that if you feel that you're just one lowly person and that no one will listen to your ethical concerns, it might be worth talking to the people around you to see whether they feel the same way—perhaps others would be willing to stand with you and argue for doing the right thing!

MODULE 16 Behaving Ethically—Learning Outcomes Revisited

16.1 Outline four strategies that you can use to create conditions that will help you behave in ways that align with your values

Challenges to your ability to behave ethically can be managed by recognizing the potential for everyday ethical challenges, considering the conditions that will help or hinder ethical behavior in the face of those challenges, creating a plan for managing ethical challenges that are likely to occur, and working to counteract the tendency of others to behave in unethical ways. We hope that after reading this section, you'll be better able to think about how you can use these strategies to help when you need to manage the everyday threats to your values!

Reflective Practice

Content Check

1. Psychologists interested in moral behavior initially focused on ideas about power and loyalty. T or F?
2. "Enablers" are conditions that help you to behave in ways that are in keeping with your values. T or F?
3. Planning in advance what you would do in an ethically challenging situation will help you to be true to your values. T or F?

Skill Check

Think Critically

4. Many of the issues confronting the country—abortion, same-sex marriage, stem cell research, and physician-assisted suicide—are often considered to be a matter of ethics, and this is why people are so passionate about them. Which of the five ideas that shape our values is most likely to be associated with our views on these issues?

Self-Reflect

Which of the five ideas that shape our values—harm, fairness, loyalty, power, and purity—is the most important in guiding your own set of core beliefs?

ANSWERS

1. F 2. T 3. T 4. Each of these issues is most closely associated with purity/sanctity.

MODULE 17

Sensation and Perception
Sensory Processes

Snake!

One of your authors was hiking in a beautiful rainforest when he had the uncanny sensation he was being watched. For several minutes, he searched fruitlessly, taking in the lush scene. There! Hanging not more than a foot from his own head was the head of a snake, staring straight at him. The snake was perfectly camouflaged, hanging motionless from an overhanging branch, looking like another green vine (this species isn't called a green vine snake for nothing).

As this story shows, sensing the world is just a first step in perceiving the world. Even though his eyes picked up the basic visual information he needed to perceive the snake, his brain couldn't put the perceptual puzzle together. Sensory information can be interpreted (and misinterpreted) in various ways, which is step two in experiencing the world. This module addresses the first step, sensation. We explore the second step, perception, in Module 20.

Kevin Schafer/Minden Pictures/Superstock

~LEARNING OUTCOMES~

After reading this module you should be able to:

17.1 Describe the relationship between sensation and perception, outline what happens in the sensory organs during transduction, and distinguish between absolute threshold and difference threshold

17.2 Identify some of the ways by which the senses reduce the amount of information sent to the brain as well as some of the factors that will influence whether we will pay attention to a stimulus

Sensory Systems—The First Step

Learning Outcome 17.1 Describe the relationship between sensation and perception, outline what happens in the sensory organs during transduction, and distinguish between absolute threshold and difference threshold

Right now, you are bathed in a swirling kaleidoscope of electromagnetic radiation, heat, pressure, vibrations, molecules, and mechanical forces. If some of this physical energy (say in the form of light, heat, or sound) strikes your senses, an instant later, you may notice a bumblebee whiz past, the warmth of the sun on your face, or a catchy new tune on the radio. In that instant, a remarkable series of events transpires as you detect, encode, and interpret sensory information. However, unless your senses translate these physical energies into a form that your brain can understand, you will experience only a void of silence and darkness. Before we examine specific senses in more detail, let's explore how the senses and selective attention together reduce the amount of information the brain must process.

The primary function of the senses is to act as biological **transducers**, devices that convert one kind of energy into

Transducers Devices that convert one kind of energy into another.

another (Fain, 2003; Goldstein & Brockmole, 2017). Through the process of **sensation**, each sense converts a specific type of physical energy from the environment into a pattern of response by the nervous system. Information arriving at the brain from the sense organs creates *sensory impressions.*

When the brain selects, organizes, and interprets sensory impressions into meaningful patterns, we speak of **perception**. Some brain areas receive visual information; others receive auditory information, and still others receive taste or touch information (see Module 9). Knowing which brain areas are active tells us, in general, what kinds of sensations that you are feeling. This knowledge is beginning to make it possible to artificially restore sight, hearing, or other senses.

In one approach, researchers used a miniature television camera to send electrical signals directly to the brain, bypassing damaged eyes and optic nerves (➤ **Figure 17.1**) (Dobelle, 2000; Warren & Normann, 2005). Using technologies such as these, people who have lost their vision are now able to "see" letters, words, and some common objects such as knives and forks (Nirenberg & Pandarinath, 2012).

It is fascinating to realize that "seeing" and "hearing" take place in your brain, not in your eyes or ears. It is also fascinating to realize that much, if not all, of this two-step sensation-perception process is unconscious; that is, we are usually aware only of the result, the *percept.* Think back to Module 2, where we learned that subjective introspection cannot help us understand much of our behavior. Pay close attention to your experience as you look away from this book, casting your gaze somewhere else in the room. Seemingly in an instant, your eyes come to rest upon some other aspect of your room: a lamp, a photo of a friend, a dirty sock, or a pile of homework (yikes!). But *how* did you do that? Your introspection almost certainly offers no trace of how your eyes did the sensing, how the messages were streamed back to your brain, or how your brain constructed your percept.

Fortunately, objective scientific methods, such as those used by *psychophysicists,* enable us to better understand the *how* of both sensation and perception.

Psychophysics

In the field of **psychophysics**, the physical properties of stimuli (such as sound waves or electromagnetic radiation)

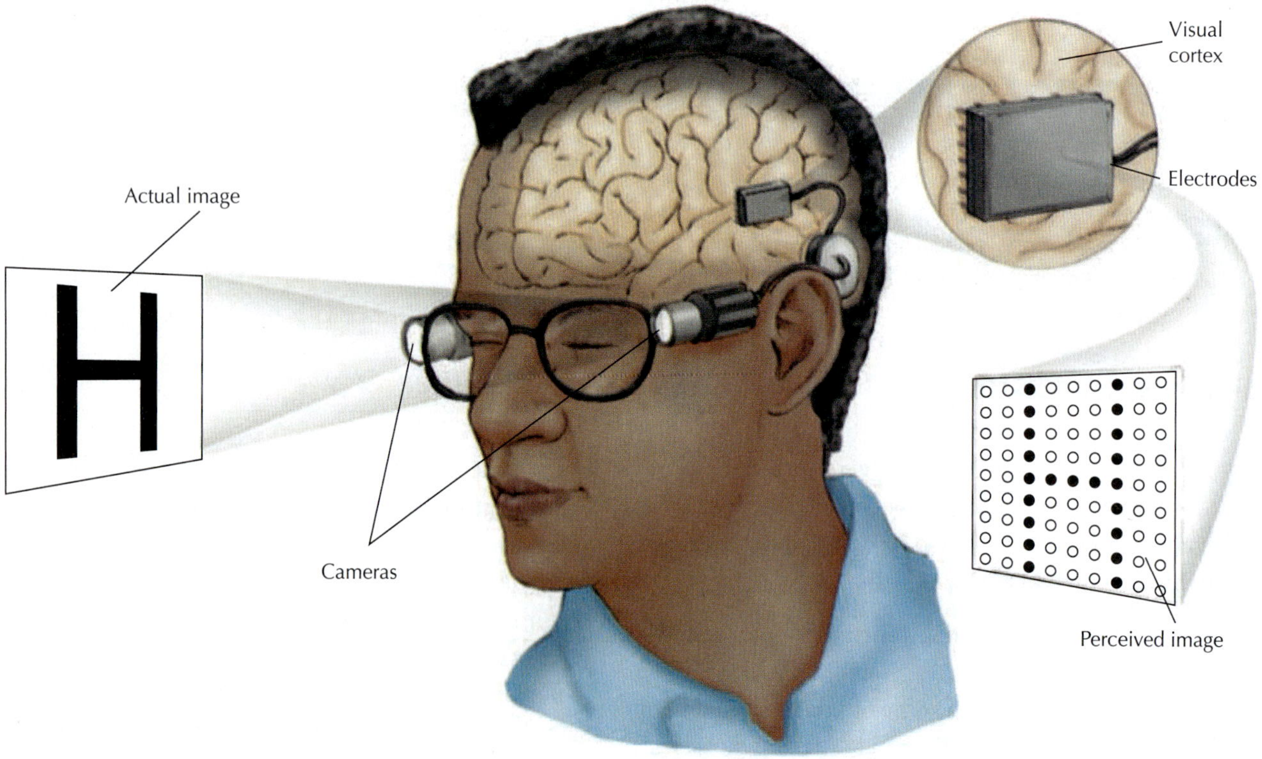

➤ **Figure 17.1**

An artificial visual system. Video cameras translate light into electrical impulses that directly stimulate the visual cortex, resulting in rudimentary visual experiences. What do you suppose this person would experience if the electrical impulses were sent to the auditory cortex instead?

Brian J. Skerry/National Geographic Image Collection

Absolute thresholds define the sensory worlds of humans and animals, sometimes with serious consequences. The endangered Florida manatee (sea cow) is a peaceful, plant-eating creature that can live for more than 60 years. Every year, many manatees are injured or even killed by boats. The problem? Manatees have poor sensitivity to the low-frequency sounds made by slow-moving boats. Current laws require boats to slow down in manatee habitats, which may actually increase the risk to these gentle creatures (Gerstein, 2002).

are measured and related to the resulting sensations that our brain constructs (such as loudness or brightness) (Lu & Dosher, 2014).

It was psychophysicists who scientifically demonstrated that energy above a certain minimum intensity is necessary for a sensation impression to arise. The **absolute threshold** for any sensory input is formally defined as the minimum amount of physical energy that can be detected 50 percent of the time. For example, very soft sounds (which could be heard if they were just a little louder) fall below the absolute threshold for human hearing. Of course, owls that hunt at night have much lower absolute thresholds for hearing.

Similarly, not every difference between two stimuli is experienced; instead, the difference must be sufficiently large. A psychophysicist studying **difference thresholds** will ask, "How different must two stimuli be before the difference becomes noticeable 50 percent of the time?" For example, if you were to put one extra grain of sugar in your coffee, would you notice a difference? How much would it take? A few grains? A half-spoonful? A spoonful?

Sensory Transduction and Selection Sensory transduction usually involves some *selection*. Consider, for example, vision, which gives us an amazingly wide window on the world. In one instant, you can view a star light-years away; in the next, you can peer into the microscopic universe of a dewdrop. Yet psychophysical research has found that vision also narrows what we can possibly observe. Like the other senses, vision acts as a *data selection system*. It selects information in order to code and send to the brain only the most important sensory information for further processing (Goldstein & Brockmole, 2017).

How does sensory data selection take place? Considerable selection occurs because sensory receptors do not transduce all the energies that they encounter. For example, a guitar transduces string vibrations into sound waves. Pluck a string, and the guitar produces a sound. However, stimuli that don't cause the string to move have no effect. If you shine a light on the string, or pour cold water on it, the guitar remains silent. (The owner of the guitar, however, might become quite loud at this point!) In a similar way, the eye transduces electromagnetic radiation, the ear transduces sound waves, and so on. Many other types of stimuli cannot be sensed directly because we lack sensory receptors to transduce their energy. For example, humans cannot sense the bioelectric fields of living creatures, but many fish have special organs that can (Caputi et al., 2013). (Do they *hear* the fields, *feel* them, or what?)

Further selection occurs because sense receptors transduce only part of their target energy range (Fain, 2003). For example, your eyes transduce only a tiny fraction of the entire range of electromagnetic energies—the part that we call the *visible spectrum*. The eyes of honeybees can transduce, and therefore see, parts of the electromagnetic spectrum invisible to us humans. Likewise, bats *shout* at a pitch too high for humans to transduce. But bats can hear their own reflected echoes. This ability, called *echolocation*, allows bats to fly in total darkness, avoid collisions, and catch insects. As you can see, our rich sensory experiences are only a small part of what *could* be sensed and what some animals *can* sense.

Doesn't extrasensory perception allow us to override the limits of our five senses? More than a third of the general public believes in the existence of *extrasensory perception*

Sensation Conversion of energy from the environment into a pattern of response by the nervous system; also, a sensory impression.

Perception Selection, organization, and interpretation of sensory input.

Psychophysics Study of how the mind interprets the physical properties of stimuli.

Absolute threshold Minimum amount of physical energy that can be detected 50 percent of the time.

Difference threshold Minimum difference in physical energy between two stimuli that can be detected 50 percent of the time.

(*ESP*), the purported ability to perceive events in ways that cannot be explained by known sensory capacities (Gray & Gallo, 2016). However, even after over 130 years of research into ESP, few psychologists share this belief (Shermer, 2011). A close look at ESP experiments often reveals serious problems of evidence, procedure, and scientific rigor (Alcock, 2010; Alcock, Burns, & Freeman, 2003; Hyman, 2007). In fact, professional magician and skeptic James Randi once offered to award a $1 million prize to anyone who could demonstrate evidence of extrasensory perception under standardized conditions. No one was able to claim the prize.

What would it take to scientifically demonstrate the existence of ESP? Quite simply, it would take a set of instructions that would allow any competent, unbiased observer to produce evidence of ESP under standardized conditions to rule out any possibility of fraud or chance (Schick & Vaughn, 2014).

Sensory Adaptation and Selection The flow of sensations to the brain is reduced in another way. Think about walking into a house in which fried liver, sauerkraut, and headcheese were just prepared for dinner. (Some dinner!) Although you might pass out at the door, people who had been in the house for some time likely wouldn't be aware of the food odors. Why? Because sensory receptors respond less over time to unchanging stimuli, a process called **sensory adaptation**.

Fortunately, the olfactory (smell) receptors adapt quickly. When exposed to a constant odor, they send fewer and fewer nerve impulses to the brain until the odor is no longer noticed. Adaptation to pressure from a wristwatch, waistband, ring, or glasses is based on the same principle. Because there is usually little reason to keep reminding the brain that a sensory input is unchanged, sensory receptors generally respond best to *changes* in stimulation. No one wants or needs to be reminded 16 hours a day that his or her shoes are on.

Feature Detection and Selection As the senses collect information, *feature detectors* in the brain also reduce the flow of sensory input by dividing the world into important **perceptual features**, or basic stimulus patterns. A **feature detector** is a cell, or collection of cells, in the cerebral cortex that responds to a specific attribute of an object. As a consequence, the brain need only further process the perceptual feature rather than the underlying sensory pattern.

The visual system, for example, has a set of feature detectors that are attuned to specific stimuli, such as lines, shapes, edges, spots, colors, and other patterns (Hubel & Wiesel, 2005). Look at ➤ **Figure 17.2** and notice how eye-catching the single vertical line is among a group of slanted lines. This effect, which is called *visual pop-out*, occurs because your visual system is highly sensitive to these perceptual features (Hsieh, Colas, & Kanwisher, 2011).

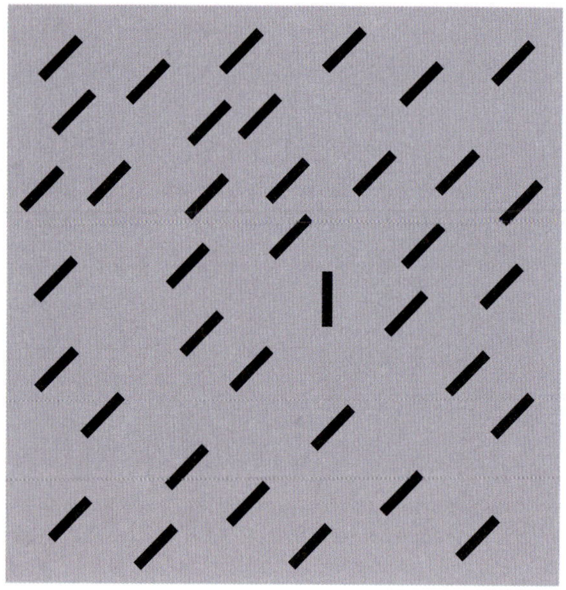

➤ **Figure 17.2**

Visual pop-out. This pop-out is so basic that babies as young as three months respond to it. (Adapted from Adler & Orprecio, 2006.)

Similarly, frog eyes are highly sensitive to small, dark, moving spots. In other words, they are "tuned" to detect bugs flying nearby (Lettvin, 1961). But the insect (spot) must be moving, or the frog's "bug detectors" won't work. A frog could starve to death surrounded by dead flies.

Although our sensitivity to perceptual features is an innate characteristic of the nervous system, it also is influenced by experiences early in life. For instance, Colin Blakemore and Graham Cooper of Cambridge University raised kittens in a room with only vertical stripes on the walls. Another set of kittens was raised seeing only horizontal stripes. When returned to normal environments, the "horizontal" cats could easily jump onto a chair, but when walking on the floor, they bumped into chair legs. "Vertical" cats, on the other hand, easily avoided chair legs, but they missed when they tried to jump to horizontal surfaces. The cats raised with vertical stripes were "blind" to horizontal lines, and the "horizontal" cats acted as if vertical lines were invisible (Blakemore & Cooper, 1970). Other experiments show an actual decrease in brain cells that are tuned to the missing features (Grobstein & Chow, 1975).

How much control do people have over sensory data selection? Is it anything like focusing attention on studying and deliberately ignoring other stuff going on around you? Good question. We have little conscious control over what energy ranges our senses can transduce or how the brain encodes perceptual features. Likewise, it is quite difficult to consciously control sensory adaptation. *Selective attention* is a different capability, one that you *can* control. Pay attention now.

Selective Attention—Tuning In and Tuning Out

Although the senses reduce a flood of sights, sounds, odors, tastes, and touch sensations to more manageable levels, the result is still too much for the brain to handle. That's why the brain further filters sensory information through *selective attention*. For example, as you sit reading this page, receptors for touch and pressure in the seat of your pants are sending nerve impulses to your brain. Although these sensations have been present all along, you were probably not aware of them until just now. This "seat-of-the-pants phenomenon" is an example of **selective attention**—voluntarily focusing on a specific sensory input. Selective attention appears to be based on the ability of brain structures to select and divert incoming sensory messages (Isbell et al., 2016). We are able to "tune in" on a single sensory message while excluding others.

Another familiar example of this is the "cocktail party effect." When you are in a group of people, surrounded by voices, you can still select and attend to the voice of the person that you are facing. Or if that person gets dull, you can eavesdrop on conversations all over the room. (Be sure to smile and nod your head occasionally!) However, no matter how interesting your companion may be, your attention will probably shift if you hear your own name spoken somewhere in the room (Koch et al., 2011). We do find what others say about us to be very interesting, don't we?

At times, we can even suffer from **inattentional blindness**, a failure to notice a stimulus because attention is focused elsewhere (Thakral, 2011). Not seeing something that is plainly before your eyes most likely occurs when your attention is narrowly focused (Bressan & Pizzighello, 2008). Inattentional blindness is vividly illustrated by a classic study in which participants were shown a film of two basketball teams, one wearing black shirts and the other wearing white. Observers were asked to watch the film closely and count how many times a basketball passed between members of one of the teams, while ignoring the other team. As observers watched and counted, a person wearing a gorilla suit walked into the middle of the basketball game, faced the camera, thumped his chest, and walked out of view. Half the observers failed to notice this rather striking event (Simons & Chabris, 1999). This effect probably explains why fans of opposing sports teams often act as if they had seen two completely different games.

In a similar way, using a cellphone while driving can cause inattentional blindness. Instead of ignoring a gorilla, you might miss seeing another car, a motorcyclist, or a pedestrian while your attention is focused on the phone. It probably goes without saying, but the more engaged you are with your cellphone while driving (like texting instead of having a conversation), the greater the problem (Murphy & Greene, 2016).

You might find it helpful to think of selective attention as a *bottleneck*, or a narrowing in the information channel that links the senses to perception. When one message enters the bottleneck, it seems to prevent others from passing through (➤ Figure 17.3). Imagine, for instance, that you are driving a car and approaching an intersection. You need to be sure that the traffic light is still green. Just as you are about

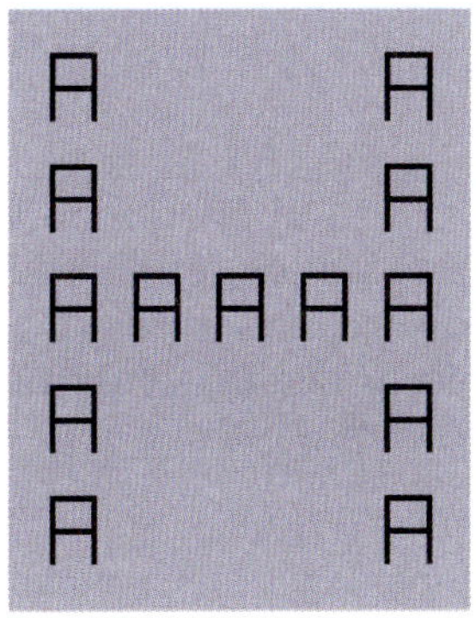

➤ **Figure 17.3**

Focusing attention. The attentional "bottleneck," or "spotlight," can be widened or narrowed. If you focus on local details in this drawing, you will see the letter *A* repeated 13 times. If you broaden your field of attention to encompass the overall pattern, you see the letter *H*.

Sensory adaptation A decrease over time in sensory response to an unchanging stimulus.

Perceptual features Basic attributes of a stimulus, such as lines, shapes, edges, or colors.

Feature detector Cells in the cortex that respond to a specific attribute of an object.

Selective attention Giving priority to a particular incoming sensory message.

Inattentional blindness A failure to notice a stimulus because attention is focused elsewhere.

to check, your passenger points to a friend at the side of the road. If you then don't notice that the light just changed to red, an accident may be seconds away.

Are some stimuli more attention-getting than others? Yes. Very *intense* stimuli usually command attention. Stimuli that are brighter, louder, or larger tend to capture attention: A gunshot would be hard to ignore. If a brightly colored hot-air balloon ever lands at your college campus, it almost certainly will draw a crowd.

Multitasking *But I'm a good multitasker. What's up with that?* Whenever we try to pay attention to more than one thing at a time, such as texting while driving, we are engaging in a *divided attention* task. While it may seem as if we are good multitaskers, the research evidence we have just reviewed indicates that we can rarely divide our attention without suffering any overall decline in performance (Koch et al., 2018).

A notable exception occurs when tasks are very well practiced, like folding laundry and eating apples. Well-practiced tasks like these can become highly *automated*, and require substantially less attention to complete (Willingham & Reiner, 2019). Automated tasks can often be successfully carried out alongside other, more attention-demanding tasks with some success, making it *seem* like you're multitasking. More than likely, though, when we think we're dividing attention to complete multiple things at once, we likely aren't. Instead, what we're doing is *task-switching*—moving our attention rapidly between each of the things that we're working on. Unfortunately, we also cannot task-switch well among tasks that demand significant attentional resources (Alzahabi, Becker, & Hambrick, 2017).

But how do the individual senses actually function? We explore that topic shortly, but first, here's a chance to pay some attention to what you've learned.

MODULE 17 Sensory Processes—Learning Outcomes Revisited

17.1 Describe the relationship between sensation and perception, outline what happens in the sensory organs during transduction, and distinguish between absolute thresholds and difference thresholds

Sensation is the process by which sensory organs take in information from the environment, while perception is the process by which the brain interprets that information. Transduction is the process by which one form of energy is converted into another. The sense organs (eyes, ears, skin, tongue) transduce various forms of energy found in the environment (electromagnetic energy from light; mechanical energy from sound) into electrical energy in the form of action potentials so that the brain can understand the information taken in by the senses. Absolute threshold refers to the minimum amount of sensory input that must be present for physical energy (light; sound) to be detected 50 percent of the time. In contrast, difference threshold refers to the minimum difference that must exist between two stimuli for that difference to be detected 50 percent of the time.

17.2 Identify some of the ways by which the senses reduce the amount of information sent to the brain as well as some of the factors that influence whether we will pay attention to a stimulus

The senses act as selective data selection systems to prevent the brain from being overwhelmed by sensory input. Some of the ways by which this happens are: a lack of specific transducers, the restricted range of transducers, sensory adaptation, and feature detection. We are most likely to attend to stimuli that are intense, that are unexpected, and that are repetitious.

Reflective Practice

Content Check

1. Sensory receptors are biological ____________, or devices for converting one type of energy to another.
2. As time passes, nerve endings in the skin under your clothes send fewer signals to the brain, and you become unable to feel your clothes. This process is called
   a. transduction
   b. difference threshold
   c. reverse attention
   d. sensory adaptation

3. Brain cells that divide the world into important features are known as feature
   a. transducers
   b. detectors
   c. pop-outs
   d. adapters
4. The conscious ability to influence what sensations we will receive is called
   a. sensory adaptation
   b. psychophysics
   c. selective attention
   d. sensory biasing
5. Which of the following stimuli are more effective at getting attention?
   a. unexpected stimuli
   b. repetitious stimuli
   c. intense stimuli
   d. all of the above

Skill Check

Think Critically

6. William James once said, "If a master surgeon were to cross the auditory and optic nerves, we would hear lightning and see thunder." Can you explain what James meant?

Self-Reflect

What if, like some other animals, you could transduce other energies? How would the sensory world in which you live change? What would it be like to be a bat? A shark? As you sit reading this book, which sensory inputs have undergone adaptation? What new inputs can you become aware of by shifting your focus of attention? Can you pay attention to more than one sensory input at once?

ANSWERS

1. transducers 2. d 3. b 4. c 5. d 6. The explanation is based on sensory localization: If a lightning flash caused rerouted messages from the eyes to activate auditory areas of the brain, we would experience a sound sensation. Likewise, if the ears transduced a thunderclap and sent impulses to the visual area, a sensation of light would occur. It is amazing that some people, called *synesthetes*, naturally experience sensory inputs in terms of other senses. For example, one synesthete experiences the number 37 as lumpy porridge, whereas for another, the taste of beef is blue (Zaraska, 2016).

MODULE 18

Sensation and Perception
Vision

The Most Important Sense?

Most people agree that vision is their most important sense. And why not? When you first open your eyes in the morning, you effortlessly become aware of the visual richness of the world around you. That visual richness obscures the fact that your eyes transduce only the tiniest fraction of the entire range of electromagnetic energies—the visible spectrum. You cannot "see" the vast majority of the electromagnetic spectrum, such as microwaves, cosmic rays, X-rays, or radio waves.

Similarly, the effortlessness with which normally sighted people can *see* obscures incredible complexity. How does sensory transduction in vision actually occur? What does it mean to need glasses? How can we see in the dark? How can we see in color? Many questions have been answered, yet many remain. Regardless, vision is an impressive sensory system, worthy of a detailed discussion.

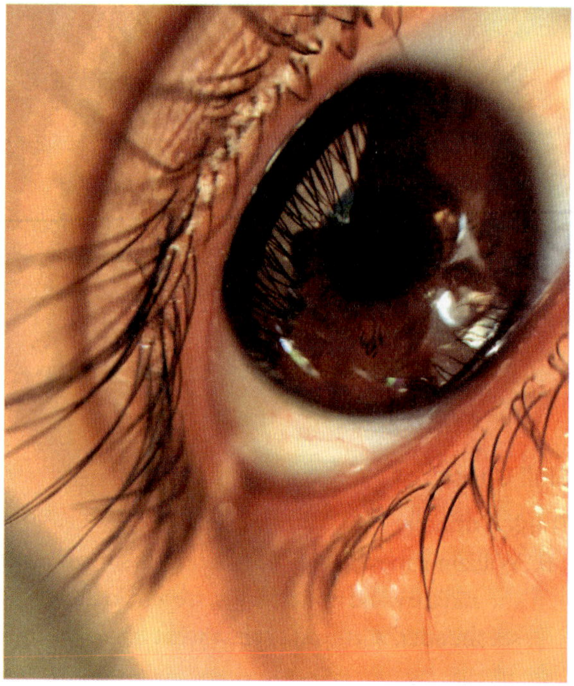

Irina Neftenova/Shutterstock.com

~LEARNING OUTCOMES~

After reading this module you should be able to:

18.1 Describe three characteristics of light that are processed by the eye, outline what is meant by accommodation in the eye, and the conditions that result from problems with accommodation, describe the two types of photoreceptors that are necessary for the process of transduction in the eye, and contrast the trichromatic and opponent-process theories of color vision

Vision—Catching Some Rays

Learning Outcome 18.1 Describe three characteristics of light that are processed by the eye, outline what is meant by accommodation in the eye, and the conditions that result from problems with accommodation, describe the two types of photoreceptors that are necessary for the process of transduction in the eye, and contrast the trichromatic and opponent-process theories of color vision

What are the basic dimensions of light and vision? The *visible spectrum*—the sliver of electromagnetic energies to which the eyes respond—is made up of a narrow range of wavelengths of electromagnetic radiation. Visible light starts at "short" wavelengths of 400 *nanometers* (nan-OM-et-ers), equal to one-billionth of a meter, which we sense as purple or violet. Successively longer light waves produce blue, green, yellow, orange, and red, which has a wavelength of 700 nanometers (➤ **Figure 18.1**).

The term **hue** refers to the various colors of light: red, orange, yellow, green, blue, indigo, and violet. As just noted,

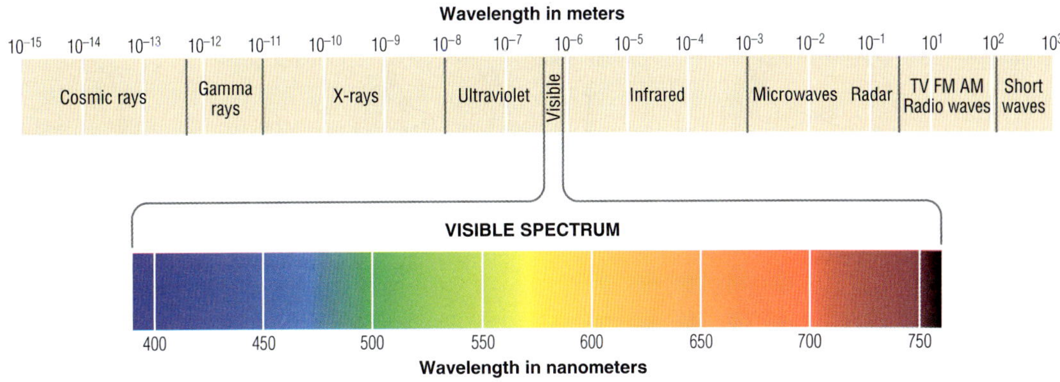

Figure 18.1
The visible spectrum.

various hues, or color sensations, correspond to the wavelength of the light that reaches our eyes (Goldstein & Brockmole, 2017). White light, in contrast, is a mixture of many wavelengths. Hues (colors) from a narrow band of wavelengths are very *saturated*, or pure. (An intense, fire-engine red is more saturated than a muddy, brick red.) A third dimension of vision, *brightness*, corresponds roughly to the amplitude, or height, of light waves. Waves of greater amplitude are taller, carry more energy, and cause the colors that we see to appear brighter or more intense. For example, the same brick red would look bright in intense, high-energy illumination and drab in dim light.

Structure of the Eye

Although the visual system is much more complex than any digital camera, both cameras and eyes have a lens to focus light rays on a light-sensitive surface at the back of an enclosed space. In a camera, it is a layer of light-sensitive pixels in the digital image sensor. In the eye, it is a layer of *photoreceptors* (light-sensitive cells) in the **retina**, which is an area about the size and thickness of a postage stamp (**Figure 18.2**).

How does the eye focus? Most focusing is done at the front of the eye by the **cornea**, a curved, transparent, protective layer that bends light inward. The **lens**, the clear structure behind the pupil that bends light toward the retina, makes additional, smaller adjustments. Your eye's focal point changes when muscles attached to the lens alter its shape. This process is called **accommodation**. In cameras, focusing is done more simply—by changing the distance between the lens and the image sensor.

Visual Problems Focusing also is affected by the shape of the eye. If your eye is too short, nearby objects will be blurred, but distant objects will be sharp. This is called **hyperopia** (HI-per-OPE-ee-ah), or farsightedness. If your eyeball is too long, images fall short of the retina and you won't be able to focus on distant objects. This results in **myopia** (my-OPE-ee-ah), or nearsightedness. When the cornea or the lens is misshapen, part of vision will be focused and part will be fuzzy. In this case, the eye has more than one focal point, a problem called **astigmatism** (ah-STIG-mah-tiz-em). All three visual defects

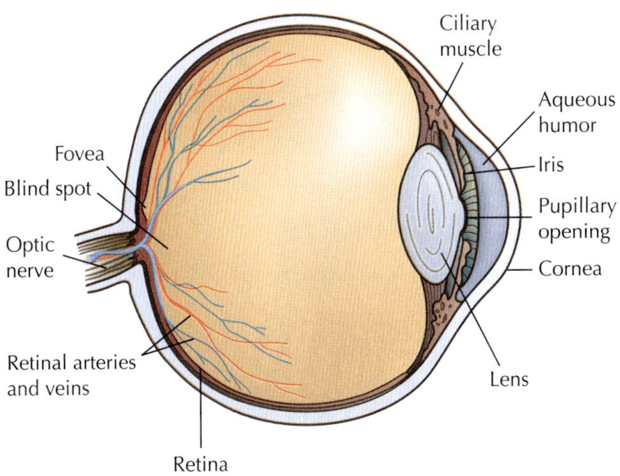

Figure 18.2
Anatomy of the eye.

Hue Color of light, as determined by its wavelength.

Retina Surface at the back of the eye onto which the lens focuses light rays.

Cornea Curved, transparent, protective layer through which light enters the eye.

Lens Clear structure behind the pupil that bends light toward the retina.

Accommodation Changes in the shape of the lens of the eye to enable the seeing of close and far objects.

Hyperopia Having difficulty focusing on nearby objects (farsightedness).

Myopia Having difficulty focusing on distant objects (nearsightedness).

Astigmatism Defects in the cornea, lens, or eye that cause some areas of vision to be out of focus.

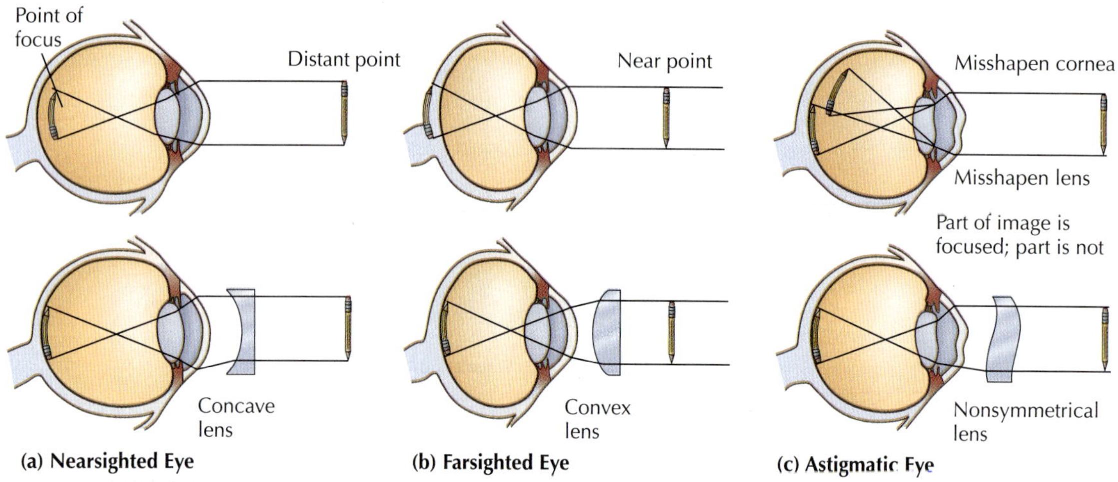

➤ **Figure 18.3**

Visual defects and corrective lenses. *(a)* A myopic (longer than usual) eye. The concave lens spreads light rays just enough to increase the eye's focal length. *(b)* A hyperopic (shorter than usual) eye. The convex lens increases refraction (bending) to focus light on the retina. *(c)* An astigmatic (lens or cornea that are not symmetrical) eye. In astigmatism, parts of vision are sharp and parts are unfocused. Lenses to correct astigmatism are nonsymmetrical.

can be corrected by placing glasses (or contact lenses) in front of the eye to change the path of light (➤ Figure 18.3).

As people age, the lens becomes less flexible and accommodating. The result is **presbyopia** (prez-bee-OPE-ee-ah), from the Latin for "old vision"—farsightedness due to aging. Perhaps you have seen a grandparent or older friend reading a newspaper at arm's length because of presbyopia. Eventually, many people need bifocals as they age. (Just like your authors. Sigh.) Bifocal lenses correct near vision *and* distance vision.

Rods and Cones

The eye has two types of photoreceptors, called *rods* and *cones* (Goldstein & Brockmole, 2017). The 5 million **cones** in each eye work best in bright light. They also produce color sensations and fine details. In contrast, the **rods**, numbering about 120 million, can't detect colors (➤ Figure 18.4). Pure rod vision is black and white. However, rods are much more sensitive to light than cones. Rods therefore allow us to see in very dim light.

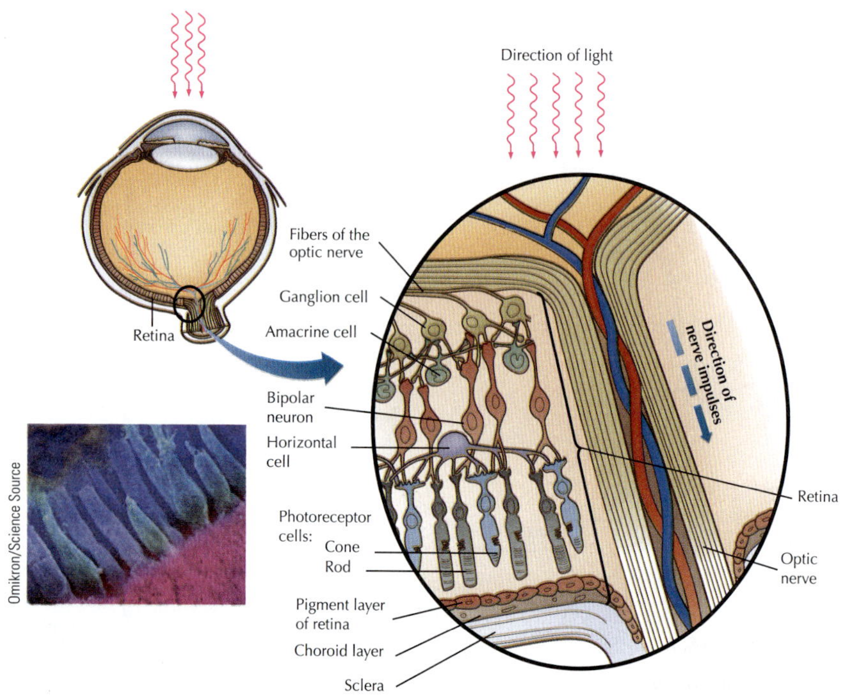

➤ **Figure 18.4**

Anatomy of the retina. Note that light does not fall directly on the rods and cones. It must first pass through the cornea, the lens, the vitreous humor (a jellylike substance that fills the eyeball), and the outer layers of the retina. Only about half of the light at the front of the eye reaches the rods and cones—testimony to the retina's amazing sensitivity. The lower-left photograph shows rods and cones as seen through an electron microscope. In the photograph, the cones are colored green and the rods blue.

➤ Figure 18.5

Experiencing the blind spot. *(a)* With your right eye closed, stare at the upper-right cross. Hold the book about 1 foot from your eye and slowly move it back and forth. You should be able to locate a position that causes the black spot to disappear. When it does, it has fallen on the blind spot. With a little practice, you can learn to make people or objects you dislike disappear too (use your new power wisely)! *(b)* Repeat the procedure described, but stare at the lower cross. When the white space falls on the blind spot, the black bar will appear to be continuous. This may help you understand why you do not usually experience a blind spot in your visual field.

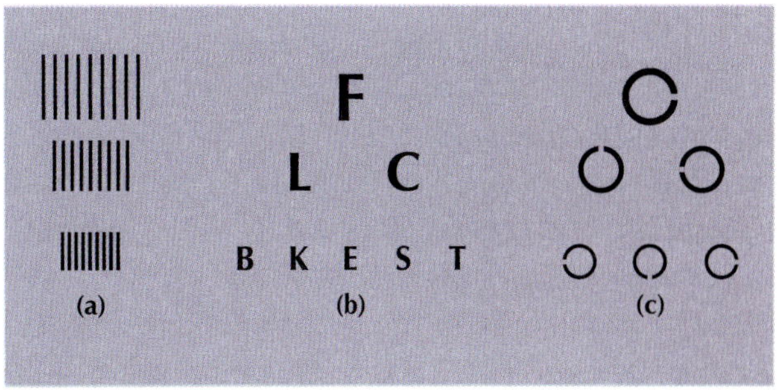

➤ Figure 18.6

Tests of visual acuity. Here are some common tests of visual acuity. In (*a*), sharpness is indicated by the smallest grating that still can be seen as individual lines. The Snellen chart (*b*) requires that you read rows of letters of diminishing size until you no longer can distinguish them. The Landolt rings (*c*) require no familiarity with letters. Simply note which side has a break in it.

It is hard to believe, but the retina has a "hole" in it: Each retina has a **blind spot** because there are no photoreceptors at the location where the **optic nerve** exits the eye to convey visual information to the brain, and blood vessels enter (Raman & Sarkar, 2016; ➤ Figure 18.5*a*). The blind spot shows that vision depends greatly on the brain. If you close one eye, some of the incoming light will fall on the blind spot of your open eye. Why isn't there a gap in your vision? The answer is that the visual cortex of the brain actively fills in the gap with patterns from surrounding areas (➤ Figure 18.5*b*). By closing one eye, you can visually "behead" other people by placing their images on your blind spot. (Just a hint for some classroom fun.) The brain can also "erase" distracting information. Roll your eyes all the way to the right and then close your right eye. You should clearly see your nose in your left eye's field of vision. Now, open your right eye again and your nose nearly disappears because your brain disregards its presence.

Visual Acuity The rods and cones also affect **visual acuity**, or sharpness (Pirson, Ie, & Langer, 2012). The cones lie mainly at the center of the eye. In fact, the **fovea** (FOE-vee-ah), a tiny spot in the center of the retina, contains only cones—about 50,000 of them. Like high-resolution digital sensors made of many small pixels, the tightly packed cones in the fovea produce the sharpest images. Normal acuity is designated as 20/20 vision: At a distance of 20 feet, you can distinguish what the average person can see at 20 feet (➤ Figure 18.6). If your vision is 20/40, you can see at 20 feet only what the average person can see at 40 feet. If your vision is 20/200, everything is a blur and you need glasses! Vision that is 20/12 means that you can see at 20 feet what the average person must be 8 feet nearer to see, indicating better than average acuity.

Peripheral Vision *What is the purpose of the rest of the retina?* Areas outside the fovea also get light, creating a large region of **peripheral (side) vision.** The rods are most numerous about 20 degrees from the center of the retina, so much of our peripheral vision is rod vision. Although rod vision is not very high resolution, the rods are quite sensitive to *movement* in peripheral vision (Yamamoto & Philbeck, 2013). To experience this characteristic of the rods, look straight ahead and hold your hand beside your head, at about 90 degrees. Wiggle your finger and slowly move your hand forward until you can detect motion. You will become aware of the movement before you can actually "see" your finger. Seeing "out of the corner of your eye" is important for sports, driving, and walking down dark alleys. People who suffer from *tunnel vision* (a loss of peripheral vision) feel as if they are wearing blinders (Godnig, 2003).

The rods also are highly responsive to dim light. Because most rods are 20 degrees to each side of the fovea, the best night vision comes from looking *next to* an object that you want to see. Test this yourself some night by looking at, and next to, a dim star.

Presbyopia Farsightedness caused by aging.

Cones Photoreceptors that are sensitive to color.

Rods Photoreceptors for dim light that produce only black and white sensations.

Blind spot Area in the retina where the optic nerve exits that contains no photoreceptor cells.

Optic nerve Structure that conveys visual information away from the retina to the brain.

Visual acuity The sharpness of visual perception.

Fovea Tiny spot in the center of the retina, containing only cones, where visual acuity is greatest.

Peripheral (side) vision Vision at the edges of the visual field.

Color Vision

How do the cones produce color sensations? The **trichromatic theory of color vision** (TRY-kro-MAT-ik) holds that there are three types of cones, each most sensitive to either red, green, or blue. Other colors result from combinations of these three.

A basic problem with the trichromatic theory is that four colors of light—red, green, blue, and yellow—seem to be primary (you can't get them by mixing other colors). Also, why is it impossible to have a reddish green or a yellowish blue? These problems led to the development of a second view, known as the **opponent-process theory of color vision**, which states that vision analyzes colors into "either-or" messages (Goldstein & Brockmole, 2017). That is, the visual system can produce messages for either red or green, yellow or blue, or black or white. Coding one color in a pair (red, for instance) seems to block the opposite message (green) from coming through. As a result, a reddish green is impossible, but a yellowish red (orange) can occur.

According to opponent-process theory, fatigue caused by making one response produces an afterimage of the opposite color as the system recovers. *Afterimages* are visual sensations that persist after a stimulus is removed—like seeing a spot after a flashbulb goes off. To see an afterimage of the type predicted by opponent-process theory, look at ➤ Figure 18.7 and follow the instructions there.

Which color theory is correct? Both! The three-color theory applies to the retina, in which three different types of cones have been found. Each contains a different type of *iodopsin* (i-oh-DOP-sin), a light-sensitive pigment that breaks down when struck by light. This triggers action potentials and sends neural messages to the brain. As predicted, each type of iodopsin is most sensitive to light in roughly the red, green, or blue region. Other colors result from combinations of these three. Thus, the three types of cones fire nerve impulses at different rates to produce various color sensations (➤ Figure 18.8).

➤ Figure 18.7

Negative afterimages. Stare at the dot near the middle of the flag for at least 30 seconds. Then look immediately at a plain sheet of white paper or a white wall. You will see the U.S. flag in its normal colors. Reduced sensitivity to yellow, green, and black in the visual system, caused by prolonged staring, results in the appearance of the complementary colors. Project the afterimage of the flag on other colored surfaces to get additional effects.

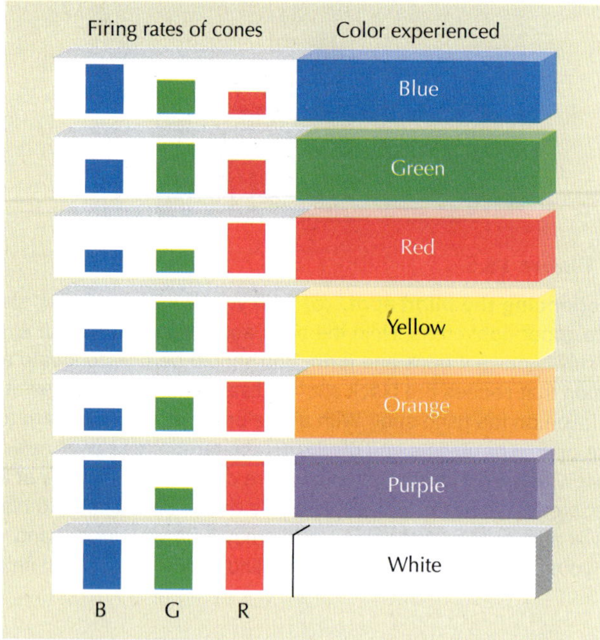

➤ Figure 18.8

Firing rates of blue, green, and red cones in response to different colors. The taller the colored bar, the higher the firing rates for that type of cone. As you can see, colors are coded by differences in the activity of all three types of cones in the normal eye. (Adapted from Goldstein & Brockmole, 2017.)

In contrast, the opponent-process theory better explains what happens further along in the retina, the optic pathways, and the brain *after* information leaves the cones (Sanes & Masland, 2015). For example, some nerve cells in the brain are excited by the color red and inhibited by the color green. So both theories are correct. One explains what happens in the cones. The other explains how color information is analyzed after messages leave the cones (Gegenfurtner & Kiper, 2003).

Color Blindness and Color Weakness A person with **color blindness** cannot perceive colors. It is as if the world were a black-and-white movie. The color-blind person either lacks cones or has cones that do not function normally (Neitz & Neitz, 2011). Such total color blindness is rare. In **color weakness,** or partial color blindness,

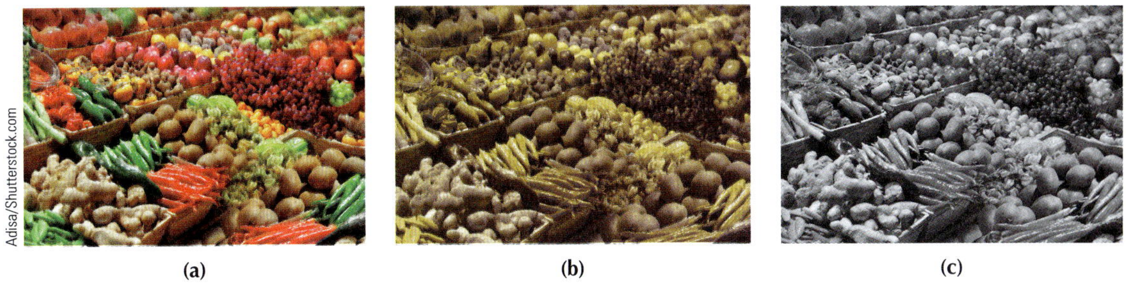

Figure 18.9

Color blindness and color weakness. *(a)* Photograph illustrates normal color vision. *(b)* Photograph is printed in blue and yellow and gives an impression of what a red–green color-blind person sees. *(c)* Photograph simulates total color blindness. If you are totally color-blind, all three photos will look nearly identical.

a person can't see certain colors (National Institutes of Health, 2020). Approximately 8 percent of Caucasian males (but fewer Asian, African, and Native-American males and fewer than 1 percent of women) are red–green color blind. These people see reds and greens as the same color, usually a yellowish brown (➤ Figure 18.9). Another type of color weakness, involving yellow and blue, is extremely rare.

It is surprising that some people reach adulthood without knowing that some colors are missing (Gündogan et al., 2005). If you can't see the number *5* or follow the dots from X to X in ➤ Figure 18.10, you might be red–green color blind.

How can color-blind individuals drive? Don't they have trouble with traffic lights? Red–green color-blind individuals have normal vision for yellow and blue, so the main problem is telling red lights from green. In practice, that's not difficult. The red light is always on top, and the green light is brighter than the red. Also, red traffic signals have yellow light mixed in with the red, and a green light is really blue-green.

Seeing in the Dark

What happens when the eyes adjust to a dark room? **Dark adaptation** is the dramatic increase in the eye's sensitivity to light that occurs after a person enters the dark (Goldstein & Brockmole, 2017). Consider walking into a movie theater. If you enter from a brightly lit lobby, you practically need to be led to your seat. Almost immediately, the **pupil**, the opening surrounded by the colored **iris**, begins to open to allow more light to enter the eye. After a short time, you can see the entire room in detail (including the couple kissing over in the corner). The retina, however, also becomes more sensitive, taking about 30 to 35 minutes of complete darkness to reach maximum visual sensitivity (➤ Figure 18.11). At that point, your eye will be 100,000 times more sensitive to light.

What causes dark adaptation? Like cones, which contain iodopsin, rods contain a light-sensitive visual pigment, *rhodopsin* (row-DOP-sin), which allows them to see in black and white. When struck by light, visual

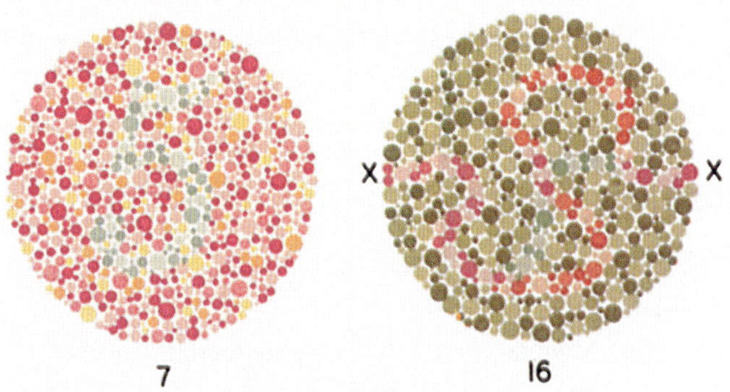

Figure 18.10

Testing for red–green color blindness. A replica of two images from the widely used Ishihara test for red–green color blindness.

Trichromatic theory of color vision A theory of color vision based on three cone types: red, green, and blue.

Opponent-process theory of color vision Proposition that color vision is based on coding things as red or green, yellow or blue, or black or white.

Color blindness A total inability to perceive color.

Color weakness An inability to distinguish some colors.

Dark adaptation Increased light sensitivity of the eye under low-light conditions.

Pupil The black opening inside the iris that allows light to enter the eye.

Iris Colored structure on the surface of the eye surrounding the pupil.

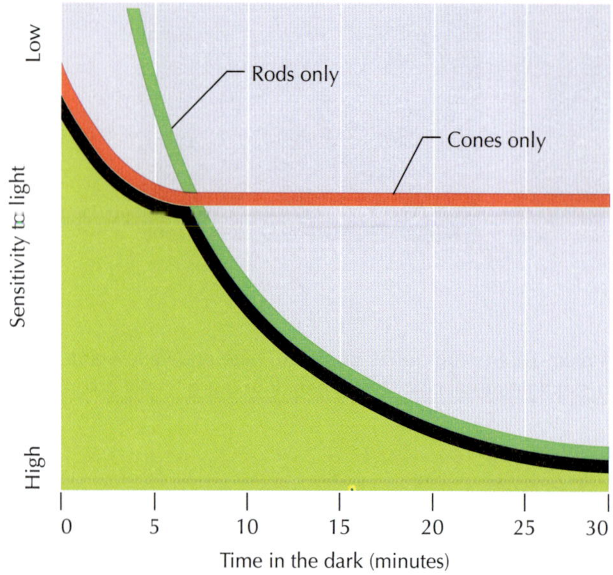

Figure 18.11

Typical time course of dark adaptation. The dark line shows how the threshold for vision lowers as a person spends time in the dark. (A lower threshold means that less light is needed for vision.) The green line shows that the cones adapt first, but they soon cease adding to light sensitivity. Rods, shown by the red line, adapt more slowly. However, they continue to add to improved night vision long after the cones are fully adapted.

pigments *bleach*, or break down chemically. The afterimages that you see after looking at the explosion of a flashbulb are a result of this bleaching. In fact, a few seconds of exposure to bright white light can completely wipe out dark adaptation. That's why you should avoid looking at oncoming headlights when you are driving at night—especially bluish-white xenon lights. To restore light sensitivity, the rhodopsin in the rods must recombine, which takes time.

The rods are *insensitive* to extremely red light. That's why submarines, airplane cockpits, and ready rooms for fighter pilots are illuminated with red light. In each case, people can move quickly from a light place into a dark one without having to adapt. Because the red light doesn't stimulate the rods, it is as if they had already spent time in the dark.

MODULE 18 Vision—Learning Outcomes Revisited

18.1 Describe three characteristics of light that are processed by the eye, outline what is meant by accommodation in the eye, and the conditions that result from problems with accommodation, describe the two types of photoreceptors that are necessary for the process of transduction in the eye, and contrast the trichromatic and opponent-process theories of color vision

The eye takes in information about hue (associated with the frequency or wavelength of the light wave), saturation (associated with the width of the band of wavelengths), and brightness (associated with the amplitude of the light wave). Accommodation refers to the eye's ability to focus, and is carried out by the lens. Four common visual defects are myopia, hyperopia, presbyopia, and astigmatism. The rods and cones are photoreceptors in the retina of the eye. The rods specialize in peripheral vision, night vision, seeing black and white, and detecting movement. The cones specialize in color vision, acuity, and daylight vision. Color vision is explained by the trichromatic theory within the retina itself, where three types of cones (red, blue, green) containing different pigments are responsible for generating action potentials. The opponent-process theory explains color vision beyond the retina, once the information about color is sent to the optic nerve.

Reflective Practice

Content Check

1. Match:

_____ Myopia	**A.** Farsightedness
_____ Hyperopia	**B.** Elongated eye
_____ Presbyopia	**C.** Misshapen cornea or lens
_____ Astigmatism	**D.** Farsightedness due to aging

2. In dim light, vision depends mainly on the _______________. In brighter light, color and fine detail are produced by the _______________.
3. The greatest visual acuity is associated with the _________ and the ________.
   a. periphery, rods
   b. periphery, cones
   c. fovea, cones
4. Colored afterimages are best explained by
   a. trichromatic theory
   b. the effects of astigmatism
   c. sensory localization
   d. opponent-process theory
5. Dark adaptation is directly related to an increase in
   a. rhodopsin
   b. astigmatism
   c. accommodation
   d. iodopsin

Skill Check

Think Critically

6. Sensory transduction in the eye takes place first in the cornea, then in the lens, and then in the retina. T or F?

Self-Reflect

Pretend that you are a beam of light. What will happen to you at each step as you pass into the eye and land on the retina? What will happen if the eye is not perfectly shaped? How will the retina know that you've arrived? How will it tell what color of light you are? What will it tell the brain about you?

ANSWERS

1. B, A, D, C 2. rods, cones 3. c 4. d 5. a 6. F. Although the cornea and lens prepare incoming light rays by bending them and focusing them on the retina, they do not change light to another form of energy. No change in the *type* of energy takes place until the retina converts light into nerve impulses.

MODULE 19

Sensation and Perception

The Nonvisual Senses

Even Pain?

We depend so much on vision that we sometimes neglect the other senses. But you need to wear earplugs for only a short time to appreciate how much we rely on hearing for communication, navigation, entertainment, and many other purposes. Similarly, skilled novelists always include descriptions of odors and tastes in their writings. Perhaps they intuitively realize that a scene is incomplete without smells and tastes. Like the other senses, the body senses also are an essential part of our sensory world. It would be very difficult to move, stay upright, or even stay alive without touch, balance, and other body senses. Even pain, which few people welcome, has its place in our lives. To appreciate pain, just imagine how much damage you might do to yourself if, for example, you could not feel any pain even though your foot was far too close to a burning campfire. Here's to the "other" senses.

Lolostock/Shutterstock.com

~LEARNING OUTCOMES~

After reading this module you should be able to:

19.1 Describe two characteristics of sound and how they are processed by the ear, contrast the frequency and place theory of hearing, and describe two forms of hearing loss

19.2 Name the two chemical senses and describe the processes of transduction in the nose and on the tongue

19.3 Name the somesthetic senses, describe the process of transduction on the skin, distinguish between the function of large and small nerve fibers in the sensation of pain, explain the gate control theory of pain, contrast the roles of the kinesthetic and vestibular systems and describe the process of transduction in the vestibular system

Hearing—Good Vibrations

Learning Outcome 19.1 Describe two characteristics of sound and how they are processed by the ear, contrast the frequency and place theory of hearing, and describe two forms of hearing loss

Rock, classical, jazz, blues, country, hip-hop—whatever your musical taste, you have undoubtedly been moved by the riches of sound. Hearing also collects information from all around the body, such as detecting the direction of approach of an unseen car (Johnstone, Nábělek, & Robertson, 2010). Vision, in all its glory, is limited to stimuli in front of the eyes.

What is the stimulus for hearing? If you throw a stone into a quiet pond, a circle of waves spreads in all directions. In much the same way, sound travels as a series of invisible waves of *compression* (peaks) and *rarefaction* (RARE-eh-fak-shun), or valleys, in the air. Any vibrating object—a tuning fork, the string of a musical instrument, or the vocal cords—will produce sound waves (rhythmic movement of air molecules). Other materials, such as fluids or solids, also can carry sound.

The *frequency* of sound waves (the number of waves per second) corresponds to the perceived **pitch** (higher or lower

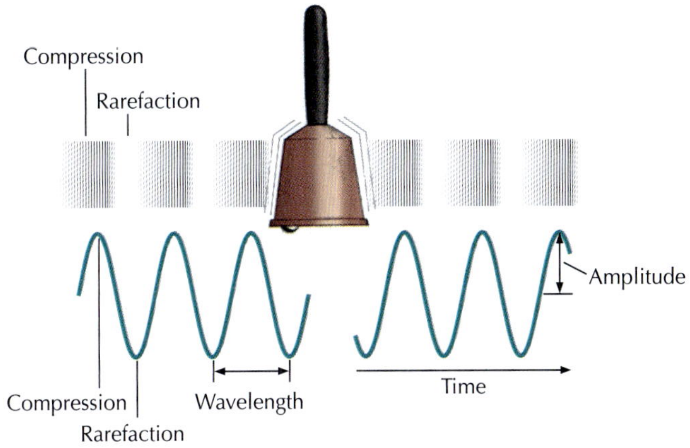

➤ **Figure 19.1**

Characteristics of sound waves. Waves of compression in the air, or vibrations, are the stimulus for hearing. The frequency (or wavelength) of sound waves determines their pitch. The amplitude determines loudness.

tone) of a sound. The *amplitude,* or physical "height," of a sound wave tells how much energy it contains. Psychologically, amplitude corresponds to sensed *loudness* or sound intensity (➤ Figure 19.1).

How We Hear Sounds

How are sounds converted to nerve impulses? Hearing involves a chain of events that begins with the *pinna* (PIN-ah), the visible, external part of the ear. In addition to being a good place to hang earrings or balance pencils, the pinna acts like a funnel to focus sounds. After they are guided into the ear canal, sound waves collide with the **eardrum** (*tympanic membrane*), setting it vibrating in response, thus transmitting them inward. This, in turn, causes three small middle ear *ossicles* (OSS-ih-kuls) or bones, the *malleus* (MAL-ee-us) or hammer, *incus* or anvil, and *stapes* (STAY-peas) or stirrup, to vibrate (➤ Figure 19.2). The ossicles link the eardrum with

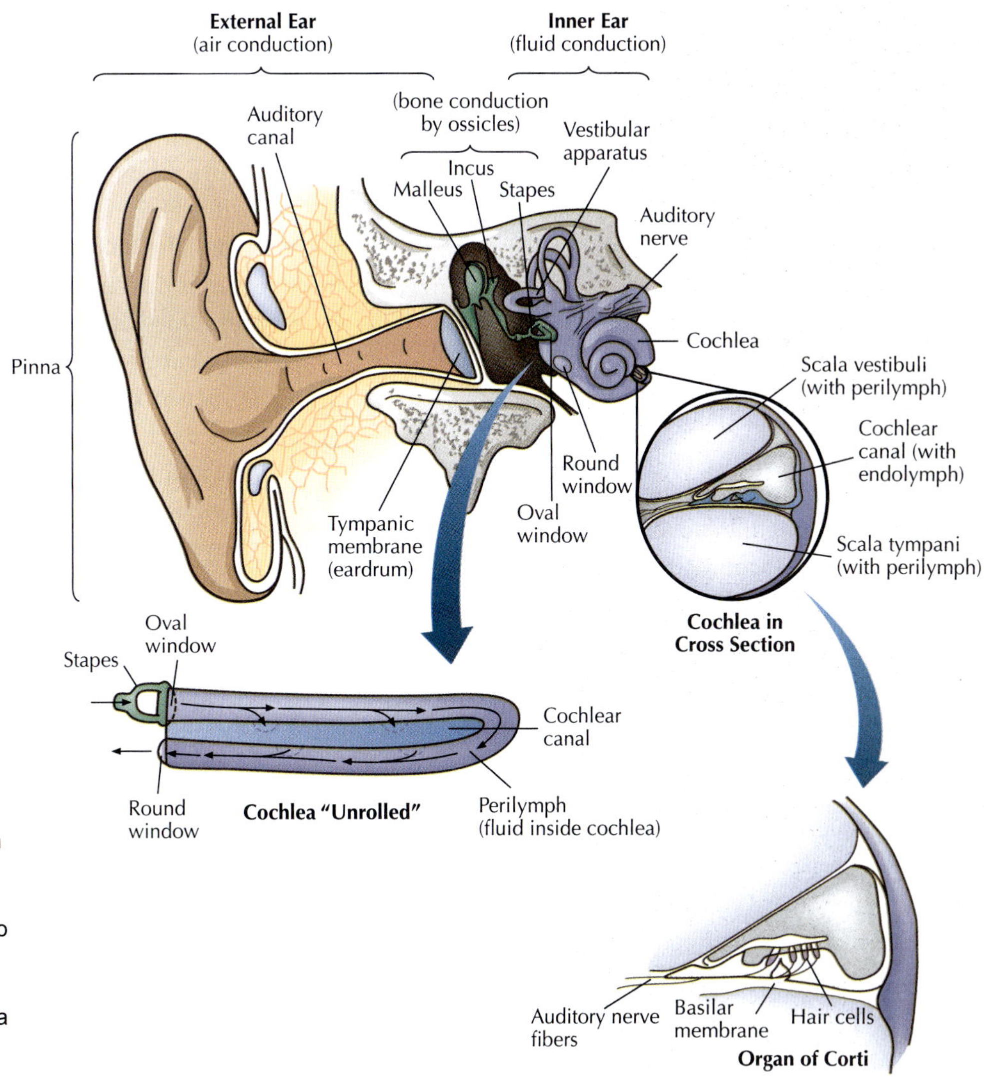

➤ **Figure 19.2**

Anatomy of the ear. The entire ear is a mechanism for transducing waves of air pressure into nerve impulses. The inset in the foreground ("Cochlea 'Unrolled'") shows that as the stapes moves the oval window, the round window bulges outward, allowing waves to ripple through fluid in the cochlea. The waves move membranes near the hair cells, causing cilia, or "bristles," on the tips of the cells to bend. The hair cells then generate nerve impulses that are carried to the brain. (See an enlarged cross section of cochlea in Figure 19.3.)

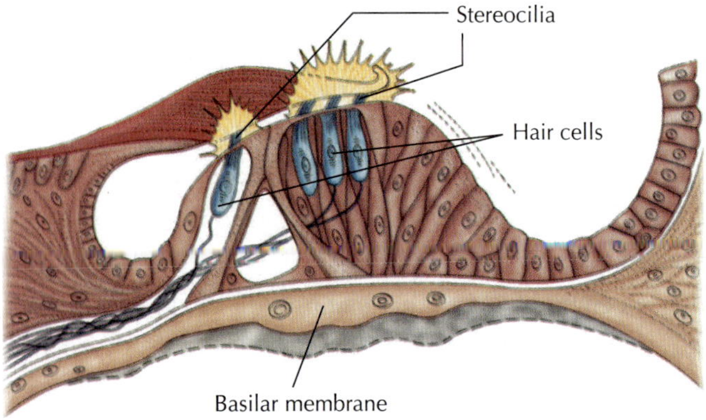

Figure 19.3

Functioning of hair cells. A closer view of the hair cells shows how movement of fluid in the cochlea causes the bristling "hairs," or cilia, to bend, generating a nerve impulse.

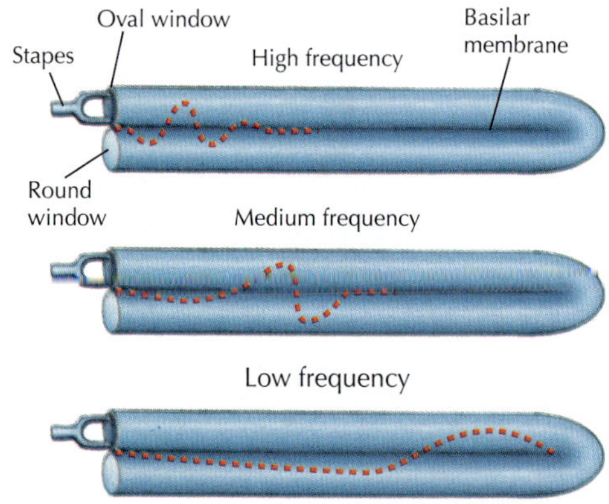

Figure 19.4

Simplified side view of the cochlea "unrolled." The basilar membrane is the elastic "roof" of the lower chamber of the cochlea. The organ of Corti, with its sensitive hair cells, rests atop the basilar membrane. The colored line shows where waves in the cochlear fluid cause the greatest deflection of the basilar membrane. (The amount of movement is exaggerated in the drawing.) Hair cells respond most in the area of greatest movement, which helps identify sound frequency.

the **cochlea** (KOCK-lee-ah), a snail-shaped organ that makes up the inner ear. The stapes is attached to a membrane on the cochlea called the *oval window*. As the oval window moves back and forth, it makes waves in a fluid inside the cochlea.

Inside the cochlea, the fluid waves trigger vibrations in the **basilar membrane**, the "floor" of the *organ of Corti* (KOR-tee). In turn, tiny **hair cells** embedded in the basilar membrane are pushed up against the *tectorial membrane*. As a consequence, a set of *stereocilia* (STER-ee-oh-SIL- ih-ah), or "bristles," atop each hair cell brush against the tectorial membrane whenever waves ripple through the fluid surrounding the organ of Corti. As the stereocilia are bent, nerve impulses are triggered, which then flow to the brain (**Figure 19.3**).

How are higher and lower sounds detected? The **frequency theory of hearing** states that as pitch rises, nerve impulses of a corresponding frequency are fed into the auditory nerve—that is, a 1,200-hertz tone produces 1,200 nerve impulses per second. (The term *hertz* refers to the number of vibrations per second.) This explains how sounds up to about 4,000 hertz reach the brain. But what about higher tones? The **place theory of hearing** states that higher and lower tones excite specific areas of the cochlea. High tones register most strongly at the base of the cochlea (near the oval window). Lower tones, on the other hand, mostly move hair cells near the narrow outer tip of the cochlea (**Figure 19.4**). Pitch is signaled by the area of the cochlea that is most strongly activated. Place theory also explains why hunters sometimes lose their hearing in a narrow pitch range. "Hunter's notch," as it is called, occurs when hair cells are damaged in the area affected by the pitch of gunfire.

Hearing Loss *Are there different types of hearing loss?* Hearing loss afflicts about 37.5 million Americans (National Institute on Deafness and Other Communication Disorders, 2016) and over 270 million people worldwide (World Health Organization, 2020). There are two common types of hearing loss. **Conductive hearing loss** occurs when the transfer of vibrations from the outer ear to the inner ear weakens. For example, the eardrums or ossicles may be damaged or immobilized by disease or injury. In many cases, conductive hearing loss can be overcome with a hearing aid, which makes sounds louder and clearer.

Sensorineural hearing loss results from damage to the inner ear hair cells or the auditory nerve. Many jobs, hobbies, and pastimes can cause **noise-induced hearing loss**, a common form of sensorineural hearing loss that occurs when very loud sounds damage fragile hair cells, as in hunter's notch (National Institute on Deafness and Other Communication Disorders, 2019).

If you work in a noisy environment or enjoy loud music, motorcycling, snowmobiling, hunting, or similar pursuits, you may be risking noise-induced hearing loss. Be forewarned: Dead hair cells are never replaced. When you abuse them, you lose them. By the time you are 65, more than 40 percent of them will be gone, mainly those that transduce high pitches (Lin et al., 2011). This explains why younger students sometimes download very high-pitched ringtones for their cellphones: If their teacher has an aging ear, the students can hear the ringtone, but their teacher cannot. (Your authors may have experienced this effect without knowing it!)

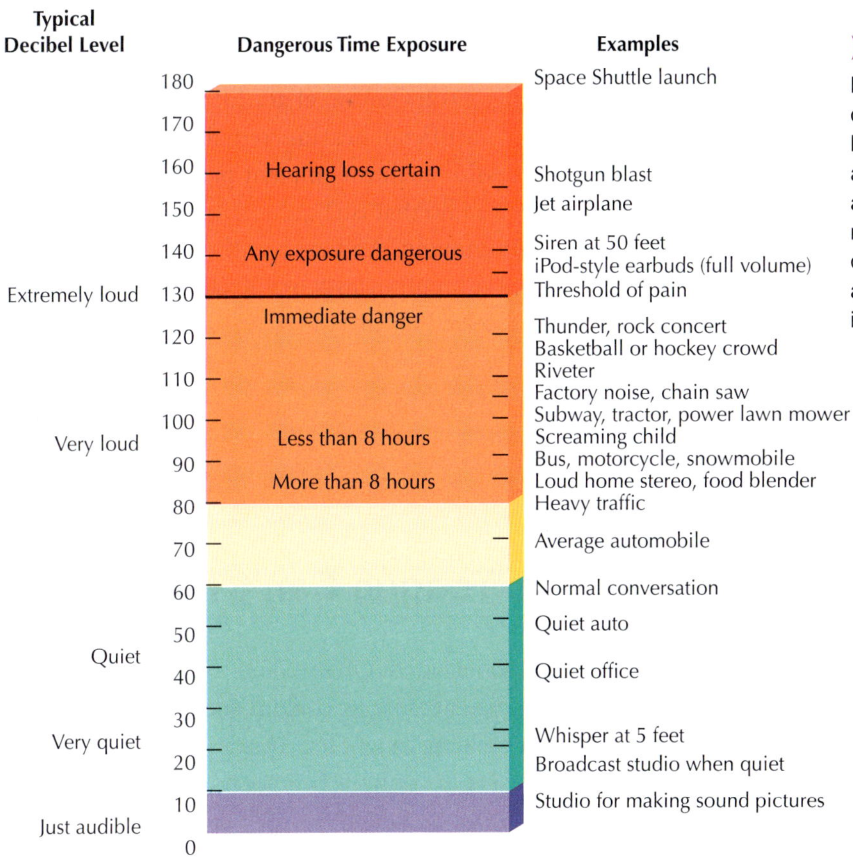

➤ **Figure 19.5**

Decibel scale. The loudness of sound is measured in decibels. The faintest sound most people can hear is little more than zero decibels. Sounds of 110 decibels are uncomfortably loud. Prolonged exposure to sounds above 85 decibels may damage the inner ear. Some music concerts, which can reach 120 decibels, have caused hearing loss in musicians and may affect audiences as well. Sounds of 130 decibels pose an immediate danger to hearing.

How loud must a sound be to be hazardous? Daily exposure to 85 decibels or more may cause permanent hearing loss (Goldstein & Brockmole, 2017). *Decibels* are a measure of sound intensity. Every 20 decibels increases the sound pressure by a factor of 10. In other words, a rock concert at 120 decibels is 1,000 times stronger than a voice at 60 decibels. Short periods at 120 decibels can cause temporary hearing loss, and even one brief exposure to 150 decibels (a jet airplane nearby) may cause permanent hearing loss. You might find it interesting to check the decibel ratings of some of your activities in ➤ Figure 19.5. Be aware that amplified music concerts, iPod-style earbuds, and car stereos also can damage your hearing.

Artificial Hearing Hearing aids are no help in cases of sensorineural hearing loss because auditory messages are blocked from reaching the brain. In many cases, however, the auditory nerve is intact. This finding has spurred the development of cochlear implants that bypass hair cells and stimulate the auditory nerves directly (➤ Figure 19.6). Wires from a microphone carry electrical signals to an external coil. A matching coil under the skin picks up the signals and carries them to one or more areas of the cochlea. The latest implants use place theory to separate higher and lower tones into separate channels. This has allowed some formerly deaf persons to hear human voices, music, and other higher-frequency sounds. About 60 percent of all multichannel implant patients can understand some spoken words and appreciate music (Leal et al., 2003; Park et al., 2011). Some deaf children with implants learn to speak.

Pitch How high or low a tone sounds.

Eardrum Membrane that vibrates in response to sound waves and transmits them inward.

Cochlea Snail-shaped organ in the inner ear that contains sensory receptors for hearing.

Basilar membrane Structure in the cochlea containing hair cells that convert sound waves into action potentials.

Hair cells Receptor cells within the cochlea that transduce vibrations into nerve impulses.

Frequency theory of hearing Proposition that pitch is decoded from the rate at which hair cells of the basilar membrane are firing.

Place theory of hearing Proposition that higher and lower tones excite specific areas of the cochlea.

Conductive hearing loss Poor transfer of sounds from the eardrum to the inner ear.

Sensorineural hearing loss Loss of hearing caused by damage to the inner-ear hair cells or auditory nerve.

Noise-induced hearing loss Damage caused by exposing the hair cells to excessively loud sounds.

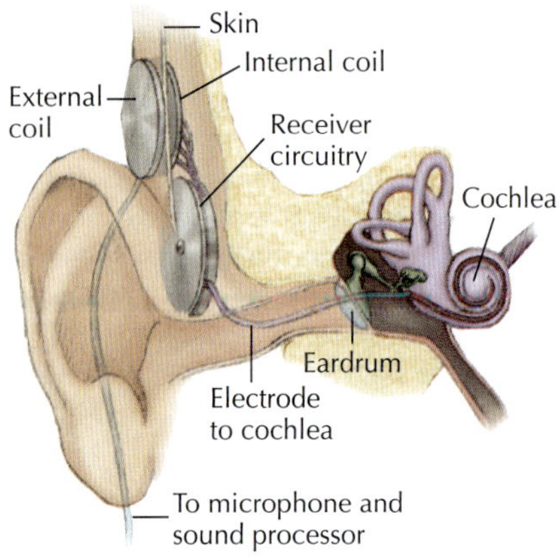

➤ **Figure 19.6**

A cochlear implant, or "artificial ear."

Those who receive a cochlear implant before age 2 have the best chance to learn spoken language at a near normal rate (Ertmer & Jung, 2012; Gordon et al., 2011).

At present, artificial hearing remains crude. All but the most successful cochlear implant patients describe the sound as "like a radio that isn't quite tuned in." But cochlear implants are improving. And even at the current level, it is hard to argue with enthusiasts like Kristen Cloud. Shortly after Kristen received an implant, she was able to hear a siren and avoid being struck by a speeding car. She says simply, "The implant saved my life."

Smell and Taste—The Nose Knows When the Tongue Can't Tell

Learning Outcome 19.2 Name the two chemical senses and describe the processes of transduction in the nose and on the tongue

Unless you are a wine taster, a perfume blender, a chef (Ramsay?), or a gourmet, you may think of **olfaction**, or smell, and **gustation**, or taste, as minor senses. You could probably survive without these *chemical senses*—receptors that respond to chemical molecules (Di Lorenzo & Youngentob, 2013). But don't be deceived—life without these senses can be difficult (Drummond, Douglas, & Olver, 2007). One person, for instance, almost died because he couldn't smell the smoke when his apartment building caught fire. Besides, olfaction and gustation add pleasure to our lives. Let's see how they work.

The Sense of Smell

Smell receptors respond to airborne molecules. As air enters the nose, it flows over roughly 5 million nerve fibers embedded in the lining of the upper nasal passages (➤ **Figure 19.7**).

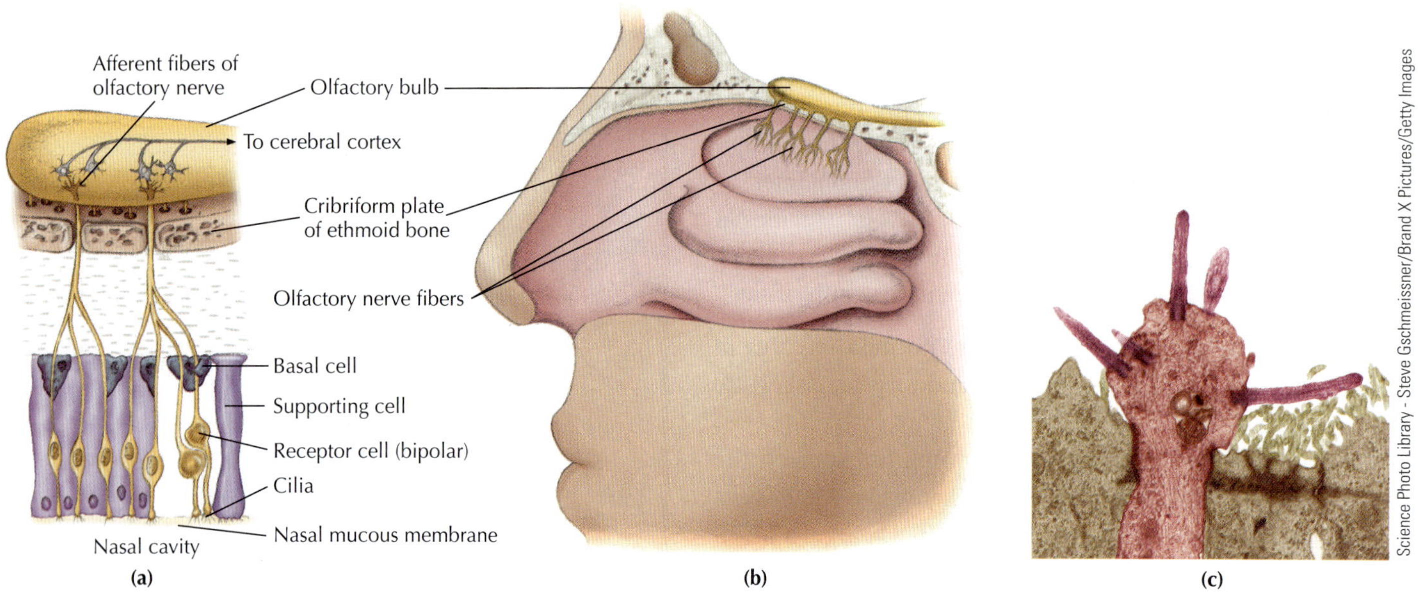

➤ **Figure 19.7**

Receptors for the sense of smell (olfaction). *(a)* Olfactory nerve fibers respond to gaseous molecules. Receptor cells are shown in cross section to the left. *(b)* Olfactory receptors are located in the upper nasal cavity. *(c)* On the right, an extreme close-up of an olfactory receptor shows fibers that sense gaseous molecules of various shapes.

Receptor proteins on the surface of the fibers are sensitive to various airborne molecules. When a fiber is stimulated, it sends signals to the brain (Dalton & Lomvardas, 2015).

How are different odors detected? This is still an unfolding mystery. One hint comes from a type of *anosmia* (an-OZE-me-ah), a sort of "smell blindness" to a single odor. Loss of sensitivity to specific types of odors suggests the presence of receptors for specific odors. Indeed, the molecules that produce a particular odor are quite similar in shape. Specific shapes produce the following types of odors: floral (flowerlike), camphoric (camphorlike), musky (have you ever smelled a sweaty musk ox?—it's like that), minty (mintlike), and etherish (like ether or cleaning fluid).

Does this mean that there are five different types of olfactory receptors? Although humans carry genes for about 1,000 types of smell receptors, only about 400 of them are expressed (Sela & Sobel, 2010). It appears that different-shaped "holes," or "pockets," exist on the surface of olfactory receptors. Like a piece fits into a puzzle, chemicals produce odors when part of a molecule matches a hole of the same shape. This is the **lock-and-key theory of olfaction**.

Furthermore, molecules trigger activity in different *combinations* of odor receptors. Thus, humans can detect at least 10,000 different odors. Just as you can make hundreds of thousands of words in English from the 26 letters of the Roman alphabet, many combinations of the 400 types of receptors are possible, resulting in many different odors. Scents also are identified, in part, by the *location* of the receptors in the nose that a particular odor activates. And finally, the *number of activated receptors* tells the brain the strength of an odor (Bensafi et al., 2004). The brain uses these distinctive patterns of messages it gets from the olfactory receptors to recognize particular scents (Sela & Sobel, 2010).

What causes anosmia? Five people out of 100 experience some degree of anosmia, including the total loss of smell (Bramerson et al., 2004). Risks include infections, allergies, and blows to the head (which may tear the olfactory nerves). Exposure to chemicals such as ammonia, paints, solvents, and hairdressing "potions" also can cause anosmia. If you value your sense of smell, be careful what you sniff (Drummond, Douglas, & Olver, 2007).

Taste and Flavors

There are at least five basic taste sensations: *sweet, salty, sour, bitter*, and *umami* (Dalton & Lomvardas, 2015). We are generally most sensitive to bitter and sour. This may have helped prevent poisonings when most humans foraged for food because bitter and sour foods are more likely to be inedible.

Umami? The Japanese word *umami* (oo-MAH-me) describes a pleasant savory or "brothy" taste associated with certain amino acids in chicken soup, some meat extracts, kelp, tuna, human milk, cheese, and soybeans. The receptors for *umami* are sensitive to glutamate, a substance found in monosodium glutamate (MSG) (Nakamura et al., 2011).

If there are only five tastes, how can there be so many different flavors? Flavors seem more varied because we include sensations of texture, temperature, smell, and even pain ("hot" chili peppers) with taste. Smell is particularly important in determining flavor (Doty, 2012). If you plug your nose and eat small bits of apple, potato, and onion, they will "taste" almost exactly alike. So do gourmet jelly beans! That's why food loses its "taste" when you have a cold. It is probably fair to say that subjective flavor is half smell.

MSG's reputation as a "flavor enhancer" likely arose because of the combination of savory odors of, say, chicken soup, with the taste of glutamate (which does not taste pleasant by itself) (Vandenbeuch et al., 2010). At the very least, we may finally know why chicken soup is such a "comfort food." But remember to smell it first!

Taste buds, clusters of taste-receptor cells, are located mainly on the top side of the tongue, especially around the edges. However, a few are found elsewhere inside the mouth (➤ Figure 19.8). As food is chewed, it dissolves and enters the taste buds, where it sets off nerve impulses to the brain (Vandenbeuch et al., 2010). Much like smell, sweet, bitter, and umami tastes appear to be based on a lock-and-key match between molecules and intricately shaped receptors. Saltiness and sourness, however, are triggered by a direct flow of charged atoms into the tips of taste cells (Dalton & Lomvardas, 2015; Lindemann, 2001).

If smell and taste are seen as minor senses, then the somesthetic senses are the unnoticed senses. Let's see why they merit our careful attention.

Olfaction Sense of smell.

Gustation Sense of taste.

Lock-and-key theory of olfaction A theory holding that odors are related to the shapes of chemical molecules.

Taste buds Receptor cells for taste.

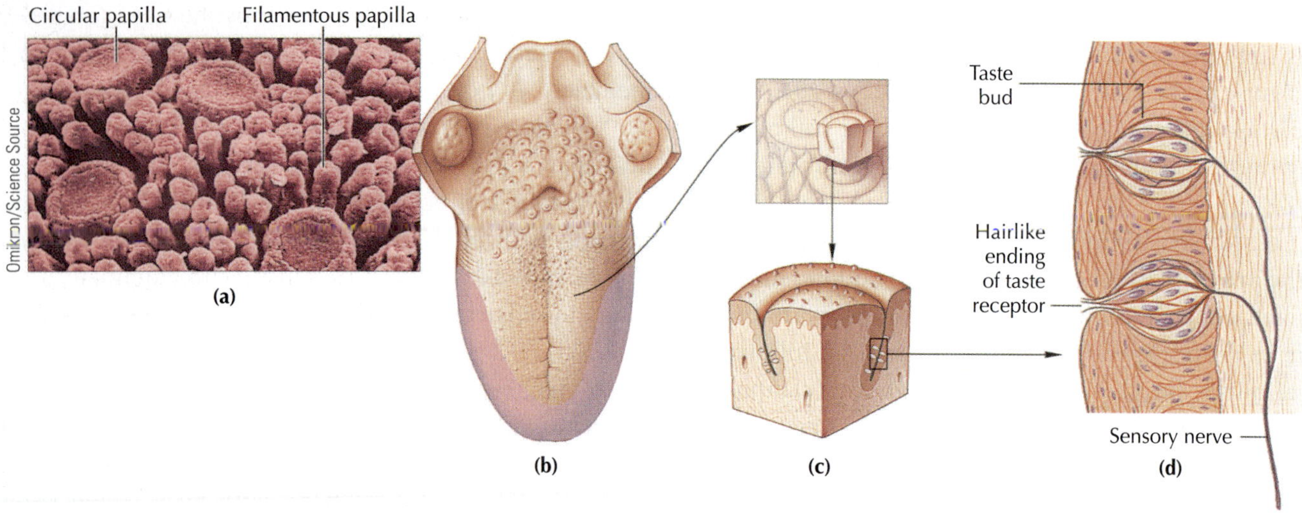

Figure 19.8

Receptors for the sense of taste. *(a)* The tongue is covered with small protrusions called *papillae. (b)* Most taste buds are found around the top edges of the tongue (shaded area). However, some are located elsewhere, including under the tongue. Stimulation of the central part of the tongue causes no taste sensations. All five primary taste sensations occur anywhere that taste buds exist. *(c)* An enlarged drawing shows that taste buds are located near the base of papillae. *(d)* Detail of a taste bud. These receptors also occur in other parts of the digestive system, such as the lining of the mouth.

The Somesthetic Senses—Flying by the Seat of Your Pants

Learning Outcome 19.3 Name the somesthetic senses, describe the process of transduction on the skin, distinguish between the function of large and small nerve fibers in the sensation of pain, explain the gate control theory of pain, contrast the roles of the kinesthetic and vestibular systems, and describe the process of transduction in the vestibular system

A gymnast "flying" through a routine on the uneven bars may rely as much on the **somesthetic senses** as on vision (*soma* means "body," *esthetic* means "feel"). Even the most routine activities, such as walking, running, or passing a sobriety test, would be impossible without the **skin senses** (touch), the **kinesthetic senses** (receptors in muscles and joints that detect body position and movement), and the **vestibular senses** (receptors in the inner ear for balance, gravity, and acceleration). Because of their importance, let's begin with the skin senses.

The Skin Senses

It's difficult to imagine what life would be like without the sense of touch, but the plight of Ian Waterman gives a hint. After an illness he suffered at 19, Waterman permanently lost all feeling below his neck. Now, in order to know the position of his body, he must be able to see it. If he moves with his eyes closed, he has no idea where he is going. If the lights go out in a room, he's in big trouble (Gallagher, 2004).

Skin receptors produce at least five different sensations: *light touch, pressure, pain, cold,* and *warmth.* Receptors with particular shapes appear to specialize somewhat in various sensations (**➤Figure 19.9**). However, free nerve endings alone can produce all five sensations (Carlson & Birkett, 2017). Altogether, the skin has about 200,000 nerve endings for temperature, 500,000 for touch and pressure, and 3 million for pain.

Does the number of receptors in an area of skin relate to its sensitivity? Yes. Your skin can be "mapped" by applying heat, cold, touch, pressure, or pain to points all over your body (Hollins, 2010). Such testing would show that the number of skin receptors varies and that sensitivity generally matches the number of receptors in a given area. Broadly speaking, important areas such as the lips, tongue, face, hands, and genitals have a higher density of receptors. Of course, the sensation that you ultimately feel will depend on brain activity.

Pain *Does the number of pain receptors also vary?* Like the other skin senses, pain receptors vary in their distribution. About 230 pain points per square centimeter (about a half-inch) are found behind the knee, 180 per centimeter on the buttocks, 60 on the pad of the thumb, and 40 on the tip of the nose. (Is it better, then, to be pinched on the nose or behind the knee? It depends on what you like!)

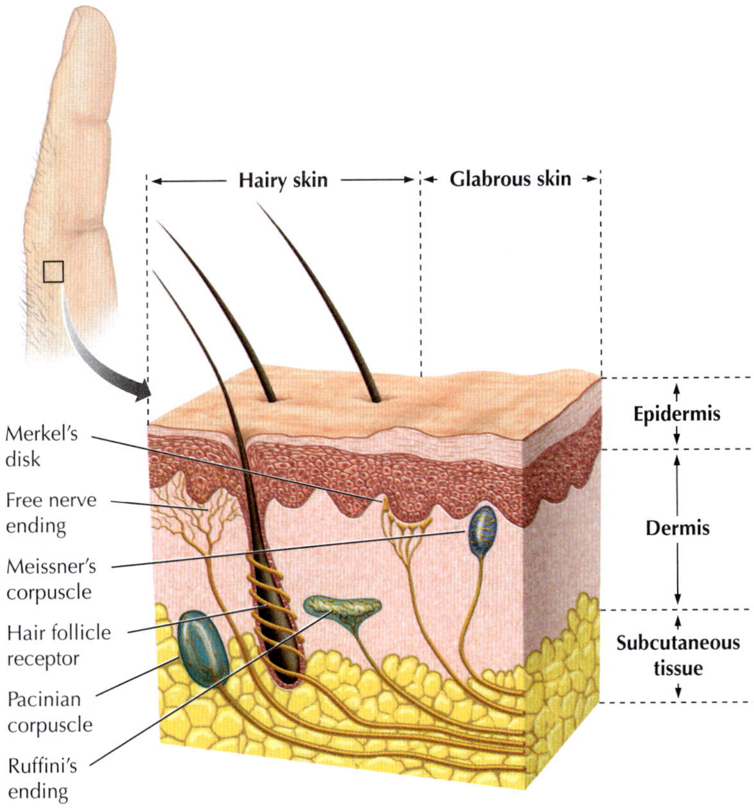

Figure 19.9

Receptors for the skin senses. The skin senses include touch, pressure, pain, cold, and warmth. This drawing shows different forms the skin receptors can take. The functions of these receptors are likely as follows: Merkel's disks sense pressure on the skin; free nerve endings sense warmth, cold, and pain; Meissner's corpuscles sense pressure; hair follicle receptors sense hair movement; Pacinian corpuscles sense pressure and vibration; and Ruffini's endings sense skin stretching (Freberg, 2021; Kalat, 2021). The feeling of being touched is likely made up of a combination of varying degrees of activity in all these receptors.

Pain carried by *large nerve fibers* is sharp, bright, and fast and seems to come from specific body areas (McMahon & Koltzenburg, 2013). This is the body's **warning system**. Give yourself a small jab with a pin and you will feel this type of pain. As you do this, notice that warning pain quickly disappears. Much as we may dislike warning pain, it is usually a signal that the body has been, or is about to be, damaged. Without warning pain, we would be unable to detect or prevent injury. Children who are born with a rare inherited insensitivity to pain repeatedly burn themselves, break bones, bite off parts of their tongues, and become ill without knowing it (Erez et al., 2010). As you might imagine, it's also hard for people with *congenital pain insensitivity* to have empathy for the pain of others (Danziger, Prkachin, & Willer, 2006).

A second type of somatic pain is carried by *small nerve fibers*. This type of pain is slower, nagging, aching, widespread, and very unpleasant (McMahon & Koltzenburg, 2013). It gets worse if the pain stimulus is repeated. This is the body's **reminding system**, which reminds the brain that the body has been injured. For instance, lower-back pain often has this quality. Sadly, the reminding system can cause agony long after an injury has healed, or in terminal illnesses, when the reminder is useless.

The Pain Gate You may have noticed that one type of pain sometimes cancels another. Ronald Melzack's (1999) **gate control theory** suggests that pain messages from the different nerve fibers pass through the same neural "gate" in the spinal cord. If the gate is "closed" by one pain message, other messages may not be able to pass through (Melzack & Katz, 2006; Moayedi & Davis, 2013).

How is the gate closed? Messages carried by large, fast nerve fibers seem to close the spinal pain gate directly. Doing so can prevent slower, "reminding system" pain from reaching the brain. Messages from small, slow fibers seem to take a different route. After going through the pain gate, they continue to a "central biasing system" in the brain. Under some

Somesthetic senses Sensations produced by the skin, muscles, joints, viscera, and organs of balance.

Skin senses The senses of touch, pressure, pain, heat, and cold.

Kinesthetic senses The senses of body movement and positioning.

Vestibular senses Perception of balance, gravity, and acceleration.

Warning system Pain based on large nerve fibers; warns that bodily damage may be occurring.

Reminding system Pain based on small nerve fibers; reminds the brain that the body has been injured.

Gate control theory A theory proposing that pain messages pass through neural "gates" in the spinal cord.

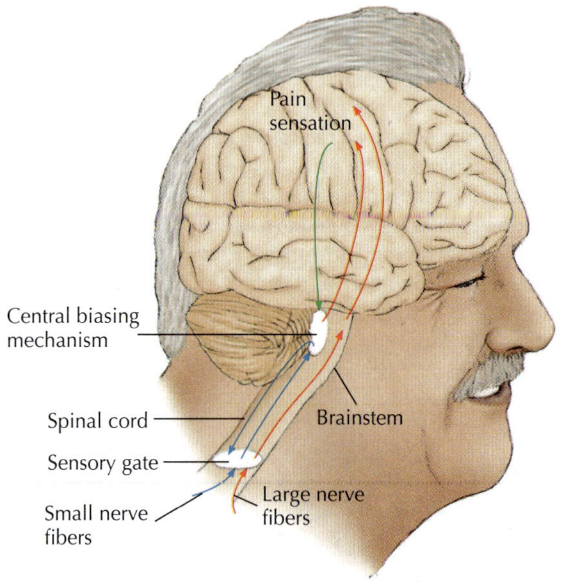

➤ Figure 19.10

A sensory gate for pain. A series of pain impulses going through the gate may prevent other pain messages from passing through. Alternatively, pain messages may relay through a "central biasing mechanism" that exerts control over the gate, closing it to other impulses.

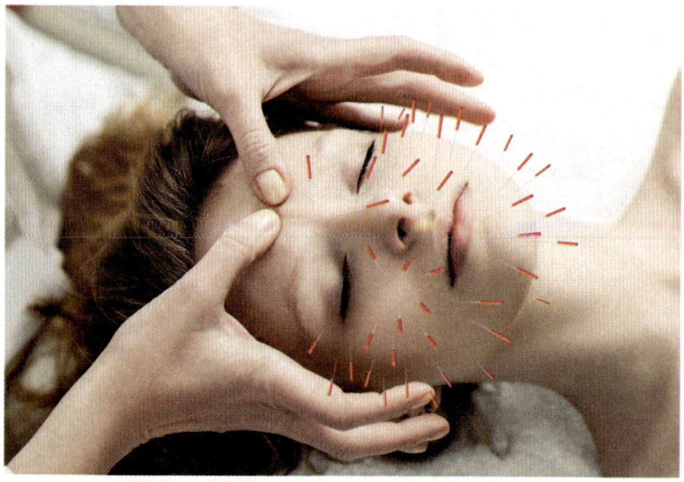

Kotin/Shutterstock.com

Acupuncture involves inserting thin, stainless steel needles into areas identified by ancient Chinese medicine. Modern research has begun to explain the painkilling effects of acupuncture, although its purported ability to cure diseases is more debatable.

circumstances, the brain then sends a message back down the spinal cord, closing the pain gates (➤ **Figure 19.10**).

Melzack believes that gate control theory may explain the painkilling effects of *acupuncture*, the Chinese medical art of relieving pain and illness by inserting thin needles into the body. As the acupuncturist's needles are twirled, heated, or electrified, they activate small pain fibers. These relay through the biasing system to close the gates to intense or chronic pain. Studies have shown that acupuncture produces short-term pain relief (Hopton, Thomas, & MacPherson, 2013; Witt et al., 2011). (However, its ability to cure illness is much more debatable.)

Pain Control Gate control theory also helps explain *counterirritation,* one widely used pain-control technique. Pain clinics use it by applying a mild electrical current to the skin. This causes only a mild tingling, but it can greatly reduce more agonizing pain (Köke et al., 2004). For more extreme pain, the electrical current can be applied directly to the spinal cord (Linderoth & Foreman, 2006).

You can use counterirritation to control your own pain (Schmelz, 2010). For instance, if you are having a tooth filled, try scratching or pinching yourself, or digging a fingernail into a knuckle, while the dentist is working. Focus your attention on the pain that you are creating, and increase it anytime the dentist's work becomes more uncomfortable or painful. This strategy may seem strange, but it works. Generations of children have used it to take the edge off a spanking.

In some cultures, people endure tattooing, stretching, cutting, and burning with little apparent pain. How do they do it? Very likely, the answer lies in relying on psychological factors that anyone can use to reduce pain, such as anxiety reduction, control, and attention (Jegindø et al., 2013). In general, unpleasant emotions such as fear and anxiety increase pain; pleasant emotions decrease it (Kerns, Sellinger, & Goodin, 2011).

Anytime you can anticipate pain (such as a trip to the doctor, dentist, or tattoo parlor), you can lower your anxiety by making sure you are *fully informed.* Be sure that everything that will happen is explained to you. In general, the more control that you *feel* over a painful stimulus, the less pain you experience (Salomons et al., 2015). To apply this principle, you might arrange a signal so your doctor, dentist, or body piercer will know when to start and stop a painful procedure. Finally, distraction also reduces pain. Instead of listening to the whirr of a dentist's drill, for example, you could imagine that you are lying in the sun at a beach, listening to the roar of the surf. Or take an iPod along and crank up your favorite MP3 tunes. At home, music also can be a good distractor from chronic pain (Garza-Villarreal, 2016).

Phantom Limb Pain and the Neuromatrix Gate control theory, however, cannot explain *phantom limb* sensations, including pain, for months or years after losing a limb (Longo, Long, & Haggard, 2012; Murray et al., 2007). Because the phantom limb feels so "real," a patient with a recently amputated leg may inadvertently try to walk on it, risking further injury. Sometimes phantom limbs feel like they are stuck in awkward positions. For instance, one man can't fall asleep on his back because his missing arm feels like it is twisted behind him.

What causes the experience of phantom limbs? Gate control theory cannot explain phantom limb pain because pain can't be coming from the missing limb (after all, it's missing!) and, therefore, cannot pass through pain gates to the brain (Hunter, Katz, & Davis, 2003). Instead, according to Ronald Melzack (Melzack, 1999; Melzack & Katz, 2006), over time, the brain creates a body image called the *neuromatrix*. This internal model of the body generates our sense of bodily self. Although amputation may remove a limb, it still exists as far as the neuromatrix is concerned.

In fact, amputees dream of intact, fully functional limbs without any phantom limb experiences. Evidently, during sleep, sensory inputs from the area of the missing limb are suppressed. In contrast, when amputees are awake, sensory inputs from the area of the missing limb conflict with the neuromatrix, which interprets the conflict as a phantom limb, complete with phantom limb pain (Alessandria et al., 2011; Giummarra et al., 2007). Functional magnetic resonance imaging (fMRI) confirms that sensory and motor areas of the brain are more active when a person feels a phantom limb (MacIver et al., 2008).

Sometimes the brain gradually reorganizes to adjust for the sensory loss (Raffin et al., 2016; Schmalzl et al., 2011). For example, a person who loses an arm first may sense a phantom arm and hand. After many years, the phantom may shrink, until only a hand is felt at the shoulder. Perhaps more vividly than others, people with phantom limbs are reminded that the sensory world that we experience is constructed, moment by moment, by our own brain activity.

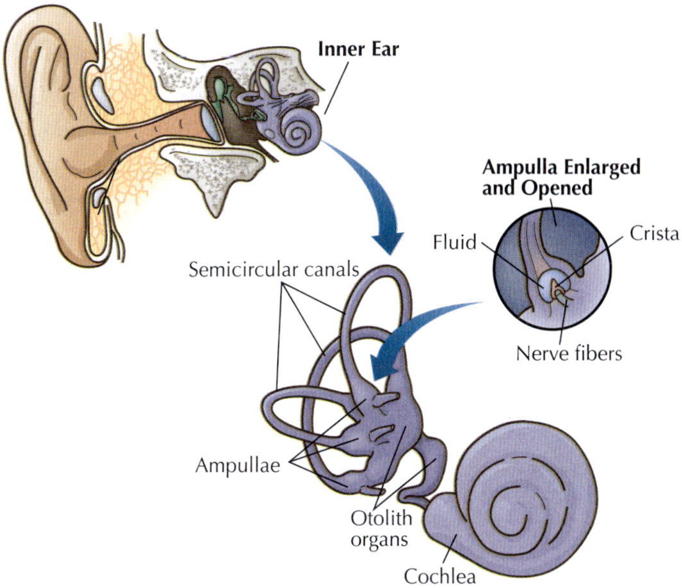

➤ **Figure 19.11**

The vestibular system.

NASA

Weightlessness presents astronauts with a real challenge in sensory adaptation. Pictured here is world-famous physicist Stephen Hawking, who was diagnosed with amyotrophic lateral sclerosis (ALS, or Lou Gehrig's disease). Before he passed away in 2018, he fulfilled a lifelong dream of experiencing weightlessness. He took a flight on the "Weightless Wonder," the official nickname that the National Aeronautics and Space Administration (NASA) gives to the high-flying airplane that provides short periods of weightlessness to train astronauts. (Its unofficial nickname, which stems from its unfortunate side effects, is the "Vomit Comet.")

The Vestibular System

Although space flight might look like fun, the likelihood of you throwing up during your first experience in orbit is about 70 percent.

Why? Weightlessness and space flight affect the vestibular system, which often causes severe motion sickness. Within the vestibular system, fluid-filled sacs called *otolith* (OH-toe-lith) *organs* are sensitive to movement, acceleration, and gravity (➤ **Figure 19.11**). The otolith organs contain tiny crystals in a soft, gelatinlike mass. The tug of gravity or rapid head movements can cause the mass to shift. This, in turn, stimulates hair-like receptor cells, allowing us to sense gravity, acceleration, and movement through space (Lackner & DiZio, 2005).

Three fluid-filled tubes—called the *semicircular canals*—are the sensory organs for balance. If you could climb inside these tubes, you would find that head movements cause the fluid to swirl about. As the fluid moves, it bends a small "flap," or "float," called the *crista*, that detects movement in the semicircular canals. The bending of each crista again stimulates hair cells and signals head rotation.

What causes motion sickness? According to **sensory conflict theory**, dizziness and nausea occur when sensations

Sensory conflict theory A theory explaining motion sickness as the result of a mismatch among information from vision, the vestibular system, and kinesthesis.

from the vestibular system don't match sensations from the eyes and body (Holly & Harmon, 2012). On solid ground, information from the vestibular system, vision, and kinesthesis usually matches. However, in a heaving, pitching boat, car, or airplane, or even playing a video game, a serious mismatch can occur—causing disorientation and heaving of another kind (Chang et al., 2012).

Why does sensory conflict cause nausea? You can probably thank (or blame) evolution. Many poisons disturb the vestibular system, vision, and the body. Therefore, we may have evolved so that we react to sensory conflict by vomiting to expel poison. The value of this reaction, however, may be little comfort to anyone who has ever been "green" and miserable with motion sickness. To minimize such conflicts, try to keep your head still, fix your vision on a distant immobile object, and lie down if you can.

MODULE 19 The Nonvisual Senses—Learning Outcomes Revisited

19.1 Describe two characteristics of sound and how they are processed by the ear, contrast the frequency and place theory of hearing, and describe two forms of hearing loss

The ear takes in information about pitch (associated with the frequency of the sound wave) and loudness (associated with the amplitude of the sound wave). Sound waves are the stimulus for hearing. They are amplified and directed by the eardrum, auditory ossicles, and oval window to the cochlea, where they are transduced by the hair cells to generate action potentials. Frequency theory (pitch corresponds to frequency of action potentials) explains how we hear tones up to 4,000 hertz; place theory (higher and lower tones are associated with excitation of different parts of the cochlea) explains it for tones above 4,000 hertz. Two basic types of hearing loss are conductive hearing loss (caused when transfer of vibration from the outer ear to the inner ear weakens) and sensorineural hearing loss (caused when there is damage to the hair cells or auditory nerve). Noise-induced hearing loss is a common form of sensorineural hearing loss caused by exposure to loud noise.

19.2 Name the two chemical senses and describe the processes of transduction in the nose and on the tongue

Olfaction (smell) and gustation (taste) are chemical senses that respond to airborne or liquefied molecules. Receptors on nerve fibers in the nose are sensitive to various chemical molecules and create action potentials when they are stimulated. The lock-and-key theory of olfaction suggests different receptors have different shaped "holes" that can bind with matching chemical molecules, creating the basis for a unique smell. In addition, the location of the olfactory receptors in the nose helps people identify various scent. There are five basic tastes: sweet, salt, sour, bitter, and umami. Sweet, bitter, and umami tastes are based on a lock-and-key coding of molecule shapes; when there is a match between receptors and the chemical molecules found in food an action potential is activated. Salty and sour tastes are triggered by a direct flow of ions into taste receptors, activating an action potential.

19.3 Name the somesthetic senses, describe the process of transduction on the skin, distinguish between the function of large and small nerve fibers in the sensation of pain, explain the gate control theory of pain, contrast the roles of the kinesthetic and vestibular systems, and describe the process of transduction in the vestibular system

The somesthetic senses include touch, the vestibular senses, and kinesthetic senses (receptors that detect muscle and joint positioning). Receptors located on the skin have particular shapes that specialize in activating action potentials for specific sensations, but nerve endings in the skin can also activate action potentials directly. Warning pain (signaled by large nerve fibers) lets the body know that the body is (or is about to be) harmed. Reminding pain (signaled by small nerve fibers) remind the body of a prior injury. Gate control theory suggests that pain messages carried by large and small nerve fibers pass through the same "gate" in the spinal cord. When pain messages from one group of nerve fibers pass through the gate, others may not be able to get through, thus explaining why one type of pain cancels out another. The kinesthetic system provides information about the location of your body parts in space through the activation of various receptors in your muscles and joints. In contrast, the vestibular system's role is to gauge the position of the body as a whole in space, and has an important role to play in balance. Sacs called otolith organs in the inner ear respond to changes in gravity, acceleration, and movement through space, stimulating hair cells that activate action potentials. Balance is maintained through fluid in the ear's semicircular canals, which stimulates hair cells that create an action potential.

Reflective Practice

Content Check

1. The frequency of a sound wave corresponds to how loud it is. T or F?
2. Sensorineural hearing loss occurs when the auditory ossicles are damaged. T or F?
3. Daily exposure to sounds with a loudness of at least ___________ decibels may cause permanent hearing loss.
4. Olfaction appears to be at least partially explained by the ______________________ theory of molecule shapes and receptor sites.
5. Which of the following is a somesthetic sense?
   a. gustation
   b. olfaction
   c. rarefaction
   d. kinesthesis
6. Warning pain is carried by __________ nerve fibers.
7. Head movements are detected primarily in the semicircular canals and gravity by the otolith organs. T or F?

Skill Check

Think Critically

8. Why do you think your voice sounds so different to you when you hear a recording of your speech?
9. Drivers are less likely to become carsick than passengers. Why do you think that drivers and passengers differ in susceptibility to motion sickness?

Self-Reflect

Close your eyes and listen to the sounds around you. As you do, try to mentally trace the events necessary to convert vibrations in the air into the sounds that you hear. What is your favorite food aroma? What is your favorite taste? Explain how you are able to sense the aroma and taste of foods. Stand on one foot with your eyes closed. Now touch the tip of your nose with your index finger. Which of the somesthetic senses did you use to perform this feat? Imagine you are on a boat ride with a friend who starts to feel queasy. What would you explain to your friend about the causes of motion sickness and what she or he can do to prevent it?

ANSWERS

1. F 2. F 3. 85 4. lock-and-key 5. d 6. large 7. T 8. The answer lies in another question: How else might vibrations from the voice reach the cochlea? Other people hear your voice only as it is carried through the air. You hear not only that sound but also vibrations conducted by the bones of your skull. 9. Drivers experience less sensory conflict because they control the car's motion. This allows them to anticipate the car's movements and to coordinate their head and eye movements with those of the car.

MODULE

20

Sensation and Perception
Perceptual Processes

Is That a Deer?

While driving at night, a woman slams on her brakes to avoid hitting a deer. As she skids to a stop, she realizes that the "deer" is actually a bush on the roadside. Such misperceptions are common. The brain must continuously find patterns in a welter of sensations. If you look closely at this pixelated photo, you can see that it is entirely made up of small individual differently colored pixels. An infant or newly sighted person might well see only a jumble of meaningless colors. But because the pixels form a familiar pattern, you should easily see the dog. How do we organize sensations into perceptions? Visual perception involves finding meaningful patterns in complex stimuli. Our brain creates our perceptions by using preexisting knowledge such as the principles of perceptual grouping and perceptual constancies to help us make sense out of sensations.

Alexey V. Smirnov/Shutterstock.com

~LEARNING OUTCOMES~

After reading this module you should be able to:

20.1 Distinguish between illusions and hallucinations, contrast bottom-up processing with top-down processing, provide some examples of top-down processing, and explain what is meant by perceptual constancies and provide three examples

20.2 Define depth perception and differentiate between monocular and binocular depth cues, giving examples of each

Perception—The Second Step

Learning Outcome 20.1 Distinguish between illusions and hallucinations, contrast bottom-up processing with top-down processing, provide some examples of top-down processing, and explain what is meant by perceptual constancies and provide three examples

Aren't you born with the ability to create perceptions out of sensations? Imagine what it would be like to have your vision restored after a lifetime of blindness. Actually, a first look at the world could be disappointing because the newfound ability to *sense* (see) the world does not guarantee that it can be *perceived.* Newly sighted persons must *learn* to identify objects, to read clocks, numbers, and letters, and to judge sizes and distances. For instance, Mr. S. B. was a cataract patient who had been blind since birth. After an operation finally restored his sight at age 52, Mr. S. B. struggled to use his vision (Gregory, 2003).

Mr. S. B. soon learned to tell time from a large clock and to read block letters that he previously had known only from touch. At a zoo, he recognized an elephant from descriptions that he had heard. However, handwriting meant nothing to

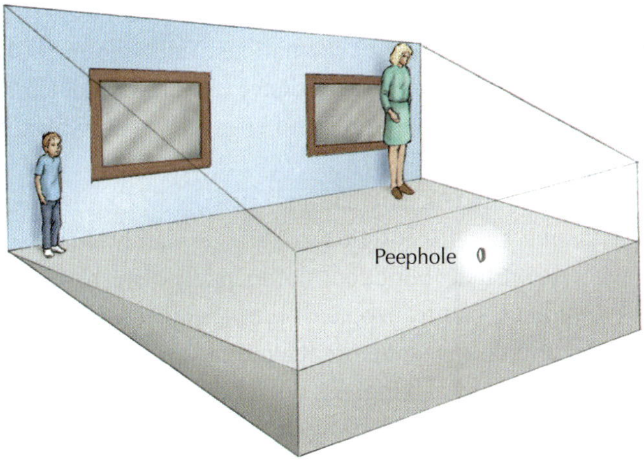

➤ **Figure 20.1**

The Ames room. From the front, the room looks normal; in reality, the right corner is very short, and the left corner is very tall. In addition, the left side of the room slants away from viewers. The diagram shows the shape of the room and reveals why people appear to get bigger as they cross the room toward the nearer, shorter right corner.

him for more than a year after he regained sight, and many objects were meaningless until he touched them. Thus, Mr. S. B. slowly learned to organize his *sensations* into meaningful *perceptions.* Cases such as those of Mr. S. B. show that your experiences are **perceptual constructions**, or mental models of external events, that *are actively created by your brain* (Goldstein & Brockmole, 2017).

While the brain automatically and continuously seeks meaningful patterns in a welter of sensations, it cannot possibly "get it right" all the time. Perceptual *misconstructions* happen often. Sometimes they are mundane, such as misperceiving a deer while driving at night. Sometimes they are more dramatic. For example, one of your authors was once approached in a supermarket by a young girl screaming, "Help! Someone is killing my father." He followed her to see two men struggling. The guy on top had his victim by the throat. Blood was everywhere. It was a murder in progress! Soon, however, it turned out that the "guy on the bottom" had passed out, hit his head, and was bleeding. The "guy on top" saw the first man fall and was loosening his collar.

Obviously, the girl misperceived what was happening to her father. Because of the dramatic influence of her words, so did your author. As this story shows, sensory information can be interpreted in various ways. The girl's description completely shaped his own initial perceptions. This perhaps is understandable. But he'll never forget the added shock that he felt when he met the "murderer." The man whom he had seen a few moments before as vicious and horrible-looking was not even a stranger. He was a neighbor whom your author had seen dozens of times before. Clearly, we don't just believe what we see. We also see what we believe.

Illusions

Perceptual misconstruction is responsible for many illusions. In an **illusion**, length, position, motion, curvature, or direction is misjudged consistently. For example, because we have seen thousands of rooms shaped roughly like a box, we habitually construct perceptions based on this assumption. This need not be true, however. An *Ames room* is a lopsided space that appears square when viewed from a certain angle (➤ **Figure 20.1**). This illusion is achieved by carefully distorting the proportions of the walls, floor, ceiling, and windows. Because the left corner of the Ames room is farther from a viewer than the right, a person standing in that corner looks very small; one standing in the nearer, shorter right corner looks very large. A person who walks from the left to the right corner will seem to "magically" grow larger.

Notice that illusions are distorted perceptions of stimuli that actually exist. In a **hallucination**, people perceive objects or events that have no external reality (Moseley, Fernyhough, & Ellison, 2013). For example, they hear voices that are not there (Gregory, 2016). If you think that you are experiencing an illusion or a hallucination, try engaging in some reality testing.

Perceptual construction A mental model of external events.

Illusion A misleading or misconstructed perception.

Hallucination Perception with no basis in reality.

Reality Testing *What do you mean by reality testing?* In any situation having an element of doubt or uncertainty, **reality testing** involves obtaining additional information to check your perceptions (Landa et al., 2006). To detect an illusion, you may have to measure a drawing or apply a straight edge to it. ➤ **Figure 20.2** shows a powerful illusion called *Fraser's spiral.* What appears to be a spiral is actually made of a series of closed circles. Most people cannot see this reality spontaneously. Instead, they must trace one of the circles carefully to confirm what is "real" in the design.

Even hallucinations can be confronted through reality testing. In contrast with illusions, hallucinations are a major symptom of psychosis, dementia, epilepsy, migraines, alcohol withdrawal, and drug intoxication (Plaze et al., 2011). They also are one of the clearest signs that a person has "lost touch with reality." Even so, if you think you see a 3-foot-tall butterfly, you can confirm that you are hallucinating by trying to touch its wings.

This is precisely what mathematician John Nash did (Nash was the subject of *A Beautiful Mind,* the winner of the 2002 Oscar for best film). Even though Nash had been diagnosed with schizophrenia, he eventually learned to use his *reality testing* to sort out which of his experiences were perceptions and which were hallucinations. Unlike John Nash, however, most people who experience full-blown hallucinations also have a limited ability to engage in reality testing (Garety & Freeman, 2013).

David Spieth/Shutterstock.com

➤ **Figure 20.2**

The limits of pure perception. Even simple designs are easily misperceived. Fraser's spiral is actually a series of concentric circles. The illusion is so powerful that people who try to trace one of the circles sometimes follow the illusory spiral and jump from one circle to the next.

Curiously, "sane hallucinations" also occur. *Charles Bonnet syndrome* is a rare condition that afflicts mainly older people who are partially blind, but not mentally disturbed. Animals, buildings, plants, people, and other objects may seem to appear and disappear before their eyes. One older woman suffering from partial blindness due to cataracts complained of seeing a young girl entering closed doors in her house (Hughes, 2013). However, people experiencing sane hallucinations can more easily tell that their hallucinations aren't real because their capacity for reality testing is not impaired.

Such unusual experiences show how powerfully the brain seeks meaningful patterns in sensory input and the role that reality testing plays in our normal perceptual experience. Let's explore the process of perceptual construction and some factors that shape or even distort it.

Bottom-Up and Top-Down Processing

Moment by moment, our perceptions are typically constructed in both *bottom-up* and *top-down* fashion. Think about the process of building a house: Raw materials, such as lumber, doors, tiles, carpets, screws, and nails, must be painstakingly fitted together. At the same time, a building plan guides how the raw materials are assembled.

Our brain builds perceptions in similar ways. In **bottom-up processing**, we start constructing at the "bottom" with raw materials—that is, we begin with small sensory units (features) and build upward to a complete perception. The reverse also occurs. In **top-down processing**, prior knowledge or expectations are used to rapidly guide the perception of meaningful wholes (Goldstein & Brockmole, 2017). If you put together a picture puzzle that you've never seen before, you are relying mainly on bottom-up processing: You must assemble small pieces until a recognizable pattern begins to emerge. Top-down processing is like putting together a puzzle that you have solved many times: after only a few pieces are in place, your past experience gives you the plan to quickly fill in the final picture.

Both types of processing are illustrated by ➤ **Figure 20.3.** Also, look ahead to Figure 20.6. The first time that you see this photo, you will probably process it from the bottom-up, picking out features until it becomes recognizable. The next time you see it, because of top-down processing, you should recognize it instantly.

➤ **Figure 20.3**

Bottom-up vs. top-down processing. Check out this abstract design. If you process it "bottom-up," likely all that you will see are three small, dark, geometric shapes near the edges. Would you like to try some top-down processing? Knowing the title of the design will allow you to apply your knowledge and see it in an entirely different way. The title? It's *Special K.* Can you see it now?

Two excellent examples of top-down perceptual construction are found in the Gestalt organizing principles and the perceptual constancies. Without these abilities, we would have a much harder time making perceptual sense out of our sensations.

Organizing Principles

How are sensations organized into perceptions? The Gestalt psychologists (see Module 3 for a brief history of Gestalt psychology) proposed that the simplest organization involves grouping some sensations into an object, or figure, that stands out against a plainer background. **Figure-ground organization** is probably inborn because it is the first perceptual ability to appear after cataract patients like Mr. S. B. regain sight. In normal figure-ground perception, only one figure is easily seen. In *reversible figures,* however, figure and ground can be switched. In ➤ Figure 20.4, it is equally possible to see either a wineglass on a dark background or two facial profiles on a light background. As you shift from one pattern to the other, you should get a clear sense of what figure-ground organization means.

➤ **Figure 20.4**

The Rubin vase. Do you see two faces in profile, or a vase?

The Gestalt psychologists identified several other principles that bring some order to your perceptions (➤ Figure 20.5):

1. **Nearness.** All other things being equal, stimuli that are near each other tend to be grouped together (Quinn, Bhatt, & Hayden, 2008). Thus, if three people stand near each other and a fourth person stands 10 feet away, the adjacent three will be seen as a group and the distant person as an outsider (see Figure 20.5*a*).
2. **Similarity.** "Birds of a feather flock together," and stimuli that are similar in size, shape, color, or form tend to be grouped together (see Figure 20.5*b*). Picture two bands marching side by side. If their uniforms are different colors, the bands will be seen as two separate groups, not as one large group.

Reality testing Obtaining additional information to check on the accuracy of perceptions.

Bottom-up processing Organizing perceptions by beginning with low-level features.

Top-down processing Perception guided by prior knowledge or expectations.

Figure-ground organization Organizing a perception so that part of a stimulus appears to stand out as an object (figure) against a less prominent background (ground).

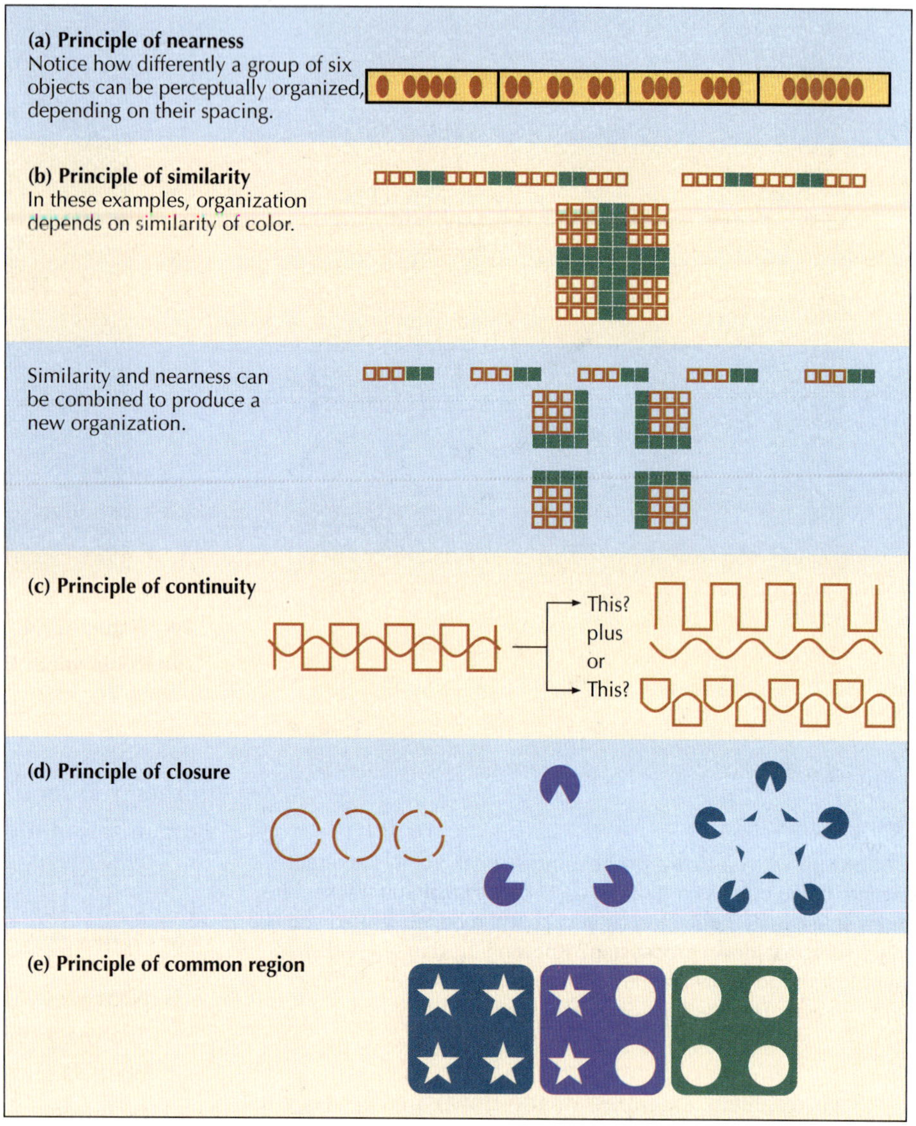

Figure 20.5
Some Gestalt organizing principles.

3. **Continuation, or continuity.** Perceptions tend toward simplicity and continuity. In Figure 20.5*c*, it is easier to visualize a wavy line on a squared-off line than it is to see a complex row of shapes.
4. **Closure.** Closure refers to the tendency to *complete* a figure so that it has a consistent overall form. Each of the drawings in Figure 20.5*d* has one or more gaps, yet each is perceived as a recognizable figure. The "shapes" that appear in the two drawings on the right in Figure 20.5*d* are *illusory figures* (implied shapes that are not bounded by an edge or an outline). Even young children see these shapes, even though they know that they are "not really there." Illusory figures reveal that our tendency to form shapes—even with minimal cues—is powerful.
5. **Common region.** As you can see in Figure 20.5*e*, stimuli that are found within a common area tend to be seen as a group (Palmer & Beck, 2007). On the basis of similarity and nearness, the stars in Figure 20.5*e* should be one group and the dots another. However, the colored backgrounds define regions that create three groups of objects (four stars, two stars plus two dots, and four dots).
6. **Contiguity.** A principle that can't be shown in Figure 20.5 is contiguity, or nearness in time *and* space. Contiguity often is responsible for the perception that one thing has *caused* another (Buehner & May, 2003). A psychologist friend of ours demonstrates this principle in class by knocking on his head with one hand while knocking on a wooden table (out of sight) with the other. The knocking sound is perfectly timed with the movements of his visible hand. This leads to the irresistible perception that his head is made of wood.

Dr. Morley Read/Shutterstock.com

➤ Figure 20.6

A challenging example of perceptual organization. Once the camouflaged insect (a species of stick insect) becomes visible, it is almost impossible to view the picture again without seeing the insect. Go ahead, try!

Clearly, the Gestalt principles offer us some basic "plans" for organizing parts of our day-to-day perceptions in top-down fashion. Take a moment and look for the camouflaged creature pictured in ➤ Figure 20.6 (no, it's not a green vine snake). Because camouflage patterns break up figure-ground organization, Mr. S. B. would have been at a total loss to find meaning in such a picture.

In a way, we are all detectives seeking patterns in what we see. In this sense, a meaningful pattern represents a **perceptual hypothesis**, or an initial plan or guess about how to organize sensations. Have you ever seen a "friend" in the distance, only to have the person turn into a stranger as you drew closer? Preexisting ideas and expectations *actively* guide our interpretation of sensations (Intaitė et al., 2013).

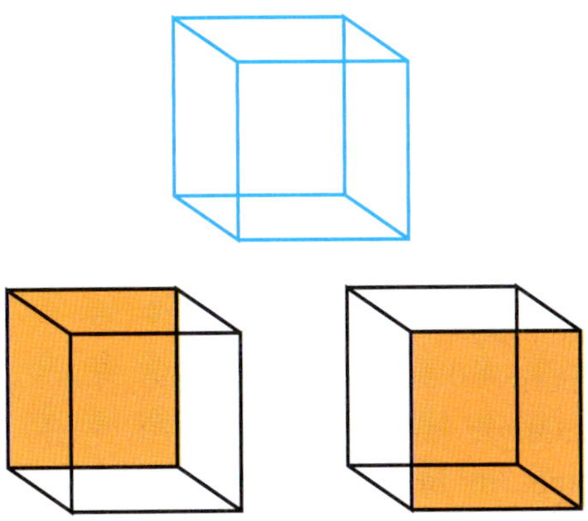

➤ Figure 20.7

The Necker cube.

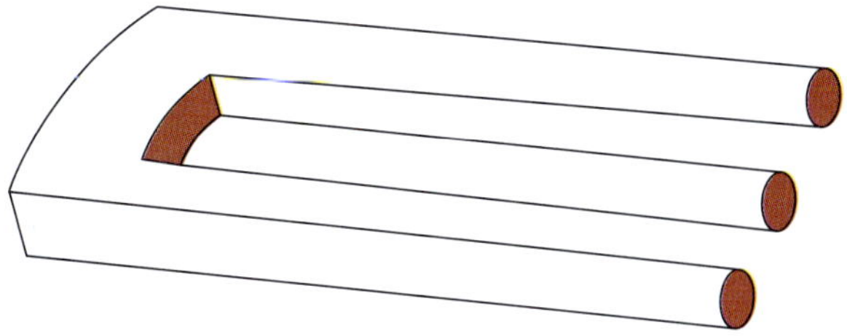

➤ Figure 20.8

An impossible figure. The "three-pronged widget."

The active, constructive nature of perception is perhaps most apparent for *ambiguous stimuli* (patterns allowing more than one interpretation). If you look at a cloud, you may discover dozens of ways to organize its contours into fanciful shapes and scenes. Even clearly defined stimuli may permit more than one interpretation. Look at the Necker cube in ➤ Figure 20.7 if you doubt that perception is an active process. Visualize the top cube as a wire box. If you stare at the cube, its organization will change. Sometimes it will seem to project upward, like the lower-left cube; other times it will project downward. The difference lies in how your brain interprets the same information. To reiterate, we actively *construct* meaningful perceptions; we do not passively record the events and stimuli around us (Intaitė et al., 2013; Rolls, 2008).

In some instances, a stimulus may offer such conflicting information that perceptual organization becomes impossible. For example, the tendency to make a three-dimensional (3-D) object out of a drawing is frustrated by the "three-pronged widget" (➤ Figure 20.8), an *impossible figure.* Such patterns cannot be organized into stable, consistent, or meaningful perceptions. If you cover either end of the drawing in Figure 20.8, it makes sense perceptually. However, a problem arises when you try to organize the entire drawing. Then, the conflicting information that it contains prevents you from constructing a stable perception.

Learning to organize his visual sensations was only one of the hurdles that Mr. S. B. faced in learning to see. In the next section, we consider some others.

Perceptual hypothesis An initial guess regarding how to organize (perceive) a stimulus pattern.

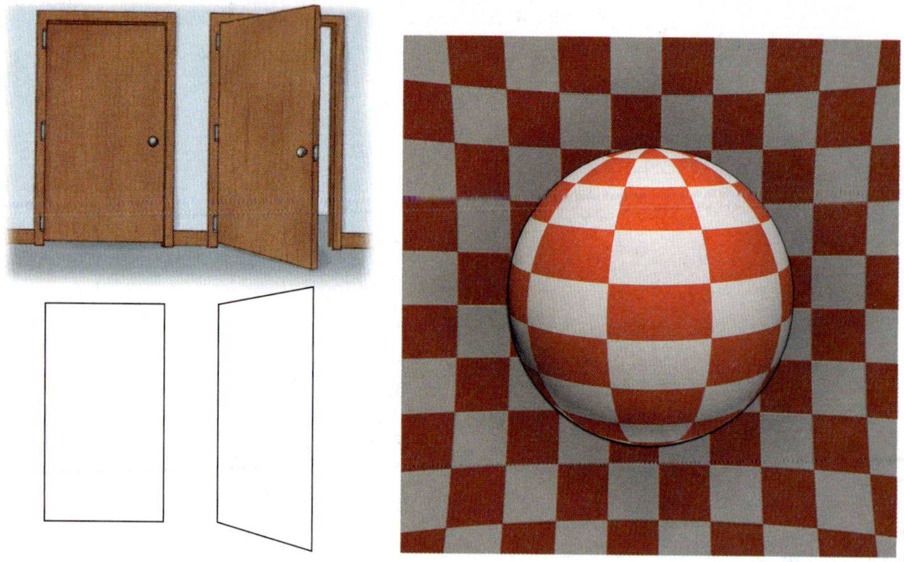

(a) (b)

Nadalina/Shutterstock.com

➤ **Figure 20.9**

Shape constancy. *(a)* When a door is open, its image actually forms a trapezoid. Shape constancy is indicated by the fact that it is still perceived as a rectangle. *(b)* With great effort, you may be able to see this design as a collection of flat shapes. However, if you maintain shape constancy, the distorted squares strongly suggest a wedge projecting out from the surface.

Perceptual Constancies

When Mr. S. B. first regained his vision, he could judge distance only in familiar situations (Gregory, 1990). One day, he was found crawling out of a hospital window to get a closer look at traffic on the street. It's easy to understand his curiosity, but he had to be restrained—his room was on the fourth floor!

Why would Mr. S. B. try to crawl out of a fourth-story window? Couldn't he at least tell distance from the size of the cars? No. You must be visually familiar with objects to use their size to judge distance. Try holding your left hand a few inches in front of your nose and your right hand at arm's length. Your right hand should appear to be about half the size of your left hand. Still, you know that your right hand did not suddenly shrink because you have seen it many times, at various distances. We call this **size constancy**: The perceived size of an object remains the same, even though the size of its image on the retina changes (Wagner, 2012).

To perceive your hand accurately, you had to draw on past experience to provide a top-down plan for constructing your perception. Some of these plans are so basic that they seem *native*, or inborn. An example is the ability to see a line on a piece of paper. Likewise, even newborn babies show some evidence of size constancy (Granrud, 2006). However, many of our perceptions are *empirical*, or based on prior experience. For instance, cars, houses, and people look like toys when seen from a great distance or from an unfamiliar perspective, such as from the top of a skyscraper. This suggests that although some size constancy is innate, it also is affected by learning (Granrud, 2009).

In **shape constancy**, the shape of an object remains stable, even though the shape of its retinal image changes. You can demonstrate shape constancy by looking at this page from directly overhead and then from an angle. Obviously, the page is rectangular, but most of the images that reach your eyes are distorted. Yet though the book's image changes, your perception of its shape remains constant (for additional examples, see ➤ Figure 20.9). On the highway, alcohol intoxication impairs size and shape constancy, adding to the accident rate among drunk drivers (Goldstein & Brockmole, 2017).

Let's say that you are outside in bright sunlight. Beside you, a friend is wearing a gray skirt and a white blouse. Suddenly a cloud shades the sun. It might seem that the blouse would grow dimmer, but it still appears to be bright white. This happens because the blouse continues to reflect a greater *proportion* of light than nearby objects. **Brightness constancy** refers to the fact that the relative brightness of objects appears to stay the same as lighting conditions change. However, this holds true only if the blouse and other objects are all illuminated by the same amount of light. You could make an area on your friend's gray skirt look whiter than the shaded blouse by shining a bright spotlight on the skirt.

To summarize, the energy patterns reaching our senses change constantly, even when they come from the same object. Size, shape, and brightness constancy rescue us from a confusing world in which objects would seem to shrink and grow, change shape as if made of rubber, and light up or fade like neon lamps.

Depth Perception—What If the World Were Flat?

Learning Outcome 20.2 Define depth perception and differentiate between monocular and binocular depth cues, giving examples of each

One particularly interesting example of perceptual construction is the brain's ability to construct a 3-D experience of the world around us (Howard, 2012). Cross your eyes, hold your head very still, and stare at a single point across the room. Your surroundings may appear to be almost flat, like a two-dimensional (2-D) painting or photograph. This is the world that neuroscientist Susan Barry, cross-eyed from birth, lived with until, at the age of 48, she learned to see in 3-D (Barry & Sacks, 2009). Now, uncross your eyes. Suddenly, the 3-D perceptual world returns. What mechanisms underlie our ability to perceive depth and space?

Depth perception is the ability to see space and to accurately judge distances. Without 3-D depth perception, a form of perceptual construction, the world would look like a flat surface. You would have great difficulty driving a car or riding a bicycle, shooting baskets, threading a needle, or simply navigating a room (Harris & Jenkin, 2011).

Mr. S. B. had trouble with depth perception after his sight was restored. Is depth perception learned? Studies done with a visual cliff suggest that depth perception is partly learned and partly innate (Witherington et al., 2005). Basically, a visual cliff is a glass-topped table (➤ **Figure 20.10**). On one side, a checkered surface lies directly beneath the glass. On the other side, the checkered surface is 4 feet below the tabletop. This makes the glass look like a tabletop on one side and a cliff, or drop-off, on the other.

To test for depth perception, 6- to 14-month-old infants were placed in the middle of the visual cliff. This gave them a choice of crawling to the shallow side or the deep side. (The glass prevented them from doing any "skydiving" if they chose the deep side.) Most infants chose the shallow side. In fact, most refused the deep side even when their mothers tried to call them toward it (Gibson & Walk, 1960).

More recent research has shown that depth perception begins to develop as early as 2 weeks of age (Yonas, Elieff, & Arterberry, 2002). It is very likely that at least a basic level of depth perception is innate. Yet the development of depth perception is not complete until about 6 months of age, suggesting that it depends on both brain maturation and individual experience (Nawrot, Mayo, & Nawrot, 2009).

Size constancy The principle that the perceived size of an object remains constant, despite changes in its retinal image.

Shape constancy The principle that the perceived shape of an object is unaffected by changes in its retinal image.

Brightness constancy The principle that the apparent (or relative) brightness of objects remains the same, so long as they are illuminated by the same amount of light.

Depth perception The ability to see 3-D space and to judge distances accurately.

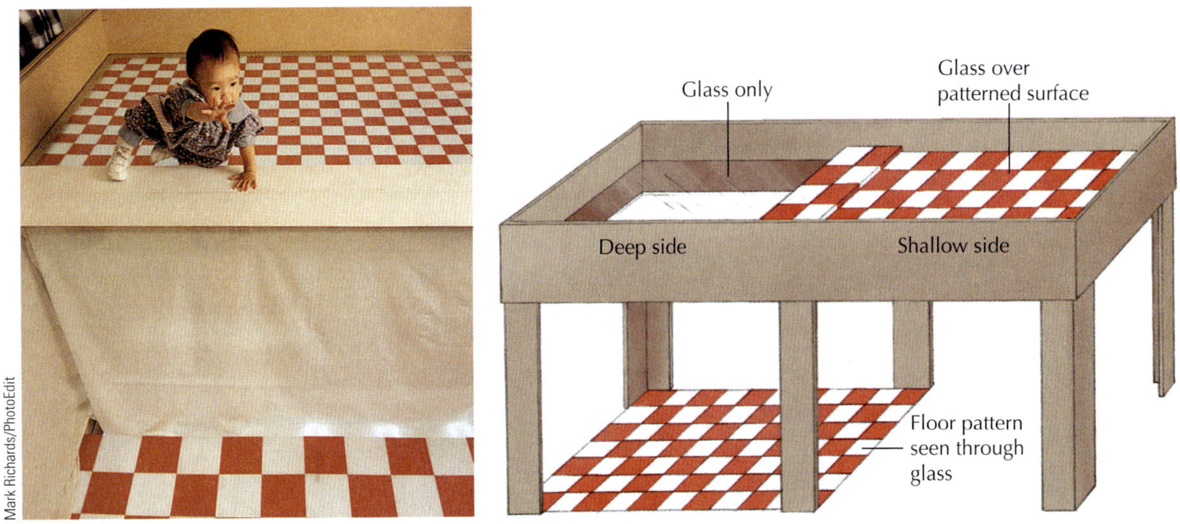

➤ **Figure 20.10**
The visual cliff. Human infants and newborn animals refuse to go over the edge of the visual cliff.

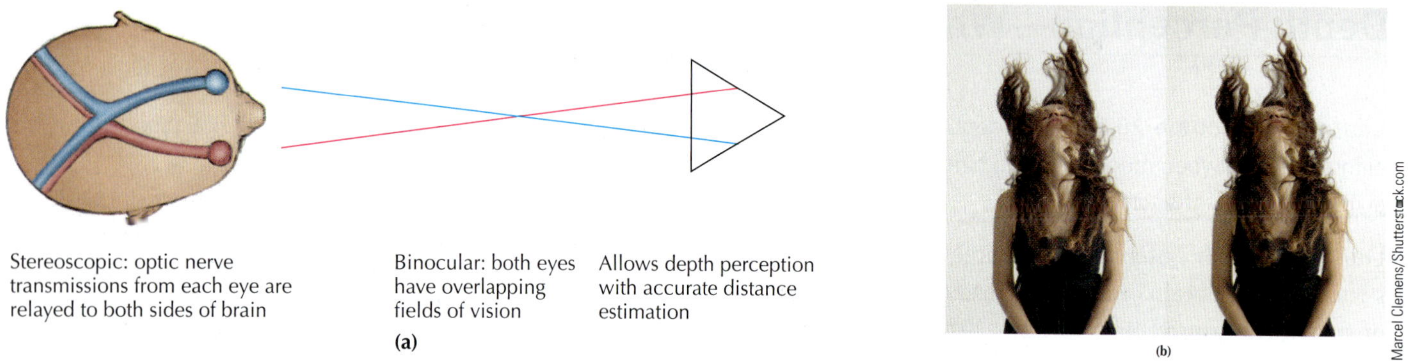

➤ **Figure 20.11**

Stereoscopic vision. *(a)* The geometry of stereoscopic vision. *(b)* The photographs show what the right and left eyes would see when viewing this person. Hold the page about 6 to 8 inches from your eyes. Allow your eyes to cross and focus on the overlapping image between the two photos. Then try to fuse the person into one image. If you are successful, the third dimension will appear like magic.

But don't some older babies crawl off tables or beds? Why would that happen? As soon as infants become active crawlers, they refuse to cross the deep side of the visual cliff. However, older infants who have just learned to walk must relearn to avoid the "deep" side of the visual cliff (Witherington et al., 2005). Besides, even babies who perceive depth may not be able to catch themselves if they slip. A lack of coordination—not an inability to see depth—probably explains most "crash landings" after about 4 months of age.

We learn to construct our perception of 3-D space by integrating information from a variety of *depth cues* (Schiller et al., 2011). **Depth cues** are features of the environment and messages from the body that supply information about distance and space. Some cues require two eyes (**binocular depth cues**), whereas others will work with just one eye (**monocular depth cues**).

Binocular Depth Cues

The most basic source of depth perception is **retinal disparity** (the difference between the images projected onto each eye). Retinal disparity is based on the fact that the eyes are about 2.5 inches apart. Because of this, each eye receives a slightly different view of the world. Try this: Put a finger in front of your eyes and as close to your nose as you can. First, close one eye and then the other, over and over again. You should notice that your finger seems to jump back and forth as you view the different images reaching each eye. However, when the two different images are fused into one overall image, **stereoscopic vision** (3-D sight) occurs (Harris & Jenkin, 2011). The result is a powerful sensation of depth (➤ Figure 20.11).

Convergence, the degree to which the eyes turn in to focus on a close object, is a second binocular depth cue. When you look at a distant object, the lines of vision from your eyes are almost parallel. You normally are not aware of it, but whenever you estimate a distance under 50 feet (as when you play catch or shoot trash can hoops with the first draft of your essay), you are using convergence. How? Muscles attached to the eyeball feed information on eye position to the brain to help it judge distance (➤ Figure 20.12).

You can feel convergence by exaggerating it: Focus on your fingertip and bring it toward your eyes until they almost cross. You can feel the muscles that control eye movement working harder and harder as your fingertip gets closer.

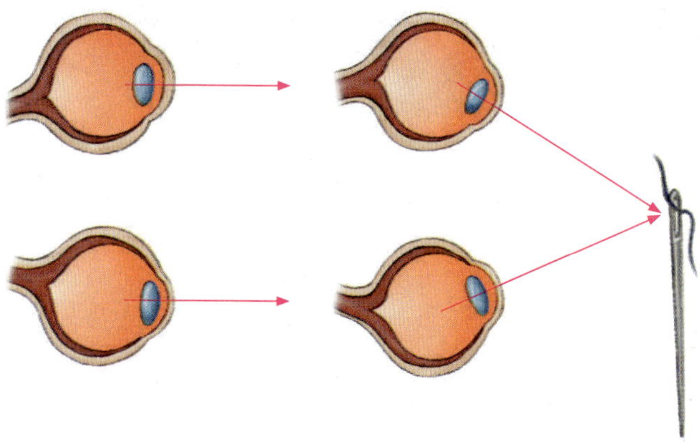

➤ **Figure 20.12**

Convergence. The eyes must converge, or turn in toward the nose, to focus on close objects. The eyes shown here are viewed from above the head.

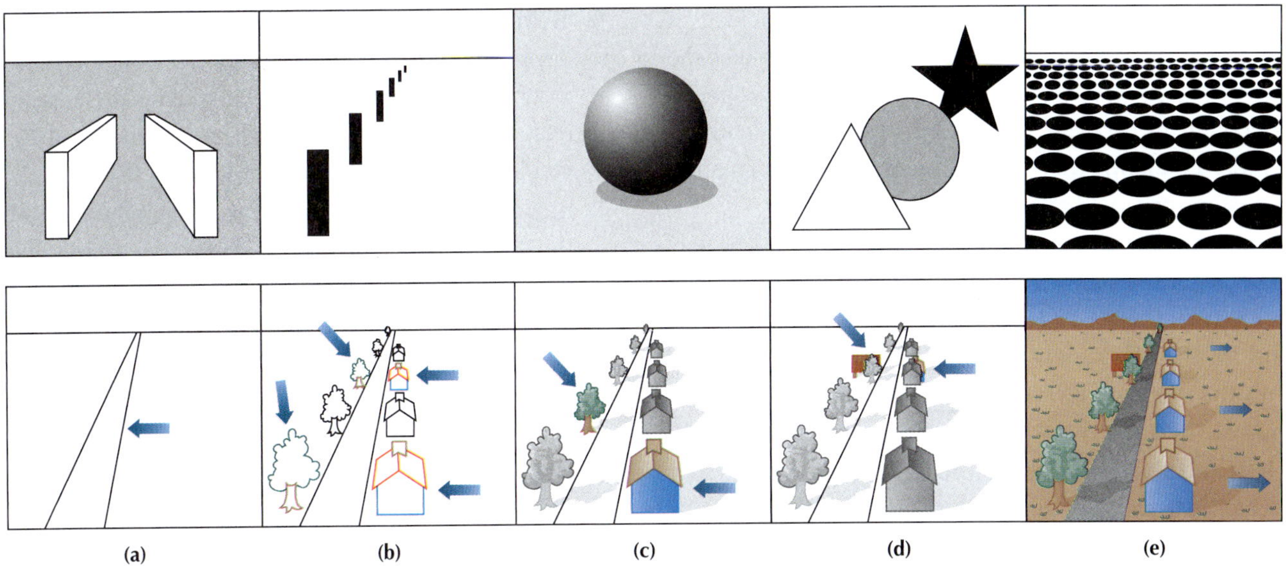

Figure 20.13

Pictorial depth cues. *(a)* Linear perspective. *(b)* Relative size. *(c)* Light and shadow. *(d)* Overlap. *(e)* Texture gradients. Drawings in the top row show fairly "pure" examples of each of the pictorial depth cues. In the bottom row, the pictorial depth cues are used to assemble a more realistic scene.

Can a person with one eye perceive depth? Yes, but not nearly as well as a person with two eyes. Try driving a car or riding a bicycle with one eye closed (not for long, please). You will find yourself braking too soon or too late, and you will have difficulty estimating your speed. ("But officer, my psychology text said to ...") Despite this, you will be able to drive, although it will be more difficult than usual. You can drive because your single eye can still use monocular depth cues.

Monocular Depth Cues

As their name implies, monocular depth cues can be perceived with just one eye. One such cue is *accommodation*, bending of the lens to focus on nearby objects. Sensations from muscles attached to each lens flow back to the brain. Changes in these sensations help us judge distances within about 4 feet of the eyes. This information is available even if you are using only one eye, so accommodation is a monocular cue. Beyond 4 feet, accommodation has limited value. Obviously, accommodation is more important to a watchmaker or a person trying to thread a needle than it is to a basketball player or someone driving an automobile. Other monocular depth cues are referred to as *pictorial depth cues* because a good movie, painting, or photograph can create a convincing sense of depth where none exists.

How is the illusion of depth created on a 2-D surface? **Pictorial depth cues** are features found in paintings, drawings, and photographs that impart information about space, depth, and distance. To understand how these cues work, imagine that you are looking outdoors through a window. If you trace everything you see onto the glass, you will have an excellent drawing, with convincing depth. If you then analyze what is on the glass, you will find the following features:

1. **Linear perspective.** This cue is based on the apparent convergence of parallel lines in the environment. If you stand between two railroad tracks, they appear to meet near the horizon, even though they actually remain parallel. Because you know that they are parallel, their convergence implies great distance (➤ **Figure 20.13*a***).

Depth cues Features of the environment and messages from the body that supply information about distance and space.

Binocular depth cues Perceptual features that impart information about distance and 3-D space that require two eyes.

Monocular depth cues Perceptual features that impart information about distance and 3-D space that require just one eye.

Retinal disparity Difference between the images projected onto each eye.

Stereoscopic vision Perception of space and depth as a result of each eye receiving different images.

Convergence Degree to which the eyes turn in to focus on a close object.

Pictorial depth cues Monocular depth cues found in paintings, drawings, and photographs that impart information about space, depth, and distance.

2. **Relative size.** If an artist wants to depict two objects of the same size at different distances, the artist makes the more distant object smaller (➤ **Figure 20.13*b***). Special effects in films create sensational illusions of depth by rapidly changing the image size of planets, airplanes, monsters, or what have you.
3. **Height in the plane.** Objects that are placed higher (i.e., closer to the horizon line) in a drawing tend to be perceived as more distant. In the upper frame of Figure 20.13*b*, the black columns look like they are receding into the distance partly because they become smaller but also because they move higher in the drawing.
4. **Light and shadow.** Most objects are lighted in ways that create clear patterns of light and shadow. Copying such patterns of light and shadow can give a 2-D design and a 3-D appearance (➤ **Figure 20.13*c***). (Also, look ahead to ➤ **Figure 20.14** for more information on light and shadow.)

➤ **Figure 20.14**

Shading and depth. When judging depth, we usually assume that light comes mainly from one direction, usually from above. Squint a little to blur the image you see here. You should perceive a collection of globes projecting outward. If you turn this page upside down, the globes should become cavities. (After Ramachandran, 1995.)

5. **Overlap.** Overlap (or *interposition*) occurs when one object partially blocks another object. Hold your hands up and ask a friend across the room which is nearer. Relative size will give the answer if one hand is much nearer to your friend than the other. But if one hand is only slightly closer than the other, your friend may not be able to tell—until you slide one hand in front of the other. Overlap then removes any doubt (**Figure 20.13*d***).
6. **Texture gradients.** Changes in texture also contribute to depth perception. If you stand in the middle of a cobblestone street, the street looks coarse near your feet. However, its texture will get smaller and finer as you look into the distance (➤ **Figure 20.13*e***).
7. **Aerial perspective.** Smog, fog, dust, and haze add to the apparent distance of an object. Because of aerial perspective, distant objects tend to be hazy, washed out in color, and lacking in detail. Aerial haze is often most noticeable when it is missing. If you have ever seen a distant mountain range on a crystal-clear day, it might have looked like it was only a few miles away. In reality, you could have been viewing the mountains through 50 miles of crystal-clear air.
8. **Relative motion.** Relative motion, also known as *motion parallax* (PAIR-ah-lax), can be seen by looking out a window and moving your head from side to side. Notice that nearby objects appear to move a sizable distance as your head moves. Trees, houses, and telephone poles that are farther away appear to move slightly in relation to the background. Distant objects such as hills, mountains, or clouds don't seem to move at all.

When combined, pictorial cues can create a powerful illusion of depth. (See ■ **Table 20.1** for a summary of all the depth cues that we have discussed here.)

TABLE 20.1 | Summary of Visual Depth Cues

Binocular Depth Cues
◗ Retinal disparity
◗ Convergence
Monocular Depth Cues
◗ Accommodation
◗ Pictorial depth cues (listed below)
Linear perspective
Relative size
Height in the picture plane
Light and shadow
Overlap
Texture gradients
Aerial perspective
Relative motion (motion parallax)

Figure 20.15

Motion parallax. The apparent motion of objects viewed during travel depends on their distance from the observer. Apparent motion can also be influenced by an observer's point of fixation. At middle distances, objects closer than the point of fixation appear to move backward; those beyond the point of fixation appear to move forward. Objects at great distances, such as the sun or moon, always appear to move forward.

Is motion parallax really a pictorial cue? Strictly speaking it is not, except in the world of 2-D movies, television, or animated cartoons. However, when parallax is present, we almost always perceive depth (Yoonessi & Baker, 2011). Much of the apparent depth in movies comes from relative motion captured by the camera. (**Figure 20.15** illustrates the defining feature of motion parallax.) Imagine that you are on a bus and watching the passing scenery (with your gaze at a right angle to the road). Under these conditions, nearby objects will appear to rush *backward*. Those farther away, such as distant mountains, will seem to move very little, or not at all. Objects that are more remote, such as the sun or moon, will appear to move in the *same* direction you are traveling. (That's why the sun appears to "follow" you when you take a stroll.)

MODULE 20 Perceptual Processes—Learning Outcomes Revisited

20.1 Distinguish between illusions and hallucinations, contrast bottom-up processing with top-down processing, provide some examples of top-down processing, and explain what is meant by perceptual constancies and provide three examples

Illusions are distorted perceptions of stimuli in the environment; the brain receives information but does not process it in a way that is faithful with reality. Hallucinations involve the perception of objects or events that do not exist. Perceptions are based on simultaneous bottom-up and top-down processing. Complete perceptions can be assembled from small sensory features in "bottom-up" processing. In contrast, preexisting knowledge is applied to sensory information in "top-down" processing to help organize features into a meaningful whole. Top-down processes are at work when we work to separate figure and ground, as well as in the interpretation of reversible and ambiguous figures. Perceptual constancies are "rules of thumb" developed by the brain as a product of years of experience interpreting the environment. They help the brain to quickly process incoming sensory information in ways that are usually accurate. Three examples are size, shape, and brightness constancy.

20.2 Define depth perception and differentiate between monocular and binocular depth cues, giving examples of each

Depth perception, the ability to see 3-D space and to judge distances accurately, depends on binocular cues (those that require two eyes) of retinal disparity and convergence. Depth perception also depends on monocular cues (those requiring one eye) that include accommodation and "pictorial" depth cues (linear perspective, relative size, height in the picture plane, light and shadow, overlap, texture gradients, and motion parallax).

Reflective Practice

Content Check

1. In top-down processing of information, individual features are analyzed and assembled into a meaningful whole. T or F?
2. At times, meaningful perceptual organization represents a(n) ________________, or "guess," which is held until the evidence contradicts it.
3. The design known as the Necker cube is a good example of an impossible figure. T or F?
4. Which among the following are subject to basic perceptual constancy?
   a. figure-ground organization
   b. size
   c. ambiguity
   d. brightness
   e. continuity
   f. closure
   g. shape
   h. nearness
5. The visual cliff is used to test for infant sensitivity to linear perspective. T or F?
6. Write an *M* or a *B* after each of the following to indicate whether it is a monocular or binocular depth cue. accommodation ______ convergence ______ retinal disparity ______ linear perspective ______ motion parallax ______ overlap ______ relative size ______

Skill Check

Think Critically

7. People who have taken psychedelic drugs, such as lysergic acid diethylamide (LSD) or mescaline, often report that the objects and people that they see appear to be changing in size, shape, and brightness. This suggests that such drugs disrupt which perceptual process?

Self-Reflect

As you look around the area where you are now, how are the Gestalt principles helping organize your perceptions? Try to find a specific example for each principle. Why are the constancies important for maintaining a stable perceptual world? Part of the rush of excitement produced by action movies and video games is based on the sense of depth that they create. Return to the list of pictorial depth cues. What cues have you seen used to portray depth? Try to think of specific examples in a movie or game that you have seen recently.

ANSWERS

1. F 2. hypothesis 3. F 4. b, d, g 5. F 6. accommodation (M), convergence (B), retinal disparity (B), linear perspective (M), motion parallax (M), overlap (M), relative size (M) 7. Perceptual constancies (size, shape, and brightness).

MODULE 21

Sensation and Perception

Perception and Objectivity

Golfing with Dad

Comstock/Stockbyte/Getty Images

One of your authors (a terrible golfer) occasionally spent the day golfing with his father (a great golfer). Imagine watching your opponent hit the ball right down the middle of the fairway over and over, while you spend much of your day looking for your lost golf ball (in the rough, forest, desert, lake—geez!). Now imagine that your opponent is always the one to find your lost ball. And so it was for your author.

In many sports, expert players are much better than beginners at paying attention to key information. Compared with novices, experts scan actions and events more quickly, and they focus on only the most meaningful information. This helps experts make decisions and react more quickly. In fact, various processes shape our perceptions, which are a far-from-perfect model of the world. Let's investigate some factors that affect the accuracy of our perceptual experiences.

~LEARNING OUTCOMES~

After reading this module you should be able to:

21.1 Describe how motives, emotions, expectations, learning, and culture alter perceptions

21.2 Outline steps that could be taken to perceive events more accurately

Perception and Experience—Believing Is Seeing

Learning Outcome 21.1 Describe how motives, emotions, expectations, learning, and culture alter perceptions

We use Gestalt organizing principles, perceptual constancies, and depth cues to construct our visual perceptions (see Module 20). All these processes, as well as others, make up the common, partly inborn, core of our perceptual abilities. In addition, we each have specific life experiences that can, in top-down fashion, affect our perceptions. For instance, what you perceive can be altered in the short run by motives, emotions, and perceptual expectancies; and in the long run by perceptual habits and culture.

Motives, Emotions, and Perception

Did you know that if you are hungry, food and even food-related words are more likely to gain your attention than non-food-related words (Werthmann et al., 2011)? Advertisers do. They are especially likely to take advantage of two motives that are widespread in our society: *anxiety* and *sex*. Everything from automobile tires to cosmetic surgery is merchandised by using sex to gain attention (Hennink-Kaminski & Reichert, 2011). Other ads combine sex with anxiety. Deodorant, soaps, toothpaste, and countless other products are pushed in ads that play on our desires to be attractive, to have "sex appeal," or to avoid embarrassment.

Our emotions can also shape our perceptions (Yiend, 2010). According to psychologist Barbara Frederickson, negative emotions generally narrow our perceptual focus, or "spotlight," which increases the likelihood of inattentional blindness. In contrast, positive emotions can broaden the scope of attention (Huntsinger, 2013). For example, positive emotions can affect how well people recognize people from other races. In recognizing faces, a consistent *other-race effect* occurs. This is a sort of "They all look alike to me" bias in perceiving persons from other racial and ethnic groups. In tests of facial recognition, people are much better at recognizing faces of their own race than others. But when people are in a positive mood, their ability to recognize people from other races improves (Blandón-Gitlin et al., 2014).

Perceptual Expectancies

What is a perceptual expectancy? If you are a runner in the starting blocks at a track meet, you are *set* to respond in a certain way. If a car backfires, runners at a track meet may "jump the gun." Likewise, past experience, motives, context, or suggestions may create a **perceptual expectancy (set)** that prepares you to perceive in a certain way. As a matter of fact, we all frequently jump the gun when perceiving. In essence, an expectancy is a perceptual hypothesis that we are *very likely* to apply to a stimulus—even if applying it is inappropriate.

Perceptual sets often lead us to see what we *expect* to see. For example, let's say while driving, you just made an illegal lane change (or texted on your cellphone!?). You then see a flashing light. For an instant, you think, "Rats, busted," and expect the police car to pull you over. But then you realize that it was just a car with a vivid turn signal. Most people have had similar experiences in which expectations altered their perceptions. To observe perceptual expectancies firsthand, perform the demonstration described in ➤ **Figure 21.1.**

Perceptual expectancies are frequently created by *suggestion.* In one study (wine snobs, take note), participants given a taste of a $90 wine reported that it tasted better than a $10 wine. In fMRI testing of the subjects, the images confirmed that brain areas related to pleasure were indeed more active when participants tasted the more expensive wine (Plassmann et al., 2008). The twist is that the same wine was served in both cases. Suggesting that the wine was expensive created a perceptual expectancy that it would taste better. And so it did (advertisers, also take note). In the same way, labeling people as "gang members," "mental patients," "queers," "illegal immigrants," "bitches," and so on is likely to distort perceptions.

Perceptual Learning: Do They See What We See?

Britain is one of the few countries in the world where people drive on the left side of the road. As you might suspect, Britons become used to this. In contrast, because of this reversal, it is not unusual for visitors from other countries to step off curbs in front of cars—after carefully looking for traffic in the *wrong* direction. As this example suggests, learning has a powerful impact on top-down processing in perception.

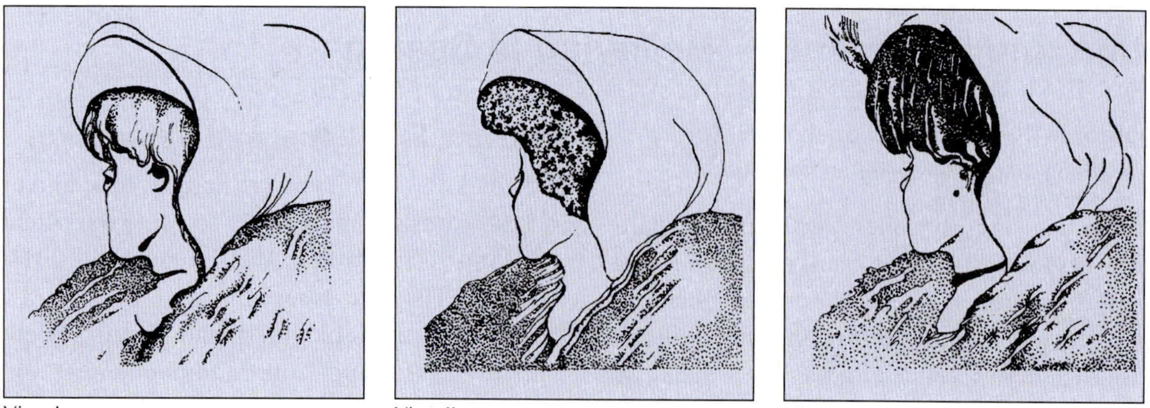

View I View II View III

➤ **Figure 21.1**

Creating perceptual expectancies. These "young woman/old woman" illustrations can be used to demonstrate perceptual expectancy. Show view I and view II to some of your friends (while covering all other views). Next, show them view III and ask them what they see. Those who saw view I should see the old woman in view III; those who saw view II should see the young woman in view III. Can you see both? (After Leeper, 1935.)

How does learning affect perception? The term **perceptual learning** refers to changes in the brain that alter how we construct sensory information into perception (Moreno et al., 2009). For example, to use a computer, you must learn to pay attention to specific stimuli, such as icons and cursors. We also learn to tell the difference between stimuli that seemed identical at first. An example is the novice chef who discovers how to tell the difference between dried basil, oregano, and tarragon. In other situations, we learn to focus on just one part of a group of stimuli. This saves us from having to process all the stimuli in the group. For instance, a football linebacker may be able to tell if the next play will be a run or a pass by watching one or two key players, rather than the entire opposing team (Gorman, Abernethy, & Farrow, 2011; Seitz & Watanabe, 2005).

In general, learning creates **perceptual habits**—ingrained patterns of organization and attention—that affect our daily experience. Stop for a moment and look at ➤ **Figure 21.2.** The face on the left looks somewhat unusual, to be sure. But the distortion seems mild—until you turn the page upside down. Viewed normally, the face looks quite grotesque. Why is there a difference? Apparently, most people have little experience with upside-down faces. Perceptual learning, therefore, has less impact on our perceptions of an upside-down face. With a face in the normal position, you know what to expect and where to look. Also, you tend to see the entire face as a recognizable pattern. When a face is inverted, we are forced to perceive its individual features separately (Caharel et al., 2006).

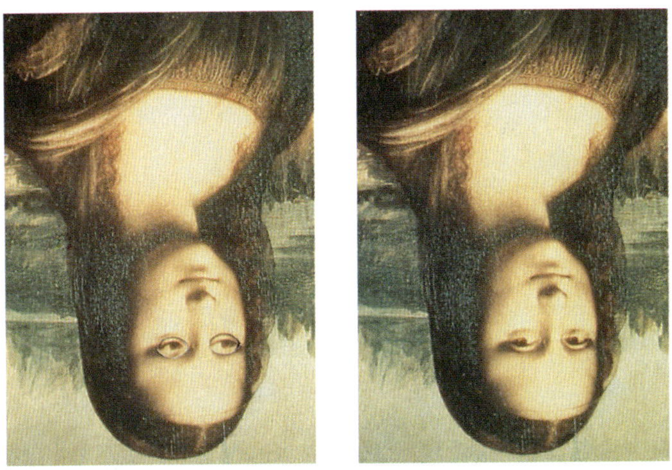

➤ **Figure 21.2**

The effects of prior experience on perception. The doctored face looks far worse when viewed right side up because it can be related to past experience.

Culture and Perception The main reason for the other-race effect we just discussed is that we typically have more experience with people from our own race. As a result, we developed perceptual habits that help us recognize different persons. For other groups, we lack the perceptual expertise needed to accurately separate one face from another (Megreya, White, & Burton, 2011; Sporer, 2001).

Okay, so maybe members of different races or ethnic groups have developed perceptual habits that lead them to see in-group faces differently, but we all see everything else the same, right? Maybe not. According to psychologist Richard Nisbett and his colleagues, based on their cultures, people often construct different perceptions of the world around them. European Americans are individualistic people who tend to focus on themselves and their sense of personal control. In contrast, East Asians are collectivist people who tend to focus on their interpersonal relationships and social responsibilities. As a consequence, European Americans tend to perceive actions in terms of internal factors ("She did it because she chose to do it"). In comparison, East Asians tend to perceive actions in terms of their social context ("He did it because it was his responsibility to his family") (Henrich, Heine, & Norenzayan, 2010; Norenzayan & Nisbett, 2000).

In one study, American and Japanese participants were shown drawings of everyday scenes, such as a farm. Later, they saw a slightly changed version of the scene and were asked to identify the differences. Some of the changes were made to the focal point, or figure, of the scene. Other changes altered the surrounding context, or ground, of the scene. Americans, it turns out, were better at detecting changes in the figure of a scene, while Japanese participants were better at finding alterations in the background (Nisbett & Miyamoto, 2005).

To explain this difference, Chua, Boland, and Nisbett (2005) presented American and Chinese participants with pictures of a figure (such as a tiger) placed on the ground (such as in a jungle) and monitored their eye-movement patterns. The Americans focused their eye movements on the figure; Chinese participants directed more eye

Perceptual expectancy (set) A readiness to perceive in a particular manner, induced by strong expectations.

Perceptual learning Changes in perception that can be attributed to prior experience; a result of changes in how the brain processes sensory information.

Perceptual habits Ingrained patterns of organization and attention that affect our daily experience.

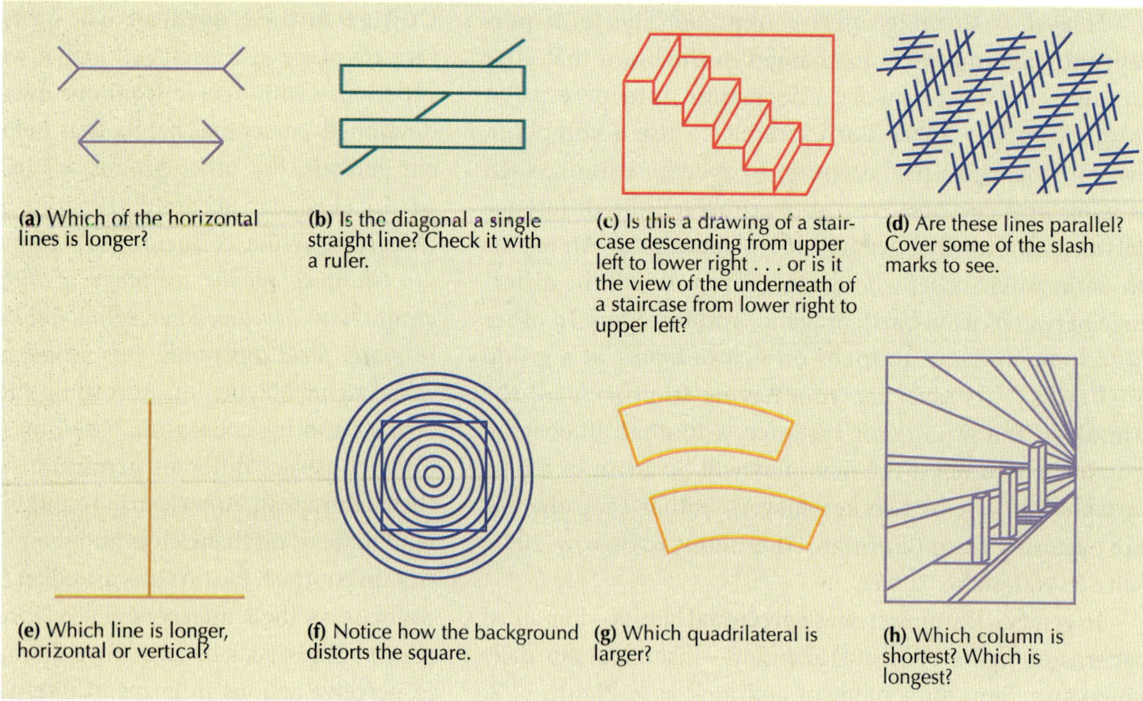

(a) Which of the horizontal lines is longer?

(b) Is the diagonal a single straight line? Check it with a ruler.

(c) Is this a drawing of a staircase descending from upper left to lower right . . . or is it the view of the underneath of a staircase from lower right to upper left?

(d) Are these lines parallel? Cover some of the slash marks to see.

(e) Which line is longer, horizontal or vertical?

(f) Notice how the background distorts the square.

(g) Which quadrilateral is larger?

(h) Which column is shortest? Which is longest?

➤ Figure 21.3
Some interesting perceptual illusions. Such illusions reveal that perceptual misconstructions are a normal part of visual perception.

movements around the ground. In other words, Westerners have a relatively narrow focus of attention, whereas Easterners have a broader focus of attention (Boduroglu, Shah, & Nisbett, 2009). Apparently, the society in which we live indeed can influence even our most basic perceptual habits (Hedden et al., 2008). This difference in perceptual style even influences the artistic and aesthetic preferences expressed in Eastern and Western art (Masuda et al., 2008).

Perceptual Learning and Perceptual Misconstruction Perceptual habits even play a role in explaining some illusions. In general, size and shape constancy, habitual eye movements, continuity, and perceptual habits combine in various ways to produce the illusions in ➤ **Figure 21.3.** Rather than attempt to explain all of them, let's focus on one deceptively simple example.

Consider the drawing in Figure 21.3*a*. This is the familiar **Müller-Lyer illusion** (MEOO-ler-LIE-er) in which the horizontal line with arrowheads appears shorter than the line with Vs. A quick measurement will show that they are the same length. How can we explain this illusion?

Evidence suggests that it is based on a lifetime of experience with the edges and corners of rooms and buildings (Deręgowski, 2013). Richard Gregory (2000) believes that you see the line with the arrowheads as if it were the nearby corner of a room joining two walls receding from it (➤ **Figure 21.4***a*). The line with the Vs (➤ **Figure 21.4***b*),

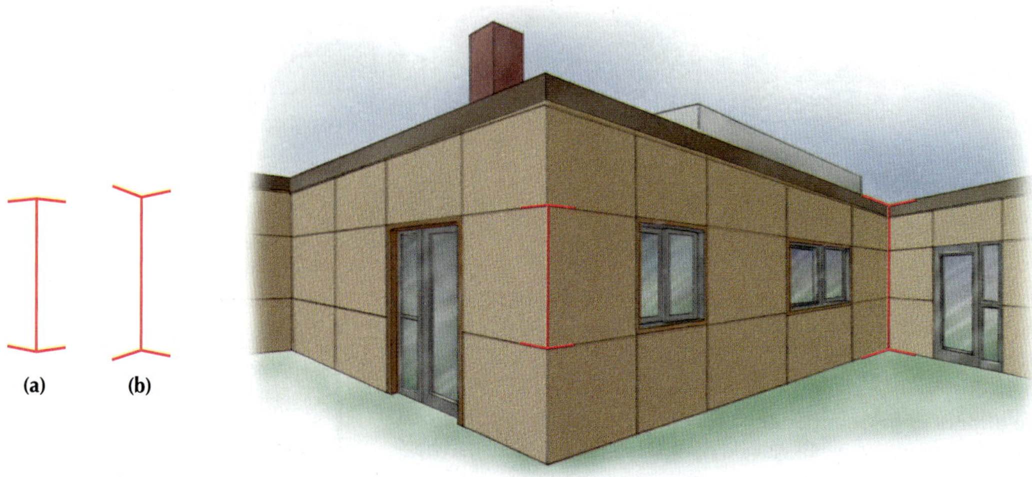

➤ Figure 21.4
The Müller-Lyer illusion. Why does line *(b)* in the Müller-Lyer illusion look longer than line *(a)*? Probably because it looks more like a distant corner than a nearer one. Because the vertical lines form images of the same length, the more "distant" line must be perceived as larger. As you can see in the drawing on the right, additional depth cues accentuate the Müller-Lyer illusion.

on the other hand, suggests the farther corner of a room or building joining two walls coming closer. [If these two lines were belly buttons, (a) would be an "outie" and (b) would be an "innie."] In other words, cues that suggest a 3-D space alter our perception of a 2-D design.

If two objects make images of the same size, the more distant object must be larger. This is known formally as *size-distance invariance* (the size of an object's image is precisely related to its distance from the eyes). Gregory believes that his concept explains the Müller-Lyer illusion. If the V-tipped line looks farther away from you than the arrowhead-tipped line, you must compensate by seeing the V-tipped line as longer. This explanation presumes that you have had years of experience with straight lines, sharp edges, and corners—a pretty safe assumption in our culture. In other words, we misconstruct the Müller-Lyer lines because of perceptual habits we acquired because we live in a "carpentered world" (Deręgowski, 2013).

Is there any way to show that past experience causes the illusion? If we could test someone who saw only curves and wavy lines as a child, we would know if experience with a "carpentered" culture is important. Fortunately, a few San bushmen, a culture from the Kalahari Desert in Africa, still live a traditional hunting-gathering life in the "round." Traditional San rarely encounter straight lines in their daily lives: Their temporary dwellings are semicircular, and the area has few straight roads or square buildings.

What happens if a San looks at the Müller-Lyer design? The typical traditional San does not experience the illusion. At most, she or he sees the V-shaped line as *slightly* longer than the other (Henrich, Heine, & Norenzayan, 2010). This seems to confirm the importance of perceptual habits in determining our view of the world.

Can perception ever be "illusion-free"? Probably not. But the next section offers some ideas on how to perceive events more accurately.

Becoming a Better Eyewitness to Life—Pay Attention!

Learning Outcome 21.2 Outline steps that could be taken to perceive events more accurately

In the courtroom, eyewitness testimony can be a key to proving guilt or innocence. The claim "I saw it with my own eyes" still carries a lot of weight with a jury. Too many jurors (unless they have taken a psychology course) tend to assume that eyewitness testimony is nearly infallible (Odinot, Wolters, & van Giezen, 2013). Even U.S. judges are vulnerable to overoptimism about eyewitness testimony (Wise et al., 2010; Wise & Safer, 2010). But, to put it bluntly, eyewitness testimony is frequently wrong (Shermer, Rose, & Hoffman, 2011). Recall, for instance, that one of your authors would have sworn in court that he had seen a murder taking place at the supermarket—*if* he hadn't received more information to correct his misperceptions.

AP Images/John-Marshall Mantel

Even in broad daylight, eyewitness testimony is untrustworthy. In 2001, an airliner crashed near Kennedy International Airport in New York. Hundreds of people saw the plane go down. Half of them said the plane was on fire. Flight recorders showed there was no fire. One witness in five saw the plane make a right turn. An equal number saw it make a left turn! As one investigator noted, the best witness may be a "kid under 12 years old who doesn't have his parents around." Adults, it seems, are swayed easily by their expectations.

What about witnesses who are certain that their perceptions were accurate? Should juries believe them? While highly confident witnesses are generally more accurate than less confident eyewitnesses, even witnesses who are completely certain are frequently wrong (Lindsay et al., 2013).

Unfortunately, perception rarely provides an "instant replay" of events. Impressions formed when a person is surprised, threatened, or under stress are especially prone to distortion (Yuille & Daylen, 1998). One study of eyewitness cases found that the *wrong person* was chosen from police lineups 25 percent of the time (Levi, 1998).

Since DNA testing became available, more than 360 people who were convicted in the United States of major

Müller-Lyer illusion Two equal-length lines tipped with inward or outward pointing Vs appear to be of different lengths.

crimes have been exonerated after serving an average of 14 *years* in prison. About 70 percent of these innocent people were convicted mainly on the basis of eyewitness testimony (Innocence Project, 2020). Psychologists are gradually convincing lawyers, judges, and police that eyewitness errors are common (Yarmey, 2010). Even so, thousands of people have been wrongfully convicted.

Wouldn't the victim of a crime remember more than a mere witness? Not necessarily. A classic study found that eyewitness accuracy is virtually the same for witnessing a crime (seeing a pocket calculator stolen) as it is for being a victim (seeing one's own watch stolen) (Hosch & Cooper, 1982). Placing more weight on the testimony of victims may be a serious mistake. In many crimes, victims fall prey to *weapon focus*, a form of inattentional blindness. Understandably, they fix their entire attention on the knife, gun, or other weapon that an attacker used. In doing so, they fail to notice details of appearance, dress, or other clues to identity (Fawcett et al., 2013). Additional factors that lower eyewitness accuracy consistently are summarized in ■ **Table 21.1**.

The Whole Human: Perceptual Accuracy

Since everyday perceptions are frequently as inaccurate or distorted as those of an emotional eyewitness, it is worth being more tolerant of the views of others and more cautious about our own objectivity. It also may encourage us to engage in more frequent *reality testing*.

If you have ever concluded that someone was angry, upset, or unfriendly without checking the accuracy of your perceptions, you have fallen into a subtle trap. Personal objectivity is an elusive quality, requiring frequent reality testing to maintain. At the very least, it pays to ask a person what she or he is feeling when you are in doubt. Clearly, most of us could learn to be better "eyewitnesses" to daily events (Siegel, 2010).

Do some people perceive things more accurately than others? Humanistic psychologist Abraham Maslow (1969)

TABLE 21.1 | Factors Affecting the Accuracy of Eyewitness Perceptions

Sources of Error	Summary of Findings
Wording of questions	An eyewitness's testimony about an event can be affected by the wording of questions that the witness is asked.
Postevent information	Eyewitness testimony about an event often reflects not only what was actually seen, but also information obtained later on.
Attitudes, expectations	An eyewitness's perception and memory for an event may be affected by his or her attitudes and expectations.
Drug intoxication	Drug (including alcohol) intoxication impairs witnesses' ability to recall events after they occur.
Cross-racial perceptions	Eyewitnesses are better at identifying members of their own race than they are at identifying people of other races.
Weapon focus	The presence of a weapon impairs an eyewitness's ability to identify the culprit's face and other personal details.
Accuracy-confidence	An eyewitness's confidence is not a good predictor of his or her accuracy.
Exposure time	The less time that an eyewitness has to observe an event, the less correctly that she or he will perceive and remember it.
Unconscious transference	Eyewitnesses sometimes identify as a culprit someone whom they have seen in another situation or context.
Color perception	Judgments of color made under monochromatic light (such as an orange streetlight) are highly unreliable.
Stress	High levels of stress impair the accuracy of eyewitness perceptions.

Source: Adapted from Wells & Olson, 2003; Yarmey, 2010.

believed that some people perceive themselves and others with unusual accuracy. Maslow characterized these people as especially alive, open, aware, and mentally healthy. He found that their perceptual styles were marked by immersion in the present; a lack of self-consciousness; freedom from selecting, criticizing, or evaluating; and a general "surrender" to experience. The kind of perception that Maslow described is like that of a mother with her newborn infant, a child at Disneyland, or two people in love.

In daily life, sensation, perception, and even selective attention often occur without conscious awareness. Furthermore, we quickly habituate, or respond less, to predictable and unchanging stimuli. **Habituation** is a type of learning—basically, we learn to cease paying attention to familiar stimuli. For instance, when you download a new song from iTunes, the music initially holds your attention all the way through. But when the song becomes "old," it may play without you really attending to it. When a stimulus is repeated *without change*, our response to it habituates, or decreases. It is interesting that creative people habituate *more slowly* than average. We might expect that they would rapidly become bored with a repeated stimulus. Instead, it seems that creative people actively attend to stimuli, even those that are repeated (Colin, Moore, & West, 1996; Runco, 2012).

The Value of Paying Attention

Whereas the average person has not reached perceptual restriction of the "if you've seen one tree, you've seen them all" variety, the fact remains that most of us look at a tree and classify it in the perceptual category of "trees in general" without appreciating the miracle standing before us. How, then, can we bring about **dishabituation**—a reversal of habituation—on a day-to-day basis? Does perceptual clarity require years of effort? Fortunately, a more immediate avenue is available. The deceptively simple key to dishabituation is this: Be reflective by paying mindful attention. The following story summarizes the importance of attention:

> One day, a man of the people said to Zen Master Ikkyu: "Master, will you please write for me some maxims of the highest wisdom?"
>
> Ikkyu immediately took his brush and wrote the word "Attention."
>
> "Is that all?" asked the man. "Will you not add something more?"
>
> Ikkyu then wrote twice running: "Attention. Attention."
>
> "Well," remarked the man rather irritably, "I really don't see much depth or subtlety in what you have just written."
>
> Then Ikkyu wrote the same word three times running: "Attention. Attention. Attention." Half-angered, the man demanded, "What does that word 'attention' mean, anyway?"
>
> And Ikkyu answered gently: "Attention means attention." (Kapleau, 1966)

Becoming a Better "Eyewitness" to Life

Here's an overview of some ideas from this module (and the other modules on sensation and perception) to help mindfully maintain and enhance perceptual awareness and accuracy:

1. *Remember that perceptions are constructions of reality.* Learn to regularly question your own perceptions. Are they accurate? Could another interpretation fit the facts? What assumptions are you making? How might your assumptions be distorting your perceptions?
2. *Break perceptual habits and interrupt habituation.* Each day, try to get away from habitual, top-down processing and do some activities in new ways. For example, take a different route when you travel to work or school. Do routine activities, such as brushing your teeth or combing your hair, with your nonpreferred hand. Try to look at friends and family members as if they are persons you just met for the first time.
3. *Seek out-of-the-ordinary experiences.* The possibilities here range from trying foods that you don't normally eat to reading opinions very different from your own. Experiences ranging from a quiet walk in the woods to a trip to an amusement park may be perceptually refreshing.
4. *Beware of perceptual sets.* Any time you pigeonhole people, objects, or events, there is a danger that your perceptions will be distorted by expectations or preexisting categories. Be especially wary of labels and stereotypes. Try to see people as individuals and events as unique, one-time occurrences.
5. *Be aware of the ways that motives and emotions influence perceptions.* It is difficult to avoid being swayed by your own interests, needs, desires, and emotions. But be aware

Habituation A decrease in perceptual response to a repeated stimulus.

Dishabituation A reversal of habituation.

of this trap and actively try to see the world through the eyes of others. Taking the other person's perspective is especially valuable in disputes or arguments. Ask yourself, "How does this look to her or him?"

6. *Make a habit of engaging in reality testing.* Actively look for additional evidence to check the accuracy of your perceptions. Ask questions, seek clarifications, and find alternate channels of information. Remember that perception is not automatically accurate. You could be wrong—we all are, frequently.
7. *Pay attention.* Make a conscious effort to pay attention to other people and your surroundings. Don't drift through life in a haze. Listen to others with full concentration. Watch their facial expressions. Make eye contact. Try to get in the habit of approaching perception as if you are going to have to testify later about what you saw and heard.

MODULE 21 Perception and Objectivity—Learning Outcomes Revisited

21.1 Describe how motives, emotions, expectations, learning, and culture alter perceptions

Motives, emotions, suggestion, and prior experience combine in various ways to create more or less long-lived perceptual sets, or expectancies. Personal motives and emotions often alter perceptions by changing the evaluation of what is seen or by altering attention to specific details. Perceptual learning and culture influences the top-down organization and interpretation of sensations.

21.2 Outline steps that could be taken to perceive events more accurately

Perceptual accuracy is enhanced by reality testing, dishabituation, and conscious efforts to pay attention. It also is valuable to break perceptual habits, to broaden frames of reference, to beware of perceptual sets, and to be aware of the ways motives and emotions influence perceptions.

Reflective Practice

Content Check

1. When a person is prepared to perceive events in a particular way, it is said that a perceptual expectancy or ____________________ exists.
2. Perceptual habits may become so ingrained that they lead us to misperceive a stimulus. T or F?
3. People around the world perceive in the same way regardless of culture. T or F?
4. Inaccuracies in eyewitness perceptions obviously occur in "real life," but they cannot be reproduced in psychology experiments. T or F?
5. Victims of crimes are more accurate eyewitnesses than impartial observers. T or F?
6. *Reality testing* is another term for dishabituation. T or F?
7. A good antidote to perceptual habituation can be found in conscious efforts to
   a. reverse sensory gating
   b. pay attention
   c. achieve visual accommodation
   d. counteract shape constancy

Skill Check

Think Critically

8. Cigarette advertisements in the United States are required to carry a warning label about the health risks of smoking. How have tobacco companies made these labels less visible?

Self-Reflect

You have almost certainly misperceived a situation at some time because of a perceptual expectancy or the influence of your motives and emotions. How were your perceptions influenced? How has perceptual learning affected your ability to safely drive a car? For example, where do you habitually look as you are driving? Because perceptions are constructions or models of external events, we should all engage in more frequent reality testing. Can you think of a recent event when a little reality testing would have saved you from misjudging a situation?

ANSWERS

1. set 2. T 3. F 4. F 5. F 6. F 7. b 8. Advertisers place health warnings in the corners of ads, where they attract the least possible attention. Also, the labels are often placed on "busy" backgrounds so they are partially camouflaged. Finally, the main images in ads are designed to be the primary focus of attention. This further distracts readers from seeing the warnings.

MODULE 22

A Psychologist's Skill Set
Effective Communication

Making Your Point

To get a sense of just how much good communication matters, consider the Global Gossip Game, run each year by several libraries around the world. A recent version of the game included more than 800 participants from all seven continents speaking six different languages. The goal of the game is to take an initial message (a recent example was "*Play is training for the unexpected*") and pass it along to players at the next participating library, translating the message as necessary. After starting in Melbourne, Australia, five versions of the original statement arrived at libraries across the United States the next day. Somehow, though, after travelling for 30 hours and across 95,000 miles, the initial message had become "I love the world," "Zombie," "Clouds travel around the world," "Glow, glow, peanut butter jelly," and "Ian needs help."

sirtravelalot/Shutterstock.com

While the results of the Global Gossip Game are funny, they also highlight the importance of clear communication. This is obviously true when messages are moving between people who may not share the same language, but it's equally important in a marriage, a social media campaign, or between coworkers in an office in Nebraska.

~LEARNING OUTCOMES~

After reading this module you should be able to:

22.1 Distinguish between verbal and nonverbal communication, outline two verbal communication methods and two verbal communication points of view, and create a plan to improve your own communication with others

Communication as a Skill—Tell Me!

Learning Outcome 22.1 Distinguish between verbal and nonverbal communication, outline two verbal communication methods and two verbal communication points of view, and create a plan to improve your own communication with others

We saw in Modules 17–21 that sensation and perception are important in determining how people see and hear the world around them. For that reason, sensory and perceptual systems play an important role in our ability to communicate with others, both nonverbally and verbally. *Nonverbal communication* refers to our perception of other people's voice, eye contact, and body language. Though humans are very sensitive to nonverbal cues (Siegman & Feldstein, 2014), in this module, we focus on *verbal communication*—the words that people use when they write or speak.

Communication is an important skill because it serves a number of purposes that are valuable in connecting us with others. For example, we use communication to persuade people to give us what we need (or want). We also use it to gather information that we need, or to provide others with information. The information that's exchanged may include facts or explanations, but it can also be more personal, relating to our thoughts, opinions, and feelings.

When you think about using verbal communication skills to meet these goals, there are two things to consider. First, there are two main *communication methods* that we use: oral (or spoken) and written. Second, there are two *communication points of view*: either we're providing information or we're receiving information. If you put those two ideas together, you'll see that there are four communication-based skills that are important to master (■ **Table 22.1**).

Mastering these skills also requires an appreciation of the many *channels* we now use for verbal communication, which include more traditional forms (written letters, books, telephone conversations, and lectures) and those that have become popular more recently (email, texting, and social media). These channels differ in terms of the level of formality that is typically considered acceptable when communicating, as well as the type of information that is appropriate for sharing and discussion.

Say What You Mean

Given the purposes that it serves, communication is critical in developing and maintaining positive personal and professional relationships. On the personal side, for example, researchers have demonstrated that conflict in marriages and parent–child relationships can often be traced back to difficulties with communication (Flora & Segrin, 2015; Gottman, 1994). In terms of your professional life, many employers are interested in hiring people who have good teamwork and leadership skills, both of which are dependent on being able to communicate well (Lussier & Achua, 2015). Let's take a closer look at how the four verbal communication skills—reading, listening, writing, and speaking—help to create positive home and work environments, and how you can improve on your own abilities in this area.

TABLE 22.1 | Forms of Communication

	Providing Information	Receiving Information
Oral/spoken communication	Speaking skills	Listening skills
Written communication	Writing skills	Reading skills

Receiving Information: Reading and Listening

Good communication depends on our ability to accurately understand the information that other people are providing. We've already spent some time talking about how to improve reading skills in Module 1. But what about listening skills? Aamodt (2016) has summarized a number of things that we should be aware of when listening to others. Some of the most important ones include:

- *Don't interrupt the speaker.* Let her finish speaking.
- *Show the speaker that you are listening through your nonverbal cues.* You should make eye contact and nod your head occasionally, and avoid nonverbal signs of disinterest such as checking your phone for new texts.
- *Keep an open mind while you are listening.* Try to listen without judging and without jumping to conclusions.
- *Ask clarifying questions* to ensure that you understand the point that's being made.
- *Focus on what's being said.* Don't be distracted by the speaker's mannerisms, his hair, his accent, or the movie that you're going to see after dinner.

Providing Information: Writing and Speaking

When you have to convey information to other people, it's important to think carefully about the message that you want to send, and the words that you'll use to make that message clear. One of the easiest ways to avoid miscommunication is to ensure that you don't use vague language. For example, if a friend says to you that he's just stepping out and won't be long, when would you expect to see him? Actual answers to that question range from 10 minutes to 3 hours, suggesting that written and spoken communication is much less likely to be misinterpreted if you are concrete in your choice of words.

However, even when you carefully choose your words, communication problems can still occur when people are not sensitive to the fact that *communication styles* can differ.

Tannen (1995) describes communication style as a person's characteristic speaking (or writing) style, and it can include features such as directness, pacing, and the extent to which we tend to use jokes, questions, or apologies when we write or speak. These styles are learned early in life and are typically guided by two important elements: the need to demonstrate power and the need to foster positive relationships. But the communication challenges that result from differing styles are not limited to misunderstandings about what has been said. To understand the far-reaching implications of communication styles, consider the following characteristics of our speech and how they can influence people's perceptions of one another and the work that they do:

The Tendency to Say "I" Versus "We" People interested in promoting relationships are more likely to speak in terms of the group ("we") rather than themselves ("I"), even when they are describing work that they did for the team *on their own.* When describing work that has been done with others, it may seem trivial whether you have a tendency to use "I" rather than "we." In reality, though, Tannen suggests that this element of conversational style can have important consequences for things such as who gets credit for a job, and whether people are perceived as being "arrogant" or "a team player."

The Tendency to Ask Questions In some environments, there's a lot of value placed on asking questions because doing so can stimulate productive discussions and help to ensure that people have a good understanding of the material. In other places, though, asking questions can have more negative consequences, including being taken as a sign of ignorance or being overly dependent.

The Tendency to Apologize or Admit Fault For some, apologies of any sort are seen as a demonstration of weakness and something to be avoided at all costs. For others, though, a communication style that demonstrates a willingness to take responsibility is very positive and demonstrates a sign of maturity. It's noteworthy, though, that in some communication styles, "apologies" are really a reflection of concern rather than an admission of guilt. For example, "I'm sorry" can often mean "I'm sorry that happened to you," rather than "I apologize for what I did." While these "ritual apologies" may help to build good relationships, Tannen has noted that people who apologize frequently (even when it is an expression of concern) can be viewed as weaker and less confident than others.

The Tendency to Be Direct The extent to which we speak in a direct manner—that is, in a fairly blunt way, without trying to "sugarcoat"—things has important implications for conversations, particularly those that involve making requests or providing criticism or feedback to others. Requests that are presented in an indirect way ("How would you like to help Sue with those reports?") rather than more directly ("Please help Sue with the reports") may be viewed as being more collegial, since they downplay power relationships. However, it's also possible that when a request is framed as a question in this way, people will not understand that they aren't really being given a choice.

Similar issues can arise when feedback is being provided on work that has been done. For example, people whose conversational style is focused more on promoting relationships may feel that it is important to begin a feedback session with praise that's aimed at what was done well, followed by areas for improvement. This approach allows the speaker to buffer the criticism that's to come. Unfortunately, it's possible that if the person receiving this type of feedback has a more direct approach to communicating, she will downplay the need for improvement (since it wasn't offered until the very end) and assume that the main point that's being made is that everything is going well (since that's how the feedback session began).

What's the Best Communication Style?

Having seen that communication styles can have important implications for how people are perceived by others, it's tempting to ask "What's the best communication style?" As you may have guessed from reading this section, though, the answer depends to some extent on the *impression that you're trying to convey*. For example, are you trying to present the impression of being in command, or are you more focused on building relationships? In addition, because communication is always two-sided, you also need to recognize that *the communication style of your partner may differ from your own, and will color his or her interpretation of your communication cues*. As a result, the "best" communication style has to take into account what you know about the person you're speaking with. Will they see your tendency to ask questions as a sign of engagement or incompetence? Will your direct style of speaking be viewed as callous or clear?

An important communication skill, then, is not just the ability to understand our own style, but to recognize that other people will have different tendencies and to consider whether it might be necessary to adjust the way we express ourselves to ensure that our goals can be met. Recognizing and responding to the diverse communication styles of others will help to minimize misunderstandings and ensure that you are being perceived by others in the way that you'd like to be seen.

MODULE 22

Effective Communication—Learning Outcomes Revisited

22.1 Distinguish between verbal and nonverbal communication, outline two verbal communication methods and two verbal communication points of view, and create a plan to improve your own communication with others

Two types of communication are nonverbal and verbal. Nonverbal communication refers to the perceptions of other's actions, such as people's tone of voice, body language, and eye contact. Verbal communication refers to words. There are two verbal communication methods we use to transmit ideas (oral and written) and two verbal communication points of view (providing information or receiving information). The four verbal communication skills that can be developed depending on your method and point of view are: speaking, listening, writing, and reading. Being mindful of the speaker and being self-aware of your own cues can improve good listening skills. Writing and speaking skills can be improved by using words that are clear and concrete. When communicating with others, keep in mind that communication styles are guided by the extent to which people want to demonstrate power versus foster positive relationships, and include things such as directness and pacing, as well as the tendency to use jokes, questions, and apologies. We hope that after reading this module, you'll be better able to think about how you can use these strategies to help you communicate with others, but always be mindful of the fact that an optimal communication style involves taking into account the style of the person to whom you are writing or speaking.

Reflective Practice

Content Check

1. The two types of communication are ______________ and ______________.
2. The two methods of verbal communication are ______________ and ______________.
3. What are the four main verbal communication skills?

Skill Check

Think Critically

4. In what situation would the tendency to apologize be beneficial? In what situations would it be less effective?

Self-Reflect

Reflect on your current communication style. Can you think of a situation—either in your personal life or at work—when your communication style has worked well? What about a situation when your communication style has been less effective? Can you remember a situation when you have experienced a "communication breakdown" with someone? What happened to cause the miscommunication?

ANSWERS

1. nonverbal and verbal 2. oral and written 3. speaking, listening, writing, reading 4. It would be beneficial to have the tendency to apologize in a situation that demonstrates you are mature and taking responsibility. It would be less effective if you apologize for something you are not responsible for, which can exhibit weakness and less confidence.

Consciousness
States of Consciousness

MODULE 23

Altered!

- In Iceland, a hiker viewing the aurora borealis enters a fully conscious state of mindfulness.
- In Brisbane, Australia, a graduate student drifts into a pleasant daydream while sitting at the back of class.
- In Boston, an aspiring actor is hypnotized to help reduce her stage fright.
- In a Paris hospital, a man lies in a deep coma after falling down a flight of stairs.
- In Iowa, a college student downs some Ritalin to help her stay awake while studying for an important exam.
- In Tucson, Arizona, one of your authors brews himself another cup of cappuccino.

Jamen Percy/Shutterstock.com

Each of these people is experiencing a different state of consciousness. Some have no choice, and others are deliberately seeking to bend their minds—to alter consciousness—in different ways, to different degrees, and for different reasons. As these examples suggest, consciousness can take many forms, some "mind blowing" and some not so much. Let's explore the varieties of conscious experience.

~LEARNING OUTCOMES~

After reading this module you should be able to:

23.1 Define consciousness and distinguish between disordered states of consciousness and altered states of consciousness

23.2 Explain how hypnosis works and describe its effects, while distinguishing between state and nonstate theories of hypnosis

23.3 Explain how meditation works and describe its effects, while distinguishing between mindfulness and concentrative meditation

States of Consciousness—The Many Faces of Awareness

Learning Outcome 23.1 Define consciousness and distinguish between disordered states of consciousness and altered states of consciousness

To be *conscious* means to be aware. **Consciousness** consists of your awareness of external events in the environment around you, as well as your awareness of your mental processes, including thoughts, memories, and feelings about your experiences and yourself (Morin, 2006; Robinson, 2008). Take, for example, that hiker's profound moment in Iceland. As Donnie absorbed the sheer magnitude of the aurora borealis, he was "blown away" by deep feelings of insignificance and awe. In that instant, he was also fully aware that he *was* experiencing a deeply moving moment. (For more about metacognition, the state of awareness of your own awareness, see Module 26.)

Although this definition of consciousness may seem obvious, it is based on your own introspective experience. While you may be the expert on *what* it feels like to be you, your subjective experience almost certainly offers no insight into *how* your brain gives rise to your consciousness or *why* you are conscious in the first place. Mind you, no one can yet satisfactorily explain the how or why of consciousness (Allen et al., 2013).

One way to appreciate the limitations of our subjective experience is to ask about other people. What does it feel like to be your mother? Or someone in a coma? What runs through a dog's mind when it sniffs other dogs? You simply can't answer these questions about *other minds* through your own subjective perspective. The difficulty of knowing other minds is one reason that the early behaviorists distrusted introspection (see Module 3).

A key challenge for psychology is to use objective studies of the brain and behavior to help us understand the mind and consciousness, which are basically subjective phenomena (Feinberg & Mallatt, 2016). Objectivity makes it possible to identify various states of consciousness and explore the role they play in our lives. This module and the three that follow summarize some of what we have learned about those different states.

Disorders of Consciousness

We spend most of our lives in **waking consciousness**, a state of clear, organized alertness. In waking consciousness, we perceive times, places, and events as real and can respond to external stimuli. But many other states of consciousness are possible. For example, brain injury can result in anything from a short-lived disorientation to a *disorder of consciousness*—a long-term lack of consciousness and responsiveness (Monti, 2012; Schnakers & Laureys, 2012).

Disorders of consciousness have traditionally been difficult to accurately diagnose (Singh et al., 2013). You simply can't ask someone in a *coma*—a state of total unresponsiveness—if he or she can hear you or feel pain. But does the lack of responsiveness mean that a person is *brain dead* (De Tanti et al., 2016)? What if the person is *locked-in*, like Kate Adamson, whom we met in Module 10? (Recall that a damaged brain stem left Kate fully aware, but almost totally unresponsive.)

Newer brain imaging methods, such as positron emission tomography (PET) and functional magnetic resonance imaging (fMRI), promise to improve the diagnosis of disorders of consciousness while also shedding light on consciousness itself. In one study, normal individuals and patients in a *persistent vegetative state*—a longer-term waking state without any signs of awareness—were administered a mildly painful stimulus. Normal individuals consciously reported feeling pain while vegetative patients did not, as expected. PET scans revealed brain activity in the midbrain, thalamus, and somatosensory cortex of both normal individuals and vegetative patients. However, only the normal individuals in this study showed activity in the frontal cortical regions, implying that these brain regions must be functional in order for someone to have a conscious experience of pain (Laureys et al., 2002).

In light of findings such as these, doctors can be more confident that patients diagnosed in a persistent vegetative state who also show no frontal cortical activity in response to pain are likely feeling no pain. At the same time, results such as these suggest that frontal lobe activity is central to conscious experience. Echoing Kate Adamson's experience of being locked-in, an fMRI investigation of patients in a persistent vegetative state showed varying degrees of frontal cortical activity in some patients. Some of them, for example, showed a frontal cortex response to hearing their own names (Bick et al., 2013).

There can be little doubt that studies such as these are beginning to improve diagnostic accuracy while illuminating the complex brain circuitry underlying our conscious experience (Askenasy & Lehmann, 2013; Långsjö et al., 2012).

Altered States of Consciousness

Many other states of conscious also differ from normal awareness, including states of consciousness related to fatigue, delirium, hypnosis, drugs, and euphoria (Chalmers, 2010). Everyone experiences at least some altered states, such as sleep, dreaming, and daydreaming. In everyday life, changes in consciousness may even accompany long-distance running, listening to music, making love, or other circumstances.

How are altered states distinguished from normal awareness? During an **altered state of consciousness (ASC)**, changes occur in the *quality* and *pattern* of mental activity. Typically, distinct shifts happen in our perceptions, emotions, memories, time sense, thoughts, feelings of self-control, and suggestibility (Hohwy & Fox, 2012). Definitions aside, just like our hiker Donnie, most people know when they have experienced an ASC. In fact, heightened self-awareness is an important feature of many ASCs (Revonsuo, Kallio, & Sikka, 2009).

Are there other causes of ASCs? In addition to the ones mentioned, we could add sensory overload (a rave, Mardi Gras crowd, or mosh pit), monotonous stimulation (such as "highway hypnotism" on long drives), unusual physical conditions (high fever, hyperventilation, dehydration, sleep loss, near-death experiences), restricted sensory input (extended periods of isolation), and many other possibilities.

Consciousness and Culture In some instances, altered states have important cultural meanings. Throughout history, people everywhere have found ways to alter their consciousness (Siegel, 2005). One dramatic example is the regular consumption of a mind-altering potion called ayahuasca. Considered a psychedelic sacrament by members of Uniao do Vegetal (UDV), a Brazilian religion, twice-monthly consumption of ayahuasca is believed to foster a deeper connection with nature, improving physical, emotional, and spiritual well-being.

Like Buddhists engaging in meditation practices, Turkish whirling dervishes entranced by their twirling dance, or New Zealand Maori priests performing nightlong rituals to communicate with the mythical period that the Aborigines call "Dreamtime," the ritual use of ayahuasca is meant to cleanse the mind and body. When they are especially intense, such experiences can bring altered awareness and personal revelation (de Rios & Grob, 2005).

People seek some altered states purely for pleasure or escape, as is often true of drug intoxication. Yet as the UDV illustrates, many cultures regard altered consciousness as a pathway to personal enlightenment. Indeed, all cultures and most religions recognize and accept some alterations of consciousness. However, the meaning given to these states varies greatly—from signs of "madness" and "possession" by spirits to life-enhancing breakthroughs. Thus, cultural conditioning greatly affects what altered states we recognize, seek, consider normal, and attain (Cardeña et al., 2011).

John Mitterer

In many cultures, rituals of healing, prayer, meditation, purification, or personal transformation at sites like this Taoist temple in Hong Kong are accompanied by altered states of consciousness.

Let's continue with a more detailed look at two interesting altered states, hypnosis and meditation, before turning our attention to sleep, dreams, and drug use and abuse in the sections that follow.

Hypnosis—Look into My Eyes

Learning Outcome 23.2 Explain how hypnosis works and describe its effects, while distinguishing between state and nonstate theories of hypnosis

"Your body is becoming heavy. You can barely keep your eyes open. You are so tired you can't move. Relax. Let go. Close your eyes and relax." These are the last words that a textbook should ever say to you, and the first a hypnotist might say. What do you know about hypnosis? Which of your beliefs are true? Which are myths? Is hypnosis real? Does it have any value?

Interest in hypnosis began in the 1700s with Austrian doctor Franz Mesmer, whose name gave us the term *mesmerize* (to hypnotize). Mesmer believed that he could cure disease with magnets. Mesmer's strange "treatments" are related to hypnosis because they relied on the power of suggestion, not magnetism (Hammond, 2013). For a time, Mesmer enjoyed quite a following. In the end, however, his

Consciousness An organism's awareness of its external environment and internal mental processes.

Waking consciousness A state of clear, organized alertness.

Altered state of consciousness (ASC) A condition of awareness distinctly different in quality or pattern from waking consciousness.

theories of "animal magnetism" were rejected, and he was branded a fraud.

Ever since, stage hypnotists have entertained us with a combination of little or no hypnosis and a bit of deception. On stage, people are unusually cooperative because they don't want to "spoil the act." As a result, they readily follow almost any instruction given by the entertainer. After volunteers loosen up and respond to a few suggestions, they find that they are suddenly the stars of the show. Audience response to the antics on stage brings out the "ham" in many people. No hypnosis is required; all the "hypnotist" needs to do is direct the action.

Like stage magicians, stage hypnotists also make liberal use of deception. One of the more impressive stage tricks is to rigidly suspend a person between two chairs. This is astounding only because the audience does not question it. Anyone can do it, as is shown in the photographs and instructions in ➤ **Figure 23.1**. Try it!

Entertainment aside, hypnosis is a real phenomenon. English surgeon James Braid coined the term hypnosis. The Greek word *hypnos* means "sleep," and Braid used it to describe the hypnotic state. Today, we know that hypnosis is *not* sleep. Confusion about this point remains because some hypnotists give the suggestion, "Sleep, sleep." However, brain activity recorded during hypnosis is different from that observed when a person is asleep or pretending to be hypnotized (Del Casale et al., 2012; Kihlstrom, 2013; Santarcangelo & Scattina, 2016).

Theories of Hypnosis

If hypnosis isn't sleep, then what is it? That's a good question. **Hypnosis** is currently defined as a state of consciousness characterized by focused attention, reduced peripheral awareness, and heightened suggestibility (Elkins et al., 2015). Notice that this definition suggests that hypnosis may be a distinct *state* of consciousness.

The best-known *state theory* of hypnosis was proposed by Ernest Hilgard (1904–2001), who argued that hypnosis causes a *dissociative state*, or "split" in awareness. To illustrate, he asked hypnotized participants to plunge one hand into a painful bath of ice water. Participants told to feel no pain said they felt none. The same participants were then asked if any part of their mind did feel pain. With their free hand, many wrote, "It hurts," or "Stop it, you're hurting me," while they continued to act pain-free (Hilgard, 1977, 1994). Thus, one part of the hypnotized person says there is no pain and acts as if there is none. Another part, which Hilgard calls the *hidden observer*, is aware of the pain but remains in the background. The **hidden observer** is a detached part of the hypnotized person's awareness that silently watches events.

In contrast, *nonstate theorists* argue that hypnosis is not a distinct state at all. Instead, it is merely a blend of conformity, relaxation, imagination, obedience, and role-playing (Lynn et al., 2015; Lynn & O'Hagen, 2009). For example, many theorists believe that all hypnosis is really self-hypnosis (*autosuggestion*). From this perspective, a hypnotist merely helps another person follow a series of suggestions. These suggestions, in turn, alter sensations, perceptions, thoughts, feelings, and behaviors (Lynn & Kirsch, 2006). Autosuggestion also plays a role in many forms of self-therapy (Yapko, 2011).

Regardless of which theoretical approach finally prevails, both views suggest that hypnosis can be explained scientifically.

The Reality of Hypnosis

How is hypnosis done? Could I be hypnotized against my will? Hypnotists use many different methods. Still, all techniques

a b

Dennis Coon

➤ **Figure 23.1**

The chair suspension trick. Arrange three chairs as shown. Have someone recline as shown. Ask him or her to lift slightly while you remove the middle chair. Accept the applause gracefully! (Concerning hypnosis and similar phenomena, the moral, of course, is "Suspend judgment until you have something solid to stand on.")

John Mitterer

To gain insight into autosuggestion, tie a string to a ring and hold the ring at eye level, near your face. Don't intentionally swing the ring. Instead, concentrate and mentally push the ring ever so slightly away from you. Then release it and let it swing back toward you. Continue to mentally push and release the ring until it is swinging freely. If the ring seems to move on its own, you used autosuggestion to influence your own behavior. Suggestions that the ring would swing caused your hand to make tiny micromuscular movements. These, in turn, caused the ring to move.

encourage a person to (1) focus attention on what is being said, (2) relax and feel tired, (3) "let go" and accept suggestions easily, and (4) use a vivid imagination (Barabasz & Watkins, 2005). Basically, you must cooperate to become hypnotized.

What does it feel like to be hypnotized? You might be surprised at some of your actions during hypnosis. You also might have mild feelings of floating, sinking, anesthesia, or separation from your body. Personal experiences vary widely. A key element in hypnosis is the **basic suggestion effect**—a tendency of hypnotized persons to carry out suggested actions as if they were involuntary. Hypnotized persons feel like their actions and experiences are *automatic*—they seem to happen without effort.

Contrary to how hypnosis is portrayed in movies, hypnotized people generally remain in control of their behavior and aware of what is going on. For instance, most people will not act out hypnotic suggestions that they consider immoral or repulsive, such as disrobing in public or harming someone (Kirsch & Lynn, 1995).

Hypnotizability *Can everyone be hypnotized?* About 75 percent of people can be hypnotized, but only 40 percent will be good hypnotic participants. People who are imaginative and prone to fantasy are often highly responsive to hypnosis (Hoeft et al., 2012). But people who lack these traits also may be hypnotized. If you are willing to be hypnotized, chances are good that you could be. Hypnosis depends more on the efforts and abilities of the hypnotized person than the skills of the hypnotist. But make no mistake: People who are hypnotized are not merely faking their responses.

Hypnotizability refers to how easily a person can become hypnotized (Elkins et al., 2015). It is measured by giving a series of suggestions and counting the number of times a person responds. The Stanford Hypnotic Susceptibility Scale, shown in **Table 23.1**, is a typical test of hypnotizability. In the test, various suggestions are made, and the person's response is noted. For instance, you might be told that your left arm is becoming more and more rigid and that it will not bend. If you can't bend your arm during the next 10 seconds, you have shown you are hypnotizable.

Effects of Hypnosis *What can (and cannot) be achieved with hypnosis?* Many abilities have been tested during hypnosis, leading to the following conclusions:

1. **Physical ability.** Hypnosis may improve some physical abilities in some sports (Tramontana, 2011), although it has no more effect on physical strength than instructions that encourage a person to make his or her best effort (Chaves, 2000).
2. **Memory.** Some evidence shows that hypnosis can enhance memory (Wester & Hammond, 2011). However, it frequently increases the number of false memories as well. For this reason, many states now bar persons from testifying in court if they were hypnotized to improve their memory of a crime that they witnessed. (For more information, see Module 32.)
3. **Amnesia.** A person told not to remember something heard during hypnosis may claim not to remember. In some instances, this may be nothing more than a deliberate attempt to avoid thinking about specific ideas. However, brief memory loss of this type does seem to occur (Barnier, McConkey, & Wright, 2004).

Hypnosis State of consciousness characterized by focused attention, deep relaxation, and heightened suggestibility.

Hidden observer A detached part of the hypnotized person's awareness that silently watches events.

Basic suggestion effect The tendency of hypnotized persons to carry out suggested actions as if they were involuntary.

Hypnotizability One's capacity for becoming hypnotized.

TABLE 23.1 | Stanford Hypnotic Susceptibility Scale

Suggested Behavior	Criterion of Passing
1. Postural sway	Falls without forcing
2. Eye closure	Closes eyes without forcing
3. Hand lowering (left)	Lowers at least 6 inches by end of 10 seconds
4. Immobilization (right arm)	Arm rises less than 1 inch in 10 seconds
5. Finger lock	Incomplete separation of fingers at end of 10 seconds
6. Arm rigidity (left arm)	Less than 2 inches of arm bending in 10 seconds
7. Hands moving together	Hands at least as close as 6 inches after 10 seconds
8. Verbal inhibition (name)	Name unspoken in 10 seconds
9. Hallucination (fly)	Any movement, grimacing, acknowledgment of effect
10. Eye catalepsy	Eyes remain closed at end of 10 seconds
11. Posthypnotic (changes chairs)	Any partial movement response
12. Amnesia test	Three or fewer items recalled

Adapted from Weitzenhoffer & Hilgard (1959).

4. **Pain relief.** Hypnosis can relieve pain (Baad-Hansen et al., 2013; Hammond, 2008; Kohen, 2011). It can be especially useful when chemical painkillers are ineffective. For instance, hypnosis can reduce phantom limb pain (Oakley, Whitman, & Halligan, 2002). (As discussed in Module 19, amputees sometimes feel phantom pain that seems to come from a missing limb.)
5. **Sensory changes.** Hypnotic suggestions concerning sensations are among the most effective. Given the proper instructions, a person can be made to smell a small bottle of ammonia and respond as if it were a wonderful perfume. It also is possible to alter color vision, hearing sensitivity, time sense, perception of illusions, and many other sensory responses.
6. Generally speaking, hypnosis is more successful at changing subjective experience than it is at modifying behaviors such as smoking or overeating. Nonetheless, like meditation, which we explore next, hypnosis is a valuable tool in a variety of settings (Yapko, 2011). It can help people relax, feel less pain, and make better progress in therapy (Lynn, Kirsch, & Rhue, 2010).

Meditation and Mindfulness—Chilling, the Healthy Way

Learning Outcome 23.3 Explain how meditation works and describe its effects, while distinguishing between mindfulness and concentrative meditation

Throughout history, meditation has been widely used as a means of altering consciousness through deep relaxation. Let's see how meditation works. **Meditation** is a mental exercise used to alter consciousness. In general, meditation heightens awareness and produces relaxation by interrupting the typical flow of thoughts, worries, and analysis. People who use meditation to reduce stress often report less daily physical tension and anxiety (Hosemans, 2015; Vago & Nakamura, 2011). Brain scans (such as PET and fMRI) reveal changes in brain activity during meditation, including the frontal lobes, suggesting that it may be a distinct state of consciousness (Brewer et al., 2011; Cahn & Polich, 2013).

Meditation takes two major forms. In **concentrative meditation**, you attend to a single focal point, such as an object, a thought, or your own breathing. In contrast, **mindfulness meditation** is "open," or expansive. In this case, you widen your attention to embrace a total, nonjudgmental awareness of the world (Hölzel et al., 2011). An example is becoming fully consciousness while walking in the wilderness with a quiet and receptive mind, just like Donnie's aurora borealis experience. Although it may not seem so, mindfulness meditation is more difficult to attain than concentrative meditation. For this reason, let's concentrate on concentrative meditation as a practical self-control method.

Performing Concentrative Meditation

How is concentrative meditation done? The basic idea is to sit still and quietly focus on some external object or on a repetitive internal stimulus, such as your own breathing or humming. Alternatively, you can silently repeat a *mantra* (a word used as the focus of attention in concentrative meditation). Typical mantras are smooth, flowing sounds that are easily repeated. A widely used mantra is the word *om*. A mantra also could be any pleasant word or a phrase from a familiar song, poem, or prayer. If other thoughts arise as you repeat a mantra, just return attention to it as often as necessary to maintain meditation.

The Relaxation Response Researcher Herbert Benson believes that the core of meditation is the **relaxation response**—an innate physiological pattern that opposes your body's fight-or-flight mechanisms (Chang, Dusek, & Benson, 2011). Benson feels, quite simply, that most of us have forgotten how to relax deeply. People in his experiments learned to produce the relaxation response by following instructions such as these:

> Sit quietly and comfortably. Close your eyes. Relax your muscles, beginning at your feet and progressing up to your head. Relax them deeply. Become aware of breathing through your nose. As you breathe out, say a word like "peace" silently to yourself. Don't worry about how successful you are in relaxing deeply. Just let relaxation happen at its own pace. Don't be surprised by distracting thoughts. When they occur, ignore them and continue repeating "peace." (Adapted from Chang, Dusek, & Benson, 2011; Hölzel et al., 2011.)

Meditation may be a good stress-control technique for people who find it difficult to "turn off" upsetting thoughts when they need to relax. In one study, a group of college students who received just 90 minutes of training in the relaxation response experienced greatly reduced stress levels (Deckro et al., 2002). The physical benefits of meditation include lowered heart rate, blood pressure, muscle tension, and other signs of stress (Zeidan et al., 2010), as well as improved immune system activity (Davidson et al., 2003).

According to Shauna Shapiro and Roger Walsh (2006), meditation has benefits beyond relaxation. Practiced regularly, meditation may foster well-being and positive mental skills such as clarity, concentration, and calm. In this sense, meditation may share much in common with psychotherapy. Indeed, research has shown that mindfulness meditation relieves a variety of psychological disorders, from insomnia to excessive anxiety. It also can reduce aggression and the use of psychoactive drugs (Brewer et al., 2011; Shapiro & Walsh, 2006). Regular meditation may even help people develop better control over their attention, heightened self-awareness, and maturity (Hodgins & Adair, 2010; Müller, Gerasimova, & Ritter, 2016).

Sensory Deprivation and Relaxation

Imagine floating in a tank of warm water, for a short while, without the least bit of muscle tension. You cannot hear anything, and it is pitch dark. You are experiencing brief *sensory deprivation*, a major reduction in the amount or variety of sensory stimulation.

What happens when stimulation is greatly reduced? A hint comes from reports by prisoners in solitary confinement, Arctic explorers, high-altitude pilots, long-distance truck drivers, and radar operators. When faced with limited or monotonous stimulation, people sometimes have bizarre sensations, dangerous lapses in attention, and wildly distorted perceptions. Intense or prolonged sensory deprivation is stressful and disorienting.

Yet, oddly enough, brief periods of sensory restriction can produce a strong relaxation response (Bood et al., 2006). An hour or two spent in a *flotation tank* can cause a large drop in blood pressure, muscle tension, chronic pain, and other signs of stress (Bood et al., 2006; Kjellgren, Buhrkall, & Norlander, 2011).

Like other forms of meditation, mild sensory deprivation also may help with more than relaxation. Deep relaxation makes people more open to suggestion, and sensory deprivation interrupts habitual behavior patterns. This can loosen belief systems, making it easier for people to quit smoking, lose weight, and reduce their use of alcohol and drugs (Suedfeld & Borrie, 1999; van Dierendonck & Te Nijenhuis, 2005). Mild sensory deprivation even shows promise as a way to stimulate creative thinking and enhance sports and music performance skills (Norlander, Bergman, & Archer, 1998, 1999; Vartanian & Suedfeld, 2011).

Meditation Mental exercise for producing relaxation or heightened awareness.

Concentrative meditation Mental exercise based on attending to a single object or thought.

Mindfulness meditation Mental exercise based on widening attention to become aware of everything experienced at any given moment.

Relaxation response The pattern of internal bodily changes that occurs at times of relaxation.

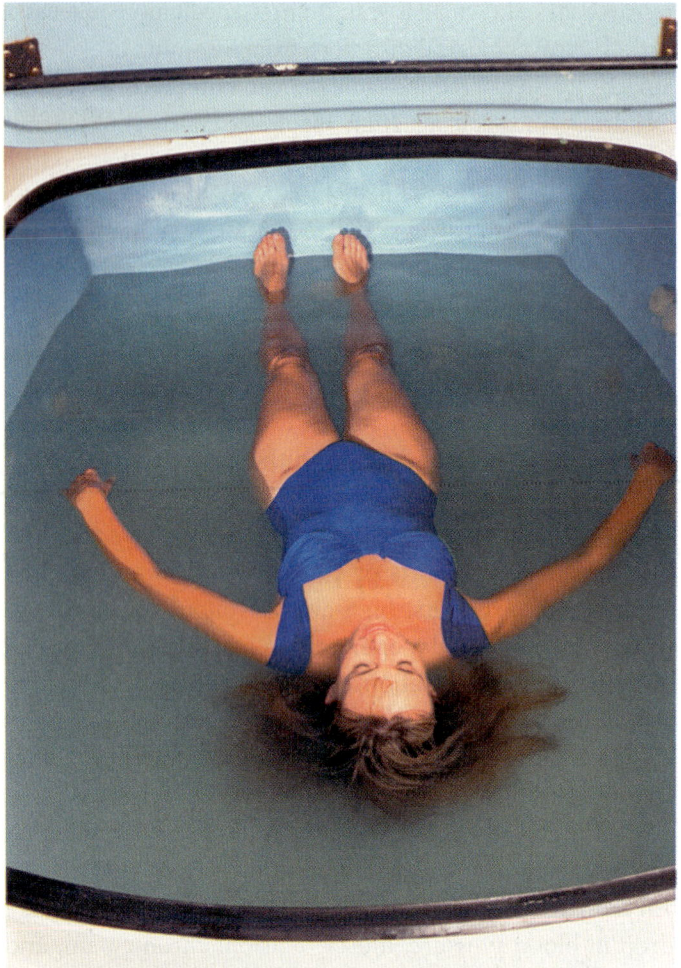

Pixtal/SuperStock

Psychologists have used small flotation tanks like this one to study the effects of mild sensory deprivation. Participants float in darkness and silence. The shallow, body-temperature water contains hundreds of pounds of Epsom salts, so participants float near the surface. Mild sensory deprivation produces deep relaxation.

Summary To summarize, research suggests that meditation, including mild sensory deprivation, is a way to elicit the relaxation response. For many people, sitting quietly and "resting" can be as effective. Similar stress reduction occurs when people set aside time daily to engage in other restful activities, such as muscle relaxation, positive daydreaming, and even leisure reading. However, if you are the type of person who finds it difficult to ignore upsetting thoughts, then concentrative meditation might be a good way to promote relaxation. Practiced regularly, meditation and mild sensory isolation may even help improve overall mental health—something almost all of us could use in our fast-paced society.

The Whole Human: Mindfulness and Well-Being

Did you "space out" anytime today? Most of us have occasional moments of reduced awareness. **Mindfulness** is the opposite of such mindless moments: It involves an open, nonjudgmental awareness of current experience. In other words, mindfulness is similar to the state that people who practice receptive meditation are trying to achieve. A person who is mindful is fully present, moment-by-moment (Hölzel et al., 2011). She or he is acutely aware of every thought, emotion, or sensation, but does not judge it or react to it. The person is fully "awake" and attuned to immediate reality, just like Donnie that day in Iceland.

Psychologists interested in positive mental states have begun to study the effects of mindfulness. For example, cancer patients who are taught mindfulness meditation have lower levels of distress and a greater sense of well-being (Jones et al., 2013). Similarly, being mindful makes it easier to quit smoking (Brewer et al., 2011). Such benefits apply to healthy people, too. In general, mindfulness is associated with self-knowledge and well-being (Ameli, 2014; Friese, Messner, & Schaffner, 2012). Anyone who has a tendency to sleepwalk through life—and that's most of us at times—would be wise to be mindful of the value of mindfulness.

Mindfulness A state of open, nonjudgmental awareness of current experience.

MODULE 23 States of Consciousness—Learning Outcomes Revisited

23.1 Define consciousness and distinguish between disordered states of consciousness and altered states of consciousness

Consciousness is a core feature of mental life consisting of sensations and perceptions of external events as well as self-awareness of mental events, including thoughts, memories, and feelings about experiences and the self. Disordered (non-normal) states of consciousness include comas and persistent vegetative states. Altered states of consciousness (ASCs) are characterized by changes in the quality and pattern of mental activity (e.g., perceptions, emotions, time sense). ASCs are especially associated with sleep and dreaming, hypnosis, meditation, and psychoactive drugs. Cultural norms affect what ASCs a person recognizes, seeks, considers normal, and attains.

23.2 Describe hypnosis, distinguishing between state and nonstate theories of hypnosis

Although not all psychologists agree, hypnosis is usually defined as a state characterized by narrowed attention, reduced peripheral awareness, and increased suggestibility. It is *not* the same as being asleep. The most common state theory of hypnosis suggests it is a dissociative state characterized by a "split" in our awareness, one part of which is a "hidden observer" that is detached from the hypnotized person's awareness and silently watches what is happening. In contrast, nonstate theories suggest hypnosis is simply a blend of conformity, relaxation, imagination, obedience, and role-playing characterized by autosuggestion. Hypnotists have individuals focus attention on their words, relax, let go, accept suggestions, and use their imagination. Feelings that accompany hypnosis include floating, sinking, and a separation from the body. Hypnosis may improve physical abilities, enhance memory, induce amnesia, relieve pain, and alter sensory experiences. Actions of the hypnotized person feel involuntary, but they are aware of what is happening and remain in control.

23.3 Describe meditation, distinguishing between mindfulness and concentrative meditation

Meditation is a mental exercise to alter consciousness. Mindfulness meditation involves observing your own thoughts and feelings without judgment. In contrast, concentrative meditation requires individuals to focus on something specific (word, mantra, breathing) to focus attention. Meditation is thought to work by bringing about the relaxation response, a calming physiological response. The major benefits of meditation are its ability to calm the body and mind, improve mental clarity, relieve some psychological disorders, and improve self-awareness and creativity.

Reflective Practice

Content Check

1. Changes in the quality and pattern of mental activity define a(n)
   - a. EEG
   - b. REM
   - c. SIDS
   - d. ASC
2. In Ernest Hilgard's dissociative state theory of hypnosis, awareness is split between normal consciousness and
   - a. disinhibition
   - b. autosuggestion
   - c. memory
   - d. the hidden observer
3. Which of the following is most likely to be achieved via hypnosis?
   - a. unusual strength
   - b. pain relief
   - c. improved memory
   - d. sleeplike brain waves
4. The focus of attention in concentrative meditation is "open," or expansive. T or F?
5. Mantras are words said silently to oneself to end a session of meditation. T or F?
6. The most immediate benefit of meditation appears to be its capacity for producing the relaxation response. T or F?

Skill Check

Think Critically

7. Regular meditators report lower levels of stress and a greater sense of well-being. What other explanations must we eliminate before this effect can be regarded as genuine?

Self-Reflect

Make a quick list of some altered states of consciousness that you have experienced. What do they have in common? How are they different? What conditions caused them? How have your beliefs about hypnosis changed after reading the preceding section? Can you think of specific examples in which hypnosis was misrepresented—for example, in movies or on television? Various activities can produce the relaxation response. When do you experience states of deep relaxation, coupled with a sense of serene awareness?

ANSWERS

1. d 2. d 3. b 4. F 5. F 6. T 7. Studies on the effects of meditation must control for the placebo effect and the fact that those who choose to learn meditation may not be a representative sample of the general population.

MODULE

24 Consciousness

Sleep and Dreams

To Sleep, Perchance to Dream

Not all animals sleep, but, like humans, those that do have powerful sleep needs. For example, dolphins must voluntarily breathe air, which means they face the choice of staying awake or drowning. A dolphin solves this problem by sleeping on just one side of its brain at a time! The other half of the brain, which remains awake, controls breathing.

Sleep is a necessity for dolphins, but how about humans? Of course, sleep will give way temporarily, especially at times of great danger. As comedian and filmmaker Woody Allen once put it, "The lion and the lamb shall lie down together, but the lamb shall not be very sleepy." What is sleep? Why do we have to sleep, anyway? What are dreams? Why do some people have trouble sleeping? Let's find out.

Pacific Stock-Design Pics/Pacific Stock-Design Pics/Superstock

~LEARNING OUTCOMES~

After reading this module you should be able to:

24.1 Describe the patterns and stages which make up a night's sleep

24.2 Explain the functions of sleep, including the functions of NREM sleep and REM sleep

24.3 Name and briefly describe three theories of dreaming

24.4 Define insomnia, outline its causes as well as some behavioral remedies, and name four other disorders associated with sleep

Sleep Patterns and Stages—The Nightly Roller Coaster

Learning Outcome 24.1 Describe the patterns and stages which make up a night's sleep

Each of us will spend some 25 years of life asleep. Because sleep is familiar, many people think they know all about it. But many commonsense beliefs about sleep are false. For example, you are not totally unresponsive during sleep. A sleeping mother may ignore a jet thundering overhead but wake at the slightest whimper of her child. Likewise, you are more likely to awaken if you hear your own name spoken instead of another. It's even possible to do simple tasks while asleep. In one experiment, people learned to avoid an electric shock by touching a switch each time a tone sounded, without waking. (This is much like the basic survival skill of turning off your alarm clock without waking.)

Let's begin to explore sleep (while awake, of course) by tackling the most basic misunderstanding of all.

Sleep Patterns

You sleep, dream occasionally, and wake up. What's to know? Sleep is not as simple as it might seem. Scientific investigation has revealed a complex and still not completely understood phenomenon. Sleep is an innate **biological rhythm** that never can be entirely ignored (Luyster et al., 2012). Rhythms of sleep and waking are usually so steady that they continue for many days, even when clocks and light–dark cycles are removed. However, under such conditions, humans eventually shift to sleep–waking cycles that average more than 24 hours (Czeisler et al., 1999; Eastman et al., 2012). This suggests that external time markers, especially light and dark, help tie our sleep rhythms to days that are exactly 24 hours long. Otherwise, many of us would drift into our own unusual sleep cycles (Kovrov et al., 2012). (Sleep cycles can be disrupted by rapid travel across time zones [jet lag] and by shift work. See Module 42.)

What is the normal range of sleep? The majority of us sleep on a familiar seven-to-eight-hour-per-night schedule. Only a small percentage are *short sleepers*, averaging five hours of sleep or fewer per night. On the other end of the scale, we find *long sleepers*, who doze nine hours or more (Grandner & Kripke, 2004). A few rare individuals can even get by on an hour or two of sleep a night—and feel perfectly fine. Urging everyone to sleep eight hours would be like advising everyone to wear medium-size shoes.

We sleep less as we get older, right? Yes, total sleep time declines throughout life. Infants spend up to 20 hours a day sleeping, usually in two- to four-hour cycles. As they mature, most children go through a nap stage and eventually settle into a steady cycle of sleeping once a day. In contrast, those older than 50 average only six hours of sleep a night. Mid-afternoon sleepiness is a natural part of the sleep cycle. Perhaps we should all continue to take an afternoon siesta. Brief, well-timed naps can help maintain alertness in people such as truck drivers and hospital interns, who often must fight to stay alert (Ficca et al., 2010).

Busy people may be tempted to sleep less. However, people on *shortened* cycles—for example, three hours of sleep to six hours awake—often can't get to sleep when the cycle calls for it. Adapting to *longer*-than-normal days is more promising. Such days can be tailored to match natural sleep patterns, which have a ratio of 2 to 1 between time awake and time asleep (16 hours awake and 8 hours asleep). For instance, one study showed that 28-hour "days" work for some people. Overall, sleep patterns may be bent and stretched, but they rarely yield entirely to human whims (Åkerstedt, 2007; Sallinen et al., 2017).

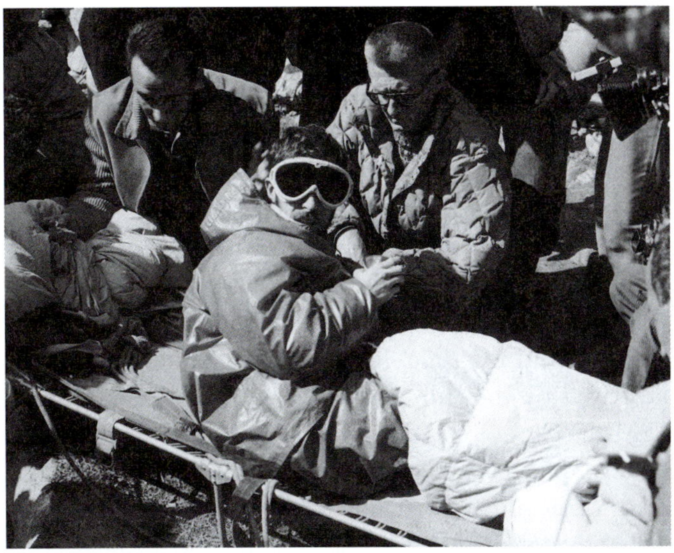

Keystone-France/Getty Images

Frenchman Michel Siffre has spent months at a time living in caves deep underground without the usual external markers of night and day. He found that without these markers, his sleep cycles tended to get longer. During one such stay, he settled into a 48-hour sleep–waking cycle.

Sleep Stages

Recordings of changes in electrical activity in the brain (brain waves) reveal that sleep also progresses through several stages every night (Pagel, 2012). When you are awake and alert, the **electroencephalograph (EEG)** (eh-LEK-tro-en-SEF-uh-lo-graf) reveals a pattern of small, fast waves called **beta waves** (➤ Figure 24.1). Immediately before sleep, the pattern shifts to larger and slower waves called **alpha waves**. (Alpha waves also occur when you are relaxed and allow your thoughts to drift.) As the eyes close, breathing becomes slow and regular, the pulse rate slows, and body temperature drops. Soon after, we descend into *slow-wave sleep* through four distinct **sleep stages**.

Biological rhythm Any repeating cycle of biological activity, such as sleep and waking cycles or changes in body temperature.

Electroencephalograph (EEG) Device that records electrical activity in the brain.

Beta waves Small, fast brain waves associated with being awake and alert.

Alpha waves Large, slow brain waves associated with relaxation and falling asleep.

Sleep stages Levels of sleep identified by brain-wave patterns and behavioral changes.

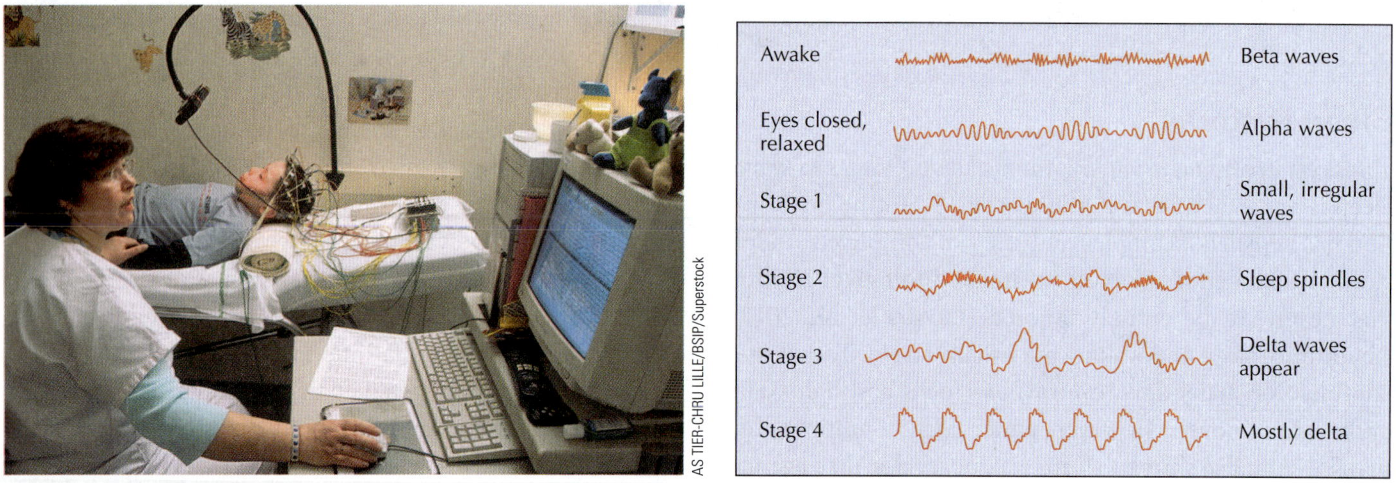

(a) (b)

Figure 24.1

Stages of sleep. *(a)* Photograph of an EEG recording session. The boy in the background is asleep. *(b)* Changes in brain-wave patterns associated with various stages of sleep. Most wave types are present at all times, but they occur more or less frequently in various sleep stages.

Stage 1 As you enter **light sleep (Stage 1 sleep)**, your heart rate slows even more. Breathing becomes more irregular. The muscles of your body relax. This may trigger a reflex muscle twitch called a *hypnic* (HIP-nik: sleep) *jerk*. (This is quite normal, so have no fear about admitting to your friends that you fell asleep with a hypnic jerk.) In Stage 1 sleep, the EEG is made up mainly of small, irregular waves, with some alpha waves. Persons awakened at this time may or may not say that they were asleep.

Stage 2 As sleep deepens, body temperature drops further. Also, the EEG begins to include **sleep spindles**, which are short bursts of distinctive brain-wave activity generated by the thalamus (Caporro et al., 2012). Sleep spindles may help prevent the sleeping brain from being aroused by external stimuli, thus marking the true boundary of sleep (Dang-Vu et al., 2010). Within a few minutes after spindles appear, most people will say they were asleep.

Stages 3 and 4 In Stage 3, very large and slow **delta waves** begin to appear. They signal a move to deeper slow-wave sleep and a further loss of consciousness. Most people reach Stage 4 **deep sleep**—the deepest level of normal sleep—in about an hour. Brain waves are almost pure slow-wave delta, and the sleeper is in a state of oblivion. If a sleeper hears a loud noise during Stage 4, he or she will wake up in a state of confusion and may not remember the noise. Stages 3 and 4 are sometimes combined into a single sleep stage (Moser et al., 2009).

REM Sleep, Dreaming, and REM Rebound There is much more to a night's sleep, however, than a simple descent into deep sleep. Fluctuations in sleep hormones cause four or five recurring cycles of deeper and lighter sleep throughout the night (Steiger, 2007; ➤ Figure 24.2). During these repeated periods of lighter sleep, a curious thing happens: the sleeper's eyes occasionally move under the eyelids. If you ever get a chance to watch a sleeping child, roommate, or spouse, you may see these **rapid eye movements (REMs)**. In addition, **REM sleep** is marked by a return of high-frequency brain waves similar to Stage 1 sleep. In fact, the brain is so active during REM sleep that it looks as if the person is awake.

In particular, brain areas associated with imagery and emotion become more active (Gujar et al., 2011). It is, therefore, likely no coincidence that REM sleep is also associated with dreaming. Although not all people remember their dreams upon awakening in the morning, people awakened during REMs report vivid dreams roughly 85 percent of the time. In fact, "nondreamers" are often surprised by their dreams when first awakened during REM sleep.

Eye movements often accompany REM dreaming. Dream that you are watching a tennis match, and you will probably move your eyes from side to side. REM sleep is easy to observe in pets, such as dogs and cats. Watch for eye and face movements and irregular breathing. (You can forget about your pet iguana, though. Reptiles show no signs of REM sleep.)

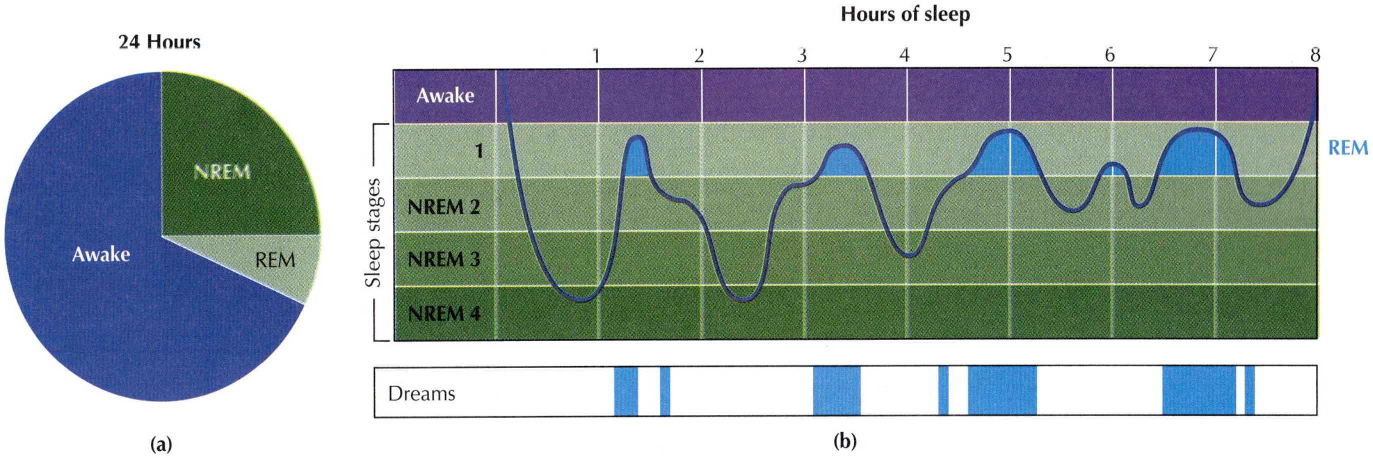

Figure 24.2

REM and NREM sleep. *(a)* Average proportion of time adults spend daily in REM sleep and NREM sleep. REM periods add up to about 20 percent of total sleep time. *(b)* Typical changes in stages of sleep during the night. Note that dreams mostly coincide with REM periods.

What else happens to the body when a person dreams? REM sleep is a time of high emotion (Gujar et al., 2011). The heart beats irregularly. Blood pressure and breathing waver. Both males and females appear to be sexually aroused. This occurs for all REM sleep, so it is not strictly related to erotic dreams.

Paradoxically, during REM sleep, your body becomes quite still, as if you were paralyzed. To understand why, imagine for a moment the results of acting out some of your recent dreams. Very likely, REM-sleep paralysis prevents some hilarious—and dangerous—nighttime escapades. When it fails, some people thrash violently, leap out of bed, and may attack their bed partners. A lack of muscle paralysis during REM sleep is called *REM behavior disorder* (Neikrug & Ancoli-Israel, 2012). One patient suffering from the disorder tied himself to his bed every night. That way, he couldn't jump up and crash into furniture or walls (Shafton, 1995).

Sometimes sleep paralysis can go a little too far. While it normally prevents us from moving during REM sleep, sleep paralysis can occur just as you begin to wake up. During such episodes, people sometimes have *hypnopompic* (hip-neh-POM-pik: "upon awakening") hallucinations, including bizarre experiences, such as sensing that an alien being is in your bedroom; feeling something pressing on your chest, suffocating you; or feeling like you are floating out of your body (D'Agostino & Limosani, 2010; Waters et al., 2016).

Although most of us shrug off these weird experiences, some people try to make sense of them. Earlier in history, people interpreted these hallucinated intruders as angels, demons, or witches and believed that their out-of-body experiences were real (Cheyne & Girard, 2009). However, as our culture changes so do our interpretations of sleep experiences. Today, for example, some people who have sleep-related hallucinations believe they have been abducted by space aliens or sexually abused (McNally & Clancy, 2005).

Swiss artist Henry Fuseli drew on hypnopompic imagery as an inspiration for his famous painting *The Nightmare.*

Superstitions and folklore often develop as attempts to explain human experiences, including some of the stranger aspects of sleep. By studying unusual experiences such as REM behavior disorder and hypnopompic hallucinations, psychologists hope to offer natural explanations for many

Light sleep (Stage 1 sleep) Marked by small, irregular brain waves and some alpha waves.

Sleep spindles Distinctive bursts of brain-wave activity that indicate a person is asleep.

Delta waves Large, slow brain waves that occur in deeper sleep (Stages 3 and 4).

Deep sleep The deepest form of normal sleep.

Rapid eye movements (REMs) Swift eye movements during sleep.

REM sleep Stage of sleep marked by rapid eye movements, high-frequency brain waves, and dreaming.

experiences that might otherwise seem supernatural or paranormal (Cheyne & Girard, 2009).

How important are REM sleep and dreaming? To answer this question, sleep expert William Dement awakened volunteers each time they entered REM sleep. Soon, their need for "dream time" grew more urgent. By the fifth night, many had to be awakened 20 or 30 times to prevent REM sleep. When the volunteers were finally allowed to sleep undisturbed, they dreamed extra amounts. This effect, called **REM rebound**, explains why alcoholics have horrible nightmares after they quit drinking. Alcohol reduces sleep quality by suppressing REM sleep, thus setting up a powerful rebound when it is withdrawn (Stein & Friedmann, 2005).

The two most basic states of sleep, then, are **non-REM (NREM) sleep**, which occurs during all four sleep stages, and REM sleep, with its associated dreaming (Rock, 2004).

Functions of Sleep—Catching a Few ZZZs

Learning Outcome 24.2 Explain the functions of sleep, including the functions of NREM sleep and REM sleep

It has long been thought that sleep helps keep the body, including the brain and immune system, healthy by regulating temperature, conserving energy, and aiding development and repair (Faraut et al., 2011; Ingiosi, Opp, & Krueger, 2013; Irwin, 2015). According to **repair/restorative theories of sleep**, lowering body metabolism and brain activity during sleep may help replenish and conserve energy and lengthen life.

The Need for Sleep

How important is the need for sleep? Very important. For example, a rare genetic disease that prevents sleep (known as *fatal familial insomnia*) always ends with stupor, coma, and death (Zhang et al., 2010). With few exceptions, four days or more without sleep becomes hell for everyone. Randy Gardner, who at age 17 went about 11 days without sleep, holds the world record. Surprisingly, Randy needed only 14 hours of sleep to recover. As Randy found, most of the symptoms of **sleep deprivation**, or sleep loss, are reversed by a single night's rest (Sallinen et al., 2008).

What are the costs of sleep loss? At various times, Randy's speech was slurred, and he couldn't concentrate, remember clearly, or name common objects (Coren, 1996). Sleep loss also typically causes trembling hands, drooping eyelids, inattention, irritability, staring, increased pain sensitivity, and general discomfort (Doran, Van Dongen, & Dinges, 2001).

Most people experience *hypersomnia* (hi-per-SOM-nee-ah), or excessive daytime sleepiness, after even a few hours of sleep loss (Centers for Disease Control, 2017b). Hypersomnia is a common problem during adolescence (Carskadon, Acebo, & Jenni, 2004; Kotagal, 2012). Rapid physical changes during puberty increase the need for sleep, even though the quality and quantity of sleep time tend to decrease during the teen years.

Most people who have not slept for a day or two can still do interesting or complex mental tasks. But they have trouble paying attention, staying alert, and doing simple or boring routines (Trujillo, Kornguth, & Schnyer, 2009). They also are susceptible to **microsleeps**, which are brief shifts in brain activity to the pattern normally recorded during sleep. Imagine placing an animal on a moving treadmill, over a pool of water. Even under these conditions, animals soon drift into repeated microsleeps. For a pilot or machine operator, this can spell disaster (Hardaway & Gregory, 2005; Sallinen et al., 2017). If a task is monotonous (such as factory work or air traffic control), no amount of sleep loss is safe.

When you drive, remember that microsleeps can lead to macro-accidents. Even if your eyes are open, you can fall asleep for a few seconds. About 72,000 crashes every year are caused by sleepiness (Centers for Disease Control, 2019b). Although coffee helps (Kamimori et al., 2005), if you are struggling to stay awake while driving, you should stop, quit fighting it, and take a short nap.

Severe sleep loss can even cause a temporary **sleep-deprivation psychosis**—a loss of contact with reality. Confusion, disorientation, delusions, and hallucinations are typical of this reaction. Fortunately, such "crazy" behavior is uncommon (Petrovsky et al., 2014; Szpak & Allen, 2012).

How can I tell how much sleep I really need? Pick a day when you feel well rested. Then sleep that night until you wake without an alarm clock. If you feel rested when you wake up, that's your natural sleep need. If you're sleeping fewer hours than you need, you're building up a sleep debt (Basner & Dinges, 2009).

Sleep and Memory

Why do we keep cycling between NREM and REM sleep throughout the night? According to one theory, NREM and REM sleep together play a role in memory formation by calming the brain and sharpening important memories (Cipolli, Mazzetti, & Plazzi, 2013). Don't expect to learn math, a foreign language, or other complex skills while asleep—especially if the snooze takes place in class (González-Vallejo et al., 2008). But do expect that a good period of sleep will help you remember what you learned the day before (Holz et al., 2012; Saxvig et al., 2008).

The Function of NREM Sleep NREM sleep is dream free about 90 percent of the time and is deepest early in the night during the first few Stage 4 periods. Your first period of Stage 1 sleep also usually lacks REMs and dreams. Later Stage 1 periods typically include a shift into REM sleep. Dreamless, slow-wave NREM sleep increases after physical exertion and may help us recover from bodily fatigue. It also appears to calm the brain, in part to begin memory consolidation during the earlier part of a night's sleep (Diekelmann & Born, 2010; Holz et al., 2012).

The basic idea is that we are bombarded by information throughout the day, which causes our neural networks to become more and more active. As a result, your brain requires more and more energy to continue functioning. Slow-wave sleep early in the night brings overall brain activation levels back down, allowing a fresh approach to the next day.

Consider for a moment the rich jumble of events that make up a day. Some experiences are worth remembering (like what you are reading right now, of course), and others are not so important (like which sock you put on first this morning). As slow-wave sleep reduces overall activation in the brain, less important experiences may fade away and be forgotten. If you wake up feeling clearer about what you studied the previous night, it might be because your brain doesn't "sweat the small stuff"!

The Function of REM Sleep *What role does REM sleep play in memory formation?* Whereas NREM sleep may calm the brain, REM sleep appears to sharpen or complete the consolidation of our memories of the previous day's more important experiences (Diekelmann & Born, 2010; Saxvig et al., 2008). During the day, when information is streaming in, the brain may be too busy to efficiently select useful memories. When the conscious brain is "off-line," we may be better able to identify and solidify important new memories. Daytime stress tends to increase REM sleep, which may rise dramatically when there is a death in the family, trouble at work, a marital conflict, or other emotionally charged events. The value of more REM sleep, then, may be that it helps us sort and retain important memories, especially memories about strategies for solving problems (Stickgold, 2013; Walker & Stickgold, 2006). This is why, after studying for a long period, you may remember more if you go to sleep rather than pulling an all-nighter. (REMember to get some REM!)

Dreams—A Royal Road?

Learning Outcome 24.3 Name and briefly describe three theories of dreaming

Here's what we know so far: Most people go into REM sleep and dream four or five times a night, at roughly 90-minute intervals. We also know that REM sleep may help us consolidate important memories. To continue our discussion of sleep, let's consider an age-old question about dreaming: How meaningful are dreams? Some theorists believe that dreams have deeply hidden meanings. Others regard dreams as nearly meaningless. Yet others hold that dreams reflect our waking thoughts, fantasies, and emotions (Hartmann, 2011). Let's examine all three views.

Psychodynamic Dream Theory

Psychodynamic theories of dreaming emphasize internal conflicts and unconscious forces (Fischer & Kächele, 2009). Interpreting dreams is such an important part of psychoanalysis that Sigmund Freud referred to them as "the royal road to the unconscious." (See Module 66.) Freud's (1900) landmark book, *The Interpretation of Dreams*, first advanced the idea that many dreams are based on **wish fulfillment**—an expression of unconscious desires. One of Freud's key proposals was that dreams express unconscious desires and

REM rebound The occurrence of extra rapid eye movement sleep following REM sleep deprivation.

Non-REM (NREM) sleep Non-rapid eye movement sleep characteristic of sleep Stages 1, 2, 3, and 4.

Repair/restorative theories of sleep Proposals that lowering body and brain activity and metabolism during sleep may help conserve energy and lengthen life.

Sleep deprivation Being prevented from getting desired or needed amounts of sleep.

Microsleep A brief shift in brain-wave patterns to those of sleep.

Sleep-deprivation psychosis A major disruption of mental and emotional functioning brought about by sleep loss.

Psychodynamic theory Any theory of behavior that emphasizes internal conflicts, motives, and unconscious forces.

Wish fulfillment Freudian belief that many dreams express unconscious desires.

According to psychodynamic theory, dream imagery often has symbolic meaning. How would you interpret this dreamlike image? The fact that dreams don't have a single unambiguous meaning is one of the shortcomings of Freudian dream theory.

conflicts as disguised **dream symbols**—images that have deeper symbolic meaning. Understanding a dream, then, requires analyzing the dream's **manifest content**, or obvious, visible meaning, to uncover its **latent content**, or hidden, symbolic meaning.

For instance, a woman who dreams of stealing her best friend's wedding ring and placing it on her own hand may be unwilling to consciously admit that she is sexually attracted to her best friend's husband. Similarly, a journey might symbolize death, and horseback riding or dancing could symbolize sexual intercourse. *Do all dreams have hidden meanings?* Probably not. Freud realized that many dreams are trivial "day residues" or carryovers from ordinary waking events. On the other hand, dreams do tend to reflect a person's current concerns, so Freud wasn't entirely wrong.

The Activation-Synthesis Hypothesis

Psychiatrists Allan Hobson and Robert McCarley have a radically different view of dreaming, called the **activation-synthesis hypothesis**. They believe that during REM sleep, several lower brain centers are "turned on" *(activated)* in more or less random fashion. However, messages from those centers are blocked from reaching the body (remember sleep paralysis?), so no movement occurs. Nevertheless, the centers continue to tell higher brain areas of their activities. Struggling to interpret this random information, the brain searches through stored memories and manufactures *(synthesizes)* a dream. Because frontal areas of the cortex, which control higher mental abilities, are mostly shut down during REM sleep, the resulting dreams are more primitive and more bizarre than daytime thoughts (Hobson, 2000, 2005).

How does that help explain dream content? According to the activation-synthesis hypothesis, dreams are usually meaningless. Let's use the classic chase dream as an example. In such dreams, we feel that we are running but not going anywhere. This occurs because the brain is told that the body is running, but it gets no feedback from the motionless legs. To try to make sense of this information, the brain creates a chase drama. A similar process probably explains dreams of floating or flying.

So dreams have no meaning? The activation-synthesis hypothesis rejects the idea that dreams are deliberate, meaningful messages from our unconscious. However, it does not rule out the possibility that we can find meaning in some dreams. Because dreams are created from memories and past experiences, parts of dreams can sometimes reflect each person's mental life, emotions, and concerns (Hobson, 2000).

Neurocognitive Dream Theory

Can't dreams just be about everyday stuff? Yes, they can. According to William Domhoff's **neurocognitive dream theory**, dreams have much in common with waking thoughts and emotions. Domhoff believes this is true because many brain areas that are active when we are awake remain active during dreaming (Domhoff, 2003, 2011). From this perspective, our dreams are a conscious expression of REM sleep processes that are sorting and storing daily experiences (Klinger, 2013; Levin & Nielsen, 2009). Speaking very loosely, it's as if the dreaming brain were reviewing messages left on voice mail to decide which are worth keeping. Thus, we shouldn't be surprised if a student who is angry at a teacher dreams of embarrassing the teacher in class, a lonely person dreams of romance, or a hungry child dreams of food. It is not necessary to seek deeper symbolic meanings to understand these dreams.

Dream Worlds

Which dream theory is the most widely accepted? Each theory has strengths and weaknesses (Hobson & Schredl, 2011; MacDuffie & Mashour, 2010). However, studies of dream content tend to support neurocognitive theory's focus on the continuity between dreams and waking thought. Rather than seeming exotic or bizarre, most dreams reflect everyday events (Domhoff & Schneider, 2008; Pesant & Zadra, 2006). For example, athletes tend to dream about the previous day's athletic activities (Erlacher & Schredl, 2004).

Nevertheless, many psychologists continue to believe that some dreams have deeper meanings (Halliday, 2010; Wilkinson, 2006). Dr. Otto Loewi, a Nobel Prize winner, provides a striking example. Loewi had spent years studying the chemical transmission of nerve impulses. A tremendous breakthrough in his research came when he dreamed of an experiment three nights in a row. On the third night, he got up after having the dream, went straight to his laboratory, and performed the crucial experiment. Loewi later said that if the experiment had occurred to him while awake, he would have rejected it.

Dreams and Creativity Loewi's experience suggests that it is possible to use dreams for your own purposes (Stickgold & Walker, 2004). The ability to take advantage of dreams for problem solving is improved if you "set" yourself before retiring for the night. Before you go to bed, try to visualize or think intently about a problem that you want to solve. Steep yourself in the problem by stating it clearly and reviewing all relevant information. Although this method is not guaranteed to lead to dreams about a novel solution or a new insight, it is certain to be an adventure.

Lucid Dreaming Creative dreaming can be further enhanced if you learn *lucid dreaming*, a relatively rare but fascinating experience (Stumbrys et al., 2012). During a **lucid dream**, a person feels as if she or he is fully awake within the dream world and capable of normal thought and action. If you ask yourself, "Could this be a dream?" and answer "Yes," you are having a lucid dream (Dresler et al., 2012). A lucid dreamer can actually change a dream *while dreaming*, potentially transforming dreaming into a "research laboratory" of sorts (Harb, Brownlow, & Ross, 2016; LaBerge, 2014).

For example, a woman who kept dreaming that she was being swallowed by a giant wave decided to try swimming the next time the wave engulfed her. She did, with great determination, and the dream evaporated. More importantly, her revised dream made her feel that she could cope with life again. For reasons such as this, people who have lucid dreams tend to feel a sense of emotional well-being (Taitz, 2011). Dream expert Allan Hobson believes that learning to voluntarily enter altered states of consciousness (through lucid dreaming or self-hypnosis, for example) has allowed him to have enlightening experiences without the risks of taking mind-altering drugs (Hobson, 2009).

We will now turn our attention to a survey of some additional sleep problems—if you are still awake.

Sleep Troubles—Some Things That Go Wrong in the Night

Learning Outcome 24.4 Define insomnia, outline its causes as well as some behavioral remedies, and name four other disorders associated with sleep

Sleep quality has taken a beating in North America. Artificial lighting, frenetic schedules, exciting pastimes, smoking, drinking, overstimulation, and many other factors have contributed to a near epidemic of sleep problems. **Sleep–wake disorders** include difficulties falling asleep, staying asleep, waking up, or any combination of these. They range from daytime sleep attacks to sleepwalking and terrifying nightmares (■ **Table 24.1**). Let's explore a few of the sleep problems that some people face.

Insomnia Disorder

No one wants to lie awake staring at the ceiling at 2 a.m. Yet, about 40 million Americans have chronic insomnia, while another 20 million have occasional problems with sleep (National Institute of Neurological Disorders and Stroke, 2019). **Insomnia** includes difficulty in getting to sleep or staying asleep (such as frequent nighttime awakenings or waking too early). Insomnia can harm people's work, health, and relationships (Ebben & Spielman, 2009).

Dream symbols Images in dreams that serve as visible signs of hidden ideas, desires, impulses, emotions, relationships, and so forth.

Manifest content (of dreams) The surface, "visible" content of a dream; dream images as the dreamer remembers them.

Latent content (of dreams) The hidden or symbolic meaning of a dream, as revealed by dream interpretation and analysis.

Activation-synthesis hypothesis Proposition that dreams are how brains process the random electrical discharges of REM sleep.

Neurocognitive dream theory Proposal that dreams reflect everyday waking thoughts and emotions.

Lucid dream A dream in which the dreamer feels awake and capable of normal thought and action.

Sleep–wake disorders Difficulties falling asleep, staying asleep, waking up, or any combination of these, such as insomnia disorder.

Insomnia Difficulty in getting to sleep or staying asleep.

TABLE 24.1 | Sleep–Wake Disorders

Insomnia disorder	Difficulty in getting to sleep or staying asleep; also, not feeling rested after sleeping.
Hypersomnolence disorder	Excessive daytime sleepiness. This can result from depression, insomnia, narcolepsy, sleep apnea, sleep drunkenness, periodic limb movements, drug abuse, and other problems.
Narcolepsy	Sudden, irresistible, daytime sleep attacks that may last anywhere from a few minutes to a half-hour. Victims may fall asleep while standing, talking, or even driving.
Breathing-related sleep disorders	Interruption in breathing during sleep. For example, during sleep, breathing stops for 20 seconds or more (sleep apnea) until the person wakes a little, gulps in air, and settles back to sleep; this cycle may be repeated hundreds of times per night.
Circadian rhythm sleep–wake disorders	A mismatch between the sleep–wake schedule demanded by a person's bodily rhythm and that demanded by the environment.
Disorders of arousal	During NREM sleep, a person engages in activities that are normally engaged in while awake, such as sleepwalking; also includes sleep terrors, partial awakenings marked by panic.
Nightmare disorder	Vivid, recurrent nightmares that significantly disturb sleep.
REM sleep behavior disorder	A failure of normal muscle paralysis, leading to violent actions during REM sleep.
Restless legs syndrome	An irresistible urge to move the legs to relieve sensations of creeping, tingling, prickling, aching, or tension.
Substance-induced sleep disorder	Disturbance of sleep because of a particular substance, such as caffeine.

Source: American Psychiatric Association (2013).

Types and Causes of Insomnia Worry, stress, and excitement can cause *temporary insomnia* and a self-defeating cycle. First, excess mental activity ("I can't stop turning things over in my mind") and heightened arousal block sleep. Then, frustration and anger over not being able to sleep cause more worry and arousal. This further delays sleep, which causes more frustration, and so on (Sunnhed & Jansson-Fröjmark, 2014). A good way to interrupt this cycle is to avoid fighting it. Get up and do something useful or satisfying when you can't sleep. (Reading a textbook might be a good choice of useful activities.) Return to bed only when you begin to feel that you are struggling to stay awake. If sleeping problems last for more than three weeks, then a diagnosis of *chronic insomnia* can be made.

Drug-dependency insomnia (sleep loss caused by withdrawal from sleeping pills) also can occur. There is real irony in the billion dollars a year that North Americans spend on sleeping pills. Many nonprescription sleeping pills have little sleep-inducing effect. Barbiturates are even worse. These prescription sedatives decrease both Stage 4 sleep and REM sleep, drastically lowering sleep quality. In addition, many users become "sleeping-pill junkies," who need an ever-greater number of pills to get to sleep. Victims must be painstakingly weaned from their sleep medicines. Otherwise, terrible nightmares and *rebound insomnia* may drive them back to drug use.

It's worth remembering that although alcohol and other depressant drugs may help a person get to sleep, they greatly reduce sleep quality (Nau & Lichstein, 2005). Even newer sleep medicines have drawbacks. Possible side effects include amnesia, impaired judgment, increased appetite, decreased sex drive, depression, and even sleepwalking, sleep eating, and sleep driving, making these drugs a temporary remedy at best.

Behavioral Remedies for Insomnia *If sleeping pills are a poor way to treat insomnia, what can be done?* It is usually better to treat insomnia with lifestyle changes and behavioral techniques (McGowan & Behar, 2013; Montgomery & Dennis, 2004). Treatment for chronic insomnia usually begins with a careful analysis of a patient's sleep habits, lifestyle, stress levels, and medical problems. All the approaches discussed in the following list are helpful for treating insomnia (Ebben & Spielman, 2009; Nau & Lichstein, 2005):

1. **Stimulus control.** Insisting on a regular schedule helps establish a firm body rhythm, greatly improving sleep. This is best achieved by exercising **stimulus control**, which refers to linking a response with specific stimuli. It is important to wake up and go to sleep at the same time each day, including weekends (Vincent, Lewycky, & Finnegan, 2008). In addition, insomniacs should avoid doing anything but sleeping when they are in bed. They are not to study, eat, watch television, read, pay the bills, worry, or even think in bed. (Lovemaking is okay, however.) In this way, only sleeping and relaxation become associated with going to bed at specific times.
2. **Sleep restriction.** Even if an entire night's sleep is missed, it is important not to sleep late in the morning, nap more than an hour, sleep during the evening, or go to bed early the following night. Instead, restricting sleep to normal bedtime hours avoids fragmenting sleep rhythms (Vincent, Lewycky, & Finnegan, 2008).
3. **Paradoxical intention.** Another helpful approach is to remove the pressures of trying to go to sleep. Instead, the goal becomes trying to keep the eyes open (in the dark) and stay awake as long as possible (Nau & Lichstein, 2005). This allows sleep to come unexpectedly and lowers performance anxiety (Taylor & Roane, 2010).
4. **Relaxation.** Some insomniacs lower their arousal before sleep by using a physical or mental strategy for relaxing, such as progressive muscle relaxation (see Module 67 for more information), meditation, or blotting out worries with calming images. It also is helpful to schedule time in the early evening to write down worries or concerns and plan what to do about them the next day in order to set them aside before going to bed.
5. **Exercise.** Strenuous exercise during the day promotes sleep (Brand et al., 2010). However, exercise within three to six hours of sleep is helpful only if it is very light.
6. **Food intake.** What you eat can affect how easily you get to sleep. Eating starchy foods increases the amount of tryptophan (TRIP-tuh-fan: an amino acid) reaching the brain. More tryptophan, in turn, increases the amount of serotonin in the brain, which is associated with relaxation, a positive mood, and sleepiness (Silber & Schmitt, 2010). Thus, to promote sleep, try eating a starchy snack, such as bread, pasta, or dry cereal. If you really want to drop the bomb on insomnia, try eating a baked potato (which may be the world's largest sleeping pill!).
7. **Stimulant avoidance.** Stimulants, such as coffee and cigarettes, should be avoided. It also is worth remembering that alcohol, although not a stimulant, impairs sleep quality.

Disorders of Arousal—Sleepwalking, Sleeptalking, and Sleepsex

Sleepsex? As strange as it may seem, many waking behaviors can be engaged in while asleep, such as driving a car, cooking, playing a musical instrument, and eating (Plazzi et al., 2005). The most common, sleepwalking, is eerie and fascinating in its own right (Banerjee & Nisbet, 2011). **Somnambulists** (som-NAM-bue-lists: those who sleepwalk) avoid obstacles, descend stairways, and on rare occasions may step out of windows or in front of automobiles. Sleepwalkers have been observed jumping into lakes, urinating in garbage pails or closets (phew!), shuffling furniture around, and even brandishing weapons (Schenck & Mahowald, 2005).

The sleepwalker's eyes are usually open, but a blank face and shuffling feet reveal that the person is still asleep. If you find someone sleepwalking, you should gently guide the person back to bed. Awakening a sleepwalker does no harm, but it is not necessary.

Does sleepwalking occur during dreaming? No. Remember that people are normally immobilized during REM sleep. EEG studies have shown that somnambulism occurs during NREM Stages 3 and 4 (Kalat, 2021; Stein & Ferber, 2001). *Sleeptalking* also occurs mostly during NREM sleep. The link with deep sleep explains why sleeptalking makes little sense and why sleepwalkers are confused and remember little when awakened.

Oh, yes, you're curious about sleepsex. *Sexsomnia* is not as exciting as it might sound. Just imagine being startled wide-awake by your bed partner, who is asleep, attempting to have sex with you (Andersen et al., 2007; Klein & Houlihan, 2010).

Nightmare Disorder and Sleep Terrors

Stage 4 sleep is also the realm of sleep terrors. These frightening episodes are quite different from ordinary nightmares. A **nightmare** is simply a bad dream that takes place during REM sleep. During a Stage 4 **sleep terror** (also

Stimulus control Linking a particular response with specific stimuli.

Somnambulists People who sleepwalk; occurs during NREM sleep.

Nightmare A bad dream that occurs during REM sleep.

Sleep terror (night terror) A state of panic during NREM sleep.

known as a **night terror**), a person suffers total panic and may hallucinate frightening dream images into the bedroom. An attack may last 15 or 20 minutes. When it is over, the person awakens drenched in sweat but only vaguely remembers the terror. Because sleep terrors occur during NREM sleep (when the body is not immobilized), victims may sit up, scream, get out of bed, or run around the room. Victims remember little afterward. (Other family members, however, may have a story to tell.) Although sleep terrors are more common in childhood, they are not uncommon in adulthood (Belicki, Chambers, & Ogilvie, 1997; Kataria, 2004).

How to Eliminate a Nightmare *Is there any way to stop a recurring nightmare?* A bad nightmare can be worse than any horror movie. It's easy to leave a theater, but we often remain trapped in terrifying dreams. Frequently occurring nightmares (one a week or more) are associated with higher levels of psychological distress (Levin & Fireman, 2002).

Nevertheless, most nightmares can be banished by following three simple steps. First, write down your nightmare, describing it in detail. Next, change the dream any way you wish, making sure to spell out the details of the new dream. The third step is *imagery rehearsal*, in which you mentally rehearse the changed dream before you fall asleep again (Krakow & Zadra, 2006). Imagery rehearsal may work because confronting upsetting dreams may reduce their impact. Or perhaps it mentally "reprograms" future dream content. In any case, the technique has helped many people (Hansen et al., 2013; Harb et al., 2012).

Sleep Apnea

Some sage once said, "Laugh and the whole world laughs with you; snore and you sleep alone." While frequent snoring is often harmless, it can signal a serious problem. A person who snores loudly, with short silences and loud gasps or snorts, may suffer from *apnea* (AP-nee-ah: interrupted breathing). In **sleep apnea**, breathing stops for periods of 20 seconds to 2 minutes. As the need for oxygen becomes intense, the person wakes a little and gulps in air. She or he then settles back to sleep. But soon, breathing stops again. This cycle is repeated hundreds of times a night. As you might guess, apnea victims are extremely sleepy during the day. They also can have a harder time functioning during the day (Grenèche et al., 2011) and, in the long run, may suffer damage to their oxygen-hungry brains (Joo et al., 2010).

What causes sleep apnea? Central sleep apnea occurs because the brain stops sending signals to the diaphragm to maintain breathing. *Obstructive sleep apnea hypopnea syndrome* is blockage of the upper air passages. One of the most effective treatments is the use of a continuous positive airway pressure (CPAP) mask to aid breathing during sleep. The resulting improvement in sleep is often followed by improved daytime function (Ferini-Strambi et al., 2013; Tregear et al., 2010). Other treatments include weight loss and surgery for breathing obstructions.

SIDS Sleep apnea is suspected as one cause of **sudden infant death syndrome (SIDS)**, or "crib death." In the "typical" crib death, a slightly premature or small baby with some signs of a cold or cough is put to bed. A short time later, parents find the child has died. A baby deprived of air will normally struggle to begin breathing again. However, SIDS babies seem to have a weak arousal reflex. This prevents them from changing positions and resuming breathing after an episode of apnea. SIDS is the leading cause of death in children between 1 month and 1 year of age (National Institute of Child Health and Human Development, 2017b).

Babies at risk for SIDS must be carefully watched for the first 6 months of life. To aid parents, a monitor may be used that sounds an alarm when breathing or pulse becomes weak. Babies at risk for SIDS are often premature; have a shrill, high-pitched cry; engage in "snoring," breath-holding, or frequent awakening at night; breathe mainly through an open mouth; or remain passive when their face rolls into a pillow or blanket. For this reason, it is wise to avoid bundling newborns or covering them with blankets or pillows.

Sleeping position is another major risk factor for SIDS. Healthy infants are best off sleeping on their backs (sides are not as good, but it's much better than facedown) (Shapiro-Mendoza et al., 2009). (However, premature babies, those with respiratory problems, and those who often vomit may need to sleep facedown. Ask a pediatrician for guidance.) Remember, "*back* to sleep" is the safest position for most infants (Ball & Volpe, 2013).

Narcolepsy

Narcolepsy (NAR-koe-lep-see), or sudden, irresistible sleep attacks, is one of the most dramatic sleep problems. Victims may fall asleep anywhere for a few minutes to a half-hour, during alert, daytime activities such as standing, talking, or even driving. Emotional excitement, especially laughter, commonly triggers narcolepsy. (Tell an especially good joke and a narcoleptic may fall asleep.) Many victims also suffer from *cataplexy* (CAT-uh-plex-see), a sudden temporary

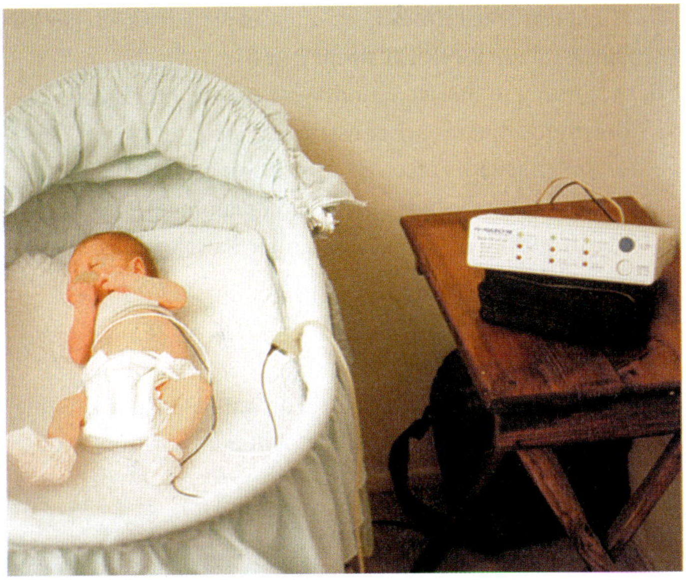

Infants at risk for SIDS are often attached to devices that monitor breathing and heart rate during sleep. An alarm sounds to alert parents if either pulse or respiration falters. SIDS rarely occurs after an infant is 1 year old. Babies, and especially those at risk for SIDS, should be placed on their backs.

paralysis of the muscles, leading to complete body collapse (Ingravallo et al., 2012). Sleep attacks and paralysis appear to occur when REM sleep intrudes into the waking state (Kalat, 2021). It's easy to understand why narcolepsy can devastate careers and relationships.

Fortunately, narcolepsy is rare. It runs in families, which suggests that it is hereditary (Chabas et al., 2003). This has been confirmed by breeding several generations of narcoleptic dogs. (These dogs, by the way, are simply outstanding at learning the trick "Roll over and play dead.") There is no known cure for narcolepsy, but a variety of drugs help reduce the frequency and intensity of attacks (Ferini-Strambi et al., 2013; Lammers et al., 2010).

Sleep apnea Disorder in which a person stops breathing during sleep.

Sudden infant death syndrome (SIDS) The sudden, unexplained death of an apparently healthy infant.

Narcolepsy A sudden, irresistible sleep attack.

MODULE 24 Sleep and Dreams—Learning Outcomes Revisited

24.1 Describe the patterns and stages which make up a night's sleep

Sleep is an innate biological rhythm of about 7–8 hours a night. This amount varies from person to person and from infancy to old age. During NREM sleep, brain waves become longer and slower, pulse rate drops and body temperature drops. NREM sleep occurs in four stages. Stage 1 is light sleep, and Stage 4 is deep sleep. The sleeper alternates between Stages 1 and 4 (passing through Stages 2 and 3) several times each night.

24.2 Explain the functions of sleep, including the functions of NREM sleep and REM sleep

NREM sleep helps the body to recover from fatigue and calms the brain to allow the process of memory consolidation to begin. Periods of REM (rapid eye movement) sleep are strongly associated with high emotion, aroused physiology, dreaming, and sleep paralysis. REM sleep is important for completing the consolidation of memories determined to be important. Lowered body metabolism and brain activity during sleep may help conserve energy and lengthen life. Moderate sleep loss affects mainly vigilance and performance on routine or boring tasks. Higher animals and people deprived of sleep experience involuntary microsleeps. Extended sleep loss can (somewhat rarely) produce a temporary sleep-deprivation psychosis.

24.3 Name and briefly describe the three theories of dreaming

The Freudian, or psychodynamic, view is that dreams express unconscious wishes, frequently disguised by dream symbols. The activation-synthesis model portrays dreaming as a random physiological process. The neurocognitive view of dreams holds that dreams are continuous with waking thoughts and emotions. Supporting the neurocognitive view, most dream content is about familiar settings, people, and actions.

24.4 Define insomnia, outline its causes as well as some behavioral remedies, and name four other disorders associated with sleep

Insomnia is defined by difficulties getting to sleep and/or staying asleep. It may be temporary or chronic. It is often caused by worry, stress, or excitement but can also be brought on by withdrawal from sleeping pills. Behavioral approaches to managing insomnia include stimulus control, sleep restriction, paradoxical intention, relaxation, exercise, monitoring food intake, and avoiding stimulants. Other sleep disorders include sleepwalking, sleeptalking, and sleepsex (which occur during NREM sleep), sleep terrors (which occur in NREM sleep) and nightmares (which occur in REM sleep), sleep apnea (interrupted breathing), which is suspected to be one cause of SIDS, and narcolepsy and cataplexy (which are caused by a sudden shift to Stage 1 REM patterns during normal waking hours).

Reflective Practice

Content Check

1. Alpha waves are to presleep drowsiness as __________ waves are to Stage 4 sleep.
2. Rapid eye movements indicate that a person is in deep sleep. T or F?
3. Sharpening memories and facilitating their storage is one function of
   a. activation-synthesis cycles
   b. REM sleep
   c. deep sleep
   d. NREM sleep
4. Which of the following is *not* a behavioral remedy for insomnia?
   a. daily hypersomnia
   b. stimulus control
   c. progressive relaxation
   d. paradoxical intention
5. Night terrors, sleepwalking, and sleeptalking all occur during Stage 1, NREM sleep. T or F?
6. According to the activation-synthesis hypothesis of dreaming, dreams are constructed from __________ to explain messages received from lower brain centers.
7. Recent research shows that lucid dreaming occurs primarily during NREM sleep or micro-awakenings. T or F?

Skill Check

Think Critically

8. The possibility of having a lucid dream raises an interesting question: If you were dreaming right now, how could you prove it?

Self-Reflect

As a counselor at a sleep clinic, how would you explain the basics of sleep and managing sleep to a new client? Do you think your dreams have symbolic meaning or reflect everyday concerns? Can dreams increase self-awareness? Almost everyone suffers from insomnia at least occasionally. Which of the techniques for combating insomnia are similar to strategies that you have discovered on your own? How many sleep–wake disorders can you name (including those listed in Table 25.1)? Have you experienced any of them?

ANSWERS

1. delta 2. F 3. b 4. a 5. F 6. memories 7. F 8. In waking consciousness, our actions have consequences that produce immediate sensory feedback. Dreams lack such external feedback. Thus, trying to walk through a wall or doing similar tests would reveal if you were dreaming.

Consciousness
Psychoactive Drugs

MODULE 25

Lucy in the Sky with Diamonds?

Many artists, writers, and musicians have celebrated the use of psychoactive drugs. Others have attributed their creativity to drug-induced experiences. Here, the artist depicts visual experiences he had while under the influence of LSD.

Unfortunately, positive images and songs about drug use obscure another, darker reality. Prescription drugs that can ease pain, induce sleep, or end depression also have a high potential for abuse. So do freely available legal drugs, such as nicotine and alcohol. Add to the mix the destruction wrought by illicit drugs, and it's little wonder that so many lives are damaged by drug abuse. This module provides an overview of commonly abused psychoactive substances.

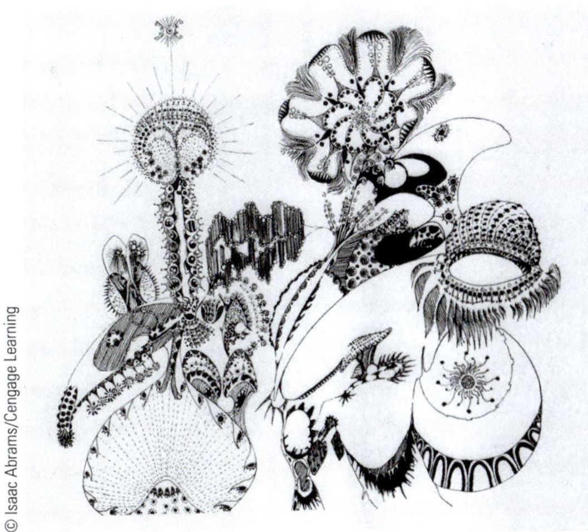

~LEARNING OUTCOMES~

After reading this module you should be able to:

25.1 Explain the action of a psychoactive drug, distinguish between recreational and instrumental drug use, and outline three reasons for drug abuse

25.2 Name five common stimulants

25.3 Name five common depressants

25.4 Name two common hallucinogens

Drug-Altered Consciousness—The High and Low of It

Learning Outcome 25.1 Explain the action of a psychoactive drug, distinguish between recreational and instrumental drug use, and outline three reasons for drug abuse

One common way to alter human consciousness is to administer a **psychoactive drug**—a substance capable of altering attention, emotion, judgment, memory, time sense, self-control, or perception. In fact, most Americans regularly use consciousness-altering drugs (don't forget, caffeine, alcohol, and nicotine are mildly psychoactive). Many psychoactive drugs can be placed on a scale ranging from stimulation to depression (➤ Figure 25.1). A **stimulant**, or *upper*, is a substance that increases activity in the body and nervous system. A **depressant**, or *downer*, does the reverse.

Patterns of Psychoactive Drug Use

In general, psychoactive drug use falls into two categories. Using a drug to address a particular issue, such as taking a painkiller for a headache, a cup of coffee to stay awake, or an antidepressant to treat depression is *instrumental* use. In contrast, *recreational* users focus on experiencing the psychoactive effects of a drug. Getting high on heroin, even though you are not in physical pain, is an example.

Psychoactive drug Any substance that can alter a person's state of consciousness.

Stimulant (upper) A substance that increases activity in the body and nervous system.

Depressant (downer) A substance that decreases activity in the body and nervous system.

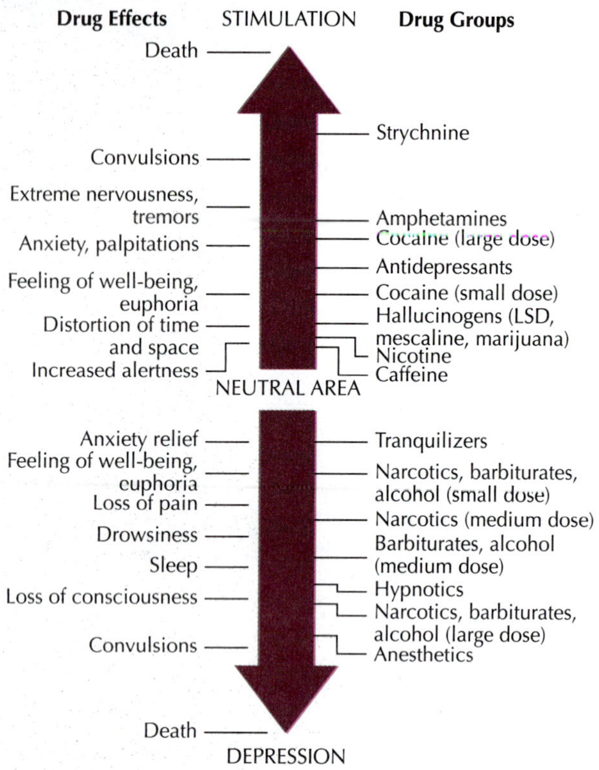

Figure 25.1

Spectrum and continuum of drug action. Many drugs can be rated on a stimulation–depression scale according to their effects on the central nervous system. Although LSD, mescaline, and cannabis are listed here, the stimulation–depression scale is less relevant to these drugs. The principal characteristic of such hallucinogens is their mind-altering quality.

Most, if not all, of the drugs discussed in this chapter have *instrumental* uses (Ksir, Hart, & Black, 2015). Some have been used for centuries in various cultures, in search of insight. Others were developed specifically to treat various mental illnesses. Still others have a variety of health benefits. For example, the main instrumental use for morphine is to control pain.

Psychoactive Drug Misuse and Abuse Psychoactive drugs are often misused. Failing to comply with a doctor's prescription, such as overmedicating oneself, is one example. Using a drug recreationally rather than instrumentally, such as using the codeine in a cough medication to get high, is another (Prus, 2017).

Isn't that just drug abuse? The term *drug abuse* is usually reserved for cases when drug misuse causes some sort of harm. Many recreational users can be classified as *experimental* users (short-term use based on curiosity) or *social-recreational* users (occasional social use for pleasure or relaxation). While these may be examples of misuse, harm is more typically associated with *intensive* use (daily use with elements of dependence) or *compulsive* use (intense use and extreme dependence), in which case the person may be diagnosed with a **substance use and addictive disorder**.

The problem, of course, is that drug misuse can easily become drug abuse (Everitt & Robbins, 2016). The key is moderation. Some people remain social drinkers for life, whereas others become alcoholics within weeks of taking their first drink (Robinson & Berridge, 2003). Because drugs such as painkillers, sleep aids, and antidepressants are easy to abuse, the more powerful psychoactive drugs are controlled substances (Goldberg, 2019). In 2018, 20.3 million Americans had a substance use disorder (Center for Behavioral Health Statistics and Quality, 2019). Drug abuse has been one of the most persistent of all social problems in Western nations.

Why is drug abuse so common? People seek drug experiences for many reasons, ranging from curiosity and a desire to belong to a group to a search for meaning or an escape from feelings of inadequacy. One study found that many adolescents who abuse drugs tend to be maladjusted, alienated, impulsive, and emotionally distressed (Masse & Tremblay, 1997). Antisocial behavior, school failure, and risky sexual behavior also are commonly associated with drug abuse (Boyd, Harris, & Knight, 2012). Such patterns make it clear that taking drugs is as much a symptom as a cause of personal and social maladjustment (Ksir, Hart, & Black, 2015).

Many abusers turn to drugs in a self-defeating attempt to cope with life. All the frequently abused drugs produce immediate feelings of pleasure. The negative consequences follow much later. This combination of immediate pleasure and delayed punishment allows abusers to feel good on demand. In time, of course, most of the pleasure goes out of drug abuse and the abuser's problems get worse. But if an abuser merely feels better (however briefly) after taking a drug, drug taking can become compulsive (Wood & Rünger, 2016).

Polydrug Abuse One more pattern of drug abuse bears mentioning: the abuse of more than one drug at the same time. According to the Florida Medical Examiners Commission (2018), *polydrug abuse* accounts for the "vast majority" of deaths due to drug overdose. When mixed, the effects of different drugs can be multiplied by a **drug interaction—** one drug enhances the effect of another—which are responsible for thousands of fatal drug overdoses every year (Goldberg, 2019). This is true whether the mixed drugs were legally or illegally obtained.

In 2016, popular music icon Prince died of an accidental fentanyl overdose, becoming the highest profile casualty to date of a drug 50 times more powerful than heroin.

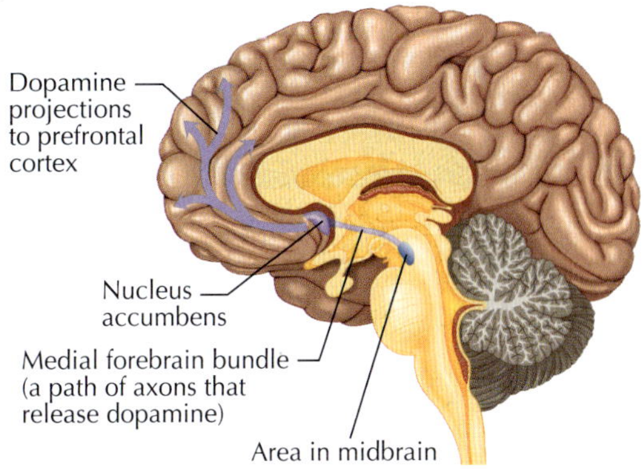

➤ **Figure 25.2**

Addiction and dopamine. Addictive drugs increase dopamine activity in the medial forebrain bundle and the nucleus accumbens, stimulating the frontal cortex and giving rise to intensified feelings of pleasure.

Psychoactive Drugs and the Brain

Psychoactive drugs generally alter consciousness by directly influencing brain activity (Maisto, Galizio, & Connors, 2018; Prus, 2017). Typically, these drugs imitate or alter the effects of neurotransmitters, the chemicals that carry messages between brain cells. Some drugs, such as MDMA (or ecstasy), amphetamines, and some antidepressants, cause more neurotransmitters to be released, increasing the activity of brain cells. Other drugs, such as cocaine, slow the removal of neurotransmitters after they are released. This prolongs the action of the neurotransmitter and typically has a stimulating effect. Other drugs, such as nicotine and opiates, directly stimulate brain cells by mimicking neurotransmitters. Alcohol and tranquilizers illustrate another possibility. These drugs affect certain types of brain cells that cause relaxation and relieve anxiety. Some drugs fill receptor sites on brain cells and block incoming messages. Other possibilities also exist, which is why drugs can have such a wide variety of effects on the brain (Julien, 2011).

Regardless, most addictive drugs stimulate the brain's reward circuitry, producing feelings of pleasure (Kalat, 2021; Prus, 2017). In particular, addictive drugs stimulate a brain region called the *nucleus accumbens* to release dopamine (DOPE-ah-meen), a neurotransmitter that results in intensified feelings of pleasure (➤ Figure 25.2; Floresco, 2015). As a result, the reward pathway signals, "That felt good. Let's do it again. Let's remember exactly how we did it." This creates a compulsion to repeat the drug experience. It's the hook that eventually snares the addict (National Institute on Drug Abuse, 2014). In the end, the addictive drug physically changes the brain's reward circuitry, making it even harder for the addict to overcome addiction (Henry et al., 2010; Niehaus, Cruz-Bermúdez & Kauer, 2009). At the same time, addiction may damage the prefrontal cortex, the brain system involved in self-control (Everitt & Robbins, 2016). Adolescents, it should be noted, are especially susceptible to addiction because the prefrontal brain systems that restrain their risk taking are not as mature as those that reward pleasure seeking (Boyd, Harris, & Knight, 2012).

Drug Dependence

Another reason that drug abuse is so common is that taking psychoactive drugs tends to create dependencies. Once you get started, it can be very difficult to stop (Calabria et al., 2010). Drug dependence falls into two broad categories (Maisto, Galizio, & Connors, 2018). When a person compulsively uses a drug to maintain bodily comfort, a **physical dependence (addiction)** exists. Addiction occurs most often with drugs that cause **withdrawal symptoms**—the physical

Substance use and addictive disorder Abuse of, or dependence on, a mood- or behavior-altering drug or equivalent.

Drug interaction A combined effect of two drugs that exceeds the addition of one drug's effects to the other.

Physical dependence (addiction) Compulsive use of a drug to maintain bodily comfort as indicated by the presence of drug tolerance and withdrawal symptoms.

Withdrawal symptoms Physical illness and discomfort after an addict stops taking a drug.

TABLE 25.1 | Comparison of Psychoactive Drugs

Name	Classification	Medical Use	Duration of Effect
Alcohol	Sedative-hypnotic	Solvent, antiseptic, sedative	1–4 hours
Amphetamines	Stimulant	Relief of mild depression, control of narcolepsy and hyperactivity	4 hours
Barbiturates	Sedative-hypnotic	Sedation, relief of high blood pressure, anticonvulsant, antianxiety	1–16 hours
Benzodiazepines	Anxiolytic (antianxiety drug)	Tranquilizer	10 minutes–8 hours
Caffeine	Stimulant	Counteract depressant drugs, treatment of migraine headaches	Varies
Cocaine	Stimulant, local anesthetic	Local anesthesia	Varied, 1–4 hours
Codeine	Narcotic	Ease pain and coughing	3–6 hours
GHB	Sedative-hypnotic	Experimental treatment of narcolepsy, alcoholism	1–3 hours
Heroin	Narcotic	Pain relief	3–6 hours
LSD	Hallucinogen	Experimental study of mental function, alcoholism	8–12 hours
Marijuana (THC)	Relaxant, euphoriant; in high doses, hallucinogen	Treatment of glaucoma and side effects of chemotherapy	2–4 hours
MDMA	Stimulant/hallucinogen	None	4–6 hours
Mescaline	Hallucinogen	None	8–12 hours
Methadone	Opioid	Pain relief	12–24 hours
Morphine	Opioid	Pain relief	3–6 hours
PCP	Anesthetic	None	4–6 hours, plus 12-hour recovery
Psilocybin	Hallucinogen	None	Varies
Tobacco (nicotine)	Stimulant	Emetic (nicotine)	Varies

Question marks indicate conflict of opinion. It should be noted that illicit drugs are frequently mixed with unknown and possibly dangerous substances and thus pose possible hazards to the user.

illness and discomfort that follows removal of a drug. Withdrawal from drugs such as alcohol, barbiturates, and opiates can cause violent, flulike symptoms, including nausea, vomiting, diarrhea, chills, sweating, and cramps. Addiction is often accompanied by a **drug tolerance**—a progressive decrease in a person's responsiveness to a drug. This leads users to take larger and larger doses to get the desired effect.

Persons who develop a **psychological dependence** feel that a drug is necessary to maintain their comfort or well-being. Usually, they intensely crave the drug and its rewarding qualities. Psychological dependence can be just as powerful as physical addiction. That's why some psychologists define

Effects Sought	Long-Term Symptoms	Physical Dependence Potential	Psychological Dependence Potential	Organic Damage Potential
Sense alteration, anxiety reduction, sociability	Cirrhosis, toxic psychosis, neurologic damage, addiction	Yes	Yes	Yes
Alertness, activeness, relieve fatigue	Loss of appetite, delusions, hallucinations, toxic psychosis	Yes	Yes	Yes
Anxiety reduction, euphoria	Addiction with severe withdrawal symptoms, possible convulsions, toxic psychosis	Yes	Yes	Yes
Anxiety relief	Irritability, confusion, depression, sleep disorders	Yes	Yes	No, but can affect fetus
Wakefulness, alertness	Insomnia, heart arrhythmias, high blood pressure	No?	Yes	Yes
Excitation, talkativeness	Depression, convulsions	Yes	Yes	Yes
Euphoria, prevent withdrawal discomfort	Addiction, constipation, loss of appetite	Yes	Yes	No
Intoxication, euphoria, relaxation	Anxiety, confusion, insomnia, hallucinations, seizures	Yes	Yes	No?
Euphoria, prevent withdrawal discomfort	Addiction, constipation, loss of appetite	Yes	Yes	No*
Insightful experiences, exhilaration, distortion of senses	May intensify existing psychosis, panic reactions	No	No?	No?
Relaxation; increased euphoria, perceptions, sociability	Possible lung cancer, other health risks	Yes	Yes	Yes?
Excitation, euphoria	Personality change, hyperthermia, liver damage	No	Yes	Yes
Insightful experiences, exhilaration, distortion of senses	May intensify existing psychosis, panic reactions	No	No?	No?
Prevent withdrawal discomfort	Addiction, constipation, loss of appetite	Yes	Yes	No
Euphoria, prevent withdrawal discomfort	Addiction, constipation, loss of appetite	Yes	Yes	No*
Euphoria	Unpredictable behavior, suspicion, hostility, psychosis	Debated	Yes	Yes
Insightful experiences, exhilaration, distortion of senses	May intensify existing psychosis, panic reactions	No	No?	No?
Alertness, calmness, sociability	Emphysema, lung cancer, mouth, and throat cancer, cardiovascular damage, loss of appetite	Yes	Yes	Yes

*Persons who inject drugs under nonsterile conditions run a high risk of contracting AIDS, hepatitis, abscesses, or circulatory disorders.

addiction as any repetitively compulsive pattern. By this definition, a person who has lost control over drug use, for whatever reason, is addicted.

Drugs of Abuse ▪ **Table 25.1** reveals that the drugs most likely to lead to physical dependence are alcohol, amphetamines, barbiturates, cocaine, codeine, heroin, methadone, morphine, and nicotine (tobacco). Using *most* of the drugs listed in Table 25.1 also can result in psychological dependence. Note also that people who take drugs intravenously are additionally at high risk for developing hepatitis and AIDS (see Module 48). The discussion that follows focuses on the drugs most often abused by students.

Stimulants—Up, Up, and Away

Learning Outcome 25.2 Name five common stimulants

Some of the most common uppers are amphetamines, cocaine, MDMA, caffeine, and nicotine.

Amphetamines

Amphetamines are synthetic stimulants. Some common street names for amphetamines are *speed*, *bennies*, *dexies*, *amp*, and *uppers*. These drugs were once widely prescribed for weight loss or depression. Today, the main instrumental medical use of amphetamines is to treat childhood hyperactivity and overdoses of depressant drugs. Illicit use of amphetamines is widespread, however, by people seeking to stay awake and those who rationalize that such drugs can improve mental or physical performance (DeSantis & Hane, 2010).

For example, Adderall and Ritalin, two popular "study drugs," are both mixes of amphetamines used to treat **attention deficit hyperactivity disorder (ADHD)**. People with ADHD have difficulty controlling their attention and are prone to displaying hyperactive and impulsive behavior (National Institute of Mental Health, 2016b). Increasing numbers of normal college students are illegally taking these drugs in the hope that they also will be able to focus better while doing schoolwork (Dodge et al., 2012).

Is it true that those drugs actually can help students study? Taking "study drugs" may produce slight improvements in problem-solving performance; however, this may be offset by a slight loss of creativity (Farah et al., 2009). Most important, all amphetamines have side effects that are worrisome, as we will see shortly.

Methamphetamine is a more potent variation of amphetamine. It can be snorted, injected, or eaten. Of the various types of amphetamine, methamphetamine has created the largest drug problem. *Bergs*, *glass*, *meth*, *crank*, or *crystal*, as it is known on the street, can be made cheaply in backyard labs and sold for massive profits. In addition to ruining lives through addiction, it has fueled a violent criminal subculture.

Amphetamines rapidly produce a drug tolerance. Most abusers quickly end up taking ever-larger doses to get the desired effect. Eventually, some users switch to injecting methamphetamine directly into the bloodstream. True "speed freaks" typically go on binges lasting several days, after which they "crash" from lack of sleep and food.

Abuse *How dangerous are amphetamines?* Large doses can cause nausea, vomiting, extremely high blood pressure, fatal heart attacks, and disabling strokes. It is important to realize that amphetamines speed up the use of the body's resources; they do not magically supply energy. After an amphetamine binge, people suffer from crippling fatigue, depression, confusion, uncontrolled irritability, and aggression. Repeated amphetamine use damages the brain. Amphetamines also can cause *amphetamine psychosis*, a loss of contact with reality. Affected users have paranoid delusions that someone is out to get them. Acting on these delusions, they may become violent, resulting in suicide, self-injury, or injury to others (Scott, 2012).

A potent, smokable form of crystal methamphetamine (also known as *ice*) has added to the risks of stimulant abuse. Like *crack*, the smokable form of cocaine (which we'll discuss next), crystal methamphetamine produces an intense high and rapidly leads to compulsive abuse and severe drug dependence.

Cocaine

Cocaine (also known as *coke*, *snow*, *blow*, *snuff*, and *flake*) is a powerful central nervous system stimulant extracted from the leaves of the coca plant. Cocaine produces feelings of alertness, euphoria, well-being, power, boundless energy, and pleasure (Julien, 2011). At the turn of the twentieth century, dozens of nonprescription potions and cure-alls contained cocaine. It was during this time that Coca-Cola was indeed the "real thing." From 1886 until 1906, when the US Pure Food and Drug Act was passed, Coca-Cola contained cocaine (since then, it has been replaced with caffeine).

How does cocaine differ from amphetamines? The two are very much alike in their effects on the central nervous system. The main difference is that amphetamine effects typically last longer than those of cocaine, which is more quickly metabolized.

Abuse *How dangerous is cocaine?* Cocaine's capacity for abuse and social damage rivals that of heroin. Rats and monkeys given free access to cocaine find it irresistible. Many, in fact, end up dying of convulsions from self-administered overdoses of the drug. Even casual or first-time users risk having convulsions, a heart attack, or a stroke. Cocaine increases the neurotransmitters *dopamine* and *norepinephrine*. Norepinephrine arouses the brain, and dopamine produces a "rush" of pleasure. This combination is so powerfully rewarding that cocaine users run a high risk of becoming compulsive abusers (Ridenour et al., 2005).

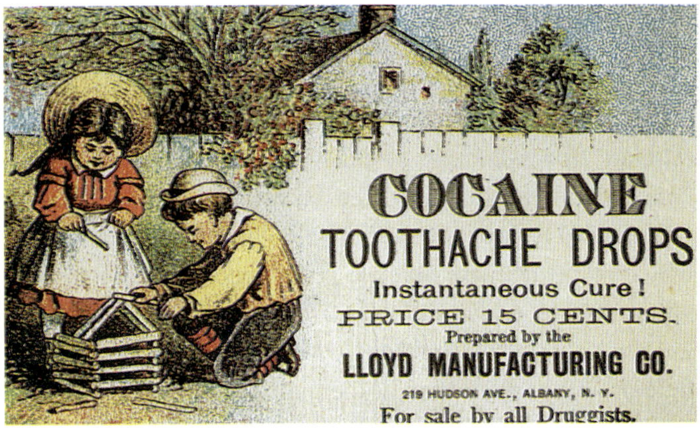

National Library of Medicine

Cocaine was the main ingredient in many nonprescription elixirs before the turn of the twentieth century. Today, cocaine is recognized as a powerful and dangerous drug. Its high potential for abuse has damaged the lives of countless users.

A person who stops using cocaine does not experience heroin-like withdrawal symptoms. Instead, the brain adapts to cocaine abuse in ways that upset its chemical balance, causing depression when cocaine is withdrawn. First, there is a jarring "crash" of mood and energy. Within a few days, the person enters a long period of fatigue, anxiety, paranoia, boredom, and **anhedonia** (an-he-DAWN-ee-ah), an inability to feel pleasure. Before long, the urge to use cocaine becomes intense. So, although cocaine does not fit the classic pattern of addiction, it is ripe for compulsive abuse. Even a person who gets through withdrawal may crave cocaine months or years later (Washton & Zweben, 2009). If cocaine were cheaper, nine out of ten users would progress to compulsive abuse. In fact, rock cocaine (*crack*, *rock*, or *roca*), which is cheaper, produces very high abuse rates.

Anyone who thinks she or he has a cocaine problem should seek advice at a drug clinic or a Cocaine Anonymous meeting. Although quitting cocaine is extremely difficult, three out of four abusers who remain in treatment succeed in breaking their dependence (Sinha et al., 2006). Hope also is on the horizon in the form of a vaccine currently undergoing clinical trials that prevents cocaine from stimulating the nervous system (Kosten et al., 2013).

MDMA

MDMA (methylenedioxymethamphetamine; also known as *ecstasy* or *molly*) is chemically similar to amphetamine. While MDMA is technically a stimulant, it is sometimes classified as a hallucinogen since it can produce hallucinations (Prus, 2017). It also produces a rush of energy, and users say it makes them feel closer to others and heightens sensory experiences.

MDMA causes brain cells to release extra amounts of dopamine (resulting in euphoria and increased energy), epinephrine (resulting in increased heart rate, blood pressure, and body temperature), and serotonin (resulting in changes in many bodily functions, such as loss of appetite and increased sexual arousal; National Institute on Drug Abuse, 2020d). Although MDMA increases sexual pleasure, it actually *diminishes* sexual performance, impairing erection in 40 percent of men and delaying orgasm in both men and women (Zemishlany, Aizenberg, & Weizman, 2001).

Abuse In 2018, over 2,500,000 Americans used MDMA (Statista, 2020). Every year, emergency room doctors see many MDMA cases, including MDMA-related deaths. Some of these incidents are caused by elevated body temperature, which can lead to collapse. MDMA users at "rave" parties try to prevent overheating by drinking water to cool themselves. This may help to a small degree, but MDMA overheating can cause kidney, heart, or liver failure, which can be fatal (National Institute on Drug Abuse, 2020d).

In addition, MDMA users are more likely to abuse alcohol and other drugs, to neglect studying, to party excessively, and to engage in risky sex (Strote, Lee, & Wechsler, 2002). Ironically, MDMA use does intensify the impact of music. We say "ironically" because the end result is often overstimulation of the brain, which can lead to a rebound depression (Iannone et al., 2006).

MDMA use also has long-term effects. Feelings of anxiety or depression can persist for months after a person stops taking MDMA. In addition, heavy users typically do not perform well in tests of learning and memory and show some signs of underlying brain damage (Quednow et al., 2006).

Caffeine

Caffeine is the most frequently used psychoactive drug in North America. (Goodnight, Seattle!) Many people have a hard time starting a day (or writing another paragraph) without a cup of coffee or tea because caffeine suppresses drowsiness and increases alertness, especially when combined with sugar (Adan & Serra-Grabulosa, 2010; Smith,

Drug tolerance Progressive decrease in a person's responsiveness to a drug.

Psychological dependence Drug dependence that is based primarily on emotional or psychological needs.

Attention deficit hyperactivity disorder (ADHD) A behavioral problem characterized by short attention span, restless movement, and impaired learning capacity.

Anhedonia An inability to feel pleasure.

Christopher, & Sutherland, 2013). Physically, caffeine can cause sweating, talkativeness, tinnitus (ringing in the ears), and hand tremors (Nehlig, 2004). Caffeine stimulates the brain by blocking chemicals that normally inhibit or slow nerve activity (Maisto, Galizio, & Connors, 2018). Its effects become apparent with doses as small as 50 milligrams, the amount found in about one-half cup of brewed coffee.

How much caffeine did you consume today? It is common to think of coffee as the major source of caffeine, but there are many others. Caffeine is found in tea, many soft drinks (especially colas and the so-called "energy drinks"), chocolate, and cocoa. Thousands of nonprescription drugs also contain caffeine, including stay-awake pills, cold remedies, and many name-brand aspirin products.

Abuse *Are there any serious drawbacks to using caffeine?* Overuse of caffeine may result in an unhealthy dependence known as *caffeinism*. Insomnia, irritability, loss of appetite, chills, racing heart, and elevated body temperature are all signs of caffeinism. Many people with these symptoms drink 15 or 20 cups of coffee a day. However, even as few as 2.5 cups of coffee a day (or the equivalent) can intensify anxiety and other psychological problems (Hogan, Hornick, & Bouchoux, 2002). People who consume even such modest amounts may experience anxiety, depression, fatigue, headaches, and flulike symptoms during withdrawal (Juliano & Griffiths, 2004).

Caffeine poses a variety of other health risks. Caffeine encourages the growth of breast cysts in women, and it may contribute to bladder cancer, heart problems, and high blood pressure. Pregnant women who consume as little as 2 cups of coffee a day increase the risk of having a miscarriage (Cnattingius et al., 2000). It is wise to remember that caffeine *is* a drug and to use it in moderation.

Nicotine

Next to caffeine and alcohol, *nicotine* is the most widely used psychoactive drug (Julien, 2011). A natural stimulant found mainly in tobacco, nicotine is so toxic that it is sometimes used to kill insects! In large doses, it causes stomach pain, vomiting and diarrhea, cold sweats, dizziness, confusion, and muscle tremors. In very large doses, nicotine may cause convulsions, respiratory failure, and death. For a nonsmoker, 50 to 75 milligrams of nicotine taken in a single dose could be lethal. (Chain-smoking a pack of cigarettes can produce this dosage.) Most first-time smokers get sick on one or two cigarettes. In contrast, regular smokers build a tolerance for nicotine. A heavy smoker may inhale several packs a day without feeling ill.

Abuse *How addictive is nicotine?* A vast array of evidence confirms that nicotine is very addictive (Dani & Balfour, 2011). Most smokers begin when they are teenagers, which is unfortunate because young people are even more vulnerable to addiction than are adults (Counotte et al., 2011). Although 35 million Americans each year want to quit smoking, more than 85 percent of them relapse, many within a week (National Institute on Drug Abuse, 2018). As humorist Mark Twain once whimsically lamented, "Giving up smoking is the easiest thing in the world. I know because I've done it thousands of times."

This should come as no surprise because withdrawal from nicotine causes headaches, sweating, cramps, insomnia, digestive upset, irritability, and a sharp craving for cigarettes. These symptoms may last from two to six weeks and may even be worse than heroin withdrawal. Just a few puffs will make that all go away until the next time the smoker works up the courage to quit.

Impact on Health *How serious are the health risks of smoking?* Smoking is the leading cause of preventable deaths worldwide. Every year, 8 million people around the globe, including about 480,000 Americans, die from tobacco use (Centers for Disease Control, 2019a; World Health Organization, 2013). Tens of millions more live diminished lives because they smoke.

A burning cigarette releases a large variety of potent *carcinogens* (car-SIN-oh-jins: cancer-causing substances). Smoking causes widespread damage to the body, leading to an increased risk of many cancers (such as lung cancer), cardiovascular diseases (such as stroke), respiratory diseases (such as chronic bronchitis), and reproductive disorders (such as decreased fertility). Together, these health risks combine to reduce the life expectancy of the average smoker by 10 to 15 years.

By the way, the same applies to chewing tobacco and snuff. A 30-minute exposure to one pinch of smokeless tobacco is equivalent to smoking three or four cigarettes. Along with all the health risks of smoking, users of smokeless tobacco also run a higher risk of developing oral cancer (Oral Cancer Foundation, 2019).

Smokers don't just risk their own health; they also endanger those who live and work nearby. Secondhand smoke causes about 7,300 lung cancer deaths and as many as 34,000 heart disease deaths each year in the United States alone. It is particularly irresponsible of smokers to expose young children, who are especially vulnerable, to secondhand smoke (American Lung Association, 2020).

Quitting Smoking *If it is so hard to quit, how do some people manage to succeed?* Whatever approach is taken, quitting smoking is not easy. It is especially difficult to try quitting alone, without any support. Many people find that using nicotine patches or gum and/or other medications, such as *bupropion*, helps them suppress their cravings during the withdrawal period (Bolt et al., 2012). The best chance of success comes when the smoker combines the desire to quit with both medication and some sort of counseling (Centers for Disease Control, 2020f).

Many smokers succeed in quitting by quitting abruptly (Lindson-Hawley et al., 2016). However, going "cold turkey" may work best only for those completely committed to quitting since it makes quitting an all-or-nothing proposition. Smokers who smoke even one cigarette after "quitting forever" tend to feel they've failed. Many figure they might just as well resume smoking. Others succeed by tapering down gradually. Those who quit gradually accept that success may take many attempts, spread over several months. Either way, you will have a better chance of success if you decide to quit *now* rather than at some time in the future, and don't delay your quit date too often (Hughes & Callas, 2011).

If you choose to taper off, the best way is *scheduled gradual reduction* (Riley et al., 2002). The key is to deliberately schedule and then gradually stretch the length of time between cigarettes. For example, the smoker might (1) delay having a first cigarette in the morning and then try to delay a little longer each day or (2) gradually reduce the total number of cigarettes smoked each day.

It is also worth noting that smoking is more than a nicotine delivery system for most smokers. The entire ritual of smoking has become a positive experience. Just holding a cigarette, dangling it between the lips, or even seeing a favorite smoking chair can give a smoker pleasure. For this reason, behavioral self-management techniques can be very useful for breaking habits such as smoking (see Module 31). In recent years, *e-cigarettes* have become popular as a way to simulate smoking either with or without delivering any nicotine. Anyone trying to quit should be prepared to make several attempts before succeeding. But the good news is that tens of millions of people have quit.

Marc Bruxelle/Shutterstock.com

Vaping. E-cigarettes are electrical devices that look and feel like cigarettes because they vaporize a smokeless mist that can mimic tobacco smoke. When they deliver no nicotine, or a reduced dose, they may help people quitting smoking by allowing the smoker to enjoy the ritual of smoking while withdrawing from nicotine. However, when they are glamorized as a smokeless way to deliver the usual dose, they become just another delivery device that must be medically regulated (Cobb & Abrams, 2011). Perhaps even more concerning is the fact that vaping is now being investigated for a potential connection to lung injuries (Shmerling, 2019).

Depressants—Down and Out

Learning Outcome 25.3 Name five common depressants

While opioids, like *heroin* and *morphine*, may be more powerful, both as drugs of abuse and as painkillers, the most widely used depressants are alcohol, barbiturates, gamma-hydroxybutyric acid (GHB), and benzodiazepine (ben-zoe-die-AZ-eh-peen) tranquilizers. Depressants are much alike in their effects. In fact, barbiturates and tranquilizers are sometimes referred to as "solid alcohol." Let's examine the properties of each.

Opioids

Raw opium, secreted by poppy seedpods, has been used for centuries to produce sleep and pain relief (Dikotter, Laamann, & Xun, 2008). Opium and the family of chemically related drugs, natural and synthetic, such as *heroin (big H, dope, horse), morphine, codeine, oxycodone*, and *fentanyl*, are now referred to as **opioids**. Also commonly referred to as *narcotics*—drugs that produce a numbing effect—the opioids are among the most addictive of all drugs.

Opioids can produce a powerful feeling of euphoria ("rush") accompanied by a reduction of anxiety, relaxation, and, of course, pain relief. At higher doses, breathing can be impaired, leading to death. Most current opioid addicts abuse prescription opioid painkillers such as oxycodone and fentanyl (Centers for Disease Control, 2020, c, d; Kolodny et al., 2015).

Another opioid, *methadone*, also bears mentioning. Opioid addicts are often treated with methadone, which reduces a narcotic's "rush," making it much easier to go through withdrawal. Methadone is often freely given to addicts as part of a **harm-reduction strategy** meant to reduce the negative consequences of addiction without requiring drug abstinence (McKeganey, 2012). Harm-reduction programs are controversial because it can seem as if they merely support substance abusers in their addiction (supplying clean needles for drug injections is another example). In reality, they are often the only hope for addicts who would otherwise cause more harm to themselves and to others (Harm Reduction International, 2020).

Barbiturates

Barbiturates are sedative drugs that depress brain activity. Common barbiturates include amobarbital, pentobarbital, secobarbital, and tuinal. On the street, they are known as *downers, blue devils, yellow jackets, lows, goofballs, reds, pink ladies, rainbows*, or *tooies*. Medically, barbiturates are used to calm patients or to induce sleep. At mild dosages, barbiturates have an effect similar to alcohol intoxication. Higher dosages can cause severe mental confusion or even hallucinations. Barbiturates are often taken in excess amounts because an initial dose may be followed by others, as the user becomes uninhibited or forgetful. Overdoses first cause a loss of consciousness followed by severe depression of the brain centers that control heartbeat and breathing. The result is often death (Grilly & Salamone, 2012).

GHB

Would you swallow a mixture of degreasing solvent and drain cleaner to get high? Apparently, a lot of people would. A mini-epidemic of GHB use has taken place in recent years, especially at nightclubs and raves. GHB (also known as *goop, scoop, max*, and *Georgia Home Boy*) is a central nervous system depressant that relaxes and sedates the body. Users describe its effects as similar to those of alcohol (Johnson & Griffiths, 2013). Mild GHB intoxication tends to produce euphoria, a desire to socialize, and a mild loss of inhibition. GHB's intoxicating effects typically last a few hours, depending on the dosage.

Abuse At lower dosages, GHB can relieve anxiety and produce relaxation. However, as the dose increases, its sedative effects may result in nausea, a loss of muscle control, and either sleep or a loss of consciousness. Potentially fatal doses of GHB are only three times the amount typically taken by users. This narrow margin of safety has led to numerous overdoses, especially when GHB was combined with alcohol. An overdose causes coma, breathing failure, and death. GHB also inhibits the gag reflex, so some users choke to death on their own vomit.

In 2000, the U.S. government classified GHB as a controlled substance, making possession a felony. Evidence increasingly suggests that GHB is addictive and a serious danger to users. Two out of three frequent users have lost consciousness after taking GHB. Chronic use leads to brain damage (Pedraza, García, & Navarro, 2009). Heavy users who stop taking GHB have withdrawal symptoms that include anxiety, agitation, tremor, delirium, and hallucinations (Miotto et al., 2001).

Tranquilizers

Tranquilizers lower anxiety and reduce tension. Doctors prescribe benzodiazepine tranquilizers to alleviate nervousness and stress. Valium is the best-known drug in this family; others are Xanax, Halcion, and Librium. Even at normal dosages, these drugs can cause drowsiness, shakiness, and confusion. When used at too high a dosage or for too long, benzodiazepines are addictive (McKim, 2013).

A drug sold under the trade name Rohypnol (ro-HIP-nol) has added to the problem of tranquilizer abuse. This drug, which is related to Valium, is cheap and 10 times more potent. It lowers inhibitions and produces relaxation or intoxication. Large doses induce short-term amnesia and sleep. *Roofies*, as they are known on the street, are odorless and tasteless. They have occasionally been used to spike drinks, which are given to the unwary. Victims of this "date rape" drug are then sexually assaulted or raped while they are unconscious (Nicoletti, 2009). (Be aware, however, that drinking too much alcohol is by far the most common prelude to date rape.)

Abuse Repeated use of barbiturates can cause physical dependence. Some abusers suffer severe emotional depression that may end in suicide. Similarly, when tranquilizers are used at too high a dosage or for too long, addiction can occur. Many people have learned the hard way that their legally prescribed tranquilizers are as dangerous as many illicit drugs (Goldberg, 2019).

Alcohol

Alcohol is the common name for ethyl alcohol, the intoxicating element in fermented and distilled liquors. Contrary to popular belief, alcohol is not a stimulant. The noisy animation at drinking parties is due to alcohol's effect as a *depressant*. Small amounts of alcohol reduce inhibitions, consequently producing feelings of relaxation and euphoria. Larger amounts cause greater impairment of the brain until the drinker loses consciousness. Alcohol also is not an aphrodisiac. Rather than enhancing sexual arousal, it usually impairs performance, especially in males. As William Shakespeare observed long ago, drink "provokes the desire, but it takes away the performance."

Some people become relaxed and friendly when they are drunk. Others become aggressive and want to argue or fight. How can the same drug have such different effects? Some people drink for pleasure. Others drink to cope with negative emotions, such as anxiety and depression. That's why alcohol abuse increases with the level of stress in people's lives. People who drink to relieve bad feelings are at great risk of becoming alcoholics (Roberto & Koob, 2009).

When a person is drunk, thinking and perception become dulled or shortsighted, a condition that has been called **alcohol myopia** (my-OH-pea-ah) (Giancola et al., 2010). Only the most obvious and immediate stimuli catch a drinker's attention. Worries and "second thoughts" that would normally restrain behavior are banished from the drinker's mind. That's why many behaviors become more extreme when a person is drunk. On college campuses, drunken students tend to have accidents, get into fights, sexually assault others, or engage in risky sex. They also destroy property and disrupt the lives of students who are trying to sleep or study (Brower, 2002).

Abuse

Alcohol, the world's favorite depressant, breeds our biggest drug problem. More than 20 million people in the United States and Canada have serious drinking problems. One American dies every 20 minutes in an alcohol-related car crash. Significant percentages of Americans of all ages abuse alcohol (➤ Figure 25.3).

It is especially worrisome to see binge drinking among adolescents and young adults. **Binge drinking** is usually defined as downing five or more drinks (four drinks for women) in a short time. Apparently, many students think it's entertaining to get completely wasted and throw up on their friends (Norman, Conner, & Stride, 2012). However, binge drinking is a serious sign of alcohol abuse (Beseler, Taylor, & Leeman, 2010). It is responsible for 1,800 U.S. college student deaths each year and thousands of trips to the emergency room (Mitka, 2009).

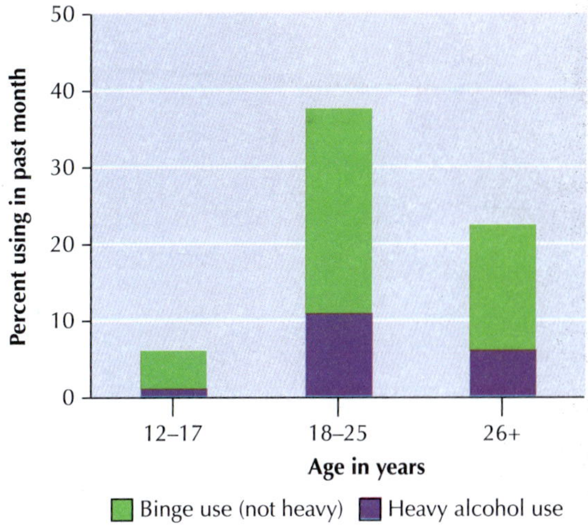

➤ **Figure 25.3**

Alcohol use in the United States. Many Americans of all ages abuse alcohol. According to this 2015 survey, almost 50 percent of young adults aged 18–25 admitted to heavy alcohol use or binge drinking in the month before the survey was administered (Center for Behavioral Health Statistics and Quality, 2019).

Binge drinking is of special concern because the brain continues to develop into the early twenties. Research has shown that teenagers and young adults who drink too much may lose as much as 10 percent of their brain power—especially their memory capacity (Brown et al., 2000). Such losses can have a long-term impact on a person's chances for success in life. In short, getting drunk is a slow but sure way to get stupid (Le Berre et al., 2014).

At Risk

Children of alcoholics and those who have other relatives who abuse alcohol are at greater risk for becoming alcohol abusers themselves. The increased risk appears to be partly genetic (Starkman, Sakharkar, & Pandey, 2012). It

Opioids Substances derived from opium (opiates) and chemically related synthetic substances that produce sleep-inducing and pain-relieving effects.

Harm-reduction strategy A treatment approach to drug addiction that seeks to reduce the negative consequences of addiction without necessarily requiring drug abstinence.

Tranquilizer A drug that lowers anxiety and reduces tension.

Alcohol myopia Shortsighted thinking and perception that occurs during alcohol intoxication.

Binge drinking Consuming five or more drinks in a short time (four for women).

riopatuca/Shutterstock.com

Binge drinking and alcohol abuse have become serious problems among college students (National Institute on Alcohol Abuse and Alcoholism, 2015).

is based on the fact that some people have stronger cravings for alcohol after they drink (Hutchison et al., 2002). Women also face some special risks. For one thing, alcohol is absorbed faster and metabolized more slowly by women's bodies. As a result, women get intoxicated from less alcohol than men. Women who drink also are more prone to liver disease, osteoporosis, and depression. Each extra drink per day adds 7 percent to a woman's risk of breast cancer (Aronson, 2003).

Recognizing Problem Drinking *What are the signs of alcohol abuse?* Because alcohol abuse is such a common problem, it is important to recognize the danger signals. If you can answer yes to even one of the following questions, you may have a problem with drinking (adapted from the College Alcohol Problems Scale, revised, in Maddock et al., 2001):

AS A RESULT OF DRINKING ALCOHOLIC BEVERAGES, I . . .

1. engaged in unplanned sexual activity.
2. drove under the influence.
3. did not use protection when engaging in sex.
4. engaged in illegal activities associated with drug use.
5. felt sad, blue, or depressed.
6. was nervous or irritable.
7. felt bad about myself.
8. had problems with appetite or sleeping.

Moderated Drinking Almost everyone has been to a party spoiled by someone who drank too much too fast. Those who avoid overdrinking have a better time, and so do their friends. But how do you avoid drinking too much? After all, as one wit once observed, "The conscience dissolves in alcohol." It takes skill to regulate drinking in social situations, where the temptation to drink can be strong. If you choose to drink, here are some guidelines that may be helpful (adapted from Doumas, Miller, & Esp, 2017; Miller & Munoz, 2005; National Institute on Alcohol Abuse and Alcoholism, 2020):

MODERATED DRINKING GUIDELINES

1. Be reflective about your drinking beforehand, plan how you will manage it, and keep track of how much you drink.
2. Drink slowly (no more than one drink an hour), eat while drinking or drink on a full stomach, and make every other drink (or more) a nonalcoholic beverage.
3. Limit drinking primarily to the first hour of a social event or party.
4. Practice how you will politely but firmly refuse drinks.
5. Learn how to relax, meet people, and socialize without relying on alcohol.

Also, remember that research has shown that you are likely to overestimate how much your fellow students are drinking (Maddock & Glanz, 2005). So don't let yourself be lured into overdrinking just because you have the (probably false) impression that other students are drinking more than you. Limiting your own drinking may help others as well. When people are tempted to drink too much, their main reason for stopping is that "other people were quitting and deciding they'd had enough" (Johnson, 2002).

Treatment Treatment for alcohol dependence begins with cutting off the supply and sobering up the person. This phase is referred to as **detoxification** (literally, "to remove poison"). It frequently produces all the symptoms of drug withdrawal and can be extremely unpleasant. The next step is to try to restore the person's health. Heavy abuse of alcohol usually causes severe damage to body organs and the nervous system. After alcoholics have "dried out" and some degree of health has been restored, they may be treated with tranquilizers, antidepressants, or psychotherapy. Unfortunately, the success of these procedures has been limited.

One mutual-help approach that has been fairly successful is Alcoholics Anonymous (AA). AA takes a spiritual approach while acting on the premise that it takes a former alcoholic to understand and help a current alcoholic. Participants at AA meetings admit that they have a problem, share feelings, and resolve to stay "dry" one day at a time. Other group members provide support for those struggling to end dependency (Teresi & Haroutunian, 2011). (Other "12-step" programs, such as Cocaine Anonymous and Narcotics Anonymous, use the same approach.)

Other groups offer a rational, nonspiritual approach to alcohol abuse that better fits the needs of some people. Examples include Rational Recovery and Secular Organizations for Sobriety (SOS). Other alternatives to AA include medical treatment, group therapy, mindfulness meditation, and individual psychotherapy (Huebner & Kantor, 2011; Jacobs-Stewart, 2010). There is a strong tendency for abusive drinkers to deny that they have a problem. The sooner they seek help, the better.

Hallucinogens—Tripping the Light Fantastic

Learning Outcome 25.4 Name two common hallucinogens

Although a **hallucinogen** (hal-LU-sin-oh-jen) is generally a mild stimulant, its main effect is to stimulate perceptions at odds with reality. The most common hallucinogens include LSD, PCP, mescaline, psilocybin, and cannabis. In fact, *cannabis* is by far the most popular illicit drug in America (Center for Behavioral Health Statistics and Quality, 2019).

LSD and PCP

The drug LSD (lysergic acid diethylamide, or *acid*) is perhaps the best-known hallucinogen. Even when taken in tiny amounts, LSD can produce hallucinations, mystical-type experiences, and psychotic-like disturbances in thinking and perception (Liechti, Dolder, & Schmid, 2016). Two other common hallucinogens are mescaline (peyote) and psilocybin (*magic mushrooms*, or *shrooms*). Incidentally, the drug PCP (phencyclidine, or *angel dust*) can have hallucinogenic effects. However, PCP, which is an anesthetic, also has stimulant and depressant effects. This potent combination can cause extreme agitation, disorientation, violence, and—too often—tragedy. Like other psychoactive drugs, all hallucinogens, including cannabis, typically affect neurotransmitter systems that carry messages between brain cells (Maisto, Galizio, & Connors, 2018).

Cannabis

Cannabis and hashish are derived from the hemp plant *Cannabis sativa*. Cannabis (also called *marijuana, pot, grass, reefer*, and *MJ*) consists of the dried leaves and flowers of the hemp plant. Hashish is a resinous material scraped from cannabis buds. The two main psychoactive chemicals in cannabis are THC (*tetrahydrocannabinol*) and CBD (*cannabidiol*).

Cannabis's psychological effects include a sense of euphoria or well-being, relaxation, altered time sense, and perceptual distortions. At very high dosages, however, paranoia, hallucinations, and delusions can occur (Ksir, Hart, & Black, 2015). All considered, cannabis intoxication is relatively subtle by comparison to drugs such as LSD or alcohol. Despite this, driving a car while high on cannabis can be hazardous (National Institute on Drug Abuse, 2020c). As a matter of fact, driving under the influence of any intoxicating drug is dangerous.

How does cannabis work? Researchers have recently discovered the *endocannabinoid system*, which is widely distributed throughout the brain (Julien, 2011). Neurons in this system communicate via neurotransmitters (such as *anandimide*) called *endocannabinoids* (the prefix *endo-* means *endogenous*, or "originating from within"). It turns out that THC and CBD, the main cannabinoids in cannabis, can also activate neurons with endocannabinoid receptors (➤ Figure 25.4).

Understanding how the endocannabinoid system affects behavior, then, may well help us better understand the effects of cannabis. Conversely, understanding the effects of cannabis may also help us better understand the functioning of the endocannabinoid system (Piomelli, 2014).

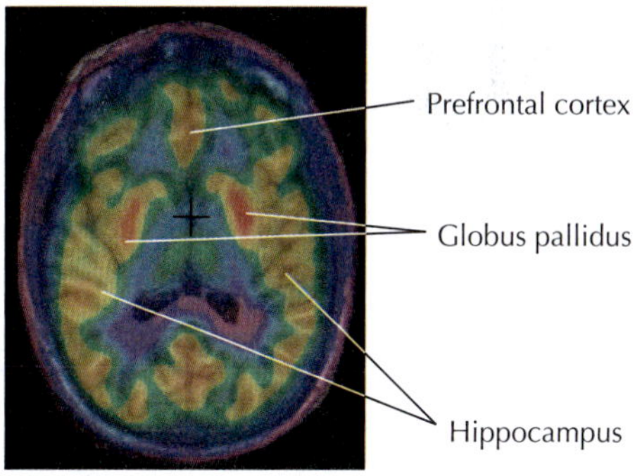

➤ **Figure 25.4**

Endocannabinoid receptors. The red and yellow areas in this PET scan show some of the areas where the brain is rich in endocannabinoid receptors. The prefrontal cortex plays a role in human consciousness, the globus pallidus is involved in the control of coordinated movement, and the hippocampus plays a role in memory. This may explain why cannabis use negatively affects memory and coordination.

Detoxification In the treatment of drug abuse, including alcoholism, the withdrawal of the patient from the drug(s) in question.

Hallucinogen Substance that stimulates perceptions at odds with reality.

Abuse *Does cannabis produce physical dependence?* Yes, according to recent studies (Filbey et al., 2009; National Institute on Drug Abuse, 2020c). Frequent users of cannabis can find it very difficult to quit, so dependence is a risk (Hasin et al., 2016). But cannabis potential for abuse lies primarily in the realm of psychological dependence, not physical addiction.

Health Risks No overdose deaths from cannabis have been reported. However, cannabis cannot be considered harmless. For about a day after a person smokes cannabis, his or her attention, coordination, and short-term memory are impaired. Frequent cannabis users show small declines in learning, memory, attention, and thinking abilities (Solowij et al., 2002). Accordingly, they score lower on IQ tests (Kuehn, 2012). In fact, many people who have stopped using cannabis say that they quit because they were bothered by short-term memory loss and concentration problems. Fortunately, IQ scores and other cognitive measures rebound about a month after a person quits using cannabis (Grant et al., 2001).

When surveyed, nonusers are healthier, earn more, and are more satisfied with their lives than people who smoke cannabis regularly (Allen & Holder, 2013; Ellickson, Martino, & Collins, 2004). In fact, cannabis use is associated with a variety of mental health problems (Buckner, Ecker, & Cohen, 2010; National Institute on Drug Abuse, 2020c). For example, chronic cannabis users are more prone to develop psychosis (Castle et al., 2012).

Cannabis' long-term effects include a number of health risks. Smoking marijuana may increase the risk of a variety of cancers, including lung, prostate, and cervical cancers (Callaghan, Allebeck, & Sidorchuk, 2013; Hashibe et al., 2005). THC may interfere with menstrual cycles and ovulation, as well as cause a higher rate of miscarriages. It also can reach the developing fetus: children whose mothers smoked cannabis during pregnancy show a lowered ability to succeed in challenging, goal-oriented activities (National Institute on Drug Abuse, 2020c; Noland et al., 2005). As is true for so many other drugs, cannabis should be avoided during pregnancy.

Medical Cannabis Is cannabis a dangerous drug or not? On the one hand, as we have just read, cannabis appears to pose a range of health risks. The U.S. government has long labeled cannabis a *Schedule 1 prohibited substance*. Classified in the most dangerous category, along with drugs such as heroin and LSD, cannabis was assumed to pose serious potential for abuse, while offering no medical benefits.

On the other hand, 33 states have legalized some instrumental uses of marijuana as a medicine, and 11 have even legalized recreational use. While the legal status of cannabis is a social policy matter best addressed by governments, it can nevertheless be helpful to examine the relevant scientific evidence that cannabis can be medically useful.

Okay, what does the evidence tell us? While the endocannabinoid system is not yet fully understood, it has been shown to influence the impact of stress and pain (Piomelli, 2014). Understandably, then, recent evidence suggests that THC is helpful in treating some forms of pain due to surgery or trauma to the body, reducing vomiting and nausea due to chemotherapy for cancer, promoting weight gain, and even lessening immune system inflammation (National Academies of Sciences, Engineering, and Medicine, 2017; Prus, 2017). Although evidence such as this may suggest that the case in favor of medical cannabis is beyond question, it is worth briefly considering the role cannabis plays in the treatment of post-traumatic stress disorder (PTSD).

PTSD is a debilitating stress reaction to traumatic events that can leave an affected person unable to function normally. Every year, over a million Americans will suffer from PTSD, including many military veterans (National Center for PTSD, 2019). We already know that the amygdala plays a key role in PTSD (Lamprecht et al., 2009), and that the endocannabinoid system moderates the functioning of the amygdala (Piomelli, 2014). It follows, then, that cannabis may help people with PTSD.

But the actual link may not be so straightforward, as suggested by research showing that people with PTSD may be vulnerable to developing a *cannabis use disorder* (Cornelius et al., 2010). In other words, while casual use may make coping with PTSD easier in the short term, it may leave a person's PTSD untreated while adding a drug abuse problem over the long term.

Fortunately, other research suggests that the key to overcoming PTSD is facing your fear (what behavior therapists call *extinction*). Cannabis makes it easier to face those fears and desensitize them in the long run (Rabinak et al., 2013). Combining existing therapies with cannabis use may turn out to be the most effective approach to treating PTSD. (See Module 63 for more information about PTSD and Module 67 for more information about systematic desensitization.)

In summary, cannabis is just like any other drug. Used indiscriminately, it may do more harm than good. Used in medically appropriate circumstances, it may do more good than harm. Hopefully, research will continue to point the way to additional effective medical uses of cannabis.

MODULE 25 Psychoactive Drugs—Learning Outcomes Revisited

25.1 Explain the action of a psychoactive drug, distinguish between recreational and instrumental drug use, and outline three reasons for drug abuse

Psychoactive drugs affect the brain in ways that alter consciousness. Most psychoactive drugs can be placed on a scale ranging from stimulant to depressant. Instrumental use of drugs refers to situations when drugs are used to address a specific issue. Recreational use of drugs refers to situations when drugs are used to experience the psychoactive effects of a drug. Recreational use may be experimental, social-recreational, intensive, or compulsive. Drug abuse is most often associated with the last two recreational uses. Psychoactive drugs are abused as a coping mechanism, to achieve the rewarding experience that drugs generate in the brain, and because the user has developed a dependency.

25.2 Name five common stimulants

Amphetamines, or synthetic stimulants (e.g., methamphetamine and "study drugs" such as Adderall and Ritalin), cocaine; a natural stimulant extracted from cocoa, MDMA/ecstasy, caffeine, and nicotine.

25.3 Name five common depressants

Opioids, or narcotics (e.g., opium, heroin, morphine, codeine, oxycodone, methadone, and fentanyl), barbiturates, or sedatives, GHB, tranquilizers (e.g., benzodiazepines such as Valium, Xanax), and alcohol.

25.4 Name two common hallucinogens

Hallucinogens such as LSD, PCP, mescaline, psilocybin, and cannabis alter sensory impressions.

Reflective Practice

Content Check

1. Addictive drugs stimulate the brain's reward circuitry by affecting
   - **a.** neurotransmitters
   - **b.** alpha waves
   - **c.** tryptophan levels
   - **d.** delta spindles
2. Which of the following drugs are known to cause physical dependence?
   - **a.** heroin
   - **b.** morphine
   - **c.** codeine
   - **d.** methadone
   - **e.** barbiturates
   - **f.** alcohol
   - **g.** cannabis
   - **h.** amphetamines
   - **i.** nicotine
   - **j.** cocaine
   - **k.** GHB
3. Amphetamine psychosis is similar to extreme ____________________, in which the individual feels threatened and suffers from delusions.
4. Cocaine is very similar to which of the following in its effects on the central nervous system?
   - **a.** Seconal
   - **b.** codeine
   - **c.** cannabis
   - **d.** amphetamine
5. MDMA and GHB are classified as depressants. T or F?
6. College students may overdrink as they try to keep up with how much they falsely imagine that their peers drink. T or F?

Skill Check

Think Critically

7. Why do you think there is such a contrast between the laws regulating marijuana and those regulating alcohol and tobacco?

Self-Reflect

What legal drugs did you use in the last year? Did any have psychoactive properties? How do psychoactive drugs differ from other substances in their potential for abuse?

ANSWERS

1. a 2. All of them 3. paranoia 4. d 5. F 6. T 7. Drug laws in Western societies reflect cultural values and historical patterns of use. Inconsistencies in the law often cannot be justified on the basis of pharmacology, health risks, or abuse potential.

MODULE 26

A Psychologist's Skill Set
Metacognition

What Do You Think of ... You?

For many years, millions of Americans have watched as men and women have tried to achieve fame on *America's Got Talent*. Some of the people who auditioned were outstanding and went on to successful careers in show business (such as Season 13 semifinalist, mentalist Aaron Crow Trent, pictured here). But some of the auditions were truly awful. What were these people thinking when they decided to perform in public? Some of them were obviously just having fun, and were well aware of their inability to carry a tune, or be funny, or juggle. But others seem genuinely unaware of their lack of talent or how to interpret audience reactions. Psychologists would likely say that these people were lacking a skill called *metacognition* (as well as talent). How are metacognitive skills related to success? Let's find out.

Kathy Hutchins/Shutterstock.com

~LEARNING OUTCOMES~

After reading this module you should be able to:

26.1 Define metacognition

26.2 Name and describe the three elements of metacognition

Thinking About Thinking—The Examined Life

Learning Outcome 26.1 Define metacognition

Metacognition is the ability to "think about thinking" (note that psychologists often refer to thoughts as *cognitions*). It includes the ability to monitor and evaluate your thought processes, understanding, and performance across different situations. In this respect it's related to *consciousness*, which was described in Module 23 as "your sensations and perceptions of external events as well as your self-awareness of mental events, including thoughts, memories, and feelings about your experiences and yourself" (Morin, 2006; Robinson, 2008).

Metacognition is also closely connected to the self-regulation skills that were discussed in Module 11, particularly the *executive functions* (Roebers & Feurer, 2015). Recall that executive functions are important in helping people to reach their goals, and one key element in that process is being able to make plans (see also Module 9). Metacognition is critical in helping you to develop effective plans and in evaluating your progress as you carry them out. As a result, it's a skill that's important in helping people to achieve both personal and professional goals.

Do You Know What You Don't Know?

Psychology has a long history of examining how accurate people are when they try to assess their thinking and behavior (Zell & Krizan, 2014). Unfortunately, the news from researchers isn't too good: In general, people are quite poor at evaluating the quality of their thinking, their understanding of material, and their skill level. To make matters worse, this inability to properly monitor what we know and how we're doing is far-reaching, influencing everything from assessments about our social, academic, and athletic skills to our judgments about how much we have understood from a textbook chapter or how long it will take to complete a task (Dunning, Heath, & Suls, 2004).

You may be asking yourself how people could be so poor at evaluating their own thinking. In tackling this question, researchers have shown that there are many things that get in the way of the ability to carry out an accurate self-assessment. According to Serra and Metcalfe (2009), the problems that we face are related to each of the three elements of metacognition: *Knowledge*, *monitoring*, and *control*.

Knowledge We think about a lot of things every day. Our thought processes can include things that are as diverse as forming an impression of a new acquaintance, considering an essay you have to write, or comparing two options on a restaurant menu. Serra and Metcalfe (2009) describe metacognitive knowledge as the information we consult when considering our thought processes. It can include what you know about your *abilities*, the *biases* you have, and what you know about the *strategies* that will help you achieve your goals.

For example, let's say that you were thinking about an essay on sleep deprivation that's due next week. Your metacognitive knowledge might include the idea that you need to get online and search for journal articles, because you understand that this general "paper-writing strategy" is more likely to result in an essay that meets your instructor's standards than simply reviewing Wikipedia pages. Metacognitive knowledge might also involve an understanding that you find the topic complicated, or the idea that you have a bias toward spending too much time reading when preparing to do a paper (because that part seems easy, and you can convince yourself that you're making progress) and that you tend to procrastinate on actually writing papers (because that task is more difficult).

Metacognitive knowledge can also be important in your personal life. For example, if you want to have good relationships with others, it would be helpful for you to be aware that you have a tendency to talk too much when you're nervous, that you're very quick to judge other people, or that you have trouble seeing things from other people's points of view. These types of strategies, biases, and abilities (and many others) are important in determining relationship quality, so it's important that you use this metacognitive knowledge when you're interacting with others.

Wow. I really should give more thought to my own thinking! It's true! Actively accessing metacognitive knowledge about how you relate to other people or perform work-related tasks is important because an awareness of this information can help as you work toward building good relationships, or plan the work that's needed to complete a school project or write a test (Zepeda et al., 2015). Of course, simply considering metacognitive knowledge isn't enough. Once you've got that information, you need to work with it, and that's where metacognitive monitoring and control come in.

Monitoring and Control Metacognitive monitoring refers to the idea that you need to track your thought processes and behaviors as they unfold, and evaluate whether they're going to allow you to meet your goals. In contrast, metacognitive control refers to a situation in which you alter or redirect your thinking and behavior because metacognitive knowledge and monitoring suggests that your current path will not allow you to meet your goals.

If we return to the sleep deprivation paper you're supposed to be writing, for example, you might ask whether you're moving too slowly with reading the research (monitoring) and might need to alter your work schedule in order to finish on time (control). Or perhaps you catch yourself when you seem to be making a snap judgment about someone you have just met (monitoring), and recognize that perhaps you should investigate their personal characteristics further (control). And if you were planning to audition for a reality show, you should be able to assess your own performance relative to a reasonable standard (monitoring), and recognize that if you're doing poorly, you may need additional practice time (control) before you go on television.

Metacognition The conscious experience of thinking about your own thinking.

The Examined Life—Worth Living?

Learning Outcome 26.2 Name and describe the three elements of metacognition

You may be wondering at this point whether poor metacognitive skills are really a big deal. In fact, difficulties with metacognition can lead to problems in many areas of your academic, personal, and professional life. For example, consider how Aysha might plan out her studying when she's preparing for a major exam. What strategies should she use to ensure that she learns the material? At what point should she leave the chapter she's working on and move on to study the next one?

The answers to these questions are important in securing a good result on the exam, and they rely on Aysha's metacognitive skills (Zepeda et al., 2015). In all likelihood, she'll use study strategies that she *thinks* will be helpful, and she'll move on when she *thinks* she's mastered the material in the chapter she's currently studying. But what if she's wrong? What if her metacognitive skills are poor, and she doesn't know that her study strategies aren't as effective as those outlined in Module 1? What if she doesn't recognize that she has a very limited understanding of the textbook material?

You can probably see where this type of poor metacognitive awareness leads: Aysha will be using strategies that are not helpful when studying, and will be likely to think—incorrectly!—that she has mastered the material that will be tested. As a result, she won't feel the need to spend any additional time studying and is likely to be very disappointed with her results.

Poor metacognitive skills have important consequences for our personal relationships as well (Myers & Wells, 2015). At one time or another, you have likely met people who don't seem to have any sense of how their behavior is impacting others. These are the people who often wind up either frustrating or intimidating those that they interact with because they don't seem able to monitor the thinking that is behind their actions, or the signals that others are sending them. A lack of self-awareness makes it difficult to forge close and supportive relationships with family, friends, and co-workers because positive interactions with others require that you consider how your thinking impacts your behavior, and assess social cues so that you can alter your thinking and behavior if it seems necessary (Rivers et al., 2012).

So if metacognitive skills are that important, how can I improve on mine? There are several things that you can do to develop your metacognitive awareness. Some of most effective strategies include the following:

- *Develop your metacognitive knowledge.* Try to become more aware of the strategies, assumptions, and biases that guide your thinking and decision-making at school, work, and in your relationships with others. Think carefully about how these tendencies can influence your behavior in particular situations, and whether there might be better ways of responding. Make sure that your thinking and decision-making make use of all of the information that you have available. Just as important, however, is that you carefully consider the information you *don't* have, but that would be useful for the task at hand. Remember that understanding what you know is only one half of the story—understanding the *limits* of what you know is the other half.
- *Develop your metacognitive monitoring processes.* When your metacognitive knowledge suggests that you're in a situation that is connected to particular strategies, biases, or assumptions, take care to monitor your thought processes and behaviors to ensure that they aren't interfering with the goals you've set for yourself.
- *Develop metacognitive control strategies.* When your metacognitive monitoring suggests that you're not on track to meet your goals, change course by altering your thought processes or your behavior.

We've seen lots of evidence to suggest that metacognition can be important across many areas of our lives. And although the psychological research demonstrates that people aren't always very good at evaluating their own thinking, the positive news is that metacognition is a skill that we can improve on with practice. There are several modules in this book that offer insight into the biases and situations that are likely to hamper the ability to judge our thinking and behavior. As you read, try to take note of them and incorporate them into your metacognitive knowledge base so that you'll be aware of them in the future. After all, no one needs more information about you than, well . . . you.

MODULE 26

Metacognition—Learning Outcomes Revisited

26.1 Define metacognition

Metacognition is the ability to think about our thinking, understanding, and performance. In general, people have poor metacognitive judgments.

26.2 Name and describe the three elements of metacognition

Three elements of metacognition are knowledge (about skills, biases, and strategies), monitoring (through tracking and evaluating thoughts and behaviors), and control (changing or redirecting thoughts and behaviors). Developing metacognitive knowledge, monitoring processes, and control strategies are important in personal and professional settings, and can help you with such things as building relationships or assessing how you might best study for exams or complete a big project.

Reflective Practice

Content Check

1. People are good at evaluating their own thinking. T or F?
2. What are the three self-assessment elements within metacognition?
3. Label the following examples as metacognitive knowledge, monitoring, or control.
   a. You set aside additional time for studying after recognizing that you won't have enough time to get through all of the chapters before your test next week.
   b. You know that you find it difficult to write tests without sufficient sleep.
   c. You notice that people tend to disengage from conversations with you when you begin complaining about how much you hate work.

Skill Check

Think Critically

4. A friend who experiences social anxiety has just begun using an online dating website in the hopes of meeting a partner. However, after a few dates, he has had little success, but feels that it must be because of the dating site he is using. Using the tips for developing better metacognitive abilities, discuss some ways you could help your friend approach this problem.

Self-Reflect

Reflect on your current metacognitive abilities. What are some ways you could improve these abilities in your personal and professional life? Do you have any current habits that may be holding you back from academic success? Are there any areas in your personal relationships that require more metacognitive thought?

ANSWERS

1. F 2. knowledge, monitoring, and control 3. a) control b) knowledge c) monitoring 4. There might be several steps that you could take to help your friend, including helping him to become more knowledgeable about his social anxiety and what triggers it (metacognitive knowledge). You might also help him to consider how important it is to be aware of how the anxiety may be affecting his dating experiences (metacognitive monitoring); for example, the people he dates may notice his anxiety and respond poorly to it. Finally, you could also help him to consider how to respond to his anxiety on a date (metacognitive control); for example, if he begins to feel anxious, he could excuse himself and practice some breathing exercises in a quiet place to calm down.

MODULE

27

Conditioning and Learning

Classical Conditioning

Pair Up!

Over the years sports apparel giant Nike has used their advertising campaigns to push important social issues. They have prominently featured athletes who were older, physically disabled, and openly HIV-positive, as well as those who have faced gender and racial discrimination in the United States and other countries. You might wonder why Nike would be interested in having their products linked with 80-year-old distance runner Walter Stack, for example, or with controversial NFL quarterback Colin Kaepernick. In this module we'll address this question by talking about *classical conditioning*—a type of learning that stems from the associations that are created when two things are repeatedly paired together. We'll see how this type of learning works and how it has important implications for our everyday behavior—including the likelihood that we'll purchase a pair of Nikes the next time we need new running shoes.

Robert Alexander/Archive Photos/Getty Images

~LEARNING OUTCOMES~

After reading this module you should be able to:

27.1 Define learning and differentiate between five types of learning

27.2 Explain how classical conditioning works, distinguish between extinction and spontaneous recovery as well as between stimulus generalization and stimulus discrimination, and name four instances of classical conditioning in everyday life

Learning—One Way or Another

Learning Outcome 27.1 Define learning and differentiate between five types of learning

Most behavior is learned. Imagine if you suddenly lost everything you had ever learned. What could you do? You would be unable to read, write, or speak. You couldn't feed yourself, find your way home, tie your shoes, or play the clarinet (assuming, of course, that you knew how to play a clarinet in the first place). Needless to say, you would be totally incapacitated.

Learning is a relatively permanent change in knowledge and/or behavior due to experience (Powell, Honey, & Symbaluk, 2017). Notice that this definition excludes both temporary changes and more permanent changes caused by motivation, fatigue, maturation, disease, injury, or drugs. Each of these can alter our understanding or behavior, but none qualifies as learning.

Types of Learning

Further, there are different types of learning (Abrahamse et al., 2016; Milton et al., 2017; Vadillo & Luque, 2013). **Associative learning** occurs whenever a person or an animal forms a simple association among various stimuli, behaviors, or both. Associative learning requires little or no awareness or thought (Everitt & Robbins, 2016). For early psychologists, such as Ivan Pavlov, John Watson, and Edward Thorndike (see Module 3), associative learning was a fairly mechanical process of "stamping in" associations between objective stimuli and objective responses, or behaviors (Henley, 2019).

There are two types of associative learning: Classical conditioning (which we'll learn about in this module) and operant (or instrumental) conditioning (which is the subject of Module 28). It is worth understanding both forms of associative learning because they help us make sense of much animal and human behavior. In later modules, we'll also discuss other ways by which people learn, including observational learning (Module 29) and cognitive learning (Module 30).

Classical Conditioning—The Nobel Drool

Learning Outcome 27.2 Explain how classical conditioning works, distinguish between extinction and spontaneous recovery as well as between stimulus generalization and stimulus discrimination, and name four instances of classical conditioning in everyday life

At the beginning of the 20th century, something happened in the lab of Russian physiologist Ivan Pavlov that gained him the Nobel Prize: His subjects drooled at him. By itself this wasn't too surprising—after all, Pavlov was studying digestion by putting dogs in harnesses and placing food on their tongues. By arranging for a tube to carry saliva from the dogs' mouths to a lever that activated a recording device, he was able to objectively measure the resulting flow of saliva.

However, after repeating his procedure many times, Pavlov noticed that his dogs began salivating *before* the food reached their mouths. Later, the dogs even began to salivate when they saw Pavlov enter the room. Now, Pavlov believed that salivation is an automatic, inherited reflex. It really shouldn't change from one day to the next. His dogs were *supposed* to salivate when he put food in their mouths, but they were *not* supposed to salivate when they merely saw him. This was a change in behavior due to experience—in other words, the dogs were learning! Because of its place in history, this form of associative learning is now called **classical conditioning** (also known as *Pavlovian conditioning* or *respondent conditioning*) (Schultz & Schultz, 2016). Pavlov was fascinated by it and began the process of determining how this type of conditioning worked.

How Classical Conditioning Works

So how did Pavlov study conditioning? To begin, he set a metronome going with a steady, constant rhythm. At first, the sound of the metronome was neutral (the dogs did not respond to it by salivating). Immediately after starting the metronome, though, he placed meat powder on the dogs' tongues, which caused reflex salivation. This sequence was repeated a number of times: Metronome, meat powder, salivation; metronome, meat powder, salivation. Eventually, as classical conditioning took place, the dogs began to salivate as soon as they heard the metronome (➤ Figure 27.1).

Learning Any relatively permanent change in knowledge or behavior that can be attributed to experience.

Associative learning The formation of simple associations between various stimuli and responses.

Classical conditioning A form of learning in which reflex responses are associated with new stimuli.

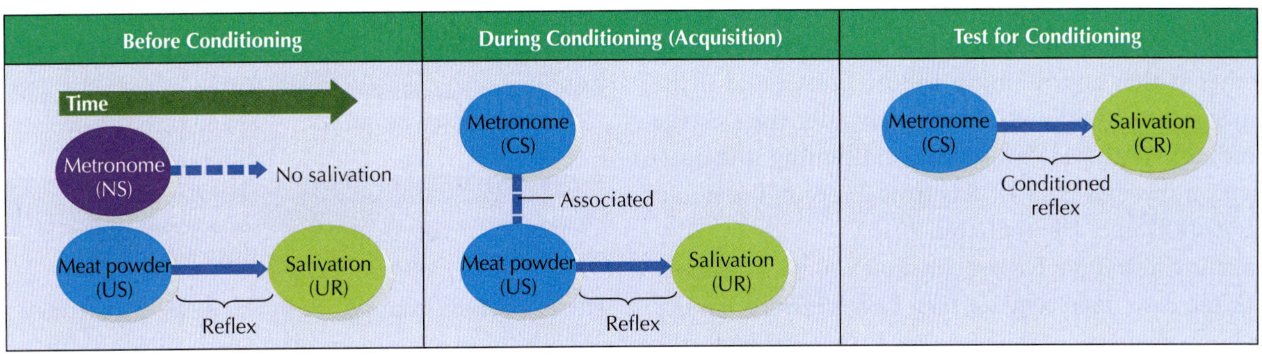

➤ **Figure 27.1**
The classical conditioning procedure.

TABLE 27.1 | Elements of Classical Conditioning

Element	Symbol	Description	Example
Unconditioned stimulus	US	A stimulus innately capable of eliciting a response	Meat powder
Unconditioned response	UR	An innate reflex response elicited by a US	Reflex salivation *to the US*
Neutral stimulus	NS	A stimulus that does not evoke the UR	Metronome *before conditioning*
Conditioned stimulus	CS	A stimulus that evokes a response because it has been repeatedly paired with a US	Metronome *after conditioning*
Conditioned response	CR	A learned response elicited by a CS	Salivation *to the CS*

Through its association with food, the metronome—which before had no effect—began to evoke the same response as food. Pavlov demonstrated this by sometimes starting the metronome *without* providing food. The dogs still salivated, even though no food had been placed in their mouths.

Psychologists use several terms to describe these events (■ Table 27.1). The meat powder is an **unconditioned stimulus (US)**—a stimulus that elicits a response without any prior experience (salivation in this case). Notice that the dog did not have to learn to respond to the US—its response is based on reflexes. Because a reflexive response like salivation is innate, or "built in," it is called an **unconditioned response (UR)**—a response to a stimulus that requires no previous experience. Reflex salivation was the UR in Pavlov's experiment.

The metronome starts out as a **neutral stimulus** (NS)—one that does not produce a specific response. In time, though, this neutral stimulus becomes a **conditioned stimulus (CS)**—a stimulus that, through pairing with an unconditioned stimulus like meat powder, comes to elicit a learned response. When hearing Pavlov's metronome also produced salivation, the dog was making a new response. Thus, salivation also had become a **conditioned response (CR)** or learned reaction (see Figure 27.1). One thing that's really important to remember is that conditioning will be most rapid if the US (meat powder) follows *immediately* after the CS (the metronome). With most classical conditioning, the optimal delay between CS and US is from ½ second to about 5 seconds (Olson & Hergenhahn, 2013).

But the CR and the UR are the same thing—salivation. If that's the case, then why do they have different names? That's a great question! The answer is that although the UR and CR are the same in this example, that isn't always the case (Kaulich et al., 2010). And sometimes even when the UR and CR seem to be the same, there are often small differences between them that are only noticeable if you're looking very closely. For example, the amount of saliva produced in response to the metronome (CR) may be less than the amount produced in response to the meat powder (UR).

It's important to note that it's not just animals who can be classically conditioned—people can learn this way as well. Let's take an example that may be familiar to some of you: If you have ever been to have your eyes checked, you may have experienced a test in which the optometrist blew a puff of air into each eye. People respond to this test with a reflexive reaction: blinking. In classical conditioning terms, a puff of air into the eye (US) will automatically cause you to blink (UR). But what if we took a neutral stimulus—say, a horn—and paired it with the puff of air going into the eye. After repeating this pairing several times, the horn (NS) would become a conditioned stimulus (CS) and it would elicit an eye blink (CR), even when the horn was no longer paired with the puff of air. Here's a summary of what's happened in this example:

Before Conditioning	Example
US → UR (reflexive response)	Puff of air → eye blink
NS → no effect	Horn → no effect
During Conditioning	**Example**
Repeatedly pair US with NS	Sound horn then deliver puff of air to eye
After Conditioning	**Example**
CS → CR	Horn → eye blink

Here's another example: Suppose a scientist named Leonard wants to condition his friend Sheldon. To observe conditioning, he could ring a bell and squirt lemon juice into Sheldon's mouth. Because lemon juice (US) reflexively causes people to salivate (UR), he could condition Sheldon to salivate to the bell (NS) by repeating this procedure several times. The bell would then become a CS that resulted in a CR (salivation). We can use this example as a way of looking at other important aspects of classical conditioning such as extinction, spontaneous recovery, generalization, and discrimination.

Extinction and Spontaneous Recovery *Once an association has been classically conditioned, will it ever go away?* If the US stops following the CS, conditioning will fade away, or extinguish. Let's return to Sheldon. If Leonard rings the bell many times and does not follow it with lemon juice, Sheldon's expectation that "bell precedes lemon juice" will weaken. As it does, he will lose his tendency to salivate when he hears the bell. Thus, **extinction (in classical conditioning)** occurs by weakening the connection between the conditioned and the unconditioned stimulus.

One thing to remember, though, is that it may take several extinction sessions to completely reverse conditioning. Let's say that Leonard rings the bell until Sheldon quits responding. It might seem that extinction is complete. However, Sheldon will probably respond to the bell again on the following day, at least at first. The return of a learned response after its apparent extinction is called **spontaneous recovery** (Revillo, Paglini, & Arias, 2014; Thanellou & Green, 2011).

Generalization After conditioning, other stimuli that are similar to the CS also may trigger a response. This is called **stimulus generalization**. In Pavlov's experiment with the dogs, he observed this quite clearly. Remember that the CS was a metronome that was set to a very specific rhythm (say, one beat per second). However, Pavlov found that the dogs would salivate to the metronome even when the rhythm was a bit faster or slower than that. Similarly, Leonard might find that Sheldon salivates to the sound of a doorbell—even though it was never used as a conditioning stimulus, the doorbell sounds enough like the bell that it can bring about the same response.

It is easy to see the value of stimulus generalization. Consider the child who burns her finger while playing with matches. Most likely, a lighted match will become a conditioned stimulus for her. Because of stimulus generalization, she also may have a healthy fear of flames from lighters, fireplaces, stoves, and so forth. As you may have guessed, though, stimulus generalization has limits. As stimuli become less like the original CS, responding decreases. If you condition a person to blink each time you play a particular note on a piano, blinking will decline as you play higher or lower notes. If the notes are *much* higher or lower, the person will not respond at all (➤ **Figure 27.2**).

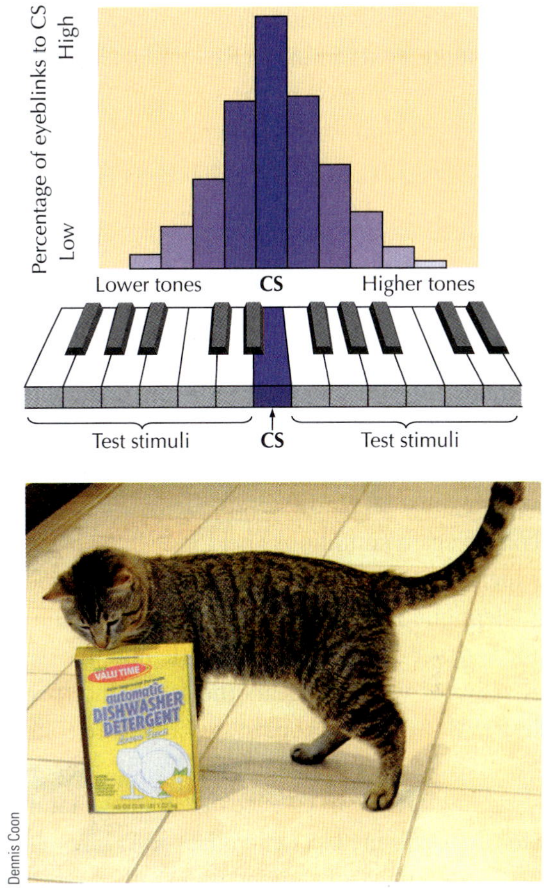

➤ **Figure 27.2**

Stimulus generalization. *(a)* Stimuli similar to the CS also elicit a response. *(b)* This cat has learned to salivate when it sees a cat food box. Because of stimulus generalization, it also salivates when shown a similar-looking detergent box.

Unconditioned stimulus (US) Something that elicits a response without any prior experience.

Unconditioned response (UR) Response to a stimulus that requires no previous experience.

Neutral stimulus (NS) A stimulus that does not evoke a response.

Conditioned stimulus (CS) Neutral stimulus that, through pairing with an unconditioned stimulus, comes to elicit a learned response.

Conditioned response (CR) Learned reaction elicited by pairing an originally neutral stimulus with an unconditioned stimulus.

Extinction (classical conditioning) Weakening of a learned response by repeatedly presenting the conditioned stimulus without the unconditioned stimulus.

Spontaneous recovery Reappearance of a learned response after its apparent extinction.

Stimulus generalization Tendency to respond to stimuli similar to a conditioned stimulus.

Discrimination Let's consider one more idea related to classical conditioning by returning to Pavlov's lab. While the dogs may have initially salivated to the sound of the metronome regardless of its rhythm (owing to generalization), Pavlov was able to teach them to be more selective in their responses. To do this, he would need to pair food with the metronome sound only when it was set to one beat per second. Any faster or slower, and the dogs would receive no food. Eventually, the dogs would become very sensitive to the rhythm being produced and would only salivate when it was one beat per second. **Stimulus discrimination**, then, is the learned ability to respond differently to a variety of similar stimuli.

We might also observe discrimination with Sheldon (who by now must be ready to explode in a big bang). Suppose Leonard again conditions Sheldon with a bell as the CS. As an experiment, he also occasionally plays the sound of a ringing telephone instead of the bell. However, the ringing telephone is never followed by the US (lemon juice). At first, Sheldon salivates when he hears the telephone (because of generalization). But after Leonard sounds the telephone several times more without any lemon juice, Sheldon will stop responding to it. Why? In essence, Sheldon's generalized response to the telephone has extinguished. As a result, he has learned to *discriminate*, or respond differently, to the bell and the telephone.

Classical Conditioning in Everyday Life

Evidence of classical conditioning is all around us. For example, we began this module by talking about Nike's decision to use Colin Kaepernick to front their ad campaign celebrating 30 years of their slogan "Just Do It." Celebrity endorsements of products are common and capitalize on the basic ideas behind classical conditioning. In this case, Nike saw Kaepernick (US) as having a strong natural association with principled behavior, and a willingness to stick up for one's beliefs even if it meant facing considerable hostility in the media (UR). So what Nike wanted when they signed Kaepernick was the opportunity to associate their products (CS) repeatedly with Kaepernick because doing so would bring about thoughts of ethical behavior and bravery in the face of opposition (CR) whenever people saw the Nike swoosh.

Food aversions provide another good example of classical conditioning in everyday life: People who have become ill after eating a particular food will often refuse to eat that food again. Here's a common example: *E. coli* is a common bacterium (US) that causes severe abdominal pain and vomiting (UR), among other less-than-pleasant symptoms. If you were to eat a burger (initially an NS) that was undercooked and contained the *E. coli* bacteria, the bacteria (US) would be paired with the burger (NS that becomes a CS), bringing about those nasty stomach problems (UR). It's not uncommon in such cases to find that people will avoid eating burgers (CS) in the future because just looking at one makes them feel sick (CR). One thing that you should note about this example is how powerful classical conditioning can be: In many cases of food aversion, effective conditioning happens after just one pairing of the US and NS!

So far, we've talked about situations when learned responses are behavioral (e.g., blinking your eyes in response to a puff of air), or physical experiences (e.g., feeling sick to your stomach). But learned responses can also be emotional (e.g., feelings of happiness or anxiety). In a very early example of this phenomenon, pioneering psychologist John B. Watson reported conditioning a young child named Little Albert to fear a white mouse by pairing the white mouse with a loud noise (Beck, Levinson, & Irons, 2009). Loud noise (US) is reflexively associated with fear (UR), but when that noise was repeatedly associated with the mouse (the NS that became the CS) Albert began to show fear (CR) in response to the mouse.

Since then, it has been widely accepted that many human phobias (FOE-bee-ahs) begin as a **conditioned emotional response (CER)**, or a learned emotional reaction to a previously neutral stimulus (Ollendick & Muris, 2015; Vriends et al., 2012) (➤ **Figure 27.3**). A *phobia* is

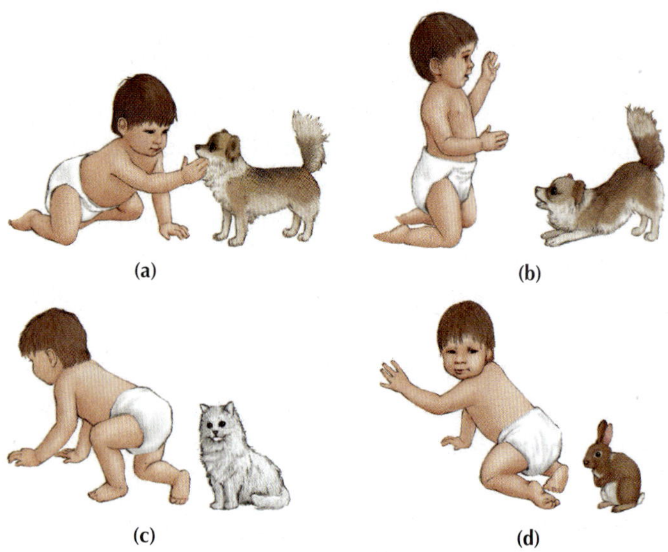

➤ **Figure 27.3**

Hypothetical example of a CER becoming a phobia. A child approaches a dog *(a)* and is frightened by it *(b)*. This fear generalizes to other household pets *(c)* and later to virtually all furry animals *(d)*.

a fear that persists even when no realistic danger exists. Fears of animals, water, heights, thunder, fire, bugs, elevators, and the like are common.

Of course, sometimes a CER can also be positive. Consider Himari, who comes from a close family and has a very good relationship with her mother. Her mother (US) is strongly associated with feelings of happiness (UR) for Himari. Together, the two of them spent many happy hours in the kitchen making shokupan bread while Himari was growing up. Eventually, for Himari the bread (NS) came to be strongly associated with her mom. When Himari grew up and went away to college, she found that even the smell of shokupan bread in a store made her feel happy and comforted. The bread (NS that became a CS) brought about those positive feelings (CR) because of its association with her mom. You may have had a similar experience: Particular smells or songs (NS that becomes CS), for example, bring about conditioned emotional responses (CER) because they have been paired with people or situations (US) from your past.

Finally, let's take a look at a situation in which conditioning is used by clinicians who are providing assistance to clients. A good example is aversion therapy, in which classical conditioning is used to help individuals overcome bad habits. Aversion therapy involves taking a US that naturally (or reflexively) elicits an aversive, or negative, response (the UR). The US is then regularly paired with a negative behavior that the client is trying to eliminate (the NS that becomes the CS). Eventually that behavior begins to elicit the negative response (CR) and clients are less inclined to engage in the behavior.

One common example of aversion therapy is the use of the drug Disulfiram for people with alcohol dependency. Here's how it works: Many people have experienced the downside caused by drinking too much alcohol: feelings of nausea, often accompanied by vomiting. This none-too-pleasant experience is based on a naturally occurring response in the body; specifically, a particularly nasty toxin (the US) that is associated with excessive alcohol consumption is responsible for all of those "hangover" symptoms (the UR). For people with an alcohol dependency, the key is to pair even a tiny amount of alcohol (the NS that becomes the CS) with the toxin that makes you feel so ill. Clinicians do this by giving their clients Disulfiram, which prevents the body from processing alcohol effectively—taking the drug therefore causes nausea and vomiting after even the smallest amount of drinking. When even tiny amounts of alcohol (the CS) are being regularly paired with the toxin (US) because of that drug, alcohol quickly begins to elicit feelings of illness (the CR) and many people who struggle with alcoholism give up their addiction.

One thing to note is that the Disulfiram is neither a stimulus nor a response here. Its importance in this example of conditioning is simply that it allows the pairing of the alcohol (NS) and the toxin (US) to happen very quickly, thus allowing the NS to become the CS. Remember that the effectiveness of classical conditioning depends to a large extent on how quickly the US (toxin) follows the CS (alcohol). Under normal circumstances (that is, without the drug being present) it would take considerable time (and a large amount of alcohol that will probably be coupled with some positive feelings!) for the toxin to build up and cause feelings of illness. For the therapy to be most effective, then, it's important that drinking becomes associated with a negative UR (feelings of illness) very quickly—Disulfiram makes that possible.

Stimulus discrimination The learned ability to respond differently to similar stimuli.

Conditioned emotional response (CER) An emotional response that has been linked to a previously nonemotional stimulus by classical conditioning.

MODULE 27 Classical Conditioning—Learning Outcomes Revisited

27.1 Define learning and differentiate between five types of learning

Learning is a relatively permanent change in knowledge or behavior due to experience. Associative learning is a simple type of learning that occurs when we form associations between stimuli, behaviors, or both. Classical conditioning and operant conditioning are two basic types of associative learning. Observational learning occurs when we imitate others and cognitive learning involves learning by thinking.

27.2 Explain how classical conditioning works, distinguish between extinction and spontaneous recovery as well as between stimulus generalization and stimulus discrimination, and name four instances of classical conditioning in everyday life

Classical conditioning, studied by Pavlov, is based on a naturally occurring association between an unconditioned stimulus (US) and an unconditioned, reflexive response (UR) that occurs in response to that US. If a neutral stimulus (NS) is consistently paired with the US, an association between the two will be established. The NS will become a conditioned stimulus (CS) that is capable of producing a conditioned response (CR).

When the CS is repeatedly presented without the US, the CR will be weakened or inhibited, and extinction will occur. After extinction seems to be complete, a rest period may lead to the temporary reappearance of a CR. This is called *spontaneous recovery*. Through stimulus generalization, stimuli similar to the CS also will produce a response. Generalization gives way to stimulus discrimination when an organism learns to respond to one stimulus, but not to similar stimuli. Food aversions can stem from classical conditioning, and celebrity endorsements for products are also usually based on classical conditioning. Emotional responses can also be the product of classical conditioning. These are referred to as conditioned emotional responses (CERs). Finally, clinicians also use classical conditioning in aversion therapy as a way to get clients to give up bad habits such as alcohol dependency.

Reflective Practice

Content Check

1. Eating homemade cookies will naturally cause people to salivate. If your mom often bakes cookies that you get to eat, your mouth will eventually start to water as soon as you smell the odor of cookies being baked. Apparently, the odor of cookies is a ____________ and your salivation is a ____________.
   a. CR, CS
   b. CS, CR
   c. CS, US
   d. UR, CS
2. The ________________ stimulus is repeatedly paired with the unconditioned stimulus and eventually becomes a conditioned stimulus.
3. After you have acquired a conditioned response, it may be weakened by
   a. spontaneous recovery
   b. stimulus generalization
   c. repeated presentation of the CS without the US
   d. repeated presentation of the CS followed by the US
4. Stimulus discrimination is the learned ability to respond differently to a variety of similar stimuli. T or F?
5. Psychologists theorize that many phobias begin when a CER generalizes to other, similar situations. T or F?

Skill Check

Think Critically

6. Lately, you have been getting a shock of static electricity every time you touch a door handle. Now, you hesitate before you approach a door handle. Can you analyze this situation in terms of classical conditioning?

Self-Reflect

US, CS, UR, CR—How will you remember these terms? First, note that we are interested in either a stimulus (S) or a response (R). Each S or R can be either conditioned (C) or unconditioned (U). If a stimulus provokes a response before any learning, then it's a US. If you have to learn to respond, then it's a CS. Does a response occur without being learned? Then it's a UR. If it has to be learned, then it's a CR.

ANSWERS

1. b 2. neutral 3. c 4. T 5. T 6. Electric shocks (the unconditioned stimulus) naturally cause people to reflexively withdraw (unconditioned response). In this case, the door handles are initially a neutral stimulus, but as they are paired repeatedly with the unconditioned stimulus (shocks), door handles become the conditioned stimulus, capable of causing the conditioned response (hesitating to touch with your hand).

MODULE 28

Conditioning and Learning
Operant Conditioning

Now That's Discrimination!

Shortly after he was put to work, the "sniffer dog" found the box. Inside, buried under other items, was the jar. Inside the jar, also buried among other items, was a USB computer memory stick. On the memory stick was the child pornography the police needed as evidence to secure a conviction. Score another victory for URL (pronounced *earl*), aka "smut mutt," one of an elite handful of dogs trained to detect electronic devices (Cabrera, 2016). Similarly trained dogs are widely used to search for a variety of odors, such as those given off by drugs, blood, explosives, currency, animals, animal parts, and even human remains. In this module we'll learn more about *operant conditioning*, a type of learning that's important in teaching sniffer dogs like URL to perform this important job.

Dragosh Co/Shutterstock.com

~LEARNING OUTCOMES~

After reading this module you should be able to:

28.1 Explain how operant conditioning works, predict how positive and negative reinforcement and punishment will impact the likelihood that a behavior will be repeated, distinguish between generalization and discrimination in operant conditioning, and explain how shaping works

28.2 Name three factors that impact the effectiveness of reinforcement and punishment, differentiate between continuous and partial schedules of reinforcement, and name the four types of partial schedules of reinforcement

28.3 Contrast primary and secondary reinforcers and briefly discuss two instances of operant conditioning in everyday life

Operant Conditioning—Send in the Reinforcements

Learning Outcome 28.1 Explain how operant conditioning works, predict how positive and negative reinforcement and punishment will impact the likelihood that a behavior will be repeated, distinguish between generalization and discrimination in operant conditioning, and explain how shaping works

In Module 27 we distinguished between two types of associative learning, classical conditioning and operant conditioning, and discussed classical conditioning in some detail. In this module we discuss operant conditioning in some detail. **Operant conditioning** (sometimes called *instrumental conditioning*) is based on the *consequences* of responding. The basic principle is simple: Acts that are followed by a

Operant (instrumental) conditioning Learning based on the positive or negative consequences of responding.

TABLE 28.1 | Comparison of Classical and Operant Conditioning

	Classical Conditioning	Operant Conditioning
Nature of response	Involuntary, reflex	Spontaneous, voluntary
Timing of learning	Occurs *before* response (CS paired with US)	Occurs *after* response (response is followed by reinforcing stimulus or event)
Role of learner	Passive (response is *elicited* by US)	Active (response is emitted)
Nature of learning	Neutral stimulus becomes a CS through association with a US	Probability of making a response is altered by consequences that follow it
Learned expectancy	US will follow CS	Response will have a specific effect

positive consequence tend to be repeated (Lefrançois, 2012). A dog is much more likely to keep searching for food under a pillow if it finds food there (positive consequence). The dog will likely stop looking there if it fails to find food (no consequence) or finds something frightening (negative consequence). Pioneer learning theorist Edward L. Thorndike called this the **law of effect**—the probability of a response is altered by the effect that it has had (Benjafield, 2015).

You may recall from Module 27 that classical conditioning is passive. It is based on naturally occurring reflexive responses, and simply "happens to" the learner when an unconditioned stimulus repeatedly follows a neutral stimulus (the neutral stimulus then becomes a conditioned stimulus). In contrast, operant conditioning requires that the learner actively "operate on" the environment; in other words, the learner needs to voluntarily emit, or produce, some kind of behavior. Thus, operant conditioning refers mainly to learning *voluntary* responses. For example, pushing buttons on a television remote control is a voluntary behavior that has the potential to become a learned operant response. When you push a particular button on the remote and gain the consequence you desire (changing channels or muting an obnoxious commercial), that behavior will be reinforced and become a learned response. (See ■ **Table 28.1** for a further comparison of classical and operant conditioning.)

Many early studies of operant conditioning in animals used an **operant conditioning chamber (Skinner box)**, which was developed by B. F. Skinner in the 1930s (Skinner, 1938; ➤ **Figure 28.1**). The walls are bare except for a metal bar and a tray into which food pellets can be dispensed. Two things increase the chances that a subject—usually a rat—will voluntarily emit the desired behavior, which is pressing the bar. First, there's not much to do in a Skinner box. Second, hunger keeps the animal motivated to seek food and actively *emit* a variety of responses.

Let's take a closer look at how operant conditioning works by considering what happens when Einstein, a smart and hungry rat, is placed in an operant conditioning chamber. For a while, Einstein walks around, grooms, sniffs at the corners, or stands on his hind legs—all typical rat behaviors. Then it happens. He places his paw on the bar to get a better view of the top of the cage. *Click!* The bar depresses, and a food pellet drops into the tray. Einstein scurries to the tray, eats the pellet, and then grooms himself. Up and exploring the cage again, he leans on the bar. *Click!* After another trip to the food tray, he returns to the bar and sniffs it, and then puts his paw on it. *Click!* Soon Einstein settles into a smooth pattern of frequent bar pressing.

Notice that Einstein did not acquire a new skill, or response, in this situation. He was already able to press the bar. In operant conditioning, the probability that various responses (like pressing a bar) will be made is influenced by the *consequences*

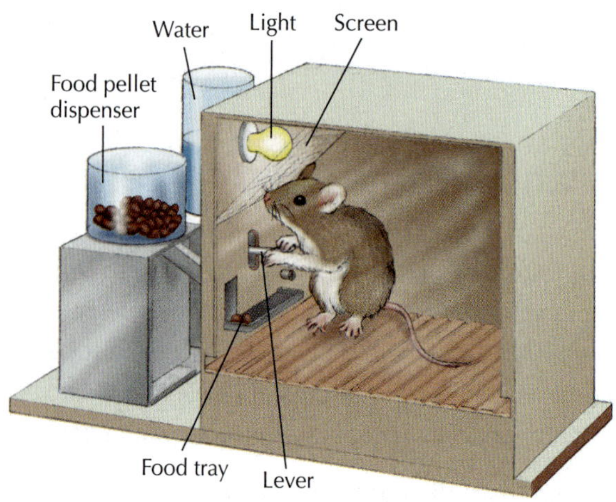

➤ **Figure 28.1**

The Skinner box. This simple device, invented by B. F. Skinner, allows careful study of operant conditioning. When the rat presses the bar, a pellet of food or a drop of water is automatically released.

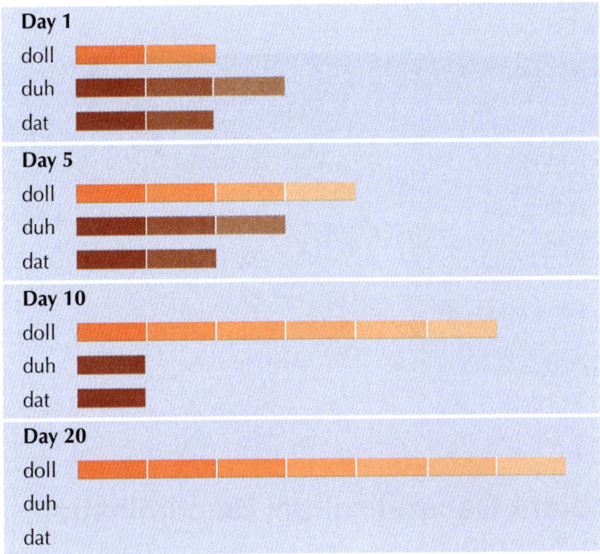

➤ **Figure 28.2**

Reinforcing language use. Assume that a child who is learning to talk points to her favorite doll and says either "doll," "duh," or "dat" when she wants it. Day 1 shows the number of times that the child uses each word to ask for the doll (each block represents one request). At first, she uses all three words interchangeably. To hasten learning, her parents decide to give her the doll only when she names it correctly. Notice how the child's behavior shifts as reinforcement is applied. By day 20, saying "doll" has become the most probable response.

of those responses. Two types of consequences are important in operant learning: reinforcement and punishment.

Reinforcement

As a practical rule of thumb, psychologists define a **reinforcer** as any event that follows a response and increases its probability of occurring again (➤ Figure 28.2). Usually, when people think about reinforcement they think about **positive reinforcement**, which occurs when a reward or other positive event follows a response. For example, giving a child praise for helping with the dishes would be an example of positive reinforcement. Similarly, providing employees with a bonus when they exceed a sales target would also serve as positive reinforcement.

Isn't reinforcement *just another term for* reward? Not exactly, because rewards do not always increase responding. If you give chocolate to a child as a "reward" for good behavior, it will work only if the child likes chocolate. What is reinforcing for one person may not be for another.

Operant learning can also be reinforced through **negative reinforcement**, which occurs when making a response is followed by removing something unpleasant from the environment of the organism. Don't be fooled by the word *negative.* Negative reinforcement also increases responding. However, it does so by ending (*negating*, or taking away) discomfort.

Let's say that you have a headache and take a Tylenol. This behavior—taking the painkiller—will be negatively reinforced if the headache stops, and you will be more likely to repeat that behavior the next time you have a headache. Likewise, a rat could be given a continuous mild shock (through the floor of its cage) that stops if the rat presses a bar. In this case, the bar press is negatively reinforcing.

Punishment

A **punisher** is an event or consequence that follows a response and makes that response less likely to happen in the future. A good example would be a young woman who drives her car very fast and receives a speeding ticket from a less-than-impressed police officer. In this situation, the voluntary behavior (or operant response)—fast driving—has been followed by an *aversive* (unpleasant) punisher (the speeding ticket). This situation is known as **positive punishment** (but usually we just say **punishment**). Again, don't be fooled by the word *positive.* Positive punishment *decreases* the likelihood that the response will occur again. However, it does so by initiating *(adding)* discomfort or other negative consequences.

Many people mistake negative reinforcement for (positive) punishment. The difference between negative reinforcement and punishment can be shown in a hypothetical example: Let's say that you live in an apartment and your neighbor's stereo is blasting so loudly that you can't concentrate on reading this book. If you pound on the wall and the volume suddenly drops (something negative has been removed) then you will have been negatively reinforced, and you will be more likely to pound on the wall

Law of effect Responses that lead to desirable effects are repeated; those that produce undesirable results are not.

Operant conditioning chamber (Skinner box) An apparatus designed to study operant conditioning in animals.

Reinforcer Any event that reliably increases the probability or frequency of responses it follows.

Positive reinforcement Occurs when a response is followed by a reward or other positive event.

Negative reinforcement Occurs when a response is followed by an end to discomfort or by the removal of an unpleasant event.

Punisher Any event that decreases the probability or frequency of responses that it follows.

Positive punishment (punishment) Any event that follows a response and *decreases* its likelihood of occurring again; the process of suppressing a response.

TABLE 28.2 | Behavioral Effects of Various Consequences

	Consequence of Making a Response	Example	Effect on Response Probability
Positive reinforcement	Good event begins	Food given	Increase
Negative reinforcement	Bad event ends	Pain stops	Increase
Positive punishment	Bad event begins	Pain begins	Decrease
Negative punishment (response cost)	Good event ends	Food removed	Decrease
Nonreinforcement	Nothing	N/A	Decrease

if the same thing happens again. Remember, any form of reinforcement makes a behavior more likely to happen in the future.

In contrast, if you pound on the wall and the volume increases (you have been positively punished) or if the neighbor comes over and pounds on you (more positive punishment), your wall pounding becomes less likely to happen if the loud music starts again. Any form of punishment makes a behavior less likely to happen in the future.

Isn't it also punishing to have privileges, money, or other positive things taken away for making a particular response? Yes. Punishment also occurs when a reinforcer or positive state of affairs is removed, such as losing privileges. This second type of punishment is called **negative punishment (response cost)**. One more time, don't be fooled by the word *negative*. Negative punishment also decreases responding. However, it does so by ending (*negating*, or taking away) something pleasant.

The best-known form of negative punishment is *time-out*, in which children are removed from situations that normally allow them to gain reinforcement (Donaldson et al., 2013). When your parents put you in time-out by sending you to your room, they denied you the reinforcement of being with the rest of your family or hanging out with your friends. For your convenience, ▪ **Table 28.2** summarizes five basic consequences of making a response.

But what if the consequences for a behavior changed over time? Would Einstein the rat stop pressing the bar if no more food arrived? Yes, but not immediately. Through **extinction (in operant conditioning)**, learned responses that are not reinforced gradually weaken. Just as acquiring an operant response takes time, so does operant extinction. For example, if a television program that you initially enjoyed watching (that is, watching was reinforced because the show was enjoyable) begins to bore you as it moves into its eighth season, then your "watching behavior" will likely be extinguished over time.

Operant Generalization, Discrimination, and Shaping

As the previous section made clear, operant conditioning depends on the consequences of a voluntarily emitted behavior. When the consequences are reinforcing, there's an increased likelihood that a behavior will occur again; when the consequences involve punishment, the likelihood of the behavior happening again decreases. However, researchers interested in operant conditioning have also noticed that even after the consequences of a specific behavior have been established, additional learning can still take place. For example, it's possible to "test the boundaries" to learn whether other, similar behaviors will bring about the same consequences, a concept referred to as *generalization*. Alternately, it's possible to discover that only a very specific behavior will generate that consequence—this is referred to as *discrimination*. The ability to discriminate exactly what behaviors will bring about particular consequences can be further used to learn more complicated sets of behaviors in a process called *shaping*. Each of these three terms—generalization, discrimination, and shaping—is discussed next.

Generalization *Is generalization the same in operant conditioning as it is in classical conditioning?* Basically, yes. We know that reinforcement and punishment will result in behavior occurring more or less frequently, respectively. However, over time it's also possible that an emitted behavior will begin to happen in situations that are similar (but not identical) to those that have been reinforced in the past. This is called **operant stimulus generalization** (but usually just **generalization**).

Assume, for instance, that your dog has begun to jump up at you whenever you are eating dinner at the kitchen table. (Bad dog!) Mind you, that's because you have been reinforcing its behavior with table scraps. (Bad owner!) The dog has learned that reinforcement tends to occur when you are at the kitchen table.

With a bit of time, though, you may find that your dog begins to jump up at you when you're sitting at the dining room table as well. Because the tables are similar, your dog will likely jump up because this response has *generalized* to other tables.

Examples of generalization can also be seen in humans. Imagine a toddler who responds with a temper tantrum when told by his father that he cannot have a chocolate bar that he has seen while waiting in a line at the grocery store. To avoid embarrassment, the father gives in and buys the chocolate bar. If temper tantrums are reinforced in this way, it's entirely possible that we will begin to see this behavior generalize to other situations, and with other people. For example, the child may have a temper tantrum at the store a few days later when told by his grandmother that he can't have a chocolate bar.

Discrimination In the previous example we saw that because jumping up at the kitchen table signaled the availability of reinforcement (table scraps) to your dog, it also began jumping up while you sat at a different table in the dining room (generalization). But if you do not feed your dog while sitting at the dining room table, the jumping response that originally generalized to it will extinguish because of *nonreinforcement*. In other words, if your dog's jumping response is consistently rewarded only in the presence of a specific table (the one in the kitchen), jumping at other tables will eventually be extinguished. Through **operant stimulus discrimination** (usually just referred to as **discrimination**), your dog has learned to differentiate between antecedent stimuli (in this case, the two tables) that signal reward and nonreward. Similarly, if the child's temper tantrum is never reinforced by the grandmother, he will quickly learn through discrimination that this behavior will only be reinforced under certain conditions (in this case, when he's with his dad).

Discrimination is aptly illustrated by the training of "sniffer" dogs like URL, who was described at the beginning of this module (Concha et al., 2014). Discrimination was used to teach URL to recognize the scent of electronic devices, distinguishing the smell of the specific chemical found in cell phones, thumb drives, and microSD cards from other chemicals. During his initial training, then, he was reinforced with food only for approaching containers baited with electronic devices.

Shaping Ultimately, people who train dogs like URL want to have the dogs go even further than just finding the device. For example, in one case an electronic sniffer dog named Iris learned to sit once she had found a device; when the handler then said "Show me," Iris would put her nose as close as possible to its location.

It seems pretty unlikely that a dog like Iris would just spontaneously show all those behaviors in the correct order. How would she ever get reinforced and learn what she was supposed to do? That's a great question. When it comes to learning behaviors that are rare or complex, the answer lies in a process called **shaping**, which is the reinforcement of behaviors that are increasingly close approximations to a desired response. Shaping depends heavily on discrimination, as the animal (or human!) begins to recognize slight changes in the way their behaviors are reinforced.

To take a closer look at shaping, let's return to our favorite rat, Einstein. Even in a barren Skinner box, it could take a long time for a rat (even one as smart as Einstein) to accidentally press the bar and get a food pellet. And that bar-pressing behavior is pretty simple—we might wait forever for more complicated chains of responses to occur. For example, you would have to wait a long time for a duck to accidentally walk out of its cage, turn on a light, play a tune on a toy piano, turn off the light, and walk back to its cage. If this is what you wanted to reward, it's entirely possible that you would never get the chance.

Instead of waiting to reinforce Einstein for pressing the bar spontaneously, we could have shaped his behavior. In general, shaping refers to a process in which a complex or rare behavior is broken down into a series of smaller steps. In the beginning, subjects (either animal or human) are reinforced for achieving a relatively simple first step. However, once they successfully achieve the second step, they are no longer reinforced for the first. Once they manage the third step in the series, they will no longer be reinforced for the second. This process continues until all of the steps have been mastered and the desired behavior has been achieved.

In the case of Einstein pressing a bar, shaping would look something like this: Assume that Einstein has not yet learned to press the bar, but our goal is to get him to do so.

Negative punishment (response cost) Removal of a positive reinforcer after a response is made.

Operant extinction The weakening or disappearance of a nonreinforced operant response.

Operant stimulus generalization The tendency to respond to stimuli similar to those that preceded reinforcement.

Operant stimulus discrimination The tendency to make an operant response when stimuli previously associated with reward are present and to withhold the response when stimuli associated with nonreward are present.

Shaping Gradually molding responses to a final desired pattern.

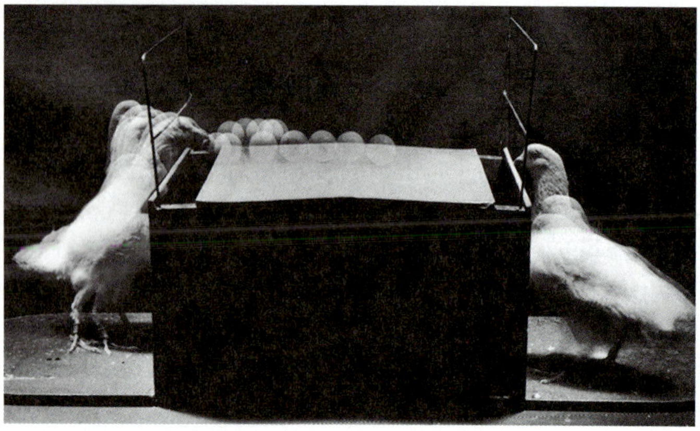

Yale Joel/Time & Life Pictures/Getty Images

belizar/Shutterstock.com

This trainer is using operant shaping to teach tricks to these seals. Fish from a cup hanging from her waist serve as reinforcers. Notice that she is using a whistle and hand signals as discriminative stimuli to control the performance.

At first, we settle for just getting him to face the bar. Any time he turns toward the bar, he is reinforced with a bit of food. Soon Einstein spends much of his time facing the bar. Next, we reinforce him every time he takes a step toward the bar. At this point, if he is just facing the bar (the first step), nothing happens. But when he faces the bar and takes a step forward (the second step), he would be reinforced with food. By gradually changing the rules about what makes a successful response, we can eventually train Einstein to approach the bar and press it. In other words, *successive approximations* (ever-closer matches) to a desired response are reinforced during shaping. Believe it or not, Skinner once taught two pigeons to play ping-pong in this way!

You should be able to see how this process of shaping depends on discrimination: Einstein needs to learn what behaviors are being reinforced at each stage, but he also needs to learn how the conditions for reinforcement change when we move from one step to another. In other words, he needs to learn how to discriminate between past behaviors that were rewarded in previous steps and those that are now being rewarded in the current step of the process.

Of course, human behavior can also be shaped (Lamb et al., 2010). Let's say that you want to exercise more often, and your ultimate goal is to run for 30 minutes three nights each week. If you were to employ shaping, you'd start by breaking this bigger goal down into a series of manageable steps. For example, during the first week, you might begin by reinforcing yourself for just going out for a walk three times. During the second week you'd up the ante, and you'd only get your reinforcement if you ran for five minutes at the beginning of each of the three walks. In the third week, there would only be a reinforcement if you ran for 10 minutes each time you went out. This process would continue until, eventually, reinforcement would only come if you were running for the full 30 minutes on each of the three nights (Watson & Tharp, 2014). In Module 31 we'll explore ways to use operant conditioning to change our behaviors in positive and productive ways.

Effectiveness of Reinforcement and Punishment—How to Make It Count

Learning Outcome 28.2 Name three factors that impact the effectiveness of reinforcement and punishment, differentiate between continuous and partial schedules of reinforcement, and name the four types of partial schedules of reinforcement

Several factors influence how effective reinforcement and punishment are during operant learning. Three of the most important factors are intensity, timing, and contingency. Let's take a closer look at each one.

Intensity

In the case of reinforcers, those that are more intense (that is, powerful) will be more likely to result in behaviors being repeated in the future. For example, recreational drugs that provide a powerfully positive high (that is, more intense reinforcement) are more likely to be used again than are those that produce only mildly pleasant feelings. Similarly, when working with a child who has been diagnosed with autism, therapists will often save the most powerful reinforcers (the ones that the child loves the most) for rewarding the behaviors that they consider most important for that child to learn.

The story is similar when it comes to punishment. Severe punishment (that is, following a response with an intensely aversive or unpleasant stimulus) can be extremely effective in stopping behavior. If 10-year-old Yuri sticks his finger in a light socket and gets a severe shock, that may be the last time he *ever* tries it. Intense punishment can permanently suppress responding, even for actions as basic as eating. However, mild punishment only temporarily *suppresses* a response. And if the response is still reinforced on occasion, mild punishment may be particularly ineffective. This fact was demonstrated in an experiment with two groups of well-trained rats who were placed in a Skinner box. Prior to the study, the rats in both groups had learned to press the bar to obtain food. As the study unfolded, one group was mildly punished with a gentle slap for each bar press, and the other group was not. It might seem that the slap would cause bar-pressing to extinguish more quickly. Yet, this was not the case, as you can see in ➤ Figure 28.3. Punishment temporarily slowed bar pressing, but it did not cause extinction. Mild punishment such as gently slapping the paws of rats or children has little permanent effect on a reinforced response.

Timing

Reinforcement and punishment are most effective when they rapidly follow a response (Powell, Honey, & Symbaluk, 2017). For rats in a Skinner box, little or no learning occurs if the delay between bar pressing and receiving food exceeds 100 seconds (➤ Figure 28.4). In general, you will be most successful if you present a reinforcer *immediately* after a response you want to change. Similarly, punishment works best when it occurs as the response is being made, or *immediately* afterward. Thus, if

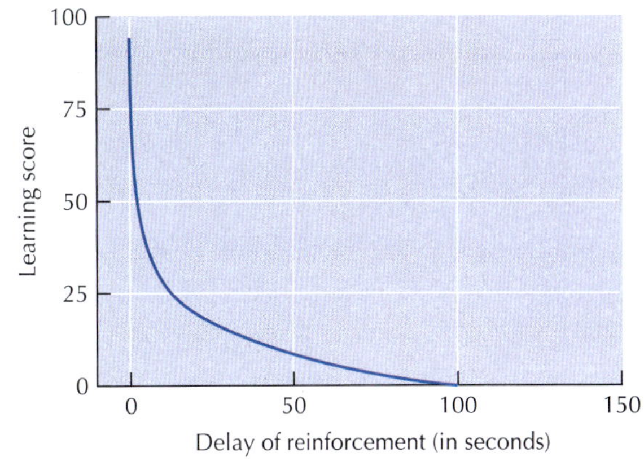

➤ **Figure 28.4**

The effect of delay of reinforcement. Notice how rapidly the learning score drops when reward is delayed. Animals learning to press a bar in a Skinner box showed no signs of learning if the food reward followed a bar press by more than 100 seconds.

simply refusing to feed your dog table scraps is not enough to stop it from jumping at you when you sit at a table, you could effectively (and humanely) punish it by spraying water on its nose immediately, each time it jumps up.

Consistency

It might seem that reinforcement and punishment would work best when they are *response contingent* (kon-TIN-jent; that is, given *only* after a desired response has occurred), and when they are given *consistently*. While these things are both true, the story is somewhat more complicated than that, especially when it comes to reinforcement. Given that's the case, we'll take some time to explore consistency in reinforcement in more detail.

Until now, we have treated reinforcement as if it were always continuous. **Continuous reinforcement** means that a reward follows every correct response. At the start, continuous reinforcement is useful for learning new responses (Chance, 2014). To teach your dog to come to you, it is best to reinforce your dog every time that it comes when called. Curiously, once your dog has learned to come when called, it is best to shift to **partial reinforcement**, in which reinforcers do *not* follow every response. Responses acquired by partial reinforcement are highly resistant to extinction, a phenomenon known as the **partial reinforcement effect** (Horsley et al., 2012; Powell, Honey, & Symbaluk, 2017).

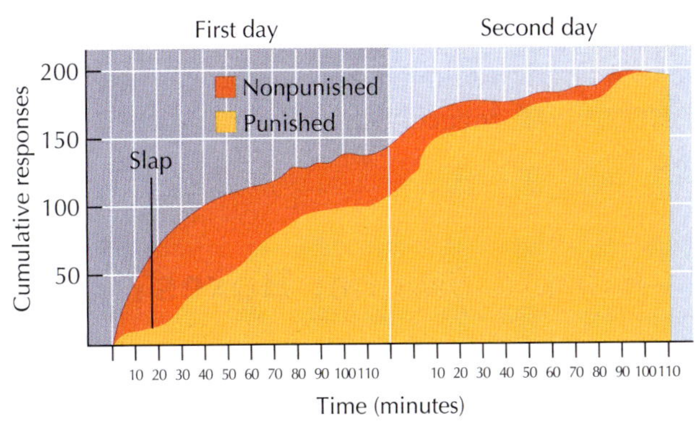

➤ **Figure 28.3**

The effect of punishment on extinction. Immediately after punishment, the rate of bar-pressing is suppressed, but by the end of the second day, the effects of punishment have disappeared. (After B. F. Skinner, 1938.)

Continuous reinforcement A pattern in which a reinforcer follows every correct response.

Partial reinforcement A pattern in which only a portion of all responses are reinforced.

Partial reinforcement effect Responses acquired with partial reinforcement are more resistant to extinction.

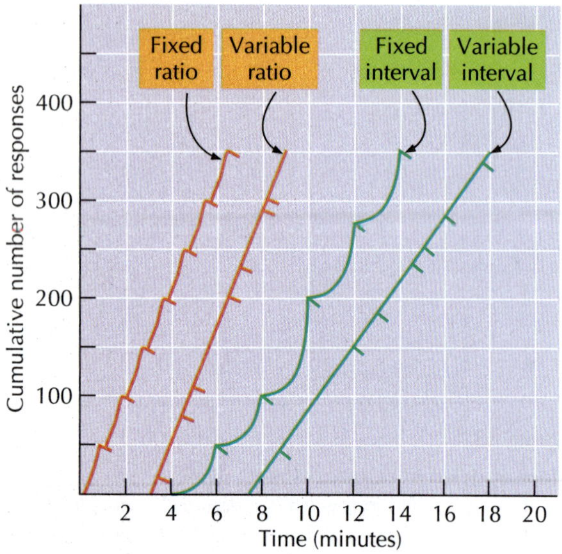

Figure 28.5

Typical response patterns for partial reinforcement schedules.

Partial reinforcement can be given on different schedules. A **schedule of reinforcement** is a protocol for determining when and how often responses will be rewarded (Chance, 2014). Let's consider the four most basic schedules: fixed ratio, variable ratio, fixed interval, and variable interval. Typical responses to each of these schedules are shown in **Figure 28.5**. Results such as these are obtained when a recorder is connected to a Skinner box. Rapid responding results in a steep line; a horizontal line indicates no response. Small tick marks on the lines show when a reinforcer was given.

Fixed Ratio (FR) Schedules In a **fixed ratio schedule**, the number of correct responses that a subject must give to receive reinforcement is predetermined (that is, fixed). For example, FR-3 means that every third response is reinforced; FR-10 means that 10 responses must be made to obtain a reinforcer. Fixed ratio schedules produce very high response rates. A hungry rat on an FR-10 schedule will quickly run off 10 responses, pause to eat, and then run off 10 more. A similar situation occurs when factory employees or farmworkers are paid on a piecework basis. When a fixed number of items must be produced for a set amount of pay, work output is high.

Variable Ratio (VR) Schedules In a **variable ratio schedule** a varying number of correct responses must be made to get a reinforcer. Instead of reinforcing every fourth response (FR-4), for example, a person or animal on a VR-4 schedule gets rewarded every fourth response *on average*. Sometimes two responses must be made to obtain a reinforcer; sometimes it's five; sometimes four; and so on. The actual number varies, but it averages out to four (in this example). VR schedules also produce high response rates.

Fixed Interval (FI) Schedules In another pattern, reinforcement is given only when a correct response is made after a set amount of time has passed. This time interval is measured from the last reinforced response. Responses made during the time interval are not reinforced. In a **fixed interval schedule**, the first correct response made after the set time period has passed is reinforced. Thus, a rat on an FI-30-second schedule has to wait 30 seconds after the last reinforced response before a bar press will pay off again. The rat can press the bar as often as it wants during the interval, but it will not be rewarded. FI schedules produce *moderate response rates*. Animals working on an FI schedule seem to display a keen sense of the passage of time (Zentall, 2010). Few responses occur just after a reinforcement is delivered, and a spurt of activity occurs just before the next reinforcement is due.

Variable Interval (VI) schedules A **variable interval schedule** is a variation on a fixed interval schedule. Here, reinforcement is given for the first correct response made after a varying time period. On a VI-30-second schedule, reinforcement is available after an interval that *averages* 30 seconds. VI schedules produce *slow, steady response rates* and tremendous resistance to extinction (Lattal, Reilly, & Kohn, 1998). If you check your text messages every now and then for an important message, your reward (getting that message) is on a VI schedule. You may have to wait a few minutes or hours. If you are like most people, you will doggedly check over and over until you get your message.

Operant Conditioning in Everyday Life—Human Skinner Boxes?

Learning Outcome 28.3 Contrast primary and secondary reinforcers and briefly discuss two instances of operant conditioning in everyday life

In this module we've tried to give you many examples of how operant conditioning is relevant in our everyday lives so that you can spot when operant principles are being used to control your behavior and the behavior of those around you. From training animals to time outs; from traffic tickets to Tylenol, operant conditioning is happening around us regularly. In this section, we'll discuss two additional

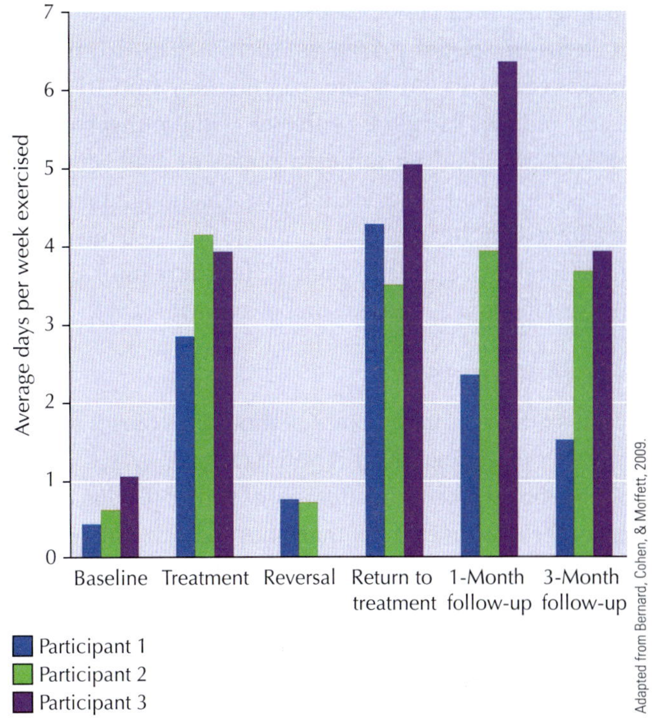

Figure 28.6

Reinforcement in a token economy. Children with cystic fibrosis (a hereditary lung disease) benefit from exercise that clears blocked airways. This graph shows the effects of using tokens to reward aerobic exercise in three children with cystic fibrosis. The number of minutes of aerobic exercise each day was measured. Tokens earned could be exchanged for rewards such as going to see a movie or staying up past bedtime. The graph shows that all three children exercised relatively infrequently without the reinforcement (*baseline* and *reversal* phases) and relatively more when the reinforcement was in place (*training* and return to *treatment* phases). It is encouraging to note that exercise rates remained heightened for months after the token economy was first implemented.

examples: the use of token economies to reinforce young children's positive behavior and the clever use of reinforcement schedules in gambling meccas around the world.

Although human learning may be reinforced by anything from a candy bar to a word of praise, a useful distinction can be made between *primary reinforcers* and *secondary reinforcers.* A **primary reinforcer** produces comfort, ends discomfort, or fills an immediate physical need: It is natural, nonlearned, and rooted in biology. Food, water, and sex are obvious examples, but psychoactive drugs such as cocaine, caffeine, and alcohol also fall in this category because they stimulate the pleasure pathways in the brain. Every time you open the refrigerator, walk to a drinking fountain, turn up the heat, or order a double latte, your actions reflect primary reinforcement (Lazenka, Legakis, & Negus, 2016; Prus, 2014).

But humans also respond to other reinforcers that are *not* rooted in biology—instead, they gain their power through learning. Money, praise, attention, approval, success, affection, grades, and the like can each serve as a learned **secondary reinforcer**. Some secondary reinforcers gain their value because they can be *exchanged* for primary reinforcers (Powell, Honey, & Symbaluk, 2017). For example, printed money obviously has little or no value of its own. You can't eat it, drink it, or sleep with it. However, it can be exchanged for food, water, lodging, and other necessities.

Secondary reinforcement is at the heart of many programs to change children's (and sometimes adults') behaviors. Such programs often rely on **token reinforcers**, which are tangible secondary reinforcers such as money, a gold star, or a poker chip. Tokens are routinely used in educational settings to promote learning, particularly with individuals who have developmental delays. For instance, tokens are often used as reinforcers to decrease undesirable behaviors (biting and self-injurious behavior) and increase desirable ones (appropriate use of speech) among children with autism. Later, the child can exchange tokens for candy, toys, or other treats.

Token Economies

Token economies, systems for managing and altering behavior through reinforcement of selected responses, have also been used with troubled children and adults in special programs and even in ordinary school classrooms (Alberto & Troutman, 2013; Maggin et al., 2011; **Figure 28.6**). In each case, the goal is to provide an immediate reward for

Schedules of reinforcement Rules or plans for determining which responses will be reinforced.

Fixed ratio (FR) schedule An arrangement where a set number of correct responses must be made to get a reinforcer. For example, a reinforcer is given for every four correct responses.

Variable ratio (VR) schedule An arrangement where a varied number of correct responses must be made to get a reinforcer. For example, a reinforcer is given after three to seven correct responses; the actual number changes randomly.

Fixed interval (FI) schedule An arrangement where a reinforcer is given only when a correct response is made after a set amount of time has passed since the last reinforced response. Responses made during the time interval are not reinforced.

Variable interval (VI) schedule An arrangement where a reinforcer is given for the first correct response made after a varied amount of time has passed since the last reinforced response. Responses made during the time interval are not reinforced.

Primary reinforcers Nonlearned reinforcers; usually those that satisfy physiological needs.

Secondary reinforcer A learned reinforcer; often one that gains reinforcing properties by association with a primary reinforcer.

Token reinforcer A tangible secondary reinforcer such as money, gold stars, poker chips, and the like.

learning. In such cases, tokens can be exchanged for bigger items or special privileges, such as trips to movies or amusement parks. At home, parents may find that tokens greatly reduce discipline problems with younger children. For example, children can earn points or gold stars during the week for good behavior. If they earn enough tokens, they are allowed on the weekend to choose one item out of a grab bag of small prizes (see Module 67 for more information on the uses of token economies in behavior therapy).

Slot Machines

Casinos offer patrons a choice of thousands of slot machines on which to gamble. And if you have ever visited a casino, you've probably seen row after row of people playing on them. One of the reasons that slot machines are such a lucrative part of the casinos' business lies in what we know about reinforcement schedules. To understand why that's the case, start by imagining that you put a dollar in a slot machine and pull the handle. A light flashes, a bell rings and—voila!—$10 spills into the tray in front of you. Now let's say that this pattern continues for several minutes. Every pull is followed by a payoff. Because you are being reinforced on a continuous schedule, you quickly "get hooked" (and begin to plan your retirement). But, alas, suddenly each pull is followed by nothing. Obviously, you would respond several times more before giving up, because extinction isn't immediate. However, when continuous reinforcement is followed by extinction, the message quickly becomes clear: No more payoffs (or early retirement).

Of course, slot machines never work on a schedule of continuous reinforcement—the casino would never make money if they did. Instead, the schedule of reinforcement looks more like this: You put a dollar in a slot machine five times without a payoff. You are just about to quit but decide to play once more. Bingo! The machine returns $20. Payoffs will continue on a partial reinforcement schedule; some pulls will bring a payout and others won't. The key point with partial reinforcement is that the timing of all payouts is variable and unpredictable. Sometimes you hit two in a row, and sometimes 20 or 30 pulls go unrewarded. Under these circumstances, how many times do you think you would continue to pull that handle before your behavior is extinguished? Because you have developed the expectation that any play may be "the one," it will be hard to resist just one more play ... and then one more ... and one more. Also, because partial reinforcement might include long periods of nonreward, it will be harder to distinguish between periods of reinforcement and extinction. It is no exaggeration to say that the clever use of partial reinforcement in casinos has left many people penniless, because such schedules make behavior very resistant to extinction (Horsley et al., 2012).

MODULE 28 Operant Conditioning—Learning Outcomes Revisited

28.1 Explain how operant conditioning works, predict how positive and negative reinforcement and punishment will impact the likelihood that a behavior will be repeated, distinguish between generalization and discrimination in operant conditioning, and explain how shaping works

Operant conditioning occurs when a voluntary action is followed by a reinforcer (which increases the frequency of the action) or a punisher (which decreases the frequency of the action). Both positive reinforcement and negative reinforcement *increase* the likelihood that a response will be repeated. Positive and negative punishment *decrease* the likelihood that the response will occur again. In generalization, an operant response tends to occur when stimuli similar to those preceding reinforcement are present. In discrimination, responses are given in the presence of discriminative stimuli associated with reinforcement and withheld in the presence of stimuli associated with nonreinforcement. By rewarding successive approximations to a particular response, behavior can be shaped into desired patterns.

28.2 Name three factors that impact the effectiveness of reinforcement and punishment, differentiate between continuous and partial schedules of reinforcement, and name the four types of partial schedules of reinforcement

The effectiveness of reinforcement and punishment is dependent upon their intensity (typically they will be more effective when they are more intense), timing (typically they will be more effective when they are delivered very soon after a behavior), and how consistently they are administered (punishment is more effective when it is administered consistently, after every behavior; however, the effectiveness of reinforcement depends on its schedule). Two basic schedules of reinforcement are continuous (after every response) or partial (only a portion of responses are reinforced). Continuous reinforcement is useful in the early stages of learning; partial reinforcement is effective after a behavior has been learned and produces greater resistance to extinction. The four most basic partial schedules of reinforcement are fixed ratio, variable ratio, fixed interval, and variable interval. Each produces a distinct pattern of responding.

28.3 Contrast primary and secondary reinforcers and briefly discuss two instances of operant conditioning in everyday life

Operant learning may be based on primary reinforcers (which are rooted in biology) and secondary reinforcers (such as tokens and social reinforcers). Primary reinforcers are "natural," physiologically based rewards. Secondary reinforcers are learned and sometimes gain their reinforcing value because they can be exchanged for primary reinforcers. Tokens and money gain their reinforcing value in this way. Operant conditioning can be seen in the use of token economies and in the partial reinforcement schedules that govern slot machines in casinos.

Reflective Practice

Content Check

1. Changing the rules in small steps so that an animal (or person) is gradually trained to respond as desired is called ____________________.
2. The schedule of reinforcement associated with playing slot machines and other types of gambling is
   a. fixed ratio
   b. variable ratio
   c. fixed interval
   d. variable interval
3. Positive reinforcers increase the rate of responding, and negative reinforcers decrease it. T or F?
4. Partial reinforcement increases resistance to extinction. T or F?
5. If you eat a pizza to satisfy your hunger pangs, pizza will serve as a:
   a. partial reinforcer
   b. primary reinforcer
   c. secondary reinforcer
   d. positive reinforcer
6. A behavior therapist at a treatment center is working with a young girl diagnosed with autism and trying to teach her to use more verbal language so that others will know what she wants. Using reinforcement, the therapist eventually gets the girl to say "food" when she wants to eat, rather than just taking food. Next, though, the therapist's goal is to get the girl to use the word "food" at home with her parents, and not just at the treatment center. The therapist wants to achieve:
   a. shaping
   b. extinction
   c. discrimination
   d. generalization

Skill Check

Think Critically

7. Using the concept of partial reinforcement, can you explain why inconsistent punishment is especially ineffective?

Self-Reflect

See if you can think of at least one everyday example of the five basic schedules of reinforcement (continuous reinforcement and the four types of partial reinforcement).

ANSWERS

1. shaping 2. b 3. F 4. T 5. b 6. d 7. An inconsistently punished response will continue to be reinforced on a partial schedule, which can make it even more resistant to extinction.

MODULE 29

Conditioning and Learning
Observational Learning

Watch It!

When Halima Aden told her family that she wanted to enter the Miss Minnesota USA pageant, they were perplexed. After all, it wasn't the kind of thing that Somali women typically did. Halima was determined to move forward with her plans, but as a Muslim woman, there were just a few issues she needed to resolve; namely, she needed to inform the pageant staff that she wasn't prepared to remove her hijab, and that she wasn't prepared to go onstage in a conventional bathing suit. As it turned out, though, neither of those things posed a problem for pageant staff.

Halima didn't win the Miss Minnesota contest, but she did sign a major modeling contract soon afterward. And these days she's not just focused on being a great model—she's also determined to be a great *role* model. By supporting other Muslim models and working as an ambassador for UNICEF, Halima wants to show young people everywhere that they can be true to their values and still be successful in the world. We can learn a great deal from watching other people, something that psychologists refer to as *observational learning*. In this module, we'll explore how this process works, and we'll discover why it's so powerful to "watch and learn."

John Parra/Getty Images Entertainment/Getty Images

~LEARNING OUTCOMES~

After reading this module you should be able to:

29.1 Define observational learning, including the three steps, the three characteristics of models we are most likely to imitate, and the connection between observational learning and operant conditioning

29.2 Name two instances of observational learning in everyday life, describe three reasons why exposure to violent media may be associated with later aggression among children and adolescents as well as the results of research examining the link between exposure to violent video games and later aggression

Observational Learning—Do as I Do, Not as I Say

Learning Outcome 29.1 Define observational learning, including the three steps, the three characteristics of models we are most likely to imitate, and the connection between observational learning and operant conditioning

Many skills are learned by what Albert Bandura (1971) calls **observational learning**—watching and imitating the actions of another person. We humans share the capacity for

antoniodiaz/Shutterstock.com

Observational learning often imparts large amounts of information that would be difficult to obtain by reading instructions or memorizing rules.

observational learning with many mammals (Tennie et al., 2010; Zentall, 2011).

The value of learning by observation is obvious: Imagine trying to learn how to perform a complex behavior such as tying a shoe or playing a piano by having someone verbally explain the steps to you. A far more effective way to learn is by observing a **model**—someone who serves as an example—and then copying their actions.

What kind of responses do we learn from observing others? Bandura believes that anything that can be learned from direct experience can also be learned by observation. Just as we can learn to perform specific actions (e.g., how to throw a football, fix a leaky faucet, or make a cake) by watching others, so too our attitudes and emotional responses (e.g., whether men and women are equally capable of effective parenting; a fear of dogs) can also be influenced by observing others.

The Three Steps of Observational Learning

Observational learning involves three steps: paying attention, remembering the model's behavior, and reproducing (or imitating) that behavior.

Paying Attention We know from Module 17 that the world is full of stimuli and that we aren't capable of attending to everything, or everyone, that we see and hear. So, what determines whether we will attend to a model and learn from their behavior?

One important factor is the *characteristics of the model.* We are more likely to pay attention to models who are in a position of authority over us, as well as those that we admire (e.g., people who have high social status, such as people who are famous or well respected). We're also more likely to attend to models who are similar to us in terms of age, sex, and interests (Bandura, 1971).

Another factor that motivates us to attend to models relates to the *characteristics of the situation.* We're more likely to watch and learn from others when we find ourselves in situations that are unfamiliar and ambiguous, or in situations when we're uncertain about our knowledge and abilities.

Remembering The second step of observational learning is that the learner must *remember* what the model did. While a beginning surgeon might be interested enough to pay close attention to an operation (the first step in observational learning), she may be unable to remember all of the steps afterward. Her inability to remember everything that she watched means that observational learning is not yet complete, since remembering allows for the third step in observational learning: imitating or reproducing the model's actions.

Reproducing/Imitating The final step in observational learning is that the learner must be able to *reproduce, or imitate,* the modeled behavior. Sometimes accurate imitation will require practice, but it's also possible that even with practice the learner will never be able to perform the behavior as well as the model. We may admire the feats of world-class musicians or athletes, for example, but most of us could never reproduce them no matter how much we practiced.

The Three Steps in Action

In a classic experiment, Bandura had children watch an adult attack a large blow-up "BoBo the Clown" doll. Some children saw an adult sit on the doll, punch it, hit it with a hammer, and kick it around the room. Others saw a movie of an adult performing these same actions. A third group saw a cartoon version of the aggression. Later, the children were frustrated by having some attractive toys taken away from them. Then they were allowed to play with the BoBo doll. Most of the children imitated the adult's attack, doing things that were very much the same as those carried out by the model (➤ **Figure 29.1**). It is interesting that the cartoon was only slightly less effective in encouraging aggression than the live adult model and the filmed model (Bandura, Ross, & Ross, 1963). The children's actions demonstrated that they had successfully completed each of the three steps of observational learning: They had

Observational learning (modeling) Learning achieved by watching and imitating the actions of another or noting the consequences of those actions.

Model (in learning) A person who serves as an example in observational learning.

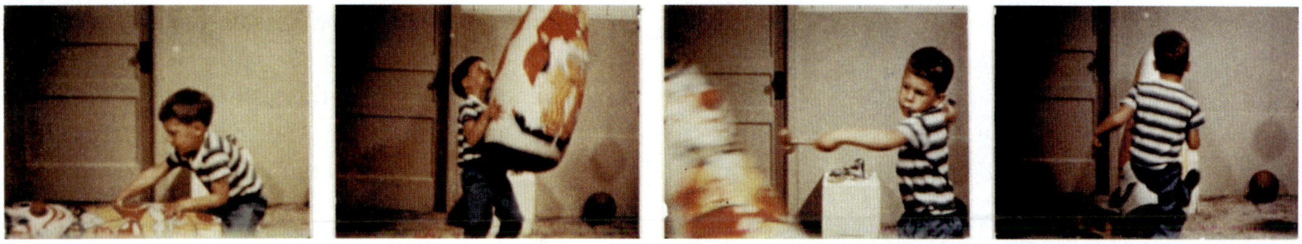

Courtesy of Albert Bandura/Stanford University

Figure 29.1

Imitating aggression. A nursery school child imitates the aggressive behavior of an adult model he has just seen in a movie.

paid attention to the model's behavior, remembered it, and then were able to reproduce it at a later time.

Bandura's study teaches us two other important points about observational learning and imitation. The first is that *not all of the behaviors that can be learned from models are positive*. In addition to the aggressive behaviors learned in this study, we know that adolescents are much more likely to begin smoking if their parents, siblings, and friends smoke (Wilkinson & Abraham, 2004).

The second lesson to take away from Bandura's study is that *learning may take place even when the model wasn't intentionally trying to teach anything*. For example, children can learn something about managing anger—including the aggressive responses seen in Bandura's study—by watching how parents deal with their frustrations over time. This can happen even though that parent isn't aware that the child is paying attention to their actions, and in spite of the parent not consciously attempting to communicate any particular message about anger management. Similarly, research has suggested that many excellent managers credit their success to their own previous managers and simply watching how they handled particular situations that emerged at work (Koch & Binnewies, 2015).

Factors Influencing Imitation

Will people always reproduce, or imitate, the behaviors learned by observation? No. In a follow-up study, Bandura (1965) recreated his original study, but in this case the children observed the model being either rewarded, punished, or receiving no consequences for their aggressive behavior toward the BoBo doll. When the children were themselves frustrated afterward, those who saw the model either rewarded or experience no consequences were far more likely to imitate the model's aggressive acts than those who saw the model being punished.

According to the results of this study, then, we learn more than just responses when we watch others: We also learn something about whether it would be a good idea to imitate what we've observed. What these findings tell us is that *observational learning only prepares us to duplicate a response*. Whether that response is actually imitated may depend on the consequences experienced by the model that we're observing. In this way, the operant learning principles that we discussed in Module 28 appear to play a role in observational learning as well. Just as the consequences of our own actions determine the likelihood of us performing those same actions again, so too is our behavior influenced by the consequences experienced by others from whom we learn.

Observational Learning in Everyday Life

Learning Outcome 29.2 Name two instances of observational learning in everyday life, describe three reasons why exposure to violent media may be associated with later aggression among children and adolescents as well as the results of research examining the link between exposure to violent video games and later aggression

Observational learning is very common in everyday life; you can probably think of a number of examples yourself. Children clearly learn a number of skills by watching others, from simple things like doing up zippers and brushing hair to more complex behaviors like using a knife and fork or tying their shoes. But people continue to learn in this

goodluz/Shutterstock.com

way as they move through adolescence and adulthood as well. For example, teenagers learn about how to drive by watching their parents or a driving instructor. After leaving school, adults can learn how to perform their jobs by observing others; in fact, observational learning is at the heart of most apprenticeships and other "hands-on" learning opportunities.

People also learn about acceptable standards of behavior in the workplace by watching how their co-workers behave. This became particularly apparent as the #metoo movement gained momentum and highlighted work environments in which harassment and disrespectful behavior was commonplace. In many instances, it appeared that newer workers had learned disrespectful and abusive behavior from those who were more experienced. The fact that this poor behavior was tolerated rather than punished meant that it continued to happen. In contrast, those individuals who may have wanted to report what was happening in these work environments quickly learned from watching other "whistle blowers" that doing so would be ignored or punished. As a result, many individuals tolerated harassment and other poor working conditions for the sake of preserving their jobs.

Collection Christophel/Alamy Stock Photo

There is no shortage of models of violence available on various media for children and adults to imitate.

Observing Media Violence

One of the most commonly discussed situations involving observational learning, though, relates to our increasing consumption of media. Specifically, there is considerable interest in what people learn from violent media (e.g., violent TV shows, movies, and video games). Earlier in this module we said that the likelihood that people will imitate behavior depends on the model's characteristics, including the extent to which they are seen as having prestige. Because this type of status is often associated with fame, and because children tend to imitate what they observe in all media (Kirsh, 2010), psychological researchers have invested a great deal of time examining the impact of media-based role models.

We know that today's children and young adults spend less time in the classroom than they do engaged with various media, including the Internet, video games, movies, television, music, and print (Rideout, Foehr, & Roberts, 2015). From social media (Anderson & Jiang, 2018) to rap music (Wingood et al., 2003) to video games (Carnagey & Anderson, 2004), children have plenty of opportunities to observe and imitate both the good and the bad (and the ugly?) that they see in the media.

Of particular concern to many people is exposure to aggression and violence. Here, the Internet is of special concern because it not only allows children to vicariously experience violence, it also allows them to directly engage in *electronic aggression* through bullying or harassment of others (Centers for Disease Control, 2017a). It should come as no surprise, then, that many parents and educators have concerns about the effects of experiencing high levels of media violence. Are they right to be worried?

By the time the average American has graduated from high school, she or he will have "witnessed" thousands of murders and countless acts of robbery, arson, bombing, torture, and beatings. But does all of this media mayhem promote the observational learning of aggression? Early studies appeared to confirm that children who watch a great deal of televised violence are more prone to behave aggressively (Anderson, Gentile, & Buckley, 2007; Miller et al., 2012).

How might media violence work to increase aggressive behavior? When describing Bandura's famous studies with the BoBo doll, we suggested that observing violence (including media violence) may teach people how to be more aggressive in real life (Kirsh, 2010; Unsworth & Ward, 2001). In addition to teaching new antisocial actions, media may disinhibit dangerous impulses that viewers already have. **Disinhibition**—the removal of inhibition—results in acting out behavior that normally would be restrained. Another possibility is that repeated exposure to media violence may result in **desensitization**—a reduction in emotional

Disinhibition The removal of inhibition; results in acting out that normally would be restrained.

Desensitization A reduction in emotional sensitivity to a stimulus.

sensitivity—making people less likely to react negatively to violence and, hence, more prone to tolerate this behavior in others and engage in it themselves (Carnagey, Anderson, & Bushman, 2007; Krahé et al., 2011).

Does the same conclusion apply to video games? Many reviews have concluded that violent video games increase aggressive behavior in children and young adults (Krahé & Möller, 2010; Miller et al., 2012). As with television, younger children appear to be especially susceptible to fantasy violence in video games (Anderson et al., 2003; Bensley & Van Eenwyk, 2001). In fact, the more personalized, intimate experience of video games may heighten their impact (Fischer, Kastenmüller, & Greitemeyer, 2010).

Unfortunately, much of the early research may have led to overly strong conclusions (Adachi & Willoughby, 2011a; Valadez & Ferguson, 2012). For example, in one earlier study, college students played a violent (*Mortal Kombat*) or nonviolent (*PGA Tournament Golf*) video game. Next, they competed with another "student" (actually an actor) in a task that allowed aggression and retaliation to take place. Students who played the violent game were much more likely to aggress by punishing their competitor (Bartholow & Anderson, 2002). However, these two games differed not only in their degree of violence, they also differed in degree of competitiveness, difficulty, and pace of action. What this means, then, is that when we find differences in aggression for people watching violent versus nonviolent games in this experiment, we don't really know whether the difference in aggression stemmed from the fact that the games differed in violent content or one of the other variables (e.g., competitiveness or difficulty). Going back to terms you learned in Module 4, competitiveness, difficulty, and pace are *extraneous variables*, and we need to control for them if we want a clear picture of how violent content (the independent variable) influences aggressive behavior (the dependent variable).

Two more recent studies have attempted to address this concern. In the first, researchers compared a violent action game (*Conan*) and a nonviolent racing game (*Fuel*) that were assessed as equally competitive, difficult, and fast-paced. In a subsequent task, college students who played the violent game were no more likely to be aggressive than those who played the nonviolent game (Adachi & Willoughby, 2011b). Taking experimental control one step further, researchers conducting the second study modified *the same game* so that it was more or less violent (Hilgard et al., 2019). Their results also suggested no effect of game violence on participants' aggression. Taken together, these studies suggest that we should not be too hasty in jumping to the conclusion that video game violence has any significant effect on aggressive behavior. Of course, it's possible that the relationship between violent video games and aggressiveness may be more complicated. For example, maybe playing violent video games only makes aggression more *likely*, but other factors (e.g., personality characteristics, family conflict, depression, and negative peer influences) ultimately affect whether hostile thoughts will be turned into actions (Ferguson & Dyck, 2012; Ferguson, Miguel, & Hartley, 2009; Valkenburg, Peter, & Walther, 2016). More research will definitely be needed before we have a clear picture of this relationship.

Parents and educators who worry that violent media are turning young people into a generation of sadistic criminals can also take heart from the correlational data shown in ➤ **Figure 29.2**. In recent years, the violent crime rate among

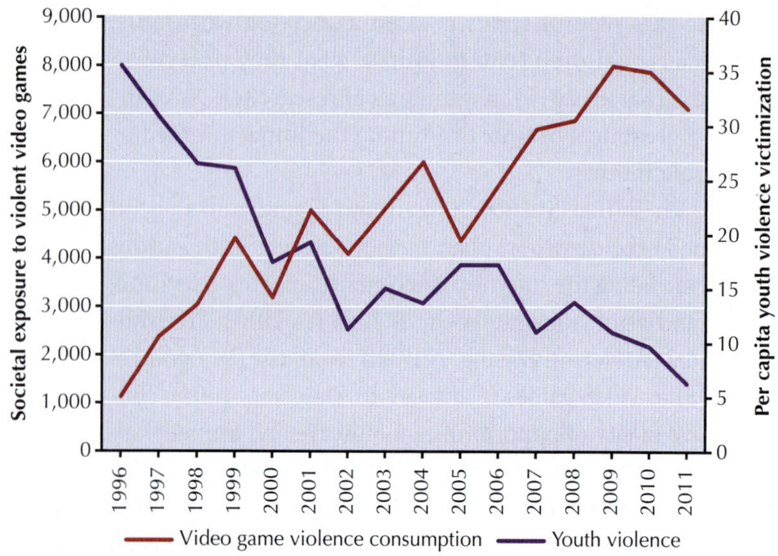

➤ **Figure 29.2**

Video game violence and youth violence rates. This graph shows that the rate of violent crimes among youth declined between the years 1996 and 2011. Yet, during the same period, exposure to violent video games increased. While correlational data such as these are not by themselves conclusive, they do help us put the issue of violence in video games into broader perspective. (Adapted from Ferguson, 2015.)

youth has declined, even as sales of violent video games have risen. However, none of this is to say that we should be unconcerned about the long-term effects of experiencing violent media, including imitation, disinhibition, and desensitization. This is especially true for younger children, who are more likely to be influenced because they don't always fully recognize that media characters and stories are fantasies (McKenna & Ossoff, 1998).

MODULE 29 Observational Learning—Learning Outcomes Revisited

29.1 Define observational learning, including the three steps, the three characteristics of models we are most likely to imitate, and the connection between observational learning and operant conditioning

Through observational learning, we can learn to perform particular actions (e.g., how to tie your shoes) as well as specific attitudes and emotional responses. Observational learning involves three steps: paying attention to the model, remembering what the model did, and being able to reproduce (imitate) the model's behavior. We are more likely to pay attention to models that we admire, who are authority figures, or who are similar to us. However, not all behaviors, attitudes, and emotions that are learned through observation are positive, and observational learning can occur even when the model did not intend to teach anything. Whether we imitate a model's behavior depends on whether the model was rewarded or punished for their actions. In this way, operant learning principles play a role in observational learning.

29.2 Name two instances of observational learning in everyday life, describe three reasons why exposure to violent media may be associated with later aggression among children and adolescents as well as the results of research examining the link between exposure to violent video games and later aggression

Observational learning is important in the workplace, where people learn acceptable standards of behavior by watching their co-workers. In addition, the media—including television, the Internet, and video games—provides powerful models from whom kids can learn through observation. Young people may learn new and aggressive and antisocial behaviors from models in the media. However, aggressive behavior may also be increased if media serves to disinhibit viewer's impulses to control aggression, or if it desensitizes people to violence. Early research suggested that playing violent video games promotes aggression; however, more recent research has suggested a more complex relationship between these two factors. It's also important to remember that much of the early research was correlational, and we cannot establish cause-and-effect relationships under such circumstances.

Reflective Practice

Content Check

1. Through observational learning we can learn
   a. behaviors
   b. attitudes
   c. emotional responses
   d. all of the above
2. Which of the following is not one of the three steps of observational learning?
   a. remembering the model's behavior
   b. judging the model's behavior
   c. paying attention to the model's behavior
   d. reproducing the model's behavior
3. The name of the researcher who carried out the studies in which children watched a model interact with a BoBo doll is __________.
4. Children only learn positive behaviors from observing others. T or F?
5. If a model is successful, or rewarded, the model's behavior is
   a. less difficult to reproduce
   b. less likely to be attended to
   c. more likely to be imitated
   d. more subject to positive transfer

6. Children who observed a live adult behave aggressively became more aggressive; those who observed movie and cartoon aggression did not. T or F?

Skill Check

Think Critically

7. A young college student secures an excellent internship working in an advertising office. During his first team meeting, the intern observes the manager ridicule one member of the team for questioning the manger's decision about how to proceed with an ad campaign. What might the intern learn by observing what happened in that meeting?

Self-Reflect

Who are some of the most powerful models for young people on social media, in your opinion? What characteristics do these models possess that make others want to imitate them? Are the models likely to be the same for males versus females?

ANSWERS

1. d 2. b 3. Bandura 4. F 5. c 6. F 7. The intern is likely to learn to keep quiet if he has concerns about the manager's decisions and not to question them, for fear of also being subject to ridicule in front of the team.

MODULE 30

Conditioning and Learning
Cognitive Learning

Think!

William Kamkwamba grew up in a rural village in Malawi. The second eldest of seven children, he had to leave school at the age of 14 because his parents were unable to afford the $80 fee. Rather than sitting idle, though, William borrowed books from the village library and set about continuing his education at home. One of the books he brought home was an 8th grade American physics textbook with a picture of a wind turbine on its cover. William was fascinated, and decided that he could use the ideas he was reading about to build a windmill that would provide power to the family home. Using plans from the book as his guide, his first windmill was constructed from a broken bicycle, a tractor fan blade, a pulley, and blue gum trees. And though people in the village initially thought he was crazy, they quickly changed their minds when they realized that the windmill was powering four light bulbs and two radios in the house.

AP Images/Taylor Jewell

William's story, told in the Netflix movie *The Boy Who Harnessed the Wind*, is a testament to the power of *cognitive learning*, which depends on our ability to think about information and solve problems. Are you interested in learning more? Read on!

~LEARNING OUTCOMES~

After reading this module you should be able to:

30.1 Define cognitive learning and outline the two main dimensions of Bloom's taxonomy

30.2 Describe four factors that affect cognitive learning

30.3 Name some instances of cognitive learning in everyday life

Cognitive Learning—Are Humans Informavores?

Learning Outcome 30.1 Define cognitive learning and outline the two main dimensions of Bloom's taxonomy

Can you imagine William Kamkwamba learning physics any other way besides using language to "digest" information? More than any other species, we humans learn through **cognitive learning**, the ability to acquire behavior, skills, and information in ways that are heavily dependent on language, memory,

Cognitive learning Higher-level learning involving language, thinking, knowing, understanding, and anticipation.

thinking, and problem solving. The emphasis on cognitive processes in this type of learning makes it very different from the associative learning described in Modules 27 and 28.

The earliest psychologists who concentrated on the cognitive aspects of learning were Gestalt theorists (see Module 3). Unlike associationists (those who focused on associative learning, like classical and operant conditioning), Gestalt psychologists firmly believed that learning requires cognition and "insight" and that it is connected to the organization of knowledge. As you might guess then, there were some significant differences of opinion between associationists and Gestalt psychologists about the nature of learning. In fact, those differences ran so deep during the early 1900s that they are now referred to as "the Learning Wars."

Today, there are two primary groups of psychologists who specialize in issues related to cognitive learning. The first is **school psychologists**. These individuals typically work in school settings. Their work is often clinical, as they take responsibility for testing students who are having school-based difficulties, designing interventions, and working with teachers and other educators to implement plans to assist students. The second group is referred to as **educational psychologists**, and they are primarily researchers who seek to understand how people best learn and how teachers can improve instruction (Snowman & McCown, 2015). In addition to carrying out research relevant to children in schools, educational psychologists might also work on research projects related to adult learners, including the most effective ways to provide training to people in the workforce.

Psychologists interested in cognitive learning focus on a number of topics. Classic early research in this area focused on basic questions related to classifying what we learn, and the processes by which we learn (Bloom, 1956). More recently, though, researchers have examined questions related to the factors that impact learning (Hattie & Donoghue, 2016). We'll take a look at both of these areas of research in the sections that follow.

What We Learn and How We Learn It: Bloom's Taxonomy

Back in the late 1940s men and women had just returned from the Second World War and many of them were interested in going to college. A special government stipend had been set up to help them with the costs, and campuses across the country were suddenly flooded with new students. Benjamin Bloom, then at the University of Chicago, found himself charged with trying to create a system of testing the educational standing of these men and women

The Cognitive Process Dimension

The Knowledge Dimension	Remember	Understand	Apply	Analyze	Evaluate	Create
Factual						
Conceptual						
Procedural						
Metacognitive						

Figure 30.1
Bloom's Taxonomy

so that they could be placed in classes that were appropriate to their current level of knowledge. The exam questions that his team developed could then be shared with colleges across the country so that these adults would be tested in a consistent way.

But Bloom's team did much more than just design a set of questions—they developed a system for thinking about cognitive learning, which is commonly referred to as **Bloom's taxonomy** (Figure 30.1). A taxonomy is a system of classification; in this case a method of classifying knowledge and learning. His team's ideas proved to be enormously successful and the initial taxonomy has now been updated to reflect ongoing thinking about the field of education (Anderson, 2013; Krathwohl, 2001). The most recent version underscores the importance of different types of knowledge (what we learn) as well as different cognitive processes (how we learn).

What We Learn: Types of Knowledge The newest version of Bloom's taxonomy describes four types of knowledge. The first is *factual knowledge* or an understanding of basic units of information (facts). An example of factual knowledge might be an understanding of the idea that associative learning includes both classical and operant conditioning.

The second type of knowledge is *conceptual.* Concepts are typically abstract ideas that often have multiple parts. Mastering conceptual knowledge requires learners to understand not just the parts, but how they fit together. Classical conditioning, described in Module 27, is a good example of a concept. It's an abstract idea that has several components (e.g., unconditioned stimulus and response; conditioned stimulus and response) and to really understand it, you'd need to not only know those four components but how they work together to foster that particular kind of learning.

The third type of knowledge is *procedural knowledge*, or knowing how to do something. An example of procedural knowledge might include how to use the principles of classical conditioning to help an alcoholic stop drinking (see Module 27).

The last type of knowledge is *metacognitive knowledge*. You may remember that we looked at metacognition in Module 26—it refers to our ability to think about and understand the limits of our own knowledge (knowing what you know and don't know!) and what learning strategies work best for us. For example, metacognitive knowledge would allow you to recognize that you sometimes struggle to understand the difference between the unconditioned and conditioned responses in classical conditioning. This type of knowledge is important to learning because it allows us to accurately assess our current understanding or skill level (and consequently know the areas in which we might need to learn more), to know what is helpful to our learning, and what we can do to improve learning when things aren't going well.

How We Learn: Cognitive Processes In addition to the types of knowledge that we can acquire, Bloom's taxonomy also addresses six ways in which we can work with that knowledge. The first is *remembering*, or being able to retrieve information from memory. The second is *understanding*, which refers to the ability to decode or establish the meaning of that information. The third process is *applying*, or using knowledge to carry out a given procedure, and the fourth is *analyzing* (working to understand the various parts that comprise a whole, and how they relate to one another). The fifth is *evaluating*, which involves using a set of criteria to judge skills and knowledge, and the sixth is *creating*, which involves using knowledge to create something totally original.

The six processes are often presented as a hierarchy, with the idea that higher-level processes (evaluating; creating) are more complex and challenging than lower-level ones (remembering and understanding). Presenting things this way has had the unfortunate consequence that teachers often feel that their lessons aren't valuable if they are focused on "lower-level" processes like remembering, and that they should consistently be designing activities that push students toward more sophisticated processes like evaluating and creating. More recently, though, educational psychologists have emphasized that the higher levels aren't really possible until the lower levels have been mastered (Hirsch, 2016). For example, it's difficult to evaluate or create something truly novel unless you first know a great deal about the subject (in other words, unless you have acquired a great deal of basic factual and conceptual knowledge that you remember and truly understand).

Factors That Influence Cognitive Learning—Creating a Nutritious Meal for an Informavore

Learning Outcome 30.2 Describe four factors that affect cognitive learning

More recent research in educational psychology has moved beyond Bloom's taxonomy to look at questions related to improving learning. In a very large-scale analysis of 80,000 studies that investigated 300 million learners, John Hattie (2017) has organized the factors that influence learning into several categories. We discuss three of them here: learner characteristics, learner strategies, and the learning environment.

Learner Characteristics A number of learner characteristics have been investigated to establish which ones might be helpful in promoting learning. According to Hattie's analysis, some of those that appear to be important across many studies include working memory (see Module 32), clinical diagnoses (e.g., ADHD, anxiety, or learning disabilities; see Modules 60–63), persistence or "grit" (see Module 56), motivation (see Modules 42–43), and self-efficacy (see Module 53). In this section we'll explore two others in a bit more detail: mindset and learning styles.

Mindset In a widely viewed TED talk, Carol Dweck of Stanford University talks about her decades-long interest in how children respond to setbacks and failure at school. Some, she argues, will push on in the face of obstacles and are determined to overcome them. In contrast, others will shrink back and simply give up. Over many years, she came to see these different response patterns as stemming from two different *mindsets* that guide our response to challenge

School psychologists Psychologists who work in schools and design interventions for students who are having difficulties.

Educational psychologists Psychologists who carry out research to better understand how people best learn and how teachers can improve instruction.

Bloom's taxonomy A system for classifying knowledge and learning.

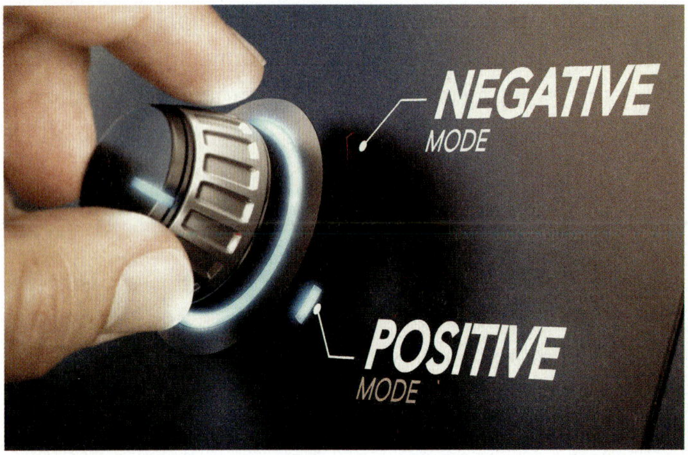

Olivier Le Moal/Shutterstock.com

(Dweck, 2008, 2017). A **growth mindset** is associated with the belief that our intelligence and talents can be developed through hard work and effort. This belief system has important consequences, including increased persistence in the face of obstacles and greater success in school and at work. In contrast, a **fixed mindset** is linked to the idea that intelligence and talents are inborn and cannot easily be changed. Someone with such a belief system is more likely to give up when the going gets rough, so it likely won't surprise you that a fixed mindset is associated with greater struggles at school and less success in the workforce. What was most exciting about Dweck's research, though, was her finding that mindset could be changed using particular classroom techniques, and that it was possible to move from having a fixed mindset to one that was more linked to growth (Dweck, 2012).

Dweck's ideas proved to be immensely popular with educators who quickly rushed to structure their classrooms in ways that would allow all learners to develop a growth mindset. Teachers began generously praising effort so that students would see the importance of continuing to try, even when circumstances were difficult. But it wasn't long before challenges to Dweck's ideas began to emerge. In particular, researchers had some difficulty replicating Dweck's positive findings regarding the ability to change children's mindset (Sisk, Burgoyne, Sun, Butler, & Macnamara, 2018).

In response, Dweck has recently spoken out in an effort to clarify her views about mindset, and the ways in which her research has been misunderstood and misused in schools (Dweck, 2016). In particular, she points to two common misconceptions that have become popular since her initial work was published:

People have a "pure" mindset that is either fixed or growth. Given the results of the early research, it seemed clear that having a growth mindset was a good thing, and having a fixed mindset was not. Unfortunately, there was a worrying trend for teachers to use mindsets to explain why students weren't succeeding ("Oh, he has a fixed mindset—that's why he's not doing well in math."). In reality, Dweck argues, everyone displays fixed and growth mindsets in different circumstances, and all of us have "triggers" that will bring on a fixed mindset. For example, how do you react when someone is much better than you at something that you really value? And how do you react to failure in different circumstances? Are there feelings of defensiveness, anger, or anxiety in some situations? A sense of being incompetent or defeated? Do you find yourself looking for excuses? Identifying those specific challenges that bring on a fixed mindset will put you on a path toward a growth mindset.

Developing a growth mindset among students is just about praising effort. Too often, Dweck argues, teachers took her research to mean that one simply needed to praise students' efforts and a growth mindset would emerge. This approach of praising effort—*even when students were not learning*—is not productive in the long run for two reasons. First, students need to know when they are not meeting a standard, and if the teacher's sole focus is on praising effort then that feedback about their learning will be absent. Second, Dweck argues that effort alone will never be enough for learning to take place—students still need to be taught a variety of strategies that they can use when things aren't going well, including the value of seeking help. Ultimately, it's using these strategies (even if you have to try a number of them!) that will help students to see the value of persisting in the face of challenge. In other words, focusing students' attention on the *process* by which learning happens—not just the effort they expend—is critical in promoting a growth mindset.

Learning Styles Another learner characteristic that has generated considerable interest among educators is *learning styles*, or the idea that people have a preferred means of receiving and processing information. Though many different types of learning styles have been proposed over the years, one of the most popular relates to the idea that people can be classified as visual, auditory, or kinesthetic learners, depending on the sensory input through which they prefer to receive new information (Willingham, 2009). Intuitively, this model has a lot of appeal. After all, we've all met people who seem to have a remarkable ability to visualize material that they've seen previously, or a remarkable "ear" for languages or music. Some people also note that they think better on their feet, or while they are moving, a preference that is associated with the kinesthetic sense.

aslysun/Shutterstock.com

Researchers and educators who subscribe to the idea of learning styles indicate that if we take note of people's preferred style and teach material to them in that way, learning will be enhanced. Many studies have investigated this claim and, like many other theories in learning research, the results have been somewhat mixed. To try to settle the matter, researchers combined the results of many studies (Pashler, McDaniel, Rohrer, & Bjork, 2008). What they observed was that learning styles did *not* appear to have any significant effect on most measures of learning (e.g., test results).

Cognitive psychologist Dan Willingham (2009) has attempted to explain why the results were so disappointing when the idea of learning styles seems to make so much sense. He argues that while it's true that some people do have a superior memory for visual images or for sounds that they hear, it's unlikely to matter for most types of cognitive learning. Why? Because the majority of information that we learn isn't stored in memory as visual images, sounds, or movement. Instead, much of what we learn—including how to add numbers, do laundry, drive a car, and cook spaghetti—is stored as abstract ideas and concepts. When this is the case, having an excellent visual or auditory memory, or having a strong kinesthetic sense, will not be of any great help when you have to retrieve the learned information from your memory. Of course, when you're learning information that *is* stored in memory as an image (e.g., what the Mona Lisa painting looks like) or as a sound (e.g., how to properly pronounce the name of the Welsh town Llanfairpwllgwyngyllgogerychwyrndrobwllllantysiliogogogoch) then people with particularly good visual or auditory memory may have an advantage when they're being tested on that material. Unfortunately, that's just not likely to be the case most of the time.

Learning Strategies

When it comes to learning, one of the most important things that educational psychologists have studied is the strategies that learners adopt when they try to master new material. Many of the most effective strategies were introduced to you in other modules (especially Module 1), and they include:

- *Spacing out your learning* over several days or weeks, rather than trying to cram everything into one session
- *Being reflective* about your learning. For example, it's important to think carefully about how the to-be-learned material "fits in" with things that you already know, and to ask yourself lots of "wh" questions as you learn (e.g., Why might that be true? When might this result not hold up? Which of these two things is likely to be more effective?)
- *Testing yourself* on the material you're learning, doing your best to mimic the exam conditions if you're going to be evaluated in a formal way
- *Using metacognitive strategies*. Remember in Module 26 we spoke about the need to be aware of your own knowledge, as well as your strengths and weaknesses when it comes to learning new things. It's also important to actively monitor your progress during learning and make adjustments (e.g., putting in more time, or spending your time differently) if your learning isn't progressing as you had hoped or planned.

Weekend Images Inc./E+/Getty Images

Growth mindset The belief that intelligence and talents can be developed through hard work and effort.

Fixed mindset The belief that intelligence and talents are inborn and cannot easily be changed.

Type of Instruction

There is little doubt that teachers can greatly affect student interest, motivation, and creativity. But what type of instruction is likely to be effective? To answer this question, psychologists have examined many methods of teaching. Two of the most basic are *direct instruction* and *discovery learning*.

In **direct instruction**, information is presented by lecture or demonstration, and students often learn through rote practice. In **discovery learning**, teachers create conditions that encourage students to discover or construct knowledge for themselves (Dean & Kuhn, 2007). ➤ **Figure 30.2** illustrates the difference. Two groups of students were taught to calculate the area of a parallelogram by multiplying the height by the length of the base. Some were encouraged to see that a "piece" of a parallelogram could be "moved" to create a rectangle. Later, they were better able to solve unusual problems in which the height times base formula didn't seem to work. Students who simply memorized a rule were confused by similar problems, suggesting that discovery can lead to a better understanding of new or unusual problems (Wertheimer, 1959).

Such findings initially led researchers to believe that direct instruction techniques led to *passive learning* (that is, students are provided with knowledge by someone who has expertise) and that a better approach to teaching was the use of techniques that promote *active learning* (in which students work to construct knowledge for themselves). And as was the case with research on mindset and learning styles, many educators quickly embraced the idea of active learning and moved quickly to design class lessons that revolved around students asking their own questions and solving problems without explicit instruction. Unfortunately, later research demonstrated that in some cases, students taught using discovery-based active learning techniques (including, for example, problem-based learning) fared *worse* on later assessments than those taught using direct instruction.

Educational psychologists have more recently tried to explain the finding that active learning techniques are not always superior, in spite of the fact that they have a great deal of appeal. After all, who doesn't like the image of students working excitedly on interesting "real-world" problems in the classroom instead of passively listening to a lesson or lecture? The difficulty with discovery learning is that it's sometimes very difficult to solve problems effectively or generate good questions about a topic when you aren't an expert. And putting students who know very little about a

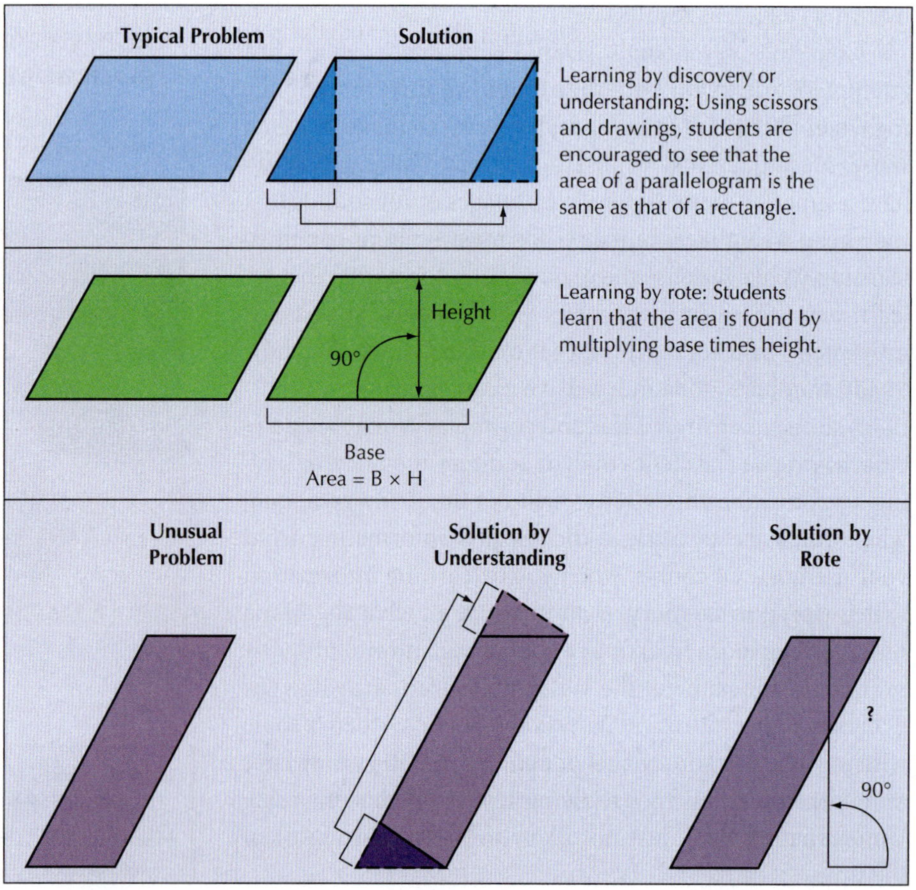

➤ **Figure 30.2**

Learning by understanding and by rote. For some types of learning, understanding may be superior, although both types of learning are useful. (After Wertheimer, 1959.)

topic into a situation where they are trying to engage in the higher-level cognitive processes of Bloom's taxonomy can be much more frustrating than rewarding. Of course, once students have developed a good working knowledge of a particular topic—usually through listening to and reading the work of experts—they will be in a much better position to solve those challenging problems and generate creative ideas.

What this research tells us is that students shouldn't be asked to stumble around trying to discover for themselves the principles of math, physics, or any other subject for that matter. The best teaching strategies are much more likely to be based on *guided discovery,* in which students are given enough guidance through direct instruction that they gain a solid understanding of foundational facts and concepts. Only then, after they have a good base of knowledge, will they be in a strong position to think productively about problems that need to be solved (Mayer, 2011; Mukherjee, 2015).

Learning Environment

Aside from the type of instruction that a teacher uses, there are other elements of the learning environment that can be important in guiding learning outcomes. Two that have received considerable attention from educational psychologists are the use of feedback and technology.

Feedback An important contributor to student learning, and research from the workforce suggests that *feedback* continues to be important in terms of driving workers' on-the-job learning and success (Harms & Roebuck, 2010). Providing feedback that is maximally effective, though, requires a good understanding of what feedback is (and what it isn't!).

One of the most important aspects of **feedback** is that it provides information about progress toward a goal (Lefrançois, 2012). If you're a comedian and your goal is to make people laugh, then feedback would come from whether your audience greets your jokes with side-splitting laughter or stony silence. If you are a tennis player and your goal is to improve your backhand, then feedback would come from whether your backhand shots cross the net and how accurately you can place them on the other side of the court.

The most helpful feedback will be delivered soon after the performance. This is why we encourage you to work through the *Knowledge Builder* questions at the end of each module and then check your answers—we want to provide you with some immediate feedback about how well you've mastered the basic ideas presented, so that you have a good sense of what to do next (move on to the next module, or go back and re-read some of the material related to questions you got wrong).

Good feedback will also be based on patterns of responses over time, rather than a single instance. Some of the exercises in *MindTap*, the online resource that accompanies this book, work on this principle by tracking your responses to similar questions over many trials and providing greater practice with concepts that are giving you trouble.

Sometimes, of course, it's not always easy to pick up on feedback because you're so focused on the task at hand (Wiggins, 2012). New teachers, for example, are often so absorbed with delivering a lesson effectively that they may fail to register student behaviors (engaged faces or lost looks) that would provide them with valuable information about their performance. This is why recorded feedback can be very helpful, regardless of whether you are learning to teach, play a musical instrument, sing, speak a second language, or deliver a speech. In sports, video replays are routinely used to provide feedback on everything from tennis serves to pick-off moves in baseball.

It's important to note that feedback is not the same thing as *advice*, even though we often use the terms interchangeably (Wiggins, 2012). The difference lies in the fact that advice doesn't provide any information about your progress toward a goal. Statements like "You should give more examples in your paper," "You need to keep your eye on the ball," or "You need to pull your shoulders back when you sing" are all good examples of advice. Though they can be helpful, they're usually much more beneficial when they're provided along with feedback, because then you'll understand why the advice is being given.

Technology Over the past two decades, technology has become very common in schools and other environments that foster cognitive learning. In general, two things have contributed to this rise of technology in the learning domain. The first is people's creative use of the Internet to promote cognitive learning. For example, the rise of YouTube has provided a new kind of "informal classroom" where people can learn about subjects that range from Renaissance literature to replacing the radiator in your car. The Internet has also paved the way for more formal classes to be offered online, allowing

Direct instruction A method of instruction in which information is presented by lecture or demonstration, and students often learn through rote practice.

Discovery learning Learning based on insight and understanding.

Feedback Information about progress toward a goal.

Nejron Photo/Shutterstock.com

students who are pursuing certificates, diplomas, or degrees to have greater flexibility to pursue their credits at a time and place that is convenient for them. And even when courses are offered in a more conventional classroom, it's common for both instructors and students to make use of the Web's vast resources to easily gather information for lessons and projects and to communicate with others in the class.

The second thing that has contributed to the rise of technology in education is the development of hardware and software that can aid in teaching and learning. For example, some technology has been designed to support students with issues that previously limited access to education (e.g., being blind or deaf). Smartboards, clickers, and PowerPoint are also examples of technological tools that, when used properly, can support learning. The literature related to the utility of such technology has been mixed, with some studies suggesting significant benefits while others indicate little value or, worse, declines in learning (Hattie, 2017). One reason that might help to explain such mixed findings is the fact that technology isn't a substitute for good teaching. To be effective, technology needs to be used in such a way that it enhances well-informed teaching practice. Using it simply to "jazz up" a lesson will not be helpful—good teaching is at the heart of successful learning.

One area that has generated particular controversy concerns the use of laptops in the classroom for note-taking. On the one hand, people argue, laptops can make taking notes more effective since people can usually type faster than they can write (and some have indicated that their typed notes are far more legible than their written ones!). This might lead to a more complete set of notes that will be of greater value when studying. On the other hand, concerns have been raised that using laptops may lead to less active information processing during a lesson, with students simply transcribing the teacher's words without really thinking about them.

So how do those competing claims stand up in the research? Two well-controlled experiments have demonstrated that taking notes on a laptop does tend to lead to more notes, and notes that more closely resemble a "transcription" of the lecture (Morehead, Dunlosky, & Rawson, 2019; Mueller & Oppenheimer, 2014). What's less clear is the impact of taking notes in this way: While one study demonstrated that taking notes on a laptop led to poorer test results than taking notes by hand, the other suggested that this was not the case. Clearly more research will be needed to settle this issue, and it may well be the case that the answer is more complex. For example, laptops may indeed be more beneficial as a note-taking strategy, but only for certain subjects or particular people.

Of course, the quality of the notes isn't the only issue. Some educators have expressed concern that allowing laptops in the classroom creates a distraction, since students often confess that they will use their laptops during class to check social media, send texts, and buy things online. If that's the case, then there's good reason to be concerned that allowing laptops in the classroom will compromise learning because of the distraction that they pose, not only for the student with the computer but also for those who are sitting around them (Sana, Weston, & Cepeda, 2013).

Cognitive Learning in Everyday Life—We Are All Life-Long Informavores

Learning Outcome 30.3 Name some instances of cognitive learning in everyday life

We've spent quite a lot of time in this module talking about cognitive learning in relation to conventional "school" settings where teachers provide instruction to learners. But cognitive learning is life-long and happens in all kinds of settings in our everyday lives. For example, it can occur when you learn something new by watching videos or reading magazines, books, newspapers, websites, or blog posts. It can also happen when you engage in everyday conversations with others, gaining new information from listening to them share their insights.

One of the messages that you should take away from the research on teaching and cognitive learning, though, is that the media will routinely make claims about research that demonstrates "the one thing" that will improve learning and help everyone reach their potential. Educators saw this with the research on mindset and learning styles, as well as the studies concerned with discovery learning and excitement about the possibilities posed by new technology.

If you read of any such claims concerning miraculous educational interventions, you would be wise to be cautious. Over the years, education has witnessed many "revolutions" that have failed to produce consistently positive results over time (Chew & Cerbin, 2017). In some respects, this shouldn't be surprising: More than ever before, educators face an increasingly diverse mix of students: "regular" students, adult learners, students who have disabilities and mental health challenges, students who speak English as a second language, and students who are juggling multiple responsibilities aside from school (Bowe, 2000). Faced with such diversity, it really shouldn't be surprising that there is no "one-size-fits-all" miracle approach to teaching that will work for everyone. Instead, we need to recognize that *almost all teaching strategies work some of the time* to enhance cognitive learning. The challenge for educational psychologists is to establish which strategies work for whom, and under what conditions (Bernstein, 2018).

Remember, though, that learning is a relatively *permanent* change in knowledge or behavior. This means that in order for learning to take place, the information that you gather needs to be stored in memory. In the next set of modules, we'll talk more about memory, and the process by which new information moves from perceptual processes like seeing and hearing to permanent storage in our memory.

MODULE 30 Cognitive Learning—Learning Outcomes Revisited

30.1 Define cognitive learning and outline the two main dimensions of Bloom's taxonomy

Cognitive learning refers to our ability to acquire skills and information using language, thinking, memory, and problem solving. Bloom's taxonomy is a classification system that organizes information about types of knowledge (factual, conceptual, procedural, and metacognitive) and the cognitive processes (remembering, understanding, applying, analyzing, evaluating, and creating) that are involved in learning.

30.2 Describe four factors that affect cognitive learning

Cognitive learning is influenced by learner characteristics (working memory, clinical diagnoses, persistence, motivation, self-efficacy, and mindset, but not learning styles), learning strategies (use of self-testing and metacognitive strategies), type of instruction (direct instruction, discovery learning, guided discovery), and the learning environment (use of feedback and technology).

30.3 Name some instances of cognitive learning in everyday life

In addition to traditional "school" settings, cognitive learning happens in many other settings (e.g., while reading for pleasure, watching a video, or engaging in everyday conversations).

Reflective Practice

Content Check

1. Which of the following is ***not*** one of the types of knowledge included in Bloom's taxonomy?
   a. conceptual
   b. metacognitive
   c. factual
   d. implicit
2. People who respond to challenge by persisting and working hard to overcome the obstacles they face are said to have:
   a. a growth mindset
   b. a fixed mindset
   c. an optimal learning style
   d. poor metacognition
3. The strong disagreement between associationists and Gestalt psychologists about how learning happens has been referred to as "The Learning Wars." T or F?
4. _______________ is a type of instruction that recognizes the importance of providing students with fundamental information about a topic and then allowing them to work on solving problems related to that topic.
5. Research related to note-taking during lectures suggests that
   a. using a laptop is superior to taking notes by hand
   b. taking notes by hand is superior to using a laptop

   c. using a laptop leads to notes that look more like a transcription of the lecture
   d. students never use laptops to check social media or send texts during lecture
6. Most educational "revolutions" have failed to produce consistently positive results over time. T or F?

Skill Check

Think Critically

7. Imagine that you're studying for your psychology exam. How could you use the well-established learning strategies outlined in this module to improve your chances of success?

Self-Reflect

Think about a subject you know a lot about, or a skill at which you really excel. Try to apply Bloom's four types of knowledge to your learning. What kind of factual knowledge is necessary to master this subject or skill? What conceptual knowledge is important? What procedural knowledge can come from learning about this subject or skill? What sort of metacognitive knowledge would someone need to consider to become an expert in this area?

ANSWERS

1. d 2. a 3. T 4. guided discovery 5. c 6. T 7. The first strategy involves spacing out your studying, so ideally you'd begin your studying early, and create a timetable that will allow you to work away at the material in small chunks over a period of time. The second strategy is to be reflective. For all of the material you study, think about how the various pieces "fit together" and how they fit in with material that you have already studied (or things that you already know). If it helps, try drawing a diagram to show how things are connected. The third strategy is self-testing, using methods that mimic what you'll have to do on the exam. If the exam will include multiple choice questions then you should practice with multiple choice questions (try MindTap!). And don't use the textbook to help during your practice test (unless it's going to be an open-book exam!). Finally, try to employ metacognitive strategies to monitor your progress and understand the gaps in your own knowledge. The self-testing from the previous step can be incredibly useful in this regard—make sure you leave yourself with enough time to go back over the areas in which you are struggling the most.

A Psychologist's Skill Set

Behavioral Self-Management

MODULE 31

A Rewarding Project

Chuck used to be out of shape. Worse, he was having a tough time motivating himself to exercise. Once Chuck decided to follow the steps outlined in this module, that changed. Now he is back on track, at least as far as his fitness is concerned. How did he do it?

Maridav/Shutterstock.com

Chuck began by targeting the number of hours per week he spent exercising. For the first week, he tracked how many hours per day he exercised (almost none, as it turned out). With this baseline in place, he set the goal of exercising an hour a week the first week, and an additional hour every week afterwards until he reached his final goal of exercising five hours a week. His fitness tracker let him easily keep track of the time spent exercising, along with the number of steps he took and calories he burned. For every hour he spent exercising, Chuck rewarded himself by watching an hour of videos on YouTube. When he didn't stick to his exercise schedule, he gave up his morning coffee at Starbucks the next day. Within a month, Chuck reached his exercise goal. (Now if only he could spend more time studying.)

~LEARNING OUTCOMES~

After reading this module you should be able to:

31.1 Create a six-step self-management plan, name four additional strategies that can help you change bad habits, and distinguish between covert sensitization and covert reinforcement

Self-Management—A Rewarding Project

Learning Outcome 31.1 Create a six-step self-management plan, name four additional strategies that can help you change bad habits, and distinguish between covert sensitization and covert reinforcement

In many ways, behavioral self-management is connected to the idea of *self-regulation*, which was discussed in Module 11. Recall that self-regulation is related to the ability to achieve our goals, and involves both internal mental processes (such as those discussed in Module 26) and external observable behaviors. In this module, we focus on the goals that are related to specific observable behaviors and how those behaviors can be altered using the principles of operant conditioning that were discussed in Module 28.

Operant conditioning offers a number of ideas that can be useful in guiding your efforts to change behaviors. For example, psychological research suggests that providing reinforcement for actions that are in line with our goals (and punishing those that are not!) can be extremely effective in helping to alter behavior.

This is an invitation to use the principles of operant conditioning to carry out a self-management project of your own—one that can help you with any behavior that's important in your relationships or the work that you do. Let's explore how to identify, track, and modify the behaviors that you want to reduce or increase in frequency (Miltenberger, 2016; Watson & Tharp, 2014).

Create a Management Plan

It is best to begin with a little reflective planning. Before getting started, you would be wise to review the basic principles of classical and operant conditioning (Modules 27 and 28) and also to look ahead to Module 67, which discusses some uses of conditioning principles in therapy. Once you're ready to proceed, you can create your own behavioral management plan, which includes the following steps:

1. **Specify a Behavioral Goal** Is there a behavior you want to eliminate altogether, such as quitting smoking or biting your nails? Perhaps you just want to *decrease* a behavior, such as watching less television. Or maybe you want to *increase* a behavior, such as exercising more or studying longer.

   Most of us find it quite difficult to suddenly completely change our behavior (hence so many broken New Year's resolutions). (Remember the principle of shaping—the reinforcement of increasingly close approximations of a desired response; see Module 28.) Instead, set realistic goals for gradual improvement over a number of successive weeks. Also, set daily goals that add up to the weekly goal for any given week.

   To increase the likelihood of meeting your goals, consider creating a **behavioral contract**. Write down the specific behavioral goal you want to achieve. Also state the rewards you will receive, privileges you will forfeit, or punishments you must accept. You and a person you trust should sign the contract.
2. **Record a Baseline** Once you have targeted a behavior, spend a week or so recording how much time you currently spend performing the target behavior. Or count the number of desired or undesired responses you make each day. You will be able to evaluate your progress against your baseline.
3. **Choose Reinforcers** If you meet your daily goal, what reward will you allow yourself? Daily rewards might be watching Netflix, eating a candy bar, socializing with friends, listening to your iPod, or whatever you enjoy. Also establish a weekly reward. A movie? A dinner out? Some time playing a computer game? A weekend hike? If you have trouble thinking of rewards, remember that anything you like to do can serve as reinforcement. This is known as the **Premack principle**, named after David Premack, the psychologist who popularized its use.

   For example, suppose you like to watch television every night and want to study more. All you need to do is to make television-watching contingent (dependent) on whether or not you meet your daily goal (study more). You might make it a rule not to watch anything until (and unless!) you have studied for an hour (or whatever length of time you choose).
4. **Record Your Progress** Keep accurate records of the amount of time spent each day on the target behavior, or the number of times you exercise, arrive late to class, eat vegetables, smoke a cigarette, study, watch television, drink a cappuccino, swear, or whatever behavior you have targeted.

   Even if you find it difficult to give and withhold rewards, **self-recording**—keeping records of response frequencies, a form of feedback—can make a difference all by itself. Reflective record keeping helps break habits (Wood & Rünger, 2016). Also, feedback can be motivating as you begin to make progress. In general, when you systematically (and honestly) observe yourself, you are more likely to engage in desired behaviors and less likely to perform undesired behaviors (Fireman, Kose, & Solomon, 2003; Watson & Tharp, 2014). As you may have noticed, this is the basic idea behind fitness trackers such as the Fitbit or goal-setting apps such as stickK.com.
5. **Reward Successes** If you meet your daily goal, collect your reward. If you fall short, be honest with yourself and skip the reward. Do the same for your weekly goal.
6. **Adjust Your Plan as You Learn More About Your Behavior** Overall progress will reinforce your attempts at self-management, so don't be dismayed by the occasional setback. Attempting to manage or alter your own behavior may be more difficult than it sounds. If you feel you need more information, have a look at *Self-directed behavior: Self-modification for personal adjustment* (Watson & Tharp. 2014). If you do try a

self-modification project but find it impossible to reach your goals, be aware that professional advice is available.

Extra Techniques to Break Bad Habits

Are there any extra tips for breaking stubborn bad habits? Breaking bad habits may be especially difficult to do. Here are some additional strategies you can add to your behavioral management plan to help you change bad habits.

- **Look for Alternate Behaviors** A good strategy for change is to try to get the same reinforcement with a new behavior. For example, Marta often tells jokes at the expense of others. Her friends sometimes feel hurt by her sharp-edged humor. Marta senses this and wants to change. What can she do? Usually, Marta's joke telling is reinforced by attention and approval. She could just as easily get the same reinforcement by giving other people praise or compliments. Making a change in her behavior should be easy because she will continue to receive the reinforcement that she seeks.
- **Break Up Response Chains** Breaking up response chains that precede an undesired behavior will help break the bad habit. The key idea is to scramble the chain of events that leads to an undesired response (Watson & Tharp, 2014). For example, Ignacio often comes home from work, logs in to his favorite role-playing game, and eats a whole bag of cookies or chips. He then takes a shower and changes clothes. By dinnertime, he has lost his appetite. Ignacio realizes he is substituting junk food for dinner. Ignacio could solve the problem by breaking the response chain that precedes dinner. For instance, he could shower immediately when he gets home or delay logging in until after dinner.
- **Reduce Cues and Antecedents** Try to avoid, narrow down, or remove stimuli that elicit the bad habit.

  Example: Brent wants to cut down on smoking. He can take many smoking cues out of his surroundings by removing ashtrays, matches, and extra cigarettes from his house, car, and office. Drug cravings are strongly related to cues conditioned to the drug, such as the odor of cigarettes. Brent can narrow antecedent stimuli even more. He could begin by smoking only in the lounge at work, never in his office or in his car. He could then limit his smoking to home. Then to only one room at home. Then to one chair at home. If he succeeds in getting this far, he may want to limit his smoking to only one unpleasant place, such as a bathroom, basement, or garage (Riley et al., 2002).
- **Use Covert Sensitization and Reward** In **covert sensitization**, aversive imagery is used to reduce the occurrence of an undesired behavior, such as smoking or overeating (Kearney, 2006; Watson & Tharp, 2014). Suppose, for example, you want to quit smoking. Every time you get the urge, repeatedly and vividly imagine yourself painfully coughing up blood or having to tell the most important person in your life that you have untreatable lung cancer and have only three months left to live. The scenes you imagine should be so *disturbing* or *disgusting* that thinking about them would temporarily make you very uncomfortable about indulging in the habit.

  Covert reinforcement—the use of positive imagery—can also be used to reinforce desired behavior (Kearney, 2006; Watson & Tharp, 2014). To make use of covert reinforcement, rehearse your target behavior mentally. Then follow each rehearsal with a vivid, rewarding image. For example, suppose that your target behavior is not smoking. Imagine that you are at a bar with your friends. You are offered a cigarette and politely refuse. Next, imagine a pleasant, reinforcing scene: Picture yourself nicotine-free. Someone you really like says to you, "Gee, you just played your best tennis ever. I've never seen you so healthy."

While actual direct self-reinforcement is the best way to alter behavior, covert or "visualized" reinforcement can have similar effects. (Direct self-reinforcement is described in Module 50.) So, while covert sensitization and reinforcement may sound as if you are "playing games with yourself," it can be a great help if you want to cut down on a bad habit (Kearney, 2006).

Behavioral contract A formal agreement stating behaviors to be changed and consequences that apply.

Premack principle Any high-frequency response can be used to contingently reinforce a low-frequency response.

Self-recording Self-management based on keeping records of response frequencies.

Covert sensitization Use of aversive imagery to reduce the occurrence of an undesired response behavior.

Covert reinforcement Using positive imagery to reinforce desired behavior.

MODULE 31

Behavioral Self-Management—Learning Outcomes Revisited

31.1 Create a six-step self-management plan, name four additional strategies that can help you change bad habits, and distinguish between covert sensitization and covert reinforcement

The six steps in formulating a self-management plan are: Specify a behavioral goal, record a baseline, choose reinforcers, record your progress, reward your progress, and adjust your plan, as required. Strategies that can help change bad habits are reinforcing alternative responses, breaking response chains, avoiding antecedent cues, and using covert sensitization and reinforcement. In covert sensitization, aversive images are used to discourage unwanted behavior. Covert reinforcement is a way to encourage desired responses by mental rehearsal. We hope that after reading this section, you'll be better able to think about how you can use these strategies to help develop a plan to manage any bad habit that you want to change!

Reflective Practice

Content Check

1. After a target behavior has been selected for reinforcement, it's a good idea to record a baseline so that you can set realistic goals for change. T or F?
2. Self-recording, even without the use of extra rewards, can bring about desired changes in target behaviors. T or F?
3. The Premack principle states that behavioral contracting can be used to reinforce changes in behavior. T or F?
4. A self-management plan should use the principle of shaping by setting a graduated series of goals. T or F?
5. Like covert sensitization, covert reinforcement of desired responses also is possible. T or F?

Skill Check

Think Critically

6. How does setting daily goals in a behavioral self-management program help maximize the effects of reinforcement?

Self-Reflect

Even if you don't expect to carry out a self-management project right now, outline a plan for changing your own behavior. Be sure to describe the behavior that you want to change, set goals, and identify reinforcers. How could you use covert sensitization and covert reinforcement to change your behavior?

ANSWERS

1. T 2. T 3. F 4. T 5. T 6. Daily performance goals and rewards reduce the delay of reinforcement, which maximizes the impact of the reinforcement.

Memory
Memory Systems

MODULE 32

My Memory Rules My Life

The more you remember, the better, right? Maybe when it comes to exams. But consider Joe, whose military service left him haunted by memories of battle. Images of combat spontaneously intrude on his thoughts while he is at work; such as the time he saw a land mine tear apart a good friend. Everyday experiences, such as smelling gas while filling up, take him back. Loud noises startle him into combat mode. He is unable to visit old comrades without being overwhelmed by painful memories. For Joe, a little more forgetfulness would be a gift (Cohen, 2006).

Or consider Jill Price's "perfect" memory: "Whenever I see a date flash on the television (or anywhere else for that matter) I automatically go back to that day and remember where I was, what I was doing, what day it fell on and on and on and on and on" (Parker, Cahill, & McGaugh, 2006, pp. 35–36; Price & Davis, 2009).

Whether memories are intensely emotional, like Joe's, or more mundane, like Jill's, who we are is determined by what we remember *and* what we forget. An interesting series of events must occur before we can say, "I remember." Don't worry. As you read this module, and others on memory and forgetting, we won't forget to share some ways to help you better remember for that next exam.

Photographee.eu/Shutterstock.com

~LEARNING OUTCOMES~

After reading this module you should be able to:

32.1 Explain the workings of the Atkinson-Shiffrin model of memory

32.2 Describe the features of short-term (or working) memory

32.3 Describe the features of long-term memory

Stages of Memory—Do You Have a Mind Like a Steel Trap? Or a Sieve?

Learning Outcome 32.1 Explain the workings of the Atkinson-Shiffrin model of memory

Memory is no passive "library of facts." Instead, human **memory** is a series of active systems that receive, store, organize, alter, and recover information (Baddeley, Eysenck, & Anderson, 2009; Sternberg, 2017). For information to be stored for a long time—like, say, between when you study and when you need to remember for an exam—it must pass through a series of memories: sensory memory, short-term memory, and long-term memory.

To pass through each memory, information must be *encoded*, *stored*, and *retrieved*. **Encoding** is the conversion of information into a form suitable for retention in memory. Once it is encoded, information must be held in memory **storage** for later use. Finally, **retrieval** involves the recovery of stored information.

If you're going to remember all of the 9,856 new terms on your next psychology exam, then you must successfully encode them in sensory memory, move them through short-term memory, and eventually retrieve them from long-term memory. These stages are summarized by the *Atkinson-Shiffrin model of memory*, shown in ➤**Figure 32.1** (Atkinson & Shiffrin, 1968; Sternberg, 2017). It is well worth tracing the series of memory events that must occur before you can pass that exam. Let's start with a quick overview.

Sensory Memory

Suppose that you sit down to memorize a few terms from this textbook for your exam next month. As you read, information is first automatically encoded in **sensory memory**, which can hold an exact copy of what you are seeing for a few seconds or less. We are normally unaware of the functioning of our sensory memories, which store information just long enough for it to be retrieved and encoded into short-term memory (Radvansky, 2017).

For instance, look at the next definition in this paragraph and then quickly close your eyes. If you are lucky, a fleeting "photocopy" of the letters will persist. **Iconic** (eye-KON-ick) **memories**—visual sensory images—are typically stored for about a half second (Clarke & Mack, 2015). Similarly, when you hear information, sensory memory stores it for up to 2 seconds as an **echoic memory**, a brief flurry of activity in the auditory system (Cheng & Lin, 2012).

If you are *selectively attending* (focusing on a selected portion of sensory input) to the terms you are studying, they most likely will be retrieved from sensory memory and encoded in short-term memory. Background events, such as a voice on the television announcing a new season of *NFL Football*, will not. However, if you are just looking at the words on the page but not paying attention (maybe you are also watching television), that does not bode well for your exam. As your elementary teacher might have commented, reading is more than just passing your eyes over the page.

Short-Term Memory

Even though you are usually unaware of your sensory memory, you cannot fail to be aware of your short-term memory. Carefully read the definition contained in the next two sentences. **Short-term memory (STM)** holds small amounts of information for short periods of time. We are consciously aware of short-term memories for a dozen seconds or so (Jonides et al., 2008). That's right—what you are aware of right now is in your short-term memory. Back to those definitions you are studying. You pay attention to what you are reading and so become aware of the definitions as they are encoded in STM.

Long-Term Memory

If STM is so short term, how do we remember for longer periods? Information that is important or meaningful is, in turn, retrieved from STM and encoded in **long-term memory (LTM)**, an unlimited capacity storage system that can hold information over lengthy periods of time. LTM contains everything you know about the world—from aardvark to zebra, math to *The Walking Dead*, facts to fantasy. Yet, there appears to be no danger of running out of room. LTM can store nearly limitless amounts of information. In fact, the more you know, the easier it becomes to add new information to memory. This is the reverse of what we would expect if LTM could be "filled up" (Goldstein, 2019). It also is one of many reasons for getting an education.

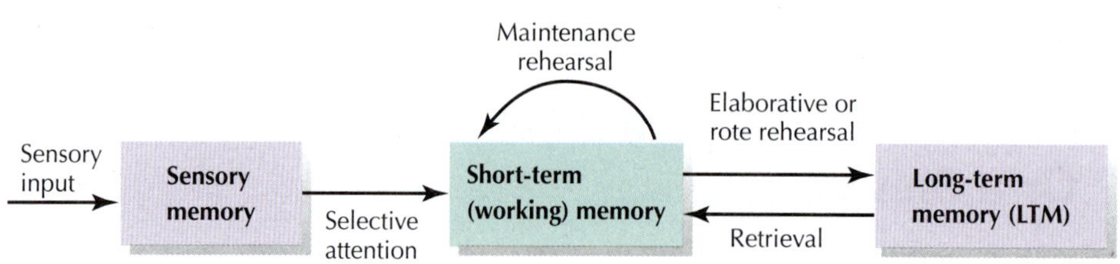

➤ **Figure 32.1**

The Atkinson-Shiffrin model. Successful long-term remembering involves three stages of memory. Sensory memory encodes and stores sensory information for a second or two. Selectively attending to that information encodes small amounts in short-term memory, where it may be processed. Any resulting meaningful information may be encoded in long-term memory, where it may be stored until it is needed, at which time it may be retrieved as needed. It is worth noting that this is a useful, but highly simplified, *model* of memory; it may not be literally true regarding what happens in the brain.

The Relationship Between STM and LTM

Although sensory memory is involved every time we store information, we are most likely to notice STM and LTM. To summarize their connection, picture a small desk (STM) at the front of a huge warehouse full of filing cabinets (LTM). As information enters the warehouse, it is first placed on the desk. Because the desk is small, it must be quickly cleared off to make room for new information. While unimportant items are simply tossed away, meaningful information is placed in the files.

When we want to use knowledge from LTM to answer a question, the information is returned to STM. Or, in our analogy, a folder is retrieved from the files (LTM) and moved to the desk (STM), where it can be used. Now that you have a general picture of memory, it is time to explore STM and LTM in more detail.

Short-Term (Working) Memory—Do You Know the Magic Number?

Learning Outcome 32.2 Describe the features of short-term (or working) memory

How are short-term memories encoded? Short-term memories can be encoded as images but most often they are encoded *phonetically* (by sound), especially when it comes to words and letters (Barry et al., 2011).

When STM combines with other mental processes, it acts like a sort of "mental scratchpad," or **working memory**, in which we do much of our thinking (Chein & Fiez, 2010; Nevo & Breznitz, 2013). Whenever you read a book, do mental arithmetic, put together a puzzle, plan a meal, or follow directions, you are using working memory (Baddeley, 2012; Prime & Jolicoeur, 2010).

To experience your short-term memory at work, answer this question: How many doors are in your house or apartment? To answer a question like this, many people form **mental images**—mental pictures—of each room and count the doorways they visualize (Ganis, 2013; Shorrock & Isaac, 2010).

Stephen Kosslyn, Thomas Ball, and Brian Reiser (1978) provided an interesting example of using images in working memory. Participants first memorized a map like the one shown in ➤ **Figure 32.2*a***. They were then asked to picture a black dot moving from one object, such as one of the trees, to another, such as the hut at the top of the island. Did people really form a working memory image to do this task? It seems that they did. As shown in Figure 32.2*b*, the time that it took to "move" the dot was directly related to actual distances on the map.

Here's another example, this time with sounds: Read the following two numbers out loud and add them together in your head: 1,874 + 3,326. Come on; give it a try. Regardless of how well you did, notice that you had to encode and store the two numbers, likely by the sound of their number names, along with any carries or other intermediate calculations, as you carried out the addition.

Storage and Rehearsal in Short-Term (Working) Memory

For how long is a short-term memory stored? That depends, because you can keep sounds active in short-term memory by repeating them over and over, a process called **maintenance rehearsal** (see Figure 7.1). You have probably used maintenance rehearsal to keep a phone number active in your mind while looking at your cell phone and dialing it. In a sense, rehearsing information (whether silently or out loud) allows you to "hear" it many times, not just once (Jarrold & Hall, 2013).

What if rehearsal is prevented, so a memory cannot be rehearsed? Without maintenance rehearsal, individual memories rapidly *decay*, or fade from STM. This feature of short-term memory prevents our minds from more permanently storing useless names, dates, telephone numbers, and other trivia.

Memory Mental system for receiving, encoding, storing, organizing, altering, and retrieving information.

Encoding (in memory) Converting information into a form to be retained in memory.

Storage (in memory) Holding information in memory for later use.

Retrieval (in memory) Recovery of stored information.

Sensory memory Fleeting storage system for sensory impressions.

Iconic memory A mental image or visual representation.

Echoic memory A brief continuation of sensory activity in the auditory system after a sound is heard.

Short-term memory (STM) Storage system used to hold small amounts of information in conscious awareness for about a dozen seconds.

Long-term memory (LTM) Unlimited capacity storage system that can hold information over lengthy periods of time.

Working memory Another name for *short-term memory*, especially as it is used for thinking and problem solving.

Mental images Mental pictures or visual depictions used in memory and thinking.

Maintenance rehearsal Repeating information over and over to keep it active in short-term memory.

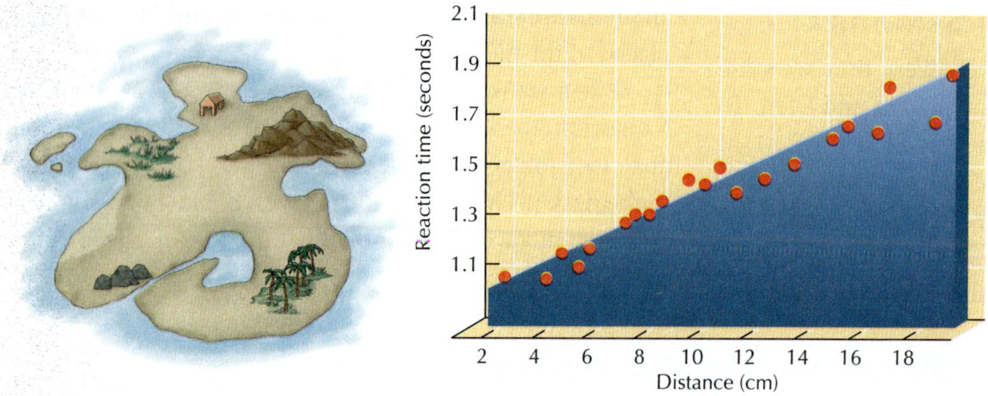

(a) (b)

Figure 32.2

Scanning mental images. (*a*) "Treasure map" similar to the one used by Kosslyn, Ball, and Reiser (1978) to study images in memory. (*b*) This graph shows how long it took participants to move a visualized spot various distances on their mental images of the map. (See text for explanation.)

In one experiment, participants heard meaningless syllables such as "xar," followed by a number such as 67. As soon as participants heard the number, they began counting backward by threes (to prevent them from rehearsing the syllable). After a delay of between 12 and 18 seconds, their memory for the syllables fell to zero (Peterson & Peterson, 1959). That's why, when you are introduced to someone, that person's name can easily slip out of STM. To avoid embarrassment, pay careful attention to the name, rehearse it several times, and try to use it in your next sentence or two, before it fades away (Radvansky, 2017).

You also have likely noticed that STM is very sensitive to *interruption*, or *displacement*. You've probably had something like this happen: A friend gives you a phone number to call, say to order a pizza. As you start to dial, your friend suddenly asks you a question. You answer and return to dialing, only to find that processing the question displaced your memory for the number. Because STM can handle only small amounts of information, it can be difficult to do more than one task at a time (Mercer & McKeown, 2010).

Isn't saying stuff to yourself over and over also a way of studying? It *is* true that the more times a short-term memory is rehearsed, the greater are its chances of being stored in LTM (Goldstein, 2019; refer to Figure 32.1). This is **rote rehearsal (rote learning)**—learning by simple repetition. But rote learning is not a very effective way to study.

Elaborative processing, which makes information more meaningful, is a far better way to form lasting memories. When encoding information for the first time, it is best to elaborate on the meaning of the information, especially by forming links between that information and memories that are already in LTM (Raposo, Han, & Dobbins, 2009). As you read, try to reflect frequently. Ask yourself "why" questions, such as, "Why would that be true?" (Toyota & Kikuchi, 2005). Also, try to relate new ideas to your own experiences and knowledge (Karpicke & Smith, 2012). If you do not already recognize this advice, consider (re?)reading Module 1 if only to elaborate on your processing of the idea of elaborative processing.

The Capacity of Short-Term (Working) Memory

How much information can be held in short-term memory? It depends on whether the information is comprised of sounds, mental images, or a combination of the two. Read the following numbers once, and then close this book and write down as many as you can in the correct order.

8 5 1 7 4 9 3

This is called a *digit-span* test—a measure of attention and short-term memory for sounds (Bowden et al., 2013). Most adults can correctly repeat about seven digits. Now try to memorize the following list, again reading it only once.

7 1 8 3 5 4 2 9 1 6 3 4

This series was likely beyond your short-term memory capacity. Psychologist George Miller (1920–2012) found that short-term memory for sounds is limited to the "magic number" of seven (plus or minus two) **information bits** (Miller, 1956). A bit is a single meaningful "piece" of information, such as a digit. It is as if short-term memory has seven "slots" or "bins" into which separate sounds can be placed. A few people can remember up to nine sounds, and for some types of information, five bits is the limit.

When all of the "slots" in STM are filled, there is no room for new information. Picture how this works at a party: Let's say your hostess begins introducing everyone who is there,

"Chun, Dasia, Sandra, Roseanna, Cholik, Shawn, Kyrene ..." *Stop,* you think to yourself. But she continues, "Nelia, Jay, Frank, Patty, Amit, Ricky." The hostess leaves, satisfied that you have met everyone. You spend the evening talking with Chun, Dasia, and Ricky, the only people whose names you remember! Thus, an *average* of seven information sounds can be stored in short-term memory (Radvansky, 2017).

Chunking Before we continue, try your short-term memory again, this time on letters. Read the following letters once, and then look away and try to write them down in the proper order.

T V I B M U S N Y M C A

Notice that there are 12 letters, or "bits" of information. If you studied the letters one at a time, this should be beyond the seven-item limit of STM. However, you may have noticed that some of the letters can be organized, or *chunked,* together. For example, you may have noticed that NY is the abbreviation for New York. If so, the two bits N and Y became one chunk. **Chunking**, then, is the process of grouping similar or meaningful information together.

Does chunking make a difference? A simple form of elaborative encoding, chunking *recodes* (reorganizes) information into units that are already in LTM. In a classic experiment that used lists like this one, people remembered best when the letters were read as familiar meaningful chunks: TV, IBM, USN, YMCA (Bower & Springston, 1970). If you recoded the letters this way, you organized them into four *chunks* of information and probably remembered the entire list. If you didn't, go back and try it again; you'll notice a big difference.

Chunking suggests that STM holds about five to seven of whatever units we are using. A single chunk could be made up of numbers, letters, words, phrases, or familiar sentences. Picture STM as a small desk again. Through chunking, we combine several items into one "stack" of information. This allows us to place seven stacks on the desk, whereas before there was room for only seven separate items.

The clear message is that creating information chunks is the key to making good use of your short-term memory (Jones, 2012). This means, for example, that it is well worthwhile to find or create meaningful chunks. While you are studying, try to find ways to link two, three, or more separate facts or ideas into larger chunks, and your short-term memory will improve. In fact, some psychologists believe that STM may actually hold only four items, unless some chunking has occurred (Jonides et al., 2008; Mathy & Feldman, 2012).

The Multimedia Principle *How about short-term memory for images?* Unlike the digit span test, there is, as yet, no standard way of measuring short-term memory span for mental images. According to one estimate, however, the average drops to about three to four bits at one time if images, rather than sounds, are stored (Taylor et al., 2017).

What we do know, however, is that people process words and mental images together better than they do words alone. This is the **multimedia principle** (Overson, 2014). When it comes to short-term memory, this means that adding mental images to short-term memory interferes less with memory for words already in STM than adding more words. If the friend who gave you the phone number of the pizza joint grinned at you and gave you a thumbs up signal instead of asking you a question as you dialed, chances are your memory for the phone number would not suffer. (See Module 36 to see how the multimedia principle can be put to good use designing memorable presentations.)

Long-Term Memory—A Blast from the Past

Learning Outcome 32.3 Describe the features of long-term memory

Are long-term memories also encoded as images or sounds? They can be. But long-term memories are typically encoded on the basis of *meaning.* For example, try to memorize this story:

> He looked outside from cramped quarters. Many unknown objects moved swiftly in blackness. Fearless companions manipulated buttons while reading complex patterns. Flat familiar homeland resembled a rubber ball. Everyone knew that only lifeless things would be found among cold mountains surrounding barren valleys. But important papers anxiously awaited their arrival for no man had ever made such big news. (Adapted from Dooling & Lachman, 1971.)

Rote rehearsal (rote learning) Learning by simple repetition.

Elaborative processing Making memories more meaningful through processing that encodes links between new information and existing memories and knowledge, either at the time of the original encoding or on subsequent retrievals.

Information bits Meaningful units of information, such as numbers, letters, words, or phrases.

Chunking Process of grouping similar or meaningful information together.

Multimedia principle The idea that people process words and mental images together better than they do words alone.

This odd story emphasizes the impact that meaning has on memory encoding. You can, of course, memorize the words without fully understanding their meaning. But people given the title of the story find it much more meaningful, and memorable, than those not given a title. See if the title helps you as much as it did them: "The First Space Trip to the Moon." In the "cramped quarters," the rest of the crew is at the controls of the space ship. The "rubber ball" is the appearance of Earth from space and the "important papers" are the newspapers waiting to report on the moon landing.

Back to your psychology exam: If you make an error in LTM, it probably will be related to meaning. For example, if you are trying to recall the phrase *test anxiety*, you are more likely to mistakenly write down *test nervousness* or *test worry* than *text anxiety* or *tent anxiety*.

Elaborative encoding offers an important way to gain meaning, by linking information currently in STM to knowledge already stored in LTM. This makes it easier to encode in LTM and, hence, remember. For example, if you can relate the definition of *test anxiety* to a memory of a time when you or a friend was nervous about taking a test, you are more likely to remember the definition.

Encoding and Culture

Culture also affects the encoding of long-term memories (Ross & Wang, 2010). For example, American culture emphasizes individuals, whereas Chinese culture emphasizes membership in groups. In one study, European-American and Chinese adults were asked to recall 20 memories from any time in their lives. As expected, American memories tended to be self-centered: Most people remembered surprising events and what they did during the events. Chinese adults, in contrast, remembered important social or historical events and their own interactions with family members, friends, and others (Wang & Conway, 2004). Thus, in the United States, personal memories tend to be about "me"; in China they tend to be about "us" (Wang, 2013).

Now that my understanding of the definitions has been encoded in LTM, all I have to do is store them until the exam, right? While you do have to retain your understanding in LTM, don't forget that, at the exam, you must be able to retrieve those definitions if necessary. Tune in later in this chapter for more on retrieval from LTM. For now, let's get back to LTM storage.

Storage in Long-Term Memory

An electrode touched the patient's brain. Immediately, she said, "Yes, sir, I think I heard a mother calling her little boy somewhere. It seemed to be something happening years ago.

After going for a walk in nature, could you remember the locations, appearances, and names of all of the plants you saw along the way? Unless you are a botanist, doing so would be quite a feat of memory. However, for indigenous peoples, such as this Piaroa Indian shaman, from Venezuela, it would be easier. Plants are very important to indigenous peoples as sources of food and medicine (Kimmerer, 2013). Since a shaman's power is strongly influenced by his knowledge of plants, he is prepared to encode and store information about plants and their uses that would be difficult for most other people to remember.

It was somebody in the neighborhood in which I live." A short time later, the electrode was applied to the same spot. Again the patient said, "Yes, I hear the same familiar sounds. It seems to be a woman calling, the same lady" (Penfield, 1958). A woman made these statements while she was undergoing brain surgery. The brain has no pain receptors, so the patient was awake while her brain was electrically stimulated (➤ **Figure 32.3**). When activated, some brain areas seemed to produce vivid memories of long-forgotten events (Jacobs, Lega, & Anderson, 2012).

Results such as those described led neurosurgeon Wilder Penfield to propose that the brain records the past like a "strip of movie film, complete with sound track" (Penfield,

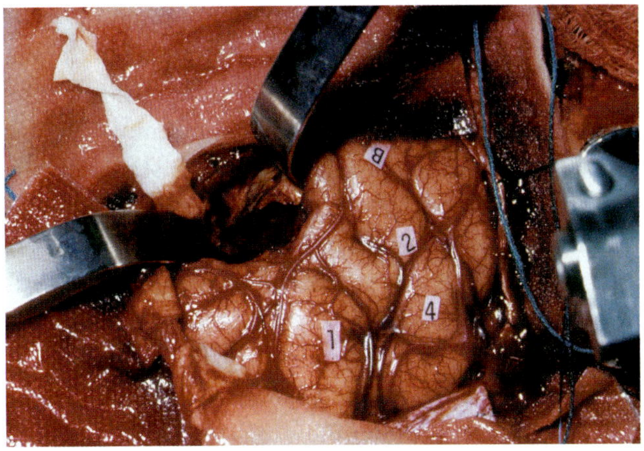

Figure 32.3

Exposed cerebral cortex of a patient undergoing brain surgery. While operating on the brains of wide-awake patients, Wilder Penfield would sometimes deliver a mild electric "shock" to the surface of the exposed cortex. In response, patients would often experience vivid memories. A critical evaluation of such reports suggests that they are more like dreams than memories. This fact raises questions about claims that long-term memories are permanent.

1957). However, as you already know, this is an exaggeration because many events never get past sensory or short-term memory. Also, most reports of memory-like experiences resemble dreams more than memories, and many are clearly imaginary. Memory experts now believe that, except for a few rare individuals, long-term memories are only relatively permanent (Goldstein, 2019).

Try It Yourself: How's Your Memory? To better appreciate the next topic, read through this list of words once and then continue reading:

bed dream blanket doze pillow nap
snore mattress alarm clock rest slumber
nod sheet bunk cot cradle groggy

False Memories

There's another reason to doubt that all our experiences are permanently recorded. Although elaborative processing is helpful when you're making meaningful connections between new information and what you already know, it also can lead to *memories* of things that never happened (Jou & Flores, 2013). Gaps in memory, which are common, may be filled in by logic, guessing, or new information (Schacter, 2012). The result is often the storage of new long-term memories as older memories might be revised or even lost (Sternberg, 2017).

To illustrate this point, Elizabeth Loftus and John Palmer (1974) showed people a filmed automobile accident. Afterward, some participants were asked to estimate how fast the cars were going when they "smashed" into one another. For others, the words "bumped," "contacted," or "hit" replaced "smashed." One week later, each person was asked, "Did you see any broken glass?" Those asked earlier about the cars that "smashed" into one another were more likely to say yes, even though no broken glass was shown in the film. The new information ("smashed") was incorporated into the original memories, elaborating them and producing a **false memory**. Such "memories" can seem accurate, but they never happened (such as remembering broken glass at an accident when there was none) (Loftus, 2003; Weinstein & Shanks, 2010).

In another study, people who had visited a Disney resort were shown several fake ads for Disney that featured Bugs Bunny. Later, about 16 percent of the people who saw these fake ads claimed that they had met Bugs at Disneyland. This is impossible, of course, because Bugs Bunny is a Warner Brothers character who would never show his face at Disneyland (Braun, Ellis, & Loftus, 2002).

Try It Yourself: Old or New? Now, without looking back to the list of words you read a few minutes ago, see if you can tell which of the following are "old" words (items from the list you read) and which are "new" words (items that weren't on the list). Mark each of the following words as old or new:

sofa sleep lamp kitchen

Contrary to what you may think you "remembered," all of the listed words are "new." None was on the original list! If you thought you "remembered" that "sleep" was on the original list, you elaborated a false memory. The word *sleep* is associated with most of the words on the original list, which creates a strong impression that you saw it before (Roediger & McDermott, 1995; Schacter, 2012).

As the preceding examples show, thoughts, inferences, and mental associations may be mistaken for true memories (Scoboria et al., 2012). False memories are a common problem in police work. For example, a witness may select a photo of a suspect from police files or see a photo in the news. Later, the witness identifies the suspect in a lineup or in court. Did the witness really remember the suspect from the scene of the crime? Or was that memory distorted by later viewing the photograph?

False memory A memory that can seem accurate but is not.

Does new information always "overwrite" existing memories? Sometimes a new memory is merely stored alongside a similar but older memory. In this case, the two memories can potentially be confused. This can make us vulnerable to **source confusion**, which occurs when the origins of a memory are misremembered (Fandakova, Shing, & Lindenberger, 2012; Rosa & Gutchess, 2011). For example, a witness to a crime might inappropriately "remember" a face when they accidentally retrieve the *wrong* memory (Ruva, McEvoy, & Bryant, 2007).

One famous example involved memory expert Donald Thomson. After appearing live on Australian television, he was accused of rape. It turns out that the victim was watching him on television when the actual rapist broke into her apartment (Schacter, 1996). She correctly remembered Thomson's face, but attributed it to the wrong *source*. Many tragic cases of mistaken identity occur this way.

To summarize, forming and using long-term memories is an active, creative, highly personal process. Our memories are colored by emotions, judgments, and quirks of personality. If you and a friend were joined at the hip and you went through life side by side, you would still have different memories. What we remember depends on what we pay attention to, what we regard as meaningful or important, how we elaborate our memory, and what we feel strongly about.

Organizing Memories

Long-term memory stores huge amounts of information during a lifetime. How are we able to quickly find specific memories? The answer is that each person's "memory index" is highly organized.

Eyewitness memories are notoriously inaccurate. By the time that witnesses are asked to testify in court, information they learned after an incident may blend into their original memories.

Does that mean that information is arranged alphabetically, as in a dictionary? Not usually. Information in LTM may be arranged according to rules, images, categories, symbols, similarity, formal meaning, or personal meaning (Baddeley, Eysenck, & Anderson, 2009). Psychologists believe that a **network model** best explains the *structure*, or organization, of memories. *Memory structure* refers to the pattern of associations among items of information. According to this view, LTM is organized as a network of linked memories.

With ➤ **Figure 32.4** in mind, assume that Erica was given two statements to which she must quickly answer yes or no: (1) *Classical conditioning was developed by Pavlov.* (2) *Classical conditioning is due to experience.* Which will she answer more quickly? Erica most likely will say yes to the statement *Classical conditioning was developed by Pavlov* faster (Collins & Quillian, 1969).

Why should this be so? When ideas are "farther" apart, it takes a longer chain of associations to connect them. The more two items are separated, the longer it takes to answer. In terms of information links, "classical conditioning" is probably "closer" to "developed by Pavlov" in Erica's "memory file." The phrases "classical conditioning" and "is due to experience" are farther apart. Remember that this has nothing to do with alphabetical order. We are talking about a system of linked meanings.

Redintegration

Memory networks also help explain a common experience: Imagine finding a picture taken on your sixth birthday. The photo serves as a **retrieval cue**, triggering the retrieval of memories of that day. Then, one memory links to another associated memory, which links to another, and another. Soon you have triggered a stream of seemingly forgotten details as link after link is activated. This process is called **redintegration** (reh-DIN-tuh-GRAY-shun).

The key idea in redintegration is that one retrieved memory serves as a retrieval cue to trigger another. As a result, an entire past experience may be reconstructed from one small recollection. Many people find that redintegration can be touched off by distinctive odors from the past—from a farm visited in childhood, Grandma's kitchen, the seashore, the perfume or aftershave of a former lover, and so on (Willander & Larsson, 2006).

The Cognitive Interview Redintegration has even been used to help improve the memory of witnesses. Imagine you are a forensic psychologist investigating a crime. Unfortunately, your witness can't remember much of what happened. What can you do to help?

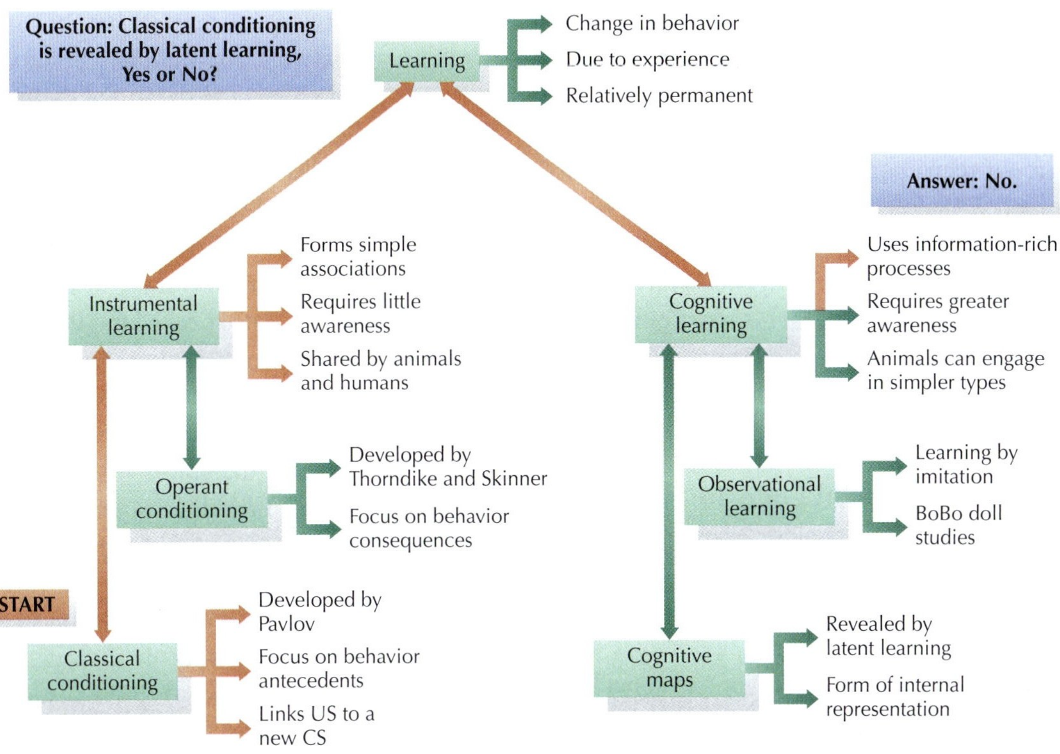

Figure 32.4

A network model of student learning. Erica, a first-year psychology major, has just finished studying for an exam on conditioning and learning. This figure presents a hypothetical network model of a part of what she just learned. Small networks of ideas such as this are probably organized into larger and larger units and higher levels of meaning.

How about hypnosis? In one case, 26 children were abducted from a school bus and held captive for ransom. Under hypnosis, the bus driver recalled the license plate number of the kidnappers' van. This memory helped break the case. Such successes seem to imply that hypnosis can improve memory. But does it?

Research has shown that hypnosis increases false memories more than it reveals true ones. In one experiment, 80 percent of the new memories produced by hypnotized subjects were *incorrect* (Dywan & Bowers, 1983). This is in part because a hypnotized person is more likely than normal to use imagination to fill in gaps in memory. Also, if a questioner asks misleading or suggestive questions, hypnotized persons tend to elaborate the questioner's information into their memories (Scoboria et al., 2002). To make matters worse, even when a memory is totally false, the hypnotized person's confidence in it can be unshakable (Burgess & Kirsch, 1999).

Thus, hypnosis sometimes uncovers more information, as it did with the bus driver (Wester & Hammond, 2011). However, in the absence of corroborating evidence, there is no sure way to tell which memories are false and which are true (Mazzoni, Heap, & Scoboria, 2010).

Is there a better way to improve eyewitness memory? To help police detectives, R. Edward Geiselman and Ron Fisher created the **cognitive interview**, a technique that uses *redintegration* to improve the memory of eyewitnesses (Fisher & Geiselman, 1987; Ginet, Py, & Colomb, 2014). The key to this approach is recreating the crime scene. Witnesses revisit the scene in their imaginations or in person. That way, aspects of the crime scene, such as sounds, smells, and objects, provide helpful retrieval cues (stimuli associated with a memory). Back in the context of the crime, the witness is encouraged to recall events in different orders and from

Source confusion (in memory) Occurs when the origins of a memory are misremembered.

Network model (of memory) A model of memory that views it as an organized system of linked information.

Retrieval cue Any information that can prompt or trigger the retrieval of particular memories. Retrieval cues usually enhance memory.

Redintegration Process by which memories are reconstructed or expanded by starting with one memory and then following chains of association to other, related memories.

Cognitive interview Use of various cues and strategies to improve the memory of eyewitnesses.

different viewpoints. Every new memory, no matter how trivial it may seem, can serve as a cue to trigger the retrieval of yet more memories.

When used properly, the cognitive interview produces 35 percent more correct information than standard questioning (Centofanti & Reece, 2006; Geiselman et al., 1986). This improvement comes without adding to the number of false memories elicited, as occurs with hypnosis (Holliday et al., 2012). The result is a procedure that is more effective in actual police work, even across cultures (Memon, Meissner, & Fraser, 2010; Stein & Memon, 2006).

From Encoding to Retrieval in Long-Term Memory

Let's get back to passing that psychology exam. On one recent exam, Jerry, another introductory psychology student, studied using rote learning, whereas Erica made extensive use of elaborative processing. ➤ **Figure 32.5** shows what their memory networks might look like for the concept of reinforcement (Module 28).

Because Jerry spent most of his time in rote rehearsal, his memory network for the concept of reinforcement is quite sparse. He managed to get the definition right. Also, during rote learning, it occurred to him that extra soldiers joining a battle also were reinforcements. In contrast, while studying, Erica asked herself how reinforcement and punishment differ and what were the kinds of reinforcement (and punishment); she also tried to think of personal examples. In addition, she checked out the difference between operant and respondent learning.

That means Erica has a better chance of doing well on the psychology exam, right? Much better. To begin, Jerry used rote learning, so his memories will be weaker because he cannot be as sure as Erica that he understood the concept of reinforcement. Also, suppose that Jerry cannot directly retrieve the definition of reinforcement during his exam. His only other hope is to remember soldiers so that redintegration might pop up the needed definition.

In sharp contrast, for Erica to successfully encode her more elaborated network, she *had* to understand the

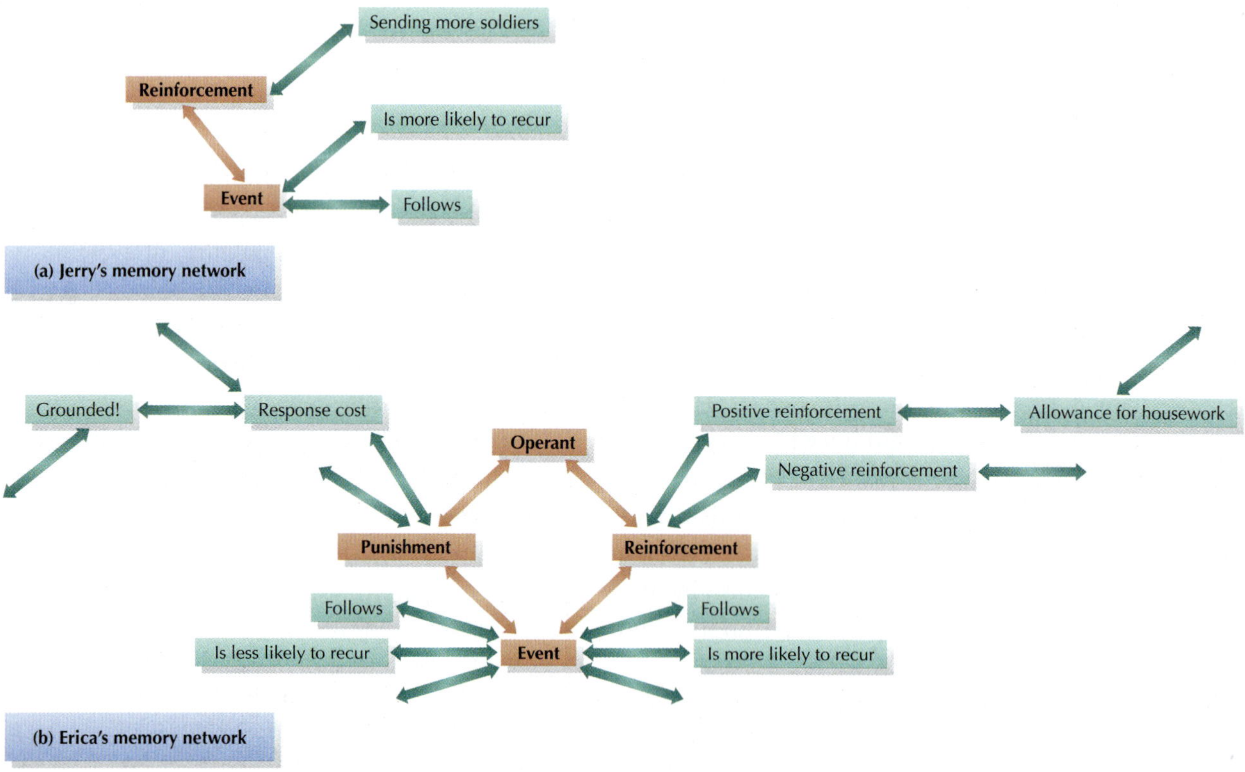

➤ **Figure 32.5**

Hypothetical networks of two students' concepts of reinforcement. Jerry is in trouble, while Erica is not. Only part of her more elaborate network is shown here. See if you can connect this fragment of Erica's network to her other fragment, shown in Figure 32.3.

concept of reinforcement. Hence, she is more likely than Jerry to directly retrieve that information if she needs it. On the off chance that Erica does not immediately remember the needed definition, she has many retrieval cues to help her. Remembering punishment, or an example of reinforcement, or even the time she got grounded, could well trigger redintegration of "reinforcement."

In summary, more elaborative processing results in more elaborate memory networks and, hence, more retrieval cues to help with redintegration. Time spent in elaborative processing is time well spent, at least if you want to do well on exams.

Types of Long-Term Memory

A curious thing happens to many people who develop amnesia. Amnesic patients may be unable to remember a telephone number, an address, or a person's name. Yet, the same patients can learn to solve complex puzzles in a normal amount of time (Cavaco et al., 2004; ➤ **Figure 32.6**). These and other observations have led many psychologists to conclude that long-term memories fall into at least two categories (Lum & Bleses, 2012). One is called *procedural memory* (or skill memory). The other is *declarative memory* (sometimes called fact memory).

Procedural Memory **Procedural memory** holds long-term memories for how to do things that require motor or performance skills, such as typing, driving, or swinging a golf club. Such memories can be fully expressed only as actions (or know-how). It is likely that skill memories are stored in "lower" brain areas, especially the basal ganglia and the cerebellum. They represent the more basic "automatic" elements of conditioning, learning, and memory (Freberg, 2021; Lum & Bleses, 2012).

Declarative Memory **Declarative memory** stores specific factual information, such as names, faces, words, dates, and ideas. Declarative memories are expressed as words or symbols. For example, knowing that *Apple* is both a fruit and a computer company is a declarative memory. Declarative memory can be further divided into *semantic memory* and *episodic memory* (Irish & Piguet, 2013; Tulving, 2002).

Semantic Memory Much of our basic factual knowledge about the world is almost totally immune to forgetting. The names of objects, the days of the week or months of the year, simple math skills, the seasons, words and language, and other general facts are all quite lasting. Such impersonal knowledge makes up a part of declarative memory called **semantic memory**, which serves as a mental dictionary or encyclopedia of basic knowledge.

Episodic Memory Semantic memory has no connection to times or places. It would be rare, for instance, to remember when and where you first learned the names of the seasons. In contrast, **episodic memory** (ep-ih-SOD-ik) is a subpart of declarative memory that stores an "autobiographical" record of personal experiences. It stores life events (or episodes) day after day, year after year. Can you remember your seventh birthday? Your first date? What you did yesterday? All are episodic memories, about the "what," "where," and "when" of our lives. More than simply storing information, they allow us to mentally travel back in time and

➤ **Figure 32.6**

The Tower of Hanoi puzzle. All the disks must be moved to the right-hand post without ever placing a larger disk on a smaller one. Only one disk may be moved at a time, and a disk must always be moved from one post to another (it cannot be held aside). An amnesic patient learned to solve the puzzle in 31 moves, the minimum possible. Even so, each time he began, he protested that he did not remember ever solving the puzzle before and that he did not know how to begin. Evidence such as this suggests that memories for skills are distinct from memories for facts.

Procedural memory That part of long-term memory for how to do things that require motor or performance skills.

Declarative memory That part of long-term memory containing specific factual information.

Semantic memory A subpart of declarative memory that records impersonal knowledge about the world.

Episodic memory A subpart of declarative memory that records personal experiences that are linked with specific times and places.

reexperience events (Moscovitch et al., 2016; Philippe, Koestner, & Lekes, 2013).

Are episodic memories as lasting as semantic memories? Either type of memory can last indefinitely. However, unless episodic memories are important, they are easily forgotten. In fact, it is the forgetting of episodic information that results in the formation of semantic memories. At first, you remembered when and where you were when you learned the names of the seasons. ("Mommy, Mommy, guess what I learned in preschool today!") Over time, you forgot the episodic details, but you will likely remember the names for the rest of your life.

How Many Types of Long-Term Memory Are There? It is likely that three types of long-term memories exist: procedural memory and two types of declarative memory, semantic and episodic (➤ **Figure 32.7**).

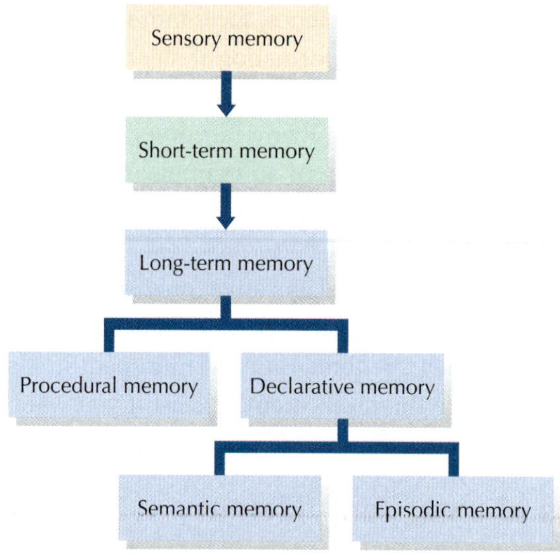

➤ **Figure 32.7**

Types of memory. In the model shown, long-term memory is divided into procedural memory (learned actions and skills) and declarative memory (stored facts). Declarative memories can be either semantic (impersonal knowledge) or episodic (personal experiences associated with specific times and places).

MODULE 32 Memory Systems—Learning Outcomes Revisited

32.1 Explain the workings of the Atkinson-Shiffrin model of memory

Memory is an active system that encodes, stores, and retrieves information. The Atkinson-Shiffrin model of memory includes three stages of memory (sensory memory, short-term or working memory, and long-term memory) that hold information for increasingly longer periods. Sensory memories are encoded as iconic memories or echoic memories. Selective attention determines what information moves from sensory memory, which is exact but very brief, on to STM. While we are normally unaware of sensory memory, we are conscious of the contents of short-term memory. Long-term memories are best encoded by meaning.

32.2 Describe the features of short-term (or working) memory

Short-term memories tend to be encoded by sound, are sensitive to interruption or displacement, and, although brief, can be prolonged through maintenance rehearsal. When STM combines with other mental processes, it acts like a sort of "mental scratchpad," or working memory. STM has a capacity of about five to seven bits of sound information, but this limit can be extended by chunking. For transferring information to LTM, rote rehearsal is less effective than elaborative processing.

32.3 Describe the features of long-term memory

Long-term memories are relatively permanent. LTM seems to have an almost unlimited storage capacity and is organized into memory networks. LTM contains procedural (skill) and declarative (fact) memories. Declarative memories can be semantic or episodic. Remembering information stored in LTM is an active process. In redintegration, memories being retrieved are reconstructed as one bit of information leads to others, which then serve as cues for further recall.

Reflective Practice

Content Check

Match: A. Sensory memory B. STM C. LTM

1. _____ Information tends to be stored phonetically
2. _____ Holds information for a few seconds or less
3. _____ Stores an iconic memory or echoic memory

4. ______ Relatively permanent, unlimited capacity
5. ______ Selective attention determines its contents
6. Elaborative processing is often responsible for creating false memories. T or F?

Skill Check

Think Critically

7. How is long-term memory helping you read this sentence?

Self-Reflect

In the United States, telephone numbers are divided into an area code (three digits) and a seven-digit number that is divided into three digits plus four more. Can you relate this practice to STM chunking? Think about how you've used your memory in the last hour. Can you identify an example of each of the following: a procedural memory, a declarative memory, a semantic memory, and an episodic memory?

ANSWERS

1. B 2. A 3. A 4. C 5. B 6. T 7. If your understanding of the meanings of the words wasn't already stored in LTM, could you read at all?

MODULE

33 Memory

Measuring Memory

On the Tip of Your Tongue?

Janelle fumed as the examination ended. She had studied hard and expected to do well. However, she was frustrated when she got to a question worth a lot of marks. She *knew* she knew the answer. It tortured her for the remainder of the exam.

Have you, too, experienced this? You read an exam question and the answer is immediately on the tip of your tongue. Yet, it doesn't come to mind. You know how this ends, right? As soon as you leave the exam, the answer "pops" into your head. (Professor, I *knew* my stuff!)

Whether you "remember" depends on how you are tested. For example, police lineups use *recognition* memory. However, unless great care is taken, false identifications are still possible. Is the lineup pictured here fair? Let's find out more about the ins and outs of measuring memory.

Rich Legg/E+/Getty Images

~LEARNING OUTCOMES~

After reading this module you should be able to:

33.1 Describe how memory is measured

Measuring Memory—The Answer Is on the Tip of My Tongue

Learning Outcome 33.1 Describe how memory is measured

You either remember something or you don't, right? Wrong. Partial memories are common, like Janelle's **tip-of-the-tongue (TOT) state**. This is the feeling that a memory is **available**—stored in your memory—and yet you cannot **access**—locate or retrieve—the complete memory (Brown, 2012).

In a classic TOT study, university students read the definitions of words such as *sextant*, *sampan*, and *ambergris*. Students who "drew a blank" and couldn't name a defined word were asked to give any other information they could. Often, they could guess the first and last letter and the number of syllables of the word they were seeking. They also gave words that sounded like or meant the same thing as the defined word (Brown & McNeill, 1966).

Closely related to the TOT state is the fact that people can often tell beforehand if they are likely to remember something. This is called the *feeling of knowing* (Thomas, Bulevich, & Dubois, 2011; Widner, Otani, & Winkelman, 2005). Feeling-of-knowing reactions are easy to observe on television game shows, where they occur just before contestants are allowed to answer.

Déjà vu, the feeling that you have already experienced a situation that you are experiencing for the first time, may be

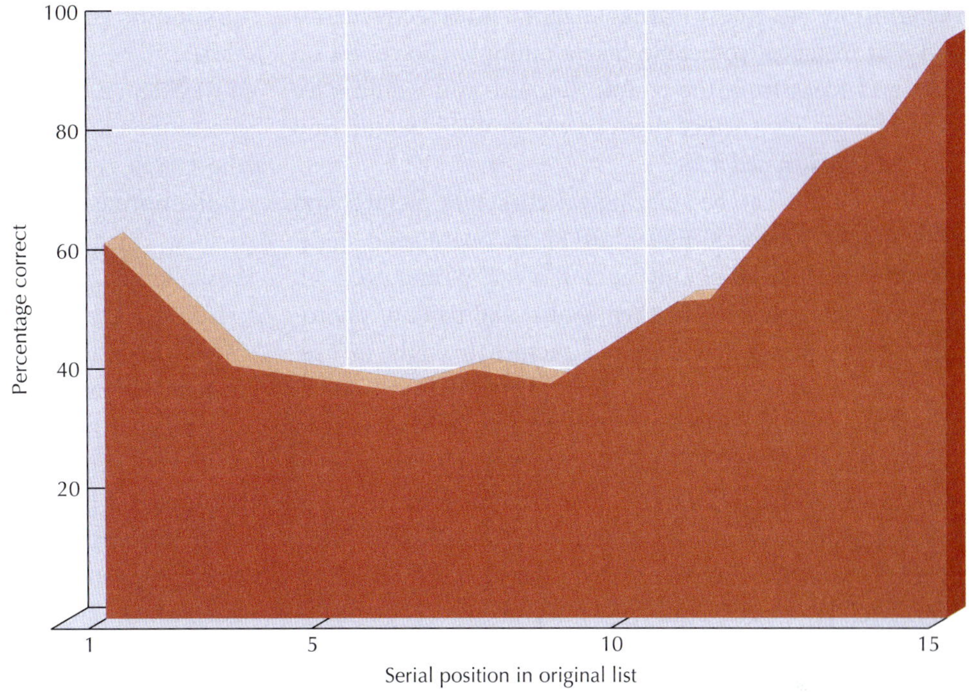

➤ **Figure 33.1**

The serial position effect. The graph shows the percentage of participants correctly recalling each item in a 15-item list. Recall is best for the first and last items. (Data from Craik, 1970.)

another example of partial memory (Brown & Marsh, 2010). If a new experience triggers vague memories of a past experience, without yielding *any* details at all, you might be left saying to yourself, "I feel like I've seen it before." The new experience seems familiar even though the older memory is too weak to rise to the level of awareness.

Because memory is not an all-or-nothing event, it can be measured in several ways. Three commonly used methods of measuring memory are *recall*, *recognition*, and *relearning*. Let's see how they differ.

Recalling Information

What is the name of your favorite song? Who won the last Super Bowl? Who wrote *Catcher in the Rye*? If you can answer these questions, you are using **recall**, a direct retrieval of facts or information with a minimum of external cues. Tests of recall often require *verbatim* (word-for-word) memory. If you study a poem until you can recite it without looking at it, you are recalling it. If you complete a fill-in-the-blank question, you are using recall. When you answer an essay question by providing facts and ideas, you also are using recall, even though you didn't learn your essay verbatim.

The order in which information is memorized has an interesting effect on recall. To experience it, try to memorize the following list, reading it only once:

bread, apples, soda, ham, cookies, rice,
lettuce, beets, mustard, cheese, oranges,
ice cream, crackers, flour, eggs

If you are like most people, it will be hardest for you to recall items from the middle of the list. ➤ **Figure 33.1** shows the results of a similar test. Notice that most errors occur with middle items of an ordered list. This is the **serial position effect** (Bonk & Healy, 2010; Gavett & Horwitz, 2012). You can remember the last items on a list because they are still in STM (short-term memory). The first items also are remembered well because they entered an "empty" STM. This allows you to rehearse the items so that they move into long-term memory. The middle items are neither held in short-term memory nor moved to long-term memory, so they are often lost.

Recognizing Information

Try to write down everything that you can remember from a class you took last year. If you actually did this, you might conclude that you had learned very little. However, a more sensitive test based on recognition could be used. In

Tip-of-the-tongue (TOT) state The feeling that a memory is available but not quite retrievable.

Availability (in memory) Memories currently stored in memory are available.

Accessibility (in memory) Memories currently stored in memory that can be retrieved when necessary are both available and accessible.

Recall Retrieval of information with a minimum of external cues.

Serial position effect When remembering an ordered list, the tendency to make the most errors with middle items.

recognition, previously learned material is correctly identified. For instance, you could take a multiple-choice test on facts and ideas from the course. Because you would have to recognize only correct answers, you probably would find that you had learned a lot.

Recognition can be amazingly accurate for pictures and photographs (Oates & Reder, 2011). In one classic study, people viewed 2,560 photographs at a rate of one every 10 seconds. Each person was then shown 280 pairs of photographs. Each pair included an "old" picture (from the first set of photos) and a similar "new" image. Participants could tell 85 to 95 percent of the time which photograph they had seen before (Haber, 1970). This finding may explain why we rarely need to see our friends' vacation photos more than once.

Recognition is usually superior to recall. That's why people so often say, "I may forget a name, but I never forget a face." (You can't recall the name but can recognize the face.) That's also why police departments use photographs or a lineup to identify criminal suspects. Witnesses who disagree when they try to recall a suspect's height, weight, age, or eye color often agree completely when they merely need to recognize the person.

Is recognition always superior? It depends greatly on the kind of *distractors* used (Flowe & Ebbese, 2007). Distractors are false items included with an item to be recognized. If distractors are very similar to the correct item, memory may be poor. A reverse problem occurs when only one choice looks like it could be correct. This can produce a *false positive*, or false sense of recognition (Clark, Rush, & Moreland, 2013).

Many hundreds of people have been put in jail on the basis of mistaken eyewitness memories (Lampinen, Neuschatz, & Cling, 2012; Wade, Green, & Nash, 2010). In some instances, witnesses have described a criminal as black, tall, or young. Then a police lineup was held in which a suspect was the only African American among whites, the only tall suspect, or the only young person. In such cases, a false identification is very likely (Steblay, 2013). To avoid tragic mistakes, it's better to have *all* the distractors look like the person witnesses described. Also, to reduce false positives, witnesses should be warned that the culprit *might not be present*. It may also be better to show witnesses one photo at a time (a sequential lineup). For each photo, the witness must decide whether the person is the culprit before another photo is shown (Mickes, Flowe, & Wixted, 2012; Wells & Olsen, 2003).

Relearning Information

In a classic experiment, a psychologist read a short passage in Greek to his son every day when the boy was between 15 months and 3 years of age. At age 8, the boy was tested to see if he remembered the Greek passage. He showed no evidence of recall or recognition. Had the psychologist stopped, he might have concluded that no memory of the Greek remained. However, the child was then asked to memorize the original passage and others of equal difficulty. This time, his earlier learning became evident. The boy memorized the passage he had heard in childhood 25 percent faster than the others (Burtt, 1941). As this experiment suggests, **relearning** is typically the most sensitive measure of memory.

When a person is tested by relearning, how do we know a memory still exists? As with the boy described, relearning is measured by a *savings score* (the amount of time saved when relearning information). Let's say that it takes you 1 hour to memorize all the names in a telephone book. (It's a small town.) Two years later, you relearn them in 45 minutes. Because you "saved" 15 minutes, your savings score would be 25 percent (15 divided by 60 times 100). Savings of this type are a good reason for studying a wide range of subjects. It may seem that learning algebra, history, or a foreign language is wasted if you don't use the knowledge immediately. But when you do need such information, you will be able to relearn it quickly.

Explicit and Implicit Memories

Who were the last three presidents of the United States? What did you have for breakfast today? What is the title of Adele's latest album? Explicit memory is used in answering each of these questions. An **explicit memory** is a past experience that is consciously brought to mind. Recall, recognition, and the tests that you take in school rely on explicit memories.

In contrast, an **implicit memory** lies outside awareness (Gopie, Craik, & Hasher, 2011). That is, we are not aware that a memory exists. For example, if you know how to type, it is apparent that you know where the letters are on the keyboard. But how many typists could correctly label blank keys in a drawing of a keyboard? Many people find that they cannot directly remember such information, even though they "know" it. Nevertheless, implicit memories—such as unconsciously knowing where the letters are on a keyboard—greatly influence our behavior (Voss, Lucas, & Paller, 2012).

Priming *How is it possible to objectively show that a memory exists outside subjective awareness?* Psychologists first noticed implicit memory while studying memory loss caused by brain injuries. Let's say, for example, that a patient

Can you label the letter keys on this blank keyboard? If you can, you probably used implicit memory to do it.

is shown a list of common words, such as *chair*, *tree*, *lamp*, *table*, and so on. Later, the patient fails to recall any words from the list.

Now, instead of asking the patient to explicitly recall the list, we could "prime" his memory by giving him the first two letters of each word. "Just say whatever word comes to mind that begins with these letters," we tell him. Of course, many words could be made from each pair of letters. For example, the first item (from "chair") would be the letters *ch*. The patient could say "child," "chalk," "chain," "check," or many other words. Instead, he says "chair," a word from the original list. The patient is not aware that he is remembering the list, but as he gives a word for each letter pair, almost all are from the list. Apparently, the letters **primed** (activated) hidden memories, which then influenced his answers.

Similar effects have been found for people with normal memories. As the preceding example implies, implicit memories are often revealed by giving a person limited cues, such as the first letter of words or partial drawings of objects. Typically, the person believes that he or she is just saying whatever comes to mind. Nevertheless, information previously seen or heard affects his or her answers (Lavigne et al., 2012).

Recognition Ability to correctly identify previously learned information.

Relearning Learning again something that was previously learned. Used to measure memory of prior learning.

Explicit memory A recollection that a person is aware of having or is consciously retrieved.

Implicit memory A recollection that a person does not know exists and is retrieved unconsciously.

Priming Facilitating the retrieval of an implicit memory by using cues to activate hidden memories.

MODULE 33 Measuring Memory—Learning Outcomes Revisited

33.1 Describe how memory is measured

The tip-of-the-tongue state shows that memory is not an all-or-nothing event. Recall, recognition, relearning, or priming may reveal memories. In recall, memories are retrieved without explicit cues, as in an essay exam. Recall of listed information often reveals a serial position effect. A common test of recognition is the multiple-choice question. In relearning, material that seems to be forgotten is learned again, and memory is revealed by a savings score. Recall, recognition, and relearning mainly measure explicit memories. Other techniques, such as priming, are necessary to reveal implicit memories.

Reflective Practice

Content Check

1. Four techniques for measuring or demonstrating memory are the following:

   ____
   ____
   ____
   ____

2. Essay tests require ________________ of facts or ideas.

3. As a measure of memory, a savings score is associated with
   a. recognition
   b. priming
   c. relearning
   d. reconstruction
4. The two most sensitive tests of explicit memory are
   a. recall and redintegration
   b. recall and relearning
   c. recognition and relearning
   d. recognition and digit-span
5. Priming is used to reveal which type of memories?
   a. explicit
   b. sensory
   c. skill
   d. implicit

Skill Check

Think Critically

6. When asked to explain why they may have failed to recall some information, people often claim it must be because the information is no longer in their memory. Why does the existence of implicit memories challenge this explanation?

Self-Reflect

Do you prefer tests based primarily on recall or recognition? Have you observed a savings effect while relearning information you studied in the past (such as in high school)? What things do you do that are based on implicit memories? For instance, how do you know which way to turn various handles in your house, apartment, or dorm? Do you have to explicitly think, "Turn it to the right," before you act?

ANSWERS

1. Recall, recognition, relearning, priming 2. recall 3. c 4. c 5. d 6. It is possible to have an implicit memory that cannot be consciously recalled. Such memories are available even though they are not consciously accessible. Such memories show that failing to recall something does not guarantee it is no longer in memory (Voss, Lucas, & Paller, 2012).

MODULE 34

Memory
Forgetting

Where's My Car?

We forget for a variety of reasons. For example, have you ever "lost" your car?

On the one hand, if you park your car in a different location in the same large parking lot every day, you may have experienced forgetting caused by *interference*. It is not so much that you *forgot* where you parked it today as that you (mis)*remembered* where you parked it some other day. Memories from yesterday, and the day before, and the day before that interfere with today's memory about your car's location.

bikeriderlondon/Shutterstock.com

On the other hand, suppose it is a special day, and you take out that special someone to a new restaurant or club to celebrate. If you had to park your car on a crowded, unfamiliar street many blocks away, and can't find it afterward, you may have experienced *encoding failure*. Perhaps you were so excited that you did not spend enough time when you got there encoding where you parked.

Before we forget to, let's explore some of the explanations for forgetting.

~LEARNING OUTCOMES~

After reading this module you should be able to:

34.1 Discuss current theories of why we forget

34.2 Describe how the brain forms and stores memories

Forgetting—Forget? Forget What?

Learning Outcome 34.1 Discuss current theories of why we forget

We don't expect sensory memories and short-term memories to remain with us for long, as they fade away or are displaced by incoming information. But when you deliberately encode and store information in long-term memory, you want it to stay there (after all, it's supposed to be *long*-term). For example, when you study for an exam, you count on your long-term memory to retain the information at least until you take your exam.

Why do we forget long-term memories? The more you know about how we "lose" memories, the better you will be able to hang on to them. Most forgetting tends to occur immediately after memorization. Herman Ebbinghaus (1885)

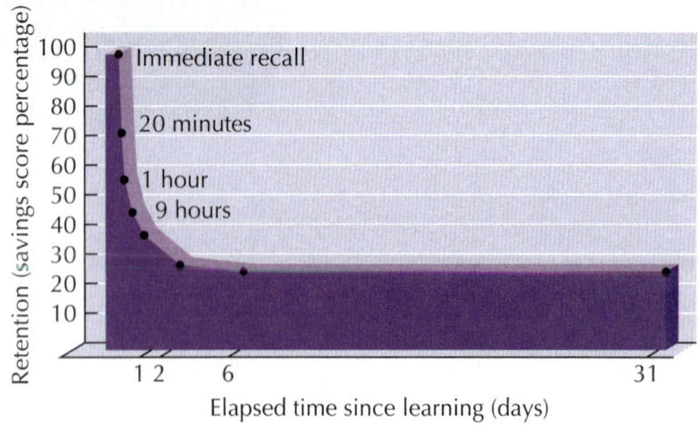

➤ **Figure 34.1**

The curve of forgetting. This graph shows the amount remembered (measured by relearning) after varying lengths of time. Notice how rapidly forgetting occurs. The material learned was nonsense syllables. Forgetting curves for meaningful information also show early losses followed by a long gradual decline, but overall, forgetting occurs much more slowly. (After Ebbinghaus, 1885.)

famously tested his own memory at various intervals after learning. To be sure that prior learning would not sway him, he memorized *nonsense syllables*. These are meaningless three-letter combinations such as *cef*, *wol*, and *gex*. The importance of using meaningless words is shown by the fact that *Vel*, *Fab*, and *Duz* are no longer used on memory tests. People who recognize these words as detergent names find them easy to remember. This is another reminder that relating new information to what you already know can improve memory.

By waiting various lengths of time before testing himself, Ebbinghaus plotted a *curve of forgetting*. This graph shows the amount of information remembered after varying lengths of time (➤ **Figure 34.1**). Notice that forgetting is rapid at first and is followed by a slow decline (Hintzman, 2005; Sternberg, 2017). The same applies to meaningful information, but the forgetting curve is stretched over a longer time. As you might expect, recent events are recalled more accurately than those from the remote past. Thus, you are more likely to remember that *Parasite* won the Best Picture Oscar for 2020 than you are to remember that *The King's Speech* won it for 2010.

As a student, you should note that a short delay between studying and taking a test minimizes forgetting. However, this is no reason for cramming. Most students make the error of only cramming. If you cram, you don't have to remember for very long, but you may not learn enough in the first place. If you use short, daily study sessions and review intensely before a test, you will get the benefit of good preparation and a minimum time lapse.

The Ebbinghaus curve shows that less than 30 percent of what is learned is remembered after only two days have passed. Is forgetting really that rapid? Not always. Meaningful information is not lost nearly as quickly as nonsense syllables. After three years, students who took a university psychology course had forgotten about 30 percent of the facts they learned. After that, little more forgetting occurred (Conway, Cohen, & Stanhope, 1992).

➤ **Figure 34.2**

Although the Ebbinghaus curve gives a general picture of forgetting from long-term memory, it doesn't explain it. For explanations, we must search further. In Module 32, we pointed out that three processes are involved in successfully remembering: Namely encoding, storage, and retrieval. Conversely, forgetting can be due to the failure of any one of these three processes.

Encoding Failure

Pick a card from the six shown in ➤ **Figure 34.2**. Look at it closely, and be sure that you can remember which card is yours.

Now, snap your fingers and look at the cards in ➤ **Figure 34.3**. Poof! Only five cards remain, and the card you chose has disappeared. Obviously, you could have selected any one of the six cards in Figure 34.2. How did we know which one to remove?

This trick is based entirely on an illusion of memory. Recall that you were asked to concentrate on one card among the six original cards. That prevented you from paying attention to the other cards, so they weren't encoded in your memory (Unsworth, Brewer, & Spillers, 2012). The five cards you see in Figure 34.3 are *all* new (none is shown in Figure 34.2). Because you couldn't find it in the "remaining five," your card seemed to disappear.

Here's another demonstration of *encoding failure*. Whose head is on a U.S. penny? Which way is it facing?

➤ **Figure 34.3**

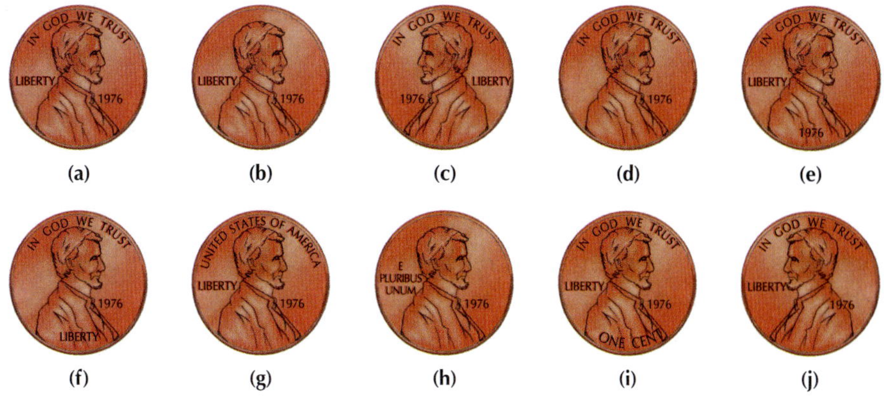

➤ **Figure 34.4**

Find the real penny. Penny A is correct but was seldom recognized. Pennies G and J were popular wrong answers. (Adapted from Nickerson & Adams, (1979). Long-term memory for a common object. *Cognitive Psychology*, 11, 287–307.)

What is written at the top of a penny? Can you accurately draw and label a penny? In an interesting experiment, Ray Nickerson and Marilyn Adams (1979) asked a large group of students to draw a penny. Few could. In fact, few could even recognize a drawing of a real penny among fakes (➤ **Figure 34.4**). Can you?

The most obvious reason for forgetting is also the most commonly overlooked. Few of us ever encode the details of a penny (or a corporate logo, for that matter; Blake, Nazarian, & Castel, 2015). Similarly, we may not encode the details of what we are reading in a book or studying for an exam. In such cases, we "forget" because of **encoding failure** (Johnson, Nessler, & Friedman, 2013). That is, a memory was never formed in the first place. If frequent forgetting or absent-mindedness bothers you, it is wise to ask yourself, "Have I been encoding the information in the first place?" By the way, if you like to study while watching television or instant messaging, beware. Dividing your attention between studying and other activities increases the likelihood of encoding failure (Johnson, Nessler, & Friedman, 2013; Unsworth, Brewer, & Spillers, 2012).

Actively focusing on the information you are learning (elaborative processing) is a good way to prevent encoding failure (Hall et al., 2007; Wong, 2015). You'll find more memory strategies in Modules 1 and 35.

College Students: They're All Alike! Encoding failure can even affect our memories of people. Imagine yourself in this situation: As you are walking on campus, a young man, who looks like a college student, approaches you and asks for directions. While you are talking, two workers carrying a door pass between you and the young man. While the door blocks your view, another man takes the place of the first. Now you are facing a different person than the one who was there just seconds earlier. If this happened to you, do you think you would notice the change? Remarkably, only half the people tested in this way noticed the switch (Simons & Levin, 1998)!

How could anyone fail to notice that one stranger was replaced by another? The people who didn't remember the first man were all older adults. College students weren't fooled by the switch. Apparently, older adults encoded the first man in very general terms as a "college student." As a result, that's all they remembered. Because his replacement also looked like a college student, they assumed he was the same person.

We all tend to categorize strangers in general terms: Is the person young or old, male or female, a member of my ethnic group or another one? This tendency is one reason that eyewitnesses are better at identifying members of their own ethnic group than persons from other groups (Wallis, Lipp, & Vanman, 2012). It may seem harsh to say so, but during brief social contacts, people really do act as if members of other ethnic groups "all look alike." Of course, this bias disappears when people get acquainted and learn more about one another as individuals (Bukach et al., 2012).

Storage Failure

One view of forgetting, **decay theory**, holds that **memory traces**—changes in neurons or brain activity—fade or weaken over time. As a result, the ability to retrieve those memories becomes more difficult. Memory decay is a factor in the loss of sensory memories and short-term memory.

Encoding failure Failure to store sufficient information to form a useful memory.

Decay theory Proposition that the strength of memories weakens over time, making them harder to retrieve.

Memory traces Physical changes in neurons or brain activity that take place when memories are stored.

Information stored in these memories initiates a flurry of activity in the brain that quickly dies out. Sensory memory and short-term memory, therefore, operate like "leaky buckets": New information constantly pours in, but it rapidly fades away and is replaced by still-newer information.

Disuse *Does decay also occur in long-term memory?* Evidence exists that memories not retrieved and "used" or rehearsed become weaker over time. That is, some long-term memory traces may fade from **disuse** (infrequent retrieval) and eventually become too weak to retrieve. However, disuse alone cannot fully explain forgetting (Della Sala, 2010). Disuse doesn't seem to account for our ability to recover seemingly forgotten memories through redintegration, relearning, and priming. It also fails to explain why some unused memories fade, whereas others are carried for life.

A third contradiction will be recognized by anyone who has spent time with the elderly. People growing senile may become so forgetful that they can't remember what happened a week ago. Unfortunately, this is often due to conditions such as *Alzheimer's disease* and other *dementias*, which slowly strangle the brain's ability to process and store information (Hanyu et al., 2010; Verma & Howard, 2012). (Memory can easily be disrupted by organic factors, including brain injuries and disorders such as Alzheimer's disease. For more information, see Module 60.)

Yet, at the same time that your Uncle Oscar's recent memories are fading, he may have vivid memories of trivial and long-forgotten events from the past. "Why, I remember it as clearly as if it were yesterday," he will say, forgetting that the story he is about to tell is one he told earlier the same day (twice). In short, disuse offers no more than a partial explanation of long-term forgetting.

Retrieval Failure

If encoding failure and storage failure don't fully explain forgetting from long-term memory, what does? If you have encoded and stored information, that leaves **retrieval failure** as a likely cause of forgetting (Della Sala, 2010; Guerin et al., 2012). Even if memories are *available* (stored in your memory), you still have to be able to *access* them (locate or retrieve them) in order to remember. For example, as we mentioned earlier, you might have had the experience of knowing that you know the answer to an exam question (you knew it was available) but being unable to retrieve it during the exam (it was inaccessible).

Cue-Dependent Forgetting One reason why retrieval may fail is that *retrieval cues* are missing when the time comes to access the information. For instance, if you were asked, "What were you doing on Monday afternoon of the third week in May, two years ago?" your reply might be, "Come on, how should I know?" However, if you were reminded, "That was the day the courthouse burned" or "That was the day Stacy had her automobile accident," you might remember immediately.

The presence of appropriate cues almost always enhances memory retrieval. As we saw previously, more elaborately encoded memories are more likely to be remembered because more retrieval cues are associated with any particular piece of information. Memory will even tend to be better if you study in the same room where you will be tested. Because this is often impossible, when you study, try to visualize the room where you will be tested. Doing so can enhance memory later (Jerabek & Standing, 1992). Similarly, people even remember better if the same odor (such as lemon or lavender) is present both when they study and are tested (Parker, Ngu, & Cassaday, 2001). In fact, odors are among the most powerful retrieval cues for emotional memories (Arshamian et al., 2013).

State-Dependent Learning Have you heard the one about the drunk who misplaced his wallet and had to get drunk again to find it? This is actually not too far-fetched. The bodily state that exists during learning also can be a strong retrieval cue for later memory, an effect known as **state-dependent learning** (Radvansky, 2017). Being very

dcwcreations/Shutterstock.com

External cues such as those found in a photograph, in a scrapbook, or during a walk through an old neighborhood often aid recall of seemingly lost memories. For this veteran, visiting the final resting place of a fallen comrade unleashed a flood of memories.

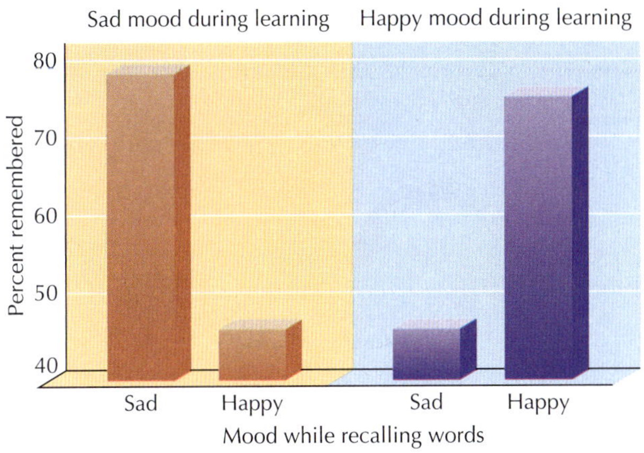

➤ **Figure 34.5**

The effect of mood on memory. Participants best remembered a list of words when their mood during testing was the same as their mood when they learned the list. (Adapted from Bower, 1981.)

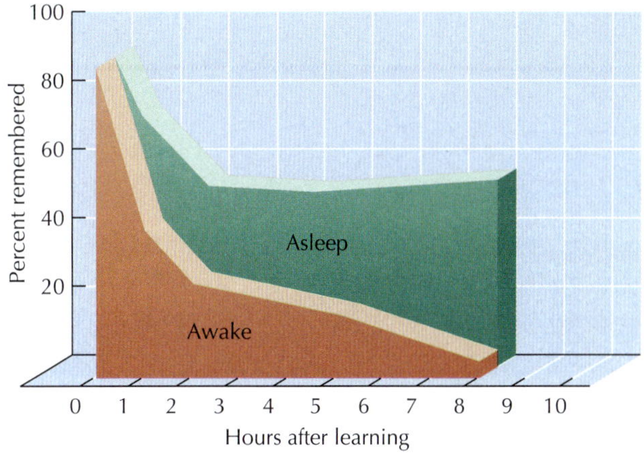

➤ **Figure 34.6**

The amount of forgetting after a period of sleep or wakefulness. Notice that sleep causes less memory loss than activity that occurs while one is awake. (After Jenkins & Dallenbach, 1924.)

thirsty, for instance, might prompt you to remember events that took place another time when you were thirsty. Because of such effects, information learned under the influence of a drug is best remembered when the drugged state occurs again (Koek, 2011; Mariani et al., 2011). (However, this is a laboratory finding. In school, it's far better to study with a clear mind in the first place.)

A similar effect applies to emotional states (Wessel & Wright, 2004; Yang & Ornstein, 2011). For instance, Gordon Bower (1981) found that people who learned a list of words while in a happy mood recalled them better when they were again happy. People who learned while they felt sad remembered best when they were sad (➤ Figure 34.5). Similarly, if you are in a happy mood, you are more likely to remember recent happy events. If you are in a bad mood, you will tend to have unpleasant memories. Such links between emotional cues and memory could explain why couples who quarrel often end up remembering—and rehashing—old arguments.

Interference

Further insight into forgetting comes from a classic experiment in which college students learned lists of nonsense syllables. After studying, students in one group slept for eight hours and were then tested for memory of the lists. A second group stayed awake for eight hours and went about business as usual. When members of the second group were tested, they remembered *less* than the group that slept (➤ Figure 34.6). This difference is based on the fact that new learning can interfere with the ability to retrieve previous learning. **Interference** refers to the tendency for new memories to impair retrieval of older memories (and the reverse). It seems to apply to both short-term and long-term memory (Radvansky, 2017; Rodríguez-Villagra et al., 2013). (Sleep can improve memory in another way: REM sleep and dreaming appear to also help us consolidate memories. See Module 24.)

It is not completely clear whether new memories alter existing long-term memory traces or whether they make it harder to retrieve earlier memories. In any case, there is no doubt that interference is a major cause of forgetting (Radvansky, 2017). In one classic study, college students who memorized 20 lists of words (one list each day) were able to recall only 15 percent of the last list. Students who learned only one list remembered 80 percent (Underwood, 1957) (➤ Figure 34.7).

The college students who studied nonsense syllables and then slept remembered more because the type of interference called retroactive interference was held to a minimum. **Retroactive interference** (RET-ro-AK-tiv) refers

Disuse (in memory) Proposition that memory traces weaken when memories are not periodically used or retrieved.

Retrieval failure Failure to access (locate) memories even though they are available (stored in memory).

State-dependent learning Memory influenced by one's physical state at the time of learning and at the time of retrieval. Improved memory occurs when the physical states match.

Interference The tendency for new memories to impair retrieval of older memories, and the reverse.

Retroactive interference The tendency for new memories to interfere with the retrieval of old memories.

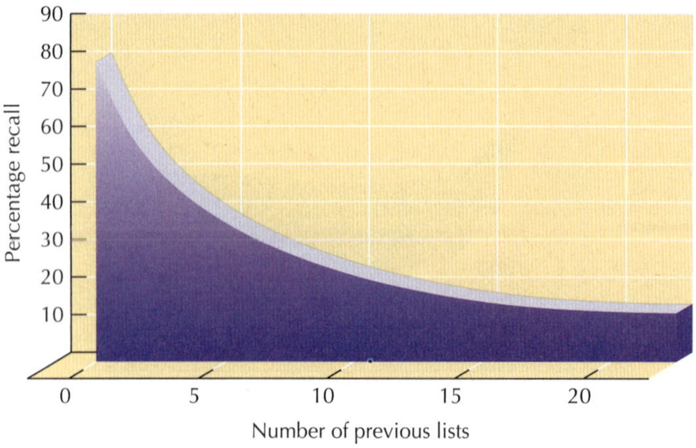

➤ **Figure 34.7**

The effects of interference on memory. The graph shows the approximate relationship between percentage recalled and number of different word lists memorized. (Adapted from Underwood, 1957.)

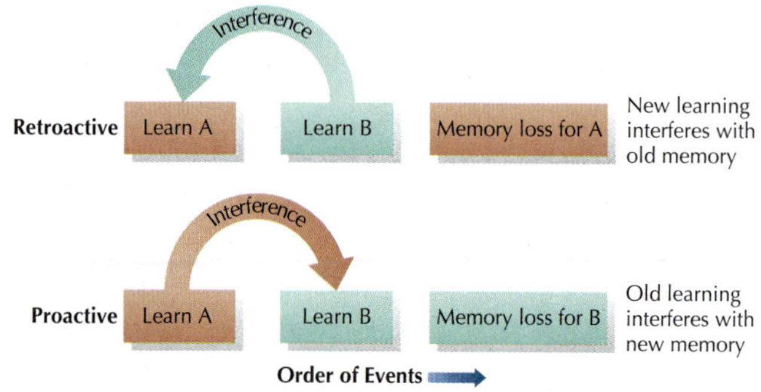

➤ **Figure 34.8**

Retroactive and proactive interference. The order of learning and testing shows whether interference is retroactive (backward) or proactive (forward).

to the tendency for new learning to inhibit retrieval of old learning. Avoiding new learning prevents retroactive interference. This doesn't exactly mean that you should hide in a closet after you study for an exam. However, you should, if possible, avoid studying other subjects until the exam. Sleeping after study can help you retain memories, and reading, writing, or even watching television may cause interference.

Retroactive interference is easily demonstrated in the laboratory by this arrangement:

Experimental group:	**Learn A**	**Learn B**	**Test A**
Control group:	**Learn A**	**Rest**	**Test A**

Imagine yourself as a member of the experimental group. In task A, you learn a list of telephone numbers. In task B, you learn a list of Social Security numbers. How do you score on a test of task A (the telephone numbers)? If you do not remember as much as the control group that learns *only* task A, then retroactive interference has occurred. The second thing learned interfered with memory of the first thing learned; the interference went "backward," or was "retroactive" (➤ **Figure 34.8**).

Proactive interference is the second type of interference. **Proactive interference** (pro-AK-tiv) occurs when prior learning inhibits recall of later learning. A test for proactive interference would take this form:

Experimental group:	**Learn A**	**Learn B**	**Test B**
Control group:	**Rest**	**Learn B**	**Test B**

Let's assume that the experimental group remembers less than the control group on a test of task B. In that case, learning task A interfered with remembering task B.

Then, proactive interference goes "forward"? Yes. For instance, if you cram for a psychology exam and then, later the same night, cram for a history exam, your memory for the second subject studied (history) will be less accurate than if you had studied only history. (Because of retroactive interference, your memory for psychology also would probably suffer.) The greater the similarity in the two subjects studied, the more interference takes place. The moral, of course, is don't procrastinate in preparing for exams. The more you can avoid competing information, the more likely you are to recall what you want to remember (Wixted, 2004).

Repression and Suppression of Memories

Take a moment and scan the events of the last few years of your life. What kinds of things most easily come to mind? Many people remember happy, positive events better than disappointments and irritations (Moore & Zoellner, 2007). This tendency is called **repression**, or motivated forgetting. Through repression, distressing, threatening, or embarrassing memories are kept buried in the unconscious. An example is provided by soldiers who have repressed some of the horrors that they saw during combat (Anderson & Huddleston, 2012).

Forgetting past failures, upsetting childhood events, the names of people you dislike, or appointments you don't want to keep may reveal repression (Goodman, Quas, & Ogle, 2010). People who are extremely sensitive to emotional events tend to use repression to protect themselves from threatening thoughts.

If I try to forget a test I failed, am I repressing it? Probably not. Repression can be distinguished from **suppression**, an active, conscious attempt to put something out of mind (Anderson et al., 2011). By not thinking about the test, you have merely suppressed a memory. If you choose, you can remember the test. Clinicians consider true repression an *unconscious* event and one of the major psychological defenses we use against emotional threats. (See Module 57 for details.) When a memory is repressed, we may be unaware that forgetting has even occurred.

Although some psychologists have questioned whether repression exists, evidence suggests that we can choose to actively suppress upsetting memories (Ceylan & Sayin, 2012; Neufeind et al., 2009). If you have experienced a painful emotional event, you will probably avoid all thoughts associated with it. This tends to keep cues out of mind that could trigger a painful memory. In time, your active suppression of the memory may become true repression.

The Recovered Memory/False Memory Debate

Many sexually abused children develop problems that persist into adulthood. In some instances, they repress all memory of the abuse. According to some psychologists, uncovering these hidden memories can be an important step toward regaining emotional health (Colangelo, 2007; Haaken & Reavey, 2010).

Although the preceding may be true, the search for repressed memories of sexual abuse has itself been a problem. Families have been torn apart by accusations of sexual abuse that later turned out to be completely false. For example, when Meredith Maran thought that she had recovered vivid memories of being molested by her father, she withdrew herself and her children from any further contact with him. It was not until nine years later that she realized that her "memories" were not true and finally apologized to her father (Maran, 2010). Things have gotten much worse for other people, as some cases have gone to court, some innocent people have gone to jail, and some actual sexual abuse victims have been accused of making false claims about their very real memories.

Why would anyone have false memories about such disturbing events? Several popular books and a few misguided therapists have actively encouraged people to find repressed memories of abuse. Hypnosis, guided visualization, suggestion, age regression, administering the so-called truth drug Amytal, and similar techniques can elicit fantasies that are mistaken for real memories. As we saw earlier, it is easy to create false memories, especially by using hypnosis (Weinstein & Shanks, 2010).

In an effort to illustrate how easy it is to create false memories, and to publicize *false memory syndrome,* memory expert Elizabeth Loftus once deliberately implanted a false memory in actor Alan Alda. As the host of the television series *Scientific American Frontiers*, he was scheduled to interview Loftus. Before the interview, Alda was asked to fill out a questionnaire about his tastes in food. When he arrived, Loftus told Alda that his answers revealed that he must once have gotten sick after eating hard-boiled eggs (which was false). Later that day, at a picnic, Alda would not eat hard-boiled eggs (Loftus, 2003).

Certainly, some memories of abuse that return to awareness are genuine and must be dealt with. However, there is little doubt that some "recovered" memories are pure fantasy. No matter how real a recovered memory may seem, it could be false, unless it can be verified by others or by court or medical records (Bernstein & Loftus, 2009; Otgaar & Smeets, 2010). The saddest thing about such claims is that they deaden public sensitivity to actual abuse. Childhood sexual abuse is widespread. Awareness of its existence must not be repressed.

Memory and the Brain—Some "Shocking" Findings

Learning Outcome 34.2 Describe how the brain forms and stores memories

One possibility overlooked in our discussion of forgetting is **amnesia**, an inability to form or retrieve memories of events due to an injury or trauma (Papanicolaou, 2006). For example, a head injury may cause a "gap" in memories preceding the accident. **Retrograde amnesia**, as this is called, involves forgetting events that occurred before an injury or trauma (MacKay & Hadley, 2009). In contrast, **anterograde amnesia** involves forgetting events that follow an injury or trauma (Dewar et al., 2010). (We discuss an example of this type of amnesia in a moment.)

Proactive interference The tendency for old memories to interfere with the retrieval of newer memories.

Repression Keeping distressing thoughts and feelings buried in the unconscious.

Suppression A conscious effort to put something out of mind or to keep it from awareness.

Amnesia Inability to form or retrieve memories of events due to an injury or trauma.

Retrograde amnesia Inability to retrieve memories of events that occurred before an injury or trauma.

Anterograde amnesia Inability to form or retrieve memories of events that occur after an injury or trauma.

Consolidation

We can explain retrograde amnesia by assuming that it takes time to form a lasting memory, a process called **consolidation** (Nadel et al., 2012). You can think of consolidation as being somewhat like writing your name in wet concrete. Once the concrete is set, the information (your name) is fairly lasting. But while the concrete is setting, the information can be wiped out (amnesia) or scribbled over (interference).

Consider a classic experiment on consolidation, in which a rat is placed on a small platform. The rat steps down to the floor and receives a painful electric shock. After one shock, the rat can be returned to the platform repeatedly, but it will not step down. Obviously, the rat remembers the shock. Would it remember if consolidation were disturbed?

Curiously, one way to prevent consolidation is to give a different kind of shock called *electroconvulsive shock (ECS).* ECS is a mild electric shock to the brain. It does not harm the animal, but it does destroy any memory that is being formed. If each painful shock (the one the animal remembers) is followed by ECS (which wipes out memories during consolidation), the rat will step down over and over. Each time, ECS erases the memory of the painful shock. (ECS has been used with humans as a psychiatric treatment for severe depression. Used in this way, electroshock therapy also causes memory loss. See Module 68.)

What would happen if ECS was given several hours after the learning? Recent memories are more easily disrupted than older memories. If enough time is allowed to pass between learning and ECS, the memory will be unaffected because consolidation is already complete. That's why people with mild head injuries lose only memories from just before the accident, whereas older memories remain intact (Baddeley, Eysenck, & Anderson, 2009). Likewise, you would forget more if you studied, stayed awake eight hours, and then slept eight hours than you would if you studied, slept eight hours, and were awake for eight hours. Either way, 16 hours would pass. However, less forgetting would occur in the second instance because more consolidation would occur before interference begins.

Where does consolidation take place in the brain? Many parts of the brain are responsible for memory, but the **hippocampus** is particularly important (Squire & Wixted, 2011). The hippocampus, part of the limbic system, acts as a sort of "switching station" between short-term and long-term memory (Moscovitch et al., 2016). The hippocampus does this, in part, by growing new neurons and by making new connections within the brain (Pan, Storm, & Xia, 2013; Zammit et al., 2017).

If the hippocampus is damaged, patients usually develop anterograde amnesia and show a striking inability to consolidate new memories. A man described by Brenda Milner (1965) provides a dramatic example. Two years after an operation damaged his hippocampus, the 29-year-old H. M. continued to give his age as 27 and reported that the operation had just taken place. His memory of events before the operation remained clear, but he found forming new long-term memories almost impossible. When his parents moved to a new house a few blocks away on the same street, he could not remember the new address. Month after month, he read the same magazines over and over without finding them familiar. If you were to meet this man, he would seem fairly normal because he still has short-term memory. But if you were to leave the room and return 15 minutes later, he would act as if he had never seen you before. Lacking the ability to form new lasting memories, he lived eternally in the present until his death in 2008 at the age of 82 (Bohbot & Corkin, 2007).

Memory, Stress, and Emotion Many people can still remember when they first learned about the terrorist attacks on New York City's World Trade Center in 2001. They can even recall lots of detail, including how they reacted. They have a **flashbulb memory** for 9/11 (Paradis et al., 2004). A flashbulb memory is an especially vivid recollection that seems to be frozen in memory at times of emotionally significant personal or public events (Lanciano, Curci, & Semin, 2010). Depending on your age, you also may have a flashbulb memory for the assassinations of John F. Kennedy or Martin Luther King, Jr., the death of Princess Diana, or one of the all-too-common mass school shootings (Curci & Luminet, 2006).

Joseph Sohm/Shutterstock.com

The 2016 presidential election was a very emotional one for many Americans. Do you have a flashbulb memory for that day? You do if you were at all involved and can still remember it like it happened yesterday. You even do if you saw the news on TV and you have clear memories of how you reacted.

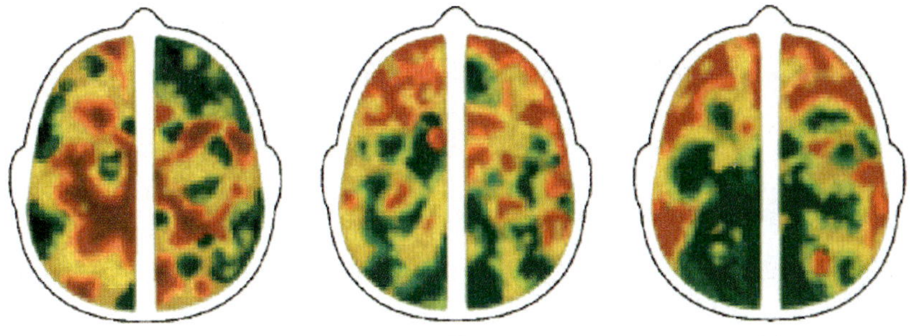

➤ **Figure 34.9**

Cortical areas involved in semantic and episodic memory. Patterns of blood flow in the cerebral cortex (wrinkled outer layer of the brain) change as areas become more or less active. Thus, blood flow can be used to draw "maps" of brain activity. This drawing, which views the brain from the top, shows the results of measuring cerebral blood flow while people were thinking about a semantic memory (*a*) or an episodic memory (*b*). In the map, green indicates areas that are more active during semantic thinking. Red shows areas of greater activity during episodic thinking. The brain in view (*c*) shows the difference in activity between views *a* and *b*. The resulting pattern suggests that the front of the cortex is related to episodic memory. Areas toward the back and sides of the cortex, especially the temporal lobes, are more associated with semantic memory (Tulving, 1989, 2002). (Copyright © Tulving, E. (1989). "Remembering and knowing the past." *American Scientist*, 77(4), 361–367. Reprinted by permission.)

Does the brain handle flashbulb memories differently? Powerfully exciting or stressful experiences activate the limbic system, a part of the brain that processes emotions. Heightened activity in the limbic system, in turn, appears to intensify memory consolidation (LaBar, 2007). As a result, flashbulb memories tend to form at times of intense emotion.

Although flashbulb memories are often related to public tragedies, memories of both positive and negative events can have "flashbulb" clarity. Would you consider any of the following to be a flashbulb memory: Your first kiss or your prom night? How about a time when you had to speak in front of a large audience? A car accident that you were in or witnessed?

The term *flashbulb memories* was first used to describe recollections that seemed to be unusually vivid and permanent (Brown & Kulik, 1977). It has become clear, however, that flashbulb memories are not particularly accurate (Tinti et al., 2014). More than anything else, what sets flashbulb memories apart is that we tend to place great *confidence* in them—even when they are wrong (Niedzwienska, 2004). Perhaps that's because we review emotionally charged events over and over and tell others about them. Also, public events such as wars, earthquakes, and elections reappear many times in the news, which highlights them in memory. Over time, flashbulb memories tend to crystallize into consistent, if not entirely accurate, landmarks in our lives (Lanciano, Curci, & Semin, 2010).

Some memories go beyond flashbulb clarity and become so intense that they may haunt a person for years. Extremely traumatic experiences, such as military combat or maltreatment as a child, can produce so much limbic system activation that the resulting memories and "flashbacks" leave a person emotionally handicapped (Bergstrom et al., 2013; Goodman, Quas, & Ogle, 2010). (To read more about post-traumatic stress disorder [PTSD], see Module 63.)

Long-Term Memory and the Brain

Somewhere within the 3-pound mass of the human brain lies all we know: ZIP codes, faces of loved ones, history, favorite melodies, the taste of an apple, and much, much more. Where is this information? According to neuroscientists, many parts of the brain become active when we form and retrieve long-term memories, but some areas are more important for different types of memory and memory processes (Squire & Wixted, 2011).

For example, brain imaging studies reveal that frontal areas of the cerebral cortex (the wrinkled outer layer of the brain) are more important in processing episodic memory. In contrast, side and back areas of cortex are more important in processing semantic memory (LePort et al., 2012; Shimotake et al., 2015; Tulving, 1989, 2002; see ➤ **Figure 34.9**). As another example, different parts of the cortex are activated when we are engaging in memory retrieval as opposed to memory suppression (Meclinger, 2010).

Consolidation Process by which relatively permanent memories are formed in the brain.

Hippocampus Part of the limbic system associated with storing memories.

Flashbulb memory Especially vivid and detailed recollection of an emotional event.

Rozilire/Shutterstock.com

An *aplysia.* The relatively simple nervous system of this sea animal allows scientists to study memory as it occurs in single neurons.

Let's summarize (and simplify greatly). Earlier, we noted that the hippocampus handles memory consolidation (Wang & Morris, 2010). Once declarative long-term memories are formed, they appear to be stored in the cortex of the brain (episodic in the front, semantic in the sides and back) (Mecklinger, 2010; Squire, 2004). Long-term procedural (skill) memories are stored in the basal ganglia and cerebellum, parts of the brain that also are responsible for muscular coordination (Freberg, 2021; Lum & Bleses, 2012).

Long-Term Potentiation *OK, that's* where, *but* how *are memories recorded in the brain?* Scientists are beginning to identify the exact ways neurons record information (Xu & Yao, 2010). Their research may eventually help the millions of persons who suffer from memory impairment (Ellis & Nathan, 2001). For example, Eric Kandel and his colleagues have studied learning in the marine snail *aplysia* (ah-PLEEZ-yah). Learning in the *aplysia* occurs when certain neurons in a circuit alter the amount of transmitter chemicals they release (Bailey & Kandel, 2004). Learning also alters the overall activity, structure, and chemistry of neurons.

Specifically, if two or more interconnected neurons become more active at the same time, the connections between them grow stronger (Kalat, 2021). This process is called **long-term potentiation**. After it occurs, an affected neuron will respond more strongly to messages from the other neurons. The brain appears to use this mechanism to form lasting memories (Blundon & Zakharenko, 2008; Kimura et al., 2012).

How has that been demonstrated? Electrically stimulating parts of the brain involved in memory, such as the hippocampus, can decrease long-term potentiation (Eckert & Racine, 2006; Ivanco & Racine, 2000). As we saw earlier, using electroconvulsive shock to overstimulate memory areas in the brains of rats interferes with long-term potentiation. It also causes memory loss—just as it does when humans are given ECS for depression.

Will researchers ever produce a "memory pill" for people with normal memory? It's a growing possibility, although one early candidate, *Ginkgo biloba*, has yielded disappointing results in research trials (Snitz et al., 2009). Yet, drugs that increase long-term potentiation also tend to improve memory (Farah et al., 2004). For example, rats administered such drugs could remember the correct path through a maze better than rats not given the drug (Wang et al., 2014). Such findings suggest that memory can be and will be artificially enhanced. However, the possibility of something like a "physics pill" or a "math pill" still seems remote.

Long-term potentiation Brain mechanism used to form lasting memories by strengthening the connection between neurons that become more active at the same time.

MODULE 34 Forgetting—Learning Outcomes Revisited

34.1 Discuss current theories of why we forget

Forgetting is most rapid immediately after learning. Failure to encode information is a common cause of "forgetting." Forgetting in sensory memory and STM is due to a failure of storage through a weakening (decay) of memory traces. STM forgetting also occurs through displacement. Decay of memory traces due to disuse may also explain some LTM losses. Failures of retrieval occur when information that resides in memory is nevertheless not retrieved. A lack of retrieval cues can produce retrieval failure. Another reason that we forget relates to interference. In retroactive interference, new learning interferes with the ability to retrieve earlier learning. Proactive interference occurs when old learning interferes with the retrieval of new learning. Finally, memories can be consciously suppressed, or they may be unconsciously repressed. Extreme caution is warranted when "recovered" memories are the only basis for believing that traumatic events, such as childhood sexual abuse, happened in the past.

34.2 Describe how the brain forms and stores memories

In the brain, memory consolidation takes place in the hippocampus. Until they are consolidated, long-term memories are easily destroyed, resulting in retrograde amnesia. After memories have been consolidated, they appear to be stored in the cortex of the brain. Lasting memories are recorded by changes in the activity, structure, and chemistry of neurons as well as in how they interconnect.

Reflective Practice

Content Check

1. Which explanation(s) best seem(s) to account for the loss of short-term memories?
   a. decay
   b. disuse
   c. repression
   d. displacement
2. When memories are available but not accessible, forgetting may be cue-dependent. T or F?
3. When learning one thing makes it more difficult to recall another, forgetting may be caused by ______________________.
4. You are asked to memorize long lists of telephone numbers. You learn a new list each day for 10 days. When tested on list three, you remember less than a person who learned only the first three lists. Your larger memory loss is probably caused by
   a. disuse
   b. retroactive interference
   c. regression
   d. proactive interference
5. If you consciously succeed at putting a painful memory out of mind, you have used
   a. redintegration
   b. suppression
   c. negative rehearsal
   d. repression
6. Retrograde amnesia results when consolidation is speeded up. T or F?

Skill Check

Think Critically

7. Based on state-dependent learning, why do you think music often strongly evokes memories?

Self-Reflect

Which of the following concepts best explains why you have missed some answers on psychology tests: Encoding failure, disuse, memory cues, interference? Do you know someone whose name you have a hard time remembering? Do you like or dislike that person? Do you think your difficulty is an instance of repression? Suppression? Interference? Retrieval failure?

ANSWERS

1. a and d 2. T 3. interference 4. b 5. b 6. F 7. Music tends to affect a person's mood, and moods tend to affect memory (Barrett et al., 2010).

MODULE 35

Memory
Exceptional Memory

Snap!

Wouldn't it to be nice to have a photographic memory? Memories would be as easy to create as snapping a timeless photo and just as easy as photos to find when you need them. OK, so maybe we mere memory mortals have to live with imperfect memories, but that's how it works for people with exceptional memories, no?

Actually, the metaphor that memory is like a photograph is not only incorrect; it is unfortunately misleading. In this module, we will see that the idea of photographic memory is more myth than reality. Exceptional or not, we all have to put serious mental effort into encoding and retrieving memories.

The good news is that, with the right motivation and some mental effort, we can all improve our memories. We'll start this module by meeting some exceptional people and conclude it by sharing some ways to immediately improve your memory skills.

MorganStudio/Shutterstock.com

~LEARNING OUTCOMES~

After reading this module you should be able to:

35.1 Describe some of the ways that memory can be "exceptional"

35.2 Outline some strategies that can improve memory

35.3 Define mnemonics and provide some examples

Exceptional Memory—Wizards of Recall

Learning Outcome 35.1 Describe some of the ways that memory can be "exceptional"

So this is not *about photographic memory, then?* Perhaps the closest we can come, in reality, is a rare type of memory called **eidetic imagery** (eye-DET-ik), which occurs when a person has visual images clear enough to be "scanned" or retained for at least 30 seconds. Internal mental images can be "viewed" mentally with the eyes closed. In contrast, eidetic images are "projected" in front of a person—that is, they are best "seen" on a plain surface, such as a blank piece of paper. In this respect, eidetic images are somewhat like the short-lived afterimages you might have after looking at a flashbulb or a brightly lit neon sign (Brang & Ramachandran, 2010). They are rare in childhood and become virtually nonexistent in adulthood (Haber & Haber, 2000).

Two Types of Exceptional Memory The occasional rare adult does have a truly exceptional memory. Some have exceptional episodic memories (for personal experiences that are linked with specific times and places) while others have exceptional semantic memories (for impersonal knowledge about the world). (You can review this distinction in Module 32.)

People with an exceptional episodic memory system (also known as *highly superior autobiographical memory*) generally have specific enlargements in the brain areas all of us use for storing episodic memories. They also tend to have normal semantic memories (LePort et al., 2012).

Before you get too jealous, consider what Jill Price has to say about her "perfect" episodic memory: "My memory has ruled my life ... Whenever I see a date flash on the television (or anywhere else for that matter), I automatically go back to that day and remember where I was, what I was doing, what day it fell on, and on and on and on and on. It is nonstop, uncontrollable, and totally exhausting ... Most have called it a gift, but I call it a burden. I run my entire life through my head every day and it drives me crazy!!!" (Parker, Cahill, & McGaugh, 2006, pp. 35–36; Price & Davis, 2009).

As you may have guessed, other people have an exceptional semantic memory system. One famous example is Mr. S., who made a living as a professional memorizer, or *mnemonist*. He regularly wowed audiences with his ability to memorize, with equal ease, long strings of digits, meaningless consonants, mathematical formulas, and poems in foreign languages. But Mr. S. displayed normal episodic memory, going so far as to describe living his life "as if in a haze" (Luria, 1968). Once again, don't be too quick to envy Mr. S.'s abilities. He had to devise ways to *forget* unimportant information—such as writing it on a piece of paper and then burning it.

What both Jill Price and Mr. S. share in common is that, unlike effortlessly "snapping a photo," they spend much of their waking life focused on their memories. In other words, exceptional memory may begin with natural ability (Yi & Qian, 2009). But it also involves high levels of motivation and the use of memory strategies, including special memory "tricks" called *mnemonics* (nee-MON-iks). Assuming that you are at least somewhat motivated to remember what you study, let's take a look at some of those strategies.

Improving Memory—Some Keys to (Memory) Success

Learning Outcome 35.2 Outline some strategies that can improve memory

To begin, you can do very little to improve your brain's ability to store long-term memories. The jury is still out on the use of drugs, herbs (such as *Ginkgo biloba*), and vitamins (such as vitamin E) to improve human memory (McDaniel, Maier, & Einstein, 2002; McGaugh & Roozendaal, 2009). However, you can immediately use meaning-based strategies to improve memory encoding and memory retrieval (Fry, 2012; Hancock, 2011). Most exceptional memorizers use these strategies to augment whatever natural talents they have. Some of their strategies are described in the remainder of this module. (See also Module 1.)

Encoding Strategies

In keeping with the (mistaken) idea that forming a memory is like snapping a photo, many students assume encoding (forming) memories *should be effortless*. So, for example, Steve was able to listen to lists of 80 digits and repeat them back without making a mistake (Ericsson & Chase, 1982). Impressive? Maybe. But easy? Not at all. Steve, a student volunteer who could remember 7 digits, spent 20 months (!) practicing memorizing ever-longer lists of digits. Ultimately, Steve was able to memorize approximately 80 digits, like this sample: 92842048050842268953990190252912807999706606574717310601080585269726026357332135.

How did Steve do it? Basically, he practiced chunking digits into meaningful groups containing three or four digits each. Steve's avid interest in long-distance running helped greatly. For instance, to him the first three digits in the preceding group represented 9 minutes and 28 seconds, a good time for a 2-mile run. When running times wouldn't work, Steve used other associations, such as ages or dates, to chunk digits (Ericsson & Chase, 1982).

Let's be clear: Steve's natural short-term memory capacity did not improve during months of practice. For example, even at the end, Steve could still memorize only seven consonants. Instead, his exceptional memory for numbers was a *skill* that he improved as he figured out new ways to chunk digits.

Also, Steve is no exception to the rule. Mr. S. worked full time as a professional memorizer. A Chinese man

Eidetic imagery The ability to retain a "projected" mental image long enough to use it as a source of information.

named Lu Chao once held the world record for reciting from memory the first 67,890 digits of the number *pi* (Hu et al., 2009). But, like other people with exceptional semantic memories, Lu Chao does not have a photographic memory. Instead he spent many years practicing, competing against other "pi memorizers," and making use of memory techniques anyone can use to improve their memories (Hu & Ericsson, 2012).

If, unlike Steve, you act on the belief that encoding memories should be effortless, you are setting yourself up for plenty of *encoding failure*. While you may never need to remember strings of 80 (or 67,890!) digits, one way to improve your memory is to be sure to more fully encode information. Following are some strategies you can use to become a better encoder.

Use Chunking to Organize Information The ability to organize information into chunks underlies expertise in many fields (Gilchrist, Cowan, & Naveh-Benjamin, 2009; Gobet, 2005). Be open to searching for good ways to better chunk customer's orders if you are a restaurant server, the playbook if you are on a football team, speeches if you are a public speaker, and so on. Don't be afraid to ask the people you work with how they manage it.

For example, assume that you must memorize the following list of words: North, man, red, spring, woman, east, autumn, yellow, summer, boy, blue, west, winter, girl, green, south. This rather difficult list could, with a little effort, be reorganized into *chunks* as follows: north-east-south-west, spring-summer-autumn-winter, red-yellow-green-blue, man-woman-boy-girl.

Organizing class notes and summarizing modules or chapters can be quite helpful (Ellis, 2016). You may even want to summarize your summaries so that the overall network of ideas becomes clearer and simpler. Summaries improve memory by encouraging better encoding of information (Anderson, 2014).

Use Mental Images Mental images, especially vivid ones, are particularly memorable (Worthen & Hunt, 2010). According to the *multimedia principle* (see Module 32), it is also better to mix words and images than to reply on words alone (Overson, 2014). For example, don't treat the figures and graphs in this textbook as unnecessary "fluff." Far from it, they can become the core of effective encodings. Try, for example, to memorize Figure 32.1 and organize your summary of Module 32 around it.

Use Elaborative Processing Let us reiterate: The more you *rehearse* (mentally review) information as you read, the better you will remember it. Even repeatedly thinking about facts helps link them together in memory. But remember that maintenance rehearsal alone is not very effective. Elaborative processing, in which you rehearse by looking for connections to existing knowledge, is far better. To learn college-level information, you must make active use of more reflective study strategies (Halonen & Santrock, 2013).

Consider Whole Versus Part Learning If you have to memorize a speech, is it better to try to learn it from beginning to end or in smaller parts like paragraphs? It depends. For fairly short, organized information, it is usually better to practice whole packages of information rather than smaller parts *(whole learning)*. Learning parts is usually better for extremely long, complicated information. In *part learning*, subparts of a larger body of information are studied (such as sections of a textbook module or chapter). To decide which approach to use, remember to study the *largest meaningful amount of information* you can at one time.

For very long or complex material, try the *progressive-part method*, by breaking a learning task into a series of short sections. At first, you study part A until it is mastered. Next, you study parts A and B; then A, B, and C; and so forth. This is a good way to learn the lines of a play, a long piece of music, or a poem (Ash & Holding, 1990). After the material is learned, you also should practice by starting at points other than A (at C, D, or B, for example). This helps prevent getting "lost" or going blank in the middle of a performance.

Beware Serial Position Whenever you must learn something in *order*, be aware of the serial position effect. As you will recall, this is the tendency to make the most errors in remembering the middle of a list. If you are introduced to a long line of people, the names you are likely to forget will be those in the middle, so you should make an extra effort to attend to them. You also should give extra practice to the middle of a list, poem, or speech.

Encode Retrieval Cues The best *retrieval cues* (stimuli that aid retrieval) are those that were present during encoding (Anderson, 2014). For example, students in one classic study had the daunting task of trying to recall a list of 600 words. As they read the list (which they did not know they would be tested on), the students gave three other words closely related in meaning to each listed word. In a test given later, the words each student supplied were used as cues to jog memory. The students recalled an astounding 90 percent of the original word list (Mantyla, 1986).

The preceding example shows, once again, that it often helps to *elaborate* on information as you learn. When you study, try to use new names, ideas, or terms in several sentences. Also, form images that include the new information and relate it to knowledge that you already have. Your goal should be to knit meaningful cues into your memory at encoding to help you retrieve information when you need it.

Overlearn Numerous studies have shown that memory is greatly improved when you *overlearn* or continue to study beyond bare mastery. After you have learned material well enough to remember it once without error, you should continue studying. Overlearning is your best insurance against going blank on a test because of nervousness.

Use Spaced Practice To keep boredom and fatigue to a minimum, try alternating short study sessions with brief rest periods. This pattern, called **spaced practice**, is generally superior to **massed practice**, in which little or no rest is given between learning sessions (Dunlosky & Rawson, 2015). By improving attention and consolidation, three 20-minute study sessions can produce more learning than 1 hour of continuous study.

Perhaps the best way to use spaced practice is to *schedule* your time. To make an effective schedule, designate times during the week before, after, and between classes when you will study particular subjects. Then treat these times just as if they are classes that you have to attend.

Retrieval Strategies

Just as it was with encoding, it is a mistake to assume retrieval should come easily. When a much-needed memory fails to pop into mind, it's time to start a deliberate *search* of memory (Sternberg, 2017).

How do you search *memory?* For example, one study found that students were most likely to recall names that eluded them if they made use of partial information (Reed & Bruce, 1982). The students were trying to answer questions such as, "He is best remembered as the scarecrow in the Judy Garland movie *The Wizard of Oz.*" (The answer is Ray Bolger.) Partial information that helped students remember included impressions about the length of the name, letter sounds within the name, similar names, and related information (such as the names of other characters in the movie). A similar helpful strategy is to go through the alphabet, trying each letter as the first sound of a name or word you are seeking.

The *cognitive interview* (described in Module 32) offers some further hints for recapturing context and jogging memories:

1. **Say or write down *everything* you can remember** that relates to the information you are seeking. Even trivial bits of information you remember can serve as a cue to bring back other information.
2. **Recall events or information in different orders.** Let your memories flow backward or out of order, or start with whatever impressed you the most.
3. **Recall from different viewpoints.** Review events by mentally standing in a different place. Or try to view information as another person would remember it. When taking a test, for instance, ask yourself what other students or your professor would remember about the topic.
4. **Mentally return to the context of encoding.** Try to mentally recreate the learning environment or relive the event. As you do, include sounds, smells, details of weather, nearby objects, other people present, what you said or thought, and how you felt as you learned the information (Milne & Bull, 2002).

The following are some more strategies to help you avoid retrieval failure:

Rely on Retrieval Practice Learning proceeds best when feedback allows you to check your progress. Feedback can help you identify ideas that need extra practice. In addition, it is rewarding to know that you have remembered or answered correctly. A prime way to provide feedback for yourself while studying is *recitation.* If you are going to remember something, eventually you have to retrieve it. *Recitation* refers to summarizing aloud while you are learning. Recitation forces you to practice retrieving information. When you are reading a textbook, you should stop frequently and try to remember what you have just read by restating it in your own words. In one classic experiment, the best memory score was earned by a group of students who spent 80 percent of their time reciting and only 20 percent reading (Gates, 1917). (Maybe students who talk to themselves aren't crazy after all.)

If you have spaced your practice and overlearned, retrieval practice in the form of review will be like icing on your study cake (Karpicke & Blunt, 2011). Reviewing shortly before an exam cuts down the time during which you must remember details that may be important for the test. When reviewing, hold the amount of new information you try to memorize to a minimum. It may be realistic to take what you have learned and add a little more to it at the last minute by cramming. But remember that more than a little new learning may interfere with what you already know.

Spaced practice A practice schedule that alternates study periods with brief rests.

Massed practice A practice schedule in which studying continues for long periods, without interruption.

Extend How Long You Remember When you are learning new information, practice retrieval repeatedly. As you do, gradually lengthen the amount of time that passes before you test yourself again. For example, if you are studying German words on flash cards, look at the first card and then move it a few cards back in the stack. Do the same with the next few cards. When you get to the first "old" card, test yourself on it and check the answer. Then, move it farther back in the stack. Do the same with other "old" cards as they come up. When "old" cards come up for the third time, put them clear to the back of the stack.

Clear Your Mind and Prepare Your Body If you are counting on successful retrieval, say when writing an exam, try to clear your mind beforehand. Don't schedule any other important events near the same time if you can help it. Remember that resting after study reduces interference. That's why your study schedule should include ample breaks between subjects and you should be well rested when you write your exam. Also remember that although it is better to *study* before eating, people who are hungry almost always score lower on memory tests (Diano et al., 2006). So Mother was right—it's a good idea to make sure that you've had a good breakfast or lunch before you take exams (Smith, Clark, & Gallagher, 1999). A cup of coffee won't hurt your test performance, either (Smith, Christopher, & Sutherland, 2013).

A Look Ahead Psychologists still have much to learn about the nature of memory and how to improve it. For now, one thing stands out clearly: People who have good memories excel at organizing meaningful information. Sometimes, however, you are faced with the need to memorize information without much inherent meaning. For example, a shopping list is just a list of more or less unrelated items. There's not much of a meaningful relationship among carrots, rolls of toilet paper, TV dinners, and Twinkies, except that you need more of them. With this in mind, you can learn how to use mnemonics to better memorize when meaning-based strategies, like those already described, are not helpful.

Mnemonics—Tricks of the (Memory) Trade

Learning Outcome 35.3 Define mnemonics and provide some examples

Imagine the poor biology or psychology student who is required to learn the names of the 12 cranial nerves (in order, of course). Although the spinal nerves connect the brain to the body through the spinal cord, the cranial nerves do so directly. Just in case you want to know, the names are olfactory, optic, oculomotor, trochlear, trigeminal, abducens, facial, vestibulocochlear, glossopharyngeal, vagus, spinal accessory, and hypoglossal.

As you might imagine, most of us find it difficult to successfully encode this list. In the absence of any obvious meaningful relationship among these terms, it is difficult to apply the memory strategies that we discussed in the previous section and tempting to resort to *rote* learning (learning by simple repetition). Fortunately, there *is* an alternative. Use a **mnemonic** (nee-MON-ik)—a strategy for enhancing memory—to impose an artificial organization on material if none is naturally present. The superiority of mnemonic learning as opposed to rote learning has been demonstrated many times (Carney & Levin, 2014; Worthen & Hunt, 2010). Here are some examples:

Create Acrostics

In an *acrostic*, the first letters of the word in a target list are used to create a sentence. Generations of students have learned the names of the spinal nerves by memorizing the sentence "**O**n **O**ld **O**lympus' **T**owering **T**op **A** **F**amous **V**ocal **G**erman **V**iewed **S**ome **H**ops." This mnemonic, which uses the first letter of each of the cranial nerves to generate a nonsense sentence, indeed produces better recall of the cranial nerves. Similarly, **S**ome **P**eople **C**an **F**ly! helps psychology students remember Piaget's stages of cognitive development: sensorimotor, preoperational, concrete operational, formal operational. Such acrostics are even more effective if you make up your own (Fry, 2012). (Try making them rhyme for an added memory boost.)

Create Mental Images

According to the multimedia principle, supplementing words with images generally improves memory. Make these images as vivid, and even bizarre, as possible (Soemer & Schwan, 2012). Bizarre images make stored information more *distinctive* and therefore easier to retrieve (Worthen & Hunt, 2010). Do note, however, that bizarre images help

Exaggerated mental images can link two words or ideas in ways that aid memory. Here, the keyword method is used to link the English word *letter* with the Spanish word *carta*.

improve mainly immediate memory, and they work best for fairly simple information (Fritz et al., 2007). Nevertheless, they can be a first step toward learning.

For example, suppose that you have to learn the names of all the bones and muscles in the human body. To remember that the jawbone is the *mandible*, you can associate it to a *man nibbling*, or maybe you can picture a *man dribbling* a basketball with his jaw (make this image as ridiculous as possible).

The Keyword Method

Let's say that you have some new vocabulary words to memorize in Spanish. You can use the **keyword method**, in which a familiar word or image is used to link two other words or items (Campos, Camino, & Pérez-Fabello, 2011; Fritz et al., 2007). To remember that the word *pajaro* (pronounced PAH-hah-ro) means "bird," you can link it to a "key" word in English: *pajaro* sounds a bit like "parked car-o." Therefore, to remember that *pajaro* means "bird," you might visualize a parked car jam-packed with birds. You should try to make this image as vivid and exaggerated as possible, with birds flapping and chirping and feathers flying everywhere. Similarly, for the word *carta* (which means "letter"), you might imagine a shopping *cart* filled with postal letters.

If you link similar keywords and images for the rest of the list, you may not remember them all, but you will get most without much more practice. As a matter of fact, if you have formed the *pajaro* and *carta* images, it will be almost impossible for you to see these words again without remembering what they mean. The keyword method is also superior when you want to work "backward" from an English word to a foreign word (Campos, Rodríguez-Pinal, & Pérez-Fabello, 2013).

Create Stories or Chains

How can mnemonics be used to remember things in order? To remember lists of ideas, objects, or words in order, try forming an exaggerated association (mental image) connecting the first item to the second and then the second to the third, and so on. To remember the following short list in order—elephant, doorknob, string, watch, rifle, oranges—picture a full-size *elephant* balanced on a *doorknob* playing with a *string* tied to him. Picture a *watch* tied to the string, and a *rifle* shooting *oranges* at the watch. This technique can be used quite successfully for lists of 20 or more items. In one test, people who used a linking mnemonic did much better at remembering lists of 15 and 22 errands (Higbee et al., 1990). Try it next time you go shopping and leave your list at home. Another helpful strategy is to make up a short story that links all the items on a list that you want to remember (McNamara & Scott, 2001; Worthen & Hunt, 2010).

The Method of Loci Ancient Greek orators had an interesting way to remember ideas in order when giving a speech, the *method of loci* (locations). They took a mental "walk" along a familiar path. As they did, they associated topics with the images of statues found along the walk. You can do the same thing by "placing" objects or ideas along the way as you mentally take a familiar walk (Radvansky, 2017).

The Pros and Cons of Mnemonics

What about a year from now? How long do these "mnemonic memories" last? Mnemonic memories work best in the short run. Later, they may be more fragile than conventional memories. That's why it's usually best to use mnemonics only during the initial stages of learning (Carney & Levin, 2003; Fry, 2012).

If you have never used mnemonics, you may still be skeptical, but give this approach a fair trial. Most people find that they can greatly extend their memory using mnemonics. But remember, like most things worthwhile, remembering takes effort (Hancock, 2011).

Mnemonic A strategy for enhancing memory.

Keyword method As an aid to memory, using a familiar word or image to link two items.

MODULE 35

Exceptional Memory—Learning Outcomes Revisited

35.1 Describe some of the ways that memory can be "exceptional"

Eidetic imagery (photographic memory) occurs when a person is able to project an image onto a blank surface. Eidetic imagery is rarely found in adults. Exceptional memory may be based on natural ability or learned strategies. Usually, it involves both.

35.2 Outline some strategies that can improve memory

Memory can be improved through better encoding strategies, such as chunking, using mental images, and elaborating, as well as whole learning, the progressive-part method, encoding retrieval cues, overlearning, and spaced practice. Memory also can be improved through better retrieval strategies, such as using active search strategies and retrieval practice, which involves feedback, recitation, and review.

35.3 Define mnemonics and provide some examples

Mnemonics use bizarre or exaggerated verbal associations and mental images to link new information with familiar memories already stored in LTM. Mnemonics include acrostics, mental imagery (including the keyword method), and stories or chains (including the method of loci). Mnemonics greatly improve immediate memory. However, conventional learning tends to create the most lasting memories.

Reflective Practice

Content Check

1. For most people, having an especially good memory is based on
   a. maintenance rehearsal
   b. elaborative processing
   c. phonetic imagery
   d. learned strategies
2. As new information is encoded, it is helpful to elaborate on its meaning and connect it to other information. T or F?
3. The cognitive interview helps people remember more by providing
   a. retrieval cues
   b. a serial position effect
   c. phonetic priming
   d. massed practice
4. Which of the following is least likely to improve a memory in the long term?
   a. using exaggerated mental images
   b. forming a chain of associations
   c. turning visual information into verbal information
   d. associating new information to information that is already known or familiar

Skill Check

Think Critically

5. What are the advantages of taking notes as you read a textbook, as opposed to underlining words in the text?
6. How are elaborative processing and using a mnemonic alike?

Self-Reflect

What kinds of information are you good at remembering? Why do you think your memory is better for those topics? Review the techniques for improving memory, and think of a specific example of how you could use each technique at school, at home, or at work. The best mnemonics are your own. As an exercise, see if you can create a better acrostic for the 12 cranial nerves. One student generated **O**ld **O**tto **O**ctavius **T**ried **T**rigonometry **A**fter **F**acing **V**ery **G**rim **V**irgin's **S**ad **H**usbands (Bloom & Lamkin, 2006).

ANSWERS

1. d 2. T 3. a 4. c 5. Properly done, note-taking is a form of elaborative processing; it encourages active reflection and facilitates the organization and selection of important ideas, and your notes can be used for review. 6. Both attempt to relate new information to information already stored in LTM that is familiar or already easy to retrieve.

A Psychologist's Skill Set

Giving Memorable Presentations

MODULE 36

Fighting PowerPoint-less Slides

AP Images/J. Scott Applewhite

In an effort to explain the U.S. Forces strategy in Afghanistan, members of the American military prepared a Microsoft PowerPoint slide for General Stanley McChrystal (pictured here). This single slide outlined 100 issues that were central to the war effort, with no fewer than 200 arrows connecting them to one another. The general, who was in charge of North Atlantic Treaty Organization (NATO) forces in the region, had just one thing to say: "When we understand that slide, we'll have won the war."

Have you, like the general, ever sat through a presentation overflowing with words or complicated diagrams? Overwhelmed by listening and reading, you probably didn't remember very much. Of course, you may also have experienced presentations that kept you on the edge of your seat, and that you remembered many months—or even years—later.

These days, it's common to give presentations at school or work that involve videos or slides made using PowerPoint, Prezi, or Keynote. Clearly, there are important technology-related skills needed to create this type of presentation. Giving a *memorable* presentation, however, requires a different set of skills altogether—skills that depend on a solid understanding of how human memory works.

~LEARNING OUTCOMES~

After reading this module you should be able to:

36.1 Define the multimedia principle, explaining the role of the visual and auditory channels, and describe the actions you can take to ensure that your audience will remember the information being communicated

From Pictures to PowerPoint—Avoid Death by PowerPoint!

Learning Outcome 36.1 Define the multimedia principle, explaining the role of the visual and auditory channels, and describe the actions you can take to ensure that your audience will remember the information being communicated

The previous four modules described human memory, including the three memory systems (sensory memory, short-term or working memory, and long-term memory) and some of the factors that contribute to remembering and forgetting. In this module, we make use of what we know about memory to describe how to give an effective multimedia presentation—that is, a presentation that includes both words (either spoken or text) and graphics (including pictures, animations, charts, or video).

One of the reasons that multimedia presentations can be so useful in conveying information is that people process words and mental images together better than they do words alone, a finding referred to as the *multimedia principle* (see Module 32). There are three important assumptions associated with this principle (Overson, 2014). The first is that people process multimedia information through two sensory channels—visual (the eyes) and auditory (the ears).

The second assumption is that people can only process a limited amount of information through either of these channels at any moment in time. For example, if you present an image or a video on the screen, the audience can only hold a portion of that graphic in working memory at one time. Similarly, when you are speaking during your presentation, the audience is only able to keep a few words in working memory.

Finally, the third assumption is that people remember information best when they *select* important information from sensory memory, *organize* it in a meaningful way in working memory, and *integrate* it with other information in long-term memory (Mayer, 2014). A memorable presentation is one that promotes active processing by helping the audience with the tasks of selecting, organizing, and integrating information.

Preparing Multimedia Presentations

Multimedia presentations are common in workplaces ranging from business to education to health care. Part of your success in the workplace, then, may rest on your ability to give a presentation that is persuasive, informative, and above all, memorable.

OK. How do I do that? Begin by noting the characteristics of your audience, such as their age and background knowledge. Understanding your audience is important because it will guide the complexity of the ideas that you present, the language that you use, and the pace at which you provide information. Audiences that are extremely knowledgeable require much less in the way of background information and will not be left behind if you move through your material at a somewhat faster pace. On the other hand, a less experienced audience will need you to move more slowly, explaining the background more thoroughly and providing examples where appropriate. If you're presenting on ideas in a field that uses a specialized professional vocabulary, it will be important to explain each term and how it relates to the main points that you're trying to make.

In terms of the multimedia part of your presentation, recall that people have a limited ability to process information through their visual and verbal channels. Remember, too, that they remember information best when they *select* information that's important from the material that enters sensory memory, *organize* it in a meaningful way while it is in working memory, and *integrate* it with other information that is in long-term memory. Let's look at how to create presentations that meet these goals (Atkinson & Mayer, 2004).

Help the Audience Select Important Information

- *Eliminate distractions.* Critically evaluate the slide design template that you have selected, as well as other features that you are using. Does the template have a very busy pattern with wild colors? Is the font easy to read? You should also ask yourself whether any animations you've selected might be distracting for the audience. For example, do you have points that are zooming onto the screen from the side, or text that bounces up and down? These kinds of animations will consume your audience's valuable processing capacity unnecessarily. Always remember that just because these features *can* be used doesn't mean that they *should* be used.
- *Eliminate anything on the slide that does not support the main point.* On individual slides, the things that you cut out may include unnecessary graphics, such as logos, backgrounds or watermarks (the images that can be seen "behind" the text), or any text that does not support the main point being made on the slide.
- *Limit yourself to a few main points per slide.* This will help limit the amount of text that's up on the screen for people to process. You can also limit the amount of text by avoiding points that are paragraphs—use the minimum number of words necessary to convey your point clearly. If you do find yourself with a large amount of text on your slide, consider splitting it into two (or more) slides.
- *Highlight the main points you want to make on each slide.* There are many ways that you can draw the audience's attention to the central point being made on a slide.

One is to use italics and colored font to draw attention to key words or phrases on the slide (but make sure that there aren't too many!). If you are contrasting two ideas, another way to visually highlight points is to use a table format that places them side-by-side, rather than two sets of bullet points.

- *Instead of a title at the top of the slide, use a headline.* A headline is written in the active voice and contains a noun and verb. Its primary purpose is to summarize, in a very limited number of words, the single overarching idea that is being conveyed by the information or graphics on the slide. People—especially those who are not very familiar with the material that you are presenting—have a better chance of remembering a short summary rather than all of the text that's on the slide. Instead of a title such as "Mnemonics," then, you may want to consider the headline "Mnemonics Help Improve Memory."

Help the Audience Organize Information

- *Keep your eye on the whole story.* As you create individual slides, it's very easy to get caught up in what information you should include on each one. Remember, though, that the entire presentation is intended to tell your audience a story. The best presentations don't begin with the creation of slides, PowerPoint, or Keynote—they begin when you map out the story's beginning (What does your audience already know?) and end (What do you want them to know by the time you're finished?), and then carefully plot the points you need to make to bridge that gap. To ensure that the story is developing smoothly, you should regularly check on the flow of the presentation as a whole by using features such as Slide Sorter in PowerPoint or Light Table in Keynote.
- *Make the structure of your points clear.* You will have noticed that each module in this book has a clear structure. The main topics have titles in very large print; if there are smaller points being made within these main topics, then their titles are written in smaller print. Using fonts of different sizes in this way helps to signal the overall structure of the information to the reader and helps them to organize it in their minds. When you create a slide that includes text, you can do the same thing: Use points and subpoints to help the audience see the underlying structure of your talk. And if you really want to emphasize structure, consider a single opening or closing slide that summarizes only the main points being made.
- *Talk over pictures.* The multimedia principle tells us that people learn better from pictures and words than they do from words alone. Because most presenters don't realize this, slides are often filled only with words. This verbal information has to be processed by the visual channel, which can quickly become overloaded when there is a lot of text on the screen. This problem is made worse when the presenter is also speaking, because the audience's attention is then trying to process the same type of information through both the visual and auditory channels! A better strategy is to use carefully selected (and high-quality) visuals that can make the point, and to narrate the text out loud for your audience (Fenesi et al., 2014). By "talking over pictures" in this way, you can capitalize on people's ability to process visual and auditory information at the same time.

Help the Audience Integrate Information

- *Help the audience make connections.* Whenever possible, help the audience to see how the information you're presenting is related to material that is already in their long-term memory. For example, you might draw their attention to how the material is similar or different to things they have seen before, how it extends what they already know, or how your topic is connected to their own personal experiences.

Practice

The final thing to remember if you want to deliver a good presentation is simple: practice, practice, practice! Practicing your talk will confirm whether you will be able to stick to the time you've been given and will help to develop your confidence. That confidence will help you to speak without stumbling over your words and present the image of someone who really understands the material. And what could be more memorable than that?

MODULE 36

Giving Memorable Presentations—Learning Outcomes Revisited

36.1 Define the multimedia principle, explaining the role of the visual and auditory channels, and describe the actions you can take to ensure that your audience will remember the information being communicated

Multimedia presentations involve both visual and auditory information. The multimedia principle states that people learn more from words and graphics together than they do from words alone. However, we can process very limited amounts of information through the auditory and visual channels at a specific time. Effective presentations consider audience demographics. You can help the audience *select* important information by eliminating irrelevant background distractions and information from slides, putting a few main points per slide and highlighting them, and using headlines rather than titles for each slide. You can help your audience *organize* information by outlining your presentation as a story, clearly structuring points, and making complementary use of the auditory and visual channels. You can help the audience *integrate* information by highlighting connections between information and external knowledge.

Reflective Practice

Content Check

1. People learn more from words alone than from words and graphics. T or F?
2. We can process unlimited multimedia information through our visual and verbal sensory channels. T or F?
3. People will remember information best when they __________ information that they consider important, __________ it in a meaningful way, and __________ it with other long-term information.

Skill Check

Think Critically

4. You are asked to give a PowerPoint presentation to a group of Grade 1 students on how to study. Now, what if you were asked to present the same topic to a group of university students? How would you tailor your presentations to suit each audience?

Self-Reflect

Think of a time you sat in a lecture and found yourself disengaged because of the professor's presentation style, tone of voice, or layout of information. Now think of a really great lecture you attended. What was it about the presentation that made this lecture engaging? How can you apply these techniques to your own presentations in the future?

ANSWERS

1. F 2. F 3. Select, organize, and integrate. 4. Considering the demographics of each audience, you could tailor language, pace of information, background knowledge, and visuals. For the Grade 1 class you should use simple language, move at a slower pace, provide less information, assume little background knowledge, and keep visuals simple and age-appropriate.

MODULE 37

Cognition and Intelligence
Modes of Thought

Hyperloop

Have you ever imagined the future of transportation? Visualize yourself reclining in a sleek pod zipping along at 700 miles per hour down a narrow low-pressure tube powered by little more than magnetic impulses and solar power. That's what Elon Musk imagined. But Musk did not stop there. He called his creative idea *Hyperloop* and set out to build it.

If anyone can do it, Musk can. After all, he is the creative genius behind *Tesla*, the company that has already revolutionized the electric automobile. Oh yes, and *SpaceX* (the first private company to successfully launch a spacecraft into orbit), dedicated to the human colonization of the planet Mars (Vance, 2015).

But *how* does Elon Musk find such elegant solutions to problems? How does he think? What *is* thinking? What does language have to do with thought? What is intelligence? What is creativity? Let's think this through.

ZUMA Press, Inc./Alamy Stock Photo

~LEARNING OUTCOMES~

After reading this module you should be able to:

37.1 Distinguish between experiential and reflective processing

37.2 Explain how imagery is used in thinking

37.3 Explain how concepts are used in thinking

37.4 Explain how language is used in thinking

What Is Thinking?—Brains over Brawn

Learning Outcome 37.1 Distinguish between experiential and reflective processing

Cognition is the process of thinking, gaining knowledge, and dealing with knowledge. At its most basic, cognition refers to *processing* a *mental representation* (internal subjective expression) of a problem or situation (Sternberg, 2017). Human cognition can take many forms, from experiential daydreaming to more reflective problem solving and reasoning. Consider, for example, the relatively reflective process of planning. Picture a television interviewer who mentally tries out several lines of questioning before beginning a live interview. By *planning* her moves, she can avoid many mistakes. Imagine planning what to study for an exam, what to say at a job interview, or how to get to your spring

Cognition Process of thinking, gaining knowledge, and dealing with knowledge.

➤ **Figure 37.1**

Experiential versus reflective processing. (*a*) An experiential processing task; (*b*) a reflective processing task. See the text for an explanation. (After Kahneman, 2011.)

break hotel. Better yet, in each of these cases, imagine what might happen if you didn't, or couldn't, plan at all.

Let's do some more experiential and reflective thinking while looking at ➤ Figure 37.1. On the left *(a)*, is this face happy or sad? Chances are that you *knew* the answer just by looking at the photo. You were engaging in more or less unconscious, effortless, and automatic **experiential processing**. Now looking at *(b)*, what is the sum of these numbers? This time, experiential processing may not have been enough; you likely had to deliberately concentrate and engage in **reflective processing** (Kahneman, 2011; Norman, 1994). (The difference between these two types of cognition is relevant to how well you understand and remember what you are learning; see Module 1.)

What do you mean when you say that experiential processing is "automatic"? Try the activity shown in ➤ Figure 37.2. Fluent readers of English usually have difficulty quickly naming the color of ink used to print the words in the bottom two rows of this figure. But why? When fluent readers look at words, they normally *read* them automatically (Moors, 2016). In this case, the task is *not* to read the words; instead, it is to *name* the ink color used to print the words. But reading words is so

➤ **Figure 37.2**

The Stroop interference task. Test yourself by naming out loud the colors in the top two rows as quickly as you can. Then name out loud the colors of the ink used to print the words in the bottom two rows. (Do not read the words themselves.) Was it harder to name the ink colors in the bottom rows?

automated that fluent readers cannot help themselves. Sooner or later, when fluent readers work through lists like these, they are likely to make some mistakes, reading out loud, for example, the word *purple* instead of naming the ink color (*green* or *red* in this example).

At the very least, fluent readers cannot speed through such lists since the *automatic* processing of word meanings is just too strong to ignore and interferes with color naming. To avoid making mistakes, fluent readers have to engage in some reflective cognition, deliberately checking responses to make sure they are not reading the color words aloud.

In a moment, we'll delve further into imagery, concepts, and language. Be aware, however, that thinking involves attention, pattern recognition, memory, decision making, intuition, knowledge, and more (Goldstein, 2019). This module is only a sample of what cognitive psychology is about.

Some Basic Units of Thought

The power of being able to mentally represent problems is dramatically illustrated by chess grand master Miguel Najdorf, who once simultaneously played 45 chess games while blindfolded. How did Najdorf do it? Like most people, he used the basic units of thought: mental images, concepts, and language (or symbols). **Mental images** are picturelike mental representations. A **concept** is a mental category for classifying things based on common features or properties. **Language** consists of words or symbols and rules for combining them. Thinking often involves all three units. For example, blindfolded chess players rely on visual images, concepts ("Game 2 begins with a strategy called an English opening"), and the notational system, or "language," of chess.

Mental Imagery—Does a Frog Have Lips?

Learning Outcome 37.2 Explain how imagery is used in thinking

Almost everyone experiences visual and auditory images. Many of us also experience imagery for movement, touch, taste, smell, and pain. Thus, mental images are often more than just "pictures." For example, your image of a bakery also may include its delicious aroma. Some people even have a rare form of imagery called **synesthesia** (sin-es-THEE-zyah). For these individuals, images cross normal sensory barriers (Craver-Lemley & Reeves, 2013; Marks, 2014). For one such person, spiced chicken tastes "pointy"; and for another, chocolate smells pink and stripey (Dixon, Smilek, & Merikle, 2004; Russell, Stevenson, & Rich, 2015).

Despite such variations, most of us use images to think, remember, and solve problems. For instance, we may use mental images to do the following:

- Make a decision or solve a problem (choose what clothes to wear; figure out how to arrange furniture in a room)
- Change feelings (think of pleasant images to get out of a bad mood; imagine yourself as thin to stay on a diet)
- Improve a skill or prepare for some action (use images to improve a tennis stroke; mentally rehearse how you will ask for a raise)
- Aid memory (picture Mr. Cook wearing a chef's hat, so you can remember his name)

Creating and Using Mental Images

To better understand our capacity to create and use mental images, let's tackle a few examples.

To begin, mental images are not flat, like photographs. Researcher Stephen Kosslyn showed this by asking people, "Does a frog have lips and a stubby tail?" Unless you often kiss frogs, you probably will tackle this question by using mental images. Most people picture a frog, "look" at its mouth, and then mentally "rotate" the frog in mental space to check its tail (Kosslyn, 1983). Mental rotation is partly based on imagined movements (➤ Figure 37.3). That is, we can mentally "pick up" an object and turn it around or even fold it (Harris, Hirsh-Pasek, & Newcombe, 2013; Wraga, Boyle, & Flynn, 2010).

Using Mental Images *How are images used to solve problems?* Let's say that you are asked, "How many ways can you use an empty egg carton?" You might begin by picturing uses you have already seen, such as sorting buttons. To give more original answers, you might assemble or invent new images. Thus, an artist may completely picture a proposed sculpture before beginning work. People with good imaging abilities tend to score higher on tests of creativity, even if they are blind (Eardley & Pring, 2007; Morrison & Wallace, 2001).

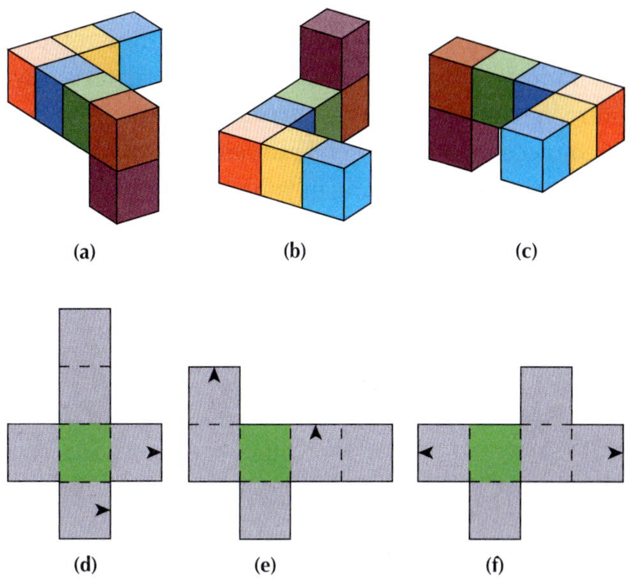

➤ **Figure 37.3**

Imagery in thinking. *(Top)* Participants were shown a drawing similar to (*a*) and drawings of how (*a*) would look in other positions, such as (*b*) and (*c*). Participants could recognize (*a*) after it had been "rotated" from its original position. However, the more (*a*) was rotated in space, the longer it took to recognize it. This result suggests that people formed a three-dimensional image of (*a*) and rotated the image to see if it matched (Shepard, 1975). *(Bottom)* Try your ability to manipulate mental images: Picture each of these shapes as a piece of paper that can be folded to make a cube. After they have been folded, on which cubes do the arrow tips meet (Kosslyn, 1985)?

"Reverse Vision" *Didn't we discuss the creation and use of mental images in the chapter on memory?* You remembered! (see Module 32). We learned that mental images are held in short-term, or working, memory. More precisely, the part of working memory that specializes in

Experiential processing Thought that is passive, effortless, and automatic.

Reflective processing Thought that is active, effortful, and controlled.

Mental images Mental pictures or visual depictions used in memory and thinking.

Concept Mental category for classifying things based on common features or properties.

Language Words or symbols, and rules for combining them, that are used for thinking and communication.

Synesthesia Experiencing one sense in terms normally associated with another sense; for example, "seeing" colors when a sound is heard.

the processing of mental images is called the *visuospatial sketch pad* (Baddeley, 2012).

Where in the brain is the visuospatial sketch pad located? Different psychological processes, like rotating a mental image in working memory, are not always easy to localize in the brain (they may actually be carried out by an interconnected collection of brain areas). Roughly speaking, then, seeing something in your "mind's eye" is similar to seeing real objects. Information from the eyes normally activates the brain's primary visual area, creating an image (➤ **Figure 37.4**). Other brain areas then help us recognize the image by relating it to stored knowledge.

When you form a mental image, the system works in reverse. Brain areas in which memories are stored send signals back to the visual cortex, where once again an image is created (Borst & Kosslyn, 2010; Zvyagintsev et al., 2013). For

The Vessel, at the Hudson Yards, New York City was designed by architect Thomas Heatherwick. Could a person lacking mental imagery design such a masterpiece? Most artists, architects, designers, sculptors, and filmmakers have excellent visual imagery.

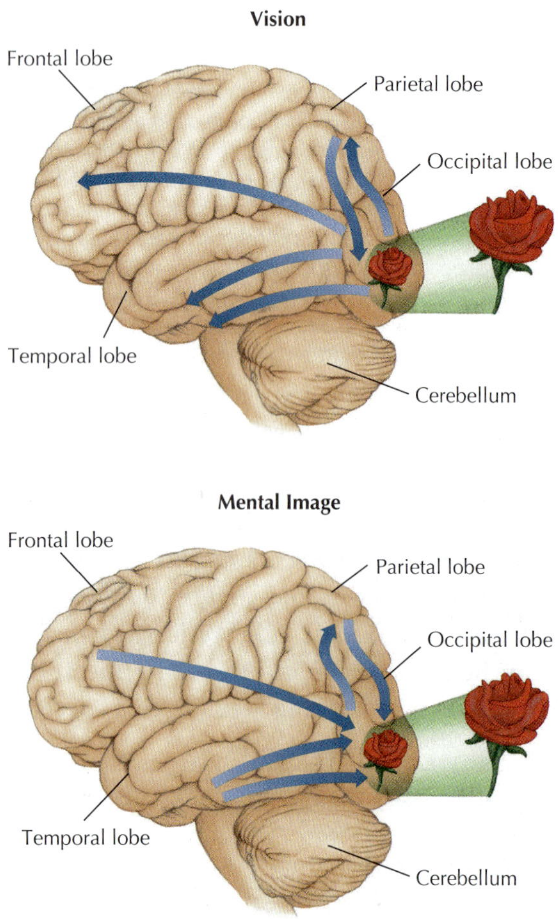

➤ **Figure 37.4**

Imagery in the brain. (*Top*) When you see a flower, its image is represented by activity in the primary visual area of the cortex at the back of the brain. Information about the flower also is relayed to other brain areas. (*Bottom*) If you form a mental image of a flower, information follows a reverse path. The result, once again, is activation of the primary visual area.

Rock climbers use kinesthetic imagery to learn climbing routes and to plan their next few moves (Naderi et al., 2018).

example, if you visualize a friend's face right now, the area of your brain that specializes in perceiving faces will become more active (Prochnow et al., 2013).

Kinesthetic Imagery In a sense, we think with our bodies as well as our brains. *Kinesthetic (motor) images* are created from muscular sensations (Grangeon, Guillot, & Collet, 2011; Olshansky et al., 2015). Such images help us think about movements and actions.

As you think and talk, kinesthetic sensations can guide the flow of ideas. For example, if a friend calls and asks you the combination of a lock you lent her, you may move your hands as if twirling the dial on the lock. Or, try answering this question: Which direction do you turn the hot-water handle in your kitchen to shut off the water? If you haven't memorized the words "leftie loosie" and "rightie tightie," you may "turn" the faucet in your imagination before answering. You may even make a turning motion with your hand before answering.

Kinesthetic images are especially important in movement-oriented skills such as music, sports, dance, skateboarding, and martial arts. An effective way to improve such skills is to practice by rehearsing kinesthetic images of yourself performing flawlessly (Anema & Dijkerman, 2013).

Concepts—I'm Positive, It's a Whatchamacallit

Learning Outcome 37.3 Explain how concepts are used in thinking

As noted previously, a *concept* is an idea that represents a category of objects or events. Concepts help us identify important features of the world. That's why experts in various areas of knowledge are good at classifying objects. Bird-watchers, tropical fish fanciers, 5-year-old dinosaur enthusiasts, and others all learn to look for identifying details that beginners tend to miss. If you are knowledgeable about a topic, such as horses, flowers, or football, you literally see things differently than less well-informed people do (Harel et al., 2010; Ross, 2006).

Forming Concepts

How are concepts learned? **Concept formation** is the process of classifying information into meaningful categories (Ashby & Maddox, 2005; Newell, 2012). At its most basic, concept formation is based on experience with *positive* and *negative instances* (examples that belong, or do not belong, to the concept category).

As adults, we often acquire concepts by learning or forming *conceptual rules*, guidelines for deciding whether objects or events belong to a concept class. For example, a triangle must be a closed shape with three sides made of straight lines. Rules are an efficient way to learn concepts, but examples remain important. It's unlikely that memorizing rules would allow a new listener to accurately categorize *rhythm and blues*, *hip-hop*, *rock*, *salsa*, *reggae*, *country*, and *rap* music.

Types of Concepts

Are there different kinds of concepts? Yes, a **conjunctive concept**, or "and concept," is defined by the presence of two or more features (Reed, 2013). In other words, an item must have "this feature *and* this feature *and* this feature." For example, a *motorcycle* must have two wheels *and* an engine *and* handlebars.

A **relational concept** is based on how an object relates to something else, or how its features relate to one another. All of the following are relational concepts: *larger*, *above*, *left*, *north*, and *upside down*. Another example is *brother*, which is defined as "a male considered in his relation to another person having the same parents."

A **disjunctive concept** has *at least one* of several possible features. These are "either/or" concepts. To belong to the category, an item must have "this feature *or* that feature *or* another feature." For example, in baseball, a *strike* is *either* a swing and a miss *or* a pitch over the plate *or* a foul ball (unless two strikes have already been called). The either/or quality of disjunctive concepts makes them harder to learn.

Prototypes When you think of the concept *bird*, do you mentally list the features of birds? Probably not. In addition to rules and features, we might use a **prototype**, or ideal

Concept formation The process of classifying information into meaningful categories.

Conjunctive concept A class of objects that have two or more features in common. (For example, to qualify as an example of the concept, an object must be both red *and* triangular.)

Relational concept A concept defined by the relationship between features of an object or between an object and its surroundings (for example, "greater than," "lopsided").

Disjunctive concept A concept defined by the presence of at least one of several possible features. (For example, to qualify, an object must be either blue *or* circular.)

Prototype An ideal model used as a prime example of a particular concept.

model, to identify concepts (Rosch, 1977; Tunney & Fernie, 2012). A robin, for example, is a prototypical bird; an ostrich is not. In other words, some items are better examples of a concept than others are (Smith, 2014). Which of the drawings in ➤ **Figure 37.5** best represents a cup? At some point, as a cup grows taller or wider, it becomes a vase or a bowl. How do we know when the line is crossed? Probably, we mentally compare objects to an "ideal" cup, like number 5. That's why it's hard to identify concepts when we can't come up with relevant prototypes (Minda & Smith, 2011).

Let's move on to explore another concept: *language*.

➤ **Figure 37.5**

Identifying prototypes. When does a cup become a bowl or a vase? Deciding if an object belongs to a conceptual class is aided by relating it to a prototype, or ideal example. Participants in one experiment chose number 5 as the "best" cup. (After Labov, 1973.)

Language—Say What?

Learning Outcome 37.4 Explain how language is used in thinking

As we have seen, thinking may occur without language. Everyone has searched for a word to express an idea that exists as a vague image or feeling. Nevertheless, most thinking relies heavily on language, because words *encode* (translate) the world into symbols that are easy to manipulate.

Linguistic Relativity: What's North of My Fork?

Our struggle at times, to express our thoughts in words, makes it clear that our thoughts influence the words we use. But might the reverse be true? Do the words we use affect our thoughts and actions? The answer appears to be "Yes." Cognitive psychologist Lera Boroditsky has reported that aboriginal children from Cape York, a remote part of northeastern Australia, can accurately point to any compass direction as early as age 5. In contrast, most Americans cannot do this even as adults (Boroditsky, 2011).

Wine tasting illustrates the encoding function of language. To communicate their experiences to others, wine connoisseurs must put taste sensations into words. The wine you see here is "Marked by deeply concentrated nuances of plum, blackberry, and currant, with a nice balance of tannins and acid, building to a spicy oak finish." (Don't try this with a soda!)

But why? According to Boroditsky, unlike English, Kuuk Thaayorre, the language of the Cape York Australian aboriginals, relies exclusively on *absolute* directional references. Like English, Kuuk Thaayorre has words for *north, south,* and so on. Unlike English, Kuuk Thaayorre lacks words for *relative* directional references, such as *left* and *right.*

For long distances, an English speaker might say, "Chicago is north of here." But for short distances, the same speaker will shift to a relative reference and might say, "My brother is sitting to my right." In contrast, a speaker of Kuuk Thaayorre always uses absolute directional references, saying things like "My friend is sitting southeast of me" and "The spoon is west of the cup." If you are a young aboriginal child, you had better master your absolute directions, or most conversations will be impossible to follow.

Another interesting consequence for speakers of Kuuk Thaayorre is how they arrange time. In one study, English speakers given a set of cards depicting a series of events (for example, a person getting older or a meal being cooked and eaten) and asked to put them in order usually arranged them from left to right. Hebrew speakers usually arranged the cards from right to left, presumably because this is the direction in which Hebrew is written. In contrast, speakers of Kuuk Thaayorre arrange temporal sequences from east to west. If the sorter is facing north, the cards are arranged from right to left, but if the sorter is facing south, the cards are arranged from left to right, and so on (Boroditsky & Gaby, 2010).

Findings like these lend support to the **linguistic relativity hypothesis**, the idea that the words we use not only reflect our thoughts but can shape them as well. So the next time you think that your future is "ahead" of you and your past is "behind," think again. For speakers of Aymara, a South American language, it is the past that is "ahead" (Miles et al., 2010). So watch your back.

Semantics

The study of meaning in words and language is known as **semantics** (Youn et al., 2016). It is here that the link between language and thought becomes most evident.

Connotative and Denotative Meaning Generally speaking, words have two types of meaning. The **denotative meaning** of words is their exact, or dictionary, definition. The **connotative meaning** is the emotional or personal meaning of words. The denotative meaning of the word *naked* (having no clothes) is the same for a nudist as it is for a movie censor, but we could expect their connotations to differ.

Connotative differences can influence how we think about issues. Would you rather eat *rare prime beef* or *bloody slab of dead cow*? The arts of *political spin* and *propaganda* often amount to manipulating connotations (Sussman, 2011). For example, as a combatant in a war, would you rather be described as a *terrorist* or a *freedom fighter* (Payne, 2009)?

Context and Meaning Word meanings also depend on context. Circle the word that does not belong in this series:

skyscraper cathedral temple prayer

If you circled *prayer,* you answered as most people do. Now try again to circle the odd item:

cathedral prayer temple skyscraper

Did you circle *skyscraper* this time? The new order subtly alters the meaning of the last word. This occurs because words get much of their meaning from *context*. For example, the word *shot* means different things when we are thinking of marksmanship, bartending, medicine, photography, or golf (Harley, 2014).

Language also plays a major role in defining ethnic communities and other social groups. Thus, language can be a bridge or a barrier between cultures. Translating languages can cause a rash of semantic problems. Perhaps a hotel in Acapulco, Mexico, can be excused for attempting to reassure tourists that their water is safe to drink by posting a sign reading, "The manager has personally passed all the water served here." However, in more important situations, such as in international business and diplomacy, avoiding semantic confusion may be vital.

Bilingualism *Wouldn't it be better to being able to speak more than one language?* It would certainly reduce the likelihood of miscommunication across cultures. But it can bring personal benefits as well. Consider, for example, **bilingualism**, the ability to speak two languages. Studies have found that students who learn to speak two languages well have better mental flexibility, general language skills, control of attention, and problem-solving abilities (Bialystok & Barac, 2012; Sorge, Toplak, & Bialystok, 2016).

Unfortunately, millions of minority American children who do not speak English at home experience *subtractive bilingualism*. Immersed in English-only classrooms, in which they are expected to "sink or swim," they usually end up losing some of their native language skills. Such children risk becoming less than fully competent in *both* their first and second languages. In addition, they tend to fall behind educationally. As they struggle with English, their grasp of arithmetic, social studies, science, and other subjects also may suffer. In short, English-only instruction can leave them poorly prepared to succeed in the majority culture (Durán, Roseth, & Hoffman, 2010; Matthews & Matthews, 2004).

For the majority of children who speak English at home, the picture can be quite different because learning a second language is almost always beneficial. It poses no threat to the child's home language and improves a variety of cognitive skills. This has been called *additive bilingualism* because learning a second language adds to a child's overall competence (Hermanto, Moreno, & Bialystok, 2012).

An approach called **two-way bilingual education** can help children benefit from bilingualism and avoid its drawbacks (Benitz, 2009; Lessow-Hurley, 2013). In such programs, majority-group children and children with limited English skills are taught part of the day in English and the rest of the day in a second language. Both majority- and minority-language speakers become fluent in two languages, and they perform as well as or better than single-language students in English and general academic abilities.

Linguistic relativity hypothesis The idea that the words we use not only reflect our thoughts but can shape them as well.

Semantics The study of meanings in words and language.

Denotative meaning The exact, dictionary definition of a word or concept; its objective meaning.

Connotative meaning The subjective, personal, or emotional meaning of a word or concept.

Bilingualism The ability to speak two languages.

Two-way bilingual education A program in which English-speaking children and children with limited English proficiency are taught some of the day in English and some in a second language.

Then why isn't two-way bilingual education more widely used? Bilingual education tends to be politically unpopular among majority-language speakers (Garcia, 2008). Language is an important sign of group membership. Even where the majority culture is highly dominant, some of its members may feel that recent immigrants and "foreign languages" are eroding their culture. Regardless, the ability to think and communicate in a second language is a wonderful gift. Given the cognitive benefits, fostering bilingualism also may turn out to be one of the best ways to improve competitiveness in our rapidly globalizing information economy.

The Structure of Language

What does it take to make a language? First, a language must provide *symbols* that stand for objects and ideas (Harley, 2014). The symbols we call words are built out of **phonemes** (FOE-neems), basic speech sounds; and **morphemes** (MOR-feems), speech sounds collected into meaningful units, such as syllables. For instance, in English, the sounds *m*, *b*, *w*, and *a* cannot form the syllable *mbwa*. In Swahili, they can. (Also see ➤ Figure 37.6.)

Next, a language must have a **grammar**, or set of rules for making sounds into words and words into sentences (Reed, 2013). One part of grammar, known as **syntax**, concerns rules for word order. Syntax is important because rearranging words almost always changes the meaning of a sentence: "Dog bites man" versus "Man bites dog."

Traditional grammar is concerned with "surface" language—the sentences we actually speak. Linguist Noam Chomsky has focused instead on the unspoken rules that we use to change core ideas into various sentences. Chomsky (1986) believes that we do not learn all the sentences we might ever say. Rather, we actively *produce* them by applying **transformation rules** to universal, core patterns. We use these rules to change a simple declarative sentence to other voices or forms (past tense, passive voice, and so forth). For example, the core sentence "Man rides horse" can be transformed to these patterns (and others):

Past: The man rode the horse.
Passive: The horse was ridden by the man.
Negative: The man did not ride the horse.
Question: Did the man ride the horse?

Children seem to be using transformation rules when they say things such as "I runned home." That is, the child applied the normal past tense rule to the irregular verb *to run*.

A true language is, therefore, *productive*—it can generate new thoughts or ideas. In fact, words can be rearranged to produce a nearly infinite number of sentences. Some are silly: "Please don't feed me to the chipmunk." Some are profound: "We hold these truths to be self-evident, that all men are created equal." In either case, the productive quality of language makes it a powerful tool for thinking.

Gestural Languages

Contrary to commonsense belief, language is not limited to speech and text. Consider the case of Ildefonso, a young man who was born deaf. At age 8, Ildefonso had never communicated with another human, except by mime. Then, at last, Ildefonso had a breakthrough: After much hard work with a sign language teacher, he understood the link between a cat and the gesture for it. At that magic moment, he grasped the idea that "cat" could be communicated to another person, just by signing the word.

American Sign Language (ASL), a gestural language, made Ildefonso's breakthrough possible. ASL is a true language, like German, Spanish, or Japanese (Liddell, 2003; Shaw & Delaporte, 2011). In fact, people who use other gestural languages, such as French Sign, Mexican Sign, or Old Kentish Sign, may not easily understand ASL (Lucas & Bayley, 2011).

Although ASL has a *spatial* grammar, syntax, and semantics all its own (➤ Figure 37.7), both speech and signing follow similar universal language patterns. Signing children pass through the stages of language development at about the same age as speaking children. Some psychologists now believe that speech evolved from gestures, far back in human and primate history (Gillespie-Lynch et al., 2014; Kendon, 2016). Gestures help us string words together as we speak (Moreno-Cabrera, 2011). Some people would have difficulty speaking with their hands tied to their sides. Do

John Mitterer

Albanian	mak, mak
Chinese	gua, gua
Dutch	rap, rap
English	quack, quack
French	coin, coin
Italian	qua, qua
Spanish	cuá, cuá
Swedish	kvack, kvack
Turkish	vak, vak

➤ **Figure 37.6**
"Vak, Vak." Animals around the world make pretty much the same sounds. Notice, however, how various languages use slightly different phonemes to express the sound that a duck makes.

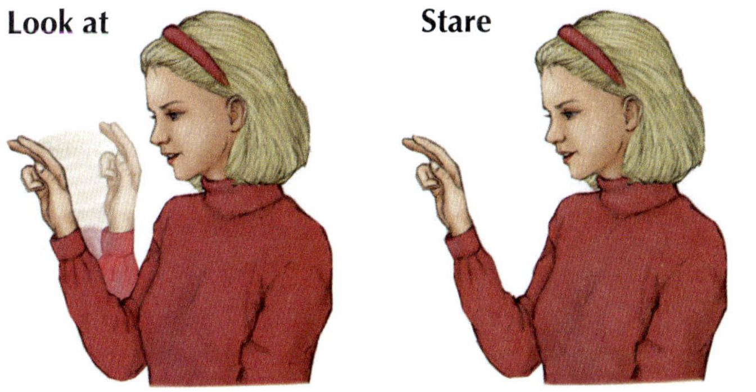

Figure 37.7

American Sign Language. ASL has only 3,000 root signs, compared with roughly 600,000 words in English. However, variations in signs make ASL a highly expressive language. For example, the sign LOOK-AT can be varied in ways to make it mean "look at me," "look at her," "look at each," "stare at," "gaze," "watch," "look for a long time," "look at again and again," "reminisce," "sightsee," "look forward to," "predict," "anticipate," "browse," and many more variations.

you ever make hand gestures when you are speaking on the phone? If so, you may be displaying a remnant of the gestural origins of language. Perhaps that's also why the same brain areas become more active when a person speaks or signs (Enrici et al., 2011).

Sign languages naturally arise out of a need to communicate visually. But they also embody a personal identity and define a distinct community. Those who "speak" sign share not just a language but a rich culture as well (West & Sutton-Spence, 2012).

Animal Language

Do animals use language? Animals in the wild definitely communicate. The cries, gestures, and mating calls of animals

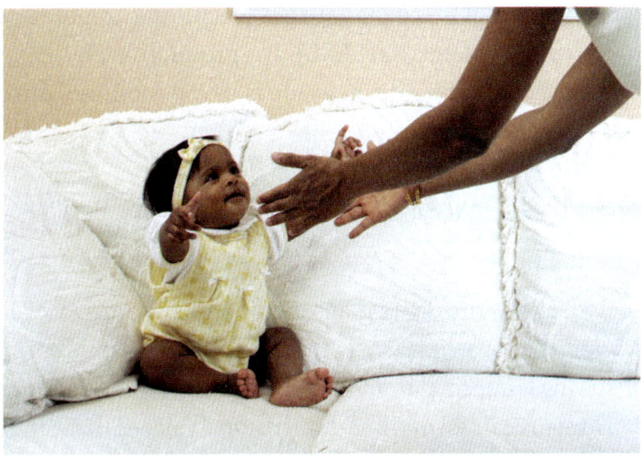

Myrleen Pearson/Alamy Stock Photo

Infants can express the idea "pick me up" in gestures before they can make the same request in words. Their progression from gestures to speech may mirror the evolution of human language abilities (Genty et al., 2009).

Michael Nichols/National Geographic Image Collection

Kanzi's language learning has been impressive. He can comprehend spoken English words. He can identify lexigram symbols when he hears corresponding words. He can use lexigrams when the objects to which they refer are absent, and he can, if asked, lead someone to the object. All these skills were acquired through observation, not conditioning (Segerdahl, Fields, & Savage-Rumbaugh, 2005).

have broad meanings immediately understood by other animals of the same species (Bradbury & Vehrencamp, 2011). For the most part, however, natural animal communication is quite limited. Even apes and monkeys make only a few dozen distinct cries, which carry messages such as "attack," "flee," or "food here." More important, animal communication lacks the productive quality of human language. For example, when a monkey gives an "eagle distress call," it always means something like, "I see an eagle." The monkey has no way of saying, "I don't see an eagle," or "Thank heavens that wasn't an eagle," or "That sucker I saw yesterday was some huge eagle" (Pinker & Jackendoff, 2005).

What about trying to teach language to animals? To this point, numerous chimps and gorillas, as well as an assortment of dolphins, sea lions, and parrots, have been taught to communicate with word symbols of various kinds (Pepperberg, 2017). The "champion" is probably a pygmy chimpanzee named Kanzi.

Phonemes Basic speech sounds of a language.

Morphemes Smallest meaningful units in a language, such as syllables or words.

Grammar A set of rules for combining language units into meaningful speech or writing.

Syntax Rules for ordering words when forming sentences.

Transformation rules Rules by which a simple declarative sentence may be changed to other voices or forms (past tense, passive voice, and so forth).

Kanzi's Lexigrams Since the 1980s, Duane Rumbaugh and Sue Savage-Rumbaugh have been teaching Kanzi to communicate by pushing buttons on a computer keyboard. Each of the 250 buttons is marked with a *lexigram*, or geometric word-symbol. Some of the lexigrams that Kanzi knows are quite abstract, like symbols for "bad" and "good" (Lyn, Franks, & Savage-Rumbaugh, 2008). Using the lexigrams, Kanzi can create primitive sentences several words long. He also can understand about 650 spoken sentences.

Kanzi's sentences consistently follow correct word order. Like a child learning language, Kanzi picked up some rules from his caregivers (Segerdahl, Fields, & Savage-Rumbaugh, 2005). However, he has developed other patterns on his own (Gillespie-Lynch et al., 2011). For example, Kanzi usually places action symbols in the order that he wants to carry them out, such as "chase tickle" or "chase hide."

In these respects, Kanzi's vocabulary and ability to invent a simple grammar are on a par with a 2-year-old's. After more than 30 years of training, Kanzi's language use is certainly noteworthy and may yet help us better understand the roots of human language (Gillespie-Lynch et al., 2014). On the other hand, as linguist Noam Chomsky insists, if chimps were biologically capable of language, they would use it on their own.

MODULE 37

Modes of Thought—Learning Outcomes Revisited

37.1 Distinguish between experiential and reflective processing

Experiential processing refers to thinking that occurs quickly and automatically, outside of awareness. Reflective processing refers to effortful, conscious thought that requires attention and concentration.

37.2 Explain how imagery is used in thinking

Mental images aid thinking by allowing us to imagine processes or outcomes in an effort to improve upon them. They can also assist with memory. The same brain areas are involved in both vision and visual imagery, and the mental images that are created are three-dimensional and can be mentally rotated. They can also be made larger or smaller in our "mind's eye." Kinesthetic images are a special type of mental imagery and are used to represent movements and actions.

37.3 Explain how concepts are used in thinking

Concepts are categories of objects or events. When faced with novel stimuli, we try to classify them using conceptual rules (which provide "boundaries" about the things that fall into that category) and prototypes (ideal models of that category). Concepts such as stereotypes can be faulty, though, leading to thinking that is overly simplistic.

37.4 Explain how language is used in thinking

Language encodes stimuli and events into symbols for easy mental manipulation during thinking. The linguistic relativity hypothesis holds that just as thought shapes language, so too, language shapes thought. Language carries meaning by combining a set of symbols according to a set of rules (grammar), which includes rules about word order (syntax). The study of word meaning in language is called *semantics*, and semantics are influenced by context. Words have denotations (dictionary definitions) and connotations (personal or emotional meanings). True languages (including complex gestural systems like ASL) are productive and can be used to generate new ideas or possibilities during thinking.

Reflective Practice

Content Check

1. Reflective processing is automatic and effortless. T or F?
2. Our reliance on imagery in thinking means that problem solving is impaired by the use of language or symbols. T or F?
3. Humans can form three-dimensional images that can be moved or rotated in mental space. T or F?

4. A *mup* is defined as anything that is small, blue, and hairy. *Mup* is a ________________ concept.
5. Stereotyping is an example of oversimplification in thinking. T or F?
6. True languages are ______________ because they can be used to generate new possibilities.
7. Noam Chomsky believes that we can create an infinite variety of sentences by applying ____________ ____________ to universal language patterns.

Skill Check

Think Critically

8. Are social stereotypes a type of concept?

Self-Reflect

Name some ways that you have used imagery in the thinking that you have done today. Write a conceptual rule for the following idea: *unicycle.* Were you able to define the concept with a rule? Would positive and negative instances help make the concept clearer for others? Just for fun, see if you can illustrate the productive quality of language by creating a sentence that no one has ever before spoken.

ANSWERS

1. F 2. F 3. T 4. conjunctive 5. T 6. productive 7. transformation rules
8. Social stereotypes are oversimplified concepts of groups of people (Le Pelley et al., 2010). Stereotypes about men, African Americans, women, conservatives, liberals, police officers, Muslims, or other groups often muddle thinking about members of the group. (See Module 73 for more information about stereotypes, prejudice, and discrimination.)

MODULE 38

Cognition and Intelligence

Problem Solving

Seal Math

Santiago got the surprise of his life. He had anchored his little motorboat 10 miles from an island and gone snorkeling. He returned to the boat only to discover that two seals had settled in for a quick nap. He climbed into his boat and immediately began to cruise toward the island at 7 miles per hour. Just then the two seals woke up, indignantly jumped into the water, and also swam toward the island. At the same instant, Santiago's friend left the island in a sailboat at 3 miles per hour, coming out to rendezvous with the motorboat. The seals swam back and forth between the motorboat and sailboat at a speed of 12 miles per hour.

A good way to start a discussion of problem solving is to solve a problem, so, how far will the seals have swum when the two boats meet?

John Mitterer

~LEARNING OUTCOMES~

After reading this module, you should be able to

38.1 Distinguish between four methods of problem solving: algorithms, understanding, heuristics, and insight

38.2 Outline some barriers that can interfere with problem solving and compare the problem solving of experts and novices

Problem Solving—Go Figure

Learning Outcome 38.1 Distinguish between four methods of problem solving: algorithms, understanding, heuristics, and insight

We all solve many problems every day. Problem solving can be as commonplace as figuring out how to make a nonpoisonous meal out of leftovers or as significant as developing a cure for cancer. No matter what form a problem takes, it is usually best faced *mindfully* (Hayes, Strosahl, & Wilson, 2012). Did you enter reflective processing mode to tackle the seals and boats problem? If you didn't immediately see the answer to this problem, try it again. (The answer is revealed in the "Insightful Solutions" section, later in this module.)

Algorithmic Solutions

For routine problems, an **algorithmic solution**—achieved by following a series of step-by-step rules—may be enough to solve the problem (Goldstein, 2019). A simple example of an *algorithm* is the steps that you used to add up the numbers in Figure 37.1 (whether you did it in your head or by using a calculator). Here's another example: If you forget the combination to your bike lock, you will be able to discover it if you systematically try all the possible combinations (this could take some time, though . . .).

Algorithmic thinking is **logical thought**—proceeding from given information to new conclusions on the basis of explicit rules. To this, we can add that logical thought may be **inductive thought**—going from specific facts or observations to general principles—or **deductive thought**—going from general principles to specific situations. Becoming a problem-solving expert in any particular field involves, at a minimum, becoming familiar with the algorithms available in that field. If you have a good background in math, you may have found an algorithmic solution to the problem of the seals and the boats. (Your authors hope you didn't. There is an easier solution.)

Solutions by Understanding

Many problems cannot be solved algorithmically. In such cases, **understanding** (deeper comprehension of a problem) is necessary. Try this problem:

> A person has an inoperable stomach tumor. A device is available that produces rays that at high intensity will destroy tissue (both healthy and diseased). How can the tumor be destroyed while minimizing damage to the surrounding tissue? (Also see the sketch in ➤ Figure 38.1.)

What does this problem show about problem solving? German psychologist Karl Duncker gave college students this problem in a classic series of studies. Duncker asked them to think aloud as they worked. He found that successful students first had to discover the *general properties* of a correct solution. A **general solution** defines the requirements for success but not in enough detail to guide further action. This phase was complete when students realized that the intensity of the rays had to be lowered on their way to the tumor. Then, in the second phase, they proposed a number of **functional solutions**, or workable solutions, and selected the best one (Duncker, 1945). (One solution is to focus weak rays on the tumor from several angles. Another is to rotate the person's body to minimize exposure of healthy tissue.)

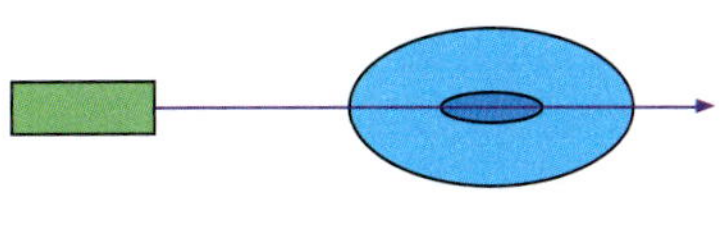

➤ **Figure 38.1**

The tumor problem. A schematic representation of Duncker's tumor problem. The dark spot represents a tumor surrounded by healthy tissue. How can the tumor be destroyed without injuring surrounding tissue? (Adapted from Duncker, 1945.)

Heuristic Solutions

"You can't get there from here," or so it often seems when facing a problem. Solving problems often benefits from a strategy. Imagine that you are traveling to Washington, DC, and decide to look up an old FBI friend, Penelope Garcia. You search an online directory and find dozens of P. Garcias listed. Of course, you could follow an algorithm such as dialing each number in alphabetical order until you found the right one.

Alternatively, you could use a **heuristic** (hew-RIS-tik)—a shortcut or "rule of thumb" for finding a solution to a problem. Typically, a heuristic *reduces the number of alternatives* that thinkers must consider (Benjafield, Smilek, & Kingstone, 2010). You could, for example, simplify the problem of looking up Penelope by randomly choosing just a few, plausible-looking entries. In this case, you would be using a **random search strategy**. This is an example of trial-and-error thinking in which some possibilities are tried, more or less randomly. "Forget it," you say to yourself. "Is there a better way I can narrow the search?" "Oh, yeah! I remember hearing that Penelope lives near work." Then you Google a map and call only the numbers with addresses in southern Washington, nearer to Quantico.

Here's another example. Amateur naturalists usually begin painfully identifying the birds, butterflies, mammals, and plants they find by mechanically (i.e., rote) searching through published field guides until they find the correct species' name and description. In time, those who persist begin to identify more and more species from memory and

Algorithmic solution A problem solution achieved by following a series of step-by-step rules.

Logical thought Drawing conclusions on the basis of formal principles of reasoning.

Inductive thought Thinking in which a general rule or principle is gathered from a series of specific examples; for instance, inferring the laws of gravity by observing many falling objects.

Deductive thought Thought that applies a general set of rules to specific situations; for example, using the laws of gravity to predict the behavior of a single falling object.

Understanding (in problem solving) A deeper comprehension of the nature of a problem.

General solution A solution that correctly states the requirements for success but not in enough detail for further action.

Functional solution A detailed, practical, and workable solution.

Heuristic Shortcut or rule of thumb for finding a solution to a problem.

Random search strategy Trying possible solutions to a problem in a more or less random order.

others based on the general properties that they have learned through experience. With enough practice, this is exactly how novices become experts in a wide variety of fields.

Expert problems solvers are good at using heuristic strategies like these:

- Try to identify how the current state of affairs differs from the desired goal. Then find steps that will reduce the difference.
- Try working backward from the desired goal to the starting point or current state.
- If you can't reach the goal directly, try to identify an intermediate goal or subproblem that at least gets you closer.
- Represent the problem in other ways—with graphs, diagrams, or analogies, for instance.
- Generate a possible solution and test it. Doing so may eliminate many alternatives, or it may clarify what is needed for a solution.

In closing, notice that although heuristics like these raise the odds of success, they do not guarantee a solution.

Insightful Solutions

A thinker who *suddenly* solves a problem has experienced **insight** (Cushen & Wiley, 2012). Insights are usually based on reorganizing a problem. This allows us to see problems in new ways and makes their solutions seem obvious (Hélie & Sun, 2010).

Let's return now to the problem of the boats and the seals. The best way to solve it is by insight. Because the boats will cover the 10-mile distance in exactly 1 hour, and the seals swim 12 miles per hour, the seals will have swum 12 miles when the boats meet. Very little math is necessary if you have insight into this problem. ➤ **Figure 38.2** lists some additional insight problems that you may want to try (the answers can be found in ■ **Table 38.1**).

The Nature of Insight Psychologist Janet Davidson (2003) believes that insight involves three abilities. The first is *selective encoding*, which refers to selecting information that is relevant to a problem while ignoring distractions. For example, consider the following problem:

> If you have white socks and black socks in your drawer, mixed in the ratio of 4 to 5, how many socks will you have to take out to ensure that you have a pair of the same color?

A person who recognizes that "mixed in a ratio of 4 to 5" is irrelevant will be more likely to come up with the correct answer of 3 socks.

Insight also relies on *selective combination*, or bringing together seemingly unrelated bits of useful information. Try this sample problem:

> With a 7-minute hourglass and an 11-minute hourglass, what is the simplest way to time boiling an egg for 15 minutes?

The answer requires using both hourglasses in combination. First, the 7-minute and the 11-minute hourglasses are started. When the 7-minute hourglass runs out, it's time to begin boiling the egg. At this point, 4 minutes remain on the 11-minute hourglass. Thus, when it runs out, it is simply turned over. When it runs out again, 15 minutes will have passed.

Water lilies

Problem: Water lilies growing in a pond double in area every 24 hours. On the first day of spring, only one lily pad is on the surface of the pond. Sixty days later, the pond is entirely covered. On what day is the pond half-covered?

Twenty dollars

Problem: Jessica and Blair both have the same amount of money. How much must Jessica give Blair so that Blair has $20 more than Jessica?

How many pets?

Problem: How many pets do you have if all of them are birds except two, all of them are cats except two, and all of them are dogs except two?

Between 2 and 3

Problem: What one mathematical symbol can you place between 2 and 3 that results in a number greater than 2 and less than 3?

One word

Problem: Rearrange the letters NEWDOOR to make one word.

➤ **Figure 38.2**
Some insight problems.

TABLE 38.1 | Solutions to Insight Problems

Water lilies: Day 59

Twenty dollars: $10

How many pets?: Three (one bird, one cat, and one dog)

Between 2 and 3: A decimal point

One word: ONE WORD (You may object that the answer is two words, but the problem called for the answer to be "one word," and it is.)

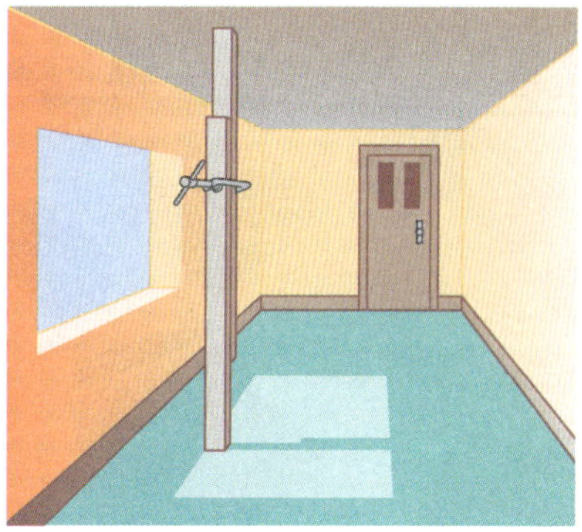

➤ **Figure 38.3**

A solution to the hat rack problem.

A third source of insights is *selective comparison*. This is the ability to compare new problems with old information or with problems already solved. A good example is the hat rack problem, in which participants must build a structure that can support an overcoat in the middle of a room. Each person is given only two long sticks and a C-clamp to work with. The solution, shown in ➤ **Figure 38.3**, is to clamp the two sticks together so that they are wedged between the floor and ceiling. If you were given this problem, you would be more likely to solve it if you first thought of how pole lamps are wedged between floor and ceiling

Common Barriers to Problem Solving—Don't Get Stuck

Learning Outcome 38.2 *Outline some barriers that can interfere with problem solving and compare the problem solving of experts and novices*

One of the most important barriers to problem solving is **fixation**, the tendency to get "hung up" on wrong solutions or to become blind to alternatives (Sternberg, 2017).

Fixations

This usually occurs when, without giving it any thought, we place unnecessary restrictions on our thinking (McCaffrey, 2012). How, for example, could you plant four small trees so that each is an equal distance from all the others? (The answer is shown in ➤ **Figure 38.4**.)

A prime example of restricted thinking is **functional fixedness**, a tendency to perceive an item only in terms of its most common use (Bernstein & Lucas, 2008). If you have ever used a dime as a screwdriver, you've overcome functional fixedness.

How does functional fixedness affect problem solving? Karl Duncker once asked students to mount a candle on a vertical board so that the candle could burn normally. He gave each student three candles, some matches, some cardboard boxes, some thumbtacks, and other items. Half of Duncker's participants received these items *inside* the cardboard boxes. The others were given all the items, including the boxes, spread out on a tabletop.

➤ **Figure 38.4**

The four trees problem. Four trees can be placed equidistant from one another by piling dirt into a mound. Three of the trees are planted equal distances apart around the base of the mound. The fourth tree is planted on the top of the mound. If you were fixated on arrangements that involve level ground, you may have been blind to this three-dimensional solution.

Insight A sudden mental reorganization of a problem that makes the solution obvious.

Fixation (in problem solving) The tendency to repeat wrong solutions or faulty responses, especially as a result of becoming blind to alternatives.

Functional fixedness Tendency to perceive an item only in terms of its most common use.

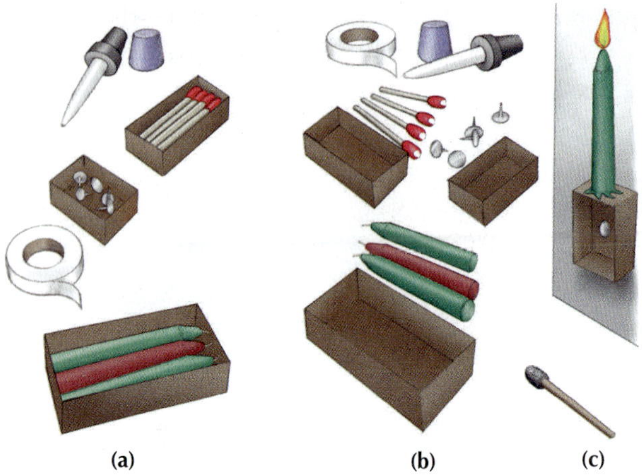

➤ **Figure 38.5**

The candle problem. Materials for solving the candle problem were given to participants in boxes (*a*) or separately (*b*). Functional fixedness caused by condition (*a*) interfered with solving the problem. The solution to the problem is shown in (*c*).

Duncker found that when the items were in the boxes, solving the problem was very difficult. Why? If students saw the boxes as *containers*, they didn't realize the boxes might be part of the solution (if you haven't guessed the solution, check ➤ Figure 38.5). Undoubtedly, we could avoid many fixations by being more flexible in categorizing the world (Kalyuga & Hanham, 2011; McCaffrey, 2012). For instance, creative thinking could be facilitated in the container problem by saying "This *could be* a box," instead of "This *is* a box."

When tested with the candle problem, 5-year-old children show no signs of functional fixedness. Apparently, this is because they have had less experience with the use of various objects. It is sometimes said that to be more creative, you should try to see the world without preconceptions, as if through the eyes of a child. In the case of functional fixedness, that may be true (German & Defeyter, 2000).

Functional fixedness is just one of the mental blocks that prevent insight (Reed, 2013). Here's an example of another: A $5 bill is placed on a table, and a stack of objects is balanced precariously on top of the bill. How can the bill be removed without touching, moving, or toppling the objects? A good answer is to split the bill on one of its sides. Gently pulling from opposite ends will tear the bill in half and remove it without toppling the objects. Many people fail to see this solution because they have learned not to destroy money (Adams, 2001). Notice again the impact of placing something in a category—in this case, "things of value" (which should not be destroyed).

Other common mental blocks can hinder problem solving:

1. **Emotional barriers:** Inhibition and fear of making a fool of oneself, fear of making a mistake, inability to tolerate ambiguity, excessive self-criticism

   Example: An architect doesn't try an unconventional design because she fears that other architects will think it is frivolous.

2. **Cultural barriers:** Values that hold that fantasy is a waste of time; that playfulness is for children only; that reason, logic, and numbers are good; that feelings, intuitions, pleasure, and humor are bad or have no value in the serious business of problem solving

   Example: A corporate manager wants to solve a business problem but becomes stern and angry when members of his marketing team joke playfully about possible solutions.

3. **Learned barriers:** Conventions about uses (functional fixedness), meanings, possibilities, taboos

   Example: A cook doesn't have any clean mixing bowls and fails to see that she could use a pot as a bowl.

4. **Perceptual barriers:** Habits leading to a failure to identify important elements of a problem

   Example: A beginning artist concentrates on drawing a vase of flowers without seeing that the "empty" spaces around the vase are part of the composition, too.

Expert and Novice Problem-Solving

So far, we have seen that problem-solving expertise is based on *acquired strategies* (learned heuristics) and specific *organized knowledge* (systematic information). Experts are better able to see the true nature of problems and to define them more flexibly in terms of general principles (Kalyuga & Hanham, 2011). For example, chess experts are much more likely than novices to have heuristics available for solving chess problems.

However, what really sets experts apart is their ability to automatically recognize *patterns* (Gorman, Abernethy, & Farrow, 2013). For example, a master chess player might recognize a particular position as one that she saw in a game played several months ago, and immediately realize what lines of play should be explored next. This helps eliminate a large number of possible moves. The chess master, therefore, wastes less time exploring unproductive pathways (Ross, 2006).

In other words, becoming a star performer does not come from some general strengthening of the mind. Chess masters don't necessarily have better memories than beginners (except for realistic chess positions) (Gobet & Simon, 1996; Goldstein, 2019; see Figure 38.6). And, typically, they don't explore more moves ahead than do lesser players.

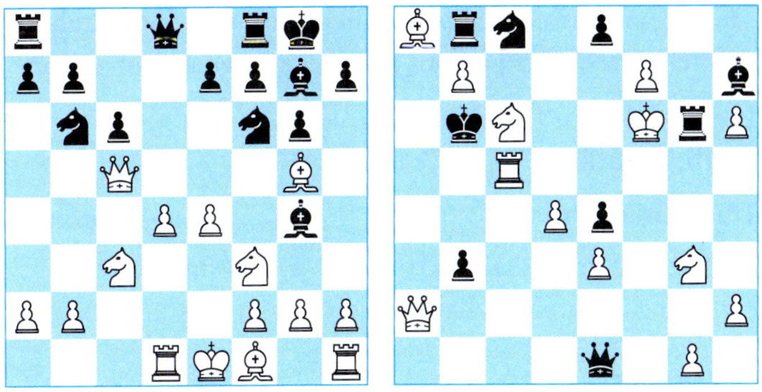

Figure 38.6

Memory for chess positions. The left chessboard shows a realistic game. The right chessboard is a random arrangement of pieces. Expert chess players can memorize the left board at a glance, yet they are no better than beginners at memorizing the random board (Ross, 2006). Expert performance at most thinking tasks is based on acquired strategies and knowledge. If you want to excel at a profession or a mental skill, plan on adding to your knowledge every day (Reed, 2013).

You might think experts are always in reflective processing mode. Oddly enough, just the opposite is true. Expertise involves more **automatic processing**, or fast, fairly effortless thinking based on experience with similar problems. Automatic processing frees "space" in short-term (working) memory, making it easier to work on the problem (Kalyuga, Renkl, & Paas, 2010). At the highest skill levels, expert performers tend to rise above rules and plans. Their decisions, thinking, and actions become rapid, fluid, and insightful (Hélie & Sun, 2010). Thus, when a chess master recognizes a pattern on the chessboard, the most desirable tactic comes to mind almost immediately. Mind you, this capacity comes at a price of time and effort. Expert chess players can automatically recognize 50,000 to 100,000 patterns, a level of skill that takes about 10 years of mindful, reflective processing to build up (Ross, 2006).

To develop expertise in a field, then, requires us to learn available heuristic solution strategies as well as to develop a deeper general understanding of the field. Throw into the mix that expertise also involves learning thousands of patterns and practicing solving many problems, and you can see that developing expertise involves years of hard work (Ericsson & Pool, 2016). Think about that the next time someone says of an expert, "She makes it look easy."

Automatic processing Fast, fairly effortless thinking; often based on experience.

MODULE 38

Problem Solving—Learning Outcomes Revisited

38.1 Distinguish between four methods of problem solving: algorithms, understanding, heuristics, and insight

Algorithmic solutions are derived by employing rule-based strategies (which might well be time-consuming). Algorithms may be inductive (from the specific to more general) or deductive (from more general to specific). Solutions by understanding usually begin with discovery of the general properties of an answer, followed by a functional solution. Problem solving using heuristics refers to the use of 'shortcuts' to narrow the search for solutions. Finally, solutions derived using insight usually involve reorganizing a problem in such a way that a rapid solution follows. Three elements of insight are selective encoding, selective combination, and selective comparison.

38.2 Outline some barriers that can interfere with problem solving and compare the problem solving of experts and novices

Problem solving can be blocked by fixations, or a tendency to get "stuck" on wrong solutions. Functional fixedness is a common fixation, and refers to a tendency to see items only in terms of their most common uses. Emotional blocks, cultural values, learned conventions, and perceptual habits can also be barriers to problem solving. Compared to novices, problem-solving experts are more likely to engage in automatic processing and pattern recognition.

Reflective Practice

Content Check

1. Insight refers to rote, or trial-and-error, problem solving. T or F?
2. The first phase in problem solving by understanding is to discover the general properties of a correct solution. T or F?
3. Problem-solving strategies that guide the search for solutions are called ______________.
4. A common element underlying insight is that information is encoded, combined, and compared
   - **a.** algorithmically
   - **b.** by rote
   - **c.** functionally
   - **d.** selectively
5. Functional fixedness is a major barrier to
   - **a.** insightful problem solving
   - **b.** using random search strategies
   - **c.** algorithmic problem solving
   - **d.** achieving fixations through problem solving
6. Organized knowledge, acquired heuristics, and the ability to recognize patterns are all characteristics of human expertise. T or F?

Skill Check

Think Critically

7. Do you think that it is true that "a problem clearly defined is a problem half solved"?

Self-Reflect

Identify at least one problem that you have solved algorithmically. Now identify a problem that you solved by understanding. Did the second problem involve finding a general solution, a functional solution, or both? What heuristics did you use to solve the problem? What is the most insightful solution that you've ever come up with? Did it involve selective encoding, combination, or comparison? Can you think of a time when you overcame functional fixedness to solve a problem?

ANSWERS

1. F 2. T 3. heuristics 4. d 5. a 6. T 7. Although this might be an overstatement, it is true that clearly defining a starting point and the desired goal can serve as a heuristic in problem solving.

MODULE 39

Cognition and Intelligence

Creative Thinking and Intuition

No One-Hit Wonders

Original ideas have changed the course of human history. Much of what we now take for granted in art, medicine, music, technology, and science was once regarded as radical or impossible. How do creative thinkers achieve the breakthroughs that advance us into new realms?

For a start, creative thinkers are usually continuously creative. Mozart produced more than 600 pieces of music. Inventor Thomas Edison held more than 1,000 patents. Emily Dickinson wrote some 1,800 poems. The 2016 Nobel Laureate in Literature, Bob Dylan, has published over 500 musical compositions. Not all of these works were masterpieces. However, a fluent outpouring of ideas fed the creative efforts of each of these geniuses.

Gary Miller/FilmMagic/Getty Images

Psychologists have learned a great deal about how creativity occurs and how to promote it. Besides noting the fluency of creative thinkers, what else have they found?

~LEARNING OUTCOMES~

After reading this module, you should be able to

39.1 Describe the nature of creative thinking and how it is measured, outline the five stages of creative problem solving and describe five characteristics associated with a creative personality

39.2 Distinguish between five issues that can lead to errors in intuitive thinking: ignoring the odds, representativeness, framing, hot cognition, and choice overload

Creative Thinking—Down Roads Less Traveled

Learning Outcome 39.1 Describe the nature of creative thinking and how it is measured, outline the five stages of creative problem solving and describe five characteristics associated with a creative personality

We have seen that problem solving may be based on algorithms, understanding, heuristics, or insight. Routine problem solving usually requires logical **convergent thinking**, where lines of thought converge on the answer. There is one correct answer and the problem is to find it.

Convergent thinking Thinking directed toward discovery of a single established correct answer; conventional thinking.

TABLE 39.1 | Convergent and Divergent Problems

Convergent Problems
What is the area of a triangle that is 3 feet wide at the base and 2 feet tall?
Erica is shorter than Zoey but taller than Carlo, and Carlo is taller than Jared. Who is the second tallest?
If you simultaneously drop a baseball and a bowling ball from a tall building, which will hit the ground first?
Divergent Problems
What objects can you think of that begin with the letters *BR*?
How could discarded aluminum cans be put to use?
Write a poem about fire and ice.

In contrast, **creativity** is the ability to combine mental elements in new and useful ways. It is usually best achieved through **divergent thinking**, in which many possibilities are developed from one starting point. (See ■ **Table 39.1** for some examples of convergent and divergent problems.) Furthermore, divergent thought tends to be **illogical thought**—intuitive, associative, or personal. Whereas problem solving is usually a consciously reflective processing activity, creativity more likely involves apparently unconscious experiential processing (Ritter, van Baaren, & Dijksterhuis, 2012).

Creative thinking also involves *fluency*, *flexibility*, and *originality*. Let's say that you would like to find creative uses for the billions of plastic containers discarded each year. The creativity of your suggestions could be rated in this way: **Fluency** is defined as the total number of suggestions that you are able to make. **Flexibility** is the number of times that you shift from one class of possible uses to another. **Originality** refers to how novel or unusual your ideas are. By counting the number of times that you showed fluency, flexibility, and originality, we could rate your creativity, or capacity for *divergent thinking* (Runco, 2012; Runco & Acar, 2012).

It is worth noting that divergent thinking is also a characteristic of **daydreams** (vivid waking fantasies). For most people, fantasy and daydreaming are associated with greater mental flexibility or creativity (Langens & Schmalt, 2002). Regardless, no matter when or how it occurs, rather than repeating learned solutions, creative thinking produces new answers, ideas, or patterns (Lewis & Lovatt, 2013).

Problem finding is another characteristic of creative thinking. Many of the problems we solve are "presented" to us—by employers, teachers, circumstances, or life in general. **Problem finding** involves actively seeking problems to solve. When you are thinking creatively, a spirit of discovery prevails: you are more likely to find unsolved problems and *choose* to tackle them. Thus, problem finding may be a more creative act than the convergent problem solving that typically follows it (Runco, 2015).

Tests of Creativity

Divergent thinking can be measured in several ways (Kaufman, 2009; Runco & Acar, 2012). In the *Unusual Uses test*, you would be asked to think of as many uses as possible for some object, such as the plastic containers mentioned previously. In the *Consequences test*, you would list the consequences that would follow a basic change in the world. For example, you might be asked, "What would happen if everyone suddenly lost their sense of balance and could no longer stay upright?" People try to list as many reactions as possible. If you were to take the *Anagrams test*, you would be given a word such as *creativity* and asked to make as many new words as possible by rearranging the letters. Each of these tests can be scored for fluency, flexibility, and originality. (For an example of other tests of divergent thinking, see ➤ **Figure 39.1**.)

Isn't creativity more than divergent thought? What if a person comes up with a large number of useless answers to a problem? Good question. Divergent thinking is an important part of creativity, but there is more to it. To be creative, the solution to a problem must be more than novel, unusual, or original. It also must be *high quality* and *relevant* to solving the original problem (Kaufman & Sternberg, 2010). This is the dividing line between a "harebrained scheme" and a "stroke of genius." In other words, the creative person brings

walter_g/Shutterstock.com

Whimsical creations such as this eyeball lightbulb make it clear that in addition to being original or novel, a creative solution must be high quality and relevant to the problem.

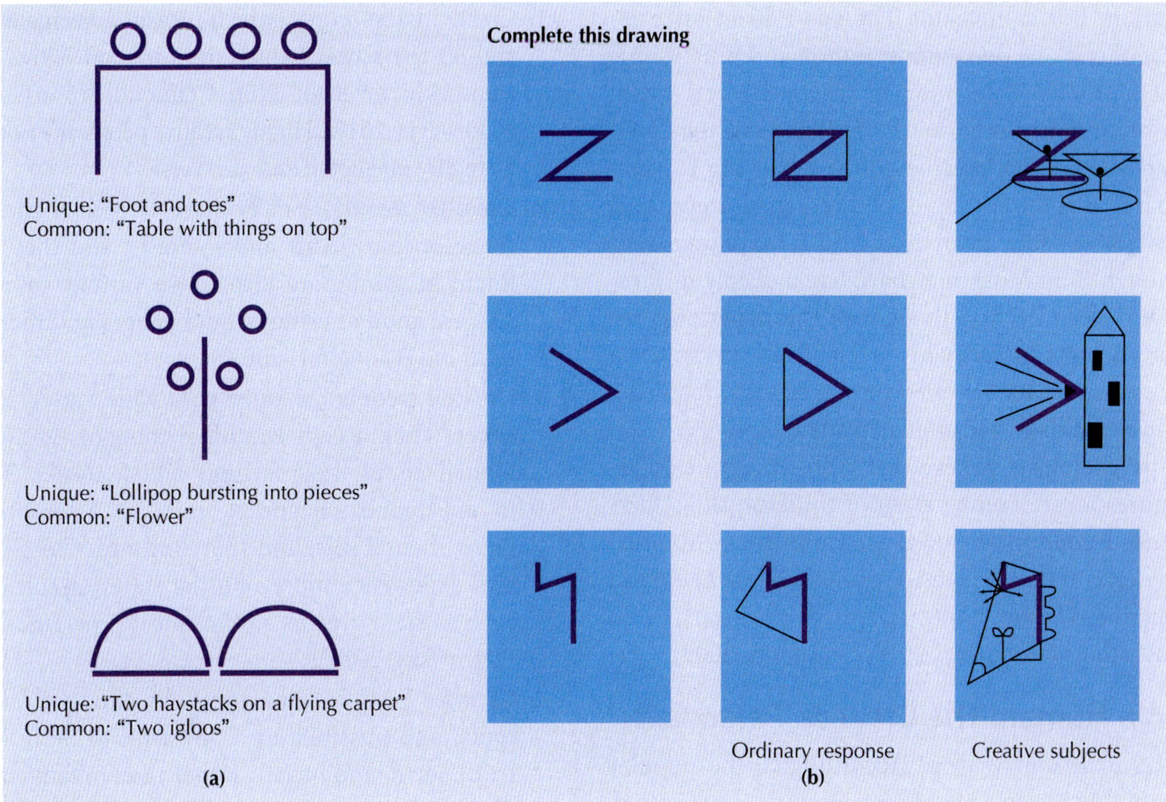

Figure 39.1

Some tests of divergent thinking. Creative responses are more original and more complex. [(*a*) Adapted from Wallach & Kogan, 1965; (*b*) adapted from Barron, 1958.]

reasoning and critical thinking to bear on new ideas once they are produced (Runco, 2012).

Stages of Creative Thought

Does creative thinking have a pattern? Typically, five stages occur during creative problem solving:

1. **Orientation.** As a first step, the person defines the problem and identifies its most important dimensions.
2. **Preparation.** It helps to be prepared *in general*, as an expert might be when first confronting a problem, but it also helps to become saturated with as much information about the *specific* problem as possible (Klein, 2013).
3. **Incubation.** Most major problems will have a period during which all attempted solutions are futile. At this point, problem solving may proceed on a subconscious level: Although the problem seems to have been set aside, it is still "cooking" in the background.
4. **Illumination.** The incubation stage is often ended by a rapid insight or series of insights. These produce the "Aha!" experience, often depicted in cartoons as a lightbulb appearing over the thinker's head.
5. **Verification.** The final step is to test and critically evaluate the solution obtained during the illumination stage. If the solution proves faulty, the thinker reverts to the stage of incubation.

Of course, creative thought is not always so neat. Nevertheless, the stages listed are a good summary of the most typical sequence of events. Perhaps the greatest misconception of the creative process is that it is all about that flash

Creativity Ability to combine mental elements in new and useful ways.

Divergent thinking Thinking that produces many ideas or alternatives; a major element in original or creative thought.

Illogical thought Thought that is intuitive, haphazard, or irrational.

Fluency In tests of creativity, *fluency* refers to the total number of solutions produced.

Flexibility In tests of creativity, *flexibility* is indicated by how many different types of solutions are produced.

Originality In tests of creativity, *originality* refers to how novel or unusual solutions are.

Daydream A vivid waking fantasy.

Problem finding The active discovery of problems to be solved.

of illumination. But as inventor Thomas Edison once remarked, "Genius is one percent inspiration and ninety-nine percent perspiration." Many hours of *orientation* and *preparation* can be overshadowed by the brilliance of the "Aha" *illumination*. Also, much creative problem solving is *incremental*. That is, it is the end result of many small steps. This is certainly true of many inventions, which build on earlier ideas. Although Elon Musk may have had a deeply inspirational insight when he first thought of the hyperloop, his subsequent attempts to *verify* his original idea by building a working example have revealed new problems, requiring more creative thinking, step after step after step.

Some psychologists believe that truly exceptional creativity requires a rare combination of thinking skills, personality, and a supportive social environment. This mix, they believe, accounts for creative giants such as Leonardo DaVinci, Sigmund Freud, Wolfgang Amadeus Mozart, Pablo Picasso, and others (Robinson, 2010; Simonton, 2009).

The Whole Human: The Creative Personality

What makes a person creative? According to the popular stereotype, highly creative people are eccentric, introverted, socially inept, unbalanced in their interests, and on the edge of madness. While most creative people are not mentally ill, and most mentally ill people are not particularly creative, there may be some truth to this stereotype, at least when it comes to mood disorders (Baas et al., 2016; Kyaga et al., 2013). Further, many of history's renowned artists, writers, poets, and composers, including Vincent Van Gogh, Edgar Allan Poe, Winston Churchill, and Ernest Hemingway, experienced pronounced mood swings.

In general, however, direct studies of creative individuals paint a very different picture (Hennessey & Amabile, 2010; Robinson, 2010):

1. Creativity test scores (which measure divergent thinking) and IQ test scores (which measure convergent thinking) are weakly correlated (Kim, Cramond, & VanTassel-Baska, 2010; Silvia, 2015). Highly creative people are not necessarily highly intelligent and vice versa.
2. Creative people usually have a greater-than-average range of knowledge and interests, and they are more fluent in combining ideas from various sources. They also are good at using mental images and metaphors in thinking (Riquelme, 2002).
3. Creative people are open to a wide variety of experiences. They accept irrational thoughts and are uninhibited about their feelings and fantasies. They tend to use broad categories, question assumptions, and break mental sets, and they find order in chaos. They also experience more unusual states of consciousness, such as lucid dreams and mystical experiences (Zink & Pietrowsky, 2013).
4. Creative people enjoy symbolic thought, ideas, concepts, and possibilities. They tend to be interested in truth, form, and beauty, rather than in fame or success. Their creative work is an end in itself (Robinson, 2010).
5. Creative people value their independence and prefer complexity. However, they are unconventional and nonconforming primarily in their work; otherwise, they do not have unusual, outlandish, or bizarre personalities.

Can creativity be learned? It is beginning to look as if some creative thinking skills can be learned. In particular, you can become more creative by practicing divergent thinking and by taking risks, asking unusual questions, analyzing ideas, and seeking odd connections between ideas (Bucher, 2011; Sternberg, 2017). (See Module 41 for more on learning creativity and innovation.)

Intuitive Thought—Mental Shortcut? or Dangerous Detour?

Learning Outcome 39.2 Distinguish between five issues that can lead to errors in intuitive thinking: ignoring the odds, representativeness, framing, hot cognition, and choice overload

You don't have to be a genius to experience flashes of insight. In fact, most people frequently experience **intuition**—quick, impulsive thought (Henry, Penner, & Eggly, 2016).

For example, think back to your least favorite teacher. (Not your current one, of course!) How long did it take you to figure out that he or she wasn't going to make your list of star teachers? Psychologist Nalini Ambady once asked people to watch video clips of teachers they did not know. After watching three 10-second segments, participants were asked to rate the teachers. Amazingly, their ratings correlated highly with year-end course evaluations made by actual students (Ambady & Rosenthal, 1993). Ambady obtained the same result when she presented an even thinner "slice" of teaching behavior, just three 2-second clips. A mere 6 seconds is all that participants needed to form intuitive judgments of the instructors' teaching!

Malcolm Gladwell (2005) argues this is not a case of hurried irrationality. Instead, it is *thin-slicing*, or quickly making sense of thin slivers of experience. Such immediate, intuitive, experiential reactions are a testament to the power of the cognitive unconscious, which is a part of the brain that does automatic, unconscious processing (Bar-Anan, Wilson, & Hassin, 2010; Wilson, 2004). Far from being irrational, intuition may be an important part of how we think (Ritter, van Baaren, & Dijksterhuis, 2012).

Rapid intuitive judgments can sometimes be as accurate as more reflective, rational consideration. The trick, of course, is figuring out when thin-slicing can be trusted and when it can't. After all, first impressions aren't always right. Have you ever had a teacher you came to appreciate only after the course was over? In many circumstances, quick impressions are most valuable when you take the time to verify them through more reflective observation (Tom, Tong, & Hesse, 2010).

Errors in Intuitive Thought

Although intuition can sometimes provide accurate answers, it also can be misleading. Two noted psychologists, Daniel Kahneman and Amos Tversky (1937–1996), have studied how we make decisions in the face of uncertainty. They found that human judgment is often seriously flawed (Kahneman, 2011; Kahneman, Slovic, & Tversky, 1982). Let's explore some common intuitive thinking errors, so that you will be better prepared to avoid them.

Underlying Odds One common error in intuitive judgment involves ignoring the **base rate**, or underlying probability of an event. People in one experiment were told that they would be given descriptions of 100 people—70 lawyers and 30 engineers. Participants were then asked to guess, without knowing anything about a person, whether she or he was an engineer or a lawyer. All correctly stated the probabilities as 70 percent for lawyer and 30 percent for engineer. Participants were then given this description:

> Eric is a 30-year-old man. He is married with no children. A man of high ability and high motivation, he promises to be quite successful in his field. He is well liked by his colleagues.

Quickly now, what are the odds Eric is a lawyer or an engineer? Notice that the description gives no new information about Eric's occupation. He could still be either an engineer or a lawyer. Therefore, the odds should again be estimated as 70–30. However, most people changed the odds to 50–50. Intuitively, it seems that Eric has an equal chance of being either an engineer or a lawyer. But this guess completely ignores the underlying odds.

Perhaps it is fortunate that we do ignore underlying odds at times. Were this not the case, how many people would get married in the face of a 50 percent divorce rate? Or how many would start high-risk businesses? On the other hand, people who smoke, drink and then drive, or skip wearing auto seatbelts ignore rather high odds of injury or illness. In many high-risk situations, ignoring base rates is the same as thinking that you are an exception to the rule.

Representativeness Another common pitfall in intuitive judgment is illustrated by the following question: which is more probable?

A. The New York Yankees will not be in the lead after the first half of the baseball season.
B. The New York Yankees will not be in the lead after the first half of the baseball season but will win their division.

People who follow baseball are likely to regard a statement like B as more probable than A (for those of you not in the know, the Yankees have historically been competitive in end-of-season and postseason play). However, this intuitive answer overlooks an important fact: the likelihood of two events occurring together must be lower than the probability of either one alone. For example, the probability of getting one head when flipping a coin is higher (one half, or 0.5) than the probability of getting two heads in a row (one fourth, or 0.25). Therefore, A (the New York Yankees will not be in the lead after the first half of the baseball season) is statistically more likely than B (the New York Yankees will not be in the lead after the first half of the baseball season *but* will win their division).

According to Tversky and Kahneman (1982), such faulty conclusions are based on the **representativeness heuristic**—that is, we tend to give a choice greater weight if it seems to be similar to other members of a class we already know. Thus, you probably compared the information about the Yankees with your general impression of the Yankees as a highly successful team. Therefore, B might seem more likely than A, even though it isn't.

Intuition Quick, impulsive thought that does not use formal logic or clear reasoning.

Base rate The basic rate at which an event occurs over time; the basic probability of an event.

Representativeness heuristic Mental shortcut of judging if something belongs in a given class based on similarity to other members.

When intuitions are unknowingly based on representativeness, the results can be disastrous. In courtrooms, for example, jurors are more likely to think that a defendant is guilty if the person appears to fit the profile of a person likely to commit a crime (Davis & Follette, 2002). For example, a young, single man from a poor neighborhood would be more likely to be judged guilty of theft than a middle-aged, married father from an affluent suburb.

Framing The most general conclusion about intuition is that the way a problem is stated, or **framed**, affects decisions (Kahneman, 2011; Tversky & Kahneman, 1981). To gain further insight into framing, try this problem:

> A couple is divorcing. Both parents seek custody of their only child, but custody can be granted to just one parent. If you had to make a decision based on the following information, to which parent would you award custody of the child?
>
> **Parent A:** Average income, average health, average working hours, reasonable rapport with the child, relatively stable social life
>
> **Parent B:** Above-average income, minor health problems, lots of work-related travel, very close relationship with the child, extremely active social life

Most people choose to award custody to Parent B, the parent who has some drawbacks but also several advantages (such as above-average income). That's because people tend to look for *positive qualities* that can be *awarded* to the child.

However, who would you choose if you were asked this question: Which parent should be denied custody? In this case, most people choose to deny custody to Parent B. Why is Parent B a good choice one moment and a poor choice the next? It's because the second question asked who should be *denied* custody. To answer this question, people tend to look for *negative qualities* that would *disqualify* a parent. As you can see, the way a question is framed can channel us down a narrow path so that we attend to only part of the information provided, rather than reflectively weighing all the pros and cons.

Usually, the *broadest* way of framing or stating a problem produces the best decisions. However, people often state problems in increasingly narrow terms until a single, seemingly "obvious" answer emerges. For example, to select a career, it would be wise to consider pay, working conditions, job satisfaction, needed skills, future employment outlook, and many other factors. Instead, such decisions are often narrowed to thoughts such as, "I like to write, so I'll be a journalist," "I want to make good money and law pays well," or "I can be creative in photography." Framing decisions so narrowly greatly increases the risk of making a poor choice. If you would like to think more critically and analytically, it is important to pay attention to how you are defining problems before you try to solve them. Remember that shortcuts to answers often short-circuit clear thinking.

Cognition and Emotion Another factor that bears mentioning is that "hot cognition"—thinking driven by emotions—also tends to affect good judgment (Lerner et al., 2015). Our emotional reactions to various possibilities can determine what intuitively seems to be the right answer. Emotions such as fear, hope, anxiety, liking, or disgust can eliminate possibilities from consideration or promote them to the top of the list (Rolls, 2014). For many people, choosing which political candidate to vote for is a good example of how emotions can cloud clear thinking. Rather than comparing candidates' records and policies, it is tempting to vote for the person we like rather than the person who is most qualified for the job.

Of course, taking action in the heat of anger, passion, or stress may not be the wisest move. It may be better to cool down a bit before picking that bar fight, running off and eloping, or immediately declining that daunting job offer (Johnson, Batey, & Holdsworth, 2009). Personal rituals, such as counting to 10, meditating for a moment, and even engaging in superstitious behaviors such as crossing your fingers before moving ahead, can be calming (Damisch, Stoberock, & Mussweiler, 2010).

Choice Overload "Venti, double-shot, sugar-free, peppermint, nonfat, double-cupped, extra hot, please." Overhearing the order while standing in line, the older woman remarked to her husband, "Don't you miss the days when all you could order was a coffee with cream and sugar?" Behind them, a young man whispered in his friend's ear, "Poor old people!" One stereotype of elderly people is that they have trouble coping with modern life. But are the elderly the only ones sometimes bewildered by tasks as "simple" as ordering a cup of coffee?

Isn't the freedom of having a wide variety of choices a good thing (Leotti, Iyengar, & Ochsner, 2010)? Maybe not. According to consumer psychologist Alexander Chernev (Chernev, Böckenholt, & Goodman, 2015), too much choice can lead to **choice overload**—difficulty making a decision in the face of many alternatives.

In one study, consumers were given an option to purchase jam. Half of them could choose from 6 different flavors; the other half had 24 flavors from which to choose. Although consumers with more choice expressed more interest, they were 10 times *less* likely to purchase *any* jam (Iyengar & Lepper, 2000). Similarly, restaurants with menus that feature a broader variety of choices often find that patrons are more likely to order from a smaller number of familiar choices (Soman, 2010). Apparently, businesses that increase the variety of their product offerings are not guaranteed increased sales (Gourville & Soman, 2005; Greifeneder, Scheibehenne, & Kleber, 2010).

It may be faintly amusing that people have trouble exercising choice in a coffee shop, grocery store, or restaurant. It's not that funny when more important issues are involved, such as choosing the best medicine or medical procedure. Imagine, for example, facing too many options when deciding whether to remove a seriously ill infant from life support (Botti, Orfali, & Iyengar, 2009).

Why are more complex choices so tough to make? Researchers have identified a number of factors, such as the complexity of the set of choices, the difficulty of the decision task, uncertainty about one's preferences, and the goal of the decision (Chernev, Böckenholt, & Goodman, 2015). Although the growing complexity of modern life may increase our freedom, our choices may be expanding beyond our capacity to cope. It's OK to order a coffee with cream and sugar sometimes.

Framing In thought, the terms in which a problem is stated or the way that it is structured.

Choice overload Difficulty making a decision in the face of many alternatives.

MODULE 39 Creative Thinking and Intuition—Learning Outcomes Revisited

39.1 Describe the nature of creative thinking and how it is measured, outline the five stages of creative problem solving, and describe five characteristics associated with a creative personality

Creative thinking requires divergent thought, characterized by fluency, flexibility, and originality. Problem finding, or actively seeking out problems to solve, is another characteristic of creative thinkers. Creativity is often measured using tests of divergent thinking, such as the Unusual Uses test and the Consequences test. Five stages often seen in creative problem solving are orientation, preparation, incubation, illumination, and verification. Studies suggest that the creative personality has a number of characteristics, most of which contradict popular stereotypes. First, only a very small correlation exists between IQ and creativity; creative people are not necessarily "intelligent," as defined by standardized tests. Second, creative people have a broad range of experiences and interests. Third, they are open to new experiences and question assumptions. Fourth, they enjoy abstract ideas and symbolic thought. Fifth, creative individuals value independence and complexity.

39.2 Distinguish between five issues that can lead to errors in intuitive thinking: ignoring the odds, representativeness, framing, hot cognition, and choice

When making decisions people often fail to consider the base rate, or probability, of events—this is referred to as ignoring the odds. The representativeness heuristic influences decisions by guiding us to give greater weight to options that seem to be similar to what we already know. Framing errors occur when we respond to how a problem is worded instead of focusing on the problem's fundamentals. Hot cognition refers to circumstances where strong emotions can distort problem solving. Choice overload occurs when we feel overwhelmed because we have too many choices.

Reflective Practice

Content Check

1. Fluency, flexibility, and originality are characteristics of
   a. convergent thought
   b. deductive thinking
   c. creative thought
   d. trial-and-error solutions
2. Reasoning and critical thinking tend to block creativity; these are noncreative qualities. T or F?
3. To be creative, an original idea also must be high quality and relevant. T or F?
4. Intelligence and creativity are highly correlated; the higher a person's IQ, the more likely he or she is to be creative. T or F?

5. Our decisions are greatly affected by the way that a problem is stated, a process called
   a. framing
   b. base rating
   c. induction
   d. selective encoding

Skill Check

Think Critically

6. A coin is flipped four times with one of the following results: (a) H T T H, (b) T T T T, (c) H H H H, (d) H H T H. Which sequence would most likely precede getting a head on the fifth coin flip?

Self-Reflect

Make up a question that would require convergent thinking to answer. Now, do the same for divergent thinking. On which of the tests of creativity described in the text do you think you would do best? (Look back if you can't remember them all.) Explain in your own words how base rates, representativeness, framing, hot cognition, and choice overload could contribute to your own thinking errors.

ANSWERS

1. c 2. F 3. T 4. F 5. a 6. None of them; the chance of getting heads on the fifth flip is the same in each case. Each time that you flip a coin, the chance of getting a head is 50 percent, no matter what happened before. However, many people intuitively think that *b* is the answer because a head is "overdue," or that *c* is correct because the coin is "on a roll" for heads.

MODULE 40

Cognition and Intelligence
Intelligence

How Intelligent Is the Idea of Intelligence?

What does it mean to say that a person such as the brilliant physicist Stephen Hawking, who died in 2018, is "intelligent"? You might assume that most psychologists agree on the meaning of this everyday word. After all, Hawking *was* a genius, right? IQ tests measure intelligence, and Hawking would score high, wouldn't he? (When Hawking was once asked about his IQ, he claimed he didn't know and joked, "People who boast about their IQ are losers.")

You might be surprised to learn that many questions about "intelligence" remain unanswered. Can intelligence be accurately measured? What does it mean to have extremely high or low intelligence? Is intelligence all about "book learning"? What about "street smarts"?

How about athletic brilliance, like the play-making abilities of remarkable athletes like LeBron James? Are we talking about another form of "intelligence" or something else altogether? Or musical brilliance, like that of Prince, who we lost in 2016?

Questions like these have fascinated psychologists for over 100 years. Let's see what we have learned to date and what is still being debated.

Mitchell Leff/Getty Images Sport/Getty Images

~LEARNING OUTCOMES~

After reading this module, you should be able to:

40.1 Define the g-factor in intelligence, and how it is measured

40.2 Distinguish between gifted individuals and those with intellectual disabilities

40.3 Define artificial intelligence, multiple intelligences, and emotional intelligence, and discuss the role of genes and the environment (including culture) in intelligence

Human Intelligence—The IQ and You

Learning Outcome 40.1 Define the g-factor in intelligence, and how it is measured

Like many important concepts in psychology, intelligence cannot be observed directly. So how can it be measured? That's the problem Alfred Binet faced in 1904 (Benjafield, 2015; Cicciola, Foschi, & Lombardo, 2014). The French Minister of Education wanted to find a way to distinguish slower students from the more capable (or the capable but lazy). In a flash of brilliance, Binet and an associate created a test made up of "intellectual" questions and problems. Next, they learned which questions an average child could answer at each age. By comparing test scores of individual children to the average score for their ages, they could tell whether a child was performing up to his or her potential (Kaplan & Saccuzzo, 2018).

Binet's approach gave rise to modern intelligence tests. At the same time, it launched an ongoing debate. Part of the debate is related to the basic difficulty of defining intelligence (Sternberg et al., 2011).

Defining Intelligence

Isn't there an accepted definition of intelligence? Broadly speaking, yes. **Intelligence** is the overall capacity to think rationally, to act purposefully, and to adapt to one's surroundings (Barber, 2010; Flynn, 2012). Beyond this, however, there is much debate about the details. According to one popular theory, the core of intelligence is an overall, or *general* (hence the "g"), mental ability called the **g-factor**. The g-factor functions by coordinating any of a large number of more specific *mental abilities* like those we have been exploring in the last eight modules, on topics such as working memory, reasoning, problem solving, and representing knowledge (Kan et al., 2013; Ziegler et al., 2011).

Here's how it works. One moment, you might face a situation that requires good working memory, imagery skill, some math, and some knowledge about geography, as you figure out how long it will take to get to a street address in a town you have never driven to before. The next moment, you might need to rely upon your knowledge of languages, some interpersonal skills, and the ability to reason about unfamiliar situations as you stop to help people at a traffic accident you come across while you are on your way. In other words, you never know just what demands life will place upon you from one moment to the next. People high in g-factor (intelligence) are good at bringing the right intellectual resources to bear on life's challenges as needed.

One more point: Some of the specific mental abilities are intellectual skills involved in **fluid intelligence (g-f)**—solving novel problems involving perceptual speed or rapid insight. Others are involved in **crystallized intelligence (g-c)**—solving problems using already acquired knowledge. By way of summary, intelligence is a complex capacity comprised of a general ability (g-factor), itself comprised of fluid (g-f) and crystal (g-c) intelligence. In turn, g-f and g-c are each comprised of a larger set of specific mental abilities (Keith & Reynolds, 2010).

As comprehensive as this may seem, it leaves many unanswered questions. *How* does the g-factor work to coordinate more specific mental abilities? Just which specific mental abilities together constitute intelligence? Is there really a g-factor or do we all possess very different, unconnected "intelligences" (Hampshire et al., 2012)? Here's another question: Intelligence has traditionally been considered a cognitive, not emotional, capacity. Is there such a thing as emotional intelligence? (To find out, read on.)

In the face of such questions, many psychologists simply accept an operational definition of intelligence by spelling out the procedures they use to measure it (Neukrug & Fawcett, 2020). Thus, by selecting items for an intelligence test, a psychologist is saying in a direct way, "This is what *I* mean by intelligence." A test that measures memory, reasoning, and verbal fluency offers a very different definition of intelligence than one that measures strength of grip, shoe size, hunting skills, or the person's best *Pokémon Go* mobile game score (Goldstein, 2019).

The Stanford-Binet

American psychologists quickly saw the value of Alfred Binet's test. By 1916, Lewis Terman and others at Stanford University had revised it for use in North America. After more revisions, the *Stanford-Binet Intelligence Scales, Fifth Edition* (SB5), continues to be widely used. The SB5 primarily is made up of age-ranked questions that get a little harder at each age level. The SB5 is appropriate for people from age 2 to 85+ years, and scores on the test are very reliable (Roid & Pomplun, 2012).

Bob Daemmrich/The Image Works

Modern intelligence tests are widely used to measure cognitive abilities. When properly administered, such tests provide one potential operational definition of intelligence.

The SB5 measures five cognitive factors (general mental abilities) thought to make up general intelligence: Fluid reasoning (roughly related to fluid intelligence), knowledge (roughly related to crystal intelligence), quantitative reasoning, visual-spatial processing, and working memory. Each factor is measured with verbal questions (those involving words and numbers) and nonverbal questions (items that use pictures and objects). If you were to take the SB5, you would be assessing your general intelligence (g-factor), verbal intelligence, nonverbal intelligence, and each of the five cognitive factors (Roid & Pomplun, 2012). Let's see what each factor looks like:

Fluid Reasoning Questions like the following are used to test fluid reasoning, the ability to reason in unfamiliar situations:

How are an apple, a plum, and a banana different from a beet?

An apprentice is to a master as a novice is to a(n) ______________.

"I knew my bag was going to be in the last place I looked, so I looked there first." What is silly or impossible about that?

Other items ask people to fill in the missing shape in a group of shapes and to tell a story that explains what's going on in a series of pictures.

Knowledge The knowledge factor assesses the person's knowledge about a wide range of topics:

Why is yeast added to bread dough?

What does "cryptic" mean?

What is silly or impossible about this picture? (For example, a bicycle has square wheels.)

Quantitative Reasoning Test items for quantitative reasoning measure a person's ability to solve problems involving numbers. Here are some samples:

If I have six marbles and you give me another one, how many marbles will I have?

Given the numbers 3, 6, 9, 12, what number would come next?

If a shirt is being sold for 50 percent of the normal price, and the price tag is $60, what is the cost of the shirt?

Visual-Spatial Processing People who have visual-spatial skills are good at putting picture puzzles together and copying geometric shapes (such as triangles, rectangles, and circles). Visual-spatial processing questions ask test-takers to reproduce patterns of blocks and choose pictures that show how a piece of paper would look if it were folded or cut. Verbal questions also can require visual-spatial abilities:

Suppose that you are going east, then turn right, then turn right again, then turn left. In what direction are you facing now?

Working Memory The working memory part of the SB5 measures the ability to use short-term memory. Some typical memory tasks include the following:

Correctly remember the order of colored beads on a stick.

After hearing several sentences, name the last word from each sentence.

Repeat a series of digits (forward or backward) after hearing them once.

The Wechsler Tests

Is the Stanford-Binet the only intelligence test? One widely used alternative is the *Wechsler Adult Intelligence Scale—Fourth Edition* (WAIS-IV). A version for children is called the *Wechsler Intelligence Scale for Children—Fifth Edition* (WISC-V). Like the Stanford-Binet, the Wechsler tests yield a single overall intelligence (g-factor) score. In addition, these tests also have separate scores for **performance (nonverbal) intelligence** and **verbal intelligence**—language- or symbol-oriented intelligence (Neukrug & Fawcett, 2020). The abilities measured by the Wechsler tests and some sample test items are listed in ▪ **Table 40.1**.

Group Tests

The SB5 and the Wechsler tests are *individual* intelligence tests, which are given to a single person by a trained

Intelligence Capacity for rational thought, purposeful action, and effective adaptation.

g-factor Measure of an individual's overall intelligence as opposed to specific abilities.

Fluid intelligence (g-f) The ability to solve novel problems involving perceptual speed or rapid insight.

Crystallized intelligence (g-c) The ability to solve problems using already acquired knowledge.

Performance (nonverbal) intelligence Intelligence measured by solving puzzles, assembling objects, completing pictures, and other nonverbal tasks.

Verbal intelligence Intelligence measured by answering questions involving vocabulary, general information, arithmetic, and other language- or symbol-oriented tasks.

TABLE 40.1 | Sample Items Similar to Those Used on the WAIS-IV

Verbal Comprehension	Sample Items or Descriptions
Similarities	In what way are a wolf and a coyote alike? In what way are a screwdriver and a chisel alike?
Vocabulary	The test consists of asking, "What is a(n) ________?" or "What does ________ mean?" The words range from more to less familiar and difficult.
Information	How many wings does a butterfly have? Who wrote *Romeo and Juliet*?
Perceptual Reasoning	
Block design	Copy designs with blocks (as shown at right). 
Matrix reasoning	Select the item that completes the matrix.
Visual puzzles	Choose the pieces that go together to form a figure.
Working Memory	
Digit span	Repeat from memory a series of digits, such as 8 5 7 0 1 3 6 2, after hearing it once.
Arithmetic	Four girls divided 28 jellybeans equally among themselves. How many jellybeans did each girl receive? If 3 peaches take 2 minutes to find and pick, how long will it take to find and pick a dozen peaches?
Processing Speed	
Symbol search	Match symbols appearing in separate groups. 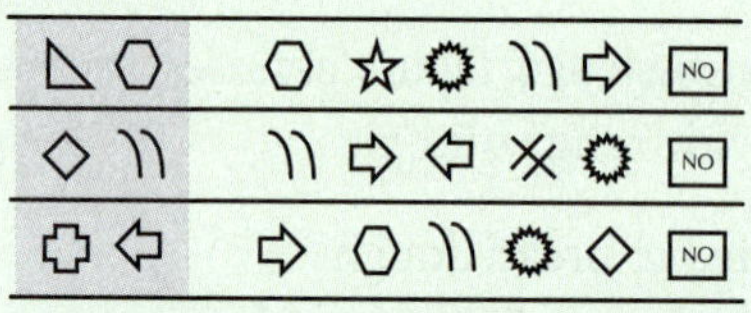
Coding	Fill in the symbols:

1	2	3	4
X	III	I	0

3	4	1	3	4	2	1	2

Items similar to those in Wechsler (2008).

specialist. In contrast, *group* intelligence tests can be given to large groups of individuals with minimal supervision. Group tests usually require people to read, to follow instructions, and to solve problems of logic, reasoning, mathematics, or spatial skills. If you're wondering if you have ever taken an intelligence test, the answer is probably yes. The well-known SAT Reasoning Test (SAT) measures aptitudes for language, math, and reasoning. The SAT is designed to predict your chances for success in college. Because it measures a number of different mental aptitudes, it also can be used to estimate general intelligence.

Intelligence Quotients

What is an IQ? Imagine that a child named Yuan can answer intelligence test questions that an average 7-year-old can answer. We could say that 7 is her **mental age** (average cognitive ability displayed by 7-year-olds). How smart is Yuan? We can't say yet, because we don't know how old she is. If she is 10, she's not very smart. If she's 5, she is very bright. To estimate a child's intelligence, then, we need to compare her mental age and her *chronological age* (age in years). When the Stanford-Binet was first used, MA (mental age) was divided by CA (chronological age). The resulting *quotient* was then multiplied by 100 to give a whole number, rather than a decimal, yielding an **intelligence quotient (IQ)**:

$$\frac{MA}{CA} \times 100 = IQ$$

In this way, children with different chronological and mental ages can be easily compared. For instance, 10-year-old Justin has a mental age of 12. Thus, his IQ is 120. Justin's friend Suke also has a mental age of 12. However, Suke's chronological age is 12, so his IQ is 100. The IQ shows that 10-year-old Justin is brighter than his 12-year-old friend Suke, even though their intellectual skills are about the same. Notice that a person's IQ will be 100 whenever mental age equals chronological age. This is why an IQ score of 100 is defined as average intelligence.

Then, does a person with an IQ score below 100 have below average intelligence? Not unless the IQ is well below 100. Average intelligence is usually defined as any score from 90 to 109. The important point is that IQ scores will be over 100 when mental age is higher than age in years. IQ scores below 100 occur when a person's age in years exceeds his or her mental age.

"The five candles represent his mental age."

Kes/CartoonStock Ltd

Deviation IQs Although the preceding discussion may give you insight into IQ scores, it's no longer necessary to directly calculate IQs. Instead, modern tests use **deviation IQs**. Tables supplied with the test are used to convert a person's relative standing in the group to an IQ score—that is, they tell how far above or below average the person's score falls. For example, if you score at the 50th percentile, half the people your age who take the test score higher than you and half score lower. In this case, your IQ score is 100. If you score at the 84th percentile, your IQ score is 115. If you score at the 97th percentile, your IQ score is 130.

Variations in Intelligence—Curved Like a Bell

Learning Outcome 40.2 Distinguish between gifted individuals and those with intellectual disabilities

The distribution (or scattering) of IQ scores approximates a bell-shaped curve or **normal distribution**—that is, most scores fall close to the average and few are found at the extremes (➤ Figure 40.1).

The Mentally Gifted

How high is the IQ of a genius? Only 2 people out of 100 score above 130 on IQ tests. These bright individuals are usually described as "gifted." Less than 0.5 percent of the population scores above 140. These people are certainly gifted, or perhaps even "geniuses." However, some psychologists reserve the term *genius* for people with even higher IQs or those who are exceptionally creative (Hallahan, Kauffman, & Pullen, 2015).

Gifted Children *Do high IQ scores in childhood predict later ability?* In a classic attempt to answer this question,

Mental age In intelligence testing, the average cognitive ability displayed by people of a given age.

Intelligence quotient (IQ) Mental age divided by chronological age times 100.

Deviation IQ An IQ obtained statistically from a person's relative standing in his or her age group—that is, how far above or below average the person's score is relative to other scores.

Normal distribution Bell-shaped curve of scores with a large number in the middle and very few on the high and low ends.

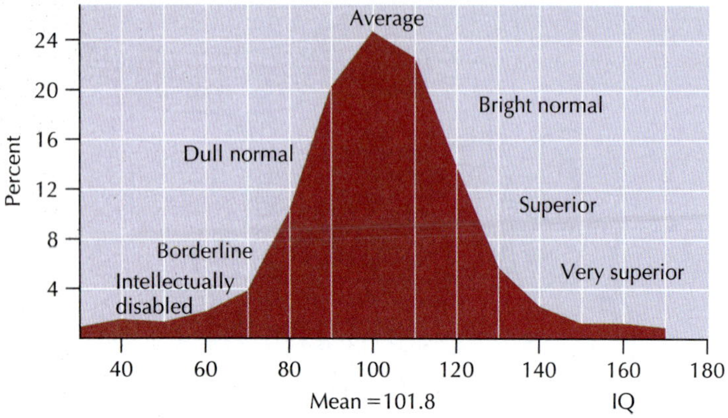

Figure 40.1

The bell curve. Distribution of Stanford-Binet Intelligence Test scores for 3,184 children. (Adapted from Terman & Merrill, 1937/1960.)

Lewis Terman followed into adulthood a gifted group of 1,500 children with IQs of 140 or more (the "Termites," as he called them). Most were quite successful. A majority finished college, earned advanced degrees, or held professional positions, and many had written books or scientific articles (Terman & Oden, 1959).

In general, the correlation between IQ scores and school grades is .50, a sizable association (Calvin et al., 2010; Mayes et al., 2009). The link would be even stronger, but motivation, special talents, off-campus learning, and many other factors also affect grades. The same is true of real-world success beyond school. IQ is also not a good predictor of success in art, music, writing, dramatics, science, and leadership. Tests of creativity are much more strongly related to achievement in these areas (Runco, 2012; Zenasni et al., 2016).

Were all the Termites superior as adults? No. Although the gifted tend to be well adjusted psychologically (Dai, 2010), some had committed crimes, were unemployable, or were unhappy misfits. Remember that a high IQ reveals *potential.* It does not guarantee success. Nor does a lower IQ guarantee failure. Nobel Prize-winning physicist Richard Feynman, whom many regard as a genius, had an IQ of 122 (Michalko, 2006).

How did Terman's more successful Termites differ from the less successful? Most of them had educated parents who valued learning and encouraged them to do the same. In general, successful gifted persons tend to have strong *intellectual determination*—a desire to know, to excel, and to persevere. Gifted or not, most successful persons tend to be *persistent* and *motivated* to learn (Reis & Renzulli, 2010; Winner, 2003). No one is paid to sit around being *capable* of achievement. What you do is always more important than what you should be able to do. That's why a child's talents are most likely to blossom when she or he is nurtured with support, encouragement, education, and effort (Reis, 2016).

Results from a recent large-scale European study are consistent with much of what Terman originally found: In general, children with higher IQs grow up into adults with higher IQs, more advanced educational achievements, and greater socioeconomic success (Fischbach et al., 2013; Schalke et al., 2013). At the same time, personality characteristics in childhood, such as optimism, studiousness, and attentiveness, are also related to adult success (Spengler et al., 2015).

Hasan Shaheed/Shutterstock.com

CREATISTA/Shutterstock.com

It is wise to remember that a child may be gifted in many ways. Many schools now offer Gifted and Talented Education programs for students who have a variety of special abilities—not just for those who score well on IQ tests.

Identifying Gifted Children *How might a parent spot an unusually bright child?* Early signs of giftedness are not always purely "intellectual." **Giftedness** can be either the possession of a high IQ or of special talents or aptitudes (Kreger Silverman, 2013). The following signs may reveal that a child is gifted: a tendency to seek out older children and adults; an early fascination with explanations and problem solving; talking in complete sentences as early as 2 or 3 years of age; an unusually good memory; precocious talent in art, music, or number skills; an early interest in books, along with early reading (often by age 3); showing kindness, understanding, and cooperation toward others (Dai, 2010; Distin, 2006).

Notice that this list goes beyond straight g-factor, or general "academic" intelligence. In fact, if artistic talent, mechanical aptitude, musical aptitude, athletic potential, and so on are considered, many children have a special "gift" of one kind or another. Limiting giftedness to a high IQ can shortchange children with special talents or potentials. This is especially true of ethnic minority children, who may be the victims of subtle biases in standardized intelligence tests. These children, as well as children with physical disabilities, are less likely to be recognized as gifted (Castellano & Frazier, 2011; Kornilov et al., 2012).

Intellectual Disability

Just as some children have exceptionally high IQs, so other children have exceptionally low IQs. A person with mental abilities far below average is termed *intellectually disabled* (the former term, *mentally retarded*, is now regarded as offensive). According to the definition listed in the American Psychiatric Association's *Diagnostic and Statistical Manual of Mental Disorders (DSM-5)*, **intellectual disability (intellectual developmental disorder)** begins at an IQ of approximately 70 or below. However, a person's ability to perform *adaptive behaviors* (basic skills such as dressing, eating, communicating, shopping, and working) is more important in evaluating this disability (American Psychiatric Association, 2013; Kirk, Gallagher, & Coleman, 2015; Murray et al., 2013).

It is important to realize that there is usually more to intellectually disabled people than what is revealed by the results of IQ testing (Treffert, 2014). In particular, they have no handicap concerning feelings. They are easily hurt by rejection, teasing, or ridicule. Likewise, they respond warmly to love and acceptance. They have a right to self-respect and a place in the community (Montreal Declaration on Intellectual Disabilities, 2004). This is especially important during childhood, when support from others adds greatly to each person's chances of becoming a well-adjusted member of society.

Savant Syndrome Some intellectually disabled individuals display a remarkable mixture of brilliance and intellectual disability. They have *savant syndrome*, a limited general intelligence accompanied by exceptional mental ability in one or more narrow areas, such as mental arithmetic, calendar calculation, art, or music (Crane et al., 2010; Young, 2005).

For example, Kim Peek, who died in 2009, could recite from memory more than 9,000 books. The model for Dustin Hoffman's character in the Academy Award-winning film *Rain Man*, Kim knew all the ZIP codes and area codes in the United States and could give accurate travel directions between any two major US cities. He also could discuss hundreds of pieces of classical music in detail and could play most of them quite well. Amazingly, though, for someone with such skills, Kim had difficulty with abstract thinking and tests of general intelligence. He was poorly coordinated and couldn't button his own clothes (Treffert, 2010).

Do savants have special mental powers not shared by most people? According to one theory, many savants have suffered some form of damage or congenital anomaly to their left cerebral hemispheres or their ability to make use of their left hemispheres, freeing them from the "distractions" of language, concepts, and higher-level thought. This allows them to focus with crystal clarity on music, drawing, prime numbers, license plates, television commercials, and other specific information (Young, 2005). Another theory holds that the performances of many savants result from intense practice. Perhaps each of us harbors embers of mental brilliance that intense practice could fan into full flame (Snyder et al., 2006; Treffert, 2014).

Although savant syndrome hasn't been fully explained, it does show that extraordinary abilities can exist apart from general intelligence.

Causes of Intellectual Disability *What causes intellectual disability?* Intellectual disability can be caused by a wide range of factors. Some of the most common are the following:

Giftedness The possession of either a high IQ or special talents or aptitudes.

Intellectual disability (intellectual developmental disorder) The presence of a developmental disability, a formal IQ score below 70, and a significant impairment of adaptive behavior.

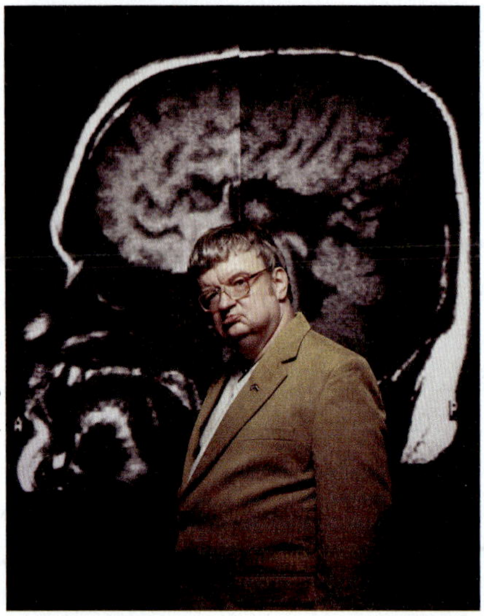

Ethan Hill/Contributor/Getty Images

This MRI of Kim's brain reveals that he was born without a corpus callosum, perhaps helping to explain his pattern of savant strengths and weaknesses.

Marcel Jancovic/Shutterstock.com

This young woman exhibits the classical features of Down syndrome, including almond-shaped eyes, a slightly protruding tongue, a stocky build, and stubby hands with deeply creased palms. Although she is mildly intellectually disabled, she is very loving and has a right to self-respect and a place in the community.

- **Genetic abnormalities.** A variety of genetic abnormalities, such as missing, extra, or defective genes, can result in an intellectual disability. For example, *Down syndrome* children have an extra 21st chromosome. This condition, also called trisomy 21, results from flaws in the parents' egg or sperm cells (National Down Syndrome Society, 2020). Although Down syndrome is *genetic*, it is not usually *hereditary* (it doesn't "run in the family"). In contrast, children with *PKU (phenylketonuria)* have an inherited inability to control a destructive chemical that builds up in their bodies (National Institute of Child Health and Human Development, 2016).
- **Fetal damage.** Fetal development can be disrupted by a variety of teratogens such as disease, infection, or drugs (Kalat, 2021; see Module 12). *Fetal alcohol syndrome (FAS)*, caused by heavy drinking during pregnancy, is, unfortunately, one of the most common causes of intellectual disability (Jones & Streissguth, 2010).
- **Birth injuries.** Birth injuries such as a lack of oxygen during delivery or an overly premature delivery also can result in intellectual disability.
- **Postnatal problems.** Malnutrition and exposure to lead, PCBs, and other toxins early in childhood also can cause organic intellectual disability (Kalat, 2021). In many cases, no known biological problem can be identified. Often, other family members also are mildly intellectually disabled. *Familial intellectual disability*, as this is called, occurs mostly in very poor households where nutrition, intellectual stimulation, medical care, and emotional support may be inadequate (Harris, 2010).

Questioning Intelligence—More Questions Than Answers?

Learning Outcome 40.3 Define artificial intelligence, multiple intelligences, and emotional intelligence, and discuss the role of genes and the environment (including culture) in intelligence

In this section, we consider some of the issues that have arisen in the study of intelligence. Most stem from questions about the traditional assumptions that intelligence can be defined in terms of a small set of general mental abilities and measured with IQ tests like the SB5 or the Wechsler scales. One criticism has been that this approach is too vague; according to researchers in the field of artificial intelligence, a better approach is to specify what we mean by intelligent behavior in enough detail that we can program computers to act intelligently. Others have wondered if maybe the traditional approach is too narrow and doesn't apply across cultures. Still others have questioned the value of defining intelligence in terms of any general intelligence factor at all. Finally, some have challenged the implicit assumption that intelligence is mainly inherited from our parents.

Artificial Intelligence

While most efforts have focused on measuring human intelligence, a small group of psychologists and computer scientists have taken an entirely different approach. Their basic idea is to build machines that display **artificial intelligence (AI)**. This usually refers to creating computer programs capable of doing things that require intelligence when done by people (Müller, 2012; Russell & Norvig, 2020).

As computer scientist Aaron Sloman explains it, "Human brains don't work by magic, so whatever it is they do should be doable by machine" (Brooks, 2009; Sloman, 2008). The resulting programs can then help us understand how people do those same things. While a robot might do a spiffy job of solving Rubik's Cube puzzles, it also can be thought of as a *computer simulation*, a program that attempts to duplicate specific human behaviors, especially thinking, decision-making, and problem solving. Here, the computer acts as a "laboratory" for testing models of cognition. If a computer program behaves as humans do (including making the same errors), then the program may be a good model of how we think.

So, how intelligent are computers? That's a complex question. Computers have been most successful in specific situations where complex skills can be converted into clearly stated rules that a computer can follow. The resulting *expert systems* can already predict the weather, analyze geological formations, diagnose disease, play chess, read, tell when to buy or sell stocks, harmonize music, and perform many other tasks better than humans (Giarratano & Riley, 2004; Mahmoodabadi et al., 2010). Consider, for example, IBM's "Watson," which outperforms expert humans at playing the television game *Jeopardy* (Markoff, 2011). Another example is Deep Blue, which beat world chess champion Garry Kasparov in 1997. (For fans of Go, AlphaGo finished off world Go champion, Lee Se-dol, in 2016.)

Source: YouTube

This robot recently held the robot world record for solving the Rubik's Cube, taking just less than 1 second. What about the fastest human, you ask? That would be China's Yusheng Du in 3.47 seconds! To what extent is the way this robot comes up with solutions helpful for understanding how humans do it?

While expert systems may perform some impressive feats, they are generally limited by the cleverness of their programmers: They must be programmed and cannot really learn on their own. A new field of artificial intelligence, *machine learning*, has sought to overcome this limitation by creating programs that gain information through learning, not programming (Jordan & Mitchell, 2015; Russell & Norvig, 2020).

How do they do that? By mimicking the human brain. Recall from Module 7 that the brain is a massive interconnected network of neurons and that the strength of the connection between any two neurons depends on how frequently the synaptic connection between those neurons is activated (Hebb's rule; Sporns, 2011). Using variations of these two general principles, computer scientists have created neural network-like computers and computer programs that learn in much the same way that human brains do. The resulting systems have shown remarkable promise in overcoming the limitations of programmed expert systems in a wide variety of applications (Christensen et al., 2017; Mangos & Hulse, 2017; Steele et al., 2017).

We will undoubtedly become able to build more and more powerful computers designed to learn from experience, like the human brain. Perhaps one day such artificial "brains" will even help us solve the riddles of the human brain and human intelligence (Resnick, 2017).

Culture and Intelligence

Let's "shift gears," something artificial intelligence systems have difficulty with. Imagine you have been asked to sort some objects into categories. Wouldn't it be smart to put the clothes, containers, implements, and foods in separate piles? Not necessarily. When individuals from the Kpelle people in Liberia were asked to sort objects, they grouped them together by function. For example, a potato (food) would be placed with a knife (implement). When the Kpelle were asked why they grouped the objects this way, they often said that was how a wise man would do it. The researchers finally asked the Kpelle, "How would a fool do it?" Only then did they sort the objects into the nice, neat categories that we Westerners prefer.

This anecdote, related by cultural psychologist Patricia Greenfield (1997), raises serious questions about general definitions of intelligence. For example, among the Cree of

Artificial intelligence (AI) Any artificial system (often a computer program) that is capable of humanlike problem solving or intelligent responding.

Northern Canada, "smart" people are those who have the skills needed to find food on the frozen tundra (Darou, 1992). For the Puluwat people in the South Pacific, "smart" means having the oceangoing navigation skills necessary to get from island to island (Sternberg, 2004). And so it goes, as each culture teaches its children how the wise man would do it, not the fool (Barber, 2010; Correa-Chávez, Rogoff, & Arauz, 2005).

Culture-Fair Intelligence Tests Cultural values, then, as well as knowledge, language patterns, and traditions, can greatly affect performance on tests designed for Western cultures (Nisbett et al., 2012; Sternberg & Grigorenko, 2005). Psychologist Jerome Kagan once remarked, "If the Wechsler and Binet scales were translated into Spanish, Swahili, and Chinese and given to every 10-year-old in Latin America, East Africa, and China, the majority would obtain IQ scores in the intellectually disabled range." Certainly, we cannot believe that children of other cultures are all intellectually disabled. The fault must lie with the test (Castles, 2012).

In view of such problems, psychologists have tried to create "culture-fair" intelligence tests that do not disadvantage certain groups. A **culture-fair test** is designed to minimize the importance of skills and knowledge that may be more common in some cultures than in others. For a sample of culture-fair test items, see ➤ Figure 40.2.

Culture-fair tests attempt to measure intelligence without being influenced by a person's verbal skills, cultural background, and educational level, to the greatest extent possible. Their value lies not just in testing people from other cultures. They also are useful for testing children in the United States who come from poor communities, rural areas, or ethnic minority families (Stephens et al., 1999). However, no intelligence test can be entirely free of cultural influences. For instance, our culture is very "visual" because children are constantly exposed to television, movies, video games, and the like. Thus, compared with children in developing countries, a child who grows up in the United States may be better prepared to take both nonverbal tests and traditional IQ tests.

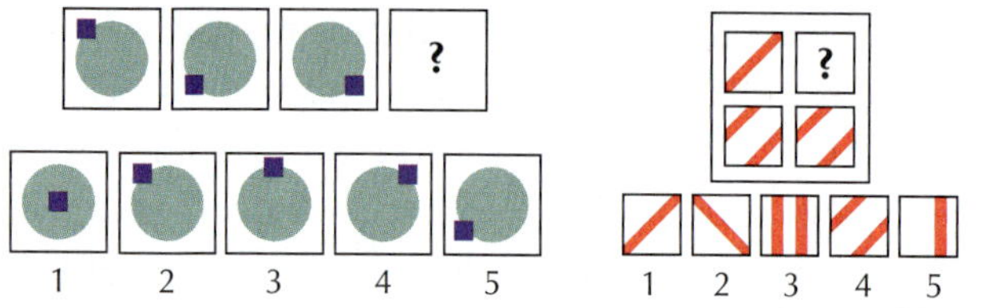

(a) Sample series problem (b) Sample matrix problem

➤ **Figure 40.2**

Sample items like those often found on culture-fair intelligence tests. (*a*) Sample series problem. Which pattern correctly continues the series of patterns shown at the top left? (Number 4.) (*b*) Sample matrix problem. Which pattern best completes the matrix of patterns shown at the top right? (Number 1.) The idea is that the ability to read and the mastery of culturally relevant knowledge should not be necessary to do well on these questions. Nevertheless, do you think that illiterate street orphans from Sao Paulo, Brazil, or aboriginals living in the Australian outback would find the items as easy to complete as you did? If not, can you think of any other truly culture-fair way to test intelligence across different cultures?

Keren Su/Getty Images

How important do you think the mental abilities assessed in modern intelligence tests are to this Dani hunter in Papua, New Guinea?

Because the concept of intelligence exhibits diversity across cultures, many psychologists have begun to stress the need to rethink the concept of intelligence itself (Greenfield, 1997; Sternberg & Grigorenko, 2005). If we are to find a truly culture-fair way to measure intelligence, we first need to identify the core cognitive skills that lie at the heart of human intelligence the world over (Gardner, 2008; Henrich, Heine, & Norenzayan, 2010).

Multiple Intelligences

Defining intelligence as a g-factor (general ability) also has been questioned. As we just noted, there may be many ways to be smart. For example, consider William, a grade-school student two years behind in reading, who shows his teacher how to solve a difficult computer-programming problem. What about his classmate, Malika, who is a poor reader but plays intricate pieces of piano music? Both of these children show clear signs of what we earlier referred to as *aptitudes*. Yet, each might score below average on a traditional IQ test. And, as we have seen, autistic savants like Kim Peek have even more extreme intellectual strengths and weaknesses. Such observations have convinced many psychologists that it is time to forge new, broader definitions of intelligence (Roberts & Lipnevich, 2012). Their basic goal is to better predict real-world success—not just the likelihood of success in school (Richardson, 2013).

One such psychologist is Howard Gardner of Harvard University. Gardner (2008, 2011) theorizes that there are nine distinctly different kinds of intelligence. These are different mental "languages" that people use for thinking. Each is listed below, with examples of pursuits that use them:

1. *Linguistic* (language abilities)—writer, lawyer, comedian
2. *Logical-mathematical* (logic and number abilities)—scientist, accountant, programmer
3. *Visual* (pictorial abilities)—engineer, inventor, artist
4. *Musical* (music abilities)—composer, musician, music critic
5. *Bodily-kinesthetic* (physical abilities)—dancer, athlete, surgeon
6. *Intrapersonal* (self-knowledge)—poet, actor, minister
7. *Interpersonal* (social abilities)—psychologist, teacher, politician
8. *Naturalist* (an ability to understand the natural environment)—biologist, medicine man, organic farmer
9. *Existential* (an ability to understand spirituality and existence)—religious leader, philosopher, motivational speaker

Most of us are probably strong in only a few types of intelligence. In contrast, geniuses like Albert Einstein seem to be able to use nearly all of the intelligences, as needed, to solve problems.

If Gardner's theory of **multiple intelligences** is correct, traditional IQ tests measure only a part of real-world intelligence—namely, linguistic, logical-mathematical, and spatial abilities (Roberts & Lipnevich, 2012). A further implication is that our schools may be wasting a lot of human potential. For example, some children might find it easier to learn math or reading if these topics were tied into art, music, dance, drama, and so on. Many schools are now using Gardner's theory to cultivate a wider range of skills and talents (Campbell, 2008).

Emotional Intelligence

Another way in which traditional IQ tests may measure only a part of real-world intelligence has been raised by proponents of **emotional intelligence**, the ability to perceive, use, and understand emotions in ourselves and others, as well as the ability to manage those feelings effectively (Caruso, Salovey, & Mayer, 2015). Being emotionally skilled can make us more flexible, adaptable, agreeable, and emotionally mature (English et al., 2012; Johnson, Batey, & Holdsworth, 2009). In addition to recognizing emotions in yourself and others, being emotionally intelligent is associated with understanding how to manage your emotions appropriately, a necessary skill in an increasingly social world.

The challenges associated with poor emotion regulation skills can be high (Sheppes, Suri, & Gross, 2015). They range from problems with health and achievement problems to poor relationships at home and difficulties at work (Joseph, Jin, Newman, & O'Boyle, 2015; Zampetakis & Moustakis, 2011; Zeidner, Matthews, & Roberts, 2012). Perhaps the greatest toll falls on children and teenagers (Alegre, 2011; Frederickson, Petrides, & Simmonds, 2012). For them, having poor emotional management skills can contribute to depression, eating disorders, unwanted pregnancy, aggression, violent crime, and poor academic performance.

Let's end this module with a look at the controversial question of how much intelligence is inherited from our parents.

IQ and Heredity

Most people are aware of a moderate similarity in the intelligence of parents and their children or between brothers and sisters. As ➤ **Figure 40.3** shows, the closer two people are on a family tree, the more alike their IQs are likely to be.

Does this indicate that intelligence is hereditary? Not necessarily. Brothers, sisters, and parents share similar environments, as well as similar genes (Grigorenko, 2005; Kaplan, 2012). To separate nature and nurture, a **twin study** may be done. Such studies compare the IQs of twins who were raised together or separated at birth. This allows us to better estimate how much heredity and environment affect intelligence.

Twin Studies Notice in Figure 40.3 that the IQ scores of fraternal twins are more alike than the IQs of ordinary

Culture-fair test A test (such as an intelligence test) designed to minimize the importance of skills and knowledge that may be more common in some cultures than in others.

Multiple intelligences Howard Gardner's theory that there are several specialized types of intellectual ability.

Emotional intelligence The ability to perceive, use, understand, and manage emotions.

Twin study A comparison of the characteristics of twins who were raised together or separated at birth; used to identify the relative impact of heredity and environment.

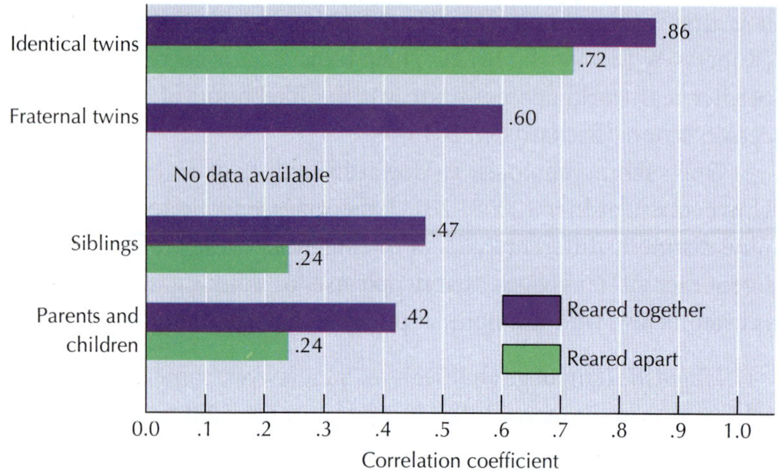

Figure 40.3

IQ as a function of genetic relatedness. Approximate correlations between IQ scores for persons with varying degrees of genetic and environmental similarity. Notice that the correlations grow smaller as the degree of genetic similarity declines. Also, note that a shared environment increases the correlations in all cases. (Adapted from McGue et al., 1993.)

brothers and sisters. **Fraternal twins** come from two separate eggs that are fertilized at the same time. They are no more genetically alike than ordinary siblings. Why, then, should the twins' IQ scores be more similar? The reason is environmental: Parents treat twins more alike than ordinary siblings, resulting in a closer match in IQs.

More striking similarities are observed with **identical twins**, who develop from a single egg and have identical genes. At the top of Figure 40.3, you can see that identical twins who grow up in the same family have highly correlated IQs. This is what we would expect with identical heredity and very similar environments. Now, let's consider what happens when identical twins are reared apart. As you can see, the correlation drops, but only from .86 to .72. Psychologists who emphasize genetics believe figures like these show that differences in adult intelligence are roughly 50 percent hereditary (Jacobs et al., 2008; Nisbett et al., 2012).

How do environmentalists interpret the figures? They point out that some separated identical twins differ by as much as 20 IQ points. In every case in which this occurs, there are large educational and environmental differences between the twins. Also, separated twins are almost always placed in homes socially and educationally similar to those of their birth parents. This would tend to inflate apparent genetic effects by making the separated twins' IQs more alike. Another frequently overlooked fact is that twins grow up in the same environment before birth (in the womb). If this environmental similarity is taken into account, intelligence would seem to be less than 50 percent hereditary (Nisbett et al., 2012; Turkheimer et al., 2003). Identical twins also tend to have similar personality traits. This suggests that heredity contributes to personality as well as intelligence. (For more information, see Module 53.)

Environmental Influences

Some evidence for an environmental view of intelligence comes from families having one adopted child and one biological child. As **Figure 40.4** shows, parents contribute genes and environment to their biological child. With an adopted child, they contribute only environment. If intelligence is highly genetic, the IQs of biological children should be more like their parents' IQs than the IQs of adopted children. However, studies show that children reared by the same mother resemble her in IQ to the same degree. It doesn't matter whether they share her genes (Kamin, 1981; Weinberg, 1989).

How much can environment alter intelligence? It depends on the quality of the environment (Nisbett et al., 2012). One way to look at environmental effects is to compare children adopted by parents of high or low *socioeconomic status (SES)*. Children who grow up in high-SES homes develop higher IQs than those reared by lower SES parents. Presumably, the higher SES homes provide an enriched environment, with better nutrition, greater educational opportunities, and other advantages (Nisbett et al., 2012).

More importantly, children adopted *out of* low-SES environments can experience great relative gains in intelligence. That is, the IQs of low-SES children may be more

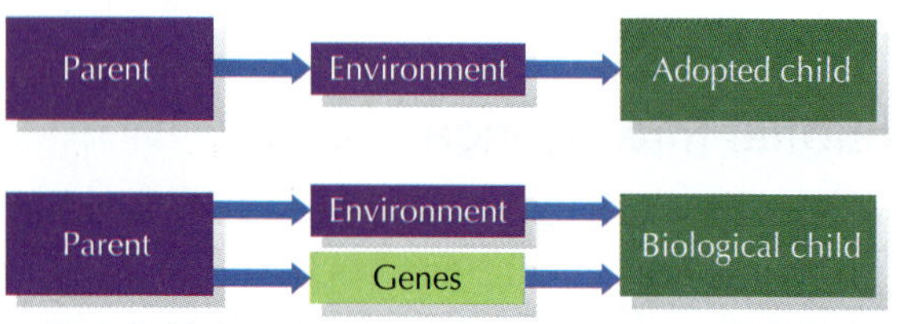

Figure 40.4

Comparison of an adopted child and a biological child reared in the same family. Adapted from Kamin, 1981.

dramatically influenced by environmental factors than the IQs of high-SES children (Henrich, Heine, & Norenzayan, 2010). In one study, striking increases in IQ occurred in 25 children who were moved from an orphanage and were eventually adopted by parents who gave them love, a family, and a stimulating home environment. Once considered intellectually disabled and unadoptable, the children gained an average of 29 IQ points. A second group of initially less intellectually disabled children, who stayed in the orphanage, lost an average of 26 IQ points (Skeels, 1966).

The Flynn Effect Many psychologists now agree that IQ scores in Western, industrialized nations have risen over the last 50 or so years (Flynn, 2012; Williams, 2013). Not by a little bit, mind you. If our grandparents scored an IQ of 100 (average, remember?) 50 years ago, they might score as low as about 70 on today's IQ tests. Conversely, if your IQ is 100 today, 50 years ago you might have scored as much as 130 on the old IQ tests. This rapid rise in IQ, referred to as the *Flynn effect* after the discoverer, New Zealand psychologist James Flynn, has occurred in far too short a time to be explained by genetics. It is more likely that the gains reflect environmental factors (Flynn, 2012; Rindermann, Becker, & Coyle, 2017).

But which factors? Flynn (2012) credits modern society, which is becoming ever more complex, demanding ever more abstract, "scientific" skills of its members. If you've ever tried to fill out an online tax form or set up a wireless network in your home, you'll understand why people may be getting better at answering IQ test questions. Video games, the Internet, and even television programming are becoming ever more complex. As a result, everyday living demands ever greater abstract cognitive effort from us. In the end, popular culture may well be inviting us to read, reflect, and problem solve more than ever before (Jaeggi et al., 2008).

Does this mean that my grandparents were intellectually disabled or that I am a genius? No. Your grandparents likely depended less on abstract reasoning than you do. For example, Flynn gives the following question that you might find on a modern IQ test: "How are dogs and rabbits alike?" (Crist & Requarth, 2012). While you might abstractly answer (correctly, according to the IQ test) that "They are both mammals," your grandparents were more likely to give a concrete, functional answer like "Dogs hunt rabbits" (which modern IQ tests are likely to score as wrong).

If this reminds you of the Kpelle people, reluctant to sort things the way a fool would, you're right. Just like people from other cultures, your grandparents did not automatically value the abstract reasoning prized in today's more complex society. Nevertheless, had they been born today, they undoubtedly would have developed abstract reasoning skills just fine. Alternatively, had you been born into their world, you undoubtedly would have, in the end, answered IQ test questions more like them. The takeaway point is that our intelligence, along with the ways we measure it, cannot easily be separated from the social and cultural context of particular places and times.

IQ and Race The likelihood that environment plays a major role in shaping intelligence is highly relevant to many of today's more important social issues. One persistent, but disputed, claim is that African Americans are genetically incapable of climbing out of poverty (Ossorio, 2011; Rushton & Jensen, 2005).

Is there any evidence for or against this claim? Historically, African-American children in the United States scored an average of about 15 points lower on standardized IQ tests than European-American children (although this gap has been reduced by one-third since 1972; Nisbett et al., 2012). As a group, Asian-American children scored above average in IQ. Could such differences be genetic? Psychologists have responded to such claims with several counterarguments.

To begin, it is no secret that, as a group, African Americans are more likely than European Americans to live in environments that are physically, educationally, and intellectually impoverished. When unequal education is part of the equation, IQs may tell us little about how heredity affects intelligence (Sternberg et al., 2011; Suzuki & Aronson, 2005). Indeed, one study found that placing poor African-American children into European-American adoptive families increased the children's IQs by an average of 13 points, bringing them into line with those of European-American children (Nisbett, 2005, 2009). That is, providing African-American children with the same environmental experiences available to European-American children erased IQ differences.

Furthermore, although IQ predicts school performance, it does not predict later career success (McClelland, 1994). In this regard, "street smarts," or what psychologist Robert Sternberg calls *practical intelligence*, may be seen by minority cultures as more important than "book learning," or what Sternberg calls *analytic intelligence* (Stemler & Sternberg, 2006; Sternberg, 2017).

Fraternal twins Twins conceived from two separate eggs.

Identical twins Twins who develop from a single egg and so share the same genes.

Most psychologists have concluded that there is no scientific evidence that group differences in average IQ are based on genetics. In fact, studies that used actual blood group testing found no significant correlations between ethnic ancestry and IQ scores. This is because it does not even make sense to talk about "races" at all—obvious external markers, like skin color, have little to do with underlying genetic differences (Bonham, Warshauer-Baker, & Collins, 2005; Sternberg, 2007). Group differences in IQ scores are based on cultural and environmental diversity as much as on heredity (Nisbett, 2009; Nisbett et al., 2012). To conclude otherwise reflects political beliefs and biases, not scientific fact.

The Whole Human: Wisdom

In the final analysis, intelligence reflects development as well as potential, nurture as well as nature (Richardson, 2013). Moreover, the fact that intelligence is partly determined by heredity tells us little of any real value. Genes are fixed at birth. Improving the environments in which children learn and grow is the main way we can ensure that they reach their full potential (Ormrod, 2014; Roberts & Lipnevich, 2012).

Perhaps most important of all, people can be intelligent without being wise. For example, a person who does well in school and on IQ tests may make a total mess of his or her life. Likewise, people can be intelligent without being creative, and clear, rational thinking can lead to correct, but uninspired, answers (Solomon, Marshall, & Gardner, 2005). In many areas of human life, wisdom represents a mixture of convergent thinking, intelligence, and reason, spiced with creativity and originality (Meeks & Jeste, 2009). People who are wise approach life with openness and tolerance (Le, 2011).

MODULE 40 Intelligence—Learning Outcomes Revisited

40.1 Define the g-factor in intelligence, and how it is measured

Intelligence refers to the general capacity (or g-factor) to act purposefully, think rationally, and adapt to the environment. G-factor, in turn, can be divided into fluid (g-f) and crystal (g-c) intelligence. One intelligence test that assesses g is the *Stanford-Binet Intelligence Scales, Fifth Edition* (SB5). A second major intelligence test is the Wechsler Scales for adults and children. Group tests can also be used to measure g. Results of these tests are expressed as an intelligence quotient (IQ), defined as mental age divided by chronological age and then multiplied by 100. The distribution of IQ scores approximates a normal distribution. Modern IQ tests no longer calculate IQs directly. Instead, the final score reported by the test is a deviation IQ.

40.2 Explain the process for identifying individuals who are gifted and those believed to have intellectual disabilities

People considered gifted tend to score above 130 on IQ tests. Intellectually gifted children often have difficulties in average classrooms and benefit from special accelerated programs. The term *intellectually disabled* is applied to those whose IQ falls below 70 and who lack various adaptive behaviors. Current classifications of intellectual disability are as follows: mild (50–55 to 70), moderate (35–40 to 50–55), severe (20–25 to 35–40), and profound (below 20–25). Chances for educational success are related to the degree of intellectual disability; however, those individuals who are able to demonstrate adaptive behaviors can make contributions to their communities and lead fulfilling lives.

40.3 Define artificial intelligence, multiple intelligences, and emotional intelligence

Artificial intelligence (AI) refers to any artificial system that can perform tasks that require intelligence when done by people. Two principal areas of AI research on particular human skills are expert systems and machine learning. Howard Gardner's theory of multiple intelligences challenges single factor theories of intelligence. Emotional intelligence is the ability to recognize and understand emotions in ourselves and others, as well as the ability to manage those feelings effectively. People who are "smart" emotionally are able to perceive, use, understand, and manage emotions. Studies of twins demonstrate that intelligence is partially determined by heredity. Heritability estimates tend to suggest that intelligence is approximately 50 percent heritable, but this is an average for the population as a whole. For any given pair of relatives, it may be higher or lower. Both adoption studies and the Flynn Effect strongly suggest that the environment makes an important contribution to intelligence. Different cultures define the mastery of different sets of skills defining intelligence.

Reflective Practice

Content Check

1. If we define intelligence by writing a test, we are using a(n) ______________________ definition.
2. By definition, a person has average intelligence when
   a. MA = CA
   b. CA = 100
   c. MA = 100
   d. MA × CA = 100
3. The distribution of IQs approximates a ______________________ (bell-shaped) curve.
4. Many cases of intellectual disability without known organic causes appear to be ______________________.
5. The claim that heredity accounts for racial differences in average IQ scores ignores environmental differences and the cultural bias inherent in standard IQ tests. T or F?
6. From a practical point of view, intelligence can most readily be increased by
   a. genetics
   b. teaching adaptive behaviors
   c. stimulating environments
   d. applying deviation IQs

Skill Check

Think Critically

7. If "intelligence" involves a g-factor coordinating a large number of more specific mental abilities, would you expect to learn that human intelligence is controlled by relatively few or relatively many genes?
8. Some people treat IQ as if it were a fixed number, permanently stamped on the forehead of each child. Why is this view in error?

Self-Reflect

If you were going to write an intelligence test, what kinds of questions would you include? How much would they resemble the questions found on the SB5, the WAIS-IV, or culture-fair tests? Can you think of any type of question that wouldn't favor the mental skills emphasized by some culture, somewhere in the world? Think of a person you know who is smart cognitively (that is, has a high IQ) but low in emotional intelligence. Think of another person who is smart cognitively *and* emotionally. How does the second person differ from the first? Which person do you think would make a better parent, friend, supervisor, roommate, or teacher? A friend says to you, "I think intelligence is entirely inherited from parents." What could you tell your friend to make sure she or he is better informed?

ANSWERS

1. operational 2. a 3. normal 4. familial 5. T 6. c 7. Most complex human qualities are controlled by many genes (i.e., they are polygenic), each having a small impact on its own. This is definitely true of human intelligence (Plomin & Deary, 2015). 8. Because one's IQ depends on the intelligence test used to measure it: Change the test and you will, to some extent, change the score. Also, heredity establishes a range of possibilities; it does not automatically preordain a person's intellectual capacities.

MODULE 41

A Psychologist's Skill Set

Creativity and Innovation

Getting a Leg Up

Struck by a boat propeller while waterskiing, college student Van Phillips had his leg severed just below the knee. His prosthetic limb (basically, a pink foam foot on the end of an aluminum tube) came with a piece of medical advice: Get used to your new "best friend." But Phillips hated his awkward artificial limb and set out to build a better prosthetic, one that would allow users to run, jump, and rebound. He considered the benefits associated with the C-shape of a cheetah's hind leg, but eventually settled on an L-shape that provided spring when weight was applied to the "heel." He tested hundreds of prototypes on himself before founding Flex-Foot, a company that produces high-quality prosthetic limbs for amputees, including Paralympic athletes. Not content to stop there, Phillips has now turned to the problem of reducing costs, so that artificial limbs can be made more widely available to landmine victims in developing countries.

filrom/iStock/Getty Images

You might think that people like Van Phillips are born with innovative minds, but research suggests that this isn't the case. In fact, we all have the skills that are needed to be creative—all it takes is a willingness to practice them.

~LEARNING OUTCOMES~

After reading this module you should be able to:

41.1 Create a plan to enhance your creativity and innovation skills

Creative Innovation—Or Is It Innovative Creativity?

Learning Outcome 41.1 Create a plan to enhance your creativity and innovation skills

Psychologists have had a longstanding interest in creativity. Some have asked how to define creativity and innovation across disciplines such as business, science, and the arts (Simonton, 2016). Others have examined this fascinating topic from diverse psychological perspectives, such as neuroscience, cognition, intelligence, and personality (Baas, Nijstad, & De Dreu, 2015; Silvia, 2015). And some have set out to assess creativity with questionnaires, standardized tests, and interview questions, and ask which people are in the best position to judge the creative worth of an idea (Galati, 2015; Silvia et al., 2012).

A significant amount of this research has focused on the conditions that enhance (or suppress) creativity (Bonnardel & Didier, 2016; Leung & Wang, 2015). For example, many studies of creativity show that it owes as much to persistence and dedication as it does to inspiration (Nijstad et al., 2010). These studies are important because they draw attention to the idea that creativity is not a trait that is fixed at birth. Instead, it is a characteristic that can be developed in positive ways and shaped by the environment in which we live.

The DNA of Innovation

At a time when the world is becoming more complex, it's no surprise that creativity and innovative thinking are increasingly seen as valuable skills. In the workforce, these skills are considered an important aspect of problem solving at many organizations. But nurturing your creative side can have benefits for your personal life as well. In fact, research indicates that people who engage in creative pursuits in their leisure time are happier and show higher levels of well-being (Cameron et al., 2013).

How can creative, innovative thinking be fostered? This is exactly what an international team of researchers asked when they spent six years interviewing some of the most innovative people in the world (Dyer, Gregersen, & Christensen, 2013). They found that these people demonstrated four key "discovery skills," which they describe in *The Innovator's DNA* project. The good news? These discovery skills can be cultivated by anyone who's willing to practice them. Let's take a closer look at what those skills are.

Make Associations *Associating* refers to our ability to connect ideas, questions, or concepts that, at first glance, seem to be completely unrelated. A good example is Steve Coleman, a jazz musician and composer who won a "genius" award from the MacArthur Foundation in 2014. Coleman creates his unique musical sound by blending music from several countries, and has even drawn on patterns derived from nature, including the pulsing patterns of the human heart.

Dyer, Gregersen, and Christensen (2013) pointed out that such unusual connections are easier to make when you've had diverse experiences or when you work with people who have had diverse experiences. (Note that the value of diversity is also discussed in Module 49.) Steve Jobs, the cofounder of Apple, understood this intuitively. He once noted that creativity was simply the process of connecting things, adding, "If you're gonna make connections which are innovative … you have to not have the same bag of experiences as everyone else does, or else you're going to make the same connections [as everybody else]."

Remember, creativity requires *divergent* thinking. To make creative associations, then, you might attempt to shift your mental "prospecting" to new areas. Try relating a problem to random words from the dictionary, for example, or to novel objects or photos. Imagine how another person would view the problem. What would a child, engineer, professor, mechanic, artist, psychologist, judge, or minister ask about it? Also, don't be afraid to ask "silly" or playful questions such as: If the problem were alive, what would it look like? If the problem were edible, how would it taste? Is any part of the problem pretty? Ugly? Stupid? Friendly? (de Bono, 1992; Michalko, 2006; Simonton, 2009).

You can also improve your ability to make novel connections by exploring a range of interests and hobbies. Finally, creative associations can be fostered when you engage with new people whose values and life experiences differ from your own. You may choose to do this by traveling to other countries, but in many American cities and towns, it's easy to find diverse others close to home or where you work. J. K. Rowling, for example, noted in a speech to the graduating class at Harvard that her experience working with a wide range of individuals at Amnesty International was valuable in the process of bringing Harry Potter to life in her books.

Ask Questions Being creative also includes a willingness to challenge conventions and a refusal to accept the status quo. This means that you should often be asking questions such as "Why?," "Why not?," and "What if?" Van Phillips provides a good example of someone who understands the value of pushing back against conventional wisdom. He didn't accept, for example, that existing prosthetics were as good as they could be. And he was willing to ask unconventional questions such as, "What if a prosthetic leg didn't have to look like a human's, but instead could look more like a cheetah's?"

Questions that force people to consider constraints can also spur innovative thinking. For example, creative solutions can sometimes emerge when we consciously work toward eliminating mental sets. A **mental set** is the tendency to perceive a problem in a way that blinds us to possible solutions. Mental sets are a major barrier to creative thinking. They usually trap us "in a box," leading us to see a problem in preconceived terms that impede our problem-solving

Mental set A predisposition to perceive or respond in a particular way.

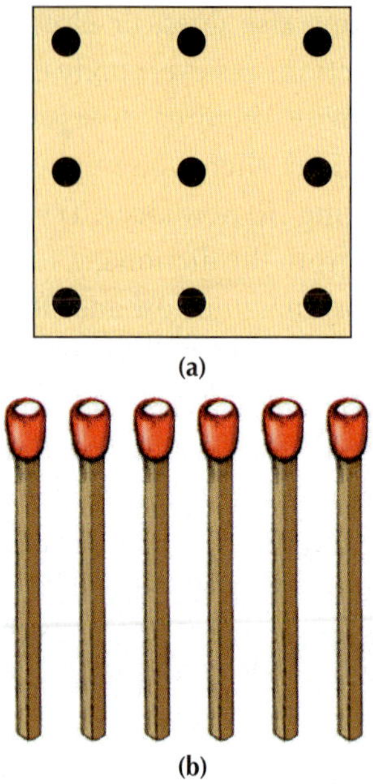

➤ **Figure 41.1**

Mental set problems. (*a*) Nine dots are arranged in a square. Can you connect them by drawing four continuous straight lines without lifting your pencil from the paper? (*b*) Six matches must be arranged to make four triangles. The triangles must be the same size, with each side equal to the length of one match.

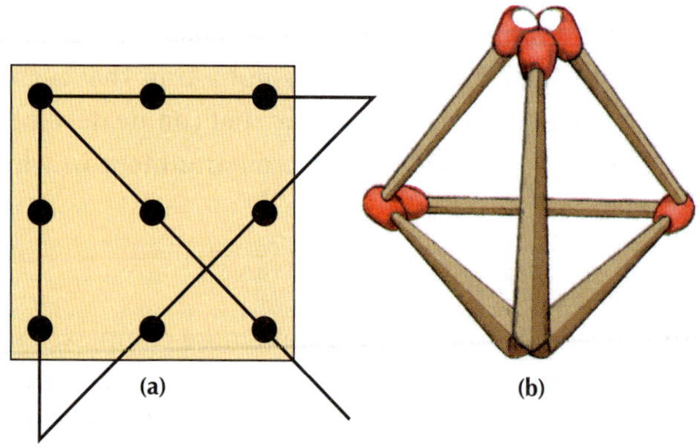

➤ **Figure 41.2**

Mental set problem solutions. (*a*) The dot problem can be solved by extending the lines beyond the square formed by the dots. Most people assume incorrectly that they may not do this. (*b*) The match problem can be solved by building a three-dimensional pyramid. Most people assume that the matches must be arranged on a flat surface. If you remembered the four-tree problem from earlier in the chapter, the match problem may have been easy to solve.

attempts (Thurson, 2008). (Fixations and functional fixedness, which were described in Module 39, are specific types of mental sets.) Try the problems pictured in ➤ **Figure 41.1**. If you have difficulty, try asking yourself what assumptions you are making. The problems are designed to demonstrate the limiting effects of a mental set. (The answers to these problems, along with an explanation of the mental sets that prevent their solution, are found in ➤ **Figure 41.2**.)

An effective way to break mental sets is to frame the problem broadly (Reed, 2013; Thurson, 2008). For instance, assume that your problem is to design a better doorway. This is likely to lead to ordinary solutions. Why not change the problem to design a better way to get through a wall? Now your solutions will be more original. Best of all might be to state the problem as follows: Find a better way to define separate areas for living and working. This could lead to truly creative solutions.

Let's say that you are leading a group that's designing a new can opener. Wisely, you ask the group to think broadly about opening in general, rather than about can openers. This was just the approach that led to the pop-top can. As the design group discussed the concept of opening, one member suggested that nature has its own openers, such as the soft seam on a pea pod. Instead of a new can-opening tool, the group invented the self-opening can (Stein, 1974).

But while it's clear that it can be useful to ask questions that will help you recognize (and avoid!) the constraints imposed by mental sets, it's interesting to note that sometimes creative ideas can also be fostered by *imposing* constraints on your thinking. For example, at a time when one company found itself in a very challenging and competitive business environment, the CEO asked the following questions: "What if we were legally prohibited from selling to our existing customers next year? How would we make money?" Thinking in terms of restrictions like this forced people at the company to think about new possibilities they might not previously have considered. Thinking in terms of restrictions is also valued at Google, where one of the nine principles of innovation is "*Creativity loves constraint.*"

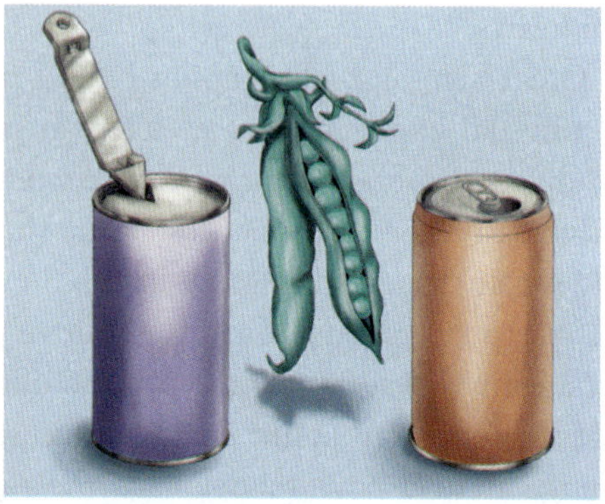

Seek Varied Input Through Networking If making associations and questioning are important in boosting creativity, then it's worth noting that both of these skills can be enhanced when you regularly exchange ideas with a wide range of people. Networking with diverse others can help you consider new questions that you might ask to challenge the status quo, and can also assist you in making new associations between ideas that at first may seem unrelated. For example, another MacArthur creative "genius," lawyer Sarah Deer, has championed the idea of bringing together diverse professionals in an effort to investigate potential reforms to the justice system that would provide greater assistance to Native American women who are victims of abuse.

Sometimes networking can simply involve having conversations with other people during social interactions. If you find yourself in this situation, try to listen without judging, but rather with the goal of widening your perspective on the world. In the workplace, though, you may find yourself working with a team to complete a project that requires creative thought. If this is the case, you may find it useful to encourage team members to use their diversity to best advantage through a process called *brainstorming*.

The essence of **brainstorming** is that producing and evaluating ideas are kept separate. This encourages the kind of divergent thinking that is promoted when you work with people who have had different experiences. In group problem solving, each person is encouraged to produce as many ideas as possible without fear of criticism (Henningsen & Henningsen, 2013). Only at the end of a brainstorming session are ideas reconsidered and evaluated. As ideas are freely generated, an interesting **cross-stimulation effect** takes place in which one participant's ideas trigger ideas from others (Brown et al., 1998; Laughlin, 2011).

Can brainstorming be applied to individual problem solving as well? Absolutely! The essential point to remember is to *suspend judgment*. Creative ideas should first be produced without regard for logic, organization, accuracy, practicality, or any other evaluation. In writing an essay, for instance, you would begin by writing ideas in any order, the more the better, just as they occur to you. Later you can go back and reorganize, rewrite, and criticize your efforts.

The basic rules for successful brainstorming are (Kaufman, 2009; Michalko, 2006; Scannell & Mulvilhill, 2012):

1. Absolutely do not criticize ideas until later in the session.
2. Modify or combine ideas freely. Don't worry about giving credit for ideas or keeping them neat. Mix them up!
3. Try to generate lots of ideas. In the early stages of brainstorming, quantity is more important than quality.
4. Let your imagination run amok! Seek unusual, remote, or wild ideas.
5. Record ideas as they occur.
6. Elaborate or improve on the most promising ideas.

Observe and Experiment Creative individuals practice their observation skills by watching the behavior of people in their everyday lives, taking note of what they do and say, what frustrates them, and what makes them happy. Often, this type of observation is combined with the questioning skills that were described earlier. After watching people, then, you might be inclined to ask yourself, "Why do they do that?," "What if they did it this way instead?," or "How does what I'm seeing differ from what I expected?" Of course, you may also want to think about taking your observations one step further. For example, Richard Branson, the CEO of Virgin, isn't just a keen observer of what's going on around him: He is well known for taking notes about everything that he sees, and every conversation that's of interest.

After observing something interesting and asking questions, you might then attempt to answer those questions in a process of experimentation. Recall from Module 2 that people interested in psychological experiments begin with questions and then develop hypotheses about what they believe will happen. Consider approaching the world with this type of hypothesis-testing mindset, which encourages you to examine your questions and hypotheses out in the world and watch to see whether the results conform to expectations. It's important to recognize that "experimenting" in this sense isn't necessarily something that's happening in a laboratory—anyone can test an idea that he or she has by simply implementing it and then evaluating the consequences.

An important thing to remember, though, is that experimenting with ideas can truly be a process of trial and error—don't be afraid to fail! When your ideas don't work or your hypotheses aren't confirmed, try to establish whether there's anything to be learned from the experience and then consider how you might use that information as you move forward. As Thomas Edison once remarked, "I haven't failed. I have simply found 10,000 ways that do not work."

Brainstorming Method of creative thinking that separates the production and evaluation of ideas.

Cross-stimulation effect In group problem solving, the tendency of one person's ideas to trigger ideas from others.

Psychology and Creativity

In promoting the importance of these four "discovery skills," the authors of *The Innovator's DNA* highlight the value of a psychology degree in fostering creativity and innovative thinking. As a discipline that places a great deal of value on observing human behavior, asking questions, testing hypotheses, and promoting engagement with diverse others, studying psychology will put you in a stronger position to live creatively both at work and at play.

MODULE 41 Creativity and Innovation—Learning Outcomes Revisited

41.1 Create a plan to enhance your creativity and innovation skills

There are several things that you can do to boost your creativity and innovation skills, including making associations between unrelated ideas, asking good questions, seeking input from others, and engaging in observation and experimentation. We hope that after reading this section, you'll be better able to think about how you can use these strategies to help boost your creative juices!

Reflective Practice

Content Check

1. Creativity has been linked to many areas of psychology, including personality and intelligence. T or F?
2. The four "discovery skills" outlined in the *Innovator's DNA* are making associations, asking questions, networking with diverse others, and observing/experimenting. T or F?
3. Creativity is diminished when we place constraints on our thinking. T or F?

Skill Check

Think Critically

4. Do you think there is any connection between your mood and your creativity?

Self-Reflect

Review the preceding pages and note which methods you could use more often to improve the quality of your thinking. Now, mentally summarize the points that you especially want to remember.

ANSWERS

1. T 2. T 3. F 4. In general, more intense moods are associated with higher creativity (Davis, 2009).

Motivation and Emotion

Overview of Motives and Emotions

MODULE 42

No Need to Tell Beyoncé

Russian novelist Leo Tolstoy once commented, "Music is the shorthand of emotion." And it's true, as any highly motivated, deeply emotional, award-winning pop singer could tell you. But there is more to motivation and emotion than getting you all excited about an upcoming concert. The words *motivation* and *emotion* derive from the Latin word *movere* (to move). Even getting out of bed in the morning can be difficult if you are unmotivated. And if you are unaware of your emotions, you will be vulnerable to health problems such as depression or addiction.

Motives provide the drumbeat of human behavior, and emotions color its rhythms. As we will see, both play complex roles in our lives. Even basic motives and emotions are not solely under the control of the body and are often influenced by external cues, expectations, learning, cultural values, and other factors. Let's explore our motives and emotions.

WENN Rights Ltd / Alamy Stock Photo

~LEARNING OUTCOMES~

After reading this module you should be able to:

42.1 Explain the role played by needs, drives, responses, goals, and incentives in shaping our motives, distinguish between biological, stimulus, and learned motives, and explain homeostasis and circadian rhythms

42.2 Explain Maslow's hierarchy of needs, including the distinction between basic needs and growth needs and the concepts of prepotency and self-actualization; also explain self-determination theory, including the distinction between intrinsic and extrinsic motivation

42.3 Discuss the four components of an emotion, list six basic emotions, and explain what makes them "basic"

Motivation—Forces That Push and Pull

Learning Outcome 42.1 Explain the role played by needs, drives, responses, goals, and incentives in shaping our motives, distinguish between biological, stimulus, and learned motives, and explain homeostasis and circadian rhythms

What are your goals? Why do you pursue them? When are you satisfied? When do you give up? These are all questions about motivation, or why we act as we do. Let's begin with a basic model of motivation and an overview of types of motives.

Motivation refers to the dynamics of behavior—the ways in which our actions are aroused, maintained, and guided (Deckers, 2014; Petri & Govern, 2013). Imagine that Christy is studying biology in the law library. Her stomach

Motivation A process that arouses, maintains, and guides behavior toward a goal.

begins to growl. She can't concentrate. She grows restless and decides to go to the cafeteria. Closed. Christy drives to a nearby fast-food outlet, where she finally eats. Her hunger satisfied, she resumes studying. Notice how Christy's food seeking was *aroused* by a physical need. Her search was *maintained* because her need was not immediately met, and her actions were *guided* by possible sources of food.

A Model of Motivation

Many motivated activities begin with a **need**, or internal deficiency. The need that aroused Christy's search was a shortage of key nutrients in her body. Needs cause a **drive** (state of bodily tension that arises from an unmet need) to develop. In Christy's case, the drive was hunger. Drives activate a **response** (an action or series of actions) designed to push us toward a **goal** (the target of motivated behavior). Reaching a goal that satisfies the need ends the chain of events. Thus, a simple model of motivation can be shown in this way:

NEED → DRIVE → RESPONSE → GOAL
(NEED REDUCTION)

Aren't needs and drives the same thing? No. The strength of needs and drives can differ (Deckers, 2014). For example, it is not unusual for older people to suffer from dehydration (a physical need for water) despite experiencing a lack of thirst (the drive to drink) (Begg, Sinclair, & Weisinger, 2012).

Now, let's observe Christy again. It's a holiday weekend. For dinner, Christy has soup, salad, a large steak, a baked potato, two pieces of cheesecake, and three cups of coffee. After dinner, she complains that she is "too full to move." Soon after, Christy's mom, Bonnie, arrives with a strawberry pie. Christy exclaims that strawberry pie is her favorite and eats three large pieces! Is this hunger? Certainly, Christy's dinner already satisfied her biological needs for food. Christy's "pie lust" illustrates that motivated behavior can be energized by the "pull" of external stimuli, as well as by the "push" of internal needs.

Incentives In addition to their ability to fill a need, some stimuli offer a "pull," or **incentive**—a reward or other stimulus that motivates behavior. Some goals are so desirable (strawberry pie, for example) that they can motivate behavior in the absence of an internal need. Other goals offer such a low incentive that they may be rejected even if they meet the internal need. Roasted grasshoppers, for instance, are nutritious. However, it is doubtful that you would eat one, unless you are a contestant on *Naked and Afraid*.

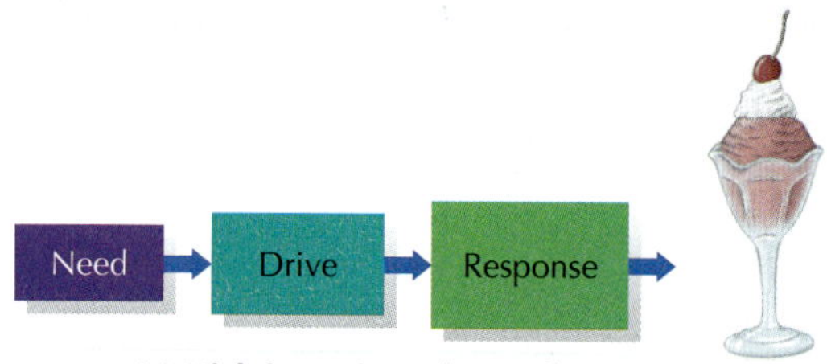

(a) High-incentive value goal

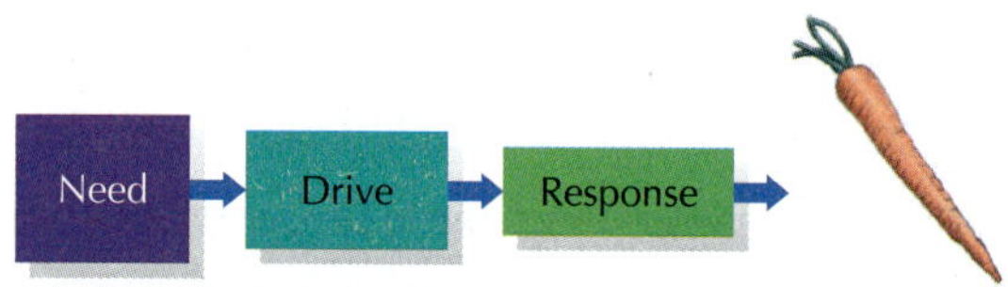

(b) Low-incentive value goal

Chad Zuber/Shutterstock.com

➤ **Figure 42.1**

Drive strength. Needs and incentives interact to determine drive strength *(above)*. (*a*) Moderate need combined with a high-incentive goal produces a strong drive. (*b*) Even when a strong need exists, drive strength may be moderate if a goal's incentive value is low. It is important to remember, however, that incentive value lies "in the eye of the beholder." No matter how hungry, few people would be able to eat the pictured roasted grasshoppers. (Does it help that they are garnished with tomato, onions, and lime?)

Usually, our actions are energized by a mixture of internal needs *and* external incentives. That's why a strong need may change an unpleasant incentive into a desired goal. Perhaps you've never eaten a grasshopper, but we'll bet you've eaten some pretty horrible leftovers when the refrigerator was empty. The incentive value of goals also helps explain motives that don't seem to come from internal needs, such as drives for success, status, or approval (➤ **Figure 42.1**).

Types of Motives Here is one way to divide motives into major categories:

1. **Biological motives** are based on innate needs that must be met for survival. The most important biological motives are hunger, thirst, pain avoidance, and the needs for air, sleep, elimination of wastes, and regulation of body temperature.

2. **Stimulus motives** express our needs for stimulation and information. Examples include activity, curiosity, exploration, manipulation, and physical contact. Although such motives also appear to be innate, they are not strictly necessary for survival.
3. **Learned motives** are based on learned needs, drives, and goals. Often social in nature, learned motives help explain many human activities, such as running for office or auditioning for *America's Got Talent.* Many learned motives are related to learned needs for power, achievement, affiliation (the need to be with others), approval, status, and security.

Biological Motives and Homeostasis

How important is air in your life? Water? Sleep? Food? Temperature regulation? Finding a restroom? For most of us, satisfying biological needs is so routine that we overlook how much of our behavior these needs guide. But exaggerate any of these needs through famine, shipwreck, poverty, near drowning, bitter cold, or drinking 10 cups of coffee, and their powerful grip on behavior becomes evident.

Biological drives are essential because they maintain *homeostasis* (HOE-me-oh-STAY-sis), or bodily equilibrium (Cooper, 2008). The term **homeostasis** means "standing steady" or "steady state." Optimal levels exist for body temperature, chemicals in the blood, blood pressure, and so forth (Goel, 2012; Petri & Govern, 2013). When the body deviates from these "ideal" levels, automatic reactions begin to restore equilibrium (Deckers, 2014). Thus, it might help to think of homeostasis as similar to a thermostat set at a particular temperature.

A (Very) Short Course on Thermostats

The thermostat in your house constantly compares the actual room temperature to a *set point,* or ideal temperature, which you can control. When room temperature falls below the set point, the heat is automatically turned on to warm the room. When the heat equals or slightly exceeds the set point, it is automatically turned off or the air conditioning is turned on. In this way, room temperature is kept in a state of equilibrium hovering around the set point.

The first reactions to disequilibrium in the human body are also automatic. For example, if you become too hot, more blood will flow through your skin and you will begin to perspire, thus lowering body temperature. We are often unaware of such changes, unless continued disequilibrium drives us to seek shade, warmth, food, or water.

Circadian Rhythms

Our needs and drives can change from moment to moment. After eating, our motivation to eat more food tends to diminish, and a few minutes in the hot sun can leave us feeling thirsty. But our motivation also can vary over longer cycles, guided by internal "biological clocks." Every 24 hours, your body undergoes a cycle of changes called a **circadian rhythm** (SUR-kay-dee-AN; *circa*: about; *diem*: a day) (Abbott, Reid, & Zee, 2015; Goel, 2012). Throughout the day, activities in the liver, kidneys, and endocrine glands undergo large changes. Body temperature, blood pressure, and amino acid levels also shift from hour to hour. These activities, and many others, peak once a day (➤ Figure 42.2).

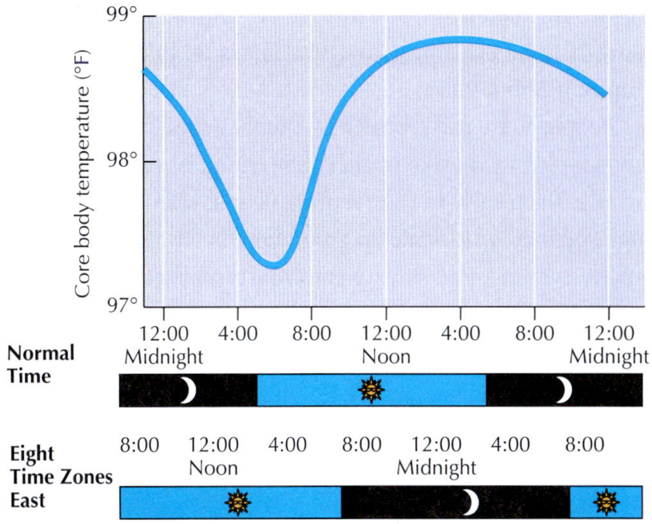

➤ **Figure 42.2**

Circadian rhythm. Core body temperature is a good indicator of a person's circadian rhythm. Rapid travel to a different time zone, shift work, depression, and illness can throw sleep and waking patterns out of synchronization with the body's core rhythm. Mismatches of this kind are very disruptive (Reinberg & Ashkenazi, 2008). Most people reach a low point two to three hours before their normal waking time. It's no wonder that both the Chernobyl and Three-Mile Island nuclear power plant accidents occurred around 4 a.m.

Need An internal deficiency that may energize behavior.

Drive A state of bodily tension, such as hunger or thirst, that arises from an unmet need.

Response Any action, glandular activity, or other identifiable behavior.

Goal The target or objective of motivated behavior.

Incentive A reward or other stimulus that motivates behavior.

Biological motives Innate motives based on biological needs.

Stimulus motives Innate needs for stimulation and information.

Learned motives Motives based on learned needs, drives, and goals.

Homeostasis The steady state of body equilibrium.

Circadian rhythm A 24-hour biological cycle found in humans and many other species.

People are usually more motivated and alert at the high point of their circadian rhythms (Bass & Takahashi, 2010; Chipman & Jin, 2009).

People with early peaks in their circadian rhythms are "day people," who wake up alert, are energetic early in the day, and fall asleep early in the evening. People with later peaks are "night people," who wake up groggy, are lively in the afternoon or early evening, and stay up late (Martynhak et al., 2010).

Lag, Shift Work, and All-Nighters Circadian rhythms are most noticeable after a major change in time schedules. Whether you take a long flight, a late shift at work, or an all-night study session, your circadian rhythms can fall "out of sync" with day–night cycles. When flying, this is most likely if you travel great distances east or west. If the peaks and valleys of your circadian rhythms fall out of phase with the sun and clocks, sleep difficulties are likely to follow (Iskra-Golec, 2016; Lazar et al., 2013). For example, you might be wide awake at midnight and feel like you're sleepwalking during the day (return to Figure 42.2). When body rhythms are disturbed, performance often suffers as well, due to the accompanying fatigue, irritability, upset stomach, and depression (Teff & Silva, 2015; Wright, Bogan, & Wyatt, 2013).

What can be done to cope with circadian rhythm disturbances? Circadian rhythms are partially controlled by variations in levels of *melatonin*, a hormone produced by the pineal gland. Normally, when light levels fall in the evening, melatonin levels rise; conversely, when light levels rise in the morning, melatonin levels fall (hence the nickname "Dracula hormone"). Because of this, taking small doses of melatonin just before bedtime for a few evenings may help synchronize circadian rhythms to the day–night cycle. (Changes in melatonin levels may partly explain the seasonal affective disorders that occur when people endure several months of long dark days. See Module 62.)

Light exposure can also help. Bright light affects the timing of body rhythms by reducing the amount of melatonin produced by the pineal gland. For this reason, a few intermittent 5-minute periods of exposure to bright light early in the morning are helpful for resetting your circadian rhythm (Dodson & Zee, 2010). In contrast, even dim light at night can upset circadian rhythms, reducing sleep quality and causing weight gain (Fonken et al., 2013).

If you are planning to "burn the midnight oil," remember that departing from your regular schedule may cost more than it's worth. You may be motivated to do as much during 1 hour in the morning as you could have done in 3 hours of work after midnight. You might just as well go to sleep 2 hours earlier.

In general, if you can anticipate an upcoming body rhythm change, it is best to *preadapt* by gradually matching your sleep–waking cycle to a new time schedule. Before traveling, for instance, you should go to sleep 1 hour later (or earlier) each day until your sleep cycle matches the time at your destination.

Motives in Perspective—A View from the Pyramid

Learning Outcome 42.2 Explain Maslow's hierarchy of needs, including the distinction between basic needs and growth needs and the concepts of prepotency and self-actualization; also explain self-determination theory, including the distinction between intrinsic and extrinsic motivation

Are all motives equally important? Abraham Maslow proposed that we humans experience a **hierarchy of needs**, in which some needs are more basic or powerful than others. (As you may recall from Module 3, Maslow called the full use of personal potential *self-actualization.*) Think about the needs that influence your own behavior. Which seems strongest? Which do you spend the most time and energy satisfying? Now look at Maslow's hierarchy (➤ **Figure 42.3**).

Note that biological needs are at the base of the pyramid. Because these needs must be met if we are to survive, they tend to be *prepotent*, or dominant over the higher needs. Maslow believed that higher, more fragile needs are expressed only after we satisfy our biological needs. That's why, when you are really hungry, you can think of little else but food. This also is true of needs for safety and security. Until they are met, we may have little interest in higher pursuits. For instance, a person who is feeling threatened might have little interest in writing poetry or even talking with friends (Noltemeyer et al., 2012). For this reason, Maslow described the first four levels of the hierarchy as **basic needs**. Other basic needs are for love and belonging (family, friendship, caring) and esteem and self-esteem (recognition and self-respect).

All the basic needs are *deficiency* motives—that is, they are activated by a *lack* of food, water, security, love, esteem, or other basic needs. At the top of the hierarchy, we

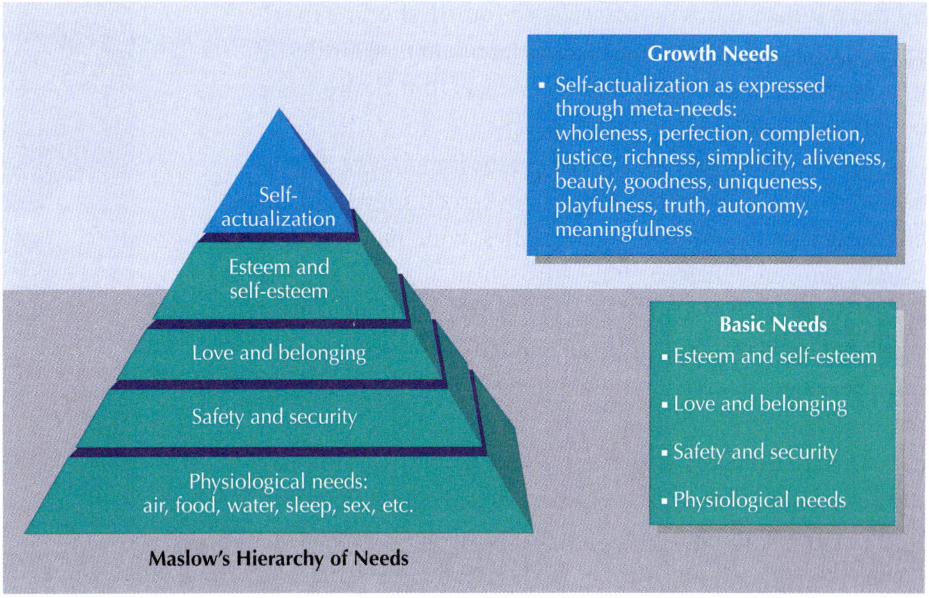

Figure 42.3

Maslow's hierarchy of needs. Maslow's hierarchy of needs. Although the pyramid illustration itself was originally developed by management theorist Keith Davis, it so well expressed the kernel of truth at the heart of Maslow's theory that it immediately became associated with Maslow himself (Bridgman, Cummings, & Ballard, 2019). Maslow believed that lower needs in the hierarchy are dominant. Basic needs must be satisfied before growth motives are fully expressed.

find **growth needs**, which are expressed as a need for self-actualization. The need for self-actualization is not based on deficiencies; rather, it is a positive, life-enhancing force for personal growth (D'Souza & Gurin, 2016). Like other humanistic psychologists, Maslow believed that people are basically good. If our basic needs are met, he said, we tend to move on to actualizing our potential (Tay & Diener, 2011).

How are needs for self-actualization expressed? Maslow called the less powerful but humanly important actualization motives *meta-needs* (return to Figure 42.3). Meta-needs are an expression of tendencies to fully develop your personal potentials (Maslow, 1970). When the meta-needs are unfulfilled, people fall into a "syndrome of decay" marked by despair, apathy, and alienation.

Michaelpuche/Shutterstock.com

Wheelchair athletes engage in vigorous competition. Maslow considered such behavior an expression of the need for self-actualization.

Maslow's point is that mere survival or comfort is usually not enough to make a full and satisfying life. It's interesting to note, in this regard, that college students who are concerned primarily with money, personal appearance, and social recognition score lower than average in vitality, self-actualization, and general well-being (Kasser, 2016; Nickerson, Diener, & Schwarz, 2011).

Maslow's hierarchy is not well documented by research, and parts of it are questionable. Despite such objections, Maslow's views help us understand and appreciate the rich interplay of human motives (Peterson & Park, 2010).

Self-Determination Theory and Intrinsic Motivation

Maslow's ideas have remained influential in psychology, prompting suggested revisions to his hierarchy of needs (Kenrick et al., 2010) and other, complementary, perspectives. *Self-determination theory* is one such perspective, sharing with Maslow a stress on the motivation to become all that you can possibly become (Ryan & Deci, 2017). According to **self-determination theory**, we are all motivated

Hierarchy of needs Maslow's classification of human motivations by order of importance from basic biological function to self-actualization.

Basic needs The first four levels of needs in Maslow's hierarchy; lower needs tend to be more potent than higher needs.

Growth needs In Maslow's hierarchy, the higher level needs associated with self-actualization.

Self-determination theory Proposes that needs for competence, autonomy, and relatedness are critical motivational needs.

by three innate motives: *competence* (our desire to experience mastery over our environment), *autonomy* (our desire to control our own lives), and *relatedness* (our desire to be connected to, and care for other people).

Self-determination theory stresses the importance of freedom of choice. When you freely choose to do something for enjoyment or to improve your abilities, your motivation is usually *intrinsic* (Olafsen et al., 2015; Ryan, Curren, & Deci, 2013). Some people cook for a living and consider it hard work. Others cook for pleasure and dream of opening a restaurant. For some people, mountain biking, gardening, writing, photography, or making jewelry is fun. For others, the same activities are drudgery that they must be paid to do. How can the same activity be *work* for one person and *play* for another?

Intrinsic motivation occurs when we act based on internal rewards without any obvious external rewards. We simply enjoy an activity or see it as an opportunity to explore, learn, and actualize our potentials. In contrast, **extrinsic motivation** stems from factors outside of the person, such as pay, grades, rewards, obligations, and approval. Most of the activities we think of as "work" are extrinsically rewarded (Murayama et al., 2017).

AUGUST Image, LLC

Intrinsically motivated people like James Cameron, feel free to explore creative solutions to problems. Best known as the director of blockbuster films such as *Titanic* and *Avatar*, Cameron has also codeveloped digital 3D cameras and remote vehicles to explore the ocean's depths.

Turning Play into Work *Don't extrinsic incentives strengthen motivation?* Yes, they can, but not always. In fact, *excessive* rewards can decrease intrinsic motivation and spontaneous interest. For instance, in one classic study, children who were lavishly rewarded for drawing with felt-tip pens later showed little interest in playing with the pens again (Greene & Lepper, 1974). Apparently, "play" can be turned into "work" by *requiring* people to do something that they would otherwise enjoy (Patall, Cooper, & Robinson, 2008). When we are coerced or "bribed" to act, we tend to feel as if we are "faking it." Employees who lack initiative and teenagers who reject school and learning are good examples of those who have such a reaction (Olafsen et al., 2015).

Intrinsic Motivation and Creativity Although salaries and bonuses may increase the amount of work done, people are not motivated solely by money. A chance to do challenging, interesting, and intrinsically rewarding work is often just as important. Work *quality* is affected more by intrinsic factors, such as personal interest and freedom of choice (Moneta, 2012; Murayama et al., 2015). When extrinsic motivation is stressed, people are less likely to solve tricky problems and come up with innovative ideas (Hennessey & Amabile, 2010).

Should extrinsic motivation always be avoided? No, but extrinsic motivation shouldn't be overused, especially with children. In general, (1) if there's no intrinsic interest in an activity to begin with, you have nothing to lose by using extrinsic rewards, (2) if basic skills are lacking, extrinsic rewards may be necessary at first, (3) extrinsic rewards can focus attention on an activity so that real interest will develop, and (4) if extrinsic rewards are used, they should be small and phased out as soon as possible (Buckworth et al., 2007; Cameron & Pierce, 2002).

Inside an Emotion—Caught in That Feeling?

Learning Outcome 42.3 Discuss the four components of an emotion, list six basic emotions, and explain what makes them "basic"

Now that we have looked at motivation, let's turn our attention to emotion. An **emotion** is a feeling state that has physiological, behavioral, and cognitive components. In other words, emotions are characterized by four components (subjective feelings; physiological arousal; behavioral changes in facial expressions, gestures, and posture; and thoughts, such as attributions and appraisals):

- **Emotional feelings:** A person's private emotional experiences are the most obvious component of emotions. This is the part of emotion with which we are usually most familiar.
- **Physiological arousal:** Emotions are also "moving." (As mentioned previously, the word *emotion* also derives from the Latin word meaning "to move.") Your body is physically aroused during emotion. A pounding heart, sweating palms, "butterflies" in the stomach, and other bodily reactions are major elements of fear, anger, joy, and other emotions. Typical *physiological changes* take place in heart rate, blood pressure, perspiration, and other bodily stirrings. Most are caused by activity in the sympathetic nervous system and by the hormones *adrenaline* and *noradrenaline,* which the adrenal glands release into the bloodstream. Such bodily stirrings are what cause us to say we were "moved" by a play, a funeral, or an act of kindness.
- **Behavioral changes:** Emotions also "move" us to behave in different ways. To begin, our emotional expressions (outward signs of what we are feeling) change to tell others what emotions we are experiencing (de Gelder, 2013). For example, when you are intensely afraid, your hands tremble, your face contorts, your posture becomes tense and defensive, and your voice changes.

Emotions are also linked to many basic **adaptive behaviors**, such as attacking, fleeing, seeking comfort, helping others, and reproducing. Such behaviors help us survive and adjust to changing conditions. Similarly, many of the goals we seek make us feel good. Many of the activities we avoid make us feel bad. We feel happy when we succeed and sad when we fail.

It also is apparent that emotions can lead to negative behavioral changes. Stage fright, or *performance anxiety*, can spoil performances. Hate, anger, contempt, disgust, and fear disrupt behavior and relationships. But more often, emotions aid survival. As social animals, it would be impossible for humans to live in groups, cooperate in raising children, and defend one another without emotions (Buss, 2019).

- **Thoughts:** Beginning in early childhood, we also *think* about our emotions. As we shall see shortly, how we think about our emotions powerfully influences how we experience them, how our physiological arousal unfolds, and how our behavior changes as a consequence. A dramatic example is provided by the process of training first responders in emergency situations, such as firefighters, police officers, members of the military, or emergency medical technicians (Dicke-Bohmann & Cox, 2015). After all, it will not help if first responders are overwhelmed by fear or anxiety when confronting an emergency. One goal of training, then, is to help first responders cope with the intense emotions usually involved in emergency situations.

Basic Emotions

How many different emotions are there? That's a tough question to answer. Let's start by noting that some emotions may be more basic than others (Ekman & Cordaro, 2011). According to Paul Ekman, there are six **basic emotions**: surprise, happiness, sadness, anger, disgust, and fear (Ekman & Friesen, 1971).

What makes these emotions "basic"? In general, our basic emotions can arise quickly and without much thought. They appear early in infancy, suggesting they are relatively unlearned. All humans, and many mammals, share these basic biological processes (Ekman & Cordaro, 2011; Izard, 2011; Panksepp & Watt, 2011). To better understand what this means, imagine that you're hiking in the woods and a growling bear steps onto the trail right in front of you. What happens next?

- **Basic emotions are fast and automatic:** Chances are, your fear level arises rather quickly and without much reflective processing. (Who thinks to herself, *Hmm, a bear. Maybe I should be afraid?*) This is an example of experiential processing (see Module 37). As we'll shortly see, basic emotions like fear are likely first processed by subcortical brain structures in the limbic system (Arnsten, Mazure, & Sinha, 2012).
- **Basic emotions develop early:** Recall from Module 13 that basic emotions develop early in infancy, unfolding mainly because of maturation (Music, 2011). Simply

Intrinsic motivation Desire to engage in a behavior based on internal rewards.

Extrinsic motivation Motivation that comes from outside of the person.

Emotion A feeling state that has physiological, cognitive, and behavioral components.

Adaptive behaviors Actions that aid attempts to survive and adapt to changing conditions.

Basic emotions According to Izard's theory, the most basic emotions are interest, joy/happiness, sadness, anger, disgust, and fear.

put, even young children show fast, automatic basic emotional responses (such as fear) to a growling bear.

- **Basic emotions are universal among humans:** It appears that people the world around, more or less independent of their cultures, experience the same basic emotions. As we discuss in Module 44, all humans make the same facial expressions. You would know instantly, just by looking, if someone from, say, the island of Java, is afraid. (It's that pesky bear again.)
- **Basic emotions are shared with other mammals:** It is highly likely that we share the experience of basic emotions with other mammals. Being growled at by a bear wouldn't feel like fun to a deer, either.

There must be more than six emotions, right? If *six* seems too few, it's because each emotion can vary in *intensity*. When you're angry, for instance, you may feel anything from simple annoyance to rage. Further, combinations of basic emotions yield new, more complex emotions. For example, mixing anger and disgust produces contempt. Other mixtures also are possible. For example, 5-year-old Tupac feels both joy and fear as he eats a cookie that he stole from Mom's cookie jar. The result? Guilt—as you may recall from your own childhood. Likewise, jealousy could be a mixture of love, anger, and fear.

A **mood** is the mildest form of emotion (➤ Figure 42.4). Moods are low-intensity emotional states that can last for many hours or even days. Moods often affect day-to-day behavior by predisposing us to act in certain ways. For example, when your neighbor Roseanne is in an irritable mood, she may react angrily to almost anything you say. When she is in a happy mood, she can easily laugh off an insult. Happy, positive moods tend to make us more adaptable in several ways. For example, when you are in a good mood, you are likely to make better decisions, and you will be more helpful, efficient, creative, and peaceful (Compton & Hoffman, 2019; Fredrickson & Branigan, 2005).

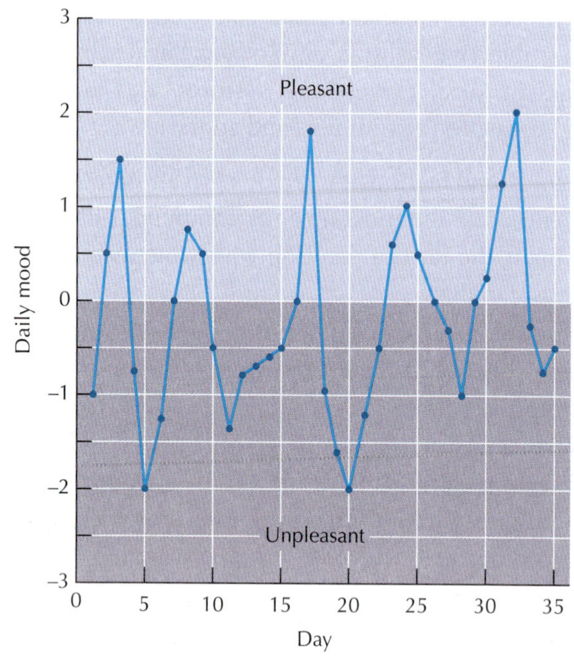

➤ Figure 42.4

Moods by the week. Folklore holds that people who work or attend school on a weekly schedule experience their lowest moods on "Blue Monday." Actually, moods generally tend to be lower for *most* weekdays than they are on weekends. The graph shown here plots the average daily moods of a group of college students over a five-week period. As you can see, many people find that their moods rise and fall on a seven-day cycle. For most students, a low point tends to occur around Monday or Tuesday and a peak on Friday or Saturday. In other words, moods are shaped by weekly schedules. (Adapted from Larsen & Kasimatis, 1990.)

Like our motives, our moods are closely tied to circadian rhythms. When your body temperature is at its daily low point, you are more likely to feel "down" emotionally. When body temperature is at its peak, your mood is likely to be positive—even if you missed a night of sleep (Boivin, Czeisler, & Waterhouse, 1997; McClung, 2011).

Mood A low-intensity, long-lasting emotional state.

MODULE 42 Overview of Motives and Emotions—Learning Outcomes Revisited

42.1 Explain the role played by needs, drives, responses, goals, and incentives in shaping our motives, list three types of motive, and explain homeostasis and circadian rhythms

Motives arouse, maintain, and guide behavior. Needs are internal deficiencies (things we lack), while a drive is a state of bodily tension that arises when needs are not met. Drives activate a response that pushes us toward a goal (usually, to address the unmet need). Incentives are rewards that can motivate behavior. The attractiveness of a goal and its ability to initiate action are related to its incentive value. Three principal types of motives are biological motives, stimulus motives, and learned motives. Most biological motives operate to maintain homeostasis, a state of equilibrium. Circadian rhythms of body activity are closely tied to sleep, activity, and energy cycles. Time zone travel, shift work, and pulling all-nighters can seriously disrupt sleep and body rhythms.

42.2 Explain Maslow's hierarchy of needs, including the distinction between basic needs and growth needs and the concepts of prepotency and self-actualization; also explain self-determination theory, including the distinction between intrinsic and extrinsic motivation

Maslow's hierarchy of needs categorizes needs as either basic or growth oriented.

Lower needs in the hierarchy are assumed to be prepotent (dominant) over higher needs. Self-actualization, the highest and most fragile need, is expressed as meta-needs. According to self-determination theory, competence, autonomy, and relatedness are the highest needs and are closely related to intrinsic motivation. In some situations, external rewards can undermine intrinsic motivation, enjoyment, and creativity.

42.3 Discuss the four components of an emotion, list six basic emotions, and explain what makes them "basic"

An emotion consists of subjective feelings: physiological arousal, behavioral changes, and thoughts. According to discrete emotions theory, there are at least six basic emotions: interest, joy/happiness, sadness, anger, disgust, and fear, which can be mixed to produce more complex emotional experiences. Basic emotions are fast and automatic, they appear early in infancy, they are universal among humans, and they are shared with other mammals.

Reflective Practice

Content Check

1. Needs provide the ________________ of motivation, whereas incentives provide the ________________.
2. The maintenance of bodily equilibrium is called thermostasis. T or F?
3. Desirable goals are motivating because they are high in ____________ value.
   a. secondary
   b. stimulus
   c. homeostatic
   d. incentive
4. The highest level of Maslow's hierarchy of needs involves
   a. meta-needs
   b. needs for safety and security
   c. needs for love and belonging
   d. extrinsic needs
5. Intrinsic motivation is often undermined in situations in which obvious external rewards are applied to a naturally enjoyable activity. T or F?
6. Emotional ______________ often communicate a person's emotional state to others.
7. Awe, remorse, and disappointment are among the basic emotions listed by Carrol Izard. T or F?

Skill Check

Think Critically

8. Many US college freshmen say that "being well-off financially" is an essential life goal and that "making more money" was a very important factor in their decision to attend college. Which meta-needs are fulfilled by "making more money"?

Self-Reflect

What effects do high- and low-incentive goals have on your behavior? Reflect on some biological, stimulus, and learned motives you have satisfied today. How did each influence your behavior? Name an activity you do that is intrinsically motivated and one that is extrinsically motivated. How do they differ? How did your most emotional moment of the past week affect your behavior, expressions, feelings, and physical state?

ANSWERS

1. push, pull 2. F 3. d 4. a 5. T 6. expressions 7. F 8. None of them

MODULE

43 Motivation and Emotion

Motivation in Detail

Jump!

Mauricio Graiki/Shutterstock.com

Where would you prefer to go on your next summer vacation? Your backyard? A week with your best friends at a cottage on a nearby lake? A shopping and museum trip to New York City? None of that will do for Natalie, who loves to skydive. If rapidly falling to Earth attracts you, you too are probably high in sensation seeking and would be interested in a vacation that includes activities such as bungee jumping, skiing, diving with sharks, and white-water rafting.

We are moved each day by a diverse array of motives, from biological motives such as hunger, to stimulus motives such as sensation seeking, to learned motives such as the need for achievement. Furthermore, our motives can be surprisingly complex. For example, while hunger might seem like a simple motive, it is still not fully understood. Grab a snack and read on to explore motivation in greater detail.

~LEARNING OUTCOMES~

After reading this module you should be able to:

43.1 Describe factors influencing hunger, overeating, weight control, and eating disorders

43.2 Explain how each of the following drives are similar to or different from hunger: thirst, pain, sex

43.3 Explain the relationship between arousal and motivation, individual differences and arousal, and discuss some ways to cope with test anxiety

43.4 Define learned motives, social motives, nAch, and need for power; and list three qualities of people high in nAch

Hunger—Pardon Me, My Hypothalamus Is Growling

Learning Outcome 43.1 Describe factors influencing hunger, overeating, weight control, and eating disorders

You get hungry, you find food, and you eat. What could be simpler? Yet, hunger is actually a complex motive. Like almost every other human motive, our hunger levels are affected by both internal bodily factors and external environmental and social ones. To understand how this works, let's begin with a survey of some of the internal factors controlling our hunger.

Internal Factors in Hunger

Don't feelings of hunger originate in the stomach? To find out, Walter Cannon and A. L. Washburn (1912) decided to see whether stomach contractions cause hunger. In an early study, Washburn trained himself to swallow a balloon, which could be inflated through an attached tube. (You, too, will do anything for science, right?) This allowed Cannon to record the movements of Washburn's stomach (➤ **Figure 43.1**).

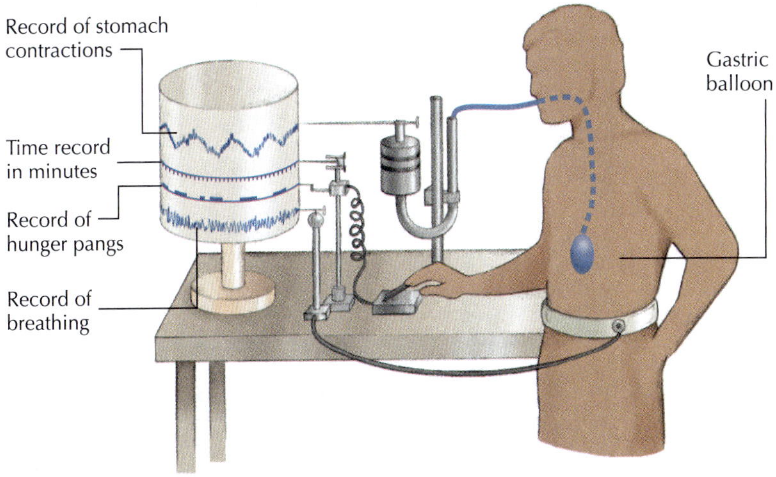

➤ **Figure 43.1**

Measuring hunger. In Walter Cannon's early study of hunger, a simple apparatus was used to simultaneously record hunger pangs and stomach contractions. (Adapted from Cannon, 1934.)

When Washburn's stomach contracted, he reported that he felt "hunger pangs." In view of this, the two scientists concluded that hunger is nothing more than the contractions of an empty stomach. (This, however, proved to be an inflated conclusion.)

For many people, hunger produces an overall feeling of weakness or shakiness, rather than a "growling" stomach. Of course, eating *does* slow when the stomach is stretched or distended (full). (Remember last Thanksgiving?) However, we now know that the stomach is not essential for feeling hunger. Even if the nerve carrying information between your stomach and brain were severed, you would still feel hungry and eat regularly (Petri & Govern, 2013).

Then what does cause hunger? Many different factors combine to promote and suppress hunger (Young, 2012). The brain receives many signals from parts of the digestive system, ranging from the tongue and stomach to the intestines and the liver.

The Brain and the Short-Term Control of Hunger

What part of the brain controls hunger? Although no single "hunger thermostat" exists, a small subcortical area of the brain called the **hypothalamus** (HI-po-THAL-ah-mus) is especially important (Young, 2012). It regulates emotional behaviors and basic biological needs, including hunger, thirst, and the sex drive (➤ Figure 43.2; see Module 10).

The hypothalamus is sensitive to levels of a variety of substances in the blood, such as sugar. It also receives neural messages from the digestive system. For example, as the levels of blood sugar (glucose) drop, the liver responds by sending nerve impulses to the brain. When combined, these signals determine whether you are hungry (Freberg, 2021; Woods & Ramsay, 2011).

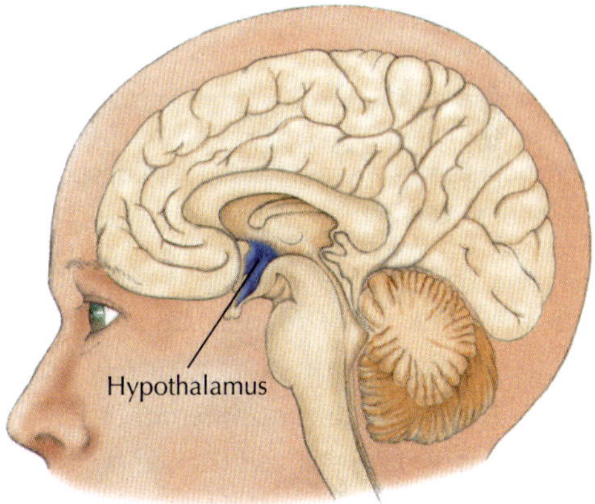

➤ **Figure 43.2**

The hypothalamus. Location of the hypothalamus in the human brain.

One part of the hypothalamus acts as a feeding "start button." If the *lateral hypothalamus* is "turned on" with an electrified probe, even a well-fed animal immediately begins eating. (The term *lateral* simply refers to the *sides* of the hypothalamus. See ➤ Figure 43.3.) If the same area is destroyed (hence no "start button"), the animal may never eat again.

The lateral hypothalamus is normally activated in a variety of ways. For example, when you are hungry, your stomach lining produces *ghrelin* (GREL-in), a hormone that activates your lateral hypothalamus (Castañeda et al., 2010). Ghrelin also activates parts of your brain involved in learning. This means you should consider studying before you eat, not immediately afterward (Diano et al., 2006).

Hypothalamus A small area of the brain that regulates emotional behaviors and basic biological needs.

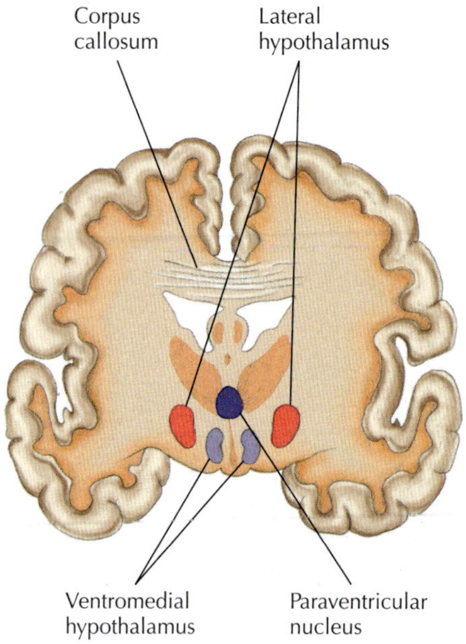

➤ Figure 43.3

Hypothalamic areas that control eating. This is a cross section through the middle of the brain (viewed from the front). Indicated areas of the hypothalamus are associated with hunger and the regulation of body weight.

Damage to the hunger satiety system in the hypothalamus can produce a very fat rat, a condition called *hypothalamic hyperphagia* (Hi-per-FAGE-yah), which means "overeating." This rat weighs 1,080 grams. (The pointer has gone completely around the dial and beyond.)

How do we know when to stop eating? A second area in the hypothalamus functions as a satiety "stop button" (Ribeiro et al., 2009). If the *ventromedial* (VENT-ro-MEE-dee-al) *hypothalamus* is destroyed (hence no "stop button"), dramatic overeating results. (*Ventromedial* refers to the bottom middle of the hypothalamus.) Rats with such damage eat until they balloon up to weights of 1,000 grams or more. A normal rat weighs about 180 grams. To put this weight gain in human terms, picture someone you know who weighs 180 pounds growing to a weight of 1,000 pounds.

A chemical called *glucagonlike peptide 1* (GLP-1) also is involved in causing eating to cease. After you eat a meal, GLP-1 is released by the intestines. From there, it travels in the bloodstream to the hypothalamus. When enough GLP-1 arrives, your desire to eat ends (Hayes, De Jonghe, & Kanoski, 2010). As you might imagine, GLP-1 pills show promise in the treatment of obesity (Hayes, 2012). By the way, it takes at least 10 minutes for the hypothalamus to respond after you begin eating. That's why you are less likely to overeat if you eat slowly, which gives your brain time to get the message that you've had enough (Liu et al., 2000).

The *paraventricular* (PAIR-uh-ven-TRICK-you-ler) *nucleus* of the hypothalamus also affects hunger (see Figure 43.3). This area helps keep blood sugar levels steady by both starting and stopping eating. The paraventricular nucleus is sensitive to a substance called *neuropeptide Y (NPY)*. If NPY is present in large amounts, an animal will eat until it cannot hold another bite (Petri & Govern, 2013). Incidentally, the hypothalamus also responds to a chemical in cannabis, which can produce intense hunger (the "munchies") (Bermudez-Silva et al., 2010).

The Brain and the Long-Term Control of Weight

In addition to determining when to start eating and when meals are over, your brain also controls your weight over long periods of time. Like a thermostat, your brain maintains a **set point** in order to control your weight over the long term. It does this by monitoring the amount of fat stored in your body in specialized *fat cells* (Gloria-Bottini, Magrini, & Bottini, 2009; Vieira & Valentine, 2009).

Your set point is the weight that you maintain when you are not trying to gain or lose weight. When your body weight goes below its set point, you will feel hungry most of the time. On the other hand, fat cells release a substance called *leptin* when your "spare tire" is well inflated. Leptin is carried in the bloodstream to the hypothalamus, where it tells us to eat less (Woods & Ramsay, 2011).

Can you change your fat set point? Your leptin levels are partly under genetic control. In rare cases, mice (and we humans) inherit a genetic defect that reduces leptin levels in the body, leading to obesity. In such cases, taking leptin can help (Berman et al., 2013). For the rest of us, the news is not so encouraging. Currently, there is no known way to lower your set point for fat because the number of fat cells remains unchanged throughout adult life (Spalding et al., 2008). To make matters worse, radical diets do not help. (But you knew that already, didn't you?) They may even raise the set point for fat (Ahima & Osei, 2004). You may not be able to lose weight by resetting your hypothalamus, but psychologists have studied more effective approaches to weight loss. We examine some later in this module.

The substances that we have reviewed here are only some of the chemical and neural signals that start and stop eating (Turenius et al., 2009). Others continue to be discovered. In time, they may make it possible to artificially influence hunger. If so, better treatments for extreme obesity and self-starvation could follow (Marco et al., 2012).

External Factors in Hunger and Obesity

As we have seen, "hunger" is affected by more than just the "push" of our biological needs for food. In fact, if internal needs alone controlled eating, fewer people would overeat (Stroebe, Papies, & Aarts, 2008). Nevertheless, roughly 65 percent of adults in the United States are currently overweight and more than one-third are obese (extremely overweight) (Fryar, Carroll, & Ogden, 2014; ➤ **Figure 43.4**). Childhood obesity has also reached epidemic proportions in the United States, having tripled in prevalence since 1980 (Ogden et al., 2010). As a result, obesity is overtaking smoking as a major cause of needless deaths (Dietz, 2015; Freedman, 2011). Let's consider some external influences on hunger and their role in obesity, a major health risk and, for many, a source of social stigma and low self-esteem.

External Eating Cues Most of us are sensitive to the "pull" of *external eating cues*, signs and signals linked with food. In cultures like ours, in which food is plentiful, eating cues add greatly to the risk of overeating (Casey et al., 2008). Many college freshmen gain weight rapidly during their first three months on campus (the famous "Frosh 15"). All-you-can-eat dining halls in the dorms and nighttime snacking appear to be the culprits (Kapinos & Yakusheva, 2011). The presence of others also can affect whether people overeat (or undereat), depending on how much everyone else is eating and how important it is to impress them (Pliner & Mann, 2004).

Taste and Plenty You may have noticed that if you eat too much of any particular food, it becomes less appealing. For example, if you are well fed, leptin dulls the tongue's sensitivity to sweet tastes (Domingos et al., 2011). If you lose your "sweet tooth" when you are full, you may have observed this effect. Overindulging a particular food can even lead to a **taste aversion**, or active dislike, for a particular food. This can happen if a food causes sickness or if it is merely associated with nausea (Chance, 2014). A friend of one of your authors once became ill after eating too many cheese Danishes (OK, way too many!) and hasn't been able to face them since.

Set point (for fat) The proportion of body fat that tends to be maintained by changes in hunger and eating.

Taste aversion An active dislike for a particular food.

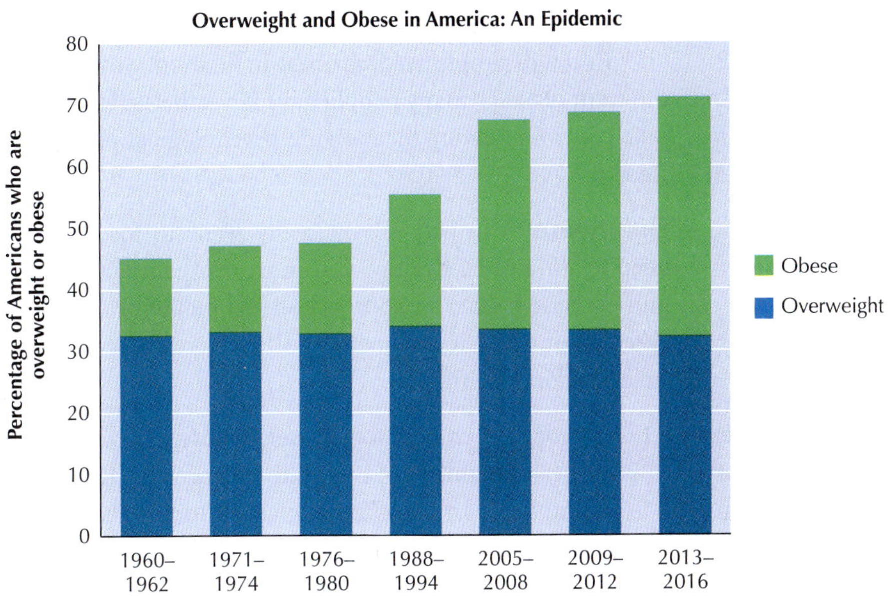

➤ **Figure 43.4**

The obesity epidemic. A near-epidemic of obesity has occurred in the United States during the last 30 years, with two-thirds of all Americans now classified as overweight or obese. (Adapted from Centers for Disease Control, 2015c; Fryar, Carroll, & Ogden, 2014.)

These shifts in taste probably help us maintain variety in our diets and even avoid severe nutritional imbalances. For example, if you go on a fad diet and eat only grapefruit, you eventually will begin to feel ill. In time, associating your discomfort with grapefruit may create an aversion to it and restore some balance to your diet.

In our society of plenty, unfortunately, shifts in taste may end up encouraging obesity. The availability of a variety of tasty foods means that we can easily shift what we eat. If you overdose on hamburgers or French fries, moving on to some cookies or chocolate cheesecake certainly won't do your body much good (Pinel, Assanand, & Lehman, 2000).

Emotional Eating *Is it true that people also overeat when they are emotionally upset?* Yes. People with weight problems are prone to overeat when they are anxious, angry, or sad (Macht & Simons, 2011). Furthermore, obese individuals are often unhappy in our fat-conscious culture. For them, overeating leads to more emotional distress and still more overeating (Lazarevich et al., 2016).

Cultural Factors Learning to think of some foods as desirable and others as revolting has a large impact on what we eat. In North America, we would never consider eating the eyes out of the steamed head of a monkey, but in some parts of the world they are considered a delicacy. By the same token, vegans and vegetarians shun eating any kind of meat. In short, cultural values greatly affect the *incentive* value of foods.

Dieting

A diet is *not* just a way to lose weight. Your current diet is defined by the types and amounts of food you regularly eat. Some diets actually encourage overeating. For instance, placing animals on a "supermarket" diet leads to gross obesity. In one classic experiment, rats were given meals of chocolate chip cookies, salami, cheese, bananas, marshmallows, milk chocolate, peanut butter, and fat. These pampered rodents overate, gaining almost three times as much weight as rats that ate only laboratory chow (Sclafani & Springer, 1976). (Rat chow is a dry mixture of several bland grains. If you were a rat, you'd probably eat more cookies than rat chow, too.)

People also are sensitive to dietary content. In general, *sweetness,* high *fat content,* and *variety* tend to encourage overeating (Dobson & Gerstner, 2010). Unfortunately, North American culture provides the worst kinds of foods for people who suffer from obesity. For example, restaurant and fast foods tend to be higher in fat and calories than meals made at home (Kessler, 2009). "Super-sized" meals are another problem. Food portions at restaurants in the United States are 25 percent larger, or more, than they are in France. Far fewer people are obese in France, most likely because they simply eat less. The French also take longer to eat a meal, which discourages overeating (Rozin et al., 2003). "Yo-yo" dieting is an added problem faced by people who want to control their weight.

The Paradox of Yo-Yo Dieting If dieting works, why are hundreds of "new" diets published each year? You can't go through life eating only grapefruit and protein. Although you will lose weight on most fad diets, you will likely gain it back when you stop dieting. In fact, many people end up weighing even more than before they dieted (Freedman, 2011). Why should this be so? Dieting (starving) slows the body's rate of metabolism (the rate at which energy is used). In effect, a dieter's body becomes highly efficient at *conserving* calories and storing them as fat (Pinel, Assanand, & Lehman, 2000).

Apparently, evolution prepared us to save energy when food is scarce and to stock up on fat when food is plentiful. Briefly starving yourself, therefore, may have little lasting effect on weight. "Yo-yo dieting," or repeatedly losing and gaining weight, is especially dangerous. Frequent changes in weight can dramatically slow the body's metabolic rate. As noted earlier, this may raise the body's set point for fat, making it harder to lose weight each time a person diets and easier to regain weight when the diet ends. Frequent weight changes also increase the risk for heart disease and premature death (Wang & Brownell, 2005). To avoid bouncing between feast and famine, a *permanent* change in eating habits and exercise is required.

To summarize, eating and overeating are related to internal and external influences—to diet, emotions, genetics, exercise, and many other factors. We live in a culture that provides inexpensive, good-tasting food everywhere, and have a brain that evolved to say, "Eat whenever food is available."

Although people become obese in different ways and for different reasons, many people have nevertheless learned to take control of eating by applying psychological principles. Read on.

Behavioral Dieting If you really want to lose weight, keep it off, and be healthy, you must overhaul your eating and exercise habits, an approach called **behavioral dieting** (Freedman, 2011; Kiernan et al., 2013). Here are some helpful behavioral techniques:

1. **Get yourself committed to weight loss.** If you are eating healthy and exercising, but still need to lose some weight, begin by committing yourself to lose that weight by restricting your calorie intake and increasing your exercise. Involve other people in your efforts. Programs such as

Overeaters Anonymous or Take Off Pounds Sensibly can be good sources of social support (Mitchell et al., 2010).

2. **Learn your eating habits by observing yourself and keeping a "diet diary."** Begin by making a complete, two-week record of when and where you eat, what you eat, and the feelings and events that occur just before and after eating. Is someone encouraging you to overeat? What are your most "dangerous" times and places for overeating?
3. **Chart your daily progress.** Record your weight, the number of calories eaten, and whether you meet your daily goal. Set realistic goals by cutting down calories gradually. Losing about a pound per week is realistic, but remember that you are changing your habits, not just dieting.
4. **Eat a balanced, healthy diet that you can stick with over the long run.** Resist thinking of dieting as a special kind of short-term, restricted-eating regime. Your *diet* is simply what you eat over the long term. According to doctor and researcher David Katz, fad diets don't work. The best way to eat is to eat healthy by minimizing intake of processed foods and meats (Katz & Meller, 2014).
5. **Incorporate exercise into your life to stay healthy over the long run.** No diet can succeed for long without an increase in exercise. To lose weight, you must use more calories than you take in. Burning just 200 extra calories a day can help prevent rebound weight gains. Add activity to your routine in every way you can think of. If you can, buy a *fitness tracker* to count the number of steps you take every day. The more frequently and vigorously you exercise, the healthier you will become and the more weight you will lose (Annesi & Marti, 2011).
6. **Learn to weaken your personal eating cues.** Once you have learned when and where you do most of your eating, avoid these situations. Try to restrict your eating to one room, and do not read, watch television, study, or talk on the phone while eating. Require yourself to interrupt what you are doing in order to eat.
7. **Don't starve yourself.** If you have trouble eating less every day, try dieting four days a week. People who diet intensely every other day lose as much as those who diet moderately every day.
8. **Develop techniques to control the act of eating.** Whenever you can, check for nutritional information and buy groceries and meals lower in calories and fat. Begin to take smaller portions. Carry to the table only what you plan to eat. Put all other food away before leaving the kitchen. Eat slowly, sip water between bites of food, leave food on your plate, and stop eating before you are completely full.
9. **Avoid snacks.** It is generally better to eat more small meals a day than fewer large ones because more calories are burned. (No, we don't mean high-calorie snacks *in addition to* meals.) If you have an impulse to snack, set a timer for 20 minutes and see if you are still hungry then. Dull your appetite by filling up on raw carrots, bouillon, water, coffee, or tea.
10. **Set a "threshold" for weight control.** Maintaining weight loss can be even more challenging than losing weight. It is easier to maintain weight loss if you set a regain limit of three pounds or fewer. In other words, if you gain more than two or three pounds, you immediately make corrections in your eating habits and amount of exercise (Kessler, 2009).

Be patient. It takes years to develop eating habits. You can expect it to take at least several months to change them. If you are unsuccessful at losing weight with these techniques, you might find it helpful to seek the aid of a psychologist familiar with behavioral weight-loss techniques.

Eating Disorders

Under the sheets of her hospital bed, Krystal looks like a skeleton. Victims of anorexia suffer devastating weight losses from severe, self-inflicted dieting (Kaye et al., 2013). If she cannot overcome her **anorexia nervosa**

Pascal Le Segretain/Getty Images

Anorexia nervosa is far more dangerous than many people realize. This haunting Italian anti-anorexia poster shows 68-pound model Isabelle Caro, who suffered from anorexia for years up until her death in 2010 at age 28. Many celebrities have struggled with eating disorders, including Karen Carpenter (who died of starvation-induced heart failure), Paula Abdul, Kirstie Alley, Fiona Apple, Victoria Beckham, Princess Diana, Tracey Gold, Janet Jackson, and Mary-Kate Olsen.

Behavioral dieting Weight reduction based on changing exercise and eating habits, rather than temporary self-starvation.

Anorexia nervosa An eating disorder characterized by a distorted body image and maintenance of unusually low body weight.

(AN-uh-REK-see-yah ner-VOH-sah: self-starvation), Krystal may die of malnutrition or other complications. Anorexia is a type of **feeding and eating disorder**—a problem managing food intake that manifests itself in forms such as a life-threatening failure to maintain sufficient body weight.

Do anorexics lose their appetite? Although a compulsive attempt to lose weight causes them to not seek or desire food, anorexics usually still feel physical hunger. Often, anorexia starts with "normal" dieting that slowly begins to dominate the person's life. In time, anorexics suffer debilitating health problems, including the highest mortality rates of all the mental illnesses (Krantz et al., 2012). ■ **Table 43.1** lists the symptoms of anorexia nervosa.

Bulimia nervosa (bue-LIHM-ee-yah) is a second major eating disorder (de Vries & Meule, 2016; Dryer, Tyson, & Kiernan, 2013). Bulimic persons gorge on food, and then vomit or take laxatives to avoid gaining weight (see Table 43.1). Bingeing without purging is a separate disorder called *binge eating disorder* (American Psychiatric Association, 2013). Bingeing and purging seriously damages health. Typical risks include sore throat, hair loss, muscle spasms, kidney damage, dehydration, tooth erosion, swollen salivary glands, menstrual irregularities, loss of sex drive, and even heart attack.

About 1 percent of all adults suffer from anorexia, along with 3 percent who are bulimic. But these are only the most serious cases. As many as 14 to 22 percent of all adolescents experience some form of disordered eating (Swanson et al., 2011).

Men and Eating Disorders While women are more prone to develop them, eating disorders are on the rise among men. More and more men also are experiencing *muscle dysmorphia*, or excessive worry about not being muscular enough (Fang & Wilhelm, 2015; Nieuwoudt et al., 2012). Currently, one-third of men say they want less body fat and another third want more muscles. As a result, many men are altering what they eat and exercising excessively (Hartmann, Greenberg, & Wilhelm, 2013). Some are going too far: About 25 percent of anorexics and bulimics are now males (Jones & Morgan, 2010; Wooldridge & Lytle, 2012).

TABLE 43.1 | Recognizing Eating Disorders

Anorexia Nervosa
▸ Refusal to maintain body weight in normal range. Body weight at 85 percent or less of normal for one's height and age.
▸ Intense fear of becoming fat or gaining weight, even though underweight.
▸ Disturbance in one's body image or perceived weight. Self-evaluation is unduly influenced by body weight. Denial of seriousness of abnormally low body weight.
▸ Purging behavior (vomiting or misuse of laxatives or diuretics).
Bulimia Nervosa
▸ Recurring binge eating. Eating—within an hour or two—an amount of food that is much larger than most people would consume. Feeling a lack of control over eating.
▸ Purging behavior (vomiting or misuse of laxatives or diuretics). Excessive exercise to prevent weight gain. Fasting to prevent weight gain.
▸ Self-evaluation is unduly influenced by body weight.

Adapted from *American Psychiatric Association* (2013).

Causes *What causes anorexia and bulimia?* People who suffer from eating disorders are extremely dissatisfied with their bodies (Trentowska, Bender, & Tuschen-Caffier, 2013). Usually, they have distorted views of themselves. Women have low self-esteem and exaggerated fears of becoming fat. Many overestimate their body size by 25 percent or more. As a result, they think they are disgustingly "fat" when in reality they are wasting away (➤ **Figure 43.5**) (Polivy & Herman, 2002).

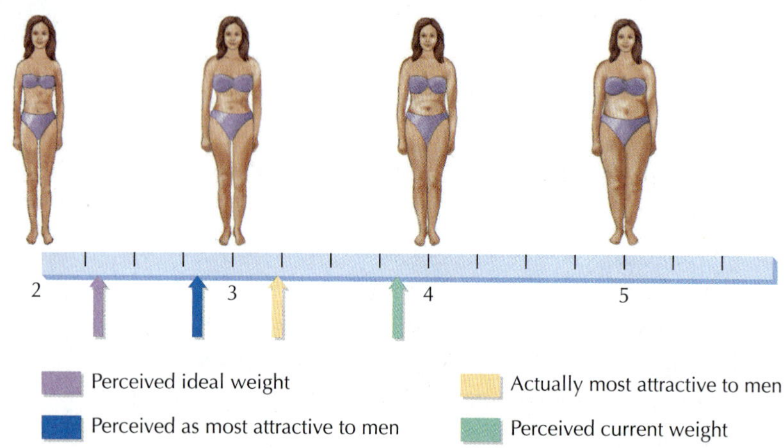

➤ **Figure 43.5**

Rating body shape. Women with abnormal eating habits were asked to rate their body shape on a scale similar to the one you see here. As a group, they chose ideal figures much thinner than what they thought their current weights were. (Most women say they want to be thinner than they currently are, but to a lesser degree than women with eating problems.) Notice that the women with eating problems chose an ideal weight that was even thinner than what they thought men prefer. This is not typical of most women. In this classic study, only women with eating problems wanted to be thinner than what they thought men find attractive (Zellner, Harner, & Adler, 1989).

Men generally think they are not muscular enough if they are not "cut" or do not have a "six-pack" (Jones & Morgan, 2010).

Many of these problems are related to the idealized body images presented in the media (Hausenblas et al., 2013). Some websites even go so far as to celebrate anorexia and bulimia (referred to by "fans" as "Ana" and "Mia"; Borzekowski et al., 2010; Juarez, Soto, & Pritchard, 2012). Girls who spend a lot of time reading fashion magazines or visiting these websites are more likely to have distorted body images and unrealistic ideas about how they compare with others (Bauer et al., 2017; Martinez-Gonzalez et al., 2003).

The popularity of fitness, exercise, and sports also has contributed to eating disorders. Today, more people are changing their diets in search of a lean, muscular look. People engaged in sports that require low body fat or extreme weight loss (such as wrestling, gymnastics, pole vaulting, high jumping, and even cycling) are particularly likely to develop eating disorders (Weltzin et al., 2005).

People with eating disorders appear to be trying to gain some measure of control. Anorexic teen girls are usually described as "perfect" daughters—helpful, considerate, conforming, and obedient. They seem to be rewarded by seeking perfect control in their lives by being perfectly slim (Keating, 2010; Slof-Op't Landt et al., 2016). People suffering from bulimia also are concerned with control (Bardone-Cone et al., 2008). Typically, they are obsessed with thoughts of weight, food, eating, and ridding themselves of food. As a result, they feel guilt, shame, self-contempt, and anxiety. Vomiting reduces their anxiety, which makes purging highly reinforcing.

Treatment Most people suffering from eating disorders do not seek help on their own. This is especially true for men because eating disorders are often perceived to be a female problem (Jones & Morgan, 2010; Weltzin et al., 2005). Typically, it takes strong urging by family or friends to get victims into treatment.

Treatment for anorexia usually begins with giving drugs to relieve obsessive fears of gaining weight. Then, a medical diet is used to restore weight and health. Next, a counselor may help patients work on the emotional conflicts that led to weight loss. For bulimia, behavioral counseling may include self-monitoring of food intake. A related cognitive-behavioral approach focuses on changing the thinking patterns and beliefs about weight and body shape that perpetuate eating disorders (Galsworthy-Francis & Allan, 2014; Waller et al., 2014).

Biological Motives Revisited—Thirst, Pain, and Sex

Learning Outcome 43.2 Explain how each of the following drives are similar to or different from hunger: thirst, pain, sex

Most biological motives work in ways that are similar to hunger. For example, thirst is only partially controlled by dryness of the mouth. If you were to take a drug that made your mouth constantly wet, or dry, your water intake would remain normal. Like hunger, thirst is regulated by separate *thirst* and *thirst satiety* systems in the hypothalamus. Also like hunger, thirst is strongly affected by learning and cultural values.

Thirst

You may not have noticed, but there are two kinds of thirst (Thornton, 2010). **Extracellular thirst** occurs when water is lost from the fluids surrounding the cells of your body. Bleeding, vomiting, diarrhea, sweating, and drinking alcohol cause this type of thirst (Petri & Govern, 2013). When a person loses both water and minerals in any of these ways—especially by perspiration—a slightly salty liquid may be more satisfying than plain water.

A second type of thirst occurs when you eat a salty meal. In this instance, your body does not lose fluid. Instead, excess salt causes fluid to be drawn out of cells. As the cells "shrink," **intracellular thirst** is triggered. Thirst of this type is best quenched by plain water (Thornton, 2010).

Pain

Not all drives are governed by circadian rhythms. While hunger, thirst, and sleepiness come and go in a fairly regular cycle each day, pain avoidance is an *episodic* (ep-ih-SOD-ik)

Feeding and eating disorder A problem managing food intake that manifests itself in forms such as a life-threatening failure to maintain sufficient body weight.

Bulimia nervosa A disorder marked by excessive eating followed by inappropriate methods of preventing weight gain.

Extracellular thirst Thirst caused by a reduction in the volume of fluids found between body cells.

Intracellular thirst Thirst triggered when fluid is drawn out of cells due to an increased concentration of salts and minerals outside the cells.

drive: It occurs in distinct episodes when bodily damage takes place or is about to occur. Most drives prompt us to actively seek a desired goal (food, drink, warmth, and so forth). Pain prompts us to *avoid* or *eliminate* sources of discomfort.

Some people feel that they must be "tough" and not show any distress. Others complain loudly at the smallest ache or pain. The first attitude raises pain tolerance, and the second lowers it. As this suggests, the drive to avoid pain is partly learned. That's why members of some societies endure cutting, burning, whipping, tattooing, and piercing of the skin that would agonize most people (Chang, 2009). (Apparently, devotees of piercing and "body art" can relate.) In general, we learn how to react to pain by observing family members, friends, and other role models (McMahon & Koltzenburg, 2013).

Sivaram V/Reuters

Tolerance for pain and the strength of a person's motivation to avoid discomfort are greatly affected by cultural practices and beliefs, such as the self-infliction of pain by this penitent at a Hindu festival.

The Sex Drive

Human sexual behavior and attitudes are discussed in detail in Module 47. For now, it is worth noting that sex is unlike most other biological motives because sex (contrary to anything your personal experience might suggest) is not necessary for *individual* survival. It is necessary, of course, for *group* survival.

The term **sex drive** refers to the strength of one's motivation to engage in sexual behavior. In lower animals, the sex drive is directly related to hormones. Female mammals (other than humans) are interested in mating only when their fertility cycles are in the stage of **estrus**, or "heat." Estrus is caused by a release of **estrogen** (one of several types of female sex hormone) into the bloodstream. Hormones are important in males as well. But in contrast to females, the normal male animal is almost always ready to mate. His sex drive is aroused primarily by the behavior and scent of a receptive female. Therefore, in many species, mating is closely tied to female fertility cycles.

How much do hormones affect human sex drives? Hormones affect the human sex drive, but not as directly as in animals (Rosenthal, M., 2013). The sex drive in men is related to the amount of **androgens** (male hormones such as testosterone) provided by the testes. When the supply of androgens dramatically increases at puberty, so does the male sex drive. Likewise, the sex drive in women is related to their estrogen levels (Hyde & DeLamater, 2014). However, "male" hormones also affect the female sex drive. In addition to estrogen, a woman's body produces small amounts of androgens. Testosterone levels decline with age, and various medical problems can lower sexual desire. In some instances, taking testosterone supplements can restore the sex drive in both men and women (Crooks & Baur, 2017).

Perhaps the most interesting fact about the sex drive is that it is largely **nonhomeostatic**—relatively independent of body need states. In humans, the sex drive can be aroused at virtually any time by almost anything. Therefore, it shows no clear relationship to deprivation (the amount of time since the drive was last satisfied). Certainly, an increase in desire may occur as time passes. But recent sexual activity does not prevent sexual desire from occurring again. Notice, too, that people may seek to arouse the sex drive as well as to reduce it. This unusual quality makes the sex drive capable of motivating a wide range of behaviors. It also explains why sex is used to sell almost everything imaginable.

Stimulus Motives—Monkey Business

Learning Outcome 43.3 Explain the relationship between arousal and motivation, individual differences and arousal, and discuss some ways to cope with test anxiety

Are you full of energy right now, or are you tired? Clearly, the level of arousal that you are experiencing is closely linked with your motivation. Are there ideal levels of arousal for different people and different activities? Let's find out.

What do you mean by arousal? *Arousal* refers to the activation of the body and nervous system. Arousal is zero at death, low during sleep, moderate during normal daily activities, and high at times of excitement, intense emotion, or panic.

Most people enjoy a steady "diet" of new movies, novels, music, fashions, games, news, websites, and adventures. Yet, *stimulus motives*, which reflect needs for information, exploration, manipulation, and sensory input, go beyond mere entertainment. Stimulus motives also help us survive. As we scan our surroundings, we constantly identify sources of food, danger, shelter, and other key details. The drive for stimulation is already present during infancy. By the time a child can walk, few things in the home have not been tasted, touched, viewed, handled, or, in the case of toys, destroyed!

Stimulus motives are readily apparent in animals as well as humans. For example, monkeys will quickly learn to solve a mechanical puzzle made up of interlocking metal pins, hooks, and latches (Butler, 1954). No food treats or other external rewards are needed to get them to explore and manipulate their surroundings. The monkeys seem to work for the sheer fun of it.

Arousal Theory

Are stimulus motives homeostatic? Yes. According to **arousal theory**, we try to keep arousal at an optimal level (Cloture, Jacobs, & van Lier, 2016; Petri & Govern, 2013). Arousal theory assumes that we become uncomfortable when arousal is too low ("I'm bored") or when it is too high, as in fear, anxiety, or panic ("The dentist will see you now"). In other words, when your level of arousal is too low or too high, you will seek ways to raise or lower it. Most adults vary music, parties, sports, conversation, sleep, surfing the web, and the like to keep arousal at moderate levels. The right mix of activities prevents boredom *and* overstimulation (Csikszentmihalyi, Abuhamdeh, & Nakamura, 2005).

Monkeys happily open locks that are placed in their cage. Because no reward is given for this activity, it provides evidence for the existence of stimulus needs.

Sensation Seekers *Sensation seeking* is a trait of people who prefer high levels of stimulation (Lynne-Landsman et al., 2011). Whether you are high or low in sensation seeking is probably based on how your body responds to new, unusual, or intense stimulation (Cservenka et al., 2013; Harden, Quinn, & Tucker-Drob, 2012). People high in sensation seeking tend to be bold, independent, and value change. They also report more sexual partners, are more likely to smoke, and prefer spicy, sour, and crunchy foods over bland foods. Low sensation seekers are orderly, nurturant, and giving, and they enjoy the company of others.

Exciting lives aside, sensation seeking has a dark side (Dunlop & Romer, 2010). High sensation seekers are more likely to engage in high-risk behaviors such as substance abuse and casual unprotected sex (Drane, Modecki, & Barber, 2017; Harden, Quinn, & Tucker-Drob, 2012).

Peak Performance

Is there an ideal level of arousal for peak performance? If we set aside individual differences, most people perform best when their arousal level is *moderate*. Let's say that you have to take an essay exam. If you are feeling sleepy or lazy (arousal level too low), your performance will suffer. If you are in a state of anxiety or panic about the test (arousal level too high), you also will perform below par. Thus, the relationship between arousal and performance forms an *inverted U function* (a curve in the shape of an upside-down U; ➤ **Figure 43.6**) (Petri & Govern, 2013).

The inverted U tells us that at very low levels of arousal, you're not sufficiently energized to perform well. Performance will improve as your arousal level increases, up to the middle of the curve. Then, it begins to drop off as you become emotional, frenzied, or disorganized. For example, imagine trying to start a car stalled on a railroad track, with

Sex drive The strength of one's motivation to engage in sexual behavior.

Estrus Changes in the sexual drives of animals that create a desire for mating; particularly used to refer to females in heat.

Estrogen Any of a number of female sex hormones.

Androgen Any of a number of male sex hormones, especially testosterone.

Nonhomeostatic drive A drive that is relatively independent of physical deprivation cycles or body need states.

Arousal theory Assumes that people prefer to maintain ideal, or comfortable, levels of arousal.

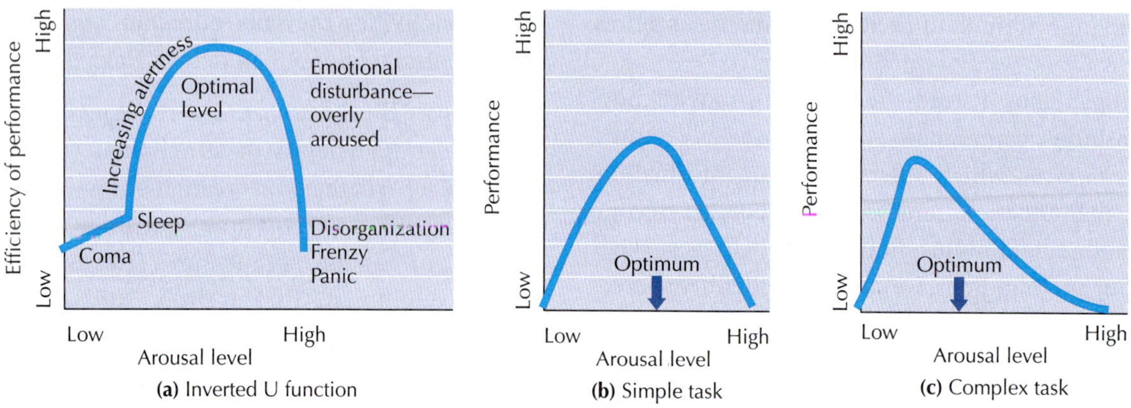

➤ **Figure 43.6**

Relationship between arousal and efficiency. (*a*) The general relationship between arousal and efficiency can be described by an inverted U curve. The optimal level of arousal or motivation is higher for a simple task (*b*) than for a complex task (*c*).

a speeding train bearing down on you. That's what the high-arousal end of the curve feels like.

Is performance always best at moderate levels of arousal? No, the ideal level of arousal depends on the complexity of a task. If a task is relatively simple, it is best for arousal to be high. When a task is more complex, your best performance will occur at lower levels of arousal. This relationship is called the **Yerkes-Dodson law** (see Figure 43.6). It applies to a wide variety of tasks and to measures of motivation other than arousal.

For example, at a track meet, it is almost impossible for sprinters to get too aroused for a race. The task is direct and simple: Run as fast as you can for a short distance. On the other hand, a golfer making a tournament-deciding putt faces a more sensitive and complex task. Excessive arousal is almost certain to hurt his or her performance. In school, students have had experience with "test anxiety," a familiar example of how too much arousal can lower performance.

Coping with Test Anxiety

Then, is it true that by learning to calm down, a person would do better on tests? Usually, but not always. To begin with, some arousal is healthy; it focuses us on the task at hand. It is only when arousal interferes with performance that we refer to anxiety. **Test anxiety** is a mixture of *heightened physiological arousal* (nervousness, sweating, pounding heart) and *excessive worry*. This combination—arousal plus worry—tends to distract students with a rush of upsetting thoughts and feelings (Conley & Lehman, 2012; Putwain & Aveyard, 2016; Sparfeldt et al., 2013). Here are some suggestions for coping with test anxiety.

Preparation *Hard work* is the most direct antidote for test anxiety. Many test-anxious students simply study too little, too late. That's why improving your study skills is a good way to reduce test anxiety (Cassady, 2004). Not studying while remaining calm simply means that you will calmly fail the test. The best solution is to *overprepare* by studying long before the "big day." Well-prepared students score higher, worry less, and are less likely to panic (Halonen & Santrock, 2013). If test anxiety is a problem for you, it would be wise to return to Module 1 and review the learning and test-taking skills described there.

Relaxation Learning to relax is another way to lower test anxiety (Bradley et al., 2010; Mowbray, 2012). (You can learn self-relaxation skills by reading Module 67.) Emotional support also helps (Stöber, 2004). If you are test anxious, discuss the problem with your professors or study for tests with a supportive classmate.

Rehearsal To reduce nervousness, rehearse how you will cope with upsetting events. Before taking a test, imagine yourself going blank, running out of time, or feeling panicked. Then, calmly plan how you will handle each situation—by keeping your attention on the task, by focusing on one question at a time, and so forth (Watson & Tharp, 2014).

Restructuring Thoughts Another helpful strategy involves listing the upsetting thoughts that you have during exams. Then, you can learn to combat these worries with calming, rational replies (Olpin & Hesson, 2021). (These are called *coping statements*; see Module 59 for more information.) Let's say you think, "I'm going to fail this test and everybody will think I'm stupid." A good reply to this upsetting thought would be to say, "If I prepare well and control my worries, I will probably pass the test. Even if I don't, it won't be the end of the world. My friends will still like me, and I can try to do better on the next test."

Students who cope well with exams usually try to do the best they can, even under difficult circumstances. Becoming a more confident test taker can actually increase your scores because it helps you remain calm. With practice, most people can learn to be less testy at test-taking time.

Learned Motives—The Pursuit of Excellence

Learning Outcome 43.4 Define learned motives, social motives, nAch, and need for power; and list three qualities of people high in nAch

Some of your friends are more interested than others in success, achievement, competition, money, possessions, status, love, approval, grades, dominance, power, or belonging to groups—all of which are *social motives* or goals. We acquire **social motives** in complex ways, through socialization and cultural conditioning (Deckers, 2014). The behavior of outstanding artists, scientists, athletes, educators, and leaders is best understood in terms of such learned needs, particularly the need for achievement.

The Need for Achievement

To many people, being "motivated" means being interested in achievement (Petri & Govern, 2013; van de Pol & Kavussanu, 2012). In other modules, we investigate aggression, helping, affiliation, seeking approval, and other social motives. For now, let's focus on the **need for achievement (nAch)**, which is a drive to excel in one's endeavors (McClelland, 1961). People with high nAch strive to do well any time they are evaluated (Steinmayr & Spinath, 2009).

Is that like the aggressive businessperson who strives for success? Not necessarily. It's true that nAch may lead to wealth and prestige, but people who are high achievers in art, music, science, or amateur sports may excel without seeking riches. Such people typically enjoy challenges and relish a chance to test their abilities.

Characteristics of People High in nAch So you want to be a success. To best achieve your goals, would it be better to be naturally talented or determined? (Yes, we know you would definitely prefer to have it *both* ways. So would we.) It probably will not surprise you to learn that, in general, drive and determination, not great natural talent, lead to exceptional success (Duckworth et al., 2007). Elite performance in music, sports, chess, the arts, and many other pursuits requires at least 10 years of dedicated practice (Ericsson & Charness, 1994; Ross, 2006). The old belief that "talent will surface" on its own is largely a myth.

How can this be? When people high in nAch tackle a task, they do so with perseverance, passion, and self-confidence (Duckworth et al., 2007; Munroe-Chandler, Hall, & Fishburne, 2008). They tend to complete difficult tasks, they earn better grades, and they tend to excel in their occupations. College students high in nAch attribute success to their own ability; they attribute failure to insufficient effort. Thus, high-nAch students are more likely to renew their efforts when they perform poorly. When the going gets tough, high achievers get going.

You may be able to improve your achievement motivation by increasing your self-confidence (Hanton, Mellalieu,

MANAN VATSYAYANA/Getty Images

Venus and Serena Williams possess high achievement motivation. They have become professional tennis champions by playing with perseverance, passion, and self-confidence.

Yerkes-Dodson law A summary of the relationships among arousal, task complexity, and performance.

Test anxiety High levels of arousal and worry that seriously impair test performance.

Social motives Learned motives acquired as part of growing up in a particular society or culture.

Need for achievement (nAch) The drive to excel in one's endeavors.

& Hall, 2004). It is easier to perform an activity or reach a goal with perseverance and passion when you believe that you can be successful. When you tackle an important task, how many of the items on the following list can you check off? To enhance self-confidence, you would be wise to do as many as possible (Watson & Tharp, 2014; Munroe-Chandler, Hall, & Fishburne, 2008):

- Set goals that are specific and challenging but attainable.
- Visualize the steps that you need to take to reach your goal.
- Advance in small steps.
- When you first acquire a skill, your goal should be to make progress in learning. Later, you can concentrate on improving your performance compared with other people.
- Get expert instruction that helps you master the skill.
- Find a skilled model (someone good at the skill) to emulate.
- Get support and encouragement from an observer.
- If you fail, regard it as a sign that you need to try harder, not that you lack ability.

Self-confidence affects motivation by influencing the challenges you will undertake, the effort you will make, and how long you will persist when things don't go well. You can be confident that self-confidence is worth cultivating.

The Need for Power

The need for achievement differs from the **need for power**, which is a desire to have impact or control over others (Lammers et al., 2016; McClelland, 1975). People with strong needs for power want their importance to be visible: They buy expensive possessions, wear prestigious clothes, and exploit relationships. In some ways, the pursuit of power and financial success is the dark side of the American dream. People whose main goal in life is to make lots of money tend to be poorly adjusted and unhappy (Kasser, 2016).

Need for power The desire to have social impact and control over others.

MODULE 43 Motivation in Detail—Learning Outcomes Revisited

43.1 Describe factors influencing hunger, overeating, weight control, and eating disorders

Hunger is influenced by a complex interplay between fullness of the stomach, blood sugar levels, metabolism in the liver, and fat stores in the body. The hypothalamus exerts the most direct control of eating, through areas that act like feeding and satiety systems. The hypothalamus is sensitive to both neural and chemical messages, which affect eating. Other factors influencing hunger are the body's set point, external eating cues, the attractiveness and variety of diet, emotions, learned taste preferences and taste aversions, and cultural values. Obesity is the result of internal and external influences, diet, emotions, genetics, and exercise. The most effective way to lose weight is behavioral dieting, which is based on techniques that change eating patterns and exercise habits. Anorexia nervosa and bulimia nervosa are two prominent eating disorders. Both tend to involve conflicts about self-image, self-control, and anxiety.

43.2 Explain how each of the following drives are similar to or different from hunger: thirst, pain, sex

Like hunger, thirst and other basic motives are affected by a number of bodily factors but are primarily under the central control of the hypothalamus. Thirst may be either intracellular or extracellular. Pain avoidance is unusual because it is episodic as opposed to cyclic. Pain avoidance and pain tolerance are partially learned. The sex drive is also unusual in that it is nonhomeostatic.

43.3 Explain the relationship between arousal and motivation, individual differences and arousal, and discuss some ways to cope with test anxiety

Drives for stimulation are partially explained by arousal theory, which states that an ideal level of bodily arousal will be maintained if possible. The desired level of arousal or stimulation varies from person to person. Optimal performance on a task usually occurs at *moderate* levels of arousal. This relationship is described by an inverted U function. The Yerkes-Dodson law further states that for simple tasks, the ideal arousal level is higher, and for complex tasks, it is lower. Test anxiety can be lessened by being prepared, by relaxing, through rehearsal, and by restructuring thoughts.

43.4 Define learned motives, social motives, nAch, and need for power; and list three qualities of people high in nAch

Learned motives, including social motives, account for much of the diversity of human motivation. Such motives are learned through socialization and cultural conditioning. People high in need for achievement (nAch) are successful in many situations due to their perseverance, passion, and self-confidence. People with a need for power seek control over others.

Reflective Practice

Content Check

1. Maintaining your body's set point for fat is closely linked with the amount of ____________ in the bloodstream.
   a. hypothalamic factor-1
   b. ventromedial peptide-1
   c. NPY
   d. leptin
2. People who frequently diet tend to benefit from practice: They lose weight more quickly each time they diet. T or F?
3. In addition to changing eating habits, a key element of behavioral dieting is
   a. exercise
   b. well-timed snacking
   c. better eating cues
   d. commitment to "starving" every day
4. Pain avoidance is a(n) ____________________ drive.
5. Exploration, manipulation, and curiosity provide evidence for the existence of ____________________ motives.
6. Complex tasks, such as taking a classroom test, tend to be disrupted by high levels of arousal, an effect predicted by
   a. sensation seeking
   b. the Yerkes-Dodson law
   c. studies of circadian arousal patterns
   d. studies of nAch
7. People high in nAch show high levels of perseverance, passion, and ____________.
   a. control
   b. intelligence
   c. self-confidence
   d. sensation seeking

Skill Check

Think Critically

8. Paloma, who is overweight, is highly sensitive to external eating cues. How might her wristwatch contribute to her overeating?

Self-Reflect

A friend of yours is yo-yo dieting. Can you explain to her or him why such dieting is ineffective? Can you summarize how behavioral dieting is done? Does arousal theory seem to explain any of your own behavior? Think of at least one time when your performance was impaired by arousal that was too low or too high. Are you high or low in your need for stimulation? Do you think you are high or low in nAch? When faced with a challenging task, are you high or low in perseverance? Passion? Self-confidence?

ANSWERS

1. d 2. F 3. a 4. episodic 5. stimulus 6. b 7. c 8. The time of day can influence eating, especially for externally cued eaters, who tend to get hungry at mealtimes, regardless of their internal needs for food.

MODULE 44

Motivation and Emotion

Emotion in Detail

Worldwide Happiness?

Picture the face of a happy person enjoying a good movie or conversation and it's easy to see that motivation and emotion are closely related. But are emotional expressions universal? Masks that are meant to be happy or joyful are strikingly similar around the world. Most have an open, upward-curved mouth and rising cheeks, with downturned outer eyebrows. Obviously, the pictured mask is meant to be warm and cuddly. Your ability to "read" its emotional message suggests that basic emotions and their expressions have universal biological roots.

Pepe Baeza/Shutterstock.com

Because emotions shape relationships and color daily activities worldwide, it is worth seeking answers to questions such as the following: How does the body respond during emotion? Do facial expressions really reveal what others are feeling? How do culture and learning affect expressions? Are there different theories of emotion? Let's look "under the mask" for some answers.

~LEARNING OUTCOMES~

After reading this module you should be able to:

44.1 Explain why "lie detectors" cannot really detect lies and describe some physiological changes that underlie emotion

44.2 Explain how accurately emotions are expressed by the face and "body language," taking into account culture and gender

44.3 Distinguish between the James-Lange, Canon-Bard, and cognitive (including discrete emotions) theories of emotion; define attribution, appraisal, and facial feedback; and outline a contemporary theory of emotion

Physiology and Emotion—Arousal and Lying

Learning Outcome 44.1 Explain why "lie detectors" cannot really detect lies and describe some physiological changes that underlie emotion

An African Bushman is frightened by a lion. A city dweller is frightened by a prowler. Will they react in much the same way? Yes. Such encounters usually produce muscle tension, a pounding heart, irritability, dryness of the throat and mouth, sweating, butterflies in the stomach, frequent urination, trembling, restlessness, sensitivity to loud noises, and numerous other body changes. These reactions are nearly universal because they are innate. As you may recall from Module 7, activity of the ANS is *automatic,* rather than voluntary (Freberg, 2021). Specifically, they are caused by the **autonomic nervous system (ANS)**—the part of the peripheral nervous system that connects the brain with internal organs and glands.

Fight or Flight

The ANS has two divisions: the sympathetic branch and the parasympathetic branch. The two branches are active at all times. Whether you are relaxed or aroused at any moment depends on the relative activity of both branches.

What does the ANS do during emotion? In general, the *sympathetic branch* activates the body for emergency action—for "fighting or fleeing." It does this by arousing some body systems and inhibiting others (➤ **Figure 44.1**). Sugar is released into the bloodstream for quick energy, the heart beats faster to supply blood to the muscles, digestion is temporarily slowed, blood flow in the skin is restricted to reduce bleeding, and so forth. Such reactions improve the chances of surviving an emergency.

The *parasympathetic branch* reverses emotional arousal, calming and relaxing the body. After a period of high emotion, the heart is slowed, the pupils return to normal size, blood pressure drops, and so forth. In addition to restoring balance, the parasympathetic system helps build up and conserve the body's energy.

The parasympathetic system responds much more slowly than the sympathetic system. That's why a pounding heart, muscle tension, and other signs of arousal don't fully settle down for 20 or 30 minutes after you feel an intense emotion, such as fear. Moreover, after a strong emotional

Autonomic nervous system (ANS) The system of nerves carrying information to and from the internal organs and glands.

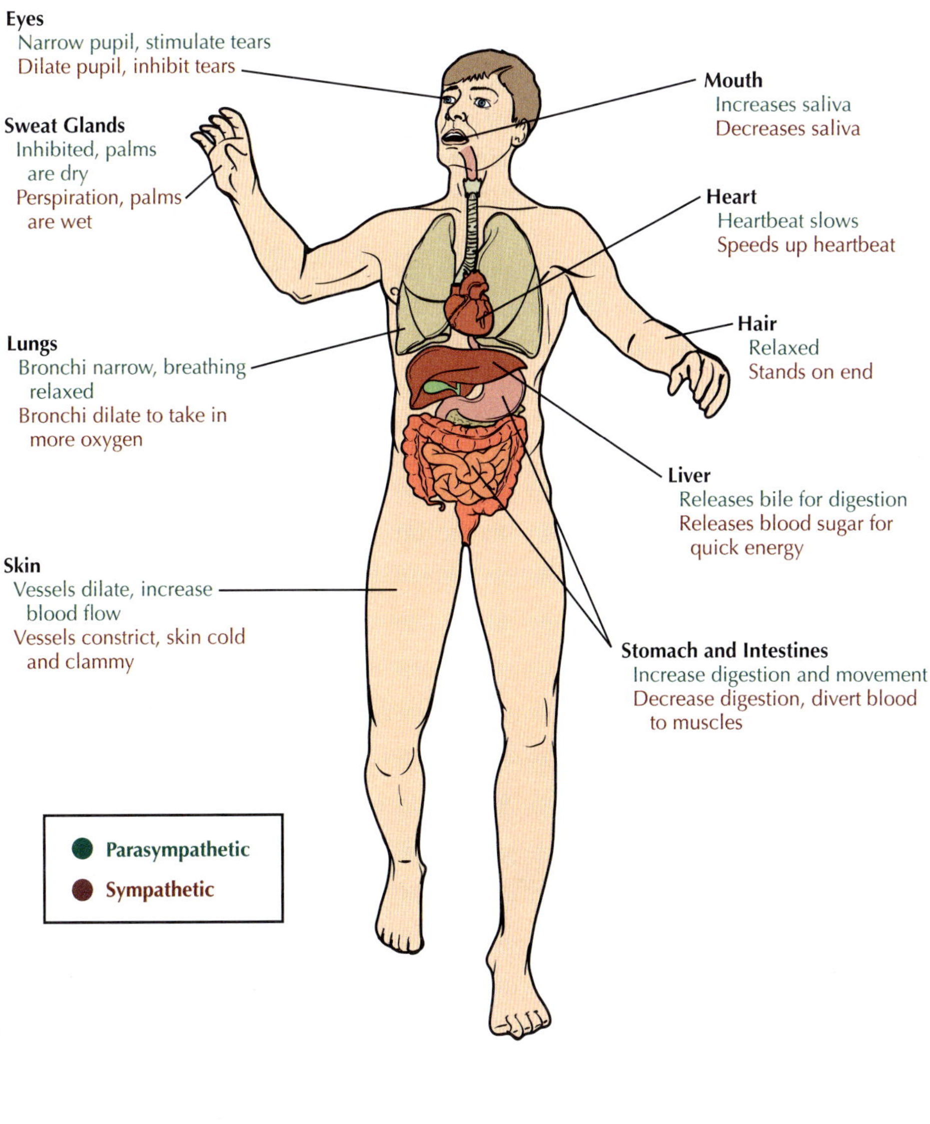

➤ **Figure 44.1**

The autonomic nervous system. The parasympathetic branch of the ANS calms and quiets the body. The sympathetic branch arouses the body and prepares it for emergency action.

shock, the parasympathetic system may overreact and lower blood pressure too much. This can cause you to become dizzy or faint after seeing something shocking, such as a horrifying accident.

Lie Detectors

You undoubtedly know that criminals are not always truthful. But what you may not know is that up to 25 percent of all wrongful convictions include false confessions as evidence (Kassin, 2005). The most popular method for detecting falsehoods measures the bodily changes that accompany emotion. Unfortunately, the accuracy of "lie detector" tests is doubtful, and they can be a serious invasion of privacy (Bunn, 2012; Meijer & Verschuere, 2010).

How do lie detectors work? The lie detector is more accurately called a **polygraph**, a word that means "many writings" (➤ **Figure 44.2**). The polygraph was invented in 1915 by psychologist William Marston, who also created the comic book character Wonder Woman, a superhero whose "magic lasso" could force people to tell the truth (Grubin & Madsen, 2005). Although popularly known as a lie detector because the police use it for that purpose, in reality, the polygraph is not a lie detector at all. A suspect is questioned while "hooked up" to a polygraph, which typically records changes in heart rate, blood pressure, breathing, and the galvanic skin response (GSR). The GSR is recorded from the hand by electrodes that measure skin conductance, or, more simply, sweating. Because the device records only general emotional arousal, it can't tell the difference between lying and fear, or anxiety and excitement (Iacono, 2008).

Couldn't an innocent but nervous person fail a polygraph test? Absolutely. In one case, a woman named Donna was arrested for violating a restraining order against Marie. Even though she claimed she was having lunch instead of harassing Marie, she failed a polygraph test (Geddes, 2008). Put yourself in her place, and it's easy to see why. Imagine the examiner asking, "Did you drive up to Marie, curse at her, and then drive away?" Because you know Marie, and you already know what you have been charged with, it's no secret that this is a critical question. What would happen to *your* heart rate, blood pressure, breathing, and perspiration under such circumstances? Psychologist David Lykken (1998, 2001) has documented many cases in which innocent people were convicted on the basis of polygraph evidence.

To minimize this problem, skilled polygraph examiners might use the **guilty knowledge test** (Hakun et al., 2009). A series of multiple-choice questions are asked; one answer is correct. For example, one question might be: "Was the gun that killed Hensley a: (a) Colt; (b) Smith & Wesson; (c) Walther PPK; or (d) Luger?" A guilty person who knew which gun she had used may show an elevated response to the correct answer. Because an innocent person couldn't know which gun was involved, she could only respond similarly to all four alternatives (Iacono, 2011).

Although proponents of lie detection claim it is 95 percent accurate, errors may occur even when questioning is done properly (Bunn, 2012). But in one study, accuracy was dramatically lowered when people thought about past emotional experiences as they answered irrelevant questions (Ben-Shakhar & Dolev, 1996). Similarly, the polygraph may be thrown off by self-inflicted pain, by tranquilizing drugs, or by people who can lie without anxiety. Worst of all, the test is much more likely to label an innocent person guilty rather than a guilty person innocent (Nahari, 2012). In studies involving real crimes, an average of one innocent person in five was rated as guilty by the lie detector (Lykken, 2001). For such reasons, the National Academy of Sciences (2003) has concluded that polygraph tests should not be used to screen employees.

Despite the lie detector's flaws, you may be tested for employment or for other reasons. Should this occur, the best advice is to remain calm; then, actively challenge the results if the machine wrongly questions your honesty.

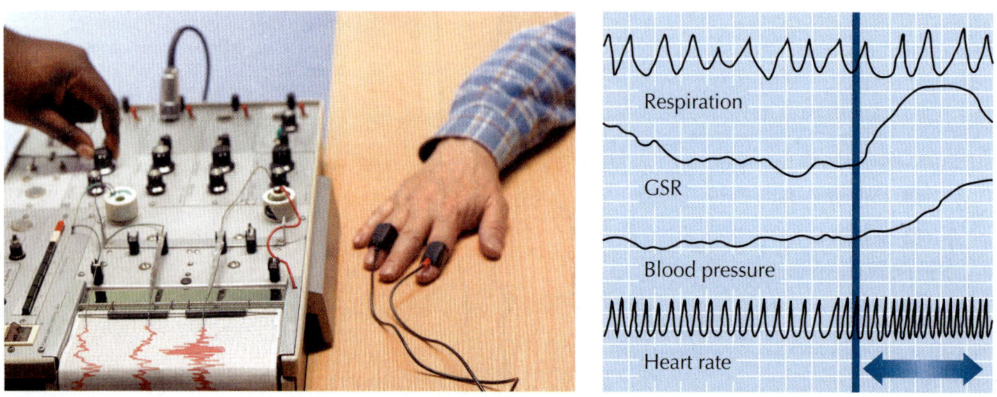

Peter Dazeley/The Image Bank/Getty Images

➤ **Figure 44.2**

Polygraph. *(photo)* A typical polygraph measures heart rate, blood pressure, respiration, and GSR. Pens mounted on the top of the machine record bodily responses on a moving strip of paper *(graph)*. Changes in the area marked by the arrow indicate emotional arousal. If such responses appear when a person answers a question, he or she may be lying, but arousal may have other causes.

Isn't there a better way to detect lies? Possibly. Harassment charges against Donna were dropped when a functional magnetic resonance imaging (fMRI) scan revealed that she was indeed telling the truth (see Module 8). Brain scans like fMRI directly measure brain activity, thus bypassing the traditional approach of measuring indirect signs of emotional arousal (Hakun et al., 2009; Lefebvre et al., 2007). For example, researchers have found that different brain areas are involved in telling a lie. Psychiatrist Daniel Langleben (2008) theorizes that a liar must inhibit telling the truth in order to lie. Thus, extra brain areas must be activated to tell a lie, which can be seen in brain images when people are lying.

Even if new methods are used, the key problem remains: How can we avoid falsely classifying liars as truth tellers and truth tellers as liars? Until that can be done with acceptable accuracy, any new technique may have no more value than the polygraph (Choi, 2015).

Emotion and the Brain

Imagine this test of willpower: Go to a zoo and place your face close to the glass in front of a rattlesnake display. Suddenly, the rattlesnake strikes at your face. Do you flinch? Even though you know that you are safe, Joseph LeDoux predicts that you cannot avoid recoiling from the attack (LeDoux, 2000, 2012).

According to LeDoux, this basic fear response is automatic and not under the control of higher brain centers (it is a form of experiential processing). Instead, the **amygdala**, a part of the *limbic system*, receives sensory information directly, before the cortex (➤ **Figure 44.3**; see Module 10 for more information). This subcortical circuit allows us to respond quickly to potential danger before we really know what's happening (Martínez-Alvarez et al., 2016). The role of the amygdala in fear may explain why people who suffer from phobias and disabling anxiety often feel afraid without knowing why (Schlund & Cataldo, 2010). Other basic emotions may also be processed first in the limbic system.

People who suffer damage to the amygdala become "blind" to emotion. An armed robber could hold a gun to a person's head and the person with damage to his or her amygdala wouldn't feel fear. Such people also are unable to "read" or understand other people's emotional expressions, especially as conveyed by their eyes (Adolphs, 2008). Many lose their ability to relate normally to friends, family, and coworkers.

Even if they are basic emotions and processed first in the limbic system, all emotions are eventually sent to the cortex where each basic emotion is associated with a distinct pattern of cortical activation (Saarimäki et al., 2016). Additional

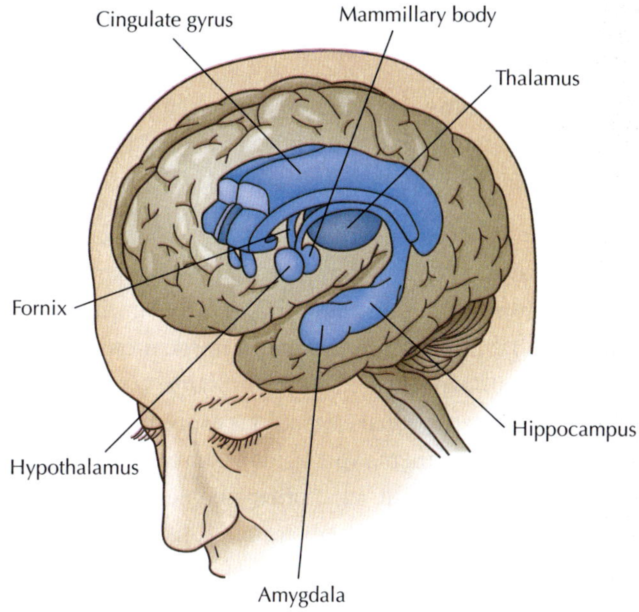

➤ **Figure 44.3**

Parts of the limbic system. Parts of the limbic system. An amygdala can be found buried beneath the temporal lobes on each side of the brain (see Module 10). The subcortical limbic system is a sort of "primitive core" of the brain strongly associated with emotion. The amygdala appears to provide "quick and dirty" processing of emotional stimuli that allows us to react involuntarily to danger.

cortical processing can be much more elaborate, giving rise to more or less complicated emotional feelings. Several interesting, and very human, curiosities arise because of this "two-layer" processing. For example, you can *feel* very afraid and yet clearly *think* that you have nothing to be afraid of. You can even have positive and negative emotions at the same time.

How is that possible? Positive emotions are processed mainly in the left hemisphere of the brain. In contrast, negative emotions are processed in the right hemisphere (Nijboer & Jellema, 2012; Simon-Thomas, Role, & Knight, 2005). In one study, people watching their favorite soccer team play well showed activity in both hemispheres but showed activity only in the right hemisphere when they were losing (Park et al., 2009).

Later, we will attempt to put all the elements of emotion together into a single picture. But first, we need to review what we just learned about physiological arousal and emotional expressions.

Polygraph A device for recording heart rate, blood pressure, respiration, and galvanic skin response; commonly called a "lie detector."

Guilty knowledge test A polygraph procedure involving testing people with facts that only a guilty person could know.

Amygdala A part of the limbic system associated with the rapid processing of emotions; especially fear.

Expressing Emotions—Making Faces and Talking Bodies

Learning Outcome 44.2 Explain how accurately emotions are expressed by the face and "body language," taking into account culture and gender

Next to our own feelings, the expressions of others are the most familiar part of emotion. Are emotional expressions a carryover from human evolution? Charles Darwin thought so. Darwin (1872) observed that angry tigers, monkeys, dogs, and humans all bare their teeth in the same way. Psychologists believe that emotional expressions evolved to communicate our feelings to others, which aids survival. Such messages give valuable hints about what other people are likely to do next (Kalat & Shiota, 2012). For instance, in one study, people were able to detect angry and scheming faces faster than happy, sad, or neutral faces (➤ **Figure 44.4**). Presumably, we are especially sensitive to threatening faces because they warn us of possible harm (Adolphs, 2008; Panksepp & Watt, 2011).

Facial Expressions

Are emotional expressions the same for all people? Basic expressions appear to be fairly universal. Facial expressions of *fear*, *anger*, *disgust*, *sadness*, *surprise*, and *happiness* (enjoyment) are fairly well recognized around the world (Dailey et al., 2010; but see Crivelli et al., 2017). Expressions of contempt and interest also may be widespread (Ekman, 1993). Notice that this list covers most of the basic emotions described previously. Children who are born blind have little opportunity to learn emotional expressions from others. Even so, they also display basic expressions in the same way as sighted people (Galati, Scherer, & Ricci-Bitti, 1997). It's also nice to note that a smile is the most universal and easily recognized facial expression of emotion.

There are more than a few facial expressions, aren't there? Yes. Your face can produce thousands of different expressions, which makes it the most expressive part of your body. Most of these are *facial blends*—a mixture of two or more basic expressions (Prodan, Orbelo, & Ross, 2007). Imagine, for example, that you just received an "F" on an unfair test. Quite likely, your eyes, eyebrows, and forehead would reveal anger, and your mouth would be turned downward in a sad frown.

Cultural Differences in Expressing Emotion

Some facial expressions are shaped by learning and may be found only in specific cultures. Among the Chinese, for example, sticking out the tongue is a gesture of surprise, not of disrespect or teasing. If a person comes from another culture, it is wise to remember that you may easily misunderstand his or her expressions. At such times, knowing the social *context* in which an expression occurs helps clarify its meaning (Carroll & Russell, 1996; Kalat & Shiota, 2012).

How many times have you expressed anger this week? If it was more than once, you're not unusual. In Western cultures, expressing anger is widely viewed as a "natural" reaction to feeling that you have been treated unfairly. Very likely this is because our culture emphasizes personal independence and free expression of individual rights and needs. In contrast, many Asian cultures place a high value on group harmony. In Asia, expressing anger in public is less common, and anger is regarded as less "natural." This is because anger tends to separate people. Thus, for many Asians, being angry is at odds with a culture that values cooperation.

Culture also influences positive emotions. In the United States, we tend to have positive feelings such as pride, happiness, and superiority, which emphasize our role as *individuals*. In Japan, positive feelings are more often linked with membership in groups (friendly feelings, closeness to others, and respect) (Markus et al., 2006).

It is common to think of emotion as an individual event. However, as you can see, emotion is shaped by cultural ideas, values, and practices (Boiger & Mesquita, 2012).

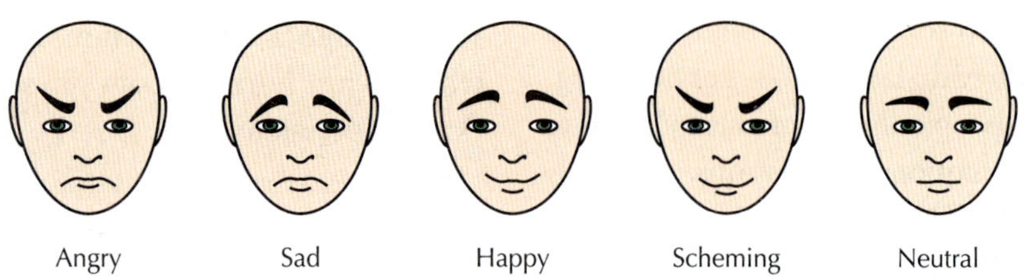

➤ **Figure 44.4**

Simplified faces. When shown groups of simplified faces (without labels), the angry and scheming faces "jumped out" at people before the sad, happy, and neutral faces. An ability to rapidly detect threatening expressions probably helped our ancestors survive. (Adapted from Tipples, Atkinson, & Young, 2002.)

Gender Differences in Expressing Emotion

Women have a reputation for being "more emotional" than men. Are they? Compared with women, men in Western cultures are more likely to have difficulty expressing their emotions (Pérusse, Boucher, & Fernet, 2012). In fact, Western men are more likely than women to experience **alexithymia** (a-LEX-ih-THIGH-me-ah), from the Latin for "can't name emotions."

According to psychologist Ronald Levant and colleagues (2006, 2009), although male babies start out life more emotionally expressive than female babies, little boys soon learn to "toughen up," beginning in early childhood. As a result, men have learned to curtail the expression of most of their emotions. Whereas girls are encouraged to express sadness, fear, shame, and guilt, boys are more likely to be allowed to express only anger and hostility (Fischer et al., 2004).

But does this mean that men experience emotions less than women? Levant believes that men who fail to express emotions over time become less aware of their own emotions and, hence, less able to name them (Levant, Allen, & Lien, 2014; Reker et al., 2010). For many men, a learned inability to express feelings or to even be aware of them is a major barrier to having close, satisfying relationships with others and also can lead to health problems, such as depression or addictive behaviors (Ogrodniczuk, Piper, & Joyce, 2011; Vanheule et al., 2010). Blunted emotions may even contribute to tragedies such as all-too-common school shootings. For many young males, anger is the only emotion they can freely feel and express.

Alfredo Estrella/AFP/Getty Images

The expression of emotion is strongly influenced by learning. As you have no doubt observed, women cry more often, longer, and more intensely than men. Men begin learning early in childhood to suppress crying—possibly to the detriment of their emotional health (Williams & Morris, 1996). Many men are especially unwilling to engage in public displays of emotion.

Body Language

Would you be offended if a friend walked up to you and said, "Hey, ugly, how are you doing?" Probably not, because such remarks are usually delivered with a big grin. The facial and body gestures of emotion speak a language all their own and add to what a person says.

Kinesics (kih-NEEZ-iks) is the study of communication through body movement, posture, gestures, and facial expressions (Goman, 2008; Hinzman & Kelly, 2013). Informally, we call it *body language*. To see a masterful use of body language, turn off the sound on a television and watch a popular entertainer or politician at work.

What kinds of messages are sent with body language? It is important to realize that cultural learning also affects the meaning of gestures. What, for instance, does it mean if you touch your thumb and first finger together to form a circle? In North America, it means "Everything is fine" or "A-okay." In France and Belgium, it means "You're worth zero." In southern Italy, it means "You're an ass!" When the layer of culturally defined meanings is removed, it is more realistic to say that body language reveals an overall emotional tone (underlying emotional state).

The body telegraphs other feelings. The most general "messages" involve *relaxation* or *tension*, and *liking* or *disliking*. Relaxation is expressed by casually positioning the arms and legs, leaning back (if sitting), and spreading the arms and legs. Liking is expressed mainly by leaning toward a person or object. Thus, body positioning can reveal feelings that would normally be concealed. Who do you "lean toward"?

Eviled/Shutterstock.com

Emotions are often unconsciously revealed by gestures and body positioning.

Alexithymia A learned difficulty expressing emotions, more common in men.

Kinesics Study of the meaning of body movements, posture, hand gestures, and facial expressions; commonly called *body language*.

Theories of Emotion—Several Ways to Fear a Bear

Learning Outcome 44.3 Distinguish between the James-Lange, Canon-Bard, and cognitive (including discrete emotions) theories of emotion; define attribution, appraisal, and facial feedback; and outline a contemporary theory of emotion

You are probably familiar with the role that emotions can play in influencing our cognitions. In Module 39, for example, we saw that "hot cognition," such as taking action in the heat of anger, can be unwise. What you may not be so familiar with is the reverse; the role that cognition plays in shaping our emotions. It turns out that we cannot fully explain adult emotions without looking into this fascinating topic. To this end, let's explore some prominent theories of emotion.

The James-Lange Theory

Let's not keep that bear waiting. Remember, you're hiking in the woods when a growling bear steps onto the trail. What will happen next? Common sense tells us that we then will feel fear, become aroused, and, consequently, run (and sweat and yell). But is this the true order of events? In the 1880s, William James and Carl Lange (LON-geh) proposed that common sense had it backward (Henley, 2019). According to the **James-Lange theory**, physiological arousal (such as increased heart rate) does not *follow* a feeling such as fear. Instead, they argued, *subjective feelings follow physiological arousal.* Thus, we see a bear, run, are aroused, and *then* feel fear as we become aware of our body reactions (➤ **Figure 44.5**).

In support, James pointed out that we frequently fail to experience an emotion until after reacting. For example, imagine that you are driving. Suddenly, a car pulls out in front of you. You swerve and skid to an abrupt halt. Only then do you notice your pounding heart, rapid breathing, and tense muscles—and recognize your fear.

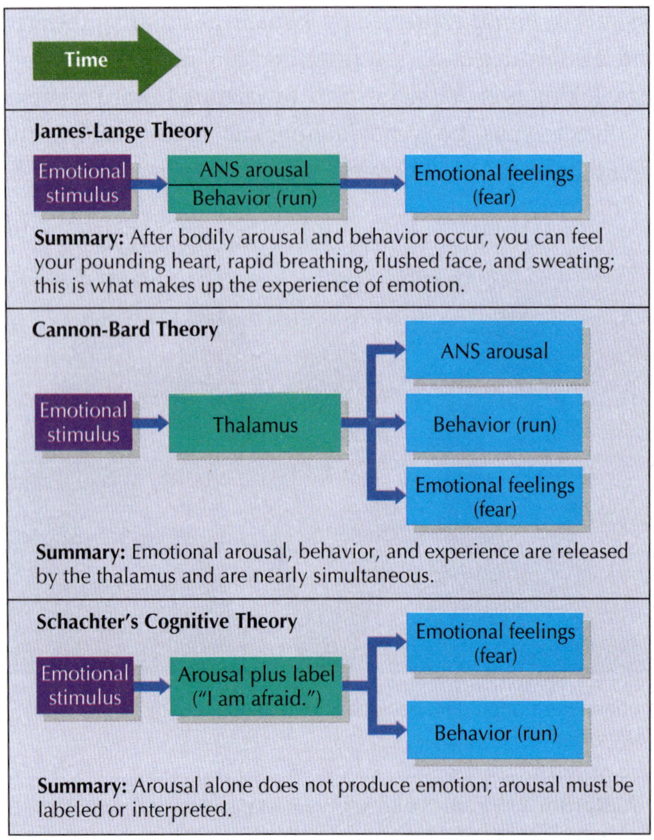

➤ **Figure 44.5**
Early theories of emotion.

The Cannon-Bard Theory

Walter Cannon (1932) and Phillip Bard disagreed with the James-Lange theory. According to the **Cannon-Bard theory**, emotional feelings and physical arousal *occur at the same time* (Cannon, 1932; Schultz & Schultz, 2016). Seeing a bear activates limbic structures in the brain, such as the amygdala, thalamus, and hypothalamus. They, in turn, alert the peripheral nervous system for action and the cortex for further reflection. The peripheral nervous system triggers a chain of events that arouses the body. The cortex produces our emotional feelings and emotional behavior. Thus, if you see a dangerous-looking bear, brain activity simultaneously produces body arousal, running, and a feeling of fear (see Figure 44.5).

Cognitive Theories of Emotion

The previous theories are concerned mostly with physiological arousal and behavioral changes. Stanley Schachter realized that cognitive factors also enter into emotion, even basic emotions. According to **Schachter's cognitive theory**, emotion occurs when we apply a particular *label* to general physiological *arousal.*

Carroll Izard's *differential emotions theory* helps explain how we come up with the label. According to Izard, the basic emotions (see Module 13), such as anger and fear, are experienced in their pure form only by young children. By the time we have reached adulthood, we have usually experienced our emotions in many different ways and have learned to interpret those emotions in a variety of ways. The collections of learned ways to interpret and label our emotions are called **emotion schemas**—learned knowledge structures combining emotional experiences and cognitive processes such as attribution or appraisal.

How does an emotion schema work? Here is one example: Five-year-old Jimmy took a ride on a huge roller coaster for the very first time and experienced pure basic fear. But his older brother Alan, who loves riding roller coasters, made fun of Jimmy's fear while his father told him to "toughen up" and reassured him that roller coasters are "fun." The second time he waited in line to ride one, Jimmy remembered that roller coasters are supposed to be fun and that his older brother loves them. He anticipated the rush of the roller coaster down the steep drops and around tight turns. This time it was not so scary. By his fifth ride, Jimmy was hooked; he now labels riding roller coasters as "a real buzz" rather than as "scary." (As we just learned in the previous section, if Jimmy's early life experiences involve too much "toughening up," he might become *alexithymic*, experiencing difficulty in naming basic fear when he experiences it. He might even toughen up so much he no longer experiences basic fear at all.)

Let's look in more detail at two major cognitive influences on the experience of emotion, *attribution* and *appraisal.*

Attribution and Emotion

One frequent way our emotion schemas interpret and label emotional experiences is through a process of **attribution**, by assigning cause to behavior—namely, by deciding which source is causing the arousal (León & Hernández, 1998; Marian & Shimamura, 2012).

Assume, for instance, that someone sneaks up behind you on a dark street and says, "Boo!" Your body is now aroused (pounding heart, sweating palms, and so on). If you attribute your arousal to a total stranger, you might label your arousal as fear; if you attribute your arousal to a close friend, you may experience surprise or delight. The label (such as anger, fear, or happiness) you apply to physiological arousal is influenced by your past experiences, the situation, and the reactions of others (see Figure 44.5).

Support for the cognitive theory of emotion comes from an experiment in which people watched a slapstick movie (Schachter & Wheeler, 1962). Before viewing the movie, everyone got an injection, but no one was told what the injection contained. One-third of the people received an arousing injection of adrenaline, one-third got a placebo (saltwater) injection, and one-third were given a tranquilizer. People who received the adrenaline rated the movie funniest and laughed the most while watching it. In contrast, those given the tranquilizer were least amused. The placebo group fell in between.

According to the cognitive theory of emotion, individuals who received adrenaline had a stirred-up body, which they then attributed to the movie, leading them to interpret their arousal as happiness and amusement. This and similar experiments make it clear that emotion is much more than just an agitated body. Perception, experience, attitudes, judgment, and many other mental factors also affect the emotions that we feel. Schachter's theory would predict, then, that if you met a bear, you would be aroused and might suddenly find yourself at full gallop. An instant later, if the bear seemed unfriendly, you might confirm your arousal as fear, and if the bear was offering to shake your "paw," you might experience happiness, amazement, and relief!

Misattribution There is, of course, no guarantee that we always make the correct attributions about our emotions. In fact, *misattributions* are more common than you might think. As an example, let's shift from a fear of bear bodies to an appreciation of bare bodies. In a classic study, male college students viewed a series of photographs of nude females while listening to an amplified heartbeat that each student believed was his own (Valins, 1967). In reality, students were listening to a recorded heartbeat carefully designed to beat *louder* and *stronger* when some (but not all) of the photos were shown.

After watching the photos, each student was asked to say which was most attractive. Students who heard the false heartbeat consistently rated photos paired with a "pounding heart" as the most attractive. In other words, when a student saw a photo and heard his heart beat louder, he (falsely) attributed his "emotion" to the photo. His attribution seems to have been, "Now that one I like!"

That seems somewhat artificial. Does it really make any difference what arousal is attributed to? Yes. Attribution theory predicts that you are most likely to "love" someone who gets you stirred up emotionally (Foster et al., 1998). This is true even when fear, anger, frustration, or rejection is part of the formula. Thus, if you want to successfully propose marriage, take your intended to the middle of a narrow, windswept suspension bridge over a deep chasm and look deeply into his or her eyes. As your beloved's heart pounds wildly (from being on the bridge, not from your irresistible charms), say,

James-Lange theory The proposition that bodily arousal leads to subjective feelings.

Cannon-Bard theory The proposition that thalamus activity causes emotions and bodily arousal to occur simultaneously.

Schachter's cognitive theory A theory stating that emotions occur when physical arousal is labeled or interpreted on the basis of experience and situational cues.

Emotion schema A learned knowledge structure combining emotional experiences and cognitive processes such as attribution or appraisal.

Attribution The act of assigning cause to behavior.

"I love you." Attribution theory predicts that your companion will conclude, "Oh, wow! I must love you, too."

Really? The preceding is not as far-fetched as it may seem. In an ingenious classic study, a female psychologist interviewed men in a park. Some were on a swaying suspension bridge, 230 feet above a river. The rest were on a solid wooden bridge just 10 feet above the ground. After the interview, the psychologist gave each man her telephone number, so he could "find out about the results" of the study. Men interviewed on the suspension bridge were much more likely to give the "lady from the park" a call (Dutton & Aron, 1974). Apparently, these men experienced heightened arousal, which they misinterpreted as attraction to the experimenter—a clear case of love at first fright! (Love is one basis for interpersonal attraction, but there are others, such as similarity and proximity. To learn more about what brings people together, see Module 72.)

Appraisal and Emotion

According to Richard Lazarus (1991a, b), the role of cognition in experiencing emotions is not restricted to making causal attributions about why arousal has occurred. The emotions you experience are also greatly influenced by your **emotional appraisal**, how you evaluate the personal meaning of a stimulus: Is it good/bad, threatening/supportive, relevant/irrelevant, and so on (Anderson & Hunter, 2012)? Emotional appraisals can be experiential and occur quickly, as with startling fear stimuli, or they can be more reflective (Bunk & Magley, 2013).

Our discussion suggests that emotion is greatly influenced by how you think about an event. For example, if another driver "cuts you off" on the highway, you could become very angry. But if you do, you will add 15 minutes of emotional upset to your day. By changing your attribution ("He probably didn't mean it") and/or your emotional appraisal ("No big deal, anyway"), you could just as easily choose to brush off the other driver's behavior—and minimize your emotional wear-and-tear (Deutschendorf, 2009). In fact, emotional appraisals have a major impact on the ability to cope with threats and stress, which may ultimately affect your health. See Module 56.

The Facial Feedback Hypothesis

Schachter and Lazarus added thinking and interpretation (cognition) to our view of emotion, but the picture still seems incomplete. What about expressions? As Charles Darwin observed, the face is central to emotion—perhaps it is more than just an "emotional billboard." Do facial expressions actually influence our felt emotions?

Psychologist Carroll Izard (1990) was among the first to suggest that the face does, indeed, affect emotion. According to Izard, emotions cause innately programmed changes in facial expression. Sensations from the face then provide cues to the brain that help us determine what emotion we are feeling. This idea is known as the **facial feedback hypothesis** (Hennenlotter et al., 2009). Stated another way, it says that having facial expressions in turn influences our private emotional experience.

Psychologist Paul Ekman takes this idea one step further. He believes that "making faces" can actually *cause* emotion (Ekman, 1993). In one study, participants were guided as they arranged their faces, muscle by muscle, into expressions of surprise, disgust, sadness, anger, fear, and happiness (➤ **Figure 44.6**). At the same time, each person's bodily reactions were monitored.

Contrary to what you might expect, "making faces" can affect the autonomic nervous system, as shown by changes in heart rate and skin temperature. In addition, each facial expression produces a different pattern of activity. An angry face, for instance, raises heart rate and skin temperature, whereas disgust lowers both (Ekman, Levenson, & Friesen, 1983). Other studies have confirmed that posed expressions alter emotions and bodily activity (Dimberg & Söderkvist, 2011; Soussignan, 2002).

In a fascinating experiment, people rated how funny they thought cartoons were while holding a pen crosswise in their mouths. Those who were told to hold the pen in their teeth thought the cartoons were funnier than did people who held the pen in their lips. Can you guess why? If you hold a pen with your teeth, you are forced to form a smile. Holding it with the lips makes a frown. As predicted by the facial feedback hypothesis,

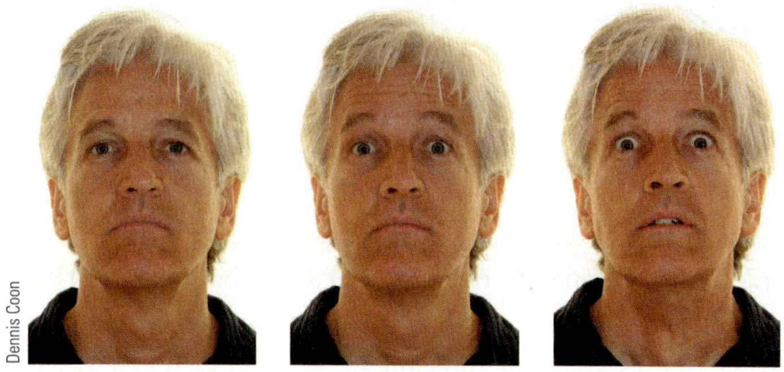

➤ **Figure 44.6**

Facial feedback and emotion. When people form facial expressions like those normally observed during emotion, emotion-like changes take place in their bodily activity (Dimberg & Söderkvist, 2011; Ekman, Levenson, & Friesen, 1983). Give it a try.

emotional experiences were influenced by the facial expressions that people made (Strack, Martin, & Stepper, 1988). Next time you're feeling sad, bite a pen! (Or, at least, make yourself smile.) It appears, then, that not only do emotions influence expressions, but expressions also influence emotions (but see Wagenmakers et al., 2016). *Do people who have Botox injected into their faces experience any less emotion?* It can certainly be uncanny to watch celebrities whose faces have been injected with Botox. (Ain't nothin' gonna move!) And it is indeed possible that they feel less emotion as a consequence. In one study, compared with normal participants, participants injected with Botox showed less brain activity as they imitated angry faces (Hennenlotter et al., 2009). And yet, reducing the facial feedback contributing to sadness may help alleviate depression (Lewis, 2012).

Suppressing Emotion *If smiling can improve a person's mood, is it a good idea to inhibit negative emotions?* According to popular media, we are supposed to be happy all the time (Hecht, 2007). However, real emotional life has its ups and downs. Have you ever been angry with a friend in public? Embarrassed by someone's behavior at a party? Disgusted by someone's table manners? Often, we try to appear less emotional than we really are, especially when we feel negative emotions. In such circumstances, people are quite good at suppressing outward signs of emotion.

However, restraining emotion can actually increase activity in the sympathetic nervous system. In other words, hiding emotion requires a lot of effort. Suppressing emotions also can impair thinking and memory as you devote energy to self-control. Thus, although suppressing emotion allows us to appear calm and collected on the outside, this cool appearance comes at a high cost (Gross, 2013). People who constantly suppress their emotions cope poorly with life and are prone to depression and other problems (Haga, Kraft, & Corby, 2010; Monde et al., 2013).

To summarize, it's usually better to manage emotions than it is to suppress them (Gross, 2013). People who express their emotions generally experience better emotional and physical health (Lumley, 2004; Pennebaker, 2004). Paying attention to our negative emotions also can lead us to think more clearly about the positive *and* the negative. The end result is better decision-making, which can increase our overall happiness in the long run (Deutschendorf, 2009).

A Contemporary Model of Emotion

To summarize, James and Lange were right that feedback from arousal and behavior adds to our emotional experiences. Cannon and Bard were right about the timing of events. Schachter showed us that cognitive attribution is important. Lazarus stressed the importance of emotional appraisal. In fact, psychologists are increasingly aware that both the *attributions* you make and how you *appraise* a situation greatly affect your emotions (Kalat & Shiota, 2012; León & Hernández, 1998). Izard focused on facial expressions. Let's put these ideas together in a single model of emotion (➤ **Figure 44.7**).

Imagine that a large, snarling bear lunges at you with its teeth bared. A modern view of your emotional reactions goes something like this: An *emotional stimulus* (the bear) is *appraised* (judged, probably experientially and quickly in this example) as a threat or other cause for emotion. Your appraisal gives rise to *ANS arousal* (your heart pounds and your body becomes stirred up). At the same time, your appraisal leads to *adaptive behavior* (you run from the bear) as it releases *innate emotional expressions* (your face twists into a mask of fear and your posture becomes tense). In addition, it triggers *cognitive labeling* and a change in consciousness that you recognize as the subjective experience of fear. (You think, *Uh oh, big trouble!* The intensity of this *emotional feeling* is directly related to the amount of ANS arousal taking place in your body.)

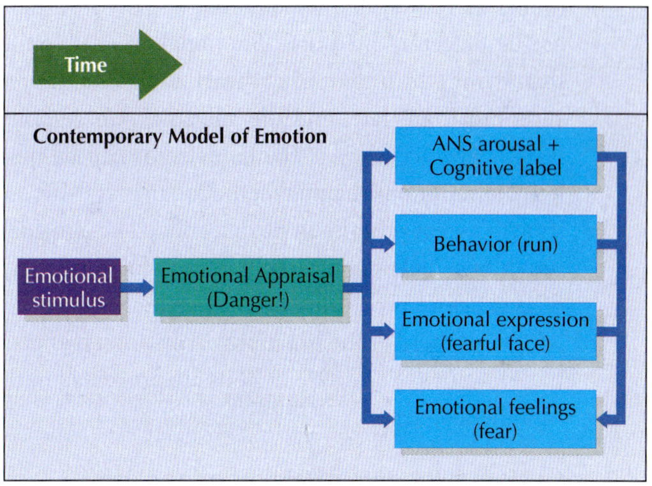

➤ **Figure 44.7**

A contemporary model of emotion. ANS arousal gives rise to cognitive labelling, behavior, facial/postural expressions, and emotional feelings. As each of these processes unfolds over time, it may, in turn, further affect arousal, behavior, expressions, and/or feelings.

Emotional appraisal Evaluating the personal meaning of a stimulus or situation.

Facial feedback hypothesis States that sensations from facial expressions help define what emotion a person feels.

Each element of emotion—ANS arousal, labeling, adaptive behavior, subjective experience, and your emotional expressions—may further alter your emotional appraisal of the situation, as well as your attributions, thoughts, judgments, and perceptions. Thus, according to the facial feedback hypothesis, your facial expression may further influence your emotion. Such changes affect each of the other reactions, which again alters your appraisal and interpretation of events. Thus, emotion may blossom, change course, or diminish as it proceeds. Note, too, that the original emotional stimulus can be external, like the attacking bear, or internal, like a memory of being chased by a bear, rejected by a lover, or praised by a friend. That's why mere thoughts and memories can make us fearful, sad, or happy (Kalat & Shiota, 2012).

A Look Ahead In Module 45, we look further at the importance of optimism. Before we continue, you might want to appraise your learning with the exercises that follow.

MODULE 44 Emotion in Detail—Learning Outcomes Revisited

44.1 Explain why "lie detectors" cannot really detect lies and describe some physiological changes that underlie emotion

Physical changes associated with emotion are caused by activity in the autonomic nervous system (ANS). The sympathetic branch of the ANS is primarily responsible for arousing the body; the parasympathetic branch is responsible for quieting it. The polygraph, or "lie detector," measures emotional arousal (rather than lying) by monitoring heart rate, blood pressure, breathing rate, and the galvanic skin response (GSR). The accuracy of the lie detector can be quite low. Newer brain-imaging methods, such as fMRI, are showing great promise in lie detection. The amygdala provides a "quick and dirty" pathway for the arousal of fear before processing by the cerebral cortex. The left hemisphere of the brain primarily processes positive emotions. Negative emotions are processed in the right hemisphere.

44.2 Explain how accurately emotions are expressed by the face and "body language," taking into account culture and gender

Basic facial expressions of fear, anger, disgust, sadness, surprise, and happiness may be universally recognized. Facial expressions of contempt and interest may be universal as well. Social context influences the meaning of facial expressions. Cultural differences in the meaning of some facial expressions also occur. Men tend to be less expressive than women. The formal study of body language is known as *kinesics*. Body gestures and movements (body language) also express feelings, mainly by communicating emotional tone rather than specific universal messages. Body positioning expresses relaxation or tension and liking or disliking.

44.3 Distinguish between the James-Lange, Canon-Bard, and cognitive (including discrete emotions) theories of emotion; define attribution, appraisal, and facial feedback; and outline a contemporary theory of emotion

Contrary to common sense, the James-Lange theory says that emotional experience follows bodily reactions. In contrast, the Cannon-Bard theory says that bodily reactions and emotional experiences occur at the same time. Schachter's cognitive theory emphasizes that labeling bodily arousal can determine what emotion you feel. According to discrete emotions theory, we learn to interpret physiological arousal through cognitive processes like memory, attribution, and appraisal, leading to the formation of emotion schemas. One of the best ways to manage emotion is to change your attributions or appraisal of an emotional situation. The facial feedback hypothesis holds that facial expressions help define the emotions that we feel. Contemporary views of emotion emphasize that all the elements of emotion are interrelated and interact with each other.

Reflective Practice

Content Check

1. Emotional arousal is closely related to activity of the ____________________ nervous system.

2. The sympathetic system prepares the body for "fight or flight" by activating the parasympathetic system. T or F?
3. What body changes are measured by a polygraph?
4. Charles Darwin held that emotional expressions aid survival for animals. T or F?
5. According to the James-Lange theory, emotional experience precedes physical arousal and emotional behavior. (We see a bear, are frightened, and run.) T or F?
6. The idea that labeling arousal helps define what emotions we experience is associated with
   a. the James-Lange theory
   b. Schachter's cognitive theory
   c. the Cannon-Bard theory
   d. Darwin's theory of innate emotional expressions
7. As you try to wiggle your ears, you keep pulling the corners of your mouth back into a smile. Each time you do, you find yourself giggling. Which of the following provides the best explanation for this reaction?
   a. attribution
   b. the Cannon-Bard theory
   c. appraisal
   d. facial feedback

Skill Check

Think Critically

8. People with high spinal injuries may feel almost no signs of physiological arousal from their bodies. Nevertheless, they still feel emotion, which can be intense at times. What theory of emotion does this observation contradict?

Self-Reflect

What did you think about lie detectors before reading this module? What do you think now? Write a list of emotions that you think you can accurately detect from facial expressions. Does your list match Paul Ekman's? Which theory seems to best explain your own emotional experiences? Try frowning or smiling for 5 minutes. Did facial feedback have any effect on your mood?

ANSWERS

1. autonomic 2. F 3. heart rate, blood pressure, breathing rate, galvanic skin response 4. T 5. F 6. b 7. d 8. The James-Lange theory and Schachter's cognitive theory. The facial feedback hypothesis also helps explain the observation.

MODULE 45

A Psychologist's Skill Set
Positivity and Optimism

Here's to the Good Life!

Michael J. Fox was only 29 years old and at the height of his acting career when he found out he had Parkinson's disease. A diagnosis like this would be devastating to many people. Not Fox. Instead, he chose to focus on the positive and the things that he *could* control, rather than those he couldn't. He has continued to act. He founded the Michael J. Fox Foundation to fund research into Parkinson's disease. He even wrote two books: *Lucky Man* and *Always Looking Up: Adventures of an Eternal Optimist*. When asked about his condition, he said: "I see possibilities in everything. For everything this disease has taken away, something of greater value has been given."

You've likely met people like Fox—relentlessly hopeful, even when the deck seems stacked against them. How do they do it? While optimism is, to some extent, part of your natural disposition, even the most pessimistic people can work toward becoming more optimistic. If you're optimistic about becoming more optimistic, read on!

Stephen Lovekin/MJF/Getty Images

~LEARNING OUTCOMES~

After reading this module you should be able to:

45.1 Explain positive psychology, optimism, and the components of your explanatory style

Optimistic?—There's Always Something to Be Happy About

Learning Outcome 45.1 Explain positive psychology, optimism, and the components of your explanatory style

Psychologists have always paid attention to the negative side of human behavior. This is easy to understand because of the pressing need to solve human problems. More recently, psychologists have also become interested in **positive psychology**, the study of human strengths, virtues, and optimal behavior (Compton & Hoffman, 2019). Many topics from positive psychology can be found in this book including empathy and helping behavior (Module 72), creativity (Modules 39 and 41), effective coping strategies (Module 57), and emotional intelligence (Module 40).

In Modules 42 and 44, we examined the role that emotions play in our lives. For researchers who are interested in positive psychology, positive emotions such as joy, hopefulness, contentment, and happiness are of particular interest.

Optimism and positive emotions are both closely connected to feelings of **subjective well-being** (Diener, 2013), which occur when people are generally satisfied with their lives, have frequent positive emotions, and relatively few negative emotions (Diener, Scollon, & Lucas, 2009; Tay & Diener, 2011).

So good and bad events predict feelings of subjective well-being? Life events themselves are not as important as a person's *explanatory style*—the way that he or she interprets those events (Seligman, 1998). And that interpretation is, in turn, influenced by many factors, such as culture, goals, values, and personality (Scollon, Koh, & Au, 2011). Most importantly, people like Michael J. Fox, who have an optimistic explanatory style, tend to have positive emotions about events—even the bad ones. As a result, they are happier and seem to negotiate life's demands more smoothly (Wong, 2011).

Ok, but sometimes things actually are *bad—surely, it's not good to assume that everything will always get better!* You're right. Optimism can have negative consequences when people fail to ground their thinking in reality. Specifically, people who demonstrate *unrealistic optimism* and refuse to see risks may not take appropriate action to deal with their problems (Weinstein, 1989). The end result is often that their difficulties worsen because they have not been addressed (Dillard, Midboe, & Klein, 2009). For example, people who always expect that things will turn out well may fail to address challenging issues that arise in their relationships, or may fail to seek early treatment for health-related concerns. Clearly there's an important line that needs to be drawn between *hopeful* thinking and *wishful* thinking.

Is optimism part of your personality? To a degree, some people are more temperamentally disposed to be upbeat and hopeful, a characteristic that researchers refer to as *dispositional optimism* (Carver & Scheier, 2014; Wrosch, Jobin, & Scheier, 2016). However, psychologist Martin Seligman has clearly established that anyone can work toward cultivating an optimistic view of life events (Seligman, 1998). In other words, optimism isn't necessarily a stable personality trait—it's a skill that you can improve upon, with a little practice. To learn why that might be important, and how you can do it, read on!

Facing Adversity

Good and bad events occur in all lives. What separates optimists and pessimists is largely a matter of attitude. Hopeful, positive people tend to see their lives in more positive terms, even when trouble comes their way. For example, optimistic people tend to find humor in disappointments. They look at setbacks as challenges. They are strengthened by losses (Lyubomirsky & Tucker, 1998).

Optimists also tend to expect that things will turn out well. In general, this motivates them to actively cope with adversity. They are less likely to be stymied by temporary setbacks and more likely to tackle their problems head on. In general, pessimists are more likely to ignore or deny problems. The result of such differences can be seen both at work and in people's personal lives. At home, optimists have relationships that last longer and are more satisfying (Neff & Geers, 2013). They also tend to do well at work, especially in jobs where setbacks are a common occurrence (Forgeard & Seligman, 2012). In terms of health, optimists are less stressed and anxious than pessimists, and are physically healthier (Carver & Scheier, 2014). In general, optimists tend to take better care of themselves, because they believe that their efforts to stay healthy will succeed (Peterson & Chang, 2003; Taylor, 2011).

Becoming More Optimistic

Sometimes I find it hard to be optimistic. Can I get better at thinking this way? Definitely. Psychological research has tested a few different ways to increase optimistic thinking. For example, simply imagining your best possible self for 5 minutes each day can lead to greater feelings of optimism (Meevissen, Peters, & Alberts, 2011; Peters, Meevissen, & Hanssen, 2013).

It is also helpful to better understand your *explanatory style* (Seligman, 1998). As we just discussed, what's important is not so much whether you experience negative or positive life events but rather how you interpret those experiences. For example, imagine that you have just received a poor midterm grade. As you try to make sense of this negative event, there are likely to be three key components of your explanation:

- **Pervasiveness.** The first relates to the *pervasiveness* of the event, or the extent to which you believe the event will impact other aspects of your life. Reacting to your poor midterm grade with the pessimistic thought "My whole life is ruined" is very different from reacting with a more optimistic one, such as "This is just one grade; the rest of my grades will be better."

Positive psychology The study of human strengths, virtues, and effective functioning.

Subjective well-being General life satisfaction, combined with frequent positive emotions and relatively few negative emotions.

- **Permanence.** A second relates to the *permanence* of the event—that is, how long you expect the conditions will last. A pessimist might look at a poor grade and think that the next exam will likely be just as bad, while an optimist thinks that the next exam will likely be much better.
- **Personal.** The third component of explanatory style relates to the extent to which you think that the event is due to something *personal* about you, as opposed to something related to your situation. A pessimist is more likely to see negative events as stemming from something unchangeable about his or her personality ("I'm just so stupid"), while an optimist is more likely to consider circumstances that can be changed ("I didn't study enough for that test").

To summarize, optimists view negative events as being limited in their effects, short term, and the result of circumstances that can be changed. Conversely, optimists view positive events as being broader in their effects, long term, and the result of stable aspects of their personality. Upon doing well on an exam, an optimist is more likely to think, "Things are going well," "I'm on a roll, exam-wise," and "I'm smart enough."

Challenging Pessimistic Explanations So, do you have an optimistic or pessimistic explanatory style? To reflect on this, take a look at the following four events (two positive and two negative) and imagine that each one has happened to you. Ask yourself why this might have happened, and if you come up with multiple reasons, then try to narrow them down to the single most important one (from Peterson et al., 1982).

Your boyfriend/girlfriend has been treating you more lovingly.

You can't get all the work done that others expect of you.

You meet a friend for lunch and s/he is behaving in a hostile way toward you.

You apply for a position that you want very badly and you get it.

Now consider the reasons you thought would lead to these events and ask yourself: Are they likely to be short or long term? Limited or far-reaching in their effects? The result of stable personality traits or temporary circumstances?

If you find that your explanatory style is somewhat pessimistic, challenge your thinking. If you can, ensure that your beliefs about the causes of events—whether positive or negative—are accurate. For example, before accepting that a poor midterm grade is the result of your intelligence, look carefully at all of the available evidence and ask yourself whether this is really true. In all likelihood it isn't, because there are bound to be many other skills that you possess, and many other times when you have been successful.

It may not always be easy to change the way that you think about the world, but psychological research has demonstrated that it is possible to change your explanatory style (Barber et al., 2005). And it's likely to be well worth the effort: Thinking carefully about the explanations that you make about events has important consequences for your health, relationships, and well-being. Clearly, we should all take heed of the advice that Henry Ford passed along in 1947: "Whether you believe you can do a thing or not, you are right."

MODULE 45 Positivity and Optimism—Learning Outcomes Revisited

45.1 Explain positive psychology, optimism, and the components of your explanatory style

The field of positive psychology focuses on people's experience of positive emotions, optimism, and subjective well-being. Well-being is affected by the way you perceive your life events. Optimism can help you overcome and grow from negative events; however, "unrealistic optimism" can cause people to ignore preventable risks. To some extent, optimism is a stable characteristic (dispositional optimism), but it is also considered a skill that can be developed. In your personal and professional life, optimism helps you approach challenges, grow and cope with adversity, have more satisfying relationships, and it leads to less stress and better health. Your explanatory style (the way you frame events) has important consequences for your health, relationships, and well-being and includes pervasiveness, permanence, and personal components.

Reflective Practice

Content Check

1. Optimism is only influenced by heredity. T or F?
2. People with an optimistic explanatory style view negative events as being short term and limited in their effects. T or F?
3. Subjective well-being refers to the idea that people are generally satisfied with their lives, have very few positive emotions, and have many negative emotions. T or F?
4. Optimism can have negative consequences when people fail to ground their thinking in reality. T or F?
5. What are the three components of explanatory style?

Skill Check

Think Critically

6. Scenario 1: You just failed a test, but you think to yourself that it will be okay, because you will try harder next time. As a result, you study much harder and receive a better grade. Scenario 2: You feel nauseous and feverish, but are trying not to think about it because you have too much schoolwork to do. You tell yourself that you can't be sick right now—if you don't think about it and avoid it, it might go away. Which of these scenarios represents the concept of "unrealistic optimism"? Why?

Self-Reflect

Reflect on your own explanatory style. Do you think you are more pessimistic or optimistic? What could you do in your personal and professional life to try to become more optimistic?

ANSWERS

1. F 2. T 3. F 4. T 5. Pervasiveness, permanence, personal 6. The second scenario is unrealistically optimistic. Ignoring or avoiding the fact that you are sick could actually make the problem worse because you may fail to take appropriate action (e.g., see a doctor, rest in bed). In contrast, if you addressed the problem appropriately, you are likely to prevent your illness from getting worse and will recover much faster.

MODULE

46 Human Sexuality

Sex and Gender

Either/Or; Neither/Nor

Chris Mosier is a remarkable athlete. He has completed three Ironman competitions, each time pushing himself hard through the grueling 2.5-mile swim, 112-mile bike race, and 26-mile run. By comparison, then, you might think that competing the New York City triathlon wouldn't be much of a challenge for Chris. The distances are much shorter than an Ironman, after all, and he'd completed that same race two years earlier. But things were different then. You see, at that time Chris Mosier was competing as a woman.

After coming out as a transgender man, Chris Mosier continued breaking down barriers that prevented LGBTQ athletes from fully participating in sports. He became the first openly transgender member of the US men's sprint duathlon team, competing at multiple World Championships. He has advocated—successfully—for changes to international rules, making sports more inclusive for all people. But perhaps most importantly, he continues to coach young athletes so that each of them can reach their full potential.

Michael Nagle/The New York Times/Redux

Chris Mosier's story is a lesson in how traditional ideas about sex and gender are changing in our society. We used to think strictly in terms of "either/or"—either male or female; masculine or feminine. Now, though, people are increasingly comfortable identifying as "neither/nor," rejecting binary categories in favor of being more fluid. To understand why, let's take a deeper dive into this fascinating area of psychology.

~LEARNING OUTCOMES~

After reading this module you should be able to:

46.1 List the four basic dimensions of biological sex and explain how hormones can influence sexual development prenatally and postnatally

46.2 Define four sexual orientations and outline their causes

46.3 Define gender identity and outline the factors that influence it

46.4 Define psychological androgyny and explain its advantages

46.5 Explain what it means for an individual to be transgender (gender variant)

Sexual Development—Circle One: *XX* or *XY*?

Learning Outcome 46.1 List the four basic dimensions of biological sex and explain how hormones can influence sexual development prenatally and postnatally

The term **sex** refers to whether you are physically, biologically female or male. Contrary to common belief, classifying a person's sex is not a simple either/or proposition. Let's begin to understand why by examining the various dimensions of what it means to be female or male.

Dimensions of Sex

What are some dimensions of sex? At the very least, classifying a person as female or male must take into account the following biological dimensions: (1) **genetic sex** (*XX* or *XY* chromosomes), (2) **hormonal sex** (predominance of estrogens or androgens), (3) **gonadal sex** (ovaries or testes), and (4) **genital sex** (clitoris and vagina in females, penis and scrotum in males). To see why sex must be defined by taking these four dimensions into account, let's trace the events involved in becoming female or male.

Genetic Sex Becoming male or female may seem simple enough. Genetic sex is determined at the instant of conception: Two ***X* chromosomes** initiate female development; an *X* chromosome plus a ***Y* chromosome** produces a male. A woman's ovum always provides an *X* chromosome because she has two *X*s in her own genetic makeup. In contrast, one-half of the male's sperm carry *X* chromosomes and the other half carry *Y*s.

Even at conception, however, variations may occur because some individuals begin life with too many or too few sex chromosomes (Crooks & Baur, 2017). For example, in *Klinefelter's syndrome*, a boy is born *XXY*, with an extra *X* chromosome. As a result, when he matures, he may appear feminine, have undersized sexual organs, and be infertile. In *Turner's syndrome,* a girl is born with only one *X* chromosome and no *Y* chromosome. As an adolescent, she may appear boyish and she also will be infertile.

Hormonal and Gonadal Sex While genetic sex stays the same throughout life, it alone does not determine biological sex. In general, sexual characteristics are also related to the effects of sex hormones before birth. (Hormones are chemical substances secreted by endocrine glands.) The **gonads** (or sex glands) affect sexual development and behavior by secreting **estrogens** (female hormones) and **androgens** (male hormones). The gonads in the male are the testes; female gonads are the ovaries. The adrenal glands (located above the kidneys) also supply sex hormones.

Everyone usually produces estrogens and androgens. Sex differences are related to the *proportion* of these hormones found in the body. In fact, prenatal development of male or female anatomy is largely due to the presence or absence of **testosterone** (tes-TOSS-teh-rone), one of the androgens, secreted mainly by the testes (LeVay & Baldwin, 2015). For the first six weeks of prenatal growth, genetically female and male embryos look identical. However, if a *Y* chromosome is present, testes develop in the embryo and supply testosterone (Knickmeyer & Baron-Cohen, 2006). This stimulates growth of the penis and other male structures (➤ **Figure 46.1**). In the absence of testosterone, the

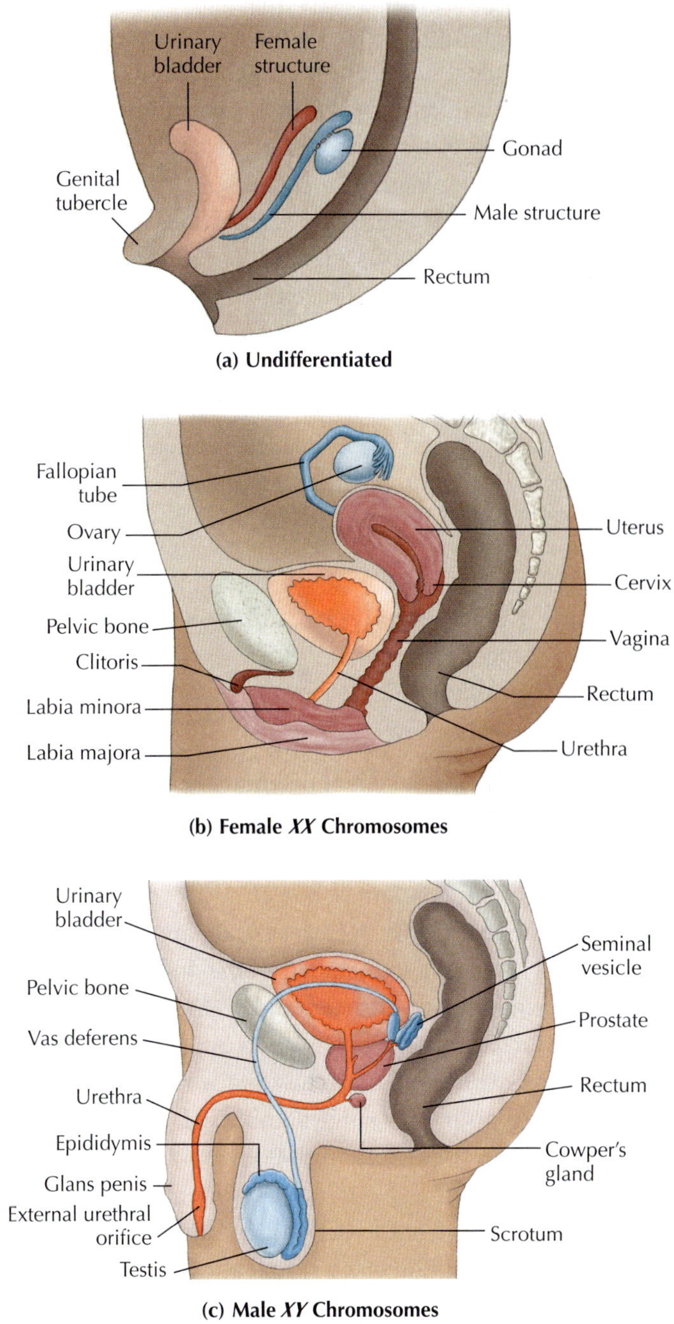

➤ **Figure 46.1**

Prenatal development of the reproductive organs. Prenatal development of the reproductive organs. Early development of ovaries or testes affects hormonal balance and alters sexual anatomy. (*a*) At first, the sex organs are the same in the human female and male. (*b*) When androgens are absent, female structures develop. (*c*) Male sex organs are produced when androgens are present.

embryo will develop female reproductive organs and genitals, regardless of genetic sex (LeVay & Baldwin, 2015). It might be said, then, that nature's primary impulse is to make a female. Without testosterone, we would all be women.

Prenatal growth does not always match genetic sex. For both genetic females and males, hormonal problems before birth may produce an **intersex person** (one who has ambiguous sexual anatomy). A genetic male won't develop male genitals if too little testosterone is available. Even if testosterone is present, an inherited *androgen insensitivity syndrome* (unresponsiveness to testosterone) may exist. Again, the result is female development (Cadet, 2011).

Similarly, androgens must be at low levels or absent for an *XX* embryo to develop as a female. For instance, a developing female may be masculinized by the anti-miscarriage drug progestin, or by a problem known as *congenital adrenal hyperplasia*. In this syndrome, the child's body produces estrogen, but a genetic abnormality causes the adrenal glands to release too much androgen. In such cases, a female child may be born with genitals that are more male than female (Kalat, 2021).

Genital Sex Mature males and females also differ in both *primary* and *secondary* sexual characteristics. **Primary sexual characteristics** refer to the sexual and reproductive organs themselves: the vagina, ovaries, and uterus in females; and the penis, testes, and scrotum in males. **Secondary sexual characteristics** are more superficial physical features that appear at puberty. These features develop in response to hormonal signals from the pituitary gland. In females, secondary sexual characteristics include breast development, broadening of the hips, and other changes in body shape. Males grow facial and body hair, and the voice deepens.

These changes signal that a person is biologically ready to reproduce. Reproductive maturity is especially evident in the female *menarche* (MEN-are-kee), the onset of menstruation. Soon after menarche, monthly ovulation begins. *Ovulation* refers to the release of ova (eggs) from the ovaries. From the first ovulation until **menopause**—the stage of life when a female stops menstruating—women can bear children.

Sexual Orientation—Who Do You Love?

Learning Outcome 46.2 Define four sexual orientations and outline their causes

Another aspect of sex is **sexual orientation**, your enduring pattern of emotional and erotic attraction. Just as physical sex does not fall neatly into two categories—male or female—sexual orientation is not always exclusively heterosexual (Carroll, 2016). **Heterosexuals** are romantically and erotically attracted to members of the opposite sex. Gay and lesbian individuals are men and women, respectively, who are attracted to people whose sex matches their own. **Bisexuals** are attracted to both men and women.

According to a growing number of psychologists, **asexuality**—a lack of attraction to both men and women—constitutes a fourth type of sexual orientation. Unlike *celibates*, who choose not to act on their sexual attractions, asexuals experience little or no sexual attraction in the first place, although they can experience sexual desire (Bogaert, 2012; Brotto et al., 2010).

About 3.4 percent of all adults regard themselves as **homosexual** or bisexual (Conron, Mimiaga, & Landers, 2010). Asexuals account for about 1 percent of adults (Bogaert, 2015). This means that over 12 million people in the United States alone are gay, lesbian, bisexual, or asexual. Millions more have a family member who is not heterosexual. It also is worth remembering that these figures are likely on the low side because many nonheterosexuals are unwilling to identify themselves as such (Bogaert, 2006).

The Stability of Sexual Orientation

Sexual orientation is a deep part of personal identity and is usually quite stable. Starting with their earliest erotic feelings, most people remember being attracted to either the opposite sex or the same sex. The chances are practically nil of an exclusively heterosexual, gay or lesbian person being "converted" from one orientation to the other (Mock & Eibach, 2012; Savin-Williams, Joyner, & Rieger, 2012).

But what about people who have had both heterosexual and homosexual relationships? The fact that sexual *orientation* is usually quite stable doesn't rule out the possibility that for some people, sexual *behavior* may change during the course of a lifetime. However, many such instances involve homosexual or asexual people who date or marry members of the opposite sex because of pressures to fit into heterosexual society. When these people realize that they are being untrue to themselves, their identity and relationships may shift. Other apparent shifts in orientation probably involve people who are basically bisexual (Mock & Eibach, 2012).

What determines a person's sexual orientation? The available evidence suggests that sexual orientation is mainly genetic and hormonal, although social, cultural, and psychological influences are also involved (LeVay, 2011; LeVay & Baldwin, 2015). Read on for a summary of two interesting theories about the origins of sexual orientation.

The Biology of Sexual Orientation Why are some people attracted to the opposite sex, whereas others prefer members of the same sex? One possibility is that sexual orientation is biologically determined and even at least partly hereditary (LeVay, 2011). One study found that if one identical twin is homosexual or bisexual, there is a 50 percent chance that the other twin is, too. Similar findings lead some researchers to estimate that sexual orientation is 30 to 70 percent genetic (Alanko et al., 2010; Mustanski, Chivers, & Bailey, 2002). Recently, the several candidates have been identified as genes that influence sexual orientation in males (Sample, 2014).

But how could homosexuality be genetically transmitted at all? At first glance, it seems that since homosexual sex does not result in genes being passed on to offspring, those genes would eventually become extinct. But maybe it is inaccurate to think of them as "gay genes." One intriguing possibility is that *sexually antagonistic selection* is at work. In other words, the same genes can be expressed differently (antagonistically) in males and females.

How so? Suppose that "gay" genes actually increase attraction to men and that they are carried by women as well as men. Now imagine a large family. The genes would tend to shift the male's sexual orientation toward men, resulting in homosexuality and *fewer* offspring. But the genes would also tend to shift the female's sexual orientation toward men. That is, they would now be especially attracted to men, with the likely result being *more* offspring. As it turns out, it has already been reported that the female relatives of homosexual men have *more* offspring than the female relatives of heterosexual men (Camperio Ciani et al., 2012). In this theory, then, the still-unidentified genes in question would result, overall, in *both* more offspring *and* male homosexuality.

Another promising approach is to focus on *epigenetics*, the study of how genes are expressed during development. Recall our previous discussion of how variations in sex hormones in the prenatal environment can dramatically influence prenatal development, resulting in conditions such as intersexuality, androgen insensitivity syndrome, and congenital adrenal hyperplasia. Along the same lines, it is entirely possible that variations in prenatal hormone levels can influence the development of sexual orientation in the fetus (LeVay, 2011).

According to the *prenatal hormonal theory of homosexuality,* some male fetuses are exposed to too little testosterone (Bogaert & Skorska, 2011). Similarly, some female fetuses are exposed to too much testosterone. These differences, in turn, can affect sexual orientation (Balthazart, 2012). Regardless, homosexuality is not caused by hormone imbalances in adulthood; the hormone levels of most gay men and lesbians are within the normal range (Banks & Gartrell, 1995).

Sex One's physical, biological classification as female or male.

Genetic sex Sex as indicated by the presence of *XX* (female) or *XY* (male) chromosomes.

Hormonal sex Sex as indicated by a preponderance of estrogens (female) or androgens (male) in the body.

Gonadal sex Sex as indicated by the presence of ovaries (female) or testes (male).

Genital sex Sex as indicated by the presence of male or female genitals.

***X* chromosome** The female chromosome contributed by the mother; produces a female when paired with another *X* chromosome and a male when paired with a *Y* chromosome.

***Y* chromosome** The male chromosome contributed by the father; produces a male when paired with an *X* chromosome. Fathers may give either an *X* or a *Y* chromosome to their offspring.

Gonads The primary sex glands—the testes in males and ovaries in females.

Estrogen Any of a number of female sex hormones.

Androgen Any of a number of male sex hormones, especially testosterone.

Testosterone A male sex hormone, secreted mainly by the testes and responsible for the development of many male sexual characteristics.

Intersex person A person who has genitals suggestive of both sexes.

Primary sexual characteristics Sex as defined by the genitals and internal reproductive organs.

Secondary sexual characteristics Sexual features other than the genitals and reproductive organs—breasts, body shape, facial hair, and so forth.

Menopause The stage of life when a female stops menstruating.

Sexual orientation Enduring pattern of attraction to members of the same and/or other sex.

Heterosexual A person romantically and erotically attracted to members of the opposite sex.

Bisexual A person romantically and erotically attracted to both men and women.

Asexual A person not romantically or erotically attracted to either men or women.

Homosexual A person romantically and erotically attracted to same-sex persons.

Hormonal differences during pregnancy may exert their effect by actually altering areas of the brain that orchestrate sexual behavior. Support for this idea comes from the finding that parts of the hypothalamus, which is connected with sexual activity, differ in size in heterosexuals and homosexuals (Kinnunen et al., 2004; LeVay, 2011). Similarly, differences in neurotransmitter levels have been detected in the hypothalamus in homosexual and heterosexual persons (Kinnunen et al., 2004).

Consistent with the biological view of sexual orientation, it is unlikely that parenting makes children homosexual. There is little difference between the development of children with gay or lesbian parents and those who have heterosexual parents (Farr, 2017; Hart, Mourot, & Aros, 2012). Most lesbians and gay men were raised by heterosexual parents, and most children raised by gay or lesbian parents become heterosexual.

Such findings tend to discredit myths about parents making children homosexual or claims that homosexuality is merely a choice. Although learning contributes to one's sexual orientation, it appears that nature strongly prepares people to be either homosexual or heterosexual. In view of this, discriminating against homosexuals is much like rejecting a person for being blue-eyed or left-handed (Smith et al., 2011).

Sexual Orientation Today

Psychologists have, for some time, accepted that homosexuality, bisexuality, and asexuality all fall within a normal range of variations in sexual orientation (Silverstein, 2009). Gay men, lesbians, and bisexuals encounter hostility because they are members of minority groups, not because there is anything inherently wrong with them (American Psychological Association, 2008).

The problems faced by lesbians and gay men tend to be related to rejection by family and discrimination in hiring and housing. Such unfair treatment is based on homophobia and heterosexism in our society (Murray, 2009; Stefurak, Taylor & Mehta, 2010). *Homophobia* refers to prejudice, fear, and dislike directed at homosexuals. *Heterosexism* is the belief that heterosexuality is better or more natural than homosexuality.

Understandably, social rejection tends to produce higher rates of anxiety, depression, and suicidal thinking among gay and lesbian people (Bostwick et al., 2014; Lester, 2006). However, anyone facing discrimination and stigma would react in much the same way (DeBord et al., 2017; Greene & Britton, 2012). When such stresses are factored out, homosexual persons are no more likely to have emotional problems than heterosexual people (Goldfried, 2001; Meyer et al., 2011).

Most homosexual people have at one time or another suffered verbal abuse—or worse—because of their sexual orientation (Doyle & Molix, 2016; Fine, 2011). Much of this rejection is based on false stereotypes about gay and lesbian people. The following points are a partial reply to such stereotypes. Gay and lesbian people:

- do not try to "convert" others to homosexuality
- are no more likely to molest children than heterosexuals
- are no more likely to be mentally ill than heterosexuals
- do not hate persons of the opposite sex
- do not, as parents, make their own children gay
- do have long-term, caring, monogamous relationships
- are no less able to contribute to society than heterosexuals

Homosexual, bisexual, and asexual people are found in all walks of life, at all social and economic levels, and in all cultural groups. They are as diverse in terms of race, ethnicity, age, parenthood, relationships, careers, health, education, politics, and sexual behavior as the heterosexual community. Perhaps as more people come to see gay and lesbian people in terms of their humanity, rather than their sexuality, the prejudices that they have faced will wane (American Psychological Association, 2008; Silverstein, 2009).

Yana Paskova/The New York Times/Redux

Contrary to the common stereotype, many lesbian and homosexual couples are in long-term, committed relationships. Tom Doyle and Bill Cornwell lived together as a married couple for over five decades. Unfortunately, when Bill died in 2016, his family legally challenged his will. As of this writing, Tom (shown here) stands to be evicted from his home of 55 years.

Gender Identity—It Begins Early

Learning Outcome 46.3 Define gender identity and outline the factors that influence it

While the term *sex* refers to your biological maleness or femaleness, **gender** refers to the cultural characteristics associated with your maleness or femaleness (Crooks & Baur, 2017). For example, if you are biologically male, do you feel and act in more masculine ways or more feminine ways? In other words, what is your **gender identity**—your subjective sense of being male or female as expressed in appearance, behavior, and attitudes?

Is your gender identity also biologically determined, or is it learned? That's a good question. In animals, clear links exist between prenatal hormones and male or female behaviors. Also, as we just saw, in humans, abnormal levels of prenatal androgens and estrogens can strongly influence the development of the body, nervous system, and later behavior patterns, such as sexual preference. Slight variations in the levels of sex hormones may subtly "sex-type" the brains of most of us before birth, altering our chances of developing feminine or masculine traits (Berenbaum, Blakemore, & Beltz, 2011). Evidence for this idea is provided by females exposed to small increases in androgens before birth. After birth, their hormones shift to female, and they are raised as girls. Nevertheless, prenatal exposure to male hormones has a relatively slight masculinizing effect. During childhood, such girls are typically "tomboys" who prefer the company of boys to girls.

Although it would be a mistake to ignore this **biological biasing effect**, most human sex-linked behaviors are influenced more by learning than is the case for animals (Helgeson, 2012). For example, during adolescence, the tomboyism of masculinized girls usually gives way to more female interests and gender characteristics (Van Volkom, 2009). In contrast, many girls who are highly feminine when they are young become more masculine in adolescence as they seek to explore the social power that comes with more masculine gender roles (Halim, Ruble, & Amodio, 2011). Cases like these make it clear that both prenatal hormones and later social factors contribute to adult gender identity.

Gender Roles

A person's gender identity usually conforms to the **gender role**, or favored pattern of behavior, expected of each sex. Traditionally, in our culture, boys are encouraged to be strong, fast, aggressive, dominant, and achieving, and females are expected to be sensitive, intuitive, passive, emotional, and "naturally" interested in child-rearing.

A look at other cultures shows that our gender roles are by no means "natural" or universal. For example, in some cultures, women do the heavy work because men are considered too weak for it (Best, 2002). In Russia, roughly 75 percent of all medical doctors are women, and women make up a large portion of the workforce. Such cross-cultural variability makes it clear that a man is no less a man if he cooks, sews, or cares for children. A woman is no less a woman if she excels in sports, succeeds in business, or works as an auto mechanic. Still, adult personality and gender identity are closely tied to cultural definitions of "masculinity" and "femininity."

John Mitterer

Is this South American less of a man because he sews? Behaviors that are considered typical and appropriate for each sex (gender roles) vary a great deal from culture to culture. Undoubtedly, some cultures magnify sex differences more than others (Carroll, 2016).

Gender Culturally constructed distinctions between male and female characteristics.

Gender identity One's personal, private sense of maleness or femaleness.

Biological biasing effect The hypothesized effect that prenatal exposure to sex hormones has on development of the body, nervous system, and later behavior patterns.

Gender role Pattern of behaviors regarded as "male" or "female" within a culture.

Despite much progress in the last 40 years, gender role stereotypes continue to have a major impact on women and men. **Gender role stereotypes** are oversimplified beliefs about what men and women are actually like. While gender roles influence how we act, gender role stereotypes, in contrast, turn gender roles into false beliefs about what men and women can and can't do.

Female Gender Role Stereotyping Are women suited to be fighter pilots, corporate presidents, military commanders, or racecar drivers? A person with strong gender role stereotypes might say, "No, because women are not sufficiently aggressive, dominant, or mechanically inclined for such roles." Yet, today's women have performed successfully in virtually all realms.

Nevertheless, gender role stereotypes persist and can be a major career obstacle. For many jobs, your chances of being hired could be reduced by your sex, be it male or female. Unequal pay for comparable work and experience also is a major problem for women (Gould, Schieder, & Geier, 2016). Overall, women earn only about 81 cents for every dollar earned by men. The rate for women of color is worse—65 cents for African-American women and a measly 58 cents for Latinas. This wage gap can cost a woman trained in a professional school as much as $2 million in lost career earnings over the course of her life. The male–female pay difference is even found among teachers in colleges, where greater awareness of gender fairness should prevail (Jaschik, 2011).

Like all stereotypes, those based on gender roles ignore the wonderful diversity of humanity. Fortunately, extreme gender stereotyping has declined somewhat in the last 20 years (Eagly et al., 2012). Just the same, in most fields, women continue to earn less money and achieve lower status than men (Brescoll, Dawson, & Uhlmann, 2010; Gould, Schieder, & Geier, 2016).

Male Gender Role Stereotyping One common gender stereotype holds that men are vulnerable to thinking with their . . . well . . . gonads. Actually, there's a bit of truth to the stereotype and more to the story. Research confirms that men may make poorer decisions about sexual behavior when they are "turned on" (Nolet et al., 2016). In one study, when compared with unaroused men, those who are sexually excited are more willing to press women to have sex (Ariely & Loewenstein, 2006). They also are more likely to engage in risky sexual behavior. When unaroused men were asked if they thought being sexually aroused might influence their sexual choices, they predicted that arousal would have little effect. (Wrong!)

Of course, women are not immune to having their heads turned by sexual passion either. However, many people see male sexual irresponsibility as part of a larger pattern that includes aggression. Some go so far as to say that men suffer from "testosterone poisoning" because men are responsible for most violence. Again, this stereotype has an element of truth. Men who have high testosterone levels are more likely to become aggressive (Mehta & Beer, 2010; Montoya et al., 2012).

Then, are high testosterone levels a problem? Not usually. For example, men with low testosterone levels may have difficulty thinking and concentrating. In such cases, testosterone supplements can help them think *more* clearly, rather than less (Fukai et al., 2010). Furthermore, older men with too little testosterone tend to have memory problems and a greater risk of developing dementia (Carcaillon et al., 2014). Finally, let's remember that we have been discussing a gender stereotype, albeit one with some truth to it. Most men, including those with high testosterone levels, keep their sexual impulses and aggressiveness within acceptable limits.

Acquiring Gender Identity

How is gender identity acquired? As stated previously, gender identity—your personal, private sense of being female or male—is at least partly learned. It begins with *labeling* ("It's a girl!" or "It's a boy!") (Eagly, 2009). Thereafter, it is shaped by **gender role socialization**—the process of learning gender behaviors (stereotyped or not) regarded as appropriate

Pat Byrnes/The New Yorker Collection/Cartoonbank.com

for one's sex in a given culture. Gender role socialization reflects all the pressures from parents, peers, and cultural forces that urge boys to "act like boys" and girls to "act like girls" (Orenstein, 2011). By the time they are 30 months of age, children are aware of gender role differences (Martin & Ruble, 2009). At 3 or 4 years of age, gender identity is usually well formed (Martin, 2011).

Historically, parents and other adults in Western countries like the United States tended to encourage boys to engage in goal-directed or **instrumental behaviors**, to be directly aggressive, to hide their emotions, and to prepare for the world of work. Girls, on the other hand, were encouraged in emotion-oriented or **expressive behaviors**, and, to a lesser degree, were socialized for indirect aggression and for motherhood (Eagly, 2009).

When parents are told that they treat boys and girls differently, many explain that the sexes are just "naturally" different. But what comes first, "natural differences" or the gender-based expectations that create them? In our culture, "male" seems—for many—to be defined as "not female"—that is, parents often have a vague fear of expressive and emotional behavior in male children. To them, such behavior implies that a boy is effeminate or a sissy. Many parents who would not be troubled if their daughters engaged in "masculine" play might be upset if their sons played with dolls or imitated "female" mannerisms (Wiseman & Davidson, 2012).

No matter what, learning gender roles begins immediately after birth. Infant girls are held more gently and treated more tenderly than boys. Both parents play more roughly with sons than with daughters (who are presumed to be more "delicate"). Later, boys are allowed to roam over a wider area without special permission. They also are expected to run errands earlier than girls. Daughters are told that they are pretty and that "nice girls don't fight." Boys are told to be strong and that "tough guys don't cry." Sons are more often urged to control their emotions, except for anger and aggression, which parents tolerate more in boys than in girls.

Toys, sports, and play are strongly sex-typed (Hardin & Greer, 2009). Parents buy dolls for girls; they buy trucks, tools, and sports equipment for boys. Fathers, especially, tend to encourage their children to play with "appropriate" sex-typed toys (Freeman, 2007). Beginning around age 3, boys start to play mostly with boys and girls play with girls. Girls tend to play indoors and near adults. They like to cooperate by playing house and other games that require lots of verbal give and take. Boys prefer superhero games and rough-and-tumble play outdoors. Thus, from an early age, males and females tend to grow up in different, gender-defined cultures (Oppliger, 2007; Shaffer & Kipp, 2014.)

Anna Om/Shutterstock.com

One study found that the mothers interacted differently with their infant sons and daughters as they played with gender-neutral toys. Mothers of girls engaged in more interpretation and conversation, whereas mothers of boys commented more and offered more instructions (Clearfield & Nelson, 2006).

By the time children reach kindergarten, they have developed a gender identity and have internalized gender roles and stereotypes. They expect that doctors, firefighters, and pilots are men and that nurses, administrative assistants, and hairdressers are women (Eagly, 2009). And why not? The workforce is still relatively segregated by sex, and children learn from what they observe. Stereotyped gender roles are even the norm in various media like TV commercials, children's picture books, and video games (Kahlenberg & Hein, 2010; Oppliger, 2007).

To summarize, gender role socialization in our society prepares children for a world in which men are expected to be instrumental, conquering, controlling, and unemotional.

Gender role stereotypes Oversimplified and widely held beliefs about the basic characteristics of men and women.

Gender role socialization The process of learning gender behaviors considered appropriate for one's sex in a given culture.

Instrumental behaviors Actions directed toward the achievement of some goal.

Expressive behaviors Actions that express or communicate emotion or personal feelings.

(In males, a restricted ability to express emotion is one of the costs of adopting a masculine gender role, at least as it is defined in North America; see Module 44.) Women, in contrast, are expected to be expressive, emotional, passive, and dependent. Thus, gender role socialization teaches us to be highly competent in some respects and handicapped in others (Levant et al., 2009).

Gender Role Strain Of course, many people find traditional gender roles acceptable and comfortable. They may even enrich many lives. Others, however, may find traditional gender roles, especially gender role stereotypes, burdensome. If you are, for example, a fiercely independent woman or a deeply emotional man, you may experience **gender role strain**—stress associated with a conflict between your personal "reality" and the expectations associated with a gender role (Levant, 2011; Levant & Powell, 2017).

Take Alexander, for example. He is always being pressured to play hockey. His father played, his brothers play, and most of his male friends play, too. But Alex doesn't like the violence and secretly wants to become a chef. It bothers him that the family TV is always tuned to hockey. His brothers tease him all the time to "man up." Lately, he has been secretly watching cooking programs on his laptop. How should Alex deal with his gender role strain? Perhaps he would benefit most if he could set aside the more stereotyped aspects of gender roles. The next section explains why.

Androgyny—A Bit of Both

Learning Outcome 46.4 Define psychological androgyny and explain its advantages

Are you aggressive, ambitious, analytical, assertive, athletic, competitive, decisive, dominant, forceful, independent, individualistic, self-reliant, and willing to take risks? If so, you are quite "masculine." Are you affectionate, cheerful, childlike, compassionate, easily flattered, gentle, gullible, loyal, sensitive, shy, soft-spoken, sympathetic, tender, understanding, warm, and yielding? If so, then you are quite "feminine." What if you have traits from both lists? In that case, you may be *androgynous.*

The two lists that you just read are from the seminal work of psychologist Sandra Bem (1974). By combining 20 traditionally "masculine" traits (like self-reliant, assertive), 20 traditionally "feminine" traits (like affectionate, gentle), and 20 neutral traits (like truthful, friendly), Bem created the *Bem Sex Role Inventory* (BSRI). (Some psychologists prefer to use the term *sex role* instead of gender role.) Next, she and her associates gave the BSRI to thousands of people, asking them to say whether each trait applied to them. Of those surveyed, 50 percent fell into traditional feminine or masculine categories, 15 percent scored higher on traits of the opposite sex, and 35 percent were androgynous, getting high scores on both feminine and masculine items.

Psychological Androgyny

The word **androgyny** (an-DROJ-ih-nee) literally means "man-woman" and refers to having both masculine and feminine traits (Helgeson, 2012). Bem is convinced that our complex society requires flexibility with respect to gender roles. She believes that it is necessary for men to also be gentle, compassionate, sensitive, and yielding and for women to

bbernard/Shutterstock.com

Robert Kneschke/Shutterstock.com

Androgynous individuals adapt more easily to both traditionally "feminine" and "masculine" situations.

also be forceful, self-reliant, independent, and ambitious—*as the situation requires.* In short, Bem thinks that more people should feel free to be more androgynous.

Adaptability Bem has shown that androgynous individuals are more adaptable. They seem especially to be less hindered by images of "feminine" or "masculine" behavior. For example, in one study, people were given the choice of doing either a "masculine" activity (oil a hinge, nail boards together, and so forth) or a "feminine" activity (prepare a baby bottle, wind yarn into a ball, and so on). Masculine men and feminine women consistently chose to do gender-appropriate activities, even when the opposite choice paid more!

Bem has concluded that masculine males have great difficulty expressing warmth, playfulness, and concern—even when they are appropriate (Bem, 1975, 1981). Masculine men, it seems, tend to view such feelings as unacceptably "feminine." Masculine men also find it hard to accept emotional support from others, particularly women (Levant, 2003). They tend to be interested in sports, have mostly male friends, and dislike feminists.

Problems faced by highly feminine women are the reverse of those faced by masculine men. Such women have trouble being independent and assertive, even when these qualities are desirable. In contrast, more androgynous individuals are higher in emotional intelligence (see Module 40) (Dean & Tate, 2016).

The Whole Human Over the years, the concept of androgyny has been variously supported, attacked, and debated. Now, as the dust begins to settle, the picture looks like this: Having "masculine" traits primarily means that a person is independent and assertive. Scoring high in "masculinity," therefore, is related to high self-esteem and to success in many situations (Moksnes & Espnes, 2012). Having "feminine" traits primarily means that a person is nurturing and interpersonally oriented. People who score high in "femininity," therefore, are more likely to seek and receive social support. They tend to experience greater social closeness with others and more happiness in marriage (Rollero, Gattino, & De Piccoli, 2013).

In the final analysis, it is worth repeating that many people remain comfortable with traditional views of gender. Nevertheless, there are advantages to possessing both "feminine" and "masculine" traits (Dean & Tate, 2016; Lefkowitz & Zeldow, 2006). In general, androgynous persons are more flexible when it comes to coping with difficult situations; they can use both instrumental and emotionally expressive capacities to enhance their lives and relationships (see ➤ **Figure 46.2**). As a consequence, androgynous persons tend to experience less gender role strain and be more satisfied with their lives.

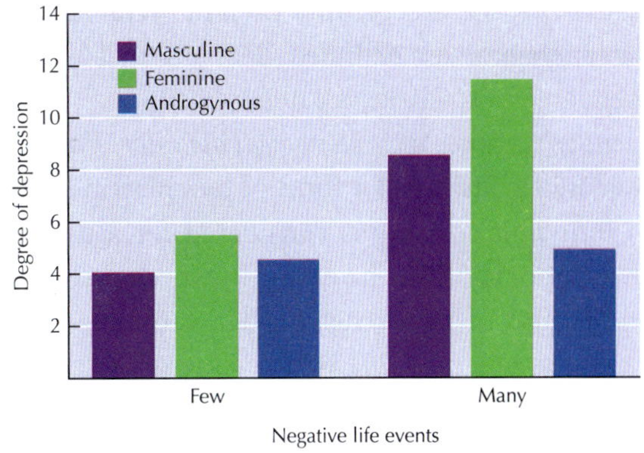

➤ **Figure 46.2**

Androgyny and stress. Another indication of the possible benefits of androgyny is found in a study of reactions to stress. When confronted with an onslaught of negative events, strongly masculine or feminine persons become more depressed than androgynous individuals do. (Adapted from Roos & Cohen, 1987.)

When Sex and Gender Do Not Match—The Binary Busters

Learning Outcome 46.5 Explain what it means for an individual to be transgender (gender variant)

As we have just learned, biological sex is not binary; it comes in shades of male and female. So, too, gender comes in shades of masculine and feminine. You will probably not be surprised, then, to learn that the relationship between sex and gender is also a rainbow of possibility (Carroll, 2016). By adulthood, most males turn out to be more or less masculine and most females turn out to be more or less feminine. At the same time, some males are quite feminine and some females are quite masculine. (Note: These variations in the relationship between sex and gender should *not* be confused with variations in sexual orientation. Many feminine men and masculine women are, nonetheless, thoroughly heterosexual.) And, like Chris Mosier, significant

Gender role strain Stress associated with any conflict between personal identity and the expectations associated with a gender role.

Androgyny The presence of both "masculine" and "feminine" traits in a single person (as masculinity and femininity are defined within one's culture).

numbers of people are **gender variant (transgender)**, in that their biological sex definitely does not match their preferred gender (Veale, Clarke, & Lomax, 2010).

Is gender variance a psychological disorder? Gender variance was once considered a form of psychiatric illness. Today, an individual usually is considered for a diagnosis of **gender dysphoria** only if he or she is experiencing extreme distress because of his or her gender variance (American Psychiatric Association, 2013). The emerging consensus is that it is better in the long run for transsexual individuals to accept who they are and for all of us to realize that some people do not neatly fit into the categories of male and female (Holmes, 2002).

In this way of thinking, the suffering of many transsexual individuals stems, not from their gender variance, but from the prejudice, hostility, and stigmatization of mainstream society. Gender-variant individuals deserve our understanding and support (Diamond, 2009; Meadow, 2011). When it comes to children, many parents try to encourage what they see as gender-appropriate behavior. Others wait and see if their children will grow into more gender-appropriate roles. Still others seek to accept and support their children's experiences. If there is a trend in the United States today, it is toward acceptance and support (Gray et al., 2016; Zeiler & Wickström, 2009).

When treatment is requested, it may include psychotherapy and, in more clear-cut cases, *sex reassignment surgery* (Imbimbo et al., 2009). Surgery can reconfigure the external appearance of the genitals while hormone treatments shift the chemical balance in the body, and a deliberate effort can be made to transform the person's sense of sexual identity. Adults who deliberately seek sex reassignment are generally happy with the results (Imbimbo et al., 2009).

Sex reassignment surgery is also becoming more common with children. Supporters of early sex assignment argue that the benefits usually outweigh the long-term psychological costs (Zeiler & Wickström, 2009). Others believe that it is better to wait until adulthood, when transsexual (and intersexual) individuals can choose for themselves whether or not to have surgery and whether to live as a man or a woman (Thyen et al., 2005).

Only time will tell which approach is more successful. Because sex and gender are complex, the best course of treatment will likely prove to be different for different people (Rathus, Nevid, & Fichner-Rathus, 2013).

Gender variant (transsexual) A condition in which a person's biological sex does not match his or her preferred gender.

Gender dysphoria Distress that may occur when gender identity does not match a person's physical sex.

MODULE 46

Sex and Gender—Learning Outcomes Revisited

46.1 List the four basic dimensions of biological sex and explain how hormones can influence sexual development prenatally and postnatally

Biological sex consists of genetic sex, gonadal sex, hormonal sex, and genital sex. Sexual development begins with genetic sex (*XX* or *XY* chromosomes) and is then influenced by prenatal hormones, particularly androgens (male sex hormones) and estrogens (female sex hormones). One type of androgen, testosterone, is needed for a male embryo to develop male structures such as a penis and testicles. Sexual development in utero may be atypical when hormones are not present at the usual levels, or when the embryo is not sensitive to those hormones. For example, androgen insensitivity syndrome, exposure to progestin, congenital adrenal hyperplasia, and similar problems may result in the development of an intersex individual. Postnatally, estrogens and androgens influence the development of different primary and secondary sexual characteristics in males and females.

46.2 Define four sexual orientations and outline their causes

Sexual orientation refers to one's degree of emotional and erotic attraction to members of the opposite sex, the same sex, both sexes, or neither sex. All four sexual orientations are part of the normal range of human variability. Sexual orientation tends to be stable over time even if sexual behaviors change. Similar factors (heredity, biology, and socialization) underlie all sexual orientations.

46.3 Define gender identity and outline the factors that influence it

Gender identity is the subjective sense of being male or female, irrespective of your biological sex. Many researchers believe that prenatal hormones exert a biological biasing effect that combines with social factors to influence gender identity. However, *gender role socialization* (that is, raising children to assume characteristics and roles that are seen as "appropriate" for their biological sex) seems to account for most observed female–male gender differences. For example, parents tend to encourage boys to behave instrumentally and girls to behave expressively behaviors. Unfortunately, gender role stereotypes often distort perceptions about the kinds of activities for which men and women are suited. Pressuring people to conform to gender stereotypes can create gender role strain.

46.4 Define psychological androgyny and explain its advantages

People who possess both masculine and feminine traits are androgynous. In our society, androgyny allows for greater adaptability to a range of situations. This flexibility is helpful in relationships and is related to greater life satisfaction.

46.5 Explain what it means for an individual to be transgender (gender variant)

Transgender, or gender-variant, individuals experience a persistent mismatch between their biological sex and their experienced gender.

Reflective Practice

Content Check

1. The four basic dimensions of biological sex are the following:

   ________, ________, ________, ________
2. All individuals normally produce both androgens and estrogens, although the proportions differ in females and males. T or F?
3. Whether a person has erotic fantasies about women or men is a strong indicator of his or her sexual orientation. T or F?
4. One's private sense of maleness or femaleness is referred to as ________ ________.
5. Traditional gender role socialization encourages ________ behavior in males.
   a. instrumental
   b. emotional
   c. expressive
   d. dependent
6. A person who is androgynous scores high on ratings of traits usually possessed by the opposite sex. T or F?

Skill Check

Think Critically

7. Could a person be androgynous in a culture where "masculine" and "feminine" traits differ greatly from those on Bem's list?

Self-Reflect

Which of your prior beliefs about sexual orientation are true? Which are false? As a child, do you think that you were encouraged to engage more in instrumental behaviors or expressive behaviors? Think of three people you know, one who is androgynous, one who is traditionally feminine, and one who is traditionally masculine. What advantages and disadvantages do you see in each collection of traits? Have you experienced gender role strain? How did you cope with it? In 2007, the American Medical Association changed its antidiscrimination policies to include transgender people. This means, for example, that doctors no longer can refuse medical treatment to transgender patients. Do you agree or disagree with this change?

ANSWERS

1. genetic sex, gonadal sex, hormonal sex, genital sex 2. T 3. T 4. gender identity 5. a 6. F 7. Yes. Being androgynous means having both masculine and feminine traits *as they are defined within one's culture.*

MODULE
47

Human Sexuality
The Human Sex Drive, Response, and Attitudes

Too Sexy?

Our sexuality is a natural part of being human; a powerful basic biological drive that underlies many of our intimate behaviors. Accordingly, we begin this module with a discussion of the human sex drive and typical patterns of sexual behavior, including the female and male sexual response.

Our sexuality is also shaped by our membership in various social groups and cultures; as shared attitudes change, so too does sexual behavior. Accordingly, we continue by exploring the explosion of sexual expressiveness in contemporary North American culture. From the ubiquitous presence of sex across the media to pornography of all types and from hook-up culture to kink, even young children are not immune. What messages, for example, do beauty pageants for children send to young girls?

Our sexuality is also a deep part of our individual identity and, hence, our intimate relationships; it is fundamentally a form of communication. We close this module, then, with some advice on how to foster sexual intimacy.

Marc Andrew Deley/Getty Images

~LEARNING OUTCOMES~

After reading this module you should be able to:

47.1 Contrast females and males in terms of their sexual response

47.2 Explain how sexual attitudes and behaviors have changed

47.3 Outline the factors that contribute to healthy sexual relationships

The Human Sex Drive and Sexual Response—Gotta Have It

Learning Outcome 47.1 Contrast females and males in terms of their sexual response

There is no question that the human **sex drive**—the strength of one's motivation to engage in sexual behavior—is extraordinarily powerful. Although it is modulated by factors such as cultural values, attitudes toward sex, and sexual experience, it is, in the end, a basic biological drive.

In lower animals, **castration** (surgical removal of the testicles or ovaries) tends to abolish sexual activity in *inexperienced* animals. In humans, the effects of male and female castration vary. At first, some people experience a loss of sex drive; in others, there is no change. (That's why castration of sex offenders does not necessarily curb their behavior.) However, after several years, almost all subjects report a decrease in sex drive unless they take hormone supplements.

The preceding observations have nothing to do with **sterilization** (surgery to make a man or woman infertile). The vast majority of women and men who choose surgical birth control (such as a tubal ligation or a vasectomy) do not lose interest in sex. If anything, they may become more sexually active when pregnancy is no longer a concern.

A capacity for sexual arousal is apparent at birth or soon after. One of the most basic sexual behaviors is **masturbation**—self-stimulation that causes sexual pleasure or orgasm. Self-stimulation has been observed in infants under 1 year of age. Researcher Alfred Kinsey even verified instances of orgasm in boys as young as 5 months old and girls as young as 4 months (Kinsey, Pomeroy, & Martin, 1948; Kinsey & Pomeroy, 1953). Kinsey also found that 2- to 5-year-old children spontaneously touch and exhibit their genitals. Although various sexual behaviors continue throughout childhood, the human sex drive normally doesn't "kick in" until the early teens. That's when the hormonal changes of *puberty* promote rapid physical growth and sexual maturity (see Module 15).

As discussed in Module 43, a male's sex drive is related to the amount of androgens (especially testosterone) supplied by the testes (Crooks & Baur, 2017). The connection can be very direct: When a man chats with a woman he finds attractive, his testosterone levels actually increase (Roney, 2003). While the sex drive in females is related to estrogen levels, testosterone also plays a role (Freberg, 2021). A woman's sex drive is closely related to the testosterone level in her bloodstream. Of course, women produce much smaller amounts of testosterone than men. But that doesn't mean their sex drive is weaker. Women's bodies are more sensitive to testosterone, and their sex drive is comparable to males.

One way to gauge the strength of the human sex drive is to chart its expression as sexual behavior. As you can see, many sexually mature men and women are sexually active at every age (see ➤ Figure 47.1).

What about masturbation? As ➤ Figure 47.2 shows, masturbation is also a regular feature of the sex lives of many people. Masturbation is an important part of the psychosexual development of most adolescents. Among other things, it provides a healthy substitute for sexual involvement at a time when young people are maturing emotionally. Approximately 70 percent of married women and men masturbate at least occasionally. Generally speaking, masturbation is valid at any age and usually has no effect on marital relationships (Herbenick et al., 2010b). Contrary to popular myths, people are not always compelled to masturbate because they lack a sexual partner (Kott, 2011). Masturbation is often just "one more item on the menu" for people with active sex lives.

Does alcohol increase the sex drive? In general, no. Alcohol is a *depressant*. As such, in small doses, it may stimulate erotic desire by lowering inhibitions. This effect no doubt

Sex drive The strength of one's motivation to engage in sexual behavior.

Castration Surgical removal of the testicles or ovaries.

Sterilization Medical procedures such as vasectomy or tubal ligation that make a man or a woman infertile.

Masturbation Producing sexual pleasure or orgasm by directly stimulating the genitals on your own body.

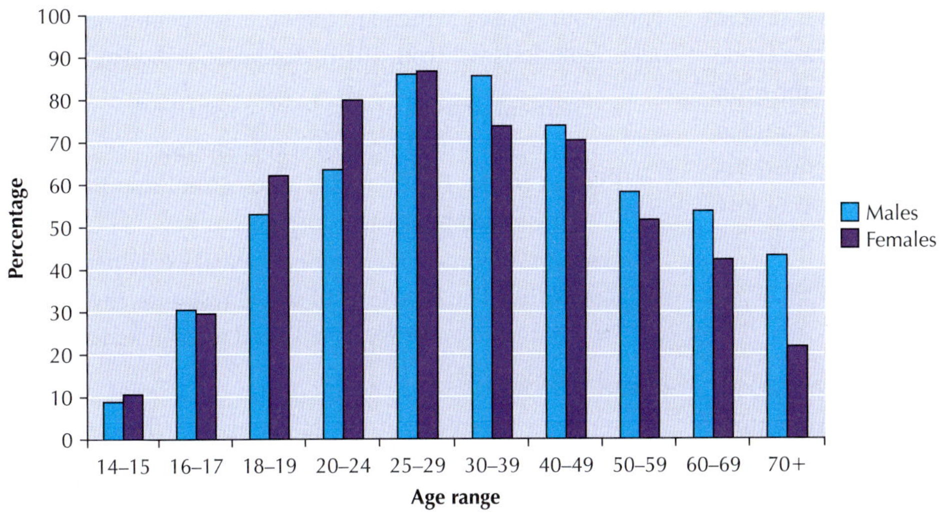

➤ **Figure 47.1**

Sexual intercourse across age. Percentage of men and women of various ages who experienced vaginal intercourse during the last month. Although percentages decline beginning as adults enter their forties, significant percentages of older people remain sexually active. (Data adapted from Herbenick et al., 2010a.)

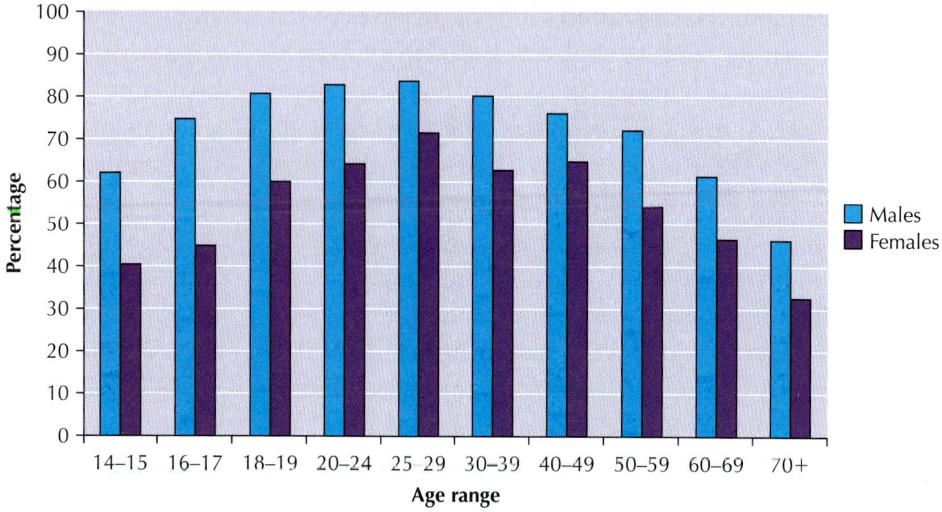

➤ **Figure 47.2**

Masturbation across age. Percentage of women and men of various ages who masturbated alone during the last year. (Data adapted from Herbenick et al., 2010a.)

accounts for alcohol's reputation as an aid to seduction. (Humorist Ogden Nash once summarized this bit of folklore by saying "Candy is dandy, but liquor is quicker.") However, in larger doses, alcohol suppresses orgasm in women and erection in men. Getting drunk *decreases* sexual desire, arousal, pleasure, and performance (Sobczak, 2009).

Numerous other drugs are reputed to be *aphrodisiacs* (af-ruh-DEEZ-ee-aks), substances that increase sexual desire or pleasure. However, like alcohol, many other drugs do not enhance and may even actually impair sexual response (McKay, 2005; Shamloul, 2010). Some examples are amphetamines, amyl nitrite, barbiturates, cocaine, MDMA, lysergic acid diethylamide (LSD), and cannabis. (It is worth noting that, around the world, many substances are believed to be aphrodisiacs, such as oysters, chocolate, powdered rhinoceros' horn, and so on. In general, these are, at best, superstitions that might produce a placebo effect.) In the end, love is the best aphrodisiac (Crooks & Baur, 2017).

What happens to the sex drive in old age? A natural decline in sex drive typically accompanies aging. This is related to a reduced output of sex hormones, especially testosterone (Carroll, 2016). However, sexual activity need not come to an end. Some people in their eighties and nineties continue to have active sex lives. The crucial factor for an extended sex life appears to be regularity and opportunity. ("Use it or lose it.") In some instances, taking testosterone supplements can restore the sex drive in both men and women (Freberg, 2021).

Human Sexual Response

Human sexual arousal is complex. It may, of course, be produced by direct stimulation of the body's **erogenous zones** (eh-ROJ-eh-nus), which means "productive of pleasure or erotic desire." Human erogenous zones include the genitals, mouth, breasts, ears, anus, and, to a lesser degree, the entire surface of the body. It is clear, however, that more than physical contact is involved: A urological or gynecological exam rarely results in any sexual arousal. Likewise, an unwanted sexual advance may produce only revulsion. Human sexual arousal obviously includes a large mental element.

The pioneering work of gynecologist William Masters and psychologist Virginia Johnson greatly expanded our understanding of sexual responses, regardless of how they are triggered (Masters & Johnson, 1966, 1970). In a series of experiments, interviews, and controlled observations, Masters and Johnson directly studied sexual intercourse and masturbation in nearly 700 males and females. This objective information has given us a much clearer picture of human sexuality.

According to Masters and Johnson, sexual response can be divided into four phases: (1) *excitement,* (2) *plateau,* (3) *orgasm,* and (4) *resolution* (➤ **Figures 47.3** and **47.4**). These four phases, which are the same for people of all sexual orientations (Carroll, 2016), can be described as follows:

Excitement phase The first level of sexual response, indicated by initial signs of sexual arousal

Plateau phase The second level of sexual response, during which physical arousal intensifies

Orgasm A climax and release of sexual excitement

Resolution The final level of sexual response, involving a return to lower levels of sexual tension and arousal

Female Response In women, the excitement phase is marked by a complex pattern of changes in the body. The vagina is prepared for intercourse, the nipples become erect, pulse rate rises, and the skin may become flushed or

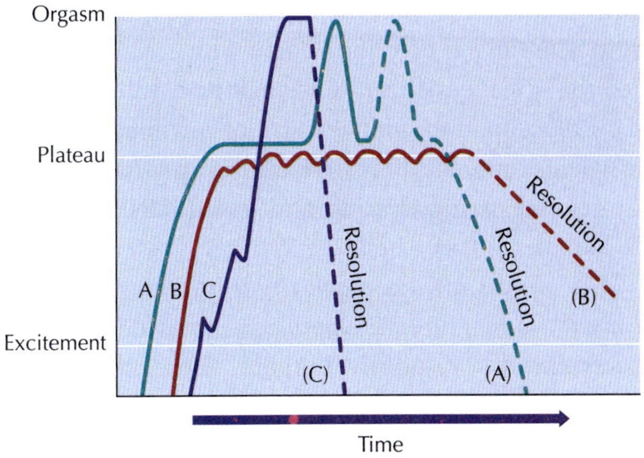

➤ **Figure 47.3**

Female sexual response cycle. The green line shows that sexual arousal rises through the excitement phase and levels off for a time during the plateau phase. Arousal peaks during orgasm and then returns to pre-excitement levels. In pattern A, arousal rises from excitement through the plateau phase and peaks in orgasm. Resolution may be immediate, or it may first include a return to the plateau phase and a second orgasm (dotted line). In pattern B, arousal is sustained at the plateau phase and slowly resolved without sexual climax. Pattern C shows a fairly rapid rise in arousal to orgasm. Little time is spent in the plateau phase, and resolution is fairly rapid. (Adapted from Carroll, 2016.)

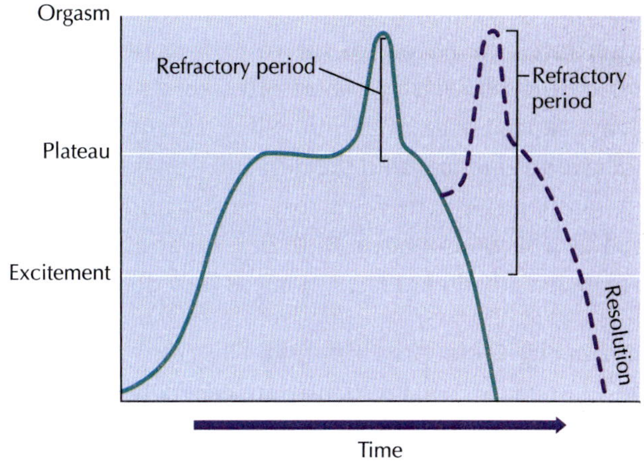

➤ **Figure 47.4**

Male sexual response cycle. The green line shows that sexual arousal rises through the excitement phase and levels off for a time during the plateau phase. Arousal peaks during orgasm and then returns to pre-excitement levels. During the refractory period, immediately after orgasm, a second sexual climax is typically impossible. However, after the refractory period has passed, there may be a return to the plateau phase, followed by a second orgasm (dotted line). (Adapted from Carroll, 2016.)

reddened. When sexual stimulation ends, the excitement phase gradually subsides. If a woman moves into the plateau phase, physical changes and subjective feelings of arousal become more intense. Sexual arousal that ends during this phase tends to ebb more slowly, which may produce considerable frustration. Occasionally, women skip the plateau phase (see Figure 47.3). For some women, this is almost always the case.

During orgasm, 3 to 10 muscular contractions of the vagina, uterus, and related structures discharge sexual tension. Orgasm is usually followed by resolution, a return to lower levels of sexual tension and arousal. After orgasm, about 15 percent of all women return to the plateau phase and may have one or more additional orgasms (Mah & Binik, 2001).

Before the work of Masters and Johnson, theorists debated whether "vaginal orgasms" are different from those derived from stimulation of the clitoris, a small, sensitive organ located above the vaginal opening. Sigmund Freud claimed that a "clitoral orgasm" is an "immature" form of female response. Because the clitoris is the female structure comparable to the penis, Freud believed that women who experienced clitoral orgasms had not fully accepted their femininity.

Masters and Johnson exploded the Freudian myth by showing that physical responses are the same no matter how an orgasm is produced (Carroll, 2016; Mah & Binik, 2001). As a matter of fact, the inner two-thirds of the vagina is relatively insensitive to touch. Most sensations during intercourse come from stimulation of the clitoris and other external areas. For most women, the clitoris is an important source of pleasurable sensations. Apparently, sensations from many sources are fused into the total experience of orgasm. Thus, to downgrade the "clitoral orgasm" ignores basic female biology (Prause, 2012).

Male Response Sexual arousal in the male is signaled by erection of the penis during the excitement phase. A rise in heart rate, increased blood flow to the genitals, enlargement of the testicles, erection of the nipples, and numerous other body changes also occur. As is true of female sexual response, continued stimulation moves the male into the plateau phase. Again, physical changes and subjective feelings of arousal become more intense. Further stimulation during the plateau phase brings about a reflex release of sexual tension, resulting in orgasm.

Erogenous zones Areas of the body that produce pleasure, provoke erotic desire, or both.

Excitement phase The first phase of sexual response, indicated by initial signs of sexual arousal.

Plateau phase The second phase of sexual response, during which physical arousal is further heightened.

Orgasm A climax and release of sexual excitement.

Resolution (in sexual response) The fourth phase of sexual response, involving a return to lower levels of sexual tension and arousal.

In the mature male, orgasm is usually accompanied by **ejaculation**—the release of sperm and seminal fluid. Afterward, it is followed by a short **refractory period**, during which a second orgasm is impossible. (Many men cannot even have an erection until the refractory phase has passed.) Only rarely is the male refractory period immediately followed by a second orgasm. Both orgasm and resolution in the male usually do not last as long as they do for females.

Comparing Male and Female Responses Although male and female sexual responses are generally quite similar, the differences that do exist can affect sexual compatibility. For example, women typically go through the sexual phases more slowly than do men. During lovemaking, 10 to 20 minutes are often required for a woman to go from excitement to orgasm. Males may experience all four stages in as little as 3 minutes. However, there is much variation, especially in women. (Note that these times refer only to intercourse, not to an entire arousal sequence.) Such differences should be kept in mind by couples seeking sexual compatibility (Carroll, 2016).

Does that mean that a couple should try to time lovemaking to promote simultaneous orgasm? Simultaneous orgasm (both partners reaching sexual climax at the same time) can undoubtedly be satisfying (Brody & Weiss, 2011). But it is usually a mistake to make it the "goal" of lovemaking because "failure" may reduce sexual enjoyment. It is more advisable for couples to seek mutual satisfaction through a combination of intercourse and erotic touching *(foreplay)* than it is to inhibit spontaneity, communication, and pleasure.

Does the slower female response just described mean that women are less sexual than men? Definitely not. During masturbation, 70 percent of females reach orgasm in 4 minutes or less. This casts serious doubt on the idea that women respond more slowly. Slower female response during intercourse probably occurs because stimulation to the clitoris is less direct. It might be said that men simply provide too little stimulation for more rapid female response, not that women are in any way inferior.

Does penis size affect female response? Contrary to popular belief, there is no relationship between penis size and male sexual potency. Think about it. If a woman's sexual satisfaction is related to her partner's attention to clitoral stimulation and foreplay, then why would his penis length matter? Besides, Masters and Johnson found that the vagina adjusts to the size of the penis and that subjective feelings of pleasure and intensity of orgasm are not related to penis size. They also found that although individual differences exist in flaccid penis size, there tends to be much less variation in size during erection. That's why erection has been called the "great equalizer." Lovemaking involves the entire body. Preoccupation with the size of a woman's breasts, a man's penis, and the like are based on myths that undermine genuine caring, sharing, and sexual satisfaction (Hyde & DeLamater, 2014).

Men almost always reach orgasm during intercourse, but many women do not. Doesn't this indicate that women are less sexually responsive? Again, the evidence argues against any lack of female sexual responsiveness. It is true that about one woman in three does not experience orgasm during the first year of marriage, and only about 30 percent regularly reach orgasm through intercourse alone. However, this does not imply lack of physical responsiveness, because 90 percent of all women reach orgasm when masturbating (Conley et al., 2011). However, women tend to place more emphasis on emotional closeness with a lover than men (Peplau, 2003). Many women also want to be active partners in lovemaking, and they want their needs and preferences to be acknowledged (Benjamin & Tlusten, 2010).

In another regard, women are clearly more responsive. Only about 5 percent of males are capable of multiple orgasms (and then only after an unavoidable refractory period). Most men are limited to a second orgasm at best. In contrast, Masters and Johnson's findings suggest that most women who regularly experience orgasm are capable of multiple orgasms (Herbenick et al., 2010a). Remember though, that only about 15 percent regularly have multiple orgasms. A woman should not automatically assume that something is wrong if she isn't orgasmic or multiorgasmic. Many women have satisfying sexual experiences even when orgasm is not involved (Komisaruk, Beyer-Flores, & Whipple, 2006; Zietsch et al., 2011).

Regardless, male and female sexual patterns are rapidly becoming more alike. ➤ **Figure 47.5** presents some of the data on sexual behavior from a major national health survey of American men and women ages 25–44. As you can see, in any given year, men and women do not differ in their average number of opposite-sex partners or in their overall pattern of sexual activity (Mosher, Chandra, & Jones, 2005). Exaggerating the differences between male and female sexuality is not only inaccurate, it can also create artificial barriers to sexual satisfaction (Conley et al., 2011; Wiederman, 2001). For example, assuming that men should always initiate sex denies the fact that women have comparable sexual interests and needs.

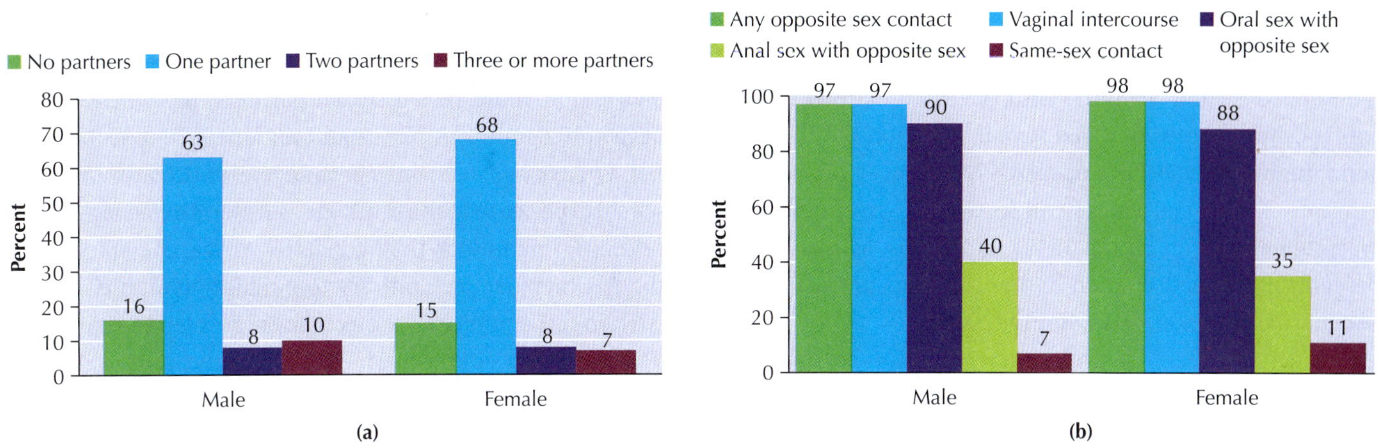

➤ **Figure 47.5**

Pattern of sexual behavior of American adults. Men and women do not differ (*a*) in their average number of sexual partners or (*b*) in their overall pattern of sexual activity. (Adapted from Mosher, Chandra, & Jones 2005).

Contemporary Sexual Attitudes and Behavior—Anything Goes?

Learning Outcome 47.2 Explain how sexual attitudes and behaviors have changed

In 1934, Cole Porter's musical, *Anything Goes,* opened on Broadway. The lyrics of the title song started like this "In olden days, a glimpse of stocking was looked on as something shocking, now heaven knows, anything goes." Porter was announcing a sexual revolution. The openness of the 1930s would indeed have shocked a person from the Victorian era. And yet the revolution didn't stop there. If a woman and a man living in the year 1934 could be transported to the present, they would, in turn, be stunned by today's North American sexual values and practices. Unmarried couples (or anyone, for that matter) having explicit sex on television; advertisements for provocative undergarments, tampons, and cures for "jock itch"; near-nudity at the beach; sexually explicit movies, hook-up culture, and, of course, the wide-open Internet—these and many other elements of contemporary culture would shock someone who was an adult in 1934.

HBO/Photofest

Even just 40 years ago, sexual portrayals in television programs seldom ventured beyond tame, gossipy melodramas. Today, series such as *Game of Thrones* and *Westworld* (shown here) frequently feature bluntly explicit sex and even sexual violence.

Has there been a "sexual revolution"? The word *revolution* suggests rapid change. Perhaps the safest conclusion is that *attitudes* toward sexuality have, indeed, undergone a revolution. For example, in a 1959 Roper poll, 88 percent of those interviewed agreed that premarital sex is wrong. By 2013, more than 70 percent of young men and women approved of premarital sex (Wilke & Saad, 2013). Similar shifts have occurred in attitudes toward homosexuality, sex education, having a baby outside of marriage, and related issues.

Contemporary Sexual Behavior

Have changing attitudes been translated into behavior? It appears that changes in sexual behavior have paralleled changes in attitudes, only more slowly and less dramatically. On the one hand, a look at social changes in the United States

Ejaculation The release of sperm and seminal fluid by the male at the time of orgasm.

Refractory period A short period after orgasm during which males are unable to again reach orgasm.

during the 1960s and early 1970s makes it clear that some fundamental alterations occurred in a relatively short time. Liberalized sexual attitudes and access to effective birth control significantly changed sexual behavior. On the other hand, many changes have occurred over longer periods. For example, traditional values call for female virginity before marriage. Yet, even by the 1940s and 1950s, as many as 75 percent of married women had engaged in premarital sex (Regnerus & Uecker, 2011; Smith, 2006).

Generally, there is greater *tolerance* for sexual activity, especially that *engaged in by others*. For example, a 1970s magazine poll found that 80 percent of all readers considered extramarital sex acceptable under some circumstances (Athenasiou, Shaver, & Tavris, 1970). But another poll found that, in practice, only about 30 percent of married persons actually had extramarital sexual experience (Rubenstein & Tavris, 1987). These are older studies, but the percentages have not changed greatly over the last 50 years (Mark, Janssen, & Milhausen, 2011). More importantly, faithfulness in marriage remains a widely shared value. In any given year, only about 4 percent of married people have sex partners other than their spouse. Americans actually seem to live up to the norm of marital fidelity quite well (Mosher, Chandra, & Jones, 2005).

Another interesting trend is the fact that people today spend as much of their adult lives (on average) alone as they do in marriage. As a result, many people are involved in nonmarried sexual relationships (Lau, 2012). This tends to increase the number of sexual partners that adults encounter. Men now report having an average of seven female sexual partners in their lifetimes, while women report four. Further, in any given year, about 17 percent of men (and 10 percent of women) reported having two or more sexual partners (Fryar et al., 2007).

All in all, there is ample evidence that sexual behavior in the United States has generally increased in the last 60 years. Although this trend has brought problems, it does not seem to represent a wholesale move toward sexual promiscuity. Even premarital intercourse does not appear to represent a major rejection of traditional values and responsible behavior. The connection between sexuality and love or affection remains strong for most people. Both premarital sex and cohabitation are still widely viewed as preludes to marriage or as temporary substitutes for it. Likewise, other changes in attitudes and behavior appear to reflect a greater acceptance of sexuality rather than a total rejection of earlier values (Crooks & Baur, 2017).

What about the rest of the world? A survey of 59 nations found that a "sexual revolution" has not occurred in most other countries (Wellings et al., 2006). People from the United States and other industrialized nations are more likely to have had two or more recent sexual partners; most people from developing countries have had only one recent sexual partner. On average, teenagers around the world have their first sexual experience at the same age as American teenagers. One finding of particular note concerns Africa, the epicenter of the AIDS epidemic. Contrary to popular opinion elsewhere, Africans are not promiscuous. They report fewer sexual partners than their counterparts in developed countries. Instead, it's likely that high rates of venereal disease in Africa result from a lack of knowledge and access to condoms.

Sex Among the Young

More recent studies of sexuality among American teenagers and young adults are consistent with our earlier conclusion that changes in attitudes and behavior reflect a greater acceptance of sexuality rather than a total rejection of earlier values. More than the "oldies" among us, younger people today are *grappling* with sexual openness. In some ways, it seems as if they are more liberal than ever; in other ways it appears that a conservative counter-movement is gathering steam. Let's look at several examples.

Casual Sex On the one hand, young people today are growing more conservative when it comes to engaging in sexual intercourse at a young age. The social upheaval that began in the 1960s led to an especially sharp rise in sexual activity among teenagers. This increase continued into the 1980s but has begun to reverse in recent years. In 1988, 60 percent of teenage males and 51 percent of teenage females had intercourse by age 19. By 2015, the rates had dropped to 43 percent for teenage males and 39 percent for teenage females. The drop is especially pronounced among younger teens (Centers for Disease Control, 2014c). It has also been accompanied by higher rates of contraceptive use and declining rates of teen pregnancy and abortion (Kost & Maddow-Zimet, 2016). By 2017, the rate of teen births reached a historic low (Centers for Disease Control, 2020e). [Nevertheless, the United States still has the highest teenage pregnancy rates among all industrialized nations (Kearney & Levine, 2012).] Apparently, as young people learn more about their sexuality, they become more likely to *delay* the age at which they first engage in sexual intercourse (Ballonoff & Brindis, 2014; Kohler, Manhart, & Lafferty, 2008).

On the other hand, younger Americans nevertheless continue to shift toward more liberal *sexual scripts* favoring casual sex (Lyons et al., 2013; Stephens, 2012; Wentland &

Reissing, 2011). A **sexual script** is a mental plan that guides sexual behavior. Such scripts influence when and where we are likely to express sexual feelings and with whom (McCormick, 2010; Ryan, 2011). They provide a "plot" for the order of events in lovemaking and they outline "approved" actions, motives, and outcomes.

According to one survey, more than half of all college students have followed a *friends with benefits* script to have sex without romantic involvement (Mongeau et al., 2013). Also common and even more casual is the *hook-up* script, in which two people having sex are more-or-less strangers (Bradshaw, Kahn, & Saville, 2010; Holman & Sillars, 2012). In contrast, traditional sexual scripts stress courtship, romance, and marriage. Sex in such relationships might be premarital, but it is still romantic (Roese et al., 2006).

As casual sexual scripts become more common, the traditional focus on intercourse is fading in favor of oral sex, which tends to be seen as less risky, more acceptable, and "not a big deal." Casual sexual scripts also are spreading to younger children. One study found that 20 percent of American ninth graders have already had oral sex and more than 30 percent intend to try it soon (Halpern-Felsher et al., 2005).

Casual sex is often viewed as easier than facing the challenges of romantic attachment and finding a lifelong partner. However, it is not without its own risks. Casual sex is usually associated with alcohol use and unsafe sexual behaviors, such as unprotected sex (Fortunato et al., 2010). Although oral sex is safer than intercourse, a significant chance of getting a sexually transmitted disease (STD) remains (Boskey, 2020). Another downside of casual sex is the letdown that can occur when one person follows a romantic script and the other follows a casual script ("He [or she] is just not that into you"). Psychological distress is also often involved (Bersamin et al., 2014). For example, young women who are having casual sex are more likely to be depressed (Grello, Welsh, & Harper, 2006).

On balance, adolescents and young adults have always engaged in experimentation and exploration. Most young people emerge unscathed if they clearly understand that their encounters are casual and if they practice safe sex. Most eventually also "graduate" to a more traditional search for love.

Internet Pornography One element of the sexual revolution about which there can be little doubt is the spread of pornography via the Internet. With the liberalization of sexual attitudes has come a glut of free pornography, always just a few clicks away. As a consequence, it is getting harder and harder (no giggling, now!) to find individuals who haven't at least taken a curious peek, as public attitudes toward porn have become more accepting (Carroll, 2016).

On the one hand, there is little reason to be concerned about spicing up a relationship with some occasional auditory/visual stimulation. Women, for example, are more likely than men to view porn with a husband or friend. On the other hand, porn use can become problematic (Wright et al., 2017). Men are more likely to view porn alone while masturbating, sometimes compulsively (Galatzer-Levy, 2012; Hald, Seaman, & Linz, 2014). Today, some 25 percent of young men worry about their porn use, and some are seeking therapy (Spenhoff et al., 2013; Woods, 2013).

What's the big deal? As one young man, Armando, put it, after the failure of two relationships, "It really messes up your mind for what sex is actually supposed to be. . . . It sets the hopes too high for normal men and women to be able to perform at that level. I believe that's causing a lot of relationship problems among my peers" (McMahon, 2014).

One way to think about porn is as a **supernormal stimulus**, which is more potent than the natural stimuli we have evolved to encounter (Ward, 2013). Idealized women and men, along with their idealized sexual encounters, may well be the processed sugar or crack cocaine of sex. In other words, porn can be so exciting that normal sex seems to pale by comparison. With excessive use, desensitization sets in. What starts out as a curiosity can, over time, become a compulsion (Griffiths, 2012).

Ollyy/Shutterstock.com

Is too much access to online pornography a problem? What do you think?

Sexual script An unspoken mental plan that defines a "plot," dialogue, and actions expected to take place in a sexual encounter.

Supernormal stimulus Any stimulus (often artificial) that is more potent than the natural stimuli that we have evolved to encounter.

Like it or not, Internet porn is here to stay. So what's a young man to do? Fortunately, many young men have already begun to address the problem themselves. Armando, for example, has joined NoFap ("fapping" is a slang term for masturbating). This online support group has helped him quit viewing porn and slowly get back to healthier relationships with real, flesh-and-blood women (McMahon, 2014).

Sexual Freedom Another major change that has occurred in sexual behavior is the growing rejection of the **double standard**, the use of different rules to judge the appropriateness of male and female sexual behavior. In the past, for example, males were largely forgiven for engaging in premarital sex. Young males who "sowed some wild oats" were widely tolerated. In fact, many were tacitly encouraged to seek casual sex as a step toward manhood. On the other hand, women who were sexually active before marriage ran the risk of being labeled "easy," "bad," or "promiscuous."

On the one hand, the ability of women (and men) more freely to express their sexuality is another positive side of changing sexual attitudes and values. As the gap between female and male sexual patterns continues to close, it is increasingly likely that an end to the double standard is in sight (Kreager & Staff, 2009; Sakaluk & Milhausen, 2012; Schleicher & Gilbert, 2005).

On the other hand, liberalized attitudes can lead to individuals feeling pressured into sexual behavior (Judson, Johnson, & Perez, 2013). Greater sexual freedom is a positive development only for those ready for it (Hatch, 2011). There is, for example, a growing recognition that young girls are being oversexualized by influences such as beauty pageants for very young girls, the stage antics of female singers such as Miley Cyrus and Nicki Minaj, and the availability of consumer goods such as padded bras for girls as young as six (Durham, 2009; Lerum & Dworkin, 2009).

Pressures to engage in sexual behaviors probably come as much from the individual as from others. Regardless, for a greater acceptance of sexuality to be constructive, people must feel that they have the right to say no, as well as the right to choose when, where, how, and with whom they will express their sexuality. As is true elsewhere, freedom must be combined with responsibility, commitment, and caring if it is to have meaning. According to the American Psychological Association (2010), unhealthy sexualization can be distinguished from healthy sexuality when one or more of the following conditions occur:

- A person is valued solely due to sexual appearance or behavior, not other characteristics.
- A person is led to narrowly equate sexual attractiveness with being "sexy."
- A person is objectified sexually (treated as an object for the gratification of other people).
- A person is inappropriately used in a sexual way by another person.

From media images to popular fashions, young girls are more likely to be oversexualized than are young boys (Roberts & Zurbriggen, 2013). Oversexualization leads young girls to see themselves as having value only as sexual objects. This results in low self-esteem, eating disorders, depression, and feelings of shame (Ward, 2004). Some studies have even shown that sexualized girls perform more poorly on intellectual activities (Hebl, King, & Lin, 2004). Most worrisome is an increasing tendency for young girls to engage in risky sexual behaviors, such as unprotected oral sex (Atwood, 2006; Hatch, 2011).

According to the American Psychological Association (2010), parents, educators, and others should encourage young girls to develop relationships based on their personalities and interests, rather than on how they look.

Looking to the Future It is unlikely that the United States will undergo a wholesale return to less sexual openness any time soon. Young people are actively engaged in "working out" what increased sexual openness, particularly for women, means to them. The emerging consensus appears to be that, while "normal" sexual behavior is defined differently by various cultures, adults typically engage in a wide variety of sexual behaviors. Apart from evolving cultural norms, it can be said that any sexual act in which consenting adults engage is "normal" if it does not hurt anyone. However, coercive and/or compulsive sexual behaviors are emotionally unhealthy. Only time will tell.

Satisfying Relationships—Keeping It Hot

Learning Outcome 47.3 Outline the factors that contribute to healthy sexual relationships

No matter the age, sex, gender, or sexual orientation, intimate sexual relationships are important parts of most people's lives. While new lovers might assume their passion will burn brightly forever, most couples find that their sexual interest and passion decline over time (Impett et al., 2008, 2010).

Is a loss of sexual interest inevitable in relationships? No. But nurturing passion does take effort, plus a willingness to resolve other types of problems in a relationship (Strong, DeVault, & Cohen, 2011). For example, conflict or anger about other issues frequently takes a toll on sexual adjustment. Conversely, couples who share positive experiences and satisfying relationships also tend to have satisfying sex lives (Algoe, Gable, & Maisel, 2010). Sex is not a performance or a skill to be mastered like playing tennis. It is a form of communication within a relationship. Couples with strong and caring relationships can usually remain passionate (Impett et al., 2010; Joel et al., 2013). Conversely, a couple with a satisfactory sex life but a poor relationship rarely stays together for long.

Bridges to Sexual Satisfaction

When disagreements arise over issues such as frequency of lovemaking, who initiates lovemaking, or what behavior is appropriate, the rule should be, "Each partner must accept the other as the final authority on his or her own feelings." Partners are urged to give feedback about their feelings by following what therapists call the "touch and ask" rule: Touching and caressing should often be followed by questions such as, "Does that feel good?," "Do you like that?," and so forth. Satisfying erotic relationships focus on enhancing sexual pleasure for both partners, not on selfish interest in one's own gratification (Carroll, 2016; Strong, DeVault, & Cohen, 2011).

When problems do arise, partners are urged to be *responsive* to each other's needs at an *emotional* level and to recognize that all sexual problems are *mutual*. "Failures" should always be shared without placing blame. It is particularly important to avoid the "numbers game"—that is, couples should avoid being influenced by statistics on the average frequency of lovemaking, by stereotypes about sexual potency, and by the media. It is especially important not to be overly influenced by the superhuman sexual exploits portrayed in pornographic media.

According to sex therapist Barry McCarthy, four elements are necessary for a continuing healthy sexual relationship:

- **Sexual anticipation.** Looking forward to lovemaking can be inhibited by routine and poor communication between partners. It is wise for busy couples to set aside time to spend together. Unexpected, spontaneous lovemaking should also be encouraged.
- **Valuing one's sexuality.** This is most likely to occur when you develop a respectful, trusting, and intimate relationship with your partner. Such relationships allow both partners to deal with negative sexual experiences when they occur.
- **Believing that you deserve sexual pleasure.** As previously noted, the essence of satisfying lovemaking is the giving and receiving of pleasure.
- **Valuing intimacy.** A sense of closeness and intimacy with one's partner helps maintain sexual desire, especially in long-term relationships (McCarthy, 1995; McCarthy & Fucito, 2005).

Intimacy and Communication

Are there any other guidelines for maintaining a healthy relationship? A study that compared happy couples with unhappy couples found that, in almost every regard, the happy couples showed superior *communication* skills.

If you really want a good relationship, you can foster intimacy and communication by doing the following (Driver & Gottman, 2004; Gottman & Krokoff, 1989; Haas et al., 2007; Joel et al., 2013):

- **Be open about feelings.** Always be ready to talk with your partner. Happy couples not only talk more, they also convey more personal feelings and show greater sensitivity to their partners' feelings. Persistent negative feelings especially need to be expressed. Avoid *gunnysacking*—saving up feelings and complaints to use as ammunition in a fight. Gunnysacking is very destructive to a relationship.

Syda Productions/Shutterstock.com

Good communication leads to good sex; poor communication leads to . . .

Double standard (in sexual behavior) Applying different standards for judging the appropriateness of male and female sexual behavior.

- **Don't be defensive.** Own your s--t. Get comfortable with saying, "I'm sorry" when it's your fault. Whenever possible, expressions of negative feelings should be given as statements of one's own feelings, not as statements of blame. It is far more constructive to say, "It makes me angry when you leave things around the house," than it is to say, "You're a slob!" Remember, too, that if you use the words *always* or *never*, you are probably mounting a character attack.
- **Don't be a "right fighter."** Constructive fights are aimed at resolving shared differences, not at establishing who is right or wrong, superior or inferior. As television's Dr. Phil likes to say, "How's that working for you?"
- **Recognize that constructive anger is appropriate.** A fight is a fight. As is the case with any other emotion in a relationship, anger should be expressed. However, it should be expressed constructively by sticking to the real issues. Destructive anger, such as "hitting below the belt" or resorting to threats, such as announcing, "This relationship is over," is damaging to relationships.
- **Try to see things through your partner's eyes.** Marital harmony is closely related to the ability to put yourself in another person's place. When a conflict arises, always pause and try to take your partner's perspective. Seeing things through your partner's eyes can be a good reminder that no one is ever totally right or wrong in a personal dispute.
- **Don't be a mind-reader.** The preceding suggestion should not be taken as an invitation to engage in mind-reading. Assuming that you know what your partner is thinking or feeling can muddle or block communication. Hostile or accusatory mind-reading, as in the following examples, can be very disruptive: "You're just looking for an excuse to criticize me, aren't you?," "You don't really want my mother to visit, or you wouldn't say that." Rather than *telling* your partner what she or he thinks, *ask* her or him.

If it seems to you that following these guidelines requires expending some serious energy, you are right. Falling in love may be as easy as falling off a log but staying in love is well worth the effort.

MODULE 47 The Human Sex Drive, Response, and Attitudes—Learning Outcomes Revisited

47.1 Contrast females and males in terms of their sexual response

Sex is a powerful biological motive that finds expression in both men and women through various sexual behaviors, such as masturbation and intercourse. The similarities between female and male sexual responses and behaviors far outweigh the differences. For example, sexual arousal for both sexes is related to the body's erogenous zones, but mental and emotional reactions are the ultimate source of sexual responsiveness. In addition, the sexual response of both men and women can be divided into four phases: excitement, plateau, orgasm, and resolution, though women move through the stages more slowly than men. Finally, men and women are similar in the average number of partners they have, and in their overall pattern of sexual activity. The frequency of sexual behavior gradually declines for both sexes with increasing age. However, many elderly persons remain sexually active, and large variations exist at all ages.

47.2 Explain how sexual attitudes and behaviors have changed

Research suggests that people's attitudes about sex, including premarital sex, have become more tolerant. There is less of a double standard around the sexual behaviors of men and women, and people now report having more sexual partners. Young people, in particular, are more likely now than in the past to engage in casual sex. People have greater access to pornography through online websites. More liberal attitudes and behaviors related to sex mean that people increasingly must deal with sexually transmitted diseases such as HIV. Other industrialized nations have followed the same pattern while the developing nations remain more conservative.

47.3 Outline the factors that contribute to healthy sexual relationships

Although solutions exist for many sexual adjustment problems, good communication and a healthy relationship are the real keys to sexual satisfaction. This includes being honest about your feelings, avoiding defensiveness, arguing constructively, trying to take your partner's perspective, and avoiding the tendency to know what your partner is thinking or feeling if you haven't asked.

Reflective Practice

Content Check

1. When exposed to erotic stimuli, men and women vary in their most common emotional reactions, but there appears to be no difference in their levels of physical arousal. T or F?
2. Some evidence suggests that sexual activity and sex drives peak later for males than for females. T or F?
3. The term ______________ ______________ describes the tendency for the sexual behavior of women and men to be judged differently.
4. Sexual adjustment is best viewed as a relationship issue, not just one partner's problem. T or F?
5. The term *gunnysacking* refers to the constructive practice of hiding anger until it is appropriate to express it. T or F?

Skill Check

Think Critically

6. Why do you think that fidelity in marriage is strongly encouraged by law and custom?
7. Who would you expect to have the most frequent sex and the most satisfying sex, hook-up couples or committed couples?

Self-Reflect

To what extent does the discussion of sexual arousal and sex drive agree with your own experiences and beliefs? What do you want to remember that you didn't know before? Based on your own observations of attitudes toward sex and patterns of sexual behavior, do you think that there has been a sexual revolution? We all make mistakes in relationships. Which mistakes have you avoided? Which would you like to avoid or correct?

ANSWERS

1. T 2. F 3. double standard 4. T 5. F 6. Through marriage laws and customs, human societies tend to foster enduring bonds between sexual partners to help ensure that children are cared for and not just produced. 7. Contrary to mass-media portrayals of sexy hook-ups, committed couples have better sex and overall well-being (Bersamin et al., 2014). Greater opportunity plus familiarity with a partner's needs and preferences probably account for these findings.

MODULE
48 Human Sexuality
Sexual Problems

33 Million

Even sex has a downside. In this module, we will face some of that downside, including the crime of rape, some of the more common sexual dysfunctions couples might experience, and atypical sexuality (the paraphilic disorders). We close this module with a discussion of sexually transmitted diseases, including HIV/AIDS. Pictured here is the AIDS Memorial Quilt, begun in 1985 to commemorate those who have died from AIDS. The photo is of the last public display of the complete quilt, in 1996. Originally, the quilt memorialized only homosexual victims. It now includes heterosexual men, women, and children, signifying that AIDS respects no boundaries. Today, it can be viewed online (https://www.aidsmemorial.org/interactive-aids-quilt) and is composed of 48,000 individual 3′ by 6′ panels (each the size of a human grave). If the quilt included panels for the more than 33,000,000 of the victims of AIDS to date, it would cover well over a quarter of all of Washington, DC.

Leonard Lessin/Science Source

~LEARNING OUTCOMES~

After reading this module you should be able to:

48.1 Define what constitutes rape, and what is meant by "rape myths"

48.2 Outline the most common sexual dysfunctions

48.3 Define what is meant by a paraphilic disorder, and provide some examples

48.4 Explain the impacts that sexually transmitted diseases have had on sexual behavior

The Crime of Rape—No Means No

Learning Outcome 48.1 Define what constitutes rape, and what is meant by "rape myths"

Many women believe that their chances of being raped are low, but the facts tell a different story (Breiding et al., 2014). Nearly 20 percent of all American women will be raped in their lifetimes. Because most rape goes unreported, the true figure is much higher. Rape refers to situations that involve penetration of the vagina or anus without the consent of the victim. Rape includes unwanted sex that results from perpetrator threats to harm the victim (or the victim's family or friends), as well as situations in which victims cannot provide consent because they are unconscious or impaired in some way. **Forcible rape**, which is distressingly common, is carried out under the threat

Forcible rape Sexual intercourse carried out against the victim's will, under the threat of violence or bodily injury.

of bodily injury. Rapists often inflict more violence on their victims than is necessary to achieve sexual domination.

Most psychologists no longer think of forcible rape as a primarily sexual act. Rather, it is an act of brutality or aggression based on the need to debase others. Many rapists impulsively take what they want, without concern for the feelings of the victim or guilt about their deed. Others harbor deep-seated resentment or outright hatred of women.

Typical aftereffects for the victim include rage, guilt, depression, loss of self-esteem, shame, sexual adjustment problems, and, in many cases, a lasting mistrust of male–female relationships. The impact is so great that most women continue to report fear, anxiety, and sexual dysfunction a year or two after being raped. Even years later, rape survivors are more likely to suffer from depression, alcohol or drug abuse, and other emotional problems.

It is important to be aware that men also can be the victims of rape, especially homosexual rape (Coxell & King, 2010). Any man who doubts the seriousness of rape should imagine himself mistakenly placed in jail, where he is violently raped (sodomized) by other inmates. There is no pleasure in rape for victims of either sex. It is truly a despicable crime.

Acquaintance Rape

Although it is commonly believed that rapists are usually strangers to their victims, nothing could be further from the truth (Breiding et al., 2014; Martin, Taft, & Resick, 2007). It has been found that 85 percent of American women who have been sexually or physically assaulted reported that the perpetrator was a husband, intimate partner, or acquaintance.

Similarly, about 20 percent of all female college students are victims of rape or attempted rape during their time at college. Roughly one-half of these rapes were **acquaintance (date) rape**, forced intercourse that occurs in the context of a date or other voluntary encounter. In other words, they were carried out by first dates, casual dates, or romantic acquaintances (Fisher, Cullen, & Daigle, 2005). But forced sex is rape, even if the rapist doesn't use a knife or become violent. The effects of rape by someone familiar can be even more devastating than those of rape committed by a stranger.

Gender Role Stereotypes and Rape Myths

Rape is related to traditional gender role socialization. Traditional feminine stereotypes include the idea that women should not show direct interest in sex. Traditional masculine stereotypes, on the other hand, include the ideas that a man should take the initiative and persist in attempts at sexual intimacy—even when the woman says no. In general, research has confirmed a link between acceptance of rape myths and sexual violence toward women (Chapleau & Oswald, 2010; Ryan, 2011).

In a classic experimental confirmation of the hypothesis that stereotyped images contribute to rape, male college students were classified as either high or low in gender role stereotyping. Each student then read one of three stories: The first described voluntary intercourse; the second depicted stranger rape; and the third described date rape. As predicted, college males high in gender role stereotyping were more aroused by the rape stories. Their arousal patterns, in fact, were similar to those found among actual rapists. Moreover, a chilling 44 percent of those tested indicated they would consider rape—especially if they could be sure of not being caught (Check & Malamuth, 1983).

Men who commit marital or date rape often believe that they have done nothing wrong. One study of college men found that many tend to blame *women* for date rape. According to them, women who are raped by an acquaintance actually wanted to have sex. A typical explanation is, "Her words were saying no, but her body was saying yes."

This is just one of several widely held beliefs that qualify as **rape myths** (Hayes, Abbott, & Cook, 2016; Suarez & Gadalla, 2010). All these statements are myths:

- A woman who appears alone in public and dresses attractively is "asking for it."
- When a woman says no, she really means yes.
- Many women who are raped actually enjoy it.
- If a woman goes home with a man on a first date, she is interested in sex.
- If a woman is sexually active, she is probably lying if she says she was raped.

Men who believe rape myths are more likely to misread a woman's resistance to unwanted sexual advances, assuming that she really means yes when she says no (Forbes, Adams-Curtis, & White, 2004). Men who believe rape myths and who have been drinking are especially likely to ignore signals that a woman wants sexual advances to stop (Chapleau & Oswald, 2010).

In view of such findings, perhaps the time has come for our culture to make it crystal clear that no means *no*. Educating men about rape myths has been one of the most successful ways of preventing sexual assault (King, 2012).

Acquaintance (date) rape Forced intercourse that occurs in the context of a date or other voluntary encounter.

Rape myths False beliefs about rape that tend to blame the victim and increase the likelihood that some men will think that rape is justified.

Sexual Dysfunctions—When Intimacy Fails

Learning Outcome 48.2 Outline the most common sexual dysfunctions

Even the best-intentioned people may nevertheless experience **sexual dysfunctions**, which are far more common than many people realize. In general, people who seek sexual counseling have one or more of the following types of problems (American Psychiatric Association, 2013; Crooks & Baur, 2017):

- **Desire disorders:** The person has either little or no sexual motivation or desire or has too much.
- **Arousal disorders:** The person desires sexual activity but does not become sexually aroused.
- **Orgasm disorders:** The person does not have orgasms or experiences orgasm too soon or too late.
- **Sexual pain disorders:** The person experiences pain that makes lovemaking uncomfortable or impossible.

There was a time when people suffered such problems in silence. However, in recent years, effective treatments have been found for many complaints (Carroll, 2016). Medical treatments or drugs (such as Viagra for men) may be helpful for sexual problems that clearly have physical causes. In other cases, counseling or psychotherapy may be the best approach. Let's briefly investigate the nature, causes, and treatments of sexual dysfunctions.

Desire Disorders

Desire disorders, like most sexual problems, must be defined in relation to a person's age, sex, partner, expectations, and sexual history. It is not at all unusual for a person to briefly lose sexual desire. Typically, erotic feelings return when anger toward a partner fades, or fatigue, illness, and similar temporary problems end. Under what circumstances, then, is loss of desire a dysfunction? First, the loss of desire must be *persistent*. Second, the person must be *troubled by it*. When these two conditions are met, **hypoactive sexual desire** is said to exist. Diminished desire can apply to both sexes. However, it is somewhat more common in women (Bitzer, Giraldi, & Pfaus, 2013; Segraves & Woodard, 2006).

Some people don't merely lack sexual desire; they are *repelled* by sex and seek to avoid it. A person who suffers from a *sexual aversion* feels fear, anxiety, or disgust about engaging in sex. Often, the afflicted person still has some erotic feelings. For example, he or she may still masturbate or have sexual fantasies. Nevertheless, the prospect of having sex with another person causes panic or revulsion. People with sexual aversions may be diagnosed with a *sexual dysfunction not otherwise specified* (American Psychiatric Association, 2013).

Sexual desire disorders are common. Possible physical causes include illness, fatigue, hormonal difficulties, and the side effects of medicines. Desire disorders also are associated with psychological factors such as depression, fearing loss of control over sexual urges, strict religious beliefs, fear of pregnancy, marital conflict, fear of closeness, and simple loss of attraction to one's partner (King, 2012).

Isn't it possible for someone to experience too much sexual desire? Yes it is. Some psychologists consider *hypersexual disorder*—an excess of sexual desire—to be a legitimate diagnosis, although it is not included in the *DSM-5* (Reid et al., 2012). Again, the excess must be *persistent* and the person must be *troubled by it*. Plagued by intense and recurrent sexual fantasies, urges, and/or behaviors, people with hypersexual disorder are sometimes described as *sex addicts* (Kafka, 2010).

Treatment Desire disorders are complex problems. Unless they have a straightforward physical cause, they are difficult to treat. Desire disorders are often deeply rooted in a person's childhood, sexual history, personality, and relationships. In such instances, counseling or psychotherapy is recommended (Crooks & Baur, 2017).

Arousal Disorders

A person with an arousal disorder experiences little or no physical arousal. Most men with an arousal disorder usually have an inability to maintain an erection but nevertheless desire sex.

Male Erectile Disorder An inability to maintain an erection for lovemaking is called **erectile disorder**. This problem, which also is known as *erectile dysfunction*, was once referred to as *impotence*. However, psychologists now discourage use of the term *impotence* because of its many negative connotations.

Erectile disorders can be primary or secondary. Men suffering from primary erectile dysfunction have never had an erection. Those who previously performed successfully but then developed a problem suffer from secondary erectile dysfunction. Either way, persistent erectile difficulties tend to be very disturbing to the man and his sexual partner (Gambescia & Weeks, 2015).

It is important to recognize that occasional erectile problems are normal. In fact, "performance demands" or overreaction to the temporary loss of an erection may generate fears and doubts that contribute to a further inhibition of arousal (Thompson & Barnes, 2012). At such times, it is particularly important for the man's partner to avoid expressing anger, disappointment, or embarrassment. Patient reassurance helps prevent the establishment of a vicious cycle.

How often must a man experience failure for a problem to exist? According to the *DSM*, erectile disorder involves a persistent difficulty of at least six months' duration, although ultimately, only the man and his partner can make this judgment (American Psychiatric Association, 2013). Repeated erectile dysfunction should therefore be distinguished from *occasional* erectile problems. Fatigue, anger, anxiety, and drinking too much alcohol can cause temporary erectile difficulties in healthy males. True erectile disorders typically persist for months or years (Rowland, 2007).

What causes erectile disorders? Roughly 40 percent of all cases are *organic,* or physically caused. The origin of the remaining cases is **psychogenic** (a result of emotional factors). Even when erectile dysfunction is organic, however, it is almost always made worse by anxiety, anger, and dejection. If a man can have an erection at times other than lovemaking (during sleep, for instance), the problem probably is not physical.

Organic erectile problems have many causes. Typical sources of trouble include alcohol or drug abuse, diabetes, vascular disease, prostate and urological disorders, neurological problems, and reactions to medication for high blood pressure, heart disease, or stomach ulcers. Erectile problems also are a normal part of aging. As men grow older, they typically experience a decline in sexual desire and arousal and an increase in sexual dysfunction (Albersen, Orabi, & Lue, 2012).

Secondary erectile disorders may be related to anxiety about sex in general, guilt because of an extramarital affair, resentment or hostility toward a sexual partner, fear of inability to perform, concerns about STDs, and similar emotions and conflicts. Often the problem starts with repeated sexual failures caused by drinking too much alcohol or by premature ejaculation. In any event, initial doubts soon become severe fears of failure—which further inhibit sexual response.

Treatment Drugs or surgery may be used in medical treatment of organic erectile disorders. The drug Viagra is successful for about 70 to 80 percent of men with erectile disorders. However, fixing the "hydraulics" of erectile problems may not be enough to end the problem. Effective treatment should also include counseling to remove fears and psychological blocks (Gambescia & Weeks, 2015). It is important for the man to also regain confidence, improve his relationship with his partner, and learn better lovemaking skills. To free him of conflicts, the man and his partner may be assigned a series of exercises to perform. This technique, called **sensate focus**, directs attention to natural sensations of pleasure and builds communication skills (Weeks & Gambescia, 2009).

In sensate focus, the couple is told to take turns caressing various parts of each other's bodies. They are further instructed to carefully avoid any genital contact. Instead, they are to concentrate on giving pleasure and on signaling what feels good to them. This takes the pressure to perform off the man and allows him to learn to give pleasure as a means of receiving it. For many men, sensate focus is a better solution than depending on an expensive drug to perform sexually.

Over a period of days or weeks, the couple proceeds to more intense physical contact involving the breasts and genitals. As inhibitions are reduced and natural arousal begins to replace fear, the successful couple moves on to mutually satisfying lovemaking.

Female Sexual Interest/Arousal Disorder Because most women with sexual arousal problems also experience a lack of sexual desire, they are usually diagnosed with **female sexual interest/arousal disorder**. Such women respond with little or no physical arousal to sexual stimulation (American Psychiatric Association, 2013). As in the male, female sexual arousal disorder may be primary or secondary. Also, it is again important to remember that all women occasionally experience inhibited arousal. In some instances, the problem may reflect nothing more than a lack of sufficient sexual stimulation before attempting lovemaking (King, 2012).

The causes of inhibited arousal in women are similar to those seen in men. Sometimes the problem is medical, being related to illness or the side effects of medicines or contraceptives. Psychological factors include anxiety, anger or hostility toward one's partner, depression, stress, or

Sexual dysfunctions Problems with sexual desire, arousal, or response.

Hypoactive sexual desire A persistent, upsetting loss of sexual desire.

Erectile disorder An inability to maintain an erection for lovemaking.

Psychogenic Having psychological origins, rather than physical causes.

Sensate focus A form of therapy that directs a couple's attention to natural sensations of sexual pleasure.

Female sexual interest/arousal disorder A lack of interest in sex, lack of physical arousal to sexual stimulation, or both.

distracting worries (Basson & Brotto, 2009). Some women can trace their arousal difficulties to frightening childhood experiences, such as molestations, incestuous relations, a harsh religious background in which sex was considered evil, or cold, unloving childhood relationships. Also common is a need to maintain control over emotions, deep-seated conflicts over being female, and extreme distrust of others, especially males.

Treatment *How does treatment proceed?* Treatment typically includes sensate focus, genital stimulation by the woman's partner, and "nondemanding" intercourse controlled by the woman (Segraves & Althof, 2002). With success in these initial stages, full, mutual, intercourse is gradually introduced. As sexual training proceeds, psychological conflicts and dynamics typically appear, and as they do, they are treated in separate counseling sessions.

Orgasm Disorders

A person suffering from an orgasm disorder either fails to reach orgasm during sexual activity or reaches orgasm too soon or too late (Regev, Zeiss, & Zeiss, 2006). Notice that such disorders are very much based on expectations. For instance, if a man experiences delayed orgasm, one couple might define it as a problem but another might welcome it. It also is worth noting again that some women rarely or never have orgasm and still find sex pleasurable (Hyde & DeLamater, 2014).

Female Orgasmic Disorder The most prevalent sexual complaint among women is a persistent inability to reach orgasm during lovemaking (McCabe, 2015). It is often clear in **female orgasmic disorder** that the woman is not completely unresponsive. Rather, she is unresponsive in the context of a relationship—she may easily reach orgasm by masturbation but not during lovemaking with her partner.

Then, couldn't the woman's partner be at fault? Sex therapists try to avoid finding fault or placing blame. However, it is true that the woman's partner must be committed to ensuring her gratification. Roughly two-thirds of all women need direct stimulation of the clitoris to reach orgasm. Therefore, some apparent instances of female orgasmic disorder can be traced to inadequate stimulation or faulty technique on the part of the woman's partner. Even when this is true, sexual adjustment difficulties are best viewed as a problem the couple shares, not just as "the woman's problem," "the man's problem," or "her partner's problem."

Treatment If we focus only on the woman, the most common source of orgasmic difficulties is overcontrol of the sexual response. Orgasm requires a degree of abandonment to erotic feelings. It is inhibited by ambivalence or hostility toward the relationship, by guilt, by fears of expressing sexual needs, and by tendencies to control and intellectualize erotic feelings. The woman is unable to let go and enjoy the flow of pleasurable sensations (Segraves & Althof, 2002).

Anorgasmic women (those who do not have orgasms) are first trained to focus on their sexual responsiveness through masturbation or vigorous stimulation by a partner. As the woman becomes consistently orgasmic in these circumstances, her responsiveness is gradually transferred to lovemaking with her partner. Couples also typically learn alternative positions and techniques of lovemaking designed to increase clitoral stimulation. At the same time, communication between partners is stressed, especially with reference to the woman's expectations, motivations, and preferences (Kelly, Strassberg, & Turner, 2006).

Delayed Ejaculation Among males, delay or absence of orgasm was once considered a rare problem. But milder forms of **delayed ejaculation** account for increasing numbers of clients seeking therapy (Foley & Gambescia, 2015). Typical background factors are strict religious training, fear of impregnating, lack of interest in the sexual partner, symbolic inability to give of oneself, unacknowledged homosexuality, or the recent occurrence of traumatic life events. Power and commitment struggles within relationships may be important added factors.

Treatment The treatment for delayed ejaculation consists of sensate focus, manual stimulation by the man's partner (which is designed to orient the male to his partner as a source of pleasure), and stimulation to the point of orgasm followed by immediate intercourse and ejaculation. Treatment also focuses on resolving personal conflicts and marital difficulties underlying the problem (Waldinger, 2009).

Premature (Early) Ejaculation **Premature ejaculation** exists when it occurs reflexively or the man cannot tolerate high levels of excitement at the plateau stage of arousal. Basically, ejaculation is premature if it consistently occurs before the man and his partner want it to occur (McMahon et al., 2013).

Do many men have difficulties with premature ejaculation? Approximately 50 percent of young adult men have problems with premature ejaculation. Theories advanced to explain it have ranged from the idea that it may represent hostility toward the man's sexual partner (because it deprives the partner of satisfaction) to the suggestion that most early male sexual experiences (such as those taking place in the backseat of a car and masturbation) tend to encourage rapid climax. Excessive arousal and anxiety over performance are usually present. Also, some men simply engage in techniques that maximize sensation and make rapid orgasm inevitable.

Ejaculation is a reflex. To control it, a man must learn to recognize the physical signals that it is about to occur. Some men have simply never learned to be aware of these signals. Whatever the causes, premature ejaculation can be a serious difficulty, especially in the context of long-term relationships (King, 2012).

Treatment The most common treatment for premature ejaculation is a "stop–start" procedure called the **squeeze technique** (Grenier & Byers, 1995). The man's sexual partner stimulates him manually until he signals that ejaculation is about to occur. The man's partner then firmly squeezes the tip of his penis to inhibit orgasm. When the man feels that he has control, stimulation is repeated. Later, the squeeze technique is used during lovemaking. Gradually, the man acquires the ability to delay orgasm sufficiently for mutually satisfactory lovemaking. During treatment, skills that improve communication between partners are developed, along with a better understanding of the male's sexual response cues (McCarthy & Fucito, 2005).

Sexual Pain Disorders

Pain in the genitals before, during, or after sexual intercourse, called *dyspareunia* (DIS-pah-ROO-nee-ah), is rare in males. In females, this problem is often related to *vaginismus* (VAJ-ih-NIS-mus), a condition in which muscle spasms of the vagina prevent intercourse (Binik, 2010). Together, these disorders constitute the major symptoms of **genito-pelvic pain/penetration disorder** (American Psychiatric Association, 2013).

Genito-pelvic pain/penetration disorder is often accompanied by obvious fear of intercourse, and where fear is absent, high levels of anxiety are present (Cherner & Reissing, 2013). This disorder, therefore, appears to often be a phobic response to intercourse. Predictably, its causes include experiences of painful intercourse, rape or other brutal and frightening sexual encounters, fear of men and of penetration, misinformation about sex (belief that it is injurious), fear of pregnancy, and fear of the specific male partner (Borg et al., 2012).

Treatment

The treatment of genito-pelvic pain/penetration disorder is similar to what might be done for a nonsexual phobia. It includes extinction of conditioned muscle spasms by progressive relaxation of the vagina, desensitization of fears of intercourse, and masturbation or manual stimulation to associate pleasure with sexual approach by the woman's partner (Bergeron & Lord, 2003). Hypnosis also has been used successfully in some cases (Roja & Roja, 2010).

Summary

Solving sexual problems can be difficult. The problems described here are rarely solved without professional help (a possible exception is premature ejaculation). If a serious sexual difficulty is not resolved in a reasonable amount of time, the aid of an appropriately trained psychologist, physician, or counselor should be sought (Rosenthal, M., 2013).

Atypical Sexual Behavior—Fifty Shades of Unusual

Learning Outcome 48.3 Define what is meant by a paraphilic disorder, and provide some examples

By strict standards (including the law in some states), almost any sexual activity other than face-to-face heterosexual intercourse between married adults is atypical or "deviant." But public standards are often at odds with private behavior. Just as the hunger drive is expressed and satisfied in many ways, the sex drive also leads to an immense range of behaviors.

Paraphilic Disorders

I just read Fifty Shades of Grey *and really liked it. Is something wrong with me?* For those of you who might not know, this is a wildly successful novel about bondage/discipline, dominance/submission, and sadism/masochism (BDSM) (Bloom & Bloom, 2012). Sexual deviance is a highly

Female orgasmic disorder A persistent inability to reach orgasm during lovemaking.

Delayed ejaculation A persistent delay or absence of orgasm during lovemaking.

Premature ejaculation Ejaculation that consistently occurs before the man and his partner want it to occur.

Squeeze technique A method for inhibiting ejaculation by compressing the tip of the penis.

Genito-pelvic pain/penetration disorder A sexual pain disorder in women involving dyspareunia (genital pain before, during, or after sexual intercourse), usually accompanied by vaginismus (muscle spasms of the vagina).

emotional subject. At one time, engaging in unusual sexual behaviors such as *sadism* (deriving sexual pleasure from inflicting pain, humiliation, or both) and *masochism* (desiring pain, humiliation, or both as part of the sex act) was viewed as evidence of a psychiatric disorder. More recently, however, we have witnessed a growing social consensus that a person engaging in unusual sexual practices does not automatically suffer from a psychiatric disorder (American Psychiatric Association, 2013).

Today, people are usually diagnosed with a **paraphilic disorder** (PAIR-eh-FIL-ick) only if it involves engaging in sexual practices *that typically cause guilt, anxiety, or discomfort for one or more participants*. For example, most sadists and masochists voluntarily associate with people who share their sexual interests. Thus, their behavior may not harm anyone, except when it is extreme. While some people may see even casual experimentation with deviant sexual behaviors as immoral or odd, and while local laws may criminalize such behaviors, psychologically, the mark of true sexual disorders is that they are compulsive and destructive.

The paraphilic disorders listed in ■ **Table 48.1** cover a wide variety of behaviors (Balon, 2016b). Two of the most common and yet misunderstood deviant sexual behaviors are pedophilia and exhibitionism.

Child Molestation The psychiatric label for child molestation is *pedophilic disorder* (American Psychiatric Association, 2013; Strickland, 2015). Child molesters, or pedophiles, are usually males, most are married, and two-thirds are fathers. Many molesters are rigid, passive, puritanical, or religious. They are often consumers of child pornography (Seto, Cantor, & Blanchard, 2006). As children, child molesters themselves were often witnesses to, or victims of, sexual abuse (Cohen et al., 2010; Nunes et al., 2013). Molesters also are often thought of as child rapists, but most molestations rarely exceed fondling (Seto, 2008, 2009).

How serious are the effects of a molestation? The impact varies widely. It is affected by how long the abuse lasts, the identity of the abuser, and whether genital sexual acts are involved. Many authorities believe that a single incident of fondling by a relative stranger is unlikely to cause severe emotional harm to a child. For most children, the event is frightening but not a lasting trauma (Rind, Tromovitch, & Bauserman, 1998). That's why parents are urged not to overreact to such incidents or to become hysterical. Doing so only further frightens the child. This by no means implies, however, that parents should ignore hints from a child that a molestation may have occurred.

Parents should watch for the following hints of trouble:

Recognizing Signs of Child Molestation

- Unusual avoidance of, or interest in, sexual matters
- Secretiveness (including about Internet access)
- Emotional disturbances such as depression, irritability, or withdrawal from family, friends, or school
- Nightmares or other sleep problems
- Misbehavior, such as unusual aggressiveness, suicidal behavior, or unusual risk-taking, such as riding a bicycle dangerously in traffic
- Loss of self-esteem or self-worth

(Adapted from American Academy of Child and Adolescent Psychiatry, 2020)

TABLE 48.1 | Paraphilic Disorders

Focus of Paraphilia	Paraphilic Disorder	Primary Symptom
Nonhuman objects	Fetishistic disorder	Sexual arousal associated with inanimate objects
	Transvestic disorder	Achieving sexual arousal by wearing clothing of the opposite sex
Nonconsenting people	Exhibitionistic disorder	"Flashing," or displaying the genitals to unwilling viewers
	Voyeuristic disorder	"Peeping," or viewing the genitals of others without their permission
	Frotteuristic disorder	Sexually touching or rubbing against a nonconsenting person, usually in a public place such as a subway
	Pedophilic disorder	Sex with children or child molesting
Pain or humiliation	Sexual masochism disorder	Desiring pain, humiliation, or both as part of the sex act
	Sexual sadism disorder	Deriving sexual pleasure from inflicting pain, humiliation, or both

Adapted from the American Psychiatric Association (2013); Durand & Barlow (2019).

How can children protect themselves? Children should be taught to shout "No!" if an adult tries to engage them in sexual activity. If children are asked to keep a secret, they should reply that they don't keep secrets. Parents and children also need to be aware that the Internet gives pedophiles an easy way to make contact with children. If an adult suggests to a child online that they could meet in person, the child should immediately tell his or her parents.

It also helps if children know the tactics typically used by molesters. Interviews with convicted sex offenders revealed the following (Elliott, Browne, & Kilcoyne, 1995; van Dam, 2006):

Tactics of Child Molesters

1. Most molesters act alone.
2. Most assaults take place in the abuser's home.
3. Many abusers gain access to the child through caretaking.
4. Children are targeted at first through bribes, gifts, and games.
5. The abuser tries to lull the child into participation through talking about sex and through persuasion. (This can take place through email or chat rooms on the Internet.)
6. The abuser then uses force, anger, threats, and bribes to gain continued compliance.

Repeated molestations, those that involve force or threats, those that are perpetuated by trusted caregivers, and incidents that exceed fondling can leave lasting emotional scars. As adults, many victims of incest or molestation develop sexual phobias. For them, lovemaking may evoke vivid and terrifying memories of the childhood victimization. Serious harm is especially likely to occur if the molester is someone whom the child deeply trusts. Molestations by parents, close relatives, teachers, priests, youth leaders, and similar persons can be profoundly damaging. In such cases, professional counseling is often needed (American Academy of Child and Adolescent Psychiatry, 2020).

Exhibitionism The psychiatric label for exhibitionism is *exhibitionistic disorder* (American Psychiatric Association, 2013). Exhibitionism, or indecent exposure, is a common disorder (Sue et al., 2016). Between one-third and two-thirds of all sexual arrests are for "flashing." Although it was long thought that exhibitionists are basically harmless, research has shown that many exhibitionists go on to commit more serious sexual crimes and other offenses (Bader et al., 2008; Firestone et al., 2006).

Exhibitionists are typically male and married, and most come from strict and repressive backgrounds. Most of them feel a deep sense of inadequacy, which produces a compulsive need to prove their "manhood" by frightening women (Murphy & Page, 2008). In general, a woman confronted by an exhibitionist can assume that his goal is to shock and alarm her. By becoming visibly upset, she actually encourages him (Sue et al., 2016).

As the preceding discussion suggests, the picture of sexual deviance that most often emerges is one of sexual inhibition and immaturity. Typically, some relatively infantile sexual expression (like pedophilia or exhibitionism) is selected because it is less threatening than more mature sexuality (Balon, 2016a).

All the paraphilic disorders, unless they are very mild, involve compulsive behavior. As a result, they tend to emotionally handicap people. There is room in contemporary society for a large array of sexual behaviors. Nevertheless, any behavior that becomes compulsive (be it eating, gambling, drug abuse, or sex) is psychologically unhealthy.

STDs and Safer Sex—Choice, Risk, and Responsibility

Learning Outcome 48.4 Explain the impacts that sexually transmitted diseases have had on sexual behavior

In general, most adults favor greater freedom of choice for themselves. When it comes to sex, however, greater choice is accompanied by greater risk. This is especially true for younger people who are exploring their sexual identities in an era of more casual sex (Wentland & Reissing, 2011).

Risk in sexual behavior often comes in the form of a **sexually transmitted disease (STD)**, an infection passed from one person to another by intimate physical contact. Sexually active people run higher risks for human papillomavirus (HPV), Chlamydia (klah-MID-ee-ah), gonorrhea, hepatitis B, herpes, syphilis, and other STDs (■ **Table 48.2**).

Paraphilic disorders Compulsive sexual behaviors that tend to emotionally handicap people, such as pedophilia, exhibitionism, fetishism, voyeurism, and so on.

Sexually transmitted disease (STD) A disease that is typically passed from one person to the next by intimate physical contact; a venereal disease.

TABLE 48.2 | Common Sexually Transmitted Diseases

STD	Male Symptoms	Female Symptoms	Prevention	Treatment
Gonorrhea	Milky discharge from urethra; painful, frequent urination	Vaginal discharge and inflammation; painful urination	Condom/safer sex practices	Antibiotics
Chlamydia	Painful urination; discharge from urethra	Painful urination; discharge from vagina; abdominal pain	Condom/safer sex practices	Antibiotics
Syphilis	Painless sores on genitals, rectum, tongue, or lips; skin rash; fever; headache; aching bones and joints	Same as in males	Condom/safer sex practices	Antibiotics
Genital herpes	Pain or itching on the penis; water blisters or open sores	Pain or itching in the genital area; water blisters or open sores	Condom/safer sex practices	Symptoms can be treated but not cured
Human papillomavirus (HPV)	Warty growths on genitals; some cancers	Same as in males	Condom/safer sex practices	Wart removal by surgery or laser, HPV vaccine for prevention
HIV/AIDS	Prolonged fatigue; swollen lymph nodes; fever lasting more than 10 days; night sweats; unexplained weight loss; purplish lesions on skin; persistent cough or sore throat; persistent colds; persistent diarrhea; easy bruising or unexplained bleeding	Same as in males	Condom/safer sex practices	Can be treated with various drugs but cannot be cured
Hepatitis B	Mild cases may have no symptoms, but infection can cause chronic liver disease, cirrhosis of the liver, or liver cancer	Same as in males	Vaccination	None available
Pelvic inflammatory disease	Does not apply	Intense pain in lower back, abdomen, or both; fever	Condom/safer sex practices	Antibiotics

Over 2.4 million new cases of Chlamydia, gonorrhea, and syphilis were reported in the United States in 2018 (Centers for Disease Control, 2019c).

Despite such statistics, many sexually active people underestimate their risk for a variety of reasons. One study of sexually active teenage girls engaging in risky sex is a case in point. Nearly 90 percent of the girls thought that they had virtually no chance of getting an STD. In reality, over the next 18 months, one in four got Chlamydia or gonorrhea (Ethier et al., 2003).

One reason for underestimating sexual risk is that people who are sexually active may have indirect contact with many other people. One study of sexual relationships at a high school in a Mid-western city found long chains of sexual contact between students. Thus, a student at the end of the chain might have had sex with only one person, but in reality, she or he had indirect contact with dozens or even hundreds of others (Bearman, Moody, & Stovel, 2004).

Another reason people underestimate their risk is that many individuals who carry STDs remain *asymptomatic* (a-SIMP-teh-mat-ik), lacking obvious symptoms. It is easy to have an infection without knowing it. Likewise, it is often impossible to tell whether a sexual partner is infectious.

Also, because most of the more common STDs are treatable, it is easy to dismiss their impact on health. But STDs such as Chlamydia or gonorrhea produce a variety of painful and embarrassing symptoms. Chlamydia can even "silently" (without symptoms) damage a woman's reproductive organs, resulting in infertility. Gonorrhea can damage the fertility of both men and women (Centers for Disease Control, 2019c).

HIV/AIDS

For many sexually active people, the *human immunodeficiency virus (HIV)* adds a whole new level of risk. Whereas most other STDs are treatable, HIV infections disable the immune system, leading to *acquired immune deficiency syndrome (AIDS)*, which can be lethal. As the immune system weakens, other "opportunistic" diseases invade the body. Most people with AIDS eventually die of multiple infections (although newer multidrug therapies have greatly improved the odds of survival).

The first symptoms of AIDS may show up as few as two months after HIV infection, but they typically don't appear for 10 years. Because of this long incubation period, infected persons often pass the HIV virus on to others without knowing it. Medical testing can detect an HIV infection. However, for at least the first six months after becoming infected, a person can test negative while carrying the virus. Even a negative test result, therefore, is no guarantee that a person is a "safe" sex partner. In fact, 25 percent of HIV-infected individuals are unaware of their infections (Nguyen et al., 2008).

HIV infections are spread by direct contact with body fluids—especially blood, semen, and vaginal secretions. The HIV virus cannot be transmitted by casual contact. People do not get HIV from shaking hands, touching or using objects touched by an HIV-infected person, eating food prepared by an infected person, or from social kissing, touching sweat or tears, sharing drinking glasses, sharing towels, and so forth.

Around the world, 38 million people are currently living with HIV/AIDS, of whom about 1.1 million live in the United States. Fortunately, the rate of new infections is slowly falling. Nevertheless, there are still 1.7 million new cases worldwide every year, including about 38,000 new cases in the United States. Despite signs of progress, AIDS could kill up to 20 million people worldwide over the next 15 years unless prevention efforts are greatly expanded (Centers for Disease Control, 2020b; United Nations Programme on HIV/AIDS, 2020).

Populations at Risk HIV can be spread by all forms of sexual intercourse, and it has affected persons of all sexual orientations. In North America, those who remain at greatest risk for HIV infection remain men who have had sex with other men (homosexual and bisexual men), people who have shared needles (for tattoos or for intravenous drug use), sexual partners of people in the preceding groups, and heterosexuals with a history of multiple partners. Thus, the vast majority of people are not at *high* risk of HIV infection. Regardless, HIV could potentially affect anyone.

Behavioral Risk Factors for STDs

Sexually active people can do much to protect their own health. It is risky to engage in the behaviors listed here with a person who has an STD:

Risky Behaviors

- Unprotected vaginal, oral, or anal sex (without a condom) with an infected partner
- Having two or more sex partners (additional partners further increase the risk)
- Sex with someone you don't know well, or with someone you know has had several partners
- Sex with someone you know injects drugs or shares drug needles and syringes (HIV/AIDS)

It's important to remember that you can't tell from external appearances if a person is infected. Many people would be surprised to learn that their partners have engaged in behavior that places them both at risk. The preceding list of high-risk behaviors can be contrasted with the following list of safer sexual practices. (Note, however, that unless a person completely abstains, sex can be made safer, but it's not risk-free.)

Safer Sex Practices

- Not having sex at all
- Having sex with one mutually faithful, uninfected partner
- Using a condom
- Discussing contraception with your partner

- Discussing your partner's sexual health prior to engaging in sex
- Being selective regarding sexual partners
- Reducing the number of sexual partners
- Not engaging in sex while intoxicated
- Not injecting drugs (HIV/AIDS)

Sexually active persons should practice safer sex until their partner's sexual history and/or health has been clearly established. Unfortunately, this message is not always getting through to those who most need to hear it. The HIV/AIDS epidemic initially triggered a sharp decrease in risky sex and an increase in monogamous relationships among gay men. Unfortunately, this trend has begun to reverse. Once again, rates for many STDs are rising among gay men. In part, this may be because new medical treatments are helping people with HIV live longer. Many victims simply do not look or act sick. This gives a false impression about the dangers of HIV infection and encourages foolish risk taking (Stevens, Bernadini, & Jemmott, 2013). Regardless, about 15 percent of new HIV infections in the United States are transmitted through heterosexual sex (Centers for Disease Control, 2020b). The focus on HIV/AIDS prevention may also have deemphasized the health impact of the other STDs.

High school and college-age students also remain too willing to engage in risky behavior (casual sex) and yet unwilling to use condoms (Bauman, Karasz, & Hamilton, 2007). A study of heterosexual adults also found that the majority did not practice safer sex with their last partner. Most of these "gamblers" knew too little about their partners to be sure that they were not taking a big risk. For many people, drinking alcohol greatly increases the likelihood of taking sexual risks (Corbin & Fromme, 2002).

Safer Sex

The threat of HIV/AIDS has forced many people to face new issues of risk and responsibility concerning STDs in general. Those who do not ensure their own safety are playing Russian roulette with their health (Essien et al., 2010). One chilling study of HIV patients who knew they were infectious found that 41 percent of those who were sexually active did not always use condoms (Sobel et al., 1996)! Thus, responsibility for "safer sex" rests with each sexually active individual. It is unwise to count on your sexual partner for protection against STDs.

Isn't it possible that practicing safer sex would be interpreted as a sign that you mistrust your lover? Those who do not ensure their own safety, or that of their partners, are gambling with their health. As is the case with other behavioral risk factors, taking precautions could, instead, be defined as a way of showing that you really care about your own health, as well as that of your partner (Essien et al., 2010).

MODULE 48 Sexual Problems—Learning Outcomes Revisited

48.1 Define what constitutes rape, and what is meant by "rape myths"

Rape refers to situations that involve penetration of the vagina or anus without the consent of the victim. Rape includes unwanted sex that results from perpetrator threats to harm the victim (or the victim's family or friends), as well as situations in which victims cannot provide consent because they are unconscious or impaired in some way. Rape myths are false beliefs grounded in traditional gender role stereotypes. One example is the (false) belief that a man should persist in attempts at sexual intimacy—even when the woman says no.

48.2 Outline the most common sexual dysfunctions

Problems with sexual function can involve desire, arousal (e.g., erectile disorder, female arousal disorder), orgasm (female orgasmic disorder, delayed ejaculation, premature ejaculation), or pain. Behavioral methods and counseling techniques have been developed to alleviate many sexual problems.

48.3 Define what is meant by a paraphilic disorder, and provide some examples

Paraphilic disorders are compulsive sexual behaviors that tend to emotionally handicap people. The paraphilic disorders include pedophilia, exhibitionism, voyeurism, frotteurism, fetishism, sexual masochism, sexual sadism, and transvestic fetishism. The most common paraphilic disorders are pedophilia and exhibitionism.

48.4 Explain the impacts that sexually transmitted diseases have had on sexual behavior

STDs and the spread of HIV/AIDS have had a sizable impact on patterns of sexual behavior, including some curtailment of risk taking. Many sexually active people continue to take unnecessary risks with their health by failing to follow safer sex practices.

Reflective Practice

Content Check

1. Rape myths are related to __________ __________ __________ __________.
2. Sensate focus is the most common treatment for premature ejaculation. T or F?
3. A person is usually diagnosed with a paraphilic disorder only if he or she is engaging in an illegal sexual act. T or F?
4. Wanting to practice safe sex is an insult to your lover. T or F?

Skill Check

Think Critically

5. Which do you think would be better suited to reducing STDs and unwanted pregnancies among adolescents: abstinence-only education programs or more comprehensive sex education programs?

Self-Reflect

To what extent do movies, music videos, and video games contribute directly to the perpetuation of rape myths? What about indirectly, by portraying gender role stereotypes? In plain language, sexual disorders can be summarized this way: The person doesn't want to do it. The person wants to do it but can't get aroused. The person wants to do it, gets aroused, but has problems with orgasm. The person wants to do it and gets aroused, but lovemaking is uncomfortable. What are the formal terms for each of these situations?

ANSWERS

1. traditional gender role stereotypes 2. F 3. F 4. F
5. More comprehensive programs are actually more effective at reducing STDs and unwanted pregnancies among adolescents (Kirby, 2008).

MODULE 49

A Psychologist's Skill Set
Diversity and Inclusion

Think Pink!

On his first day of grade 9, Charles McNeill wore a pink polo shirt to school. Outside, bullies called him a homosexual and threatened to beat him up until two grade 12 boys intervened. But the older boys weren't satisfied with putting an end to the harassment. They bought 50 pink shirts from a discount store and went online to encourage their friends to buy one and wear it to school the following day. But it wasn't 50 kids who showed up in pink the next morning. It was hundreds, some of them dressed in pink from head to toe. What began as a one-day event at a single school eventually became Anti-Bullying Day, marked annually in several countries around the world and supported by the United Nations. It's a day set aside each year to celebrate our differences, and to consider the importance of tolerance.

Leonard Lessin/Science Source

Most people publicly support policies of equality and fairness. Yet many still have lingering biases and negative images of people seen as being "different." Is it possible to work toward greater acceptance and harmony among people who appear to be so different? Let's find out.

~LEARNING OUTCOMES~

After reading this module you should be able to:

49.1 Explain how diversity and inclusion are relevant to everyday life

Living with Diversity—A Rich Tapestry

Learning Outcome 49.1 Explain how diversity and inclusion are relevant to everyday life

Today's society is more like a "tossed salad" than a cultural "melting pot." Differences can relate to sexual orientation, but they can also be connected to other personal characteristics such as age, sex, (dis)ability, race, political beliefs, social class, mental health, or religion.

Rather than expecting everyone to be alike, psychologists believe that we must learn to respect and appreciate our differences. To help us reach a point where this is possible, psychologists study diversity. Important questions guiding this research include (American Psychological Association, 2017c): What do we know about discrimination and stereotyping? How do we foster kindness, compassion, and the acknowledgment of differences without negative judgment? How do we protect people from the harmful effects of exclusion and marginalization? How do we promote a society that celebrates inclusion, diversity, and genuine equality?

Throughout this book, we draw your attention to some of the answers that psychologists have provided to these questions. Module 73, for example, explores research by social psychologists interested in understanding prejudice and discrimination. And several modules demonstrate the negative consequences of intolerance toward a variety of specific groups, including older adults (Module 15), people who are poor (Module 56), individuals who have been diagnosed with mental illness (Module 60), those with different political beliefs (Module 73), and various racial and ethnic groups (Module 73). The negative consequences of intolerance include people being unable to reach their potential, feelings of depression and anxiety, and—in the worst case—suicide.

Tolerance and Acceptance

It's no secret that the United States is becoming more diverse every year. For example, according to US Census Bureau, by 2060 the number of senior citizens will have doubled and this country will become a nation of minorities, with no single racial or ethnic group making up 50 percent of the population (Colby & Ortman, 2016). Add to this the growing acceptance of women into traditionally male roles and people of different sexual orientations into society at large. These are just some examples of the changing face of America, but they raise a point worth thinking about: It will become increasingly important to have skills that allow you to get along with a variety of people, some of whom may appear—at least at first glance—to be quite different than you.

These population trends mean that your classroom and workplace will become more diverse, but psychologists have found that this type of diversity has many benefits. For example, research from the world of work has suggested that groups with diverse membership are much better at solving complex problems. This is likely because bringing together people with a range of experiences helps to promote the creative and divergent thinking that was discussed in Module 41 (Homan et al., 2015). How, though, can we start to build skills that encourage tolerance and inclusion? It all begins with an attitude of openness.

Being Open to Openness

What do you mean by openness? At the core of successfully navigating relationships with diverse others is accepting the value of *openness to the other*, or the ability to genuinely appreciate those who differ from us. It is important to remember that being open to someone else does not mean that you have to agree with that person or turn your back on your own values. How can you work toward improving your skill at building positive open relationships with a variety of different people? Here are a few suggestions:

Seek Individuating Information

A good way to develop a sense of openness is to get to know individuals from different groups (Inzlicht, Gutsell, & Legault, 2012; Roets & Van Hiel, 2011). We often apply stereotypes when we have only minimal information about a person, but one way to avoid this is to seek **individuating information**—information that helps us see a person as an individual rather than as a member of a group (Jussim, Crawford, & Rubinstein, 2015; Lan Yeung & Kashima, 2010). When you meet individuals from various backgrounds, focus on the *person*, not the *label*.

A good example of the effects of individuating information comes from a Canadian study of English-speaking students in a French-language program. Students who were "immersed" (spent most of their waking hours with French Canadians) became more positive toward them. Immersed students were more likely to say they had come to appreciate and like French Canadians; they were more willing to meet and interact with them; and they saw themselves as less different from French Canadians (Lambert, 1987).

Don't Fall Prey to Just-World Beliefs

Do you believe that the world is basically fair and that people generally get what they deserve? It may not be obvious, but such beliefs can *reduce* the tolerance we feel for other groups (Bizer, Hart, & Jekogian, 2012; Hafer & Sutton, 2016). As an

Individuating information Information that helps define a person as an individual, rather than as a member of a group or social category.

example, suppose you happen to notice Adnan, a member of a visible minority, cleaning the toilets at the airport. **Just-world beliefs**—beliefs that people generally get what they deserve—might lead you to assume that Adnan wouldn't be in this job if he could not qualify for a better job.

The reality is often very different. As a result of discrimination, social conditions, and circumstances (such as recent immigration), many members of minorities are forced to occupy lower socioeconomic positions (Whitley & Kite, 2010). Assuming that Adnan is not motivated enough or not intelligent enough overlooks the possibility that, say, discrimination in hiring has made it very difficult for him to find a better job. This bit of faulty thinking can reduce feelings of acceptance toward minorities, and amounts to blaming people who are *victims* for their problems. Surprisingly often, people like Adnan are highly educated *and* highly motivated to take whatever work is available. Just ask Adnan.

Be Aware of Self-Fulfilling Prophecies As noted elsewhere (see, for example, Module 71), people tend to act in accordance with the behavior expected by others. If you hold strong opinions about members of various groups, a vicious cycle can occur. When you meet someone who is different from yourself, you may treat him or her in a way that is consistent with your initial opinions. If the other person is influenced by your behavior, he or she may act in ways that seem to match your stereotype. For example, a person who believes that members of a particular minority group are hostile and unfriendly will probably treat people in that group in ways that provoke a hostile and unfriendly response. This creates a **self-fulfilling prophecy**—an expectation that prompts people to act in ways that make the expectation come true—in turn reinforcing their belief in the initial expectation.

Look for Commonalities We live in a society that puts a premium on competition and individual effort. One problem with this is that competing with others fosters desires to minimize and overcome them. When we cooperate with others, we tend to share their joys and suffer when they are in distress (Kassin, Fein, & Markus, 2021). If we don't find ways to cooperate and live in greater harmony, everyone will suffer. That, if nothing else, is one thing that we all have in common. Everyone knows what it feels like to be different. Greater tolerance comes from remembering those times.

Set an Example for Others People who act in a tolerant fashion can serve as models of tolerance for others, as illustrated by the story about Anti-Bullying Day with which we began this module. Another example is the use of newsletters to promote understanding at an ethnically diverse high school in Houston, Texas. Students wrote stories for the newsletter about situations in which cooperation led to better understanding. For instance, a story about a Hispanic-Anglo friendship in a sports team had this headline: "Don't judge somebody until you know them. The color of their skin doesn't matter." Other stories emphasized the willingness of students to get acquainted with people from other ethnic groups and the new perceptions they had of their abilities. After just five months of modeling tolerance, hostility between campus ethnic groups was significantly reduced (McAlister et al., 2000).

Remember, Different Does Not Mean Less Than Some conflicts between groups cannot be avoided. What *can* be avoided is unnecessary **social competition**—rivalry among groups, each of which regards itself as superior to others. The concept of social competition refers to the fact that some individuals seek to enhance their self-esteem by identifying with a group. However, this works only if the group can be seen as superior to others. Because of social competition, groups tend to view themselves as better than their rivals (Branscombe & Baron, 2017).

In one survey, every major ethnic group in the United States rated itself as better than any other group (Njeri, 1991)! A person who has high self-esteem does not need to treat others as inferior in order to feel good about himself or herself. Similarly, it is not necessary to degrade other groups in order to feel positive about one's own group identity (Fowers & Davidov, 2006).

Living comfortably in a diverse society means being open to other groups. Getting acquainted with a person who is different from you can be a wonderful learning experience (Matsumoto & Juang, 2017). No one group has all the answers or the best ways of doing things, but being inclusive and celebrating human differences can enrich our communities and workplaces, as well as being personally rewarding (Fowers & Davidov, 2006).

Just-world beliefs Beliefs that people generally get what they deserve.

Self-fulfilling prophecy An expectation that prompts people to act in ways that make the expectation come true.

Social competition Rivalry among groups, each of which regards itself as superior to others.

MODULE 49

Diversity and Inclusion—Learning Outcomes Revisited

49.1 Explain how diversity and inclusion are relevant to everyday life

Psychologists believe that we must learn to appreciate and respect differences between individuals because developing tolerance in the workplace and other social settings facilitates better problem solving and creative thinking. Positive relations with diverse others are promoted when we remember to seek individuating information, avoid just-world beliefs and self-fulfilling prophecies, look for commonalities, set a good example for others, and remember that different does not mean inferior. Besides, intolerance of diversity can lead to feelings of depression, anxiety, and, in extreme cases, suicide.

Reflective Practice

Skill Check

1. Individuating information helps us see a person as an individual rather than as a member of a group. T or F?
2. A self-fulfilling prophecy occurs when one expects something to happen and the opposite occurs, reinforcing their initial belief. T or F?
3. Just-world beliefs are based on the assumption that people generally get what they deserve. T or F?
4. Social competition refers to the idea that certain groups view themselves as inferior to others. T or F?

Skill Check

Think Critically

5. You are in the workplace and your coworker is hesitant about collaborating with an international company. Your coworker asks for your opinion. What advice can you give her, based on what you now know from this chapter?

Self-Reflect

Which strategies do you already use to avoid intolerant behaviors? How could you apply the other strategies mentioned in this module to become more inclusive?

ANSWERS

1. T 2. F 3. T 4. F 5. You might tell your coworker that diversity promotes creativity and effective problem solving which would benefit your company. As well, remind her of biases we sometimes hold that prevent positive relationships from developing between people (e.g., belief in a just world; self-fulfilling prophecies). Finally you can set an example for your colleague by looking for commonalities between the two companies (e.g., related to their workers, company values).

MODULE 50

Personality

Overview of Personality

Same Old Shinobu

As he walked toward his former college student, Shinobu, James wondered what he would be like. After all, it had been almost 15 years since the day Shinobu graduated and moved back to Japan. Fifteen years since James last saw him. And now here they were, at the same academic conference. Although James worried that Shinobu might have changed, he was, on the contrary, more his "old self" than ever.

Have you had a similar experience? After years of separation, it is always intriguing to see an old friend. You probably will be delighted to discover that the semi-stranger before you is still the person you once knew. It is exactly this core of consistency that psychologists have in mind when they use the term *personality*. But how is *personality* defined and measured? Read on to find out.

iofoto/Shutterstock.com

~LEARNING OUTCOMES~

After reading this module you should be able to:

50.1 Define what psychologists mean by the term *personality*, explaining its relation to personality traits, types, self-concept, and self-esteem, and name four basic perspectives on personality

50.2 Outline four ways in which personality can be measured

The Psychology of Personality—Do You Have Personality?

Learning Outcome 50.1 Define what psychologists mean by the term *personality,* explaining its relation to traits, types, self-concept, and self-esteem, and name four basic perspectives on personality

It's obvious that we all frequently use the term *personality.* But if you think that personality means "charm," "charisma," or "style," you have misused the term. Psychologists regard **personality** as a person's unique long-term pattern of thinking, emotions, and behavior (Schultz & Schultz, 2017). In other words, personality refers to the consistency in who you are, have been, and will become. It also refers to the special blend of talents, values, hopes, loves, hates, and habits that makes each of us a unique person.

Psychologists use a large number of concepts and theories to explain personality. It might be wise, therefore, to start with a few key ideas to help you keep your bearings as you read on.

Traits

We use the idea of traits every day to talk about personality. For instance, Daryl is *sociable*, *orderly*, and *intelligent*. His sister Hollie is *shy*, *sensitive*, and *creative*. Personality traits such as these can be quite stable (Allemand, Steiger, & Hill, 2013; Rantanen et al., 2007). Think about how little your best friends have changed in the last 5 years. It would be strange indeed to feel like you were talking with a different person every time you met a friend or an acquaintance. In general, then, a **personality trait** is a stable quality that a person shows in most situations (Mõttus, Johnson, & Deary, 2012).

Typically, traits are inferred from behavior. If you see Daryl talking to strangers—first at a supermarket and later at a party—you might infer that he is "sociable." Once personality traits are identified, they can be used to predict future behavior. For example, noting that Daryl is outgoing might lead you to predict that he will be sociable at school or at work. In fact, such consistencies can span many years.

Traits even influence our health as well as our marital and occupational success (Donnellan et al., 2012; Strickhouser, Zell, & Krizan, 2017). For example, who do you think will be more successful in her chosen career: Melissa, who is conscientious, or Erica, who is not (Brown et al., 2011; Ng & Feldman, 2010)?

a katz/Shutterstock.com

Psychologists and employers are especially interested in the personality traits of individuals who hold high-risk, high-stress positions concerning public safety, such as police, firefighters, air traffic controllers, and nuclear power plant employees.

Types

Have you ever asked the question, "What type of person is she (or he)?" A **personality type** refers to people who have *several traits in common* (Larsen & Buss, 2014). Informally, your own thinking might include categories such as the executive type, the athletic type, the motherly type, the hip-hop type, the techno geek, and so forth. If you tried to define these informal types, you would probably list a different collection of traits for each one.

How valid is it to speak of personality "types"? Over the years, psychologists have proposed many ways to categorize personalities into types. For example, Swiss psychiatrist Carl Jung famously proposed that people are either *introverts* or *extroverts.* An **introvert** is a shy, reserved person whose attention is usually focused inward. An **extrovert** is a bold, outgoing person whose attention is usually directed outward. These terms are so widely used that you may think of yourself and your friends as being one type or the other. However, knowing if someone is extroverted or introverted tells you little about how conscientious she is, or how kind or open to new ideas he is. In short, two categories (or even several) are often inadequate to fully capture differences in personality (Ashton, 2108). That's why rating people on a list of traits tends to be more informative than classifying them into two or three types (Engler, 2014).

Even though types tend to oversimplify personality, they do have value. Most often, types are a shorthand way to label people who have several key traits in common. For example, in Module 58, we discuss hardy personalities. Hardy people are unusually resistant to stress (see ➤ **Figure 50.1**). Similarly, in Module 63, you will read about unhealthy personality types such as the paranoid personality, the dependent personality, and the antisocial personality. Each problem type is defined by a specific collection of traits that are not adaptive.

Self-Concept

Self-concepts provide another way of understanding personality. Your **self-concept** consists of all your ideas, perceptions, stories, and feelings about who you are. It is the mental "picture" that you have of your own personality (Fite et al., 2017; Ritchie et al., 2011).

We creatively build our self-concepts out of daily experiences. Then we slowly revise them as we have new experiences. Once a stable self-concept exists, it tends to guide what we pay attention to, remember, and think about. Because of this, self-concepts can greatly affect our behavior and personal adjustment—especially when they are inaccurate. For instance, Alesha is a student who thinks she is stupid, worthless, and a failure, despite getting good grades. With such an inaccurate self-concept, she tends to be depressed regardless of how well she does (Coelho, Marchante, & Jimerson, 2017).

Personality A person's unique and relatively stable patterns of thinking, emotions, and behavior.

Personality trait Stable quality that a person shows in most situations.

Personality type A style of personality defined by a group of related traits.

Introvert A person whose attention is focused inward; a shy, reserved, self-focused person.

Extrovert A person whose attention is directed outward; a bold, outgoing person.

Self-concept The perception of one's own personality traits.

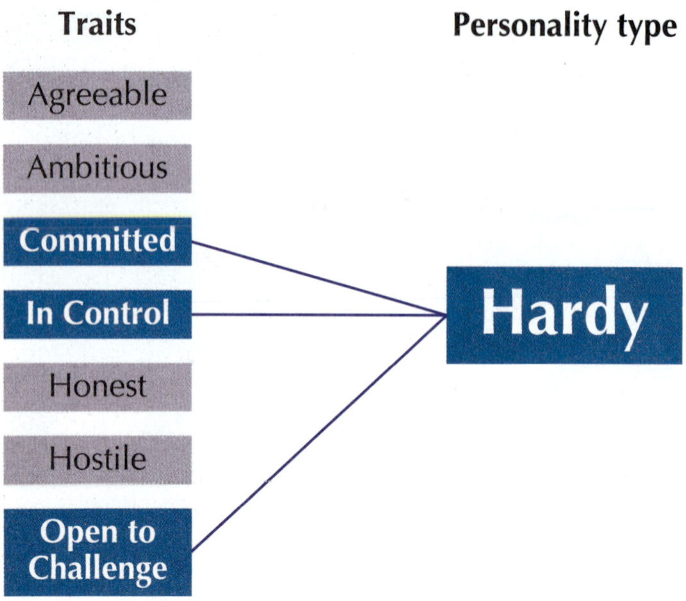

➤ **Figure 50.1**

Personality types. Personality types are defined by the presence of several specific traits. For example, several possible personality traits are shown in the left column. A person who has a hardy personality typically possesses all or most of the highlighted traits. Hardy persons are especially resistant to stress (see Module 58).

Self-Esteem

In addition to having a faulty self-concept, Alesha has low self-esteem (a negative self-evaluation). A person with high **self-esteem** is confident, proud, and self-respecting. One who has low self-esteem is insecure, lacking in confidence, and self-critical. Like Alesha, people with low self-esteem are usually anxious and unhappy. People who have low self-esteem typically also suffer from poor self-knowledge. Their self-concepts are inconsistent, inaccurate, and confused.

Self-concepts can be remarkably consistent. In an interesting study, old people were asked how they had changed over the years. Almost all thought that they were essentially the same person they were when they were young (Troll & Skaff, 1997). Nelson Mandela thought of himself as a highly committed human rights activist for his entire adult life, until his death in 2013 at the age of 95.

Self-esteem tends to rise when we experience success or praise. It also buffers us against negative experiences. A person who is competent and effective and who is loved, admired, and respected by others will almost always have high self-esteem (Baumeister et al., 2003; Coelho, Marchante, & Jimerson, 2017).

What if you "think you're hot," but you're not? For many people it's not so much a matter of an overly positive self-evaluation as much as a fragile one. Genuine self-esteem is based on an accurate appraisal of your strengths and weaknesses. A positive self-evaluation that is not securely held is unhealthy (Kernis & Lakey, 2010; Zeigler-Hill et al., 2016). Someone with fragile self-esteem may at first seem confident but can quickly become defensive when challenged.

Self-Esteem and Culture: Hotshot or Team Player?

The reasons for having high self-esteem can also vary across cultures.

For example, you and some friends are playing soccer. Your team wins, in part because you make some good plays. After the game, you bask in the glow of having performed well. You don't want to brag about being a hotshot, but your self-esteem gets a boost from your personal success.

In Japan, Shinobu (yup, *that* Shinobu) and some of his friends are playing soccer. His team wins, in part because he makes some good plays. After the game, Shinobu is happy because his team did well. However, Shinobu also dwells on the ways in which he let his team down. He thinks about how he could improve, and he resolves to be a better team player.

These sketches illustrate a basic difference in Eastern and Western psychology. In individualistic cultures such as the United States, self-esteem is frequently based on personal success and outstanding performance (Buss, 2012; Ross et al., 2005). For us, the path to higher self-esteem lies in self-enhancement. We are pumped up by our successes and tend to downplay our faults and failures.

Asian cultures frequently place a greater emphasis on collectivism or interdependence among people. For them, self-esteem is based on a secure sense of belonging to social groups. As a result, people in Asian cultures are more apt to engage in self-criticism (Kitayama, Markus, & Kurokawa, 2000; Tafarodi et al., 2011). By correcting personal faults, they add to the well-being of the group. And, when the *group* succeeds, individual members feel better about themselves, which raises their self-esteem.

Perhaps self-esteem is still based on success in both Eastern and Western cultures (Brown et al., 2009). However, it is fascinating that cultures define success in such different ways (Buss, 2012; Schmitt & Allik, 2005).

TABLE 50.1 | Comparison of Personality Theories

	Trait Theories	Psychoanalytic Theory	Humanistic Theories	Behaviorist and Social Learning Theories
Role of inheritance (genetics)	Maximized	Stressed	Minimized	Minimized
Role of environment	Recognized	Recognized	Maximized	Maximized
View of human nature	Neutral	Negative	Positive	Neutral
Is behavior free or determined?	Determined	Determined	Free will	Determined
Principal motives	Depends on one's traits	Sex and aggression	Self-actualization	Drives of all kinds
Personality structure	Traits	Id, ego, superego	Self	Habits, expectancies
Role of unconscious	Minimized	Maximized	Minimized	Practically nonexistent
Conception of conscience	Traits of honesty, etc.	Superego	Ideal self, valuing process	Self-reinforcement, punishment history
Developmental emphasis	Combined effects of heredity and environment	Psychosexual stages	Development of self-image	Critical learning situations, identification, and imitation
Barriers to personal growth	Unhealthy traits	Unconscious conflicts, fixations	Conditions of worth, incongruence	Maladaptive habits, unhealthy environment

The Whole Human: Personality Theories

As you can already see, it would be easy to get lost without a framework for understanding the richness of human personality. How do our thoughts, actions, and feelings relate to one another? How does personality develop? Why do some people suffer from psychological problems? How can they be helped? To answer such questions, psychologists have created a dazzling array of theories. A **personality theory** is a system of concepts, assumptions, ideas, and principles proposed to explain personality (Burger, 2019). Although many detailed personality theories have been put forward, they can be categorized into four broad perspectives:

1. **Trait theories** attempt to learn what traits make up personality and how they relate to actual behavior.
2. **Psychodynamic theories** focus on the inner workings of personality, especially internal conflicts and struggles.
3. **Humanistic theories** stress private, subjective experience and personal growth.
4. **Behaviorist and social learning theories** place importance on the external environment and on the effects of conditioning and learning. Social learning theories attribute differences in personality to socialization, expectations, and mental processes.

Which of the personality perspectives is right? To date, each of these broad personality perspectives has added to our understanding by providing a sort of lens through which human behavior can be viewed. Nevertheless, broad perspectives can't be fully proved or disproved. We can only ask, "Does the evidence tend to support or disconfirm a particular theory?" Yet, although perspectives are neither true nor false, their implications or predictions may be helpful. The best way to judge a perspective, then, is in terms of its usefulness. Does the perspective adequately explain behavior? Does it stimulate new research? Does it suggest how to treat psychological disorders? Each perspective has fared differently in these areas (Cervone & Pervin, 2013). ■ **Table 50.1** provides an overview of the four principal approaches to personality.

Self-esteem Regarding oneself as a worthwhile person; a positive evaluation of oneself.

Personality theory A system of concepts, assumptions, ideas, and principles used to understand and explain personality.

In the final analysis, the challenge now facing personality theorists is how to integrate the four major perspectives into a unified, systematic explanation of personality (Mayer, 2005; McAdams & Pals, 2006). With these broad perspectives in mind, let's explore some of the ways psychologists have attempted to assess personality.

Personality Assessment—Psychological Yardsticks

Learning Outcome 50.2 Outline four ways in which personality can be measured

Measuring personality can help predict how people will behave at work, at school, and in therapy. However, painting a detailed picture can be a challenge. Psychologists use interviews, observation, questionnaires, and projective tests to assess personality (Engler, 2014). Like the four personality theories, each method of measuring personality has strengths and limitations. For this reason, they are often used in combination.

Formal personality measures are refinements of more casual ways of judging a person. At one time or another, you have probably "sized up" a potential date, friend, or roommate by engaging in conversation (interview). Perhaps you have had the following conversation with a friend: "When I'm delayed, I get mad. Do you?" (questionnaire). Maybe you watch your professors when they are angry or embarrassed to learn what they are "really" like when they're caught off-guard (observation). Or possibly you have noticed that when you say, "I think people feel . . .," you may be expressing your own feelings (projection). Let's see how psychologists apply each of these methods to probe personality.

Interviews

In an **interview**, direct questioning is used to learn about a person's life history, personality traits, or current mental state (Craig, 2013; Murphy & Dillon, 2015). In an **unstructured interview**, conversation is informal and topics are taken up freely as they arise. In a **structured interview**, information is gathered by asking a planned series of questions.

How are interviews used? Interviews are used to select people for jobs, college, or special programs; to study the dynamics of personality; and to identify personality disturbances. Interviews also provide information for counseling or therapy. For instance, a counselor might ask a depressed person, "Have you ever contemplated suicide? What were the circumstances?" The counselor might then follow by asking, "How did you feel about it?" or, "How is what you are now feeling different from what you felt then?"

In addition to providing information, interviews make it possible to observe a person's tone of voice, hand gestures, posture, and facial expressions. Such "body language" cues are important because they may radically alter the message sent, as when a person claims to be "completely calm" but trembles uncontrollably.

Limitations Interviews can give rapid insight into personality, but they have limitations. For one thing, interviewers can be swayed by preconceptions. A person identified as a "housewife," "college student," "high school athlete," "punk," "geek," or "ski bum" may be misjudged because of an interviewer's personal biases (Forgas, 2011). Second, an interviewer's own personality, gender, or ethnicity may influence a client's behavior. When this occurs, it can accentuate or distort the person's apparent traits (Kaplan & Saccuzzo, 2018). A third problem is that people sometimes try to deceive interviewers. For example, a person accused of a crime might try to avoid punishment by pretending to be mentally disabled.

A fourth problem is the **halo effect**, which is the tendency to generalize a favorable (or unfavorable) impression to an entire personality (Hartung et al., 2010). Because of the halo effect, a person who is likable or physically attractive may be rated more mature, intelligent, or mentally healthy than she or he actually is. The halo effect is something to keep in mind at job interviews.

g-stockstudio/Shutterstock.com

What is your impression of this person awaiting a job interview? If you think that he looks friendly, attractive, or neat, your other perceptions of him might be altered by that impression. Interviewers are often influenced by the halo effect (see text).

Even with their limitations, interviews are a respected method of assessment. In many cases, interviews are the first step in evaluating personality and an essential prelude to therapy. Nevertheless, interviews are usually not revealing enough and must be supplemented by other measures and tests (Murphy & Dillon, 2015; Meyer et al., 2001).

Direct Observation and Rating Scales

Are you fascinated by airports, bus depots, parks, taverns, subway stations, or other public places? Many people relish a chance to observe the actions of others. When used for assessment, looking at behavior by **direct observation** is a simple extension of this natural interest in "people watching." For instance, a psychologist might arrange to observe a disturbed child as she plays with other children. Is the child withdrawn? Does she become hostile or aggressive without warning? By careful observation, the psychologist can identify the girl's personality traits and clarify the nature of her problems.

Wouldn't observation be subject to the same problems of misperception as an interview? Yes. Misperceptions can be a difficulty, which is why rating scales are sometimes used (➤ Figure 50.2). A **rating scale** is a list of personality traits or aspects of behavior that can be used to evaluate a person (Siefert, 2010). Rating scales limit the chance that some traits will be overlooked while others are exaggerated (Synhorst et al., 2005). Perhaps they should be a standard procedure for choosing a roommate, spouse, or lover!

An alternative approach is to do a **behavioral assessment** by counting the frequency of specific behaviors (Cipani & Schock, 2010). In this case, observers record *actions,* not what traits they think a person has. For example, a psychologist working with hospitalized psychiatric patients might note the frequency of a patient's aggression, self-care, speech, and unusual behaviors. Behavioral assessments also can be used to probe thought processes. In one study, for example, couples were assessed while talking with each other about their sexuality. Couples with sexual difficulties were

Interview (personality) A face-to-face meeting held for the purpose of gaining information about an individual's personal history, personality traits, current psychological state, and so forth.

Unstructured interview An interview in which conversation is informal and topics are taken up freely as they arise.

Structured interview An interview that follows a prearranged plan, usually a series of planned questions.

Halo effect The tendency to generalize a favorable or unfavorable particular impression to unrelated details of personality.

Direct observation Assessing behavior through direct surveillance.

Rating scale A list of personality traits or aspects of behavior on which a person is rated.

Behavioral assessment Recording the frequency of various behaviors.

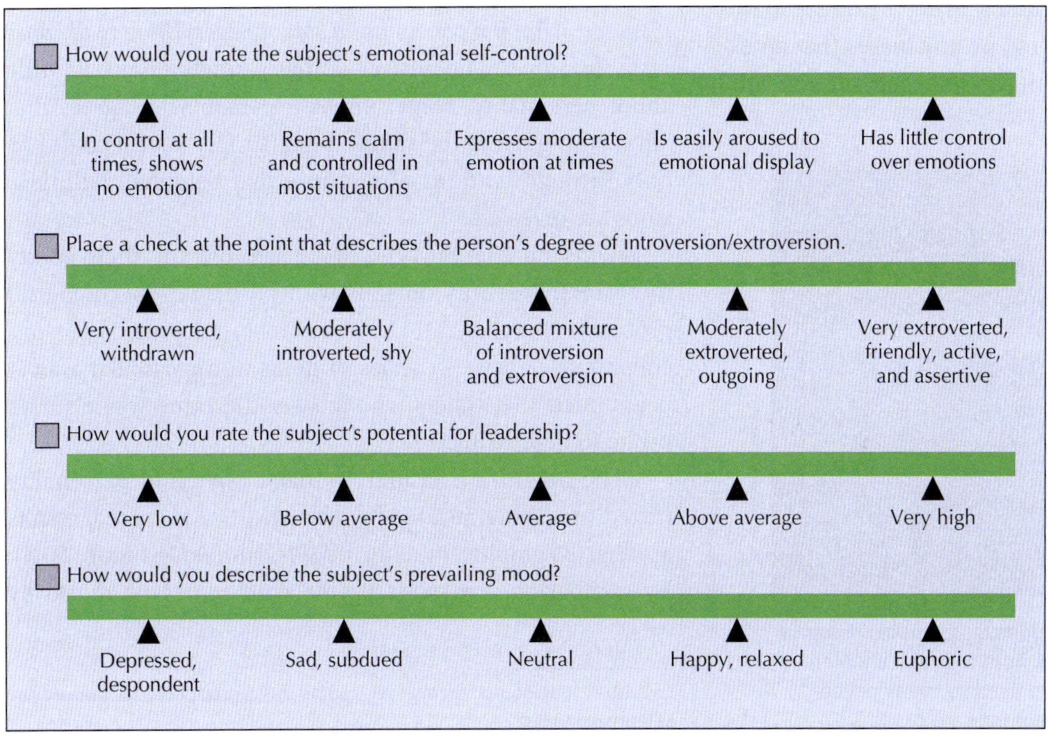

➤ **Figure 50.2**

Sample rating scale items. To understand how the scale works, imagine someone you know well. Where would you place check marks on each of the scales to rate that person's characteristics?

less likely to be receptive to discussing their sexuality and more likely to blame each other than were couples with no sexual difficulties (Kelly, Strassberg, & Turner, 2006).

Situational Testing In a **situational test**, a type of direct observation, real-life conditions are simulated so that a person's spontaneous reactions can be observed. Such tests assume that the best way to learn how people react is to put them in realistic situations and watch what happens. Situational tests expose people to frustration, temptation, pressure, boredom, or other conditions capable of revealing personality characteristics (De Leng et al., 2016). Some popular reality TV programs, such as *Naked and Afraid, Survivor,* and *The Amazing Race* bear some similarity to situational tests—which may account for their ability to attract millions of viewers.

How are situational tests done? An interesting example of situational testing is the judgmental firearms training provided by many police departments. At times, police officers must make split-second decisions about using their weapons. A mistake could be fatal. In a typical "shoot–don't shoot" test, actors play the part of armed criminals. As various high-risk scenes are acted out live or online, officers must decide to shoot or hold their fire.

Personality Questionnaires

A **personality questionnaire** is a paper-and-pencil test designed to reveal personality characteristics. Questionnaires are more objective than interviews or observation. (An **objective test** gives the same score when different people score it.) Questions, administration, and scoring are all standardized, so that scores are unaffected by any biases that an examiner may have. A good test must also be reliable and valid (Kaplan & Saccuzzo, 2018). A test has **reliability** if it yields stable scores over time—that is, if it yields close to the same score each time that it is given to the same person. A test has **validity** if it measures the trait it was designed to. Unfortunately, many personality tests that you will encounter, such as those in magazines or on the Internet, have little or no validity. Finally, an objective test benefits from extensive **norms**, standards used to compare an individual's performance on a test with that of others.

Dozens of personality tests are available, including the *Guilford-Zimmerman Temperament Survey* (GZTS), the *California Psychological Inventory* (CPI), the *Eysenck Personality Questionnaire* (EPQ), the *Sixteen Personality Factor Questionnaire* (16 PF), and the *Neuroticism, Extraversion, Openness Personality Inventory* (NEO-PI), which is based on the Big 5 theory. One of the best-known and most widely used standardized tests is the **Minnesota Multiphasic Personality Inventory** (MMPI). The current version, the MMPI-2, is composed of 567 items to which a test taker must respond "true" or "false" (Butcher, 2011). Items include statements such as the following:

Everything tastes the same.
I am very normal, sexually.
I like birds.
I usually daydream in the afternoon.
Mostly, I stay away from other people.
Someone has been trying to hurt me.
Sometimes I think strange thoughts.*

How can these items show anything about personality? For instance, what if a person has a cold, so everything really does taste the same? The answer is that a single item tells little about personality. For example, a person who agrees that "Everything tastes the same" might simply have a cold. It is only through *patterns* of response that personality dimensions are revealed.

Items on the MMPI-2 were selected for their ability to correctly identify persons with particular psychological problems (Butcher, 2011). For instance, if depressed persons consistently answer a series of items in a particular way, it is assumed that others who answer the same way also are prone to depression.

The MMPI-2 measures 10 major aspects of personality (listed in ■ Table 50.2). After the MMPI-2 is scored, results are charted graphically as an *MMPI-2 profile* (➤ Figure 50.3). By comparing a person's profile with scores produced by

Larry St. Pierre/Shutterstock.com

A police special tactics team undergoes a judgmental firearms training exercise to protect students from a school shooter. Variations on this situational test are used by many police departments. All officers must score a passing grade.

*MMPI-2 statements themselves cannot be reproduced, to protect the validity of the test.

TABLE 50.2 | MMPI-2 Basic Clinical Subscales

1. **Hs—Hypochondriasis.** Exaggerated concern about one's physical health
2. **D—Depression.** Feelings of worthlessness, hopelessness, and pessimism
3. **Hy—Hysteria.** The presence of physical complaints for which no physical basis can be established
4. **Pd—Psychopathic deviate.** Emotional shallowness in relationships and a disregard for social and moral standards
5. **Mf—Masculinity/femininity.** One's degree of traditional "masculine" aggressiveness or "feminine" sensitivity
6. **Pa—Paranoia.** Extreme suspiciousness and feelings of persecution
7. **Pt—Psychasthenia.** The presence of obsessive worries, irrational fears (phobias), and compulsive (ritualistic) actions
8. **Sc—Schizophrenia.** Emotional withdrawal and unusual or bizarre thinking and actions
9. **Ma—Mania.** Emotional excitability, manic moods or behavior, and excessive activity
10. **Si—Social introversion.** One's tendency to be socially withdrawn

typical, normal adults, a psychologist can identify various personality disorders. Additional scales can identify substance abuse, eating disorders, repression, anger, cynicism, low self-esteem, family problems, inability to function in a job, and other problems (Butcher, 2011).

How accurate is the MMPI-2? Personality questionnaires are accurate only if people tell the truth about themselves. Because of this, the MMPI-2 has additional *validity scales* that reveal whether a person's scores should be discarded. The validity scales detect attempts by test takers to "fake good" (make themselves look good) or "fake bad" (make it look like they have problems) (Scherbaum et al., 2013).

Situational test Simulating real-life conditions so that a person's reactions may be directly observed.

Personality questionnaire A paper-and-pencil test consisting of questions that reveal aspects of personality.

Objective test A test that gives the same score when different people score it.

Reliability Stability of test scores over time.

Validity Degree to which a test measures the trait that it was designed to.

Norm Standard used to compare an individual's performance on a test with that of others.

Minnesota Multiphasic Personality Inventory A standardized test designed to identify problem areas of functioning in an individual's personality.

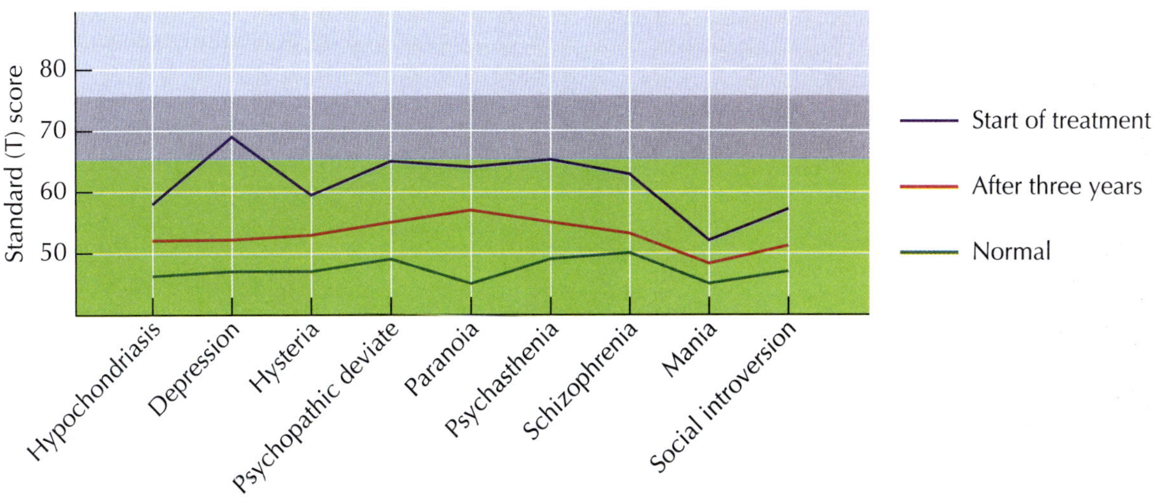

➤ **Figure 50.3**

MMPI-2 profiles. The MMPI-2 can even track progress in therapy. At the start of treatment, the scores of a group of severely troubled individuals were elevated on most of the individual scales. (Note that the masculinity/femininity scores are not included.) After 3 years of therapy, their scores have declined significantly and are much more similar to normal scores, which usually fall in the 45–50 range. An unusually low score (40 and below) also may reveal personality characteristics or problems. (Adapted from Gordon, 2001.)

Other scales uncover defensiveness or tendencies to exaggerate shortcomings and troubles. When taking the MMPI-2, it is best to answer honestly and not try to second-guess the test.

A clinical psychologist trying to decide whether a person has emotional problems would be wise to take more than the MMPI-2 into account. Test scores are informative, but they can incorrectly label some people (Kaplan & Saccuzzo, 2018). Fortunately, clinical judgments usually rely on information from interviews, tests, and other sources. Also, despite their limitations, it is reassuring to note that psychological assessments are at least as accurate as commonly used medical tests (Neukrug & Fawcett, 2020).

Projective Tests of Personality

Projective tests take a different approach to personality. Interviews, observation, rating scales, and inventories try to directly identify overt, observable traits. By contrast, projective tests seek to uncover deeply hidden or *unconscious* wishes, thoughts, and needs (Burger, 2015; McGrath & Carroll, 2012).

As a child, you may have delighted in finding faces and objects in cloud formations. Or perhaps you have learned something about your friends' personalities from their reactions to movies or paintings. If so, you have some insight into the rationale for projective tests. In **projective tests**, a person is asked to describe ambiguous or unstructured stimuli or make up stories about them. Describing an unambiguous stimulus (a picture of an automobile, for example) tells little about your personality. But when you are faced with an unstructured stimulus, you must organize what you see in terms of your own life experiences. Everyone sees something different in a projective test, and what is perceived can reveal the inner workings of personality.

Projective tests have no right or wrong answers, which makes them difficult to fake. Moreover, projective tests can be a rich source of information because responses are not restricted to simple true/false or yes/no answers.

The Rorschach Inkblot Test *Is the inkblot test a projective technique?* The **Rorschach Inkblot Test** (ROAR-shock) is one of the oldest and most widely used projective tests. Developed by Swiss psychologist Hermann Rorschach in the 1920s, it consists of 10 standardized inkblots forming complex, irregular shapes.

How does the test work? First, a person is shown each blot and asked to describe what she or he sees in it (➤ **Figure 50.4**). Later, the psychologist may return to a blot, asking the person to identify specific sections of it, to expand previous descriptions, or to give new impressions about what it contains. Obvious differences in content—such as "blood dripping from a dagger" versus "flowers blooming in a basket"—are important for identifying personal conflicts and fantasies. But surprisingly, content is less important than what parts of the inkblot are used to organize images. These factors allow psychologists to detect emotional disturbances by observing how a person perceives the world (Bornstein, 2012; Kishimoto et al., 2016). Schizophrenia and other psychotic disorders are associated with severe disturbances in thinking and perception (see Module 61). Such disturbances are usually readily apparent during projective testing (Moore et al., 2013).

The Thematic Apperception Test Another popular projective test is the **Thematic Apperception Test (TAT)**, developed by personality theorist Henry Murray (1893–1988).

➤ **Figure 50.4**

The Rorschach. Inkblots similar to those used on the Rorschach. What do you see?

How does the TAT differ from the Rorschach? The TAT consists of 20 sketches depicting various scenes and life situations (➤ **Figure 50.5**). During testing, a person is shown each sketch and asked to make up a story about the people in it. Later, the person looks at each sketch a second or a third time and elaborates on previous stories or creates new stories.

To score the TAT, a psychologist analyzes the content of the stories. Interpretations focus on how people feel, how they interact, what events led up to the incidents depicted in the sketch, and how the story will end. For example, TAT stories told by bereaved college students typically include themes of death, grief, and coping with loss (Balk et al., 1998).

A psychologist might also count how many times the central figure in a TAT story is angry, overlooked, apathetic, jealous, or threatened. A student wrote the following story to describe Figure 50.5:

> The girl has been seeing this guy her mother doesn't like. The mother is telling her that she better not see him again. The mother says, "He's just like your father." The mother and father are divorced. The mother is smiling because she thinks she is right. But she doesn't really know what the girl wants. The girl is going to see the guy again, anyway.

As this example implies, the TAT is especially good at revealing feelings about social situations and relationships (Jenkins, Dobbs, & Leeper, 2015; Serfass & Sherman, 2013).

➤ **Figure 50.5**

The Thematic Apperception Test. This is a picture like those used for the TAT. If you wish to simulate the test, tell a story that explains what led up to the pictured situation, what is happening now, and how the action will end.

Limitations of Projective Testing Although projective tests have been popular, their validity is open to question (Ackerman, Lewis, & Taylor, 2014; Bornstein, 2012). Objectivity and reliability (consistency) also are low for different users of the TAT and Rorschach. Note that after a person interprets an ambiguous stimulus, the scorer must interpret the person's (sometimes) ambiguous responses. In a sense, the interpretation of a projective test may be a projective test for the scorer!

Despite their drawbacks, projective tests still have value (McGrath & Carroll, 2012). This is especially true when they are used as part of a *test battery* (collection of assessment devices and interviews). In the hands of a skilled clinician, projective tests can be a good way to detect major conflicts, to get clients to talk about upsetting topics, and to set goals for therapy (Garcia-Barrera et al., 2013).

Projective tests Personality tests that use ambiguous or unstructured stimuli.

Rorschach Inkblot Test Projective test that consists of complex, irregular monochromatic shapes.

Thematic Apperception Test (TAT) A projective test consisting of 20 different scenes and life situations about which respondents make up stories.

MODULE 50 Overview of Personality—Learning Outcomes Revisited

50.1 Define what psychologists mean by the term *personality*, explaining its relation to personality traits, types, self-concept, and self-esteem, and name four basic perspectives on personality

Personality refers to a person's consistent and unique patterns of thinking, emotion, and behavior. Personality traits are lasting personal qualities that are inferred from behavior. Personality types group people into categories on the basis of shared traits. Behavior is influenced by self-concept, which is a perception of one's own personality traits. A positive self-evaluation leads to high self-esteem. Low self-esteem is associated with stress, unhappiness, and depression. Four theories put forward to explain personality include trait theories, psychodynamic theory, humanistic theories, and behaviorist theories (including social learning theory).

50.2 Outline four ways in which personality can be measured

Techniques typically used for personality assessment are interviews, observation, questionnaires, and projective tests. Structured and unstructured interviews provide much information, but they are subject to interviewer bias and misperceptions. The halo effect may also reduce the accuracy of an interview. Direct observation, sometimes involving situational tests, behavioral assessment, or the use of rating scales, allows evaluation of a person's actual behavior. Personality questionnaires, such as the *Minnesota Multiphasic Personality Inventory-2 (MMPI-2)*, are objective and reliable, but their validity is open to question. Projective tests ask a person to project thoughts or feelings onto an ambiguous stimulus or unstructured situation. Two well-known examples are the *Rorschach Inkblot Test* and the *Thematic Apperception Test (TAT)*. Projective tests are low in validity and objectivity. Nevertheless, they are considered useful by many clinicians, particularly as part of a test battery.

Reflective Practice

Content Check

1. An individual's perception of his or her own personality constitutes that person's ____________________.
2. The halo effect can be a serious problem in accurate personality assessment that is based on
   a. projective testing
   b. behavioral recording
   c. interviewing
   d. the TAT
3. Doing a behavioral assessment requires direct observation of the person's actions or a direct report of the person's thoughts. T or F?
4. A test is considered valid if it consistently yields the same score when the same person takes it on different occasions. T or F?
5. Which of the following is considered the most objective measure of personality?
   a. rating scales
   b. personality questionnaires
   c. projective tests
   d. TAT
6. The use of ambiguous stimuli is most characteristic of
   a. interviews
   b. projective tests
   c. personality inventories
   d. direct observation

Skill Check

Think Critically

7. Projective testing would be of greatest interest to which type of personality theorist?

Self-Reflect

See if you can define or describe the following terms in your own words: *personality, character, trait, type, self-concept, self-esteem.* How do *you* assess personality? Do you informally use any of the methods described in this module?

ANSWERS

1. self-concept 2. c 3. T 4. F 5. b 6. b 7. Psychodynamic, because projective testing is designed to uncover unconscious thoughts, feelings, and conflicts.

Personality
Trait Theories

MODULE 51

Conscientious Drivers Rarely Do This!

Sam is a good guy and a great friend. He's talkative, curious, and good-natured. Conscientious? Not so much. Sam's more likely to be found socializing at the local students' pub than studying at the library.

Trait theories seek to describe personality in terms of a small number of underlying personality traits or factors, like the adjectives we used to describe Sam. The trait approach is currently the dominant method for studying personality. Of the various trait theories, the *Big Five theory* is currently the most influential. According to this theory, all personalities can be described as varying along five key factors: *extroversion, agreeableness, conscientiousness, neuroticism,* and *openness to experience.*

Knowing where a person stands on the "Big Five" personality traits helps predict his or her behavior. For example, people who score high on conscientiousness tend to be safe drivers who are less likely to have automobile accidents (Sam, Sam, what have you done! lol).

Thomas Barrat/Shutterstock.com

~LEARNING OUTCOMES~

After reading this module you should be able to:

51.1 Outline the trait approach to understanding personality

The Trait Approach—Describe Yourself in 18,000 Words or Less

Learning Outcome 51.1 Outline the trait approach to understanding personality

Take a moment to read through ■ **Table 51.1** and check the traits that describe your personality. Don't worry if some of your key traits aren't in the table. More than 18,000 English words refer to personal characteristics. Are the traits you checked of equal importance? Are some stronger or more basic than others? Do any overlap? For example, if you checked "dominant," did you also check "confident" and "bold"? Answers to these questions would interest a trait theorist.

To better understand personality, *trait theorists* attempt to analyze, classify, and interrelate traits. In addition, trait theorists often think of traits as *biological predispositions,*

TABLE 51.1 | Adjective Checklist

Check the traits that you feel are characteristic of your personality. Are some more basic than others?			
Aggressive	Organized	Ambitious	Clever
Confident	Loyal	Generous	Calm
Warm	Bold	Cautious	Reliable
Sensitive	Mature	Talented	Jealous
Sociable	Honest	Funny	Religious
Dominant	Dull	Accurate	Nervous
Humble	Uninhibited	Visionary	Cheerful
Thoughtful	Serious	Helpful	Emotional
Orderly	Anxious	Conforming	Good-natured
Liberal	Curious	Optimistic	Kind
Meek	Neighborly	Passionate	Compulsive

a hereditary readiness of humans to behave in particular ways. (We encountered this idea before, in Module 63, in which humans were described as having a biological predisposition to learn language.)

Hereditary or not, traits are stable dispositions that a person shows in most situations (Mõttus, Johnson, & Deary, 2012). For example, if you are usually friendly, optimistic, and cautious, these qualities are traits of your personality.

What if I am also sometimes shy, pessimistic, or uninhibited? The original three qualities are still traits so long as they are most *typical* of your behavior. Let's say that Lin's old boyfriend Winston approaches most situations with optimism but tends to expect the worst each time he applies for a job. If his pessimism is limited to this situation or just a few others, it is still accurate and useful to describe him as an optimistic person.

Predicting Behavior

As we have noted, separating people into broad types, such as "introvert" or "extrovert," may oversimplify personality. However, introversion/extroversion also can be thought of as a trait. Knowing how you rate on this single dimension allows us to predict how you will behave in a variety of settings. How, for example, do you prefer to meet people—face-to-face or through the Internet? Researchers have found that students high in the trait of introversion are more likely to prefer the Internet because they find it easier to talk with people online (Mitchell et al., 2011; Rice & Markey, 2009). Other interesting links exist between traits and behavior. For a "dark" example, read on.

The Dark Triad: Oh, Oh, Seven Ian Fleming's character, James Bond, is undoubtedly the most famous fictional spy of all time, having appeared in 24 official Bond films since 1962. But suppose that he was real and was your boyfriend, husband, brother, or best friend. Very cool, no? Maybe not. According to psychologist Peter Jonason and his colleagues, Bond is a charming, manipulative, cold-blooded killer who is comfortable operating outside the law. He is also an impeccable dresser who casually beds women as it suits him (Jonason et al., 2012).

There are no real people like 007, right? Don't be so sure. See ■ **Table 51.2** to rate yourself on the "Dirty Dozen" (Jonason & Webster, 2010). A high score on the first four questions is associated with the trait of *Machiavellianism*, a willingness to manipulate others. A high score on the middle four questions is associated with the trait of *psychopathy*, an impulsive lack of empathy for others. A high score on the last four questions is associated with the trait of *narcissism*, a self-centeredness often based on feelings of superiority. Taken together, these three interrelated traits make up the *dark triad* (Furnham, Richards, & Paulhus, 2013).

Aren't these traits signs of mental illness? In Module 60, we will discuss personality disorders such as narcissistic personality disorder. Individuals with these disorders typically express dark triad traits, *but to the extreme*. In contrast,

TABLE 51.2 | The Dirty Dozen

On a scale where 1 means strongly disagree and 5 means strongly agree, circle the number which best describes how well you think each of the following statements applies to you.					
	Strongly disagree			Strongly agree	
1. I tend to manipulate others to get my way.	1	2	3	4	5
2. I have used deceit or lied to get my way.	1	2	3	4	5
3. I have used flattery to get my way.	1	2	3	4	5
4. I tend to exploit others toward my own end.	1	2	3	4	5
5. I tend to lack remorse.	1	2	3	4	5
6. I tend to be unconcerned with the morality of my actions.	1	2	3	4	5
7. I tend to be callous or insensitive.	1	2	3	4	5
8. I tend to be cynical.	1	2	3	4	5
9. I tend to want others to admire me.	1	2	3	4	5
10. I tend to want others to pay attention to me.	1	2	3	4	5
11. I tend to seek prestige or status.	1	2	3	4	5
12. I tend to expect special favors from others.	1	2	3	4	5

these traits are **subclinical** in many dark triad personalities, and hence not extreme enough to qualify for a diagnosis.

As you might imagine, dark personalities tend to be men who are risk takers and are more likely to smoke, drink, and do drugs (Jonason, Koenig, & Tost, 2010). Although these "bad boys" also tend to be promiscuous and indiscriminate in their choice of sex partners, women find them strangely attractive (Aitken, Lyons, & Jonason, 2013; Carter, Campbell, & Muncer, 2014). (It is worth noting that some women also have dark triad personalities [Jonason & Lavertu, 2017].)

You think you know someone like that? Try using the Dirty Dozen to rate that person. If the scores are high, you might just have identified a real-life dark personality. Oh, oh.

Classifying Traits

Are there different types of traits? Yes. Psychologist Gordon Allport (1897–1967) distinguished between *central traits* and *secondary traits.*

Central and Secondary Traits

How do central and secondary traits differ? **Central traits** are the basic building blocks of personality. A surprisingly small number of central traits can capture the essence of a person. For instance, just six traits would provide a good description of Jacintha's personality: dominant, sociable, honest, cheerful, intelligent, and optimistic. When college students were asked to describe someone they knew well, they mentioned an average of seven central traits (Allport, 1961).

Secondary traits are more superficial personal qualities, such as food preferences, attitudes, political opinions, musical tastes, and so forth. In Allport's terms, a personality description might therefore include the following items:

Name: Jane Doe

Age: 22

Central traits: Possessive, autonomous, artistic, dramatic, self-centered, trusting

Secondary traits: Prefers colorful clothes, likes to work alone, politically liberal, always late

Source and Surface Traits

How can you tell whether a personality trait is central or secondary? Raymond B. Cattell (1906–1998) tried to answer this question by directly studying the traits of a large number of people. Cattell began by measuring visible features of personality, which he called **surface traits**. Soon, Cattell noticed that these surface

Subclinical (traits) Qualities of individuals that are not extreme enough to merit a psychiatric diagnosis.

Central traits The core traits that characterize an individual personality.

Secondary traits Traits that are inconsistent or relatively superficial.

Surface traits The visible or observable traits of one's personality.

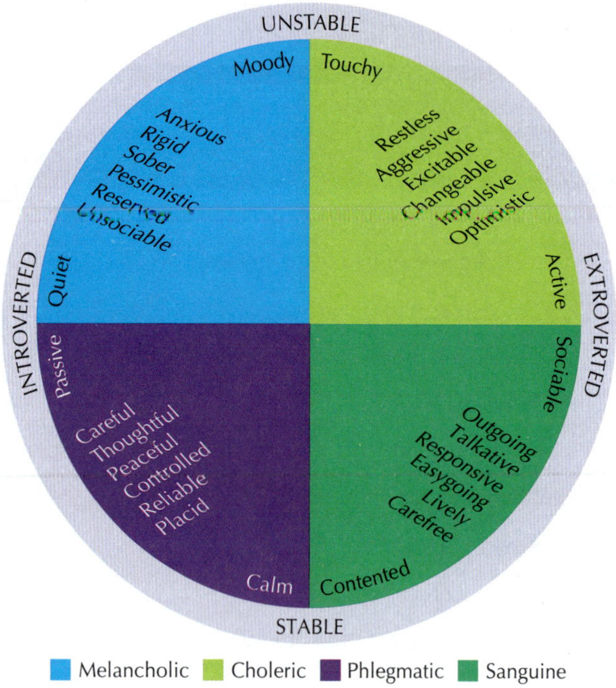

➤ **Figure 51.1**

Eysenck's two-factor theory of personality. English psychologist Hans Eysenck (1916–1997) proposed that many personality traits are related to whether you are mainly introverted or extroverted and whether you tend to be emotionally stable or unstable (highly emotional). These characteristics, in turn, are related to four basic types of temperament first recognized by the early Greeks. The types are *melancholic* (sad, gloomy), *choleric* (hot-tempered, irritable), *phlegmatic* (sluggish, calm), and *sanguine* (cheerful, hopeful). (Adapted from Eysenck, 1981.)

traits often appeared together in groups. In fact, some traits clustered together so often that they seemed to represent a single, more basic trait. Cattell called these deeper characteristics, or dimensions, **source traits (factors)** (Cattell, 1965). They are the core of an individual's personality.

How do source traits differ from Allport's central traits? Allport classified traits subjectively, and it's possible that he was wrong at times. To look for connections among traits, Cattell used **factor analysis**, a statistical technique used to correlate multiple measurements and identify general underlying factors. For example, he found that imaginative people are almost always inventive, original, curious, creative, innovative, and ingenious. If you are an imaginative person, we automatically know that you have several other traits. Thus, *imaginative* is a source trait, or factor. For example, ➤ **Figure 51.1** shows one of the first trait theories, composed of two factors, introversion–extroversion and emotionally stable–unstable.

Cattell (1973) identified 16 source traits. According to him, all 16 are needed to fully describe a personality. Source traits are measured by the *Sixteen Personality Factor Questionnaire* (often referred to as the *16 PF*). Like many personality tests, the 16 PF can be used to produce a *trait profile*, a graph of a person's score on each trait. Trait profiles draw a "picture" of individual personalities, which makes it easier to compare them (➤ **Figure 51.2**).

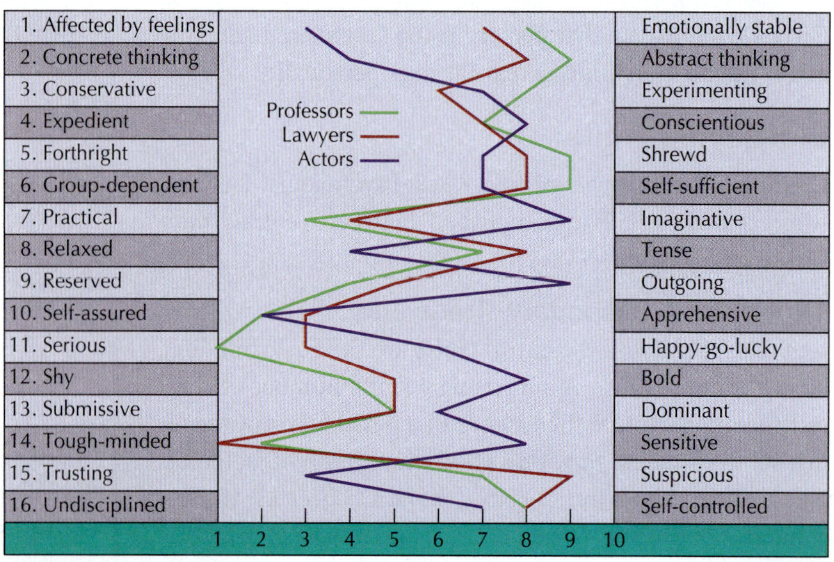

➤ **Figure 51.2**

Hypothetical 16 PF profiles. The 16 source traits measured by Cattell's (1973) 16 PF are listed beside the graph. Scores can be plotted as a profile for an individual or a group. The hypothetical profiles shown here are group averages for college professors, lawyers, and professional actors. Notice the similarities between professors and lawyers and the differences between these two groups and professional actors. (Of course, your authors may only be expressing the common stereotype that professors and lawyers are more reserved abstract thinkers than actors or that actors are less emotionally stable and more happy-go-lucky than professors and lawyers. What do you think?)

The Big Five

Noel is outgoing and friendly, conscientious, even-tempered, and curious. His brother Joel is reserved, hostile, irresponsible, temperamental, and uninterested in ideas. You will be spending a week in a space capsule with either Noel or Joel. Who would you choose? If the answer seems obvious, it's because Noel and Joel were described with the **Big Five personality traits**, a theory that only a handful of characteristics account for most individual differences in personality.

Five Key Dimensions The "Big Five" traits shown in ➤ Figure 51.3 attempt to reduce Cattell's 16 factors to just five factors, or source traits (McCrae & Costa, 2013; Noftle & Fleeson, 2010). The Big Five may be the best answer of all to the question: What is the essence of human personality?

If you would like to compare the personalities of two people, try rating them informally on the five dimensions shown in Figure 51.3. For *extroversion,* rate how introverted or extroverted each person is. *Agreeableness* refers to how friendly, nurturant, and caring a person is, as opposed to cold, indifferent, self-centered, or spiteful. A person who is *conscientious* is self-disciplined, responsible, and achieving. People low on this factor are irresponsible, careless, and undependable. *Neuroticism* refers to negative, upsetting emotions. People who are high in neuroticism tend to be anxious, emotionally "sour," irritable, and unhappy. Finally, people who rate high on *openness to experience* are creative and open to new ideas (Ashcraft, 2015).

The beauty of the Big Five theory is that almost any trait that you can name will be related to one of these five factors. If you were selecting a college roommate, hiring an employee, or answering a post at a singles site, you would probably want to know all the personal dimensions covered by the Big Five.

Source traits (factors) Basic underlying traits, or dimensions, of personality; each source trait is reflected in a number of surface traits.

Factor analysis A statistical technique used to correlate multiple measurements and identify general underlying factors.

Big Five personality traits Theory that only a handful of characteristics account for most individual differences in personality.

Extroversion										
Loner Quiet Passive Reserved	Low	1	2	3	4	5	6	7	High	Joiner Talkative Active Affectionate

Agreeableness										
Suspicious Critical Ruthless Irritable	Low	1	2	3	4	5	6	7	High	Trusting Lenient Soft-hearted Good-natured

Conscientiousness										
Negligent Lazy Disorganized Late	Low	1	2	3	4	5	6	7	High	Conscientious Hard-working Well-organized Punctual

Neuroticism										
Calm Even-tempered Comfortable Unemotional	Low	1	2	3	4	5	6	7	High	Worried Temperamental Self-conscious Emotional

Openness to Experience										
Down-to-earth Uncreative Conventional Uncurious	Low	1	2	3	4	5	6	7	High	Imaginative Creative Original Curious

➤ **Figure 51.3**

The Big Five. According to the five-factor model, basic differences in personality can be "boiled down" to the dimensions shown here. Rate yourself on each factor. The five-factor model answers these essential questions about a person: Is she or he extroverted or introverted? Agreeable or difficult? Conscientious or irresponsible? Emotionally stable or unstable? Curious or uncreative? These dimensions cover a large measure of what we might want to know about someone's personality. (Trait descriptions adapted from McCrae & Costa, 2001.)

The Big Five traits have been related to different brain systems and chemicals (DeYoung et al., 2010; Nettle, 2008). They also predict how people will act in various circumstances (Heidemeier & Göritz, 2016; Sutin & Costa, 2010). For example, people who score high in conscientiousness tend to perform well at work, do well in school, and rarely have automobile accidents (Brown et al., 2010; Chamorro-Premuzic & Furnham, 2003). They are healthier and even live longer (Hampson et al., 2013; Martin, Friedman, & Schwartz, 2007).

Which Personality Are You (and Which Is Best)?

Does that mean some Big Five trait scores are better than others? According to the *Big Five theory,* your rating on each of five basic personality traits, or factors, gives a good overall description of your personality. Try rating yourself (see Figure 51.2). How well do you think your ratings describe you? When you were rating yourself, did you notice that some of the traits don't seem very attractive? After all, who would want to score low in *Extroversion*? What could be good about being a quiet, passive, and reserved loner? In other words, aren't some personality patterns better than others?

You might be surprised to learn that there is no single "best" personality pattern. For example, extroverts tend to earn more during their careers than introverts, and they have more sexual partners. But they also are more likely to take risks than introverts (and to land in the hospital with an injury). Extroverts also are more likely to divorce. Because of this, extroverted men are less likely to live with their children. In other words, extroversion tends to open the doors to some life experiences, and introversion opens doors to others (Cain, 2012; Nettle, 2005).

The same is true for *agreeableness.* Agreeable people attract more friends and enjoy strong social support from others. But agreeable people often put the interests of friends and family ahead of their own. This can leave such people at a disadvantage. To do creative, artistic work or to succeed in the business world often involves putting your own interests first (Nettle, 2008).

How about conscientiousness? Up to a point, conscientiousness is associated with high achievement. However, having impossibly high standards, a trait called *perfectionism,* can be a problem. As you might expect, college students who are perfectionists tend to get good grades. Yet some students cross the line into maladaptive perfectionism, which typically *lowers* performance at school and elsewhere (Weiner & Carton, 2012). Authentic Navajo rugs always have a flaw in their intricate designs. Navajo weavers intentionally make a "mistake" in each rug as a reminder that humans are not perfect. There is a lesson in this: It is not always necessary, or even desirable, to be "perfect." To learn from your experiences, you must feel free to make mistakes. Success, in the long run, is more often based on seeking "excellence" rather than "perfection" (Enns, Cox, & Clara, 2005).

Except for very extreme personality patterns, which are often maladaptive, most "personalities" involve a mix of costs and benefits (Turiano et al., 2013). We all face the task of pursuing life experiences that best suit our own unique personality patterns (Nettle, 2008).

MODULE 51 Trait Theories—Learning Outcomes Revisited

51.1 Outline the trait approach to understanding personality

Trait theories identify qualities that are most lasting or characteristic of a person. Allport made a useful distinction between central and secondary traits. Cattell's theory attributes visible surface traits to the existence of 16 underlying source traits. Source traits are measured by the *Sixteen Personality Factor Questionnaire* (16 PF). The five-factor model identifies five universal dimensions of personality: extroversion, agreeableness, conscientiousness, neuroticism, and openness to experience.

Reflective Practice

Content Check

1. Eysenck's early trait theory was composed of two factors, emotional stability–instability and ____________.
2. Traits are stable dispositions that a person shows in most ____________.
3. Central traits are those shared by most members of a culture. T or F?
4. Cattell believes that clusters of ____________ traits reveal the presence of underlying ____________ traits.

5. Which of the following is *not* one of the Big Five personality traits?
   a. submissiveness
   b. agreeableness
   c. extroversion
   d. neuroticism

Skill Check

Think Critically

6. Can you think of a Big Five trait besides conscientiousness that might be related to academic achievement?

Self-Reflect

List six or seven traits that best describe your personality. Which system of traits seems to best match your list, Allport's, Cattell's, or the Big Five? Choose a prominent trait from your list. Does its expression seem to be influenced by specific situations? Do you think that heredity contributed to the trait?

ANSWERS

1. introversion–extroversion 2. situations 3. F 4. surface, source 5. a
6. In one study, conscientiousness was positively related to academic performance, as you might expect. Students high in neuroticism also were better academic performers, but only if they were not too stressed (Kappe & van der Flier, 2010).

MODULE 52

Personality

Psychodynamic and Humanistic Theories

The Why of Personality

Meghan is self-conscious around strangers. You could almost say she is shy. This has been a life-long personality trait. But *why*, she often wonders. So, too, do psychodynamic theorists, who are not content with studying traits. Instead, they try to probe under the surface of personality—to learn what drives, conflicts, and energies animate us. A psychodynamic theorist would explain Meghan's shyness in terms of hidden, or *unconscious*, thoughts, needs, and emotions.

While humanistic theorists also seek to explain personality, they tend to focus on *conscious* thoughts, needs, and emotions. For example, humanists consider self-image a central determinant of behavior and personal adjustment. Humanistic theories also pay special attention to the fuller use of human potentials, and they help bring balance to our overall views of personality. A humanist might ask what it is about the attitudes Meghan holds regarding herself that makes her feel self-conscious.

So, which is it, Meghan? Let's look into it.

Shai Halud/Shutterstock.com

~LEARNING OUTCOMES~

After reading this module you should be able to:

52.1 Describe how psychodynamic theories explain personality

52.2 Describe how humanistic theories explain personality

Psychoanalytic Theory—Id Came to Me in a Dream

Learning Outcome 52.1 Describe how psychodynamic theories explain personality

As we discussed in Module 3, **psychoanalytic theory**, the first, and best-known, psychodynamic approach, grew out of the work of Sigmund Freud, a Viennese physician. As a doctor, Freud was fascinated by patients whose problems seemed to be more emotional than physical. From about 1890 until his death in 1939, Freud developed a theory of personality that deeply influenced modern thought (Schultz & Schultz, 2017; Tauber, 2010). Let's consider some of its main features.

The Structure of Personality

How did Freud view personality? Freud's model portrays personality as a dynamic system directed by three mental structures: the *id*, the *ego*, and the *superego*. According to Freud, most behavior involves activity of all three systems.

The Id The **id** contains primitive drives present at birth. The id operates on the **pleasure principle**. It is self-serving, irrational, impulsive, and totally unconscious—that is, it seeks to avoid pain and freely express pleasure-seeking urges of all kinds. If we were solely under control of the id, the world would be chaotic beyond belief.

The id acts as a power source for the entire **psyche** (SIGH-key), or personality. This energy, called **libido** (lih-BEE-doe), flows from **Eros**, the life instincts. According to Freud, libido underlies our efforts to survive, as well as our sexual desires and pleasure seeking. Freud also described **Thanatos**, the "death" instinct—although today it is more often thought of as an impulse toward aggression and destructive urges. Freud offered humanity's long history of wars and violence as evidence of such urges. Most id energies, then, are aimed at discharging tensions related to sex and aggression.

Rykoff Collection/Corbis Historical/Getty Images

Freud considered personality an expression of two conflicting forces, life instincts and the death instinct. Both are symbolized in this drawing by Allan Gilbert. (If you don't immediately see the death symbolism, move farther away from the drawing.)

The Ego The **ego** is sometimes described as the "executive" because it makes decisions about how to direct energies supplied by the id. The id is like a blind warrior whose power is awesome, but who must rely on others to give it orders. The id can only form mental images of things that it desires. The ego wins the power to direct behavior by relating the desires of the id to external reality.

Are there other differences between the ego and the id? Yes. Recall that the id operates on the pleasure principle. The ego, in contrast, is guided by the **reality principle**. The ego is the system of thinking, planning, problem solving, and deciding. It is in conscious control of the personality and often delays action until it is practical or appropriate.

The Superego *What is the role of the superego?* The **superego** represents moral conscience by acting as a judge or censor for the thoughts and actions of the ego. One part of the superego, called the **conscience**, reflects actions for which a person has been punished. When standards of the conscience are not met, you are punished internally by *guilt* feelings.

A second part of the superego is the **ego ideal**. The ego ideal reflects all behavior that one's parents approved or rewarded. The ego ideal is a source of goals and aspirations. When its standards are met, we feel *pride*.

The superego acts as an "internalized parent" to bring behavior under control. In Freudian terms, a person with a weak superego will be a delinquent, criminal, or antisocial personality. In contrast, an overly strict or harsh superego may cause inhibition, rigidity, or unbearable guilt.

Psychoanalytic theory Freudian theory of personality that emphasizes unconscious forces and conflicts.

Id Component of Freud's personality theory containing primitive drives present at birth.

Pleasure principle According to Freud, the id's drive to avoid pain and seek what feels good.

Psyche The mind, mental life, and personality as a whole.

Libido In Freudian theory, the force, primarily pleasure oriented, that energizes the personality.

Eros Freud's name for the "life instincts."

Thanatos The death instinct postulated by Freud.

Ego According to Freud, the decision-making part of personality that operates on the reality principle.

Reality principle Delaying action (or pleasure) until it is appropriate.

Superego According to Freud, the part of personality that represents moral conscience

Conscience The part of the superego that causes guilt when its standards are not met.

Ego ideal The part of the superego representing ideal behavior; a source of pride when its standards are met.

The Dynamics of Personality

How do the id, ego, and superego interact? Freud didn't picture the id, ego, and superego as parts of the brain or as "little people" running the human psyche. Instead, they are conflicting mental processes. Freud theorized a delicate balance of power among the three. For example, the id's demands for immediate pleasure often clash with the superego's moral restrictions. Perhaps an example will help clarify the role of each part of the personality.

Freud in a Nutshell

Let's say that you are sexually attracted to an acquaintance. The id clamors for immediate satisfaction of its sexual desires but is opposed by the superego (which finds the very thought of sex shocking). The id says, "Go for it!" The superego icily replies, "Never even think that again!" And what does the ego say? The ego says, "Hold on—I have a plan!"

This is, of course, a drastic oversimplification, but it does capture the core of Freudian thinking. To reduce tension, the ego could begin actions leading to friendship, romance, courtship, and marriage. If the id is unusually powerful, the ego may give in and attempt a seduction. If the superego prevails, the ego may be forced to *displace* or *sublimate* sexual energies to other activities (sports, music, dancing, push-ups, cold showers). According to Freud, internal struggles and rechanneled energies typify most personality functioning.

Is the ego always caught in the middle? Basically, yes, and the pressures on it can be intense. In addition to meeting the conflicting demands of the id and superego, the overworked ego must deal with external reality.

According to Freud, you feel anxiety when your ego is threatened or overwhelmed. Impulses from the id cause **neurotic anxiety** when the ego can barely keep them under control. Threats of punishment from the superego cause **moral anxiety**. Each person develops habitual ways of calming these anxieties, and many resort to using *ego-defense mechanisms* to lessen internal conflicts. Defense mechanisms are mental processes that deny, distort, or otherwise block out sources of threat and anxiety. (The ego defense mechanisms that Freud identified are used as a form of protection against stress, anxiety, and threatening events. See Module 57.)

Levels of Awareness Like other psychodynamic theorists, Freud believed that our behavior often expresses unconscious (or hidden) forces. The **unconscious** holds repressed memories and emotions, plus the instinctual drives of the id. It is interesting that modern scientists have found brain circuits that do, in fact, seem to underlie repression and the triggering of unconscious emotions and memories (Berlin, 2011; Stevens, 2016).

Even though they are beyond awareness, unconscious thoughts, feelings, or urges may slip into behavior in disguised or symbolic form (Reason, 2000; yes, these are *Freudian slips*). For example, if you meet someone you would like to know better, you may unconsciously leave a book or a jacket at that person's house to ensure another meeting.

Are the actions of the ego and superego also unconscious, like the id? At times, yes, but they also operate on two other levels of awareness (➤ **Figure 52.1**). The **conscious** level includes everything that you are aware of at a given moment, including thoughts, perceptions, feelings, and memories. The **preconscious** contains material that can be easily brought to awareness. If you stop to think about a time when you felt angry or rejected, you are moving this memory from the preconscious to the conscious level of awareness.

The superego's activities also reveal differing levels of awareness. At times, we consciously try to live up to moral codes or standards. Yet, at other times, a person may feel guilty without knowing why. Psychoanalytic theory credits such guilt to unconscious workings of the superego. Indeed, Freud believed that the unconscious origins of many feelings cannot be easily brought to awareness.

Personality Development

How does psychoanalytic theory explain personality development? Freud theorized that the core of personality develops before age 6 in a series of **psychosexual stages**. Freud believed that erotic urges in childhood have lasting effects on development (Ashcraft, 2015). As you might expect, this is a controversial idea. However, Freud used the terms *sex* and *erotic* very broadly to refer to many physical sources of pleasure.

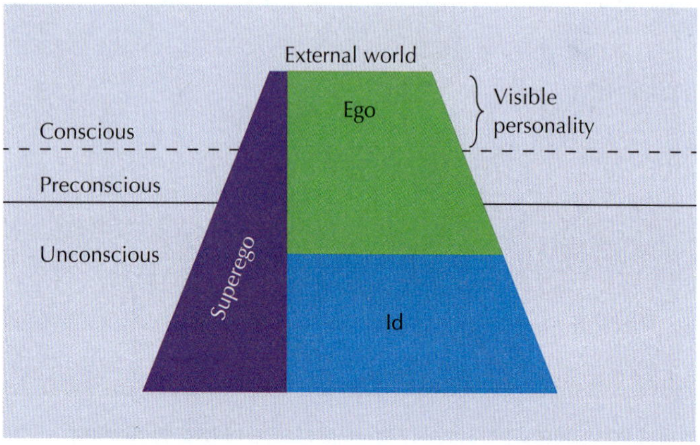

➤ **Figure 52.1**

Freud's levels of consciousness. The approximate relationship between the id, ego, and superego, and the levels of awareness.

Freud identified five psychosexual stages, *oral, anal, phallic, latency,* and *genital.* At each stage except latency, a different part of the body becomes a child's primary **erogenous zone**—an area capable of producing pleasure. Each area then serves as the main source of pleasure, frustration, and self-expression. Freud believed that many adult personality traits can be traced to fixations in one or more of the stages.

What is a fixation? A **fixation** is an unresolved conflict or emotional hang-up caused by overindulgence or frustration. As we describe the psychosexual stages, you'll see why Freud considered fixations important.

The Oral Stage During the first year of life, the **oral stage**, most of an infant's pleasure comes from stimulation of the mouth. If a child is overfed or frustrated, oral traits may be created. Adult expressions of oral needs include gum chewing, nail biting, smoking, kissing, overeating, and alcoholism.

What if there is an oral fixation? Fixation early in the oral stage produces an **oral-dependent personality**. Oral-dependent persons are gullible (they swallow things easily!) and passive and need lots of attention (they want to be mothered and showered with gifts). Frustrations later in the oral stage may cause aggression, often in the form of biting. Fixations here create cynical, **oral-aggressive** adults who exploit others. They also like to argue. ("Biting sarcasm" is their forte!)

The Anal Stage Between the ages of 1 and 3, the **anal stage**, the child's attention shifts to the anus and the process of elimination. When parents attempt toilet training, the child can gain approval or express rebellion or aggression by "holding on" or by "letting go." Therefore, harsh or lenient toilet training can cause an anal fixation that may lock such responses into personality. Freud described a "holding-on," or **anal-retentive personality**, as obstinate, stingy, orderly, and compulsively clean. (If someone accuses you of being "anal," blame Freud.) The "letting-go," or **anal-expulsive personality**, is disorderly, destructive, cruel, or messy.

Was Freud's ever-present cigar a sign of an oral fixation? Was it a phallic symbol? Was it both? Or was it neither? Once, when he was asked, Freud himself apparently replied, "Sometimes a cigar is just a cigar." An inability to say for sure is one of the shortcomings of psychoanalytic theory.

The Phallic Stage Between the ages of 3 and 6, the **phallic stage**, psychosexual attention shifts to the genitals. Freud theorized that fixations developed in this psychosexual stage result in adults with a **phallic personality**, characterized by vanity, exhibitionism, sensitive pride, and narcissism (self-love).

During the phallic stage, increased sexual interest causes the child to be physically attracted to the parent of the opposite sex. In males, this attraction leads to an **Oedipus complex**. In it, the boy aggressively competes with his father for the affection of his mother. Freud believed that the male child feels threatened by the father (specifically, the boy fears castration). To ease his anxieties, the boy must *identify* with the father. Their rivalry ends when the boy seeks to become more like his father. As he does, he begins to accept the father's values and forms a conscience (Kupfersmid, 2012).

Neurotic anxiety Apprehension felt when the ego struggles to control id impulses.

Moral anxiety Apprehension felt when thoughts, impulses, or actions conflict with the superego's standards.

Unconscious Contents of the mind that are beyond awareness, especially impulses and desires.

Conscious The region of the mind that includes all mental contents that a person is aware of at any given moment.

Preconscious An area of the mind containing information that can be voluntarily brought to awareness.

Psychosexual stages How Freud classifies a period of development.

Erogenous zone Any body area that produces pleasurable sensations.

Fixation A lasting conflict developed as a result of frustration or overindulgence.

Oral stage The period when infants are preoccupied with the mouth as a source of pleasure and means of expression.

Oral-dependent personality A person who wants to passively receive attention, gifts, love, and so forth.

Oral-aggressive personality A person who uses the mouth to express hostility by shouting, cursing, biting, and so forth. Also, one who actively exploits others.

Anal stage Period of psychosexual development where pleasure focuses on the anus, according to Freud.

Anal-retentive personality A person who is obstinate, stingy, or compulsive and who generally has difficulty "letting go."

Anal-expulsive personality A disorderly, destructive, cruel, or messy person.

Phallic stage Period of development in which psychosexual interest focuses on the penis or clitoris, according to Freud.

Phallic personality A person who is vain, exhibitionistic, sensitive, and narcissistic.

Oedipus complex According to Freud, a young boy's sexual interest in his mother accompanied by competitive aggression toward his father.

What about the female child? Girls experience an **Electra complex**. In this case, the girl loves her father and competes with her mother. However, according to Freud, the girl identifies with the mother more gradually.

Freud believed that females already feel castrated. Because of this, they are less driven to identify with their mothers than boys are with their fathers. This, he said, is less effective in creating a conscience. This particular part of Freudian thought has been thoroughly—and rightfully—rejected by modern experts in the psychology of women. It is better understood as a reflection of the male-dominated times in which Freud lived.

The Latency Stage According to Freud, there is a period of latency from age 6 to puberty. **Latency** is not so much a stage as it is a quiet time during which psychosexual development is dormant. Freud's belief that psychosexual development is "on hold" at this time is hard to accept. Nevertheless, Freud saw latency as a relatively quiet time compared with the stormy first 6 years of life.

The Genital Stage At puberty, an upswing in sexual energies activates all the unresolved conflicts of earlier years. This upsurge, according to Freud, is the reason that adolescence can be filled with emotion and turmoil. The **genital stage** begins at puberty. It is marked, during adolescence, by a growing capacity for responsible social–sexual relationships. The genital stage ends with a mature capacity for love and the realization of full adult sexuality.

Critical Comments *Is Freudian theory still widely accepted?* Although few psychologists wholeheartedly embrace Freud's theory today, it remains influential for several reasons. First, it pioneered the general idea of unconscious processes. Contemporary psychodynamic theorists generally agree that some part of the human mind is unconscious and yet plays an important role in shaping human behavior, even if they do not share Freud's (over?) focus on the motivating power of sex and death (Epstein, 2003). Other motives and cognitive factors are today seen as having equal importance.

Second, the general idea that critical events during the first years of life help shape adult personality remains widely accepted. For example, Freud was among the first to propose that development proceeds through a series of stages (Shaffer, 2009). (Erik Erikson's psycho*social* stages, which cover development from birth to old age, are a modern offshoot of Freudian thinking. See Module 15.)

However, when it comes to the details, Freud clearly was often wrong. His portrayal of the elementary school years (latency) as free from sexuality and unimportant for personality development is hard to believe. His idea of the role of a stern or threatening father in the development of a strong conscience in males also has been challenged. Studies show that a son is more likely to develop a strong conscience if his father is affectionate and accepting rather than stern and punishing.

In addition, Freud's ideas on the development of women have been thoroughly discredited (Hyde & Else-Quest, 2013). For example, Freud has been heavily criticized for his views of patients who believed that they were sexually molested as children (Marcel, 2005). Freud assumed that such events were merely childhood fantasies. This view led to a longstanding tendency to disbelieve children who have been molested and women who have been raped (Brannon, 2011).

Another important criticism is that Freud's concepts are almost impossible to verify scientifically. His theories provide numerous ways to explain almost any thought, action, or feeling *after* it has occurred. However, they lead to few predictions, which makes their claims difficult to test. Although more criticisms of Freud could be listed, the fact remains that much of what he said has an element of truth (Moran, F., 2010; Tauber, 2010).

The Neo-Freudians

Freud's ideas quickly attracted a brilliant following, including his daughter, Anna. Some, known as *neo-Freudians* (*neo* means "new"), created their own opposing theories that stressed the role of cultural and social factors in the development of the personality. The full story of other psychodynamic theories must await your first course in personality. For now, let's sample the views of two neo-Freudians, Alfred Adler and Carl Jung.

Adler (1870–1937) Adler believed that we are social creatures governed by social urges, not by biological instincts (Carlson & Maniacci, 2012). In Adler's view, the main driving force in personality is a **striving for superiority**. This striving, he said, is a struggle to overcome imperfections, an upward drive for competence, completion, and mastery of shortcomings.

What motivates "striving for superiority"? Adler believed that we all experience feelings of inferiority. This occurs mainly because we begin life as small, weak, and relatively powerless children surrounded by larger and more powerful adults. Feelings of inferiority may also come from our personal limitations. The struggle for superiority arises from such feelings. The failure of this struggle can lead to an **inferiority complex**, characterized by a chronic lack of self-worth along with self-doubt (Schultz & Schultz, 2017).

Carl Jung (1875–1961) Like Freud, Jung (pronounced *Yoong*) called the conscious part of the personality the *ego.* However, he further noted that a *persona,* or "mask," exists between the ego and the outside world. The **persona** is the "public self" presented to others. It is most apparent when we adopt particular roles or hide our deeper feelings. As mentioned in Module 50, Jung believed that actions of the ego may reflect attitudes of **introversion** (in which energy is directed inward) or of **extroversion** (in which energy is directed outward).

Was Jung's view of the unconscious the same as Freud's? Jung used the term *personal unconscious* to refer to what Freud simply called the unconscious. The **personal unconscious** is a mental storehouse for a single individual's experiences, feelings, and memories. But Jung also described a **collective unconscious**, a deeper mental storehouse for unconscious ideas and images shared by all humans. Jung believed that, from the beginning of time, all humans have had experiences with birth, death, power, god figures, mother and father figures, animals, the earth, energy, evil, rebirth, and so on. According to Jung, such universals create **archetypes** (ARE-keh-types), original ideas, images, or patterns (Rutter & Singer, 2015).

Archetypes, found in the collective unconscious, are unconscious images that cause us to respond emotionally to symbols of birth, death, energy, animals, evil, and the like (Engler, 2014). Jung believed that he detected symbols of such archetypes in the art, religion, myths, and dreams of every culture and age.

Humanistic Theory—Peak Experiences and Personal Growth

Learning Outcome 52.2 Describe how humanistic theories explain personality

Humanism focuses on human experience, problems, potentials, and ideals. As we saw in Module 3, the core of humanism is a positive image of humans as creative beings capable of **free will**—an ability to choose that is not determined by genetics, learning, or unconscious forces. In short, humanists seek ways to encourage our potentials to blossom.

Humanism is sometimes called a "third force" in that it is opposed to both psychodynamic and behaviorist theories of personality. Humanism is a reaction to the pessimism of psychoanalytic theory. It rejects the Freudian view of personality as a battleground for instincts and unconscious forces. Instead, humanists view **human nature**—the traits, qualities, potentials, and behavior patterns most characteristic of the human species—as inherently good. Humanists also oppose the machinelike overtones of the behaviorist view of human nature (which we discuss in Module 53). We are not, humanists say, merely a bundle of moldable responses.

To a humanist, the person you are today is largely the product of all the choices that you have made. Humanists also emphasize immediate **subjective experience**—private perceptions of reality—rather than prior learning. They believe that there are as many "real worlds" as there are people. To understand behavior, we must learn how a person subjectively views the world—what is "real" for her or him.

Who are the major humanistic theorists? Many psychologists have added to the humanistic tradition. Of these, the best known are Abraham Maslow (1908–1970) and Carl Rogers (1902–1987). Because Maslow's idea of self-actualization was introduced in Module 42, let's begin with a more detailed look at this facet of his thinking.

Electra complex A girl's sexual attraction to her father and feelings of rivalry with her mother.

Latency (in Freudian theory) According to Freud, a period in childhood when psychosexual development is more or less interrupted.

Genital stage Period of psychosexual development in which sexual pleasure focuses on sexual relations, according to Freud.

Striving for superiority According to Alfred Adler, this basic drive propels us toward perfection.

Inferiority complex Arises when feelings of inferiority become overwhelming; negative pattern characterized by a chronic lack of self-worth along with self-doubt.

Persona The "mask" or public self presented to others.

Introversion An ego attitude in which energy is mainly directed inward.

Extroversion An ego attitude in which energy is mainly directed outward.

Personal unconscious A mental storehouse for an individual's unconscious thoughts.

Collective unconscious According to Carl Jung, a mental storehouse for unconscious ideas and images shared by all humans.

Archetype According to Carl Jung, a universal idea, image, or pattern found in the collective unconscious.

Humanism An approach that focuses on human experience, problems, potentials, and ideals.

Free will The ability to freely make choices that are not controlled by genetics, learning, or unconscious forces.

Human nature Those traits, qualities, potentials, and behavior patterns most characteristic of the human species.

Subjective experience Reality as it is perceived and interpreted, not as it exists objectively.

Abraham Maslow and Self-Actualization

Abraham Maslow became interested in people who were living unusually effective lives (Hoffman, 2008). How were they different? To find an answer, Maslow began by studying the lives of great men and women from history, such as Albert Einstein, William James, Jane Addams, Eleanor Roosevelt, Abraham Lincoln, John Muir, and Walt Whitman. From there, he moved on to directly study living artists, writers, poets, and other creative individuals.

Along the way, Maslow's thinking changed radically. At first, he studied only people of obvious creativity or high achievement. However, it eventually became clear that anyone could live a rich, creative, and satisfying life (D'Souza & Gurin, 2016). Maslow referred to the process of fully developing personal potentials as **self-actualization** (Maslow, 1954). The heart of self-actualization is a continuous search for personal fulfillment (Ivtzan et al., 2013; Peterson & Park, 2010).

Characteristics of Self-Actualizers A *self-actualizer* is a person who is living creatively and fully using his or her potential. In his studies, Maslow found that self-actualizers share many similarities. Whether famous or unknown, well-schooled or uneducated, rich or poor, self-actualizers tend to fit the following profile:

1. **Efficient perceptions of reality.** Self-actualizers are able to judge situations correctly and honestly. They are very sensitive to the fake and dishonest.
2. **Comfortable acceptance of self, others, and nature.** Self-actualizers accept their own human nature, with all its flaws. The shortcomings of others and the contradictions of the human condition are accepted with humor and tolerance.
3. **Spontaneity.** Maslow's subjects extended their creativity into everyday activities. Actualizers tend to be unusually alive, engaged, and spontaneous.
4. **Task centering.** Most of Maslow's subjects had a mission to fulfill in life or some task or problem outside themselves to pursue. Humanitarians such as Albert Schweitzer and Mother Teresa represent this quality.
5. **Autonomy.** Self-actualizers are free from reliance on external authorities or other people. They tend to be resourceful and independent.
6. **Continued freshness of appreciation.** The self-actualizer seems to constantly renew appreciation of life's basic goodness. A sunset or a flower is experienced as intensely time after time as it was first experienced. Self-actualizers have an "innocence of vision," like that of an artist or child.
7. **Fellowship with humanity.** Maslow's subjects felt a deep identification with others and the human situation in general.
8. **Profound interpersonal relationships.** The interpersonal relationships of self-actualizers are marked by deep, loving bonds.
9. **Comfort with solitude.** Despite their satisfying relationships with others, self-actualizing persons value solitude and are comfortable being alone.
10. **Nonhostile sense of humor.** This refers to the wonderful capacity to laugh at oneself. It also describes the kind of humor possessed by a man like Abraham Lincoln. Lincoln probably almost never made a joke that hurt anybody. His wry comments were a gentle prodding of human shortcomings.
11. **Peak experiences.** All of Maslow's subjects reported the frequent occurrence of **peak experiences**, or temporary moments of self-actualization. These occasions were marked by feelings of ecstasy, harmony, and deep meaning. Self-actualizers reported feeling at one with the universe, stronger and calmer than ever before.

In summary, self-actualizers feel safe, nonanxious, accepted, loved, loving, and alive.

Although Maslow tried to investigate self-actualization empirically, his choice of people for study was subjective. Undoubtedly, one can make full use of personal potential in many ways. Maslow's primary contribution was to draw our attention to the possibility of lifelong personal growth (Peterson & Park, 2010).

What steps can be taken to promote self-actualization? Maslow found no magic formula for leading a more creative life. Self-actualization is primarily a *process,* not a goal or an end point. As such, it requires hard work, patience, and commitment. Nevertheless, some helpful suggestions can be gleaned from his writings (Maslow, 1954, 1967, 1971). Here are some ways to begin:

1. **Be willing to change.** Continually ask yourself, "Am I living in a way that is deeply satisfying to me and that truly expresses me?" If not, be prepared to make changes in your life.
2. **Take responsibility.** You can become an architect of self by acting as if you are personally responsible for every aspect of your life. Avoid the habit of blaming others for your own shortcomings.
3. **Examine your motives.** Self-discovery involves an element of risk. If your behavior is restricted by a desire for safety or security, it may be time to test some limits.

4. **Experience honestly and directly.** Wishful thinking is another barrier to personal growth. Self-actualizers trust themselves enough to accept all kinds of information without distorting it to fit their fears and desires. Try to see yourself as others do.
5. **Use your positive experiences.** Maslow considered peak experiences temporary moments of self-actualization. Therefore, you might actively repeat activities that have caused feelings of awe, amazement, exaltation, renewal, reverence, humility, fulfillment, or joy in you.
6. **Be prepared to be different.** Maslow felt that everyone has a potential for "greatness," but most fear becoming everything that they might become. As part of personal growth, be prepared to trust your own impulses and feelings; don't automatically judge yourself by the standards of others.
7. **Get involved.** With few exceptions, self-actualizers tend to have a mission or "calling" in life. For these people, "work" is not done just to fill deficiency needs, but to satisfy higher yearnings for truth, beauty, community, and meaning. Turn your attention to problems outside yourself.
8. **Assess your progress.** There is no final point at which one becomes self-actualized. It's important to gauge your progress frequently and to renew your efforts. If you feel bored at school, at a job, or in a relationship, consider it a challenge. Have you been taking responsibility for your own personal growth?

The Whole Human: Thriving

It could be said that self-actualizing people are thriving, not just surviving. Like Maslow, proponents of positive psychology have tried to scientifically study positive personality traits that contribute to happiness and well-being (Ryan & Deci, 2017). Although their work does not always fall within the humanistic tradition, their findings are relevant here.

Martin Seligman, Christopher Peterson, and others have identified six human strengths that contribute to well-being and life satisfaction. Each strength is expressed by the positive personality traits listed here (Peterson & Seligman, 2004):

- **Wisdom and knowledge:** Creativity, curiosity, open-mindedness, love of learning, perspective
- **Courage:** Bravery, persistence, integrity, vitality
- **Humanity:** Love, kindness, social intelligence
- **Justice:** Citizenship, fairness, leadership
- **Temperance:** Forgiveness, humility, prudence, self-control
- **Transcendence:** Appreciation of beauty and excellence, gratitude, hope, humor, spirituality

These characteristics, combined with Maslow's descriptions of self-actualizers, provide a good guide to the characteristics that help people live happy, meaningful lives.

Carl Rogers's Self Theory

Another well-known humanist, Carl Rogers, also emphasized the human capacity for inner peace and happiness (Elliott & Farber, 2010). The **fully functioning person**, he said, lives in harmony with his or her deepest feelings and impulses. Such people are open to their experiences, and they trust their inner urges and intuitions (Rogers, 1961). Rogers believed that this attitude is most likely to occur when a person receives ample amounts of love and acceptance from others.

Personality Structure and Dynamics

Rogers's theory emphasizes the **self**, a flexible and changing perception of personal identity. Much behavior can be understood as an attempt to maintain consistency between our *self-image* and our actions. (Your **self-image** is a total subjective perception of your body and personality.) For example, people who think of themselves as kind tend to be considerate in most situations.

Let's say that I know a person who thinks she is kind, but she really isn't. How does that fit Rogers's theory? According to Rogers, we allow into awareness experiences that match our self-image, where they gradually change the self. Information or feelings inconsistent with the self-image are said to be incongruent. Thus, a person who thinks she is kind but really isn't is in a state of **incongruence**. In other words, there is a discrepancy between her experiences and her self-image. As another example, it would be incongruent to believe that you are a person who "never gets angry" if you spend much of each day seething inside.

Self-actualization The process of fully developing personal potentials.

Peak experiences Temporary moments of self-actualization.

Fully functioning person A person living in harmony with her or his deepest feelings, impulses, and intuitions.

Self A continuously evolving conception of one's personal identity.

Self-image Total subjective perception of one's body and personality (another term for self-concept).

Incongruence A state that exists when there is a discrepancy between one's experiences and self-image or between one's self-image and ideal self.

Experiences seriously incongruent with the self-image can be threatening and are often distorted or denied conscious recognition. Blocking, denying, or distorting experiences prevents the self from changing. This creates a gap between the self-image and reality (Ryckman, 2013). As the self-image grows more unrealistic, the *incongruent person* becomes confused, vulnerable, dissatisfied, or seriously maladjusted (➤ **Figure 52.2**). In line with Rogers's observations, a study of college students confirmed that being *authentic* is vital for healthy functioning—that is, we need to feel that our behavior accurately expresses who we are (Human et al., 2014; Wenzel & Lucas-Thompson, 2012). Please note, however, that being authentic doesn't mean that you can do whatever you want. Being true to yourself is no excuse for acting irresponsibly or ignoring the feelings of others (Kernis & Goldman, 2005).

When your self-image is consistent with what you really think, feel, do, and experience, you are best able to actualize your potential. Rogers also considered it essential to have congruence between the self-image and the **ideal self**. The ideal self is similar to Freud's ego ideal. It is an image of the person that you would most like to be (Przybylski et al., 2012).

Is it really incongruent not to live up to your ideal self? Rogers was aware that we never fully attain our ideals. Nevertheless, the greater the gap between the way you see yourself and the way you would like to be, the more tension and anxiety you will experience.

Rogers emphasized that to maximize our potentials, we must accept information about ourselves as honestly as possible. In accord with his thinking, researchers have found that people with a close match between their self-image and ideal self tend to be socially poised, confident, and resourceful. Those with a poor match tend to be depressed, anxious, and insecure (Boldero et al., 2005).

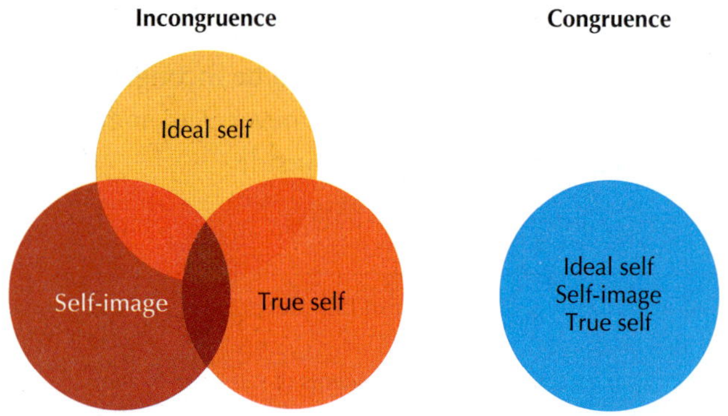

➤ **Figure 52.2**

Incongruence versus congruence. Incongruence occurs when there is a mismatch between any of these three entities: the ideal self (the person you would like to be), your self-image (the person you think you are), and the true self (the person you actually are). Self-esteem suffers when there is a large difference between one's ideal self and self-image. Anxiety and defensiveness are common when the self-image does not match the true self.

Possible Selves According to psychologists Hazel Markus and Paula Nurius (1986), our current ideal self is only one of a number of **possible selves**—persons that we could become or are afraid of becoming. Consider William, an intellectually gifted African-American student. He simultaneously welcomes the possible self who continues to broaden his intellectual horizons and fears the possible self of the stereotyped gangsta wearing baggy pants (Frazier, 2012). Like William, you may have pondered many possible personal identities.

For example, you may know these two student stereotypes: the carefree party animal and the conscientious bookworm. Perhaps you even think of yourself as one or the other. Is there any truth to these (stereo)types? Can you change your story?

In general, our personality traits are relatively stable characteristics (McAdams & Pals, 2006). As a result, a person high in the Big Five traits of extroversion and agreeableness tends to embrace a carefree college lifestyle. In comparison, someone high in conscientiousness will find it easier to hit the books (McGregor, McAdams, & Little, 2006).

Does that mean a partier can't become a bookworm (or vice versa)? It depends: Do you mean over a week? Or a lifetime? Personality traits do slowly change as we age (Mõttus, Johnson, & Deary, 2012). In particular, we tend to become more agreeable, conscientious, and emotionally stable as we grow older (Roberts & Mroczek, 2008).

Oh, you need to change by the end of the semester? That's a taller order (Hudson & Fraley, 2015). In that case, you might want to try telling yourself stories about the better student that you could become (Lee et al., 2016). The *narrative approach* to personality asserts that our personalities are shaped by the stories that we tell about ourselves (Frazier, 2012; McAdams & McLean, 2013). In other words, alternative life stories are not just fantasies or daydreams. They actually influence who we are and who we become.

So, if you feel that you are being too careless and carefree at school, start imagining yourself studying more, getting to classes on time, and getting good grades. Listen to the stories of successful students and use them to revise your own story. Visit your campus counseling center to learn more about how to succeed at school. In other words, imagine yourself as a bit more of a bookworm. (Don't worry, your carefree nature won't desert you!)

If you feel you are too conscientious and working too hard, imagine yourself going out with friends more often. Listen to the stories of your extroverted classmates. Imagine the benefits of balancing work and play in your life. If you are shy or perfectionistic, visit your campus counseling center to learn how to become more sociable or relaxed. And, again, don't worry: Having more fun won't make you irresponsible.

Whatever possible self you choose to pursue, you are more likely to become what you imagine if you elaborate your story, making it more detailed and "real" as you gradually adopt new patterns. You *can* create a new narrative identity for yourself (Bauer, McAdams, & Pals, 2008; Nelson et al., 2012).

Possible selves translate our hopes, fears, fantasies, and goals into specific images of who we *could* be (Barreto & Frazier, 2012; Oyserman et al., 2004). Of course, almost everyone over age 30 has probably felt the anguish of realizing that some cherished possible selves will never be realized. Nevertheless, there is value in asking yourself not just "Who am I?" but also "Who would I like to become?"

Humanistic View of Development

Why do mirrors, photographs, video cameras, and the reactions of others hold such fascination and threat for many people? Carl Rogers's theory suggests that it is because they provide information about one's self. The development of a self-image depends greatly on information from the environment. It begins with a sorting of perceptions and feelings: my body, my toes, my nose, I want, I like, I am, and so on. Soon, it expands to include self-evaluation: I am a good person, I did something bad just now, and so forth.

How does development of the self contribute to later personality functioning? Rogers believed that positive and negative evaluations by others cause children to develop internal standards of evaluation called **conditions of worth**. In other words, we learn that some actions win our parents' love and approval, whereas others are rejected. More important, parents may label some *feelings* as bad or wrong. For example, a child might be told that it is wrong to feel angry toward a brother or sister—even when anger is justified. Likewise, a little boy might be told that he must not cry or show fear, two very normal emotions.

Learning to evaluate some experiences or feelings as "good" and others as "bad" is directly related to a later capacity for self-esteem, positive self-evaluation, or **positive self-regard**, to use Rogers's term. To think of yourself as a good, lovable, worthwhile person, your behavior and experiences must match your internal conditions of worth. The problem is that this can cause incongruence by leading to the denial of many true feelings and experiences.

To put it simply, Rogers blamed many adult emotional problems on attempts to live by the standards of others (Ashcraft, 2015). He believed that congruence and self-actualization are encouraged by replacing conditions of worth with **organismic valuing**, a natural, undistorted, full-body reaction to an experience. Organismic valuing is a direct, gut-level response to life that avoids the filtering and distortion of incongruence. It involves trusting one's own feelings and perceptions. Rogers felt that organismic valuing most likely develops when children (or adults) receive **unconditional positive regard**—complete, unqualified acceptance of another person as he or she is—when they are "prized" as worthwhile human beings, just for being themselves, without any conditions or strings attached. Although this may be a luxury that few people enjoy, we are more likely to move toward our ideal selves if we receive affirmation and support from a close partner (Drigotas, 2002; Righetti, Rusbult, & Finkenauer, 2010).

Ideal self An idealized image of oneself (the person that one would like to be).

Possible selves A collection of thoughts, beliefs, feelings, and images concerning the person that one could become.

Conditions of worth Internal standards used to judge the value of one's thoughts, actions, feelings, or experiences.

Positive self-regard Thinking of oneself as a good, lovable, worthwhile person.

Organismic valuing A natural, undistorted, full-body reaction to an experience.

Unconditional positive regard Complete, unqualified acceptance of another person as he or she is.

MODULE 52 Psychoanalytic and Humanistic Theories—Learning Outcomes Revisited

52.1 Describe how psychodynamic theories explain personality

Like other psychodynamic approaches, Sigmund Freud's psychoanalytic theory emphasizes unconscious forces and conflicts within the personality. In Freud's theory, personality is made up of the id, ego, and superego. Libido, derived from the life instincts, is the primary energy running the personality. Conflicts within the personality may cause neurotic anxiety or moral anxiety and motivate us to use ego-defense mechanisms. The personality operates on three levels: the conscious, preconscious, and unconscious. The Freudian view of personality development is based on a series of psychosexual stages: the oral, anal, phallic, latency, and genital stages. According to Freud, fixation at any stage can leave a lasting imprint on personality. Neo-Freudian theorists accepted the broad features of Freudian psychology, but developed their own views. Two prominent neo-Freudians are Alfred Adler and Carl Jung.

52.2 Describe how humanistic theories explain personality

Humanistic theories stress subjective experience, free will, self-actualization, and positive models of human nature. Abraham Maslow found that self-actualizers share characteristics that range from efficient perceptions of reality to frequent peak experiences. Positive psychologists have identified six human strengths that contribute to well-being and life satisfaction: wisdom and knowledge, courage, humanity, justice, temperance, and transcendence. Carl Rogers viewed the self as an entity that emerges from personal experience. We tend to become aware of experiences that match our self-image and exclude those that are incongruent with it. The incongruent person has a highly unrealistic self-image, a mismatch between the self-image and the ideal self, or both. The congruent or fully functioning person is flexible and open to experiences and feelings. Like the ideal self, possible selves help us become the person we would like to become. As parents apply conditions of worth to children's behavior, thoughts, and feelings, children begin to do the same. Internalized conditions of worth then contribute to incongruence that disrupts the organismic valuing process.

Reflective Practice

Content Check

1. Freud stated that the mind functions on three levels: the conscious, the unconscious, and the
   - **a.** psyche
   - **b.** preconscious
   - **c.** superego
   - **d.** subconscious
2. List the three divisions of personality postulated by Freud: ________ ________ ________
3. Freud's view of personality development is based on the concept of ____________________ stages.
4. Humanists view human nature as basically good, and they emphasize the effects of subjective learning and unconscious choice. T or F?
5. Maslow thought of peak experiences as temporary moments of
   - **a.** congruence
   - **b.** positive self-regard
   - **c.** self-actualization
   - **d.** self-reinforcement
6. According to Rogers, a close match between the self-image and the ideal self creates a condition called incongruence. T or F?
7. Carl Rogers believed that personal growth is encouraged when conditions of worth are replaced by
   - **a.** self-efficacy
   - **b.** instrumental worth
   - **c.** latency
   - **d.** organismic valuing

Skill Check

Think Critically

8. What role would your "possible selves" have in the choice of a college major?

Self-Reflect

Try to think of at least one time when your thoughts, feelings, or actions seemed to reflect the workings of each of the following: the id, the ego, and the superego. Do you know anyone who seems to have oral, anal, or phallic personality traits? Do you think Freud's concept of fixation explains their characteristics? Do you know anyone who seems to be making especially good use of his or her personal potential? Does that person fit Maslow's profile of a self-actualizer? How much difference do you think there is among your self-image, your ideal self, and your true self?

ANSWERS

1. b 2. id, ego, superego 3. psychosexual 4. F 5. c 6. F 7. d 8. Career decisions almost always involve, in part, picturing oneself occupying various occupational roles. Such possible "future selves" play a role in many of the major decisions we make (Masters & Holley, 2006).

MODULE 53

Personality

Behavioral and Social Learning Theories

A Boy Named Sue

Suzanne Tucker/Shutterstock.com

Why is little Sue so aggressive? His daddy named him Sue after an old country song. Freud believed that aggressive urges are "instinctual." Unlike psychodynamic and humanistic theorists, behavioral theories assume that personal characteristics such as aggressiveness are learned. Could Sue's aggression be the result of observational learning, harsh punishment, or prior reinforcement?

Sue will tell you himself that his name always triggers giggles from girls. Boys always laugh at and taunt him. The resulting fights are, to Sue, an inevitable part of his life. So why did his father name him Sue, you ask? To toughen him up, the dirty, mangy dog said, before he abandoned his family when Sue turned three.

All kidding aside, behavioral and social learning theories are based on scientific research, which makes them especially powerful ways of looking at personality and developing therapies to help people change, if they should so desire.

~LEARNING OUTCOMES~

After reading this module you should be able to:

53.1 Describe how behaviorists and social learning theorists explain personality

53.2 Describe how heredity and the environment affect personality

Learning Theories of Personality—Habit I Seen You Before?

Learning Outcome 53.1 Describe how behaviorists and social learning theorists explain personality

After exploring psychodynamic theories, you might be relieved to know that behavioral theorists explain personality through straightforward concepts, such as learning, reinforcement, and imitation. Behaviorists have shown repeatedly that children can *learn* things like kindness, hostility, generosity, or destructiveness. What does this have to do with personality? Everything, according to the behavioral viewpoint.

Behavioral personality theories emphasize that personality is no more (or less) than a collection of relatively stable learned behavior patterns. (For a discussion of *leadership* as a collection of relatively stable and definitely learnable, behavior patterns, see Module 54.) Personality, like other learned behavior, is acquired through classical and operant conditioning, observational learning, reinforcement, extinction, generalization, and discrimination. When Mother says, "It's not nice to make mud pies with Mommy's blender. If we want to grow up to be a big girl, we won't do it again, will we?" she is shaping her daughter's personality.

Strict *learning theorists* reject the idea that personality is made up of traits. They would assert, for instance, that there is no such thing as a *trait* of "honesty" (Mischel, 2004).

Certainly some people are honest and others are not. How can honesty not be a trait? Remember, for many trait theorists, traits are biological dispositions. According to learning theorists, they are, instead, stable learned responses. If his parents consistently reward little Alexander for honesty, he is more likely to become an honest adult. If his parents are less scrupulous, Alexander might well grow up differently (Schultz & Schultz, 2017).

Learning theorists also stress the external causes, or **situational determinants**, of actions. Knowing that someone is honest does not automatically allow us to predict whether that person will be honest in a specific situation (Carter, 2013). It would not be unusual, for example, to find that a person honored for returning a lost wallet had cheated on a test, bought a term paper, or broken the speed limit. If you were to ask a learning theorist, "Are you an honest person?" the reply might be, "In what situation?"

A good example of how situations can influence behavior is a study in which people were intentionally overpaid for doing an assigned task. Under normal circumstances, 80 percent kept the extra money without mentioning it. But as few as 17 percent were dishonest if the situation were altered. For instance, if people thought the money was coming out of the pocket of the person doing the study, far fewer were dishonest (Bersoff, 1999). Thus, situations always interact with our prior learning to activate behavior.

Digital Vision/Photodisc/Getty Images

Seventy-five percent of American college students admit that they have been academically dishonest in one way or another. What can be done about these high rates of dishonesty? The behavioral perspective holds that honesty is determined as much by circumstances as it is by personality. In line with this, simple measures such as announcing in classes that integrity codes will be enforced can significantly reduce cheating. Using multiple forms of exams and web-based plagiarism software and educating students about plagiarism also tend to deter dishonesty (Altschuler, 2001; McKeever, 2006).

How Situations Affect Behavior

Situations vary greatly in their impact. Some are powerful. Others are trivial and have little effect on behavior. The more powerful the situation, the easier it is to see what is meant by *situational determinants*. For example, each of the following situations would undoubtedly have a strong influence on your behavior: An armed person walks into your classroom; you accidentally sit on a lighted cigarette; you find your lover in bed with your best friend. Yet, even these situations could provoke very different reactions from different personalities. That's why behavior is always a product of both prior learning and the situations in which we find ourselves (Mischel & Shoda, 2010; Mischel, Shoda, & Smith, 2008).

Ultimately, what is predictable about personality is that we respond in fairly consistent ways to certain situations. Consider, for example, two people who are easily angered: One person might get angry when she is delayed (for example, in traffic or a checkout line), but not when she misplaces something at home; the other person might get angry whenever she misplaces things but not when she is delayed. Overall, the two women are equally prone to anger, but their anger tends to occur in different patterns and different situations (Mischel, 2004).

Personality = Habitual Behavior

How do learning theorists view the structure of personality? The behavioral view of personality can be illustrated with an early theory proposed by John Dollard and Neal Miller (1950). In their view, learned behavior patterns, or **habits**, make up the structure of personality. As for the dynamics of personality, habits are governed by four elements of learning: *drive*, *cue*, *response*, and *reward*. A *drive* is any stimulus strong enough to goad a person to action (such as hunger, pain, lust, frustration, or fear). *Cues* are signals from the environment. These signals guide *responses* (actions) so that they are most likely to bring about *reward* (positive reinforcement).

How does that relate to personality? Let's say that a child named Amina is frustrated by her older brother, Kelvin, who takes a toy from her. Amina could respond in several ways: She could throw a temper tantrum, hit Kelvin, tell her mother, and so forth. The response that she chooses is guided by available cues and the previous effects of each response. If telling her mother has paid off in the past, and her mother is present, telling may be Amina's immediate response. If a different set of cues exists (if her mother is absent, or if Kelvin looks particularly menacing), Amina may select some other response. To an outside observer, Amina's actions seem to reflect her personality. To a learning theorist, they simply express the combined effects of drive, cue, response, and reward. Behavioral theories have contributed greatly to the creation of therapies for various psychological problems and disorders. See the discussion of behavior therapy in Module 67.

Doesn't this analysis leave out a lot? Yes. Learning theorists originally set out to provide a simple, clear model of personality. But they eventually had to face a fact that they previously tended to set aside: People think. Contemporary behavioral psychologists—whose views include perception, thinking, expectations, and other mental events—are called *social learning theorists*. Learning principles, modeling, thought patterns, perceptions, expectations, beliefs, goals, emotions, and social relationships are combined in **social learning theory** to explain personality (Brauer & Tittle, 2012; Mischel, Shoda, & Smith, 2008).

Social Learning Theory

The "cognitive behaviorism" of social learning theory can be illustrated by three classic concepts proposed by Julian Rotter: the psychological situation, expectancy, and reinforcement value (Rotter & Hochreich, 1975). Let's examine each.

Someone trips you. How do you respond? Your reaction probably depends on whether you think it was planned or an accident. It is not enough to know the setting in which a person responds. We also need to know the person's **psychological situation** (how the person interprets or defines the situation). As another example, let's say that you score low on an exam. Do you consider it a challenge to work harder, a sign that you should drop the class, or an excuse to get drunk? Again, your interpretation is important.

Our actions are affected by an **expectancy**, or anticipation, that making a response will lead to reinforcement. To continue the example, if working harder has paid off in the past, it is a likely reaction to a low test score. But to predict your response, we also would have to know if you *expect* your efforts to pay off in the present situation. In fact, expected reinforcement may be more important than actual past reinforcement. And what about the *value* you attach to grades, school success, or personal ability? The third concept, **reinforcement value**, states that we attach different subjective values to various activities or rewards. You will likely choose to study harder if passing your courses and obtaining a degree is highly valued. This, too, must be taken into account to understand personality.

Self-Efficacy An ability to control your own life is the essence of what it means to be human (Corey & Corey, 2014). Because of this, Albert Bandura believes that one of the most important expectancies we develop concerns **self-efficacy** (EF-uh-keh-see)—a capacity for producing a desired result. Believing that our actions will produce desired results influences the activities and environments that we choose (Bandura, 2001; Schultz & Schultz, 2017). You're attracted to someone in your anthropology class. Will you ask him or her out? You're beginning to consider a career in psychology. Will you take the courses that you need to get into graduate school? You'd like to exercise more on the weekends. Will you join a hiking club? In these and countless other situations, efficacy beliefs play a key role in shaping our lives (Byrne, Barry, & Petry, 2012; Prat-Sala & Redford, 2012).

Behavioral personality theory Any model of personality that emphasizes learning and observable behavior.

Situational determinants External conditions that strongly influence behavior.

Habit A deeply ingrained, learned pattern of behavior.

Social learning theory A theory that combines learning principles with cognitive processes, socialization, and modeling, to explain behavior, including personality.

Psychological situation A situation as it is perceived and interpreted by an individual, not as it exists objectively.

Expectancy Anticipation about the effect that a response will have, especially regarding reinforcement.

Reinforcement value The subjective value that a person attaches to a particular activity or reinforcer.

Self-efficacy Belief in your capacity to produce a desired result.

John Mitterer

Fishing on Marco Island. We can reward ourselves through self-reinforcement for personal achievements and other "good" behavior. (At least that's the theory, right?)

Blend Images/Shutterstock.com

Adult personality is influenced by identification with parents and imitation of their behavior.

Self-Reinforcement One more idea deserves mention. At times, we all evaluate our actions and may reward ourselves with special privileges or treats for "good behavior." With this in mind, social learning theory adds the concept of self-reinforcement to the behaviorist view. **Self-reinforcement** refers to praising or rewarding yourself for having made a particular response (such as completing a school assignment). Thus, habits of self-praise and self-blame become an important part of personality (Schultz & Schultz, 2017). In fact, self-reinforcement can be thought of as the social learning theorist's counterpart to the superego.

Self-reinforcement is closely related to high self-esteem. The reverse also is true: Mildly depressed college students tend to have low rates of self-reinforcement. It is not known if low self-reinforcement leads to depression, or the reverse. In either case, higher rates of self-reinforcement are associated with less depression and greater life satisfaction (Seybolt & Wagner, 1997). From a behavioral viewpoint, there is value in learning to be "good to yourself."

Behaviorist View of Development

How do learning theorists account for personality development? Learning theorists tend to agree with Freud that the first six years are crucial for personality development, but for different reasons. Rather than thinking in terms of psychosexual urges and fixations, they ask, "What makes early learning experiences like toilet training so lasting in their effects?" Their answer is that childhood is a time of urgent drives, powerful rewards and punishments, and crushing frustrations. These forces combine to shape the core of personality (Shaffer, 2009).

Social reinforcement, which is based on praise, attention, or approval from others, is especially important (Brauer & Tittle, 2012). One obvious example involves learning socially defined "male" and "female" gender roles—which, in turn, affects personality (Cervone & Pervin, 2013).

Personality and Gender *What does it mean to have a "masculine" or "feminine" personality?* From birth onward, children are labeled as boys or girls and encouraged to learn appropriate **gender roles**—the pattern of behaviors regarded as "male" or "female" within a culture (Fine, 2011; Orenstein, 2011). According to social learning theory, identification and imitation contribute greatly to personality development and to sex training. **Identification** refers to the child's emotional attachment to admired adults, especially those who provide love and care. Identification typically encourages **imitation**, a desire to act like the admired person. Many "male" or "female" traits come from children's attempts to imitate a same-sex parent with whom they identify (Helgeson, 2012).

If children are around parents of both sexes, why don't they imitate behavior typical of the opposite sex as well as of the same sex? You may recall (from Module 29) that learning takes place vicariously as well as directly. This means that we can learn without direct reward by observing and remembering the actions of others. But the actions that we choose to imitate depend on their outcomes. For example, boys and girls have equal chances to observe adults and other children acting aggressively. However, girls are less likely than boys to imitate directly aggressive behavior (shouting at or hitting another person). Instead, girls are more likely to rely on indirectly aggressive behavior (excluding others from friendship, spreading rumors). This could be because expressing direct aggression is considered inappropriate for girls.

As a consequence, girls do not as often see direct female aggression rewarded or approved (Field et al., 2009). In other words, "girlfighting" is likely a culturally reinforced pattern (Brown, 2005). It is intriguing that over the last few years, girls have become more willing to engage in direct aggression as popular culture presents more and more images of directly aggressive women (Artz, 2005; Taylor & Ruiz, 2013).

We have considered only a few examples of the links between social learning and personality. Nevertheless, the connection is unmistakable. When parents accept their children and give them affection, the children become sociable, positive, and emotionally stable and they have high self-esteem. When parents are rejecting, punishing, sarcastic, humiliating, or neglectful, their children become hostile, unresponsive, unstable, and dependent and have impaired self-esteem (Cervone & Pervin, 2013; Triandis & Suh, 2002).

Traits and Situations—The Great Debate

Learning Outcome 53.2 Describe how heredity and the environment affect personality

Personality theorists have long grappled with the relative roles of nature and nurture in shaping personalities. Some theories, such as trait theory and psychoanalytic theory, stress the role of inherited biological predispositions, whereas others, including humanist and behavioral theories, stress the role of learning and life experiences. Let's look at the roles that heredity and biological predispositions (nature) and environmental situations (nurture) play in forming personality.

Do We Inherit Personality?

Even newborn babies differ in temperament, which implies that it is hereditary. (See Module 12.) **Temperament**, the "raw material" from which personalities are formed, refers to the general pattern of attention, arousal, and mood that is evident from birth, such as biological predispositions to be sensitive, irritable, and distractible and to display a typical mood (Shiner et al., 2012). Temperament has a large impact on how infants interact with their parents.

At what age are personality traits firmly established? Personality starts to stabilize at around age 3 and continues to "harden" well past age 50 (Briley & Tucker-Drob, 2017; Hopwood et al., 2011). However, personality slowly matures during old age, as most people continue to become more conscientious, agreeable, and emotionally stable (Roberts & Mroczek, 2008). It appears that stereotypes of the "grumpy old man" and "cranky old woman" are largely unfounded. At the same time, extroversion and openness slowly decline with advancing age (Wortman, Lucas, & Donnellan, 2012).

Does the stability of personality traits mean that they are affected by heredity? Some breeds of dogs have reputations for being friendly, aggressive, intelligent, calm, or emotional. Such differences fall in the realm of **behavioral genetics**, the study of inherited behavioral traits. We know that facial features, eye color, body type, and many other physical characteristics are inherited. So are many of our behavioral dispositions (Kalat, 2021). Genetic studies have shown that intelligence, language, some mental disorders, temperament, and other complex qualities are influenced by heredity. Behavioral genetic research has helped us better understand the hereditary origins of intellectual disability (see Module 40) and psychological disorders (see Module 60). In view of such findings, it wouldn't be a surprise to find that genes affect personality as well (Briley & Tucker-Drob, 2017).

Wouldn't comparing the personalities of identical twins help answer the question? It would indeed—especially if the twins were separated at birth or soon after.

Twins and Traits: The Amazing Twins For several decades, psychologists at the University of Minnesota have been studying identical twins who grew up in different homes. Medical and psychological tests reveal that reunited twins are very much alike, even when they are reared apart (Bouchard, 2004; Segal, 2012). If one twin excels at art,

Self-reinforcement Praising or rewarding oneself for having made a particular response (such as completing a school assignment).

Social reinforcement Praise, attention, approval, and/or affection from others.

Gender roles Pattern of behaviors regarded as "male" or "female" within a culture.

Identification Feeling emotionally connected to a person and seeing oneself as like him or her.

Imitation An attempt to match one's own behavior to another person's behavior.

Temperament General pattern of attention, arousal, and mood that is evident from birth.

Behavioral genetics The study of inherited behavioral traits and tendencies.

music, dance, drama, or athletics, the other is likely to as well—despite wide differences in childhood environment. They may even be similar in voice quality, facial gestures, hand movements, and nervous tics, such as nail biting.

It is, however, wise to be cautious about some reports of extraordinary similarities in reunited twins. Many reunited twins in the Minnesota study (the Minnesota Twins?) have displayed similarities far beyond what would be expected on the basis of heredity (Segal, 2012). The "Jim twins," James Lewis and James Springer, are one famous example. Both Jims had married and divorced women named Linda. Both had undergone police training. One named his firstborn son James Allan—and the other named *his* firstborn son James Alan. Both drove Chevrolets and vacationed at the same beach each summer. Both listed carpentry and mechanical drawing among their hobbies. Both had built benches around trees in their yards, and so forth (Holden, 1980).

Are all identical twins so, well, identical? No, they aren't. Consider identical twins Carolyn Spiro and Pamela Spiro Wagner who, unlike the "Jim twins," lived together throughout their childhood. While in sixth grade, they found out that President Kennedy had been assassinated. Carolyn wasn't sure why everyone was so upset. Pamela heard voices announcing that she was responsible for his death. After years of hiding her voices from everyone, Pamela tried to commit suicide while the twins were attending Brown University. She was diagnosed with schizophrenia. Never to be cured, she has gone on to write award-winning poetry. Carolyn eventually became a Harvard psychiatrist (Spiro Wagner & Spiro, 2005). Some twins reared apart appear very similar; some reared together appear rather different.

So why are some identical twins, like the Jim twins, so much alike even if they were reared apart? Although genetics is important, it is preposterous to suggest that there are child-naming genes and bench-building genes. How, then, do we explain the eerie similarities in some separated twins' lives? Imagine that you were separated at birth from a twin brother or sister. If you were reunited with your twin today, what would you do? Quite likely, you would spend the next several days comparing every imaginable detail of your lives. Under such circumstances, it is virtually certain that you and your twin would notice and compile a long list of similarities. ("Wow! I use the same brand of toothpaste you do!") Yet, two unrelated persons of the same age, sex, and race could probably rival your list—*if* they were as motivated to find similarities.

In fact, one study compared twins with unrelated pairs of students. The unrelated pairs, who were the same age and sex, were almost as alike as the twins. They had highly similar political beliefs, musical interests, religious preferences, job histories, hobbies, favorite foods, and so on (Wyatt et al., 1984). Why were the unrelated students so similar? Basically, it's because people of the same age and sex live in the same historical times and select from similar societal options. As just one example, in nearly every elementary school classroom, you will find several children with the same first name.

It appears then that many of the seemingly "astounding" coincidences shared by reunited twins may be yet another example of confirmation bias, described in Module 2. Reunited twins tend to notice the similarities and ignore the differences.

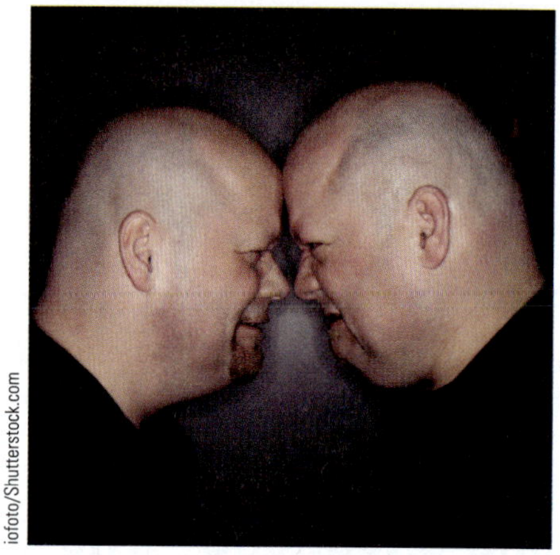

How similar are the identical twins pictured above? While the "Jim twins" are very similar despite being reared apart, Carolyn Spiro and Pamela Spiro Wagner are very different despite being reared together. Their stories illustrate the complex interplay of forces that shape our adult personalities.

Summary Studies of twins make it clear that heredity has a sizable effect on each of us. All told, it seems reasonable to conclude that heredity is responsible for about 25 to 50 percent of the variation in many personality traits (Briley & Tucker-Drob, 2017; Kandler, 2012). Notice, however, that the same figures imply that personality is shaped as much by environment as it is by biological predispositions (Johnson et al., 2009).

Each personality, then, is a unique blend of heredity and environment, nature and nurture, biology and culture. We are not—thank goodness—genetically programmed robots whose behavior and personality traits are "wired in" for life. Where you go in life is the result of the choices that you make. Although these choices are influenced by inherited tendencies, they are not merely a product of your genes (Funder, 2010).

Personality and Environment

Sally was always quite calm and peaceful. Then one day in a bar, she decked a man who was harassing her. How could that happen? Before we try to provide an answer, take a moment to answer the questions that follow. Doing so will add to your understanding of a long-running controversy in the psychology of personality.

Rate Yourself: How Do You View Personality?

1. My friends' actions are fairly consistent from day to day and in different situations. T or F?
2. Whether a person is honest or dishonest, kind or cruel, a hero or a coward depends mainly on circumstances. T or F?
3. Most people I have known for several years have pretty much the same personalities now as they did when I first met them. T or F?
4. People in some professions (such as teachers, lawyers, or doctors) seem so much alike because their work requires that they act in particular ways. T or F?
5. One of the first things that I would want to know about a potential roommate is what the person's personality is like. T or F?
6. I believe that immediate circumstances usually determine how people act at any given time. T or F?
7. To be comfortable in a particular job, a person's personality must match the nature of the work. T or F?
8. Almost anyone would be polite at a wedding reception; it doesn't matter what kind of personality the person has. T or F?

Now count the number of times you marked true for the odd-numbered items. Do the same for the even-numbered items. If you agreed with most of the odd-numbered items, you tend to view behavior as strongly influenced by personality traits or lasting personal dispositions, whether biological or learned. If you agreed with most of the even-numbered items, you view behavior as strongly influenced by external situations and circumstances.

What if I answered true about equally for odd and even items? Then you place equal weight on traits and situations as ways to explain behavior. This is the view now held by many personality psychologists (Funder, 2010; Mischel, Shoda, & Smith, 2008).

Does that mean that to predict how a person will act, it is better to focus on both personality traits and external circumstances? Yes, it's best to take both into account. Because personality *traits* are consistent, they can predict such things as job performance, dangerous driving, or a successful marriage (Burger, 2019). Yet, as we mentioned earlier, *situations* also greatly influence our behavior. A person's normally calm demeanor, for example, might become aggressive only because of an unusual and extreme situation.

Trait–Situation Interactions It would be unusual for you to dance at a movie or read a book at a football game. Likewise, few people sleep in roller coasters or tell off-color jokes at funerals. However, your personality traits may predict whether you choose to read a book, go to a movie, or attend a football game in the first place. Typically, traits *interact* with situations to determine how we will act (Mischel, 2004).

In a **trait–situation interaction**, external circumstances influence the expression of a personality trait. For instance, imagine what would happen if you moved from a church to a classroom to a party to a football game. As the setting changed, you would probably become louder and more boisterous. This change would show situational effects on behavior. At the same time, your personality traits also would be apparent: If you were quieter than average in church and class, you would probably be quieter than average in the other settings, too.

Trait–situation interaction The influence that external settings or circumstances have on the expression of personality traits.

MODULE 53 Behavioral and Social Learning Theories—Learning Outcomes Revisited

53.1 Describe how behaviorists and social learning theorists explain personality

Behavioral theories of personality emphasize learning, conditioning, and immediate effects of the environment (situational determinants). Learning theorists Dollard and Miller consider habits the basic core of personality. Habits express the combined effects of drive, cue, response, and reward. Social learning theory adds cognitive elements, such as perception, thinking, and understanding to the behavioral view of personality. Social learning theory is exemplified by Julian Rotter's concepts of the psychological situation, expectancies, and reinforcement value. Identification and imitation are of particular importance in learning to be "male" or "female."

53.2 Describe how heredity and the environment affect personality

Temperament refers to the hereditary and physiological aspects of one's emotional nature. Behavioral genetics and studies of identical twins suggest that heredity contributes significantly to adult personality traits. Biological predispositions (traits) interact with environment (situations) to explain our behavior.

Reflective Practice

Content Check

1. Learning theorists believe that personality "traits" really are ____________________ that are acquired through prior learning. They also emphasize ____________________ determinants of behavior.
2. Dollard and Miller consider cues the basic structure of personality. T or F?
3. To explain behavior, social learning theorists include mental elements, such as ____________________ (the anticipation that a response will lead to reinforcement).
4. Self-reinforcement is to behaviorist theory as superego is to psychoanalytic theory. T or F?
5. In addition to basic rewards and punishments, a child's personality also is shaped by ____________________ reinforcement.
6. Although personality ____________________ are consistent, ____________________ also influence behavior.

Skill Check

Think Critically

7. Rotter's concept of *reinforcement value* is closely related to a motivational principle discussed in Module 42. Can you name it?

Self-Reflect

Some people love to shop; others hate it. How have the psychological situation, expectancy, and reinforcement value affected your willingness to "shop 'til you drop"? One way to describe personality is in terms of a set of "if–then" rules that relate situations to traits (Kammrath, Mendoza-Denton, & Mischel, 2005). For example, Winston has a trait of independence. But he is not independent in every situation. Here are some if–then rules for Winston: *If* Winston is working at home, *then* he is independent. *If* Winston is being hassled at work, *then* he is very independent. *If* Winston has to go for a medical checkup, *then* he is not very independent. Can you write some if–then rules that describe your personality?

ANSWERS

1. habits, situational 2. F 3. expectancies 4. T 5. social 6. traits, situations
7. Incentive value

MODULE 54

A Psychologist's Skill Set
Leadership

Born to Lead?

Jonathan Ferrar is a true leader. That much was already clear when he was growing up in Brooklyn's Sunset Park. As a teenager, he recognized that his low-income neighborhood was home to significant environmental risks: three power plants, a sludge transfer facility, dozens of industrial sites, and a major highway carrying 200,000 cars and trucks each day. He learned about the effects on residents' health—above-average rates of lung cancer and respiratory illnesses.

Some people might resign themselves to accepting the situation, but not Jonathan. Instead, he worked for Uprose, an environmental not-for-profit agency. He testified in front of the Environmental Protection Agency about the risk of storm surges brought on by climate change. He warned that they could unleash toxic waste into the air and water from the industrial waterfront in his community. Sadly, he was proven right when Hurricane Sandy smashed into the New York coastline 18 months later. Jonathan has also organized the annual New York City Climate Justice Youth Summit so that young people can have a voice in political discussions about the environment.

Photo Courtesy The Barron Prize

Are people born leaders, or can each of us develop these skills? If you want to know the answer, we'll lead you there.

~LEARNING OUTCOMES~

After reading this module you should be able to:

54.1 Explain the characteristics of effective leaders

Leaders—Born or Made?

Learning Outcome 54.1 Explain the characteristics of effective leaders

Most early leadership research focused on the personality of the successful leader. It was generally accepted that good leaders possessed certain personality traits that enabled them to effectively manage teams (Northouse, 2016). Psychologists focused on traits such as self-confidence, intelligence, extroversion, persistence, and responsibility, although they also examined traits that are more closely connected to building relationships, such as sociability, cooperativeness, and emotional intelligence.

Does that mean people are either "born leaders" or they are not? Just as with early theories of personality, early *trait-based approaches* to leadership assumed that traits were inborn. More recently, however, psychologists studying leadership have begun to think of traits as relatively stable learned *behavior* patterns. (The same is true of personality psychologists. See Module 53.) This *behavioral approach* to leadership refocused research on leadership behaviors, the role of environmental circumstances, and how to "learn" leadership.

The behavioral approach examines what successful leaders actually say and do. In general, two groups of behaviors appear to be important. The first is related to managing tasks. Here, the focus is on the extent to which leaders can manage time, define responsibilities, and delegate appropriately. The second group of behaviors relates to managing people, and involves actions that build a sense of trust, respect, and liking among members of a team (Northouse, 2016).

Studying leadership behaviors is also connected to an interest in the leadership environment and the extent to which different leadership behaviors are more or less effective under different circumstances. For example, more recent research has examined how different leadership characteristics are more or less helpful when working in different cultures, or in different types of organizations (Aktas, Gelfand, & Hanges, 2016).

Most importantly, the behavioral approach to leadership also suggests the possibility that people can be taught to be good leaders. After all, if leadership traits are relatively stable learned behavior patterns, it should be possible to learn those patterns, or skills, and how to identify which skills are most appropriate for various leadership situations (Day et al., 2014; Middlehurst, 2015). What are the skills that people should develop to improve their leadership abilities? Read on so that you can lead on …

Becoming a Good Leader

Employers value employees with leadership potential because these individuals can take the initiative and advance projects of importance to an organization. Good leaders also help to develop the skills of their team members, thus developing a strong pool of talent. But leadership skills can be helpful in your personal life as well. For example, maybe you'll become active in community-based causes that matter to you (like Jonathan Ferrar). Or perhaps you will take on a mentoring role by coaching or teaching others. Taking a leadership role in this way helps to build strong and healthy communities, and often provides a great deal of personal satisfaction.

In spite of their importance, employers have noted that graduating students have weak leadership skills (Radermacher & Walia, 2013). Similarly, graduating students often don't feel as confident about their leadership abilities as they do about other skills. This may be because leadership skills are not readily developed through course assignments, unlike many of the other skills described in this book. Instead, students often indicate that leadership abilities are fostered through extracurricular activities, such as clubs, varsity sports, and student government. Students may also hone their leadership skills through work that they perform either for pay or as volunteers (Desmarais et al., 2013).

What are the leadership skills that I should consider developing while completing my studies? There is no simple answer since different leadership skills may be more or less effective, depending on the situation. In their research with effective college student leaders, however, Kouzes and Posner (2014) identified the following abilities as being important:

Be Inspiring and Commit to a Shared Vision Getting others to support your leadership requires that you have a clear sense of the values that guide you (see Module 16), and that you work toward understanding the values of other members of the group. Values are important in promoting commitment, because people will always work harder on projects that appeal to their fundamental beliefs (Kouzes & Posner, 2014). As a result, good leaders will work toward finding common ground among the values of the people they work with so that all members of the team feel dedicated to the work that needs to be done. Establishing shared values for the group is a process that requires input from all members. It may take some time to achieve consensus and considerable skill in negotiating to find compromises. Ultimately, though, it's a good use of time because group members will feel as though they have been heard, and are more likely to buy into the approach that's being adopted to move a project forward.

Ultimately, though, defining the shared values of a group is unhelpful unless a leader acts in ways that are in keeping with those values (Northouse, 2016). People will be unlikely to follow someone who "talks the talk" but isn't prepared to "walk the walk." For this reason, it's important to pay close attention to your own behavior: Are your actions in keeping with the group's goals and shared values? It's also important that you seek feedback about how your actions are affecting the team's performance. Though it isn't always easy to hear what others have to say about your performance, keep in mind that good leadership is promoted through self-awareness and metacognition (Module 26), which are both enhanced when you solicit the views of other people.

Be Innovative and Challenge the Process The skills associated with creativity and innovation are an important part of a leader's toolbox, as is the ability to recognize when those skills are necessary to bring about change (see Module 41). It's important to note that leadership isn't about changing things just because you can—it's about creating change that will improve the situation.

To determine whether change is necessary, good leaders continually ask why things are done in a particular way, and whether doing things differently would lead to improvement. Moreover, they recognize and draw upon the strengths and insights of other group members, who often have had diverse experiences that can help to fuel the creative process needed for change (see Module 49 for the benefits associated with diversity).

When a team faces big challenges, wise leaders break the problem down into smaller, more manageable pieces. This lessens the chances that group members will be overwhelmed and lose the motivation needed to continue. Generating "small wins" can also be helpful in building momentum behind the effort to bring about change. People are more likely to get behind an effort that is heading in the right direction.

Of course, challenging the process may also result in failures. When they happen, try to learn from the experience rather than being defeated by it. Good leaders are active learners, and have a strong belief in the idea that things can be turned around (Burbach, Matkin, & Fritz, 2004). They are also optimistic and show great resilience in the face of setbacks. What's more, they will work to develop these characteristics among other group members, so that they can provide each other with support when necessary.

Promote Strong Relationships and Individual Talent A group's success is enhanced when leaders work to foster positive relationships and a sense of responsibility for one another (Kouzes & Posner, 2014). Leaders can do this by listening carefully, showing an interest in others' concerns and circumstances, and by trusting team members to do their job rather than continually trying to take control and micromanage. Efforts to build a team can also be advanced when leaders create a climate in which members can get to know one another as individuals, and when tasks are structured in such a way that the goals allow people to work together cooperatively, rather than in isolation.

It's important, too, to recognize the unique talents of people on the team and to help them develop these abilities. Encouraging self-confidence through effective coaching can be extremely helpful in this regard. Good mentoring involves setting clear goals for people on your team and providing clear and consistent feedback. Providing feedback can be challenging, since people will sometimes take it as criticism. For this reason, it's useful to consider the following tips when providing assessments to people that you work with:

- Give feedback that focuses on the person's behaviors rather than their character.
- Whenever possible, provide concrete examples that provide some basis for your comments so that people can see how you have drawn your conclusions.
- Be selective—a few well-chosen suggestions are more likely to be acted upon than a very large number, which people may find overwhelming.
- Present your suggestions so that they will invite a dialogue by stating your thoughts and asking for their reaction.
- Pay careful attention to people's responses to your feedback, including nonverbal cues that might provide insight into their reactions to your suggestions.

Finally, it's important to make sure that, as a leader, you take time to note and celebrate the team's successes. Celebrations don't need to be big and expensive; sometimes they can simply take the form of a congratulatory email that recognizes a job well done. And always remember that a leader can go a long way with team members by remembering two small words: Thank you.

MODULE 54 Leadership—Learning Outcomes Revisited

54.1 Explain the characteristics of effective leaders

Leadership skills are beneficial in the workplace because they can be used to promote organizational goals. Leadership skills also benefit your personal life, because taking on leadership roles can bring great personal satisfaction. To be an effective leader one must inspire and commit to shared values, ask questions, seek feedback, welcome innovation, be a creative problem solver, be optimistic, and promote team success and individual talents.

Reflective Practice

Content Check

1. Different people, cultures, and organizations benefit from different leadership styles. T or F?
2. Employers value leadership because they prefer one person to do the work of many. T or F?
3. Employers report recent graduates to be deficient in leadership abilities. T or F?

Skill Check

Think Critically

4. In the following scenario, identify effective and ineffective leadership practices and provide suggestions to improve ineffective strategies: You are evaluating your peer following a presentation she gave. You tell her that the pace of her speech could have been slower. You add that the presentation was unclear, and because you want to save time, you offer to email a list of other suggestions to her later on.

Self-Reflect

Consider the recommended skills that can increase your leadership ability. Are there any areas in which you perform particularly well? Are there areas you could improve upon? How could improving these skills benefit your personal and professional life?

ANSWERS

1. T 2. F 3. T 4. Effective: Focusing on speech as behavioral criticism instead of framing comment toward the peer's character. Ineffective: Giving vague criticism such as "unclear," and emailing a list of suggestions. Emailing a list could be overwhelming and does not encourage dialogue with your peer. Improvements: Give concrete examples of a part of your peer's presentation that was unclear, make notes that outline a few important criticisms, and welcome her feedback in person so you can respond to her reactions and feelings about your comments.

MODULE 55

Health Psychology
Overview of Health Psychology

Sandy Gets Sick

What a year! Sandy barely managed to survive the rush of make-or-break term papers, projects, and classroom presentations. Sleep deprivation, gallons of coffee, junk food, and equal portions of cramming and complaining had carried her through finals. She was off for a summer of gymnastics, a sport she had grown to love after emigrating to the United States. At last she could stretch out, relax, and have some fun. Or could she? Just four days after school ended, Sandy got a bad cold, followed by bronchitis that lasted for nearly a month.

Sandy's term from heck (well, that's not exactly what *she* called it) illustrates what happens when personal habits, stress, and health collide. Though the timing of her cold might have been a coincidence, odds are it wasn't. Periods of stress are frequently followed by illness.

In this module, we explore how our health is affected by a variety of behavioral health risks, including stress.

Alex Emanuel Koch/Shutterstock.com

~LEARNING OUTCOMES~

After reading this module you should be able to:

55.1 Explain how cognition and behavior affect health

55.2 Identify the central role stress plays in our health

Health Psychology—Here's to Your Good Health

Learning Outcome 55.1 Explain how cognition and behavior affect health

Western medicine was dominated by the *medical model* for centuries (Engel, 2012; Middleton, 2015). From this perspective, the body is a complex biological machine. When it functions well, it is healthy; when it breaks down it becomes ill (and takes *you* down with it). Moreover, physical illnesses call for physical treatments (Sick? Take your medicine). In the medical model, *any* impact of the mind on health is dismissed as a mere placebo effect. (To remind yourself about placebo effects, see Module 4.)

Most psychologists reject the medical model as too simplistic, preferring instead the *biopsychosocial model* that we first encountered in Module 3. From the biopsychosocial perspective, both disease and health are better understood as being influenced by biological, psychological, *and* social processes (Lane, 2014; Saxbe, 2017). While some medical practitioners may still undervalue the effect the mind has on health and illness, health psychologists accept that health is a state of physical *and* psychological well-being that we can *actively* attain and maintain (Oakley, 2004). When it comes to illness, it is becoming clear that medicine works best when people *understand* their medical condition and its treatment (Benedetti, 2009; Moerman, 2002).

Consider our intrepid gymnast, Sandy. She has a weak right elbow and has just reinjured it during training. Her physiotherapist firmly wrapped her elbow with kinesiology tape and advised her to take a week or two off training to allow for some healing to take place. Instead, Sandy took off the tape and began training especially hard for an upcoming competition. If her elbow troubles worsen, of course Sandy should consult her physiotherapist. But a health psychologist might well advise her to change her cognitions by revaluating her stubborn determination to train at all costs, or rethink the pros and cons of following in her mother's footsteps as a champion gymnast. Other possibilities include learning more advanced gymnastic techniques to put less stress on her elbows or changing her diet to one that strengthens muscles.

Health psychology, then, aims to use cognitive and behavioral principles to prevent illness and promote well-being (Hales, 2021). Health psychologists may work with doctors in the allied field of **behavioral medicine**. Together, they apply psychology to manage medical problems, such as diabetes or asthma. Their interests include pain control, helping people cope with chronic illness, stress-related diseases, self-screening for diseases (such as breast cancer), and similar topics (Brannon, Feist, & Updegraff, 2021; Davis et al., 2015).

Lifestyle Diseases and Behavioral Risk Factors

Most of us agree that our health is priceless. Yet, many diseases and well over half of all deaths each year in North America can be traced to our unhealthy behaviors (Danaei et al., 2009). A century ago, most people died primarily from external factors, such as infectious diseases and unavoidable injuries. Today, more people than ever are dying from **lifestyle diseases**, which involve risky, health-damaging behaviors (Kozica et al., 2012). Examples include heart disease, stroke, HIV/AIDS, and lung cancer (➤ **Figure 55.1**). Clearly, some behaviors promote health, whereas others risk illness and death (Hales, 2021). As a poet once put it, "If you don't take care of yourself, the undertaker will overtake that responsibility for you."

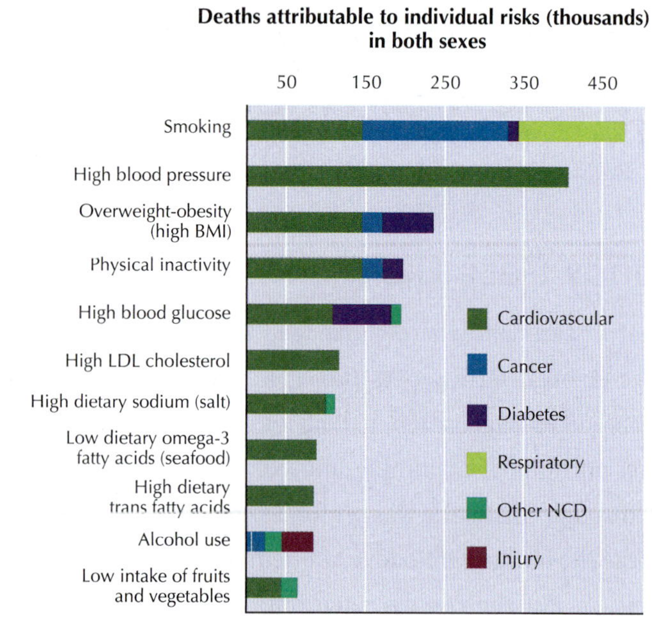

➤ **Figure 55.1**

Causes of preventable deaths in the United States. The leading causes of preventable deaths in the United States are tobacco and alcohol consumption, along with poor diet and exercise habits. Together they account for over half of all premature deaths and cause no end of day-to-day health problems. (Data adapted from Centers for Disease Control, 2018a. NCD = noncommunicable diseases.)

What are some unhealthy behaviors? While many external causes of illness are beyond our control, many subjective factors, such as behavioral risks, can be controlled and even reversed. **Behavioral risk factors** are actions people choose to take that increase the chances of disease, injury, or early death. For example, more than 480,000 Americans die every year from smoking-related diseases—about 20 percent of all deaths, regardless of the cause (Centers for Disease Control, 2019a).

Similarly, roughly two-thirds of all American adults are overweight. Of those, half are extremely overweight, or *obese* (Flegal et al., 2010). A person who is overweight at age 20 can expect to lose 5 to 20 years of life expectancy (Fontaine et al., 2003). In fact, being overweight may soon overtake smoking as the main cause of preventable death (Danaei et al., 2009).

Each of the following factors is a major behavioral risk (Brannon, Feist, & Updegraff, 2021): high levels of stress, untreated high blood pressure, cigarette smoking, abuse of alcohol or other drugs, overeating, inadequate exercise, unsafe sexual behavior, exposure to toxic substances, violence, excess sun exposure, reckless driving, and disregarding personal safety (avoidable accidents). About 70 percent

TABLE 55.1 | Percentage of U.S. High School Students Who Engage in Health-Endangering Behaviors in 2017

Risky Behavior	Percentage
Rode with drinking driver (previous 30 days)	16.5
Were in a physical fight (previous 12 months)	23.6
Carried a weapon (previous 30 days)	15.7
Binge drinking of alcohol (previous 30 days)	13.5
Used cannabis (previous 30 days)	19.8
Engaged in sexual intercourse (previous 90 days)	28.7
Did not use any method to prevent pregnancy (during last intercourse)	13.8
Smoked cigarettes (previous 30 days)	8.8
Did not have any fruit or 100% fruit juice (previous 7 days)	5.6
Did not have any vegetables, excluding fried potatoes (previous 7 days)	7.2
Played 3 or more hours of video games (average school day)	43.0

Source: Centers for Disease Control, 2018b.

of all medical costs are related to just six of these factors—smoking, alcohol abuse, drug abuse, poor diet, insufficient exercise, and risky sexual practices (Brannon, Feist, & Updegraff, 2021; Orleans, Gruman, & Hollendonner, 1999). (Risky sex is discussed in Module 48.)

The personal habits that you have by the time you are 18 or 19 greatly affect your health, happiness, and life expectancy years later (Gurung, 2014). ■ **Table 55.1** shows the percentage of American high school students who engaged in various kinds of risky behaviors in 2017. (It is well worth noting that these results were the lowest recorded since this particular record-keeping program was first instituted in 1991.)

Specific risk factors are not the only concern. Some people have a general **disease-prone personality** that leaves them depressed, anxious, hostile, and frequently ill (Meyer, 2014). In contrast, people who are intellectually resourceful, compassionate, optimistic, and nonhostile tend to enjoy good health (Li et al., 2009; Taylor, 2021). Depression, in particular, is likely to damage health (Gleason et al., 2013; Hales, 2021). People who are depressed in turn eat poorly, sleep poorly, rarely exercise, fail to use seat belts in cars, smoke more, and so on.

Killer Lifestyles In your mind's eye, fast-forward an imaginary film of your life all the way to old age. Do it twice—once with a lifestyle including a large number of behavioral risk factors, and again without them. It should be obvious that many small risks can add up, dramatically raising the chance of illness. If stress is a frequent part of your life, visualize your body seething with emotion, day after day. If you smoke, picture a lifetime's worth of cigarette smoke blown through your lungs in a week. If you drink, take a lifetime of alcohol's assaults on the brain, stomach, and liver and squeeze them into a month. If you eat a high-fat, high-cholesterol diet, fast-forward a lifetime of heart-stopping plaque clogging your arteries. Your body would be poisoned, ravaged, and soon dead.

We don't mean to sermonize. We just want to remind you that risk factors make a huge difference. To make matters worse, unhealthy lifestyles almost always create multiple risks—that is, people who smoke also are likely to drink excessively. Those who overeat usually do not get enough exercise, and so on (Lippke, Nigg, & Maddock, 2012). Even infectious diseases are often linked to behavioral risks. For example, pneumonia and other infections occur at higher rates in people who have cancer, heart disease, lung disease, or liver disease. Thus, many deaths attributed to infections can be traced back to smoking, poor diet, or alcohol abuse (Mokdad et al., 2004).

Reducing Behavioral Risk Factors

To prevent disease, health psychologists first try to reduce behavioral risk factors. In many cases, lifestyle diseases can be prevented by making specific, minor changes in behavior. For example, small adjustments in how food is prepared can greatly influence health (Mills et al., 2017). For instance,

Health psychology Study of how cognitive and behavioral principles can be used to prevent illness and promote physical well-being.

Behavioral medicine A medical specialty focused on the study of nonbiological factors influencing physical health and illness.

Lifestyle disease A disease related to health-damaging personal habits.

Behavioral risk factors Behaviors that increase the chances of disease, injury, or premature death.

Disease-prone personality A personality type associated with poor health, marked by persistent negative emotions, including anxiety, depression, and hostility.

Tom Wang/Shutterstock.com

Boiarkina Marina/Shutterstock.com

In the long run, behavioral risk factors and lifestyles do make a difference in health and life expectancy.

hypertension (high blood pressure) can be deadly. Yet, consuming less salt (sodium) can help fend off this "silent killer." Losing weight, using alcohol sparingly, and getting more exercise will also help (Edenfield & Blumenthal, 2011).

You probably won't be surprised to learn that many people fail to engage in health-promoting behaviors until ill health forces it upon them. For example, 75 million Americans have hypertension (Koçkaya & Wertheimer, 2011). A friend of one of your authors commented about his recent heart attack, "I guess that's my wake-up call. Time to lose some weight, exercise more, and eat healthier. I want to be around while my grandchildren grow up."

What may surprise you is that despite being diagnosed, many people *still* don't change the habits that led to their illnesses. Change can be hard (Gainforth, West, & Michie, 2015). All the medicine in the world might not be enough to restore health without changes in cognition and behavior. For example, according to one estimate, although 78 percent of people with hypertension know about it, only 68 percent of diagnosed patients are treated, and of those, only 38 percent *comply* with their treatment regimens. Overall, only 29 percent of all people with hypertension are receiving optimal treatment. If 100 percent of people with hypertension complied fully with their treatments, the rate of hypertension would drop by 32 percent, meaning that 8.5 million fewer Americans would need treatment in any given year, resulting in yearly savings of $72 billion (Koçkaya & Wertheimer, 2011).

Early Prevention Of the behavioral risks we have discussed, smoking is the largest preventable cause of death and the single most lethal factor (Centers for Disease Control, 2019a). As such, it illustrates the prospect for preventing illness.

What have health psychologists done to lessen the risks of smoking? Attempts to "immunize" youths against pressures to start smoking are a good example. When humorist Mark Twain said, "Giving up smoking is the easiest thing in the world. I know because I've done it thousands of times," he stated a basic truth—only 1 smoker in 10 has long-term success at quitting (Krall, Garvey, & Garcia, 2002; García-Rodríguez et al., 2013). Thus, the best way to deal with smoking is to prevent it before it becomes a lifelong habit. For example, prevention programs in schools discourage smoking with quizzes about smoking, multimedia presentations, antismoking art contests, poster and T-shirt giveaways, antismoking pamphlets for parents, and questions for students to ask their parents (Flynn et al., 2011; Prokhorov et al., 2010). Such efforts are designed to persuade kids that smoking is dangerous and "uncool."

Some antismoking programs include **refusal skills training**. In such training, youths learn to resist pressures to begin smoking (or using other drugs). For example, junior high students can roleplay ways to resist smoking pressures from peers, adults, and cigarette ads. Similar methods can be applied to other health risks, such as sexually transmitted diseases and teen pregnancy (Wandersman & Florin, 2003; Witkiewitz et al., 2011).

Many health programs also teach students general life skills. The idea is to give kids skills that will help them cope with day-to-day stresses. That way, they will be less tempted to escape problems through drug use or other destructive behaviors. **Life skills training** includes practice in stress reduction, self-protection, decision-making, goal setting, self-control, and social skills (Allen & Williams, 2012; Corey & Corey, 2014).

Community Health and Social Media In addition to early prevention, health psychologists have had some success with **community health campaigns**. These are community-wide education projects designed to lessen major risk factors (Hawe, 2015; Lounsbury & Mitchell, 2009). Health campaigns inform people of risks such as stress, alcohol abuse, high blood pressure, high cholesterol, smoking, sexually transmitted diseases, or excessive sun exposure. This is followed by efforts to motivate people to change their behavior (Miller & Prentice, 2016). Campaigns sometimes provide *role models* (positive examples) who show people how to improve their own health. They also direct people to services for health screening, advice, and treatment. Health campaigns may reach people through mass media, public schools, health fairs, workplaces, or self-help programs.

Recently, *social media* have become increasingly important as tools for bringing cost-effective health information to large numbers people, as well as fostering behavioral change (Moller et al., 2017). (See Module 76 for a discussion of *social norms marketing* and *personalized normalized feedback*, two promising social media approaches to fostering effective behavioral change.)

Mr. Exen/Shutterstock.com

Too many people diagnosed with lifestyle illnesses, such as this smoker with severe emphysema, fail to comply with their doctor's instructions. Changing long-standing risky behaviors usually involves more than just telling people what they need to do differently. One major goal of health psychology is to find ways to increase compliance with doctor's advice.

Increasing Subjective Well-Being and Health-Promoting Behaviors

In addition to removing specific risk factors, psychologists are interested in getting people to increase behaviors that promote health. Health is not just an absence of disease (Diener & Chan, 2011; Diener, 2013). People who are truly healthy enjoy a positive state of *subjective well-being*. Maintaining subjective well-being is a lifelong pursuit and, hopefully, a labor of love. People who attain subjective well-being are both physically and psychologically healthy (Wrosch, Jobin, & Scheier, 2016). They are happy, optimistic, self-confident individuals who can bounce back emotionally from adversity. People who enjoy a sense of well-being also have supportive relationships with others, do meaningful work, and live in a clean environment. (Many of these aspects of subjective well-being are addressed elsewhere in this book. See Module 45 for more on positivity and optimism.)

Health-promoting behaviors include obvious practices such as getting regular exercise, controlling smoking and alcohol use, maintaining a balanced diet, getting good medical care, and managing stress (Zarcadoolas, Pleasant, & Greer, 2006). In one study, the risk of dying during a 10-year period was cut by 65 percent for adults who were careful about diet, alcohol, exercise, and smoking (Knoops et al., 2004).

Health-promoting behaviors don't have to be restrictive or burdensome. For instance, maintaining a healthy diet doesn't mean surviving on tofu and wheatgrass. The healthiest people in the study just mentioned ate a tasty "Mediterranean diet" higher in fruit, vegetables, and fish and lower in red meat and dairy products. Likewise, you don't need to exercise like an Olympic athlete to benefit from physical activity (Portugal et al., 2013). All you need is 30 minutes of exercise (the equivalent of a brisk walk) three or four times a week. Almost everyone can fit such "lifestyle physical activity" into his or her schedule (Pescatello, 2001).

What about alcohol? Moderation in drinking doesn't mean that you must be a teetotaler. Consuming one or two alcoholic drinks per day is generally safe for most people, especially if you remain alcohol-free two or three days a week. A glass of red wine daily may even be healthy (Anekonda, 2006). However, having three or more drinks a day greatly increases the risk for stroke, cirrhosis of the liver, cancer, high blood pressure, heart disorders, and other diseases (Knoops et al., 2004; Lamont et al., 2011).

To summarize, a small number of behavioral patterns account for many common health problems (Centers for Disease Control, 2018a; Straub, 2012). ▪ **Table 55.2** lists several major ways to promote good health. To explore an interesting social factor that may underlie common health problems, read on.

Social Networks and Healthy Behaviors Would you like to eat better, exercise more, or quit smoking? Researchers Nicholas Christakis and James Fowler believe that they know why it can be difficult to alter unhealthy behaviors. Often, social factors are a barrier to change. Unhealthy behaviors such as overeating or smoking seem to spread almost like a "mental virus" (Christakis & Fowler, 2009; Lyons, 2011).

Refusal skills training A program that teaches youths how to resist pressures to begin smoking (also can be applied to other drugs and health risks).

Life skills training A program that teaches stress reduction, self-protection, decision-making, self-control, and social skills.

Community health campaign A community-wide education program that provides information about how to lessen risk factors and promote health.

TABLE 55.2 | Major Health-Promoting Behaviors

Source	Desirable Behaviors
Tobacco	Do not smoke; do not use smokeless tobacco.
Nutrition	Eat a balanced, low-fat diet; have appropriate caloric intake; maintain a healthy body weight.
Exercise	Engage in at least 30 minutes of aerobic exercise 5 days per week.
Blood pressure	Lower blood pressure with diet and exercise or medicine if necessary.
Alcohol and drugs	Drink no more than two drinks per day; abstain from using drugs.
Sleep and relaxation	Avoid sleep deprivation; provide for periods of relaxation every day.
Sex	Practice safer sex; avoid unplanned pregnancy.
Injury	Curb dangerous driving habits; use seat belts; minimize sun exposure; forgo dangerous activities.
Stress	Learn stress management; lower hostility.

One study of social contagion found that people were 57 percent more likely to become obese if they had a friend who became obese first (Christakis & Fowler, 2007). Similarly, smokers tend to "hang out" with other smokers (Christakis & Fowler, 2008). Another study found that spending time with drinkers increases alcohol consumption (Ali & Dwyer, 2010). Apparently, we tend to flock together with like-minded people and adopt many of their habits (Barnett et al., 2013; Miller & Prentice, 2016).

Does that mean I am doomed to be unhealthy if my family and friends have unhealthy habits? Not necessarily. Social networks also can spread healthy behaviors (Fowler & Christakis, 2010). If one smoker in a group of smokers quits, others are more likely to follow suit. If your spouse quits smoking, you are 67 percent more likely to quit. If a good friend quits smoking, your chances of abandoning tobacco go up by 36 percent (Christakis & Fowler, 2008). The growing social unpopularity of smoking may be the best explanation of why fewer and fewer American adults (now only 15 percent) still smoke (Centers for Disease Control, 2019a).

Tony Arruza/The Image Bank Unreleased/Getty Images

If you are a smoker, do your friends also smoke? Are your family members fast-food junkies just like you? Are your friends all drinkers?

The implication? Don't wait for your friends or family to adopt healthier habits. Take the lead and inspire them to join you. Failing that, start hanging out with a healthier crowd. You might catch something healthy.

Stress and Health

Learning Outcome 55.2 Identify the central role stress plays in our health

Health psychology pays special attention to the effect that stress has on health and illness. Although stress can be a major behavioral risk factor if it is prolonged or severe, it isn't always bad. As Canadian stress research pioneer Hans Selye (SEL-yay) (1976) observed, "To be totally without stress is to be dead." That's because **stress** is the pressure or demand placed on an organism to adjust or adapt. Unpleasant events such as work pressures, marital problems, or financial woes are naturally stressful. But so are travel, sports, a new job, rock climbing, dating, and other positive activities. Even if you aren't a thrill seeker, a healthy lifestyle may include a fair amount of *eustress* (good stress). Activities that provoke "good stress" are usually challenging, rewarding, and energizing.

Regardless of whether it is triggered by a pleasant or an unpleasant event, the *stress reaction* begins with the same autonomic nervous system (ANS) arousal that occurs during emotion. Imagine that you are standing at the top of a wind-whipped ski jump for the first time. Internally, you experience a rapid surge in your heart rate, blood pressure, respiration, muscle tension, and other ANS responses. *Short-term* stresses of this kind can be uncomfortable, but they rarely do any damage. (Your landing might, however.) *Long-term* stresses are another matter entirely.

General Adaptation Syndrome

The impact of long-term stresses can be understood by examining the body's defenses against stress, a pattern known as **general adaptation syndrome** (GAS). GAS is a series of three stages of stress response to prolonged stress. Selye (1976) noticed that the first symptoms of almost any disease or trauma (poisoning, infection, injury, or stress) are almost identical. The body responds in much the same way to any stress, be it infection, failure, embarrassment, a new job, trouble at school, or a stormy romance.

How does the body respond to stress? The GAS consists of three stages: an alarm reaction, a stage of resistance, and a stage of exhaustion (➤ Figure 55.2; Selye, 1976).

Alarm Reaction In the **alarm reaction**, your body mobilizes its resources to cope with added stress. The pituitary gland signals the adrenal glands to produce more adrenaline, noradrenaline, and cortisol. As these stress hormones are dumped into the bloodstream, some bodily processes are speeded up and others are slowed. This allows bodily resources to be applied where they are needed.

We should all be thankful that our bodies automatically respond to emergencies. But brilliant as this emergency system is, it also can cause problems. In the first phase of the alarm reaction, people have symptoms such as headache, fever, fatigue, sore muscles, shortness of breath, diarrhea, upset stomach, loss of appetite, and a lack of energy. Notice that these also are the symptoms of being sick, of stressful travel, of high-altitude sickness, of final exams week, and (possibly) of falling in love!

Stage of Resistance During the **stage of resistance**, bodily adjustments to stress stabilize. As the body's defenses come into balance, symptoms of the alarm reaction disappear. Outwardly, everything seems normal. However, this appearance of normality comes at a high cost. The body is better able to cope with the original stressor, but its resistance to other stresses is lowered. For example, animals placed in extreme cold become more resistant to the cold but more susceptible to infection. It is during the stage of resistance that the first signs of psychosomatic disorders (physical disorders triggered by psychological factors) begin to appear.

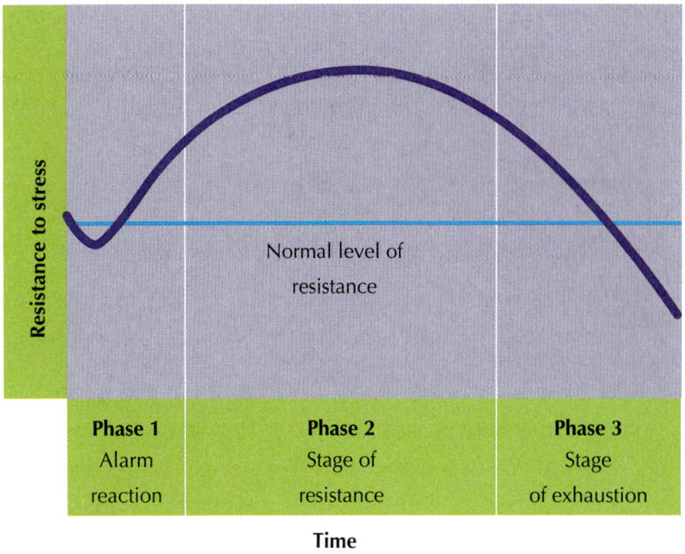

➤ Figure 55.2

General adaptation syndrome (GAS). During the initial alarm reaction to stress, resistance falls below normal. It rises again as body resources are mobilized, and it remains high during the stage of resistance. Eventually, resistance falls again as the stage of exhaustion is reached. (Based on Selye, 1976.)

Stage of Exhaustion Continued stress leads to a **stage of exhaustion**, in which the body's resources are drained and stress hormones are depleted. Some of the typical signs

Stress Pressure or demand placed on an organism to adjust or adapt.

General adaptation syndrome Three-stage model of stress response, consisting of alarm, resistance, and exhaustion.

Alarm reaction The first stage of the general adaptation syndrome, during which body resources are mobilized to cope with a stressor.

Stage of resistance The second stage of the general adaptation syndrome, during which the body adjustments to stress stabilize, but at a high physical cost.

Stage of exhaustion The third stage of the general adaptation syndrome, at which time the body's resources are exhausted and serious health consequences occur.

or symptoms of impending exhaustion include the following (Friedman, 2002; Gurung, 2014; Hales, 2021):

Emotional signs: Anxiety, apathy, irritability, mental fatigue

Behavioral signs: Avoidance of responsibilities and relationships, extreme or self-destructive behavior, self-neglect, poor judgment

Physical signs: Excessive worry about illness, frequent illness, exhaustion, overuse of medicines, physical ailments and complaints

GAS may sound melodramatic if you are young and healthy, or if you've never endured prolonged stress. However, do not take stress lightly. Unless a way of relieving stress is found, the result will be a psychosomatic disease, a serious loss of health, or complete collapse. When Selye examined animals in the later stages of GAS, he found that their adrenal glands were enlarged and discolored. Intense shrinkage of internal organs, such as the thymus, spleen, and lymph nodes, was evident, and many animals had stomach ulcers. In addition to such direct effects, stress can disrupt the body's immune system.

Subbotina Anna/Shutterstock.com

Stress and negative emotions lower immune system activity and increase inflammation. This, in turn, raises our vulnerability to infection, worsens illness, and delays recovery.

Understanding stress and learning to control it can improve not only your health, but also your quality of life (Allen, Carlson, & Ham, 2007). (For these reasons, a discussion of stress and stress management can be found in Modules 56–59.)

MODULE 55 Overview of Health Psychology—Learning Outcomes Revisited

55.1 How do cognition and behavior affect health?

Health psychologists are interested in how cognition and behavior help maintain and promote health. Studies of health and illness have identified several behavioral risk factors that have a major effect on general health and life expectancy. At a minimum, it is important to maintain health-promoting cognitions and behaviors with respect to diet, alcohol, exercise, and smoking. Health psychologists have pioneered efforts to prevent the development of unhealthy habits and to improve well-being through community health campaigns and social media. Maintaining good health is a personal responsibility, not a matter of luck. Wellness is based on minimizing risk factors and engaging in health-promoting behaviors.

55.2 Identify the central role stress plays in our health

Stress is the mental and physical condition that occurs when we adjust or adapt to the environment. Stress is a normal part of life; however, it also is a major risk factor for illness and disease. The body reacts to stress in a series of stages called *general adaptation syndrome (GAS)*. The stages of GAS are alarm, resistance, and exhaustion. Bodily reactions in GAS follow the pattern observed in the development of psychosomatic disorders.

Reflective Practice

Content Check

1. With respect to health, which of the following is *not* a major behavioral risk factor?
   a. overexercise
   b. cigarette smoking
   c. stress
   d. high blood pressure
2. Lifestyle diseases related to just six behaviors account for 70 percent of all medical costs. These behaviors are

smoking, alcohol abuse, drug abuse, poor diet, insufficient exercise, and

a. driving too fast
b. excessive sun exposure
c. unsafe sex
d. exposure to toxins

3. The disease-prone personality is marked by ______________, anxiety, and hostility.
4. Health psychologists tend to prefer ______________ rather than modifying habits (like smoking) that become difficult to break once they are established.
5. The first signs of psychosomatic disorders begin to appear during the stage of

a. alarm
b. exhaustion
c. resistance
d. appraisal

Skill Check

Think Critically

6. The general public is increasingly well informed about health risks and healthful behavior. Can you apply the concept of reinforcement to explain why so many people fail to act on this information?

Self-Reflect

Make a list of the major behavioral risk factors that apply to you. Are you laying the foundation for a lifestyle disease? Which of the health-promoting behaviors listed in Table 55.2 would you like to increase? If you were designing a community health campaign, who would you use as role models of healthful behavior? Are you experiencing any signs of GAS? (Not a joke, guys ☺) What are they?

ANSWERS

1. a 2. c 3. depression 4. prevention 5. c 6. Many unhealthy behaviors result in immediate reinforcement, while the benefits of healthy behaviors may be delayed by months or years, greatly lessening the immediate rewards for healthful behavior (Watson & Tharp, 2014).

MODULE

56 Health Psychology
Stressors

The Luckiest Girl in the World

Halfpoint/Shutterstock.com

Darya was the luckiest girl in the world. After marrying her sweetheart, they enjoyed a spectacular honeymoon in Jamaica. Now they were moving to a new apartment to begin their lives together. So why was she feeling run over by a truck?

What Darya was learning firsthand is that prolonged or severe stress can lead to health problems, even if it is triggered by positive events. Over the last few months, she had experienced quite a few major life changes. It had all added up, and now she had a bad cough and a fever.

We begin this module with the commonsense idea that stressful events "happen to" people. Although this is sometimes the case, more often stress is a matter of how we perceive events and react to them. We also explore some of the factors that determine the intensity of a stressor and close with a look at some different types of stressors, including frustration and conflict.

~LEARNING OUTCOMES~

After reading this module you should be able to:

56.1 Explain the concept of a stressor, and outline factors that determine its severity

56.2 Distinguish among different types of stressors

Stressors—Threats or Thrills?

Learning Outcome 56.1 Explain the concept of a stressor, and outline factors that determine its severity

A **stressor** is a specific condition or event that challenges or threatens a person. It goes almost without saying that some events are more likely to be stressors than others.

But what makes an event a stressor? It might seem that stressful events "happen to" us. Sometimes this is true, but as noted in Module 44, our emotions are greatly affected by how we appraise situations. That's why some people are distressed by events that others view as a thrill or a challenge (*eustress*). Ultimately, stress depends on how you perceive a situation. Our friend Akihito would find it stressful to listen to five of his son's hip-hop CDs in a row. His son Takashi would find it stressful to listen to *one* of his father's opera CDs. To know if you are stressed, we must know what meaning you place on events. As we will see in a moment, whenever a stressor is appraised as a *threat* (potentially harmful), a powerful stress reaction follows (Lazarus, 1991a,b; Smith & Kirby, 2011).

Appraising Stressors

You have been selected to give a speech to 300 people. Or a doctor tells you that you must undergo a dangerous and painful operation. Or the one true love of your life walks out the door. What would be your cognitive and emotional response to these events?

According to Richard Lazarus (1991a,b), there are two important steps in dealing with a threat. The first is **primary appraisal**, in which you decide whether a situation is relevant or irrelevant, positive or threatening. In essence, this step answers the question, "Am I okay or in trouble?" Then, you make a **secondary appraisal**, in which you assess your resources and choose a way to meet the threat or challenge. ("What can I do about this situation?")

Thus, the way a situation is "sized up" greatly affects our ability to cope with it (➤ **Figure 56.1**; Gomes, Faria, & Lopes, 2016). Public speaking, for instance, can be appraised as an intense threat or as a chance to perform. Emphasizing the threat—by imagining failure, rejection, or embarrassment—obviously invites disaster (Tripp et al., 2011). That's why it's valuable to learn to think in ways that ward off the body's stress response (Bliese, Edwards, & Sonnentag, 2017). (Some strategies for controlling upsetting thoughts are described in Module 59.)

Several factors contribute to the appraised intensity of any given threat. In most day-to-day situations, perceived threat has to do with the idea of *control*. We are particularly prone to feel stressed when we can't—or think we can't—control our immediate environment. In short, a *perceived* lack of control is just as threatening as a real lack of control. For example, college students who feel overloaded experience stress even though their workload may not be any heavier than that of their classmates (Jacobs & Dodd, 2003).

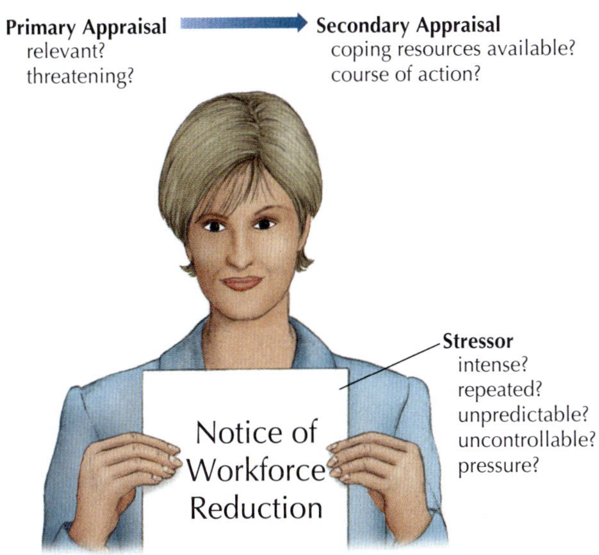

➤ **Figure 56.1**

The origins of stress. Stress is the product of an interchange between a person and the environment.

A sense of control also comes from believing you can reach desired goals. It is threatening to feel that we lack *competence* to cope with life's demands (Bandura, 2001; Leiter, Gascón, & Martínez-Jarreta, 2010).

Unpredictability is another important factor. Police officers, for instance, suffer from a high rate of stress-related diseases. The threat of injury or death—plus occasional confrontations with angry, drunk, or hostile citizens—takes a toll. A major factor is the *unpredictable* nature of police work. An officer who stops a car to issue a traffic ticket never knows if a cooperative citizen or an armed gang member is waiting inside.

A revealing study shows how unpredictability adds to stress. In a series of 1-minute trials, college students breathed air through a mask. On random (i.e., unpredictable) trials, the air contained 20 percent more carbon dioxide (CO_2) than normal. If you were to inhale this air, you would feel anxious, stressed, and a little like you were suffocating. Students tested this way hated the "surprise" doses of CO_2. They found it much less stressful to be told in advance which trials would include a choking whiff of CO_2 (Lejuez et al., 2000).

Pressure is another element of stress, especially job stress. *Pressure* occurs when a person must meet *urgent* external demands or expectations (Szollos, 2009). For example, we feel pressured when activities must be sped up, when deadlines must be met, when extra work is added, or when we must work near maximum capacity for long periods. Most students who have survived final exams are familiar with the effects of pressure.

What if I set deadlines for myself? Does the source of the pressure make a difference? It can certainly help since that would tend to increase your sense of self-control (Brough, Drummond, & Biggs, 2017; Leiter, Gascón, & Martínez-Jarreta, 2010). In one study, nurses with a high sense of

Stressor Specific condition or event that challenges or threatens a person.

Primary appraisal Deciding if a situation is relevant to oneself and if it is a threat.

Secondary appraisal Deciding how to cope with a threat or challenge.

Jason Patterson/The New Yorker Collection/Cartoonbank.com

control (e.g., over the pacing of work and the physical arrangement of the working environment) were less likely to get sick, either physically or mentally, than nurses with a low sense of control (Ganster, Fox, & Dwyer, 2001).

To summarize, when emotional "shocks" are *uncontrollable, unpredictable,* and linked to *pressure,* stress is magnified and damage is likely to result. At work, people face many of these sources of stress every day (Bliese, Edwards, & Sonnentag, 2017). (See ■ **Table 56.1** for a list of the most common sources of stress at work.) In fact, chronic job stress sometimes results in *burnout.*

Burnout When workers are physically, mentally, and emotionally drained, they may experience **burnout** (Leiter, Gascón, & Martínez-Jarreta, 2010). When people become burned out, they experience emotional exhaustion, cynicism or detachment, and feelings of reduced personal accomplishment.

Burnout may occur in any job, but it is a special problem in emotionally demanding helping professions, such as nursing, teaching, social work, childcare, counseling, or police work (Ray et al., 2013). Also, people who are more passionate about their work are more vulnerable to burnout (Turgoose et al., 2017; Vallerand, 2010). If we wish to keep caring people in the helping professions, it may be necessary to adjust workloads, rewards, and the amount of control people have in their jobs (Leiter & Maslach, 2005).

Can college students experience burnout? Yes, they can (Parker & Salmela-Aro, 2011). If you have a negative attitude toward your studies and feel that your college workload is too heavy, you may be vulnerable to burnout (Jacobs & Dodd, 2003). On the other hand, if you have a positive attitude toward your studies, participate in extracurricular activities, and enjoy good social support from your friends, keep it up!

TABLE 56.1 | The Top 10 Work Stresses

Work Stress	Rank
Low salary	1
Lack of opportunity for growth	2
Workload too heavy	3
Hours too long	4
Job expectations uncertain	5
Job expectations unrealistic	6
Work interferes with personal time	7
Job insecurity	8
Lack of participation in decision-making	9
Inflexible hours	10

Source: Data from American Psychological Association (2012).

Poverty and Health

The phenomenon of *relative poverty* is a good example of how changing your appraisal may make a big difference in your life. To be clear, being poor is no fun. It probably won't surprise you to learn it's no good for your health, either (Fuller-Rowell, Evans, & Ong, 2012). In general, the poorer people are, the more their health suffers and the lower is their life expectancy. According to the World Bank (2018), in 2015, 736 *million* people around the world lived in *absolute poverty,* surviving on less than the international poverty line of $1.90 a day. Tragically, absolute poverty wreaks havoc on people's health. But that's not the whole story. For example, physician Stephen Bezruchka has shown that Greeks earn, on average, less than half of what Americans earn and yet they have a longer life expectancy (Bezruchka as cited in Sapolsky, 2005).

How could this be? One possibility is suggested by a study that found poorer women in California are more likely to die if they live in better-off neighborhoods than if they live in poorer neighborhoods (Winkleby, Ahn, & Cubbin, 2006). Apparently, being constantly reminded that you are relatively poor piles on an extra measure of stress (Bjornstrom, 2011; Fritzell et al., 2015).

Relative poverty is not the whole story, though, since even better-off Americans are not as healthy as their counterparts in other developed countries (Weir, 2013). Instead, income inequality itself may prove to be a chronic social stressor (Cushing et al., 2015). The United States currently has the largest income inequality in the developed world. Rich or poor, living in a "rat race" where we are all in competition with each other seems to lessen trust and weaken the American social fabric. As a result, we all, to some degree, pay a price with our health.

No one should pretend that relative poverty in the United States is anywhere near as big a problem as absolute poverty around the world. Nevertheless, it is a growing problem in the United States as the gap between the rich and poor continues to widen (Emerson, 2009; Oishi, Kesebir, & Diener, 2011).

What should I do if I always feel poor? That may be part of the reason why you are reading this book. First, commit to changing your circumstances through education and hard work. That's called *problem-focused coping* (you'll read about it in Module 57). In the meantime, remember Lazarus's (1991a,b) point about appraisal: Something is a stressor only if you *think* it is one. A realistic appraisal of your situation may reveal that you are "richer" than you think. Maybe the best things in life are not all free, but why make yourself sick comparing yourself to people much better off than you (Wilkinson & Pickett, 2009)?

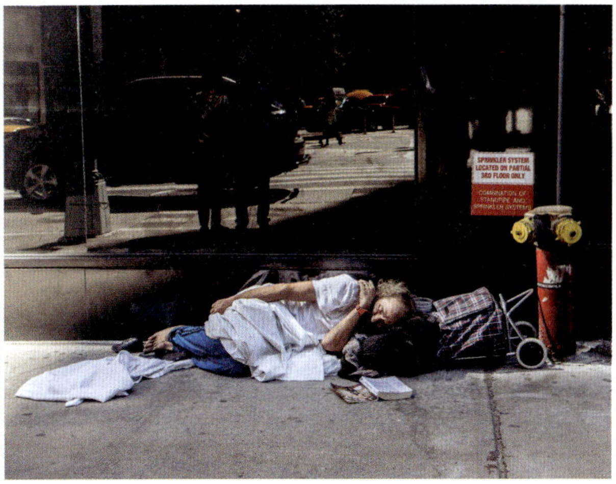
ULU_BIRD/Shutterstock.com

Although being poor in the United States may mean living above an absolute poverty level, it also means constantly living with the stress of dramatic income inequality (Wilkinson & Pickett, 2009).

Types of Stressors—The Good, the Bad, and the Ugly

Learning Outcome 56.2 Distinguish among different types of stressors

From major life events, such as getting married or moving to another country, to minor hassles, such as getting cut off by the car in front of you or having too many things to do, and from frustrations to conflicts, almost anything can become a stressor under the right circumstances. Let's look at stressors in more detail.

Life Events and Stress

Disaster, depression, and sorrow often precede illness (Harrington, 2013). More surprising is the finding that *life changes*—both good *and* bad (*and* ugly?)—can increase susceptibility to accidents or illness. Major changes in our surroundings or routines require us to be on guard and ready to react. Over long periods, this can be quite stressful.

How can I tell if I am subjecting myself to too much stress? Psychiatrist Thomas Holmes and graduate student Richard Rahe developed the first rating scale to estimate the health hazards we face when stresses add up (Holmes & Rahe, 1967). Still widely used today, a version of the **Social Readjustment Rating Scale (SRRS)** is reprinted in ■ **Table 56.2** (Miller & Rahe, 1997; Woods, Racine, & Klump, 2010). Notice that the impact of life events is expressed in *life change units (LCUs)* (numerical values assigned to each life event).

Why is going on vacation on the list? Positive life events can be stressful as well. (For example, marriage rates a 50 and Christmas a 30, even though they usually are happy events.) Even a change in social activities rates 27 LCUs, whether the change is due to an improvement or a decline. A stressful adjustment may be required in either case. To use the SRRS, add up the LCUs for all the life events you have experienced during the last year and compare the total to the following standards:

0–150: No significant problems
150–199: Mild life crisis (33 percent chance of illness)
200–299: Moderate life crisis (50 percent chance of illness)
300 or more: Major life crisis (80 percent chance of illness)

You have a higher chance of illness or accident when your LCU total exceeds 300 points. Other stressful events—

Burnout A work-related condition of mental, physical, and emotional exhaustion.

Social Readjustment Rating Scale (SRRS) A scale that rates the impact of various life events on the likelihood of illness.

TABLE 56.2 | Social Readjustment Rating Scale

Rank	Life Event	Life Change Units	Rank	Life Event	Life Change Units
1	Death of spouse or child	119	23	Mortgage or loan greater than $10,000	44
2	Divorce	98	24	Change in responsibilities at work	43
3	Death of close family member	92	25	Change in living conditions	42
4	Marital separation	79	26	Change in residence	41
5	Fired from work	79	27	Begin or end school	38
6	Major personal injury or illness	77	28	Trouble with in-laws	38
7	Jail term	75	29	Outstanding personal achievement	37
8	Death of close friend	70	30	Change in work hours or conditions	36
9	Pregnancy	66	31	Change in schools	35
10	Major business readjustment	62	32	Christmas	30
11	Foreclosure on a mortgage or loan	61	33	Trouble with boss	29
12	Gain of new family member	57	34	Change in recreation	29
13	Marital reconciliation	57	35	Mortgage or loan less than $10,000	28
14	Change in health or behavior of family member	56	36	Change in personal habits	27
15	Change in financial state	56	37	Change in eating habits	27
16	Retirement	54	38	Change in social activities	27
17	Change to different line of work	51	39	Change in number of family get-togethers	26
18	Change in number of arguments with spouse	51	40	Change in sleeping habits	26
19	Marriage	50	41	Vacation	25
20	Spouse begins or ends work	46	42	Change in church activities	22
21	Sexual difficulties	45	43	Minor violations of the law	22
22	Child leaving home	44			

Source: Reprinted from Miller & Rahe (1997).

such as entering college, changing majors, or experiencing a breakup in a steady relationship—also affect the health of college students.

Since people differ greatly in their reactions to the same event, stress scales like the SRRS at best provide a rough index of stress. Nevertheless, research has shown that if your stress level is too high, an adjustment in your activities or lifestyle may be needed. In one classic study, people were deliberately exposed to the virus that causes common colds. The results were nothing to sneeze at: If a person had a high stress score, she or he was much more likely to actually get a cold (Cohen, Tyrrell, & Smith, 1993). In view of such findings, higher levels of stress should be taken seriously (Hales, 2021).

The Hazards of Hassles

There must be more to stress than major life changes. Isn't there a link between ongoing stresses and health? In addition to having a direct impact, major life events spawn countless daily frustrations and irritations (Henderson, Roberto, & Kamo, 2010). Also, many of us face ongoing stresses at work or at home that do not involve major life changes (Pett & Johnson, 2005). Such minor but frequent stresses are called **hassles (microstressors)**. Some common hassles faced by college students include too many things to do, not enough money for housing, feeling discriminated against, people making gender jokes, communication problems with friends, driving to school, people making fun of their religion, fear of losing valuables, work schedule, getting into shape, and parents' expectations (Pett & Johnson, 2005).

In a year-long study, 100 men and women recorded the hassles they endured. Participants also reported on their physical and mental health. Frequent and severe hassles turned out to be better predictors of day-to-day health than major life events. However, major life events did predict changes in health one or two years after the events took place. It appears that daily hassles are closely linked to immediate health and psychological well-being (Crowther et al., 2001). Major life changes have more of a long-term impact and exacerbate the effects of daily hassles (Woods, Racine, & Klump, 2010).

Acculturative Stress: Stranger in a Strange Land

One way to guarantee that you will experience a large number of life changes and hassles is to live in a foreign culture. Around the world, an increasing number of emigrants and refugees must adapt to dramatic changes in language, dress, values, and social customs. For many, the result is a period of culture shock or **acculturative stress**—stress caused by adapting to a foreign culture. Typical reactions to acculturative stress are anxiety, hostility, depression, alienation, physical illness, or identity confusion (Castañeda et al., 2015). For many young immigrants, acculturative stress is a major source of mental health problems (Claudat, White, & Warren, 2016; Sirin et al., 2013).

The severity of acculturative stress is related in part to how a person adapts to a new culture. Here are four main patterns (Fox, Thayer, & Wadhwa, 2017; Sam & Berry, 2010):

The Washington Post/Getty Images

One of the best antidotes for acculturative stress is a society that tolerates or even celebrates ethnic diversity. While some people find it hard to accept new immigrants, the fact is, nearly everyone's family tree includes people who, like this Syrian family, had the courage to become strangers in a strange land.

Integration: Maintain your old cultural identity but participate in the new culture.

Separation: Maintain your old cultural identity and avoid contact with the new culture.

Assimilation: Adopt the new culture as your own and have contact with its members.

Marginalization: Reject your old culture, but suffer rejection by members of the new culture.

To illustrate each pattern, let's consider a family that has immigrated to the United States from the imaginary country of Heinleinia:

> The father favors integration. He is learning English and wants to get involved in American life. At the same time, he is a leader in the Heinleinian-American community and spends much of his leisure time with other Heinleinian Americans. His level of acculturative stress is low.
>
> The mother speaks only the Heinleinian language and interacts only with other Heinleinian Americans. She remains almost completely separate from American society. Her stress level is high.
>
> The teenage daughter is annoyed by hearing Heinleinian spoken at home, by her mother's serving only Heinleinian food, and by having to spend her leisure time with her extended Heinleinian family. She would prefer to speak English and to be with her American friends. Her desire to assimilate creates moderate stress.

Hassle (microstressor) Any distressing, day-to-day annoyance.

Acculturative stress Stress caused by the many changes and adaptations required when a person moves to a foreign culture.

The son doesn't particularly value his Heinleinian heritage, yet his schoolmates reject him because he speaks with a Heinleinian accent. He feels trapped between two cultures. His position is marginal, and his stress level is high.

To summarize, those who feel marginalized tend to be highly stressed; those who seek to remain separate also are highly stressed; those who pursue integration into their new culture are minimally stressed; and those who assimilate are moderately stressed. As you can see, integration and assimilation are the best options. However, a big benefit of assimilating is that people who embrace their new culture experience fewer social difficulties. For many, this justifies the stress of adopting new customs and cultural values (Gurung, 2014; Sam & Berry, 2010).

Frustration

Frustration is a negative emotional state that occurs when people are prevented from reaching desired goals. If your goal of finding a parking space is blocked by another car, you may be frustrated and experience stress.

Obstacles of many kinds cause frustration. A useful distinction can be made between external and personal sources of frustration. *External frustration* is based on conditions outside a person that impede progress toward a goal. The following are external frustrations: getting stuck with a flat tire, having a marriage proposal rejected, finding the cupboard bare when you go to get your poor dog a bone, and being chased out of the house by your starving dog. In other words, external frustrations are based on *delays*, *failure*, *rejection*, *loss*, and other direct blocking of motivated behavior.

Notice that external obstacles can be either *social* (slow drivers, tall people in theaters, people who cut in line) or *nonsocial* (stuck doors, a dead battery, rain on the day of the baseball game). If you ask your friends what has frustrated them recently, most will probably mention someone's behavior ("My sister wore one of my dresses when I wanted to wear it," "My supervisor is unfair," or "My history teacher grades too hard"). As social animals, we humans are highly sensitive to social sources of frustration (Taylor, 2012). That's probably why unfair treatment associated with racial or ethnic prejudice is a major source of frustration and stress in the lives of many African Americans and other minority group members (Brondolo et al., 2011; Gurung, 2014).

Frustration usually increases as the *strength*, *urgency*, or *importance* of a blocked motive increases. An escape artist submerged in a tank of water and bound with 200 pounds of chain would become *quite* frustrated if a trick lock jammed. Remember, too, that motivation becomes stronger as we near a goal. As a result, frustration is more intense when a person runs into an obstacle when very close to a goal. If you've ever missed an A grade by five points, you were probably very frustrated. If you've missed an A by one point—well, frustration builds character, right?

A final factor affecting frustration is summarized by the old phrase "the straw that broke the camel's back." The effects of *repeated* frustrations can accumulate until a small irritation sets off an unexpectedly violent response. A case in point is the fact that people with long daily commutes are more likely to display "road rage" (angry, aggressive driving) (Sansone & Sansone, 2010).

Personal frustrations are based on personal characteristics. If you are 4 feet tall and aspire to be a professional basketball player, you very likely will be frustrated. If you want to go to medical school but can earn only D grades, you likewise will be frustrated. In both examples, frustration is based on personal limitations (yet failure may be *perceived* as externally caused).

Does frustration always cause aggression? Aren't there other reactions? Although the connection is strong, frustration does not always incite aggression. More often, frustration is met first with *persistence*, often in the form of more vigorous efforts and varied responses (➤ **Figure 56.2**). For

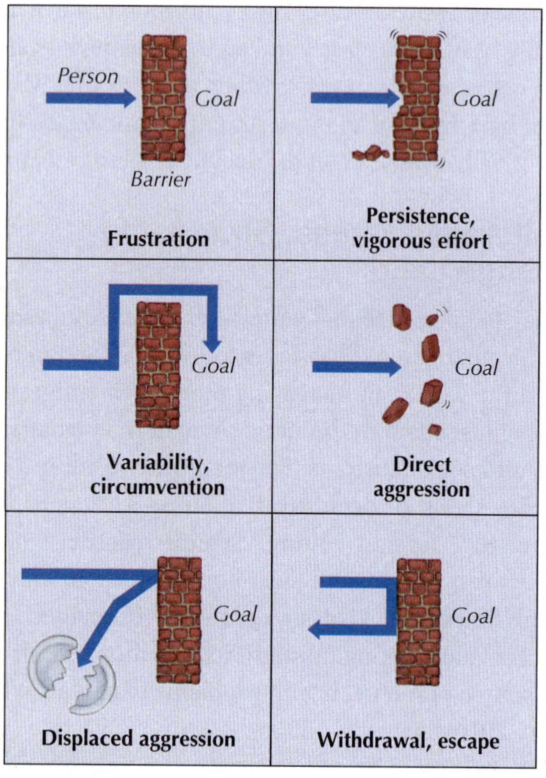

➤ **Figure 56.2**
Common reactions to frustration.

example, if you put your last dollar in a vending machine and pressing the button has no effect, you probably will press harder and faster (vigorous effort). Then, you will press all the other buttons (varied response). Persistence may help you reach your goal by getting *around* a barrier. However, if the machine *still* refuses to deliver or return your dollar, you may become aggressive and kick the machine (or at least tell it what you think of it).

Persistence can be very adaptive. Overcoming a barrier ends the frustration and allows the need or motive to be satisfied. The same is true of aggression that removes or destroys a barrier. Picture a small band of nomadic humans, parched by thirst but separated from a water hole by a menacing animal. It is easy to see that attacking the animal may ensure their survival. In modern society, such direct aggression is seldom acceptable. If you find a long line at the drinking fountain, aggression is hardly appropriate. Because direct aggression is discouraged, it is frequently *displaced* (Reijntjes et al., 2013b).

How is aggression displaced? Directing aggression toward a source of frustration may be impossible, or it may be too dangerous. If you are frustrated by your boss at work or by a teacher at school, the cost of direct aggression may be too high (losing your job or failing a class). Instead, the aggression may be displaced, or redirected, toward whomever or whatever is available. Targets of **displaced aggression** tend to be safer, or less likely to retaliate, than the original source of frustration. At one time or another, you have probably lashed out at a friend or relative who was not the real cause of your annoyance. As this suggests, excessive anger over a minor irritation is a common form of displaced aggression (Miller et al., 2003).

Psychologists attribute much hostility to displaced aggression. A disturbing example is the finding that unemployment and divorce are associated with increased child abuse (Weissman, Jogerst, & Dawson, 2003). In a pattern known as **scapegoating**, a person or a group is blamed for conditions not of their making. A *scapegoat* is a person who has become a habitual target of displaced aggression. Despite recent progress, many minority groups continue to face hostility based on scapegoating (Vasquez, Lickel, & Hennigan, 2010). Think, for example, about the hostility expressed toward illegal immigrants during times of economic hardship. In many communities, layoffs and job losses are closely linked to increased violence (Glick, 2008). Or, think about the hostility expressed toward anyone who looks even vaguely "foreign" right after a terrorist attack in the United States and Europe.

Iakov Filimonov/Shutterstock.com

Paintball seems to bring out aggressive impulses in many players. Wild shootouts are part of the fun, but are some players displacing aggressive urges related to frustration in other areas of their lives?

I have a friend who dropped out of school to hitchhike around the country. He seemed very frustrated before he quit. What type of response to frustration is that? Another major reaction to frustration is escape, or withdrawal. It is stressful and unpleasant to be frustrated. If other reactions do not reduce frustration, a person may try to escape. **Escape** may mean actually leaving a source of frustration (dropping out of school, quitting a job, leaving an unhappy marriage), or it may mean getting away psychologically. Two common forms of psychological escape are feigned apathy (pretending not to care) and the use of drugs such as cocaine, alcohol, cannabis, or opioids. Notice that these are examples of ineffective *emotion-focused coping* (see Module 57).

Coping with Frustration In a classic experiment, a psychologist studying frustration placed rats on a small platform at the top of a tall pole. Then, he forced them to jump off the platform toward two elevated doors, one locked and the other unlocked. If the rat chose the correct door, it swung open and the rat landed safely on another platform. Rats that chose the locked door bounced off it and fell into a net far below them.

The problem of choosing the open door was made unsolvable and very frustrating by randomly alternating which door was locked. After a time, most rats adopted a

Frustration A negative emotional state that occurs when one is prevented from reaching a goal.

Displaced aggression Redirecting aggression to a target other than the actual source of one's frustration.

Scapegoating Blaming a person or a group of people for conditions not of their making.

Escape Reducing discomfort by leaving frustrating situations or by psychologically withdrawing from them.

stereotyped response—that is, they chose the same door every time. This door was then permanently locked. All the rats had to do was jump to the other door to avoid a fall, but time after time, they bounced off the locked door (Maier, 1949).

Isn't that an example of persistence? No. Persistence that is *inflexible* can turn into "stupid," stereotyped behavior like that of a rat on a jumping platform. When dealing with frustration, you must know when to quit and establish a new direction. Here are some suggestions to help you avoid needless frustration:

1. Try to identify the source of your frustration. Is it external or personal?
2. Is the source of frustration something that can be changed? How hard would you have to work to change it? Is it under your control at all?
3. If the source of your frustration can be changed or removed, are the necessary efforts worth it?

The answers to these questions help determine whether persistence will be futile. There is value in learning to accept gracefully those things that cannot be changed.

Conflict

Conflict occurs whenever a person must choose between contradictory needs, desires, motives, or demands. Choosing between college and work, marriage and single life, or study and failure are common conflicts. There are three basic forms of conflict. As we will see, each has its own properties (➤ **Figure 56.3**).

➤ **Figure 56.3**

Three basic forms of conflict. For this woman, choosing between pie and ice cream is a minor approach–approach conflict; choosing between paying higher rent and moving is an avoidance–avoidance conflict; and deciding whether to take a job that will require weekend work is an approach–avoidance conflict.

Approach–Approach Conflicts Having to choose between two positive, or desirable, alternatives poses an **approach–approach conflict**. Choosing between tutti-frutti-coconut-mocha-champagne ice and orange-marmalade-peanut-butter-coffee swirl at the ice cream parlor may throw you into a temporary conflict. However, if you really like both choices, your decision will be quick. Even when more important decisions are at stake, approach–approach conflicts tend to be the easiest to resolve. The old fable about the mule that died of thirst and starvation while standing between a bucket of water and a bucket of oats is obviously unrealistic. When both options are positive, the scales of decision are easily tipped in one direction or the other.

Avoidance–Avoidance Conflicts Being forced to choose between two negative, or undesirable, alternatives creates an **avoidance–avoidance conflict**. A person in an avoidance conflict is caught between "the devil and the deep blue sea," "the frying pan and the fire," or "a rock and a hard place." In real life, avoidance–avoidance conflicts involve dilemmas such as choosing between unwanted pregnancy and abortion, the dentist and tooth decay, a monotonous job and poverty, or dorm food and starvation.

Suppose that I consider any pregnancy sacred and not to be tampered with. Or, suppose that I don't object to abortion. Like many other stressful situations, these examples can be defined as conflicts only on the basis of personal needs and values. If a woman would not consider abortion under any circumstances, she experiences no conflict. If she wants to end a pregnancy and does not object to abortion, she also experiences no conflict.

Avoidance conflicts often have a "damned if you do, damned if you don't" quality. In other words, both choices are negative, but *not choosing* may be impossible or equally undesirable. To illustrate, imagine the plight of a person trapped in a hotel fire 20 stories from the ground. Should she jump from the window and almost surely die on the pavement? Or, should she try to dash through the flames and almost surely die of smoke inhalation and burns? When faced with a choice such as this, it is easy to see why people often *freeze*, finding it impossible to decide or take action. In actual disasters of this sort, people are often found dead in their rooms, victims of an inability to take action.

Indecision, inaction, and freezing are not the only reactions to avoidance–avoidance conflicts. Because avoidance conflicts are stressful and difficult to solve, people sometimes pull out of them entirely. This reaction, called *leaving the field*, is another form of escape. It may explain the behavior of a student who could not attend school unless he worked. However, if he worked, he could not earn passing grades. His solution after much conflict and indecision? He joined the navy.

Approach–Avoidance Conflicts Approach–avoidance conflicts also are difficult to resolve. In some ways, they are more troublesome than avoidance conflicts because people seldom escape them. A person in an **approach–avoidance conflict** is "caught" by being attracted to, and repelled by, the same goal or activity. Attraction keeps the person in the situation, but its negative aspects cause turmoil and distress. For example, a high school student arrives to pick up his date for the first time. He is met at the door by her father, who is a professional wrestler—7 feet tall, 300 pounds, and entirely covered with hair. The father gives the boy a crushing handshake and growls that he will break him in half if the girl is not home on time. The student considers the girl attractive and has a good time. But does he ask her out again? It depends on the relative strength of his attraction and his fear. Almost certainly he will feel ambivalent about asking her out again, knowing that another encounter with her father awaits him.

Ambivalence (mixed positive and negative feelings) is a central characteristic of approach–avoidance conflicts. **Ambivalence** is usually translated into *partial approach* (Miller, 1944). Because the student in our example is still attracted to the girl, he may spend time with her at school and elsewhere. But he may not actually date her again. Some more realistic examples of approach–avoidance conflicts are planning to marry someone your parents strongly disapprove of, wanting to be in a play but suffering stage fright, wanting to buy a car but not wanting to make monthly payments, and wanting to eat when you're already overweight. Many of life's important decisions have approach–avoidance dimensions.

Multiple Conflicts *Aren't real-life conflicts more complex than the ones described here?* Yes. Conflicts are rarely as clear-cut as those described. People in conflict are usually faced with several dilemmas at once, so several types of conflict may be intermingled. In real life, it is common to face **multiple approach–avoidance conflicts**, in which you are simultaneously attracted to and repelled by each of several alternatives. For example, you are offered two jobs: One is in a good city and pays well but offers poor hours and dull work; the other is in a city you don't like so much and pays poorly but offers interesting work and excellent hours. Which do you select? Situations like these are more typical of the choices that we must usually make. The options are neither completely positive nor completely negative.

As with single approach–avoidance conflicts, people faced with multiple approach–avoidance conflicts tend to feel ambivalent about each choice. This causes them to *vacillate,* or waver, between the alternatives. Just as you are about to choose one such alternative, its undesirable aspects tend to loom large. What do you do? You swing back toward the other choice. If you have ever been romantically attracted to two people at once—each having qualities you like and dislike—then you have probably experienced vacillation. Another example that may be familiar is trying to decide between two college majors, each with advantages and disadvantages.

When multiple approach–avoidance conflicts involve major life decisions, such as choosing a career, a school, a mate, or a job, they can add greatly to the amount of stress we experience.

Managing Conflicts

How can I handle conflicts more effectively? Most of the suggestions made earlier concerning frustration also apply to conflicts. However, here are some additional things to remember when you are in conflict or must make a difficult decision:

1. Don't be hasty when making important decisions. Hasty decisions are often regretted. Even if you do make a faulty decision, it will trouble you less if you know that you did everything possible to avoid a mistake.
2. Try out important decisions *partially* when possible. If you are thinking about moving to a new town, try to spend a few days there first. If you are choosing between colleges, do the same. If classes are in progress, sit in on some. If you want to learn to scuba dive, rent equipment for a reasonable length of time before buying.
3. Look for workable compromises. Again, it is important to get all the available information. If you think that you have only one or two alternatives and they are undesirable or

Conflict A stressful condition that occurs when a person must choose between incompatible or contradictory alternatives.

Approach-approach conflict Choosing between two positive, desirable, alternatives.

Avoidance-avoidance conflict Choosing between two negative, undesirable alternatives.

Approach–avoidance conflict Being attracted to and repelled by the same goal or activity.

Ambivalence Mixed positive and negative feelings or simultaneous attraction and repulsion.

Multiple approach–avoidance conflict Being simultaneously attracted to and repelled by each of several alternatives.

unbearable, seek the aid of a teacher, counselor, minister, or social service agency. You may be overlooking possible alternatives that these people will know about.

4. When all else fails, make a decision and live with it. Indecision and conflict exact a high cost. Sometimes it is best to select a course of action and stick with it, unless it is obviously wrong after you have started it.

Conflicts are a normal part of life. With practice, you can learn to manage many of the conflicts that you will face.

MODULE 56 Stressors—Learning Outcomes Revisited

56.1 Explain the concept of a stressor, and outline factors that determine its severity

A stressor is a condition or event that challenges or threatens a person. Making a primary appraisal greatly affects our emotional responses to a situation. Stress is intensified when a situation is appraised as a threat. During a secondary appraisal, we select a way to manage stress. Stress also is intensified when a person does not feel competent to cope with it. Stress is more damaging in situations involving a lack of control, unpredictability of the stressor, and pressure. In work settings, prolonged stress can lead to burnout.

56.2 Distinguish among different types of stressors

Stress scales like the *Social Readjustment Rating Scale (SRRS)* indicate that multiple life changes tend to increase long-range susceptibility to accident or illness. Immediate physical and psychological health is more closely related to the intensity and severity of daily hassles (microstressors). Acculturative stress arises during adaptation to a foreign culture. Four acculturative patterns are integration, separation, assimilation, and marginalization. Frustration is the negative emotional state that occurs when progress toward a goal is blocked. External frustrations are based on delay, failure, rejection, loss, and other direct blocking of motives. Personal frustration is related to personal characteristics over which one has little control. Major behavioral reactions to frustration include persistence, more vigorous responding, circumvention, direct aggression, displaced aggression (including scapegoating), and escape or withdrawal. Three basic types of conflict are approach–approach, avoidance–avoidance, and approach–avoidance. Approach–approach conflicts are usually the easiest to resolve. Avoidance–avoidance conflicts are difficult to resolve and are characterized by inaction, indecision, freezing, and a desire to escape (called *leaving the field*). People usually remain in approach–avoidance conflicts but fail to fully resolve them. Approach–avoidance conflicts are associated with ambivalence and partial approach. Vacillation is a common reaction to multiple approach–avoidance conflicts.

Reflective Practice

Content Check

1. According to Richard Lazarus, choosing a way to meet a threat or challenge takes place during the ____________ ____________.
   a. primary stress reaction
   b. secondary stress reaction
   c. primary appraisal
   d. secondary appraisal
2. Stress tends to be greatest when a situation is appraised as a(n) ____________ and a person does not feel ____________ to cope with the situation.
3. Emotional exhaustion, cynicism, and reduced accomplishment are characteristics of job ____________.
4. The SRRS appears to predict long-range changes in health, whereas the frequency and severity of daily microstressors are closely related to immediate ratings of health. T or F?
5. Which of the following is *not* a common reaction to frustration?
   a. ambivalence
   b. aggression
   c. displaced aggression
   d. persistence
6. Displaced aggression is closely related to the pattern of behavior known as
   a. scapegoating
   b. leaving the field
   c. stereotyped responding
   d. burnout

7. You would be most likely to experience vacillation if you found yourself in
   a. an approach–approach conflict
   b. an avoidance–avoidance conflict
   c. a multiple approach–avoidance conflict
   d. an escape situation

Skill Check

Think Critically

8. Being frustrated is unpleasant. If some action, including aggression, ends frustration, why might we expect the action to be repeated on other occasions?

Self-Reflect

Do you think there is more of a connection between major life events and your health? Or have you observed more of a connection between microstressors and your health? Suppose that you moved to a foreign country. How much acculturative stress do you think you would face? Which pattern of adaptation do you think you would adopt? Think of a time when you were frustrated. What was your goal? What prevented you from reaching it? Was your frustration external or personal? Have you ever displaced aggression? Why did you choose another target for your hostility? Review the major types of conflict and think of a conflict you have faced that illustrates each type.

ANSWERS

1. d 2. threat, competent 3. burnout 4. T 5. a 6. a 7. c 8. If a response ends discomfort, the response has been negatively reinforced. This makes it more likely to occur in the future (see Module 28).

MODULE 57

Health Psychology
Coping with Stress

Malala's Triumph

There can be no doubt that Malala Yousafzai experienced a trauma. In 2012, while a 15-year-old student in northwest Pakistan, she was shot in the head by a religious extremist who believed that girls should not be educated. Not only did she survive, she has thrived as a global symbol of the power of education. Less than a year later, addressing the United Nations, she asserted, "They thought that the bullets would silence us, but they failed. The terrorists thought they would change my aims and stop my ambitions. But nothing changed in my life except this: Weakness, fear, and hopelessness died. Strength, power, and courage was born" (Schifrin, 2013).

Xinhua/Alamy Stock Photo

Stressful and threatening experiences often produce anxiety. Let's examine how we cope with this unpleasant state, including an examination of various defense mechanisms that shield us from anxiety. You'll also find an interesting perspective on helplessness and depression in this module, with a special section on the "college blues."

~LEARNING OUTCOMES~

After reading this module you should be able to:

57.1 Differentiate between problem-focused and emotion-focused coping

57.2 Define defense mechanisms and give several examples

57.3 Explain how to cope with feelings of helplessness and depression

Coping Styles—Making the Best of It

Learning Outcome 57.1 Differentiate between problem-focused and emotion-focused coping

You have appraised a situation as stressful. What will you do next? You have two major choices. Both involve thinking and acting in ways that help us handle stress (Gardner et al., 2017; Smith & Kirby, 2011). **Problem-focused coping** aims at managing or correcting the distressing situation. Some examples are making a plan of action or concentrating on your next step. In contrast, in **emotion-focused coping**, we try to control our emotional reactions to the situation. For example, a distressed person may calm or distract herself by listening to music, taking a walk to relax, or seeking emotional support from others.

In general, problem-focused coping tends to be especially useful when you are facing a controllable stressor—that is, a situation you can actually do something about. Emotion-focused efforts are best suited to managing your reaction to stressors you cannot control (Folkman & Moskowitz, 2004; Smith & Kirby, 2011).

Couldn't both types of coping occur together? Yes. Sometimes the two types of coping aid one another. For instance, quieting your emotions may make it easier for you to find a way to solve a problem. Say, for example, that you feel anxious as you step in front of your class to give a presentation. If you take a few deep breaths to reduce your anxiety (emotion-focused coping), you will be better able to glance over your notes to improve your delivery (problem-focused coping).

It is also possible for coping efforts to clash. For instance, if you have to make a difficult decision, you may suffer intense emotional distress. In such circumstances, it is tempting to make a quick, unreflective choice, just to end the suffering (Arnsten, Mazure, & Sinha, 2012). Doing so may allow you to cope with your emotions, but it short-changes problem-focused coping.

So far, our discussion has focused on everyday stresses. How do people react to the extreme stresses imposed by war, violence, or disaster? Read on. . . .

Coping with Traumatic Stress

Traumatic experiences produce psychological injury or intense emotional pain. Victims of **traumatic stresses**, such as war, torture, rape, assassination, plane crashes, natural disasters, and street violence, may suffer from nightmares, flashbacks, insomnia, irritability, nervousness, grief, emotional numbing, and depression (Durand & Barlow, 2019; Sue et al., 2017). For example, the annual parade of tornadoes and hurricanes, along with the resulting chaos, are undoubtedly traumatically stressful events.

People who personally witness or survive a disaster are most affected by traumatic stress. For instance, 20 percent of the people who lived close to the World Trade Center in New York City suffered serious stress disorders after the 9/11 terrorist attack (Galea et al., 2002). Yet even those who experience horror at a distance may be traumatized (Galea & Resnick, 2005). In fact, 44 percent of US adults who only saw the 9/11 attacks on television had at least some stress symptoms (Schuster et al., 2001). For example, Americans faced elevated risks of hypertension and heart problems for three years after 9/11 (Holman et al., 2008). Indirect exposure to such terrorist attacks, coupled with the ongoing risk of more attacks, has ensured that many people will suffer ongoing stress into the foreseeable future (Marshall et al., 2007).

Traumatic stress produces feelings of helplessness and vulnerability. Victims realize that disaster could strike again without warning. In addition to feeling threatened, many victims sense that they are losing control of their lives (Fields & Margolin, 2001; Ford, 2012; Kearney & Trull, 2018).

What can people do about such reactions? Psychologists recommend the following:

- Identify what you are feeling and talk to others about your fears and concerns.
- Think about the skills that have helped you overcome adversity in the past and apply them to the present situation.
- Continue to do the things that you enjoy and that make life meaningful.
- Get support from others. This is a major element in recovery from all traumatic events.
- Give yourself time to heal. Fortunately, most people are more resilient than they think.

When traumatic stresses are severe or repeated, some people have even more serious symptoms (Durand & Barlow, 2019). They suffer from crippling anxiety or become emotionally numb. Typically, they can't stop thinking about the disturbing event, they anxiously avoid anything associated with the event, and they are constantly fearful or nervous. Such reactions can leave victims emotionally handicapped for months or years after a disaster. The consequences can last a lifetime for children who are the victims of trauma (Gillespie & Nemeroff, 2007; Salloum & Overstreet, 2012). (These are also the symptoms of *stress disorders*, which are discussed in Module 63.) If you feel that you are having trouble coping with a severe emotional shock, consider seeking help from a psychologist or other professional (American Psychological Association, 2020; Bisson et al., 2007).

Problem-focused coping Directly managing or remedying a stressful or threatening situation.

Emotion-focused coping Managing or controlling one's emotional reaction to a stressful or threatening situation.

Traumatic stresses Extreme events that cause psychological injury or intense emotional pain.

Psychological Defense—Mental Gymnastics?

Learning Outcome 57.2 Define defense mechanisms and give several examples

Threatening situations tend to produce **anxiety**. When you are anxious, you feel tense, uneasy, apprehensive, worried, and vulnerable. This unpleasant state can lead to emotion-focused coping that is defensive in nature (Kramer et al., 2010). Psychodynamic psychologists have identified various defense mechanisms that allow us to reduce anxiety caused by stressful situations or our own shortcomings (Sue et al., 2017). You might not always be aware of it, but you have probably used several of the defenses described here. (Severe anxiety can be extremely disruptive. It is the basis for some of the most common psychological disorders. See Module 63.)

What are psychological defense mechanisms, and how do they reduce anxiety? A **defense mechanism** is a protective behavior that reduces anxiety. Many of the defenses were first identified by Sigmund Freud, who assumed they operate *unconsciously*. Often, defense mechanisms create large blind spots in awareness. For instance, you might know an extremely stingy person who is completely unaware that he is a tightwad.

Everyone has at one time or another used defense mechanisms. Let's consider some of the most common; a more complete listing is given in ■ **Table 57.1** (Sue et al., 2017).

Denial

One of the most basic defenses is **denial**—protecting oneself from an unpleasant reality by refusing to accept it or believe it. We are prone to deny death, illness, and similar painful and threatening events. For instance, if you were told that you had only three months to live, how would you react? Your first thoughts might be, "Aw, come on, someone must have mixed up the X-rays," or, "The doctor must be mistaken," or simply, "It can't be true!" Similar denial and disbelief are common reactions to the unexpected death of a friend or relative: "It's just not real. I don't believe it!"

Repression

Freud noticed that his patients had tremendous difficulty recalling shocking or traumatic events from childhood. It seemed that powerful forces were holding these painful memories from awareness. Freud called this **repression**, and said that we use it to protect ourselves by blocking out threatening thoughts and impulses. Feelings of hostility toward a family member, the names of people we dislike, and past failures are common targets of repression. Research

TABLE 57.1 | Psychological Defense Mechanisms

Compensation	Counteracting a real or imagined weakness by emphasizing desirable traits or seeking to excel in the area of weakness or in other areas
Denial	Protecting oneself from an unpleasant reality by refusing to acknowledge or perceive it
Displacement (sublimation)	Diverting a thought or behavior from its natural target toward a less threatening one
Fantasy	Fulfilling unmet desires in imagined achievements or activities
Identification	Taking on some of the characteristics of an admired person, usually as a way to compensate for perceived personal weaknesses or faults
Intellectualization	Separating emotion from a threatening or anxiety-provoking situation by talking or thinking about it in impersonal "intellectual" terms
Isolation	Separating contradictory thoughts or feelings into "logic-tight" mental compartments so that they do not come into conflict
Projection	Attributing one's own feelings, shortcomings, or unacceptable impulses to others
Rationalization	Creating false but plausible excuses to justify unacceptable behavior
Reaction formation	Preventing dangerous impulses from being expressed in behavior by exaggerating opposite behavior
Regression	Retreating to an earlier level of development or to earlier, less demanding habits or situations
Repression	Keeping distressing thoughts and feelings buried in the unconscious

suggests that you are most likely to repress information that threatens your self-image (Axmacher et al., 2010).

Reaction Formation

In a **reaction formation**, impulses are not just repressed; they also are held in check by exaggerating opposite behavior. For example, a mother who unconsciously resents her children may, through reaction formation, become absurdly overprotective and overindulgent. Her real thoughts of "I hate them" and "I wish they were gone" are replaced by "I love them" and "I don't know what I would do without them." The mother's hostile impulses are traded for "smother" love so that she won't have to admit that she really hates her children. Thus, the basic idea in a reaction formation is that the individual acts out an opposite behavior to block threatening impulses or feelings.

Regression

In its broadest meaning, **regression** refers to any return to earlier, less demanding situations or habits. Most parents who have a second child have to put up with at least some regression by the older child. Threatened by a new rival for affection, an older child may regress to childish speech, bed-wetting, or infantile play after the new baby arrives. If you've ever seen a child get homesick at summer camp or on a vacation, you've observed regression. The child wants to go home, where it's "safe." An adult who throws a temper tantrum or a married adult who "goes home to mother" also is regressing.

Projection

Projection is an unconscious process that protects us from the anxiety that we would feel if we were to discern our faults. A person who is projecting tends to see his or her own feelings, shortcomings, or unacceptable impulses in others. **Projection** lowers anxiety by exaggerating negative traits in others. This justifies one's own actions and directs attention away from personal failings.

One of your authors once worked for a greedy shop owner who cheated many of his customers. This same man considered himself a pillar of the community and very moral and religious. How did he justify to himself his greed and dishonesty? He believed that everyone who entered his store was bent on cheating *him* any way they could. In reality, few, if any, of his customers shared his motives, but he projected his own greed and dishonesty onto them.

Rationalization

Every teacher is familiar with this strange phenomenon: On the day of an exam, an incredible wave of disasters sweeps through the city. Mothers, fathers, sisters, brothers, aunts, uncles, grandparents, friends, relatives, and pets of students become ill or die. Motors suddenly fall out of cars. Books are lost or stolen. Alarm clocks go belly-up and ring no more. All manner of computer equipment malfunctions.

The making of excuses comes from a natural tendency to explain our behavior. **Rationalization** refers to justifying personal actions by giving plausible "rational" but false reasons for them. When the explanation you give for your behavior is reasonable and plausible—but not the real reason—you are *rationalizing.*

All the defense mechanisms described seem pretty undesirable. Do they have a positive side? People who overuse defense mechanisms become less adaptable because they consume great amounts of emotional energy to control anxiety and maintain an unrealistic self-image. Defense mechanisms do have value, though. Often, they help keep us from being overwhelmed by immediate threats. This can provide time for a person to learn to cope in a more effective, problem-focused manner. If you recognize some of your own behavior in the descriptions here, it is hardly a sign that you are hopelessly defensive. As noted earlier, most people occasionally use defense mechanisms (Diehl et al., 2014).

Two defense mechanisms that have a decidedly more positive quality are compensation and displacement.

Compensation

Compensatory reactions are defenses against feelings of inferiority. **Compensation** occurs when a person with a defect or weakness (real or imagined) goes to unusual lengths to

Anxiety Apprehension, dread, or uneasiness similar to fear but based on an unclear threat.

Defense mechanism In Freud's personality theory, a protective behavior that reduces anxiety.

Denial Protecting oneself from an unpleasant reality by refusing to acknowledge or perceive it.

Repression Keeping distressing thoughts and feelings buried in the unconscious.

Reaction formation Preventing dangerous impulses from being expressed in behavior by exaggerating opposite behavior.

Regression Retreating to an earlier level of development or to earlier, less demanding habits or situations.

Projection Attributing one's own feelings, shortcomings, or unacceptable impulses to others.

Rationalization Creating false but plausible excuses to justify unacceptable behavior.

Compensation Counteracting a real or imagined weakness by emphasizing desirable traits or seeking to excel in the area of weakness or in other areas.

overcome the weakness or to excel in other areas. One of the pioneers of "pumping iron" was Jack LaLanne, who opened the first modern health club in America. LaLanne made a successful career out of bodybuilding in spite of the fact that he was thin and sickly as a young man. Perhaps it would be more accurate to say because he was thin and sickly. You can find dozens of examples of compensation at work. A childhood stutterer may excel in debate at college. As a child, Helen Keller was unable to see or hear, but she became an outstanding thinker and writer. Perhaps Ray Charles, Stevie Wonder, Andrea Bocelli, and other blind entertainers were drawn to music because of their disability.

Displacement

When we divert a thought or behavior from its natural target toward a less threatening one, we are engaged in **displacement**, which is also referred to as sublimation (sub-lih-MAY-shun). Freud believed that art, music, dance, poetry, scientific investigation, and other creative activities could serve to rechannel sexual energies into productive behavior. Freud also felt that almost any strong desire could be displaced. For example, a very aggressive person may find social acceptance as a professional soldier, boxer, or football player. Greed may be refined into a successful business career. Lying may be displaced into storytelling, creative writing, or politics.

A_Lesik/Shutterstock.com

For some competitors—and fans—mixed martial arts may well allow sublimation of aggressive urges. *Call of Duty*, *Overwatch*, and similar first-person shooter computer games may serve the same purpose.

Sexual motives appear to be the most easily and widely sublimated (Moran, F., 2010). Freud would have had a field day with such modern pastimes as surfing, motorcycle riding, automobile racing, and dancing to or playing rock music, to name but a few. People enjoy each of these activities for a multitude of reasons, but it is hard to overlook the rich sexual symbolism apparent in each.

Learned Helplessness and Depression—Is There Hope?

Learning Outcome 57.3 Explain how to cope with feelings of helplessness and depression

What would happen if a person's defenses failed or if the person appraised a threatening situation as hopeless? Martin Seligman studied the case of a young Marine who seemed to have adapted to the stresses of being held prisoner during the Vietnam War. The Marine's health was related to a promise made by his captors: If he cooperated, they said, he would be released on a certain date. As the date approached, his spirits soared. Then came a devastating blow. He had been deceived. His captors had no intention of ever releasing him. He immediately lapsed into a deep depression, refused to eat or drink, and died shortly thereafter.

That seems like an extreme example. Does anything similar occur outside concentration camps and wartime scenarios? Apparently so. For example, researchers in San Antonio, Texas, asked older people if they were hopeful about the future. Those who answered "No" died at elevated rates (Stern, Dhanda, & Hazuda, 2001).

Learned Helplessness

To explain such patterns, psychologists have focused on the concept of **learned helplessness**, a belief that one cannot control the outcome of events such as an inability to overcome obstacles and avoid aversive stimuli (Maier & Seligman, 2016; Seligman, 1989). To observe learned helplessness, let's see what happens when animals are tested in a shuttle box (➤ **Figure 57.1**). If placed in one side of a divided box, dogs quickly learn to leap to the other side to escape an electric shock. If they are given a warning before the shock occurs (for example, a light that dims), most dogs learn to avoid the shock by leaping the barrier before the shock arrives. This is true of most dogs, but not those who have learned to feel helpless (Overmier & LoLordo, 1998).

How is a dog made to feel helpless? Before being tested in the shuttle box, a dog can be placed in a harness (from which the dog cannot escape) and then given several painful shocks. The animal is helpless to prevent these shocks. When placed in the shuttle box, dogs prepared in this way

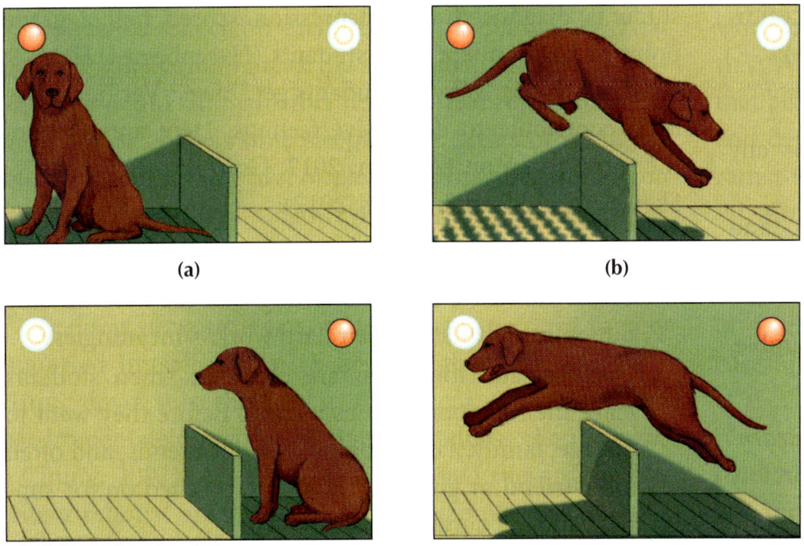

(a) (b) (c) (d)

Figure 57.1

Learned helplessness. In the normal course of escape and avoidance learning, a light dims shortly before the floor is electrified (*a*). Because the light does not yet have meaning for the dog, the dog receives a shock (noninjurious, by the way) and leaps the barrier (*b*). Dogs soon learn to watch for the dimming of the light (*c*) and to jump before receiving a shock (*d*). Dogs made to feel "helpless" rarely even learn to escape shock, much less to avoid it.

react to the first shock by crouching, howling, and whining. None of them try to escape. They helplessly resign themselves to their fate. After all, they have already learned that there is nothing they can do about getting shocked.

As the shuttle box experiments suggest, helplessness is a psychological state that occurs when events *do not appear to be controllable* (Maier & Seligman, 2016). Helplessness also afflicts humans (Domjan, 2015; Reivich et al., 2013). It is a common reaction to repeated failure and to unpredictable or unavoidable punishment. A prime example is college students who feel helpless about their schoolwork. Such students tend to procrastinate, give up easily, and drop out of school (Perry, 2003).

Where humans are concerned, attributions (discussed in Module 44) have a large effect on helplessness. Persons who are made to feel helpless in one situation are more likely to act helpless in other situations if they attribute their failure to *lasting, general* factors. An example would be concluding "I must be stupid" after doing poorly on a test in a biology class. In contrast, attributing a low score to specific factors in the situation ("I'm not too good at the type of test my biology professor uses" or "I'm not very interested in biology") tends to prevent learned helplessness from spreading (Peterson & Vaidya, 2001; Prochaska & Norcross, 2014).

Depression

Seligman and others have pointed out the similarities between learned helplessness and **depression**. Both are marked by feelings of despondency, powerlessness, and hopelessness. "Helpless" animals display decreased activity, lowered aggression, blunted appetite, and a loss of sex drive. Humans suffer from similar effects and also tend to see themselves as failing, even when they're not (Brown & Barlow, 2017; LoLordo, 2001).

Depression is one of the most widespread emotional problems. While it undoubtedly has many causes, learned helplessness seems to explain many cases. For example, Seligman (1972) describes the fate of Archie, a 15-year-old boy. For Archie, school is an unending series of shocks and failures. Other students treat him as if he's stupid; in class, he rarely answers questions because he doesn't know some of the words. He feels knocked down everywhere he turns. These may not be electric shocks, but they are certainly emotional "shocks," and Archie has learned to feel helpless to prevent them. When he leaves school, his chances of success are poor. He has learned to passively endure whatever shocks life has in store for him. Archie is not alone in this regard. Hopelessness is almost always a major element of depression (Durand & Barlow, 2019; Reivich et al., 2013).

Recognizing Depression Most people know, obviously enough, when they are "down." But depression is a complex problem that takes many forms and has many causes (see Module 62). You should assume that more than a minor

Displacement Diverting a thought or behavior from its natural target toward a less threatening one.

Learned helplessness Belief that one cannot control the outcome of events.

Depression A state of despondency marked by feelings of powerlessness and hopelessness.

6. Learned helplessness tends to occur when events appear to be
   a. frustrating
   b. in conflict
   c. uncontrollable
   d. problem focused
7. Frequent self-criticism and self-blame are a natural consequence of doing college work. T or F?

Skill Check

Think Critically

8. Learned helplessness is closely related to which of the factors that determine the severity of stress?

Self-Reflect

What type of coping do you tend to use when you face a stressor such as public speaking or taking an important exam? We tend to be blind to our own reliance on defense mechanisms. See if you can think of one example of each defense that you have observed yourself or someone else using. Have you ever felt helpless in a particular situation? What caused you to feel that way? Imagine that a friend of yours is suffering from the college blues. What advice would you give your friend?

ANSWERS

1. F 2. c 3. F 4. a, g 5. learned helplessness 6. c 7. F 8. Feelings of incompetence and lack of control.

MODULE 58

Health Psychology
Stress and Health

Type A

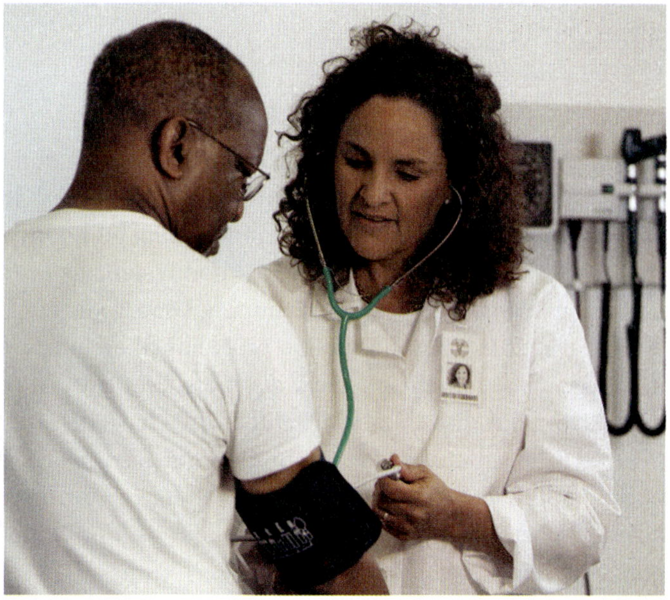
Ariel Skelley/Blend Images/SuperStock

Have you ever become ill after facing a stressful final exam period? Or gotten sick after experiencing one or more positive life events, like getting married? Was it a coincidence? Maybe you even got accused of faking it, of being a *hypochondriac*, or of having a *psychosomatic* problem and needing a psychiatrist. Antoine, a college wide receiver, got teased when his teammates found out he had chronic high blood pressure. They even nicknamed him "Type A."

What do all of these terms mean? Psychologists have now firmly established that stress affects our bodily health. Let's begin to see how this powerful mind–body connection is explained by the field of *psychoneuroimmunology*. (Try dropping that word into a conversation sometime if you want to see a stress reaction!)

We also explore some factors that limit the health risks we face. Because we live in a fast-paced and often stressful society, these are topics worth stressing.

~LEARNING OUTCOMES~

After reading this module you should be able to:

58.1 Explain the relationship between stress, health, and disease

Stress and Health—Unmasking a Hidden Killer

Learning Outcome 58.1 Explain the relationship between stress, health, and disease

How can stress result in a physical illness? An answer can be found in your body's immune system, which mobilizes defenses (such as white blood cells) against invading microbes and other disease agents. The immune system is regulated, in part, by the brain. Because of this link, stress and upsetting emotions can affect the immune system in ways that increase susceptibility to disease (Janusek, Cooper, & Mathews, 2012; Zachariae, 2009). By the way, the study of links among behavior, stress, disease, and the immune system is called **psychoneuroimmunology** (Clark & Fessler, 2014; Daruna, 2012).

Studies show that the immune system is weakened in students during major exam times, as you may already have unfortunately discovered. Immunity is also lowered by divorce, bereavement, a troubled marriage, job loss, poor sleep, depression, and similar stresses (Motivala & Irwin, 2007; Segerstrom & Miller, 2004). Lowered immunity explains why the "double whammy" of getting sick when you are trying to cope with prolonged or severe stress is so common (Pedersen, Bovbjerg, & Zachariae, 2011). Stress causes the body to release substances that increase inflammation. This is part of the body's self-protective response to threats, but it can prolong infections and delay healing (Kiecolt-Glaser, 2010).

Psychosomatic Disorders

Prolonged stress reactions are closely related to a large number of psychosomatic (SIKE-oh-so-MAT-ik) illnesses. In **psychosomatic disorders** (*psyche:* mind; *soma:* body), psychological factors contribute to actual bodily damage or to damaging changes in bodily functioning (Bourgeois et al., 2009; Fava, 2016). Psychosomatic problems, therefore, are not the same as *somatic symptom disorders*. People with somatic symptom disorders *imagine* that they have diseases. (The term *hypochondriac* refers to a person who mistakes normal bodily processes as illness; see Module 63 for more details.) There is nothing imaginary about asthma, a migraine headache, or high blood pressure.

The most common psychosomatic problems are gastrointestinal and respiratory (stomach pain and asthma, for example), but many others exist. Typical problems include eczema (skin rash), hives, migraine headaches, rheumatoid arthritis, hypertension (high blood pressure), colitis (ulceration of the colon), and heart disease. And these are only the major problems. Many lesser health complaints also are stress related. Typical examples include sore muscles, headaches, neckaches, backaches, indigestion, constipation, chronic diarrhea, fatigue, insomnia, premenstrual problems, and sexual dysfunctions (Taylor, 2021). Severe psychosomatic disorders can even be fatal. Thus, the person who says, "Oh, it's *just* psychosomatic" doesn't understand how serious stress-related diseases really are.

Could reducing stress help prevent illness? Exactly. Various psychological approaches, such as support groups, relaxation exercises, guided imagery, and stress-management training, can actually boost immune system functioning (Kottler & Chen, 2011). By doing so, they help promote and restore health. For example, stress management reduced the severity of cold and flu symptoms in a group of university students (Reid, Mackinnon, & Drummond, 2001).

There is even evidence that stress management can improve the chances of survival in people with life-threatening diseases, such as cancer, heart disease, and HIV/AIDS. With some successes to encourage them, psychologists are now searching for the best combination of treatments to help people resist disease (Phillips et al., 2012; Schneiderman et al., 2001). For more detail about how to manage your stress, see Module 59.

An interesting technique called *biofeedback* may also be helpful for some psychosomatic complaints. The next section explains how.

Biofeedback Psychologists have discovered that people can learn to control bodily activities once thought to be involuntary. This is done by applying informational feedback to bodily control, a process called **biofeedback**. If you were asked to raise the temperature of your right hand, you probably couldn't because you wouldn't know if you were succeeding. To make your task easier, a sensitive thermometer could be attached to your hand. The thermometer could be wired so that an increase in temperature would activate a signal light. Then, all you would have to do is try to keep the light on as much as possible. With practice and the help of biofeedback, you could learn to raise your hand temperature at will.

Biofeedback holds promise as a way to treat some psychosomatic problems. For instance, people have been trained to prevent migraine headaches with biofeedback. Sensors are taped to patients' hands and foreheads. Patients then learn to redirect blood flow away from the head to their extremities. Because migraine headaches involve excessive blood flow to the head, biofeedback helps patients reduce the frequency of their headaches (Larsson et al., 2005; Stokes & Lappin, 2010).

Biofeedback also can help relieve muscle-tension headaches and chronic pain (Sielski, Rief, & Glombiewski, 2017; Sousa et al., 2009). It shows promise for lowering blood pressure and controlling heart rhythms (Olsson et al., 2010; Peira, Fredrikson, & Pourtois, 2014). The technique has been used with some success to control epileptic seizures and hyperactivity in children (Demos, 2005). Insomnia also responds to biofeedback therapy (McLay & Spira, 2009).

How does biofeedback work? Some researchers believe that many of its benefits arise from *general relaxation*. Others stress that the method simply acts as a "mirror" to help a person perform tasks involving *self-regulation*. Just as a mirror does not comb your hair, and a bathroom scale does not reduce your body weight, biofeedback does not do anything by itself. It can, however, provide information needed for people to make desired changes in their behavior.

War Archive/Alamy Stock Photo

In biofeedback training, normally uncontrollable bodily processes are monitored and processed electronically. A signal is then routed back to the patient through headphones, signal lights, or other means. This man's brainwaves are being measured and visually displayed. He could use this visual feedback to control his brainwaves in order to relax.

Personality and Health

It would be a mistake to assume that stress is the sole cause of psychosomatic diseases. Genetic differences, organ weaknesses, and learned reactions to stress combine to do damage. Personality also enters the picture.

The Type A Personality

Aren't there Type A personalities who are at a higher risk of heart disease? There has certainly been a lot of publicity around the possible existence of a "cardiac personality"—a person at high risk for heart disease. In an early study of heart problems, two cardiologists, Meyer Friedman and Ray Rosenman, classified people as either a *Type A personality*, someone who runs a high risk for heart attack, or a *Type B personality*, someone who is unlikely to have a heart attack. In an eight-year follow-up, they found more than twice the rate of heart disease in Type As than in Type Bs (Friedman & Rosenman, 1983). Health researchers have also identified the *Type D* personality, someone who is worried, expresses many negative emotions, and is disease-prone (Meyer, 2014).

According to Friedman and Rosenman, Type A people are hard driving, ambitious, highly competitive, achievement oriented, and striving. Type A people believe that with enough effort they can overcome any obstacle, and they "push" themselves accordingly. Perhaps the most telltale signs of a Type A personality are time urgency and chronic anger or hostility. Type As hurry from one activity to another, racing the clock in self-imposed urgency. As they do, they feel a constant sense of frustration and anger.

At first, research appeared to support the idea of a "cardiac personality." Subsequent research has not. Some researchers have found that only feelings of anger and hostility are reliably related to an increased risk for heart attack (Brydon et al., 2010; Bunde & Suls, 2006). The most damaging pattern may occur in hostile persons who keep their anger "bottled up." Such people seethe with anger but don't express it outwardly. This increases their pulse rate and blood pressure and puts a tremendous strain on the heart (Bongard, al'Absi, & Lovallo, 1998; Lemogne et al., 2010; Smith & Traupman, 2011).

Most recently, other researchers have failed to find any relationship between the so-called Type A behavior pattern and coronary heart disease (Kastytis et al., 2015; Petticrew, Lee, & McKee, 2012). As a result, many psychologists are now skeptical of the distinction between Type A, Type B, and Type D personalities.

As we mentioned in Module 50, theories of personality types are often oversimplifications. If there is one bit of wisdom to take away from this discussion, it is that if you frequently feel angry and hostile toward others, consider this advice from Redford Williams (1989): Reducing hostility

Donald Reilly/The New Yorker Collection/Cartoon Bank

Psychoneuroimmunology Study of the links among behavior, stress, disease, and the immune system.

Psychosomatic disorders Illnesses in which psychological factors contribute to bodily damage or to damaging changes in bodily functioning.

Biofeedback Information given to a person about his or her ongoing bodily activities; aids voluntary regulation of bodily states.

involves three goals. First, you must stop mistrusting the motives of others. Second, you must find ways to reduce how often you feel anger, indignation, irritation, and rage. Third, you must learn to be kinder and more considerate. It is entirely possible to succeed in life without sacrificing your health or happiness in the process.

The Hardy Personality One more personality type bears mentioning. Psychologist Salvatore Maddi has studied people who have a **hardy personality**. Such people seem to be unusually resistant to stress (Maddi, 2013; Sandvik et al., 2013). The first study of hardiness began with two groups of managers at a large utility company. All the managers held high-stress positions. Yet, some tended to get sick after stressful events, whereas others were rarely ill.

How did the people who were thriving differ from their "stressed-out" colleagues? The main difference was that the hardy group seemed to hold a worldview that consisted of three traits (Maddi, 2013; Maddi et al., 2009):

1. They had a sense of personal *commitment* to self, work, family, and other stabilizing values.
2. They felt that they had *control* over their lives and their work.
3. They had a tendency to see life as a series of *challenges* rather than as a series of threats or problems.

How do such traits protect people from the effects of stress? Persons strong in terms of *commitment* find ways to turn whatever they are doing into something that seems interesting and important. They tend to get involved rather than feel alienated.

Persons strong in terms of *control* believe that more often than not, they can influence the course of events around them. This prevents them from passively seeing themselves as victims of circumstance.

Finally, people strong in terms of *challenge* find fulfillment in continual growth. They seek to learn from their experiences rather than accept easy comfort, security, and routine. Indeed, many "negative" experiences can enhance personal growth—if you have support from others and the skills needed to cope with challenge (Garrosa et al., 2008; Stix, 2011).

A Look Ahead The work that we have reviewed here has drawn new attention to the fact that each of us has a personal responsibility for maintaining and promoting health. In Module 59, we look at what you can do to better cope with stress and the health risks that it entails. But first, the following questions may help you earn a healthy grade on your next psychology test.

Hardy personality A personality style associated with superior stress resistance.

MODULE 58 Stress and Health—Learning Outcomes Revisited

58.1 Explain the relationship between stress, health, and disease

Studies of psychoneuroimmunology show that stress lowers the body's resistance to disease by weakening the immune system. Intense or prolonged stress may cause damage in the form of psychosomatic problems. During biofeedback training, bodily processes are monitored and converted to a signal that tells what the body is doing. Biofeedback allows people to alleviate some psychosomatic illnesses by altering bodily activities. People who are angry and hostile may be prone to having heart attacks. People who have the traits of a hardy personality seem to be unusually resistant to stress.

Reflective Practice

Content Check

1. Students taking stressful final exams are more susceptible to the cold virus, a pattern best explained by the concept of
   a. the disease-prone personality
   b. psychoneuroimmunology
   c. emotion-focused coping
   d. reaction formation
2. Ulcers, migraine headaches, and hypochondria frequently are all psychosomatic disorders. T or F?
3. Two major elements of biofeedback training appear to be relaxation and self-regulation. T or F?

4. Evidence suggests that the most important feature of the Type A personality is a sense of time urgency rather than feelings of anger and hostility. T or F?
5. A sense of commitment, challenge, and control characterizes the hardy personality. T or F?

Skill Check

Think Critically

6. People with a hardy personality type appear to be especially resistant to which of the problems discussed in Module 57?

Self-Reflect

Mindy complains about her health all the time, but she seems to be just fine. An acquaintance of Mindy's dismisses her problems by saying, "Oh, she's not really sick. It's just psychosomatic." What's wrong with this use of the term *psychosomatic*? Do you think you are basically a hostile? To what extent do you possess traits of the hardy personality?

ANSWERS

1. b 2. F 3. T 4. F 5. T 6. Learned helplessness

MODULE
59

A Psychologist's Skill Set
Stress Management

Send Silence Packing

Abandoned backpacks—1,100 of them—were scattered across the grass on campus, and college students who were passing stopped to look. They didn't need to ask where the owners were, though. The signs next to the bags told them everything they needed to know.

Send Silence Packing is a traveling art exhibition that has moved between more than 100 campuses in the United States during the past decade. Each of the backpacks represents a student who takes his or her life at an American college each year. Many of these students commit suicide because they are overwhelmed by the pressure that comes with the desire to succeed at school, to be liked by their peers, and to manage other responsibilities, including work. They may feel unable to cope with the stress they experience, but are often reluctant to speak up and seek help for fear of appearing weak. But the message that the backpacks provide is clear: Suffering in silence when you are feeling stressed and overwhelmed is not the answer. And while dealing with stress is not easy, there are things that you can do to make things more manageable. Let's take a closer look.

Richard Levine/Alamy Stock Photo

~LEARNING OUTCOMES~

After reading this module you should be able to:

59.1 Explain stress management and three approaches to stress management

De-Stress—Here's to Your Good Health!

Learning Outcome 59.1 Explain stress management and three approaches to stress management

Stress management is the use of cognitive and behavioral strategies to reduce stress and improve coping skills. We have seen in Modules 55–58 that working to minimize stress is helpful, given that psychologists have provided considerable evidence of its negative effects. These modules also outlined the extensive psychological literature concerning coping as a means of managing stress. Psychological research has gone much further in terms of promoting our understanding of stress, though. For example, psychologists have begun to document the unique effects of different kinds of stress, such as the acculturative stress demonstrated by new immigrants (Suh et al., 2016) and the post-traumatic stress experienced after events such as natural disasters, rape, terrorist attacks, and military deployment (Post et al., 2015). They have also examined how the effects of stressors change across the lifespan (Jamieson & Mendes, 2016) and as a function of our genes and physiology (Belsky et al., 2015). Finally, newer research has begun to examine whether stressful events can have positive consequences (e.g., post-traumatic growth; Tsai et al., 2015), as well as the effectiveness of alternative forms of treating stress-related responses, such as virtual reality, drugs that blunt the emotions associated with traumatic memories, and Internet-based therapy (Lane et al., 2015; Morina et al., 2015).

Stress, then, can have a number of negative consequences that are likely to affect your own life, as well as your relationships with others. In addition to doing physical damage to your body (e.g., increased risk of cardiovascular problems), stress can also be at the root of psychological issues such as anxiety and depression. But the effects of stress aren't restricted to your physical and psychological well-being. Stress can also prove damaging to your relationships, both at home and at work. People under stress can appear more unmotivated, defensive, short-tempered, or withdrawn than they would be otherwise. Such behaviors can create tension between people, resulting in strained relationships.

I can't help feeling stressed—I have three midterms next week! Is there anything I can do to manage my stress better? Obviously, the simplest way of coping with stress is to modify or remove its source—by leaving a stressful job or a bad relationship, for example. As you point out, though, this is often impossible; there's simply no way to avoid those midterms!

You can begin to manage your stress by recognizing that stress triggers *bodily effects, ineffective behavior,* and *upsetting thoughts* (➤ **Figure 59.1**). All of these effects are important, but each one may require different techniques to effectively manage the stressor. Of course, not all of them will be effective for all people, but you should try them out to see what works for you.

Managing Bodily Effects

Much of the immediate discomfort of stress is caused by fight-or-flight physical responses. The body is ready to act, with tight muscles and a pounding heart. If action is prevented, we merely remain "uptight." A sensible remedy is to learn a reliable, drug-free way to relax.

Exercise Stress-based arousal can be dissipated by using the body. Any full-body exercise can be effective. Swimming, dancing, jumping rope, yoga, most other sports, and especially walking are additional valuable outlets. Regular exercise alters hormones, circulation, muscle tone, and several other aspects of physical functioning. Together, such changes can reduce anxiety and lower the risks for disease (Brannon, Feist, & Updegraff, 2021; Edenfield & Blumenthal, 2011).

Be sure to choose activities that are vigorous enough to relieve tension, yet enjoyable enough to be done repeatedly. Exercising for stress management is most effective when it is done daily. As little as 30 minutes of total exercise per day, even if it occurs in short 10- to 20-minute sessions, can improve mood and energy (Hansen, Stevens, & Coast, 2001).

Stress management The application of cognitive and behavioral strategies to reduce stress and improve coping skills.

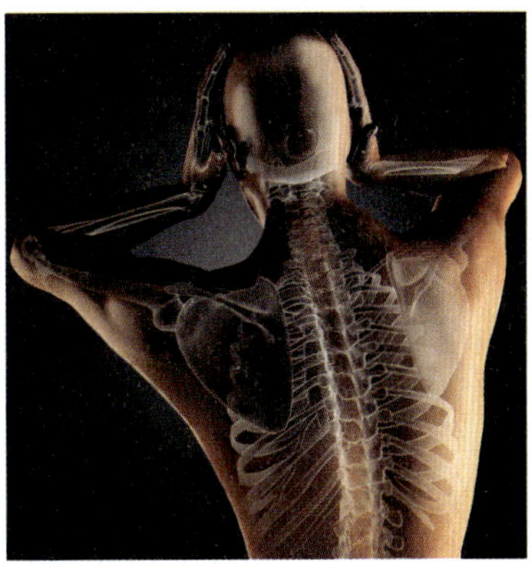

Bodily Reactions
- Fight-or-flight response
- Tight muscles
- Pounding heart
- Shallow breathing
- Poor sleep
- Tiredness
- Stress-based illness
- Poor digestion

Ineffective Behavior
- Too fast-paced
- Too disorganized
- Too unbalanced
- Unrealistic
- Indecisive
- Avoidant
- Inefficient
- Aggressive

Upsetting Thoughts
- Negative self-statements
- Fearful
- Worried
- Distracted
- Obsessive
- Excessively body aware
- Health fears
- Self-doubt

➤ **Figure 59.1**
Effects of stress on body, behavior, and thought.

Meditation Many stress counselors recommend meditation for quieting the body and promoting relaxation. Meditation is one of the most effective ways to relax (Sears & Kraus, 2009; Zeidan et al., 2010). Be aware that listening to or playing music, taking nature walks, enjoying hobbies, and the like can be meditative. Anything that reliably interrupts upsetting thoughts and promotes relaxation can be helpful. For now, it is enough to state that meditation is easy to learn—taking an expensive commercial course is unnecessary. To learn more about meditation and its effects, read Module 23.

Progressive Relaxation It is possible to relax systematically, completely, and by choice. The basic idea of **progressive relaxation** is to tighten all the muscles in a given area of your body (the arms, for instance) and then voluntarily relax them. By first tensing and relaxing each area of the body (also called the tension–release method), you can learn what muscle tension feels like. Then, when each area is relaxed, the change is more noticeable and more controllable. In this way, it is possible, with practice, to greatly reduce tension. To learn the details of how this is done, consult Module 67.

Guided Imagery In a technique called **guided imagery**, people visualize images that are calming, relaxing, or beneficial in other ways. Relaxation, for instance, can be promoted by visualizing peaceful scenes. Pick several places where you feel safe, calm, and at ease. Typical locations might be a beach or lake, the woods, floating on an air mattress in a warm pool, or lying in the sun at a quiet park. To relax, vividly imagine yourself in one of these locations. In the visualized scene, you should be alone and in a comfortable position. It is important to visualize the scene as realistically as possible. Try to feel, taste, smell, hear, and see what you would experience in the calming scene. Practice forming such images several times a day for about five minutes each time. When your scenes become familiar and detailed, they can be used to reduce anxiety and encourage relaxation.

Modifying Ineffective Behavior

Stress is often made worse by our misguided responses to it. The following suggestions may help you deal with stress more effectively:

Slow Down Remember that stress can be self-generated. Try to deliberately do things at a slower pace—especially if your pace has speeded up over the years. Tell yourself, "What counts most is not if I get there first, but if I get there at all," or "My goal is distance, not speed."

Strike a Balance Work, school, family, friends, interests, hobbies, recreation, community, church—a satisfying life has many important elements. Damaging stress often comes from letting one element—especially work or school—get blown out of proportion. Your goal should be quality in life, not quantity. Try to strike a balance between challenging "good stress" and relaxation. Remember, when you are "doing nothing," you are doing something very important: Set aside time for "me acts" such as loafing, browsing, puttering, playing, and napping.

Recognize and Accept Your Limits Many of us set unrealistic and perfectionist goals. Given that no one can ever be perfect, this attitude leaves many people feeling inadequate, no matter how well they have performed. Set gradual, achievable goals for yourself. Also, set realistic limits on what you try to do on any given day. Learn to say no to added demands or responsibilities.

Seek Social Support Close, positive relationships with others—**social support**—facilitate good health and morale (Ai et al., 2013; Winfree & Jiang, 2010). People with close, supportive relationships have better immune responses and better health (Smith, Ruiz, & Uchino, 2004; Taylor & Master, 2011). Apparently, support from family, friends, and even pets serves as a buffer to cushion the impact of stressful events (Allen, Blascovich, & Mendes, 2002).

Write About Your Feelings If you don't have someone you can talk to about stressful events, you might try expressing your thoughts and feelings in writing. Several studies have found that students who write about their upsetting experiences, thoughts, and feelings are better able to cope with stress. They also experience fewer illnesses, and they get better grades (Smyth & Pennebaker, 2008). Writing about your feelings tends to leave your mind clearer. This makes it easier to pay attention to life's challenges and come up with effective coping strategies. Thus, after you write about your feelings, it helps to make specific plans for coping with upsetting experiences (Klein & Boals, 2001; Smyth, Pennebaker, & Arigo, 2012).

As an alternative, you might want to try writing about positive experiences. In one study, college students who wrote about intensely positive experiences had fewer illnesses over the next three months. Writing just 20 minutes a day for three days improved the students' moods and had a surprisingly long-lasting effect on their health (Burton & King, 2004).

Counteracting Upsetting Thoughts

Assume that you are taking a test. Suddenly you realize that you are running short of time. If you say to yourself, "Oh no, this is terrible, I've blown it now," your body's response will probably be sweating, tenseness, and a knot in your stomach. On the other hand, if you say, "I should have watched the time, but getting upset won't help; I'll just take one question at a time," your stress level will be much lower.

As stated previously, stress is greatly affected by the views that we take of events. Physical symptoms and a tendency to make poor decisions are increased by negative thoughts or "self-talk." In many cases, what you say to yourself can mean the difference between coping and collapsing (Smith & Kirby, 2011).

Coping Statements Psychologist Donald Meichenbaum has popularized a technique called **stress inoculation**. In it, clients learn to fight fear and anxiety with an internal monologue of positive coping statements. First, clients learn to identify and monitor **negative self-statements**—self-critical thoughts that increase anxiety. Negative thoughts are a problem because they tend to directly elevate physical arousal. To counter this effect, clients learn to replace negative statements with coping statements from a supplied list. Eventually, they are encouraged to make their own lists (Meichenbaum, 2009).

How are coping statements applied? **Coping statements** are reassuring and self-enhancing. They are used to block out, or counteract, negative self-talk in stressful situations. Before giving a short speech, for instance, you would replace "I'm scared," "I can't do this," "My mind will go blank and I'll panic," or "I'll sound stupid and boring" with "I'll give my speech on something I like," or "I'll breathe deeply before I start my speech," or "My pounding heart just means I'm psyched up to do my best." Additional examples of coping statements follow:

Preparing for Stressful Situations

I'll just take things one step at a time.

If I get nervous, I'll just pause a moment.

Tomorrow, I'll be done with it.

I've managed to do this before.

What exactly do I have to do?

Confronting Stressful Situations

Relax, this can't really hurt me.

Stay organized; focus on the task.

There's no hurry; take it step by step.

Nobody's perfect; I'll just do my best.

It will be over soon; just be calm.

Meichenbaum cautions that saying the "right" things to yourself may not be enough to improve stress tolerance. You must practice this approach in actual stress situations. Also, it is important to develop your own personal list of coping statements by finding what works for you. Ultimately, the value of learning this, and other stress-management skills, ties back into the idea that much stress is self-generated. Knowing that you can manage a demanding situation is in itself a major antidote for stress. In one study, college students who learned stress inoculation not only had less anxiety and depression, but better self-esteem as well (Schiraldi & Brown, 2001).

Lighten Up It's also worth noting again the value of positive emotions. Happiness, laughter, and delight tend to strengthen immune system response. Doing things that make you happy also can protect your health (Diener & Chan, 2011; Rosenkranz et al., 2003).

Humor is especially worth cultivating as a way to reduce stress. A good sense of humor can lower your distress/stress reaction to difficult events (Morrison, 2012). In addition, an ability to laugh at life's ups and downs is associated with better immunity to disease (Earleywine, 2011). Don't be afraid to laugh at yourself and at the many ways that we humans make things difficult for ourselves. You've probably heard the following advice about everyday stresses: "Don't sweat the small stuff" and "It's all small stuff." Humor is one of the best antidotes for anxiety and emotional distress because it helps put things into perspective (Crawford & Caltabiano, 2011; Kuiper & McHale, 2009). The vast majority of events are only as stressful as you allow them to be. Have some fun. It's perfectly healthy.

Progressive relaxation A method for producing deep relaxation of all parts of the body.

Guided imagery Intentional visualization of images that are calming, relaxing, or beneficial in other ways.

Social support Close, positive relationships with other people.

Stress inoculation Use of positive coping statements to control fear and anxiety.

Negative self-statements Self-critical thoughts that increase anxiety and lower performance.

Coping statements Reassuring, self-enhancing statements that are used to stop self-critical thinking.

MODULE 59

Stress Management—Learning Outcomes Revisited

59.1 Explain stress management and three approaches to stress management

Psychologists have studied many aspects of stress besides its negative effects and effective coping strategies. Recent research has focused on different types of stress, the role of genetics and physiology, developmental changes in stress responses, and new forms of treatment. Stress-management techniques focus on one of three areas: bodily effects, ineffective behavior, and upsetting thoughts. All of the following are good ways to manage bodily reactions to stress: Exercise, meditation, progressive relaxation, and guided imagery. To minimize ineffective behavior when you are stressed, you can slow down, get organized, balance work and relaxation, accept your limits, seek social support, and write about your feelings. Learning to use coping statements is a good way to combat upsetting thoughts.

Reflective Practice

Content Check

1. Exercise, meditation, and progressive relaxation are considered effective ways to counter negative self-statements. T or F?
2. A person using progressive relaxation for stress management is most likely trying to control which component of stress?
   a. bodily reactions
   b. upsetting thoughts
   c. ineffective behavior
   d. the primary appraisal
3. Research shows that social support from family and friends has little effect on the health consequences of stress. T or F?
4. While taking a stressful classroom test, you say to yourself, "Stay organized, focus on the task." It's obvious that you are using a
   a. guided image
   b. coping statement
   c. defense mechanism
   d. guided relaxation

Skill Check

Think Critically

5. Steve always feels extremely pressured when the due date arrives for his major term papers. How could he reduce stress in such instances?

Self-Reflect

If you were going to put together a "toolkit" for stress management, what items would you include?

ANSWERS

1. F 2. a 3. F 4. b 5. The stress associated with doing term papers can be almost completely eliminated by breaking up a long-term assignment into many small daily or weekly assignments (Anderson, 2014; Ariely & Wertenbroch, 2002). Students who habitually procrastinate are often amazed at how pleasant college work can be once they renounce "brinkmanship" (pushing things off to the limits of tolerance).

MODULE 60

Psychological Disorders
Defining Psychopathology

Break In or Break Down?

James was busted trying to break in to the Federal Bureau of Investigation (FBI). This account of the episode makes it clear he had suffered another breakdown: "James said he was overwhelmed lately with feelings of apprehension and fear that he and someone important were about to be harmed. He could not specify why he felt this way, but he was sure he had special information that the President of the United States was going to be harmed soon and that he, James, would also be harmed because he knew of the plot. These feelings eventually became so strong that James felt he had to leave his apartment and warn someone at the FBI office. James said he thought the police were going to kill him because they were agents responsible for the plot against the president" (Kearney & Trull, 2018, p. 360).

Is James mentally ill? How is mental illness defined, categorized, and diagnosed? What causes mental illness? Let's tackle these important questions.

gary718/Shutterstock.com

~LEARNING OUTCOMES~

After reading this module you should be able to:

60.1 Name four ways of considering whether behavior is abnormal

60.2 Explain how psychological disorders are classified

60.3 Explain how psychological disorders are diagnosed

60.4 Describe some causes of mental disorders and the importance of the stress-vulnerability model

Normality—What's Normal?

Learning Outcome 60.1 Name four ways of considering whether behavior is abnormal

The statistics are grim. The direct cost of treating people who seek help for mental illness is almost $60 billion a year. Add the indirect costs, such as lost earnings, and the total exceeds $315 billion a year. Hidden behind the dollar signs is the immense human cost. James's case is but one hint of the magnitude of mental health problems. About 19 percent of American adults suffer from a diagnosable mental disorder in any given year (Kessler, 2010; National Institute of Mental Health, 2018). In 2016, nearly 45,000 Americans committed suicide. Most of them had a diagnosable mental disorder (National Alliance on Mental Illness, 2019; National Institute of Mental Health, 2018).

To draw the line between normal behavior and a mental disorder, we must weigh some complex issues. We'll explore some of them in this modules and the three that follow, as well as an array of psychological problems.

A **mental disorder** is a significant impairment in psychological functioning, such as schizophrenia or major depression. The scientific study of mental disorders is known as **psychopathology**, although the term can also refer to mental disorders themselves and to behavior patterns that make people unhappy and impair their personal growth (Sue et al., 2017). Even though these definitions may seem obvious, to seriously classify people as mentally unhealthy raises complex and age-old issues (Luyten & Blatt, 2011). The conservative, churchgoing housewife down the street might be flagrantly psychotic and a lethal danger to her children. The reclusive eccentric who hangs out at the park could be the sanest person in town.

Let's begin with the idea of statistical abnormality, which some psychologists use to define normality more objectively. **Statistical abnormality** refers to scoring very high or low on some dimension, such as intelligence, anxiety, or depression. Anxiety, for example, is a feature of several psychological disorders. To measure it, we could create a test to learn how many people show low, medium, or high levels of anxiety. Usually, the results of such tests will form a *normal* (bell-shaped) *curve*. (*Normal* here refers only to the *shape* of the curve.) Notice that most people score near the middle of a normal curve; very few have extremely high or low scores (➤ **Figure 60.1**). A person who deviates from the average by being highly anxious is, by definition, statistically abnormal. So, too, is a person who never feels anxiety.

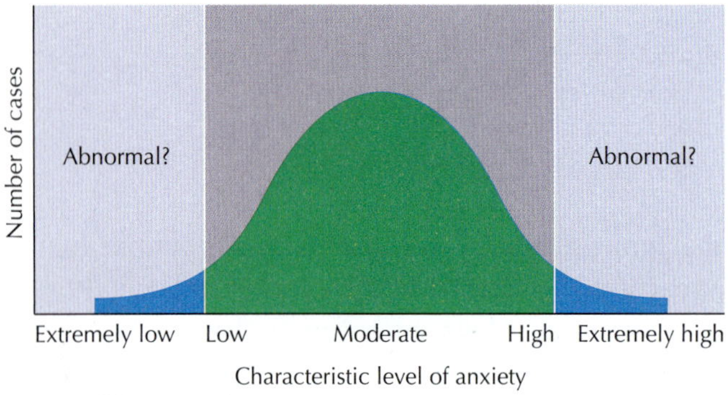

➤ **Figure 60.1**

The normal curve and abnormality. The number of people displaying a personal characteristic may help define what is statistically abnormal.

Eugenio Marongiu/Shutterstock.com

Performing a mildly abnormal behavior is a good way to get a sense of how social norms define "normality." Here's your assignment: Do something strange in public and observe how people react. (Please don't do anything dangerous or offensive—and don't get arrested!) Try walking around campus on a sunny day carrying an open umbrella. Or stick one finger in your nose and another in your ear and walk through a shopping mall. Better yet, wear an animal mask for a day (no, not Halloween!). As we have noted, social nonconformity is just one facet of abnormal behavior. Nevertheless, actions that are regarded as "strange" within a particular culture are often the first sign to others that a person has a problem.

But what if a statistically abnormal person is functioning well? Right. If people with statistically abnormal levels of anxiety are nevertheless functioning well in their lives, why label them mentally ill? Statistical definitions also can't tell us *where to draw the line* between normality and abnormality. For example, we could obtain the average frequency of sexual intercourse for persons of a particular age, sex, sexual orientation, and marital status. Clearly, a person who feels driven to have sex dozens of times a day has a problem. But as we move back toward the norm, we face the problem of drawing lines. How often does a normal behavior have to occur before it becomes abnormal? As you can see, statistical boundary lines tend to be somewhat arbitrary (Comer, 2018).

Another approach is to focus on the nonconformity that may be associated with some disorders. **Social nonconformity** refers to disobeying public standards for acceptable conduct. Extreme nonconformity can lead to destructive, self-destructive, or illegal behavior. (Think, for instance, of a drug abuser or a prostitute.)

Once again, we must be careful to separate unhealthy nonconformity from creative lifestyles. Many eccentric "characters" are charming and emotionally stable. Note, too, that strictly following social norms is no guarantee of mental health. In some cases, psychopathology involves rigid conformity.

Julio Cesar Aguilar/AFP/Getty Images

Social nonconformity does not automatically indicate psychopathology. For example, meet Maria Jose Cristerna, a mother of four and a former lawyer. She is the current Guinness Book of World Records record holder for the most body piercings and tattoos. Nonconformist? You bet. Mentally ill? Definitely not.

Furthermore, before we can even begin to judge a behavior as abnormal or nonconforming, we must also consider the *situational context* (social situation, behavioral setting, or general circumstances) in which it occurs. Is it abnormal to stand outside and water a lawn with a hose? It depends on whether it is raining. Is it nonconforming for a grown man to remove his pants and expose himself to another man or woman in a place of business? It depends on whether the other person is a bank clerk or a doctor.

Almost any imaginable behavior can be considered normal in some contexts. For example, in 2003, a man sawed off his own arm. Mind you, Aaron Ralston was rock climbing when he fell into a crevasse, trapping his arm between two boulders. After five days of trying to free his arm, and nearing unconsciousness, he did what he needed to do to survive (Ralston, 2004).

As implied by our earlier discussion of social norms, culture is one of the most influential contexts in which any behavior is judged (Kirmayer & Ryder, 2016; Whitbourne & Halgin, 2013). In some cultures, it is considered normal to defecate or urinate in public or to appear naked in public. In our culture, such behaviors would be considered unusual or abnormal. In some Muslim cultures, women who remain completely housebound are considered normal, even virtuous. In some Western cultures, they might be suspected of suffering from a disorder called agoraphobia. (Agoraphobia is described in Module 63.)

Thus, *cultural relativity* (the idea that judgments are made relative to the values of one's culture) can affect the definitions of psychological disorders. Still, *all* cultures classify people as abnormal if they fail to communicate with others or are consistently unpredictable in their actions. Yet another approach is to characterize psychopathology by *subjective discomfort* (private feelings of pain, unhappiness, or emotional distress).

But couldn't a person experience serious distress without psychopathology, and couldn't someone be seriously disturbed without feeling discomfort? Yes on both counts. People who have, for example, lost a loved one or lived through a natural disaster such as a massive wildfire normally take some time to overcome their distress. Also, psychopathology doesn't always cause personal anguish. A person suffering from mania might feel elated and "on top of the world." A *lack* of discomfort may actually reveal a problem. For example, if you showed no signs of grief or distress after the violent death of a close friend, we might suspect psychopathology. In practice, though, subjective discomfort explains most instances in which people voluntarily seek professional help.

Mental Disorders Are Maladaptive

If abnormality is so hard to define, how are judgments of psychopathology made? As you can see, categorizing someone as mentally ill is far from "cut and dried." Although the standards we have discussed thus far are *relative*,

Mental disorder A significant impairment in psychological functioning.

Psychopathology The scientific study of mental, emotional, and behavioral disorders; the term is also used to refer to maladaptive behavior.

Statistical abnormality Abnormality defined on the basis of an extreme score on some dimension, such as IQ or anxiety.

Social nonconformity Failure to conform to societal norms or the usual minimum standards for social conduct.

psychopathological behavior does have a core feature: It is **maladaptive**. Rather than helping people cope successfully, maladaptive behavior arises from an underlying psychological or biological dysfunction that makes it more difficult for them to meet the demands of day-to-day life (American Psychiatric Association, 2013). Maladaptive behavior most often results in serious psychological discomfort, disability, and/or *loss of control* of thoughts, behaviors, or feelings, such as James's overwhelming sense of impending doom.

For example, gambling is not a problem if people bet for entertainment and can maintain self-control. However, compulsive gambling is a sign of psychopathology. Hearing uncontrollable voices is a prime example of what it means to lose control of one's thoughts. In the most extreme cases, people become a danger to themselves or others, which is clearly maladaptive.

In practice, deciding that a person needs help usually occurs when the person *does something* (assaults a person, hallucinates, stares into space, collects too many old pizza cartons, and so forth) that *annoys* or *gains the attention* of a person in a *position of power* in the person's life (an employer, teacher, parent, spouse, or the person himself or herself). That person then does something about it. The person may voluntarily seek help, the person may be urged to see a psychologist, a police officer may be called, or a relative may start commitment proceedings.

Abnormal Behavior and the Law

Commitment proceedings are legal proceedings that may result in the finding of **insanity**, which is a legal, not a psychological, term (Fuller, 2012). It refers to an inability to manage one's affairs or foresee the consequences of one's actions. People who are declared insane are not legally responsible for their actions. If necessary, they can be involuntarily committed to a mental hospital.

Legally, insanity is established by testimony from *expert witnesses* (psychologists and psychiatrists) recognized by a court of law as qualified to give opinions on a specific topic. Involuntary commitments happen most often when people are brought to emergency rooms or are arrested for committing a crime. People who are involuntarily committed are usually judged to be a danger to themselves or to others, or they are severely intellectually disabled.

What is the insanity defense? Someone accused of a crime may argue that he or she is *not guilty by reason of insanity*. In practice, this means that the accused, due to a diagnosable mental disorder, was unable to realize that what he or she did was wrong (Gowensmith, Murrie, & Boccaccini, 2013).

You may be surprised to learn that being diagnosed with a mental disorder does not automatically imply a successful insanity defense. For example, someone diagnosed with, say, an anxiety disorder who commits murder might nevertheless be well aware that murder is against the law. In fact, very few criminal trials end with this verdict (Fuller, 2012; Martin & Weiss, 2010).

What if someone suffered brain damage that caused them to engage in illegal behaviors? Good question. Someone with brain damage or an intellectual disability such as autism could plead *not guilty by reason of diminished responsibility* (Jones et al., 2013). For example, as Mr. P grew older, his interest in child pornography also grew. By the age of 40, he had begun seeking out sexual contacts with his young stepdaughter and at massage parlors. He was arrested and sent to a rehabilitation clinic, where he proceeded to seek sexual contacts with the staff and clients, despite not wanting to go to prison. All along, he maintained that he knew he was in the wrong but couldn't stop himself. A magnetic resonance imaging (MRI) scan (see Module 8) revealed a large tumor growing in a part of his brain responsible for impulse control. When it was removed, his abnormal sexual behavior disappeared as well. A few years later, he started collecting child pornography again. Another MRI confirmed that the tumor had returned (Burns & Swerdlow, 2003).

With the rise of brain-scanning technologies, cases like this have become more common (Fabian, 2011). Such cases also raise serious questions about the plea of *not guilty by reason of diminished responsibility*. Should Mr. P. be set free? Should his sentence be reduced? Is it ever appropriate to blame the person, and not his or her brain? What do you think?

Classifying Mental Disorders—Problems by the Book

Learning Outcome 60.2 Explain how psychological disorders are classified

In North America, mental disorders are generally classified by using the most recent version of the *DSM*, the *Diagnostic and Statistical Manual of Mental Disorders (5th Edition)*. (In Europe, the ICD-11 is generally used for the same purpose [World Health Organization, 2018].) The *DSM-5* influences most activities in American mental health settings—from diagnosis to therapy to insurance company billing (American Psychiatric Association, 2013). As even a quick scan of the

DSM-5 makes clear, a wide variety of psychological disorders are currently diagnosed and treated; hundreds of specific disorders are organized into over 20 major categories.

A partial list of major categories and specific disorders can be found in ■ **Table 60.1**. Many of the disorders on this list are described in the next three modules. (Others are discussed elsewhere in this book: sleep–wake disorders in Module 24, problems with drug abuse and dependence in Module 25, eating disorders in Module 43, and sexual disorders in Modules 46 and 48.)

Comorbidity

In addition, many disturbed people are **comorbid**—that is, they suffer from more than one mental disorder at the same time. One way that comorbidity develops is when a *primary* problem causes *secondary* problems. For example, someone experiencing a prolonged and deep depression might start taking drugs (legal or otherwise) for treatment and become addicted, complicating the primary mood disorder with a secondary, substance use disorder (Fenton et al., 2012).

According to sociologist Ronald Kessler, more than 40 percent of all people with mental disorders are comorbid (Kessler, 2010). Not only does comorbidity increase these people's misery, it also makes it much more difficult for healthcare providers to diagnose and treat them.

Mental Illness in Other Cultures

As you might well imagine, different cultures around the world have identified their own *culture-bound syndromes* you won't find in the *DSM-5* (Barlow, Durand, & Hofmann, 2021; López & Guarnaccia, 2000; Teo & Gaw, 2010). For example, men in some parts of Asia sometimes run *amok* after they have been insulted. After a period of brooding, they erupt into an outburst of violent, aggressive, or homicidal behavior randomly directed at people and objects. (Yes, this is the origin of the familiar expression "to run amok.") Can *amok* be understood within the framework of the *DSM-5* as a *brief psychotic disorder*?

As another example, in Japan, adolescents or young adults who refuse to leave their parents' homes for months at a time are experiencing *hikikomori*, an extreme form of social withdrawal. Is *hikikomori* a variation of the *DSM-5* disorder *agoraphobia*?

It is clear that people everywhere have a need to label and categorize troubled behavior. With some cultural sensitivity, it is often possible to understand these unusual experiences (Flaskerud, 2009; Ross, Schroeder, & Ness, 2013). By the way, culture-bound syndromes occur in all societies. For example, American psychologists Pamela Keel and Kelly Klump believe that the eating disorder *bulimia nervosa* is primarily a syndrome of Western cultures such as the United States (Keel & Klump, 2003).

Beware Medical Student's Disease We hope that you have not already fallen prey to "medical student's disease." Medical students, it seems, have a predictable tendency to notice in themselves the symptoms of each dreaded disease they study. As a psychology student, you may notice what seem to be abnormal tendencies in your own behavior. If so, don't panic. In most instances, this shows only that pathological behavior is an *exaggeration* of normal defenses and reactions, not that your behavior is abnormal. Keep this in mind as you read on.

The Fluidity of Psychiatric Categories

You might be surprised to learn that definitions of mental disorders change over time. For example, when the *DSM-I* was first published in 1952, *neurosis* was included. The term was dropped in later editions because it is too imprecise. Even though *neurosis* is an outdated term, you may still hear it used to loosely refer to problems involving excessive anxiety. Similarly, *homosexuality* was omitted as a disorder in 1974.

Published in 2013, the *DSM-5* reflects recent scientific advances and cultural changes (American Psychiatric Association, 2013; Birgegård, Norring, & Clinton, 2012). Regardless, the process leading up to publication of the *DSM-5* was controversial (Frances, 2012; Marecek & Gavey, 2013). Perhaps the most important, and certainly the most contentious, change has been the proliferation of disorders. The original *DSM* contained about 100 disorders; today, it contains over 350.

Critics charge that more and more previously "normal" people are being categorized as "mentally ill" (Frances, 2012; Lane, 2009). For example, *attention deficit hyperactivity disorder (ADHD)* was not a disorder in the original *DSM*. Since its inclusion, it has become one of the most widely diagnosed disorders among young boys, prompting critics to decry the disorder as "pathologizing boyhood" (Bruchmüller, Margraf, & Schneider, 2012).

Maladaptive behavior Behavior arising from an underlying psychological or biological dysfunction that makes it difficult to adapt to the environment and meet the demands of day-to-day life.

Insanity A legal term that refers to a mental inability to manage one's affairs or to be aware of the consequences of one's actions.

Comorbidity (in mental disorders) The simultaneous presence in a person of two or more mental disorders.

TABLE 60.1 | Major *DSM-5* Categories of Psychopathology

Problem	Primary Symptom	Typical Signs of Trouble	Examples
Neurodevelopmental disorders	Impairment of nervous system development before adulthood	You have intellectual, communication, attentional, or motor problems that emerge early in your life.	Intellectual developmental disorder, Autism spectrum disorder, Attention deficit/hyperactivity disorder
Schizophrenia spectrum and other psychotic disorders	Loss of contact with reality	You hear or see things that others don't; your mind has been playing tricks on you.	Delusional disorder, Schizophrenia, Brief psychotic disorder
Bipolar and related disorders	Alternating mania and depression	You feel depressed, or you talk too loud and too fast and have a rush of ideas and feelings that others think are unreasonable.	Cyclothymic disorder, Bipolar I disorder, Bipolar II disorder
Depressive disorders	Depression	You feel sad and hopeless.	Persistent depressive disorder (dysthymia), Major depressive disorder, Postpartum depression, Seasonal affective disorder
Anxiety disorders	High anxiety or anxiety-related distortions of behavior	You have anxiety attacks and feel like you are going to die; or you are afraid to do things that most people can do.	Generalized anxiety disorder, Panic disorder, Agoraphobia, Specific phobia, Social anxiety disorder
Obsessive-compulsive and related disorders	Unnecessarily repetitious behavior	You spend unusual amounts of time doing things such as washing your hands or counting your heartbeats.	Obsessive compulsive disorder, Hoarding disorder
Trauma- and stressor-related disorders	Difficulty dealing with a traumatic or stressful event	You persistently re-experience a traumatic event; you have an exceptionally strong negative reaction to a traumatic event such as becoming highly anxious, depressed, or, being unable to sleep.	Adjustment disorder, Acute stress disorder, Post-traumatic stress disorder
Dissociative disorders	Amnesia, feelings of unreality, multiple identities	There are major gaps in your memory of events; you feel like you are a robot or a stranger to yourself; others tell you that you have done things that you don't remember doing.	Dissociative amnesia, Dissociative identity disorder
Somatic symptom disorders	Body complaints without an organic (physical) basis	You feel physically sick, but your doctor says nothing is wrong with you; you suffer from pain that has no physical basis; or you are preoccupied with thoughts about being sick.	Somatic symptom disorder, Factitious disorder, Conversion disorder
Feeding and eating disorders	Disturbance of food intake into the body	You eat nonfood items (pica) or have difficulty eating enough food to remain healthy.	Anorexia nervosa, Bulimia nervosa, Binge eating disorder
Elimination disorders	Disturbance of waste elimination from the body	You have trouble controlling the elimination of urine (enuresis) or feces (encopresis).	Enuresis, Encopresis

TABLE 60.1 | Major *DSM-5* Categories of Psychopathology (*Continued*)

Problem	Primary Symptom	Typical Signs of Trouble	Examples
Sleep–wake disorders	Troubles falling asleep, staying asleep, or waking up	You have difficulty getting a healthy night's sleep; you snore, have nightmares, or fall asleep inappropriately (narcolepsy).	Insomnia disorder, Hypersomnolence disorder, Narcolepsy, Nightmare disorder
Sexual dysfunctions	Problems in sexual adjustment	You have problems with sexual desire, arousal, orgasm, or pain.	Erectile disorder, Female sexual interest/arousal disorder, Genito-pelvic pain/penetration disorder, Male hypoactive sexual desire disorder
Gender dysphoria	Disturbed gender identity	You feel that you are a man trapped in a woman's body (or the reverse).	Gender dysphoria
Disruptive, impulse control and conduct disorders	Difficulties of self-control	You are defiant and aggressive; you set fires (pyromania) or are a chronic thief (kleptomania).	Oppositional defiant disorder, Intermittent explosive disorder, Pyromania, Kleptomania
Substance use and addictive disorders	Disturbances related to drug abuse or dependence as well as other addictive behaviors	You have been drinking too much, using illegal drugs, taking prescription drugs more often than you should, or gambling too much.	Opioid use disorder, Stimulant use disorder, Alcohol use disorder, Tobacco use disorder, Gambling disorder
Neurocognitive disorders	Impairment of nervous system development while in adulthood	Your ability to think and remember has suffered a dramatic decline in adulthood.	Delirium, Neurocognitive disorder due to Alzheimer's disease, Neurocognitive disorder due to Parkinson's disease, Neurocognitive disorder due to HIV infection
Personality disorders	Unhealthy personality patterns	Your behavior patterns repeatedly cause problems at work, at school, and in your relationships with others.	Antisocial personality disorder, Borderline personality disorder
Paraphilic disorders	Deviant sexual behavior	You can gain sexual satisfaction only by engaging in highly atypical sexual behavior.	Pedophilic disorder, Exhibitionistic disorder, Voyeuristic disorder, Fetishistic disorder

Sources: American Psychiatric Association, 2013; Durand & Barlow, 2019; Sue et al., 2017.

A related concern is that psychiatric labels are getting easier and easier to apply. For example, changes to the *DSM-5* make it easier to label someone whose husband died as suffering from *major depressive disorder* rather than grief (Frances, 2012).

At the same time, some changes are more widely accepted. For example, after considerable debate, the now-outdated term *gender identity disorder* appears in the *DSM-5* as *gender dysphoria* (American Psychiatric Association, 2013; De Cuypere, Knudson, & Bockting, 2011). Opponents of the old terminology argued that many people whose physical sex does not match their gender identity are well adjusted and should not be labeled as "disordered" (Hein & Berger, 2012). The new label better reflects this idea because it applies only to individuals who are deeply troubled by their gender variance.

Hopefully the updated *DSM-5* will result in better diagnoses and treatments for those of us who need help.

The Impact of Psychiatric Labels

In case you haven't yet realized it, labeling someone mentally ill is serious business. A fascinating classic study carried out by psychologist David Rosenhan illustrates the impact of psychiatric labeling. Rosenhan and several volunteers had themselves committed to mental hospitals as "schizophrenics" (Rosenhan, 1973). After being admitted, each of these "pseudopatients" dropped all pretense of mental illness. Yet, even though they acted completely normal, none of the researchers was ever recognized by hospital *staff* as a phony patient. Real patients were not so easily fooled: It was not unusual for a patient to say to one of the researchers, "You're not crazy, you're checking up on the hospital!" or "You're a journalist."

To record his observations, Rosenhan took notes by carefully jotting things on a small piece of paper hidden in his hand. However, he soon learned that stealth was totally unnecessary. Rosenhan simply walked around with a clipboard, recording observations. No one questioned this behavior. Rosenhan's note-taking was just regarded as another symptom of his "illness." This observation clarifies why staff members failed to detect the fake patients. Because they were in a mental ward and because they had been *labeled* schizophrenic, anything the pseudopatients did was seen as a symptom of psychopathology.

To fully appreciate the implications of Rosenhan's study, imagine being falsely labeled "schizophrenic." Now imagine struggling to prove to people that you are actually normal when even denying you are "crazy" just becomes more proof of how crazy you really are. As Rosenhan's study implies, it is better to label *problems* than to label people. Think of the difference in impact between saying, "You are experiencing a serious psychological disorder" and "You're a schizophrenic." Which statement would you prefer to have said about yourself?

The Oppressive Side of Psychiatric Labels An added problem with psychiatric labeling is that it frequently leads to prejudice and discrimination—that is, the mentally ill in our culture are often *stigmatized* (rejected and disgraced). People who have been labeled mentally ill (at any time in their lives) are less likely to be hired. They also tend to be denied housing and are more likely to be falsely accused of crimes. Sadly, the fear of stigmatization, including self-stigmatization, is one major reason many people do not seek help for their mental illness (Mojtabai et al., 2011). Thus, people who are grappling with mental illness may be harmed by social stigma as well as by their immediate psychological problems (Oexle et al., 2017).

Everyone has felt or acted "crazy" during brief periods of stress or high emotion. People with psychological disorders may have problems that are more severe or long-lasting than most of us experience. Otherwise, though, they may not be that different from the rest of us. The terms used to describe mental illness are meant to aid communication about human problems. But as we have just seen, the dangers of labeling, including stigmatization, mean that if psychiatric labels are used carelessly or maliciously, they can oppress people.

Can you give an example? Sure. In the mid-1800s, slaves who tried to escape were sometimes labeled as suffering from "drapetomania," a mental "disorder" that causes slaves to run away (Wakefield, 1992). The "cure"? Amputation of the toes. As this example suggests, psychiatric terms are easily abused. Historically, some have been applied to culturally disapproved behaviors that are not mental disorders. Another of our personal favorites is the long-outdated diagnosis of "anarchia," a form of insanity that leads one to seek a more democratic society (Brown, 1990).

All of the following sexual behaviors were considered mental disorders not that long ago: childhood masturbation, lack of vaginal orgasm, homosexuality, and nymphomania (a woman with a healthy sexual appetite) (Wakefield, 1992). Modern critics suggest that labeling, for example, homosexuality as a deviant form of sexuality amounts to nothing more than using medical labels as a way to justify prejudice.

Even today, stereotypes of race, gender, and social class continue to affect the definitions of various disorders (Mizock & Harkins, 2011; Poland & Caplan, 2004). Gender is probably the most common source of bias in judging normality because standards tend to be based on males (Fine, 2010; Nolen-Hoeksema, 2020). According to psychologist Paula Caplan, women are penalized both for ignoring female stereotypes and for conforming to them. If a woman is independent, aggressive, and unemotional, she may be considered "overmasculinized." Yet a woman who is vain, emotional, irrational, and dependent on others (all "feminine" traits in our culture) may be classified as having a personality disorder. Indeed, a majority of persons classified as having dependent personality disorder are women. In view of this, Caplan asks, why isn't there a category called "delusional dominating personality disorder" for obnoxious men (Caplan, 1995)?

Because biases and prejudices can influence perceptions of disorder and normality, it is worth being extra cautious before you leap to conclusions about or label the mental health of others (American Psychiatric Association, 2013). *Animal-mask-wearing disorder?* They might be doing an assignment for their psychology class!

Diagnosing Mental Illness—Attaching a Label to the Person

Learning Outcome 60.3 Explain how psychological disorders are diagnosed

Like physical illness, mental illness is typically diagnosed by assessing the presence and/or absence of a number of symptoms (Barlow, Durand, & Hoffman, 2021). Consider the diagnosis of *major depressive episode.* Of course, one of the symptoms is being in a depressed (sad, empty, or hopeless) mood. But almost everybody gets a little depressed from time to time. This symptom won't qualify for this diagnosis unless the mood is unusually intense and has gone nearly all day, every day, for at least two weeks. Furthermore, there are eight additional main symptoms to consider, such as loss of interest or pleasure, difficulties with sleep, fatigue or loss of energy, and thoughts of suicide. At least five of these nine main symptoms must have occurred nearly all day, every day, for at least two weeks.

To complicate matters, some symptoms may go unnoticed by the person being diagnosed only to be uncovered by the diagnosing clinician (such symptoms are sometimes referred to as *signs*). For example, Jasper complained to a clinical psychologist about feeling depressed and suicidal but made no mention of sleep problems or fatigue, which were added to Jasper's symptom list only after the clinician completed a careful assessment.

At the same time, there can't have been any *manic episodes* (or else this may be bipolar disorder) and no drug use (or this may be a *substance use disorder*). A further complicating factor is the potential presence of other symptoms not usually part of the diagnosis under consideration. Although depressed people do not typically report psychotic symptoms such as *hallucinations*, it is not unheard of and may indicate comorbidity.

In reality, diagnosing a *major depressive episode* is substantially more complicated than we have portrayed here. It takes a skilled practitioner to make accurate diagnoses. This is critical since treatments are only as good as the diagnoses they are based on (Sue et al., 2017).

Types of Symptoms

As you begin to think about the symptoms underlying mental illness, you might find it helpful to distinguish between *positive* and *negative symptoms* (Rollins et al., 2010). *Positive symptoms,* such as delusions and hallucinations, are excesses or exaggerations compared to normal behavior. People who suffer from **delusions** hold strong false beliefs that they insist are true, regardless of how much the facts contradict them. An example is a 34-year-old woman who was convinced that she would become "President of the United States of the World" (Mendelson & Goes, 2011).

Hallucinations are imaginary perceptions, such as seeing, hearing, or smelling things that don't exist in the real world. The most common hallucination is hearing voices. Sometimes these voices command patients to hurt themselves or others and, unfortunately, sometimes they obey (Birchwood et al., 2014).

In contrast, *negative symptoms* are absences or deficiencies compared to normal behavior. Sometimes patients may be apathetic or display a lack of emotion—*flat affect*—a condition in which the face is frozen in a blank expression. Brain images from patients with "frozen faces" reveal that their brains process emotions abnormally (Lepage et al., 2011). Similarly, a reduced capacity to communicate verbally is a common symptom of some disorders such as psychosis. In fact, psychotic speech can be so garbled and chaotic that it sometimes sounds like a "word salad."

It is one thing to identify symptoms or to diagnose a mental disorder; it is another matter entirely to understand what causes it. While much mystery still remains, in the next section we begin by describing the general factors that underlie all mental illnesses.

Causes of Mental Illness—What Went Wrong?

Learning Outcome 60.4 Describe some causes of mental disorders and the importance of the stress-vulnerability model

Like different physical diseases, different mental illnesses undoubtedly have different underlying causes. Regardless, a small number of general factors underlie all illnesses, mental or otherwise. In the modules on health psychology we stressed the *biopsychosocial* model. As you surely recall

Delusion Strongly held thought or belief that is at odds with reality.
Hallucination Perception with no basis in reality.

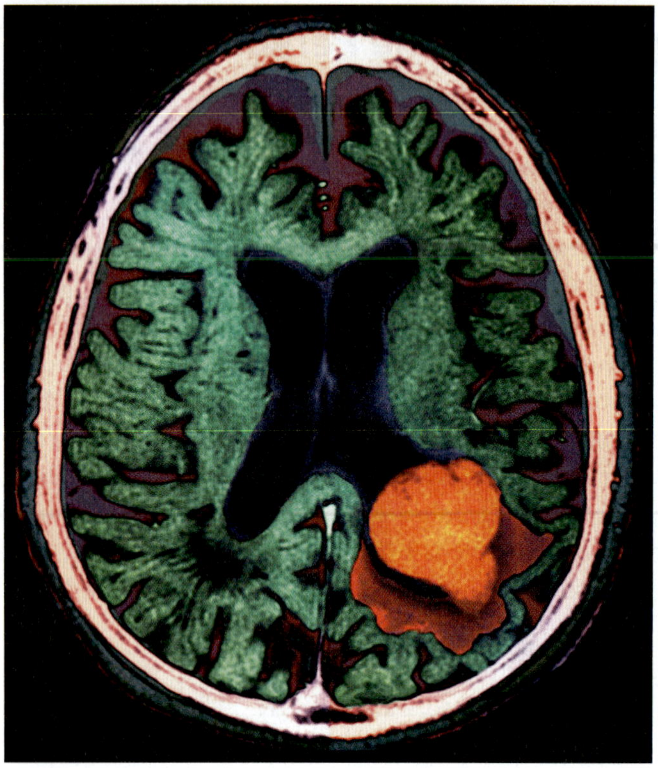

Zephyr/Science Source

This MRI scan of a human brain (viewed from the top) reveals a tumor (dark spot). Mental disorders, like Mr. P's abnormal sexual behaviors, sometimes have organic causes of this sort. However, in many instances, no obvious organic damage can be found.

(right?), combinations of biological, psychological, and/or social factors can underlie both poor and good health. In the same vein, biological, psychological, and/or social factors play a role in mental illness (Yim et al., 2015).

Biological Factors

A variety of mental illnesses are directly associated with biological factors such as genetic defects, very low birth weight, chronic physical illness or disability, exposure to toxic chemicals or drugs, or head injuries. Mr. P's abnormal sexual behaviors clearly arose due to a tumor in his brain.

Similarly, poisoning by chemicals such as lead or mercury can damage the brain, causing intellectual disability, hallucinations, delusions, and a loss of emotional control (Kern et al., 2012). Children with high levels of lead in their blood are more likely to be arrested as adults for criminal offenses (Wright et al., 2008). That is why the current lead poisoning crisis centered in Flint, Michigan, is so frightening to parents. On a much larger scale, "poisoning" of another type, in the form of drug abuse, also can produce deviant behavior and psychotic symptoms (American Psychiatric Association, 2013).

In general, problems directly related to nervous system damage that arise before adulthood, such as *autism*, are termed **neurodevelopmental disorders**. For example, Down syndrome, a form of intellectual disability, is caused by a genetic defect. It is also known as trisomy 21 because the defect involves an extra 21st chromosome (Module 40).

Problems not arising until adulthood, such as *Parkinson's disease*, are termed **neurocognitive disorders**. These are often serious mental impairments in old age caused by deterioration of the brain. In these disorders, we see major disturbances in memory, reasoning, judgment, impulse control, and personality (Treves & Korczyn, 2012). This combination usually leaves people confused, suspicious, apathetic, or withdrawn. Some common causes of neurocognitive disorders are circulatory problems, repeated strokes, or general shrinkage and atrophy of the brain.

Alzheimer's disease (ALLS-hi-merz) is the most common neurocognitive disorder. Alzheimer's victims slowly lose the ability to work, cook, drive, read, write, or do arithmetic. Eventually, they are mute and bedridden. Alzheimer's disease appears to be related to unusual webs and tangles in the brain that damage areas important for memory and learning (Hanyu et al., 2010; Irish et al., 2018). Genetic factors can increase the risk of developing this devastating disease (Treves & Korczyn, 2012).

The Genetics of Mental Illness A variety of mental disorders from narcolepsy to schizophrenia run in families, likely indicating the involvement of an inherited genetic factor. For

Ryan Garza/ZUMA Press/Newscom

The Mad Hatter, from Lewis Carroll's *Alice's Adventures in Wonderland*, was modeled after an occupational disease of the 18th and 19th centuries. In that era, hat makers were heavily exposed to mercury used in the preparation of felt. Consequently, many suffered brain damage and became psychotic, or "mad" (Kety, 1979). Such environmental exposure to toxic chemicals remains a problem to this day. Unacceptably high concentrations of lead in water supplies are currently plaguing the mostly poor families living in cities such as Flint, Michigan.

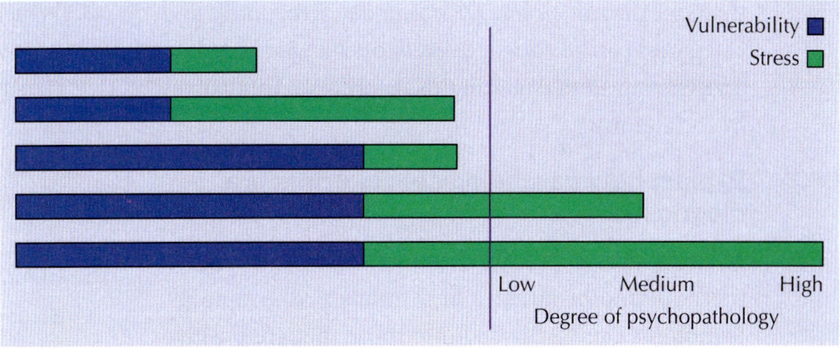

➤ **Figure 60.2**

The Stress-vulnerability model. Various combinations of vulnerability and stress may produce psychological problems. The top bar shows low vulnerability and low stress. The result? No problem. The same is true of the next bar down, in which low vulnerability is combined with moderate stress. Even high vulnerability (third bar) may not lead to problems if stress levels remain low. However, when high vulnerability combines with moderate or high stress (bottom two bars), the person "crosses the line" and suffers from psychopathology.

example, one recent study identified 128 gene variations associated with schizophrenia (Schizophrenia Working Group of the Psychiatric Genomics Consortium, 2014). While any progress in understanding schizophrenia is welcome, this still leaves researchers with more questions than answers (Sharma et al., 2016). How do particular genes, once they are identified, affect the brain? Do they modify brain structure? Do they alter neurotransmitter function? Most importantly, does any of this lead to new therapies for schizophrenia?

Our current understanding of the genetics of most mental illnesses is, like our understanding of schizophrenia, a work in progress (e.g., Halmai et al., 2013). Nevertheless, genetic analyses will undoubtedly continue to contribute to our rapidly expanding knowledge of the causes of mental illness.

Psychosocial Factors

A variety of psychosocial factors also are associated with a variety of mental illnesses. Relevant psychological factors include stress; psychological trauma; learning disorders; and lack of knowledge, control, or mastery. Contributing family factors include parents who are immature, mentally disturbed, criminal, or abusive; severe marital strife; extremely poor child discipline; and disordered family communication patterns. Relevant social conditions include poverty, stressful living conditions, homelessness, social disorganization, and overcrowding. Of these, the most important are stress and early **psychological trauma**—a psychological injury or shock.

The Stress-Vulnerability Model Most psychologists now accept that most mental illnesses are caused by a blend of environmental, psychosocial stress, and inherited vulnerability (Jones & Fernyhough, 2007; Yim et al., 2015). This type of explanation is called the **stress-vulnerability model** (or the *diathesis-stress* model) (see ➤ **Figure 60.2**).

Neurodevelopmental disorders Psychopathologies due to various forms of damage to the nervous system arising before adulthood.

Neurocognitive disorders Psychopathologies due to various forms of damage to the nervous system not arising until adulthood.

Alzheimer's disease Age-related condition characterized by memory loss, confusion, and increasing loss of mental abilities.

Psychological trauma A psychological injury or shock, such as that caused by violence, abuse, neglect, separation, etc.

Stress-vulnerability (diathesis-stress) model A model that attributes mental illness to a combination of environmental stress and inherited susceptibility.

MODULE 60 Defining Psychopathology—Learning Outcomes Revisited

60.1 Name four ways of considering whether behavior is abnormal

When deciding whether behavior is abnormal, we can consider statistical abnormality, nonconformity, subjective discomfort, and the extent to which the behavior may be considered maladaptive .

60.2 Explain how psychological disorders are classified

Psychological problems are classified by using the *Diagnostic and Statistical Manual of Mental Disorders (5th Edition) (DSM-5)*, and it is possible for people to be comorbid (i.e., exhibiting symptoms that fit more than one disorder). The *DSM* is updated regularly, and categories can be added, deleted, or changed based on an evolving understanding of disorders and changes in social norms.

60.3 Explain how psychological disorders are diagnosed

Mental illness is typically diagnosed by confirming the presence and/or absence of a number of symptoms. Symptoms can be divided into those that are positive (i.e., exaggeration compared to normal behavior) and those that are negative (i.e., deficit compared to normal behavior).

60.4 Describe some causes of mental disorders and the importance of the stress-vulnerability model

Some mental disorders are due to known injuries or diseases of the brain, such as poisoning and drug abuse. Neurocognitive disorders, such as Alzheimer's disease, strike in old age. Psychosocial factors that contribute to psychopathology include psychological factors, family factors, and social conditions. A promising explanation for many mental illnesses is the stress-vulnerability model, which emphasizes a combination of inherited susceptibility and environmental stress.

Reflective Practice

Content Check

1. One of the most powerful contexts in which judgments of normality and abnormality are made is
   - **a.** the family
   - **b.** occupational settings
   - **c.** religious systems
   - **d.** culture
2. The core feature of abnormal behavior is that it is
   - **a.** statistically unusual
   - **b.** maladaptive
   - **c.** socially nonconforming
   - **d.** a source of subjective discomfort
3. Which of the following is a *legal* concept?
   - **a.** neurosis
   - **b.** psychosis
   - **c.** drapetomania
   - **d.** insanity
4. *Comorbidity* is said to occur when a person suffers from ______________.
5. Mental illness is typically diagnosed by confirming the
   - **a.** absence of symptoms
   - **b.** presence of symptoms
   - **c.** presence of atypical symptoms
   - **d.** all of the above
6. According to the stress-vulnerability model, mental illness is caused by a blend of environmental stress and
   - **a.** lack of knowledge
   - **b.** inherited susceptibility
   - **c.** brain damage
   - **d.** psychological trauma

Skill Check

Think Critically

7. Many states began to restrict the use of the insanity defense after John Hinckley, Jr., who tried to assassinate President Ronald Reagan in 1981, was found not guilty by reason of insanity. What does this trend reveal about insanity?

Self-Reflect

Think of an instance of abnormal behavior that you have witnessed. By what formal standards would the behavior be regarded as abnormal? In every society? Was the behavior maladaptive in any way? How are the mentally ill stigmatized in movies and television dramas? Can you think of any positive portrayals (such as the film *A Beautiful Mind*)? How do you think such portrayals affect attitudes about mental disorders?

ANSWERS

1. d 2. b 3. d 4. more than one disorder 5. d 6. b 7. It emphasizes that insanity is a legal concept, not a psychiatric diagnosis. Laws reflect community standards. When those standards change, lawmakers may seek to alter definitions of legal responsibility.

MODULE 61

Psychological Disorders

Psychotic Disorders

Edna

Edna has problems. Here is a part of her intake interview:

"*Dr.:* Tell me, how do you feel?
Patient: London's bell is a long, long dock. Hee! Hee! *(Giggles uncontrollably.)*
Dr.: Do you know where you are now?
Patient: D___n! S___t on you all who rip into my internals! The grudgerometer will take care of you all! *(Shouting)* I am the Queen, see my magic, I shall turn you all into smidgelings forever!
Dr.: Your husband is concerned about you. Do you know his name?
Patient: *(Stands, walks to and faces the wall)* Who am I, who are we, who are you, who are they *(turns)* I . . . I . . . I . . . I! *(Makes grotesque faces.)*" (Suinn, 1975*).

Elnur/Shutterstock.com

If you observed such symptoms, would you be concerned? Of course you would, and rightly so. Edna is suffering from an extreme form of schizophrenia marked by silliness, laughter, and bizarre or obscene behavior. How about the woman pictured here? While not all of the psychotic disorders are this extreme, they all involve a break with reality, placing them among the most dramatic and serious of all mental problems. Let's take a closer look at some major psychotic disorders.

~LEARNING OUTCOMES~

After reading this module you should be able to:

61.1 Describe the general characteristics of psychotic disorders

61.2 Outline the specific characteristics of delusional disorders

61.3 Outline the specific characteristics of schizophrenia and describe its causes

Psychotic Disorders—Loss of Contact

Learning Outcome 61.1 Describe the general characteristics of psychotic disorders

At their core, the **psychoses** (psycho*sis*, singular; psycho*ses*, plural) involve a loss of contact with shared views of

*From *Fundamentals of Behavior Pathology* by R. M. Suinn. Copyright © 1975. Reprinted by permission of John Wiley & Sons, Inc.

Psychosis A withdrawal from reality marked by hallucinations and delusions, disturbed thoughts and emotions, and personality disorganization.

TABLE 61.1 | *DSM-5* Classification of Schizophrenia Spectrum and Other Psychotic Disorders

Problem	Typical Signs of Trouble
Delusional disorder	You have some deeply held and bizarre but false beliefs.
Schizophrenia	Your personality has disintegrated; you have hallucinations, delusions, or both.
Brief psychotic disorder	You suffer a sudden, but short-lived loss of contact with reality.

Sources: American Psychiatric Association, 2013; Durand & Barlow, 2019; Sue et al., 2017.

Eric Audras/Getty Images

A psychotic individual in a state mental hospital.

reality (Durand & Barlow, 2019). Psychosis can occur in a variety of mental illnesses including Alzheimer's disease, bipolar disorder, and drug use disorder. In this section, however, we will focus on two major types of **schizophrenia spectrum and other psychotic disorders**: *delusional disorders* and *schizophrenia* (see ■ **Table 61.1**). These diagnoses are usually applied only after psychotic disturbances are evident for weeks or months (American Psychiatric Association, 2013; Sue et al., 2017).

Psychoses are characterized by one or more of the following: delusions, hallucinations, disturbed thought and/or speech, disturbed motor behavior, or social/emotional isolation. Typically, psychotic patients cannot control their thoughts, emotions, and/or actions. Psychotic disorders are severely disabling. They also are among the most difficult to treat. Drug therapies offer some hope; however, many psychotic individuals end up in prison or committed to a mental hospital.

Delusional Disorders—An Enemy Behind Every Tree

Learning Outcome 61.2 Outline the specific characteristics of delusional disorders

People with delusional disorders usually do *not* suffer from hallucinations, disturbed motor behavior, emotional excesses, or personality disintegration. Even so, their break with reality is unmistakable. The main symptom of a **delusional disorder** is the presence of deeply held false beliefs. While many different delusions are possible, most people with delusional disorder can be categorized into these types (American Psychiatric Association, 2013; Sue et al., 2017):

- **Erotomanic type:** In this disorder, people have erotic delusions that they are loved by another person, especially by someone famous or of higher status. As you might imagine, some celebrity stalkers suffer from erotomania.
- **Grandiose type:** In this case, people suffer from the delusion that they have some great, unrecognized talent, knowledge, or insight. They also may believe that they have a special relationship with an important person or with God, or that they are a famous person. (If the famous person is alive, the deluded person regards her or him as an imposter.)
- **Jealous type:** An example of this type of delusion would be having an all-consuming, but unfounded, belief that your spouse or lover is unfaithful.
- **Persecutory type:** Delusions of persecution involve the belief that you are being conspired against, cheated, spied on, followed, poisoned, maligned, or harassed.
- **Somatic type:** People suffering from somatic delusions typically believe that their bodies are diseased or rotting, infested with insects or parasites, or that parts of their bodies are defective.

Although false and sometimes far-fetched, these delusions tend to be about experiences that could conceivably occur in real life. In other types of psychosis, such as Edna's schizophrenia, delusions tend to be more bizarre (Brown & Barlow, 2017). For example, a person with schizophrenia might believe that space aliens have replaced all his internal organs with electronic monitoring devices. In contrast, people with ordinary delusions merely believe that someone is trying to steal their money, that they are being deceived by a lover, that the FBI is watching them, and the like.

Paranoid Psychosis

The most common delusional disorder, **paranoid psychosis**, centers on delusions of persecution. Many self-styled reformers, crank letter writers, conspiracy theorists, and the like suffer paranoid delusions. Paranoid individuals often believe that they are being cheated, spied on, followed, poisoned, harassed, or plotted against. Usually they are intensely suspicious, believing that they must be on guard at all times.

The evidence that such people find to support their beliefs generally fails to persuade others. Every detail of the paranoid person's existence is woven into a private version of "what's really going on." For instance, buzzing during a telephone conversation may be interpreted as "someone listening," or a stranger who comes to the door asking for directions may be seen as "really trying to get information."

It is difficult to treat people suffering from paranoid delusions because it is almost impossible for them to accept that they need help. Anyone who suggests that they have a problem is quickly incorporated into the "conspiracy" to "persecute" them. Consequently, paranoid people frequently lead lonely, isolated, and humorless lives dominated by constant suspicion and hostility.

Although paranoid people are not necessarily dangerous to others, they can be. People who believe that the Mafia, "government agents," terrorists, or a street gang is slowly closing in on them may be moved to violence by their irrational fears. Imagine that a stranger comes to the door to ask a paranoid person for directions. If the stranger has his hand in his coat pocket, he could become the target of a paranoid attempt at "self-defense."

Delusional disorders, fortunately, are rare. By far the most common form of psychosis is schizophrenia. Let's explore schizophrenia in more detail and see how it differs from a delusional disorder.

Schizophrenia—Shattered Reality

Learning Outcome 61.3 Outline the specific characteristics of schizophrenia and describe its causes

Do people with schizophrenia have two personalities? No. How many times have you heard people say something like, "Laurence was so warm and friendly yesterday, but today he's as cold as ice. He's so schizophrenic that I don't know how to react." Such statements show how often the term *schizophrenic* is misused. As we will see in Module 63, a person who displays two or more *integrated* personalities has a dissociative disorder and is *not* schizophrenic. Neither, of course, is a person like Laurence, whose behavior is merely inconsistent.

Symptoms of Schizophrenia

In any given year, one person in 100 has **schizophrenia** (SKIT-soh-FREN-ee-uh), a disorder characterized by disturbances in thought, perceptions, emotions, and behavior (National Institute of Mental Health, 2017). In schizophrenia, these disturbances are so severe that a person's thoughts, actions, and emotions are no longer coordinated, resulting in *personality disintegration* along with a consequent break with reality.

Disturbed Thinking Many schizophrenic symptoms appear to be related to problems with *selective attention*. In other words, it is hard for people with schizophrenia to focus on one item of information at a time. Having an impaired "sensory filter" in their brains may be why they are overwhelmed by a jumble of thoughts, sensations, images, and feelings (Cellard et al., 2010; Heinrichs, 2001).

Positive symptoms such as delusions also frequently occur in schizophrenia. Paranoid delusions are especially common. As in paranoid delusional disorders, **paranoia** in schizophrenia centers on delusions of grandeur and persecution. However, schizophrenics with paranoia also hallucinate, and their delusions are generally more bizarre and unconvincing than those in a delusional disorder (Corcoran, 2010; Freeman & Garety, 2004). Schizophrenic delusions may include the idea that the person's thoughts and actions are being controlled, that thoughts are being broadcast (so others can hear them), that thoughts have been "inserted"

Schizophrenia spectrum and other psychotic disorders Severe mental disorders characterized by delusions, hallucinations, disturbed thought and/or speech, disturbed motor behavior, and/or retreat from reality.

Delusional disorder A psychosis marked by severe delusions of grandeur, jealousy, persecution, or similar preoccupations.

Paranoid psychosis A delusional disorder centered especially on delusions of persecution.

Schizophrenia Severe disorder characterized by disturbances in thought, perceptions, emotions, and behavior.

Paranoia A symptom marked by a preoccupation with delusions related to a single theme, especially grandeur or persecution.

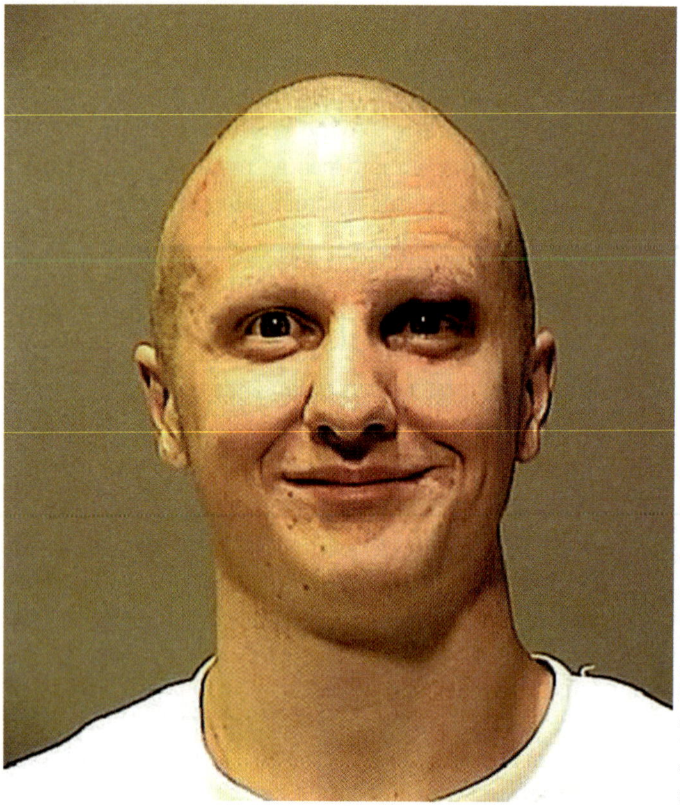

In 2011, Jared Lee Loughner went on a shooting rampage in Tucson, Arizona, severely injuring his intended target, US Representative Gabrielle Giffords. Of the other 18 people he shot, 12 died of their wounds. Diagnosed with paranoid schizophrenia, he was nevertheless found competent to stand trial. He was convicted and sentenced to life in prison.

into the person's mind, or that thoughts have been removed. Schizophrenics whose predominant symptom is paranoia are sometimes referred to as *paranoid schizophrenics*.

Disturbed Perception Another positive symptom, hallucinations, is also characteristic of schizophrenia. While the most common *hallucinations* center on hearing voices, psychotic people may feel "insects crawling under their skin," taste "poisons" in their food, or smell "gas" that their "enemies" are using to "get" them. Sensory changes, such as anesthesia (numbness, or a loss of sensation) or extreme sensitivity to heat, cold, pain, or touch also can occur.

Unfortunately, thinking that God, the government, or "cosmic rays from space" are controlling their minds, or that someone is trying to poison them, people suffering from paranoid schizophrenia may feel forced to commit violence to "protect" themselves. An example is James Huberty, who in 1984 brutally murdered 21 people at a McDonald's restaurant in San Ysidro, California. Huberty, who had paranoid schizophrenia, felt persecuted and cheated by life. Shortly before he announced to his wife that he was "going hunting humans," Huberty had been hearing *command hallucinations* (Birchwood et al., 2014).

How dangerous are the mentally ill? Horrific crimes, such as the San Ysidro murders, publicized by sensationalized media reports, lead many people to believe that the mentally ill are dangerous. Unfortunately, there is an element of truth to this belief (Markowitz, 2011; Walters, 2011). At the same time, the pattern of results is more complex than such a simple generalization suggests. For example, according to one large study, mentally ill individuals who are substance abusers *are* more prone to violence than normal individuals. What can be lost when reading the previous sentence is that most mentally ill individuals are not substance abusers and are not more prone to violence than normal individuals (Monahan et al., 2001). Similarly, while people with psychotic disorders are more prone to violence, it is usually only when they are *actively psychotic* and *currently* experiencing psychotic symptoms (Douglas, Guy, & Hart, 2009).

In fact, the risk of violence from mental patients is many times lower than that from persons who have the following attributes: young, male, poor, and intoxicated (Corrigan & Watson, 2005). It is also worth noting that the mentally ill are more often the victims of violence than are normal individuals; this is particularly true of mentally ill homeless individuals (Markowitz, 2011).

Disturbed Emotions During a psychotic episode, the emotions of a person with schizophrenia may also become very inappropriate or blunted. For instance, if a person with schizophrenia is told his mother just died, he may smile, giggle, or become wildly elated or hyperemotional. But sometimes psychotic patients may be depressed or apathetic, displaying no emotion at all (the negative symptom of *flat affect*).

Disturbed Behavior Schizophrenia also often involves withdrawal from contact with others, apathy, loss of interest in external activities, a breakdown of personal habits, and an inability to deal with daily events (Neufeld et al., 2003; Ziv, Leiser, & Levine, 2011).

Schizophrenics sometimes display **catatonia**, remaining *mute* (not speaking) while holding odd postures for hours or even days at a time (Tandon et al., 2013). These periods of stupor may be similar to the tendency to "freeze" at times of great emergency or panic. Catatonic individuals appear to be struggling desperately to control their inner turmoil (Fink, 2013). One sign of this is the fact that stupor may occasionally give way to agitated outbursts or violent behavior. As you might imagine, catatonic patients

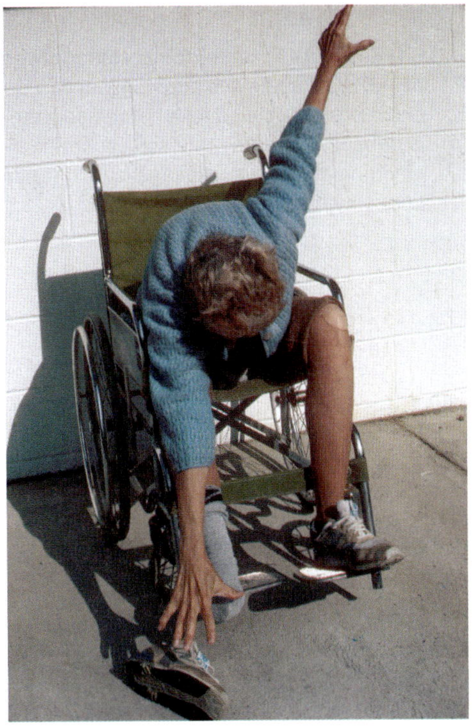

Catatonia, with its rigid postures and stupor, is recognized by the *DSM-5* as a disorder of its own. It also can occur along with schizophrenia, bipolar disorder, depression, and several other conditions, including drug abuse (Tandon et al., 2013).

are difficult to "reach." Schizophrenics whose predominant symptom is catatonia are sometimes referred to as *catatonic schizophrenics*.

Disorganized Schizophrenia Not all of these symptoms are equally prominent in every schizophrenic. Similarly, the different symptoms in any individual can become more or less prominent over time. For these reasons, the various manifestations of schizophrenia are referred to as *schizophrenia spectrum disorders* (American Psychiatric Association, 2013). However, when a person's personality disintegration is almost complete and thinking, perception, feeling, and behavior are *all* highly disorganized, the result comes close to matching the stereotyped images of "madness" seen in movies. Such schizophrenics are sometimes referred to as *disorganized* or *hebephrenic*.

We started this section with an interview with Edna, who was diagnosed as a disorganized schizophrenic. After admission to a mental hospital, Edna was placed in the women's ward where she proceeded to masturbate. Occasionally, she would scream or shout obscenities. At other times, she giggled to herself. She was known to attack other patients. She began to complain that her uterus was attached to Moscow, Russia, by a pipeline that communists were using to invade (Suinn, 1975).

Such extreme schizophrenia typically develops in adolescence or young adulthood. As with most disorganized schizophrenics, Edna's chances of improvement are limited, and her social impairment is extreme (American Psychiatric Association, 2013).

Causes of Schizophrenia

An increased risk of developing schizophrenia may begin at birth or even before. Women who are exposed to the influenza (flu) virus or to rubella (German measles) during the middle of pregnancy have children who are more likely to become schizophrenic (Barlow, Durand, & Hofmann, 2021; Vuillermot et al., 2010). Malnutrition during pregnancy and complications at the time of birth can have a similar impact. Such events likely disturb brain development, leaving people more vulnerable to a psychotic break with reality (Walker et al., 2004).

Psychosocial Factors in Schizophrenia *What about psychosocial factors?* Often the victims of schizophrenia were exposed to a psychological trauma, such as sexual abuse, death, divorce, separation, or other stresses in childhood (Walker et al., 2004). Living in a troubled family is a related risk factor. In a disturbed family setting, stressful relationships, communication patterns, and negative emotions prevail. Deviant communication patterns cause anxiety, confusion, anger, conflict, and turmoil. Typically, disturbed families interact in ways that are laden with guilt, prying, criticism, negativity, and emotional attacks (Bressi, Albonetti, & Razzoli, 1998; Davison & Neale, 2006).

Although they are attractive, psychosocial explanations alone are not enough to account for schizophrenia. For example, when the children of schizophrenic parents are raised away from their chaotic homes, they still are more likely to become psychotic (Walker et al., 2004).

Heredity and Schizophrenia *Does that mean that heredity affects the risk of developing schizophrenia?* There is now little doubt that heredity is a factor in schizophrenia (Gejman, Sanders, & Duan, 2010). It appears that some individuals inherit a *potential* for developing schizophrenia. They are, in other words, more *vulnerable* to the disorder (Levy et al., 2010; Walker et al., 2004).

How has that been shown? If one identical twin becomes schizophrenic (remember, identical twins have identical genes), then the other twin has a *48 percent* chance of

Catatonia A disorder marked by stupor, rigidity, unresponsiveness, posturing, mutism, and sometimes agitated, purposeless behavior.

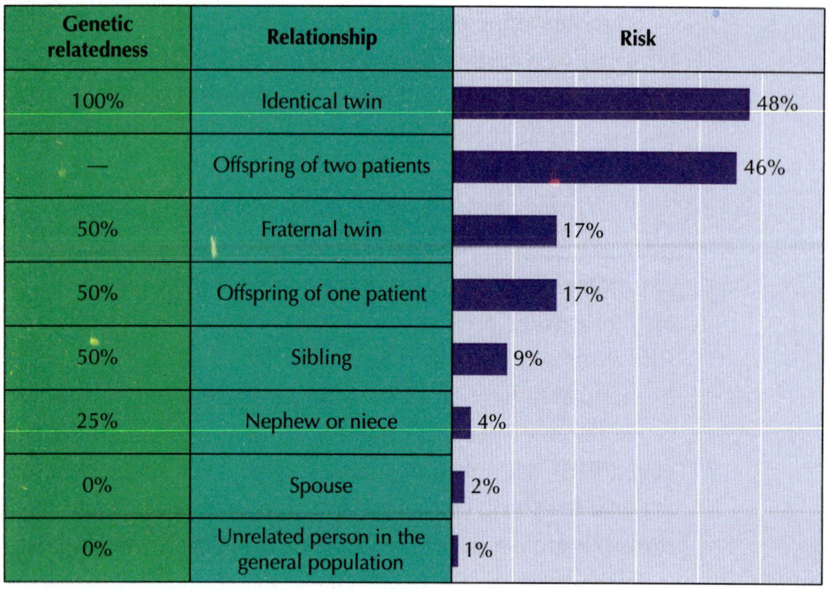

➤ Figure 61.1

Lifetime risk of developing schizophrenia. The risk of developing schizophrenia over a person's lifetime is associated with how closely the person is genetically related to a schizophrenic. A shared environment also increases the risk. (Estimates from Lenzenweger & Gottesman, 1994.)

also becoming schizophrenic (Insel, 2010; Lenzenweger & Gottesman, 1994). The figure for twins can be compared with the risk of schizophrenia for the population in general, which is 1 percent. (See ➤ **Figure 61.1** for other relationships.) In general, schizophrenia is clearly more common among close relatives and tends to run in families. There's even a case on record of *four* identical quadruplets *all* developing schizophrenia (Mirsky et al., 2000). In light of such evidence, researchers are beginning to search for specific genes related to schizophrenia (Curtis et al., 2011; Schwab & Wildenauer, 2013).

A problem exists with current genetic explanations of schizophrenia: Very few people with schizophrenia have children (Bundy, Stahl, & MacCabe, 2011). How could a genetic defect be passed from one generation to the next if afflicted people don't reproduce? One possibility is suggested by the fact that the older a man is (even if he doesn't suffer from schizophrenia) when he fathers a child, the more likely it is that the child will develop schizophrenia (Helenius, Munk-Jørgensen, & Steinhausen, 2012). Apparently, genetic mutations occur in aging male reproductive cells and increase the risk of disturbed brain development, leading to schizophrenia (as well as other medical problems) (Sipos et al., 2004).

Neurotransmitters and Schizophrenia One way that disturbed brain development might result in a vulnerability to schizophrenia is by damaging normal neurotransmitter functions. For example, drugs such as amphetamine and lysergic acid diethylamide (LSD) produce effects that partially mimic the symptoms of schizophrenia. Also, the same drugs (phenothiazines) used to treat LSD overdoses tend to alleviate psychotic symptoms. Observations such as these suggest that schizophrenic people may be on a sort of drug trip caused by their own brains.

One likely candidate is *dopamine* (DOPE-ah-meen), an important neurotransmitter naturally found in the brain (➤ **Figure 61.2**). In schizophrenia, dopamine receptors in one part of the brain appear to become super-responsive to normal amounts of dopamine, triggering a flood of

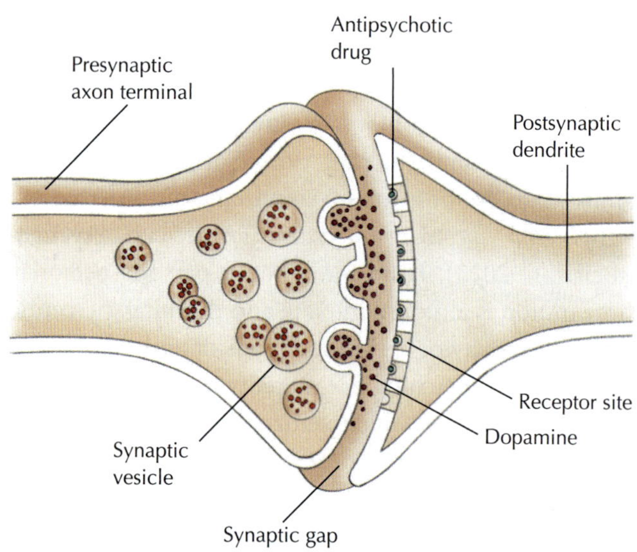

➤ Figure 61.2

Dopamine and schizophrenia. Dopamine normally crosses the synapse between two neurons, activating the second cell. Antipsychotic drugs bind to the same receptor sites as does dopamine, blocking its action. In people suffering from schizophrenia, a reduction in dopamine activity can quiet a person's agitation and psychotic symptoms.

unrelated thoughts, feelings, and perceptions, which may account for the positive symptoms (voices, hallucinations, and delusions) of schizophrenia (Citrome, 2011; Madras, 2013).

The neurotransmitter glutamate also appears to be related to schizophrenia. People who take the hallucinogenic drug phencyclidine (PCP, or angel dust) have symptoms that closely mimic schizophrenia (Javitt et al., 2012). This occurs because PCP affects *glutamate*, another neurotransmitter that influences brain activity in areas that control emotions, cognition, and sensory information (Citrome, 2011; Volk et al., 2015). Another tantalizing connection is the fact that stress alters glutamate levels, which in turn alters dopamine systems (Holloway et al., 2013; Moghaddam, 2002).

The story is far from complete, but it appears that abnormalities in dopamine, glutamate, and other neurotransmitters partly explain the devastating symptoms of schizophrenia (Walker et al., 2004).

The Brain and Schizophrenia Another way that disturbed brain development might result in a brain-based vulnerability to schizophrenia is by disrupting overall brain structure and/or function. For example, structural brain imaging methods have revealed that the brains of schizophrenics are shrunk, or atrophied (Bora et al., 2011; see Module 8). ➤ **Figure 61.3** shows a computed tomography (CT) scan of the brain of John Hinckley, Jr., who shot President Ronald Reagan and three other men in 1981. In the ensuing trial, Hinckley was declared insane. As you can see, his brain had wider than normal surface fissuring. Similarly, magnetic resonance imaging (MRI) scans indicate that schizophrenic people tend to have enlarged ventricles (fluid-filled spaces within the brain), again suggesting that surrounding brain tissue has withered (Andreasen et al., 2011; Barkataki et al., 2006).

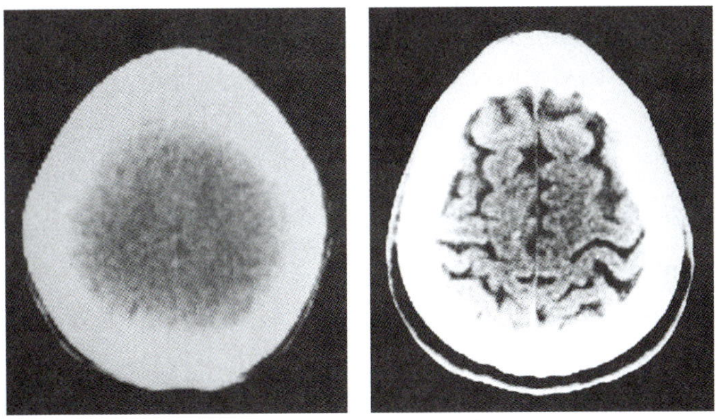

Dennis Brack/Black Star

➤ **Figure 61.3**

Brain fissures and schizophrenia. *(Left)* A CT scan of a normal 25-year-old's brain. In most young adults, the surface folds of the brain are pressed together too tightly to be seen. *(Right)* A CT scan of would-be presidential assassin John Hinckley, Jr., taken when he was 25. The image shows widened fissures in the wrinkled surface of Hinckley's brain. As a person ages, the surface folds of the brain normally become more visible. Pronounced brain fissuring in young adults may be a sign of schizophrenia, chronic alcoholism, or other problems.

One possible explanation is that the schizophrenic brain may be unable to continually create new neurons to replace old ones that have died. In contrast, normal brains continue to produce new neurons throughout life (a process referred to as neurogenesis; see Module 7). It is telling that the affected areas are crucial for regulating motivation, emotion, perception, actions, and attention (DeCarolis & Eisch, 2010; Inta, Meyer-Lindenberg, & Gass, 2011; Kawada et al., 2009).

Other methods provide images of brain activity, including positron emission tomography (PET) scans. To make a PET scan, a radioactive sugar solution is injected into a vein. When the sugar reaches the brain, an electronic device measures how much is used in each area. These data are then translated into a color map, or scan, of brain activity (➤ **Figure 61.4**). Researchers are finding patterns in such scans that are consistently linked with schizophrenia, affective disorders, and other problems. For instance, activity tends to be abnormally low in the frontal lobes of the schizophrenic brain (Barlow, Durand, & Hofmann, 2021; Roffman et al., 2011). In the future, PET scans may be used to accurately diagnose schizophrenia. For now, such scans show that there is a clear abnormality in schizophrenic brain activity.

The Stress-Vulnerability Model

Most psychologists today accept that the *stress-vulnerability model* (see Module 60) best fits our current understanding of psychotic disorders such as schizophrenia. It takes this form: Anyone subjected to enough stress may be pushed to a psychotic break. (*Battlefield psychosis* is an example of such a phenomenon.) However, some people inherit a difference in brain chemistry or brain structure/function that makes them more susceptible to developing psychotic disorders, even when experiencing normal life stresses. Thus, the right mix of environmental stress and inherited potential brings about mind-altering changes in the brain (Pruessner et al., 2017; Walker et al., 2004).

Despite advances in our understanding, psychosis remains a mystery. Let's hope that recent progress toward a cure for schizophrenia will continue.

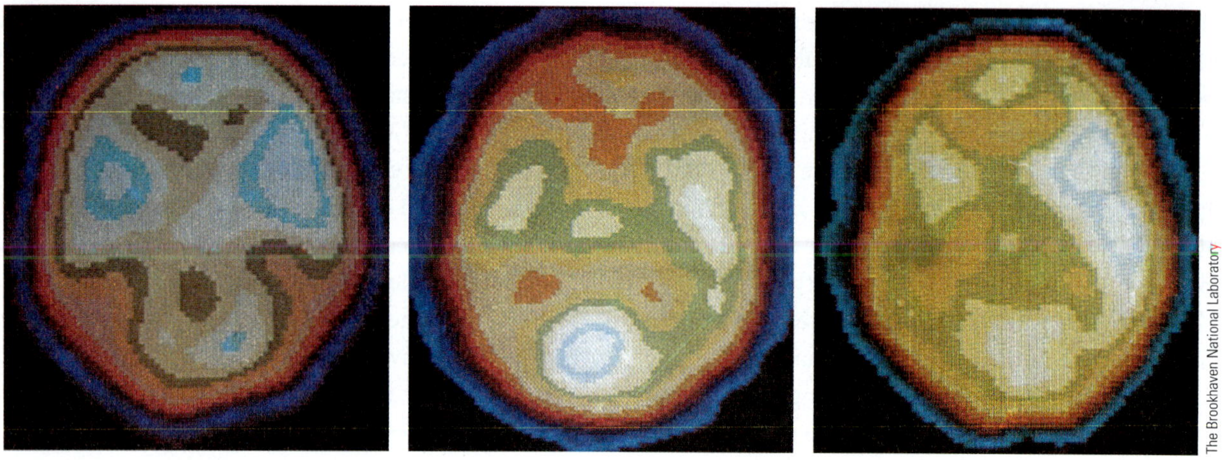

Figure 61.4

Patterns of activity in normal and abnormal brains. In the PET scans of the human brain shown here, red, pink, and orange indicate lower levels of brain activity; white and blue indicate higher activity levels. Notice that activity in the schizophrenic brain is quite low in the frontal lobes (top area of each scan; Velakoulis & Pantelis, 1996). Activity in the manic-depressive brain is low in the left-brain hemisphere and high in the right-brain hemisphere. The reverse is more often true of the schizophrenic brain. Researchers are trying to identify consistent patterns like these to aid the diagnosis of mental disorders.

MODULE 61 Psychotic Disorders—Learning Outcomes Revisited

61.1 Describe the general characteristics of psychotic disorders

Psychosis is a break in contact with reality that is marked by delusions, hallucinations, sensory changes, disturbed emotions, disturbed communication, and personality disintegration.

61.2 Outline the specific characteristics of delusional disorders

Delusional disorders are almost totally based on the presence of deeply held false beliefs of grandeur, persecution, infidelity, romantic attraction, or physical disease. Paranoid psychosis is the most common delusional disorder. Paranoid persons may be violent if they believe that they are threatened.

61.3 Outline the specific characteristics of schizophrenia and describe its causes

Schizophrenia spectrum disorder involves varying degrees of abnormal cognition (delusions, paranoia), perceptions (hallucinations), abnormal mood (flat or inappropriate affect), abnormal behavior (inability to cope, catatonia), and a disintegrated personality.

Environmental factors that increase the risk for schizophrenia include viral infection or malnutrition during the mother's pregnancy and birth complications. Psychosocial factors include early psychological trauma and a disturbed family environment. Heredity is a major factor in schizophrenia. Recent biochemical studies have focused on the neurotransmitters glutamate and dopamine and their receptor sites. The stress-vulnerability model currently offers the best general explanation for schizophrenia.

Reflective Practice

Content Check

1. People are said to have "retreated from reality" when they suffer from ________________.
   - **a.** psychotic disorders
   - **b.** schizophrenia
   - **c.** delusional disorder
   - **d.** all of the above
2. Angela wrongly believes that her body is "rotting away." She is suffering from ______________.
   - **a.** depressive hallucinations
   - **b.** a delusion
   - **c.** flat affect
   - **d.** Alzheimer's disease

3. Colin, who has suffered a psychotic break, is hearing voices. This symptom is referred to as ____________.
   a. flat affect
   b. a hallucination
   c. a word salad
   d. an organic delusion
4. Hallucinations and personality disintegration are principal features of schizophrenia. T or F?
5. Psychosocial explanations of schizophrenia emphasize emotional trauma and
   a. manic parents
   b. schizoaffective interactions
   c. psychedelic interactions
   d. disturbed family relationships
6. Biochemical explanations of schizophrenia have focused on disturbed functioning of ______________ in the brain.
   a. radioactive sugar
   b. webs and tangles
   c. PCP
   d. dopamine and glutamate

Skill Check

Think Critically

7. Enlarged surface fissures and ventricles are frequently found in the brains of chronic schizophrenics. Why is it a mistake to conclude that such features cause schizophrenia?

Self-Reflect

If you were asked to play the role of a paranoid person for a theater production, what symptoms would you emphasize? You have been asked to explain the causes of schizophrenia to the parents of a schizophrenic teenager. What would you tell them?

ANSWERS

1. d 2. b 3. b 4. T 5. d 6. d 7. Correlation does not confirm causation. Structural brain abnormalities are merely *correlated* with schizophrenia. They could be additional symptoms, rather than causes, of the disorder.

MODULE
62

Psychological Disorders
Mood Disorders

Mood Swings

Eakachai Leesin/Shutterstock.com

For some people, minor bouts of depression are as common as colds. But extreme swings of mood can be as disabling as a serious physical illness. In fact, depression can be deadly because depressed persons may be suicidal. It is difficult to imagine how bleak and hopeless the world looks to a person who is deeply depressed.

By the same token, it can be "crazy" to ride a wave of true mania. Manic patients may go bankrupt in a matter of days, get arrested, or go on a binge of promiscuous sex and then have to deal with the consequences of their actions. In the most severe cases of depression and mania, the person may even lose touch with reality and display psychotic symptoms.

Unfortunately, mood disorders have resisted adequate explanation and treatment. Nevertheless, scientific progress continues to be made, so let's explore mood disorders and their causes.

~LEARNING OUTCOMES~

After reading this module you should be able to:

62.1 Describe the general characteristics of mood disorders, the specific characteristics of depression and bipolar disorders, and the causes of mood disorders, including their risk factors

62.2 Explain why people commit suicide

Mood Disorders—Peaks and Valleys

Learning Outcome 62.1 Describe the general characteristics of mood disorders, the specific characteristics of depression and bipolar disorders, and the causes of mood disorders, including their risk factors

Psychologists have come to realize that *mood disorders*—the presence of unusual disturbances in the emotions—are among the most serious of all psychological conditions. In any given year, roughly 9.9 percent of the US population suffers from a mood disorder (National Institute of Mental Health, 2018). Two general types of mood disorder are *depressive disorders* and *bipolar disorders* (see ■ **Table 62.1**).

Depressive Disorders

In **depressive disorders**, sadness and despondency are exaggerated, prolonged, or unreasonable. Signs of a depressive disorder are dejection, hopelessness, and an inability to feel pleasure or to take interest in anything. Other common symptoms are fatigue, disturbed sleep and eating patterns, feelings of worthlessness, a very negative self-image, and thoughts of suicide.

Some depressive disorders are long-lasting but relatively moderate. If a person is mildly depressed for at least two years, the problem is called a **persistent depressive disorder (dysthymia)** (dis-THY-mee-ah). Even at this level,

TABLE 62.1 | *DSM-5* Classification of Mood Disorders

Problem	Typical Signs of Trouble
Depressive Disorders	
Persistent depressive disorder (dysthymia)	You feel down and depressed more days than not; your self-esteem and energy levels have been low for many months.
Major depressive disorder	You feel extremely sad, worthless, fatigued, and empty; you are unable to feel pleasure; you are having thoughts of suicide.
Bipolar and Related Disorders	
Cyclothymic disorder	You have been experiencing upsetting emotional ups and downs for many months.
Bipolar I disorder	At times, you have little need for sleep, you can't stop talking, your mind races, and everything you do is of immense importance; at other times, you feel extremely sad, worthless, and empty.
Bipolar II disorder	Most of the time, you feel extremely sad, worthless, fatigued, and empty; however, at times, you feel unusually good, cheerful, energetic, or "high."

Sources: American Psychiatric Association, 2013; Durand & Barlow, 2019; Sue et al., 2017.

depressive disorders can be debilitating. However, major depressions are much more damaging.

In a **major depressive disorder**, the depression is much deeper. Everything looks bleak and hopeless. The person has feelings of failure, worthlessness, and total despair. In serious cases of depression, it is impossible for a person to function at work or at school. Sometimes, depressed individuals cannot even feed or dress themselves. The suffering is intense, and the person may become extremely subdued, withdrawn, or intensely suicidal. Suicide attempted during the depths of a major depression is rarely a "cry for help." Usually, the person intends to succeed and may give no prior warning.

Bipolar and Related Disorders

When depression alternates with periods of *mania*, one of the **bipolar and related disorders** is involved (American Psychiatric Association, 2016; Ellison-Wright & Bullmore, 2010). During a **manic episode**, the person is loud, elated, hyperactive, grandiose, and agitated.

A long-lasting but relatively moderate alternation between depression and mania is a **cyclothymic disorder** (SIKE-lo-THY-mik). Like depressive disorders, however, major bipolar disorders are much more severe. In a **bipolar I disorder**, people experience both extreme mania and deep depression. During periods of depression, the person is deeply despondent and possibly suicidal.

In a **bipolar II disorder**, the person is mostly sad and guilt ridden but has had one or more mildly manic episodes (called *hypomania*). That is, in a bipolar II disorder, both mania and depression occur, but the person's mania is not as extreme as in a bipolar I disorder. Bipolar II patients who are hypomanic usually just manage to irritate everyone around them. They are excessively cheerful, aggressive, or irritable, and they may brag, talk too fast, interrupt conversations, or spend too much money (Nolen-Hoeksema, 2020).

Causes of Mood Disorders

Some scientists are focusing on the biology of mood changes. They are interested in disturbed transmitter function, especially *serotonin*, *noradrenaline*, and *dopamine* levels.

Depressive disorders Class of disorders marked by chronic feelings of sadness and despondency.

Persistent depressive disorder (dysthymia) Moderate depression that persists for two years or more.

Major depressive disorder Mood disorder in which the person has suffered one or more intense episodes of depression.

Bipolar and related disorders Mood disorders characterized by alternating periods of mania and depression.

Manic episode Period of abnormally excessive energy and elation.

Cyclothymic disorder Moderate manic and depressive behavior that persists for two years or more.

Bipolar I disorder A mood disorder in which a person has episodes of mania (excited, hyperactive, energetic, or grandiose behavior) and also periods of deep depression.

Bipolar II disorder A mood disorder in which a person is mostly depressed (sad, despondent, guilt-ridden) but also has had one or more episodes of mild mania (hypomania).

The findings are incomplete, but progress has been made. For example, the chemical lithium carbonate can be effective for treating some cases of bipolar depression (Malhi & Outhred, 2016).

Other researchers seek psychological explanations. Psychoanalytic theory, for instance, holds that depression is caused by repressed anger turned inward as self-blame and self-hate. As discussed in Module 57, behavioral theories of depression emphasize learned helplessness (Durand & Barlow, 2019; Reivich et al., 2013). Cognitive psychologists believe that self-criticism and negative, distorted, or self-defeating thoughts underlie many cases of depression. (This view is discussed in Module 66.)

Clearly, life stresses trigger many mood disorders (Calabrese et al., 2009). This is especially true for people who have personality traits and thinking patterns that make them vulnerable to depression (Weber et al., 2012).

Gender and Depression Overall, women are about twice as likely as men to experience depression (Kuehner, 2017). Hormonal fluctuations likely play a role in cases of depression involving pregnancy, menstruation, and menopause (Lokuge et al., 2011). Nevertheless, researchers believe that social and environmental conditions are the main reason for this difference (Jack & Ali, 2010; McGuinness, Dyer, & Wade, 2012).

Psychosocial factors that contribute to women's greater risk for depression include conflicts about birth control and pregnancy, work and parenting, and the strain of providing emotional support for others. Marital strife, sexual and physical abuse, and poverty also are factors. Nationwide, women and children are most likely to live in poverty. As a result, poor women frequently suffer the stresses associated with single parenthood, loss of control over their lives, poor housing, and dangerous neighborhoods (Estefan, Coulter, & VandeWeerd, 2016; Grant et al., 2011; Stoppard & McMullen, 2003).

Postpartum Depression One source of women's depression is fairly easy to identify. After pregnancy and childbirth, many women face an elevated risk of becoming depressed (Phillips et al., 2010). An estimated 25 to 50 percent of women experience *maternity blues,* a mild depression that usually lasts from one to two days after childbirth. For most women, brief, mild bouts of crying, fitful sleep, tension, anger, and/or irritability are a normal part of adjusting to childbirth.

For some women, maternity blues can be the beginning of a persistent depressive disorder or even major depressive disorder. Roughly 13 percent of all women who give birth develop **postpartum depression**, a moderately severe depression that begins within three months following childbirth. Typical signs of postpartum depression are mood swings, despondency, feelings of inadequacy, an inability to cope with the new baby, and an increased risk of self-harm (Healey et al., 2013; National Institute of Mental Health, 2020). Unlike other types of depression, postpartum depression also features unusually high levels of restlessness and difficulty concentrating (Bernstein et al., 2008). Depression of this kind may last anywhere from two months to about a year. Women are not the only ones to suffer when postpartum depression strikes. A depressed mother can seriously affect her child's development (Cooper & Murray, 2001; Tikotzky et al., 2012).

Stress and anxiety before birth and negative attitudes toward child-rearing increase the risk of postpartum depression (Phillips et al., 2010; Yim, 2015). A troubled marriage and lack of support from the father also are danger signs. Part of the problem may be hormonal: After a woman gives birth, her estrogen levels can drop, altering her mood (Fernandez, Grizzell, & Wecker, 2013). Educating new parents about the importance of supporting one another may reduce the risk of depression. Groups where new mothers can discuss their feelings also are helpful. If depression is severe or long-lasting, new mothers should seek professional help.

Biology and Depression *Is heredity involved in major mood disorders?* Yes, especially in bipolar disorders (Ciobanu et al., 2016; Curtis et al., 2011). As a case in point, if one identical twin is depressed, the other has a 67 percent chance of suffering depression, too. For fraternal twins, the probability is 19 percent. This difference may be related to the finding that people who have a particular version of a gene are more likely to become depressed when they are stressed (Halmai et al., 2013). As we have noted, psychological causes are important in many cases of depression. But for major mood disorders, biological factors seem to play a larger role. Surprisingly, one additional source of depression is related to the seasons.

Seasonal Affective Disorder (SAD) Unless you have experienced "cabin fever" in the far north in the winter, you may be surprised to learn that the rhythms of the seasons underlie **seasonal affective disorder (SAD)**, or depression that occurs only during the fall and winter months (now known as *major depressive disorder with seasonal pattern*). Almost anyone can get a little depressed when days are short, dark, and cold. But when a person's symptoms are lasting and disabling, the problem may be SAD.

Starting in the fall, people with SAD sleep longer, but more poorly. During the day they feel tired and drowsy, and they tend to overeat. With each passing day, they become sadder, anxious, irritable, and socially withdrawn (Rosenthal, N. E., 2013). Although their depressions are usually not severe, many victims of SAD face each winter with a sense of foreboding. SAD is especially prevalent in northern latitudes (think of countries such as Sweden and Canada), where days are very short during the winter. For instance, 9 percent of those who live in Alaska experience SAD compared to 1 percent in Florida (Melrose, 2015).

Seasonal depressions are related to the release of more melatonin during the winter. This hormone, which is secreted by the pineal gland in the brain, regulates the body's response to changing light conditions (Delavest et al., 2012). That's why 80 percent of SAD patients can be helped by a remedy called **phototherapy**, which involves exposing SAD patients to one or more hours of very bright fluorescent light each day. This is best done early in the morning, where it simulates dawn in the summer (Rosenthal, 2013; Vandewalle et al., 2011). (In addition to its role in producing SAD, melatonin regulates normal circadian rhythms. See Module 42.)

Image Point Fr/Shutterstock.com

An hour or more of bright white or blue light a day can dramatically reduce the symptoms of SAD. Treatment is usually necessary from fall through spring. Light therapy is best done early in the morning, when it simulates dawn in the summer (Avery et al., 2001).

Suicide—Too Permanent a Solution?

Learning Outcome 62.2 Explain why people commit suicide

No discussion of depression would be complete without exploring suicide. Talk show host Phil Donahue once commented that "suicide is a permanent solution to a temporary problem." Why suicide? The best explanation may simply come from a look at the conditions that precede it.

Is it mostly depressed people who attempt suicide? A diagnosable mental disorder (usually depression or substance use disorder) is a factor in 90 percent of all suicides. However, the following are also risk factors: a prior suicide attempt; a family history of suicidal behavior; the availability of a firearm; feelings of hopelessness or worthlessness; antisocial, impulsive, or aggressive behavior; severe anxiety, panic attacks, shame, humiliation, failure, or rejection (Burón et al., 2016; Joiner, 2010; National Alliance on Mental Illness, 2019).

Anyone may temporarily reach a state of depression severe enough to impulsively attempt suicide. Most dangerous for the average person are times of divorce, separation, rejection, failure, and bereavement. Among ethnic adolescents, loss of face, acculturative stress, racism, and discrimination have been identified as additional risk factors (Goldston et al., 2008).

Such situations can seem intolerable and motivate an intense desire to escape, to obtain relief, or to die. Typically, suicidal people isolate themselves from others; feel worthless, helpless, and misunderstood; and want to die (Britton et al., 2008; Heisel, Flett, & Hewitt, 2003).

Factors Affecting Suicide Rates Suicide rates in the United States reveal some general patterns:

- **Sex.** Although four times as many men *complete* suicide, women make more attempts. While men typically use a gun or an equally fatal method, women most often attempt a drug overdose, so there's a better chance of help arriving before death occurs (Denney et al., 2009; National Institute of Mental Health, 2018).
- **Ethnicity.** Caucasians generally have higher suicide rates than non-Caucasians (National Institute of Mental Health, 2018). Sadly, the suicide rate among Native Americans is by far the highest in the country (Goldston et al., 2008).

Postpartum depression A mild to moderately severe depression that begins within three months following childbirth.

Seasonal affective disorder (SAD) Depression that occurs only during fall and winter; presumably related to decreased exposure to sunlight.

Phototherapy A treatment for SAD that involves exposure to bright, full-spectrum light.

➤ **Figure 62.1**

The slippery slope of suicide. Suicidal behavior usually progresses from suicidal thoughts, to threats, to attempts. A person is unlikely to make an attempt without first making threats. Thus, suicide threats should be taken seriously (Leenaars, Lester, & Wenckstern, 2005).

- **Age.** Although most suicide victims are white males over 45, suicide rates among younger people are of special concern. Suicide is the second-leading cause of death among 10- to 34-year-olds (National Institute of Mental Health, 2018). School is a factor in some youth suicides, as are illegal drug or alcohol use, chronic health problems, and interpersonal difficulties (Barlow, Durand, & Hofmann, 2021; Garlow, Purselle, & Heninger, 2007).
- **Marital status.** Married individuals have lower suicide rates than divorced, widowed, or single persons, at least among men (Denney et al., 2009).

Suicide Threats *Is it true that people who talk about or threaten suicide are rarely the ones who try it?* Actually, all suicide threats should be taken seriously. Eighty percent of potential suicides give warning beforehand (see ➤ **Figure 62.1**). Some warning signs, especially if they are observed in combination, are: direct threats to commit suicide, preoccupation with death, depression/hopelessness, rage/anger or seeking revenge, aggressive risk taking, alcohol/drug use, withdrawal from contact with others, no sense of purpose in life, sudden swings in mood, personality change, gift giving of prized possessions, and recent occurrence of a life crisis or an emotional shock (Centers for Disease Control, 2020g; Leenaars, Lester, & Wenckstern, 2005).

How to Help *What should I do if someone hints that he or she is thinking about suicide?* Suicidal persons often feel misunderstood. You should offer support, acceptance, and legitimate caring. Try to accept and understand the feelings the person is expressing. It is completely acceptable to ask, "Are you thinking of suicide?" Establishing communication with suicidal persons may be enough to carry them through a difficult time. You also may find it helpful to get day-by-day commitments from them to meet for lunch, share a ride, and the like. Such small commitments can be enough to tip the scales when a person is alone and thinking about suicide.

If a suicide attempt seems to be imminent, remember, most cities have mental health crisis intervention teams or centers for suicide prevention trained to talk with suicidal persons over the phone (Spencer-Thomas & Jahn, 2012). Give a person who seems to be suicidal the number of one of these services. Urge the person to call you or the other number if she or he becomes frightened or impulsive. Better yet, help the person make an appointment to get psychological treatment (Kleiman, Miller, & Riskind, 2012; Weishaar, 2006). If the person shares a *specific, workable plan*, and the means to carry it out, you should accompany that person to the emergency ward of a hospital.

Needless to say, you should call for the police or a rescue unit immediately if a person is in the act of attempting suicide or if a drug has already been taken. The majority of suicide attempts come at temporary low points in a person's life and may never be repeated. Get involved—you may save a life!

MODULE 62 Mood Disorders—Learning Outcomes Revisited

62.1 Describe the general characteristics of mood disorders, the specific characteristics of depression and bipolar disorders, and the causes of mood disorders, including their risk factors

Mood disorders primarily involve disturbances of mood or emotion, producing manic or depressive states. Severe mood disorders may include psychotic features. In a persistent depressive disorder (dysthymia), depression is long-lasting but moderate. In contrast, major depressive disorder involves extreme sadness and despondency. Bipolar disorders combine mania and depression. In a cyclothymic disorder, people suffer from long-lasting, though moderate, swings between depression and elation. In a bipolar I disorder, the person fluctuates between severe mania and severe depression. In a bipolar II disorder, the person is mostly depressed but has had periods of mild mania. Mood disorders are partially explained by genetic vulnerability and changes in brain chemistry. Mood disorders also are partially explained by psychological factors such as loss, anger, learned helplessness, stress, and self-defeating thinking patterns. Gender is one important risk factor. Women are more likely than men to become depressed owing to hormonal fluctuations and stressful social and environmental conditions (including childbirth, which can lead to postpartum depression). Another risk factor is time of year. Seasonal affective disorder (SAD), which occurs during the winter months, is another common form of depression. SAD is typically treated with phototherapy.

62.2 Explain why people commit suicide

In individual cases, the potential for suicide is best identified by a desire to escape, unbearable psychological pain, and frustrated psychological needs. Suicide is statistically related to such factors as sex, ethnicity, age, and marital status.

Reflective Practice

Content Check

1. Dysthymic disorder is to depression as cyclothymic disorder is to bipolar disorder. T or F?
2. Learned helplessness is emphasized by ____________ theories of depression.
   a. humanistic
   b. biological
   c. behaviorist
   d. psychoanalytic
3. The drug lithium carbonate has been shown to be an effective treatment for anxiety disorders. T or F?
4. The *maternity blues* and *postpartum depression* are the same thing. T or F?
5. The risk that a person may attempt suicide is greatest if the person has
   a. a concrete, workable plan
   b. had a recent life crisis
   c. withdrawn from contact with others
   d. frustrated psychological needs

Skill Check

Think Critically

6. How might relationships contribute to the higher rates of depression experienced by women?

Self-Reflect

Have you ever suffered a bout of the "blues" or got "on a roll"? What is the difference between normal mood swings and a mood disorder? You're working a suicide hotline, and you take a call from a very distressed young man. What risk factors will you look for as he tells you about his anguish?

ANSWERS

1. T 2. c 3. F 4. F 5. a 6. Women tend to be more focused on relationships than men are. When listing the stresses in their lives, depressed women consistently report higher rates of relationship problems, such as loss of a friend, spouse, or lover; problems getting along with others; and illnesses suffered by people they care about. Depressed men tend to mention issues such as job loss, legal problems, and work problems (Cambron, Acitelli, & Pettit, 2009).

MODULE 63

Psychological Disorders

Anxiety, Anxiety-Related, and Personality Disorders

High Anxiety

Imagine that you are waiting to find out whether you have a serious illness. It would be quite normal for you to experience some fear or *anxiety*—feelings of apprehension, dread, or uneasiness. However, people who suffer from extreme anxiety are miserable most of the time, and their behavior can become distorted and self-defeating.

Anxiety can arise in many ways. It can be generalized and unrelated to any particular life stressor. It may also be triggered by specific events, such as the annual US tornado season, which upsets many lives. In the aftermath of such disasters, many survivors suffer from stress reactions that can affect them for years. In this module, we begin by discussing anxiety and anxiety-related disorders and why they occur.

You probably know someone whose personality characteristics make life difficult for her or him. Imagine that person's traits becoming more extreme. If they did, the person would have a personality disorder, our final topic in this module.

Anton Oparin/Alamy Stock Photo

~LEARNING OUTCOMES~

After reading this module you should be able to:

63.1 Describe the general characteristics of anxiety disorders and explain how psychological theories account for those disorders

63.2 Name and briefly describe some important anxiety-related disorders

63.3 Describe the general characteristics of personality disorders, and the specific features of antisocial personality disorder

Anxiety Disorders—When Anxiety Rules

Learning Outcome 63.1 Describe the general characteristics of anxiety disorders and explain how psychological theories account for those disorders

If anxiety is a normal emotion, when does it signify a problem? Anxiety becomes a problem when it becomes so intense that it prevents people from doing what they want or need to do. Usually their anxieties are out of control—they simply cannot stop worrying. People with anxiety disorders feel threatened and don't know what to do about it. They struggle to control themselves but remain ineffective and unhappy (Cisler et al., 2010; Sheppes, Suri, & Gross, 2015).

An example is a college student named Jian, who became unbearably anxious when he took exams. By the time Jian went to see a counselor, he had skipped several tests and was in danger of flunking out of school. In general, people with anxiety problems like Jian's display the following characteristics:

- High levels of anxiety, restrictive, self-defeating behavior patterns, or both
- A tendency to use elaborate defense mechanisms or avoidance responses to get through the day. (Excessive use of psychological defense mechanisms is a feature of many anxiety disorders. See Module 57)
- Pervasive feelings of stress, insecurity, inferiority, and dissatisfaction with life

Some Anxiety Disorders

Particular **anxiety disorders** involve feelings of *panic*. Others take the form of *phobias* (irrational fears) or just overwhelming anxiety and nervousness. In most *anxiety disorders*, distress seems greatly out of proportion to a person's circumstances. For example, consider the following description of Adrian H:

> She becomes very anxious that her children "might have been hurt or killed if they were out of the neighborhood playing and she hadn't heard from them in a couple of hours." She also worries all the time about her job performance and her relationships with men. Adrian believes that men rarely call back after a date or two because "they can sense I'm not a fun person." She never really relaxes, has difficulty focusing at work, has frequent headaches, and suffers from insomnia. (Adapted from Brown & Barlow, 2017.)

Distress like Adrian H's is a key ingredient of the anxiety disorders. In any given year, roughly 19 percent of the adult population suffers from an anxiety disorder (National Institute of Mental Health, 2018). To deepen your understanding, let's directly examine the anxiety disorders (■ **Table 63.1**).

Generalized Anxiety Disorder

A person with a **generalized anxiety disorder** experiences nearly constant, exaggerated worries. He or she has been extremely anxious and worried for at least six months. Sufferers typically complain of sweating, a racing heart, clammy hands, dizziness, upset stomach, rapid breathing, irritability, and poor concentration. Overall, more women than men have these symptoms (Brown & Barlow, 2017).

Was Adrian H's problem a generalized anxiety disorder? Yes. However, if she also experienced *anxiety attacks,* then she would likely be diagnosed with panic disorder (Batelaan et al., 2010).

TABLE 63.1 | *DSM-5* Classification of Anxiety Disorders

Type of Disorder	Typical Signs of Trouble
Anxiety Disorders	
Generalized anxiety disorder	You have been extremely anxious or worried for six months.
Panic disorder	You are anxious much of the time and have sudden panic attacks. You are afraid that your attacks might occur in public places, so you rarely leave home.
Agoraphobia	You fear that something extremely embarrassing will happen if you leave home (but you don't have panic attacks).
Specific phobia	You have an intense fear of particular objects, activities, or locations.
Social anxiety disorder	You fear social situations in which people can watch, criticize, embarrass, or humiliate you.

Sources: American Psychiatric Association, 2013; Durand & Barlow, 2019; Sue et al., 2017.

Panic Disorder

In a **panic disorder**, people are highly anxious and also feel sudden, intense, unexpected panic. During a *panic attack*, victims experience chest pain, a racing heart, dizziness, choking, feelings of unreality, trembling, or fears of losing control. Many believe that they are having a heart attack, are going insane, or are about to die. Needless to say, this pattern leaves victims unhappy and uncomfortable much of the time. Again, the majority of people who suffer from panic disorder are women (Cannon et al., 2013).

Imagine that you are trapped in your stateroom on a sinking ocean liner (the Titanic?). The room fills with water. When only a small air space remains near the ceiling and you are gasping for air, you'll know what a panic attack feels like.

Agoraphobia

Agoraphobia (ah-go-rah-FOBE-ee-ah) is an excessive, irrational fear of being in public places. It usually involves the *fear that something extremely threatening*

Anxiety disorders Class of disorders marked by feelings of excessive apprehension and worry.

Generalized anxiety disorder Psychological disorder characterized by nearly constant, exaggerated worries.

Panic disorder Chronic state of anxiety, with brief moments of sudden, intense, unexpected panic.

Agoraphobia The fear that something extremely embarrassing will happen if one leaves the house or enters an unfamiliar situation; excessive, irrational fear of being in public places.

will happen in public, such as a panic attack, dizziness, diarrhea, or shortness of breath. Going outside the home alone, being in a crowd, standing in line, crossing a bridge, or riding in a car can be impossible for an agoraphobic person. As a result, some agoraphobics are prisoners in their own homes (American Psychiatric Association, 2013).

Although they are considered to be separate disorders, agoraphobia and panic attacks can occur together in the same individual. About 4.2 percent of all adults suffer from agoraphobia (with or without panic) during their lifetime (Grant et al., 2006).

Social Anxiety Disorder These disorders are intense, irrational fears that a person cannot shake off, even when there is no real danger. In a **social anxiety disorder**, people fear situations in which they can be scrutinized, evaluated, or humiliated by others. This leads them to avoid certain social situations, such as eating, writing, using the restroom, or speaking in public. When such situations cannot be avoided, people endure them with intense anxiety or distress. It is common for them to have uncomfortable physical symptoms, such as a pounding heart, shaking hands, sweating, diarrhea, mental confusion, and blushing. Social anxiety disorders greatly impair a person's ability to work, attend school, and form personal relationships (American Psychiatric Association, 2013). About 7 percent of all adults are affected by social anxiety disorders in a given year (American Psychiatric Association, 2017).

Specific Phobia In a **specific phobia**, the person's fear, anxiety, and avoidance are focused on specific objects, activities, or situations (Ipser, Singh, & Stein, 2013). Specific phobias can be linked to nearly any object or situation (Stinson et al., 2007). People affected by phobias recognize that their fears are unreasonable, but they cannot control them. For example, a person with a spider phobia would find it impossible to ignore a picture of a spider, even though a photograph can't bite anyone (Lipka, Miltner, & Straube, 2011). About 7–9 percent of all adults have a specific phobic disorder in any given year (American Psychiatric Association, 2017).

The most common specific phobias among Americans are phobias of insects, birds, snakes, or other animals, including, of course, arachnophobia (fear of spiders) and zoophobia (fear of all animals). Other "popular" phobias, in descending order of prevalence, are acrophobia (fear of heights), astraphobia (fear of storms, thunder, lightning), aquaphobia (fear of being on or in water), aviophobia (fear of airplanes), claustrophobia (fear of closed spaces), and agoraphobia (fear of crowds).

By combining the appropriate root word with the word "phobia," any number of fears can be named. Some include triskaidekaphobia (fear of the number 13), xenophobia (fear of strangers), and hematophobia (fear of blood). One of your authors' favorites is coulrophobia (fear of clowns).

Almost everyone has a few mild phobias, such as fear of heights, closed spaces, or bugs and crawly things. True phobias may lead to overwhelming fear, vomiting, wild climbing and running, or fainting. For a phobic disorder to exist, the person's fear must disrupt his or her daily life. Phobic persons are so threatened that they will go to almost any length to avoid the feared object or situation, such as driving 50 miles out of the way to avoid crossing a bridge.

Some Causes of Anxiety Disorders

What causes anxiety disorders? Anxiety disorders may be best explained by the stress-vulnerability model. Susceptibility to anxiety disorders appears to be partly inherited (Rachman, 2013). Studies show that being high-strung, nervous, or emotional runs in families. For example, 60 percent of children born to parents suffering from panic disorder have a fearful, inhibited temperament. Such children are irritable and wary as infants, shy and fearful as toddlers, and quiet and cautious introverts in elementary school. By the time they reach adulthood, they are at high risk for anxiety problems, such as panic attacks (Barlow, 2000; Barlow, Durand, & Hofmann, 2021).

There are at least four major psychological perspectives on the causes of anxiety disorders. These are (1) the *psychodynamic* approach, (2) the *humanistic-existential* approach, (3) the *behavioral* approach, and (4) the *cognitive* approach.

Psychodynamic Approach The term *psychodynamic* refers to internal motives, conflicts, unconscious forces, and other dynamics of mental life. Freud was the first to propose a psychodynamic explanation for what he called "neurosis." According to Freud, disturbances like those we have described represent a raging conflict among subparts of the personality—the id, ego, and superego.

Freud emphasized that intense anxiety can be caused by forbidden id impulses for sex or aggression that threaten to break through into behavior. The person constantly fears doing something "crazy" or forbidden. She or he also may be tortured by guilt, which the superego uses to suppress forbidden impulses. Caught in the middle, the ego is eventually overwhelmed. This forces the person to use rigid defense mechanisms and misguided, inflexible behavior to prevent a disastrous loss of control (see Module 57).

Humanistic-Existential Approaches Humanistic theories emphasize subjective experience, human problems, and personal potentials. Humanistic psychologist Carl Rogers regarded disorders of emotion, including anxiety disorders, as the result of a faulty self-image (Rogers, 1959). Rogers believed that anxious individuals have built up unrealistic mental images of themselves. This leaves them vulnerable to contradictory information. Let's say, for example, that an essential part of Cheyenne's self-image is that she is highly intelligent. If Cheyenne does poorly in school, she may begin to deny or distort her perceptions of herself and the situation. Should Cheyenne's anxiety become severe, she may resort to using defense mechanisms. Anxiety attacks, or similar symptoms, also may result from threats to her self-image. These symptoms, in turn, might become new threats that provoke further distortions. Soon, she could fall into a vicious cycle of maladjustment and anxiety that feeds on itself.

Existentialism focuses on elemental problems of existence, such as death, meaning, choice, and responsibility. *Existential anxiety* is the unavoidable anguish that comes from knowing that we are personally responsible for our lives even as we face life's empty and impersonal void. According to existential psychologists, we must courageously face existential anxiety by taking *responsibility* for our choices if life is to have meaning. Adolescents may experience considerable existential anxiety as they develop their identity (Berman, Weems, & Stickle, 2006).

If we collapse in the face of existential anxiety by failing to make life-enhancing choices, we risk living in "bad faith" and losing our way in life. Existential psychologists believe that unhealthy anxiety reflects a loss of *meaning* in life. That is, making choices that don't truly reflect what you value, feel, and believe can make you sick.

Behavioral Approach Behaviorist approaches emphasize overt, observable behavior, and the effects of learning and conditioning. Behaviorists assume that the "symptoms" of anxiety disorders are learned, just as other behaviors are learned. You might recall from Module 28, for instance, that phobias can be acquired through classical conditioning. Similarly, panic attacks may reflect conditioned emotional responses that generalize to new situations. One point on which all theorists agree is that disordered behavior is ultimately self-defeating because it makes the person more miserable in the long run, even though it temporarily lowers anxiety.

But if the person becomes more miserable in the long run, how does the pattern get started? The behavioral explanation is that self-defeating behavior begins with avoidance learning (described in Module 30). Avoidance learning occurs when making a response delays or prevents the onset of a painful or unpleasant stimulus. Here's a quick review to refresh your memory:

> An animal is placed in a special cage. After a few minutes a light comes on, followed a moment later by a painful shock. Quickly, the animal escapes into a second chamber. After a few minutes, a light comes on in this chamber, and the shock is repeated. Soon the animal learns to avoid pain by moving before the shock occurs. Once an animal learns to avoid the shock, it can be turned off altogether. A well-trained animal may avoid the nonexistent shock indefinitely if the light keeps turning on.

The same analysis can be applied to human behavior. A behaviorist would say that the powerful reward of immediate relief from anxiety keeps self-defeating avoidance behaviors alive. This view, known as the **anxiety reduction hypothesis**, seems to explain why the behavior patterns that we have discussed often look very "stupid" to outside observers.

Cognitive Approach The cognitive view is that distorted thinking causes people to magnify ordinary threats and failures, leading to distress (Steinman et al., 2013). For example, Bonnie, who is socially phobic, constantly has upsetting thoughts about being evaluated at school. Like other social phobics, Bonnie is a perfectionist excessively concerned about making mistakes. She also perceives criticism when none exists. If Bonnie expects that a social situation will focus too much attention on her, she avoids it (Brown & Barlow, 2017). Even when socially phobic persons are successful, distorted thoughts lead them to believe they have failed. In short, changing the thinking patterns of anxious individuals like Bonnie can greatly lessen their fears (Arch et al., 2013).

Implications All four psychological explanations probably contain an element of truth. For this reason, understanding anxiety disorders may be aided by combining parts of each perspective. Each viewpoint also suggests a different approach to treatment. Because many possibilities exist, therapy is discussed in later modules.

Social anxiety disorder An intense, irrational fear of being observed, evaluated, embarrassed, or humiliated by others in social situations.

Specific phobia Persistent fear and avoidance of a specific object or situation.

Anxiety reduction hypothesis Explains the self-defeating nature of avoidance responses as a result of the reinforcing effects of relief from anxiety.

Anxiety-Related Disorders—Also Anxious?

Learning Outcome 63.2 Name and briefly describe some important anxiety-related disorders

We began this module by examining the *anxiety disorders*. Let's now turn our attention to several types of disorders that are in some way related to anxiety: *obsessive-compulsive and related disorders, trauma- and stressor-related disorders, dissociative disorders*, and *somatic symptom and related disorders* (■ Table 63.2).

Obsessive-Compulsive and Related Disorders

While the *DSM-5* now categorizes obsessive-compulsive and related disorders separately from the anxiety disorders, at first glance they appear to involve coping with anxiety. The **obsessive-compulsive and related disorders** involve extreme preoccupations with certain thoughts and compulsive performance of certain behaviors.

People who suffer from **obsessive-compulsive disorder (OCD)** are preoccupied daily with distressing, repetitive thoughts and urges to perform certain rituals. You have probably experienced a mild obsessional thought, such as a song or stupid commercial jingle that repeats over and over in your mind. This may be irritating, but it's usually not terribly disturbing. True obsessions are images or thoughts that force their way into awareness against a person's will. They are so disturbing that they cause intense anxiety. The main types of obsessions are (1) about being "dirty" or "unclean," (2) about whether one has performed some action (such as locking the door), (3) about putting things "in order," and (4) about taboo thoughts or actions (such as one's spouse being poisoned or committing immoral acts). A related disorder, **hoarding disorder**, is about excessively collecting various things (Rasmussen, Eisen, & Greenberg, 2013).

TABLE 63.2 | *DSM-5* Classification of Anxiety-Related Disorders

Type of Disorder	Typical Signs of Trouble
Obsessive-Compulsive Disorders	
Obsessive-compulsive disorder	Your thoughts make you extremely nervous, and you rigidly repeat certain actions or routines.
Hoarding disorder	You collect things and have difficulty throwing or giving them away.
Trauma- and Stressor-Related Disorders	
Adjustment disorder	A normal life event has triggered troublesome anxiety, apathy, or depression.
Acute stress disorder	You are tormented for less than a month by the emotional aftereffects of horrible events that you have experienced.
Post-traumatic stress disorder	You are tormented for more than a month by the emotional aftereffects of horrible events that you have experienced.
Dissociative Disorders	
Dissociative amnesia	You can't remember your name, address, or past. In extreme (fugue) cases, you took a sudden, unplanned trip and are confused about who you are.
Dissociative identity disorder	You have two or more separate identities or personality states.
Somatic Symptom and Related Disorders	
Somatic symptom disorder	You are preoccupied with bodily functions and disease.
Factitious disorder (Munchausen syndrome)	You are deliberately faking medical problems to gain attention.
Conversion disorder	You are "converting" severe emotional conflicts into symptoms that closely resemble a physical disability.

Sources: American Psychiatric Association, 2013; Durand & Barlow, 2019; Sue et al., 2017.

Roger Bamber/Alamy Stock Photo

Hoarders are obsessive about collecting things, which they also have great difficulty discarding (Hayward & Coles, 2009).

The traditional view of OCD (let's call it *OCD theory*) is that *obsessions* give rise to *compulsions*, irrational acts that a person feels driven to repeat. The idea is that compulsive acts help control or block out anxiety caused by an obsession. For example, a minister who finds profanities popping into her mind might start compulsively counting her heartbeat. Doing this would prevent her from thinking "dirty" words. Some compulsive people are *checkers* or *cleaners*. For instance, a young mother who repeatedly pictures a knife plunging into her baby might check once an hour to make sure that all the knives in her house are locked away.

Of course, not all obsessive-compulsive disorders are so dramatic. Many simply involve extreme orderliness and rigid routine. Compulsive attention to detail and rigid following of rules help keep activities totally under control and make the highly anxious person feel more secure (Challacombe, Oldfield, & Salkovskis, 2011). (If such patterns are longstanding but less intense, they are classified as *personality disorders*, which we will shortly discuss in more detail.)

Causes of OCD Achieving a fuller understanding of the obsessive-compulsive and related disorders will undoubtedly require considerable effort and creativity. Let's focus on one remarkably creative theory, *COD theory*, which sets the traditional view of OCD on its head (Gillan & Sahakian, 2015). Imagine a *cleaner*, a patient who feels "contaminated" from touching ordinary objects because "germs are everywhere," driven to wash his hands hundreds of times a day. As we just saw, traditional OCD theory holds that the *obsession* (fear of germs) leads to a *compulsive* attempt to cope (handwashing).

According to COD theory, the problem actually begins with the compulsion. In our example, the patient begins to wash his hands more and more often. In order to explain to himself *why* he is washing his hands so often, he speculates that it must be because he is afraid of germs. Hence *COD*: The *compulsion* leads to the *obsession* (Gillan & Robbins, 2014).

How does that work? Repeated often, behaviors that start out as conscious, reflective decisions eventually become automatic, unconscious habits (Wood & Rünger, 2016). Many of our daily activities have long ago become habitual: buttoning our shirts, brushing our teeth, washing our hands, and so forth. What if the parts of your brain involved in forming habits malfunctioned, occasionally forming exceptionally strong habits, or *compulsions*? In effect, our cleaner starts habitually washing his hands a lot and adopts the germ explanation in a desperate attempt to explain, to himself, *why* he is washing his hands so much. (If you enjoy a challenge, go back to Module 2 and reread the section on the failings of introspection. Notice the similarity?)

COD theory has a lot going for it. Similar reasoning has already been applied to other types of compulsive behavior, such as drug addiction (Everitt & Robbins, 2016). Also, the brain structures involved in exercising conscious control over habits (i.e., resisting habits) are the same structures that appear to be abnormal in OCD patients. Furthermore, medical and behavioral methods designed to weaken habit formation have shown promise in reducing OCD symptoms (Gillan & Robbins, 2014).

Trauma- and Stressor-Related Disorders

If a situation causes distress, anxiety, or fear, we tend to "put it behind us" and avoid it in the future. This is a normal survival instinct. But what happens if we experience traumas or stresses outside our ability to cope? **Trauma- and stressor-related disorders** are behavior patterns also associated with high levels of fear or anxiety brought on by experiencing traumatic stresses.

Obsessive-compulsive and related disorders Extreme preoccupations with certain thoughts and compulsive performance of certain behaviors.

Obsessive-compulsive disorder (OCD) An extreme preoccupation with certain thoughts and compulsive performance of certain behaviors.

Hoarding disorder Excessively collecting various things.

Trauma- and stressor-related disorders Behavior patterns brought on by traumatic stresses.

How is this different from an anxiety disorder? The outward symptoms are similar. However, people suffering from anxiety disorders seem to generate their own misery, regardless of what's happening around them. They feel that they must be on guard against *future* threats that *could happen* at any time (Butcher, Mineka, & Hooley, 2010). In contrast, trauma- and stressor related disorders are caused by a person's specific life circumstances and may improve as life circumstances improve (Kramer et al., 2010).

Do stress and trauma problems cause a "nervous breakdown"? People suffering from *trauma- and stressor-related disorders* may be miserable, but they rarely experience a "breakdown." Actually, the term *nervous breakdown* has no formal meaning. Nevertheless, a problem known as an *adjustment disorder* does come close to being something of a breakdown.

An **adjustment disorder** occurs when ordinary stresses push people beyond their ability to cope with life. Examples of such stresses are a job loss, intense marital strife, and chronic physical illness. People suffering from an adjustment disorder may be extremely irritable, anxious, apathetic, or depressed. They also have trouble sleeping, lose their appetite, and suffer from various physical complaints. Often their problems can be relieved by rest, sedation, supportive counseling, and a chance to "talk through" their fears and anxieties (Ben-Itzhak et al., 2012).

More extreme reactions can occur when traumas or stresses fall outside the range of normal human experience, such as floods, tornadoes, earthquakes, or horrible accidents. They affect many political hostages; combat veterans; prisoners of war; victims of terrorism, torture, violent crime, child molestation, rape, or domestic violence; and people who have witnessed a death or serious injury (Hughes et al., 2011; Polusny et al., 2011).

Symptoms of more extreme stress disorders include repeated reliving of the traumatic event, avoidance of reminders of the event, and blunted emotions. Also common are insomnia, nightmares, wariness, poor concentration, irritability, and explosive anger or aggression. If such reactions last *less* than a month after a traumatic event, the problem is called an **acute stress disorder**. If they last *more* than a month, the person is suffering from **post-traumatic stress disorder (PTSD)** (Gupta, 2013; Sue et al., 2017).

About 3.6 percent of American adults suffer from PTSD in any given year (National Institute of Mental Health, 2018). Sadly, up to 20 percent of military veterans returning from wars develop PTSD, including soldiers involved in combat in the Middle East (Rosen et al., 2012; Salisbury & Burker, 2011). The constant threat of death and the gruesome sights and sounds of war take a terrible toll.

Dissociative Disorders

A person with one of the **dissociative disorders** experiences a disintegration of consciousness, memory, or self-identity. He or she may have temporary amnesia or multiple personalities. Also included in this category are frightening episodes of depersonalization, in which people feel like they are outside their bodies, are behaving like robots, or are lost in a dream world. In *dissociative disorders*, we see striking episodes of *amnesia, fugue,* or *multiple identity.*

Dissociative amnesia is an inability to recall one's name, address, or past. In extreme cases, a person with dissociative amnesia may experience a **dissociative fugue** (fewg), which involves sudden, unplanned travel away from home and confusion about personal identity. In such cases, forgetting personal identity and fleeing unpleasant situations appear to be defenses against intolerable anxiety. A person suffering from a **dissociative identity disorder** has two or more separate identities or personality states. (Don't forget that identity disorders are not the same as schizophrenia. See Module 61.)

One famous and dramatic example of multiple identities is described in the book *Sybil* (Schreiber, 1973). Sybil reportedly had 16 different personality states. Each identity had a distinct voice, vocabulary, and posture. One personality could play the piano, but the others (including Sybil herself) could not.

When an identity other than Sybil was in control, Sybil experienced a "time lapse," or memory blackout. Sybil's amnesia and alternate identities first appeared during childhood. As a girl, she was beaten, locked in closets, perversely tortured, sexually abused, and almost killed. Sybil's first dissociations allowed her to escape by creating another person who would suffer torture in her place. Identity disorders often begin with unbearable childhood experiences, like those that Sybil endured. A history of childhood trauma, especially sexual abuse, is found in a high percentage of persons whose personalities split into multiple identities (McLewin & Muller, 2006).

Flamboyant cases such as Sybil's have led some experts to question the existence of multiple personalities (Boysen & VanBergen, 2013; Piper, 2008). However, a majority of psychologists continue to believe that multiple identity is a real, if rare, problem (Boysen, 2011; Dell, 2009).

Somatic Symptom and Related Disorders

Have you ever known someone who appeared healthy but seemed to constantly worry about disease? These people are preoccupied with bodily functions, such as their heartbeat, breathing, or digestion. Minor physical problems—even a small sore or an occasional cough—may convince them that they have cancer or some other dreaded disease. Typically, they can't give up their fears of illness, even if doctors find no medical basis for their complaints (Dimsdale, 2011). (Don't confuse somatoform disorders with psychosomatic illnesses, which occur when stress causes real physical damage to the body. See Module 58.) **Somatic symptom and related disorders** occur when a person has physical symptoms that mimic disease or injury (e.g., paralysis, blindness, illness, chronic pain) for which there is no identifiable physical cause. In such cases, psychological factors appear to explain the symptoms.

Are you describing hypochondria? Partly. **Somatic symptom disorder** ("body-form" disorder) is a *DSM-5* disorder combining the features of three "older" disorders, *hypochondriasis* (HI-po-kon-DRY-uh-sis), *somatization disorder*, and *pain disorder* (American Psychiatric Association, 2013). People with this disorder typically display some combination of the following: (1) interpreting normal bodily sensations as proof that they have a terrible disease (hypochondria), (2) expressing their anxieties through various bodily complaints, and (3) experiencing disabling pain that has no identifiable physical basis. Such individuals may suffer from problems such as vomiting or nausea, shortness of breath, difficulty swallowing, or painful menstrual periods. Typically, the person feels ill much of the time and visits doctors repeatedly. Most sufferers take medicines or other treatments, but no physical cause can be found for their distress. (Read on for a related disorder with a curious twist.)

Factitious Disorder: Sick of Being Sick At 14, Ben was in the hospital again for his sinus problem. Since the age of 8, he had undergone 40 surgeries. In addition, he had been diagnosed at various times with bipolar disorder, oppositional defiant disorder, and ADHD. Ben was taking 19 different medications, and his mother said that she desperately wanted him to be "healed." She sought numerous tests and never missed an appointment. But at long last, it became clear that there was nothing wrong with Ben. Left alone with doctors, Ben revealed that he was "sick of being sick."

In reality, it was Ben's mother who was sick. She was eventually diagnosed as suffering from **factitious disorder** (Awadallah et al., 2005). The factitious disorder is *imposed on self* (in *Munchausen syndrome*) if the person fakes his or her own medical problems, and *imposed on another* (in *Munchausen by proxy syndrome*) if the person fakes the medical problems of someone in his or her care. As in Ben's case, most people with Munchausen by proxy syndrome are mothers who fabricate their children's illnesses (Day & Moseley, 2010; Ferrara et al., 2013). Sometimes they even deliberately harm their children. For example, one mother injected her son with 7-Up (Reisner, 2006).

But why? People who suffer from factitious disorder appear to have a pathological need to seek attention and sympathy from medical professionals. They also may win praise for being health conscious or a good parent (Day & Moseley, 2010).

Conversion Disorder In another rare disorder, **conversion disorder**, severe emotional conflicts are "converted" into symptoms that actually disturb physical functioning or closely resemble a physical disability. For instance, a soldier might become deaf or lame or develop "glove anesthesia" just before a battle.

Glove anesthesia? Glove anesthesia is a loss of sensitivity in the areas of the skin that would normally be covered by a glove. Glove anesthesia shows that conversion symptoms often contradict known medical facts. The system of nerves in the hands does not form a glove-like pattern and could not cause such symptoms (➤ **Figure 63.1**).

If symptoms disappear when a victim is asleep, hypnotized, or anesthetized, a conversion reaction must be suspected (Russo et al., 1998). Another sign to note is that victims of conversion reactions are strangely unconcerned about suddenly being disabled.

Adjustment disorder Emotional disturbance caused by ongoing stressors within the range of common experience.

Acute stress disorder A psychological disturbance lasting up to one month following stresses that would produce anxiety in anyone who experienced them.

Post-traumatic stress disorder (PTSD) Pattern of unwanted memories, nightmares, and flashbacks following a traumatic event for more than a month.

Dissociative disorders Class of psychological disorders involving disintegration of consciousness, memory, or self-identity.

Dissociative amnesia Loss of memory (partial or complete) for important information related to personal identity.

Dissociative fugue Sudden travel away from home, plus confusion about one's personal identity.

Dissociative identity disorder Presence of two or more distinct personalities (multiple personality).

Somatic symptom and related disorders Physical symptoms that mimic disease or injury (e.g., paralysis, blindness, illness, or chronic pain) for which there is no identifiable physical cause.

Somatic symptom disorder Exhibiting the characteristics of a disease or injury without an identifiable physical cause.

Factitious disorder (Munchausen syndrome) To gain attention, an affected person fakes his or her medical problems or those of someone in his or her care.

Conversion disorder A bodily symptom that mimics a physical disability but is actually caused by anxiety or emotional distress.

Figure 63.1

Glove anesthesia. *(Left)* "Glove anesthesia" is a conversion reaction involving loss of feeling in areas of the hand that would be covered by a glove *(a)*. If the "anesthesia" were physically caused, it would follow the pattern shown in *(b)*. *(Right)* To test for organic paralysis of the arm, an examiner can suddenly extend the arm, stretching the muscles. A conversion reaction is indicated if the arm pulls back involuntarily. (Adapted from Weintraub, 1983.)

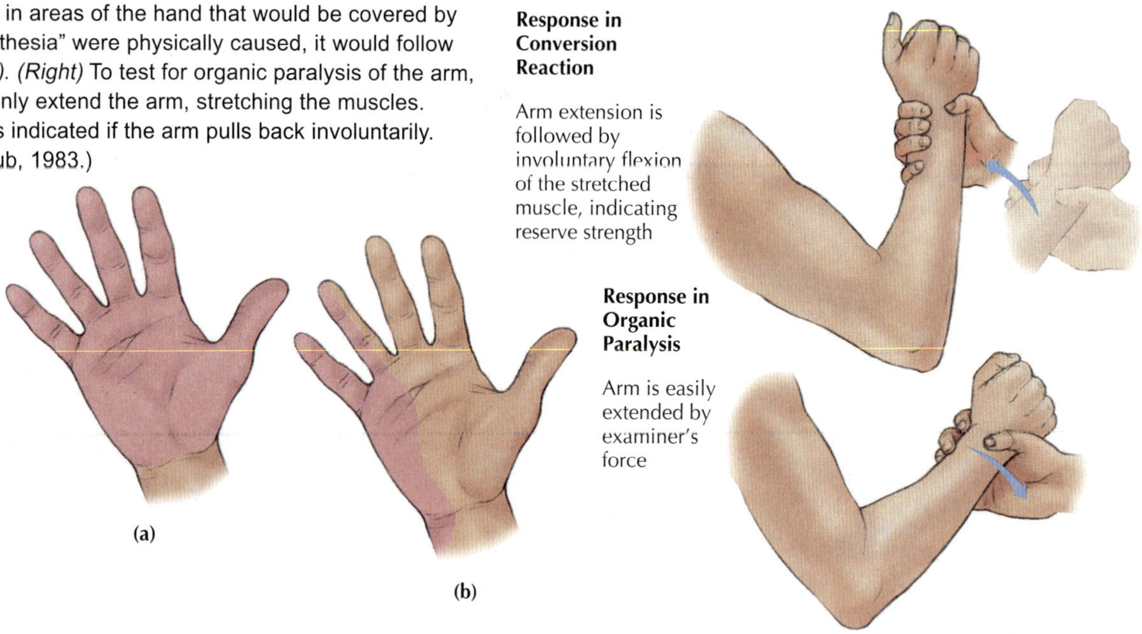

Personality Disorders—Blueprints for Maladjustment

Learning Outcome 63.3 Describe the general characteristics of personality disorders, and the specific features of antisocial personality disorder

"I want to end it all," Michelle declared, "No one loves me" (Kearney & Trull, 2018, p. 290). At 23, Michelle had already tried to kill herself six times, this time by downing a lot of aspirin. She is always very dramatic and impulsive, frequently binging on drugs, sex, or food. Her violent mood swings make for turbulent relationships with other people. She once clung to a friend's leg until she agreed to stay for dinner; another time, she destroyed a wall with a hammer in a fit of anger because her professor gave her a low grade. Michelle has a condition called *borderline personality disorder.*

Maladaptive Personality Patterns

Personality disorders are long-standing, inflexible ways of behaving that create a variety of problems. For example, people with a *paranoid personality disorder* are suspicious, hypersensitive, and wary of others. *Narcissistic persons* need constant admiration and are lost in fantasies of power, wealth, brilliance, beauty, or love. Celebrities appear more likely to be narcissistic than noncelebrities, perhaps because they receive so much attention (Young & Pinsky, 2006). The *dependent personality* suffers from extremely low self-confidence. Dependent persons allow others to run their lives, and they place everyone else's needs ahead of their own. People with a *histrionic personality disorder* constantly seek attention by dramatizing their emotions and actions.

Typically, patterns such as the ones just described begin during adolescence or even childhood. Thus, *personality disorders* are deeply rooted and usually span many years. The list of personality disorders is long (■ **Table 63.3**), so let's focus on the antisocial personality now.

Antisocial Personality Disorder

What are the characteristics of an antisocial personality? A person with an **antisocial personality disorder** displays unusual remorselessness, a lack of empathy, or disregard for social conventions. Simply put, he or she lacks a conscience. Such people are impulsive, selfish, dishonest, emotionally shallow, and manipulative (Visser et al., 2010). They are poorly socialized and seem to be incapable of feeling guilt, shame, fear, loyalty, or love (American Psychiatric Association, 2013). Antisocial persons are sometimes called *psychopaths,* although it may be more accurate to think of psychopathy as an extreme form of antisocial personality disorder (Riser & Kosson, 2013).

Are psychopaths dangerous? Psychopaths tend to have a long history of conflict with society. Many are delinquents or criminals who may be a threat to the general public (Bateman

TABLE 63.3 | *DSM-5* Classification of Personality Disorders

Type of Personality Disorder	Typical Signs of Trouble
Paranoid	You deeply distrust others and are suspiciousness of their motives, which you perceive as insulting or threatening.
Schizoid	You feel very little emotion and can't form close personal relationships with others.
Schizotypal	You are a loner, you engage in extremely odd behavior, and your thought patterns are bizarre, but you are not actively psychotic.
Antisocial	You are irresponsible, lack guilt or remorse, and engage in antisocial behavior, such as aggression, deceit, or recklessness.
Borderline	Your self-image, moods, and impulses are erratic, and you are extremely sensitive to any hint of criticism, rejection, or abandonment by others.
Histrionic	You are dramatic and flamboyant; you exaggerate your emotions to get attention from others.
Narcissistic	You think that you are wonderful, brilliant, important, and worthy of constant admiration.
Avoidant	You are timid and uncomfortable in social situations and fear evaluation.
Dependent	You lack confidence, and you are extremely submissive and rely on others excessively (clinging).
Obsessive-compulsive	You demand order, perfection, control, and rigid routine at all times.

Sources: American Psychiatric Association, 2013; Durand & Barlow, 2019; Sue et al., 2017.

& Fonagy, 2012; Lobbestael, Cima, & Arntz, 2013). However, psychopaths are rarely the crazed murderers that you may have seen portrayed in the media. In fact, many psychopaths are charming at first. Their friends only gradually become aware of the psychopath's lying and self-serving manipulation.

One study found that psychopaths are blind to signs of disgust in others. This may add to their capacity for cruelty and their ability to use others (Kosson et al., 2002). Many successful businesspersons, entertainers, politicians, and other seemingly normal people have psychopathic leanings. Basically, antisocial persons, who are usually men, coldly use others and cheat their way through life (Alegria et al., 2013).

Causes *What causes psychopathy?* Typically, people with antisocial personalities showed similar problems in childhood (then usually referred to as *conduct disorder*; Burt et al., 2007). Adult psychopaths also display subtle neurological problems (➤ **Figure 63.2**). For example, they have unusual brainwave patterns that suggest underarousal of the brain. This may explain why psychopaths tend to be thrill seekers. Quite likely, they are searching for stimulation strong enough to overcome their chronic underarousal and feelings of "boredom" (Hare, 2006; Pemment, 2013).

In a revealing study, psychopaths were shown extremely grisly and unpleasant photographs of mutilations. The photos were so upsetting that they visibly startled normal people.

Halfdark/Getty Images

Many prison inmates have been diagnosed with antisocial personality disorder (Bateman & Fonagy, 2012).

Personality disorders Long-standing, inflexible ways of behaving that create a variety of problems.

Antisocial personality disorder Unusual remorselessness, lack of empathy, or disregard for social conventions.

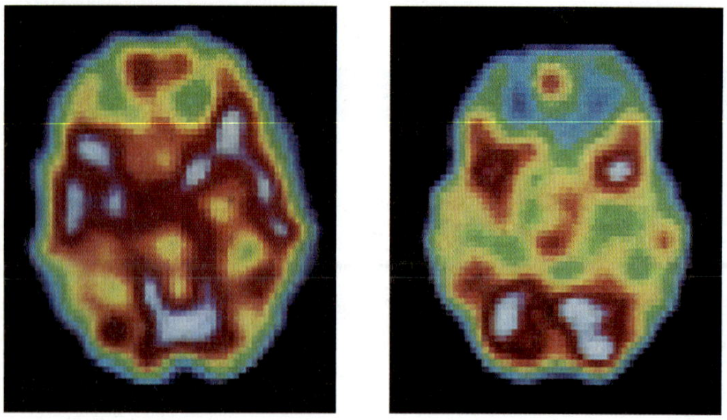

Figure 63.2

The psychopathic brain. Using PET scans, Canadian psychologist Robert Hare found that the normally functioning brain *(left)* lights up with activity when a person sees emotion-laden words such as "maggot" or "cancer." But the brain of a psychopath *(right)* remains inactive, especially in areas associated with feelings and self-control. When Dr. Hare showed the right image to several neurologists, one asked, "Is this person from Mars?"

The psychopaths, however, showed no startle response to the photos (Levenston et al., 2000). (They didn't "bat an eyelash.") Those with antisocial personalities might therefore be described as *emotionally cold*. They simply do not feel normal pangs of conscience, guilt, or anxiety, perhaps explaining their ability to calmly lie, cheat, steal, or take advantage of others (Blair et al., 2006).

Can psychopathy be treated? Antisocial personality disorders are rarely treated with success (Bateman & Fonagy, 2012). All too often, psychopaths manipulate therapy, just like any other situation. If it is to their advantage to act "cured," they will do so. However, they return to their former behavior patterns as soon as possible. On a more positive note, antisocial behavior does tend to decline somewhat after age 40, even without treatment, because people tend to become more "mellow" as they age (Black, 2015).

A Look Ahead Treatments for psychological problems range from counseling and psychotherapy to mental hospitalization and drug therapy. Because they vary greatly, a complete discussion of therapies is found in Modules 65–68. For now, it's worth noting that many milder mental disorders can be treated successfully. Even major disorders may respond well to drugs and other techniques. It is wrong to fear "former mental patients" or to exclude them from work, friendships, and other social situations. A struggle with major depression or a psychotic episode does not inevitably lead to lifelong dysfunction. Too often, however, it does lead to unnecessary rejection based on groundless fears (Elkington et al., 2012; Sarason & Sarason, 2005).

Let's conclude by noting, like many other things in life, overcoming mental illness is challenging and requires a tremendous amount of determination. What can you do to improve your ability to persevere when things get difficult? Consider reading Module 64 for some answers.

MODULE 63 Anxiety, Anxiety-Related, and Personality Disorders—Learning Outcomes Revisited

63.1 Describe the general characteristics of anxiety disorders and explain how psychological theories account for those disorders

Anxiety disorders are characterized by high levels of anxiety, rigid defense mechanisms, and self-defeating behavior patterns. Anxiety disorders include generalized anxiety disorder, panic disorder, and a variety of phobias. The psychodynamic approach emphasizes unconscious conflicts as the cause of disabling anxiety. The humanistic approach emphasizes the effects of a faulty self-image. The behaviorists emphasize the effects of previous learning, particularly avoidance learning. Cognitive theories of anxiety focus on distorted thinking and being fearful of others' attention and judgments.

63.2 Name and briefly describe some important anxiety-related disorders

The obsessive-compulsive and related disorders include obsessive-compulsive disorder and hoarding disorder. COD theory proposes that compulsions give rise to obsessions. Trauma- and stressor-related disorders include adjustment disorder, acute stress disorder, and post-traumatic stress disorder. Dissociative disorders may take the form of amnesia, fugue, or multiple identities. Somatic symptom and related disorders center on physical complaints that mimic disease or disability. Three examples are somatic symptom disorder, factitious disorder (Munchausen syndrome and Munchausen by proxy), and conversion disorder.

63.3 Describe the general characteristics of personality disorders, and the specific features of antisocial personality disorder

Personality disorders are persistent, maladaptive personality patterns. Antisocial personalities seem to lack a conscience. They are emotionally unresponsive, manipulative, shallow, and dishonest. Psychopathy may be an extreme form of antisocial personality disorder.

Reflective Practice

Content Check

1. Disabling anxiety over ordinary life stresses is characteristic of which of the following disorders?
   a. PTSD
   b. agoraphobia
   c. hypochondriasis
   d. adjustment disorder
2. Panic disorder can occur with or without agoraphobia, but agoraphobia cannot occur alone, without the presence of a panic disorder. T or F?
3. According to the ____________ view, anxiety disorders are the end result of a loss of meaning.
   a. psychodynamic
   b. humanistic
   c. behaviorist
   d. cognitive
4. The symptoms of acute stress disorders last less than one month; post-traumatic stress disorder (PTSD) lasts more than one month. T or F?
5. Amnesia, multiple identities, and depersonalization are ____________________.
   a. mood disorders
   b. somatic symptom disorders
   c. psychoses
   d. dissociative disorders
6. Which of the following is *not* a dissociative disorder?
   a. fugue
   b. amnesia
   c. conversion disorder
   d. multiple identities
7. Antisocial personality disorders are difficult to treat, but typically, antisocial behavior declines a year or two after adolescence. T or F?

Skill Check

Think Critically

8. In this module, we met Ben's mother, who was deliberately faking her son's "illnesses." How did she get away with it? Wouldn't doctors figure out that something was fishy with Ben long before he had 40 surgeries for a faked sinus disorder?

Self-Reflect

Which of the anxiety disorders would you *least* want to suffer from? Why? Which of the psychological explanations of anxiety disorders do you find most convincing? What minor obsessions or compulsions have you experienced? Many of the qualities that define personality disorders exist to a minor degree in normal personalities. Try to think of a person you know who has some of the characteristics described for each type of personality disorder.

ANSWERS

1. d 2. F 3. b 4. T 5. d 6. c 7. F 8. No one doctor tolerates false symptoms for long. Once a doctor refuses further treatment, the factitious disorder sufferer moves on to another. Also, more than one doctor is often being seen.

MODULE 64

A Psychologist's Skill Set

Perseverance

Grit

At first, there may not seem to be much that's similar about these two photos. One shows a group of new cadets at West Point, the elite training academy for officers in the US military. The other is a photo of contestants in the Scripp's National Spelling Bee. Competitors move through eight stressful rounds, spelling words such as "pipsissewa," "sprachgefühl," and "myrmo therene" before a winner emerges.

If you look past the obvious differences in the pictures, though, you'll discover that there's an important similarity between these two groups: In both cases, successful individuals are very likely to possess a characteristic that psychologist Angela Duckworth refers to as "grit"—having the passion and perseverance to pursue a very long-term goal (Duckworth, Peterson, Matthews, & Kelly, 2007). How gritty are *you*? And how can you develop true grit? Read on!

Drew Angerer/Getty Images News/Getty Images

Alex Wong/Getty Images News/Getty Images

~LEARNING OUTCOMES~

After reading this module you should be able to:

64.1 Create a plan to improve your "grit" and perseverance

Perseverance—True Grit?

Learning Outcome 64.1 Create a plan to improve your "grit" and perseverance

As we've seen throughout the modules on psychological disorders, overcoming mental health challenges is typically a long journey that requires a great deal of commitment, and perseverance is likely to be a key component of success. But there are many other aspects of our personal and professional lives that also require the ability to "stick to it" when the going gets tough. Surprisingly, Duckworth has found in multiple studies that grit is often a better predictor of success than intelligence, or the kind of natural ability that inspires awe whenever we watch someone who seems to be a "gifted" athlete, musician, artist, or mathematician. Even better, Duckworth argues that grit isn't a characteristic that's fixed; instead, she makes the case that it's a skill that anyone can work at.

Measuring Grit

Grit can be measured with rating scales that are composed of statements like:

- New ideas and projects sometimes distract me from previous ones.
- Setbacks don't discourage me. I don't give up easily.

The above two statements are the first two items from Angela Duckworth's 10-item *Grit Scale*. (Go to http://angeladuckworth.com/grit-scale/ to complete the entire scale and have it automatically scored. Higher scores indicate higher levels of grit.)

My grit score wasn't very high. Can I get grittier? Given how important grit is in predicting success, it's good to know that it's a skill that anyone can work on. Psychological research suggests that "gritty" individuals possess four important characteristics: interest, practice, purpose, and hope. Working at them will help you to develop your passions and improve your performance over the long term.

Interest

Individuals who score high on the grit scale have very well developed interests that have evolved over a long period of time. This passion may start as a hobby, or as a pastime to which people just devote a few hours each week. Over time, though, as they become more knowledgeable and experienced, a real interest in this activity develops and this drives the desire to keep working at it.

But I haven't really developed a passion like that for anything. . . . According to Duckworth, for most young adults that's likely to be true, and it's nothing to worry about. In fact, she has taken issue with people who casually suggest that everyone should just "follow their passion." The trouble with framing it that way, she argues, is that it might lead you to believe that your passion exists out there in the world and that your job is to just go out, discover its location, and bring it home with you.

Clearly this isn't the way people develop strong interests. A better approach is to open yourself up to trying new things that have some appeal for you. You need to give yourself permission to explore things that are of interest, try them for a period of time and, if they don't really grab you, move on and try something else. The key thing is balance: While exploration is not a bad thing, it's important to keep in mind the human tendency toward novelty. Left to their own devices, people experience a strong pull toward the next fad, or the newest craze. To really improve your level of grit, there will be times when you'll need to think hard about leaving behind something in which you've developed some expertise. To improve the chances of persevering, one strategy is to "substitute nuance for novelty."

What this means is that instead of dropping an activity that you're getting good at to pursue the latest craze, you may want to ask yourself whether it might be better to work at improving your ability to perform smaller elements of that activity. For example, an artist who had developed some expertise in making stained glass might decide that he was going to work a little harder on one very specific element of his technique—perhaps his ability to solder the pieces of glass together with smooth seams—rather than just packing up and moving on to doing something completely different.

Practice

After developing a keen interest in something, the second stage of developing grit is *deliberate practice*. According to Anders Ericsson at Florida State University, deliberate practice is focused on gathering useful feedback to help you recognize your weaknesses and then using that information to improve specific aspects of your performance. Ericsson has written about the three F's: *focus*, *feedback*, and *fix it* (Ericsson & Pool, 2016). The first of these, focus, refers to the idea that practice will only be helpful if you're really concentrating on what you're doing. According to Ericsson, amateurs tend to daydream or think about more pleasant things when they're practicing—especially when that practice is physically strenuous or mentally challenging. But unless you're using the practice time to very consciously think about what you're doing (and how closely you're approximating your best work), you won't improve very much. It's far better to practice in a very focused way for a shorter period of time than to work longer while expending less effort.

The second F—feedback—emphasizes the importance of having an expert watch your performance and provide advice about what you can do to improve. These days it's not unusual for people to learn to do something by reading a book or watching videos on YouTube. In some cases, we may take classes with others in our efforts to get better at something. These things will all help, but none of them is a substitute for having someone who is very skilled focus specifically on you and explain what it is you need to do to move your performance to the next level.

Finally, Ericsson emphasizes the importance of taking the feedback and fixing your weaknesses. In some cases, this will require you to try different methods until you find something that will help you to address those things that need improvement.

Truthfully, deliberate practice is really, really challenging. It involves putting a lot of time and energy into improving your technique, and even people with a great deal of passion and interest will tell you that it's incredibly effortful. Duckworth once asked US Olympic gold-medal swimmer Rowdy Gaines whether he loved to practice, and his answer will sound familiar to anyone who has committed themselves to improving on a skill they care about: "Are you asking me if I love getting up at four in the morning, jumping into a cold pool, and swimming laps looking at a black line on the bottom, at the very edge of my physical ability where my lungs are screaming for oxygen and my arms feel like they're about to fall off? No, I don't, but I love the whole thing. You know, I have a passion for the whole sport."

Purpose and Hope

The final two aspects of grit, purpose and hope, draw on the idea that truly committing to something that's of interest to you—and all of the deliberate practice that's required to improve—is much easier when you see a greater purpose in your actions, and when you possess a sufficient level of hope to carry you through setbacks. When Duckworth talks about feeling a sense of purpose, she's referring to a strong sense that what you're doing matters to others, as well as yourself. Someone committed to playing the piano may feel that their music will bring pleasure to others who listen, while gritty hockey players might believe that their efforts on the ice matter to both their teammates and the people who come to watch the games. And while hope is the last of Duckworth's four characteristics of grit, she emphasizes that it's the one that's necessary throughout the process of developing your passions. Without it, she argues, people would simply give up on their efforts at improvement whenever they encountered an obstacle or felt that they weren't getting better.

The moral of the story? Continue looking for the things that inspire you to work hard and feel satisfied. And when you feel frustrated and want to give up, think about what basketball great Michael Jordan had to say about "true grit": *I have failed over and over and over again in my life. And that is why I succeed.*

MODULE 64 Perseverance—Learning Outcomes Revisited

64.1 Create a plan to improve your "grit" and perseverance

In psychology, "grit" refers to having the passion and perseverance to pursue a long-term goal, and is associated with four characteristics: interest, (deliberate) practice, purpose, and hope. Improving your level of grit requires that people engage in deliberate practice when you are pursuing a goal. Deliberate practice involves staying focused during training, seeking feedback from experts, and then working to correct problems that have been identified. Fostering a sense of hope will allow you to overcome the obstacles that inevitably occur when we are working toward important goals. We hope that after reading this section, you'll be better able to think about how you can use these strategies to help enhance your "grittiness"!

Reflective Practice

Content Check

1. Grit has been shown to be a better predictor of success than other things, including intelligence and "natural ability." T or F?
2. It's better to practice for longer periods of time—even if you aren't fully focused on the task—than it is to practice for shorter periods while concentrating carefully. T or F?
3. Which of the following is *not* a characteristic of "gritty" individuals?
   a. interest
   b. unbiased thinking
   c. practice
   d. hope
4. People who love what they're doing will always enjoy deliberate practice. T or F?
5. What are the three F's of deliberate practice?
   a. focus, feedback, fervor
   b. feedback, faith, focus
   c. faith, focus, fix it
   d. focus, feedback, fix it

Skill Check

Think Critically

6. These days there are lots of different ways that you can learn to do something. What are the limitations of classes and online video training when you're trying to develop expertise in a particular skill?

Self-Reflect

What activities have you tried out of genuine interest? Have you persevered with any of them, engaging in the kind of deliberate practice that Ericsson discusses? If you haven't yet discovered a passion for something, can you think of anything that you'd like to try?

ANSWERS

1. T 2. F 3. b 4. F 5. d 6. These learning techniques can be very helpful when you're first beginning to learn a skill; however, as you get better you will eventually need to seek out individualized feedback from a true expert who will be able to provide very specific, detailed information about your technique, and how you might improve.

MODULE 65

Therapies

Treating Psychological Distress

Like a Duck

Stanley stared through the blinds in his professor's office at the ducks, quacking away on the campus pond. His teacher was surprised. Stanley's excellent work in class and his healthy, casual appearance left her unprepared when he murmured, "I feel like I'm losing my mind." He told her about working hard to hide a world of crippling fear, anxiety, and depression. At work, he was deathly afraid to talk to coworkers and customers. Several disastrous romances had left him terrified of women. As Stanley described his own personal hell, it became clear he felt like the ducks outside, appearing peaceful on the surface, but madly paddling underneath.

This module offers an overview of methods used to alleviate problems like Stanley's. We begin with a look at the origins of modern therapy and identify both the ways contemporary psychotherapies differ and the core features all successful therapies share.

Tracy Whiteside/Shutterstock.com

~LEARNING OUTCOMES~

After reading this module you should be able to:

65.1 Describe some historical approaches to psychotherapy

65.2 Outline the ways contemporary psychotherapies differ

65.3 Describe how various psychotherapies are effective and what they have in common

Origins of Therapy—Bored Out of Your Skull

Learning Outcome 65.1 Describe some historical approaches to psychotherapy

Fortunately, the odds are that you will *not* experience problems as serious as those of Stanley, the student we just met. But if you did, what help is available? In most cases, it would be some form of **psychotherapy**, any psychological technique that can bring about positive changes in personality, behavior, or personal adjustment. It might, as with Stanley, also include a medical therapy.

Early treatments for mental problems give good reasons to appreciate modern therapies (Sharf, 2016). Archaeological findings dating to the Stone Age suggest that most premodern approaches were marked by fear and superstitious belief in spirits, demons, witchcraft, and magic (McNamara, 2011). If Stanley had been unlucky enough to be born several thousand years ago, his "treatment" might have left him feeling "bored." One of the more dramatic "cures" practiced by primitive "therapists" was a process called *trepanning* (treh-PAN-ing), also sometimes spelled *trephining* (Terry, 2006). In modern usage, trepanning is any surgical procedure in which a hole is bored in the skull. In the hands of primitive therapists, it meant boring, chipping, or bashing

Primitive "treatment" for mental disorders sometimes took the form of boring a hole in the skull. This example shows signs of healing, which means the patient actually survived the treatment. Many didn't.

(Left) Many early asylums were no more than prisons, with inmates held in chains. *(Right)* One late-19th-century "treatment" was based on swinging the patient in a harness—presumably to calm the patient's nerves.

holes in the skull. Presumably, this was done to relieve pressure or release the spirits "possessing" the patient.

Stanley would not have been much better off during the Middle Ages. Then, treatments for mental illness in Europe focused on *demonology*, the study of demons and persons plagued by them. Medieval "therapists" commonly blamed abnormal behavior on supernatural forces, such as possession by the devil, or on curses from witches and wizards. As a cure, they used exorcism to "cast out evil spirits." For the fortunate, exorcism was a religious ritual. More often, physical torture was used to make the body an inhospitable place for the devil to reside.

Modern analyses of "demonic possession" suggest that many victims may have been suffering from epilepsy, schizophrenia, dissociative disorders, Tourette's syndrome, and depression (McNamara, 2011; Mirsky & Duncan, 2005; Thase, 2006; van der Hart, Lierens, & Goodwin, 1996). Thus, many people "treated" by demonologists may have been doubly victimized.

Then, in 1793, a French doctor named Philippe Pinel changed the Bicêtre Asylum in Paris from a squalid "madhouse" into a mental hospital by unchaining the inmates (Schuster, Hoertel, & Limosin, 2011). Finally, the emotionally disturbed were regarded as "mentally ill" and given more compassionate treatment. The process of improving care continues to this day.

When was psychotherapy developed? In contrast to medical therapies, which are physical in nature, the first true *psychotherapy*, was created by Sigmund Freud little more than 100 years ago (Borch-Jacobsen & Shamdasani, 2011). As a physician in Vienna, Freud was intrigued by cases of *hysteria*. People suffering from hysteria have physical symptoms (such as paralysis or numbness) for which no physical causes can be found. (Such problems are now called *somatic symptom disorders*, as discussed in Module 63.)

Freud slowly became convinced that hysteria was related to deeply hidden unconscious conflicts and developed *psychoanalysis*, his "talking cure," to help patients gain insight into those conflicts (Strenger, 2016). In this way, Freud became the first *psychotherapist*.

Psychotherapy Since Freud

Over the years, psychoanalysis has evolved into a rich variety of psychotherapies. Some have retained Freudian elements while others were inspired by other psychological perspectives. Along the way, psychotherapists have discovered that therapy is *not* equally effective for all problems. Chances of improvement are fairly good for phobias, low self-esteem, some sexual problems, and marital conflicts. Further, some forms of therapy are more effective for some types of problems. More complex problems can be difficult to solve and, as in Stanley's case, may require medical treatment as well. The most extreme cases may not respond to psychotherapy at all, leaving a medical therapy as the only viable treatment option.

In short, it is often unrealistic to expect psychotherapy to undo a person's entire past. For many people, the major

Psychotherapy Any psychological technique used to facilitate positive changes in a person's personality, behavior, or adjustment.

benefit of psychotherapy is that it provides comfort, support, and a way to make constructive changes (Compton & Hoffman, 2019). Yet even when problems are severe, therapy may help a person gain a new perspective or learn behaviors to better cope with life. Psychotherapy can be hard work for both clients and therapists, but when it succeeds, few activities are more worthwhile.

It's also a mistake to think that psychotherapy is useful only to solve problems or end a crisis. Even if a person is already doing well, therapy can be a way to promote personal growth (Trull & Prinstein, 2013). Therapists are also developing ways to help people use their personal strengths. Rather than trying to fix what is "wrong" with a person, they seek to nurture positive traits and actively solve problems (Compton & Hoffman, 2019). ■ **Table 65.1** lists some of the elements of positive mental health that therapists seek to restore or promote.

In Modules 66, 67, and 68, we look in depth at five main types of modern therapy: Four contemporary approaches to psychotherapy (psychodynamic, humanistic, cognitive, and behavior psychotherapies), along with medical therapies. Before then, let's get an overview of the various forms that the contemporary psychotherapies can take.

TABLE 65.1 | Elements of Positive Mental Health

Personal autonomy and independence
A sense of identity
Feelings of personal worth
Skilled interpersonal communication
Sensitivity, nurturance, and trust
Genuineness and honesty with self and others
Self-control and personal responsibility
Committed and loving personal relationships
Capacity to forgive others and oneself
Personal values and a purpose in life
Self-awareness and motivation for personal growth
Adaptive coping strategies for managing stresses and crises
Fulfillment and satisfaction in work
Good habits of physical health

Source: Adapted from Compton & Hoffman, 2019.

Dimensions of Therapy—The Many Paths to Health

Learning Outcome 65.2 Outline the ways contemporary psychotherapies differ

Psychotherapy began as a form of one-on-one dialogue between therapists and their clients meant to yield insight. Today, therapists have many approaches from which to choose and, as we will see, each therapy emphasizes different concepts and methods. For this reason, the best approach for a particular person or problem may vary. The terms in the list that follows describe some basic dimensions of various psychotherapies (Corsini & Wedding, 2019; Prochaska & Norcross, 2014; Sharf, 2016):

- **Insight versus action therapy:** Does the therapy aim to bring clients to a deeper understanding of their thoughts, emotions, and behavior? Or is it designed to bring about direct changes in troublesome thoughts, habits, feelings, or behavior without seeking insight into their origins or meanings?
- **Nondirective versus directive therapy:** Does the therapist provide strong guidance and advice? Or does the therapist assist clients, who are responsible for solving their own problems?
- **Open-ended versus time-limited therapy:** Is the therapy allotted a time limit or not?
- **Individual versus group therapy:** Does the therapy involve one therapist with one client? Or can several clients participate at the same time?
- **Face-to-face versus distance therapy:** Will the therapist and client meet face-to-face, or will they communicate over the telephone or the Internet?

Notice that more than one dimension can apply to a particular therapy. For example, it is possible to have an action, directive, open-ended group therapy meeting via the Internet or an insight, nondirective, individual, time-limited therapy meeting face-to-face. In what follows, we explore these dimensions of therapies in a bit more detail.

Insight Versus Action Therapy

Freud's initial intent in developing psychoanalysis was to provide patients with an **insight therapy** that could resolve psychological problems by gaining a conscious understanding of previously unconscious psychodynamic conflicts. A psychoanalyst might use free association and dream analysis to enable Stanley to realize that his anxieties originate, say, in an unconscious fear of dying. Stanley was approaching the age at which his namesake uncle Stanley died prematurely of a heart attack 22 years ago. Psychoanalysts expect this insight will "discharge" Stanley's unconscious pressures and alleviate his general sense of anxiety.

In contrast, **action therapies** generally focus on directly changing troubling thoughts and behaviors. We will shortly explore some extreme action therapies, the *behavioral therapies*. A behavioral therapist would spend little time on *why* Stanley felt anxious; rather she might help Stanley learn some relaxation techniques to directly relieve his anxieties whenever they get too strong. We encounter psychoanalysis and the humanistic *insight* therapies in Module 66, and the cognitive and behavioral *action* therapies in Module 67.

Directive Versus Nondirective Therapy

Psychoanalysis is a **directive therapy**, in which the therapist leads the patient through the therapeutic process. Based on his analysis of Stanley's free associations and dreams, his psychoanalyst might *direct* Stanley's awareness toward his unconscious fear of dying. Without this direction, Stanley might *resist* gaining the insight needed to overcome his anxiety.

In a **nondirective therapy** the role of the therapist is to create the conditions under which the client can resolve his or her psychological issues. For example, in *client-centered therapy*, it would be assumed that Stanley must articulate his own problems and actively seek to resolve them himself. His nondirective therapist's role is to support him in his growing understanding, not to tell Stanley what is "wrong" with him or how to "fix it." We further explore nondirective and directive therapies in Module 66.

Open-Ended Versus Time-Limited Therapy

Traditional psychoanalysis was open-ended, calling for three to five therapy sessions a week, often for many years. Today, most patients in psychoanalysis are seen only once or twice per week, but treatment may still go on for years.

Today, most psychodynamic therapists have switched to doing time-limited, **brief psychodynamic therapy**, which tends to use direct questioning to reveal unconscious conflicts (Binder & Betan, 2013). Modern therapists also actively provoke emotional reactions that will lower defenses and provide insights. It is interesting that brief therapy appears to accelerate recovery. Patients seem to realize that they need to get to the heart of their problems quickly (Lemma, Target, & Fonagy, 2011).

Interpersonal Psychotherapy

One example of a brief dynamic therapy is **interpersonal psychotherapy (IPT)**, which was first developed to help depressed people improve their relationships with others (Teyber & McClure, 2017). Research has confirmed that IPT is effective for depressive disorders, as well as eating disorders, substance abuse, PTSD, and personality disorders (Cuijpers et al., 2011; Fiore et al., 2008; Hoffart, 2005; Lenze & Potts, 2017; Markowitz, 2017; Talbot & Gamble, 2008).

Liona's therapy is a good example of IPT (Brown & Barlow, 2017). Liona was suffering from depression that a therapist helped her trace to a conflict with her parents. When her father was absent, Liona adopted the role of her mother's protector and friend. However, when her father was home, she was expected to resume her role as a daughter. She was angry with her father for frequently abandoning her mother and upset about having to switch roles so often. Liona's IPT sessions (which sometimes included her mother) focused on clarifying Liona's family roles. Her mood improved a lot after her mother urged her to "stick to being herself."

Individual Versus Group Therapy

Many psychotherapies can be adapted for use in groups (Corey, 2017). Surprisingly, **group therapy**—psychotherapy done with several unrelated clients—has turned out to be just as cost-effective as individual therapy and even has some special advantages (Burlingame, Fuhriman, & Mosier, 2003; Wroe & Wise, 2012).

Insight therapy Any therapy that stresses the importance of understanding the origins of a psychological disorder, usually unresolved unconscious conflicts.

Action therapy Any therapy that stresses directly changing troublesome thoughts and/or behaviors without regard for their origins, unconscious or otherwise.

Directive therapy Any therapy that stresses the need for the therapist to lead the patient toward a resolution of his or her psychological distress.

Nondirective therapy Any therapy in which the therapist supports the client while the client gains insight into his or her own problems and their resolution.

Brief psychodynamic therapy A modern therapy based on psychoanalytic theory but designed to produce insights more quickly.

Interpersonal psychotherapy (IPT) A brief dynamic psychotherapy designed to help people by improving their relationships with other people.

Group therapy Psychological treatment involving several unrelated clients.

A group therapy session. Group members offer mutual support while sharing problems and insights.

What are the advantages of group therapy? In group therapy, a person can *act out* or directly experience problems. Doing so often produces insights that might not occur from merely talking about an issue. In addition, other group members with similar problems can offer support and useful input. Group therapy is especially good for helping people understand their personal relationships (Corey, 2017; McCluskey, 2002). For reasons such as these, several specialized groups have emerged. Because they range from Alcoholics Anonymous (AA) to Marriage Encounter, we share only a few examples.

Psychodrama One of the first group therapies was developed by Jacob Moreno (1953), who called his technique *psychodrama*. In **psychodrama**, clients act out personal conflicts with others who play supporting roles (McVea, Gow, & Lowe, 2011; Schermer, 2015). Through role-playing, the client reenacts incidents that cause problems in real life. For example, Don, a disturbed teenager, might act out a typical family fight, with the therapist playing his father and with other clients playing his mother, brothers, and sisters. Moreno believed that insights gained in this way transfer to real-life situations.

Therapists using psychodrama often find that role reversals are helpful. A **role reversal** involves taking the part of another person to learn how he or she feels. For instance, Don might role-play his father or mother to better understand *their* feelings. A related method is the **mirror technique**, in which a client observes another person reenact his or her behavior. Thus, Don might briefly join the group and watch as another group member plays his role. This would allow him to see himself as others see him. Later, the group may summarize what happened and reflect on its meaning.

Family and Couples Therapy Family relationships are the source of great pleasure and, all too often, great pain. In **family therapy**, a group of related individuals focuses on improving interpersonal dynamics and communication to resolve the problems of each family member. This is called *couples therapy* when children are not involved (Scheinkman, 2008). Family and couples therapy tends to be time-limited and focused on specific problems, such as frequent fights or a depressed teenager. For some types of problems, family therapy may be superior to other approaches (Eisler et al., 2007; Wiebe & Johnson, 2016).

Family therapists believe that a problem experienced by one family member is the whole family's problem (Teyber & McClure, 2017). If the entire pattern of behavior in a family doesn't change, improvements in any individual family member may not last. Family members, therefore, work together to improve communication, change destructive patterns, and see themselves and each other in new ways (Goldenberg & Goldenberg, 2013; Griffin, 2002).

Does the therapist work with the whole family at once? Family therapists treat the family as a unit, but they may not meet with the entire family at each session (Eisler et al., 2007). If a family crisis is at hand, the therapist may first try to identify the most resourceful family members who can help solve the immediate problem.

Face-to-Face Versus Distance Therapy

While it is generally preferable to meet with a therapist face-to-face, it is not always possible. Today, psychological services are available in the home through radio, television, telephone, and the Internet (Silverman, 2013). Not only is this generally less expensive, it also makes therapy available to people who, for a variety of reasons, cannot easily attend a traditional face-to-face session.

Mass Media Therapists By now, you have probably heard a phone-in radio psychologist or watched one on television. Participants typically describe problems ranging from child abuse to phobias and sexual adjustment to depression. The media psychologist then offers reassurance, advice, or suggestions for getting help. Such programs may seem harmless, but they raise some important questions. For instance, is it reasonable to give advice without knowing anything about a person's background? Could the advice do harm? What good can a psychologist do in three minutes, or even an hour?

In their own defense, mass media psychologists point out that listeners and viewers may learn solutions to their problems by hearing others talk. Many also stress that their work is educational, not therapeutic. Nevertheless, the question arises: When does advice become therapy? The American Psychological Association urges media psychologists to discuss problems only of a general nature and not to actually counsel anyone.

Telephone and Internet Therapists Of course, mass media psychologists must entertain as well as educate. Most actual distance therapy, however, is conducted one-on-one via telephone or the Internet. Regardless of how a therapist and client communicate, perhaps the *key* feature of successful therapy is the establishment of an effective relationship between therapist and client. This could be a problem if, for example, only texting is used. Smiley faces and text message shorthand are poor substitutes for real human interaction, which includes interpersonal cues such as facial expressions and body language. ☺ LOL. Similarly, brief email messages are no way to make a diagnosis. However, the Internet also makes it possible to create two-way audio–video links. Conducting therapy this way lacks the close personal contact of face-to-face interaction, but it also removes many of the objections to doing therapy at a distance (Gros et al., 2013).

It is worth noting that distance therapy does have some distinct advantages and disadvantages. For one thing, clients can more easily remain anonymous. Thus, a person who might hesitate to see a psychologist can seek help privately by phone or online. (But beware that email counseling may not be completely confidential and could be intercepted and misused.) Of special concern is the fact that distance therapists may or may not be trained professionals. Even if they are, questions exist about whether a psychologist licensed in one state can legally do therapy in another state via the telephone or the Internet.

In closing, under the right circumstances, distance therapy can be successful (Bauer et al., 2011; Brenes, Ingram, & Danhauer, 2011). For example, telephone counseling helps people quit smoking (Rabius, Wiatrek, & McAlister, 2012). Other studies have shown that depressed people, substance abusers, as well as people with social phobia and panic disorder benefit from Internet therapy (Carlbring et al., 2007; Hermes & Rosenheck, 2016; Klein, Richards, & Austin, 2006; Titov, 2011).

AF archive/Alamy Stock Photo

Popular TV psychologist Phillip McGraw was awarded a President's Citation from the APA for his work in publicizing mental health issues (Meyers, 2006). Media psychologists have been urged to educate without actually doing therapy on the air. Some overstep this boundary, however. Do you think Dr. Phil ever goes too far?

Summary For a summary of major differences among the psychotherapies discussed in this module, as well as in Modules 66 and 67, see ■ **Table 65.2**. To add to your understanding, let's ask whether the psychotherapies work and what, if anything, all successful psychotherapies have in common.

Psychodrama A therapy in which clients act out personal conflicts and feelings in the presence of others who play supporting roles.

Role reversal Taking the role of another person to learn how one's own behavior appears from the other person's perspective.

Mirror technique Observing another person reenact one's own behavior, like a character in a play; designed to help persons see themselves more clearly.

Family therapy Treatment of a group of related individuals that focuses on interpersonal dynamics and communication.

TABLE 65.2 | Comparison of Psychotherapies

	Insight or Action?	Nondirective or Directive?	Individual or Group?	Therapy's Strength
Psychoanalysis	Insight	Directive	Individual	Searching honesty
Brief psychodynamic therapy	Insight	Directive	Individual	Productive use of conflict
Client-centered therapy	Insight	Nondirective	Both	Acceptance, empathy

(*Continued*)

TABLE 65.2 | (Continued)

	Insight or Action?	Nondirective or Directive?	Individual or Group?	Therapy's Strength
Existential therapy	Insight	Both	Individual	Personal empowerment
Gestalt therapy	Insight	Directive	Both	Focus on immediate awareness
Behavior therapy	Action	Directive	Both	Observable changes in behavior
Cognitive therapy	Action	Directive	Individual	Constructive guidance
Rational-emotive behavior therapy	Action	Directive	Individual	Clarity of thinking and goals
Psychodrama	Insight	Directive	Group	Constructive reenactments
Family therapy	Both	Directive	Group	Shared responsibility for problems

Sources: Adapted from Corsini & Wedding, 2019; Prochaska & Norcross, 2014.

Therapies—An Overview

Learning Outcome 65.3 Describe how various psychotherapies are effective and what they have in common

Effectiveness of Psychotherapy

OK. So how effective is psychotherapy? In 1952, British psychologist Hans Eysenck published the first systematic attempt to empirically answer this question. His answer sent shockwaves through psychology when he found that psychotherapy produces no more improvement in patients than doing nothing (Eysenck, 1952, 1994). Apparently, psychotherapy, and in particular, psychoanalysis, took so long that patients experienced a **spontaneous remission** of symptoms—improvement due to the mere passage of time.

How seriously should the possibility of spontaneous remission be taken? An old joke among doctors is that a cold lasts a week without treatment and seven days with it. Perhaps the same is true of therapy. It's true that problems ranging from hyperactivity to anxiety often improve with the passage of time.

Further, this is not the only problem we face when evaluating the effectiveness of therapies. In one national survey, nine out of ten people who have sought mental health care say their lives improved as a result of the treatment (Howard et al., 2001; Kotkin, Daviet, & Gurin, 1996). Unfortunately, you can't just take people's word for it. Someone who feels better after six months of therapy may have experienced a spontaneous remission. Or perhaps the crisis that triggered the therapy is now nearly forgotten. Or maybe some sort of **therapy placebo effect** has occurred, in which improvement is based on a client's belief that therapy will help. Also, it's possible that the person has received help from other people, such as family, friends, or clergy.

To find out if a therapy works, we could randomly place clients in an experimental group that receives therapy and a control group that does not. When this is done, the control group may show some improvement, even without receiving therapy (Lambert & Ogles, 2002; Schuck, Keijsers, & Rinck, 2011). Thus, we can conclude that the therapy is effective only if people in the experimental group improve more than those in the control group.

But isn't it unethical to withhold treatment from someone who really needs therapy? That's right. One way to deal with this is to use a *waiting-list control group.* In this case, people who are waiting to see a therapist are compared with those who receive therapy. Later, those on the waiting list also eventually receive therapy.

Empirically Supported Therapies

The real value of Eysenck's critique of the effectiveness of psychoanalysis is that it encouraged psychologists to try new ideas and techniques. Researchers began to ask, "When psychotherapy works, why does it work? Which parts of it are essential and which are unnecessary?" Some research has addressed the risk factors that predispose individuals to mental health problems (Giletta et al., 2015), as well as factors that promote resilience, and help to buffer people against such problems (Ehret, Joormann, & Berking, 2015).

Research has also been carried out to examine whether particular treatments are effective. In some cases, the American Psychological Association has designated treatments as *empirically supported*, meaning that there is a body of research that consistently supports their effectiveness in dealing with a specific form of psychopathology (American Psychological Association, 2006; Tolin et al., 2015). For example, behavioral, cognitive, and drug therapies are most helpful in treating obsessive-compulsive disorder.

Of course, whether treatments are successful or not depends on factors such as therapist characteristics (Holdsworth, Brown, Bowen, & Howat, 2014), client characteristics (Wiltink et al., 2016), and the therapist–client relationship (sometimes called the therapeutic alliance; Bartle-Haring et al., 2016). Based on their findings, researchers have increasingly noted the importance of tailoring treatments to individuals, leading to new research on the effectiveness of personalized treatments (Schneider, Arch, & Walitzky-Taylor, 2015).

Also, results vary in individual cases. For some people, therapy is immensely helpful; for others, it is unsuccessful. Overall, it is effective for more people than not. Speaking more subjectively, a real success, in which a person's life is changed for the better, can be worth the frustration of several cases in which little progress is made.

To summarize, hundreds of studies show a strong pattern of positive effects for psychotherapy, counseling, and other psychological treatments (Barlow, Boswell, & Thompson-Hollands, 2013; Shedler, 2010). In addition, studies have revealed that some therapies work best for specific problems (Bradley et al., 2005; Eddy et al., 2004). For example, behavioral, cognitive, and drug therapies are most helpful in treating obsessive-compulsive disorder.

Core Features of Psychotherapy

What, if anything, do all psychotherapies have in common, regardless of what form they take? Psychotherapies of various types share all or most of the following goals: understanding a client's perspective; to help the client restore hope, courage, and optimism; gain insight; resolve conflicts; improve one's sense of self; change unacceptable patterns of behavior; find purpose; mend interpersonal relations; and learn to approach problems rationally (Frank & Frank, 2004; Trull & Prinstein, 2013). To accomplish these goals, psychotherapies offer the following:

1. Perhaps more than any other single factor, effective therapy provides a **therapeutic alliance**, a *caring relationship* that unites the client and therapist as they work together to solve the client's problems. The strength of this alliance has a major impact on whether therapy succeeds (Arnow et al., 2013; Bartle-Haring et al., 2016; Constantino et al., 2017). The basis for this relationship is emotional rapport, warmth, friendship, understanding, acceptance, and empathy (Crisp, 2014).
2. Therapy offers a *protected setting* in which emotional *catharsis* (release) can take place. It is a sanctuary in which the client is free to express fears, anxieties, and personal secrets without fearing rejection or loss of confidentiality.
3. All therapies to some extent offer an *explanation* or *rationale* for the client's suffering. In addition, they propose a line of action that will end this suffering.
4. Therapy provides clients with a *new perspective* about themselves and their situations and a chance to practice *new behaviors* (Prochaska & Norcross, 2014). Insights gained during therapy can bring about lasting changes in clients' lives (Grande et al., 2003).

Therapy and Culture Understanding another person's perspective is especially important when cultural differences may create a barrier between a client and therapist (Jun, 2010; La Roche & Lustig, 2013).

For example, at the age of 23, the patient was clearly suffering from *ifufunyane*, a form of bewitchment common in the Xhosa culture of South Africa. However, he was treated at a local hospital by psychiatrists, who said he had schizophrenia and gave him antipsychotic drugs. The drugs helped, but his family shunned his fancy medical treatment and took him to a traditional healer, who gave him herbs for his ifufunyane. Unfortunately, he got worse and was readmitted to the hospital. This time, the psychiatrists

Spontaneous remission Improvement of symptoms due to the mere passage of time.

Therapy placebo effect Improvement caused not by the actual process of therapy but by a client's expectation that therapy will help.

Therapeutic alliance A caring relationship that unites a therapist and a client in working to solve the client's problems.

Culturally skilled therapist A therapist who has the awareness, knowledge, and skills necessary to treat clients from diverse cultural backgrounds.

included the patient's family in his treatment. Together, they agreed to treat him with a combination of antipsychotic drugs *and* traditional herbs. This time, the patient got much better and his ifufunyane was alleviated, too (Niehaus et al., 2005).

As this example illustrates, a **culturally skilled therapist** is trained to work with clients from various cultural backgrounds. To be culturally skilled, a counselor must be able to do all of the following (American Psychological Association, 2017c; Brammer, 2012; Comas-Diaz, 2012):

- Adapt traditional theories and techniques to meet the needs of clients from non-European ethnic or racial groups.
- Be aware of his or her own cultural values and biases.
- Establish rapport with a person from a different cultural background.
- Be open to cultural differences without resorting to stereotypes.
- Treat members of racial or ethnic communities as individuals.
- Be aware of a client's ethnic identity and degree of acculturation to the majority society.
- Use existing helping resources within a cultural group to support efforts to resolve problems.

Cultural awareness has helped broaden our ideas about mental health and optimal development (Brammer, 2012). It also is worth remembering that cultural barriers apply to communication in all areas of life, not just therapy. Although such differences can be challenging, they also are frequently enriching (Fowers & Davidov, 2006).

MODULE 65 Treating Psychological Distress—Learning Outcomes Revisited

65.1 Describe some historical approaches to psychotherapy

Early approaches to mental illness were dominated by superstition and moral condemnation. Demonology attributed mental disturbance to demonic possession and prescribed exorcism as the cure. More humane treatment began in 1793 with the work of Philippe Pinel in Paris. Sigmund Freud developed psychoanalysis, the first psychotherapy, little more than 120 years ago.

65.2 Outline the ways contemporary psychotherapies differ

All psychotherapy aims to facilitate positive changes in personality, behavior, or adjustment. Psychotherapies may be classified as insight, action, nondirective, directive, and combinations of these. Psychotherapies may be open-ended or time-limited. Brief psychodynamic therapy (which relies on psychoanalytic theory but is brief and focused) is as effective as other major therapies. One example is interpersonal psychotherapy. Psychotherapies may be conducted with individuals or groups. In psychodrama, individuals enact roles and incidents resembling their real-life problems. In family therapy, the family group is treated as a unit. Many therapies may be effectively conducted either face-to-face or at a distance, via telephone and the Internet.

65.3 Describe how various psychotherapies are effective and what they have in common

Psychotherapies that have significant research that supports their effectiveness are referred to as empirically supported treatments. Research into the effectiveness of therapies must take many factors into account, including spontaneous remission, therapy placebo effects, risk and resilience factors, and therapist and client characteristics. Psychotherapy is generally effective, although some forms of therapy are better than others for dealing with some psychological issues. Most modern psychotherapies are based on a therapeutic alliance, a protected setting, catharsis, insights, new perspectives, and a chance to practice new behaviors. The culturally skilled counselor must be able to establish rapport with a person from a different cultural background and adapt traditional theories and techniques to meet the needs of clients from non-European ethnic groups.

Reflective Practice

Content Check

Match:

_______ **1.** Directive therapies	**A.** Change behavior
_______ **2.** Action therapies	**B.** Place responsibility on the client
_______ **3.** Insight therapies	**C.** The client is guided strongly
_______ **4.** Nondirective therapies	**D.** Seek understanding

5. In psychodrama, people attempt to form meaningful wholes out of disjointed thoughts, feelings, and actions. T or F?

6. The mirror technique is frequently used in
- **a.** exposure therapy
- **b.** psychodrama
- **c.** family therapy
- **d.** ECT

7. To date, the most acceptable type of "distance therapy" is
- **a.** media psychology
- **b.** commercial telephone counseling
- **c.** emoticon-based therapy
- **d.** based on two-way audio and video links

8. Emotional rapport, warmth, understanding, acceptance, and empathy are the core of
- **a.** the therapeutic alliance
- **b.** large-group awareness training
- **c.** role reversals
- **d.** action therapy

9. Culturally skilled therapists do all but one of the following. Which one does *not* apply?
- **a.** Are aware of the client's degree of acculturation
- **b.** Use helping resources within the client's cultural group
- **c.** Adapt standard techniques to match cultural stereotypes
- **d.** Are aware of their own cultural values

Skill Check

Think Critically

10. In your opinion, do psychologists have a duty to protect others who may be harmed by their clients? For example, if a patient has homicidal fantasies about his ex-wife, should she be informed?

Self-Reflect

The use of trepanning, demonology, and exorcism all implied that the mentally ill were "cursed." To what extent are the mentally ill rejected and stigmatized today? Can you think of any personal experiences of spontaneous remission (times when a psychological issue resolved itself without any intervention on your part)? Make a list describing what you think it means to be mentally healthy. How well does your list match the items in Table 65.1? What lies at the "heart" of psychotherapy? How would you describe it to a friend?

ANSWERS

1. C 2. A 3. D 4. B 5. F 6. b 7. d 8. a 9. c 10. According to the law, there is a duty to protect others when a therapist could, with little effort, prevent serious harm. However, this duty can conflict with a client's rights to confidentiality and with client–therapist trust. Therapists often must make difficult choices in such situations.

MODULE 66

Therapies

Psychodynamic, Humanistic, and Cognitive Therapies

The Talking Cures

Prisma Bildagentur AG/Alamy Stock Photo

Imagine lying back on a couch, talking about whatever comes to mind. That's just how psychotherapy got started, on this famous couch with Sigmund Freud sitting out of sight, taking notes, and offering interpretations. This procedure was supposed to encourage a free flow of thoughts and images from the unconscious.

When most people picture psychotherapists at work, they imagine them talking with their clients. Let's sample a variety of talk-oriented approaches. Psychodynamic therapies, of which Freudian psychoanalysis was the first, tend to stress the need to gain insight into the *unconscious* forces assumed to control us all. While humanistic therapies also are insight therapies, they focus on helping clients gain deeper insight into their *conscious* thoughts, emotions, and behavior. In contrast to both psychodynamic and humanistic therapies, cognitive therapies tend to be less concerned with insight than with helping people change harmful thinking patterns. Let's start with some insight.

~LEARNING OUTCOMES~

After reading this module you should be able to:

66.1 Briefly discuss Freudian psychoanalysis and explain why it is no longer a common therapy

66.2 Describe three major humanistic therapies

66.3 Explain how cognitive therapy changes thoughts and emotions; also describe some contemporary forms of cognitive and cognitive behavioral therapy

Psychodynamic Therapies—The Talking Cure

Learning Outcome 66.1 Briefly discuss Freudian psychoanalysis and explain why it is no longer a common therapy

How did Freud treat psychological problems? Freud's theory stressed that "neurosis" and "hysteria" are caused by repressed memories, motives, and conflicts—particularly those stemming from instinctual drives for sex and aggression. Although they are hidden, these forces remain active in the personality and cause some people to develop rigid ego defenses and compulsive, self-defeating behavior. Thus, the main goal of

psychoanalysis is to reduce internal conflicts that lead to emotional suffering (Aron & Starr, 2013).

Psychoanalysis

Freud developed four basic techniques to uncover the unconscious roots of neurosis (Freud, 1949): *free association, dream analysis, analysis of resistance,* and *analysis of transference.*

Free Association The basis for **free association** is saying whatever comes to mind without worrying whether ideas are painful, embarrassing, or illogical. Thoughts are simply allowed to move freely from one idea to the next, without self-censorship. The purpose of free association is to lower defenses so that unconscious thoughts and feelings can emerge (Lavin, 2012; Spence et al., 2009).

Dream Analysis Freud believed that dreams disguise consciously unacceptable feelings and forbidden desires in dream form (Fischer & Kächele, 2009; Klösch & Holzinger, 2014). The psychoanalyst can use this "royal road to the unconscious" to help the patient work past the obvious, visible meaning of the dream (its *manifest content*) to uncover the hidden, symbolic meaning (its *latent content*). This is achieved by analyzing *dream symbols* (images that have personal or emotional meanings; see Module 24).

Suppose that a young man dreams of pulling a pistol from his waistband and aiming at a target as his wife watches. The pistol repeatedly fails to discharge, and the man's wife laughs at him. Freud might have seen this as an indication of repressed feelings of sexual impotence, with the gun serving as a disguised image of the penis.

Analysis of Resistance A central concern of psychoanalysis is the fact that patients who come to analysis for help nevertheless often *resist* changing when it is necessary to become healthier (Levenson, 2012). For example, when free associating or describing dreams, patients may resist talking about or thinking about certain topics. Such **resistances**—blockages in the flow of insights and ideas—reveal particularly important unconscious conflicts. As analysts become aware of resistances, they bring them to the patient's awareness so the patient can deal with them realistically. Rather than being roadblocks in therapy, resistances can be clues and challenges (Plakun, 2012).

Analysis of Transference **Transference** is the tendency to "transfer" feelings to a therapist similar to those that the patient had for important persons in his or her past. At times, for example, the patient may act as if the analyst is a rejecting father, an unloving or overprotective mother, or a former lover. As the patient reexperiences repressed emotions, the therapist can help the patient recognize and understand them. Troubled persons often provoke anger, rejection, boredom, criticism, and other negative reactions from others. Effective therapists learn to avoid reacting like others and playing the patient's habitual resistance and transference games. This, too, contributes to therapeutic change (Aron & Starr, 2013).

Psychoanalysis Today

What is the status of psychoanalysis today? Psychoanalysis made a major contribution to modern therapies by highlighting the importance of unconscious conflicts (Borch-Jacobsen & Shamdasani, 2011; Strenger, 2016). Since the development of psychoanalysis, however, psychotherapy has undergone dramatic change beginning with Freud's own followers, the neo-Freudians (see Module 52). Today, a wide variety of psychotherapeutic options are available, and traditional psychoanalysts are relatively hard to find (Cortina, 2016).

Also, traditional psychoanalysis took a long time and considerable effort. This resulted in the development of newer, more streamlined dynamic therapies, in part due to questions about whether traditional psychoanalysis "works." In a classic criticism, Hans Eysenck (1994) suggested that psychoanalysis simply takes so long that patients experience a **spontaneous remission** of symptoms—improvement due to the mere passage of time.

How seriously should the possibility of spontaneous remission be taken? It's true that problems ranging from hyperactivity to anxiety do improve with the passage of time. Regardless, researchers have confirmed that psychoanalysis and related psychotherapies do, in fact, produce improvement in a majority of patients (see Module 65).

The real value of Eysenck's critique is that it encouraged psychologists to try new ideas and techniques. Researchers

Psychoanalysis A Freudian therapy that emphasizes the use of free association, dream interpretation, resistances, and transference to uncover unconscious conflicts.

Free association The psychoanalytic technique of encouraging a patient to say whatever comes to mind without censoring.

Resistance Blockage in the flow of free association around topics the client avoids thinking or talking about.

Transference The tendency of patients to transfer to a therapist feelings that correspond to those the patient had for important persons in his or her past.

Spontaneous remission Improvement of symptoms due to the mere passage of time.

began to ask, "When psychoanalysis works, why does it work? Which parts of it are essential and which are unnecessary?" Modern therapists have given surprisingly varied answers to these questions. Let's explore some of them.

Humanistic Therapies—Liberating Human Potential

Learning Outcome 66.2 Describe three major humanistic therapies

Better self-knowledge was the goal of traditional psychoanalysis. However, Freud claimed that his patients could expect only to change their "hysterical misery into common unhappiness"! Unlike psychoanalysts, humanistic therapists are more optimistic and believe that humans have a natural urge to seek health and self-growth. Most assume that it is possible for people to use their potentials fully and live rich, rewarding lives. Here, we discuss three of the most popular humanistic therapies: client-centered therapy, existential therapy, and Gestalt therapy.

Client-Centered Therapy

What is client-centered therapy? How is it different from psychoanalysis? Whereas psychoanalysis is directive and based on insights from the *un*conscious, **client-centered therapy** (or person-centered therapy) is *non*directive and based on insights from *conscious* thoughts and feelings (Brodley, 2006; Cain, 2014; Murphy & Joseph, 2016). (Rogers preferred the term *client* since *patient* implies that a person is sick and needs to be cured.)

The *client* being treated speaks without direction, judgment, or interpretation from the therapist. The psychoanalyst tends to take a position of authority, stating what dreams, thoughts, or memories "mean." In contrast, Carl Rogers (1902–1987), who originated client-centered therapy, believed that what is right or valuable for the therapist may be wrong for the client (Rogers, 1959).

Consequently, in client-centered therapy, therapists do not try to "fix" clients. Instead, clients must actively seek to solve their problems because they determine what will be discussed during each session (Cooper & McLeod, 2011). The therapist's job is to create a safe "atmosphere of growth" by providing opportunities for change.

How do therapists create such an atmosphere? Rogers believed that effective therapists maintain four basic conditions. First, the therapist offers the client **unconditional positive regard**, or complete, unqualified acceptance of another person as he or she is. The therapist refuses to react with shock, dismay, or disapproval to anything the client says or feels. Total acceptance by the therapist is the first step to self-acceptance by the client.

Psychotherapist Carl Rogers (1902–1987), who originated client-centered therapy.

Photo Credit Doug Land, 1983, Copyright Natalie Rogers

Second, the therapist attempts to achieve genuine **empathy** by trying to see the world through the client's eyes and feeling some part of what the client is feeling (Grant, 2010).

As a third essential condition, the therapist strives for **authenticity** (to be genuine and honest). The therapist must not hide behind a professional role. Rogers believed that phony fronts destroy the growth atmosphere sought in client-centered therapy.

Fourth, the therapist does not make interpretations, propose solutions, or offer advice. Instead, the therapist relies on **reflection**—rephrasing, summarizing, or repeating—the client's thoughts and feelings. This enables the therapist to act as a psychological "mirror" so clients can see themselves more clearly. Rogers theorized that a person armed with a realistic self-image and greater self-acceptance will gradually discover solutions to life's problems.

Existential Therapy

According to the existentialists, "being in the world" (existence) creates deep existential anxiety. Each of us must deal with universal human challenges such as the realities of *death*, the fact that we are *free* to create our private world by making choices, *isolation* on a vast and indifferent planet, and most of all, we must confront feelings of *meaninglessness* (Craig, 2012).

What do these concerns have to do with psychotherapy? **Existential therapy** focuses on the "ultimate concerns" of existence, such as meaning, choice, and responsibility (Vontress, 2013). Like client-centered therapy, it promotes self-knowledge (Adams, 2016). However, there are important differences. Client-centered therapy seeks to uncover a "true self" hidden behind a screen of defenses. In contrast, existential therapy emphasizes free will, the human ability to make choices. Accordingly, existential therapists believe you can *choose to become* the person you want to be. Existential therapists try to give clients the *courage* to make rewarding and socially constructive choices.

One example of existential therapy is Victor Frankl's *logotherapy,* which emphasizes the need to find and maintain meaning in life. Frankl (1904–1997) based his approach on experiences that he had as a prisoner in a Nazi concentration camp. In the camp, Frankl saw countless prisoners break down as they were stripped of all hope and human dignity (Frankl, 1955). Those who survived with their sanity did so because they managed to hang on to a sense of meaning *(logos).* Even in less dire circumstances, a sense of purpose in life adds greatly to psychological well-being (Prochaska & Norcross, 2014).

What does the existential therapist do? The therapist helps clients discover self-imposed limitations in personal identity. To be successful, the client must fully accept the challenge of changing his or her life (Bretherton & Orner, 2004). It is interesting that Buddhists seek a similar state that they call "radical acceptance" (Brach, 2003).

A key aspect of existential therapy is *confrontation,* in which clients are challenged to be mindful of their values and choices and to take responsibility for the quality of their existence (Claessens, 2009). An important part of confrontation is the unique, intense, here-and-now *encounter* between two human beings. When existential therapy is successful, it brings about a renewed sense of purpose and a reappraisal of what's important in life. Some clients even experience an emotional rebirth, as if they had survived a close brush with death.

Gestalt Therapy

Gestalt therapy is based on the idea that perception, or *awareness,* is disjointed and incomplete in maladjusted persons. The German word *Gestalt* means "whole" or "complete." **Gestalt therapy** helps people rebuild thinking, feeling, and acting into connected wholes. This is achieved by expanding personal awareness; by accepting responsibility for one's thoughts, feelings, and actions; and by filling in gaps in experience (Brownell, 2016).

What are "gaps in experience"? Gestalt therapists believe that we often shy away from expressing or "owning" upsetting feelings. This creates a gap in self-awareness that may become a barrier to personal growth. For example, a person who feels anger after the death of a parent might go for years without fully expressing it. Threatening gaps like this may impair emotional health.

The Gestalt approach is more directive than client-centered or existential therapy, and it is less insight-oriented, instead emphasizing immediate experience. Working either one-on-one or in a group setting, the Gestalt therapist encourages clients to become more aware of their moment-to-moment thoughts, perceptions, and emotions (Frew, 2013). Rather than discussing *why* clients feel guilt, anger, fear, or boredom, the therapist encourages them to have these feelings in the "here and now" and become fully aware of them. The therapist promotes awareness by drawing attention to a client's posture, voice, eye movements, and hand gestures. Clients also may be asked to exaggerate vague feelings until they become clear. Gestalt therapists believe that expressing such feelings allows people to "take care of unfinished business" and break through emotional impasses (Truscott, 2014).

Gestalt therapy is often associated with the work of Fritz Perls (1969). According to Perls, emotional health comes from knowing what you *want* to do, not dwelling on what you *should* do, *ought* to do, or *should want* to do (Wheeler & Axelsson, 2015). In other words, emotional health comes from taking full responsibility for one's feelings and actions. For example, it means changing "I can't" to "I won't," or "I must" to "I choose to."

Client-centered (person-centered) therapy Individual being treated talks without direction, judgment, or interpretation from the therapist.

Unconditional positive regard Complete, unqualified acceptance of another person as he or she is.

Empathy A capacity for taking another's point of view; the ability to feel what another is feeling.

Authenticity In Carl Rogers's terms, the ability of a therapist to be genuine and honest about his or her own feelings.

Reflection In client-centered therapy, the process of rephrasing or repeating thoughts and feelings expressed by clients so they can become aware of what they are saying.

Existential therapy An insight therapy that focuses on the elemental problems of existence, such as death, meaning, choice, and responsibility; emphasizes making courageous life choices.

Gestalt therapy An approach that focuses on immediate experience and awareness to help clients rebuild thinking, feeling, and acting into connected wholes; emphasizes the integration of fragmented experiences.

How does Gestalt therapy help people discover their real wants? Above all else, Gestalt therapy emphasizes *present* experience (Levin, 2010; Yontef, 2007). Clients are urged to stop intellectualizing and talking *about* feelings. Instead, they learn to live now; live here; stop imagining; experience the real; stop unnecessary thinking; taste and see; express rather than explain, justify, or judge; give in to unpleasantness and pain just as to pleasure; and surrender to being as you are. Gestalt therapists believe that, paradoxically, the best way to change is to become who you really are (Wheeler & Axelsson, 2015).

Cognitive Therapies—Think Positive!

Learning Outcome 66.3 Explain how cognitive therapy changes thoughts and emotions; also describe some contemporary forms of cognitive and cognitive behavioral therapy

Influential American psychiatrist Aaron Beck (1967) launched a revolution in psychotherapy when he proposed that people could alleviate their depression by actively modifying their conscious thoughts and feelings. Whereas psychodynamic and humanistic therapies generally seek to foster insight into unconscious motives, **cognitive therapy** generally helps clients change conscious maladaptive thoughts, beliefs, and feeling patterns (Power, 2010; Rosner, 2012).

For example, Josephine is a hoarder whose home is crammed full with things she has acquired over two decades. If she seeks help from a therapist concerned with insight, she will try to better understand why she began collecting stuff. In contrast, if she seeks help from a cognitive therapist, she may spend little time examining her past. Instead, she will work to actively change her thoughts and beliefs about hoarding. With either approach, the goal is to give up hoarding. Further, in practice, humanistic therapies often also result in active change, and cognitive therapies often also yield deeper insight.

Cognitive therapy has been successfully used as a remedy for many problems, ranging from generalized anxiety disorder and posttraumatic stress disorder (PTSD) to marital distress and anger (Butler et al., 2006). For example, hypochondria can be greatly reduced by changing a client's thoughts and beliefs about intrusive imagery (McManus et al., 2015). Cognitive therapy has been especially successful in treating depression (Eisendrath et al., 2014).

Cognitive Therapy for Depression

As you may recall from Module 62, cognitive psychologists believe that negative, self-defeating thoughts underlie depression. According to Aaron Beck (1967, 1991), depressed persons see themselves, the world, and the future in negative terms because of several major distortions in thinking. The first is **selective perception**, which refers to perceiving only certain stimuli in a larger array. If five good things and two bad things happen during the day, depressed people focus only on the bad. A second thinking error in depression is **overgeneralization**, the tendency to think that an upsetting event applies to other, unrelated situations. An example would be Stanley's considering himself a total failure or completely worthless if he were to lose a part-time job or fail a test. To complete the picture, depressed persons tend to magnify the importance of undesirable events by engaging in **all-or-nothing thinking**. They see events as completely good or bad, right or wrong, and themselves as either successful or failing miserably (Lam & Mok, 2008).

How do cognitive therapists alter such patterns? Cognitive therapists make a step-by-step effort to correct negative thoughts that lead to depression or similar problems. At first, clients are taught to recognize and keep track of their own thoughts. The client and therapist then look for ideas and beliefs that cause depression, anger, and avoidance (Segal, Williams, & Teasdale, 2013). Next, clients are asked to gather information to test their beliefs. For instance, a depressed person might list his or her activities for a week. The list is then used to challenge all-or-nothing thoughts, such as "I had a terrible week" or "I'm a complete failure." With more coaching, clients learn to alter their thoughts in ways that improve their moods, actions, and relationships.

Cognitive therapy is at least as effective as drugs for treating many cases of depression (Lopez & Basco, 2015). Also, people who have adopted new thinking patterns are less likely to become depressed again—a benefit that drugs can't impart (Eisendrath et al., 2014; Eisendrath, Chartier, & McLane, 2011).

In an alternative approach, cognitive therapists look for an *absence* of effective coping skills and thinking patterns, not for the *presence* of self-defeating thoughts (Dobson, Backs-Dermott, & Dozois, 2000). The aim is to teach clients how to cope with anger, depression, shyness, stress, and similar problems. Stress inoculation, which was described in Module 59, is a good example of this approach.

Cognitive therapy is a rapidly expanding specialty. Before we leave the topic, let's explore another widely used cognitive therapy.

Rational-Emotive Behavior Therapy

An important pioneer of cognitive behavior therapy, Albert Ellis (1913–2007), founded rational-emotive behavior therapy. **Rational-emotive behavior therapy (REBT)** attempts to change self-defeating thoughts that cause emotional problems. According to Ellis, the basic idea of REBT is as easy as A-B-C (Ellis, 1995; Ellis & Ellis, 2011). Ellis assumed that people become unhappy and develop self-defeating habits because they have unrealistic or faulty *beliefs*.

How are beliefs important? Ellis analyzed problems in this way: The letter A stands for an *activating experience*, which the person assumes to be the cause of C, an *emotional consequence*. For instance, a person who is rejected (the activating experience) feels depressed, threatened, or hurt (the consequence). REBT shows the client that the real problem is what comes between A and C: B, which is the client's irrational and unrealistic *beliefs*. In this example, an unrealistic belief leading to unnecessary suffering is: "I must be loved and approved by everyone at all times." REBT holds that events do not *cause* us to have feelings. We feel as we do because of our beliefs (Dryden, 2011; Kottler & Shepard, 2015). (Notice that this REBT explanation of emotional distress is related to the effects of emotional appraisals. See Module 44.)

Irrational Beliefs—Which Ones Do You Hold?

REBT therapists have identified numerous beliefs that commonly lead to emotional upsets and conflicts. See if you recognize any of the following irrational beliefs (Dryden, 2011; Ellis & Ellis, 2011; Teyber & McClure, 2017):

1. I must be loved and approved by almost every significant person in my life or it's awful and I'm worthless.
   Example: "One of my classmates doesn't seem to like me. I must be a big loser."
2. I should be completely competent and achieving in all ways to be a worthwhile person.
   Example: "I don't understand my physics class. I guess I really am just stupid."
3. It's terribly upsetting when things don't go my way.
   Example: "I should have gotten a B in that class. The teacher is a total creep."
4. It's not my fault I'm unhappy; I can't control my emotional reactions.
   Example: "You make me feel awful. I would be happy if it weren't for you."
5. I should never forget it if something unpleasant happens.
   Example: "I'll never forget the time my boss insulted me. I think about it every day at work."
6. It is easier to avoid difficulties and responsibilities than to face them.
   Example: "I don't know why my girlfriend is angry. Maybe it will just pass if I ignore it."
7. A lot of people I have to deal with are bad. I should severely punish them for it.
   Example: "The students renting next door are such a pain. I'm going to play my stereo even louder the next time they complain."
8. I should depend on others who are stronger than me.
   Example: "I couldn't survive if she left me."
9. Because something once strongly affected me, it will do so forever.
   Example: "My girlfriend dumped me during my junior year in college. I can never trust a woman again."
10. There is always a perfectly obvious solution to human problems, and it is immoral if this solution is not put into practice.
    Example: "I'm so depressed about politics in this country. It all seems hopeless."*

If any of the listed beliefs sound familiar, you may be creating unnecessary emotional distress for yourself by holding on to unrealistic expectations. Ellis (1979; Ellis & Ellis, 2011) says that most irrational beliefs come from three core ideas, each of which is unrealistic:

1. I *must* perform well and be approved of by significant others. If I don't, then it is awful, I cannot stand it, and I am a rotten person.
2. You *must* treat me fairly. When you don't, it is horrible, and I cannot bear it.
3. Conditions *must* be the way I want them to be. It is terrible when they are not, and I cannot stand living in such an awful world.

Cognitive therapy Treatment of emotional and behavioral problems by changing maladaptive thoughts, beliefs, and feeling.

Selective perception Perceiving only certain stimuli among a larger array of possibilities.

Overgeneralization Blowing a single event out of proportion by extending it to a large number of unrelated situations.

All-or-nothing thinking Classifying objects or events as absolutely right or wrong, good or bad, acceptable or unacceptable, and so forth.

Rational-emotive behavior therapy (REBT) Type of treatment designed to identify and change self-defeating thoughts.

It's easy to see that such beliefs can lead to much grief and needless suffering in a less-than-perfect world. Rational-emotive behavior therapists are very directive in their attempts to change a client's irrational beliefs and "self-talk." The therapist may directly attack clients' logic, challenge their thinking, confront them with evidence contrary to their beliefs, and even assign "homework." Here, for instance, are some examples of statements that dispute irrational beliefs (adapted from Dryden, 2011; Ellis & Ellis, 2011; Kottler & Shepard, 2015):

- "Where is the evidence that you are a loser just because you didn't do well this one time?"
- "Who said the world should be fair? That's your rule."
- "What are you telling yourself to make yourself feel so upset?"
- "Is it really terrible that things aren't working out as you would like? Or is it just inconvenient?"

Many of us would probably do well to give up our irrational beliefs. Improved self-acceptance and a better tolerance of daily annoyances are the benefits of doing so.

Gambling Disorder As an example, let's consider gambling disorder. Seventeen-year-old Jonathan just lost his shirt again. This time, he did it playing online blackjack. Jonathan started out making $5 bets and then doubled his bet over and over. Surely, he thought, his luck would eventually change. However, he ran out of money after just eight straight losing hands, having lost more than $1,000. Last week, he lost a lot of money playing Texas Hold 'Em. Now Jonathan is in tears—he has lost most of his summer earnings, and he is worried about having to drop out of school and tell his parents about his losses. Jonathan has had to admit that he is part of the growing ranks of underage gambling addicts (Dixon et al., 2016; Volberg, 2012).

Like many problem gamblers, Jonathan suffers from several cognitive distortions related to gambling. Here are some mistaken beliefs about gambling (adapted from Toneatto, 2002; Wickwire, Whelan, & Meyers, 2010):

Magnified gambling skill: Your self-confidence is exaggerated, despite the fact that you lose persistently.

Attribution errors: You ascribe your wins to skill but blame your losses on bad luck.

Gambler's fallacy: You believe that a string of losses soon must be followed by wins.

Selective memory: You remember your wins but forget your losses.

Comstock/Stockbyte/Getty Images

Gambling addiction is a growing problem among young people (LaBrie & Shaffer, 2007).

Overinterpretation of cues: You put too much faith in irrelevant cues such as bodily sensations or a feeling that your next bet will be a winner.

Luck as a trait: You believe that you are a lucky person in general.

Probability biases: You have incorrect beliefs about randomness and chance events.

Do you have any of these mistaken beliefs? Taken together, Jonathan's cognitive distortions created an *illusion of control*—that is, he believed if he worked hard enough, he could figure out how to win. Fortunately, a cognitive therapist helped Jonathan *cognitively restructure* his beliefs. He now no longer believes that he can control chance events. Jonathan still gambles a bit, but he does so only recreationally, keeping his losses within his budget and enjoying himself in the process.

Cognitive Behavior Therapy

One last point. Before we go on to explore behavior therapies in Module 67: Did you notice that the B in REBT stands for "behavior"? Today, most therapists realize that changing maladaptive thoughts and doing the same for maladaptive behaviors can be done simultaneously. **Cognitive behavior therapy (CBT)** combines cognitive and behavioral therapies to optimize treatment outcomes (Farmer & Chapman, 2016). For example, compulsive hoarders respond well to therapy when it *both* corrects distorted thinking about hoarding *and* actively modifies hoarding behavior (Steketee et al., 2010). In fact, CBT is currently the most popular approach to nonmedical therapy (Pilgrim, 2011).

Thought Stopping One interesting CBT technique is **thought stopping**, which involves interrupting or preventing upsetting thoughts (Bakker, 2009). Behavior therapists and cognitive behavior therapists accept that thoughts are covert behaviors. And just like overt behaviors, thoughts can be reinforced or punished.

Think of times when you have repeatedly "put yourself down" mentally or when you have been preoccupied by needless worries, fears, or other negative and upsetting thoughts. If you want to gain control over such thoughts, thought stopping may help you do it. You can interrupt the thoughts by telling yourself "Stop" when the thought occurs.

Another simple thought-stopping technique uses mild physical punishment to suppress upsetting mental images and internal "talk." Simply place a large, flat rubber band around your wrist. As you go through the day, apply this rule: Each time you catch yourself thinking the upsetting image or thought, pull the rubber band away from your wrist and snap it. You need not make this terribly painful. Its value lies in drawing your attention to how often you form negative thoughts and in interrupting the flow of thoughts.

Anyway, onward to the behavior therapies.

Cognitive behavior therapy (CBT) Any therapy that combines elements of cognitive therapy and behavior therapy.

Thought stopping Use of aversive stimuli to interrupt or prevent upsetting thoughts.

MODULE 66 Psychodynamic, Humanistic, and Cognitive Therapies—Learning Outcomes Revisited

66.1 Briefly discuss Freudian psychoanalysis and explain why it is no longer a common therapy

The psychoanalyst uses free association, dream analysis, and analysis of resistance and transference to reveal health-producing insights. As the first true psychotherapy, Freud's psychoanalysis gave rise to modern psychodynamic therapies, although traditional psychoanalysts are now hard to find because psychoanalysis is both time-consuming and expensive. Some critics argue that traditional psychoanalysis receives credit for spontaneous remissions of symptoms. However, psychoanalysis is successful for many patients.

66.2 Describe three major humanistic therapies

Client-centered (or person-centered) therapy is nondirective, based on insights gained from conscious thoughts and feelings, and dedicated to creating an atmosphere of growth. Unconditional positive regard, empathy, authenticity, and reflection are combined to give the client a chance to solve his or her own problems. Existential therapies focus on the end result of the choices one makes in life. Clients are encouraged through confrontation and encounter to exercise free will and to take responsibility for their choices. Gestalt therapy emphasizes immediate awareness of thoughts and feelings. Its goal is to rebuild thinking, feeling, and acting into connected wholes and to help clients break through emotional blockages.

66.3 Explain how cognitive therapy changes thoughts and emotions; also describe some contemporary forms of cognitive and cognitive behavioral therapy

Cognitive therapy emphasizes changing thought patterns that underlie emotional or behavioral problems. Its goals are to correct distorted thinking, teach improved coping skills, or both. Aaron Beck's cognitive therapy focuses on changing several major distortions in thinking: selective perception, overgeneralization, and all-or-nothing thinking. In Albert Ellis's variation of cognitive therapy, called rational-emotive behavior therapy (REBT), clients learn to recognize and challenge the irrational beliefs that are at the core of their maladaptive thinking patterns. Cognitive and behavior therapies can be combined, resulting in cognitive behavior therapy (CBT). Thought-stopping is a useful CBT technique.

Reflective Practice

Content Check

1. In psychoanalysis, an emotional attachment to the therapist is called ________.

Match:

2. Client-centered therapy — **A.** Changing thought patterns
3. Gestalt therapy — **B.** Unconditional positive regard
4. Existential therapy — **C.** Gaps in awareness
5. REBT — **D.** Choice and becoming

6. The Gestalt therapist tries to *reflect* a client's thoughts and feelings. T or F?
7. Confrontation and encounter are concepts of existential therapy. T or F?
8. The B in the A-B-C of REBT stands for
   - **a.** behavior
   - **b.** belief
   - **c.** being
   - **d.** Beck

Skill Check

Think Critically

9. According to Freud's concept of *transference,* patients "transfer" their feelings onto the psychoanalyst. In light of this idea, to what might the term *countertransference* refer?
10. How might using the term *patient* affect the relationship between an individual and a therapist?

Self-Reflect

Try to free associate (aloud) for 10 minutes. Did anything interesting surface? You are going to play the role of a therapist for a classroom demonstration. How would you act if you were a psychoanalyst? A client-centered therapist? A Gestalt therapist? A rational-emotive behavior therapist? A cognitive behavior therapist? We all occasionally engage in negative thinking. Can you remember a time recently when you engaged in selective perception? Overgeneralization? All-or-nothing thinking?

ANSWERS

1. transference 2. B 3. C 4. D 5. A 6. T 7. T 8. b 9. Psychoanalysts (and therapists in general) also are human. They may transfer their own unresolved, unconscious feelings onto their patients. This sometimes complicates the therapeutic process (Bunnell, 2016). 10. The terms *doctor* and *patient* imply a large gap in status and authority between the individual and his or her therapist. Client-centered or person-centered therapy attempts to narrow this gap by making the person the final authority concerning solutions to his or her problems. Also, the word *patient* implies that a person is "sick" and needs to be "cured." Many regard this as an inappropriate way to think about human problems.

Therapies
Behavior Therapies

MODULE 67

Testing Her Wings

Shanika had a big problem. It wasn't the free Caribbean vacation she unexpectedly won in a contest so much as her fear of flying there in the first place. Realizing that she should have done it years ago, she enrolled in a program designed to help her overcome her fear. Little did she know that phobias like hers responded well to a behavior therapy called systematic desensitization.

John Lund/Marc Romanelli/Blend Images/Corbis

In just a few weeks, her program eased her fear of flying by combining systematic desensitization, relaxation, group support, and lots of direct exposure to airliners. She was amazed at how calm she was when her program concluded with an actual brief flight so that participants could "test their wings."

Behavior therapists seek to directly change behavior patterns so that people can function more comfortably and effectively. This module describes some innovative and successful behavioral therapies, including systematic desensitization.

~LEARNING OUTCOMES~

After reading this module you should be able to:

67.1 Contrast behavior and insight therapies, and describe some behavioral change techniques derived from classical conditioning

67.2 Describe some behavioral change techniques derived from operant conditioning

Therapies Based on Classical Conditioning—Healing by Learning

Learning Outcome 67.1 Contrast behavior and insight therapies, and describe some behavioral change techniques derived from classical conditioning

In general, how does behavior therapy work? A breakthrough occurred when psychologists realized they could use learning principles to solve human problems. **Behavior therapy** is an action therapy that uses learning principles to make constructive changes in behavior. Unlike psychoanalysts, behavior therapists believe that deep insight into one's problems is often unnecessary for improvement. Instead, they try to directly alter troublesome actions and thoughts. Shanika didn't need to probe into her past or her emotions and conflicts; she simply wanted to overcome her fear of flying.

Behavior therapy Any therapy designed to actively change behavior.

Sidney Harris/www.CartoonStock.com

Behavior therapists assume that people have *learned* to be the way they are. If they have learned responses that cause problems, then they can change them by *relearning* more appropriate behaviors. Broadly speaking, **behavior modification** refers to any use of classical or operant conditioning to directly alter human behavior (Miltenberger, 2016; Spiegler, 2016). (Some therapists prefer to call this approach *applied behavior analysis.*) Behavioral therapies include aversion therapy, systematic desensitization, token economies, and other techniques (Spiegler, 2013a, b).

How does classical conditioning work? Perhaps a brief review would be helpful. Classical conditioning is a form of learning in which simple responses (especially reflexes) are associated with new stimuli. In classical conditioning, a neutral stimulus is followed by an *unconditioned stimulus (US)* that consistently produces an unlearned reaction, called the *unconditioned response (UR).* Eventually, the previously neutral stimulus begins to produce this response directly. The response is then called a *conditioned response (CR),* and the stimulus becomes a *conditioned stimulus (CS).* Thus, for a child, the sight of a hypodermic needle (CS) is followed by an injection (US), which causes anxiety or fear (UR). Eventually, the sight of a hypodermic (the CS) may produce anxiety or fear (a CR) *before* the child gets an injection. (For a more thorough review of classical conditioning, return to Modules 27 and 28.)

What does classical conditioning have to do with behavior modification? Classical conditioning can be used, for example, to associate discomfort with a bad habit. More powerful versions of this approach are called aversion therapy.

Aversion Therapy

Imagine that you are eating an apple. Suddenly, you discover that you just bit a large green worm in half. You vomit. Months later, you cannot eat an apple without feeling ill. It's apparent that you have developed a conditioned aversion to apples. (A *conditioned aversion* is a learned dislike or negative emotional response to some stimulus.)

In **aversion therapy**, an individual learns to associate a strong aversion to an unwanted behavior such as smoking, drinking, or gambling (Miltenberger, 2016). Aversion therapy has been used to treat hiccups, sneezing, stuttering, vomiting, nail-biting, bed-wetting, compulsive hair-pulling, alcoholism, and the smoking of tobacco, cannabis, or crack cocaine. Actually, aversive conditioning happens every day. For example, not many physicians who treat lung cancer patients are smokers, nor do many emergency room doctors drive without using their seat belts (Eifert & Lejuez, 2000).

Puffing Up an Aversion The fact that nicotine is toxic makes it easy to create an aversion that helps people give up smoking. Behavior therapists have found that electric shock, nauseating drugs, and similar aversive stimuli are not required to make smokers uncomfortable. All that is needed is for the smoker to smoke—rapidly, for a long time, at a forced pace. During *rapid smoking*, clients are told to smoke continuously, taking a puff every 6 to 8 seconds. Rapid smoking continues until the smoker is miserable and can stand it no more. By then, most people are thinking, "I never want to see another cigarette for the rest of my life."

Rapid smoking has long been known as an effective behavior therapy for smoking (Gifford & Shoenberger, 2009). Nevertheless, anyone tempted to try rapid smoking should realize that it is very unpleasant. Without the help of a therapist, most people quit too soon for the procedure to succeed. In addition, rapid smoking can be dangerous. It should be done only with professional supervision. (Covert sensitization, an alternative method that is more practical, is described in Module 31.)

Aversive Therapy for Drinking Another excellent example of aversion therapy was pioneered by Roger Vogler and his associates (1977). Vogler worked with alcoholics who were unable to stop drinking and for whom aversion therapy was a last chance. While drinking an alcoholic beverage, clients receive a painful (although not injurious) electric shock to the hand. Most of the time, these shocks occur as the client is beginning to take a drink of alcohol.

These *response-contingent shocks* (shocks that are linked to a response) obviously take the pleasure out of drinking. Shocks also cause the alcohol abuser to develop a conditioned aversion to drinking. Normally, the misery caused by alcohol abuse comes long after the act of drinking—too late to have much effect. But if alcohol can be linked with *immediate* discomfort, then drinking will begin to make the individual very uncomfortable.

Is it really acceptable to treat clients this way? People are often disturbed (shocked?) by such methods. However, clients usually *volunteer* for aversion therapy because it helps them overcome a destructive habit. Indeed, commercial aversion programs for overeating, smoking, and alcohol abuse have attracted many willing customers. More important, aversion therapy can be justified by its benefits. Many people prefer the short-term discomfort of aversion therapy to the long-term pain caused by a lifetime of struggling with a maladaptive habit.

Exposure Therapy

Can behavior therapy be used to treat phobias, fears, and anxieties? Another behavioral technique, *exposure therapy*, can be used to help people unlearn phobias (intense, unrealistic fears), strong anxieties, obsessions, and compulsions (Abramowitz, Deacon, Whiteside, 2012; Abramowitz & Jacoby, 2015). For example, each of these people might be a candidate: a teacher with stage fright; a student with test anxiety; a newlywed with an aversion to sexual intimacy; a person with hoarding disorder, or a person like Shanika, who is afraid of flying. **Exposure therapy** relies on the fact that classically conditioned responses can be extinguished.

Systematic Desensitization

Suppose that a behavior therapist wanted to help Kal-El overcome his fear of heights (acrophobia). How might she proceed? Assuming that Kal-El's fear of heights is a *conditioned emotional response*, it should be possible to extinguish that fear response by repeatedly exposing him to heights. Simply forcing Kal-El to go out onto a balcony on the top (35th) floor of his apartment building could be a psychological disaster (after all, Kal-El is a ground floor kind of guy). The behavior therapist (and Kal-El) might be better off avoiding *flooding* Kal-El with anxiety and instead using **systematic desensitization**—a guided reduction in fear, anxiety, or aversion attained by gradually approaching a feared stimulus while maintaining relaxation (Head & Gross, 2009).

The key to desensitization is relaxation. To inhibit fear, you must *learn* to relax. One way to voluntarily relax is by using the **tension-release method**. To achieve deep-muscle relaxation, try the following exercise:

> Tense the muscles in your right arm until they tremble. Hold them tight as you slowly count to 10 and then let go. Allow your hand and arm to go limp and to relax completely. Repeat the procedure. Releasing tension two or three times will allow you to feel whether your arm muscles have relaxed. Repeat the tension-release procedure with your left arm. Compare it with your right arm. Repeat until the left arm is equally relaxed. Apply the tension-release technique to your right leg, to your left leg, to your abdomen, and then to your chest and shoulders. Clench and release your chin, neck, and throat. Wrinkle and release your forehead and scalp. Tighten and release your mouth and face muscles. As a last step, curl your toes and tense your feet and then release.

If you followed these instructions, you should be noticeably more relaxed than you were before you began. Practice the tension-release method until you can achieve complete relaxation quickly (5 to 10 minutes). After you have practiced relaxation once a day for a week or two, you will begin to be able to tell when your body (or a group of muscles) is tense. Also, you will begin to be able to relax on command. This is a valuable skill that you can apply in any situation that makes you feel tense or anxious.

While Kal-El learns to voluntarily relax, he and the therapist can also construct his **fear hierarchy**—a list of at least 10 fear-provoking situations related to his fear of heights, arranged from least disturbing to most frightening.

Kal-El would then begin by trying to perform the least disturbing item on his fear of heights hierarchy, which might be (1) Stand on a chair. The first item is repeated until Kal-El feels no anxiety. Any change from complete relaxation is a signal that Kal-El must relax again before continuing. Slowly, Kal-El moves up the hierarchy: (2) Climb to the top of a small stepladder, (3) Look down one flight of stairs, and so on, until the last item, (20) Stand on the balcony on the top floor, is performed without fear.

As stated previously, working through his fear hierarchy in a safe, relaxed setting allows Kal-El to gradually undergo *extinction* of his conditioned fear response. Systematic desensitization also involves **reciprocal inhibition**—using one emotional state to block another (Heriot & Pritchard, 2004;

Behavior modification (applied behavior analysis) The application of learning principles to change human behavior, especially maladaptive behavior.

Aversion therapy Treatment to reduce unwanted behavior by pairing it with an unpleasant stimulus.

Exposure therapy Alleviating fears and phobias (conditioned emotional responses) by using classical conditioning extinction.

Systematic desensitization A reduction in fear, anxiety, or aversion brought about by planned exposure to aversive stimuli.

Tension-release method A procedure for systematically achieving deep relaxation of the body.

Fear hierarchy A list of fears, arranged from least fearful to most fearful, for use in systematic desensitization.

Reciprocal inhibition The presence of one emotional state can inhibit the occurrence of another, such as joy preventing fear or anxiety inhibiting pleasure.

Trull & Prinstein, 2013). For instance, it is impossible to be anxious and relaxed at the same time. If we can get Kal-El onto the building staircase in a relaxed state, his anxiety and fear will be further inhibited. Repeated visits to the staircase should cause fear to disappear in this situation. When Kal-El has conquered his fear, we can say that *desensitization* has occurred.

For many phobias, desensitization works best when people are directly exposed to the stimuli and situations they fear (Bourne, 2010; Miltenberger, 2016). For something like a simple spider phobia, this exposure can even be done in groups and may be completed in a single session (Müller et al., 2011).

Vicarious Desensitization *What if it's not practical to directly act out the steps of a fear hierarchy?* For a fear of heights, the steps of the fear hierarchy might be acted out, just as Kal-El did. However, if this is impractical, as it might be in the case of a fear of flying, the problem can be handled by having clients observe *models* who are performing the feared behavior (Bourne, 2010; Eifert & Lejuez, 2000; ➤ Figure 67.1). A model is a person (either live or filmed) who serves as an example for observational learning. If such **vicarious desensitization**—secondhand learning—can't be used, there is yet another option. Fortunately, desensitization works almost as well when a person *vividly imagines* each step in the hierarchy (Lang, 2016; Yahnke, Sheikh, & Beckman, 2003). If the steps can be visualized without anxiety, fear in the actual situation is reduced. Because imagining feared stimuli can be done at a therapist's office, it is the most common way of doing desensitization.

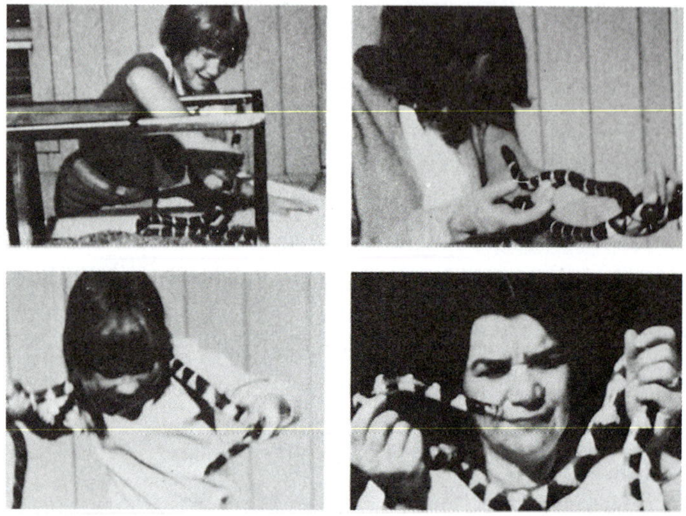

Albert Bandura/Stanford University

➤ **Figure 67.1**

Treatment of a snake phobia by vicarious desensitization. These classic photographs show models interacting with snakes. To overcome their own fears, phobic subjects observed the models (Bandura, Blanchard, & Ritter, 1969).

Virtual Reality Exposure In an important recent development, psychologists are now using virtual reality to treat phobias. Virtual reality is a computer-generated, three-dimensional "world" that viewers enter by wearing a head-mounted video display. **Virtual reality exposure** presents computerized fear stimuli to clients in a realistic yet carefully controlled fashion (Anderson, Edwards, & Goodnight, 2017; Motraghi et al., 2014). It has already been used to treat fears of flying, driving, and public speaking as well as acrophobia, claustrophobia, and spider phobias (Meyerbröker & Emmelkamp, 2010; Müller et al., 2011; ➤ Figure 67.2). Virtual reality exposure also has been used to create immersive distracting environments for helping patients reduce the experience of pain (Keefe et al., 2012).

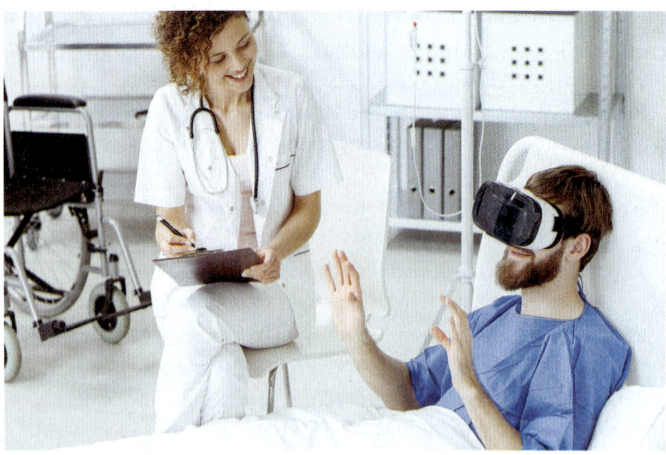

Photographee.eu/Shutterstock.com

Photographs used with permission from University of Southern California Institute for Creative Technologies

➤ **Figure 67.2**

Treatment of PTSD with virtual reality. (*Left*) A person in the head-mounted display explores a virtual reality system used to expose people to feared stimuli. (*Right*) A computer image from a virtual Iraq or Afghanistan. Veterans suffering from post-traumatic stress disorder (PTSD) can reexperience their traumas. For example, someone whose checkpoint was suddenly attacked by a carload of terrorists can relive that moment, complete with sights, sounds, vibrations, and even smells. Successive exposures result in a reduction of PTSD symptoms (Reger et al., 2016; Rizzo et al., 2015).

Exposure therapy has been one of the most successful behavior therapies. A relatively new technique may provide yet another way to lower fears, anxieties, and psychological pain.

Eye Movement Desensitization Traumatic events produce painful memories. Disturbing flashbacks often haunt victims of accidents, disasters, molestations, muggings, rapes, or emotional abuse. To help ease traumatic memories and post-traumatic stress, Dr. Francine Shapiro developed **eye movement desensitization and reprocessing (EMDR)**.

In a typical EMDR session, the client is asked to visualize the images that most upset her or him. At the same time, a pencil (or other object) is moved rapidly from side to side in front of the person's eyes. Watching the moving object causes the person's eyes to dart swiftly back and forth. After about 30 seconds, clients describe any memories, feelings, and thoughts that emerged and discuss them with the therapist. These steps are repeated until troubling thoughts and emotions no longer surface (Hensley, 2016).

Several studies suggest that EMDR lowers anxieties and takes the pain out of traumatic memories (Fleming, 2012; Shapiro, 2012). However, EMDR is controversial. Some question, for example, whether eye movements add anything to the treatment (Jeffries & Davis, 2013). The apparent success of EMDR may simply be based on gradual exposure to upsetting stimuli, as in other forms of exposure therapy (Albright & Thyer, 2010). On the other hand, some researchers continue to find that EMDR is superior to traditional therapies (Oren & Solomon, 2012; Tarquinio et al., 2012).

Is EMDR a breakthrough? Given the frequency of traumas in modern society, it shouldn't be long before we find out.

Operant Therapies—All the World Is a Skinner Box?

Learning Outcome 67.2 Describe some behavioral change techniques derived from operant conditioning

Aversion therapy and desensitization are based on classical conditioning. Where does operant conditioning fit in? As you may recall, *operant conditioning* refers to learning based on the consequences of making a response. Behavior therapists most often use the following operant principles to deal with human behavior:

1. **Positive reinforcement.** Responses that are followed by reinforcement tend to occur more frequently. If children whine and get attention, they will whine more frequently. If you get straight *A*s in your psychology class, you may become a psychology major.
2. **Nonreinforcement and extinction.** A response that is not followed by reinforcement will occur less frequently. If a response is not followed by reward after it has been repeated many times, it will extinguish entirely. After winning 3 times, you pull the handle on a slot machine 30 times more without a payoff. What do you do? You go away. So does the response of handle pulling (for that particular machine, at any rate).
3. **Punishment.** If a response is followed by discomfort or an undesirable effect, the response will be suppressed (but not necessarily extinguished).
4. **Shaping.** Shaping means reinforcing actions that are closer and closer approximations to a desired response. For example, to reward an intellectually challenged child for saying "ball," you might begin by reinforcing the child for saying anything that starts with a *b* sound.
5. **Stimulus control.** Responses tend to come under the control of the situation in which they occur. If you set your clock 10 minutes ahead, it may be easier to leave the house on time in the morning. Your departure is under the stimulus control of the clock, even though you know that it is fast.
6. **Time out.** A time-out procedure usually involves removing the individual from a situation in which reinforcement occurs. Time-out is a variation of punishment: It prevents reward from following an undesirable response. For example, children who fight with each other can be sent to separate rooms and allowed out only when they are able to behave more calmly. (For a more thorough review of operant learning, return to Modules 28 and 31.)

Vicarious desensitization A reduction in fear or anxiety that takes place vicariously ("secondhand") when a client watches models perform the feared behavior.

Virtual reality exposure Use of computer-generated images to present fear stimuli while responding to a viewer's head movements and other input.

Eye movement desensitization and reprocessing (EMDR) A technique for reducing fear or anxiety; based on holding upsetting thoughts in mind while rapidly moving the eyes from side to side.

As simple as these principles may seem, they have been used very effectively to overcome difficulties in work, home, school, and industrial settings. Let's see how.

Nonreinforcement and Operant Extinction

Fourteen-year-old Terrel periodically appeared in the nude in the activity room of a training center for disturbed adolescents. This behavior always generated a great deal of attention from staff and other patients. As an experiment, the next time he appeared nude, counselors and other staff members greeted him normally and then ignored him. Attention from other patients rapidly subsided. Sheepishly, he returned to his room and dressed. Over time his inappropriate nudity was completely extinguished. *In this example, what learning principles did the therapist use?* The therapist used *nonreinforcement* to produce *operant extinction*. The most frequently occurring human behaviors lead to some form of reward. An undesirable response can be eliminated by *identifying* and *removing* the rewards that maintain it. But like Terrel, people don't always do things for food, money, or other obvious rewards. Most of the rewards maintaining human behavior are subtler. *Attention*, *approval*, and *concern* are common yet powerful reinforcers for humans (➤ **Figure 67.3**).

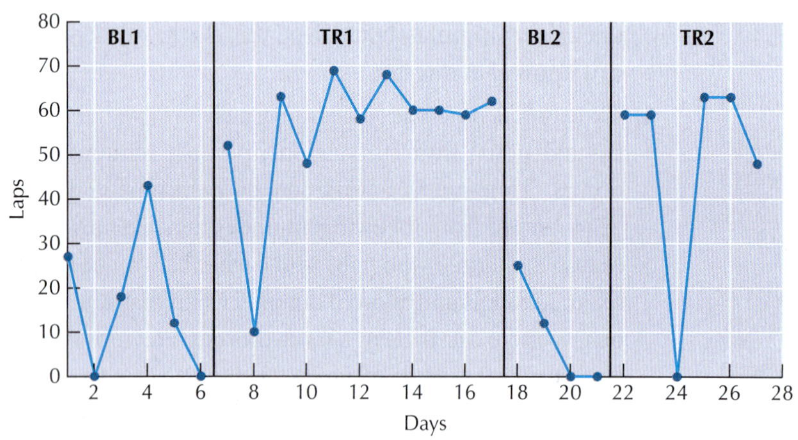

➤ **Figure 67.3**

Token reinforcers and behavioral change. Adults with intellectual disabilities often struggle with their weight. Paul is overweight and diabetic yet does not get enough exercise. The graph shows the number of laps Paul walks around a short track during an exercise period each day. During baseline periods (BL1 and BL2) he walks fewer laps than during token reinforcer (TR1 and TR2) periods, when he is awarded one token for each lap. After walking, Paul is allowed to exchange his tokens for treats such as Gatorade and Gatorade chews. (Adapted from Krentz, Miltenberger, & Valbuena, 2016.)

Reinforcement and Token Economies

Unlike Terrel, whose problem behavior occurred too frequently, desired behavior sometimes does not occur frequently enough. For example, Paul is an adult with intellectual disabilities who struggles with his weight. Even though Paul is overweight and diabetic, he does not get enough exercise.

What can be done to increase desired behaviors, like Paul's exercise? One widely used approach is based on *tokens* (symbolic rewards that can be exchanged for real rewards). Tokens may be printed slips of paper, check marks, points, or gold stars. Whatever form they take, tokens serve as rewards because they may be exchanged for candy, food, cigarettes, recreation, or privileges, such as private time with a therapist, outings, or watching TV.

By using tokens, positive responses can be *immediately rewarded*. For maximum impact, therapists select specific *target behaviors* (actions or other behaviors that the therapist seeks to modify). Target behaviors are then reinforced with tokens. Using tokens to reinforcing walking, Paul's target behavior, was effective (see Figure 67.3).

Tokens are used in mental hospitals, halfway houses, schools for the intellectually disabled, programs for delinquents, and ordinary classrooms. They usually produce improvements in behavior (Krentz, Miltenberger, & Valbuena, 2016; Maggin et al., 2011). (Tokens provide an effective way to change behavior because they are secondary reinforcers. See Module 28.)

The full-scale use of tokens in an institutional setting produces a *token economy*. In a **token economy**, patients are rewarded with tokens for a wide range of socially desirable or productive activities (Spiegler, 2016), and they must *pay* tokens to receive privileges and when they engage in problem behaviors (➤ **Figure 67.4**). For example, tokens are given to patients who dress themselves, take required medication, arrive for meals on time, and so on. Constructive activities, such as gardening, cooking, or cleaning, also may earn tokens. Patients must *exchange* tokens for meals and private rooms, movies, passes, off-ward activities, and other privileges. They are *charged* tokens for disrobing in public, talking to themselves, fighting, crying, and similar target behaviors (Morisse et al., 1996; Spiegler, 2016).

Token economies can radically change a patient's overall adjustment and morale. Patients are given an incentive to change, and they are

OXNARD DAY TREATMENT CENTER
CREDIT INCENTIVE SYSTEM

EARN CREDITS BY		SPEND CREDITS FOR	
MONITOR DAILY	15	COFFEE	5
MENU PLANNING CHAIRMAN	50	LUNCH	10
PARTICIPATE	5	EXCEPT THURSDAY	15
BUY FOOD AT STORE	10	BUS TRIP	5
COOK FOR/PREPARE LUNCH	5	BOWLING	8
WIPE OFF KITCHEN TABLE	3	GROUP THERAPY	5
WASH DISHES	5–10	PRIVATE STAFF TIME	5
DRY AND PUT AWAY DISHES	5	DAY OFF	5–20
MAKE COFFEE AND CLEAN URN	15	WINDOW SHOPPING	5
CLEAN REFRIGERATOR	20	REVIEW WITH DR.	10
ATTEND PLANNING CONFERENCE	1	DOING OWN THING	1
OT PREPARATION	1–5	LATE 1 PER EVERY 10 MIN	
COMPLETE OT PROJECT	5	PRESCRIPTION FROM DR.	10
RETURN OT PROJECT	2		
DUST AND POLISH TABLES	5		
PUT AWAY GROCERIES	3		
CLEAN TABLE	5		
CLEAN 6 ASH TRAYS	2		
CLEAN SINK	5		
CARRY OUT CUPS & BOTTLES	5		
CLEAN CHAIRS	5		
CLEAN KITCHEN CUPBOARDS	5		
ASSIST STAFF	5		
ARRANGE MAGAZINES NEATLY	3		
BEING ON TIME	5		
MONITOR-ANN			

Figure 67.4

Token economy. Shown here is a token used in one token economy system. In this instance, the token is a card that records the number of credits earned by a patient. Also pictured is a list of credit values for various activities. Tokens may be exchanged for items or for privileges listed on the board. (After photographs by Robert P. Liberman.)

held responsible for their actions. The use of tokens may seem manipulative, but it empowers patients. Many "hopelessly" intellectually disabled, mentally ill, and delinquent people have been returned to productive lives by means of token economies (Boerke & Reitman, 2011).

By the time they are ready to leave, patients may be earning tokens on a weekly basis for maintaining sane, responsible, and productive behavior (Miltenberger, 2016). Typically, the most effective token economies are those that gradually switch from tokens to *social rewards* such as praise, recognition, and approval. Such rewards are what patients will receive when they return to their family, friends, and community.

Token economy Behavior modification in which desired behaviors earn objects that can be exchanged for positive reinforcers.

MODULE 67 Behavior Therapies—Learning Outcomes Revisited

67.1 Contrast behavior and insight therapies, and describe some behavioral change techniques derived from classical conditioning

Behavior therapists assume that insight is unnecessary to change behavior. Instead, they use the learning principles of classical and/or operant conditioning to directly change human behavior. In aversion therapy, classical conditioning is used to associate maladaptive behavior (such as smoking or drinking) with pain or other aversive events to inhibit undesirable responses. In desensitization, a form of exposure therapy, gradual adaptation and reciprocal inhibition break the link between fear and particular situations. Typical steps in desensitization are the following: Construct a fear hierarchy; learn to produce total relaxation; and perform items on the hierarchy (from least to most disturbing). Desensitization may be carried out with real settings or it may be done by vividly imagining the fear hierarchy or by watching models perform the feared responses. In some cases, virtual reality exposure can be used to present fear stimuli in a controlled manner. Eye movement desensitization and reprocessing (EMDR) shows promise as a treatment for traumatic memories and stress disorders. At present, however, EMDR is controversial.

67.2 Describe some behavioral change techniques derived from operant conditioning

Operant principles, such as positive reinforcement, nonreinforcement, extinction, punishment, shaping, stimulus control, and time out, are used to extinguish undesirable responses and to promote constructive behavior. Nonreward can extinguish troublesome behaviors. Often, this is done by simply identifying and eliminating reinforcers, particularly attention and social approval. To apply positive reinforcement and operant shaping, tokens are often used to reinforce selected target behaviors. Full-scale use of tokens in an institutional setting produces a token economy. Toward the end of a token economy program, patients are shifted to social rewards such as recognition and approval.

Reflective Practice

Content Check

1. Shock or a nauseating drug plays what role in conditioning an aversion?
   a. conditioned stimulus
   b. unconditioned response
   c. unconditioned stimulus
   d. conditioned response
2. When desensitization is carried out through the use of live or filmed models, it is called
   a. cognitive therapy
   b. systematic desensitization
   c. covert desensitization
   d. vicarious desensitization
3. Systematic desensitization has three basic steps: constructing a hierarchy, flooding the person with anxiety, and imagining relaxation. T or F?
4. In EMDR therapy, computer-generated virtual reality images are used to expose clients to fear-provoking stimuli. T or F?
5. Behavior modification programs aimed at extinction of an undesirable behavior typically use what operant principles?
   a. punishment and stimulus control
   b. punishment and shaping
   c. nonreinforcement and time-out
   d. stimulus control and time-out
6. Attention can be a powerful ___________ for humans.

Skill Check

Think Critically

7. A natural form of desensitization often takes place in hospitals. Can you guess what it is?

Self-Reflect

Can you describe three problems for which you think behavior therapy would be an appropriate treatment? Have you ever become naturally desensitized to a stimulus or situation that at first made you anxious (for instance, heights, public speaking, or driving on freeways)? How would you explain your reduced fear? See if you can give a personal example of how the following principles have affected your behavior: positive reinforcement, extinction, punishment, shaping, stimulus control, and time-out.

ANSWERS

1. c 2. d 3. F 4. F 5. c 6. reinforcer 7. Doctors and nurses learn to relax and remain calm at the sight of blood and other bodily fluids because of their frequent exposure to them.

MODULE 68

Therapies
Medical Therapies

When Talk Won't Do

Psychotherapy can be used to treat many mental disorders, but it may not always be successful. How can you talk someone through their illness if they are suffering a complete psychotic break from reality? Besides, if the primary problem is due to, say, a biochemical imbalance in the brain, wouldn't it be better to treat the imbalance itself, perhaps with medication? For reasons like these, severe mental disorders, such as schizophrenia or major depressive disorders, are more often treated medically—although combinations of medication and psychotherapy can often be helpful (Beck et al., 2009; Trull & Prinstein, 2013).

With appropriate treatment, many seriously mentally ill individuals have gone on to lead happy and productive lives. The work of artist Rodger Casier illustrates the value of psychiatric care. Despite having a form of schizophrenia, Casier produced artwork, like his *Self-Portrait* shown here, that has received public acclaim and has been featured in professional journals.

Courtesy of Roger Casier

~LEARNING OUTCOMES~

After reading this module you should be able to:

68.1 Explain how psychiatrists treat psychological disorders, and describe some of the different approaches they use

Medical Therapies—Psychiatric Care

Learning Outcome 68.1 Explain how psychiatrists treat psychological disorders, and describe some of the different approaches they use

Three main types of **somatic therapy**, or physical body therapy, are *pharmacotherapy (drug therapies), brain stimulation therapy*, and *psychosurgery*. Somatic therapy is often done in the context of psychiatric hospitalization. All somatic approaches have a strong medical slant and are typically administered by psychiatrists, who are trained as medical doctors.

Drug Therapies

The atmosphere in psychiatric wards and mental hospitals changed radically in the mid-1950s with the widespread adoption of **pharmacotherapy** (FAR-meh-koe-THER-eh-pea),

Somatic therapy Any bodily therapy, such as drug therapy, electroconvulsive therapy, or psychosurgery.

Pharmacotherapy (FAR-meh-koe-THER-eh-pea) The use of drugs to treat psychopathology.

TABLE 68.1 | Some Commonly Prescribed Psychiatric Drugs

Class	Examples (trade names)	Effects	Main Mode(s) of Action
Antipsychotics (major tranquilizers)	Clozaril, Haldol, Mellaril, Fanapt, Risperdal, Thorazine	Reduce agitation, delusions, hallucinations, thought disorders	Reduce effects of dopamine; lesser effects on norepinephrine, serotonin, and acetylcholine
Antianxiety medications (anxiolytics or minor tranquilizers)	Ativan, Klonopin, Librium, Valium, Xanax	Reduce anxiety, tension, fear	Enhance effects of gamma-aminobutyric acid (GABA)
Antidepressants	Brintellix, Effexor, Elavil, Emsam, Nardil, Prozac, Zoloft, Tofranil, Wellbutrin	Counteract depression, Some antidepressants also counteract anxiety	Enhance effects of serotonin, dopamine, norepinephrine, or any combination
Mood stabilizers	Lithobid (Lithium)	Counteract bipolar disorder, reduce suicidal tendencies	Currently unclear
Stimulants	Adderall, Concerta, Dexedrine, Ritalin,	Counteract attention deficit hyperactivity disorder, narcolepsy	Enhance effects of norepinephrine; lesser effects on dopamine

Sources: Adapted from Advokat, 2014; Prus, 2017.

the use of drugs to treat psychopathology (Prus, 2017). Today, a bewildering variety of drugs are used to combat a wide range of problems from the discomforts of milder psychological disorders to the disabling effects of the anxiety disorders, major mood disorders, and even schizophrenia (Maisto, Galizio, & Connors, 2018).

What sort of drugs are used in pharmacotherapy? Five major types of drugs are used. (See ■ **Table 68.1** for examples of each class of drugs.) All achieve their effects by influencing the activity of different brain neurotransmitters (Kalat, 2021):

- **Antipsychotic drugs** (major tranquilizers), such as Risperdal, have tranquilizing effects and reduce hallucinations and delusions.
- **Antianxiety drugs** (anxiolytics [ANG-zee-eh LIT-iks] or minor tranquillizers), such as Valium, produce relaxation or reduce anxiety.
- **Antidepressant drugs**, such as Prozac, are mood-elevating drugs that combat depression.
- **Mood stabilizers**, such as Lithobid (lithium), are mood-leveling drugs that level out the extreme mood swings of bipolar disorder.
- **Stimulants**, such as Ritalin, are arousing drugs that paradoxically calm attention deficit hyperactivity disorder.

Are drugs a valid approach to treatment? Definitely. Drugs have shortened hospital stays, and they have greatly improved the chances that people will recover from major psychological disorders. Drug therapy also has made it possible for many people to return to the community, where they can be treated on an outpatient basis.

Limitations of Drug Therapy Regardless of their benefits, all drugs involve risks. For example, some antipsychotics, when taken for long periods, can cause sexual side effects such as erectile dysfunction and loss of sexual desire (Prus, 2017). Similarly, although the drug clozapine (Clozaril) can relieve the symptoms of schizophrenia, 2 out of 100 patients taking the drug suffer from a potentially fatal blood disease (Mustafa, 2013).

Is the risk worth it? Many experts think it is because chronic schizophrenia robs people of almost everything that makes life worth living. It's possible, of course, that newer drugs will improve the risk/benefit ratio in the treatment of severe problems like schizophrenia. For example, the antipsychotics risperidone (Risperdal) and olanzapine (Zyprexa) appear to be as effective as clozapine, without the same degree of lethal risk.

An additional problem is that each of the specific drugs that make up each major category of pharmacotherapy has different effects. For example, the antidepressant Prozac is an SSRI (selective serotonin reuptake inhibitor) that improves the availability of the neurotransmitter *serotonin,* while Effexor is an SNRI (serotonin-norepinephrine reuptake inhibitor) that has comparable effects on both serotonin and norepinephrine. Unfortunately, there is no easy way to determine beforehand which is the best specific drug, dosage, or combination of drugs for any given patient. Prescription, therefore, often becomes a frustrating trial-and-error process.

Even the best new drugs are not cure-alls. They help some people and relieve some problems, but not all. As noted earlier, for many, if not most, mental disorders, a combination of medication and psychotherapy is often very helpful (Kamenov et al., 2017; Oestergaard & Møldrup, 2011). Nevertheless, where schizophrenia and major mood disorders are concerned, drugs will undoubtedly remain the primary mode of treatment (Leucht et al., 2011; Vasa, Carlino, & Pine, 2006).

Brain Stimulation Therapy

In contrast to drug therapies, brain stimulation therapies achieve their effects by altering the electrical activity of the brain.

Electroconvulsive therapy **Electroconvulsive therapy** (ECT) is the first, and most dramatic, of the brain stimulation therapies. Widely used since the 1940s, it remains controversial to this day (Case et al., 2013; Choy, Farber, & Kellner, 2017). Although ECT is mainly used to treat depression, it is still occasionally used to treat some other disorders (Cusin et al., 2013; Weiss, Allan, & Greenaway, 2012). In ECT, a 150-volt electrical current is applied to the brain for slightly less than a second. This rather drastic medical treatment for depression triggers a seizure and causes the patient to lose consciousness for a short time. Muscle relaxants and sedative drugs are given before ECT to soften its impact. Treatments are given in a series of sessions spread over several weeks or months.

How does shock help? It is the seizure activity—not the shock—that is believed to be helpful. Proponents of ECT claim that shock-induced seizures alter or "reset" the biochemical and hormonal balance in the brain and body, bringing an end to severe depression and suicidal behavior as well as improving long-term quality of life (Fochtmann, 2016; McCall et al., 2006). Critics have charged that ECT works only by confusing patients so that they can't remember why they were depressed.

Not all professionals support the use of ECT. However, most experts seem to agree on the following: (1) At best, ECT produces only temporary improvement—it gets the patient out of a bad spot, but it must be combined with other treatments; (2) ECT can cause memory loss in some patients (Sienaert et al., 2010); (3) ECT should be used only after other treatments have failed; and (4) to lower the chance of a relapse, ECT should be followed by antidepressant drugs (McCall et al., 2011). All told, ECT is considered by many to be a valid treatment for selected cases of depression—especially when it rapidly ends wildly self-destructive or suicidal behavior (Medda et al., 2009). It's interesting to note that most ECT patients feel that the treatment helped them. Most, in fact, would have it done again (Bernstein et al., 1998; Smith et al., 2009).

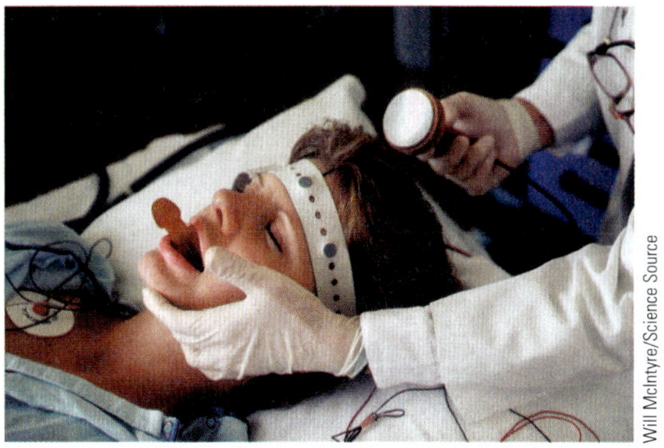

In ECT, electrodes are attached to the head and a brief electrical current is passed through the brain. ECT is used in the treatment of severe depression.

Deep Brain Stimulation Unlike ECT, **deep brain stimulation (DBS)** requires surgery to implant electrodes that allow for electrical stimulation of precisely targeted brain regions. In some studies, depressed patients who hadn't benefited from drug therapy and ECT improved when a specific brain region was stimulated (Johansson et al., 2013; Kennedy et al., 2011). Also, unlike ECT, DBS can be used to treat disorders other than depression, such as obsessive-compulsive disorder (Haq et al., 2010). (Electrical stimulation of the brain is one of several methods used to

Antipsychotic drugs (major tranquilizers) Medications that may alleviate hallucinations and delusional thinking associated with mental disorders.

Antianxiety drugs (anxiolytics or minor tranquilizers) (ANG-zee-eh LIT-ik) Medications that produce relaxation or reduce anxiety.

Antidepressant drugs Medications that combat depression by affecting the levels or activity of neurotransmitters.

Mood stabilizers Medications that combat bipolar disorder by leveling mood swings.

Stimulants (as drugs to treat ADHD) Medications used to calm attention deficit hyperactivity disorder even though they arouse the nervous system.

Electroconvulsive therapy (ECT) Treatment for severe depression in which electrical current is applied to the brain, causing a seizure.

Deep brain stimulation (DBS) Electrical stimulation of precisely targeted brain regions; a surgical procedure is necessary to implant electrodes in the brain that allow for the stimulation.

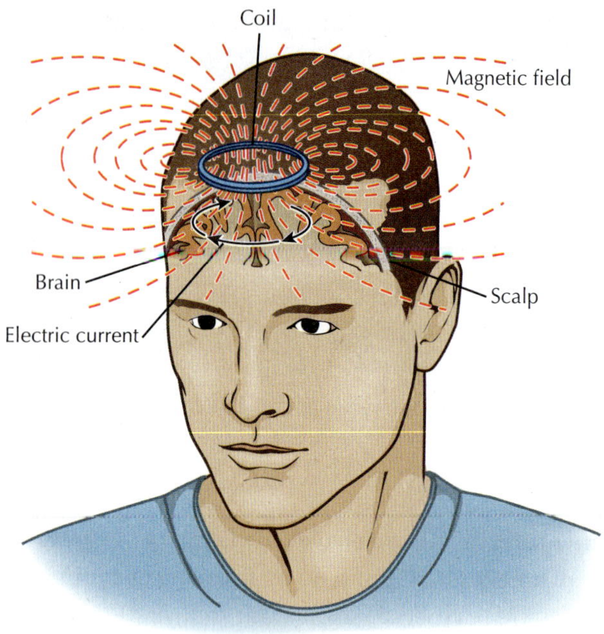

➤ **Figure 68.1**

Transcranial Magnetic Stimulation (TMS). TMS uses a small coil held near the surface of the scalp to create magnetic pulses that induce electrical activity in the underlying brain tissue. The result is a temporary blockage of normal brain activity. TMS can be used to study brain function and has already been applied as a medical therapy (Mantovani et al., 2010).

investigate the brain's inner workings. For more information, see Module 8.)

Transcranial Magnetic Stimulation Neuroscience research continues to probe the functioning of the brain and its various parts in ever-greater detail. As a result, more precisely targeted medical therapies with fewer side effects continue to be discovered (Aleman, 2013; Barr et al., 2013). For example, a promising new technique called **transcranial magnetic stimulation (TMS)** uses magnetic pulses to temporarily block activity in specific parts of the brain (➤ **Figure 68.1**).

By applying TMS to parts of the frontal lobe, Paulo Boggio and his colleagues (2010) were able to change the way that people made decisions while gambling. It is not a long stretch to imagine that this technique might become a powerful adjunct therapy to cognitive therapy when treating compulsive gambling (Ladouceur, Lachance, & Fournier, 2009). Similarly, patients with obsessive-compulsive disorder have shown marked improvement when TMS disrupted brain areas involved in compulsive behavior (Mantovani et al., 2010).

Psychosurgery

Psychosurgery—any surgical alteration of the brain intended to treat a psychological disorder—is the most extreme medical treatment. The oldest and most radical psychosurgery is the lobotomy. In *prefrontal lobotomy*, the frontal lobes are surgically disconnected from other brain areas. This procedure was supposed to calm persons who didn't respond to any other type of treatment.

When the lobotomy was first introduced in the 1940s, there were enthusiastic claims for its success. But later studies suggested that some patients were calmed, some showed no change, and some became mental "vegetables." Lobotomies also produced a high rate of other undesirable side effects, such as seizures, blunted emotions, major personality changes, and stupor. About the same time that such problems became apparent, the first antipsychotic drugs became available. Soon after, the lobotomy was abandoned (Raz, 2013).

To what extent is psychosurgery used now? Psychosurgery is still considered valid by many neurosurgeons. However, most now use *deep lesioning,* in which small target areas are destroyed in the brain's interior. The appeal of deep lesioning is that it can have value as a remedy for some very specific disorders. For instance, patients suffering from a severe type of obsessive-compulsive disorder may be helped by psychosurgery (Anderson & Booker, 2006; Greenspan et al., 2008). (Deep lesioning is another method used to study the brain. See Module 8.)

It is worth remembering that psychosurgery cannot be reversed. Whereas a drug can be given or taken away and electrical stimulation can be turned off, you can't take back psychosurgery. Critics argue that psychosurgery should be banned altogether; others continue to report success with brain surgery. Nevertheless, it may have value as a remedy for some very specific and severe disorders (Lévêque, 2014; Sachdev & Chen, 2009).

Hospitalization

In 2017, about 7.5 percent of all Americans received inpatient treatment for a mental health problem (National Institute of Mental Health, 2018). **Psychiatric hospitalization** involves placing a person in a protected setting where medical therapy is provided. Hospitalization by itself can be a form of treatment. Staying in a hospital takes patients out of situations that may be sustaining their problems. For example, people with drug addictions may find it nearly impossible to resist the temptations for drug abuse in their daily lives. Hospitalization can help them make a clean break from their self-destructive behavior patterns (André et al., 2003).

At their best, hospitals are sanctuaries that provide diagnosis, support, refuge, and therapy. This is frequently true of psychiatric units in general hospitals and private psychiatric hospitals. At its worst, confinement to an institution can be a brutal experience that leaves people less prepared to face the world than when they arrived. This is more often the case in large state mental hospitals. In most instances, hospitals are best used as a last resort, after other forms of treatment within the community have been exhausted (Trull & Prinstein, 2013).

Another trend in treatment is *partial hospitalization* (Bales & Bateman, 2012). In this approach, some patients spend their days in the hospital but go home at night. Others attend therapy sessions during the evening. A major advantage of partial hospitalization is that patients can go home and practice what they've been learning. Overall, partial hospitalization can be just as effective as full hospitalization (Drymalski & Washburn, 2011; Kiser, Heston, & Paavola, 2006).

Deinstitutionalization In the last 70 years in the United States, the population in large mental hospitals has dropped by two-thirds. This is largely a result of **deinstitutionalization**, or reduced use of full-time commitment to mental institutions (Hudson, 2016). Long-term "institutionalization" can lead to dependency, isolation, and continued emotional disturbance (Novella, 2010). Deinstitutionalization was meant to remedy this problem.

How successful has deinstitutionalization been? In truth, its success has been limited (Paulson, 2012). Many states reduced mental hospital populations primarily to save money. The upsetting result is that many chronic patients have been discharged to hostile communities without adequate care. Many former patients have joined the ranks of the homeless. Others are repeatedly jailed for minor crimes. Sadly, patients who trade hospitalization for unemployment, homelessness, and social isolation all too often end up rehospitalized, in jail, or even as suicides (Hudson, 2016; Markowitz, 2011).

Large psychiatric hospitals may no longer be warehouses for society's unwanted, but many former patients are no better off in bleak nursing homes, single-room hotels, board-and-care homes, shelters, or jails. For example, almost 170,000 mentally ill Americans are currently homeless and almost 385,000 are currently in prison or jail (Treatment Advocacy Center, 2018). These figures suggest that the streets and jails are replacing psychiatric hospitals as our society's "solution" for mental illness (Markowitz, 2011). Yet, ironically, high-quality care is available in almost every community. As much as anything, a simple lack of money prevents large numbers of people from getting the help they need.

Halfway houses may be a better way to ease a patient's return to the community (Soyez & Broekaert, 2003). A **halfway house** is a short-term group-living facility for people making the transition from an institution (psychiatric hospital, prison, and so forth) to independent living. Typically, halfway houses offer supervision and support, without being as restricted and medically oriented as hospitals. They also keep people near their families. Most important, halfway houses can ease a person's return to "normal" life and reduce chances of being readmitted to a hospital (Davidson et al., 2010).

Community Mental Health Programs

Community mental health centers, which offer a wide range of mental health services and psychiatric care, are a bright spot in the area of mental health care (Kloos et al., 2021).

Eric Audras/ONOKY/Getty Images

Depending on the quality of the institution, hospitalization may be a refuge or a brutalizing experience. Many state "asylums" or psychiatric hospitals are antiquated and in need of drastic improvement.

Transcranial magnetic stimulation (TMS) A device that uses magnetic pulses to temporarily block activity in specific parts of the brain.

Psychosurgery Any surgical alteration of the brain designed to bring about desirable behavioral or emotional changes.

Psychiatric hospitalization Placing a person in a protected, therapeutic environment staffed by mental health professionals.

Deinstitutionalization The reduced use of full-time commitment to mental institutions to treat mental disorders.

Halfway house A community-based facility for individuals making the transition from an institution (psychiatric hospital, prison, and so forth) to independent living.

Community mental health center A facility offering a wide range of mental health services, such as prevention, counseling, consultation, and crisis intervention.

AP Images/David Goldman

A well-run halfway house can be a humane and cost-effective way to ease former patients back into the community.

Such centers try to help people avoid hospitalization, find answers to mental health problems, and improve mental health literacy (Jorm, 2012; Mark et al., 2013). Typically, they do this by providing short-term treatment, counseling, outpatient care, emergency services, and suicide prevention.

Mental health centers also are concerned with *prevention*. Consultation, education, and **crisis intervention** (skilled management of a psychological emergency) are used to prevent problems before they become serious. Also, some centers attempt to raise the general level of mental health in a community by combating unemployment, delinquency, and drug abuse (Mancini & Wyrick-Waugh, 2013).

Have community mental health centers succeeded in meeting their goals? In practice, they have concentrated much more on providing clinical services than they have on preventing problems. This appears to be primarily the result of wavering government support (translation: money). Overall, community mental health centers have succeeded in making psychological services more accessible than ever. Many of their programs rely on **paraprofessionals**, individuals who work in a near-professional capacity under the supervision of more highly trained staff. Some paraprofessionals are ex-addicts, ex-alcoholics, or ex-patients who have "been there." Many more are persons (paid or volunteer) who have skills in tutoring, crafts, or counseling or who are simply warm, understanding, and skilled at communication. Often, paraprofessionals are more approachable than doctors. This encourages people to seek mental health services that they might otherwise be reluctant to use (Farrand et al., 2009).

Crisis intervention The skilled management of a psychological emergency.

Paraprofessional An individual who works in a near-professional capacity under the supervision of a more highly trained person.

MODULE 68 Medical Therapies—Learning Outcomes Revisited

68.1 Explain how psychiatrists treat psychological disorders, and describe some of the different approaches they use

Three medical, or somatic, approaches to treatment are pharmacotherapy, brain stimulation therapy (including electroconvulsive therapy [ECT]), and psychosurgery. Hospitalization, including partial hospitalization, involves placing a person in a protected setting where medical therapy is provided. Community mental health centers seek to avoid or minimize mental hospitalization. They also seek to prevent mental health problems through education, consultation, and crisis intervention.

Reflective Practice

Content Check

1. Major tranquilizers also are known as
   a. anxiolytics
   b. antipsychotics
   c. antidepressants
   d. prefrontal sedatives
2. ECT is a modern form of pharmacotherapy. T or F?
3. Currently, the frontal lobotomy is the most widely used form of psychosurgery. T or F?
4. Deinstitutionalization is an advanced form of partial hospitalization. T or F?

Skill Check

Think Critically

5. Residents of Berkeley, California, once voted on a referendum to ban the use of ECT within city limits. Do you think that the use of certain psychiatric treatments should be controlled by law?

Self-Reflect

Keeping in mind that all therapies, and especially medical therapies, have side effects (see, e.g., Casselle, 2009), when is it appropriate to use a medical therapy to treat someone with a mental illness? Why not use psychotherapy instead? Why might you choose to combine medical therapy and psychotherapy methods? Can you frame your reasons in terms of the stress–vulnerability model introduced in Module 60?

ANSWERS

1. b 2. F 3. F 4. F 5. The question of *who* can prescribe drugs, perform surgery, and administer ECT *is* controlled by law. However, psychiatrists strongly object to residents, city councils, or government agencies making *medical* decisions.

MODULE 69

A Psychologist's Skill Set

Managing Mental Health

Learning to Say Shhhh

Consider this list: Angelina Jolie, Owen Wilson, Adele, Daniel Radcliffe, Eminem, Robert Downey Jr., and Ellen DeGeneres. What do all these people have in common? If you said that it's a list of famous people who have been praised for their acting and music, you'd only be partly correct. It's also a list of A-list celebrities who have talked openly about their struggles with mental health issues, including depression, anxiety, eating disorders, and addictions. Many of them have also been upfront about the treatments that have helped them to deal with those difficult issues. Some, like singer Ellie Goulding, have opted for medication. Others, like Ke$ha, have sought counseling. And even Captain America—actor Chris Evans—has reported that he uses a form of *thought stopping*, silently saying "Shhhh" to himself when things get overwhelming.

Photos 12/Alamy Stock Photo

Experiencing mental health problems creates significant challenges for people, but what's often overlooked is that getting help for these problems can be equally difficult. What are some of the options that you can try on your own? And if professional help is needed, where can you go? If you need some help to help yourself—or others that you know—read on!

~LEARNING OUTCOMES~

After reading this module you should be able to:

69.1 Explain how to help yourself and others face mental health issues

How Am I?—Can't Complain

Learning Outcome 69.1 Explain how to help yourself and others face mental health issues

We all want to be healthy, strong, and self-reliant. And we often have other people in our lives—children, family, friends, or colleagues—who depend on us. Not wanting to let anyone down, if we are asked, "How are you?" we are prone to respond, "Can't complain."

Admitting you have a problem can be incredibly difficult, but some of the most important skills that we can possess are a self-awareness of our own mental health and, additionally, a willingness to ask for help when we need it. Sometimes all we need is a caring individual to help us work through a problem. Other times we may need more professional help. Mental health issues are common in the United States. Chances are good that at some point you, a friend, or a family member will benefit from mental health services of one kind or another. About 13 percent of all Americans receive treatment for a mental health problem every year (National Institute of Mental Health, 2017).

By the way, we are not counseling you to run for help at the least sign of trouble. By all means, be strong and deal with the issue yourself if you feel that you can (Martin & Pear, 2011; Watson & Tharp, 2014). For example, in Module 31, we shared some behavioral self-management skills that can be helpful with a variety of mental health issues. Further, many of the therapeutic techniques described in Modules 66 and 67 can be adapted for self-management. Thought stopping (yo, Captain America!) and desensitization are two good examples.

Talking About Problems: Basic Counseling Skills

If you decide to ask someone else for advice, be on the lookout for their ability to use basic counseling skills when talking with you. Alternately, while you may not currently be experiencing any mental health problems, perhaps you have a friend who is. If someone close to you asks to talk about his or her troubles, it helps to be prepared. Several general helping skills can be distilled from the various approaches to therapy. Keep these points in mind if you are ever called on to comfort a person in distress, such as a troubled friend or relative (Kottler & Shepard, 2015; Neukrug, 2014; Sharf, 2016) (■ **Table 69.1**).

Be an Active Listener People frequently talk "at" each other without really listening. A person with problems needs to be heard. Make a sincere effort to listen to and understand the person. Try to accept the person's message without judging it or leaping to conclusions. Let the person know you are listening, through eye contact, posture, your tone of voice, and your replies (Kottler & Shepard, 2015).

Reflect Thoughts and Feelings One of the best things that you can do when offering support to another person is to give feedback by simply restating what is said. This also is a good way to encourage a person to talk. If your friend seems to be at a loss for words, *restate* or *paraphrase* his or her last sentence. Here's an example:

Friend: I'm really down about school. I can't get interested in any of my classes. I flunked my Spanish test, and somebody stole my notebook for psychology.

You: So you're really upset about school?

Friend: Yeah, and my parents are hassling me about my grades again.

You: You're feeling pressured by your parents?

Friend: Yeah.

As simple as this sounds, it is very helpful to someone trying to sort out feelings. Try it. If nothing else, you'll develop a reputation as a fantastic conversationalist!

Don't Be Afraid of Silence Counselors tend to wait longer before responding than do people in everyday conversations. Pauses of 5 seconds or more are not unusual, and interrupting is rare. Listening patiently lets the person feel unhurried and encourages her or him to speak freely.

Ask Open-Ended Questions Because your goal is to encourage free expression, *open-ended questions* tend to be the most helpful. A *closed question* is one that can be answered yes or no. Open-ended questions call for an open-ended reply. Say, for example, that a friend tells you, "I feel like my boss has it in for me at work." A closed question would be, "Oh, yeah? So, are you going to quit?" Open-ended questions such as, "Do you want to talk about it?" or "How do you feel about it?" are more likely to be helpful.

Clarify Problems People who have a clear idea of what is wrong in their lives are more likely to discover solutions. Try to understand the problem from the person's point of view.

TABLE 69.1 | Helping Behaviors

To help another person gain insight into a personal problem, it is valuable to keep the following comparisons in mind:

Behaviors That Help	Behaviors That Hinder
Active listening	Probing painful topics
Acceptance	Judging/moralizing
Reflecting feelings	Criticism
Open-ended questioning	Threats
Supportive statements	Rejection
Respect	Ridicule/sarcasm
Patience	Impatience
Genuineness	Placing blame
Paraphrasing	Opinionated statements

Sources: Adapted from Corey, 2017; Kottler & Shepard, 2015; Sharf, 2016.

As you do, check your understanding often. For example, you might ask, "Are you saying that you feel depressed just at school? Or in general?" Remember, a problem well defined is often half solved.

Focus on Feelings Feelings are neither right nor wrong. By focusing on feelings, you can encourage the outpouring of emotion that is the basis for catharsis. Passing judgment on what is said just makes people defensive. For example, a friend confides that he has failed a test. Perhaps you know that he studies very little. If you say, "Just study more and you will do better," he will probably become defensive or hostile. Much more can be accomplished by saying, "You must feel very frustrated" or simply, "How do you feel about it?"

Avoid Giving Advice Many people mistakenly think that they must solve problems for others. Remember that your goal is to provide understanding and support, not solutions. Of course, it is reasonable to give advice when you are asked for it, but beware of the trap of the "Why don't you . . . ? Yes, but . . ." game. According to psychotherapist Eric Berne (1964), this "game" follows a pattern: Someone says, "I have this problem." You say, "Why don't you do this?" The person replies, "Yes, but . . ." and then tells you why your suggestion won't work. If you make a new suggestion, the reply once again will be, "Yes, but. . . ." Obviously, the person either knows more about his or her personal situation than you do, or he or she has reasons for avoiding your advice. The student described earlier knows that he needs to study. His problem is to understand why he doesn't *want* to study.

Accept the Person's Frame of Reference Because we all live in different psychological worlds, there is no "correct" view of a life situation. Try to resist imposing your views on the problems of others. A person who feels that his or her viewpoint has been understood feels freer to examine it objectively and to question it.

Maintain Confidentiality Your efforts to help will be wasted if you fail to respect the privacy of someone who has confided in you. Put yourself in the person's place. Don't gossip.

The points just made help define the qualities of a helping relationship. They also emphasize that each of us can supply two of the greatest mental health resources available at any cost: friendship and honest communication. However, in closing, it is important to remember that only a licensed professional possesses the full set of skills necessary to counsel more serious mental health issues. The *instant* you realize that your problem is beyond your friend's ability to properly address, or that your friend's problem is beyond your ability to address, look for, or help your friend, find a more qualified counselor. Seeking more professional counseling is not a sign of failure for either you or your friend; it is a testimony to your own wisdom. Although your textbook authors are psychologists, we are not licensed counselors and quite frequently refer students to our college counseling centers.

Getting Counseling

In some cases, mental health challenges are best managed with the support of a professional. In this section, we review some basic information about things to consider should you decide to seek counseling for yourself.

Seeking Professional Help—When, Where, and How? *How would I know if I should seek professional help at some point in my life?* Although this question has no simple answer, the following guidelines may be helpful:

1. If your level of psychological discomfort (unhappiness, anxiety, or depression, for example) is comparable to a level of physical discomfort that would cause you to see a doctor or dentist, you should consider seeing a psychologist or a psychiatrist.
2. Another signal to watch for is significant changes in behavior, such as the quality of your work (or schoolwork), your rate of absenteeism, your use of drugs (including alcohol), or your relationships with others.
3. Perhaps you have urged a friend or relative to seek professional help and were dismayed because he or she refused to do so. If *you* find friends or relatives making a similar suggestion, recognize that they may be seeing things more clearly than you are.
4. If you have persistent or disturbing suicidal thoughts or impulses, seek help immediately.

Locating a Therapist *If I wanted to talk to a therapist, how would I find one?* Here are some suggestions that can help you get started:

1. **Your family physician.** Your family physician, if you have one, often will be able to help you find the help you are seeking.
2. **Colleges and universities.** If you are a student, don't overlook counseling services offered by a student health center or special student counseling facilities.
3. **Workplaces.** If you have a job, check with your employer. Some employers have employee assistance

programs that offer confidential free or low-cost therapy for employees.

4. **Community or county mental health centers.** Most counties and many cities offer public mental health services. (These are listed in the phone book or can be found by searching the Internet.) Public mental health centers usually provide counseling and therapy services directly, and they can refer you to private therapists.
5. **Mental health associations.** Many cities have mental health associations organized by concerned citizens. Groups such as these usually keep listings of qualified therapists and other services and programs in the community.
6. **The Yellow Pages.** Psychologists are listed in the telephone book or on the Internet under "Psychologists," or in some cases under "Counseling Services." Psychiatrists are generally listed as a subheading under "Physicians." Counselors are usually found under the heading "Marriage and Family Counselors." These listings will usually put you in touch with individuals in private practice.
7. **Crisis hotlines.** A typical crisis hotline is a phone service staffed by volunteers. These people are trained to provide information concerning a wide range of mental health problems. They also have lists of organizations, services, and other resources in the community where you can go for help.

■ Table 69.2 summarizes the sources for psychotherapy, counseling, and referrals we have discussed as well as some additional possibilities.

Options *How would I know what kind of a therapist to see? How would I pick one?* The choice between a psychiatrist and a psychologist is somewhat arbitrary. Both are trained to do psychotherapy and can be equally effective as therapists. Although a psychiatrist can administer somatic therapy and prescribe drugs, so can psychologists in New Mexico, Louisiana, Illinois, and Iowa, along with psychologists in the US military (Munsey, 2006). A psychologist also can work in conjunction with a physician if such services are needed.

Be aware that most health insurance plans will pay for psychological services. If fees are a problem, keep in mind that many therapists charge on a sliding scale, or ability-to-pay basis, and that community mental health centers almost always charge on that basis as well. In one way or another, help is almost always available for anyone who needs it.

Some communities and college campuses have counseling services staffed by sympathetic paraprofessionals or peer counselors. These services are free or very low-cost. As mentioned previously, paraprofessionals are people who work in a near-professional capacity under professional supervision. **Peer counselors** are nonprofessional persons who have learned basic counseling skills. There is a natural tendency, perhaps, to doubt the abilities of paraprofessionals. However, paraprofessional counselors are often as effective as professionals (Farrand et al., 2009).

Also, don't overlook **self-help groups**, which can add valuable support to professional treatment. Members of a self-help group typically share a particular type of problem, such as eating disorders, alcoholism, or coping with an alcoholic parent. Self-help groups offer members mutual support and a chance to discuss problems. In many instances, helping others also serves as therapy for those who give help. For some problems, self-help groups may be the best choice of all (Dadich, 2010; Galanter et al., 2005).

Qualifications You can usually find out about a therapist's qualifications simply by asking. A reputable therapist will be glad to reveal his or her background. If you have any doubts, credentials may be checked and other helpful information

TABLE 69.2 | Mental Health Resources

- Family doctors (for referrals to mental health professionals)
- Mental health specialists, such as psychiatrists, psychologists, social workers, and mental health counselors
- Religious leaders/counselors
- Health maintenance organizations (HMOs)
- Community mental health centers
- Hospital psychiatry departments and outpatient clinics
- University- or medical school-affiliated programs
- State hospital outpatient clinics
- Family service/social agencies
- Private clinics and facilities
- Employee assistance programs
- Local medical, psychiatric, or psychological societies

Sources: Adapted from Corey, 2017; Kottler & Shepard, 2015; Sharf, 2016.

Peer counselor A nonprofessional person who has learned basic counseling skills.

Self-help group A group of people who share a particular type of problem and provide mutual support to one another.

can be obtained from local branches of any of the following organizations. You also can browse the websites listed here:

American Association for Marriage and Family Therapy (www.aamft.org)
American Family Therapy Academy (www.afta.org)
American Psychiatric Association (www.psych.org)
American Psychological Association (www.apa.org)
Association of Humanistic Psychology (www.ahpweb.org)
Canadian Psychiatric Association (www.cpa-apc.org)
Canadian Psychological Association (www.cpa.ca)
National Mental Health Association (www.nmha.org)

The question of how to pick a particular therapist remains. The best way is to start with a short consultation with a respected psychiatrist, psychologist, or counselor. This allows the person that you consult to evaluate your difficulty and recommend a type of therapy, or a therapist who is likely to be helpful. As an alternative, you might ask the person teaching this course for a referral.

Evaluating a Therapist *How would I know a therapist is being effective?* A balanced look at psychotherapies suggests that all techniques can be equally successful. However, all *therapists* are not equally successful. Former clients consistently rate the person doing the therapy as more important than the type of therapy used (Elliott & Williams, 2003).

Ask yourself if you feel you are establishing a *therapeutic alliance* with your therapist. A therapist who is working *with* you is usually willing to use whatever method seems most helpful for a client. He or she also can be evaluated on personal characteristics of warmth, integrity, sincerity, and empathy (Okiishi et al., 2003; Prochaska & Norcross, 2014). The *relationship* between a client and therapist is the therapist's most basic tool (Hubble, Duncan, & Miller, 1999; Prochaska & Norcross, 2014). This is why you must trust and easily relate to a therapist for therapy to be effective. Here are some danger signals to watch for in psychotherapy:

- Sexual advances by a therapist
- A therapist who makes repeated verbal threats or is physically aggressive
- A therapist who is excessively blaming, belittling, hostile, or controlling
- A therapist who makes excessive small talk; talks repeatedly about his or her own problems
- A therapist who encourages prolonged dependence on him or her
- A therapist who demands absolute trust or tells the client not to discuss therapy with anyone else

An especially important part of the therapeutic alliance is agreement about the goals of therapy (Bartle-Haring et al., 2016). It is therefore a good idea to think about what you want to accomplish by entering therapy. Write down your goals and discuss them with your therapist during the first session. Your first meeting with a therapist should also answer all of the following questions:

- Will the information I reveal in therapy remain completely confidential?
- What risks do I face if I begin therapy?
- How long do you expect treatment to last?
- What form of treatment do you expect to use?
- Are there alternatives to therapy that might help me as much or more?

It's always tempting to avoid facing personal problems. With this in mind, you should give a therapist a fair chance and not give up too easily. But don't hesitate to change therapists or to terminate therapy if you lose confidence in the therapist or if you don't relate well to the therapist as a person.

MODULE 69 Managing Mental Health—Learning Outcomes Revisited

69.1 Explain how to help yourself and others face mental health issues

There are many things that you can do to help when listening to someone else describe their mental health issues. These include: being an active listener, reflecting the person's thoughts and feelings, welcoming silence, asking open-ended questions, clarifying problems, focusing on feelings, avoiding advice, accepting their frame of reference, and maintaining their confidence. There are many places to find counselors, including university and community health centers, family doctors, crisis hotlines, and the Yellow Pages. There are various types of counseling options, including psychologists, psychiatrists, peer counselors, and self-help groups. Practical considerations such as cost and qualifications enter into choosing a therapist. However, the therapist's personal characteristics are of equal importance.

Reflective Practice

Content Check

1. Listening to people talk about their problems is usually more helpful than offering them your advice. T or F?
2. Instead of judging people who ask you for help, it is better to
   a. accept their frame of reference
   b. tell them what to do
   c. tell them about your problems
   d. avoid focusing on feelings
3. Persistent emotional discomfort is a clear sign that professional psychological counseling should be sought. T or F?
4. Community mental health centers rarely offer counseling or therapy themselves; they only do referrals. T or F?
5. In many instances, a therapist's personal qualities have more of an effect on the outcome of therapy than the type of therapy used. T or F?

Skill Check

Think Critically

6. Would it be acceptable for a therapist to urge a client to break all ties with a troublesome family member?

Self-Reflect

Review Modules 31 and 67. How could you use covert sensitization, thought stopping, and covert reinforcement to change your behavior? Just for practice, make a fear hierarchy for a situation that you find frightening. Does vividly picturing items in the hierarchy make you tense or anxious? If so, can you intentionally relax using the tension-release method? Which of the basic counseling skills would improve your ability to help a person in distress (or even just have an engaging conversation)? Take some time to find out what mental health services are available to you.

ANSWERS

1. T 2. a 3. T 4. F 5. T 6. Such decisions must be made by clients themselves. Therapists can help clients evaluate important decisions and feelings about significant persons in their lives. However, actively urging a client to sever a relationship borders on unethical behavior.

MODULE 70

Social Psychology
Social Behavior and Cognition

Call 'Em Like You See 'Em

They see eye to eye on almost everything. And why not? They've been best friends since childhood. They attended school together, hung out with the same friends, and double-dated together. On sports, though, Jimarcus and Jim Bob could not be any more different. They are famous among their friends for never seeing a play the same way.

According to Australian psychologist Pascal Molenberghs, Jimarcus and Jim Bob are typical sports fans. When he scanned the brains of fans watching their teams compete, he found that fans of opposing teams don't just think differently about what they see, they literally *see* things differently (Molenberghs et al., 2013).

Like the rest of us, Jimarcus and Jim Bob are social beings. Our behaviors, our thoughts, our feelings, and even our perceptions are strongly influenced by our social worlds. In this, and the next few modules, we will look at some ways that we think about social situations and some ways in which we influence others.

Jon Feingersh/Getty Images

~LEARNING OUTCOMES~

After reading this module you should be able to:

70.1 Define two types of social roles, group structure, group cohesiveness, social norms, social status, and social power

70.2 Explain social comparison theory, attribution theory, the fundamental attribution error, and the actor–observer bias

70.3 Define attitudes and explain how they are acquired and changed

70.4 Explain when persuasion is most effective and discuss cognitive dissonance

Humans in a Social Context—Mind Your Manners

Learning Outcome 70.1 Define two types of social roles, group structure, group cohesiveness, social norms, social status, and social power

Social psychology is the study of how individuals think and behave in social situations—that is, in the presence, actual or implied, of others (Baumeister & Bushman, 2021). Every day, there is a fascinating interplay between our own behavior and that of the people around us. We are born into organized societies. Established values, expectations, and behavior patterns are present when we arrive. So, too, is **culture**, an ongoing pattern of life that is passed from one generation to the next. To appreciate the impact of society and culture, think about how you have been affected by language, marriage customs, concepts of ownership, and sex roles (Matsumoto & Juang, 2017).

Social Roles

We all belong to many overlapping social groups, and in each, we occupy a *position* in the *structure* of the group. A **social role** is a pattern of behavior expected of a person in a social position (Baumeister & Bushman, 2021). For instance, playing the role of mother, boss, or student involves different sets of behaviors and expectations. Some roles are *ascribed* (they are assigned to a person or are not under personal control): Male or female, son, adolescent, inmate. *Achieved roles* are voluntarily attained by special effort: Spouse, teacher, scientist, bandleader, criminal.

What effect does role-playing have on behavior? Roles streamline daily interactions by allowing us to anticipate what others will do. When a person is acting as a doctor, mother, clerk, or police officer, we expect certain behaviors.

However, roles can have a negative side, too. In the infamous Stanford prison experiment, Phil Zimbardo at Stanford University paid normal healthy male college students to play the role of either "prisoners" or "guards" in a simulated prison (Drury et al., 2012; Haney, Banks, & Zimbardo, 1973). Within a few days, the "guards" clamped down with increasing brutality. Surprisingly quickly, the fake convicts looked like real prisoners: They were dejected, traumatized, passive, and dehumanized. After six days, the experiment had to be halted.

What happened? We tend to think of people as inherently good or bad. But students in the Stanford prison study were randomly assigned to be prisoners or guards. Regardless, according to the researchers, the ascribed social roles—prisoner and guard—were so powerful that in just a few days, the experiment became "reality" for those involved.

According to critics, however, the social roles in the prison experiment were not as powerful as the researchers claimed. Instead, it appears that the researchers actively biased the students to behave the way they did (Bartels, 2015). (Return to Module 4 where we discussed *researcher bias*.) Thus, we cannot know how much of the behavior of the students was triggered by the social roles they were asked to play and how much was triggered by the biases created by the experimenters.

Although this criticism of the original Haney, Banks, and Zimbardo (1973) experiment is now widely accepted by psychologists, the image of decent students turned into brutal "prison guards" or "dehumanized prisoners" nevertheless captured both the popular imagination and an important kernel of truth: That people *can* be changed by the social roles ascribed to them. Comparable, better-controlled studies have since confirmed the power of social roles to change people's behavior, although the effects are usually rather less dramatic than originally reported (Haslam & Reicher, 2006; Lovibond, Mithiran, & Adams, 1979).

Many people also experience **role conflicts**, in which two or more roles make conflicting demands on them (Gordon et al., 2012; Memili et al., 2015). Consider, for example, a teacher who must flunk a close friend's son, a mother who has a demanding full-time job, or a soccer coach whose daughter is on the team but isn't a very good athlete. Likewise, the clashing demands of work, family, and school create role conflicts for many students (Senécal, Julien, & Guay, 2003). Role conflicts at work (such as being a good team player versus being a strong manager) can lead to job burnout and negative health outcomes (Pomaki, Supeli, & Verhoeven, 2007; Schmidt et al., 2014).

Group Structure, Cohesion, and Norms

Are there other dimensions of group membership? Two other important dimensions of any group are its structure and its cohesiveness (Forsyth, 2014). **Group structure** consists of the network of roles, communication pathways, and power

dotshock/Shutterstock.com

Ascribed roles have a powerful impact on social behavior. What kinds of behavior do you expect from your teachers or your coaches? What behaviors do they expect from you? What happens if either of you fails to match the other's expectations?

Social psychology Study of how individuals think and behave in social situations.

Culture An ongoing pattern of life, characterizing a society at a given point in history.

Social role Expected behavior patterns associated with particular social positions (such as daughter, worker, or student).

Role conflict Trying to occupy two or more roles that make conflicting demands on behavior.

Group structure The network of roles, communication pathways, and power in a group.

in a group. Organized groups such as an army or an athletic team have a high degree of structure. Informal friendship groups may or may not be very structured.

Group cohesiveness refers to the degree of attraction among group members or the strength of their desire to remain in the group. Members of cohesive groups literally stick together: They tend to stand or sit close together, they pay more attention to one another, and they show more signs of mutual affection. Also, their behavior tends to be closely coordinated (Lin & Peng, 2010). Cohesiveness is the basis for much of the power that groups exert over us. Therapy groups, businesses, sports teams, and the like seek to increase cohesion because it helps people work together better (Boyd et al., 2014; Casey-Campbell & Martens, 2009).

In-Groups Cohesiveness is particularly strong for **in-groups**—groups with which a person mainly identifies. Very likely, your own in-groups are defined by a combination of prominent social dimensions, such as nationality, ethnicity, age, education, religion, income, political values, gender, sexual orientation, and so forth. In-group membership helps define who we are socially. Predictably, we tend to attribute positive characteristics to our in-group and negative qualities to **out-groups**—groups with which we do not identify. We also tend to exaggerate differences between members of out-groups and our own groups. This sort of "us-and-them" thinking seems to be a basic fact of social life. It also sets the stage for conflict between groups and for racial and ethnic prejudice—topics we will explore in Module 73.

Wrapped in ever-expanding social networks, we are never far from other people. They are always right beside us, just around the next corner, or only a phone call or text message away. Nevertheless, a little solitude can be healthy. In fact, many of history's most creative and spiritual individuals have found insight in their solitude (Flowers, 2011; Storr, 1988). Quiet time for reflection does seem to be associated with creativity, spiritual growth, problem solving, and self-discovery (Knafo, 2012; Long et al., 2003).

Social Status and Social Power In addition to defining roles, a person's social position within groups affects his or her prestige and dominance in those groups. **Social status** refers to the degree to which other group members respect and admire a person, while **social power** refers to the degree to which a person possesses the capacity to control the behavior of other group members (Hays, 2013). A person can be high in both social status and social power (such as a popular chief of police), high in one but not the other (such as a famous actor, who may be accorded high social status while having little social power), or be low in both (like most homeless people). Incidentally, men generally prefer social power over status while women generally prefer status over power (Hays, 2013).

While higher social power obviously bestows special privileges, so too can higher social status (Albrecht & Albrecht, 2011). For example, in one experiment, a man walked into several bakeries and asked for a pastry while claiming that he did not have enough money to pay for it. Half the time he was well dressed, and the rest of the time he was poorly dressed. If the man was polite when he asked, he was equally likely to be given a free pastry no matter how he was dressed (95 percent versus 90 percent). However, if he was impolite when he asked, he was much less likely to get a pastry if he was poorly dressed than if he was well dressed (75 percent versus 20 percent) (Guéguen & Pascual, 2003).

You don't have to be in a bakery for this to work. In most situations, we are more likely to comply with a request made by a high-status (well-dressed) person (Guéguen & Lamy, 2012). Perhaps the better treatment given people with higher social power or status, even when they are impolite, explains some of our society's preoccupation with expensive clothes, cars, and other social power and status symbols.

Norms We also are greatly affected by group norms (Matsumoto & Juang, 2017; Miller & Prentice, 2016). A **norm** is a widely accepted (but often unspoken) standard for appropriate behavior. If you have the slightest doubt about the power of norms, try this test: Walk into a crowded supermarket, get in a checkout line, and begin singing loudly in your fullest voice. Are you the 1 person in 100 who could actually do this?

The impact of norms is shown by a classic study of littering. The question was, "Does the amount of trash in an area affect littering?" To find out, people were given flyers as they walked into a public parking garage. As you can see in ➤ **Figure 70.1**, the more litter there was on the floor, the more likely people were to add to it by dropping their flyer. Apparently, seeing that others had already littered implied a lax norm about whether littering is acceptable. The moral? The cleaner a public area is kept, the less likely people are to "trash" it (Cialdini, Reno, & Kallgren, 1990; Göckeritz et al., 2010).

In the next section, we'll see that the people around us affect not only how we behave, they also influence how we think about ourselves and others. For example, one common way that we understand ourselves is by comparing ourselves to others, a process called . . . wait for it . . . *social comparison* (Brakel et al., 2011).

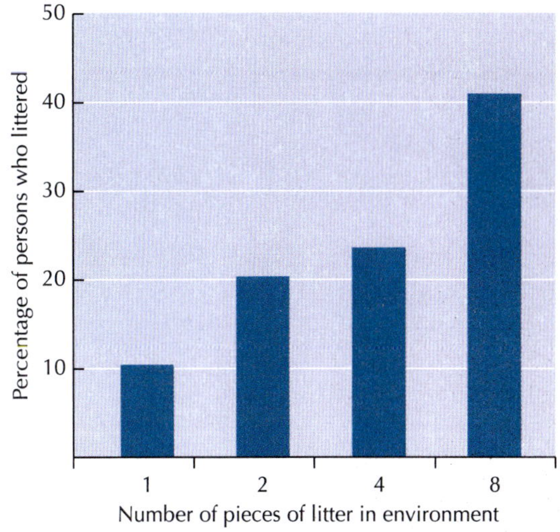

➤ **Figure 70.1**

Results of an experiment on norms concerning littering. The prior existence of litter in a public setting implies that littering is acceptable. This encourages others to "trash" the area. (From Cialdini, Reno, & Kallgren, 1990.)

Social Cognition—Behind Our Masks

Learning Outcome 70.2 Explain social comparison theory, attribution theory, the fundamental attribution error, and the actor–observer bias

Social cognition is the process of thinking about ourselves and others in a social context (Happé, Cook, & Bird, 2017; Shook, 2013). Despite the fact that we are immersed in social relationships with other people all the time and can freely *observe* their behavior, as well as our own, *understanding* that behavior is another matter entirely. For example, we know Jimarcus and Jim Bob see sports differently, but *why*?

In the next few sections, we'll consider some examples of social cognition. We begin with *social comparison*. We then move on to consider the process of *attribution*, one way that we understand the behavior of other people. Finally, we look at *attitudes* and how we form them.

Social Comparison

If you want to know how heavy you are, you simply get on a scale. But how do you know if you are a good athlete, worker, parent, or friend? How do you know if your views on politics, religion, or music are unusual or widely shared? When there are no objective standards, the only available yardstick is provided by comparing yourself with others (Baumeister & Bushman, 2021; Dvash et al., 2010).

Social psychologist Leon Festinger (1919–1989) theorized that group membership fills needs for **social comparison**—comparing your own actions, feelings, opinions, or abilities to those of others. Have you ever "compared notes" with other students after taking an exam? ("How did you do?" "Wasn't that last question hard?") If you have, you were satisfying a need for social comparison (Festinger, 1957; Johnson & Lammers, 2012).

Group cohesiveness The degree of attraction among group members or their commitment to remaining in the group.

In-group A group with which a person identifies.

Out-group A group with which a person does not identify.

Social status The degree of prestige, admiration, and respect accorded to a member of a group.

Social power The degree to which a group member can control, alter, or influence the behavior of another group member.

Norm A widely accepted (but often unspoken) standard of conduct for appropriate behavior.

Social cognition The process of thinking about ourselves and others in a social context.

Social comparison Making judgments about ourselves through comparison with others.

Visions of America, LLC/Alamy Stock Photo

Have you ever gone to a high school class reunion? Do you keep track of your high school classmates on social media (Cramer, Song, & Drent, 2016)? Apparently, it's hard to resist comparing yourself with former classmates to see how you are doing in life.

Typically, we don't make social comparisons randomly or on some absolute scale. Meaningful evaluations are based on comparing yourself with people of similar backgrounds, abilities, and circumstances (Stapel & Marx, 2007). To illustrate, let's ask a student named Wendy if she is a good tennis player. If Wendy compares herself with a professional, the answer will be "no." But this tells us little about her *relative* ability. Within her tennis group, Wendy is regarded as an excellent player. On a fair scale of comparison, Wendy knows that she is good, and she takes pride in her tennis skills. In the same way, thinking of yourself as successful, talented, responsible, or fairly paid depends entirely on whom you choose for comparison. Thus, a desire for social comparison provides a motive for associating with others and influences which groups we join (Johnson & Stapel, 2010; Strickhouser & Zell, 2015).

Let's shift gears now to examine another form of social cognition. Vonda just insulted Sutchai. But why? Why did Nick change his college major? Why does Kirti talk so fast when she's around men? In answering such questions, we *attribute* people's behavior to various causes. Whether we are right or wrong about the causes of their behavior, our conclusions affect how *we* act. To learn how we fill in the "person behind the mask," let's explore the making of attributions.

Attribution Theory

Every day, we must guess how people will act, often from small shreds of evidence. We do this through a form of social cognition called **attribution**. As we observe others, we make attributions about them. For example, two people enter a restaurant and order different meals. Nell tastes her food and then salts it. Bert salts his food before he tastes it. How would you explain their behavior? In Nell's case, you might assume that the *food* needed salt. If so, you have attributed her actions to an *external cause* (one that lies outside a person). With Bert, you might be more inclined to conclude that he must really *like* salt. If so, the cause of his behavior is internal. *Internal causes*, such as needs, personality traits, and Bert's taste for salt, lie within the person. (Attributing your own bodily arousal to various sources can also have a large impact on the emotions you feel. See Module 44.)

What effects do such interpretations have? It is difficult to fully understand social behavior without considering the attributions that we make. For instance, let's say that at the last five parties you've attended, you've seen a woman named Macy. Based on this, you assume that Macy likes to socialize. You see Macy at yet another gathering and mention that she seems to like parties. She says, "Actually, I am very shy and really hate these parties, but I keep coming to overcome my shyness. My counselor says I need to practice being social, so I keep attending these dumb events. How am I doing?"

We seldom know the real reasons for others' actions. That's why we tend to infer causes from *circumstances*. However, in doing so, we often make mistakes like the one with Macy. The most common error is to attribute the actions of others to internal causes (Hooper et al., 2015; Moran, Jolly, & Mitchell, 2014). This mistake is called the **fundamental attribution error**. We tend to think that the

Kathy Hutchins /Shutterstock.com

In 2013, Tom Hanks was the most trusted person in the United States, according to a *Reader's Digest* poll, ranking above many politicians, judges, religious leaders, and sports figures. Is Tom Hanks actually *that* trustworthy? Or is it that he has played many trustworthy characters in popular films? We are more prone than you might think to attribute to actors the personality traits of the characters they play (Tal-Or & Papirman, 2007).

actions of others have internal causes even if, in reality, they are caused by external forces or circumstances. One amusing example of this error is the tendency of people to attribute the actions of actors playing a role to their personalities rather than the obvious external cause (that they are playing a character) (Tal-Or & Papirman, 2007).

Where our own behavior is concerned, we are more likely to think that external causes explain our actions. In other words, an **actor–observer bias** is present in how we explain behavior. As *observers,* we attribute the behavior of others to their wants, motives, and personality traits (this is the fundamental attribution error). As *actors,* however, we tend to find external explanations for our own behavior (Aronson et al., 2015; Gordon & Kaplar, 2002).

No doubt you chose your major in school because of what it has to offer. Other students choose *their* majors because of the kind of people they are. Other people who don't leave tips in restaurants are cheapskates. If you don't leave a tip, it's because the service was bad. And, of course, other people are always late because they are irresponsible. You are late because you were held up by events beyond your control.

As you can see, attribution theory summarizes much of how we think about ourselves and others, including the errors that we tend to make.

Attitudes—Got Attitude?

Learning Outcome 70.3 Define attitudes and explain how they are acquired and changed

Our tastes, friendships, votes, preferences, goals, and behavior in many other situations are all touched by attitudes (Baumeister & Bushman, 2021).

What, specifically, is an attitude? An **attitude** is a positive or negative perception of people, objects, or issues. Attitudes summarize your *evaluation* of objects (Bohner & Dickel, 2010). As a result, they predict or direct future actions.

Attitudes are expressed through beliefs, emotions, and actions. The *belief component* of an attitude is what you believe about a particular object or issue. The *emotional component* consists of your feelings toward the attitudinal object. The *action component* refers to your behaviors toward various people, objects, or institutions.

Consider, for example, your attitude toward gun control. You will have beliefs about whether gun control would affect rates of crime or violence. You will respond emotionally to guns, finding them either attractive and desirable or threatening and destructive. And you will have a tendency to seek out or avoid gun ownership. The action component of your attitude may well include support of organizations that urge or oppose gun control. As you can see, attitudes orient us to the social world. In doing so, they prepare us to act in certain ways (Forgas, Cooper, & Crano, 2010; Jackson, 2011). (For another example, see ➤ **Figure 70.2**.)

Forming Attitudes

How do people acquire attitudes? Attitudes are acquired in several basic ways. Sometimes attitudes come from *direct contact* (personal experience) with the object of the attitude—such as opposing pollution when a nearby factory ruins your favorite river (Ajzen, 2005). Some attitudes are simply formed through *chance conditioning* (learning that takes place by luck or coincidence) (Albarracín, Johnson, & Zanna, 2005). Let's say, for instance, that you have had three encounters in your lifetime with psychologists. If all three were negative, you might take an unduly dim view of psychology. In the same way, people often develop strong attitudes toward cities, foods, or parts of the country on the basis of one or two unusually good or bad experiences (Ledgerwood & Trope, 2010).

Attitudes also are learned through *interaction with others*—such as discussion with people holding a particular attitude. For instance, if three of your good friends are volunteers at a local recycling center and you talk with them about their beliefs, you may well come to favor recycling, too. More generally, there is little doubt that many of our attitudes are influenced by *group membership.* In most groups, pressures to conform shape our attitudes, just as they do our behavior. *Child rearing* (the effects of parental values, beliefs, and practices) also affects attitudes (Bartram, 2006; Guidetti et al., 2012). For example, if both parents belong to

Attribution The process of making inferences about the causes of one's own behavior, and that of others.

Fundamental attribution error Tendency to attribute behavior to internal causes without regard to situational influences.

Actor–observer bias The tendency to attribute the behavior of others to internal causes while attributing one's own behavior to external causes (situations and circumstances).

Attitude Positive or negative perception of people, objects, or issues.

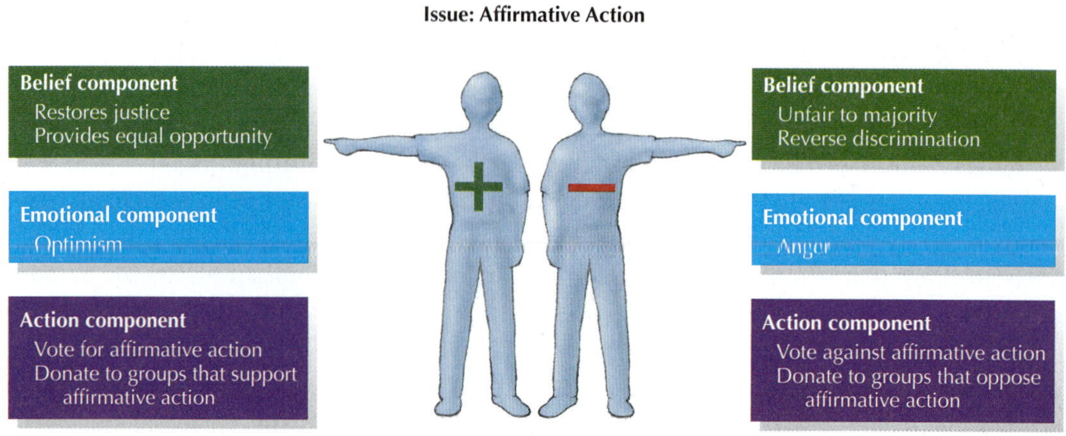

Figure 70.2
Elements of positive and negative attitudes toward affirmative action.

Chip Somodevilla/Getty Images News/Getty Images

Attitudes are an important dimension of social behavior. Attitudes are often greatly influenced by the attitudes of parents and the groups to which they belong.

the same political party, chances are that their children will belong to that party as adults.

Finally, there is no doubt that attitudes are influenced by the media, such as newspapers, television, and the Internet (Mahler, Beckerley, & Vogel, 2010). Every day, we are coaxed, persuaded, and skillfully manipulated by messages in various media. Teenagers today spend at least 70 hours a week immersed in media, such as television, video games, movies, the Internet, music, and print (but not time spent at school or at homework!). Eight-to-twelve-year-olds spend at least 40 hours in similar ways (Rideout, 2015).

The information thus channeled into homes has a powerful impact. For instance, frequent television viewers mistrust others and overestimate their own chances of being harmed. This suggests that a steady diet of television violence leads some people to develop a *mean worldview*, in which they regard the world as a dangerous and threatening place (Nellis & Savage, 2012). (For more on media and observational learning, see Module 29.)

Attitudes and Behavior

Why are some attitudes acted on, whereas others are not? To answer this question, let's consider an example. Assume that a woman named Lorraine knows that automobiles are expensive to operate and add to air pollution. Besides, she hates smog. Why would Lorraine continue to drive to work every day? It is probably because the *immediate consequences* of our actions weigh heavily on the choices we make. No matter what Lorraine's attitude may be, it is difficult for her to resist the immediate convenience of driving.

Our expectations of how *others will evaluate* our actions also are important. Lorraine may resist taking public transit to work for fear that her coworkers will be critical of her environmental stand. By taking this factor into account, researchers have been able to predict family planning choices, alcohol use by teenagers, reenlistment in the National Guard, voting on a solar power initiative, and so forth (Cialdini, 2009). Finally, we must not overlook the effects of longstanding *habits* (Oskamp & Schultz, 2005). Let's say that after years of driving to work Lorraine finally vows to shift to public transit. Two months later, it would not be unusual if she found herself driving again because of habit, despite her good intentions.

In short, there are often large differences between attitudes and behavior—particularly between privately held attitudes and public behavior (Johnson & Boynton, 2010). However, barriers to action typically fall when a person holds an attitude with *conviction*. If you have *conviction* about an issue, it evokes strong feelings, you are reluctant to change it, you think about it and discuss it often, and you are knowledgeable about it (Howe & Krosnick, 2017; Rucker et al., 2014).

Attitude Change—When the Seekers Went Public

Learning Outcome 70.4 Explain when persuasion is most effective and discuss cognitive dissonance

Although attitudes are fairly stable, they do change (Forgas, Cooper, & Crano, 2010; Izuma, 2013). Some attitude change can be understood in terms of a **reference group**—any group that an individual uses as a standard for social comparison. It is not necessary to have face-to-face contact with other people for them to be a reference group. It depends instead on with whom you identify or whose attitudes and values you care about (Ajzen, 2005; Larimer et al., 2011).

In the 1930s, Theodore Newcomb studied real-life attitude change among students at Bennington College (Alwin, Cohen, & Newcomb, 1991). Most students came from conservative homes, but Bennington was a very liberal school. Newcomb found that most students shifted significantly toward more liberal attitudes during their four years at Bennington. Those who didn't change kept their parents and hometown friends as primary reference groups. Those who did change identified primarily with the campus community. Notice that all students could count the college and their families as *membership* groups. However, one group or the other tended to become their point of reference.

Persuasion

What about advertising and other direct attempts to change attitudes? Are they effective? **Persuasion** is any deliberate attempt to change attitudes or beliefs through information and arguments (Gass & Seiter, 2014; Perloff, 2010). Businesses, politicians, and others who seek to persuade us obviously believe that attitudes can be changed. Billions of dollars are spent yearly on advertising in the United States and Canada alone. Persuasion can range from the daily blitz of media commercials to personal discussion among friends. In most cases, the success or failure of persuasion can be understood if we consider the *communicator,* the *message,* and the *audience.*

arindambanerjee/Shutterstock.com

Are you likely to be swayed by this group's message? Successful persuasion is related to the characteristics of the communicator, the message, and the audience.

wavebreakmedia/Shutterstock.com

Do you exercise regularly? Like students in the Bennington study, your intentions to exercise are probably influenced by the exercise habits of your reference groups (Ajzen, 2005; Terry & Hogg, 1996).

At a community meeting, let's say that you have a chance to promote an issue important to you (for or against building a new mall nearby, for instance). Whom should you choose to make the presentation, and how should that person present it? Research suggests that attitude change is encouraged when certain conditions are met. You should have little trouble seeing how the following principles are applied to sell everything from underarm deodorants to presidents (Aronson et al., 2015; Oskamp & Schultz, 2005; Perloff, 2010):

1. The communicator is likable, expressive, trustworthy, an expert on the topic, and similar to the audience in some respect.
2. The communicator appears to have nothing to gain if the audience accepts the message.

Reference group Any group that an individual uses as a standard for social comparison.

Persuasion A deliberate attempt to change attitudes or beliefs with information and arguments.

Cognitive dissonance Psychological state of having related ideas or perceptions that are inconsistent.

3. The message appeals to emotions, particularly to fear or anxiety.
4. The message also provides a clear course of action that will, if followed, reduce fear or produce personally desirable results.
5. The message states clear-cut conclusions.
6. The message is backed up by facts and statistics.
7. The message is repeated as frequently as possible.
8. Both sides of the argument are presented, in the case of a well-informed audience.
9. Only one side of the argument is presented, in the case of a poorly informed audience.

As we have just seen, we sometimes change our attitudes in response to external persuasion (Gass & Seiter, 2014). Sometimes, however, the internal process of *cognitive dissonance* also can lead to attitude change.

Cognitive Dissonance Theory

What happens if people act in ways that are inconsistent with their attitudes or self-images? Cognitions are thoughts. *Dissonance* means clashing. The influential theory of **cognitive dissonance** states that contradicting or inconsistent thoughts cause a psychological state of discomfort—that is, we have a need for *consistency* in our thoughts, perceptions, and images of ourselves (Cooper, 2007; Festinger, 1957). Inconsistency, then, can motivate people to make their thoughts or attitudes agree with their actions (Gawronski, 2012).

For example, smokers are told on every pack that cigarettes endanger their lives. They light up and smoke anyway. How do they resolve the tension between this information and their actions? They could quit smoking, but it may be easier to convince themselves that smoking is not really so dangerous. To do this, a smoker might seek examples of heavy smokers who have lived long lives, spend time with other smokers, and avoid information about the link between smoking and cancer; or he or she might just suppress thoughts of the health consequences altogether (Kneer, Glock, & Rieger, 2012). According to cognitive dissonance theory, we also tend to reject new information that contradicts ideas that we already hold. We're all guilty of this "don't bother me with the facts, my mind is made up" strategy at times.

A famous example of cognitive dissonance in action involves a woman named Mrs. Keech, who claimed she was in communication with beings on a planet called Clarion (Festinger, 1957). The messages foretold the destruction of North America. Mrs. Keech and her followers, the Seekers, were to be rescued by a flying saucer. The news media became involved and reported on the proceedings. When nothing happened, the Seekers suffered a bitter and embarrassing disappointment.

Did the group break up then? Amazingly, instead of breaking up, the Seekers became *more* convinced than ever before that they were right. Mrs. Keech announced that she had received a new message explaining that the Seekers had saved the world. Before, the Seekers were uninterested in persuading other people that the world was coming to an end. Now they called newspapers and radio stations to convince others of their accomplishment.

Why did their belief in Mrs. Keech's messages increase after the world failed to end? Why did the group suddenly become interested in convincing others that they were right? Cognitive dissonance theory explains that after publicly committing themselves to their beliefs, they had a strong need to maintain consistency (Tavris & Aronson, 2007). In effect, convincing others was a way of adding proof that they were correct (■ **Table 70.1**).

Cognitive dissonance also underlies attempts to convince *ourselves* that we've done the right thing. Have you ever noticed how, once you've made a choice, it can be irksome to notice something positive about a rejected alternative (I should have bought the *blue* shirt; it had nicer buttons)? Welcome to *buyer's regret* (Godoy et al., 2010). To minimize such dissonance, we tend to emphasize positive aspects of what we choose, while downgrading other alternatives. Thus, you are more likely to think that your college courses will be good *after* you have registered than before making a commitment.

Acting contrary to one's attitudes doesn't always bring about change. How does cognitive dissonance explain that? The amount of justification for acting contrary to your attitudes and beliefs affects how much dissonance you feel. (*Justification* is the degree to which a person's actions are explained by rewards or other circumstances.) In a classic study, college students did an extremely boring task (turning wooden pegs on a board) for a *long* time. Afterward, they were asked to help lure others into the experiment by pretending that the task was interesting and enjoyable. Students paid $20 for lying to others did not change their own negative opinion of the task: "That was *really* boring!" Those who were paid only $1 later rated the task as "pleasant" and "interesting." How can we explain these results? Apparently,

TABLE 70.1 | Strategies for Reducing Cognitive Dissonance

LeShawn, who is a college student, has always thought of himself as an environmental activist. Recently, LeShawn "inherited" a car from his parents, who were replacing the family "barge." In the past, LeShawn biked or used public transportation to get around. His parents' old car is an antiquated gas-guzzler, but he has begun to drive it every day. How might LeShawn reduce the cognitive dissonance created by the clash between his environmentalism and his use of an inefficient automobile?

Strategy	Example
Change your attitude.	"Cars are not really a major environmental problem."
Add consonant thoughts.	"This is an old car, so keeping it on the road makes good use of the resources that were consumed when it was manufactured."
Change the importance of the dissonant thoughts.	"It's more important for me to support the environmental movement politically than it is to worry about how I get to school and work."
Reduce the amount of perceived choice.	"My schedule has become too hectic. I really can't afford to bike or take the bus anymore."
Change your behavior.	"I'm only going to use the car when it's impossible to bike or take the bus."

Source: Franzoi, 2002.

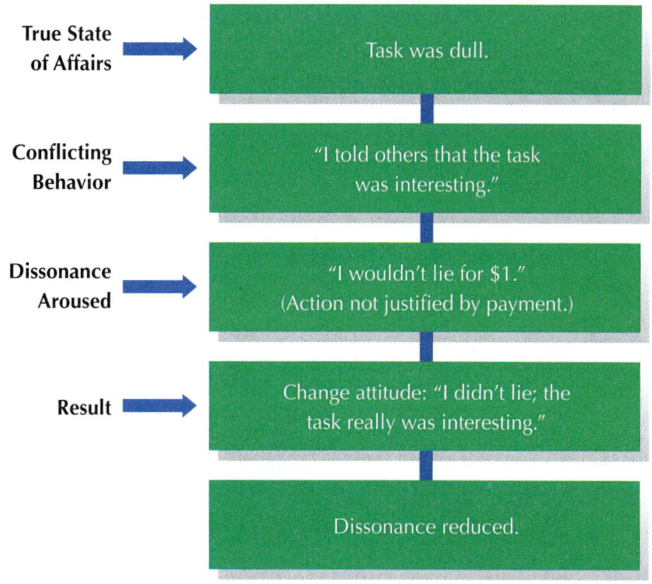

Figure 70.3

Cognitive dissonance. Summary of the Festinger and Carlsmith (1959) study from the viewpoint of a person experiencing cognitive dissonance. (Adapted from Franzoi, 2002.)

students paid $20 experienced no dissonance. These students could reassure themselves that anybody would tell a little white lie for $20. Those paid $1 were faced with the conflicting thoughts: "I lied" and "I had no good reason to do it." Rather than admit to themselves that they had lied, these students changed their attitude toward what they had done (Festinger & Carlsmith, 1959; see **Figure 70.3**).

MODULE 70 Social Behavior and Social Cognition—Learning Outcomes Revisited

70.1 Define two types of social roles, group structure, group cohesiveness, social norms, social status, and social power

Social psychology studies humans as social animals enmeshed in complex networks of social and cultural contexts. Membership in groups, and social situations in general, strongly influence how people behave, think, and feel. Social roles, which may be achieved or ascribed, define one's position in groups and particular behavior patterns associated with those social roles. When two or more contradictory roles are held, role conflicts may occur. *Group structure* refers to the organization of roles, communication pathways, and power within a group. *Group cohesiveness* is basically the degree of attraction among group members. Positions within groups typically carry higher or lower levels of social status, power, or both. High social power and/or status is associated with special privileges and respect. Norms are standards of conduct enforced (formally or informally) by groups.

70.2 Explain social comparison theory, attribution theory, the fundamental attribution error, and the actor–observer bias

Social comparison theory holds that we affiliate to evaluate our actions, feelings, and abilities. Attribution theory is concerned with how we make inferences about behavior. The fundamental attribution error is to ascribe the actions of others to internal causes. Because of actor–observer differences, we tend to attribute our own behavior to external causes.

70.3 Define attitudes and explain how they are acquired and changed

Attitudes are learned dispositions made up of a belief component, an emotional component, and an action component. Attitudes may be formed by direct contact, interaction with others, child-rearing practices, and group pressures. Peer group influences, reference group membership, the media, and chance conditioning also appear to be important in attitude formation.

70.4 Explain when persuasion is most effective and discuss cognitive dissonance

Changing reference groups can change attitudes. Effective persuasion occurs when characteristics of the communicator, the message, and the audience are well matched. In general, a likable and believable communicator who repeats a credible message that arouses emotion in the audience and states clear-cut conclusions will be persuasive. Maintaining and changing attitudes is closely related to cognitive dissonance and our need to be consistent in our thoughts and actions. We are motivated to reduce dissonance when it occurs, often by changing inconsistent beliefs or attitudes.

Reflective Practice

Content Check

1. Social psychology is the study of how people behave in ______________________.
2. *Social status* refers to a set of expected behaviors associated with a social position. T or F?
3. Social comparisons are made pretty much at random. T or F?
4. The fundamental attribution error is to attribute the actions of others to internal causes. T or F?
5. Which of the following is associated with attitude formation?
   - **a.** group membership
   - **b.** mass media
   - **c.** chance conditioning
   - **d.** childrearing
   - **e.** all of the preceding
   - **f.** a and d only
6. In presenting a persuasive message, it is best to give both sides of the argument if the audience is already well informed on the topic. T or F?
7. The amount of cognitive dissonance a person feels is related to how much ______________ exists for his or her actions.
   - **a.** reciprocity
   - **b.** justification
   - **c.** chance conditioning
   - **d.** reference

Skill Check

Think Critically

8. Cognitive dissonance theory predicts that false confessions obtained during brainwashing are not likely to bring about lasting changes in attitudes. Why?

Self-Reflect

What are the most prominent roles you play? What conflicts do they create? How has social comparison affected your behavior? How often do you commit the fundamental attribution error? Try to think of a specific personal example that illustrates the concept. Which of the various sources of attitudes best explain your own attitudes? How would you explain cognitive dissonance theory to a person who knows nothing about it?

ANSWERS

1. social situations or the presence of others 2. F 3. F 4. T 5. e 6. T 7. b 8. Because there is strong justification for such actions. As a result, little cognitive dissonance is created when a prisoner makes statements that contradict his or her beliefs.

Social Psychology
Social Influence

MODULE
71

Question Authority?

Explaining people's behavior often comes down to understanding various forms of social influence. It is one thing to notice, for example, the similarities in the clothes worn by this group of friends. It is another thing entirely to understand why they are all dressed the same way. Is this an example of conformity; did these friends spontaneously and freely change their behavior to bring it into agreement with each other? Or is it an example of obedience to the commands of some authority?

What are the limits of your willingness to comply with the requests of strangers or with the commands of authorities? How much should you resist attempts at coercion? You've probably seen a bumper sticker that says "Question Authority." Actually, that's not bad advice if it means "Think Critically." When, though, is it appropriate to comply with or to resist authority? These are essential questions about how we are affected by social influence.

oneinchpunch/Shutterstock.com

~LEARNING OUTCOMES~

After reading this module you should be able to:

71.1 Define social influence, and discuss five forms it can take, from weakest to strongest

71.2 Distinguish between assertive, aggressive, and non-assertive behavior

Social Influence—Follow the Leader

Learning Outcome 71.1 Define social influence, and discuss five forms it can take, from weakest to strongest

No topic lies nearer the heart of social psychology than **social influence**—changes in behavior induced by the actions of others. When people interact, they almost always affect one another's behavior (Baer, Cialdini, & Lueth, 2012; Kassin, Fein, & Markus, 2021). For example, in a classic experiment, various numbers of people stood on a busy New York City street. On cue, they all looked at a sixth-floor window across the street. A camera recorded how many passersby also stopped to stare. The larger the influencing group, the more people were swayed to join in staring at the window (Milgram, Bickman, & Berkowitz, 1969).

Are there different kinds of social influence? Social influence ranges from milder to stronger. The gentlest form of social influence is *mere presence* (changing behavior just because other people are nearby). We *conform* when we spontaneously change our behavior to bring it into agreement with others. Compliance is a more directed form of social influence.

Social influence Changes in a person's behavior induced by the presence or actions of others.

We *comply* when we change our behavior in response to another person who has little or no social power or authority. Obedience is an even stronger form of social influence. We *obey* when we change our behavior in direct response to the demands of an authority. The strongest form of social influence is *coercion*, or changing behavior because you are forced to.

Mere Presence

Suppose that you just happened to be alone in a room, picking your nose. (We know, none of us would do that, right?) Would you continue if a stranger entered the room? **Mere presence** refers to the tendency for people to change their behavior just because of the presence of other people. (You *would* quit picking your nose, wouldn't you?) Let's explore some of the ways that mere presence can induce us to modify our behavior.

Imagine that you are pedaling your bike when another rider pulls up beside you. Will you pick up your pace? Slow down? Completely ignore the other rider? In 1898, psychologist Norman Triplett's investigation of just such a social situation was the first published social psychology experiment (Strubbe, 2005). According to Triplett, you are more likely to speed up. This is **social facilitation**, the tendency to perform better when in the presence of others (Cole, Barrett, & Griffiths, 2011).

Does mere presence always improve performance? No. If you are confident in your abilities, your behavior will most likely be facilitated in the presence of others. If you are not, your performance is more likely to be impaired (Uziel, 2007). Another classic study focused on college students shooting pool at a student union. Good players who were confident (sharks?) normally made 71 percent of their shots. Their accuracy improved to 80 percent when others were watching them. Less confident, average players (marks?) who normally made 36 percent of their shots dropped to 25 percent accuracy when someone was watching them (Michaels et al., 1982).

Social loafing is another consequence of having other people nearby. People tend to exert less effort (loaf) when they are part of a group than they do when they are solely responsible for their work (Ferrari & Pychyl, 2012; Hall & Buzwell, 2013). In one study, people playing tug-of-war while blindfolded pulled harder if they thought they were competing alone. When they thought others were on their team, they made less of an effort (Ingham et al., 1974).

Conformity

Whereas mere presence can influence our behavior in a variety of ways, conformity involves a more specific response to the presence of others. We show **conformity** when we bring our behavior into agreement with perceived social norms. When Harry met Sally, they fell in love and were not shy about expressing themselves around campus. Increasingly, Sally noticed other students staring at her and Harry when they were, well, expressing their love. Although they never made a conscious decision to conform, in another week their publicly intimate moments were a thing of the past. Perhaps the most basic of all group norms is, as Harry and Sally discovered, "Thou shalt conform." Like it or not, life is filled with instances of conformity (Carlson & Settle, 2016; Suhay, 2015).

As mentioned earlier, all groups have unspoken norms. The broadest norms, defined by society as a whole, establish "normal" or acceptable behavior in most situations. Comparing hairstyles, habits of speech, dress, eating habits, and social customs in two or more cultures makes it clear that we all conform to social norms. In fact, a degree of uniformity is necessary if we are to interact comfortably. Imagine being totally unable to anticipate the actions of others. In stores, schools, and homes, this would be frustrating and disturbing. On the highways, it would be lethal.

The Asch Experiment *How strong are group pressures for conformity?* One of the first experiments on conformity was staged by Solomon Asch (1907–1996). To fully appreciate it, imagine yourself as a participant. Assume that you are seated at a table with six other students. Your task is actually quite simple: You are shown three lines on a card, and you must select the line that matches a "standard" line (➤ Figure 71.1).

As the testing begins, each person announces an answer for the first card. When your turn comes, you agree with the others. "This isn't hard at all," you say to yourself. For several more trials, your answers agree with those of the group. Then comes a shock. All six people announce that line 1 matches the standard, and you were about to say line 2 matches. Suddenly you feel alone and upset. You nervously look at the lines again. The room falls silent. Everyone seems to be staring at you. The experimenter awaits your answer. Do you yield to the group?

In this study, the other "students" were all actors who gave the wrong answer on about a third of the trials to

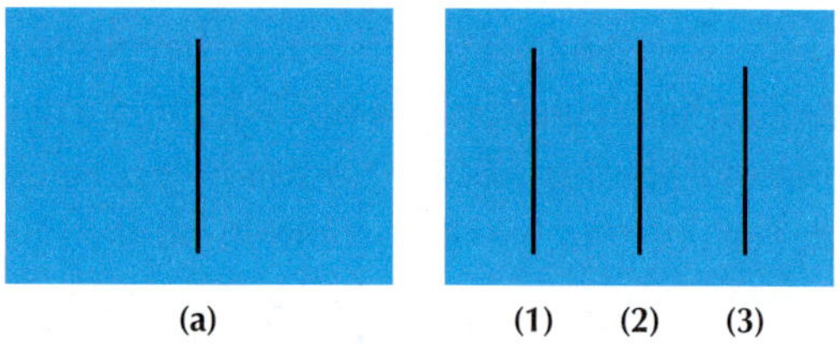

➤ **Figure 71.1**
Stimuli used in Asch's conformity experiments.

create group pressure (Asch, 1956). Real students conformed to the group on about one-third of the critical trials. Of those tested, 75 percent yielded at least once. People who were tested alone erred in less than 1 percent of their judgments. Clearly, those who yielded to group pressures were denying what their eyes told them.

Are some people more susceptible to group pressures than others? People with high needs for structure or certainty are more likely to conform. So are people who are anxious, low in self-confidence, or concerned with the approval of others. People who live in cultures that emphasize group cooperation (such as many Asian cultures) also are more likely to conform (Bond & Smith, 1996; Fu et al., 2007).

Group Factors in Conformity *How do groups enforce norms?* In most groups, we have been rewarded with acceptance and approval for conformity and threatened with rejection or ridicule for nonconformity. These reactions are called *group sanctions.* Negative sanctions range from laughter, staring, or social disapproval to complete rejection or formal exclusion. If you've ever felt the sudden chill of disapproval by others, you understand the power of group sanctions—just as Harry and Sally did.

The more important group membership is to a person, the more he or she will be influenced by other group members (Stein, 2017). The risk of being rejected can be a threat to our sense of personal identity (Baer, Cialdini, & Lueth, 2012). That's why the Asch experiments are impressive. Because these were only temporary groups, sanctions were informal and rejection had no lasting importance. Just the same, the power of the group was evident.

What other factors, besides importance of the group, affect the degree of conformity? In the sidewalk experiment described previously, we noted that large groups had more influence. In Asch's face-to-face groups, the size of the majority also made a difference, but a surprisingly small one. Even more important than the size of the majority is its *unanimity* (total agreement). Having at least one person in your corner can greatly reduce pressures to conform. If you can find at least one other person who sees things as you do, you can be relatively secure in your opposition to other viewpoints. Incidentally, the Internet now makes it much easier to find that other like-minded person.

Groupthink Yale psychologist Irving Janis (1918–1990) first proposed the concept of groupthink in an attempt to understand a series of disastrous decisions made by government officials (Janis, 1989, 2007). The core of **groupthink** is misguided loyalty—an urge by decision makers to maintain each other's approval, even at the cost of critical thinking (Singer, 2005). Group members are hesitant to "rock the boat," question sloppy thinking, or tolerate alternative views. This self-censorship leads people to believe that they agree more than they actually do (Matusitz & Breen, 2012; Tsintsadze-Maass & Maass, 2014).

Groupthink has been blamed for contributing to many crises, such as the invasion and occupation of Iraq and the *Columbia* space shuttle disaster in 2003 (Houghton, 2008; Post, 2011; Schafer & Crichlow, 2010). More recently, groupthink has been implicated in the failure of Penn State University administrators to deal appropriately with a long-standing pattern of child sexual abuse by then-Penn State football coach Gerry Sandusky (Wagner, 2013).

To prevent groupthink, group leaders should take the following steps (Janis, 2007; Schafer & Crichlow, 2010):

- Define each group member's role as a "critical evaluator."
- Avoid revealing any personal preferences in the beginning. State the problem factually, without bias.
- Invite a group member or outside person to play devil's advocate. Make it clear that group members will be held accountable for decisions.
- Encourage open inquiry and a search for alternate solutions.

In addition, Janis suggested that a "second-chance" meeting should be held to reevaluate important decisions—that is, each decision should be reached twice.

In fairness to our decision makers, it is worth noting that the presence of too many alternatives can lead to *deadlock,* which can delay taking necessary action (Kowert, 2002). Regardless, in an age clouded by the threat of war, global warming, and terrorism, even stronger solutions to the problem of groupthink would be welcome. Perhaps we should form a group to think about it!

Compliance

Pressures to "fit in" and conform are usually indirect. In contrast, the term **compliance** refers to situations in which

Mere presence The tendency for people to change their behavior just because of the presence of other people.

Social facilitation Tendency to perform better when in the presence of others.

Social loafing Exerting less effort when performing a specific task with a group than when alone.

Conformity Matching behavior and appearance to perceived social norms.

Groupthink Flawed decision-making in which a collection of individuals favors conformity over critical analysis.

Compliance Bending to the requests of a person who has little or no authority or other form of social power.

one person bends to the requests of another person who has little or no authority (Cialdini, 2009). These more direct pressures to comply are quite common and more powerful than you might think (Bohns, 2016). You *passively comply* when, for example, you suffer, without protest, someone smoking near you in a nonsmoking zone or talking loudly while you are trying to study in the library. You *actively comply* when, for example, you hand over your cell phone to a stranger who asks to borrow it to make a call or lend money to a coworker who requests it to buy a cappuccino.

What determines whether a person will comply with a request? Many factors could be listed, but three stand out as especially interesting (Cialdini & Griskevicius, 2010). We are more likely to comply with a request if it:

1. Comes from someone we *know* rather than a stranger
2. Is *consistent* with our previous actions
3. Allows us to *reciprocate* a prior gift, favor, or service

These factors allow us to better understand several strategies that can be used to gain compliance. Because strangers must work harder to gain compliance, salespeople depend heavily on appealing to your tendency to be *consistent* and to *reciprocate*.

The Foot-in-the-Door Effect People who sell door-to-door have long recognized that once they get a foot in the door, a sale is almost a sure thing. To state the **foot-in-the-door effect** more formally, a person who first agrees to a small request is, to be *consistent*, later more likely to comply with a larger demand (Guéguen et al., 2016; Pascual et al., 2013). For instance, if someone asked you to put a large, ugly sign in your front yard to promote safe driving, you would probably refuse. If, however, you had first agreed to put a small sign in your window, you would later be much more likely to allow the big sign in your yard.

kagemusha/Shutterstock.com

Would you be willing to help this young woman carry her books to a nearby desk? What if she subsequently asked you to carry them across campus to her car? If you did, you might have fallen victim to the foot-in-the-door effect. (That is unless you were attracted to her and were trying to get your own foot in the door!)

The Door-in-the-Face Effect Let's say that a neighbor comes to your door and asks you to feed his dogs, water his plants, and mow his yard while he is out of town for a month. This is quite a major request—one that most people would probably turn down. Feeling only slightly guilty, you tell your neighbor that you're sorry but you can't help him. Now, what if the same neighbor returns the next day and asks if you would at least pick up his mail while he is gone. Chances are very good that you would honor this request, even if you might have originally turned it down, too.

Psychologist Robert Cialdini coined the term **door-in-the-face effect** to describe the tendency for a person who has refused a major request to agree to a smaller request. In other words, after a person has turned down a major request ("slammed the door in your face"), he or she may be more willing to comply with a lesser demand. This strategy works because a person who abandons a large request appears to have given up something. In response, many people feel that they must *reciprocate* by giving in to the smaller request (Cialdini, 2009; Meineri et al., 2016). In fact, a good way to get another person to comply with a request is to first do a small favor for the person.

The Lowball Technique Anyone who has purchased an automobile will recognize a third way of inducing compliance. Automobile dealers are notorious for convincing customers to buy cars by offering "lowball" prices that undercut the competition. The dealer first gets the customer to agree to buy at an attractively low price. Then, once the customer is committed, various techniques are used to bump the price up before the sale is concluded.

The **lowball technique** consists of getting a person committed to act and then making the terms of acting less desirable (Pascual et al., 2016). In this case, because you have already complied with a large request, it would be *inconsistent* to deny the follow-on, smaller additional request. Here's another example: A fellow student asks to borrow $25 for a day. This seems reasonable, and you agree. However, once you have given your classmate the money, he explains that it would be easier to repay you after payday, in two weeks. If you agree, you've succumbed to the lowball technique. Here's another example: Let's say that you ask someone to give you a ride to school in the morning. Only after the person has agreed do you tell her that you have to be there at 6 a.m.

Obedience

If ordered to do so, would you shock a man with a heart condition who is screaming and asking to be released? Certainly, few people would obey. Or would they? In Nazi Germany, obedient soldiers (who were once average citizens) helped slaughter more than 6 million people in concentration camps. Do such inhumane acts reflect deep character flaws? Are they the acts of heartless psychopaths or crazed killers? Or are they simply the result of obedience to authority? These are questions that puzzled social psychologist Stanley Milgram (1965) when he began a provocative series of studies on **obedience**, a special type of compliance to the demands of an *authority*.

How did Milgram study obedience? As was true of the Asch experiments, Milgram's research is best appreciated by imagining yourself as a participant. Place yourself in the following situation.

Milgram's Obedience Studies Imagine answering a newspaper ad to take part in a "learning" experiment at Yale University. When you arrive, a coin is flipped, and a second participant, a pleasant-looking man in his fifties, is designated the "learner." By chance, you have become the "teacher."

Your task is to read aloud a list of word pairs. The learner's task is to memorize them. You are to punish him by using electric shocks. The learner is taken to an adjacent room, and you watch as he is seated in an "electric chair" apparatus. Electrodes are attached to his wrists. You are then escorted to your position in front of a "shock generator." On this device is a row of 30 switches marked from 15 to 450 volts. Corresponding labels range from "Slight Shock" to "Extreme Intensity Shock" and, finally, "Danger: Severe Shock." Your instructions are to shock the learner each time he makes a mistake. You must begin with 15 volts and then move one switch (15 volts) higher for each additional mistake (➤ **Figure 71.2**).

The experiment begins, and the learner soon makes his first error. You flip a switch. More mistakes. Rapidly, you reach the 75-volt level. The learner moans after each shock. At 100 volts, he complains that he has a heart condition. At 150 volts, he says he no longer wants to continue and demands to be released. At 300 volts, he screams and says he no longer can give answers.

At some point, you begin to protest to the experimenter. "That man has a heart condition," you say. "I'm not going to kill that man." The experimenter says, "Please continue." Another shock and another scream from the learner and you say, "You mean I've got to keep going up the scale? No, sir. I'm not going to give him 450 volts!" The experimenter says, "The experiment requires that you continue." For a time, the learner refuses to answer any more questions and screams with each shock. Then he falls chillingly silent for the rest of the experiment (Milgram, 1965; Perry, 2013).

It's hard to believe many people would do this. What happened? Milgram also doubted that many people would obey his orders. When he polled a group of psychiatrists before the experiment, they predicted that less than 1 percent of those tested would obey. The astounding fact is that 65 percent obeyed completely by going all the way to the

Foot-in-the-door effect The tendency for a person who has first complied with a small request to be more likely later to fulfill a larger request.

Door-in-the-face effect The tendency for a person who has refused a major request to subsequently be more likely to comply with a minor request.

Lowball technique A strategy in which commitment is gained first to reasonable or desirable terms, which are then made less reasonable or desirable.

Obedience Compliance with a request from an authority figure.

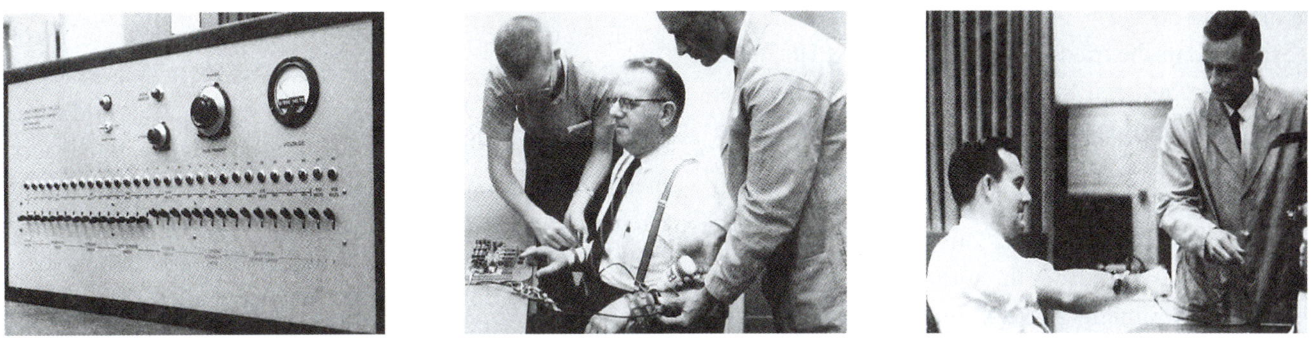

➤ **Figure 71.2**

Milgram's obedience study. Scenes from Stanley Milgram's study of obedience: the "shock generator," strapping a "learner" into his chair, and a "teacher" being told to administer a severe shock to the learner.

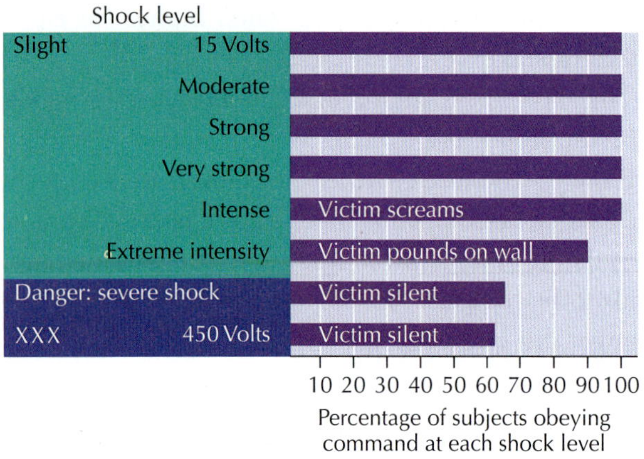

Figure 71.3

Results of Milgram's obedience experiment. Only a minority of participants refused to provide shocks, even at the most extreme intensities. The first substantial drop in obedience occurred at the 300-volt level (Milgram, 1963).

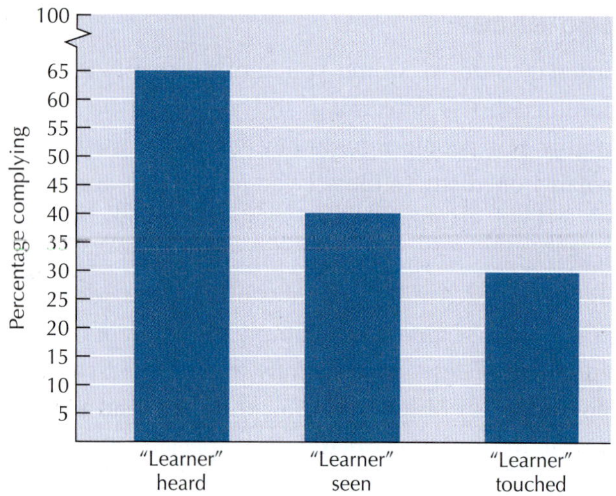

Figure 71.4

Obedience as a function of physical distance. Physical distance from the "learner" had a significant effect on the percentage of participants obeying orders.

450-volt level. Virtually no one stopped short of 300 volts ("Severe Shock") (➤ **Figure 71.3**).

Was the learner injured? The "learner" was actually an actor who turned a tape recorder on and off in the shock room. No shocks were ever administered, but the dilemma for the "teacher" was quite real. Participants protested, sweated, trembled, stuttered, bit their lips, and laughed nervously. Clearly, they were disturbed by what they were doing. Nevertheless, most obeyed the experimenter's orders.

Milgram's Follow-up *Why did so many people obey?* Some have suggested that the prestige of Yale University added to participants' willingness to obey. Could it be that they assumed the professor running the experiment would not really allow anyone to be hurt? To test this possibility, the study was rerun in a shabby office building in nearby Bridgeport, Connecticut. Under these conditions, fewer people obeyed (48 percent), but the reduction was relatively minor.

Milgram was disturbed by the willingness of people to knuckle under to authority and senselessly shock someone. In later experiments, he tried to reduce obedience. He found that the distance between the teacher and the learner was important. When participants were in the *same room* as the learner, only 40 percent obeyed fully. When they were *face-to-face* with the learner and were required to force his hand down on a simulated "shock plate," only 30 percent obeyed (➤ **Figure 71.4**). Distance from the authority also had an effect. When the experimenter gave his orders over the phone, only 22 percent obeyed.

Implications *Surely people wouldn't act the same way if Milgram's research was repeated today, right?* Don't be so sure. Psychologist Jerry Burger of Santa Clara University recently partially replicated Milgram's study and obtained very similar results (Burger, 2009). Milgram's research raises nagging questions about our willingness to commit antisocial or inhumane acts commanded by a "legitimate authority." The excuse so often given by war criminals—"I was only following orders"—takes on new meaning in this light. Milgram suggested that when directions come from an authority, people rationalize that they are not personally responsible for their actions.

Criticisms of Milgram's experiments include condemnation that his experiments were deeply unethical, actively biased the "teachers" to behave the way they did (remember the criticisms of the Stanford prison experiment?), and failed to consider alternative explanations, such as the likelihood that followers obey because they agree with the authority (Griggs, 2017; Haslam, Reicher, & Birney, 2016; Perry, 2013).

Even if blind obedience isn't the only, or even the main, cause, the reality is that in locales as diverse as Cambodia, Rwanda, Bosnia, Vietnam, Darfur, Sri Lanka, Iraq, and Syria, obedience to authority likely played a role in "sanctioned massacres" of chilling proportions (Mastroianni, 2015). Even in everyday life, crimes of obedience are common (Zimbardo, 2007). In order to keep their jobs, many people obey orders to do things that they know are dishonest, unethical, or harmful (Hinrichs, 2007).

Isn't that an overly negative view of obedience? Obedience to authority is obviously necessary and desirable in many circumstances. Just the same, as C. P. Snow (1961) observed, "When you think of the long and gloomy history of man, you will find more hideous crimes have been committed in the name of obedience than in the name of rebellion." With this in mind, let's end on a more positive note. In one of his experiments, Milgram found that group support can greatly reduce destructive obedience. When real participants saw two other "teachers" (both actors) resist orders and walk out of the experiment, only 10 percent continued to obey. Thus, a personal act of courage or moral fortitude by one or two members of a group may free others to disobey misguided or unjust authority.

Coercion

We close this section on social influence by examining some forms of *coercion*, the most extreme type of social influence. You are being subjected to **coercion** if you are forced to change your beliefs or your behavior against your will (Baumeister & Bushman, 2021; Moghaddam, 2013).

If you're a history enthusiast, you may associate *brainwashing* with techniques used by the Communist Chinese on prisoners during the Korean War (Jowett, 2006). Through various types of "thought reform," the Chinese were able to coerce some prisoners to sign false confessions.

Brainwashing *How does brainwashing differ from other persuasive techniques?* As we have noted, advertisers, politicians, educators, religious organizations, and others actively seek to alter attitudes and opinions. To an extent, their persuasive efforts resemble brainwashing, but there is an important difference: **Brainwashing**, or forced attitude change, requires a captive audience. If you are offended by a television commercial, you can tune it out. Prisoners are completely at the mercy of their captors. Complete control over the environment allows a degree of psychological manipulation that would be impossible in a normal setting.

How does captivity facilitate coercion? Brainwashing typically begins by making the target person feel completely helpless. Physical and psychological abuse, lack of sleep, humiliation, and isolation serve to *unfreeze*, or loosen, former values and beliefs. When exhaustion, pressure, and fear become unbearable, *change* occurs as the person begins to abandon former beliefs. Prisoners who reach the breaking point may sign a false confession or cooperate to gain relief. When they do, they are suddenly rewarded with praise, privileges, food, or rest. From that point on, a mixture of hope and fear plus pressures to conform serve to *refreeze* (solidify) new attitudes (Taylor, 2004).

How permanent are changes coerced by brainwashing? In most cases, the dramatic shift in attitudes brought about by brainwashing is temporary. Most "converted" prisoners who returned to the United States after the Korean War eventually reverted to their original beliefs. Nevertheless, brainwashing can be powerful, as shown by the success of cults in recruiting new members.

Cults Exhorted by their leader, some 900 members of the Reverend Jim Jones's People's Temple picked up paper cups and drank purple Flavor Aid laced with the deadly poison cyanide. Some even forced their own children to join in. The People's Temple is a classic example of a **cult**, an authoritarian group in which the leader's personality is more important than the beliefs he or she preaches.

Psychologically, the mass suicide at Jonestown in 1978 is not so incredible as it might seem (Dein & Littlewood, 2005; Moore, 2009). The inhabitants of Jonestown were isolated in the jungles of Guyana, intimidated by guards, and lulled with sedatives. They were also cut off from friends and

Coercion Being forced to change your beliefs or your behavior against your will.

Brainwashing Engineered or forced attitude change involving a captive audience.

Cult A group that professes great devotion to some person and follows that person almost without question; cult members are typically victimized by their leaders in various ways.

Bettmann/Getty Images

Aftermath of the mass suicide at Jonestown. How do cult-like groups recruit new devotees?

relatives and totally accustomed to obeying rigid rules of conduct, which primed them for Jones's final "loyalty test."

Most psychologists regard "prophet" Warren Jeffs's FLDS Church to be a current example of a cult. Cult members give their allegiance to this person, who is regarded as infallible, and they follow his or her dictates without question. Almost always, cult members are victimized by their leaders in one way or another. Jeffs, for example, is currently serving a 20-year prison sentence for multiple child rapes.

If a lesson is to be learned from such destructive cults, it is this: All true spiritual leaders have taught love and compassion. They also encourage followers to question their beliefs and to reach their own conclusions about how to live. In contrast, destructive cults show how dangerous it is to trade personal independence and critical thinking for security (Cowan & Bromley, 2008; Goldberg, 2001).

Assertiveness—Stand Up for Your Rights

Learning Outcome 71.2 Distinguish between assertive, aggressive, and nonassertive behavior

Most of us have been rewarded for compliant, obedient, or "good" behavior, first as children and later as adults. Perhaps this is why so many people find it difficult to assert themselves (Hauck, 2011). Or perhaps not asserting yourself is related to anxiety about "making a scene" or feeling disliked by others. Whatever the causes, some people suffer anguish in any situation requiring poise, self-confidence, or self-assertion. Have you ever done any of the following: Hesitated to question an error on a restaurant bill because you were afraid of making a scene? Backed out of asking for a raise or a change in working conditions? Said yes when you wanted to say no? Been afraid to question a grade that seemed unfair?

If you have ever had difficulty asserting yourself in similar situations, it might be worth practicing how to be self-assertive (Tavakoli et al., 2009; Wolpe, 1974). The first step is to convince yourself of three basic rights: You have the right to refuse, to request, and to right a wrong. **Self-assertion** involves standing up for these rights by speaking out on your own behalf.

AP Images/Jeff Widener

Associated Press photographer Jeff Widener snapped this timeless photo of a lone protester literally standing up on his own behalf while he halted a column of tanks during the 1989 pro-democracy rallies in Tiananmen Square in Beijing, China. How many of us would find the courage to assert ourselves against such direct expressions of authority?

Is self-assertion just getting things your own way? Not at all. A basic distinction can be made between *self-assertion* and *aggressive behavior*. Self-assertion is a direct, honest expression of feelings and desires. It is not exclusively self-serving. People who are nonassertive are usually patient to a fault. Sometimes their pent-up anger explodes with unexpected fury, which can damage relationships. In contrast to assertive behavior, *aggression* involves hurting another person or achieving one's goals at the expense of another. Aggression does not take into account the feelings or rights of others. It is an attempt to get one's own way no matter what. Assertion techniques emphasize firmness, not attack (■ **Table 71.1**).

The basic idea is that each assertive action is practiced until it can be repeated even under stress. For example, let's say it really angers you when a store clerk waits on several people who arrived after you did. To improve your assertiveness in this situation, you would begin by *rehearsing* the dialogue, posture, and gestures you would use to confront the clerk or the other customer. Working in front of a mirror can be very helpful. If possible, you should *role-play* the scene with a friend. Be sure to have your friend take the part of a really aggressive or irresponsible clerk as well as a cooperative one. Rehearsal and role-playing also should be used when you expect a possible confrontation with someone—for example, if you are going to ask for a raise, challenge a grade, or confront a landlord.

Is that all there is to it? No. Another important principle is *overlearning* (practice that continues after initial mastery of a skill). When you rehearse or role-play assertive behavior, it is essential to continue to practice until your responses

TABLE 71.1 | Comparison of Assertive, Aggressive, and Nonassertive Behavior

	Actor	Receiver of Behavior
Nonassertive behavior	Self-denying, inhibited, hurt, and anxious; lets others make choices; goals not achieved	Feels sympathy, guilt, or contempt for actor; achieves goals at actor's expense
Aggressive behavior	Achieves goals at others' expense; expresses feelings, but hurts others; chooses for others or puts them down	Feels hurt, defensive, humiliated, or taken advantage of; does not meet own needs
Assertive behavior	Self-enhancing; acts in own best interests; expresses feelings; respects rights of others; goals usually achieved; self-respect maintained	Needs respected and feelings expressed; may achieve goal; self-worth maintained

become almost automatic. This helps prevent you from getting flustered in the actual situation.

To summarize, self-assertion does not supply instant poise, confidence, or self-assurance. However, it is a way of combating anxieties associated with life in an impersonal and sometimes intimidating society (Sarkova et al., 2013). If you are interested in more information, you can consult a book titled *Your Perfect Right* by Alberti and Emmons (2008).

Self-assertion A direct, honest expression of feelings and desires.

MODULE 71 Social Influence—Learning Outcomes Revisited

71.1 Define social influence, and discuss five forms it can take, from weakest to strongest

Social influence refers to alterations in behavior brought about by the behavior of others. Social influence ranges from milder (mere presence, conformity, and compliance) to stronger (obedience and coercion). The mere presence of others may facilitate (or inhibit) performance. People may also engage in social loafing, working less hard when they are part of a group. Virtually everyone conforms to a variety of broad social and cultural norms. Conformity pressures also exist within smaller groups. The Asch experiments demonstrated that group sanctions encourage conformity. *Groupthink* refers to compulsive conformity in group decision-making. Group members who succumb to groupthink seek to maintain each other's approval, even at the cost of critical thinking. Compliance with direct requests from a person who has little or no authority is another means by which behavior is influenced. Compliance may be active or passive. Three strategies for gaining compliance are the foot-in-the-door technique, the door-in-the-face approach, and the lowball technique. Research suggests that people are excessively obedient to authority. Obedience in Milgram's studies decreased when the victim was in the same room, when the victim and participant were face to face, when the authority figure was absent, and when others refused to obey. Coercion involves forcing people to change their beliefs or behavior against their will. Three steps in brainwashing (forced attitude change) are unfreezing, changing, and refreezing attitudes and beliefs. Cults are groups that rely on coercion.

71.2 Distinguish between assertive, aggressive, and nonassertive behavior

Self-assertion involves standing up for yourself; aggression involves achieving your goals at the expense of another; and nonassertion involves denying your own needs and yielding to others.

Reflective Practice

Content Check

1. The mere presence of others always improves performance. T or F?
2. Participants in Solomon Asch's conformity study yielded on about 75 percent of the critical trials. T or F?
3. Nonconformity is punished by negative group ____________________.
4. The term *compliance* refers to situations in which a person complies with commands made by a person who has authority. T or F?
5. Obedience in Milgram's experiments was related to
   a. distance between learner and teacher
   b. distance between experimenter and teacher
   c. obedience of other teachers
   d. all of these
6. Brainwashing differs from other persuasive attempts in that brainwashing requires a ____________________ ____________________.
7. In assertiveness training, people learn techniques for getting their way in social situations and angry interchanges. T or F?

Skill Check

Think Critically

8. Is it possible to be completely nonconforming—that is, to not conform to some group norm?
9. Modern warfare allows killing to take place impersonally and at a distance. How does this relate to Milgram's experiments?

Self-Reflect

Have you ever encountered a social loafer? (*You* were never one, right?) How did you react? Identify a recent time when you conformed in some way. How did norms, group pressure, sanctions, and unanimity contribute to your tendency to conform? You would like to persuade people to donate to a deserving charity. How, specifically, could you use compliance techniques to get people to donate? Are you surprised that so many people obeyed orders in Milgram's experiments? Do you think you would have obeyed? How actively do you question authority? To what extent are governments entitled to use coercion to modify the attitudes or behavior of their citizens? Pick a specific instance when you could have been more assertive. How would you handle the situation if it occurs again?

ANSWERS

1. F 2. F 3. sanctions 4. F 5. d 6. captive audience 7. F 8. A person who did not follow at least some norms concerning normal social behavior very likely would be perceived as extremely bizarre, disturbed, or psychotic. 9. There is a big difference between killing someone in hand-to-hand combat and killing someone by lining up images on a video screen. Milgram's research suggests that it is easier for a person to follow orders to kill another human when the victim is at a distance and removed from personal contact.

MODULE 72

Social Psychology
Prosocial Behavior

The "Snuggle" for Survival

One common misunderstanding of human nature is that we are engaged in a perennial struggle for survival against one another. In fact, we cooperate with the people around us at least as much as we are in conflict with them. Although at times you want to be left alone, the fact is that we humans are social animals. Imagine if you were deprived of all contact with your family and friends. You would probably find it painfully lonely and disorienting. If deprived of all human contact, you might have difficulty even surviving.

The various forms of *prosocial behavior* all involve having a positive effect on people around us. From the desire for intimacy with family to the impulse to help strangers, we are drawn to other people. What brings people together to help each other, to seek friendship, and to find love? Let's further explore the "snuggle" for survival.

Martin Barraud/Caiaimage/Getty Images

~LEARNING OUTCOMES~

After reading this module you should be able to:

72.1 Explain why we affiliate, describe factors influencing interpersonal attraction, and discuss self-disclosure

72.2 Explain how interpersonal attraction and love differ, how adult relationships are rooted in childhood, and outline how evolutionary psychology views human mating patterns

72.3 Outline the decision points and factors influencing our willingness to help other people

Affiliation and Attraction—Come Together

Learning Outcome 72.1 Explain why we affiliate, describe factors influencing interpersonal attraction, and discuss self-disclosure

Prosocial behavior is any behavior that has a positive impact on other people. (In contrast, *antisocial behavior* is any behavior that has a negative impact on other people.) We are social beings with a **need to affiliate**—a need to associate with other people—rooted in basic human desires to get and to give approval, support, friendship, and love (Baumeister & Bushman, 2021). We also affiliate to help us think about ourselves by comparing ourselves with others (see Module 70). We even seek the company of others to alleviate fear or anxiety.

Don't people also affiliate out of attraction for one another? Of course they do. Let's see why.

Prosocial behavior Any behavior that has a positive impact on other people.

Need to affiliate The desire to associate with other people.

Interpersonal Attraction

Interpersonal attraction—affinity to another person—is the basis for most voluntary social relationships (Berscheid, 2010; Finkel & Eastwick, 2015). To form friendships, we must first identify potential friends and then get to know them. Deciding whether you would like to get to know another person can happen very quickly, sometimes within just minutes of meeting (Grant-Jacob, 2016). That may be because you don't usually randomly choose people to encounter.

Finding Potential Friends

What initially attracts people to each other? "Birds of a feather flock together." "Familiarity breeds contempt." "Opposites attract." Are these statements true? At best, the folklore is a mixture of fact and fiction. As you might expect, we look for friends and lovers who will be kind and understanding and who appear to have attractive personalities (Bradbury & Karney, 2010; Park & Lennon, 2008). Let's explore some other factors that influence our initial attraction to people.

Familiarity In general, we are attracted to people with whom we are familiar (Reis et al., 2011). (That's one reason actors costarring in movies often become romantically involved.) In fact, our choice of friends (and even lovers) is based more on *physical proximity* (nearness) than we might care to believe. Proximity promotes attraction by increasing the *frequency of contact* between people.

The closer people live to each other, the more likely they are to become friends. Likewise, lovers like to think they have found the "one and only" person in the universe for them. In reality, they have probably found the best match in a 5-mile radius (Reis et al., 2011). Marriages are not made in heaven—they are made in local schools, businesses, churches, bars, clubs, and neighborhoods.

In short, there does seem to be a "boy-next-door" or "girl-next-door" effect in romantic attraction, and a "folks-next-door" effect in friendship. Notice, however, that the Internet is making it increasingly easier to stay in constant "virtual contact," which is leading to more and more long-distance friendships and romances (Aron, 2012; Whyte & Torgler, 2017).

Similarity In everything from casual acquaintance to marriage, similar people are attracted to each other (Montoya & Horton, 2013). *Similarity* refers to how alike you are to another person in background, age, sex, interests, attitudes, ethnicity, beliefs, and so forth.

Take a moment to make a list of your closest friends. What do they have in common (other than the joy of knowing you)? It is likely that their ages are similar to yours and you are of the same sex and ethnicity. There will be exceptions, of course. They also likely share common interests, attitudes, and beliefs. And why not? It's reinforcing to see our beliefs and attitudes shared by others. It shows we are "right" and reveals that they are clever people as well!

So similarity also influences mate selection? Yes. In choosing a mate, we tend to marry someone who is like us in almost every way, a pattern called *homogamy* (huh-MOG-ah-me) (Kalmijn, 2010; Schramm et al., 2012). Studies show that married couples are highly similar in age, education, ethnicity, and religion. To a lesser degree, they also are similar in attitudes and opinions, mental abilities, status, height, weight, and eye color. In case you're wondering, homogamy also applies to unmarried couples who are living together (Blackwell & Lichter, 2004).

Physical Attractiveness People who are *physically attractive* are regarded as good-looking by others. Beautiful people are generally rated as more appealing than average. This is due, in part, to the *halo effect*, a tendency to generalize a favorable impression to unrelated personal characteristics. Because of it, we assume that attractive people also are likable, intelligent, warm, witty, mentally healthy, and socially skilled. Basically, we act as if "what is beautiful is good" (Lorenzo, Biesanz, & Human, 2010).

In reality, physical attractiveness has little or no connection to intelligence, talents, or abilities. Perhaps that's why beauty affects mainly our initial interest in getting to know others (Keller & Young, 1996). Later, more meaningful qualities gain in importance. As you discover that someone has a good personality, he or she will start looking even more attractive to you. It takes more than appearance to make a lasting relationship (Berscheid, 2010; Lewandowski, Aron, & Gee, 2007; Reis et al., 2011).

Reciprocity *Okay, so he or she is someone with whom you are familiar, appears to share a lot in common with you, and is even hot. What else do you need to know before taking it to the next level?* Well, it would be nice to know if he or she also is the least bit into you (Greitemeyer, 2010; Montoya & Horton, 2012). In fact, **reciprocity**, which occurs when people respond to each other in similar ways, may be the most important factor influencing the development of relationships. Most people find it easier to reciprocate someone else's overtures than to be the initiator (Montoya & Insko, 2008). That way, at least the embarrassment of an outright rejection can be avoided.

Getting to Know One Another: Self-Disclosure

Once initial contact has been made, it's time to get to know each other. This is done mainly through the process of **self-disclosure** as you begin to share private thoughts and feelings and reveal yourself to others. To get acquainted, you must be willing to talk about more than just the weather, sports, or nuclear physics. In general, as friends talk, they gradually deepen their level of liking, trust, and self-disclosure (Sprecher, Treger, & Wondra, 2013; Sprecher & Treger, 2015). We more often reveal ourselves to people we like than to those we find unattractive. Disclosure also requires a degree of trust. Many people play it safe, or "close to the vest," with people they do not know well. Indeed, self-disclosure is governed by unspoken rules about what's acceptable (Phillips, Rothbard, & Dumas, 2009).

Moderate self-disclosure leads to increased reciprocity. In contrast, *overdisclosure* exceeds what is appropriate for a relationship or social situation, giving rise to suspicion and reducing attraction. For example, imagine standing in line at a store and having the stranger in front of you say, "Lately I've been thinking about how I really feel about myself. I think I'm pretty well adjusted, but I occasionally have some questions about my sexual adequacy."

When self-disclosure proceeds at a moderate pace, it builds trust, intimacy, reciprocity, and positive feelings. When it is too rapid or inappropriate, we are likely to "back off" and wonder about the person's motives. It's interesting to note that on the Internet (and especially on social networking sites such as Facebook), people often feel freer to express their true feelings, which can lead to personal growth and genuine, face-to-face friendships. However, it also can lead to some very dramatic overdisclosures (Jiang, Bazarova, & Hancock, 2013; Special & Li-Barber, 2012).

EXImages/Alamy Stock Photo

Overdisclosure is a staple of many reality television shows such as *Catfish* and *90 Day Fiancé*. Participants frequently reveal intimate details about their personal lives, including private family matters, sex and dating, physical or sexual abuse, major embarrassments, and criminal activities. Viewers probably find such intimate disclosures entertaining, rather than threatening, because they don't have to reciprocate.

Interpersonal Attraction and Love—The Love Triangle

Learning Outcome 72.2 Explain how interpersonal attraction and love differ, how adult relationships are rooted in childhood, and outline how evolutionary psychology views human mating patterns

Interpersonal attraction comes in degrees. Casual friendships tend to be based on liking, while deeper friendships and romantic relationships are usually based on various forms of love. According to psychologist Robert Sternberg's (1988) *triangular theory of love*, different forms of love arise from different combinations of three basic components (➤ **Figure 72.1**):

Intimacy refers to feelings of connectedness and affection.

Passion refers to deep emotional and/or sexual feelings.

Commitment involves the determination to stay in a long-term relationship with another person.

How does this triangle work? Try it for yourself. Think of a person to whom you are attracted. Refer to ■ **Table 72.1** as you ask yourself three yes/no questions: Do I feel intimate with this person? Do I feel passion for this person? Am I committed to this person? Find the kind of love that fits

Interpersonal attraction Social attraction to another person.

Reciprocity A mutual exchange of feelings, thoughts, or things between people.

Self-disclosure The process of revealing private thoughts, feelings, and one's personal history to others.

Intimacy Feelings of connectedness and affection for another person.

Passion Deep emotional and/or sexual feelings for another person.

Commitment The determination to stay in a long-term relationship with another person.

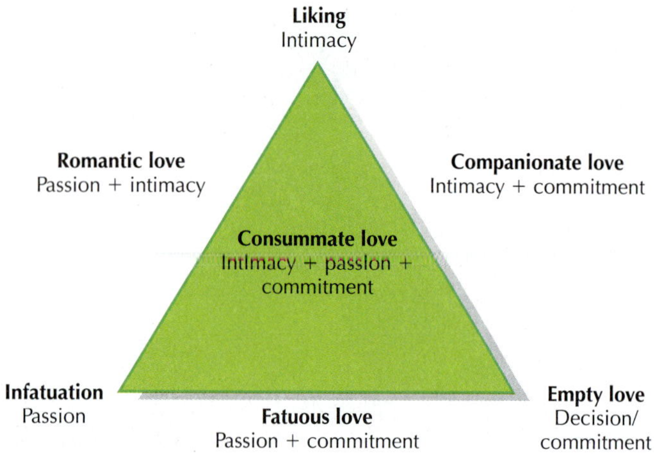

➤ **Figure 72.1**

The triangle of love. Each of the three basic components of love (intimacy, passion, and commitment) appears at one corner of the triangle and is associated with a form of love. Pairs of components and their associated form of love appear on lines of the triangle. Consummate love, which involves all three components, is pictured at the center of the triangle. (Adapted from Sternberg, 1988.)

TABLE 72.1 | Sternberg's Triangular Theory of Love

Combinations of intimacy, passion, and commitment

Type of Love	Intimacy	Passion	Commitment
Nonlove			
Liking	Yes		
Infatuated love		Yes	
Empty love			Yes
Romantic love	Yes	Yes	
Companionate love	Yes		Yes
Fatuous love		Yes	Yes
Consummate love	Yes	Yes	Yes

Source: Sternberg (1988).

your answers. For example, if you answered *yes* to intimacy but *no* to passion and commitment, you **like** that person; you are friends.

Romantic love, in contrast, is based on intimacy, as well as high levels of passion: Emotional arousal, sexual desire, or both (Marazziti & Baroni, 2012). You are experiencing romantic love as you are "falling in love" (Grant-Jacob, 2016). Romantic love differs from friendship in another interesting way. In contrast to simple liking, romantic love usually involves deep *mutual absorption*. In other words, lovers (unlike friends) attend almost exclusively to one another (Riela et al., 2010).

Alternatively, if you answered *yes* to intimacy and commitment but *no* to passion, then you are feeling **companionate love**. This form of love is more common among couples who have been together for a long time. Such couples often describe themselves as "being in love" rather than "falling in love" (Riela et al., 2010).

Does that mean that the most complete form of love is consummate love? You've got it! We experience **consummate love** when we feel intimacy and passion for another person, *and* we are strongly committed to him or her.

Interpersonal Attraction, Love, and Attachment

Another factor influencing adult interpersonal attraction and love has its roots deep in childhood (see Module 13). There is growing evidence that our early attachments to caregivers can have a lasting impact on how we relate to others (Millings et al., 2013; Vrtička & Vuilleumier, 2012). For example, studies of dating couples have identified secure, avoidant, and ambivalent attachment patterns similar to those seen in early child development (Brumbaugh & Fraley, 2010; Lavy, Mikulincer, & Shaver, 2010). Nationally, about 60 percent of all adults have a secure attachment style, 25 percent are avoidant, and 10 percent have ambivalent attachment styles (Mickelson, Kessler, & Shaver, 1997).

How can I figure out my attachment style? Read the following statements and see which best describes your adult relationships:

Secure Attachment Style

In general, I think most other people are well-intentioned and trustworthy.
I find it relatively easy to get close to others.
I am comfortable relying on others and having others depend on me.
I don't worry much about being abandoned by others.
I am comfortable when other people want to get close to me emotionally.

Avoidant Attachment Style

I tend to pull back when things don't go well in a relationship.
I am somewhat skeptical about the idea of true love.
I have difficulty trusting my partner in a romantic relationship.
Other people tend to be too eager to seek commitment from me.
I get a little nervous if anyone gets too close emotionally.

Ambivalent Attachment Style

I have often felt misunderstood and unappreciated in my romantic relationships.

My friends and lovers have been somewhat unreliable.

I love my romantic partner but I worry that she or he doesn't really love me.

I would like to be closer to my romantic partner, but I'm not sure I trust her or him.

Do any of the preceding statements sound familiar? If so, they may describe your adult attachment style (Manning et al., 2017; Simpson & Rholes, 2017). Do you see any similarities between your present relationships and your attachment experiences as a child?

Most adults have a *secure attachment style* that is marked by caring, intimacy, supportiveness, and understanding in love relationships. Secure people regard themselves as friendly, good-natured, and likable. They think of others as generally well-intentioned, reliable, and trustworthy. People with a secure attachment style find it relatively easy to get close to others. They are comfortable depending on others and having others depend on them. In general, they don't worry too much about being abandoned or about having someone become too emotionally close to them. Most people prefer to have a secure partner, whatever their own style might be (Keren & Mayseless, 2013).

However, it's not unusual to have an *avoidant attachment style* that reflects a fear of intimacy and a tendency to resist commitment to others. Avoidant people tend to pull back when things don't go well in a relationship. The avoidant person is suspicious, aloof, and skeptical about love. She or he tends to see others as either unreliable or overly eager to commit to a relationship. As a result, avoidant people find it hard to completely trust and depend on others, and they get nervous when anyone gets too close emotionally. Basically, they avoid intimacy (Juhl, Sand, & Routledge, 2012; Lavy, Mikulincer, & Shaver, 2010).

An *ambivalent attachment style* is marked by mixed feelings about love and friendship. Conflicting feelings of affection, anger, emotional turmoil, physical attraction, and doubt result in an unsettled, ambivalent state. Often, ambivalent people regard themselves as misunderstood and unappreciated. Ambivalent people worry that their romantic partners don't really love them or may leave them. Although they want to be extremely close to their partners, they are also preoccupied with doubts about the partner's dependability and trustworthiness (DeWall et al., 2011).

How could emotional attachments early in life affect adult relationships? It appears that we use early attachment experiences to build mental models about affectionate relationships. Later, we use these models as a sort of blueprint for forming, maintaining, and breaking bonds of love and affection (Sroufe et al., 2005). It is fascinating to think that our relationships may be influenced by events early in childhood. Could the source of adult mating patterns reach even farther back?

Evolution and Mate Selection

Evolutionary psychology is the study of the evolutionary origins of human behavior patterns (Brown & Cross, 2017; Geher, 2014). Many psychologists believe that evolution left an imprint on men and women that influences everything from sexual attraction and infidelity to jealousy and divorce. According to David Buss, the key to understanding human mating patterns is to understand how evolved behavior patterns guide our choices (Buss, 2019).

In a study of 37 cultures on six continents, Buss found the following patterns: Compared with women, men are more interested in casual sex; they prefer younger, more physically attractive partners; and they get more jealous over real or imagined sexual infidelities than they do over a loss of emotional commitment. Compared with men, women prefer slightly older partners who appear to be industrious, higher in status, or economically successful; women are more upset by a partner who becomes emotionally involved with someone else, rather than one who is sexually unfaithful (Buss, 2019; Regan et al., 2000; ➤ **Figure 72.2**).

Why do such differences exist? Buss and others believe that mating preferences evolved in response to the differing reproductive challenges faced by men and women (Buss, 2019; Frederick & Fales, 2016). As a rule, women must invest more time and energy in reproduction and nurturing their young than men. Consequently, women evolved an interest in whether their partners will stay with them and whether their mates have the resources to provide for their children.

Liking A relationship based on intimacy, but lacking passion and commitment.

Romantic love Love that is associated with high levels of interpersonal attraction, heightened arousal, mutual absorption, and sexual desire.

Companionate love A form of love characterized by intimacy and commitment, but not passion.

Consummate love A form of love characterized by intimacy, passion, and commitment.

Evolutionary psychology The study of the evolutionary origins of human behavior patterns.

Figure 72.2

Potential dating partners. What do people look for when considering potential dating partners? Here are the results of a study in which personal ads were placed in newspapers. As you can see, men were more influenced by looks and women by success (Goode, 1996).

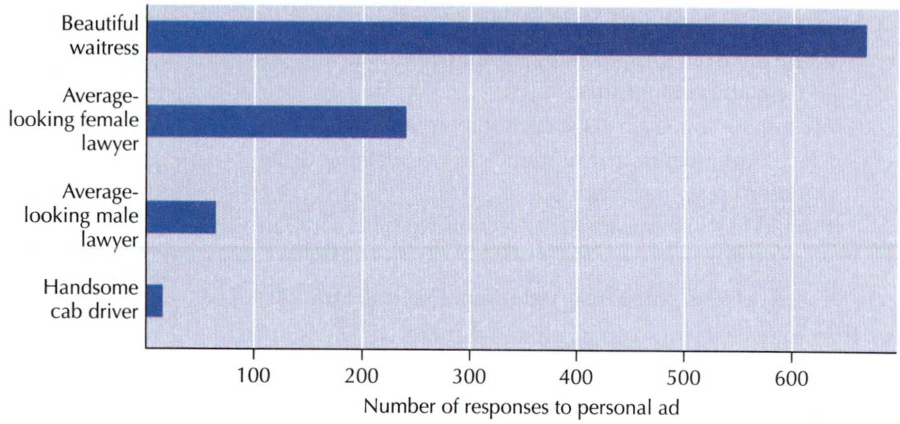

Rob Marmion/Shutterstock.com

According to evolutionary psychologists, women tend to be concerned with whether mates will devote time and resources to a relationship. Men place more emphasis on physical attractiveness and sexual fidelity.

In contrast, the reproductive success of men depends on their mates' fertility. Men, therefore, tend to look for health, youth, and beauty in a prospective mate as signs of suitability for reproduction. Evolutionary theory further proposes that the male emphasis on mates' sexual fidelity is based on concerns about the paternity of offspring. From a biological perspective, men do not benefit from investing resources in children they did not sire (Geher, 2014).

Although some evidence supports the evolutionary view of mating, it is important to remember that evolved mating tendencies are subtle at best and easily overruled by other factors. Some mating patterns may simply reflect the fact that men still tend to control the power and resources in most societies (Fine, 2011). Also, early research may be misleading because women tend to give "polite" answers to questions about jealousy. Privately, they may be just as furious about a mate's sexual infidelity as any man (Harris, 2004).

Whatever the outcome of the debate about evolution and mate selection, it is important to remember this: Potential mates are rated as most attractive if they are kind, secure, intelligent, and supportive (Klohnen & Luo, 2003; Regan et al., 2000). These qualities are love's greatest allies.

Helping Strangers—The Ultimate Kindness

Learning Outcome 72.3 Outline the decision points and factors influencing our willingness to help other people

It is entirely understandable to act kindly toward people to whom you're attracted or with whom you are friends or lovers. But what about total strangers? Showing kindness to strangers, especially when they are in need, is perhaps the most tender of prosocial acts (Mikulincer & Shaver, 2010).

Every year, awards are given to people who risk their lives while saving the lives of others. These heroes are typically honored for saving people from fires, drowning, animal attacks, electrocution, and suffocation. In the aftermath of terrorist attacks, many heroic first responders, including private citizens, rush to help the victims, demonstrating once again the prosocial side of human nature.

The majority of people who perform such heroic acts are men, perhaps because of the physical dangers involved. However, other heroic, prosocial acts also save lives and involve personal risk. Examples are kidney donors, Peace Corps volunteers, and Doctors Without Borders volunteers. In such endeavors, we find as many women as men, and often more. It is important to remember, perhaps, that sensational and highly visible acts of heroism are only one of many ways in which people engage in selfless, altruistic behavior (Becker & Eagly, 2004). People who serve as community volunteers, tutors, coaches, blood donors, and the like don't just help others. Often, their efforts contribute to their own personal growth. Thus, it can be said that "We do well by doing good" (Piliavin & Siegl, 2015).

But do we always help? Over the years, the popular media have circulated a number of dispiriting accounts of people failing to help, even in dire circumstances. Among psychologists, one famous example is the 1964 murder of Kitty Genovese in New York City. According to media report at the times, although as many as 38 people watched as her assailant repeatedly attacked her, no one offered her any assistance. As the entire country recoiled at the horror, people immediately blamed the whole affair on the alienation of city life.

Popular media reports undoubtedly oversensationalize such cases, making it difficult to sort fact from fiction (but that is a topic for another module—Module 6 on information literacy, to be precise). The facts of the Kitty Genovese case, for example, are much less dramatic than the sensationalized version portrayed in popular media reports of the day and ever since (Griggs, 2015; Manning, Levine, & Collins, 2007). So too, the uncharitable view of large cities as breeding grounds for urban apathy has been largely discredited (Gallo, 2015).

Nevertheless, psychological research inspired by the Kitty Genovese murder has since shown that there is a kernel of truth to these assertions. Although it is true that urban living can be dehumanizing, this does not fully explain such *bystander apathy* (the unwillingness of bystanders to offer help during emergencies; this also is referred to as the **bystander effect**). According to landmark work by psychologists John Darley and Bibb Latané (1968), failure to help is related to the number of people present. Over the years, many studies have shown that when *more* potential helpers are present, the *less* likely are people to help (Fischer et al., 2011; Hortensius & de Gelder, 2014).

Why would people be less willing to help when others are present? Basically, we are likely to assume that *someone else* will help. The dynamics of this effect are easily illustrated: Suppose that two motorists have stalled at the roadside, one on a sparsely traveled country road and the other on a busy freeway. Who gets help first?

On the freeway, where hundreds of cars pass every minute, each driver can assume that someone else will help. Personal responsibility for helping is spread so thin that no one takes action. On the country road, one of the first few people to drive by will probably stop because the responsibility is clearly theirs. In general, Darley and Latané assume that bystanders are not apathetic or uncaring: they are inhibited by the presence of others.

AP Images/Mark Lennihan

Does this person lying on the ground need help? What factors determine whether a person in trouble will receive help in an emergency? Surprisingly, the presence of more potential helpers tends to lower the chances that help will be given.

Bystander Intervention

People must pass through four decision points before giving help. First, they must notice that something is happening. Next, they must define the event as an emergency. Then they must take responsibility. Finally, they must select a course of action (➤ Figure 72.3). Laboratory experiments have shown that each step can be influenced by the presence of other people.

Noticing What would happen if you fainted and collapsed on the sidewalk? Would someone stop to help? Would people think you were drunk? Would they even notice you? Darley and Latané suggest that if the sidewalk is crowded, few people will even see you. This has nothing to do with people blocking each other's vision. Instead, it is related to widely accepted norms against staring at others in public. People in crowds typically "keep their eyes to themselves."

Is there any way to show that this is a factor in bystander apathy? To test this idea, students were asked to fill out a questionnaire either alone or in a room full of people. As the students worked, a thick cloud of smoke was blown into the room through a vent.

Bystander effect (bystander apathy) The unwillingness of bystanders to offer help during emergencies or to become involved in others' problems.

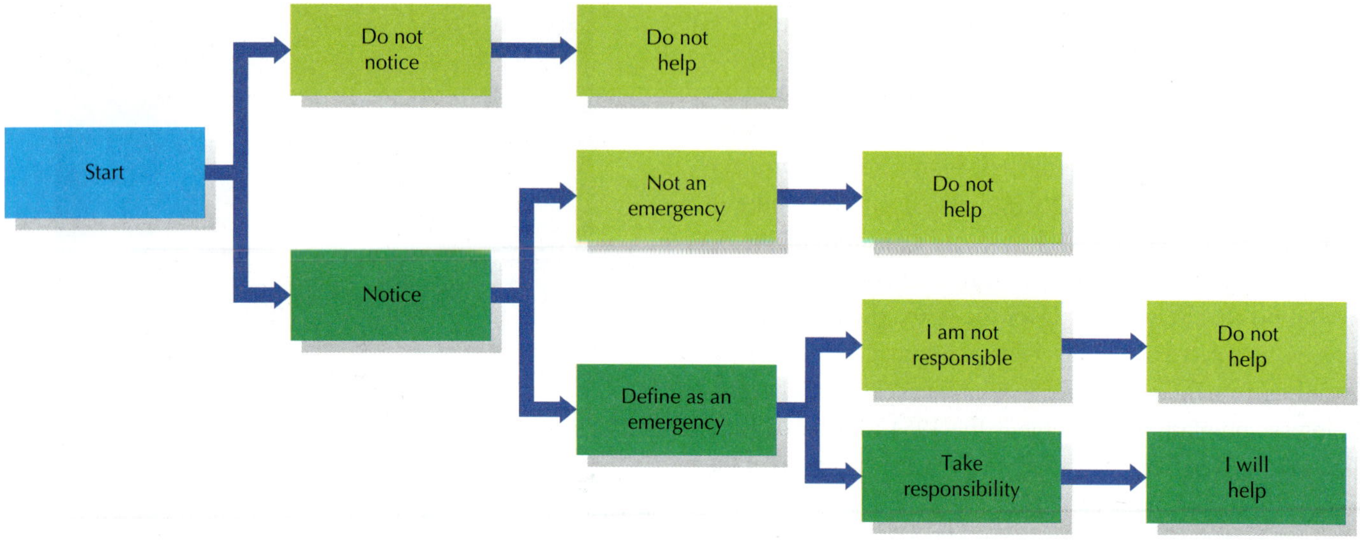

Figure 72.3

Steps involved in offering help. This decision tree summarizes the steps a person must take before making a commitment to offer help, according to Latané and Darley's model.

Most students left alone in the room noticed the smoke immediately. Few of the people in groups noticed the smoke until it became difficult to see through it. Participants working in groups politely kept their eyes on their papers and avoided looking at others (or the smoke). In contrast, those who were alone scanned the room from time to time.

Defining an Emergency The smoke-filled room also shows the influence others have on defining a situation as an emergency. When participants in groups finally noticed the smoke, they cast sidelong glances at others in the room. (Remember *social comparison*?) Apparently, they were searching for clues to help interpret what was happening. No one wanted to overreact or act like a fool if there was no emergency. However, as participants coolly surveyed the reactions of others, they were themselves being watched. In real emergencies, people sometimes "fake each other out" and underestimate the need for action because each person attempts to appear calm. In short, until someone acts, no one does.

Taking Responsibility Perhaps the most crucial step in helping is assuming responsibility. In this case, groups limit helping by causing a **diffusion of responsibility**—spreading responsibility among several people (Plötner et al., 2015).

Is that like the unwillingness of drivers to offer help on a crowded freeway? Exactly. It is the feeling that no one is personally responsible for helping. This problem was demonstrated in an experiment in which students participated in a group discussion over an intercom system. However, each group had only one real participant; the others were tape-recorded actors. Each participant was placed in a separate room (supposedly to maintain confidentiality), and discussions of college life were begun. During the discussion, one of the "students" simulated an epileptic-like seizure and called out for help. In some cases, participants thought they were alone with the seizure victim. Others believed they were members of three- or six-person groups.

People who thought they were alone with the "victim" of this staged emergency reported it immediately or tried to help. Some participants in the three-person groups failed to respond, and those who did were slower. In the six-person groups, over a third of the participants took no action at all. People in this experiment were obviously faced with a conflict like that in many real emergencies: Should they be helpful and responsible, or should they mind their own business? Many were influenced toward inaction by the presence of others.

People do help in some emergencies. How are these different? Helping behavior is complex and influenced by many variables (Baumeister & Bushman, 2021). One naturalistic experiment staged in a New York City subway gives a hint of the kinds of things that may be important. When a "victim" (actor) "passed out" in a subway car, he received more help when carrying a cane than when carrying a liquor bottle (Piliavin, Rodin, & Piliavin, 1969). To better answer the question, we need to consider some factors not included in Latané and Darley's account of helping.

Who Will Help Whom?

Higher costs (such as possible embarrassment, great effort, and especially personal risk) almost always decrease helping (Zoccola et al., 2011). In one study, the presence of an extra, passive bystander doing nothing to help actually *increased* the likelihood of people stopping to help in a potentially dangerous situation (Fischer & Greitemeyer, 2013).

Regardless of risk, many studies suggest that when we see a person in trouble, it tends to cause *heightened arousal* (Batson, 2010; Dovidio et al., 2006). This aroused, keyed-up feeling can motivate us to give aid, but only if the rewards of helping outweigh the costs. In addition to general arousal, potential helpers may also feel **empathic arousal**. This means they empathize with the person in need or feel some of the person's pain, fear, or anguish. Helping is much more likely when we are able to take the perspective of others and feel sympathy for their plight (Batson & Powell, 2003; Myers & Hodges, 2013). Empathic arousal is especially likely to motivate helping when the person in need seems to be similar to ourselves (Guéguen, Martin, & Meineri, 2011; Batson, 2010). In fact, a feeling of connection to the victim may be one of the most important factors in encouraging helping.

This, perhaps, is why being in a good mood also increases helping. When we are feeling successful, happy, or fortunate, we also may feel more connected to others (Dovidio & Penner, 2001; Lamy, Fischer-Lokou, & Guéguen, 2012). In summary, there is a strong **empathy–helping relationship**: We are most likely to help someone in need when we "feel for" that person and experience emotions such as empathy, sympathy, and compassion (Batson, 2006, 2010).

People who see others helping are more likely to offer help themselves. Also, people who give help in one situation tend to perceive themselves as helpful people. This change in self-image encourages them to help in other situations. One more point is that norms of fairness encourage us to help others who have helped us (Dovidio & Penner, 2001). For all these reasons, helping others not only assists them directly, it encourages others to help too.

"Devictimize" Yourself If you should find yourself in need of help during an emergency, what can you do to avoid being a victim of bystander apathy? The work we have reviewed here suggests that you should make sure that you are noticed, that people realize there's an emergency, and that they need to take action. Being noticed can be promoted in some situations by shouting "Fire!" Bystanders who might run away from a robbery or an assault may rush to see where the fire is. At the very least, remember not to just scream. Instead, you should call out "Help!" or "I need help right now." Whenever possible, define your situation for bystanders. Say, for instance, "I'm being attacked—call the police!" Or, "Stop that man, he has my purse." You also can directly assign responsibility to a bystander by pointing to someone and saying, "You, call the police" or "I'm injured, I need you to call an ambulance."

Diffusion of responsibility Spreading the responsibility to act among several people; reduces the likelihood that help will be given to a person in need.

Empathic arousal Emotion that occurs when you feel some of another person's pain, fear, or anguish.

Empathy–helping relationship The observation that we are most likely to help someone else when we feel emotions such as empathy and compassion.

MODULE 72 Prosocial Behavior—Learning Outcomes Revisited

72.1 Explain why we affiliate, describe factors influencing interpersonal attraction, and discuss self-disclosure

Affiliation is tied to needs for approval, support, friendship, love, and information. Also, affiliation can reduce anxiety. Initial interpersonal attractiveness is increased by familiarity, similarity, physical attractiveness, and reciprocity. Self-disclosure follows a reciprocity norm: Low levels of self-disclosure are met with low levels in return; moderate self-disclosure elicits more personal replies. However, overdisclosure tends to inhibit self-disclosure by others.

72.2 Explain how interpersonal attraction and love differ, how adult relationships are rooted in childhood, and outline how evolutionary psychology views human mating patterns

According to Sternberg's triangular theory of love, liking involves a desire for intimacy with another person, while love involves desiring intimacy as well as passion and/or commitment. Romantic love is based on feelings of both intimacy and passion. Romantic love is also associated with greater mutual absorption between people. Companionate love involves feelings of both intimacy and commitment. Consummate love, involving intimacy, passion, *and* commitment, is the most complete form of love. Adult love relationships tend to mirror patterns of emotional attachment observed in infancy and early childhood. Secure, avoidant, and ambivalent patterns can be defined on the basis of how a person approaches romantic and affectionate relationships with others. Evolutionary psychology attributes human mating patterns to the differing reproductive challenges faced by men and women during the course of evolution.

72.3 Outline the decision points and factors influencing our willingness to help other people

Four decision points must be passed before a person gives help: noticing, defining an emergency, taking responsibility, and selecting a course of action. Helping is less likely at each point when other potential helpers are present. Helping is encouraged by general arousal, empathic arousal, being in a good mood, low effort or risk, and perceived similarity between the victim and the helper. For several reasons, giving help tends to encourage others to help, too.

Reflective Practice

Content Check

1. Interpersonal attraction is increased by all but one of the following. (Which does *not* fit?)
   a. familiarity
   b. reciprocity
   c. similarity
   d. social costs
2. High levels of self-disclosure are reciprocated in most social encounters. T or F?
3. In Sternberg's triangular theory, infatuated love involves commitment but not passion or intimacy. T or F?
4. The most striking finding about marriage patterns is that most people choose mates whose personalities are quite unlike their own. T or F?
5. ________________ behavior refers to actions that are constructive, altruistic, or helpful to others.
6. People are more likely to help another who is in trouble if
   a. many other helpers are present
   b. a diffusion of responsibility occurs
   c. they experience empathic arousal
   d. desensitization takes place

Skill Check

Think Critically

7. How has the Internet altered the effects of proximity on interpersonal attraction?

Self-Reflect

How has social comparison affected your behavior? Has it influenced with whom you associate? Think of three close friends. Which of the attraction factors described earlier apply to your friendships? To what extent does Sternberg's triangular theory of love apply to your own relationships? An elderly woman is at the side of the road, trying to change a flat tire. She obviously needs help. You are approaching her in your car. What must happen before you are likely to stop and help her?

ANSWERS

1. d 2. F 3. F 4. F 5. prosocial 6. c 7. As mentioned earlier, the Internet makes actual physical proximity less crucial in interpersonal attraction because frequent contact is possible even at great distances. Internet romances are a good example of this possibility.

Social Psychology
Antisocial Behavior

MODULE
73

The Struggle for Survival

It might seem that the horrors of war and the ravages of terrorism would lead to a worldwide revulsion for killing. Yet, violent and aggressive behavior remains so commonplace it is often viewed as entertainment. Aggression is only one form of *antisocial behavior*, all of which involve having a negative effect on people around us. For example, while love and friendship bring people together, prejudice and discrimination, which are marked by suspicion, fear, or hatred, have the opposite effect.

How "natural" is aggressive behavior? What causes aggression? Can violence be reduced? What are the origins of prejudice and discrimination? How can such hurtful attitudes be reduced? Around the world, we are becoming ever more interdependent. At the same time, it is becoming easier for even a "lone wolf" to cause widespread damage. Finding answers to questions like those posed here becomes even more important. If nothing else, we owe it to the victims, past and future.

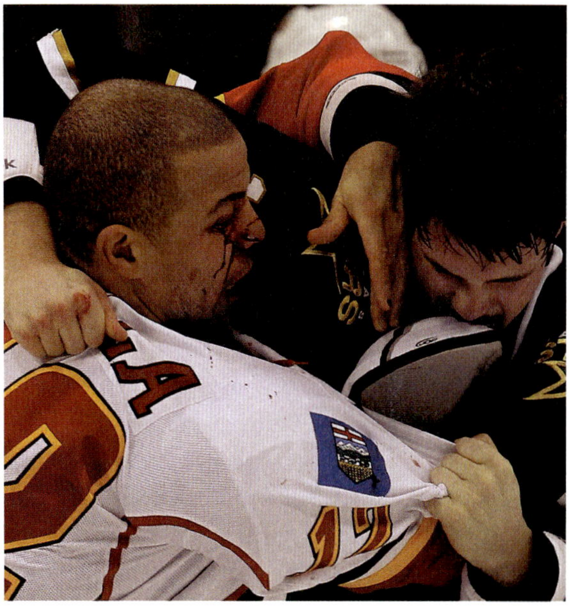
Ronald Martinez/Getty Images Sport Classic/Getty Images

~LEARNING OUTCOMES~

After reading this module you should be able to:

73.1 Define biological explanations of aggression, the frustration–aggression hypothesis, aggression cues, social learning theories of aggression, and how aggression can be reduced

73.2 Discuss prejudice, the forms it can take, its causes, and the authoritarian personality

73.3 Outline the role of status, superordinate goals, and mutual interdependence in reducing prejudice and intergroup conflict

Aggression—The World's Most Dangerous Animal

Learning Outcome 73.1 Define biological explanations of aggression, the frustration–aggression hypothesis, aggression cues, social learning theories of aggression, and how aggression can be reduced

Our understanding of social behavior would be incomplete without examining **antisocial behavior**—any behavior that has a negative impact on other people. Bluntly put, we humans are capable of hatred and cruelty as well as love and kindness. Let's begin with **aggression**, which refers to any action carried out with the intention of harming another person. The human capacity for aggression is staggering.

Antisocial behavior Any behavior that has a negative impact on other people.

Aggression Any action carried out with the intention of harming another person.

More than 180 million humans were killed by other humans (an average of nearly one person every 18 seconds) during the 20th century (Pinker, 2011). War, homicide, riots, family violence, assassination, rape, assault, forcible robbery, and other violent acts offer sad testimony to the realities of human aggression (Shaver & Mikulincer, 2011).

Bullying It is worth noting that aggression can be expressed in many ways, from the truly horrific, such as ethnic cleansing and gangland executions, to the more mundane, such as harassment and the one-finger salute. As an example, one pervasive form is **bullying**, defined as any behavior that deliberately and repeatedly exposes a person to negative experiences (Powell & Ladd, 2010). Bullies tend to deal with everyday situations by resorting to aggression. Bullying can be *verbal* (name-calling, insults, teasing) or *physical* (hitting, pushing, confining), and it can also be *direct* ("in your face") or *indirect* (intentional exclusion, spreading rumors). Whereas male bullies are more likely than females to engage in direct physical aggression, female bullies tend to specialize in indirect verbal aggression (Field et al., 2009).

Bullying is a worldwide phenomenon. It occurs among all age groups and in all settings. It can even be found online, in the form of *cyberbullying* (Bonanno & Hymel, 2013). Childhood bullying can have long-term consequences for the mental health of both bullies and their victims (Sansone, Leung, & Wiederman, 2013; Miehls, 2017). Adolescent and adult bullying can lead to serious violence, including murder and suicide.

What causes aggression such as bullying? Aggression has many potential causes (DeWall & Anderson, 2011). Let's look at some of the major possibilities.

Biology and Aggression

Some theorists argue that humans are naturally aggressive, having inherited a "killer instinct" from our animal ancestors (Buss, 2019). While this idea has intuitive appeal, many psychologists question it (Rhee & Waldman, 2011). Just labeling a behavior as due to an **instinct**—an innate impulse that directs or motivates behavior—does little to explain it. More important, we are left with the question of why some individuals or human groups (the Arapesh, the Senoi, the Navajo, the Eskimo, and others) show little hostility or aggression. And, thankfully, the vast majority of humans do *not* kill or harm others.

Nevertheless, aggression does have biological roots (Rhee & Waldman, 2011). Physiological studies have shown that some brain areas are capable of triggering or ending aggressive behavior. Also, researchers have found a relationship between aggression and such physical factors as hypoglycemia (low blood sugar), allergies, alcohol and drug use, and specific brain injuries and diseases. For both men and women, higher levels of the hormone testosterone may be associated with more aggressive behavior (Mehta & Beer, 2010; Montoya et al., 2012). Perhaps because of their higher testosterone levels, men are more likely to engage in physical aggression than women (Anderson & Bushman, 2002).

New York Daily News/Getty Images

Road rage and some freeway shootings may be a reaction to the stress and frustration of traffic congestion. The fact that automobiles provide anonymity, or a loss of personal identity, also may encourage aggressive actions that would not otherwise occur.

The effects of alcohol and other drugs provide another indication of the role of the brain and biology in violence and aggression. A variety of studies show that alcohol is involved in large percentages of murders and violent crimes. Intoxicating drugs also seem to lower inhibitions to act aggressively—often with tragic results (Banks et al., 2017; Lundholm et al., 2013).

Regardless, none of these biological factors can be considered a direct *cause* of aggression. Instead, they probably lower the threshold for aggression, making hostile behavior more likely to occur (Tackett & Krueger, 2011). The fact that we are biologically *capable* of aggression does not mean that aggression is inevitable or "part of human nature." Humans are fully capable of learning to inhibit aggression. For example, the Quakers and the Amish, who live in this country's increasingly violent culture, adopt nonviolence as a way of life.

Frustration and Aggression

Step on a dog's tail and you may get nipped. Frustrate a human and you may get insulted. As we also discuss in Module 56, frustration tends to lead to aggression, a relationship known as the **frustration–aggression hypothesis**.

Does frustration always produce aggression? Although the connection is strong, a moment's thought will show that frustration does not *always* lead to aggression. Frustration, for instance, may lead to stereotyped responses or perhaps to a state of "learned helplessness" (see Module 57). Also, aggression can occur in the absence of frustration. This possibility is illustrated by sports spectators who start fights, throw bottles, tear down goalposts, and so forth—after their team has *won.*

Aversive Stimuli Frustration probably encourages aggression because it is uncomfortable. Various *aversive stimuli,* which produce discomfort or displeasure, can heighten hostility and aggression (Morgan, 2005; Simister & Cooper, 2005; ➤ Figure 73.1). Examples include insults, high air temperatures, pain, and even disgusting scenes or odors. Such stimuli probably raise overall arousal levels so that we become more sensitive to *aggression cues*—signals that are associated with aggression (Schwenzer, 2008). Aversive stimuli also tend to activate ideas, memories, and expressions associated with anger and aggression (Morgan, 2005).

Some cues for aggression are internal (angry thoughts, for instance). Many are external: Certain words, actions, and gestures made by others are strongly associated with aggressive responses. A raised middle finger, for instance, is an almost universal invitation to aggression in North America. Weapons serve as particularly strong cues for aggressive behavior in virtually every possible situation. The implication of this *weapons effect* seems to be that the symbols and trappings of aggression encourage aggression. A prime example is the fact that murders are more likely to occur in homes in which guns are kept (Siegel et al., 2013).

Social Learning and Aggression

One of the most widely accepted explanations of aggression is also the simplest. **Social learning theory** holds that we learn to be aggressive by observing aggression in others (Bandura, 2001; Lefrançois, 2012). Social learning theory combines learning principles with cognitive processes, socialization, and modeling to explain behavior. According to this view, there is no instinctive human programming for fistfighting, pipe bombing, knife wielding, gun loading, 95-mile-an-hour "beanballs," or other violent or aggressive behaviors. Hence, aggression must be learned (➤ Figure 73.2). Is it any wonder that people who were victims of violence during childhood are more likely to become violent themselves (Murrell, Christoff, & Henning, 2007)?

Social learning theorists predict that people growing up in nonaggressive cultures will themselves be nonaggressive. Those raised in a culture with aggressive models and heroes will learn aggressive responses. Considered in such terms, it is no wonder that the United States has become one of the more violent countries. More than 1,206,000 violent crimes occurred in the United States during 2018 (Federal Bureau

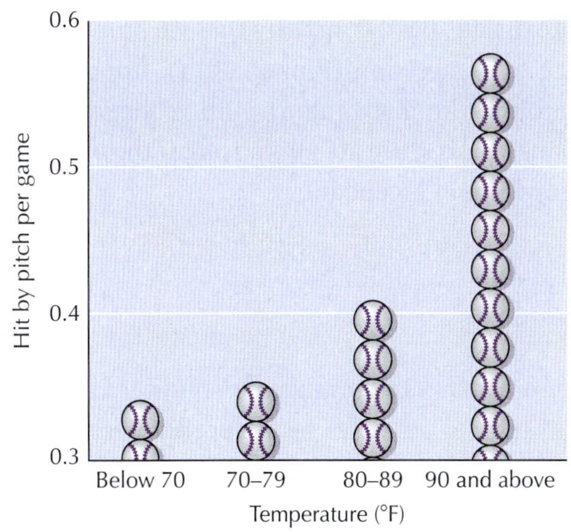

➤ **Figure 73.1**

Hit batters as a function of temperature. Personal discomfort caused by aversive (unpleasant) stimuli can make aggressive behavior more likely. For example, studies of crime rates show that the incidence of highly aggressive behavior, such as murder, rape, and assault, rises as the air temperature goes from warm to hot to sweltering (Anderson, 1989). The results you see here further support the heat–aggression link. The graph shows that there is a strong association between the temperatures at major league baseball games and the number of batters hit by a pitch during those games. When the temperature goes over 90°, watch out for that fastball (Reifman, Larrick, & Fein, 1991)!

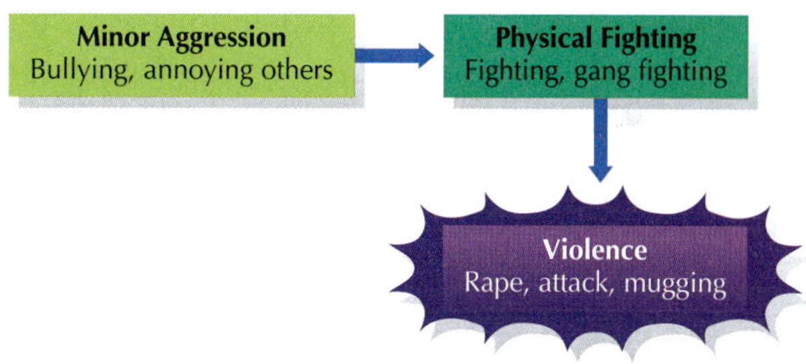

➤ **Figure 73.2**

Progression of aggression. Violent behavior among delinquent boys doesn't appear overnight. Usually, their capacity for violence develops slowly as they move from minor aggression to increasingly brutal acts. Overall aggression increases dramatically in early adolescence as boys gain physical strength and more access to weapons (after Loeber & Hay, 1997).

Bullying The deliberate and repeated use of aggression (whether verbal or physical, direct or indirect) as a tactic for dealing with everyday situations.

Instinct Innate impulse that directs or motivates behavior.

Frustration–aggression hypothesis States that frustration tends to lead to aggression.

Social learning theory A theory that combines learning principles with cognitive processes, socialization, and modeling, to explain behavior.

of Investigation, 2019). Up to 49 percent of US households own at least one firearm (Agresti, Smith, & Reynolds, 2020). Children and adults are treated to an almost nonstop parade of aggressive models, in the media as well as in actual behavior. We are, without a doubt, an aggressive culture. (See Module 29 to review evidence that media exposure to violence may play a role in the social learning of aggressive behavior.)

Preventing Aggression

What can be done about aggression? Social learning theory implies that "aggression begets aggression" and "kindness begets kindness." For example, children who are physically abused at home, those who suffer severe physical punishment, and those who merely witness violence in the community or in the media are more likely to be involved in fighting, aggressive play, and antisocial behavior at school (Bartholow, Sestir, & Davis, 2005). Similarly, experiences of prosocial behaviors (consisting of actions toward others that are helpful, constructive, or altruistic) reduce aggression by increasing helping, cooperation, charity, and brotherhood (Greitemeyer et al., 2012; Velez et al., 2016). Accordingly, one way to lower aggression may be to reduce exposure to violence, as well as increasing our exposure to prosocial behaviors (Meier & Wilkowski, 2013).

Anger Management On a personal level, psychologists have succeeded in teaching some people to control their anger and aggressive impulses (Meier & Wilkowski, 2013; Nay, 2014). Like strengthening a muscle, self-control improves with practice (Denson et al., 2011). (Anger management is a form of *self-regulation*; see Module 11.)

Also, in Module 57 we encountered the distinction between *emotion-focused* and *problem-focused* coping. Responding to an upsetting situation by giving into anger is often an ineffective emotion-focused coping strategy. It is usually better to learn to remain calm by using a problem-focused coping strategy, such as defining upsetting situations as *problems to be solved*. Therefore, to limit anger, people are taught to do the following:

1. Define the problem as precisely as possible.
2. Make a list of possible solutions.
3. Rank the likely success of each solution.
4. Choose a solution and try it.
5. Assess how successful the solution was, and make adjustments if necessary.

It also helps to learn how to avoid problematic situations or think differently about them in the first place, as well as learning how to let go of anger (Tafrate & Kassinove, 2009). Taking steps such as these has helped many people to lessen tendencies toward child abuse, family violence, and other destructive outbursts (Hall, 2009; Miltenberger, 2016).

The Better Angels of Our Nature

Let's close with some possible good news. Harvard University psychologist Steven Pinker has suggested that if you compare the amount of violence in the modern world with the more distant past, it appears that we humans are losing our taste for aggression (Pinker, 2011). Improving human rights around the globe, along with reductions in slavery, executions, and torture are all signs that "the better angels of our nature" are in ascendancy.

Prejudice—Attitudes That Injure

Learning Outcome 73.2 Discuss prejudice, the forms it can take, its causes, and the authoritarian personality

Love and friendship bring people together. Prejudice, which is marked by suspicion, fear, or hatred, has the opposite effect. **Prejudice**, an all-too-common part of daily life, is a negative attitude toward an entire group of people (Biernat & Danaher, 2013). Stereotyping, prejudice, and discrimination directed against people based solely on their race is **racism**. If the sole basis is gender, that is **sexism**, and if the sole basis is age, that is **ageism**. **Heterosexism** is based solely on the belief that heterosexuality is better or more natural than homosexuality. (It is worth noting that even when prejudices are positive, they oversimplify individuals.) What are the different forms and origins of prejudice? How can prejudice and hurtful attitudes be reduced? Psychologists have provided valuable insights into these questions.

Forms of Prejudice

Distinguished psychologist Gordon Allport (1958) concluded that there are two important sources of prejudice. *Personal prejudice* arises when members of another ethnic group are perceived as a threat to one's own interests. For example, members of another group may be viewed as competitors for jobs. *Group prejudice* arises when a person conforms to group norms. Let's say, for instance, that you have no personal reason for disliking out-group members. Nevertheless, your friends, coworkers, or relatives expect it of you.

When group prejudice becomes institutionalized in the policies of organizations such as police departments, schools, or governments, it is generally referred to as **systemic prejudice** or, more specifically, systemic racism, sexism, ageism, or heterosexism, depending on the group affected (Harrell & Medford, 2012).

Prejudice is easy to notice when it is *explicit* and out in the open (Payne et al., 2010). However, because many people realize that crude and obvious explicit prejudice is no longer socially acceptable, the public expression of explicit prejudice has become much less common. As a consequence, prejudice is now often disguised as **symbolic prejudice**—the expression of prejudice in subtly veiled forms (Anderson, 2010; Neville et al., 2013). For example, modern racists must find ways to rationalize their prejudice so that it seems to be based on issues other than raw racism. One common way to disguise racism, then, is to offer subtly racist opinions framed in terms of topics such as affirmative action, busing, immigration, crime, and so on.

In a similar vein, suppose a European-American candidate and an equally qualified African-American candidate apply for a job. Both are only moderately qualified for the position. If the person making the hiring decision is European-American, who gets the job? As you might guess, the European-American candidate is much more likely to be hired. In other words, the European-American candidate will be given "the benefit of the doubt" about his or her abilities, whereas the African-American candidate won't.

People making such decisions often believe that they aren't being prejudiced, but they nevertheless unconsciously discriminate against minorities (Berg, 2013). While it is an admirable step, making a conscious decision to forsake prejudice does not immediately eliminate **implicit prejudice**—unconscious prejudiced thoughts and feelings about members of other groups (Anderson, 2010; Nosek, Greenwald, & Banaji, 2005; Waller, Lampman, & Lupfer-Johnson, 2012).

Discrimination Because it is so prevalent and damaging, let's focus on racism (Miller & Garran, 2008). Both racial prejudice and racism lead to **discrimination**—unfair actions toward people based on stereotyping and prejudice (Kassin, Fein, & Markus, 2021). Discrimination prevents people from doing things they should be able to do, such as buying a house, getting a job, or attending a high-quality school (Whitley & Kite, 2010). For example, in many cities, African Americans have been the targets of "racial profiling," in which police stop them without reason. Sometimes, they are merely questioned, but many are cited for minor infractions, such as a cracked taillight or an illegal lane change. For many law-abiding citizens, being detained in this manner is a rude awakening (Plous, 2003). It's also one reason many African Americans and other minority people in the United States distrust police and the legal system (Dovidio et al., 2002). As distinguished African-American psychologist Kenneth Clark said, "Racial prejudice . . . debases all human beings—those who are its victims, those who victimize, and in quite subtle ways, those who are merely accessories."

Becoming Prejudiced

How do prejudices develop? One major theory suggests that prejudice is a form of *scapegoating* (blaming a person or a group for the actions of others or for conditions not of their making). Scapegoating is a type of *displaced aggression* in which hostilities triggered by frustration are redirected at "safer" targets (Glick, 2008; Reijntjes et al., 2013a). One interesting classic test of this hypothesis was conducted at a summer camp for young men. The men were given a difficult test that they were sure to fail. In addition, completing the test caused them to miss a trip to the movies, which was normally the high point of their weekly entertainment. Attitudes toward Mexicans and Japanese were measured before the test and after the men had failed the test and missed the movie. Participants in this study, all European Americans, consistently rated members of the two ethnic groups lower after being frustrated (Miller & Bugelski, 1948). This effect has been easy to observe since the September 11, 2001, terrorist attacks in the United States, as people who look "foreign" have become targets for displaced anger and hostility (Ahluwalia & Pellettiere, 2010).

At times, the development of prejudice (like other attitudes) can be traced to direct experiences with members

Prejudice Positive or negative attitude toward an entire group of people.

Racism Stereotyping, prejudice, and discrimination directed against someone based solely on their race.

Sexism Stereotyping, prejudice, and discrimination directed against someone based solely on their gender.

Ageism Stereotyping, prejudice, and discrimination directed against someone based solely on their age.

Heterosexism Stereotyping, prejudice, and discrimination directed against someone based solely on the belief that heterosexuality is better or more natural than homosexuality.

Systemic prejudice Prejudice that has become institutionalized (that is, it is reflected in government policy, schools, and so forth) and that is enforced by the existing social power structure.

Symbolic prejudice Prejudice that is expressed in a disguised fashion.

Implicit prejudice Unconscious prejudiced thoughts and feelings about members of other groups.

Discrimination (in social behavior) Unfair actions based on stereotyping and prejudice.

of the rejected group. A child who is repeatedly bullied by members of a particular ethnic group might develop a lifelong dislike for all members of the group. Yet even subtle influences, such as parents' attitudes, the depiction of people in books and on television, and exposure to children of other races can have an impact. By the time they are three years old, many children show signs of race bias (Katz, 2003). Sadly, once prejudices are established, they prevent us from accepting more positive experiences that could reverse the damage (Jackson, 2011).

The Prejudiced Personality

Other research suggests that prejudice can be a general personality characteristic. Theodor Adorno and his associates (1950) described what they called the *authoritarian personality*. These researchers started out by studying anti-Semitism. In the process, they found that people who are prejudiced against one group tend to be prejudiced against *all* out-groups (Hodson, MacInnis, & Busseri, 2017; Kteily, Sidanius, & Levin, 2011).

What are the characteristics of the prejudice-prone personality? The **authoritarian personality** is marked by rigidity, inhibition, prejudice, and oversimplification (black-and-white thinking, so to speak). In addition, authoritarians exhibit *right-wing authoritarianism*, placing a highly value on social conformity. Authoritarians also tend to be very *ethnocentric*. **Ethnocentrism** refers to placing one's own group "at the center," usually by rejecting all other groups. In fact, authoritarians have a general *social dominance orientation* and think they are superior to everyone who is different, not just other ethnic groups (Bilewicz, 2017; Duckitt & Sibley, 2010).

To measure these qualities, the *F scale* was created (the *F* stands for *fascism*). This scale is made up of statements such as the ones that follow—to which authoritarians readily agree (Adorno et al., 1950):

Authoritarian Beliefs

- Obedience and respect for authority are the most important virtues that children should learn.
- People can be divided into two distinct classes: the weak and the strong.
- If people would talk less and work more, everybody would be better off.
- What this country needs most, more than laws and political programs, is a few courageous, tireless, devoted leaders, in whom the people can put their faith.
- Nobody ever learns anything really important except through suffering.
- Every person should have complete faith in some supernatural power whose decisions are obeyed without question.
- Certain religious sects that refuse to salute the flag should be forced to conform to such patriotic action or else be abolished.

As you can see, authoritarians are rather close-minded (Butler, 2000; Roets & Van Hiel, 2011). As children, many were severely punished. As a result, they learned to fear authority (and to covet it) at an early age. In general, people are more likely to express authoritarian beliefs when they feel threatened. One example would be calling for more severe punishment in schools when the economy is bad and job insecurities are high.

Although it may appear that the F scale is slanted toward politically conservative authoritarians, rigid and authoritarian personalities can be found at both ends of the political scale (Pettigrew, 2016). It may be better, therefore, to describe rigid and intolerant thinking as **dogmatism**, an unwarranted certainty in matters of belief or opinion. Dogmatic people find it difficult to change their beliefs, even when the evidence contradicts them (Peterson et al., 2016; White-Ajmani & Bursik, 2011).

Even if we discount the obvious bigotry of the authoritarian personality, racial prejudice runs deep in many nations. Let's probe deeper into the roots of such prejudiced behavior.

Intergroup Conflict—The Roots of Prejudice

Learning Outcome 73.3 Outline the role of status, superordinate goals, and mutual interdependence in reducing prejudice and intergroup conflict

What can be done about prejudice and intergroup conflict? An unfortunate byproduct of group membership is that it often limits contact with people in other groups (Hodson & Hewstone, 2013). In addition, groups themselves may come into conflict. Both situations tend to foster hatred and prejudice toward the out-group (Kassin, Fein, & Markus, 2021).

Shared beliefs concerning *superiority*, *injustice*, *vulnerability*, and *distrust* are common triggers for hostility between groups. Pick almost any group in conflict with others and you will find people thinking along these lines: "We are special people who are superior to other groups, but we have been unjustly exploited, wronged, or humiliated [superiority and injustice]. Other groups are a threat to us [vulnerability]. They are dishonest and have repeatedly betrayed us [distrust]. Naturally, we are hostile toward them. They don't deserve our respect or cooperation" (Eidelson & Eidelson, 2003; Whitley & Kite, 2010).

Racial stereotypes are common in sports. For example, a study confirmed that many people actually believe that "white men can't jump." This stereotype implies that black basketball players are naturally superior in athletic ability. White players, in contrast, are falsely perceived as smarter and harder working. Such stereotypes set up expectations that distort the perceptions of fans, coaches, and sportswriters. The resulting misperceptions, in turn, help perpetuate the stereotypes (Stone, Perry, & Darley, 1997).

In addition to hostile beliefs about other groups, conflicts are almost always amplified by stereotyped images of out-group members (Crandall et al., 2011; Pereira, Estramiana, & Gallo, 2010).

What exactly is a stereotype? **Social stereotypes** are oversimplified images of people in various groups. There is a good chance that you have stereotyped images of some of the following: African Americans, European Americans, Hispanics, Jews, women, Christians, old people, men, Asian Americans, blue-collar workers, Southerners, politicians, business executives, teenagers, or billionaires. In general, the top three categories on which most stereotypes are based are sex, age, and race (Fiske et al., 2002).

During times of war, social stereotypes can become oversimplified to the point of *dehumanizing* the enemy. Dehumanizing others makes it seem that they *deserve* hatred, even death (Leidner et al., 2010; Waytz, Epley, & Cacioppo, 2010). Undoubtedly, this provides a degree of emotional insulation that makes it easier for soldiers to harm other people. However, it also makes terrorism, torture, murder, and genocide possible.

Stereotypes tend to simplify people into "us" and "them" categories. Aside from the fact that they always oversimplify, stereotypes may include a mixture of *positive* or *negative* qualities. Even though stereotypes sometimes include positive traits, they are mainly used to demean and control people. That's why no one likes to be stereotyped. Being forced into a small, distorted social "box" is limiting and insulting. Stereotypes rob people of their individuality (Kteily, Hodson, & Bruneau, 2016; Maddox, 2004).

Note, too, that when a prejudiced person meets a pleasant or likable member of a rejected group, the out-group member tends to be perceived as "an exception to the rule," not as evidence against the stereotype. This allows prejudiced people to avoid changing their stereotyped beliefs (Asgari, Dasgupta, & Stout, 2012).

Self-Stereotyping and Stereotype Threat It is especially troubling when people begin to *self-stereotype*, halfway believing the stereotypes applied to them, or at least worrying about how they appear in the presence of stereotypers (Schmader, Croft, & Whitehead, 2014; Tine & Gotlieb, 2013).

Consider Bill, a retired aircraft mechanic, who has agreed to talk to a group of high school students about the early days of commercial aviation. During his talk, Bill is concerned that any slip in his memory will confirm stereotypes about older people being forgetful. Because he is anxious and preoccupied about possible memory lapses, Bill actually "chokes," suffering problems with his memory (Jordano & Touron, 2017; Mazerolle et al., 2012).

As Bill's example suggests, negative stereotypes can have a self-fulfilling quality. This is especially true of situations in which a person's abilities are evaluated. For example, African-American and other minority group students must often cope with negative stereotypes about their academic abilities (Steele & Aronson, 1995; Owens & Massey, 2011). Could such stereotypes actually impair school performance?

Psychologist Claude Steele has amassed evidence that victims of stereotyping tend to feel **stereotype threat**. They can feel threatened when they think they are being judged in terms of a stereotype. The anxiety that this causes can then lower performance, seemingly confirming the stereotype (Spencer, Logel, & Davies, 2016). An experiment that Steele did demonstrates this effect. In the study, African-American and European-American college students took a very difficult verbal test. Some students were told that the test measured *academic ability*. Others were told that the test was a laboratory *problem-solving task* unrelated

Authoritarian personality A personality pattern characterized by rigidity, inhibition, prejudice, and an excessive concern with power, authority, and obedience.

Ethnocentrism Placing one's own group or race at the center—that is, tending to reject all other groups but one's own.

Dogmatism An unwarranted positiveness or certainty in matters of belief or opinion.

Social stereotypes Oversimplified images of the traits of individuals who belong to a particular social group.

Stereotype threat The anxiety caused by the fear of being judged in terms of a stereotype.

to ability. In the ability condition, African-American students performed worse than European-Americans. In the problem-solving condition, they performed the same as European-Americans (Steele, 1997; Steele & Aronson, 1995). A similar effect occurs with women, who score lower on math, engineering, and finance tests after being reminded of the stereotype that "women aren't good at math" (Cadaret et al., 2017; Carr & Steele, 2010).

In light of such findings, Steele and others are currently working on ways to combat stereotype threat, so that all students can use their potentials more fully (Alter et al., 2010; Bowe et al., 2017; Bowen, Wegmann, & Webber, 2013). Without stereotypes, there would be far less hate, prejudice, exclusion, and conflict.

Experiments in Prejudice

How do stereotypes and intergroup tensions develop? Two experiments, both in unlikely settings and both using children as participants, offer some insight into these problems.

What is it like to be discriminated against? In a unique experiment, elementary school teacher Jane Elliott sought to give her pupils direct experience with prejudice. On the first day of the experiment, Elliott announced that brown-eyed children were to sit in the back of the room, and that they could not use the drinking fountain. Blue-eyed children were given extra recess time and got to use the fountain and leave first for lunch. At lunch, brown-eyed children were prevented from taking second helpings because they would "just waste it." Brown-eyed and blue-eyed children were kept from mingling, and the blue-eyed children were told they were "cleaner" and "smarter" (Peters, 1971).

Barcroft Media/Getty Images

Are these children of different "races"? Yes, this *is* a trick question. Only skin color differentiates these nonidentical twins. The odds, by the way, of mixed-race parents having a pair of twins like these two are one in a million. How fair will it be when these two children experience differential treatment based solely on their skin color?

Eye color might seem like a trivial basis for creating prejudices. However, people use primarily skin color to make decisions about the race of another person (Glenn, 2009). Surely this is just as superficial a way of judging people as using eye color, especially given recent biological evidence that it does not even make genetic sense to talk about "races" (Richeson & Sommers, 2016).

At first, Elliott made an effort to constantly criticize and belittle the brown-eyed children. To her surprise, the blue-eyed children rapidly joined in and were soon outdoing her in the viciousness of their attacks. The blue-eyed children began to feel superior, and the brown-eyed children felt just plain awful. Fights broke out. Test scores of the brown-eyed children fell.

How lasting were the effects of this experiment? The effects were short-lived because, two days later, the children's roles were reversed. Before long, the same destructive effects occurred again, but this time in reverse. The implications of this experiment are unmistakable. In less than one day it was possible to get children to hate each other because of eye color and **status inequalities**—differences in power, prestige, or privileges. Certainly the effects of a lifetime of real-life racial or ethnic prejudice are infinitely more powerful and destructive. Racism is a major source of stress in the lives of many people of color. Over time, prejudice can have a negative impact on a person's physical and emotional health (Brondolo et al., 2011).

Political Prejudice in America

As research suggests, it is easy to create prejudice. Pick any simplistic way to divide a group of people into "us" and "them" and popularize it. That's what teacher Jane Elliott did when she divided her class into the brown-eyed kids and the blue-eyed kids. In no time at all, the groups were prejudiced against each other.

But that was just an experiment. It couldn't happen in the real world, right? According to psychologists Conor Seyle and Matthew Newman (2006), we are witnessing just such a real-world example in the United States today. In order to graphically convey the outcome of the presidential vote in the 2000 election, *USA TODAY* created a state-by-state map, color-coded red and blue, to denote states that had voted for the Republican candidate or the Democratic candidate.

Just a few years later, "red" and "blue" has become a national shorthand for dividing Americans into opposing camps. The "reds" are supposed to be Republican, conservative, middle-class, rural, religious, and live in the American heartland. The "blues" are supposed to be Democrat, liberal, upper-class, urban, nonreligious, and live on the coasts. The result is that the complex American social world is reduced to two oversimplified stereotypes, leading to an increase in between-group prejudice (Binning et al., 2010; Edgerly, 2015).

This oversimplification ignores the fact that, in many states, the presidential votes are very close. Thus, a state that is "red" by 51 percent is nevertheless 49 percent "blue." Besides, many different combinations exist. How do you categorize someone from California (a "blue" state) who is an economic conservative, attends church occasionally, lives in San Francisco, supports gay marriage, and yet votes Republican?

According to Seyle & Newman (2006), a better approach is to recognize that the United States is made of a full spectrum of political, social, religious, and economic views and that most Americans are "purple." Thinking this way also highlights the fact that Americans of all political persuasions share more similarities than they do differences when compared with the citizens of other countries. This more tolerant, less polarizing view of America is reflected in the "purple America" map (Gastner, Shalizi, & Newman, 2005). "Thinking purple" just might result in a more productive national discussion about the important issues facing the United States today.

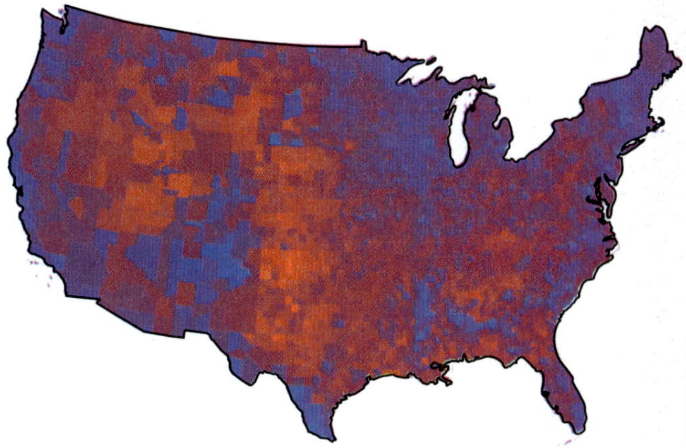

Figure 73.3

Purple America map. Counties within states voting more than 70 percent Republican appear in red; areas voting more than 70 percent Democratic appear in blue. Shades of purple represent intermediate percentages of voters. Source: http://www-personal.umich.edu/~mejn/election/2016/. 2016 M. E. J. Newman.

However, this is not the whole answer. As we noted earlier, there is often a disconnect between attitudes and actual behavior. Changing beliefs can be quite superficial if prejudiced behavior doesn't change as well.

Combating Prejudice

What can be done to combat prejudice? Progress has been made through attempts to educate the general public about the lack of justification for prejudice. Changing the belief component of an attitude is one of the most direct means of changing the entire attitude. Thus, when people are made aware that members of various racial and ethnic groups share the same goals, ambitions, feelings, and frustrations as they do, intergroup relations may be improved (Moskowitz & Li, 2011).

Many school districts in the United States require students to wear uniforms. Appearance (including gang colors) is one of the major reasons that kids treat each other differently. Uniforms help minimize status inequalities and in-group/out-group distinctions (Sanchez, Yoxsimer, & Hill, 2012).

Several lines of thought (including cognitive dissonance theory) suggest that more frequent *equal-status contact* between groups in conflict should more completely reduce prejudice and stereotyping (Koschate & van Dick, 2011; Pettigrew, 2016). *Equal-status contact* refers to interacting on an equal footing, without obvious differences in power or status. In various studies, mixed-race groups have been formed at work, in the laboratory, and at schools. The conclusion from such research is that personal contact with a disliked group tends to induce friendly behavior, respect, and liking (Abrams et al., 2017). However, these benefits are most pervasive when personal contact is cooperative and on an equal footing (Moskowitz & Li, 2011).

Superordinate Goals Let's now consider a revealing study done with 11-year-old boys. When the boys arrived at a summer camp, they were split into two groups and housed in separate cabins. At first, the groups were kept apart to build up separate identities and friendships. Soon each group had a flag and a name (the "Rattlers" and the "Eagles"), and each had staked out its territory. At this point, the two groups were placed in competition with each other. After several clashes, dislike between the groups bordered on hatred: The boys baited each other, started fights, and raided each other's cabins (Sherif et al., 1961).

Status inequalities Differences in the power, prestige, or privileges of two or more people or groups.

Were they allowed to go home hating each other? As an experiment in reducing intergroup conflict, and to prevent the boys from remaining enemies, various strategies to reduce tensions were tried. Holding meetings between group leaders did nothing. When the groups were invited to eat together, the event turned into a free-for-all. Finally, emergencies that required *cooperation* among members of both groups were staged at the camp. For example, the water supply was damaged so that all the boys had to work together to repair it. These emergencies created **superordinate goals** that exceeded or overrode the lesser competitive goals. Creating this and other superordinate goals helped restore peace between the two groups.

Cooperation and shared goals seem to help reduce conflict by encouraging people in opposing groups to see themselves as members of a single, larger group (Gaertner et al., 2000; Pettigrew, 2016). Superordinate goals, in other words, have a "we're all in the same boat" effect on perceptions of group membership. The power of superordinate goals can be seen in the unity that prevailed in the United States (and throughout much of the rest of the world) for months after the September 11 terrorist attacks. Superordinate goals also are an important factor in helping peacekeepers constructively engage with people from other nationalities (Boniecki & Britt, 2003; Whitley & Kite, 2010).

Can such goals exist on a global scale? One example might be a desire to deal with the current global energy crisis. Another is the need to preserve the natural environment on a global scale. Still another is the continuing threat posed by terrorism and religious extremism. Politically, such goals may be far from universal. But their superordinate quality is clearly evident.

"Jigsaw" Classrooms Contrary to the hopes of many, integrating public schools often has little positive effect on racial prejudice. In fact, prejudice may be made worse, and the self-esteem of minority students frequently decreases (Aronson, 2012; Binder et al., 2009).

If integrated schools provide equal-status contact, shouldn't prejudice be reduced? Theoretically, yes. But in practice, minority-group children often enter schools unprepared to compete on an equal footing. The competitive nature of schools almost guarantees that children will *not* learn to like and understand each other.

With the preceding in mind, social psychologist Elliot Aronson pioneered a way to apply superordinate goals to ordinary classrooms. According to Aronson, such goals are effective because they create **mutual interdependence**—that is, people must depend on one another to meet each person's goals. When individual needs are linked, cooperation is encouraged (Güth, Levati, & von Wangenheim, 2010; Pettigrew, 2016).

Monkey Business Images/Shutterstock.com

In a "jigsaw" classroom, children help each other prepare for tests. As they teach each other what they know, the children learn to cooperate and to respect the unique strengths of each individual.

How has that idea been applied? Aronson has created "jigsaw" classrooms that emphasize cooperation rather than competition. The term *jigsaw* refers to the pieces of a jigsaw puzzle. In a **jigsaw classroom**, each child is given a "piece" of the information needed to complete a project or prepare for a test.

In a typical session, children are divided into groups of five or six and given a topic to study for a later exam. Each child is given his or her "piece" of information and asked to learn it. For example, one child might have information on Thomas Edison's invention of the light bulb; another, facts about his invention of the long-playing phonograph record; and a third, information about Edison's childhood. After the children have learned their parts, they teach them to others in the group. Even the most competitive children quickly realize that they cannot do well without the aid of everyone in the group. Each child makes a unique and essential contribution, so the children learn to listen to and respect themselves and each other (Crone & Portillo, 2013).

Does the jigsaw method work? Compared with children in traditional classrooms, children in jigsaw groups are less prejudiced, they like their classmates more, they have more positive attitudes toward school, their grades improve, and their self-esteem increases (Aronson, 2012; Walker & Crogan, 1998). Such results are quite encouraging.

To summarize, prejudice will be reduced when the following happens:

- Members of different groups have equal status *within the situation* that brings them together.
- Members of all groups seek a common goal.
- Group members must cooperate to reach the goal.
- Group members spend enough time together for cross-group friendships to develop.

Superordinate goal A goal that exceeds or overrides all others; a goal that renders other goals relatively less important.

Mutual interdependence A condition in which two or more people must depend on one another to meet each person's needs or goals.

Jigsaw classroom A method of reducing prejudice; each student receives only part of the information needed to complete a project or prepare for a test, encouraging all students to work together to achieve their goal.

MODULE 73 Antisocial Behavior—Learning Outcomes Revisited

73.1 Define biological explanations of aggression, the frustration–aggression hypothesis, aggression cues, social learning theories of aggression, and how aggression can be reduced

Aggression is a fact of life that occurs in many forms. Nevertheless, humans are not inevitably aggressive. Biological explanations of aggression emphasize brain mechanisms and physical factors that lower the threshold for aggression. According to the frustration–aggression hypothesis, frustration and aggression are closely linked. Frustration is only one of many aversive stimuli that can arouse a person and make aggression more likely. Aggression is especially likely to occur when aggression cues are present. Social learning theory has focused attention on the role of aggressive models in the development of aggressive behavior. Aggression can be reduced by reducing exposure to violence, increasing exposure to prosocial acts, and teaching anger control.

73.2 Discuss prejudice, the forms it can take, its causes, and the authoritarian personality

Prejudice, a negative attitude held toward members of various out-groups, can be expressed explicitly, systemically, symbolically, and implicitly. One theory attributes prejudice to scapegoating. A second account says that prejudices may be held for personal reasons (personal prejudice) or simply through adherence to group norms (group prejudice). Prejudiced individuals tend to have an authoritarian or dogmatic personality, characterized by rigidity, inhibition, intolerance, oversimplification, and ethnocentrism.

73.3 Outline the role of status, superordinate goals, and mutual interdependence in reducing prejudice and intergroup conflict

Intergroup conflict gives rise to hostility and the formation of social stereotypes. Stereotypes and self-stereotyping rob people of their individuality and can even dehumanize them. Status inequalities tend to build prejudice. Equal-status contact tends to reduce it. Shared superordinate goals are a key to reducing intergroup conflict. On a smaller scale, jigsaw classrooms (which encourage cooperation through mutual interdependence) have been shown to be an effective way of combating prejudice.

Reflective Practice

Content Check

1. Social learning theorists view aggression as primarily related to biological instincts. T or F?
2. Heavy exposure to media results in lowered emotional sensitivity to violence. T or F?
3. Some expressions of prejudice can be thought of as scapegoating or
   a. displaced aggression
   b. empathic arousal
   c. reference group reversal
   d. external attribution
4. The authoritarian personality tends to be prejudiced against all out-groups, a quality referred to as
   ______________________.
5. The term *symbolic prejudice* refers to racism or prejudice that is expressed in disguised or hidden form. T or F?

6. Jigsaw classrooms use ____________________ to create mutual interdependence.
   a. social competition
   b. just-world beliefs
   c. self-fulfilling prophecies
   d. superordinate goals

Skill Check

Think Critically

7. In court trials, defense lawyers sometimes try to identify and eliminate prospective jurors who have authoritarian personality traits. Can you guess why?

Self-Reflect

Which concepts or theories do you think best explain your own aggressive actions? Does the most rigid person you know match the profile of the authoritarian personality? Stereotypes exist for many social categories, even ordinary ones such as "college student" or "unmarried young adult." What stereotypes do you think you face in daily life? Do they generate stereotype threat in you? The director of a youth recreation center is concerned about the amount of conflict she is seeing between boys and girls from different racial and ethnic groups. What advice can you give the director?

ANSWERS

1. F 2. T 3. a 4. ethnocentrism 5. T 6. d 7. Authoritarians tend to believe that punishment is effective so they are more likely to vote for conviction.

MODULE 74

A Psychologist's Skill Set
Teamwork

Pull Together

After a massive earthquake left Haiti devastated in 2010, two former US Marines—Jake Wood and William McNulty—decided that they wanted to help. Along with six other veterans and first responders, they provided assistance to Haitians in remote regions that were getting little aid. Realizing that many former members of the US Armed Forces possess important skills that are desperately needed after natural disasters, they set about organizing a team that could provide help under these difficult circumstances. This was the beginning of Team Rubicon, an organization that brings veterans together to assist others.

Polaris Images/Nepal/Newscom

It may surprise you to know that as much as they help others, members of Team Rubicon also help each other: After their years spent in uniform come to an end, the challenges of returning to civilian life are difficult, and the support they receive from other members of the military can be invaluable. The "team" has now grown to include thousands of past members of the US Forces. They volunteer their time to work on community-based projects with organizations such as Habitat for Humanity, as well as disaster relief efforts in remote corners of the world such as India and Ecuador. Together, these men and women accomplish a great deal of important work. But they're not just a group of individuals working on the same project. Instead, they function as a team. What's the difference, you ask? Let's find out.

~LEARNING OUTCOMES~

After reading this module you should be able to:

74.1 Explain how to become a better team member

Teamwork—The Dream Team

Learning Outcome 74.1 Explain how to become a better team member

In Modules 70–73, we examined topics that broadly relate to social psychology—the area of psychology that is most closely aligned to our relationships with other people. In this module, we focus on the importance of those relationships when people have to work together in teams to accomplish a goal.

Isn't "team" just another word for "group"? According to psychologists, a *team* is a special kind of group. While group work involves multiple people working toward a common goal, teams are characterized by their *interdependence*:

Members of groups can often work on their own, in parallel, and then bring their individual contributions together at the end to construct the final product. In contrast, group work involves multiple people working toward a common goal, but group members can often work on their own and then bring their individual contributions together at the end to construct the final product. In contrast, teams are characterized by their *interdependence*: Members of teams have to actively work together at all stages of the project. Progress toward the goal depends on each member of the team providing their expertise that, in turn, enables the others to complete their own tasks more effectively (West, 2012).

Considerable research has been carried out in the area of teamwork by psychologists in many areas, including social and personality psychologists, industrial/organizational psychologists (psychologists who study people at work and in organizations; see Module 75), and cognitive psychologists. Collectively, they have addressed a number of questions including, for example, the costs and benefits of working in teams (rather than individually), cross-cultural differences in perceptions of teamwork, and developmental changes in teams that work together over long periods of time (Caligiuri & Lundby, 2015; Hackman, 2002; Salas et al., 2015). More recently, rapid improvements in technology have led to increased interest among psychologists about virtual collaboration, and how to ensure success among teams that may never meet face-to-face (Gilson et al., 2015).

In addition to these questions, there's also a large body of literature that addresses the characteristics of both effective and dysfunctional teams, and much of that research examines the role of team members' characteristics and abilities in contributing to positive outcomes. Psychological research has suggested that effective teamwork draws on several skills, including communication, leadership, problem solving, working with diverse others, creativity, emotional intelligence, and integrity (most of which have been discussed in the *Psychologist's Skill Set* modules in this book!) (Levi, 2017). If a potential employer asks you to talk about your ability to work as part of a team during an interview, then it's useful to have considered your answer in terms of all of these skills. Even better, try to have ready some concrete examples of experiences that you can use to clearly demonstrate that you have these abilities!

Benefiting from Teamwork

When most people think about teamwork, their minds immediately jump to the workplace. They think about teams working together to plan an event, launch a product, or solve a difficult problem. And the literature supports the idea that effective teams are a valuable resource for any organization: A group of people who work well together often creates a synergistic effect, accomplishing more than could be done by each of the team members on their own.

But being a good "team player" isn't just relevant to our working life; these skills are also important in personal relationships as well. Consider, for example, how teamwork is relevant when romantic partners are raising a child, or when siblings are providing care for an elderly parent (Tolkacheva, van Groenou, & Tilburg, 2014). Consider, too, that teamwork may be necessary for volunteer work and community service projects that you choose to undertake when you are committed to a particular cause.

Becoming a Team Player

If teamwork skills are important across so many aspects of your life, how can you work to improve them? We've already mentioned that good teamwork draws on a number of other skills (e.g., communication, problem solving, and an openness to working with diverse others), so it's important to work on your abilities in these areas. But according to Amy Edmundson at Harvard Business School, there are a number of other things that you can consider if you want to make valuable contributions to a team (Edmondson, 2012):

Help to Create Ground Rules. Setting up norms that team members understand and agree with is important in ensuring that all members of the team understand what's expected of them (and others!).

Help to Ensure That Everyone Participates. It's easy sometimes to assume that the right way to proceed is coming from the person who's speaking the loudest. However, making this type of assumption means that you may often miss out on the valuable opinions of those who are more introverted, or people who just need a bit more time to think things through before responding. There are a number of ways to avoid this problem, but one of the simplest is to just make sure that you go around the table and ask for each person's opinion before making a decision. Of course, for this strategy to work, it's also important to create a climate in which everyone feels that their contributions to the team will be valued and considered.

Don't Assume That Everyone Knows What You Do. Explicitly sharing what you know means that everyone "begins on the same page," and that the project is much more likely to proceed smoothly.

Model the Behavior You Want to See. It's an age-old truism that you should treat other people the way that you want to be treated. When you work closely with others, this is particularly important. If characteristics such as openness, acceptance, conscientiousness, and reliability are important to you, then make sure you demonstrate those same characteristics when you interact with other members of the team.

MODULE 74 Teamwork—Learning Outcomes Revisited

74.1 Explain how to become a better team member

Teams differ from groups because in teams, members are more dependent on one another to achieve a goal. Numerous skills are important to being a good team member, including communication, leadership, emotional intelligence, and integrity. Teamwork is important at work, but can also be important in relationships with family and friends. There are a number of things that you can do to improve your ability to function well in a team environment, including creating ground rules, ensuring that everyone participates, providing important information to all members of the team, and modeling the behavior that you want to see from others.

Reflective Practice

Content Check

1. Teamwork and group work are essentially the same thing. T or F?
2. One of the most important things that characterizes teams is that its members are interdependent. T or F?
3. Which of the following skills are important to teamwork?
   a. communication
   b. problem solving
   c. emotional intelligence
   d. a, b, and c are all important
4. Teamwork is important in the workplace, but is unlikely to be relevant in your personal or family life. T or F?

Skill Check

Think Critically

5. What are some of the strategies that you could use to make sure that all members of a team have an opportunity to offer their opinion in a meeting?

Self-Reflect

Do you consider yourself to be a good "team player," or are you someone who prefers to work alone? Given that so many workplaces require teamwork these days, what skills might you need to work on to improve your ability to work well as part of a team?

ANSWERS

1. F 2. T 3. d 4. F 5. In addition to being supportive and systematically giving all team members the opportunity to speak (by going around the table and asking for each person's opinion, for example), the team may also want to consider circulating a list of questions or issues before the meeting so that people can consider what they'd like to say in advance. This may be particularly helpful for people who aren't always good at "thinking on their feet."

MODULE

75

Applied Psychology

Industrial/Organizational Psychology

Punching the Clock

Have you ever had a job that made you feel like a cog in a machine? Charlie Chaplin captured this feeling in his 1936 film *Modern Times*. Fortunately, the world of work has changed since Chaplin's day. Consider Armando, a software engineer working long hours developing a novel way to predict hurricanes for a satellite weather system. His work efficiency cannot easily be measured or improved. Instead, Armando's success depends on his own initiative, creativity, and commitment to his work. Armando quit his last job because it made him feel like he was "punching the clock," which is something he does not want to do.

Do you believe that you should live to work or work to live? Whatever your attitude, the simple fact is that most adults work for a living. Whether you are already employed or plan to begin a career after college, it helps to know something about the psychology of work and organizations.

Chaplin/United Artists/The Kobal Collection/Picture Desk

~LEARNING OUTCOMES~

After reading this module you should be able to:

75.1 Define applied psychology, I/O psychology, and three leadership styles, and explain some issues underlying job satisfaction and organizational culture

75.2 Describe the methods companies use to hire personnel as well as retain them

Organizational Psychology—Psychology at Work

Learning Outcome 75.1 Define applied psychology, I/O psychology, and three leadership styles, and explain some issues underlying job satisfaction and organizational culture

Applied psychology refers to the use of psychological principles and research methods to solve practical problems. The largest applied areas are clinical and counseling psychology, but there are many others, such as community psychology, educational psychology, military psychology, consumer psychology, sports psychology, health psychology, and space psychology.

Industrial/organizational (I/O) psychology, the study of people at work and in organizations, is one of the most important applied areas (Aamodt, 2016; Bryan & Vinchur, 2013). The efforts of I/O psychologists likely will affect how you are selected for a job and tested, trained, or evaluated for promotion. Most I/O psychologists are employed by the government, industry, and businesses. Typically, they work in two major areas: (1) studying jobs to identify underlying skills, which can then guide efforts to select people and train them for those jobs (the *industrial* part), and (2) studying organizations to understand how to create structures and company cultures that will improve performance (the *organizational* part). To get a better idea of what I/O psychologists do, examine ■ **Table 75.1**. As you can see, their interests are quite varied.

A key person in any organization is its leader (Humphrey, 2014; Lussier & Achua, 2015). Family therapist and rabbi Edwin Friedman once remarked, "Leadership can be thought of as a capacity to define oneself to others in a way that clarifies and expands a vision of the future." (Can leadership be learned? See Module 54.) How do great business leaders inspire their followers?

Theory X Leadership

One of the earliest attempts to improve worker efficiency was made in 1923 by Frederick Taylor, an engineer. To speed up production, Taylor standardized work routines and stressed careful planning, control, and orderliness. Today, versions of Taylor's approach are classified as **Theory X leadership (scientific management)**. Using time-and-motion studies, task analysis, job specialization, assembly lines, pay schedules, and the like, scientific management seeks to increase productivity (Crowley et al., 2010; Paton, 2013).

TABLE 75.1 | Topics of Special Interest to Industrial/Organizational Psychologists

Absenteeism	Minority workers
Decision-making	Pay schedules
Design of organizations	Personnel selection
Employee stress	Personnel training
Employee turnover	Productivity
Interviewing	Promotion
Job enrichment	Task analysis
Job satisfaction	Task design
Labor relations	Work behavior
Leadership	Work environment
Machine design	Work motivation
Management styles	Worker evaluation

It also sounds like scientific management treats people as if they were machines. Is that true? To some extent it is. In Taylor's day, many large companies were manufacturers with giant assembly lines. People had to be efficient cogs in the manufacturing machinery. Leaders who follow Theory X have a task orientation, focusing on the work to be done, rather than a person orientation, focusing on the people doing the work. As such, they tend to assume that workers must be goaded or guided into being productive. Many psychologists working in business, of course, are concerned with improving **work efficiency**, defined as maximum output at lowest cost. As a result, they alter conditions that they believe will affect workers (such as time schedules, work quotas, bonuses, and so on). Some might even occasionally wish that people would act like well-oiled machines.

However, most psychologists working in business recognize that psychological efficiency is just as important as work efficiency. **Psychological efficiency** refers to maintaining good morale, labor relations, employee satisfaction, and similar aspects of work behavior. Leadership styles that ignore or mishandle the human element can be devastatingly costly. Studies have consistently found that happy workers are productive workers (Dik, Byrne, & Steger, 2013; Lavy & Littman-Ovadia, 2017).

Theory Y Leadership

The term *Theory X* was coined by psychologist Douglas McGregor (1960) as a way to distinguish the leadership style associated with scientific management from *Theory Y*, a newer approach, which emphasizes human relations at work.

How is this approach different? **Theory Y leaders** have a person orientation rather than a task orientation and tend to assume that workers enjoy autonomy and are willing to accept responsibility. They also assume that a worker's needs and goals can be meshed with the company's goals and that people are not naturally passive or lazy. In short, Theory Y

Applied psychology The use of psychological principles and research methods to solve practical problems.

Industrial/organizational (I/O) psychology A field that focuses on the psychology of work and on behavior within organizations.

Theory X leadership (scientific management) An approach to leadership that emphasizes work efficiency.

Work efficiency Maximum output (productivity) at lowest cost.

Psychological efficiency Maintenance of good morale, labor relations, employee satisfaction, and similar aspects of work behavior.

Theory Y leadership A leadership style that emphasizes human relations at work and that views people as industrious, responsible, and interested in challenging work.

assumes that people are industrious, creative, and rewarded by challenging work. It appears that given the proper conditions of freedom and responsibility, many people *will* work hard to gain competence and use their talents.

Leadership and Gender *Aren't women more person-oriented than men? And doesn't that imply that women would make better Theory Y leaders?* Good thinking. As person-oriented Theory Y leadership styles have become more popular, cracks have begun to appear in the glass ceiling, the invisible barrier that has historically prevented women from moving into leadership positions (Diehl & Dzubinski, 2016). Today, women are slowly gaining acceptance as leaders (Eagly, 2013; Şahin, Gürbüz, & Şeşen, 2017). The proportion of American organizations with female CEOs is also slowly increasing (Martin, 2007). And some studies have shown that companies with more women in leadership roles perform better financially and when managing their employees (Krishnan & Park, 2005; Melero, 2011).

Yet, according to psychologist Alice Eagly, women continue to face unique challenges including those created by a clash between leadership stereotypes and stereotypes of women (Brescoll, Dawson, & Uhlmann, 2010; Eagly & Carli, 2007). On the one hand, most people expect good leaders to be *agentic*: independent, confident, ambitious, objective, dominant, and forceful. On the other hand, they expect women to be more *communal*: dependent, caring, nurturing, tender, sensitive, and sympathetic. According to traditional gender role stereotypes (see Module 46), it is men who are agentic (and therefore better) leaders, despite evidence to the contrary (Eagly, 2013).

What does this mean for a woman who moves into a leadership role? If she practices communal, Theory Y leadership, she is seen as weak. She is "not tough enough" or does not "have the right stuff" to be a leader. Yet, if she acts more assertively and confidently, she is scorned for "trying to be a man" (Kark & Eagly, 2010). This conflict has been perfectly expressed by Carly Fiorina, former CEO of Hewlett-Packard, who wrote, "In the chat rooms around Silicon Valley . . . I was routinely referred to as either a 'bimbo' or a 'bitch'—too soft or too hard, and presumptuous, besides" (Fiorina, 2006, p. 173).

As traditional gender stereotypes fade, and as Theory Y leadership styles gain wider acceptance, perhaps women will add shattering the glass ceiling to their many other successes (Kaiser & Wallace, 2016).

Transformational Leadership Today's harsh economic realities often require more of leaders than a person-oriented Theory Y style. **Transformational leadership** seeks to transform employees to exceed expectations and look beyond self-interest to help the organization better compete (Guay, 2013; Şahin, Gürbüz, & Şeşen, 2017). The transformational leader achieves these goals in four ways:

Martin Haas/Shutterstock.com

As the CEO of Hewlett-Packard, past presidential candidate Carly Fiorina constantly faced the incongruity between leadership stereotypes and stereotypes of women (Fiorina, 2006).

1. **Idealized influence:** Employees are encouraged to work ethically, emphasizing values such as trust.
2. **Inspirational motivation:** Employees are inspired to see their work as meaningful and challenging.
3. **Intellectual stimulation:** Employees are empowered to "think outside the box" to find new solutions to problems.
4. **Individualized consideration:** Employees' individual needs, goals, and abilities are valued; appropriate professional development is available as required.

Leadership Strategies

Two techniques that make Theory Y and transformational leadership methods effective are *shared leadership* and *management by objectives*. In **shared leadership (participative management)**, employees at all levels are directly involved in decision-making and problem solving (Neubert et al., 2015; Pearce, Manz, & Sims, 2009). By taking part in decisions that affect them, employees come to see work as a cooperative effort—not as something imposed on them by an egotistical leader. The benefits include greater productivity, more involvement in work, greater job satisfaction, and less job-related stress (Pearce, Conger, & Locke, 2007; Raes et al., 2013).

What is management by objectives? In **management by objectives**, workers are given specific goals to meet so they can tell whether they are doing a good job (Antoni, 2005). Typical objectives include reaching a certain sales total, making a certain number of items, or reducing waste by a specific percentage. In any case, workers are free to choose (within limits) how they will achieve their goals. As a result, they feel more independent and take personal responsibility for their work. Workers are especially productive when they receive feedback about their progress toward goals. Clearly, people like to know what the target is and whether they are succeeding.

Many companies also give *groups* of workers even greater freedom and responsibility. This is typically done by creating self-managed teams. A **self-managed team** is a group of employees who work together toward shared goals. Self-managed teams can typically choose their own methods of achieving results, so long as they are effective. Self-managed teams tend to make good use of the strengths and talents of individual employees. As a consequence, workers in self-managed teams are much more likely to feel that they are being treated fairly at work and to develop a positive team atmosphere (Chansler, Swamidass, & Cammann, 2003; Gilboa & Tal-Shmotkin, 2012). Self-managed teams also promote new ideas and improve motivation. Most of all, they encourage cooperation and teamwork within organizations (Markova & Perry, 2014).

How can workers below the management level be involved more in their work? One answer is the use of **quality circles**, voluntary discussion groups that seek ways to solve business problems and improve efficiency (Aamodt, 2016). In contrast to self-managed teams, quality circles usually do not have the power to put their suggestions into practice directly. But good ideas speak for themselves, and many are adopted by company leaders. Quality circles do have limitations, but nevertheless, studies verify that greater personal involvement can lead to better performance and job satisfaction (Pereira & Osburn, 2007).

Job Satisfaction

It often makes perfect sense to apply Theory X methods to work. However, doing so without taking worker needs into account can be a case of winning the battle while losing the war—that is, immediate productivity may be enhanced while job satisfaction is lowered. And when job satisfaction is low, absenteeism skyrockets, morale falls, and there is a high rate of employee turnover, leading to higher training costs and inefficiency (Silla & Gamero, 2014; Wright & Bonett, 2007).

Understandably, many of the methods used by enlightened Theory Y leaders ultimately improve **job satisfaction**—the degree to which a person is pleased with his or her work. Job satisfaction is well worth cultivating because positive attitudes are associated with more cooperation, better performance, a greater willingness to help others, more creative problem solving, and less absenteeism (Bowling, 2010; Judge et al., 2017).

Monkey Business Images/Shutterstock.com

Shared leadership techniques encourage employees at all levels to become involved in decision-making. Quite often, this arrangement leads to greater job satisfaction.

Transformational leadership Leadership aimed at transforming employees to exceed expectations and look beyond self-interest to help the organization better compete.

Shared leadership (participative management) A leadership approach that allows employees at all levels to participate in decision-making.

Management by objectives A management technique in which employees are given specific goals to meet in their work.

Self-managed team A work group that has a high degree of freedom with respect to how it achieves its goals.

Quality circle An employee discussion group that makes suggestions for improving quality and solving business problems.

Job satisfaction The degree to which a person is comfortable with or satisfied with his or her work.

Under what conditions is job satisfaction highest? Basically, job satisfaction comes from a good fit between work and a person's interests, abilities, needs, and expectations. The major factors determining job satisfaction are noted in the following list. Think of a job that you have held. It's likely that the more these factors were present, the higher was your job satisfaction (Aamodt, 2016; Landy & Conte, 2009).

1. My job meets my expectations. Y or N?
2. My needs, values, and wants are met by my job. Y or N?
3. The tasks I have to do are enjoyable. Y or N?
4. I enjoy my supervisors and coworkers. Y or N?
5. My coworkers are outwardly happy. Y or N?
6. I am rewarded fairly for doing a good job. Y or N?
7. I have a chance to grow and be challenged. Y or N?

We should note that job satisfaction is not entirely a matter of work conditions. Anyone who has ever been employed has probably encountered at least one perpetually grumpy coworker. In other words, workers don't leave their personalities at home. Happy people are more often happy at work, and they are more likely to focus on what's good about their job rather than what's bad. Understandably, the most productive employees are those who are happy at work (Aamodt, 2016; Brown, Charlwood, & Spencer, 2012). This connection can be seen clearly when employees are allowed to participate in various forms of *flexible work*.

Flexible Work If you've ever worked "9 to 5" in an office, you know that traditional time schedules can be confining. They also doom many workers to a daily battle with rush-hour traffic. To improve worker morale, I/O psychologists recommend the use of a variety of flexible work arrangements, of which the best known is **flextime**, or flexible working hours (Kossek & Michel, 2011). The basic idea of flextime is that starting and quitting times are flexible, so long as employees are present during a core work period. For example, employees might be allowed to arrive between 7:30 a.m. and 10:30 a.m. and depart between 3:30 p.m. and 6:30 p.m. In a common variation called a *compressed workweek*, employees might work fewer days, but put in more hours per day so that the number of hours per week stay the same.

Daxiao Productions/Shutterstock.com

Connecting with work through the Internet makes it possible to telecommute, or work from home while still interacting with office-mates (Golden, Veiga, & Simsek, 2006).

With **flexplace** (also called *telework* or *telecommuting*), work is done outside the workplace, usually at home (Lautsch, Kossek, & Eaton, 2009; Nätti & Häikiö, 2012).

Is flexible work really an improvement? Generally speaking, yes (Yang & Zheng, 2011). For example, flextime typically has a positive effect on workers' productivity, job satisfaction, absenteeism, and comfort with their work schedules (Thompson, Payne, & Taylor, 2015). Similarly, flexplace is especially effective when it allows valued employees to maintain homes in other cities rather than being forced to move to the company's location (Atkin & Lau, 2007). Psychologists theorize that flexible work lowers stress and increases feelings of independence, both of which increase productivity and job satisfaction (Beckmann, Cornelissen, & Kräkel, 2017).

Of course, not everyone wants a compressed workweek or to work from home. Ideally, flexible working arrangements should fit the needs of employees (Rudolph & Baltes, 2017; Troup & Rose, 2012). Regardless, most large organizations now use flexible work arrangements. Perhaps we can conclude that it is better, when possible, to bend working arrangements instead of people.

Job Enrichment For years, the trend in business and industry was to make work more streamlined and efficient and to tie better pay to better work. Ample evidence now shows that incentives such as bonuses, earned time off, and profit sharing can increase productivity. However, far too many jobs are routine, repetitive, boring, and unfulfilling. To combat the discontent this can breed, many psychologists recommend a strategy called *job enrichment*.

Job enrichment involves making a job more personally rewarding, interesting, or intrinsically motivating. Large corporations such as IBM, Maytag, Western Electric, Chrysler, and Polaroid have used job enrichment with great success. It usually leads to lower production costs, increased job satisfaction, reduced boredom, and less absenteeism (Gregory, Albritton, & Osmonbekov, 2010).

How is job enrichment done? Merely assigning a person more tasks is usually not enriching. Overloaded workers just feel stressed, and they tend to make more errors. Instead, job enrichment applies many of the principles that we have discussed. Usually, it involves removing some of the controls and restrictions on employees, thus giving them greater freedom, choice, and authority. In some cases, employees also switch to doing a complete cycle of work—that is, they complete an entire item or project instead of doing an isolated part of a larger process. Whenever possible, workers are given direct feedback about their work or progress.

True job enrichment increases workers' feeling of *empowerment* and *knowledge*—that is, workers are encouraged to continuously learn and exercise a broad range of options, skills, and information related to their occupations (Gregory, Albritton, & Osmonbekov, 2010; Sessa & London, 2006). In short, most people enjoy being good at what they do. (Job enrichment can be thought of as a way of increasing intrinsic motivation. See Module 42.)

Organizational Culture

Businesses and other organizations, whether they are large or small, develop distinct cultures. **Organizational culture** refers to the blend of customs, beliefs, values, attitudes, and rituals that give each organization its unique "flavor" (Chamorro-Premuzic & Furnham, 2010). Organizational culture includes such things as how people are hired and trained, disciplined, and dismissed. It encompasses how employees dress, communicate, resolve conflicts, share power, identify with organizational goals and values, negotiate contracts, and celebrate special occasions.

People who fit well into a particular organization tend to contribute to its success in ways that are not specifically part of their job description. For example, they are helpful, conscientious, and courteous. They also display good sportsmanship by avoiding pettiness, gossiping, complaining, and making small problems into big ones. Like good citizens, the best workers keep themselves informed about organizational issues by attending meetings and taking part in discussions. Workers with these characteristics display what could be called **organizational citizenship**. Understandably, managers and employers highly value workers who are good organizational citizens (Woods & West, 2020).

Desk Rage and Healthy Organizations

Like road rage on the highways, "desk rage," or workplace anger, is a frequent occurrence and, at times, erupts into workplace violence (Niven, Sprigg, & Armitage, 2013). It's not difficult to understand the common triggers for workplace anger: intense anger triggered by job-related stresses (such as feeling that one has been treated unfairly), perceived threats to one's self-esteem, and work-related conflicts with others (Einarsen & Hoel, 2008; Spector, 2012).

What can be done about anger and aggression at work? Most larger companies now offer mental health services to troubled employees and trauma counseling if violence erupts in the workplace. More important, healthy organizations actively promote the well-being of people. They do this by openly confronting problems, empowering employees, and encouraging participation, cooperation, and full use of human potential. Healthy organizations also support well-being in the following ways (Hodson & Sullivan, 2012; Martinko, Douglas, & Harvey, 2006):

- Rather than always complaining and blaming, group members express sincere gratitude for the efforts of others.
- Everyone makes mistakes. The culture in caring organizations includes a capacity to forgive.
- Everyone needs encouragement at times. Encouragement can inspire workers and give them hope, confidence, and courage.
- Showing sensitivity to others can dramatically change the work environment. Sensitivity can take the form of expressing interest in others and in how they are doing. It also includes respecting the privacy of others.
- Compassion for others is a good antidote for destructive competitiveness and petty game playing.
- People have very different needs, values, and experiences. Tolerance and respect for the dignity of others goes a long way toward maintaining individual well-being.

The economic pressures that organizations face can lead to hostile and competitive work environments. However, even in economically difficult times, the productivity and quality of life at work are closely intertwined. Effective organizations seek to optimize both. For example, companies who pay more attention to the quality of life at work generally suffer fewer productivity losses if they are forced to downsize (i.e., reduce the size of their workforce; Iverson & Zatzick, 2011).

Flextime A work schedule that allows flexible starting and quitting times.

Flexplace (telecommuting) An approach to flexible work that involves working at a location away from the office, but using a computer to stay connected throughout the workday.

Job enrichment Making a job more personally rewarding, interesting, or intrinsically motivating; typically involves increasing worker knowledge.

Organizational culture The blend of customs, beliefs, values, attitudes, and rituals within an organization.

Organizational citizenship Making positive contributions to the success of an organization in ways that go beyond one's job description.

Personnel Psychology—Hiring Right

Learning Outcome 75.2 Describe the methods companies use to hire personnel as well as retain them

Companies also can enhance their chances of success by hiring the right employees in the first place. **Personnel psychology** is concerned with the testing, selection, placement, and promotion of employees (Campbell, 2013; Woods & West, 2020). At present, nine out of ten people are or will be employed in business or industry. Thus, nearly everyone who holds a job is placed under the "psychological microscope" of personnel selection sooner or later. Clearly, it is valuable to know how selection for hiring and promotion is done.

Job Analysis

How do personnel psychologists select employees? Personnel selection begins with **job analysis**, a detailed description of the skills, knowledge, and activities required by a particular job (Paquette & Heitzman, 2014; Sackett, Walmsley, & Laczo, 2013). A job analysis may be done by interviewing expert workers or supervisors, giving them questionnaires, directly observing work, or identifying *critical incidents.* **Critical incidents** are situations with which competent employees must be able to cope. The ability to deal calmly with a mechanical emergency, for example, is a critical incident for airline pilots. Once job requirements are known, psychologists can state what skills, aptitudes, and interests are needed. In addition, some psychologists are now doing a broader "work analysis." In this case, they try to identify general characteristics that a person must have to succeed in a variety of work roles, rather than in just a specific job (DuVernet, Dierdorff, & Wilson, 2015).

MixPix/Alamy Stock Photo

Analyzing complex skills has also been valuable to the US Navy. When million-dollar aircraft and the lives of pilots are at stake, it makes good sense to do as much training and research as possible on the ground. Navy psychologists use flight simulators such as the one pictured here to analyze the complex skills needed to fly jet fighters. Skills can then be taught without risk on the ground. The CAE P-8 Poseidon simulator shown here uses a computer to generate full-color images that respond realistically to a pilot's use of the controls.

Selection Procedures

After desirable skills and traits are identified, the next step is to learn who has them. Today, the methods most often used for evaluating job candidates include collecting *biodata,* conducting *interviews,* giving *standardized psychological tests,* and employing the *assessment center* approach. Let's see what each entails.

Biodata As simple as it may seem, one good way to predict job success is to collect detailed biographical information (**biodata**) from applicants (Schultz & Schultz, 2010). The idea behind biodata is that looking at past behavior is a good way to predict future behavior. By learning in detail about a person's life, it is often possible to determine whether the person is suited for a particular type of work (Schmitt & Golubovich, 2013).

Some of the most useful items of biodata include past athletic interests, academic achievements, scientific interests, extracurricular activities, religious activities, social popularity, conflict with brothers and sisters, attitudes toward school, and parents' socioeconomic status (Woods & West, 2020). (It is worth pointing out that there are civil liberty and privacy concerns relating to the collection of sensitive biodata.) Such facts tell quite a lot about personality, interests, and abilities. In addition to past experiences, a person's recent life activities also help predict job success. For instance, you might think that college grades are unimportant, but college grade point average (GPA) predicts success in many types of work (Sackett & Lievens, 2008).

Interviews The traditional personal interview is still one of the most popular ways to select people for jobs or promotions. In a **personal interview**, job applicants are questioned about their qualifications. At the same time, interviewers gain an impression of the applicant's personality (Chamorro-Premuzic & Furnham, 2010). (Or personalities—but that's another story!)

As discussed in Module 50, interviews are subject to the halo effect and similar problems. (Recall that the *halo effect* is the tendency of interviewers to extend favorable or unfavorable impressions to unrelated aspects of an individual's personality, such as his or her appearance.) In addition, interviewees actively engage in *impression management,* seeking to portray a positive image to interviewers (Kleinmann & Klehe, 2011).

It is for reasons such as these that psychologists continue to look for ways to improve the accuracy of interviews. For instance, some studies suggest that interviews can be improved by giving them more structure (Levashina et al., 2014; Sackett & Lievens, 2008). For example, each job candidate should be asked the same questions. However, even with their limitations, interviews can be a valid and effective way of predicting how people will perform on the job (Hodson & Sullivan, 2012).

Psychological Testing *What kinds of tests do personnel psychologists use?* General mental ability tests (intelligence tests) tell a great deal about a person's chances of succeeding in various jobs (Aamodt, 2016; Schmidt & Hunter, 1998). So do general personality tests (described in Module 50; Hough & Connelly, 2013). In addition, personnel psychologists often use **vocational interest tests**. These tests assess people's interests and match them to interests found among successful workers in various occupations (Van Iddekinge, Putka, & Campbell, 2011). Tests such as the *Kuder Occupational Interest Survey* and the *Strong-Campbell Interest Inventory* probe interests with items like the following:

> I would prefer to: a. visit a museum b. read a good book c. take a walk outdoors

Interest inventories typically measure six major themes identified by John Holland (■ **Table 75.2**). If you take an interest test and your choices match those of people in a given occupation, it is assumed that you, too, would be comfortable doing the work they do (Meireles & Primi, 2015).

TABLE 75.2 | Vocational Interest Themes

Themes	Sample College Majors	Sample Occupations
Realistic	Agriculture	Mechanic
Investigative	Physics	Chemist
Artistic	Music	Writer
Social	Education	Counselor
Enterprising	Business	Sales
Conventional	Economics	Clerk

Source: Holland (1997).

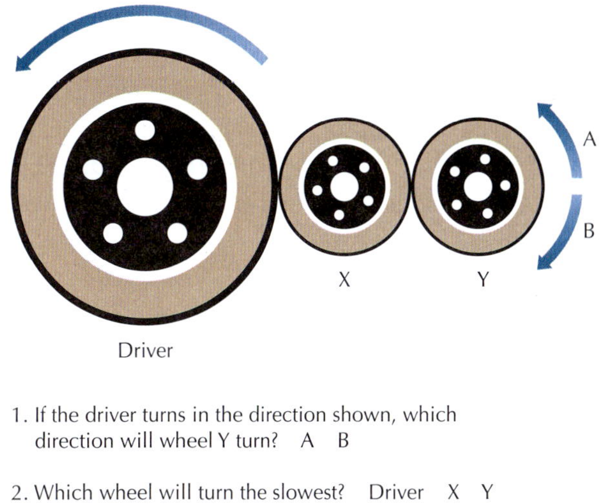

➤ **Figure 75.1**

Testing mechanical aptitude. Sample questions like those found on tests of mechanical aptitude. (The answers are A and the Driver.)

Aptitude tests are another mainstay of personnel psychology. Such tests rate a person's potential to learn tasks or skills used in various occupations. Tests exist for clerical, verbal, mechanical, artistic, legal, and medical aptitudes, plus many others (➤ **Figure 75.1**). For example, tests of clerical aptitude emphasize the capacity to do rapid, precise, and accurate office work. One section of a clerical aptitude test, therefore, might ask a person to mark all the identical numbers and names in a long list of pairs like those shown here:

49837266	49832766
Global Widgets, Inc.	Global Wigets, Inc.
874583725	874583725
Sevanden Corp.	Sevanden Corp.
Cengage Publishing	Cengage Puhlishing

Personnel psychology A branch of industrial/organizational psychology concerned with testing, selection, placement, and promotion of employees.

Job analysis A detailed description of the skills, knowledge, and activities required by a particular job.

Critical incidents Situations that arise in a job with which a competent worker must be able to cope.

Biodata Detailed biographical information about a job applicant.

Personal interview Formal or informal questioning of job applicants to learn their qualifications and to gain an impression of their personalities.

Vocational interest test A paper-and-pencil test that assesses a person's interests and matches them to interests found among successful workers in various occupations.

Aptitude test An evaluation that rates a person's potential to learn skills required by various occupations.

After college, chances are good that you will encounter an *assessment center.* Many large organizations use **assessment centers** to do in-depth evaluations of job candidates. This approach has become so popular that the list of businesses using it—Ford, IBM, Kodak, Exxon, Sears, and thousands of others—reads like a corporate *Who's Who.*

How do assessment centers differ from the selection methods already described? Assessment centers are primarily used to fill management and executive positions. First, applicants are tested and interviewed. Then, they are observed and evaluated in simulated work situations. Specifically, **situational judgment tests** are used to present difficult but realistic work situations to applicants (Christian, Edwards, & Bradley, 2010; Pollard & Cooper-Thomas, 2015). For example, in one exercise, applicants are given an **in-basket test** that simulates the decision-making challenges executives face. The test consists of a basket full of memos, requests, and typical business problems. Each applicant is asked to quickly read all the materials and to take appropriate action.

In another situational test, applicants take part in a **leaderless group discussion**. This is a test of leadership that simulates group decision-making and problem solving. While the group grapples with a realistic business problem, "clerks" bring in price changes, notices about delayed supplies, and so forth. By observing applicants, it is possible to evaluate leadership skills and to see how job candidates cope with stress (Chamorro-Premuzic & Furnham, 2010). (Situational tests are also used to investigate personality differences. See Module 50.)

How well does this approach work? Assessment centers have had considerable success in predicting performance in a variety of jobs, careers, and advanced positions (Chamorro-Premuzic & Furnham, 2010).

Performance Appraisal

Many of the same procedures used to hire employees can also be used to periodically (usually yearly) evaluate the performance of employees after they have been hired (DeNisi & Murphy, 2017). The results can be used in a variety of ways designed to improve employee job performance. This might include providing employees with feedback, setting goals, and determining appropriate rewards or punishments.

One popular approach is **360° feedback**, the evaluation of employee performance from a variety of perspectives. Although implementations of 360° feedback can vary considerably from company to company, it is fair to say that the key feature of most implementations is a set of anonymous numerical ratings collected from different company stakeholders. Some examples include the employee's managers, coworkers, subordinates, customers, and even the employee. Appraising an employee's performance in this way is more likely to reveal strengths or weaknesses not readily apparent from single-perspective evaluations, such as more traditional manager-only appraisals (Bracken, Rose, & Church, 2016).

Although we have only scratched the surface of industrial/organizational psychology, it is time to move on to look at another applied area of great personal relevance. Before we begin, here's a chance to enhance your learning.

Assessment center A program set up within an organization to conduct in-depth evaluations of job candidates.

Situational judgment test Presenting realistic work situations to applicants in order to observe their skills and reactions.

In-basket test A testing procedure that simulates the individual decision-making challenges that executives face.

Leaderless group discussion A test of leadership that simulates group decision-making and problem solving.

360° feedback Evaluation of employee performance, mainly anonymous numerical ratings, collected from different perspectives.

MODULE 75 Industrial/Organizational Psychology—Learning Outcomes Revisited

75.1 Define applied psychology, I/O psychology, and three leadership styles, and explain some issues underlying job satisfaction and organizational culture

The term *applied psychology* refers to the use of psychological principles and research to solve practical problems. Industrial/organizational psychologists enhance the quality of work by studying jobs to better match people to them and by studying organizational structures and culture to improve worker performance. Three basic leadership styles are Theory X (scientific management), Theory Y (human relations approaches), and transformational (thinking outside the box). Theory X is mostly concerned with work efficiency, Theory Y emphasizes psychological efficiency, and transformational leadership emphasizes the corporate need to compete. Theory Y and transformational leadership methods include shared leadership (participative management), management by objectives, self-managed teams, and quality circles. Job satisfaction influences productivity, absenteeism, morale, employee turnover, and other factors that affect business efficiency. Job satisfaction comes from a good fit between work and a person's interests, abilities, needs, and expectations. Job enrichment tends to increase job satisfaction.

75.2 Describe the methods companies use to hire personnel as well as retain them

To match people with jobs, personnel psychologists combine job analysis with selection procedures, such as gathering biodata, interviewing, giving standardized psychological tests, and using assessment centers. 360° feedback is popular for evaluating existing employees.

Reflective Practice

Content Check

1. Theory X leadership, or scientific management, is concerned primarily with improving ______________ ______________.
2. Shared leadership management is often a feature of businesses with leaders who adhere to Theory Y or transformational management. T or F?
3. For the majority of workers, job satisfaction is almost exclusively related to the amount of pay received. T or F?
4. Job enrichment is a direct expression of scientific management principles. T or F?
5. Identifying critical work incidents is sometimes included in a thorough ______________ ______________.
6. A leaderless group discussion is most closely associated with which approach to employee selection?
   a. aptitude testing
   b. personal interviews
   c. job analysis
   d. assessment center

Skill Check

Think Critically

7. In what area of human behavior other than work would a careful task analysis be helpful?

Self-Reflect

If you were leading people in a business setting, which of the leadership concepts do you think you would be most likely to use? Do you think women can make effective leaders? In business? In politics? Think of a job that you know a lot about. Could job enrichment be applied to this work? What would you do to increase job satisfaction for people doing similar work? Which of the various ways of evaluating job applicants do you regard as most valid? Which would you prefer to have applied to yourself?

ANSWERS

1. work (or task) efficiency 2. T 3. F 4. F 5. job analysis 6. d 7. One such area is sports psychology. As described in Module 77, sports skills can be broken into subparts so that key elements can be identified and taught. Such methods are an extension of techniques first used for job analyses. To a large extent, attempts to identify the characteristics of effective teaching also rely on task analysis.

MODULE 76

Applied Psychology

Environmental Psychology

Environmental Melancholia

TSpider/Shutterstock.com

Climate change, environmental degradation, pollution, dying oceans, species extinction, and human overpopulation, all on a global scale. What was once inconceivable has become a real possibility: The death of dear old Mother Earth. Once the realm of science fiction, now entrepreneurs like Elon Musk are deadly serious about escaping looming human extinction by colonizing Mars.

Yet despite the fact that we all have good reason to worry, according to environmental psychologist Susan Clayton most experts are surprised by how weak the public response has been (Gregoire, 2016). What about you? Are you distressed about the state of the environment? Feel helpless to do anything useful? Experience a sense of loss? Are you in denial? You may be experiencing *environmental melancholia,* an unresolved sadness about the destruction of our natural environment (Lertzman, 2015). One of the goals of environmental psychology is to figure out how to convert our passive melancholia about the environment into more active, constructive channels.

~LEARNING OUTCOMES~

After reading this module you should be able to:

76.1 Discuss the effects natural, physical, and social environments have on humans

76.2 Discuss the effects humans have on the natural environment

Environmental Influences on Behavior—No Talking!

Learning Outcome 76.1 Discuss the effects natural, physical, and social environments have on humans

Environmental psychology is the specialty concerned with the relationship between environments and human behavior (Winter & Koger, 2010). Environmental psychologists are interested in both **social environments**, defined by groups of people, such as a dance, business meeting, or party, and **physical environments**, whether constructed or natural. They also give special attention to **behavioral settings**, smaller areas within an environment whose use is well defined, such as an office, locker room, church, casino, or classroom. As you have

TABLE 76.1 | Topics of Special Interest to Environmental Psychologists

Architectural design	Noise
Behavioral settings	Personal space
Cognitive maps	Personality and environment
Constructed environments	Pollution
Crowding	Privacy
Energy conservation	Proxemics
Environmental stressors	Resource management
Heat	Territoriality
Human ecology	Urban planning
Littering	Vandalism
Natural environment	

no doubt noticed, various environments and behavioral settings tend to "demand" certain actions. Consider, for example, the difference between a library and a campus center lounge. Try having an animated discussion at the library sometime (No talking!)

Other major interests of environmental psychologists are crowding, stressful environments, architectural design, environmental protection, and many related topics (■ **Table 76.1**). One of the more "personal" topics in environmental psychology concerns the efforts we make to regulate the space around our bodies.

Personal Space

The next time you are talking with an acquaintance, move in closer and watch the reaction. Most people show signs of discomfort and step back to reestablish their original distance. Those who hold their ground may turn to the side, look away, or position an arm in front of themselves as a barrier. If you persistently edge toward your subjects, it should be easy to move them back several feet.

In this case, your mere (and close) presence amounted to an invasion of that person's **personal space**, an area surrounding the body that is regarded as private and subject to personal control (Novelli, Drury, & Reicher, 2010). Basically, personal space extends "I" or "me" boundaries past the skin to the immediate environment. Personal space also is illustrated by the fact that many train commuters prefer to stand up if it means that they can avoid sitting too close to strangers (Evans & Wener, 2007).

Spatial Norms The systematic study of the human use of space is called *proxemics* (prok-SEE-miks) (Matsumoto, Hwang, & Frank, 2016). Proxemics has revealed that unspoken spatial norms govern personal space. Such norms may explain why people who feel offended by another person sometimes say, "Get out of my face."

Would approaching "too close" work with a good friend? Possibly not. Norms governing comfortable or acceptable distances vary according to relationships as well as activities. Hall (1966) identified four basic zones: *intimate, personal, social,* and *public* distance (➤ **Figure 76.1**).

Environmental psychology The formal study of how environments affect behavior.

Social environment An environment defined by a group of people and their activities or interrelationships (such as a parade, revival meeting, or sports event).

Physical environments Natural settings, such as forests and beaches, as well as environments built by humans, such as buildings, ships, and cities.

Behavioral setting A smaller area within an environment whose use is well defined, such as a bus depot, waiting room, or lounge.

Personal space An area surrounding the body that is regarded as private and subject to personal control.

➤ **Figure 76.1**

Spatial zones. Typical spatial zones (in feet) for face-to-face interactions in North America. Often, we must stand within intimate distance of others in crowds, buses, subways, elevators, and other public places. At such times, privacy is maintained by avoiding eye contact, by standing shoulder to shoulder or back to back, and by positioning a purse, bag, package, or coat as a barrier to spatial intrusions.

Cultural differences also affect spatial norms (Beaulieu, 2004). In many Middle Eastern countries, people hold their faces only inches apart while talking. In Western Europe, the English sit closer together when conversing than do the French. The Dutch, on the other hand, sit farther apart than the French (Remland, Jones, & Brinkman, 1991). The following distances apply to face-to-face interactions in North America:

1. **Intimate distance.** For most North Americans, intimate space extends about 18 inches out from the skin. Entry within this space (face to face) is reserved for special people or special circumstances. Lovemaking, comforting others, and cuddling children all take place within this space.
2. **Personal distance.** This is the distance maintained in comfortable interaction with friends. It extends from about 18 inches to 4 feet from the body. Personal distance basically keeps people within "arm's length" of each other.
3. **Social distance.** Impersonal business and casual social gatherings take place in a range of about 4 to 12 feet. This distance eliminates most touching, and it formalizes conversation by requiring greater voice projection. "Important people" in many business offices use the imposing width of their desks to maintain social distance. (A big smelly cigar helps, too.)
4. **Public distance.** This is the distance at which formal interactions occur (about 12 feet or more from the body). When people are separated by more than 12 feet, they look "flat," and they must raise their voices to speak to one another. Formal speeches, lectures, business meetings, and the like are conducted at public distance.

Because spatial behavior is very consistent, you can learn about your relationship to others by observing the distance that you comfortably hold between yourselves. But remember to be aware of cultural differences. When two people of different nationalities have different norms for personal space, an amusing "dance" may occur. Both are likely to be uncomfortable when talking. One tries to move closer and the other keeps moving back. This can lead to misunderstandings in which one person feels that the other is being too familiar, yet at the same time, the person moving closer feels rejected (Beaulieu, 2004).

John Mitterer

Graffiti, one of the blights of urban life, is an obvious form of territorial marking.

Territoriality Personal space extends to areas that we claim as our "territory." **Territorial behavior** refers to actions that define a space as one's own or that protect it from intruders (Costa, 2012). For example, in the library, you might protect your space with a coat, handbag, book, or other personal belonging. "Saving a place" at a theater or a beach also demonstrates the tendency to identify a space as "ours." Even sports teams are territorial, usually showing a home team advantage by playing better on their own home territory (Swartz & Arce, 2014).

Respect for the temporary ownership of space also is widespread. It is not unusual for a person to "take over" an entire table or study room by looking annoyed when others intrude. Your own personal territory may include your room, specific seats in many of your classes, or a particular table in the campus center or library that "belongs" to you and your friends.

Researchers have found that the more attached you are to an area, the more likely you are to adorn it with obvious **territorial markers** that signal your "ownership." Typical markers include decorations, plants, photographs, or posters. College dorms and business offices are prime places to observe this type of territorial marking. It is interesting to note that obvious territorial markers, such as fences (even if small), parked cars, lawn furniture, exterior lights, and security signs can help create a more *defensible space* by deterring crime (Reynald & Elffers, 2009). The "gated communities" that have sprung up in many cities are a good example.

Environmental Influences on Behavior

Much of our behavior is influenced, in part, by specific types of environments. For example, a variety of environmental factors influence the amount of vandalism and other crime that occurs in public places (Brown & Devlin, 2003; Hipp et al., 2013; Welsh, Mudge, & Farrington, 2010). For example, in every city, more assaults and burglaries take place near the few restaurants or bars where likely offenders tend to hang out (Buchanan, 2008).

Research on such environmental factors is often applied to the design of local environments, such as public spaces. For example, many shopping malls and department stores are designed like mazes. Their twisting pathways encourage shoppers to linger and wander while looking at merchandise. (Oddly enough, raised flowerbeds around signs help protect them because people resist trampling the flowers to get to the signs.) Or consider the public restroom. Many architects now "harden" and "de-opportunize" public restrooms by adding elements such as doorless toilet stalls and tiled walls to discourage vandalism and graffiti.

Given the personal impact of environments, it is important to know how we are affected by stressful or unhealthy settings, such as large cities. Traffic congestion, pollution, crime, and impersonality are urban problems that immediately come to mind. To this list, psychologists have added crowding, overstimulation, and noise as major sources of urban stress. Psychological research has begun to clarify the impact of each of these conditions on human functioning (Malan et al., 2008; Thomas, 2013).

This fly is a good example of modern washroom design. It isn't real; it is painted onto this urinal at Amsterdam's Schiphol Airport. Men tend to aim at the "fly" and hence are more accurate when they urinate. The result is much cleaner men's washrooms.

Crowding Nowhere are the effects of urbanization more evident than in the teeming cities of many underdeveloped nations (Malan et al., 2012). Closer to home, the jammed buses, subways, and living quarters of our own large cities are ample testimony to the stresses of crowding.

Is there any way to assess the effect that crowding has on people? One approach is to study the effects of overcrowding among animals. Although the results of animal experiments cannot be considered conclusive for humans, they point to some disturbing effects.

In an influential classic experiment, John Calhoun (1962) let a group of laboratory rats breed without limit in a confined space. Calhoun provided plenty of food, water, and nesting material for the rats. All that the rats lacked was space. At its peak, the colony numbered 80 rats; yet it was housed in a cage designed to comfortably hold about 50. Overcrowding in the cage was heightened by the actions of the two most dominant males. These rascals staked out private territory at opposite ends of the cage, gathered harems of eight to ten females, and prospered. Their actions forced the remaining rats into a small, severely crowded middle area.

What effect did crowding have on the animals? A high rate of pathological behavior developed in both males and females. Females gave up nest building and caring for their young. Pregnancies decreased, and infant mortality ran extremely high. Many of the animals became indiscriminately aggressive and went on rampaging attacks against others. Abnormal sexual behavior was rampant, with some animals displaying hypersexuality and others total sexual passivity. Many of the animals died, apparently from stress-caused diseases. The link between these problems and overcrowding is unmistakable.

But does that apply to humans? Many of the same pathological behaviors can be observed in crowded inner-city ghettos. It is, therefore, tempting to assume that violence, social disorganization, and declining birthrates as seen in these areas are directly related to crowding. However, the connection has not been so clearly demonstrated with humans (Evans et al., 2010). People living in the inner city suffer disadvantages in nutrition, education, income, and health care. These conditions, more than crowding, may deserve the blame for pathological behaviors. In fact, most

Territorial behavior Any behavior that tends to define a space as one's own or that protects it from intruders.

Territorial markers Objects and other signals whose placement indicates to others the "ownership" or control of a particular area.

Times Square in New York, New Year's Eve, 2019, BC (before COVID). High densities do not automatically produce feelings of crowding. The nature of the situation and the relationships among crowd members are also important.

laboratory studies using human subjects have failed to produce any serious ill effects by crowding people into small places.

Most likely this is because *crowding* is a psychological condition that is separate from **density**—the number of people in a given space. **Crowding** refers to subjective feelings of being overstimulated by social inputs or a loss of privacy. Whether high density is experienced as crowding may depend on the relationships among those involved. In an elevator, subway, or prison, high densities may be uncomfortable. In contrast, a musical concert, party, or reunion may be most pleasant at high density levels. Thus, physical crowding may interact with situations to intensify existing stresses or pleasures (Evans, Lercher, & Kofler, 2002).

However, when crowding causes a *loss of control* over one's immediate social environment, stress and health problems are likely to result (Solari & Mare, 2012; Steiner & Wooldredge, 2009). Stress probably explains why death rates increase among prison inmates and mental hospital patients who live in crowded conditions. Even milder instances of crowding can have a negative impact. People who live in crowded conditions often become more aggressive or guarded and withdrawn from others (Regoeczi, 2008).

Attentional Overload One unmistakable consequence of high densities and crowding is a state that psychologist Stanley Milgram called **attentional overload.** This is a stressful condition that occurs when sensory stimulation, information, and social contacts make excessive demands on attention. Large cities, in particular, tend to bombard residents with continuous input resulting in sensory and cognitive overload.

Milgram (1970) believed that city dwellers learn to prevent attentional overload by engaging only in brief, superficial social contacts, by ignoring nonessential events, and by fending off others with cold and unfriendly expressions. In short, many city dwellers find that a degree of callousness is essential for survival (Wilson & Kennedy, 2006). Thus, a blunting of sensitivity to the needs of others may be one of the more serious costs of urban stresses and crowding.

As described next, noise also contributes to the sensory assault that many people endure in urban environments.

Noise Pollution *How serious are the effects of daily exposure to noise?* A classic study of children attending schools near Los Angeles International Airport suggests that constant noise can be quite damaging. Children from the noisy schools were compared with similar students attending schools farther from the airport (Cohen et al., 1981). The comparison students were from families of similar social and economic makeup. Testing showed that children attending the noisy schools had higher blood pressure than those from the quieter schools. They were more likely to give up attempts to solve a difficult puzzle. And they were poorer at proofreading a printed paragraph—a task that requires close attention and concentration. Other studies of children living near other airports or in noisy neighborhoods have found similar signs of stress, poor reading skills, and other damaging effects (Evans, 2006; Linting et al., 2013; Sörqvist, 2010).

The tendency of the noise-battered children to give up or become distracted is a serious handicap. It may even reveal a state of *learned helplessness* (described in Module 57) caused by daily, uncontrollable blasts of sound. Even if such damage proves to be temporary, it is clear that **noise pollution**—annoying and intrusive sound—is a major source of environmental stress.

Environmental Problem Solving

How do psychologists find solutions to problems such as overcrowding, pollution, and overuse of resources? Solutions can more easily be found by doing an **environmental assessment** to see how an environment influences the behavior and perceptions of the people using it. For example, anyone who has ever lived in a college dorm knows that, at times, it can be quite a "crazy house." In one well-known environmental assessment, Baum and Valins (1977) found that students housed in long, narrow, corridor-design dormitories often feel crowded and stressed. The crowded students tended to withdraw from others and even made more trips to the campus health center than students living in less-crowded buildings.

Through **architectural psychology**, the study of the effects that buildings have on behavior, psychologists are often able to suggest design changes that solve or avoid problems (Zeisel, 2006). For example, Baum and Valins (1979) studied two basic dorm arrangements. One dorm had a long corridor with one central bathroom. As a result, residents were constantly forced into contact with one another. The other dorm had rooms clustered in threes. Each of these suites shared a small bathroom. Even though the amount of space available to each student was the same in both dorms, students in the long-corridor dorm reported feeling more crowded. They also made fewer friends in their dorm and showed greater signs of withdrawing from social contact.

What sort of solution does this suggest? A later study showed that small architectural changes can greatly reduce stress in high-density living conditions. Baum and Davis (1980) compared students living in a long-corridor dorm housing 40 students with those living in an altered dorm where the hallway was divided in half, with unlocked doors, and three center bedrooms were turned into a lounge area (➤ Figure 76.2). At the end of the term, students living in the divided dorm reported less stress from crowding. They also formed more friendships and were more open to social contacts. In comparison, students in the long-corridor dorm felt more crowded, stressed, and unfriendly, and they kept their doors shut much more frequently—presumably because they "wanted to be alone."

Similar improvements have been made by altering the interior design of businesses, schools, apartment buildings, mental hospitals, and prisons. In general, the more spaces that one must pass through to get from one part of a building to another, the less stressed and crowded people feel (Evans, Lepore, & Schroeder, 1996; Zeisel, 2006). We have had room here only to hint at the creative and highly useful work being done in environmental psychology. Although many environmental problems remain, it is encouraging to see that behavioral solutions exist for at least some of them. Surely, creating and maintaining healthy environments is one of the major challenges facing coming generations (Des Jardins, 2013; Lertzman, 2015).

Space Habitats Nowhere are the demands on applied psychology greater than in space flight. Every machine, tool, and environment in a spacecraft must be carefully adapted for human use (Mulavara et al., 2010). The same goes for life on the International Space Station. Residents are restricted to tiny living quarters with little privacy for months at a time. These conditions, and other sources of stress, make it clear that the design of space habitats must take many human needs into account. For instance, researchers have learned that astronauts prefer rooms that clearly define "up" and "down"—even in the weightlessness of space. This can

Density The number of people in a given space or, inversely, the amount of space available to each person.

Crowding A subjective feeling of being overstimulated by a loss of privacy or by the nearness of others (especially when social contact with them is unavoidable).

Attentional overload A stressful condition caused when sensory stimulation, information, and social contacts make excessive demands on attention.

Noise pollution Stressful and intrusive noise; usually artificially generated by machinery, but also includes sounds made by animals and humans.

Environmental assessment The measurement and analysis of the effects that an environment has on the behavior and perceptions of people within that environment.

Architectural psychology The study of the effects that buildings have on behavior and the design of buildings using behavioral principles.

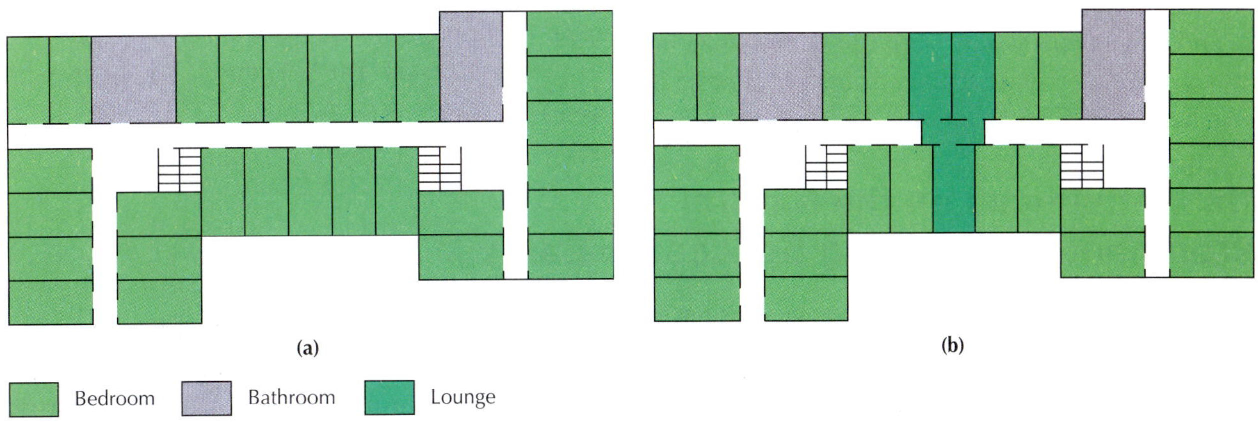

➤ **Figure 76.2**

An architectural solution for crowding. Psychologists divided a dorm hall like that shown in the left diagram *(a)* into two shorter halls separated by unlocked doors and a lounge area *(b)*. This simple change minimized unwanted social contacts and greatly reduced feelings of crowding among dorm residents. (Adapted from Baum & Davis, 1980.)

N.A.S.A./SIPA/Newscom/Sipa Press

The International Space Station provides a habitat in which men and women can live and work in space for extended periods. Solving the behavioral problems of living in space will be an important step toward human exploration of the solar system.

be done by color-coding walls, floors, and ceilings and by orienting furniture and controls so they all face the "ceiling" (Suedfeld & Steel, 2000).

Ideally, there should be some flexibility in the use of living and work areas inside a space station. Behavior patterns change over time, and being able to control one's environment helps lower stress. At the same time, people need stability. Regular exercise, for instance, is both physically and psychologically necessary. Similarly, psychologists have found that eating becomes an important high point in monotonous environments. Eating at least one meal together each day can help keep crew members working as a social unit.

Sleep cycles must be carefully controlled in space to avoid disrupting body rhythms (Kanas & Manzey, 2008; Suedfeld & Steel, 2000). In past space missions, some astronauts found that they couldn't sleep while other crew members continued to work and talk. Problems with sleep can be worsened by the constant noise on a space station. At first, such noise is annoying. It can be difficult to get used to it and, after weeks or months, it can become a serious stressor. Researchers are experimenting with various earmuffs, eyeshades, and sleeping arrangements to alleviate such difficulties.

Sensory Restriction Sensory monotony can also be a problem in space—even the magnificent vistas of Earth become repetitive (Kanas & Manzey, 2008). (How many times would you have to see the North American continent before you lost interest?)

Researchers are developing stimulus environments that use music, movies, and other diversions to combat monotony and boredom. Again, they are trying to provide choice and control for space crews. Studies of confined living in the Arctic and elsewhere make it clear that one person's symphony is another's grating noise. Where music is concerned, individual earphones may be all that is required to avoid problems.

Most people in restricted environments find that they prefer solitary pastimes such as reading, listening to music, looking out windows, writing, and watching films or television. As much as anything, this preference may again show the need for privacy. Reading or listening to music is a good way to psychologically withdraw from the group. Experiences with confining environments on Earth (such as Biosphere 2) suggest that including live animals and plants in space habitats could reduce stress and boredom (Suedfeld & Steel, 2000).

Life on Spaceship Earth

It is curiously fitting that the dazzling technology of space travel has highlighted the inevitable importance of human behavior. Here on Earth, as in space, we cannot count on cleverly designed machines or technology alone to solve problems. The threat of nuclear war, social conflict, crime, prejudice, infectious disease, overpopulation, environmental damage, famine, homicide, economic disaster, and most other major problems facing us are behavioral.

Will spaceship Earth endure? It's the psychological question we turn to next.

Human Influences on the Natural Environment—Sustaining Spaceship Earth

Learning Outcome 76.2 Discuss the effects humans have on the natural environment

Overpopulation and its environmental impact are surely among the most serious problems facing the world today. The world population has exploded in the last 150 years to more than 7.3 billion people today (➤ **Figure 76.3**). It may reach 9.7 billion by 2050 (United Nations, 2019).

All that human activity drastically changes the natural environment (Miller & Spoolman, 2016). We burn fossil fuels, destroy forests, use chemical products, and strip, clear, and farm the land. In doing so, we alter natural cycles, animal populations, and the very face of the Earth. The long-range impact of such activities is already becoming evident through global warming, the extinction of plants and

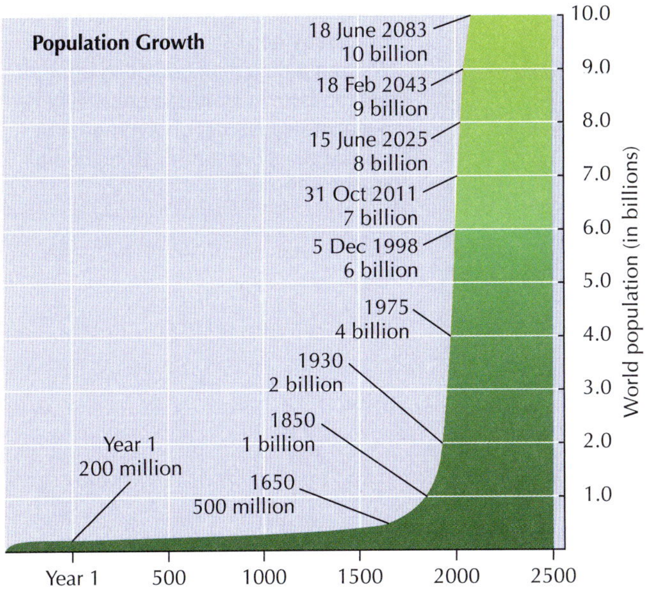

Figure 76.3

World population growth. Population growth has exploded since 1850 and already exceeds 7 billion. Overpopulation and rapid population growth are closely connected with environmental damage, international tensions, and rapid depletion of nonrenewable resources. Some demographers predict that if population growth is not limited voluntarily before it reaches 10 billion, it will be limited by widespread food shortages, disease, infant mortality, and early death (Global Footprint Network, 2020a; United Nations, 2019).

animals, a hole in the ozone layer, and polluted land, air, water, and oceans (Winter & Koger, 2010).

On a smaller scale, there is plenty of evidence that unchecked environmental damage will be costly to our children

AP Images/Itsuo Inouye

In March 2011, a Japanese nuclear reactor leaked radiation into the environment when it suffered a catastrophic failure in reaction to a giant earthquake and tsunami. Major environmental catastrophes like this one have become depressingly common. As the late Carl Sagan once said, "When you look closely, you find so many things going wrong with the environment, you are forced to reassess the hypothesis of intelligent life on Earth."

and descendants. For example, exposure to toxic hazards, such as radiation, pesticides, and industrial chemicals, leads to an elevated risk of physical and mental disease (Evans, 2006).

How many more people can the forests, oceans, cropland, and atmosphere of this world support? Resource consumption can be measured as an **ecological footprint**, the amount of land and water area required to replenish the resources that a human population consumes.

Multiply the average individual's ecological footprint by a bit over 7.7 billion, the current world population, and you get a giant *world footprint*, covering the surface area of our entire planet, with another .7 Earths to boot. For every year of human resource consumption, it will *already* take Earth 1.7 years to recover (Global Footprint Network, 2020a). By 2030, we could well be using two Earths worth of resources every year. How is our one Earth to cope? As we saw at the beginning of this module, humans are already consuming more than the Earth can regenerate (Global Footprint Network, 2020a). Industrialized nations, in particular, are consuming world resources at an alarming rate. North America, for instance, has an ecological footprint about 10 times larger than that of Asia or Africa.

A worldwide ecological crisis is brewing, and humans must change course to avoid vast human misery and permanent damage (Moran, E. F., 2010). Of course, corporations and governments do much environmental damage. Thus, many of the solutions require changes in politics and policies. Ultimately, the solutions also require changes in individual behavior. Most of the environmental problems that we face can be traced back to the individual human tendency to overuse natural resources (Global Footprint Network, 2020a; Huang & Rust, 2011). In the face of projected shortages and squandered resources, what can be done to encourage both the reduction of consumption and greater reliance on recycling and reuse on a personal level?

Conservation

Try as you might to reduce your use of resources (such as electricity), you may find it difficult (Stall-Meadows & Hebert, 2011). Learning about environmental problems and pro-environment values at home, school, and work has been one of the most effective ways to encourage pro-environmental behavior (Carrico & Riemer, 2011; Matthies, Selge, & Klöckner, 2012). Still, as environmental psychologists have

Ecological footprint The amount of land and water area required to replenish the resources that a human population consumes.

What will it cost the world to provide for a baby born since the year 2000? Without a major conservation effort, a person born in North America will over a lifetime consume, on average, the resources shown here ("Bringing up Baby," 1999).

found, a lack of *feedback* and *control* remain major barriers (McCalley, de Vries, & Midden, 2011; Winter & Koger, 2010).

Feedback About Conservation Efforts Imagine learning that you suffer from high blood pressure and decide to lower it. Yet you have no way to measure your blood pressure as required and, hence, no immediate and direct way of telling if your efforts are successful. Until recently, this was the situation with conservation.

For example, feedback about electricity use (such as the monthly electricity bill) usually arrives long after the temptation to turn up the heat or to leave lights on. Psychologists aware of this problem have shown that lower energy bills result from simply giving families and work groups daily feedback about their use of gas or electricity (Carrico & Riemer, 2011). But now *smart meters* can provide continuous feedback about energy usage to both consumers and their energy suppliers (U.S. Department of Energy, 2017).

As another example, recycling typically increases when families, work groups, dorms, and the like are given feedback on a periodic basis about how much they recycled (Kim, Oah, & Dickinson, 2005). In one study, signs were placed on recycling containers on a college campus. The signs showed how many aluminum cans had been deposited in the previous week. This simple procedure increased recycling by 65 percent (Larson, Houlihan, & Goernert, 1995).

Effective feedback about overall resource use also is finally becoming widely available as several organizations provide *ecological footprint calculators,* websites that allow individuals to calculate (and therefore track) their individual overall resource consumption (Global Footprint Network, 2020a,b). Similarly, with growing public concern over global warming, many people can now calculate their individual **carbon footprint**, the volume of greenhouse gases their individual consumption adds to the atmosphere (The Nature Conservancy, 2016).

Control and Conservation Of course, feedback without control is still not optimal. Fortunately many of the same technologies that provide feedback also allow individuals greater control over their conservation efforts. For example, programmable home thermostats and energy-saving settings on appliances and electronics make it possible for conservation-conscious consumers to control their energy consumption more precisely. It is now easier than ever to conserve energy (by installing energy-efficient lights, for example) and see an immediate reduction in your carbon footprint.

sunsetman/Shutterstock.com

People are much more likely to recycle if proper attention is given to psychological factors that promote recycling behavior. For example, these recycling bins are designed to make efficient recycling easier.

At the same time, corporations and public utilities can use up-to-date information to offer incentives, such as monetary rewards, for energy conservation. Electricity utilities have begun, for example, to offer electricity at lower prices during periods of low demand. Savvy consumers not only can more easily conserve electricity, but they also can save even more money by, say, running their dishwasher in the evening rather than during the day.

Similarly, anything that makes recycling more convenient or worthwhile doing helps put people in control. A good example is cities that offer curbside pickup of household recyclables. Another is businesses that help customers recycle old computers, printers, and the like. Requiring refundable deposits on glass bottles is a good example of using incentives to increase recycling.

On campus, simply putting marked containers in classrooms is also helpful (Duffy & Verges, 2009).

It is even becoming more possible and popular to offset some *carbon debt*—by planting trees, for example. Prompt and accurate information and feedback about energy use are making it possible to aspire to a *carbon-neutral lifestyle,* in which your energy consumption is reduced and the remainder offset so that your overall impact on global warming is zero.

Persuasion One last point. All the knowledge, feedback, and control in the world won't much matter to a person with little or no motivation to conserve resources or recycle. For this reason, we also need to consider how best to persuade people to participate. Even people who believe that recycling is worthwhile are likely to regard it as a boring task. Thus, people are most likely to begin and continue recycling if they emphasize the sense of satisfaction that they get from contributing to the environment (Nigbur, Lyons, & Uzzell, 2010).

To date, there have been many different types of media campaigns designed to get people engaged. Often, these campaigns seek to highlight the costs and benefits of environmentalism. While such approaches produce results, more needs to be done. Fortunately, the widespread use of social media is beginning to allow more custom-tailored approaches.

Social norms marketing seeks to change attitudes by making social norms more explicit in order to encourage compliance. What would you do if you received a Twitter tweet or Facebook post that read, "Seventy-seven percent of your neighbors report taking shorter showers to conserve energy" (Miller & Prentice, 2016, p. 340)? A more precisely targeted approach, **personalized normative feedback**, seeks to change attitudes by comparing feedback about individual performance with the relevant social norms. A sample tweet or post might be "Did you know that you use more water every week than eighty percent of your neighbors?" Both of these *social norms-based approaches* are proving to be powerful new tools in the battle for Earth (Ferraro, Miranda, & Price, 2011; Ferraro & Price, 2013; Miller & Prentice, 2016).

Social Dilemmas

Why is it so difficult to get people to take better care of the environment? A pattern of behavior called a *social dilemma* contributes to many environmental problems. A **social dilemma** is any social situation that rewards actions that have undesired effects in the long run (Van Lange et al., 2013; Van Vugt, 2009). In a typical social dilemma, no one individual intentionally acts against the group interest, but if many people act alike, collective harm is done. For example, the rapid transit systems in many large cities are underused. At the same time, the roads are jammed. Why?

Carbon footprint The volume of greenhouse gases individual consumption adds to the atmosphere.

Social norms marketing A persuasion technique that seeks to change attitudes by making explicit relevant social norms in order to foster compliance.

Personalized normative feedback A persuasion technique that seeks to change attitudes by comparing feedback about individual performance with relevant social norms in order to foster compliance.

Social dilemma A social situation that tends to provide immediate rewards for actions that will have undesired effects in the long run.

Too many individuals decide that it is convenient to own and drive a separate car (to run errands and so on). However, each person's behavior affects the welfare of others. Because everyone wants to drive for "convenience," driving becomes inconvenient: The mass of cars in most cities causes irritating traffic snarls and a lack of parking spaces. It also contributes to pollution and global warming. Each car owner has been drawn into a dilemma.

The Tragedy of the Commons Social dilemmas are especially damaging when we are enticed into overuse of scarce resources that must be shared by many people. Again, each person acts in his or her self-interest but, collectively, everyone ends up suffering. Ecologist Garrett Hardin (1968) calls such situations the **tragedy of the commons**. An example that we have already discussed in this book is the lack of individual incentives to conserve gasoline, water, or electricity. Whenever personal comfort or convenience is involved, it is highly tempting to "let others worry about it." Yet in the long run, everyone stands to lose (Ansari, Wijen, & Gray, 2013; Van Vugt, 2009).

Why does such misguided behavior so often prevail? Again, we see a social dilemma at work: If one person pollutes a river or trashes the roadside, it has little noticeable effect. But as many people do the same, problems that affect everyone quickly mount. Throwing away one plastic bag may seem inconsequential, but across the world, hundreds of billions of plastic bags are used every year, and it takes hundreds of years for the environment to recycle them. Plastic bags are major polluters of the world's oceans.

As another example, consider the farmer who applies pesticides to a crop to save it from insect damage. The farmer benefits immediately. However, if other farmers follow suit, the local water system may be permanently damaged. In most cases of environmental pollution, immediate individual benefits are gained for polluting, but the major, long-term collective costs are delayed. What can we do to avoid such dilemmas?

Escaping Dilemmas Persuasion and education have been used with some success to get individuals and businesses to voluntarily reduce destructive activities. Effective appeals may be based on self-interest (cost savings), the collective good (protecting one's own children and future generations), or simply a personal desire to take better care of the planet (Pelletier, Baxter, & Huta, 2011; Winter & Koger, 2010). It really helps if conservation is seen as a group effort. There is evidence that in most social dilemmas, people are more likely to restrain themselves when they believe that others will, too (Kugler & Bornstein, 2013; Nigbur, Lyons, & Uzzell, 2010). Otherwise, they are likely to think, "Why should I be a sucker? I don't think anyone else is going to conserve" (fuel, electricity, water, paper, or whatever).

In some cases, it is possible to dismantle social dilemmas by rearranging rewards and costs. For example, many companies are tempted to pollute because it saves them money and increases profits. To reverse the situation, a pollution tax could be levied so that it would cost more, not less, for a business to pollute. Likewise, incentives could be offered for responsible behavior. An example is the rebates offered for installing insulation or buying energy-efficient appliances (Schmuck & Vlek, 2003). Another is offering lower electricity rates for shifting use to off-peak times (U.S. Department of Energy, 2017).

Some problems may be harder to solve: What, for instance, can be done about truck drivers who cause dangerous traffic jams because they will not pull over on narrow roads? How can littering be discouraged or prevented? How would you make carpooling or using public transportation the first choice for most people? How could people simply be encouraged to stagger their departure times to and from work? All these and more are social dilemmas that need solving. It is important that we not fall into the trap of ignoring them (van Dijk, Parks, & van Lange, 2013).

Tragedy of the commons A social dilemma in which individuals, each acting in his or her immediate self-interest, overuse a scarce group resource.

MODULE 76 Environmental Psychology—Learning Outcomes Revisited

76.1 Discuss the effects natural, physical, and social environments have on humans

Environmental psychologists are interested in behavioral settings, physical and social environments, sustainability, and human territoriality, among other topics. The nature of many relationships is revealed by your personal space, the distance you are comfortable maintaining between yourself and another person. Territorial behaviors, including territorial markers, are used to define a space as one's own or to protect it from intruders. Environmental problems such as crowding, overstimulation, and noise are major sources of urban stress. Animal experiments indicate that excessive crowding can be unhealthy. However, human research shows that psychological feelings of crowding do not always correspond to density. One major consequence of crowding is attentional overload. Noise pollution is a major source of environmental stress. Environmental psychologists offer solutions to many practical problems—from noise pollution to architectural design. Their work often begins with a careful environmental assessment. Space habitats must be designed with special attention to the numerous human factor issues raised by space flight.

76.2 Discuss the effects humans have on the natural environment

The origins of many environmental disasters lie in overpopulation and overconsumption. Providing control and feedback about resource use is an effective way to promote conservation and recycling. Persuasive messages about conservation are more effective when they reference social norms. Social dilemmas, such as the tragedy of the commons, arise when people are enticed into overuse of scarce, shared resources.

Reflective Practice

Content Check

1. If two people position themselves 5 feet apart while conversing, they are separated by a gap referred to as ________________ distance.
2. Although male rats in Calhoun's crowded animal colony became quite pathological, female rats continued to behave in a relatively normal fashion. T or F?
3. Milgram believed that many city dwellers prevent attentional overload by limiting themselves to superficial social contacts. T or F?
4. Performing an environmental ________________ might be a good prelude to redesigning college classrooms to make them more comfortable and conducive to learning.
5. Researchers have learned that astronauts don't really care if living quarters have clearly defined "up" and "down" orientations. T or F?
6. Using smart meters and ecological footprint calculators to provide feedback is one effective approach for bringing about energy conservation. T or F?
7. So far, the most successful approach for bringing about energy conservation is to add monetary penalties to monthly bills for excessive consumption. T or F?

Skill Check

Think Critically

8. Many of the most damaging changes to the environment being caused by humans will not be felt until sometime in the future. How does this complicate the problem of preserving environmental quality?

Self-Reflect

What forms of territorial behavior are you aware of in your own actions? Have you ever experienced a stressful level of crowding? Was density or control the key factor? Have you ever calculated your carbon footprint? Why not try it? You might be surprised by what you find. Would it get you more involved in conservation to be given regular feedback about your conservation activities? About those of your social reference groups?

ANSWERS

1. social 2. F 3. T 4. assessment 5. F 6. T 7. F 8. Delay of consequences (rewards, benefits, costs, and punishments) tends to reduce their impact on immediate behavior.

MODULE 77

Applied Psychology

The Psychology of Law, Community Psychology, and Sports Psychology

Enough for the Death Penalty?

In May 2015, a jury convicted Boston Marathon bomber Dzhokhar Tsarnaev of brutally murdering three spectators and wounding at least 260 others. After months of often heartbreaking testimony, the jury reached their verdict—guilty, with a recommendation to sentence Tsarnaev to death by lethal injection for his crime. When most people think about psychology and the law, they think about *Criminal Minds*. Yet, understanding the minds of jurors is at least as important to the legal process.

Jane Flavell Collins/EPA/Newscom

Three of the best places to see psychology in action are in a courthouse, in a classroom, and at sporting events. These settings are all capable of bringing out some of the best and worst of human behavior. It is worth applying psychology to foster the best rather than the worst. Let's begin with a look at the psychology of juries.

~LEARNING OUTCOMES~

After reading this module you should be able to:

77.1 Define the psychology of law, scientific jury selection, and death-qualified juries

77.2 Discuss how community psychology can improve communities

77.3 Define sports psychology, task analysis, motor skills, and peak performance

Psychology and Law—Judging Juries

Learning Outcome 77.1 Define the psychology of law, scientific jury selection, and death-qualified juries

Jury trials are often fascinating studies in human behavior. Does the defendant's appearance affect the jury's decision? Do the personality characteristics or attitudes of jurors influence how they vote? These and many more questions have been investigated by psychologists interested in law. Specifically, the **psychology of law** is the study of the behavioral dimensions of the legal system (Greene & Heilbrun, 2014; see ■ **Table 77.1**).

Jury Behavior

When a case goes to trial, jurors must listen to days or weeks of testimony and then decide guilt or innocence. How do they reach their decision? Psychologists use **mock juries**, or simulated juries, to probe such questions (Bornstein, 2017).

TABLE 77.1 | Topics of Special Interest in the Psychology of Law

Arbitration	Juror attitudes
Attitudes toward law	Jury decisions
Bail setting	Jury selection
Capital punishment	Mediation
Conflict resolution	Memory
Criminal personality	Parole board decisions
Diversion programs	Police selection
Effects of parole	Police stress
Expert testimony	Police training
Eyewitness testimony	Polygraph accuracy
Forensic hypnosis	Sentencing decisions
Insanity plea	White-collar crime

In some mock juries, volunteers are simply given written evidence and arguments to read before making a decision. Others watch videotaped trials staged by actors. Either way, studying the behavior of mock juries helps us understand what determines how real jurors vote (Pezdek, Avila-Mora, & Sperry, 2010).

Some of the findings of jury research are unsettling (Peoples et al., 2012). Studies show that jurors are rarely able to put aside their biases, attitudes, and values while making a decision (Buck & Warren, 2010; Stawiski, Dykema-Engblade, & Tindale, 2012). For example, appearance can be unduly influential (just like interpersonal attraction; see Module 72). Jurors are less likely to find attractive defendants guilty (on the basis of the same evidence) than unattractive defendants. In one mock jury study, defendants were less likely to be convicted if they were wearing eyeglasses than if they were not. Presumably, eyeglasses imply intelligence and, hence, that the defendant wouldn't do anything as foolish as commit the crime for which she was on trial (Brown, Henriquez, & Groscup, 2008).

Another problem is that jurors are not very good at separating evidence from other information, such as their perceptions of the defendant, attorneys, witnesses, and what they think the judge wants. For example, if complex scientific evidence is presented, jurors tend to be swayed more by the expertise of the witness than by the evidence itself (Cooper, Bennett, & Sukel, 1996; Hans et al., 2011). Similarly, today's jurors place too much confidence in DNA evidence because crime-solving programs such as *CSI* and *Forensic Files* make it seem simple (Meyers, 2007).

Furthermore, jurors who have been exposed to pretrial publicity tend to inappropriately incorporate that information into their jury deliberations, often without being aware that it has happened (Ruva, McEvoy, & Bryant, 2007). Similarly, the jurors' final verdict is influenced by inadmissible evidence, such as mention of a defendant's prior conviction. When jurors are told to ignore information that slips out in court (even if it is "stricken from the record"), they find it very hard to do so. A related problem occurs when jurors take into account the severity of the punishment that a defendant faces (Sales & Hafemeister, 1985). Jurors are not supposed to let this affect their verdict, but many do.

A final area of difficulty arises because jurors usually cannot suspend judgment until all the evidence is presented. Typically, they form an opinion early in the trial. It then becomes difficult for them to fairly judge evidence that contradicts that opinion.

Problems like these are troubling in a legal system that prides itself on fairness. However, all is not lost. The more severe the crime and the more clear-cut the evidence, the less a jury's quirks affect the verdict. Although it is far from perfect, the jury system works reasonably well in most cases (Greene & Heilbrun, 2014).

Jury Selection

In many cases, the composition of a jury has a major effect on the verdict of a trial (Kovera & Cutler, 2013). Before a trial begins, opposing attorneys are allowed to disqualify potential jurors who may be biased. For example, a person who knows anyone connected with the trial can be excluded. Beyond this, attorneys try to use jury selection to remove people who may cause trouble for them (Morrison, DeVaul-Fetters, & Gawronski, 2016). For instance, juries composed of women are more likely to vote for conviction in child sexual assault trials (Eigenberg et al., 2012; Golding et al., 2007).

Only a limited number of potential jurors can be excused. As a result, many attorneys ask psychologists for help in identifying people who will favor or harm their efforts. In **scientific jury selection**, social science

Psychology of law The study of the psychological and behavioral dimensions of the legal system.

Mock jury A group that realistically simulates a courtroom jury.

Scientific jury selection Using social science principles to choose members of a jury.

principles are applied to the process of choosing a jury (Lieberman, 2011). Several techniques are typically used. As a first step, *demographic information* may be collected for each juror. Much can be guessed by knowing a juror's age, sex, race, occupation, education, political affiliation, religion, and socioeconomic status. Most of this information is available from public records, including social media (Nance, 2015).

To supplement demographic information, a *community survey* may be done to find out how local citizens feel about the case. The assumption is that jurors probably have attitudes similar to people with backgrounds like their own. Although talking with potential jurors outside the courtroom is not permitted, other information networks are available. For instance, a psychologist may interview relatives, acquaintances, neighbors, and coworkers of potential jurors.

Back in court, psychologists also often watch for *authoritarian personality* traits in potential jurors. Authoritarians tend to believe that punishment is effective, and they are more likely to vote for conviction (Devine et al., 2001). (Authoritarian personality traits are also related to ethnocentrism and racial prejudice. See Module 73.) At the same time, the psychologist typically observes potential jurors' *nonverbal behavior.* The idea is to try to learn from body language which side the person favors.

In the well-publicized case of O.J. Simpson, who was accused of brutally killing his wife and her friend, a majority of African Americans thought that Simpson was innocent during the early stages of the trial. In contrast, the majority of European Americans thought that he was guilty. The opinions of both groups changed little over the course of the year-long trial. (Simpson was eventually acquitted, but he later lost a civil lawsuit brought by the victims' families.) The fact that emerging evidence and arguments had little effect on what people believed shows why jury makeup can sometimes decide the outcome of a trial (Cohn et al., 2009).

Cases such as Simpson's raise troubling ethical questions. Wealthy clients have the advantage of scientific jury selection—something that most people cannot afford. Attorneys, of course, can't be blamed for trying to improve their odds of winning a case. And because both sides help select jurors, the net effect in most instances is probably a more balanced jury. At its worst, jury analysis leads to unjust verdicts. At its best, it helps to identify and remove only people who would be highly biased (Kovera & Cutler, 2013).

Death-Qualified Juries In the United States, murder trials may require a special jury—one made up of people who are not opposed to the death penalty. That way, jurors are capable of voting for the death penalty if they think that it is justified.

Death-qualified juries may be a necessity for the death penalty to have meaning. However, psychologists have discovered that the makeup of such juries tends to be biased. Specifically, death-qualified juries are likely to contain a disproportionate number of people who are male, white, high income, conservative, and authoritarian. Given the same facts, jurors who favor the death penalty are more likely to read criminal intent into a defendant's actions and are much more likely than average to convict a defendant (Butler, 2007; Summers, Hayward, & Miller, 2010).

Could death-qualified juries be too willing to convict? It is nearly impossible to say how often the bias inherent in death-qualified juries results in bad verdicts. However, the possibility that some innocent persons have been executed may be one of the inevitable costs of using death as the ultimate punishment.

Jury research is perhaps the most direct link between psychology and law, but there are others. Psychologists evaluate people for sanity hearings, do counseling in prisons, profile criminals, advise lawmakers on public policy, help select and train police cadets, and more (Greene & Heilbrun, 2014; Wrightsman & Fulero, 2009). In the future, it is quite likely that psychology will have a growing impact on law and the courts.

Community Psychology—An Ounce of Prevention

Learning Outcome 77.2 Discuss how community psychology can improve communities

In February of 2018, Nikolas Cruz walked into Marjory Stoneman Douglas school in Parkland, Florida. Using a semi-automatic rifle, it took him only six minutes to kill three members of staff and fourteen students. In the days that followed, there was a great deal of discussion about this tragedy, and what to do about the problem of gun-related violence in schools. Two clear approaches emerged as people discussed and debated the events that had transpired in Florida. The first assumes an *individual* focus. In the case of Parkland, this approach would involve looking back in time and examining Nikolas Cruz's behavior (e.g., his disturbing posts on social media) and state of mental health, and questioning whether he should have been referred for therapy, and what type of therapy might have been helpful. This approach is at the heart of the modules that focus on psychopathology (see Modules 60–63) and psychotherapy (see

Modules 65–68). Often, the strategies and therapies that define this approach are *reactive*; that is, they are adopted *after* a problem has been identified. In addition, this model often views our ability to change as dependent on the expertise of professionals, including clinicians and medical doctors.

The second approach to the issue of gun violence in schools is very different, and is best characterized by the surviving students. Many of these young people did not respond with quiet grief and fear, as one might expect after witnessing such a tragedy. Instead, they stood up and loudly demanded political change. With the support of many Americans, students marched and held rallies, they took to social media using the tag #NeverAgain, and they met with politicians and journalists. Each time, they spoke powerfully about the need to change state and federal laws in ways that would prevent gun-related violence in the future. This second approach, with its focus on *communities* rather than individuals, is in keeping with a branch of psychology referred to as **community psychology**.

From Individuals to Societies

Community psychology is a relatively new area of study whose beginnings in the United States can be traced back to the 1960s. At that time, a group of clinical psychologists gathered together and discussed their shared interest in developing an activist approach to health-related challenges—one that would move beyond traditional psychotherapy (Bond, Serrano-García, Keys, & Shinn, 2017). Given the roots of community psychology, it won't surprise you to learn that psychologists who work in this area tackle health-related challenges quite differently than clinicians. First, their efforts are aimed at moving beyond individuals to influence health at the level of groups, including organizations, neighborhoods, and societies. Second, they emphasize not just social factors, but also the cultural, economic, environmental, and political forces that shape our health. Third, community psychology is squarely focused on empowering people to bring about the change that they wish to see, rather than waiting for experts to step in on their behalf. And finally, the field is defined by the need to be *proactive* rather than reactive, emphasizing the benefits that come from preventing health-related problems rather than trying to manage them afterward.

Jeff Malet/Washington/DC/United States of America/Newscom

Over the past 50 years, community psychologists have participated in a number of successful initiatives that have had a positive impact on the health and well-being of people around the world. In the United States, for example, community psychologists played an important role in large-scale national changes related to smoking and the use of tobacco (Pokorny, Jason, & Schoeny, 2003). But there are many smaller-scale initiatives that have also benefitted from the input of community psychologists. For example, community psychologists have worked on initiatives that promote environmental awareness and sustainability (Browne & Bishop, 2011; Sun & Han, 2018) and rural development (Landini, 2015), as well as positive experiences in schools (McMahon, 2018), healthcare facilities (Franz, Skinner, & Murphy, 2017), and the military (O'Neal, Mallette, & Mancini, 2018). And these are just a small number of the areas where community psychologists are making a difference—each day, they make important contributions to efforts that are aimed at improving the health of communities across the country and around the globe (■ **Table 77.2**).

TABLE 77.2 | Topics of Special Interest to Community Psychologists

AIDS/HIV prevention	Homelessness
Disabilities	Mental health resources
Education outcomes	Multiculturalism and inclusion
Environmental sustainability	Poverty
Gender and sexuality	Substance Abuse
Globalization	Rural development
Health care	Well-being

Community psychology A branch of psychology that goes beyond an individual focus and integrates social, cultural, economic, political, environmental, and international influences to promote positive change, health, and empowerment at individual and systemic levels.

How do community psychologists contribute to these efforts? That's a great question! In some cases, they get involved in designing, implementing, and evaluating community-based programs. This might involve working with non-profit agencies, governments, and other organizations, helping them to establish what approaches are most likely to be successful in achieving their goals, putting those plans into action, and measuring success in ways that make sense in that situation. They can also work as consultants, assisting groups in their efforts to promote positive community-based change. And finally, many community psychologists work in colleges and universities helping to educate the next generation of community activists—people just like you!

Sports Psychology—Psyched!

Learning Outcome 77.3 Define sports psychology, task analysis, motor skills, and peak performance

Sports psychology is the study of the behavioral dimensions of sports performance (Cox, 2012; Davis, 2016). As almost all serious athletes soon learn, peak performance requires more than physical training. Mental and emotional "conditioning" also are important. Recognizing this fact, many teams, both professional and amateur, now include psychologists on their staffs. On any given day, a sports psychologist might teach an athlete how to relax, how to ignore distractions, or how to cope with emotions. The sports psychologist also might provide personal counseling for handling performance-lowering stresses and conflicts (LeUnes, 2008). Other psychologists are interested in studying factors that affect athletic achievement, such as skill learning, the personality profiles of champion athletes, the effects of spectators, and related topics (■ **Table 77.3**). In short, sports psychologists seek to understand and improve sports performance and to enhance the benefits of participating in sports (Cox, 2012; Davis, 2016).

TABLE 77.3 | Topics of Special Interest to Sports Psychologists

Achievement motivation	Hypnosis
Athletic personality	Mental practice
Athletic task analysis	Motor learning
Coaching styles	Peak performance
Competition	Positive visualization
Control of attention	Self-regulation
Coping strategies	Skill acquisition
Emotions and performance	Social facilitation
Exercise and mental health	Stress reduction
Goal setting	Team cooperation
Group (team) dynamics	Training procedures

Sports often provide valuable information on human behavior in general. For example, one study of adolescents found a link between sports participation and physical self-esteem that in turn was linked with overall self-esteem (Bowker, 2006). In other research, psychologists have learned that such benefits are most likely to occur when competition, rejection, criticism, and the "one-winner mentality" are minimized. When working with children in sports, it is also important to emphasize fair play, intrinsic rewards, self-control of emotions, independence, and self-reliance.

Adults, of course, also may benefit from sports through reduced stress, better self-image, and improved general health (Khan et al., 2012; Williams, 2010). Runners, for instance, experience lower levels of tension, anxiety, fatigue, and depression than are found in the nonrunning population.

Since the advent of sports psychology, our understanding of sports and expert performance has developed by leaps and bounds. An ability to do detailed studies of complex skills has been one of the major contributions. In a **task analysis**, sports skills are broken into subparts so that key elements can be identified and taught (Hewit, Cronin, & Hume, 2012). Such methods are an extension of techniques first used for job analyses, as described in Module 75.

For example, it doesn't take much to be off target in the Olympic sport of marksmanship. The object here is to hit a bull's-eye the size of a dime at the end of a 165-foot-long shooting range. Nevertheless, an average of 50 bull's-eyes out of 60 shots is not unusual in international competition (prone position).

What does it take—beyond keen eyes and steady hands—to achieve such accuracy? The answer is surprising. Sports psychologists have found that top shooters

Boston Globe/Getty Images

Testing by psychologists has shown that umpires can call balls and strikes more accurately if they stand behind the outside corner of the home plate. This position supplies better height and distance information because umpires are able to see pitches pass in front of the batter (Ford et al., 1999).

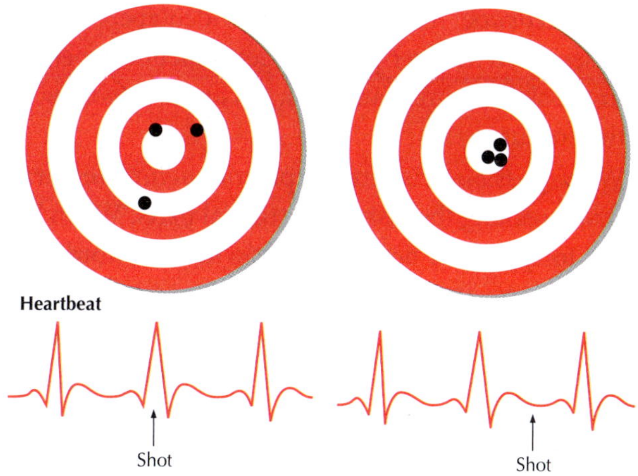

➤ **Figure 77.1**

Accuracy of target shooting as a function of heartbeats. The target on the left shows what happens when a shooter fires during the heart's contraction. Higher scores, as shown by the three shots on the right, are more likely when shots are taken between heartbeats. (Adapted from Pelton, 1983.)

consistently squeeze the trigger *between* heartbeats (➤ **Figure 77.1**). Apparently, the tiny tremor induced by a heartbeat is enough to send the shot astray (Pelton, 1983). Without careful psychological study, it is doubtful that this element of marksmanship would have been identified. Now that its importance is known, competitors have begun to use various techniques—from relaxation training to biofeedback—to steady and control their heartbeats. In the future, the best shooters may be those who set their sights on mastering their hearts.

Motor Skills Sports psychologists are very interested in how we learn motor skills (Hodges & Williams, 2012). A **motor skill** is a series of actions molded into a smooth and efficient performance. Typing, walking, pole-vaulting, shooting baskets, playing golf, driving a car, writing, and skiing are all motor skills.

A basketball player may never make exactly the same shot twice in a game. This makes it almost impossible to practice every shot that might occur. How, then, do athletes become skillful? Typically, athletic performances involve learning *motor programs.* A **motor program** is a mental plan or model of what a skilled movement should be like. Motor programs allow an athlete—or a person simply walking across a room—to perform complex movements that fit changing conditions. If, for example, you have learned a "bike-riding" motor program, you can easily ride bicycles of different sizes and types on a large variety of surfaces.

Throughout life, you will face the challenge of learning new motor skills. How can psychology make your learning more effective? Studies of sports skills suggest that you should keep the following points in mind for optimal skill learning (Karageorgis & Terry, 2011; Williams, 2010):

1. Begin by observing and imitating a *skilled model.* Modeling provides a good mental picture of the skill. At this point, try simply to grasp a visual image of the skilled movement.
2. Learn *verbal rules* to back up motor learning. Such rules are usually most helpful in the early phases of skill learning. When first learning cross-country skiing, for example, it is helpful to say, "left arm, right foot, right arm, left foot." Later, as a skill becomes more automated, internal speech may actually get in the way.
3. Practice should be as *lifelike* as possible, so artificial cues and responses do not become a part of the skill. A competitive diver should practice on the board, not on a trampoline. If you want to learn to ski, try to practice on snow, not straw.

Sports psychology The study of the psychological and behavioral dimensions of sports performance.

Task analysis Breaking complex skills into their subparts.

Motor skill A series of actions molded into a smooth and efficient performance.

Motor program A mental plan or model that guides skilled movement.

4. Get *feedback* from a mirror, videotape, coach, or observer. Whenever possible, get someone experienced in the skill to direct attention to *correct responses* when they occur.
5. When possible, it is better to practice *natural units* rather than breaking the task into artificial parts. When learning to type, it is better to start with real words rather than nonsense syllables.

The last point leads to one more suggestion. Research has shown that **mental practice**, or merely imagining a skilled performance, can aid learning. This technique seems to help by refining motor programs. Although mental practice is not superior to actual practice, it can be a powerful adjunct to actual practice (Caliari, 2008; Frank, Land, & Schack, 2016; Smith & Wakefield, 2016).

The Whole Human: Peak Performance

One of the most interesting topics in sports psychology is the phenomenon of *peak performance*. During **peak performance**, physical, mental, and emotional states are harmonious and optimal (Bourne & Healy, 2014). Many athletes report episodes during which they felt almost as if they were in a trance. The experience also has been called *flow* because the athlete becomes one with his or her performance and flows with it. At such times, athletes experience intense concentration, detachment, a lack of fatigue and pain, a subjective slowing of time, and feelings of unusual power and control (Dietrich & Stoll, 2010; Hartley, 2012). It is at just such times that "personal bests" tend to occur.

A curious aspect of flow is that it cannot be forced to happen. In fact, if a person stops to think about it, the flow state goes away. Psychologists are now seeking to identify conditions that facilitate peak performance and the unusual mental state that usually accompanies it (Harmison, 2011).

Even though flow may be an elusive state, there is much that athletes and coaches can do mentally to improve performance (Rijken et al., 2016; Williams, 2010). A starting point is to make sure that their arousal level is *appropriate* for the task at hand. For a sprinter at a track meet, that may mean elevating arousal to a very high level. For example, the sprinter could try to become angry by picturing a rival cheating. For a golfer or a gymnast, lowering arousal may be crucial, in order to avoid "choking" during a big event. One way of controlling arousal is to go through a *fixed routine* before each game or event. Athletes also learn to use *imagery and relaxation techniques* to adjust their degree of arousal (LeUnes, 2008). (Many of the mental strategies developed by sports psychologists are an extension of stress inoculation techniques. See Module 59.)

Imaging techniques can be used to *focus attention* on the athlete's task and to *mentally rehearse* it beforehand (Gould et al., 2014). For example, golf great Jack Nicklaus "watches a movie" in his head before each shot. During events, athletes learn to *use cognitive-behavioral strategies to guide their efforts* in a supportive, positive way (Johnson et al., 2004). For instance, instead of berating herself for being behind in a match, a soccer player could use the time between points to savor a good shot or put an error out of her mind. In general, athletes benefit from avoiding negative, self-critical thoughts that distract them and undermine their confidence (Cox, 2012). Finally, top athletes tend to use more *self-regulation strategies,* in which they evaluate their performance and make adjustments to keep it at optimum levels (Edwards & Polman, 2012; Puente & Anshel, 2010).

At present, sports psychology is a young field and still much more an art than a science. Nevertheless, interest in the field is rapidly expanding.

A Look Ahead

Although we have sampled several major areas of applied psychology, by no means are they the only applied specialties. Others that immediately come to mind are military psychology and human factors psychology. The upcoming *Psychologist's Skill Set* module revisits the world of I/O psychology to ask, "What steps can be taken to prepare for postgraduate training or a job search?"

Mental practice Imagining a skilled performance to aid learning.

Peak performance A performance during which physical, mental, and emotional states are harmonious and optimal.

MODULE 77

The Psychology of Law, Community Psychology, and Sports Psychology—Learning Outcomes Revisited

77.1 Define the psychology of law, scientific jury selection, and death-qualified juries

The psychology of law includes studies of courtroom behavior and other topics that pertain to the legal system. Psychologists also serve various consulting and counseling roles in legal, law enforcement, and criminal justice settings. Studies of mock juries show that jury decisions are often far from objective. Scientific jury selection is used in attempts to choose jurors who have particular characteristics. In some instances, this may result in juries that have a particular bias or that do not represent the community as a whole. A bias toward convicting defendants is characteristic of many death-qualified juries.

77.2 Discuss how community psychology can improve communities

Community psychology focuses on communities rather than individuals, focusing on the health of groups like organizations, neighborhoods, and societies. Community psychologists go beyond social factors, emphasizing the cultural, economic, environmental, and political forces that shape our health. A community psychology approach to health empowers people to bring about the changes that they want to see, rather than waiting for experts to step in and help. Community psychology emphasizes the need to be proactive in preventing health problems rather than trying to manage them after-the-fact.

77.3 Define sports psychology, task analysis, motor skills, and peak performance

Sports psychologists seek to enhance sports performance and the benefits of sports participation. A task analysis of sports skills is a major tool for improving coaching and performance. A motor skill is a nonverbal response chain assembled into a smooth performance. Motor skills are guided by internal mental models called motor programs. Motor skills are refined through direct practice, but mental practice also can contribute to improvement. During moments of peak performance, physical, mental, and emotional states are optimal. Top performers in sports often use a variety of self-regulation strategies to focus their attention and maintain optimal levels of arousal.

Reflective Practice

Content Check

1. Despite their many limitations, one thing that jurors are good at is setting aside inadmissible evidence. T or F?
2. Which of the following is *not* commonly used by psychologists to aid jury selection?
   a. mock testimony
   b. information networks
   c. community surveys
   d. demographic data
3. Community psychology emphasizes the importance of economic, environmental, and political forces in relation to our health. T or F?
4. Rather than relying on experts, community psychologists emphasize the importance of empowering ________________ to bring about change.
5. Community psychologists stress the importance of being reactive rather than proactive. T or F?
6. The flow experience is closely linked with instances of __________ performance.

Skill Check

Think Critically

7. When an athlete follows a set routine before an event, what source of stress has she or he eliminated?

Self-Reflect

What advice would you give a person who is about to serve on a jury if she or he wants to render an impartial decision? One major health issue in the United States is childhood obesity. How might a community psychologist approach this problem? How could you apply the concepts of task analysis, mental practice, and peak performance to a sport in which you are interested?

ANSWERS

1. F 2. b 3. T 4. people 5. F 6. peak 7. As discussed in Module 56, stress is reduced when a person feels in control of a situation. Following a routine helps athletes maintain a sense of order and control so that they are not excessively aroused when the time comes to perform.

MODULE 78

A Psychologist's Skill Set

Career Preparation

Next Steps

If you've been reading this textbook as a first-year student, chances are that the end of your degree still seems a long way off, and worrying about securing a job is probably the last thing on your mind. The reality, though, is that it's never too early to start preparing for the steps that will follow graduation. Whether you think you will pursue additional education or look for work, it's often the case that your degree is only one of the things that will be of interest to the people evaluating your application. Many employers are interested in hiring people with relevant experience, even for entry-level jobs: They want to know that you have the *skills* that are needed to be successful, as well as a good understanding of the facts and theories that have been presented in your textbooks. The same is often true for postgraduate programs, where skills such as communication, critical thinking, and the ability to work with others are essential. As a result, it's important to start thinking in advance about building your skill set so that you will be in a strong position to be competitive with your applications, and to distinguish yourself from others. What's the best way to do this? Read on and we'll give you a roadmap to direct those next steps.

Rawpixel.com/Shutterstock.com

~LEARNING OUTCOMES~

After reading this module you should be able to:

78.1 Outline the steps you can take to prepare for postgraduate training or a job search

Where Are You Going—More School or Work?

Learning Outcome 78.1 Outline the steps you can take to prepare for postgraduate training or a job search

There are a number of things that you can do while you're at college that will assist you in making an informed decision about a career path that you'll find rewarding. Below we provide a number of suggestions for getting you started. Because the process of building the skills that you'll need can be time consuming, we can't emphasize enough the importance of starting early.

Investigate Potential Career Paths Now

At this stage of your search, you should definitely make use of on-campus resources such as a career services office, but the Internet can also be a rich source of information about potential jobs. Some of the following sites are useful, though not all of them are exclusively for psychology majors:

- careersinpsychology.org
- apa.org/action/careers
- onetonline.org
- insidecareerinfo.com

As you review information about potential careers, some questions that you should be asking yourself include:

- What does a typical day look like? What are the main tasks that would occupy your time? Ask yourself whether the job looks like it will be a good fit for you in terms of your interests, values, and personality.
- What qualifications are needed for this job? Where can these be obtained, how long will it take, and how much is it likely to cost? Are internships available?
- What is the demand like for this particular career—will there be many jobs available when you finish your education? And is the demand greater in some areas of the country than others?
- What kind of compensation can you expect? Are there working conditions (e.g., weekend work, extensive travel) that you should be aware of? It's important to get a clear sense of whether this job will provide you with the kind of lifestyle that you'd like to have.

You can learn a great deal about particular jobs by searching career-relevant websites, but another way to gather information is to engage in *informational interviews*. Informational interviews are very different from a typical employment interview because their sole purpose is not to land you a job but rather to allow you to gather job-related information from someone who is currently employed in a field that's of interest to you (Fiske, 2015). Typically, you would make contact with this person via email and set up a time to speak to them for a maximum of 20 to 30 minutes (either in person, on the phone, or via Skype).

While it's not a formal interview for a job, you should nevertheless carry yourself in a very professional way during an informational interview: Email correspondence should have a formal, businesslike tone and be free of errors. Write out and rehearse your questions about the job ahead of time, and dress professionally. Use your time efficiently, and do not go over the agreed-upon amount of time. And don't forget that afterward, it's always a good idea to follow up with a note of thanks (Hettich & Landrum, 2014).

Find Out About Necessary Skills

We've discussed several career-related skills in the *Psychologist's Skill Set* modules of this book. One helpful way of organizing these skills in your mind is to think about them in terms of Five Cs:

- *Communication* obviously includes your oral and written skills (see Module 22). But don't forget that nonverbal communication is also important. People who are skilled at nonverbal communication are very aware of their own body language and tone of voice, and how those things may be interpreted by the people around them. They are also sensitive to the nonverbal cues of others, "reading" signals that might indicate someone is upset, bored, confused, or enthusiastic. In this respect, nonverbal communication is closely linked to emotional intelligence.
- *Critical thinking* skills are wide ranging, and include recognizing problems, evaluating the value and reliability of information (information literacy), and developing or assessing potential solutions (see Module 6). Critical thinking also includes the ability to think about issues from multiple points of view, as well as your metacognitive skills. You may recall from Module 26 that metacognition refers to your ability to monitor your own knowledge and performance, and to recognize when you might need additional information, or when you might need to change your strategy to accomplish a goal.
- *Collaboration* skills are those that relate to your ability to work with others. They include broad skills such as teamwork and leadership skills (see Modules 54 and 74), but as we mentioned in those modules, strong teamwork and leadership abilities depend on a host of other skills, such as integrity, communication, and the ability to work with diverse others (see Modules 16, 22, and 49).
- *Creativity* is an important skill set in many jobs, even those that are not closely connected to the arts. Because creativity is so closely linked to innovation and problem solving (see Module 41), it is highly valued by employers in many different fields.
- *Character* is a broad category of skills that include a number of personal characteristics that are important for both your personal and professional life. We have discussed a number of them in the Skills in Action modules, including self-regulation and self-management, the ability to work with diverse others, and ethics and integrity.

Assess Your Current Skill Set and Your Characteristics

Once you have established what skills you are likely to need for your chosen career path, it's a good idea to do an assessment of your own skills and consider where the gaps are in relation to what's needed. Many tools are available online and through most campus career services centers. Remember that if you rate yourself as being high on a particular skill, you should be able to back up your evaluation with experiences you've had that have allowed you to develop it (Cook, 2013). Students are often inclined to think about their work-related experiences when they think about skill development, but don't forget that course-based assignments and activities can also be valuable. For example, giving presentations or writing papers that have been favorably evaluated by your instructors could be used as evidence of your communication abilities.

Aside from your skills, you should also consider evaluating aspects of your character that are likely to have an influence on your satisfaction with a particular career path (Bolles, 2016). Your values and personality traits are important here, as are the kinds of people whose company you enjoy. The surroundings in which you feel happiest are also important to consider. For example, are you most comfortable working in an organized, structured environment? How do you feel about a high degree of supervision? What about noise level? Flexible hours?

Many students underestimate the importance of these elements of the working environment, focusing instead on issues such as salary and vacation time. However, working with people that you do not like or under conditions that you find challenging will almost certainly make you very unhappy over the long term. When considering potential career paths, then, always think carefully about how well the job will fit with what you know about yourself, and the lifestyle that you hope to have.

Work to Develop Necessary Skills

If there are skills that you feel you will eventually need, but on which you consider yourself to be weak, ask yourself what experiences you could engage in that would help you to build these skills. Consider the possibilities presented by relevant community work and volunteer experiences, as well as opportunities that may be connected to course credit (e.g., service-learning courses and study abroad programs). Getting involved in extracurricular activities such as sports teams, campus clubs, and student government may also provide a solid foundation for the development of a variety of skills.

Document Key Learning Experiences

Because you'll do many interesting things during the course of your degree, it's important that you begin to record your key learning experiences, and how each one has developed your skills and contributed to your personal growth. You can keep track of them in a career-related journal, or you can document your experiences and skills more formally in a **portfolio**.

While portfolios used to resemble a large scrapbook with printed examples of people's accomplishments and work, they are now increasingly created in a digital format. These newer **e-portfolios** can showcase examples of your work as well as relevant photos, videos, and links to websites (Light, Chen, & Ittelson, 2012). One of the most common e-portfolio platforms is LinkedIn, a professional networking website that is increasingly used by employers to recruit new talent. Users create profiles and build professional connections by following the online activities of other users and companies. Pathbrite (pathbrite.com) is another excellent tool for creating an e-portfolio that can be sent to prospective employers along with your resume.

Examine Your Digital Footprint

Aside from providing you with an additional tool to market yourself to prospective employers, e-portfolios also have another benefit: They can help you to begin the process of creating a professional *digital footprint*. The term digital footprint refers to all of the information that is available about you on the Internet. Do you know what you would find if you typed your name and some basic information about yourself (e.g., your college and the city where you live) into a search engine? For many students, such a search would primarily reveal their participation in social media sites such as Facebook, Twitter, Snapchat, and Instagram. Now ask yourself whether you'd be happy for potential employers to find that information when they carried out this type of online search.

One firm reported that in a study of 275 human resources professionals, more than 75% indicated that they actively research potential candidates online. Perhaps more relevant is the fact that of those who carried out Internet-based searches, approximately 70% decided *not* to hire someone based on what they found on the web (Cross-Tab, 2010). The moral of the story? Take care to manage your digital footprint, and if you are concerned about any of the hits that are revealed in a Google search about you, then remove those pages and work toward replacing them with web-based content that's more in keeping with what you'd like an employer to see.

We realize that the prospect of moving into the world of work is likely to be a bit intimidating for many students. However, if you start early and take a bit of time during your degree to do some job-based research and planning, you'll put yourself in a strong position to secure an interesting and satisfying career after you graduate. Good Luck!

Portfolio A collection of printed examples of a person's accomplishments and work.

e-Portfolio A digital, rather than hardcopy, portfolio.

MODULE 78 Career Preparation— Learning Outcomes Revisited

78.1 Outline the steps you can take to prepare for postgraduate training or a job search

Begin the process of researching careers early in your degree, making use of resources such as your campus career services office, career-related sites on the Internet, and informational interviewing. Determine the skills that are necessary for jobs that interest you and assess yourself on these skills. If you believe that you need to develop any of them further to make yourself competitive, consider what types of experiences would help you to do so. Begin to build a portfolio or e-portfolio. Manage your digital footprint carefully. Remove any web-based material about you that you would not want a potential employer to find, and work to create digital content that is professional (e.g., LinkedIn profile, e-portfolio).

Reflective Practice

Content Check

1. It's helpful to begin thinking about a potential career early, since developing the necessary skills may take time. T or F?
2. Informational interviews are often used to secure a job in a field of interest to you. T or F?
3. Which of the following is *not* one of the skills included in the Five Cs?
   a. communication
   b. creativity
   c. cheerfulness
   d. critical thinking
   e. character
4. It is important to manage your digital footprint carefully because employers are increasingly likely to search for you online to gather information about you. T or F?

Skill Check

Think Critically

5. Leadership is a skill that employers often value, but that is difficult to develop in a college classroom or through coursework. What are some activities that you can engage in during your college years that might help you to develop your leadership abilities?

Self-Reflect

What skills do you think you are most likely to need in the career you're planning to pursue? What kinds of personality characteristics are likely to be relevant if you want to work in that field?

ANSWERS

1. T 2. F 3. c 4. T 5. Leadership skills can often be developed through volunteer or service-learning experiences (e.g., helping to organize a fundraiser for a community-based organization). On-campus activities can also be helpful in developing these skills (e.g., taking on a leadership role in a club or student government). Finally, if the type of leadership that is relevant to your career goals involves mentoring, then consider how you might get involved in an organization that promotes activities of this kind (e.g., working at a kid's camp or coaching a team; working for an organization such as Big Brothers/Big Sisters). (For more on leadership skills, see Module 54.)

MODULE 79

A Psychologist's Skill Set

Appendix: Behavioral Statistics

A Stretch for Samantha and Grandma

GWImages/Shutterstock.com

Samantha almost decided to avoid majoring in psychology when she found out she needed to take a statistics course to graduate. "I want to work with people, not numbers," she insisted to anyone who would listen. But her attitude started to change as she began to get more involved in a research project exploring the effect of stretching exercises on the quality of sleep in older people. After all, her beloved grandma was troubled by insomnia, and Samantha hoped to use what she learned from her research to advise elders how to get a better night's sleep.

Thankfully, Samantha's curiosity about exercise and the quality of sleep in older people, in particular, and human behavior in general, was stronger than her fear of statistics. By the time she got to her third year and began to design research projects and collect data, she understood that the results of psychological studies are often expressed as numbers, which psychologists must summarize and interpret before they have any meaning. Let's follow Samantha to get an overview of how statistics are used in psychology.

~LEARNING OUTCOMES~

After reading this module you should be able to:

79.1 Define some basic descriptive statistics, convert raw data into frequency distributions, and graph the data as histograms or polygons

79.2 Define and calculate these measures of central tendency: mean, median, mode

79.3 Define and calculate these measures of variability: range, normal curve, standard deviation, standard score

79.4 Discuss the use of correlations in psychology, including scatter diagrams, correlation coefficients, prediction, and correlation vs. causality

79.5 Discuss inferential statistics, including samples, populations, and statistical significance

Descriptive Statistics—Psychology by the Numbers

Learning Outcome 79.1 Define some basic descriptive statistics, convert raw data into frequency distributions, and graph the data as histograms or polygons

Statistics bring greater clarity and precision to psychological thought and research (Gravetter, Wallnau, & Forzano, 2021). In fact, it is difficult to make scientific arguments about human behavior without depending on statistics. Psychologists depend on two major types of statistics. **Descriptive statistics** summarize or "boil down" data collected from research participants so the results become more meaningful and easier to communicate to others. In comparison, **inferential statistics** are used for extending experimental conclusions from samples to larger populations. Psychologists must often base decisions on limited data. Such decisions are much easier to make with the help of inferential statistics.

Let's begin with a look at three basic types of descriptive statistics: *graphical statistics,* measures of *central tendency,* and measures of *variability.*

Graphical Statistics

Graphical statistics present numbers pictorially, so they are easier to visualize. At one point, Samantha got a chance to administer a short questionnaire to measure sleep quality in a group of elderly retirees. She planned to eventually use the scores from this questionnaire to select participants with poor sleep quality for further study. ■ **Table 79.1** shows the sleep quality scores she obtained from 100 retirees.

With such disorganized data, it is hard to form an overall picture of the differences in sleep quality. But by using a *frequency distribution,* large amounts of information can be neatly organized and summarized. A **frequency distribution** is made by breaking down the entire range of possible scores into classes of equal size. Next, the number of scores falling into each class is recorded. In ■ **Table 79.2**, Samantha's raw data from Table 79.1 have been condensed into a frequency distribution. Notice how much clearer the pattern of sleep quality scores for the entire group becomes.

Frequency distributions are often shown *graphically* to make them more "visual." A **frequency histogram**, or graph of a frequency distribution, is made by labeling class intervals on the *abscissa* (x-axis, or horizontal line) and frequencies (the number of scores in each class) on the *ordinate* (y-axis, or vertical line). Next, bars are drawn for each class interval; the height of each bar is determined by the number of scores in each class (➤ **Figure 79.1**). An alternative way of graphing scores is the more familiar **frequency polygon** (➤ **Figure 79.2**). Here, points are placed at the center of each class interval to indicate the number of scores. Then the dots are connected by straight lines.

TABLE 79.1 | Raw Sleep Quality Scores

55	86	52	17	61	57	84	51	16	64
22	56	25	38	35	24	54	26	37	38
52	42	59	26	21	55	40	59	25	57
91	27	38	53	19	93	25	39	52	56
66	14	18	63	59	68	12	19	62	45
47	98	88	72	50	49	96	89	71	66
50	44	71	57	90	53	41	72	56	93
57	38	55	49	87	59	36	56	48	70
33	69	50	50	60	35	67	51	50	52
11	73	46	16	67	13	71	47	25	77

TABLE 79.2 | Frequency Distribution of Sleep Quality Scores

Class Interval	Number of Elders
0–19	10
20–39	20
40–59	40
60–79	20
80–99	10

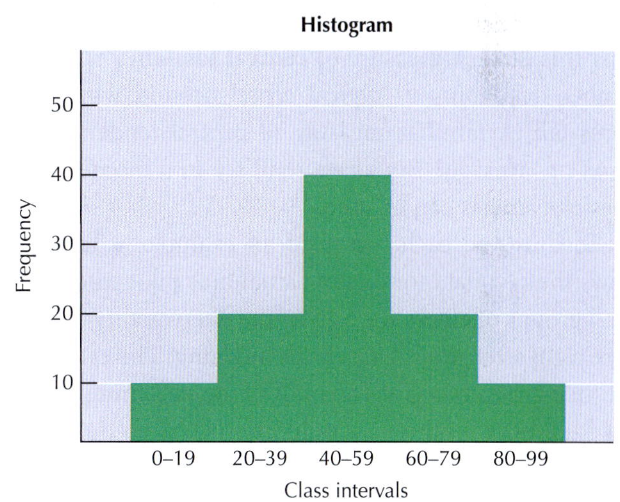

➤ **Figure 79.1**

Frequency histogram. A frequency histogram of the sleep quality scores contained in Table 79.2.

Descriptive statistics Mathematical techniques used to describe and summarize numeric data.

Inferential statistics Mathematical method for extending experimental conclusions from samples to larger populations.

Graphical statistics Techniques for presenting numbers pictorially, often by plotting them on a graph.

Frequency distribution A table that divides an entire range of scores into a series of classes and then records the number of scores that fall into each class.

Frequency histogram A graph of a frequency distribution in which the number of scores falling in each class is represented by vertical bars.

Frequency polygon A graph of a frequency distribution in which the number of scores falling in each class is represented by points on a line.

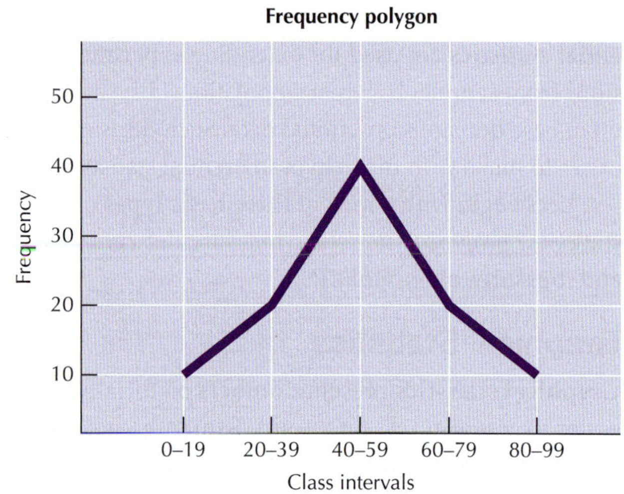

Figure 79.2

Frequency polygon. A frequency polygon of the sleep quality scores contained in Table 79.2.

Measures of Central Tendency—In the Middle

Learning Outcome 79.2 Define and calculate these measures of central tendency: mean, median, mode

Notice in Table 79.2 that more of Samantha's sleep quality scores fall in the range 40–59 than elsewhere. How can we show this fact? A measure of **central tendency** is simply a number describing a "typical score" around which other scores fall. A familiar measure of central tendency is the *mean,* or "average." But as we shall see in a moment, other types of averages can be used.

To illustrate each, we need an example: ■ **Table 79.3** shows the raw data for one of Samantha's pilot studies. Two small groups of elders were given the sleep quality questionnaire right after waking up in the morning. The evening before, one group was given an hour of the stretching exercises that Samantha predicted should improve sleep quality. The second group watched television for an hour. Is there a difference in concentration scores between the two groups? It's difficult to tell without computing an average.

The Mean As one type of "average," the **mean** is calculated by adding all the scores for each group and then dividing by the total number of scores. Notice in Table 79.3 that the means reveal a difference between the two groups.

The mean is sensitive to extremely high or low scores in a distribution. For this reason, it is not always the best measure of central tendency. (Imagine how distorted it would be to calculate average yearly incomes from a small sample of people that happened to include a billionaire, such as Oprah Winfrey.) In such cases, the middle score in a group of scores—called the *median*—is used instead.

The Median The **median** is found by arranging scores from highest to lowest and then selecting the score that falls in the middle. In other words, half the values in a group of scores fall below the median and half fall above it. Consider, for example, the following weights obtained from a small class of college students: 105, 111, 123, 126, 148, 151, 154, 162, 182. The median for the group is 148, the middle score. Of course, if there is an even number of scores, there will be no middle score. This problem is handled by averaging the two scores that "share" the middle spot. This procedure yields a single number to serve as the median. (See the bottom panel of Table 79.3.)

The Mode A final measure of central tendency is the **mode**, which is simply the most frequently occurring score in a group of scores. If you were to take the time to count the scores in Table 79.3, you would find that the mode of Group 1 is 65 and the mode of Group 2 is 60. Although the mode is usually easy to obtain, it can be an unreliable measure, especially in a small group of scores. The mode's advantage is that it gives the score actually obtained by the greatest number of people.

Measures of Variability—Differences 'R Us

Learning Outcome 79.3 Define and calculate these measures of variability: range, normal curve, standard deviation, standard score

Let's say that a researcher discovers two drugs that lower anxiety in agitated patients. However, let's also assume that one drug consistently lowers anxiety by moderate

TABLE 79.3 | Raw Sleep Quality Scores After Sleep Preceded by Engaged in Stretching Exercises or Watching Television

Participant	Group 1 Stretches	Group 2 Television
1	65	54
2	67	60
3	73	63
4	65	33
5	58	56
6	55	60
7	70	60
8	69	31
9	60	62
10	68	61
Sum	650	540
Mean	65	54
Median	66	60

$$\text{Mean} = \frac{\Sigma X}{N} \text{ or } \frac{\text{sum of all scores, } X}{\text{number of scores}}$$

$$\text{Mean Group 1} = \frac{65 + 67 + 73 + 65 + 58 + 55 + 70 + 69 + 60 + 68}{10} = \frac{650}{10} = 65$$

$$\text{Mean Group 2} = \frac{54 + 60 + 63 + 33 + 56 + 60 + 60 + 31 + 62 + 61}{10} = \frac{540}{10} = 54$$

Median = the middle score or the mean of the two middle scores*

$$\text{Median Group 1} = 55\ 58\ 60\ 65\ \boxed{65\ 67}\ 68\ 69\ 70\ 73 = \frac{65 + 67}{2} = 66$$

$$\text{Median Group 2} = 31\ 33\ 54\ 56\ \boxed{60\ 60}\ 60\ 61\ 62\ 63 = \frac{60 + 60}{2} = 60$$

* $\boxed{\quad}$ Indicates middle score(s).

amounts, whereas the second sometimes lowers it by large amounts, sometimes has no effect, or may even increase anxiety in some patients. Overall, there is no difference in the *average* (mean) amount of anxiety reduction. Even so, an important difference exists between the two drugs. As this example shows, it is not enough to simply know the average score in a distribution. Usually, we would also want to know if scores are grouped closely together or scattered widely.

Measures of **variability** provide a single number that tells how "spread out" scores are. When the scores are widely spread, this number gets larger. When they are close together, it gets smaller. If you look again at the example in Table 79.3, you will notice that the scores within each group vary widely. How can we show this fact?

The Range The simplest way would be to use the **range**, which is the difference between the highest and lowest scores. In Group 1 of our study, the highest score is 73, and the lowest is 55; thus, the range is 18 (73 − 55 = 18). In Group 2, the highest score is 63, and the lowest is 31; this makes the range 32. Scores in Group 2 are more spread out (are more variable) than those in Group 1.

The Standard Deviation A better measure of variability is the **standard deviation (SD)**—an index of how much a typical score differs from the mean of a group of scores. To obtain the SD, we find the deviation (or difference) of each score from the mean and then square it (multiply it by itself). These squared deviations are then added and averaged (the total is divided by the number of deviations). Taking the square root of this average yields the SD (■ **Table 79.4**). Notice again that the variability for Group 1 (5.4) is less than that for Group 2 (where the SD is 11.3).

Central tendency The tendency for a majority of scores to fall in the midrange of possible values.

Mean A measure of central tendency calculated by adding a group of scores and then dividing by the total number of scores.

Median A measure of central tendency found by arranging scores from the highest to the lowest and selecting the score that falls in the middle—that is, half the values in a group of scores fall above the median and half fall below it.

Mode A measure of central tendency found by identifying the most frequently occurring score in a group of scores.

Variability The tendency for a group of scores to differ in value. Measures of variability indicate the degree to which a group of scores differs from one another.

Range The difference between the highest and lowest scores in a group of scores.

Standard deviation A statistical index of how much a typical score differs from the mean of a group of scores.

TABLE 79.4 | Computation of the SD

Group 1 Mean = 65		
Score Mean	Deviation (d)	Deviation Squared (d^2)
65 − 65 =	0	0
67 − 65 =	2	4
73 − 65 =	8	64
65 − 65 =	0	0
58 − 65 =	−7	49
55 − 65 =	−10	100
70 − 65 =	5	25
69 − 65 =	4	16
60 − 65 =	−5	25
68 − 65 =	3	9
		292

$$SD = \sqrt{\frac{\text{sum of } d^2}{n}} = \sqrt{\frac{292}{10}} = \sqrt{29.2} = 5.4$$

Group 2 Mean = 54		
Score Mean	Deviation (d)	Deviation Squared (d^2)
54 − 54 =	0	0
60 − 54 =	6	36
63 − 54 =	9	81
33 − 54 =	−21	441
56 − 54 =	2	4
60 − 54 =	6	36
60 − 54 =	6	36
31 − 54 =	−23	529
62 − 54 =	8	64
61 − 54 =	7	49
		1276

$$SD = \sqrt{\frac{\text{sum of } d^2}{n}} = \sqrt{\frac{1276}{10}} = \sqrt{127.6} = 11.3$$

Standard Scores

A particular advantage of the SD is that it can be used to "standardize" scores in a way that gives them greater meaning. For example, Samantha and her classmate, Rahul, both took psychology midterms, but in different classes. Samantha earned a score of 118, and Rahul scored 110. Who did better? It is impossible to tell for sure without knowing what the average score was on each test and whether Samantha and Rahul scored at the top, middle, or bottom of their classes. We would like to have one number that gives all this information. A number that does this is the *z-score.*

To convert an original score to a **z-score**, we subtract the mean from the score. The resulting number is then divided by the SD for that group of scores. To illustrate, Rahul had a score of 110 in a class with a mean of 100 and an SD of 10. Therefore, his z-score is +1.0 (■ **Table 79.5**). Samantha's score of 118 came from a class having a mean of 100 and an SD of 18; thus, her z-score is also +1.0 (see Table 79.5). Originally, it looked as if Samantha did better on her midterm than Rahul. But we now see that, relatively speaking, their scores were equivalent. Compared with other students, each was an equal distance above average.

TABLE 79.5 | Computation of a z-score

$$Z = \frac{X - \overline{X}}{SD} = \text{or } \frac{\text{score} - \text{mean}}{\text{standard deviation}}$$

$$\textbf{Rahul: } Z = \frac{110 - 100}{10} = \frac{+10}{10} = +1.0$$

$$\textbf{Samantha: } Z = \frac{118 - 100}{18} = \frac{+18}{18} = +1.0$$

The Normal Curve

When chance events are recorded, we find that some outcomes have a high probability and occur very often, others have a lower probability and occur infrequently, and still others have little probability and occur rarely. As a result, the distribution (or tally) of chance events typically resembles a *normal curve* (➤ **Figure 79.3**). A **normal curve** is bell-shaped, with a large number of scores in the middle, tapering to very few extremely high and low scores. Most psychological traits or events are determined by the action of a large number of factors. Therefore, like chance events, measures of psychological variables tend to roughly match a normal curve. For example, direct measurement has shown such characteristics as height, memory span, and intelligence to be distributed approximately along a normal curve. In other words, many people have average height, memory ability, and intelligence. However, as we move above or below average, fewer and fewer people are found.

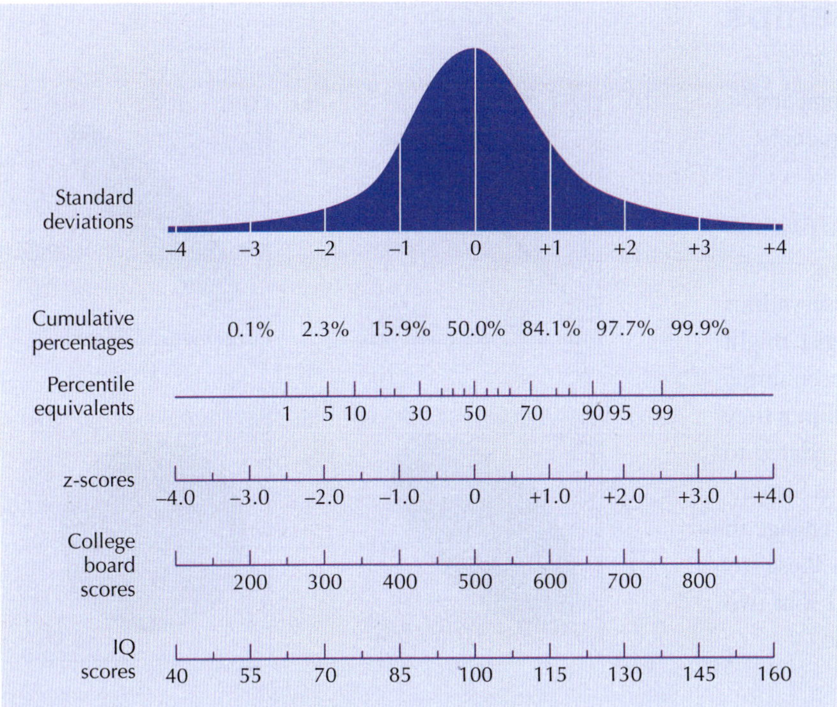

Figure 79.3

The normal curve. The normal curve is an idealized mathematical model. However, many measurements in psychology closely approximate a normal curve. The scales shown here show the relationship of SDs, z-scores, and other measures to the curve.

It is fortunate that so many psychological variables tend to form a normal curve because much is known about the curve. One valuable property concerns the relationship between the SD and the normal curve. Specifically, the SD measures offset proportions of the curve above and below the mean. For example, in Figure 79.3, notice that roughly 68 percent of all cases (84.1 – 15.9 = 68.2) fall between one SD above and below the mean (±1 SD); 95 percent of all cases fall between ±2 SD; and 99 percent of the cases can be found within ±3 SD from the mean. This is generally true whether we're talking about IQ scores, memory scores, heights, or whatever.

TABLE 79.6 | Computation of a z-score

z-Score	Percentage of Area to the Left of This Value	Percentage of Area to the Right of This Value
−3.0 SD	00.1	99.9
−2.5 SD	00.6	99.4
−2.0 SD	02.3	97.7
−1.5 SD	06.7	93.3
−1.0 SD	15.9	84.1
−0.5 SD	30.9	69.1
0.0 SD	50.0	50.0
+0.5 SD	69.1	30.9
+1.0 SD	84.1	15.9
+1.5 SD	93.3	06.7
+2.0 SD	97.7	02.3
+2.5 SD	99.4	00.6
+3.0 SD	99.9	00.1

■ **Table 79.6** gives a more complete account of the relationship between z-scores and the percentage of cases found in a particular area of the normal curve. Notice, for example, that 93.3 percent of all cases fall below a z-score of +1.5. A z-score of 1.5 on a test (no matter what the original, or "raw," score was) would be a good performance because roughly 93 percent of all scores fall below this mark. Relationships between the SD (or z-scores) and the normal curve do not change. This makes it possible to compare various tests or groups of scores if they come from distributions that are approximately normal.

z-score A number that tells how many standard deviations above or below the mean a score is.

Normal curve A bell-shaped distribution, with a large number of scores in the middle, tapering to very few extremely high and low scores.

Correlation—Rating Relationships

Learning Outcome 79.4 Discuss the use of correlations in psychology, including scatter diagrams, correlation coefficients, prediction, and correlation vs. causality

As we noted in Module 5, many of the statements that psychologists make about behavior do not result from using experimental methods. Rather, they come from keen observations and measures of existing phenomena. A psychologist might note, for example, that the higher a couple's socioeconomic and educational status, the smaller the number of children they are likely to have. Or that grades in high school are related to how well a person is likely to do in college. Or even, as Samantha found, that elders with poor sleep quality who engage in stretching exercises are also better able to sleep. In these instances, we are dealing with a **correlation**—the fact that two variables are varying together in some orderly fashion.

Relationships

Psychologists are very interested in detecting relationships between events: Are children from single-parent families more likely to misbehave at school? Is wealth related to happiness? Is there a relationship between childhood exposure to the Internet and IQ at age 20? Is the chance of having a heart attack related to having a hostile personality? All of these questions are about correlation (Jackson, 2017).

The simplest way of visualizing a correlation is to construct a **scatter diagram**. In a scatter diagram, two measures (grades in high school and grades in college, for instance) are obtained. One measure is indicated by the *x*-axis and the second by the *y*-axis. The scatter diagram plots the intersection (crossing) of each pair of measurements as a single point. Many such measurement pairs give pictures like those shown in ➤ **Figure 79.4**.

Figure 79.4 also shows scatter diagrams of three basic kinds of relationships between variables (or measures):

- **Positive correlation:** Graphs a, b, and c show *positive relationships* of varying strength. As you can see, in a **positive correlation**, increases in the X measure (or score) are matched by increases on the Y measure (or score). An example would be finding that higher IQ scores (X) are associated with higher college grades (Y).
- **Zero correlation:** A **zero correlation** suggests that no relationship exists between two measures (see graph d). This might be the result of comparing participants' hat sizes (X) to their college grades (Y).
- **Negative correlation:** Graphs e and f both show a **negative correlation**. Notice that as values of one measure increase, those of the second become smaller. An example might be the relationship between the amount of alcohol consumed and scores on a test of coordination: Higher alcohol levels are correlated with lower coordination scores.

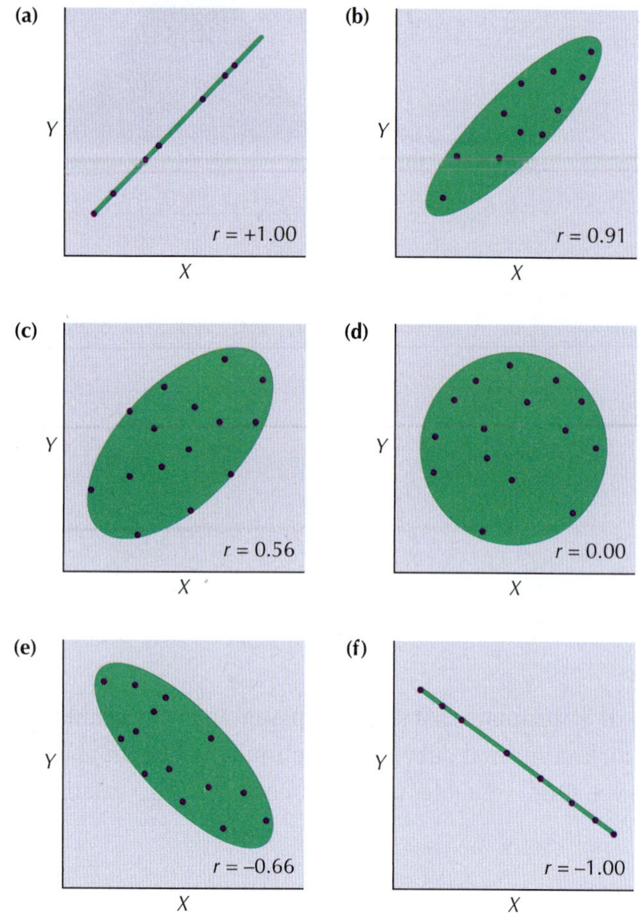

➤ **Figure 79.4**

Scatter diagrams. Scatter diagrams showing various degrees of relationship for a positive, zero, and negative correlation.

The Correlation Coefficient

The strength of a correlation can also be expressed as a **coefficient of correlation**. This coefficient is simply a number falling somewhere between +1.00 and −1.00. If the number is zero or close to zero, it indicates a weak or nonexistent relationship. If the number is +1.00, a **perfect positive correlation** exists; if the number is −1.00, a **perfect negative correlation** has been discovered. The most commonly used correlation coefficient is called the Pearson *r*. Calculation of the Pearson *r* is relatively simple, as shown in ▪ **Table 79.7**. (The numbers shown are hypothetical.)

As stated in Module 5, correlations in psychology are rarely perfect. Most fall somewhere between 0 and ±1. The closer the

TABLE 79.7 | IQ and Grade Point Average for Computing Pearson *r*

Student No.	IQ (*X*)	Grade Point Average (*Y*)	*X* Score Squared (X^2)	*Y* Score Squared (Y^2)	*X* Times *Y* (*XY*)
1	110	1.0	12,100	1.00	110.0
2	112	1.6	12,544	2.56	179.2
3	118	1.2	13,924	1.44	141.6
4	119	2.1	14,161	4.41	249.9
5	122	2.6	14,884	6.76	317.2
6	125	1.8	15,625	3.24	225.0
7	127	2.6	16,124	6.76	330.2
8	130	2.0	16,900	4.00	260.0
9	132	3.2	17,424	10.24	422.4
10	134	2.6	17,956	6.76	348.4
11	136	3.0	18,496	9.00	408.0
12	138	3.6	19,044	12.96	496.8
Total	1503	27.3	189,187	69.13	3488.7

$$r = \frac{\Sigma XY - \dfrac{(\Sigma X)(\Sigma Y)}{N}}{\sqrt{\left[\Sigma X^2 - \dfrac{(\Sigma X)^2}{N}\right]\left[\Sigma Y^2 - \dfrac{(\Sigma Y)^2}{N}\right]}}$$

$$= \frac{3488.7 - \dfrac{1503(27.3)}{12}}{\sqrt{\left[189{,}187 - \dfrac{(1503)^2}{2}\right]\left[69.132\dfrac{(27.3)^2}{12}\right]}}$$

$$= \frac{69.375}{81.088} = 0.856 = 0.86$$

correlation coefficient is to +1.00 or −1.00, the stronger the relationship. An interesting example of some typical correlations is provided by a study that compared the IQs of adopted children with the IQs of their biological mothers. At age 4, the children's IQs correlated at .28 with their biological mothers' IQs. By age 7, the correlation was .35. And by age 13, it had grown to .38. Over time, the IQs of adopted children become more similar to the IQs of their biological mothers.

Correlations often provide highly useful information. For instance, it is valuable to know that there is a correlation between cigarette smoking and lung cancer rates. Another example is the fact that higher consumption of alcohol during pregnancy is correlated with lower birth weight and a higher rate of birth defects. There is a correlation between

Correlation The existence of a consistent, systematic relationship between two events, measures, or variables.

Scatter diagram A graph that plots the intersection of paired measures—that is, the points at which paired *X* and *Y* measures cross.

Positive correlation A mathematical relationship in which increases in one measure are matched by increases in the other (or decreases correspond with decreases).

Zero correlation The absence of a (linear) mathematical relationship between two measures.

Negative correlation A mathematical relationship in which increases in one measure are matched by decreases in the other.

Coefficient of correlation A statistical index ranging from −1.00 to +1.00 that indicates the direction and degree of correlation.

Perfect positive correlation A mathematical relationship in which the correlation between two measures is +1.00.

Perfect negative correlation A mathematical relationship in which the correlation between two measures is −1.00.

the number of recent life stresses experienced and the likelihood of emotional disturbance. Many more examples could be cited, but the point is, correlations help us identify relationships that are worth knowing.

Prediction *But why is that?* Correlations are particularly valuable for making *predictions.* If we know that two measures are correlated and we know a person's score on one measure, we can predict his or her score on the other. For example, most colleges have formulas that use multiple correlations to decide which applicants have the best chances for success. Usually, the formula includes such predictors as high school grade point average (GPA), teacher ratings, extracurricular activities, and scores on the *SAT Reasoning Test* or some similar test. Although no single predictor is perfectly correlated with success in college, the various predictors together correlate highly and provide a useful technique for screening applicants.

There is an interesting "trick" that you can do with correlations that you may find useful. It works like this: If you *square* the correlation coefficient (multiply r by itself), you will get the **percent of variance**, or amount of variation in scores, accounted for by the correlation. For example, the correlation between IQ scores and college grade point average is .5. Multiplying .5 times .5 gives .25, or 25 percent. This means that 25 percent of the variation in college grades is accounted for by knowing IQ scores. In other words, with a correlation of .5, college grades are "squeezed" into an oval, like the one shown in graph C of Figure 79.4. IQ scores take away some of the possible variation in corresponding grade point averages. If no correlation existed between IQ and grades, grades would be completely free to vary, as shown in graph D of Figure 79.4.

Along the same line, a correlation of +1.00 or −1.00 means that 100 percent of the variation in the Y measure is accounted for by knowing the X measure: If you know a person's X score, you can tell exactly what the Y score is. An example that comes close to this state of affairs is the high correlation (.86) between the IQs of identical twins. In any group of identical twins, 74 percent of the variation in the *Y* twins' IQs is accounted for by knowing the IQs of their siblings (the *X* twins).

Squaring correlations to obtain the percent of variance accounted for is a useful tool for interpreting the correlations encountered in the media and the psychological literature. For example, sweeping pronouncements about relationships are occasionally made on the basis of correlations in the .25 to .30 range, even though the values mean that only 6 to 9 percent of the variance is accounted for by the observed correlation. Such correlations may document relationships worth noting, but they are rarely something to get excited about.

Correlation and Causation It is important to reiterate that finding a correlation between two measures does not automatically demonstrate **causation**, that one variable is causing the other. When a correlation exists, the best we can say is that two variables are related. Of course, this does not mean that it is impossible for two correlated variables to have a cause-and-effect relationship. Rather, it means that we cannot *conclude,* solely on the basis of correlation, that a causal link exists. To gain greater confidence that a cause-and-effect relationship exists, an experiment must be performed (as explained in Module 4).

Often, two correlated measures are related as a result of the influence of a third variable. For example, we might observe that the more hours students devote to studying, the better their grades. Although it is tempting to conclude that more studying produces (causes) better grades, it is possible (indeed, it is probable) that grades and the amount of study time are both related to the student's amount of motivation or interest.

The difference between cause-and-effect data and data that reveal a relationship of unknown origin is one that should not be forgotten. Because we rarely run experiments in daily life, the information on which we act is largely correlational. This should make us humbler and more tentative in the confidence with which we make pronouncements about human behavior.

Inferential Statistics—Significant Numbers

Learning Outcome 79.5 Discuss inferential statistics, including samples, populations, and statistical significance

You would like to know whether boys are more aggressive than girls. You observe a group of 5-year-old boys and girls on a playground. After collecting data for a week, you find that the boys committed more aggressive acts than the girls. Could this difference just be a meaningless fluctuation in aggression? Or does it show conclusively that boys are more aggressive than girls? Inferential statistics were created to answer such questions (Gravetter, Wallnau, & Forzano, 2021).

Let's say that a researcher studies the effects of a new therapy on a small group of depressed individuals. Is she or he interested only in these particular individuals? Usually not, because except in rare instances, psychologists seek to discover general laws of behavior that apply widely to humans and animals (Babbie, 2016). Undoubtedly, the researcher would like to know whether the therapy holds any promise for all depressed people. As stated earlier, inferential statistics are techniques that allow us to make inferences—that is, they allow us to generalize from the behavior of small groups of participants to that of the larger groups they represent.

Samples and Populations

In any scientific study, we would prefer to observe the entire set, or **population**, of participants, objects, or events of interest. However, this is usually impossible or impractical. Observing all terrorists, all cancer patients, or all mothers-in-law could be both impractical (because all are large populations) and impossible (because people change political views, may be unaware of having cancer, and change their status as relatives). In such cases, a **sample** (a smaller cross section of a population) is selected, and observations of the sample are used to draw conclusions about the entire population.

For any sample to be meaningful, it must be **representative**—that is, the sample group must truly reflect the membership and characteristics of the larger population. In Samantha's pilot study of sleep quality, it would be essential for the sample of 20 people to be representative of the general population. A very important aspect of representative samples is that their members are chosen by **random selection**. In other words, each member of the population must have an equal chance of being included in the sample.

Significant Differences

In Samantha's sleep quality experiment, she found that the average sleep quality score was higher for the group given the stretching exercises than it was for the one that watched TV. Certainly this result is interesting, but could it have occurred by chance? If two groups were repeatedly tested (with neither receiving any exercise or TV), their average sleep quality scores would sometimes differ. How much must two means differ before we can consider the difference "real" (not due to chance)?

Tests of **statistical significance** provide an estimate of how often experimental results could have occurred by chance alone. The results of a significance test are stated as a probability. This probability gives the odds that the observed difference was due to chance. In psychology, any experimental result that could have occurred by chance 5 times (or less) out of 100 (in other words, a probability of .05 or less) is considered *significant.* In Samantha's sleep quality and exercise experiment, the probability turned out to be .025 ($p = .025$) that the group means would differ as much as they did by chance alone. This allows Samantha to conclude with reasonable certainty that the exercise actually did improve sleep quality scores.

Percent of variance A portion of the total amount of variation in a group of scores.

Causation The act of causing some effect.

Population An entire group of animals, people, or objects belonging to a particular category (for example, all college students or all married women).

Sample A smaller subpart of a population.

Representative sample A small, randomly selected part of a larger population that accurately reflects characteristics of the whole population.

Random selection Choosing a sample so that each member of the population has an equal chance of being included in the sample.

Statistical significance The degree to which an event (such as the results of an experiment) is unlikely to have occurred by chance alone.

MODULE 79 Appendix: Behavioral Statistics—Learning Outcomes Revisited

79.1 Define some basic descriptive statistics, convert raw data into frequency distributions, and graph the data as histograms or polygons

Descriptive statistics organize and summarize numbers. Summarizing numbers visually, by using various types of graphs such as frequency histograms and polygons, makes it easier to see trends and patterns in the results of psychological investigations.

79.2 Define and calculate these measures of central tendency: mean, median, mode

Measures of central tendency define the "typical score" in a group of scores. The mean is found by adding all the scores in a group and then dividing by the total number of scores. The median is found by arranging a group of scores from the highest to the lowest and selecting the middle score. The mode is the score that occurs most frequently in a group of scores.

79.3 Define and calculate these measures of variability: range, normal curve, standard deviation, standard score

Measures of variability provide a number that shows how much scores vary. The range is the difference between the highest score and the lowest score in a group of scores. The standard deviation (SD) shows how much, on average, all the scores in a group differ from the mean. To express an original score as a standard score (or z-score), you must subtract the mean from the score and then divide the result by the SD. Standard scores (z-scores) tell, in SD units, how far above or below the mean a score is. This allows meaningful comparisons between scores from different groups. Scores that form a normal curve are easy to interpret because the properties of the normal curve are well known.

79.4 Discuss the use of correlations in psychology, including scatter diagrams, correlation coefficients, prediction, and correlation vs. causality

Pairs of scores that vary together in an orderly fashion are said to be correlated. The relationship between two variables or measures can be positive or negative. Correlation coefficients tell how strongly two groups of scores are related. If a correlation is high enough, knowing a person's score on one measure allows us to predict his or her score on the second measure. Correlation alone does not demonstrate cause-and-effect links between variables or measures.

79.5 Discuss inferential statistics, including samples, populations, and statistical significance

Inferential statistics are used to make decisions, to generalize from samples, and to draw conclusions from data. Most studies in psychology are based on samples. Findings from representative samples are assumed to also apply to entire populations. In psychology experiments, differences in the average performance of groups could occur purely by chance. Tests of statistical significance tell us if the observed differences between groups are common or rare. If a difference is large enough to be improbable, it suggests that the results did not occur by chance alone.

Reflective Practice

Content Check

1. Three measures of central tendency are the mean, the median, and the ________________.
2. As a measure of variability, the standard deviation is defined as the difference between the highest and lowest scores. T or F?
3. A z-score of −1 tells us that a score fell one standard deviation below the mean in a group of scores. T or F?
4. A scatter diagram can be used to plot and visualize a(n) ________________ between two groups of scores.
5. It is important to remember that correlation does not demonstrate ________________.
6. In inferential statistics, observations of a ________________ are used to make inferences and draw conclusions about an entire ________________.
7. A representative sample can be obtained by selecting members of the sample at ________________.
8. If the results of an experiment could have occurred by chance alone fewer than 25 times out of 100, the result is considered statistically significant. T or F?

Skill Check

Think Critically

9. Suppose that it was found that sleeping with your clothes on correlates with waking up with a headache. Could you conclude that sleeping with your clothes on causes headaches?

Self-Reflect

How would you feel about receiving your scores on classroom tests in the form of z-scores? Do you think the distribution of scores in Samantha's study of sleep quality in elderly people would form a normal curve? Why or why not? See if you can identify at least one positive relationship and one negative relationship involving human behavior that you have observed. How strong do you think the correlation would be in each case? What correlation coefficient would you expect to see? If you were trying to test whether a drug causes birth defects, what level of statistical significance would you use? If you were doing a psychology experiment, with what level would you be comfortable?

ANSWERS

1. mode 2. F 3. T 4. correlation 5. causation 6. sample, population 7. random 8. F 9. No. To reiterate, correlation does not prove causality. It is more likely that a third factor is causing *both* the sleeping with the clothes on at night *and* the headaches (too much alcohol, anyone?).

References

Aamodt, M. G. (2016). *Industrial/organizational psychology: An applied approach* (8th ed.). Boston, MA: Cengage Learning.

Abbott, K. R., & Sherratt, T. N. (2011). The evolution of superstition through optimal use of incomplete information. *Animal Behaviour, 82*(1), 85–92. doi:10.1016/j.anbehav.2011.04.002

Abbott, S. M., Reid, K. J., et al. (2015). Circadian rhythm sleep-wake disorders. *Psychiatric Clinics of North America, 38*(4), 805–823. doi:10.1016/j.psc.2015.07.012

Abdollahi, A., & Talib, M. A. (2015). Emotional intelligence as a mediator between rumination and suicidal ideation among depressed inpatients: The moderating role of suicidal history. *Psychiatry Research, 228*(3), 591–597. doi:10.1016/j.psychres.2015.05.046

Abrahamse, E., Braem, S., et al. (2016). Grounding cognitive control in associative learning. *Psychological Bulletin, 142*(7), 693–728. doi:10.1037/bul0000047

Abramowitz, J. S., & Jacoby, R. J. (2015). Obsessive-compulsive and related disorders: A critical review of the new diagnostic class. *Annual Review of Clinical Psychology, 11*, 165–186. doi:10.1146/annurev-clinpsy-032813-153713

Abramowitz, J. S., Deacon, B. J., & Whiteside, S. P. H. (2012). *Exposure therapy for anxiety: Principles and practice.* New York, NY: Guilford.

Abrams, D., Van de Vyver, J., et al. (2017, February 16). Does terror defeat contact? Intergroup contact and prejudice toward Muslims before and after the London bombings. *Peace & Conflict: Journal of Peace Psychology*, n.p. doi:10.1037/pac0000167

Ackerman, S. J., Lewis, K. C., & Taylor, A. E. (2014). The Thematic Apperception Test: A performance-based assessment technique. In R. P. Archer & S. R. Smith (Eds.), *Personality assessment* (2nd ed., pp. 371–400). New York, NY: Routledge/Taylor & Francis.

Adachi, P. J., & Willoughby, T. (2011a). The effect of violent video games on aggression: Is it more than just the violence? *Aggression & Violent Behavior, 16*(1), 55–62. doi:10.1016/j.avb.2010.12.002

Adachi, P. J., & Willoughby, T. (2011b). The effect of video game competition and violence on aggressive behavior: Which characteristic has the greatest influence? *Psychology of Violence, 1*(4), 259–274. doi:10.1037/a0024908

Adamaszek, M., D'Agata, F., et al. (2016, Aug 2). Consensus paper: Cerebellum and emotion. *Cerebellum*, n.p. doi:org.proxy.library.brocku.ca/10.1007/s12311-016-0815-8

Adams, J. (2001). *Conceptual blockbusting* (4th ed.). New York, NY: Basic Books.

Adams, M. (2016). Existential therapy as a skills-learning process. *Existential Analysis, 27*(1), 58–69.

Adamson, K. (2004). *Kate's journey: Triumph over adversity.* Redondo Beach, CA: Nosmada Press.

Adan, A., & Serra-Grabulosa, J. P. (2010). Effects of caffeine and glucose, alone and combined, on cognitive performance. *Human Psychopharmacology: Clinical & Experimental, 25*(4), 310–317. doi:10.1002/hup.1115

Adler, S. A., & Orprecio, J. (2006). The eyes have it: Visual pop-out in infants and adults. *Developmental Science, 9*, 189–206. doi:10.1111/j.1467-7687.2006.00479.x

Adolph, K. E., & Berger, S. E. (2011). Physical and motor development. In M. H. Bornstein & M. E. Lamb (Eds.), *Cognitive development: An advanced textbook* (pp. 257–318). New York, NY: Psychology Press.

Adolphs, R. (2008). Fear, faces, and the human amygdala. *Current Opinion in Neurobiology, 18*(2), 166–172. doi:10.1016/j.conb.2008.06.006

Adorno, T. W., Frenkel-Brunswik, E., et al. (1950). *The authoritarian personality.* New York, NY: Harper.

Advokat, C. D. (2014). *Julien's primer of drug action.* (13th ed.). New York, NY: Worth.

Afifi, T. O., Brownridge, D. A., et al. (2006). Physical punishment, childhood abuse, and psychiatric disorders. *Child Abuse & Neglect, 30*(10), 1093–1103. doi:10.1016/j.chiabu.2006.04.006

Agresti, J. D., Smith, R. K., & Reynolds, W. T. (2020). Gun control facts. *Just Facts.* Retrieved July 19, 2020 from www.justfacts.com/guncontrol.asp

Agrigoroaei, S., & Lachman, M. E. (2011). Cognitive functioning in midlife and old age: Combined effects of psychosocial and behavioral factors. *Journals of Gerontology, 66B*, 130–140. doi:10.1093/geronb/gbr017

Ahern, A. L., Bennett, K. M., & Hetherington, M. M. (2008). Internalization of the ultra-thin ideal: Positive implicit associations with underweight fashion models are associated with drive for thinness in young women. *Eating Disorders: Journal of Treatment & Prevention, 16*(4), 294–307. doi:10.1080/10640260802115852

Ahima. R. S., & Osei, S. Y. (2004). Leptin signaling. *Physiology & Behavior, 81*, 223–241. doi:10.1016/j.physbeh.2004.02.014s

Ahluwalia, M. K., & Pellettiere, L. (2010). Sikh men post-9/11: Misidentification, discrimination, and coping. *Asian American Journal of Psychology, 1*(4), 303–314. doi:10.1037/a0022156

Ai, A. L., Huang, B., et al. (2013). Religious attendance and major depression among Asian Americans from a national database: The mediation of social support. *Psychology of Religion & Spirituality, 5*(2), 78–89. doi:10.1037/a0030625

Ainsworth, M. D. (1989). Attachments beyond infancy. *American Psychologist, 44*(4), 709–716.

Aitken, S. J., Lyons, M., & Jonason, P. K. (2013). Dads or cads? Women's strategic decisions in the mating game. *Personality & Individual Differences, 55*(2), 118–122. doi:10.1016/j.paid.2013.02.017

Ajzen, I. (2005). *Attitudes, personality and behaviour* (2nd ed.). New York, NY: McGraw-Hill.

Åkerstedt, T. (2007). Altered sleep/wake patterns and mental performance. *Physiology & Behavior, 90*(2–3), 209–218. doi:10.1016/j.physbeh.2006.09.007

Aktas, M., Gelfand, M., & Hanges, P. (2016). Cultural tightness–looseness and perceptions of effective leadership. *Journal of Cross-Cultural Psychology, 47*, 294–309. doi:10.1177/0022022115606802

Al Yacoub, A. A. (1997, December). How Muslim Arab parents in Western Pennsylvania view the influence of American TV on their children's morality. *Dissertation Abstracts International Section A, 58.*

Alanko, K., Santtila, P., et al. (2010). Common genetic effects of gender atypical behavior in childhood and sexual orientation in adulthood: A study of Finnish twins. *Archives of Sexual Behavior, 39*(1), 81–92. doi:10.1007/s10508-008-9457-3

Albarracín, D., Johnson, B. T., & Zanna, M. P. (Eds.). (2005). *The handbook of attitudes.* Mahwah, NJ: Erlbaum.

Albersen, M., Orabi, H., & Lue, T. F. (2012). Evaluation and treatment of erectile dysfunction in the aging male: A mini-review. *Gerontology, 58*(1), 3–14. doi:10.1159/000329598

Alberti, R., & Emmons, M. (2008). *Your perfect right* (9th ed.). San Luis Obispo, CA: Impact.

Alberto, P. A., & Troutman, A. C. (2013). *Applied behavior analysis for teachers* (9th ed.). Englewood Cliffs, NJ: Prentice Hall.

Albrecht, C. M., & Albrecht, D. E. (2011). Social status, adolescent behavior, and educational attainment. *Sociological Spectrum, 31*(1), 114–137. doi:10.1080/02732173.2011.525698

Albright, D. L., & Thyer, B. (2010). Does EMDR reduce post-traumatic stress disorder symptomatology in combat veterans? *Behavioral Interventions, 25*(1), 1–19. doi:10.1002/bin.295

Alcock, J. E. (2010). The parapsychologist's lament. In S. Krippner & H. L. Friedman (Eds.), *Mysterious minds: The neurobiology of psychics, mediums, and other extraordinary people* (pp. 35–43). Santa Barbara, CA: Praeger.

Alcock, J. E., Burns, J., & Freeman, A. (2003). *Psi wars: Getting to grips with the paranormal.* Exeter, UK: Imprint Academic Press.

Alegre, A. (2011). Parenting styles and children's emotional intelligence: What do we know? *The Family Journal, 19*(1), 56–62. doi:10.1177/1066480710387486

Alegria, A. A., Blanco, C., et al. (2013). Sex differences in antisocial personality disorder: Results from the National Epidemiological Survey on Alcohol and Related Conditions. *Personality Disorders: Theory, Research, & Treatment, 4*(3), 214–222. doi:10.1037/a0031681

Aleman, A. (2013). Use of repetitive transcranial magnetic stimulation for treatment in psychiatry. *Clinical Psychopharmacology & Neuroscience, 11*(2), 53–59. doi:10.9758/cpn.2013.11.2.53

Alessandria, M., Vetrugno, R., et al. (2011). Normal body scheme and absent phantom limb experience in amputees while dreaming. *Consciousness & Cognition, 20*(4), 1831–1834. doi:10.1016/j.concog.2011.06.013

Algoe, S. B., Gable, S. L., & Maisel, N. (2010). It's the little things: Gratitude as a booster shot for romantic relationships. *Personal Relationships, 17*(2), 217–233.

Ali, M. M., & Dwyer, D. S. (2010). Social network effects in alcohol consumption among adolescents. *Addictive Behaviors, 35*(4), 337–342. doi:10.1016/j.addbeh.2009.12.002

Allemand, M., Steiger, A. E., & Hill, P. L. (2013). Stability of personality traits in adulthood: Mechanisms and implications. *Geropsych: Journal of Gerontopsychology & Geriatric Psychiatry, 26*(1), 5–13. doi:10.1024/1662-9647/a000080

Allen, A. K., Wilkins, K., et al. (2013). Conscious thoughts from reflex-like processes: A new experimental paradigm for consciousness research. *Consciousness & Cognition, 22*(4), 1318–1331.

Allen, D., Carlson, D., & Ham, C. (2007). Well-being: New paradigms of wellness-inspiring positive health outcomes and renewing hope. *American Journal of Health Promotion, 21*(3), 1–9.

Allen, H. L., Estrada, K., et al. (2010): Hundreds of variants clustered in genomic loci and biological pathways affect human height. *Nature, 467*, 832–838.

Allen, J. L., Lavallee, K. L., et al. (2010). DSM-IV criteria for childhood separation anxiety disorder: Informant, age, and sex differences. *Journal of Anxiety Disorders, 24*(8), 946–952. doi:10.1016/j.janxdis.2010.06.022

Allen, J., & Holder, M. D. (2013). Marijuana use and well-being in university students. *Journal of Happiness Studies, 15*(2), 301–321. doi:10.1007/s10902-013-9423-1

Allen, K., Blascovich, J., & Mendes, W. B. (2002). Cardiovascular reactivity in the presence of pets, friends, and spouses: The truth about cats and dogs. *Psychosomatic Medicine, 64*(5), 727–739.

Allen, M., Mabry, E., & McKelton, D. (1998). Impact of juror attitudes about the death penalty on juror evaluations of guilt and punishment: A meta-analysis. *Law & Human Behavior, 22*(6), 715–731.

Allen, T. T., & Williams, L. D. (2012). An approach to life skills group work with youth in transition to independent living: Theoretical, practice, and operational considerations. *Residential Treatment for Children & Youth, 29*(4), 324–342. doi:10.1080/ 0886571X.2012.725375

Allport, G. W. (1958). *The nature of prejudice.* Garden City, NY: Anchor Books, Doubleday.

Allport, G. W. (1961). *Pattern and growth in personality.* New York, NY: Holt, Rinehart, & Winston.

Alstermark, B., & Ekerot, C. (2013). The lateral reticular nucleus: A precerebellar centre providing the cerebellum with overview and integration of motor functions at systems level. A new hypothesis. *Journal of Physiology, 591*(22), 5453–5458. doi:10.1113/jphysiol.2013.256669

Altemeyer, B. (2004). Highly dominating, highly authoritarian personalities. *Journal of Social Psychology, 144*(4), 421–447. doi:10.3200/SOCP.144.4.421-448

Alter, A. L., Aronson, J., et al. (2010). Rising to the threat: Reducing stereotype threat by reframing the threat as a challenge. *Journal of Experimental Social Psychology, 46*, 166–171. doi:10.1016/j.jesp.2009.09.014

Altschuler, G. C. (2001). Battling the cheats. *The New York Times*: Education, January 7, 15.

Alwin, D. F., Cohen, R. L., & Newcomb, T. M. (1991). *Political attitudes over the life span: The Bennington women after fifty years.* Madison, WI: University of Wisconsin Press.

Aly, A., Macdonald, S., et al. (2017). Introduction to the special issue: Terrorist online propaganda and radicalization. *Studies in Conflict & Terrorism, 40*(1), 1–9. doi:10.1080/105 7610X.2016.1157402

Alzahabi, R., Becker, M. W., & Hambrick, D. Z. (2017). Investigating the relationship between media multitasking and processes involved in task-switching. *Journal of Experimental Psychology: Human Perception and Performance, 43*(11), 1872–1894. doi:10.1037/xhp0000412

Ambady, N., & R. Rosenthal, R. (1993). Half a minute: Predicting teacher evaluations from thin slices of nonverbal behavior and physical attractiveness. *Journal of Personality & Social Psychology, 64*, 431–441. doi:10.1037/0022-3514.64.3.431

Ameli, R. (2014). *25 lessons in mindfulness: Now time for healthy living.* Washington, DC: American Psychological Association. doi:10.1037/14257-000

American Academy of Child and Adolescent Psychiatry. (2020). *Child sexual abuse.* Retrieved July 19, 2020, from https://www.aacap.org/AACAP/Families_and_Youth/Facts_for_Families/FFF-Guide/Child-Sexual-Abuse-009.aspx

American Lung Association. (2020). *Health effects of secondhand smoke.* Retrieved July 19, 2020, from https://www.lung.org/quit-smoking/smoking-facts/health-effects/secondhand-smoke

American Psychiatric Association. (2013). *Diagnostic and statistical manual of mental disorders* (5th ed.). Washington, DC: American Psychiatric Association.

American Psychiatric Association. (2017). *What are anxiety disorders?* Retrieved August 13, 2020, from https://www.psychiatry.org/patients-families/anxiety-disorders/what-are-anxiety-disorders

American Psychological Association. (2006). Evidence-based practice in psychology. *American Psychologist, 61*, 271–285. doi:10.1037/0003-066X.61.4.271

American Psychological Association. (2008). *Sexual orientation and homosexuality.* Retrieved June 17, 2020, from www.apa.org/topics/lgbt/orientation.pdf

American Psychological Association. (2009). *Civic engagement.* Retrieved June 17, 2020, from http://www.apa.org/education/undergrad/civic-engagement.aspx

American Psychological Association. (2010). *Report of the APA Task Force on the sexualization of girls.* Retrieved June 17, 2020, from www.apa.org/pi/women/programs/girls/report-full.pdf

American Psychological Association. (2012). *Workplace survey.* Retrieved June 18, 2020, from https://www.apa.org/news/press/releases/phwa/workplace-survey.pdf

American Psychological Association. (2013). *APA guidelines for the undergraduate major, version 2.0.* Retrieved June 16, 2020, from https://www.apa.org/ed/precollege/about/undergraduate-major

American Psychological Association. (2017a). *2017: APA member profiles.* Retrieved June 18, 2020, from https://www.apa.org/workforce/publications/17-member-profiles/tables.pdf

American Psychological Association. (2017b). *Ethical principles of psychologists and code of conduct: Including 2010 and 2016 amendments.* Retrieved June 17, 2020, from www.apa.org/ethics/code/index.aspx

American Psychological Association. (2017c). *Multicultural guidelines: An ecological approach to context, identity, and intersectionality.* Retrieved August 6, 2020, from http://www.apa.org/about/policy/multicultural-guidelines.pdf

American Psychological Association. (2018). *2007–16: Demographics of the U.S. psychology workforce.* Retrieved June 17, 2020, from https://www.apa.org/workforce/publications/16-demographics/

American Psychological Association. (2020). *Psychologist locator.* Retrieved June 17, 2020, from http://locator.apa.org

Ancis, J. R., Chen, Y., & Schultz, D. (2004). Diagnostic challenges and the so-called culture-bound syndromes. In J. R. Ancis (Ed.), *Culturally responsive interventions: Innovative approaches to working with diverse populations* (pp. 213–222). New York, NY: Brunner-Routledge.

Andersen, M. L., Poyares, D., et al. (2007). Sexsomnia: Abnormal sexual behavior during sleep. *Brain Research Reviews, 56*(2), 271–282. doi:10.1016/j.brainresrev.2007.06.005

Anderson, C. A. (1989). Temperature and aggression. *Psychological Bulletin, 106*, 74–96. doi:10.1037/0033-2909.106.1.74

Anderson, C. A., & Bushman, B. J. (2002). Human aggression. *Annual Review of Psychology, 53*, 27–51. doi:10.1146/annurev.psych.53.100901.135231

Anderson, C. A., Berkowitz, L., et al.(2003). The influence of media violence on youth. *Psychological Science in the Public Interest, 4*, 81–100. doi:10.1111/j.1529-1006.2003.pspi_1433.x

Anderson, C. A., Gentile, D. A., & Buckley, K. E. (2007). *Violent video game effects on children and adolescents: Theory, research, and public policy.* New York, NY: Oxford University Press.

Anderson, K. J. (2010). *Benign bigotry: The psychology of subtle prejudice.* New York, NY: Cambridge University Press.

Anderson, M. C., & Huddleston, E. (2012). Towards a cognitive neurobiological model of motivated forgetting. In R. F. Belli (Ed.), *True and false recovered memories: Toward a reconciliation of the debate* (pp. 53–120). New York, NY: Springer. doi:10.1007/978-1-4614-1195-6_3

Anderson, M. C., Reinholz, J., et al. (2011). Intentional suppression of unwanted memories grows more difficult as we age. *Psychology & Aging, 26*(2), 397–405. doi:10.1037/a0022505

Anderson, M., & Jiang, J. (2018). Teens, *Social Media & Technology 2018.* Retrieved July 23, 2020, from https://www.pewinternet.org/2018/05/31/teens-social-media-technology-2018/

Anderson, P. L., Edwards, S. M., & Goodnight, J. R. (2017). Virtual reality and exposure group therapy for social anxiety disorder: Results from a 4–6 year follow-up. *Cognitive Therapy & Research, 41*(2), 230–236. doi:10.1007/s10608-016-9820-y

Anderson, S. W., & Booker, M. B. (2006). Cognitive behavioral therapy versus psychosurgery for refractory obsessive-compulsive disorder. *Journal of Neuropsychiatry & Clinical Neurosciences, 18*(1), 129. doi:10.1176/appi.neuropsych.18.1.129

Anderson, S., & Hunter, S. C. (2012). Cognitive appraisals, emotional reactions, and their associations with three forms of peer-victimization. *Psicothema, 24*(4), 621–627.

André, C., Jaber-Filho, J. A., et al. (2003). Predictors of recovery following involuntary hospitalization of violent substance abuse patients. *The American Journal on Addictions, 12*(1), 84–89. doi:10.1080/10550490390143394

Andreasen, N. C., Nopoulos, P., et al. (2011). Progressive brain change in schizophrenia: A prospective longitudinal study of first-episode schizophrenia. *Biological Psychiatry, 70*(7), 672–679. doi:10.1016/j.biopsych.2011.05.017

Anekonda, T. S. (2006). Resveratrol: A boon for treating Alzheimer's disease? *Brain Research Reviews, 52*(2), 316–326. doi:10.1016/j.brainresrev.2006.04.004

Anema, H. A., & Dijkerman, H. (2013). Motor and kinesthetic imagery. In S. Lacey & R. Lawson (Eds.), *Multisensory imagery* (pp. 93–113). New York, NY: Springer. doi:10.1007/978-1-4614-5879-1_6

Annesi, J. J., & Marti, C. N. (2011). Path analysis of exercise treatment-induced changes in psychological factors leading to weight loss. *Psychology & Health, 26*(8), 1081–1098. doi:10.1080/08870446.2010.534167

Ansari, S., Wijen, F., & Gray, B. (2013). Constructing a climate change logic: An institutional perspective on the "tragedy of the commons." *Organization Science, 24*(4), 1014-1040. doi:10.1287/orsc.1120.0799

Anthony, J. S., Clayton, K. E., & Zusho, A. (2013). An investigation of students' self-regulated learning strategies: Students' qualitative and quantitative accounts of their learning strategies. *Journal of Cognitive Education & Psychology, 12*(3), 359–373. doi:10.1891/1945-8959.12.3.359

Antoni, C. (2005). Management by objectives: An effective tool for teamwork? *International Journal of Human Resource Management, 16*(2), 174–184.

Apperly, I. A. (2012). What is "theory of mind"? Concepts, cognitive processes and individual differences. *Quarterly Journal of Experimental Psychology, 65*(5), 825–839. doi:10.1080/17470218.2012.676055

Aradillas, E., Libon, D. J., & Schwartzman, R. J. (2011). Acute loss of spatial navigational skills in a case of a right posterior hippocampus stroke. *Journal of the Neurological Sciences, 308*(1–2), 144–146. doi:10.1016/j.jns.2011.06.026

Arch, J. J., Ayers, C. R., et al. (2013). Randomized clinical trial of adapted mindfulness-based stress reduction versus group cognitive behavioral therapy for heterogeneous anxiety disorders. *Behaviour Research & Therapy, 51*(4–5), 185–196. doi:10.1016/j.brat.2013.01.003

Ardila, A., Bernal, B., et al. (2016). The role of Wernicke's area in language comprehension. *Psychology & Neuroscience, 9*(3), 340–343. doi:10.1037/pne0000060

Ariely, D., & Loewenstein, G. (2006). The heat of the moment: The effect of sexual arousal on sexual decision making. *Journal of Behavioral Decision Making, 19*(2), 87–98.

Ariely, D., & Wertenbroch, K. (2002). Procrastination, deadlines, and performance: Self-control by precommitment. *Psychological Science, 13*(3), 219–224. doi:10.1111/1467-9280.00441

Arnett, J. J. (2011). The cultural psychology of a new life stage. In L. A. Jensen (Ed.), *Emerging adulthood(s): The cultural psychology of a new life stage* (pp. 255–275). New York, NY: Oxford University Press.

Arnett, J. J. (2016). Does emerging adulthood theory apply across social classes? National data on a persistent question. *Emerging Adulthood, 4*(4), 227–235. doi:10.1177/2167696815613000

Arnow, B. A., Steidtmann, D., et al. (2013). The relationship between the therapeutic alliance and treatment outcome in two distinct psychotherapies for chronic depression. *Journal of Consulting & Clinical Psychology, 81*(4), 627–638. doi:10.1037/a0031530

Arnsten, A., Mazure, C. M., & Sinha, R. (2012). This is your brain on meltdown. *Scientific American, 306,* 48–53. doi:10.1038/scientificamerican0412-48

Aron, A. (2012). Online dating: The current status—and beyond. *Psychological Science in the Public Interest, 13*(1), 1–2. doi:10.1177/1529100612438173

Aron, A., Fisher, H. E., et al. (2008). Falling in love. In S. Sprecher, A. Wenzel, & J. Harvey (Eds.), *Handbook of relationship initiation* (pp. 315–336). New York, NY: Psychology Press.

Aron, L., & Starr, K. (2013). *A psychotherapy for the people: Toward a progressive psychoanalysis.* New York, NY: Routledge.

Aronson, E. (2012). *The social animal* (11th ed.). New York, NY: Worth.

Aronson, E., Wilson, T. D., & Akert, R. M. (2015). *Social psychology* (9th ed.). Englewood Cliffs, NJ: Prentice Hall.

Aronson, K. (2003). Alcohol: A recently identified risk factor for breast cancer. *Canadian Medical Association Journal, 168*(9), 1147–1148.

Arshamian, A., Iannilli, E., et al. (2013). The functional neuroanatomy of odor evoked autobiographical memories cued by odors and words. *Neuropsychologia, 51*(1), 123–131. doi:10.1016/j.neuropsychologia.2012.10.023

Artz, S. (2005). To die for: Violent adolescent girls' search for male attention. In D. J. Pepler, K. C. Madsen, et al. (Eds.), *The development and treatment of girlhood aggression* (pp. 137–160). Mahwah, NJ: Erlbaum.

Asch, S. E. (1956). Studies of independence and conformity: A minority of one against a unanimous majority. *Psychological Monographs, 70*(9, Whole No. 416). doi:10.1037/h0093718

Aselton, P. (2012). Sources of stress and coping in American college students who have been diagnosed with depression. *Journal of Child & Adolescent Psychiatric Nursing, 25*(3), 119–123. doi:10.1111/j.1744-6171.2012.00341.x

Asgari, S., Dasgupta, N., & Stout, J. G. (2012). When do counterstereotypic ingroup members inspire versus deflate? The effect of successful professional women on young women's leadership self-concept. *Personality & Social Psychology Bulletin, 38*(3), 370–383. doi:10.1177/0146167211431968

Ash, D. W., & Holding, D. H. (1990). Backward versus forward chaining in the acquisition of a keyboard skill. *Human Factors, 32*(2), 139–146. doi:10.1177/001872089003200202

Ashby, F. G., & Maddox, W. T. (2005). Human category learning. *Annual Review of Psychology, 56,* 149–178. doi:10.1146/annurev.psych.56.091103.070217

Ashcraft, D. (2015). *Personality theories workbook* (6th ed.). Boston, MA: Cengage Learning.

Ashton, M. C. (2013). *Individual differences and personality* (2nd ed.). San Diego, CA: Elsevier.

Askenasy, J., & Lehmann, J. (2013). Consciousness, brain, neuroplasticity. *Frontiers in Psychology, 4,* 412. doi:10.3389/fpsyg.2013.00142

Asmundson, G. J. G., & Taylor, S. (2005). *It's not all in your head.* London, UK: Psychology Press.

Asthana, H. S. (2015). Wilhelm Wundt. *Psychological Studies, 60*(2), 244–248. doi:10.1007/s12646-014-0295-1

Athenasiou, R., Shaver, P., & Tavris, C. (1970). Sex. *Psychology Today, 4*(2), 37–52.

Atkin, D. J., & Lau, T. Y. (2007). Information technology and organizational telework. In C. A. Lin & D. J. Atkin (Eds.), *Communication technology and social change: Theory and implications* (pp. 79–100). Mahwah, NJ: Erlbaum.

Atkinson, C., & Mayer, R. E. (2004). *Five ways to reduce PowerPoint overload.* Retrieved July 19, 2020, from https://johnsonedl7200.weebly.com/five-ways-to-reduce-powerpoint-overload-by-cliff-atkinson-and-richard-e-mayer.html

Atkinson, R. C., & Shiffrin, R. M. (1968). Human memory: A proposed system and its control processes. In K. W. Spence & J. T. Spence (Eds.), *The psychology of learning and motivation* (Vol. 2, pp. 742–775). London, UK: Academic Press. doi:10.1016/S0079-7421(08)60422-3

Atwood, J. D. (2006). Mommy's little angel, daddy's little girl: Do you know what your pre-teens are doing? *American Journal of Family Therapy, 34*(5), 447–467.

Au, S., & Stavinoha, P. L. (2008). *Stress-free potty training: A commonsense guide to finding the right approach for your child.* New York, NY: AMACOM.

Aucoin, K. J., Frick, P. J., & Bodin, S. D. (2006). Corporal punishment and child adjustment. *Journal of Applied Developmental Psychology, 27*(6), 527–541.

Ausubel, D. P. (1978). In defense of advance organizers: A reply to the critics. *Review of Educational Research, 48,* 251–257.

Avery, D. H., Eder, D. N., et al. (2001). Dawn simulation and bright light in the treatment of SAD. *Biological Psychiatry, 50*(3), 205–216. doi:10.1016/S0006-3223(01)01200-8

Avolio, B. J., Walumbwa, F. O., & Weber, T. J. (2009). Leadership: Current theories, research, and future directions. *Annual Review of Psychology, 60,* 421–449.

Awadallah, N., Vaughan, A., et al. (2005). Munchausen by proxy: A case, chart series, and literature review of older victims. *Child Abuse & Neglect, 29*(8), 931–941. doi:10.1016/j.chiabu.2004.11.007

Axmacher, N., Do Lam, A. T., et al. (2010). Natural memory beyond the storage model: Repression, trauma, and the construction of a personal past. *Frontiers in Human Neuroscience, 4,* 211. doi:10.3389/fnhum.2010.00211

Ayal, S., Gino, F., et al. (2015). Three principles to REVISE people's unethical behavior. *Perspectives on Psychological Science, 10*(6), 738–741. doi:10.1177/1745691615598512

Ayman, R., & Korabik, K. (2010). Leadership: Why gender and culture matter. *American Psychologist, 65*(3), 157–170.

Azadyecta, M. (2011). Relationship between hardiness and parenting styles among high school girls of Tehran. *Psychological Research, 14*(1), 65–78.

Baad-Hansen, L., Abrahamsen, R., et al. (2013). Somatosensory sensitivity in patients with persistent idiopathic orofacial pain is associated with pain relief from hypnosis and relaxation. *Clinical Journal of Pain, 29*(6), 518–526.

Baas, M., Nijstad, B. A., et al. (2016). Mad genius revisited: Vulnerability to psychopathology, biobehavioral approach-avoidance, and creativity. *Psychological Bulletin, 142*(6), 668–692. doi:10.1037/bul0000049

Baas, M., Nijstad, B. A., & De Dreu, C. K. (2015). The cognitive, emotional and neural correlates of creativity. *Frontiers in Human Neuroscience, 9,* 275. doi:10.3389/fnhum.2015.00275

Babbie, E. R. (2016). *The practice of social research* (14th ed.). Boston, MA: Cengage Learning.

Baddeley, A. (2012). Working memory: Theories, models, and controversies. *Annual Review of Psychology, 63,* 1–29. doi:10.1146/annurev-psych-120710-100422

Baddeley, A., Eysenck, M. W., & Anderson, M. C. (2009). *Memory.* Hove, UK: Psychology Press.

Bader, S. M., Schoeneman-Morris, K. A., et al. (2008). Exhibitionism: Findings from a Midwestern police contact sample. *International Journal of Offender Therapy & Comparative Criminology, 52*(3), 270–279. doi:10.1177/0306624X07307122

Baer, N., Cialdini, R. B., & Lueth, N. (2012). *Influence: Science and practice: The Comic.* Highland Park, IL: Roundtable.

Bailey, C. H., & Kandel, E. R. (2004). Synaptic growth and the persistence of long-term memory: A molecular perspective. In M. S. Gazzaniga (Ed.), *The cognitive neurosciences* (3rd ed., pp. 647–663). Cambridge, MA: MIT Press.

Baillargeon, R. (1991). Reasoning about the height and location of a hidden object in 4.5- and 6.5-month-old infants. *Cognition, 38*(1), 13–42. doi:10.1016/0010-0277(91)90021-U

Baillargeon, R. (2004). Infants' reasoning about hidden objects: Evidence for event-general and event-specific expectations. *Developmental Science, 7*(4), 391–424. doi:10.1111/j.1467-7687.2004.00357.x

Baillargeon, R., De Vos, J., & Graber, M. (1989). Location memory in 8-month-old infants in a nonsearch AB task. *Cognitive Development, 4,* 345–367. doi:10.1016/S0885-2014(89)90040-3

Baillargeon, R., Scott, R. M., & Bian, L. (2016). Psychological reasoning in infancy. *Annual Review of Psychology, 67,* 159–186. doi:10.1146/annurev-psych-010213-115033

Baker, S. C., & Serdikoff, S. L. (2013). Addressing the role of animal research in psychology. In D. S. Dunn, R. A. R. Gurung, et al. (Eds.), *Controversy in the psychology classroom: Using hot topics to foster critical thinking* (pp. 105–112). Washington, DC: American Psychological Association. doi:10.1037/14038-007

Bakker, G. M. (2009). In defence of thought stopping. *Clinical Psychologist, 13*(2), 59–68. doi:10.1080/13284200902810452

Bales, D., & Bateman, A. W. (2012). Partial hospitalization settings. In A. W. Bateman & P. Fonagy (Eds.), *Handbook of mentalizing in mental health practice,* (pp. 197–226). Arlington, VA: American Psychiatric Publishing.

Balk, D. E., Lampe, S., et al. (1998). TAT results in a longitudinal study of bereaved college students. *Death Studies, 22*(1), 3–21. doi:10.1080/074811898201704

Ball, H. L., & Volpe, L. E. (2013). Sudden Infant Death Syndrome (SIDS) risk reduction and infant sleep location: Moving the discussion forward. *Social Science & Medicine, 79,* 84–91. doi:10.1016/j.socscimed.2012.03.025

Ballonoff, S. A., & Brindis, C. D. (2014). Adolescent school-based sex education: Using developmental neuroscience to guide new directions for policy and practice. *Sexuality Research & Social Policy: A Journal of the NSRC,* doi:10.1007/s13178-014-0147-8

Balon, R. (2016a). Exhibitionistic disorder. In R. Balon (Ed.), *Practical guide to paraphilia and paraphilic disorders* (pp. 77–91). doi:10.1007/978-3-319-42650-1_6

Balon, R. (Ed.). (2016b). *Practical guide to paraphilia and paraphilic disorders.* Cham, Switzerland: Springer International Publishing. doi:10.1007/978-3-319-42650-1

Balthazart, J. (2012). *Biology of homosexuality.* New York, NY: Oxford University Press.

Bandura, A. (1971). *Social learning theory.* New York, NY: General Learning Press.

Bandura, A. (2001). Social cognitive theory: An agentic perspective. *Annual Review of Psychology, 52,* 1–26. doi:10.1146/annurev.psych.52.1.1

Bandura, A., Blanchard, E. B., & Ritter, B. (1969). Relative efficacy of desensitization and modeling approaches for inducing behavioral, affective, and attitudinal changes. *Journal of Personality & Social Psychology, 13*(3), 173–199. doi:10.1037/h0028276

Bandura, A., Ross, D., & Ross, S. A. (1963). Vicarious reinforcement and imitative learning. *Journal of Abnormal & Social Psychology, 67,* 601–607. doi:10.1037/h0045550

Banerjee, D., & Nisbet, A. (2011). Sleepwalking. *Sleep Medicine Clinics, 6*(4), 401–416. doi:10.1016/j.jsmc.2011.07.001

Banich, M. T., & Compton, R. J. (2018). *Cognitive neuroscience* (4th ed.). Boston, MA: Cengage Learning.

Banks, A., & Gartrell, N. K. (1995). Hormones and sexual orientation: A questionable link. *Journal of Homosexuality, 28*(3–4), 247–268.

Banks, G., Hadenfeldt, K., et al. (2017, February 16). Gun violence and substance abuse. *Aggression & Violent Behavior,* n.p. doi:10.1016/j.avb.2017.02.002

Barabasz, A., & Watkins, J. G. (2005). *Hypnotherapeutic techniques* (2nd ed.). Washington, DC: Taylor & Francis.

Bar-Anan, Y., Wilson, T. D., & Hassin, R. R. (2010). Inaccurate self-knowledge formation as a result of automatic behavior. *Journal of Experimental Social Psychology, 46*(6), 884–894. doi:10.1016/j.jesp.2010.07.007

Barber, J. P., Abrams, M. J., et al. (2005). Explanatory style change in supportive-expressive dynamic therapy. *Journal of Clinical Psychology, 61*(3), 257–268. doi:10.1002/jclp.20114

Barber, N. (2010). Applying the concept of adaptation to societal differences in intelligence. *Cross-Cultural Research, 44*(2), 116–150. doi:10.1177/1069397109358041

Bardone-Cone, A. M., Joiner, Jr., T. E., et al. (2008). Examining a psychosocial interactive model of binge eating and vomiting in women with bulimia nervosa and subthreshold bulimia nervosa. *Behaviour Research & Therapy, 46*(7), 887–894. doi:10.1016/j.brat.2008.04.003

Barkan, R., Ayal, S., et al. (2012). The pot calling the kettle black: Distancing response to ethical dissonance. *Journal of Experimental Psychology: General, 141,* 757–773. doi: 10.1037/a0027588

Barkataki, I., Kumari, V., et al. (2006). Volumetric structural brain abnormalities in men with schizophrenia or antisocial personality disorder. *Behavioural Brain Research, 169*(2), 239–247. doi:10.1016/j.bbr.2006.01.009

Barlow, D. H. (2000). Unraveling the mysteries of anxiety and its disorders from the perspective of emotion theory. *American Psychologist, 55,* 1247–1263. doi:10.1037/0003-066X.55.11.1247

Barlow, D. H., Boswell, J. F., & Thompson-Hollands, J. (2013). Eysenck, Strupp, and 50 years of psychotherapy research: A personal perspective. *Psychotherapy, 50*(1), 77–87. doi:10.1037/a0031096

Barlow, D. H., & Hofmann, S. G. (2021). *Abnormal psychology: An integrative approach* (9th ed.). Boston, MA: Cengage Learning.

Barnett, J., Behnke, S. H., et al. (2007). In case of ethical dilemma, break glass: Commentary on ethical decision making in practice. *Professional Psychology: Research & Practice, 38*(1), 7–12. doi:10.1037/0735-7028.38.1.7

Barnett, N. P., Ott, M. Q., et al. (2013). Peer associations for substance use and exercise in a college student social network. *Health Psychology, 33*(10), 1134–1142. doi:10.1037/a0034687

Barnier, A. J., McConkey, K. M., & Wright, J. (2004). Posthypnotic amnesia for autobiographical episodes: Influencing memory accessibility and quality. *International Journal of Clinical & Experimental Hypnosis, 52*(3), 260–279. doi:10.1080/0020714049052351

Baron, R. A., Byrne, D., & Branscombe, N. R. (2012). *Mastering social psychology* (13th ed.). Boston, MA: Pearson/Allyn & Bacon.

Barr, M. S., Farzan, F., et al. (2013). Can repetitive magnetic stimulation improve cognition in schizophrenia? Pilot data from a randomized controlled trial. *Biological Psychiatry, 73*(6), 510–517. doi:10.1016/j.biopsych.2012.08.020

Barratt, B. B. (2013). *What is psychoanalysis? 100 years after Freud's "secret committee."* New York, NY: Taylor & Francis.

Barreto, M. L., & Frazier, L. D. (2012). Coping with life events through possible selves. *Journal of Applied Social Psychology, 42*(7), 1785–1810. doi:10.1111/j.1559-1816.2012.00918.x

Barrett, F. S., Grimm, K. J., et al. (2010). Music-evoked nostalgia: Affect, memory, and personality. *Emotion, 10*(3), 390–403. doi:10.1037/a0019006

Barron, F. (1958). The psychology of imagination. *Scientific American, 199*(3), 150–170. doi:10.1038/scientificamerican0958-150

Barrouillet, P. (2015). Theories of cognitive development: From Piaget to today. *Developmental Review, 38,* 1–12. doi:10.1016/j.dr.2015.07.004

Barrowcliff, A. L., & Haddock, G. (2006). The relationship between command hallucinations and factors of compliance: A critical review of the literature. *Journal of Forensic Psychiatry & Psychology, 17*(2), 266–298. doi:10.1080/14789940500485078

Barry, J. G., Sabisch, B., et al. (2011). Encoding: The keystone to efficient functioning of verbal short-term memory. *Neuropsychologia, 49*(13), 3636–3647. doi:10.1016/j.neuropsychologia.2011.09.018

Barry, S. R., & Sacks, O. (2009). *Fixing my gaze.* New York, NY: Basic Books.

Bartels, J. M. (2015). The Stanford prison experiment in introductory psychology textbooks: A content analysis. *Psychology Learning & Teaching, 14*(1), 36–50. doi:10.1177/1475725714568007

Bartholow, B. D., & Anderson, C. A. (2002). Effects of violent video games on aggressive behavior. *Journal of Experimental Social Psychology, 38*(3), 283–290. doi:10.1006/jesp.2001.1502

Bartholow, B. D., Sestir, M. A., & Davis, E. B. (2005). Correlates and consequences of exposure to video game violence: Hostile personality, empathy, and aggressive behavior. *Personality & Social Psychology Bulletin, 31*(11), 1573–1586. doi:10.1177/0146167205277205

Bartle-Haring, S., Shannon, S., et al. (2016). Therapist differentiation and couple clients' perceptions of therapeutic alliance. *Journal of Marital & Family Therapy*, Feb 29. doi:10.1111/jmft.12157

Bartram, B. (2006). An examination of perceptions of parental influence on attitudes to language learning. *Educational Research, 48*(2), 211–222. doi:10.1080/00131880600732298

Basner, M., & Dinges, D. (2009). Dubious bargain: Trading sleep for Leno and Letterman. *Sleep, 32*(6), 747–752.

Bass, J., & Takahashi, J. S. (2010). Circadian integration of metabolism and energetics. *Science, 330*(6009), 1349–1354. doi:10.1126/science.1195027

Basson, R., & Brotto, L. A. (2009). Disorders of sexual desire and subjective arousal in women. In R. Balon & R. T. Segraves (Eds.), *Clinical manual of sexual disorders* (pp. 119–159). Arlington, VA: American Psychiatric Publishing.

Batelaan, N. M., de Graaf, R., et al. (2010). The course of panic attacks in individuals with panic disorder and subthreshold panic disorder: A population-based study. *Journal of Affective Disorders, 121*(1–2), 30–38. doi:10.1016/j.jad.2009.05.003

Bateman, A. W., & Fonagy, P. (2012). Antisocial personality disorder. In A. W. Bateman & P. Fonagy (Eds.), *Handbook of mentalizing in mental health practice* (pp. 289–308). Arlington, VA: American Psychiatric Publishing.

Batson, C. D. (2006). "Not all self-interest after all": Economics of empathy-induced altruism. In D. De Cremer, M. Zeelenberg, et al. (Eds.), *Social psychology and economics* (pp. 281–299). Mahwah, NJ: Erlbaum.

Batson, C. D. (2010). Empathy-induced altruistic motivation. In M. Mikulincer & P. R. Shaver (Eds.), *Prosocial motives, emotions, and behavior: The better angels of our nature* (pp. 15–34). Washington, DC: American Psychological Association. doi:10.1037/12061-001

Batson, C. D., & Powell, A. A. (2003). Altruism and prosocial behavior. In T. Millon & M. J. Lerner (Eds.), *Handbook of psychology: Personality and social psychology* (Vol. 5, pp. 463–484). New York, NY: Wiley.

Bauer, A., Schneider, S., et al. (2017). Selective visual attention towards oneself and associated state body satisfaction: An eye-tracking study in adolescents with different types of eating disorders. *Journal of Abnormal Child Psychology,* n.p. doi:10.1007/s10802-017-0263-z

Bauer, J. J., McAdams, D. P., & Pals, J. L. (2008). Narrative identity and eudaimonic well-being. *Journal of Happiness Studies, 9*(1), 81–104. doi:10.1007/s10902-006-9021-6

Bauer, S., Wolf, M., et al. (2011). The effectiveness of Internet chat groups in relapse prevention after inpatient psychotherapy. *Psychotherapy Research, 21*(2), 219–226. doi:10.1080/10503307.2010.547530

Baugh, C. M., Stamm, J. M., et al. (2012). Chronic traumatic encephalopathy: Neurodegeneration following repetitive concussive and subconcussive brain trauma. *Brain Imaging & Behavior, 6*(2), 244–254. doi:10.1007/s11682-012-9164-5

Baum, A., & Davis, G. E. (1980). Reducing the stress of high-density living: An architectural intervention. *Journal of Personality & Social Psychology, 38,* 471–481.

Baum, A., & Valins, S. (1979). Architectural mediation of residential density and control: Crowding and the regulation of social contact. *Advances in Experimental & Social Psychology, 12,* 131–175.

Baum, A., & Valins, S. (Eds.). (1977). *Human response to crowding: Studies of the effects of residential group size.* Mahwah, NJ: Erlbaum.

Bauman, L. J., Karasz, A., & Hamilton, A. (2007). Understanding failure of condom use intention among adolescents: Completing an intensive preventive intervention. *Journal of Adolescent Research, 22*(3), 248–274.

Baumeister, R. F. (2015). Conquer yourself, conquer the world. *Scientific American, 312*(4), 60–65.

Baumeister, R. F., & Bushman, B. (2021). *Social psychology and human nature* (5th ed.). Boston, MA: Cengage Learning.

Baumeister, R. F., Campbell, J. D., et al. (2003). Does high self-esteem cause better performance, interpersonal success, happiness, or healthier lifestyles? *Psychological Science in the Public Interest, 4*(1), 1–44. doi:10.1111/1529-1006.01431

Baumrind, D. (1991). The influence of parenting style on adolescent competence and substance use. *Journal of Early Adolescence, 11*(1), 56–95. doi:10.1177/0272431691111004

Baumrind, D. (2005). Patterns of parental authority and adolescent autonomy. In J. Smetana (Ed.), *New directions for child development: Changes in parental authority during adolescence* (pp. 61–69). San Francisco: Jossey-Bass.

Bayne, R., & Jinks, G. (2013). *Applied psychology: Research, practice and new directions* (2nd ed.). Thousand Oaks: Sage.

Beans, D. R. (2009). *Integrative endocrinology.* New York, NY: Routledge.

Bearman, P. S., Moody, J., & Stovel, K. (2004). Chains of affection: The structure of adolescent romantic and sexual networks. *American Journal of Sociology, 110*(1), 44–91.

Beaulieu, C. M. J. (2004). Intercultural study of personal space: A case study. *Journal of Applied Social Psychology, 34*(4), 794–805.

Beck, A. T. (1991). Cognitive therapy. *American Psychologist, 46*(4), 368–375. doi:10.1037/0003-066X.46.4.368

Beck, H. P., Levinson, S., & Irons, G. (2009). Finding little Albert: A journey to John B. Watson's infant laboratory. *American Psychologist, 64*(7), 605–614. doi:10.1037/a0017234

Becker, S. W., & Eagly, A. H. (2004). The heroism of women and men. *American Psychologist, 59*(3), 163–178.

Beckmann, M., Cornelissen, T., et al. (2017). Self-managed working time and employee effort: Theory and evidence. *Journal of Economic Behavior & Organization, 133,* 285–302. doi:10.1016/j.jebo.2016.11.013

Bedny, M., Pascual-Leone, A., et al. (2012). A sensitive period for language in the visual cortex: Distinct patterns of plasticity in congenitally versus late blind adults. *Brain & Language, 122*(3), 162–170. doi:10.1016/j.bandl.2011.10.005

Beeber, L. S., Chazan-Cohen, R., et al. (2007). The Early Promotion and Intervention Research Consortium (E-PIRC): Five approaches to improving infant/toddler mental health in Early Head Start. *Infant Mental Health Journal, 28*(2), 130–150. doi:10.1002/imhj.20126

Begg, D. P., Sinclair, A. J., & Weisinger, R. S. (2012). Thirst deficits in aged rats are reversed by dietary omega-3 fatty acid supplementation. *Neurobiology of Aging, 33*(10), 2422–2430. doi:10.1016/j.neurobiolaging.2011.12.001

Behne, T., Liszkowski, U., et al. (2012). Twelve-month-olds' comprehension and production of pointing. *British Journal of Developmental Psychology, 30*(3), 359–375. doi:10.1111/j.2044-835X.2011.02043.x

Beirne-Smith, M., Patton, J., & Shannon, K. (2006). *Mental retardation: An introduction to intellectual disability* (7th ed.). Englewood Cliffs, NJ: Prentice Hall.

Bekinschtein, T. A., Shalom, D. E., et al. (2009). Classical conditioning in the vegetative and minimally conscious state. *Nature Neuroscience, 12*, 1343–1349. doi:10.1038/nn.2391

Belicki, K., Chambers, E., & Ogilvie, R. (1997). Sleep quality and nightmares. *Sleep Research, 26*, 637.

Belsky, J., Ruttle, P. L., et al. (2015). Early adversity, elevated stress physiology, accelerated sexual maturation, and poor health in females. *Developmental Psychology, 51*(6), 816–822. doi:10.1037/dev0000017

Bem, S. L. (1974). The measurement of psychological androgyny. *Journal of Consulting & Clinical Psychology, 42*(2), 155–162. doi:10.1037/h0036215

Bem, S. L. (1975). Androgyny vs. the tight little lives of fluffy women and chesty men. *Psychology Today, 31*, 58–62.

Bem, S. L. (1981). Gender schema theory. A cognitive account of sex typing. *Psychological Review, 88*, 354–364.

Ben Abdallah, N. M.-B., Slomianka, L., et al. (2010). Early age-related changes in adult hippocampal neurogenesis in C57 mice. *Neurobiology of Aging, 31*(1), 151–161. doi:10.1016/j.neurobiolaging.2008.03.002

Benedetti, F. (2009). *Placebo effects: Understanding the mechanisms in health and disease.* New York, NY: Oxford University Press.

Benitz, L. (2009). Becoming biliterate: A study of two-way bilingual immersion education. *Journal of Language, Identity, & Education, 8*(1), 54–57. doi:10.1080/15348450802620001

Ben-Itzhak, S., Bluvstein, I., et al. (2012). The effectiveness of brief versus intermediate duration psychodynamic psychotherapy in the treatment of adjustment disorder. *Journal of Contemporary Psychotherapy, 42*(4), 249–256. doi:10.1007/s10879-012-9208-6

Benjafield, J. G. (2015). *A history of psychology* (4th ed.). New York, NY: Oxford University Press.

Benjafield, J. G., Smilek, D., & Kingstone, A. (2010). *Cognition* (4th ed.). New York, NY: Oxford University Press.

Benjamin, O., & Tlusten, D. (2010). Intimacy and/or degradation: Heterosexual images of togetherness and women's embracement of pornography. *Sexualities, 13*(5), 599–623.

Benloucif, S., Bennett, E. L., & Rosenzweig, M. R. (1995). Norepinephrine and neural plasticity: The effects of xylamine on experience-induced changes in brain weight, memory, and behavior. *Neurobiology of Learning & Memory, 63*(1), 33–42. doi:10.1006/nlme.1995.1003

Bennett, P. (2011). *Abnormal and clinical psychology* (3rd ed.). New York, NY: McGraw-Hill.

Bensafi, M., Zelano, C., et al. (2004). Olfaction: From sniff to percept. In M. S. Gazzaniga (Ed.), *The cognitive neurosciences* (3rd ed., pp. 259–280). Cambridge, MA: MIT Press.

Ben-Shakhar, G., & Dolev, K. (1996). Psychophysiological detection through the guilty knowledge technique: Effect of mental countermeasures. *Journal of Applied Psychology, 81*(3), 273–281. doi:10.1037/0021-9010.81.3.273

Bensley, L., & Van Eenwyk, J. (2001). Video games and real-life aggression. *Journal of Adolescent Health, 29*(4), 244–257. doi:10.1016/S1054-139X(01)00239-7

Berenbaum, S. A., Blakemore, J., & Beltz, A. M. (2011). A role for biology in gender-related behavior. *Sex Roles, 64*(11–12), 804–825. doi:10.1007/s11199-011-9990-8

Berg, J. (2013). Opposition to pro-immigrant public policy: Symbolic racism and group threat. *Sociological Inquiry, 83*(1), 1–31. doi:10.1111/j.1475-682x.2012.00437.x

Bergeron, S., & Lord, M. J. (2003). The integration of pelvi-perineal reeducation and cognitive-behavioral therapy in the multidisciplinary treatment of the sexual pain disorders. *Sexual & Relationship Therapy, 18*, 135–141.

Bergstrom, H. C., McDonald, C. G., et al. (2013). Neurons activated during fear memory consolidation and reconsolidation are mapped to a common and new topography in the lateral amygdala. *Brain Topography, 26*(3), 468–478. doi:10.1007/s10548-012-0266-6

Berlin, H. A. (2011). The neural basis of the dynamic unconscious. *Neuropsychoanalysis, 13*(1), 5–31.

Berman, M. G., Yourganov, G., et al. (2013). Dimensionality of brain networks linked to life-long individual differences in self-control. *Nature Communications, 4*, 1373. doi:10.1038/ncomms2374

Berman, S. L., Weems, C. F., & Stickle, T. R. (2006). Existential anxiety in adolescents: Prevalence, structure, association with psychological symptoms and identity development. *Journal of Youth & Adolescence, 35*(3), 303–310. doi:10.1007/s10964-006-9032-y

Berman, S. M., Paz-Filho, G., et al. (2013). Effects of leptin deficiency and replacement on cerebellar response to food-related cues. *Cerebellum, 12*(1), 59–67. doi:10.1007/s12311-012-0360-z

Bermudez-Silva, F. J., Viveros, M. P., et al. (2010). The endocannabinoid system, eating behavior and energy homeostasis: The end or a new beginning? *Pharmacology, Biochemistry & Behavior, 95*(4), 375–382. doi:10.1016/j.pbb.2010.03.012

Bernard, R. S., Cohen, L. L., & Moffett, K. (2009). A token economy for exercise adherence in pediatric cystic fibrosis: A single-subject analysis. *Journal of Pediatric Psychology, 34*(4), 354–365. doi:10.1093/jpepsy/jsn101

Berne, E. (1964). *Games people play*. New York, NY: Grove.

Bernstein, H. J., Beale M. D., et al. (1998). Patient attitudes about ECT after treatment. *Psychiatric Annals, 28*(9), 524–527.

Bernstein, D. A., & Lucas, S. G. (2008): *Functional fixedness in problem solving.* In L. T. Benjamin (Ed.), *Favorite activities for the teaching of psychology* (pp. 143–144). Washington, DC: American Psychological Association.

Bernstein, D. M., & Loftus, E. F. (2009). How to tell if a particular memory is true or false. *Perspectives on Psychological Science, 4*(4), 370–374. doi:10.1111/j.1745-6924.2009.01140.x

Bernstein, I. H., Rush, A. J., et al. (2008). Symptom features of postpartum depression: Are they distinct? *Depression & Anxiety, 25*(1), 20–26.

Bernthal, M. J. (2008). How viewing professional wrestling may affect children. *The Sport Journal, 6*(3). Retrieved July 19, 2020, from https://thesportjournal.org/article/how-viewing-professional-wrestling-may-affect-children/

Berry, J. W., Phinney, J. S., et al. (2005). *Immigrant youth in cultural transition.* Mahwah, NJ: Erlbaum.

Bersamin, M. M., Zamboanga, B. L., et al. (2014). Risky business: Is there an association between casual sex and mental health among emerging adults? *Journal of Sex Research, 51*(1), 43–51. doi:10.1080/00224499.2013.772088

Berscheid, E. (2010). Love in the fourth dimension. *Annual Review of Psychology, 61*, 1–25. doi:10.1146/annurev.psych.093008.100318

Berscheid, E., & Regan, P. (2005). *The psychology of interpersonal relationships.* Englewood Cliffs, NJ: Prentice Hall.

Bersoff, D. M. (1999). Why good people sometimes do bad things: Motivated reasoning and unethical behavior. *Personality & Social Psychology Bulletin, 25*(1), 28–39. doi:10.1177/0146167299025001003

Beseler, C. L., Taylor, L. A., & Leeman, R. F. (2010). An item-response theory analysis of DSM-IV alcohol-use disorder criteria and "binge" drinking in undergraduates. *Journal of Studies on Alcohol & Drugs, 71*(3), 418–423.

Best, D. (2002). Cross-cultural gender roles. In J. Worell (Ed.), *Encyclopedia of women and gender* (pp. 279–290). New York, NY: Oxford University Press.

Beyer, M., Gerlach, F. M., et al. (2003). The development of quality circles/peer review groups as a tool for quality improvement in Europe: Results of a survey in 26 European countries. *Family Practice, 20*, 443–451.

Beyers, W., & Seiffge-Krenke, I. (2010). Does identity precede intimacy? Testing Erikson's theory on romantic development in emerging adults of the 21st century. *Journal of Adolescent Research, 25*(3), 387–415. doi:10.1177/0743558410361370

Bialystok, E., & Barac, R. R. (2012). Emerging bilingualism: Dissociating advantages for metalinguistic awareness and executive control. *Cognition, 122*(1), 67–73. doi:10.1016/j.cognition.2011.08.003

Bick, A. S., Leker, R. R., et al. (2013). Implementing novel imaging methods for improved diagnosis of disorder of consciousness patients. *Journal of the Neurological Sciences, 334*(1), 130–138. doi:10.1016/j.jns.2013.08.009

Biernat, M., & Danaher, K. (2013). Prejudice. In H. Tennen, J. Suls, et al. (Eds.), *Handbook of psychology* (Vol. 5): *Personality and social psychology* (2nd ed., pp. 341–367). New York, NY: Wiley.

Bilewicz, M., Soral, W., et al. (2017). When authoritarians confront prejudice. Differential effects of SDO and RWA on support for hate-speech prohibition. *Political Psychology, 38*(1), 87–99. doi:10.1111/pops.12313

Binder, J. L., & Betan, E. J. (2013). Essential activities in a session of brief dynamic/interpersonal psychotherapy. *Psychotherapy, 50*(3), 428–432. doi:10.1037/a0032521

Binder, J., Zagefka, H., et al. (2009). Does contact reduce prejudice or does prejudice reduce contact? A longitudinal test of the contact hypothesis among majority and minority groups in three European countries. *Journal of Personality & Social Psychology, 96*(4), 843–856. doi:10.1037/a0013470

Binik, Y. M. (2010). The DSM diagnostic criteria for dyspareunia. *Archives of Sexual Behavior, 39*(2), 292–303. doi:10.1007/s10508-009-9563-x

Binning, K. R., Sherman, D. K., et al. (2010). Seeing the other side: Reducing political partisanship via self-affirmation in the 2008 presidential election. *Analyses of Social Issues & Public Policy,* (1), 276–292. doi:10.1111/j.1530-2415.2010.01210.x

Birchwood, M., Michail, M., et al. (2014). Cognitive behaviour therapy to prevent harmful compliance with command hallucinations (COMMAND): A randomised controlled trial. *The Lancet Psychiatry, 1*(1), 23–33. doi:10.1016/S2215-0366(14)70247-0

Birgegård, A., Norring, C., & Clinton, D. (2012). DSM-IV versus DSM-5: Implementation of proposed DSM-5 criteria in a large naturalistic database. *International Journal of Eating Disorders, 45*(3), 353–361. doi:10.1002/eat.20968

Biro, F. M., Galvez, M. P., et al. (2010). Pubertal assessment method and baseline characteristics in a mixed longitudinal study of girls. *Pediatrics, 126*(3), e583–e590. doi:10.1542/peds.2009-3079

Bisson, J. I., Ehlers, A., et al. (2007). Psychological treatments for chronic post-traumatic stress disorder: Systematic review and meta-analysis. *British Journal of Psychiatry, 190*(2), 97–104. doi:10.1192/bjp.bp.106.021402

Bitzer, J., Giraldi, A., & Pfaus, J. (2013). Sexual desire and hypoactive sexual desire disorder in women. Introduction and overview. Standard operating procedure (SOP Part 1). *Journal of Sexual Medicine, 10*(1), 36–49. doi:10.1111/j.1743-6109.2012.02818.x

Bizer, G. Y., Hart, J., & Jekogian, A. M. (2012). Belief in a just world and social dominance orientation: Evidence for a mediational pathway predicting negative attitudes and discrimination against individuals with mental illness. *Personality & Individual Differences, 52*(3), 428–432. doi:10.1016/j.paid.2011.11.002

Bjorklund, D. F., & Causey, K. B. (2017). *Children's thinking* (6th ed.). Boston, MA: Cengage Learning.

Bjorklund, D. F., & Hernández Blasi, C. (2012). *Child and adolescent development*. Boston, MA: Cengage Learning.

Bjornstrom, E. E. (2011). An examination of the relationship between neighborhood income inequality, social resources, and obesity in Los Angeles County. *American Journal of Health Promotion, 26*(2), 109–115. doi:10.4278/ajhp.100326-QUAN-93

Black, D. W. (2015). The natural history of antisocial personality disorder. *Canadian Journal of Psychiatry, 60*(7), 309–314.

Blackmore, S. (2000). First person: Into the unknown. *New Scientist, Nov 4*, 55.

Blackwell, B. (2012). Obituary: Jose Manuel Rodriguez Delgado. *Neuropsychopharmacology, 37*(13), 2883–2884.

Blackwell, D. L., & Lichter, D. T. (2004). Homogamy among dating, cohabiting, and married couples. *Sociological Quarterly, 45*(4), 719–737. doi:10.1111/j.1533-8525.2004.tb02311.x

Blair, K. S., Richell, R. A., et al. (2006). They know the words, but not the music: Affective and semantic priming in individuals with psychopathy. *Biological Psychology, 73*(2), 114–123. doi:10.1016/j.biopsycho.2005.12.006

Blake, A. B., Nazarian, M., et al. (2015). The Apple of the mind's eye: Everyday attention, metamemory, and reconstructive memory for the Apple logo. *Quarterly Journal of Experimental Psychology, 68*(5), 858–865. doi:10.1080/17470218

Blakemore, C., & Cooper, G. (1970). Development of the brain depends on the visual environment. *Nature, 228*, 477–478. doi:10.1038/228477a0

Blanchard, E. B., Kuhn, E., et al. (2004). Studies of the vicarious traumatization of college students by the September 11th attacks: Effects of proximity, exposure and connectedness. *Behaviour Research & Therapy, 42*(2), 191–205.

Blandón-Gitlin, I., Pezdek, K., et al. (2014). Oxytocin eliminates the own-race bias in face recognition memory. *Brain Research, 1580*, 180–187. doi10.1016/j.brainres.2013.07.015

Bliese, P. D., Edwards, J. R., et al. (2017). Stress and well-being at work: A century of empirical trends reflecting theoretical and societal influences. *Journal of Applied Psychology, 102*(3), 389–402. doi:10.1037/apl0000109

Bloom, C. M., & Lamkin, D. M. (2006). The Olympian struggle to remember the cranial nerves: Mnemonics and student success. *Teaching of Psychology, 33*(2), 128–129. doi:1207/s15328023top3302_8

Bloom, L., & Bloom, C. (2012). What's so special about *Fifty Shades of Gray?* Retrieved July 19, 2020, from https://www.psychologytoday.com/us/blog/stronger-the-broken-places/201212/whats-so-special-about-fifty-shades-gray

Blundon, J. A., & Zakharenko, S. S. (2008). Dissecting the components of long-term potentiation. *The Neuroscientist, 14*(6), 598–608.

Bodner, E. (2009). On the origins of ageism among older and younger adults. *International Psychogeriatrics, 21*(6), 1003–1014. doi:10.1017/S104161020999055X

Boduroglu, A., Shah, P., & Nisbett, R. E. (2009). Cultural differences in allocation of attention in visual information processing. *Journal of Cross-Cultural Psychology, 40*(3), 349–360. doi:10.1177/0022022108331005

Boergers, J., Spirito, A., & Donaldson, D. (1998). Reasons for adolescent suicide attempts. *Journal of the American Academy of Child & Adolescent Psychiatry, 37*(12), 1287–1293. doi:10.1097/00004583-199812000-00012

Boerke, K. W., & Reitman, D. (2011). Token economies. In W. W. Fisher, C. C. Piazza, et al. (Eds.), *Handbook of applied behavior analysis* (pp. 370–382). New York, NY: Guilford.

Bogaert, A. F. (2006). Toward a conceptual understanding of asexuality. *Review of General Psychology, 10*, 241–250.

Bogaert, A. F. (2012). *Understanding asexuality*. Lanham, MD: Rowman & Littlefield.

Bogaert, A. F. (2015). Asexuality: What it is and why it matters. *Journal of Sex Research, 52*(4), 362–379. doi:10.1080/00224499.2015.1015713

Bogaert, A. F., & Skorska, M. (2011). Sexual orientation, fraternal birth order, and the maternal immune hypothesis: A review. *Frontiers in Neuroendocrinology, 32*(2), 247–254. doi:10.1016/j.yfrne.2011.02.004

Boggio, P. S., Campanhã, C., et al. (2010). Modulation of decision-making in a gambling task in older adults with transcranial direct current stimulation. *European Journal of Neuroscience, 31*(3), 593–597. doi:10.1111/j.1460-9568.2010.07080.x

Bohbot, V., & Corkin, S. (2007). Posterior parahippocampal place learning in H.M. *Hippocampus, 17*(9), 863–872. doi:10.1002/hipo.20313

Bohner, G., & Dickel, N. (2010). Attitudes and attitude change. *Annual Review of Psychology, 62*, 391–417. doi:10.1146/annurev.psych.121208.131609

Bohns, V. K. (2016). (Mis)understanding our influence over others: A review of the underestimation-of-compliance effect. *Current Directions in Psychological Science, 25*(2), 119–123. doi:10.1177/0963721415628011

Boiger, M., & Mesquita, B. (2012). The construction of emotion in interactions, relationships, and cultures. *Emotion Review, 4*(3), 221–229. doi:10.1177/1754073912439765

Boivin, D. B., Czeisler, C. A., & Waterhouse, J. W. (1997). Complex interaction of the sleep-wake cycle and circadian phase modulates mood in healthy subjects. *Archives of General Psychiatry, 54*(2), 145–152. doi:10.1001/archpsyc.1997.01830140055010

Boldero, J. M., Moretti, M. M., et al. (2005). Self-discrepancies and negative affect: A primer on when to look for specificity and how to find it. *Australian Journal of Psychology, 57*(3), 139–147. doi:10.1080/00049530500048730

Bolles, R. N. (2016). *What color is your parachute?* New York, NY: Ten Speed Press.

Bolt, D. M., Piper, M. E., et al. (2012). Why two smoking cessation agents work better than one: Role of craving suppression. *Journal of Consulting & Clinical Psychology, 80*(1), 54–65. doi:10.1037/a0026366

Bonanno, R. A., & Hymel, S. (2013). Cyber bullying and internalizing difficulties: Above and beyond the impact of traditional forms of bullying. *Journal of Youth & Adolescence, 42*, 685–697. doi:10.1007/s10964-013-9937-1

Bond, M. A., Serrano-García, I., E., et al. (2017). *APA handbook of community psychology: Theoretical foundations, core concepts, and emerging challenges, Vol. 1.* Washington DC: American Psychological Association.

Bond, R., & Smith, P. B. (1996). Culture and conformity: A meta-analysis of studies using Asch's (1952, 1956) line judgment task. *Psychological Bulletin, 119*(1), 111–137. doi:10.1037/0033-2909.119.1.111

Bongard, S., al'Absi, M., & Lovallo, W. R. (1998). Interactive effects of trait hostility and anger expression on cardiovascular reactivity in young men. *International Journal of Psychophysiology, 28*(2), 181–191. doi:10.1016/S0167-8760(97)00095-0

Bonham, V., Warshauer-Baker, E., & Collins, F. S. (2005). Race and ethnicity in the genome era: The complexity of the constructs. *American Psychologist, 60*(1), 9–15. doi:10.1037/0003-066X.60.1.9

Boniecki, K. A., & Britt, T. W. (2003). Prejudice and the peacekeeper. In T. W. Britt & A. B. Adler (Eds.), *The psychology of the peacekeeper: Lessons from the field* (pp. 53–70). Westport, CT: Praeger.

Bonk, W. J., & Healy, A. F. (2010). Learning and memory for sequences of pictures, words, and spatial locations: An exploration of serial position effects. *American Journal of Psychology, 123*(2), 137–168.

Bonnardel, N., & Didier, J. (2016). Enhancing creativity in the educational design context: An exploration of the effects of design project-oriented methods on students' evocation processes and creative output. *Journal of Cognitive Education & Psychology, 15*(1), 80–101. doi:10.1891/1945-8959.15.1.80

Bood, S., Sundequist, U., et al. (2006). Eliciting the relaxation response with the help of flotation-REST (Restricted Environmental Stimulation Technique) in patients with stress-related ailments. *International Journal of Stress Management, 13*(2), 154–175. doi:10.1037/1072-5245.13.2.154

Bora, E., Fornito, A., et al. (2011). Neuroanatomical abnormalities in schizophrenia: A multimodal voxelwise meta-analysis and meta-regression analysis. *Schizophrenia Research, 127*(1), 46–57. doi:10.1016/j.schres.2010.12.020

Borch-Jacobsen, M., & Shamdasani, S. (2011). *The Freud files: An inquiry into the history of psychoanalysis*. London, UK: Cambridge University Press.

Borg, C., Peters, M. L., et al. (2012). Vaginismus: Heightened harm avoidance and pain catastrophizing cognitions. *Journal of Sexual Medicine, 9*(2), 558–567. doi:10.1111/j.1743-6109.2011.02535.x

Bornstein, B. H. (2017). Jury simulation research: Pros, cons, trends, and alternatives. In M. B. Kovera (Ed.), *The psychol ogy of juries* (pp. 207–226). Washington, DC: American Psychological Association. doi:10.1037/0000026-010

Bornstein, R. F. (2012). Rorschach score validation as a model for 21st-century personality assessment. *Journal of Personality Assessment, 94*(1), 26–38. doi:10.1080/00223891.2011.627961

Boroditsky, L. (2011). How language shapes thought. *Scientific American, February*, 62–65. doi:10.1038/scientificamerican0211-62

Boroditsky, L., & Gaby, A. (2010). Remembrances of times east: Absolute spatial representations of time in an Australian Aboriginal community. *Psychological Science, 21*(11), 1635–1639. doi:10.1177/0956797610386621

Borst, G., & Kosslyn, S. M. (2010). Fear selectively modulates visual mental imagery and visual perception. *Quarterly Journal of Experimental Psychology, 63*(5), 833–839. doi:10.1080/17470211003602420

Borzekowski, D. L. G., Schenk, S., et al. (2010). e-Ana and e-Mia: A content analysis of pro–eating disorder web sites. *American Journal of Public Health, 100*(8), 1526–1534.

Boskey, E. (2020). *Is oral sex really safe sex?* Retrieved July 19, 2020, from https://www.verywellhealth.com/is-oral-sex-safe-sex-3133091

Bostwick, W. B., Boyd, C. J., et al. (2014). Discrimination and mental health among lesbian, gay, and bisexual adults in the United States. *American Journal of Orthopsychiatry, 84*(1), 35–45. doi:10.1037/h0098851

Botti, S., Orfali, K., & Iyengar, S. S. (2009). Tragic choices: Autonomy and emotional responses to medical decisions. *Journal of Consumer Research, 36*(3), 337–352. doi:10.1086/598969

Bouchard, T. J. Jr. (2004). Genetic influence on human psychological traits: A survey. *Current Directions in Psychological Science, 13*(4), 148–151. doi:10.1111/j.0963-7214.2004.00295.x

Boudry, M., Blancke, S., & Pigliucci, M. (2015). What makes weird beliefs thrive? The epidemiology of pseudoscience. *Philosophical Psychology, 28*(8), 1177–1198. doi: 10.1080/09515089.2014.971946

Bourgeois, J. A., Kahn, D., et al. (2009). *Casebook of psychosomatic medicine*. Washington, DC: American Psychiatric Publishing.

Bourne, E. J. (2010). *The anxiety & phobia workbook* (5th ed.). Oakland, CA: New Harbinger.

Bourne, L. R., & Healy, A. F. (2014). *Train your mind for peak performance: A science-based approach for achieving your goals.* Washington,

DC: American Psychological Association. doi:10.1037/14319-000

Bowden, S. C., Petrauskas, V. M., et al. (2013). Exploring the dimensionality of Digit Span. *Assessment, 20*(2), 188–198. doi:10.1177/1073191112457016

Bowe, A. G., Desjardins, C. D., et al. (2017). Urban elementary single-sex math classrooms: Mitigating stereotype threat for African American girls. *Urban Education, 52*(3), 370–398. doi:10.1177/0042085915574521

Bowe, F. (2000). *Universal Design in education: Teaching nontraditional students.* Westport, CT: Bergin & Garvey.

Bowen, N. K., Wegmann, K. M., & Webber, K. C. (2013). Enhancing a brief writing intervention to combat stereotype threat among middle-school students. *Journal of Educational Psychology, 105*(2), 427–435. doi:10.1037/a0031177

Bower, G. H. (1981). Mood and memory. *American Psychologist, 36,* 129–148. doi:10.1037/0003-066X.36.2.129

Bower, G. H., & Springston, F. (1970). Pauses as recoding points in letter series. *Journal of Experimental Psychology, 83,* 421–430. doi:10.1037/h0028863

Bowker, A. (2006). The relationship between sports participation and self-esteem during early adolescence. *Canadian Journal of Behavioural Science, 38*(3), 214–229.

Bowling, N. A. (2010). Effects of job satisfaction and conscientiousness on extra-role behaviors. *Journal of Business & Psychology, 25*(1), 119–130.

Boyd, J., Harris, S., & Knight, J. R. (2012). Screening and brief interventions for the addiction syndrome: Considering the vulnerability of adolescence. In H. Shaffer, D. A. LaPlante, et al. (Eds.), *APA addiction syndrome handbook* (Vol. 2): *Recovery, prevention, and other issues* (pp. 169–194). Washington, DC: American Psychological Association. doi:10.1037/13750-008

Boyd, M., Kim, M., et al. (2014). Perceived motivational team climate in relation to task and social cohesion among male college athletes. *Journal of Applied Social Psychology, 44*(2), 115–123. doi:10.1111/jasp.12210

Boysen, G. A. (2011). The scientific status of childhood dissociative identity disorder: A review of published research. *Psychotherapy & Psychosomatics, 80*(6), 329–334. doi:10.1159/000323403

Boysen, G. A., & VanBergen, A. (2013). A review of published research on adult dissociative identity disorder: 2000–2010. *Journal of Nervous & Mental Disease, 201*(1), 5–11. doi:10.1097/NMD.0b013e31827aaf81

Brach, T. (2003). *Radical acceptance.* New York, NY: Bantam Books.

Bracken, D. W., Rose, D. S., et al. (2016). The evolution and devolution of 360° feedback. *Industrial & Organizational Psychology: Perspectives on Science & Practice, 9*(4), 761–794. doi:10.1017/iop.2016.93

Bradbury, J. W., & Vehrencamp, S. L. (2011). *Principles of animal communication* (2nd ed.). Sunderland, MA: Sinauer.

Bradbury, T. N., & Karney, B. R. (2010). *Intimate relationships.* New York, NY: Norton.

Bradley, R. T., McCraty, R., et al. (2010). Emotion self-regulation, psychophysiological coherence, and test anxiety: Results from an experiment using electrophysiological measures. *Applied Psychophysiology & Biofeedback, 35*(4), 261–283. doi:10.1007/s10484-010-9134-x

Bradley, R., Greene, J., et al. (2005). A multidimensional meta-analysis of psychotherapy for PTSD. *American Journal of Psychiatry, 162*(2), 214–227. doi:10.1176/appi.ajp.162.2.214

Bradshaw, C., Kahn, A. S., & Saville, B. K. (2010). To hook up or date: Which gender benefits? *Sex Roles, 62*(9–10), 661–669.

Brainerd, C. J. (2003). Jean Piaget, learning research, and American education. In B. J. Zimmerman & D. H. Schunk (Eds.), *Educational psychology: A century of contributions* (pp. 251–287). Mahwah, NJ: Erlbaum.

Brakel, T. M., Dijkstra, A., et al. (2011). Impact of social comparison on cancer survivors' quality of life: An experimental field study. *Health Psychology, 31,* 660–670. doi:10.1037/a0026572

Bramerson, A., Johansson, L., et al. (2004). Prevalence of olfactory dysfunction: The Skovde population-based study. *Laryngoscope, 114*(4), 733–737. doi:10.1097/00005537-200404000-00026

Brammer, R. (2012). *Diversity in counseling* (2nd ed.). Boston, MA: Cengage Learning.

Brand, S., Gerber, M., et al. (2010). High exercise levels are related to favorable sleep patterns and psychological functioning in adolescents: A comparison of athletes and controls. *Journal of Adolescent Health, 46*(2), 133–141. doi:10.1016/j.jadohealth.2009.06.018

Brang, D., & Ramachandran, V. S. (2010). Visual field heterogeneity, laterality, and eidetic imagery in synesthesia. *Neurocase, 16*(2), 169–174. doi:10.1080/13554790903339645

Brannon, L. (2011). *Gender: Psychological perspectives.* Boston, MA: Pearson/Allyn & Bacon.

Brannon, L., Feist, J., & Updegraff, J. (2021). *Health psychology: An introduction to behavior and health* (10th ed.). Boston, MA: Cengage Learning.

Branscombe, N. R., & Baron, R. A. (2017). *Social psychology.* New York, NY: Pearson.

Brauer, J. R., & Tittle, C. R. (2012). Social learning theory and human reinforcement. *Sociological Spectrum, 32*(2), 157–177. doi:10.1080/02732173.2012.646160

Braun, K. A., Ellis, R., & Loftus, E. F. (2002). Make my memory: How advertising can change memories of the past. *Psychology & Marketing, 19,* 1–23. doi:10.1002/mar.1000

Breedlove, S. M., Watson, N. V., et al. (2013). *Biological psychology: An introduction to behavioral and cognitive neuroscience* (7th ed.). Sunderland, MA: Sinauer Associates.

Breiding, M. G., Smith, S. G., et al. (2014). *Prevalence and characteristics of sexual violence, stalking, and intimate partner violence victimization—National Intimate Partner and Sexual Violence Survey, United States, 2011.* Retrieved July 19, 2020, from www.cdc.gov/mmwr/preview/mmwrhtml/ss6308a1.htm

Brenes, G. A., Ingram, C. W., & Danhauer, S. C. (2011). Benefits and challenges of conducting psychotherapy by telephone. *Professional Psychology: Research & Practice, 42*(6), 543–549. doi:10.1037/a0026135

Brescoll, V. L., Dawson, E., & Uhlmann, E. L. (2010). Hard won and easily lost: The fragile status of leaders in gender-stereotype-incongruent occupations. *Psychological Science, 21*(11), 1640–1642.

Bressan, P., & Pizzighello, S. (2008). The attentional cost of inattentional blindness. *Cognition, 106*(1), 370–383. doi:10.1016/j.cognition.2007.03.001

Bressi, C., Albonetti, S., & Razzoli, E. (1998). "Communication deviance" and schizophrenia. *New Trends in Experimental & Clinical Psychiatry, 14*(1), 33–39.

Bretherton, R., & Orner, R. J. (2004). Positive psychology and psychotherapy: An existential approach. In P. A. Linley & S. Joseph (Eds.), *Positive psychology in practice* (pp. 420–430). New York, NY: Wiley.

Brevers, D., Dan, B., et al. (2011). Sport superstition: Mediation of psychological tension on non-professional sportsmen's superstitious rituals. *Journal of Sport Behavior, 34*(1), 3–24.

Bridges, K. M. B. (1932). Emotional development in early infancy. *Child Development, 3,* 324–341. doi:10.2307/1125359

Brewer, J. A., Mallik, S., et al. (2011). Mindfulness training for smoking cessation: Results from a randomized controlled trial. *Drug & Alcohol Dependence, 119*(1–2), 72–80. doi:10.1016/j.drugalcdep.2011.05.027

Bridgett, D. J., Gartstein, M. A., et al. (2009). Maternal and contextual influences and the effect of temperament development during infancy on parenting in toddlerhood. *Infant Behavior & Development, 32*(1), 103–116. doi:10.1016/j.infbeh.2008.10.007

Briley, D. A., & Tucker-Drob, E. M. (2017). Comparing the developmental genetics of cognition and personality over the life span. *Journal of Personality, 85*(1), 51–64. doi:10.1111/jopy.12186

Bringing Up Baby. (1999). *Sierra,* Jan–Feb, 17.

Britton, P. C., Duberstein, P. R., et al. (2008). Reasons for living, hopelessness, and suicide ideation among depressed adults 50 years or older. *American Journal of Geriatric Psychiatry, 16*(9), 736–741. doi:10.1097/JGP.0b013e31817b609a

Brodley, B. T. (2006). Nondirectivity in client-centered therapy. *Person-Centered & Experiential Psychotherapies, 5*(1), 36–52.

Brody, S., & Weiss, P. (2011). Simultaneous penile–vaginal intercourse orgasm is associated with satisfaction (sexual, life, partnership, and mental health). *Journal of Sexual Medicine, 8*(3), 734–741. doi:10.1111/j.1743-6109.2010.02149.x

Brondolo, E., ver Halen, N., et al. (2011). Racism as a psychosocial stressor. In R. J. Contrada & A. Baum (Eds.), *The handbook of stress science: Biology, psychology, and health* (pp. 167–184). New York, NY: Springer.

Brooks, M. (2009). Rise of the robogeeks. *New Scientist, 2697,* 34–36.

Brotto, L.A., Knudson, G., et al. (2010). Asexuality: A mixed-methods approach. *Archives of Sexual Behavior, 39*(3), 599–618.

Brower, A. M. (2002). Are college students alcoholics? *Journal of American College Health, 50*(5), 253–255. doi:10.1080/07448480209595716

Brown, A. S. (2012). *The tip of the tongue state.* New York, NY: Psychology Press.

Brown, A. S., & Marsh, E. J. (2010). Digging into déjà vu: Recent research on possible mechanisms. In B. H. Ross (Ed.), *The psychology of learning and motivation: Advances in research and theory* (Vol. 53, pp. 33–62). San Diego, CA: Elsevier. doi:10.1016/S0079-7421(10)53002-0

Brown, A., Charlwood, A., & Spencer, D. A. (2012). Not all that it might seem: Why job satisfaction is worth studying despite it being a poor summary measure of job quality. *Work, Employment & Society, 26*(6), 1007–1018. doi:10.1177/0950017012461837

Brown, G., & Devlin, A. S. (2003). Vandalism: Environmental and social factors. *Journal of College Student Development, 44*(4), 502–516.

Brown, G. R., & Cross, C. P. (2017). Evolutionary approaches to human psychology. In J. Call, G. M. Burghardt, et al. (Eds.), *APA handbook of comparative psychology: Basic concepts, methods, neural substrate, and behavior* (Vol. 1, pp. 299–313). Washington, DC: American Psychological Association. doi:10.1037/0000011-015

Brown, J. D. (2010). High self-esteem buffers negative feedback: Once more with feeling. *Cognition & Emotion, 24*(8), 1389–1404. doi:10.1080/02699930903504405

Brown, J. D., Cai, H., et al. (2009). Cultural similarities in self-esteem functioning: East is east and west is west, but sometimes the twain do meet. *Journal of Cross-Cultural Psychology, 40*(1), 140–157. doi:10.1177/0022022108326280

Brown, L. M. (2005). *Girlfighting: Betrayal and rejection among girls.* New York, NY: New York University Press.

Brown, M. J., Henriquez, E., & Groscup, J. (2008). The effects of eyeglasses and race on juror decisions involving a violent crime. *American Journal of Forensic Psychology, 26*(2), 25–43.

Brown, P. (1990). The name game. *Journal of Mind and Behavior, 11,* 385–406.

Brown, R., & Kulik, J. (1977). Flashbulb memories. *Cognition, 5,* 73–99. doi:10.1016/0010-0277(77)90018-X

Brown, R., & McNeill, D. (1966). The "tip of the tongue" phenomenon. *Journal of Verbal Learning & Verbal Behavior, 5,* 325–337. doi:10.1016/S0022-5371(66)80040-3

Brown, S. A., Tapert, S. F., et al. (2000). Neurocognitive functioning of adolescents: Effects of protracted alcohol use. *Alcoholism: Clinical & Experimental Research, 24*(2), 164–171. doi:10.1111/j.1530-0277.2000.tb04586.x

Brown, S. D., Lent, R. W., et al. (2011). Social cognitive career theory, conscientiousness, and work performance: A meta-analytic path analysis. *Journal of Vocational Behavior, 79*(1), 81–90. doi:10.1016/j.jvb.2010.11.009

Brown, T. A., & Barlow, D. H. (2017). *Casebook in abnormal psychology* (5th ed.). Boston, MA: Cengage Learning.

Brown, V., Tumeo, M., Larey, T. S., et al. (1998). Modeling cognitive interactions during group brainstorming. *Small Group Research, 29*(4), 495–526.

Browne, A. L., & Bishop, B. J. (2011). Chasing our tails: Psychological, institutional and societal paradoxes in natural resource management, sustainability, and climate change in Australia. *American Journal of Community Psychology, 47,* 354–361. doi:10.1007/s10464-010-9390-1

Browne, N., & Keeley, S. (2010). *Asking the right questions* (9th ed.). Englewood Cliffs, NJ: Prentice Hall.

Brownell, P. (2016). Contemporary Gestalt therapy. In Cain, D. J., Keenan, K., & Rubin, S. (Eds.), *Humanistic psychotherapies: Handbook of research and practice* (2nd ed., pp. 219–250). Washington, DC: American Psychological Association. doi:10.1037/14775-008

Bruchmüller, K., Margraf, J., & Schneider, S. (2012). Is ADHD diagnosed in accord with diagnostic criteria? Overdiagnosis and influence of client gender on diagnosis. *Journal of Consulting & Clinical Psychology, 80*(1), 128–138. doi:10.1037/a0026582

Bruehl, S. S., Burns, J. W., et al. (2012). What do plasma beta-endorphin levels reveal about endogenous opioid analgesic function? *European Journal of Pain, 16*(3), 370–380. doi:10.1002/j.1532-2149.2011.00021.x

Brumbaugh, C. C., & Fraley, R. C. (2010). Adult attachment and dating strategies: How do insecure people attract mates? *Personal Relationships, 17*(4), 599–614.

Bruner, J. (1973). *Going beyond the information given.* New York, NY: Norton.

Bruner, J. (1983). *Child's talk.* New York, NY: Norton.

Bryan, L., & Vinchur, A. J. (2013). *Industrial-organizational psychology.* In D. K. Freedheim & I. B. Weiner (Eds.), *Handbook of psychology* (Vol. 1): *History of psychology* (2nd ed., pp. 407–428). New York, NY: Wiley.

Brydon, L., Strike, P. C., et al. (2010). Hostility and physiological responses to laboratory stress in acute coronary syndrome patients. *Journal of Psychosomatic Research, 68*(2), 109–116. doi:10.1016/j.jpsychores.2009.06.007

Buchanan, M. (2008). Sin cities: The geometry of crime. *New Scientist, 2654* (April 30), 36–39.

Bucher, S. G. (2011). *344 questions: The creative person's do-it-yourself guide to insight, survival, and artistic fulfillment.* Berkeley, CA: New Riders Publishing.

Buck, J. A., & Warren, A. R. (2010). Expert testimony in recovered memory trials: Effects on mock jurors' opinions, deliberations and verdicts. *Applied Cognitive Psychology, 24*(4), 495–512.

Buckner, J. D., Ecker, A. H., & Cohen, A. S. (2010). Mental health problems and interest in marijuana treatment among marijuana-using college students. *Addictive Behaviors, 35*(9), 826–833. doi:10.1016/j.addbeh.2010.04.001

Buckworth, J., Lee, R. E., et al. (2007). Decomposing intrinsic and extrinsic motivation for exercise: Application to stages of motivational readiness. *Psychology of Sport & Exercise, 8*(4), 441–461. doi:10.1016/j.psychsport.2006.06.007

Budney, A. J., & Hughes, J. R. (2006). The cannabis withdrawal syndrome. *Current Opinion in Psychiatry, 19*(3), 233–238. doi:10.1097/01.yco.0000218592.00689.e5

Buehner, M. J., & May, J. (2003). Rethinking temporal contiguity and the judgement of causality: Effects of prior knowledge, experience, and reinforcement procedure. *Quarterly Journal of Experimental Psychology: A Human Experimental Psychology, 56*(5), 865–890. doi:10.1080/02724980244000675

Bukach, C. M., Cottle, J., et al. (2012). Individuation experience predicts other-race effects in holistic processing for both Caucasian and Black participants. *Cognition, 123,* 319–324. doi:10.1016/j.cognition.2012.02.007

Buller, D. J. (2005). *Adapting minds: Evolutionary psychology and the persistent quest for human nature.* Cambridge, MA: MIT Press.

Bunde, J., & Suls, J. (2006). A quantitative analysis of the relationship between the Cook-Medley hostility scale and traditional coronary artery disease risk factors. *Health Psychology, 25*(4), 493–500. doi:10.1037/0278-6133.25.4.493

Bundy, H., Stahl, D., & MacCabe, J. H. (2011). A systematic review and meta-analysis of the fertility of patients with schizophrenia and their unaffected relatives. *Acta Psychiatrica Scandinavica, 123*(2), 98–106. doi:10.1111/j.1600-0447.2010.01623.x

Bunk, J. A., & Magley, V. J. (2013). The role of appraisals and emotions in understanding experiences of workplace incivility. *Journal of Occupational Health Psychology, 18*(1), 87–105. doi:10.1037/a0030987

Bunn, G. C. (2012). *The truth machine: A social history of the lie detector.* Baltimore, MD: Johns Hopkins University Press.

Bunnell, D. W. (2016). Gender socialization, countertransference and the treatment of men with eating disorders. *Clinical Social Work Journal, 44*(1), 99–104. doi:10.1007/s10615-015-0564-z

Burbach, M. E., Matkin, G. S., & Fritz, S. M. (2004). Teaching critical thinking in an introductory leadership course utilizing active learning strategies: A confirmatory study. *College Student Journal, 38*(3), 482–493.

Burchinal, M., Skinner, D., & Reznick, J. S. (2010). European American and African American Mothers' beliefs about parenting and disciplining infants: A mixed method analysis. *Parenting: Science & Practice, 10,* 79–96. doi:10.1080/15295190903212604

Burger, J. M. (2009). Replicating Milgram: Would people still obey today? *American Psychologist, 64*(1), 1–11. doi:10.1037/a0010932

Burger, J. M. (2019). *Personality* (10th ed.). Boston, MA: Cengage Learning.

Burgess, C. A., & Kirsch, I. (1999). Expectancy information as a moderator of the effects of hypnosis on memory. *Contemporary Hypnosis, 16*(1), 22–31. doi:10.1002/ch.146

Burlingame, G. M., Fuhriman, A., & Mosier, J. (2003). The differential effectiveness of group psychotherapy: A meta-analytic perspective. *Group Dynamics: Theory, Research, & Practice, 7*(1), 3–12. doi:10.1037/1089-2699.7.1.3

Burns, J. M., & Swerdlow, R. H. (2003). Right orbitofrontal tumor with pedophilia symptom and constructional apraxia sign. *Archives of Neurology, 60*(3), 437–440. doi:10.1001/archneur.60.3.437

Burón, P., Jimenez-Trevino, L., et al. (2016). Reasons for attempted suicide in Europe: Prevalence, associated factors, and risk of repetition. *Archives of Suicide Research, 20*(1), 45–58. doi:10.1080/13811118.2015.10 04481

Burt, S. A., McGue, M., et al. (2007). The different origins of stability and change in antisocial personality disorder symptoms. *Psychological Medicine, 37*(1), 27–38. doi:10.1017/S0033291706009020

Burton, C. M., & King, L. A. (2004). The health benefits of writing about intensely positive experiences. *Journal of Research in Personality, 38*(2), 150–163. doi:10.1016/S0092-6566(03)00058-8

Burtt, H. E. (1941). An experimental study of early childhood memory: Final report. *Journal of General Psychology, 58,* 435–439.

Bushnell, M. C., Villemure, C., & Duncan, G. H. (2004). Psychophysical and neurophysiological studies of pain modulation by attention. In D. D. Price & M. C. Bushnell (Eds.), *Psychological methods of pain control: Basic science and clinical perspectives* (pp. 99–116). Seattle, WA: IASP Press.

Buss, A. H. (2012). *Pathways to individuality: Evolution and development of personality traits.* Washington, DC: American Psychological Association.

Buss, D. M. (2007). The evolution of human mating. *Acta Psychologica Sinica, 39*(3), 502–512.

Buss, D. M. (2019). *Evolutionary psychology: The new science of the mind* (6th ed.). Boston, MA: Psychology Press.

Butcher, J. N. (2011). *A beginner's guide to the MMPI-2* (3rd ed.). Washington, DC: American Psychological Association.

Butcher, J. N., Mineka, S., & Hooley, J. (2010). *Abnormal psychology* (14th ed.). Boston, MA: Allyn & Bacon.

Butler, A. C., Chapman, J. E., et al. (2006). The empirical status of cognitive-behavioral therapy: A review of meta-analyses. *Clinical Psychology Review, 26*(1), 17–31. doi:10.1016/j.cpr.2005.07.003

Butler, B. (2007). The role of death qualification in capital trials involving juvenile defendants. *Journal of Applied Social Psychology, 37*(3), 549–560.

Butler, J. C. (2000). Personality and emotional correlates of right-wing authoritarianism. *Social Behavior & Personality, 28*(1), 1–14. doi:10.2224/sbp.2000.28.1.1

Butler, R. (1954). Curiosity in monkeys. *Scientific American, 190*(18), 70–75. doi:10.1038/scientificamerican0254-70

Byrne, S., Barry, D., & Petry, N. M. (2012). Predictors of weight loss success: Exercise vs. dietary self-efficacy and treatment attendance. *Appetite, 58*(2), 695–698. doi:10.1016/j.appet.2012.01.005

Byrne, J. S., & O'Brien, E. J. (2014). Interpersonal views of narcissism and authentic high self-esteem: It is not all about you. *Psychological Reports, 115*(1), 243–260. doi:10.2466/21.09.PR0.115c15z9

Byrnes, J. P., Miller, D. C., & Schafer, W. D. (1999). Gender differences in risk taking: A meta-analysis. *Psychological Bulletin, 125*(3), 367–383.

Cabrera, A. (2016). Pound puppy turned police "porn dog." *CNN.* Retrieved July 19, 2020, from www.cnn.com/2016/09/05/us/police-dog-sniffs-out-flash-drives-in-porn-cases

Cadaret, M. C., Hartung, P. J., et al. (2017). Stereotype threat as a barrier to women entering engineering careers. *Journal of Vocational Behavior, 99,* 40–51. doi:10.1016/j. jvb.2016.12.002

Cadet, P. (2011). Androgen insensitivity syndrome with male sex-of-living. *Archives of Sexual Behavior, 40*(6), 1101–1102. doi:10.1007/s10508-011-9823-4

Cadinu, M., Maass, A., et al. (2005). Why do women underperform under stereotype threat? Evidence for the role of negative thinking. *Psychological Science, 16*(7), 572–578. doi:10.1111/j.0956-7976.2005.01577.x

Caharel, S., Fiori, N., et al. (2006). The effects of inversion and eye displacements of familiar and unknown faces on early and late-stage ERPs. *International Journal of Psychophysiology, 62*(1), 141–151. doi:10.1016/j.ijpsycho.2006.03.002

Cahn, B., & Polich, J. (2013). Meditation states and traits: EEG, ERP, and neuroimaging studies. *Psychology of Consciousness: Theory, Research, & Practice, 1*(S), 48–96. doi:10.1037/2326-5523.1.S.48

Cain, D. J. (2014). Person-centered therapy. In G. R. VandenBos, E. Meidenbauer, et al. (Eds.), *Psychotherapy theories & techniques: A reader* (pp. 251–259). Washington, DC: American Psychological Association. doi:10.1037/14295-027

Cain, S. (2012). *Quiet: The power of introverts in a world that can't stop talking.* New York, NY: Crown Publishers/Random House.

Calabrese, F., Molteni, R., et al. (2009). Neuronal plasticity: A link between stress and mood disorders. *Psychoneuroendocrinology, 34*(Suppl. 1), S208–S216. doi:10.1016/j.psyneuen.2009.05.014

Calabria, B., Degenhardt, L., et al. (2010). Systematic review of prospective studies investigating "remission" from amphetamine, cannabis, cocaine, or opioid dependence. *Addictive Behaviors, 35*(8), 741–749. doi:10.1016/j.addbeh.2010.03.019

Calhoun, J. B. (1962). A "behavioral sink." In E. L. Bliss (Ed.), *Roots of behavior* (pp. 295–315). New York, NY: Harper & Row.

Caliari, P. (2008). Enhancing forehand acquisition in table tennis: The role of mental practice. *Journal of Applied Sport Psychology, 20*(1), 88–96.

Caligiuri, P., & Lundby, K. (2015). Developing cross-cultural competencies through global teams. In J. L. Wildman & R. L. Griffith (Eds.), *Leading global teams* (pp. 123–139). New York, NY: Springer.

Callaghan, R. C., Allebeck, P., & Sidorchuk, A. (2013). Marijuana use and risk of lung cancer: A 40-year cohort study. *Cancer Causes & Control, 24*(10), 1811–1820.

Calvin, C. M., Fernandes, C., et al. (2010). Sex, intelligence, and educational achievement in a national cohort of over 175,000 11-year-old schoolchildren in England. *Intelligence, 38*(4), 424–432.

Calzada, E. J., Fernandez, Y., & Cortes, D. E. (2010). Incorporating the cultural value of respeto into a framework of Latino parenting. *Cultural Diversity & Ethnic Minority Psychology, 16*(1), 77–86. doi:10.1037/a0016071

Cambron, M. J., Acitelli, L. K., & Pettit, J. W. (2009). Explaining gender differences in depression: An interpersonal contingent self-esteem perspective. *Sex Roles, 61*(11–12), 751–761. doi:10.1007/s11199-009-9616-6

Cameron, H. A., & Glover, L. R. (2015). Adult neurogenesis: Beyond learning and memory. *Annual Review of Psychology, 66*, 53–81. doi:10.1146/annurev-psych-010814-015006

Cameron, J., & Pierce, W. D. (2002). *Rewards and intrinsic motivation: Resolving the controversy.* Westport, CO: Bergin & Garvey.

Cameron, M., Crane, N., et al. (2013). Promoting well-being through creativity: How arts and public health can learn from each other. *Perspectives in Public Health, 133*(1), 52–59. doi:10.1177/1757913912466951

Campbell, B. (2008). *Handbook of differentiated instruction using the multiple intelligences.* Boston, MA: Pearson/Allyn & Bacon.

Campbell, J. P. (2013). Assessment in industrial and organizational psychology: An overview. In K. F. Geisinger, B. A. Bracken, et al. (Eds.), *APA handbook of testing and assessment in psychology* (Vol. 1): *Test theory and testing and assessment in industrial and organizational psychology* (pp. 355–395). Washington, DC: American Psychological Association. doi:10.1037/14047-022

Camperio Ciani, A. S., Fontanesi, L., et al. (2012). Factors associated with higher fecundity in female maternal relatives of homosexual men. *Journal of Sexual Medicine, 9*(11), 2878–2887. doi:10.1111/j.1743-6109.2012.02785.x

Campo, M., Laborde, S., & Weckemann, S. (2015). Emotional intelligence training: Implications for performance and health. In A. M. Columbus (Ed.), *Advances in psychology research* (Vol. 101, pp. 75–92).

Campos, A., Camino, E., & Pérez-Fabello, M. (2011). Using the keyword mnemonics method among adult learners. *Educational Gerontology, 37*(4), 327–335. doi:10.1080/03601271003608886

Campos, A., Rodríguez-Pinal, M. D., & Pérez-Fabello, M. (2013). Receptive and productive recall with the keyword mnemonics in bilingual students. *Current Psychology.* doi:10.1007/s12144-013-9197-y

Canadian Psychological Association. (2020). Careers in and related to psychology. Retrieved April 26, 2020, from http://www.cpa.ca/students/career/careersinpsychology/

Cannon, D. M., Klaver, J. M., et al. (2013). Gender-specific abnormalities in the serotonin transporter system in panic disorder. *International Journal of Neuropsychopharmacology, 16*(4), 733–743. doi:10.1017/S1461145712000776

Cannon, W. B. (1932). *The wisdom of the body.* New York, NY: Norton.

Cannon, W. B. (1934). Hunger and thirst. In C. Murchinson (Ed.), *Handbook of general experimental psychology* (pp. 247–263). Worcester, MA: Clark University Press. doi:10.1037/11374-005

Cannon, W. B., & Washburn, A. L. (1912). An explanation of hunger. *American Journal of Physiology, 29*, 441–454.

Caplan, P. J. (1995). *They say you're crazy.* Reading, MA: Addison-Wesley.

Caporro, M., Haneef, Z., et al. (2012). Functional MRI of sleep spindles and K-complexes. *Clinical Neurophysiology, 123*(2), 303–309. doi:10.1016/j.clinph.2011.06.018

Caputi, A. A., Aguilera, P. A., et al. (2013). On the haptic nature of the active electric sense of fish. *Brain Research, 1536*, 27–43. doi:10.1016/j.brainres.2013.05.028

Carcaillon, L., Brailly-Tabard, S., et al. (2014). Low testosterone and the risk of dementia in elderly men: Impact of age and education. *Alzheimer's & Dementia, 10*(5), S306–S314. doi:10.1016/j.jalz.2013.06.006

Cardeña, E., Winkelman, M., et al. (Eds.). (2011). *Altering consciousness: Multidisciplinary perspectives* (Vol. 1): *History, culture and the humanities.* Westport, CT: Praeger.

Carlbring, P., Gunnarsdóttir, M., et al. (2007). Treatment of social phobia: Randomized trial of Internet-delivered cognitive-behavioural therapy with telephone support. *British Journal of Psychiatry, 190*(2), 123–128. doi:10.1192/bjp.bp.105.020107

Carlson, J., & Maniacci, M. P. (Eds.) (2012). *Alfred Adler revisited.* New York, NY: Routledge.

Carlson, N. R., & Birkett, M. A. (2017). *Physiology of behavior* (12th ed.). Boston, MA: Allyn & Bacon.

Carlson, T. N., & Settle, J. E. (2016). Political chameleons: An exploration of conformity in political discussions. *Political Behavior, 38*(4), 817–859. doi:10.1007/s11109-016-9335-y

Carnagey, N. L., & Anderson, C. A. (2004). Violent video game exposure and aggression: A literature review. *Minerva Psichiatrica, 45*(1), 1–18.

Carnagey, N. L., Anderson, C. A., & Bushman, B. J. (2007). The effect of video game violence on physiological desensitization to real-life violence. *Journal of Experimental Social Psychology, 43*(3), 489–496. doi:10.1016/j.jesp.2006.05.003

Carney, R. N., & Levin, J. R. (2003). Promoting higher-order learning benefits by building lower-order mnemonic connections. *Applied Cognitive Psychology, 17*(5), 563–575. doi:10.1002/acp.889

Carney, R. N., & Levin, J. R. (2014). Learning more about and with the face–name mnemonic strategy. *Applied Cognitive Psychology, 28*(4), 569–578. doi:10.1002/acp.3036

Carr, P. B., & Steele, C. M. (2010). Stereotype threat affects financial decision making. *Psychological Science, 21*(10), 1411–1416. doi:10.1177/0956797610384146

Carrico, A. R., & Riemer, M. (2011). Motivating energy conservation in the workplace: An evaluation of the use of group-level feedback and peer education. *Journal of Environmental Psychology, 31*(1), 1–13. doi:10.1016/j.jenvp.2010.11.004

Carroll, D. W. (2008). *Psychology of language* (5th ed.). Boston, MA: Cengage Learning.

Carroll, J. L. (2016). *Sexuality now: Embracing diversity* (5th ed.). Boston, MA: Cengage Learning.

Carroll, J. M., & Russell, J. A. (1996). Do facial expressions signal specific emotions? Judging emotion from the face in context. *Journal of Personality & Social Psychology, 70*(2), 205–218. doi:10.1037/0022-3514.70.2.205

Carroll, J. S., Padilla-Walker, L. M., et al. (2008). Generation XXX: Pornography acceptance and use among emerging adults. *Journal of Adolescent Research, 23*(1), 6–30. doi:10.1177/0743558407306348

Carskadon, M. A., Acebo, C., & Jenni, O. C. (2004). Regulation of adolescent sleep: Implications for behavior. *Annals of the New York Academy of Science, 1021*, 276–291. doi:10.1196/annals.1308.032

Carstensen, L. L., & DeLiema, M. (2018). The positivity effect: A negativity bias in youth fades with age. *Current Opinion in Behavioral Sciences, 19*, 7–12. doi:10.1016/j.cobeha.2017.07.009

Carter, D. A., Simkins, B. J., & Simpson, W. G. (2003). Corporate governance, board diversity, and firm value. *Financial Review, 38*, 33–53.

Carter, G., Campbell, A. C., & Muncer, S. (2014). The dark triad personality: Attractiveness to women. *Personality & Individual Differences, 56*, 57–61. doi:10.1016/j.paid.2013.08.021

Carter, M. J. (2013). Advancing identity theory: Examining the relationship between activated identities and behavior in different social contexts. *Social Psychology Quarterly, 76*(3), 203–223.

Caruso, D. R., Salovey, P., & Mayer, J. D. (2015). The ability model of emotional intelligence. In S. Joseph (Ed.), *Positive psychology in practice: Promoting human flourishing in work, health, education, and everyday life* (2nd ed., pp. 545–558). New York, NY: Wiley.

Carver, C. S., & Scheier, M. F. (2014). Dispositional optimism. *Trends in Cognitive Sciences, 18*, 293–299. doi:10.1016/j.tics.2014.02.003

Case, B. G., Bertollo, D. N., et al. (2013). Declining use of electroconvulsive therapy in United States general hospitals. *Biological Psychiatry, 73*(2), 119–126. doi:10.1016/j.biopsych.2012.09.005

Casey, A. A., Elliott, M., et al. (2008). Impact of the food environment and physical activity environment on behaviors and weight status in rural U.S. Communities. *Preventive Medicine, 47*(6), 600–604. doi:10.1016/j.ypmed.2008.10.001

Casey-Campbell, M., & Martens, M. L. (2009). Sticking it all together: A critical assessment of the group cohesion–performance literature. *International Journal of Management Reviews, 11*(2), 223–246. doi:10.1111/j.1468-2370.2008.00239.x

Caspi, A., Roberts, B. W., & Shiner, R. L. (2005). Personality development: Stability and change. *Annual Review of Psychology, 56*, 453–484. doi:10.1146/annurev.psych.55.090902.141913

Cassady, J. C. (2004). The influence of cognitive test anxiety across the learning-testing cycle. *Learning & Instruction, 14*(6), 569–592.

Casselle, G. (2009). What is it really like to have electroconvulsive therapy? *Journal of ECT, 25*(4), 289. doi:10.1097/YCT.0b013e3181a59f97

Cassimatis, N. L. (2012). Artificial intelligence and cognitive modeling have the same problem. In P. Wang & B. Goertzel (Eds.), *Theoretical foundations of artificial general intelligence* (pp. 11–24). Amsterdam: Atlantis Press. doi:10.2991/978-94-91216-62-6_2

Castañeda, H., Holmes, S. M., et al. (2015). Immigration as a social determinant of health. *Annual Review of Public Health, 36*, 375–392. doi:10.1146/annurev-publhealth-032013-182419

Castañeda, T. R., Tong, J., et al. (2010). Ghrelin in the regulation of body weight and metabolism. *Frontiers in Neuroendocrinology, 31*(1), 44–60. doi:10.1016/j.yfrne.2009.10.008

Castellano, J. A., & Frazier, A. D. (Eds.). (2011). *Special populations in gifted education: Understanding our most able students from diverse backgrounds.* Waco, TX: Prufrock Press.

Castle, D., Murray, R., et al. (Eds.). (2012). *Marijuana and madness* (2nd ed.). London, UK: Cambridge University Press.

Castles, E. E. (2012). *Inventing intelligence: How America came to worship IQ.* Santa Barbara, CA: Praeger.

Castro, J., Gila, A., et al. (2004). Perfectionism dimensions in children and adolescents with anorexia nervosa. *Journal of Adolescent Health, 35*(5), 392–398. doi:10.1016/j.jadohealth.2003.11.094

Castro-Schilo, L., & Kee, D. W. (2010). Gender differences in the relationship between emotional intelligence and right hemisphere lateralization for facial processing. *Brain & Cognition, 73*(1), 62–67. doi:10.1016/j.bandc.2010.03.003

Cattell, R. B. (1965). *The scientific analysis of personality*. Baltimore, MD: Penguin.

Cattell, R. B. (1973). Personality pinned down. *Psychology Today*, July, 40–46.

Caulfield, M. (2017). *Web literacy for student fact-checkers*. Retrieved December 14, 2020, from https://open.umn.edu/opentextbooks/textbooks/454

Cavaco, S., Anderson, S. W., et al. (2004). The scope of preserved procedural memory in amnesia. *Brain: A Journal of Neurology, 127*(8), 1853–1867. doi:10.1093/brain/awh208

Cavanaugh, J. C., & Blanchard-Fields, F. (2015). *Adult development and aging* (7th ed.). Boston, MA: Cengage Learning.

Cavazotte, F., Moreno, V., & Hickmann, M. (2012). Effects of leader intelligence, personality and emotional intelligence on transformational leadership and managerial performance. *The Leadership Quarterly, 23*(3), 443–455. doi:10.1016/j.leaqua.2011.10.003

Cellard, C., Lefèbvre, A.-A., et al. (2010). An examination of the relative contribution of saturation and selective attention to memory deficits in patients with recent-onset schizophrenia and their unaffected parents. *Journal of Abnormal Psychology, 119*(1), 60–70. doi:10.1037/a0018397

Center for Behavioral Health Statistics and Quality. (2019). *Key substance use and mental health indicators in the United States: Results from the 2018 National Survey on Drug Use and Health*. Retrieved July 6, 2020, from https://www.samhsa.gov/data/sites/default/files/cbhsq-reports/NSDUHNationalFindingsReport2018/NSDUHNationalFindingsReport2018.pdf

Center on the Developing Child at Harvard University. (2011). *Building the brain's "air traffic control" system: How early experiences shape the development of executive function*. Retrieved July 19, 2020, from https://developingchild.harvard.edu/resources/building-the-brains-air-traffic-control-system-how-early-experiences-shape-the-development-of-executive-function/b

Centers for Disease Control. (2017a). *Electronic aggression*. Retrieved July 19, 2020, from https://www.cdc.gov/violenceprevention/youthviolence/electronicaggression/

Centers for Disease Control. (2017b). *Many workers get too little sleep*. Retrieved July 20, 2020, from https://www.cdc.gov/niosh/updates/upd-03-03-17.html

Centers for Disease Control. (2018a). *Health, United States, 2018*. Retrieved July 19, 2020, from https://www.cdc.gov/nchs/data/hus/hus18.pdf

Centers for Disease Control. (2018b). *Youth Risk Behavior Surveillance–United States, 2017*. Retrieved July 19, 2020, from https://www.cdc.gov/healthyyouth/data/yrbs/pdf/2017/ss6708.pdf

Centers for Disease Control. (2019a). *Current cigarette smoking among adults in the United State*. Retrieved July 19, 2020, from https://www.cdc.gov/tobacco/data_statistics/fact_sheets/adult_data/cig_smoking/index.htm

Centers for Disease Control. (2019b). *Drowsy driving: Asleep at the wheel*. Retrieved July 19, 2020, from www.cdc.gov/Features/dsDrowsyDriving/index.html

Centers for Disease Control. (2019c). *Sexually transmitted disease surveillance 2018*. Retrieved July 20, 2020, from https://www.cdc.gov/std/stats18/default.htm

Centers for Disease Control. (2020a). *Fragile X Syndrome (FXS)*. Retrieved July 20, 2020, from www.cdc.gov/ncbddd/fxs/data.html

Centers for Disease Control. (2020b). *HIV in the United States: At a glance*. Retrieved July 20, 2020, from https://www.cdc.gov/hiv/statistics/overview/ataglance.html

Centers for Disease Control. (2020c). *Injury prevention & control: Opioid overdose*. Retrieved July 20, 2020, from www.cdc.gov/drugoverdose

Centers for Disease Control. (2020d). *Opioid overdose*. Retrieved July 29, 2020, from https://www.cdc.gov/drugoverdose/index.html

Centers for Disease Control. (2020e). *Reproductive health: Teen pregnancy*. Retrieved July 20, 2020, from http://www.cdc.gov/teenpregnancy/index.htm

Centers for Disease Control. (2020f). *Smoking cessation*. Retrieved July 20, 2020, from https://www.cdc.gov/tobacco/quit_smoking/index.htm

Centers for Disease Control. (2020g). *Violence prevention: Suicide*. Retrieved July 19, 2020, from https://www.cdc.gov/violenceprevention/suicide/fastfact.html

Centofanti, A. T., & Reece, J. (2006). The cognitive interview and its effect on misleading postevent information. *Psychology, Crime & Law, 12*(6), 669–683. doi:10.1080/10683160600558394

Cervone, D., & Pervin, L. A. (2013). *Personality: Theory & research* (12th ed.). New York, NY: Wiley.

Ceylan, M., & Sayin, A. (2012). Neurobiology of repression: A hypothetical interpretation. *Integrative Psychological & Behavioral Science, 46*(3), 395–409. doi:10.1007/s12124-012-9197-8

Chabas, D., Taheri, S., et al. (2003). The genetics of narcolepsy. *Annual Review of Genomics & Human Genetics, 4*, 459–483. doi:10.1146/annurev.genom.4.070802.110432

Chaffee, J. (2019). *Thinking critically* (12th ed.). Boston, MA: Cengage Learning.

Challacombe, F., Oldfield, V. B., & Salkovskis, P. M. (2011). *Break free from OCD: Overcoming obsessive compulsive disorder using CBT*. London, UK: Vermillion.

Chalmers. D. J. (2010). *The character of consciousness*. New York, NY: Oxford University Press.

Chambers, R. (2013). Adult hippocampal neurogenesis in the pathogenesis of addiction and dual diagnosis disorders. *Drug & Alcohol Dependence, 130*, 1–12. doi:10.1016/j.drugalcdep.2012.12.005

Chamorro-Premuzic, T., & Furnham, A. (2003). Personality predicts academic performance. *Journal of Research in Personality, 37*(4), 319–338. doi:10.1016/S0092-6566(02)00578-0

Chamorro-Premuzic, T., & Furnham, A. (2010). *The psychology of personnel selection*. New York, NY: Cambridge University Press.

Chance, P. (2014). *Learning and behavior* (7th ed.). Boston, MA: Cengage Learning.

Chang, B., Dusek, J. A., & Benson, H. (2011). Psychobiological changes from relaxation response elicitation: Long-term practitioners vs. novices. *Psychosomatics: Journal of Consultation Liaison Psychiatry, 52*(6), 550–559.

Chang, C., Pan, W., et al. (2012). Postural activity and motion sickness during video game play in children and adults. *Experimental Brain Research, 217*(2), 299–309. doi:10.1007/s00221-011-2993-4

Chang, J.-H. (2009). Chronic pain: Cultural sensitivity to pain. In S. Eshun & R. A. R. Gurung (Eds.), *Culture and mental health: Sociocultural influences, theory, and practice* (pp. 71–89). New York, NY: Wiley-Blackwell. doi:10.1002/9781444305807

Chansler, P. A., Swamidass, P. M., & Cammann, C. (2003). Self-managing work teams: An empirical study of group cohesiveness in "natural work groups" at a Harley-Davidson Motor Company plant. *Small Group Research, 34*(1), 101–120.

Chapleau, K. M., & Oswald, D. L. (2010). Power, sex, and rape myth acceptance: Testing two models of rape proclivity. *Journal of Sex Research, 47*(1), 66–78.

Charmaraman, L., & Grossman, J. M. (2010). Importance of race and ethnicity: An exploration of Asian, Black, Latino, and multiracial adolescent identity. *Cultural Diversity & Ethnic Minority Psychology, 16*(2), 144–151. doi:10.1037/a0018668

Chaves, J. F. (2000). Hypnosis. In A. Kazdin (Ed.), *Encyclopedia of psychology* (Vol. 4, pp. 211–216). Washington, DC: American Psychological Association.

Cheah, C. L., Leung, C. Y., & Zhou, N. (2013). Understanding "tiger parenting" through the perceptions of Chinese immigrant mothers: Can Chinese and U.S. parenting coexist? *Asian American Journal of Psychology, 4*(1), 30–40. doi:10.1037/a0031217

Check, J. V., & Malamuth, N. M. (1983). Sex role stereotyping and reactions to depictions of stranger versus acquaintance rape. *Journal of Personality & Social Psychology, 45*, 344–356.

Chein, J. M., & Fiez, J. A. (2010). Evaluating models of working memory through the effects of concurrent irrelevant information. *Journal of Experimental Psychology: General, 139*(1), 117–137. doi:10.1037/a0018200

Chen, C., Lin, Y., & Hsiao, C. (2012). Celebrity endorsement for sporting events using classical conditioning. *International Journal of Sports Marketing & Sponsorship, 13*(3), 209–219.

Cheng, C., & Lin, Y. (2012). The effects of aging on lifetime of auditory sensory memory in humans. *Biological Psychology, 89*(2), 306–312. doi:10.1016/j.biopsycho.2011.11.003

Cherner, R. A., & Reissing, E. D. (2013). A comparative study of sexual function, behavior, and cognitions of women with lifelong vaginismus. *Archives of Sexual Behavior, 42*(8), 1605–1614. doi:10.1007/s10508-013-0111-3

Chernev, A., Böckenholt, U., et al. (2015). Choice overload: A conceptual review and meta-analysis. *Journal of Consumer Psychology, 25*(2), 333–358. doi:10.1016/j.jcps.2014.08.002

Chess, S., & Thomas, A. (1986). *Know your child*. New York, NY: Basic.

Cheyne, J. A., & Girard, T. A. (2009). The body unbound: Vestibular-motor hallucinations and out-of-body experiences. *Cortex, 45*(2), 201–215. doi:10.1016/j.cortex.2007.05.002

Chipman, M., & Jin, Y. L. (2009). Drowsy drivers: The effect of light and circadian rhythm on crash occurrence. *Safety Science, 47*(10), 1364–1370. doi:10.1016/j.ssci.2009.03.005

Choi, O. (2015). Using fMRI for lie detection: Ready for court? In K. J. Weiss & Watson, C. (Eds.), *Psychiatric expert testimony: Emerging applications* (pp. 84–101). New York, NY: Oxford University Press. doi:10.1093/med/9780199346592.003.0006

Chomsky, N. (1986). *Knowledge of language*. New York, NY: Praeger.

Choy, M. M., Farber, K. G., et al. (2017). Electroconvulsive therapy (ECT) in the news: "Balance" leads to bias. *Journal of ECT, 33*(1), 1–2. doi:10.1097/YCT.0000000000000376

Christakis, N. A., & Fowler, J. H. (2007). The spread of obesity in a large social network over 32 years. *New England Journal of Medicine, 357*(4), 370–379.

Christakis, N. A., & Fowler, J. H. (2008). The collective dynamics of smoking in a large social network. *New England Journal of Medicine, 358*(21), 2249–2258. doi:10.1056/NEJMsa0706154

Christakis, N. A., & Fowler, J. H. (2009). *Connected: The surprising power of our social networks and how they shape our lives*. New York, NY: Little, Brown.

Christensen, K., Nørskov, S., et al. (2017). In search of new product ideas: Identifying ideas in online communities by machine learning and text mining. *Creativity and Innovation Management*. Retrieved July 20, 2020, from https://pure.au.dk/portal/files/143667296/Christensen_2017_In_search_of_new_product_ideas.pdf

Christian, M. S., Edwards, B. D., & Bradley, J. C. (2010). Situational judgment tests: Constructs assessed and a meta-analysis of their criterion-related validities. *Personnel Psychology, 63*(1), 83–117.

Chua, A. (2011). *Battle hymn of the tiger mother*. New York, NY: Penguin

Chua, H. F., Boland, J. E., & Nisbett, R. E. (2005). Cultural variation in eye movements during scene perception. *Proceedings of the National Academy of Sciences, 102*(35), 12629–12633. doi:10.1073/pnas.0506162102

Cialdini, R. B. (2009). *Influence: Science and practice* (5th ed.). Boston, MA: Allyn & Bacon.

Cialdini, R. B., & Griskevicius, V. (2010). Social influence. In R. F. Baumeister & E. J. Finkel (Eds.), *Advanced social*

psychology: The state of the science (pp. 385–417). New York, NY: Oxford University Press.

Cialdini, R. B., Reno, R. R., & Kallgren, C. A. (1990). A focus theory of normative conduct: Recycling the concept of norms to reduce littering in public places. *Journal of Personality & Social Psychology, 58*(6), 1015–1026. doi:10.1037/0022-3514.58.6.1015

Cicchetti, D. (2016). Socioemotional, personality, and biological development: Illustrations from a multilevel developmental psychopathology perspective on child maltreatment. *Annual Review of Psychology, 67*, 187–211. doi:10.1146/annurev-psych-122414-033259

Cicciola, E., Foschi, R., et al. (2014). Making up intelligence scales: De Sanctis's and Binet's tests, 1905 and after. *History of Psychology, 17*(3), 223–236. doi:10.1037/a0033740

Ciobanu, L. G., Sachdev, P. S., et al. (2016). Differential gene expression in brain and peripheral tissues in depression across the life span: A review of replicated findings. *Neuroscience & Biobehavioral Reviews, 71*, 281–293. doi:10.1016/j.neubiorev.2016.08.018

Cipolli, C., Mazzetti, M., & Plazzi, G. (2013). Sleep-dependent memory consolidation in patients with sleep disorders. *Sleep Medicine Reviews, 17*(2), 91–103. doi:10.1016/j.smrv.2012.01.004

Cisler, J. M., Olatunji, B. O., et al. (2010). Emotion regulation and the anxiety disorders: An integrative review. *Journal of Psychopathology & Behavioral Assessment, 32*(1), 68–82. doi:10.1007/s10862-009-9161-1

Citrome, L. (2011). Neurochemical models of schizophrenia: Transcending dopamine. *Annals of Clinical Psychiatry, 23*(4), S10–S14.

Claessens, M. (2009). Mindfulness and existential therapy. *Existential Analysis, 20*(1), 109–119.

Clark, J. A., & Fessler, D. M. T. (2014). Recontextualizing the behavioral immune system within psychoneuroimmunology. *Evolutionary Behavioral Sciences, 8*(4), 235–243. doi:10.1037/ebs0000024

Clark, S. E., Rush, R. A., & Moreland, M. B. (2013). Constructing the lineup: Law, reform, theory, and data. In B. L. Cutler (Ed.), *Reform of eyewitness identification procedures* (pp. 87–112). Washington, DC: American Psychological Association. doi:10.1037/14094-005

Clarke, J., & Mack, A. (2015). Iconic memory for natural scenes: Evidence using a modified change-detection procedure. *Visual Cognition, 23*(7), 917–938. doi:10.1080/13506285.2015. 1103826

Claudat, K., White, E. K., & Warren, C. S. (2016). Acculturative stress, self-esteem, and eating pathology in Latina and Asian American female college students. *Journal of Clinical Psychology, 72*(1), 88–100. doi:10.1002/jclp.22234

Clayton, N. S. (2017). Episodic-like memory and mental time travel in animals. In J. Call, G. M. Burghardt, et al. (Eds.), *APA handbook of comparative psychology: Basic concepts, methods, neural substrate, and behavior: Perception, learning, and cognition* (Vol. 2, pp. 227–243). Washington, DC: American Psychological Association.

Clayton, A. H., & Hamilton, D. V. (2009). Female orgasmic disorder. In R. Balon & R. T. Segraves (Eds.), *Clinical manual of sexual disorders* (pp. 251–271). Arlington, VA: American Psychiatric Publishing.

Clearfield, M. W., & Nelson, N. M. (2006). Sex differences in mothers' speech and play behavior with 6-, 9-, and 14-month-old infants. *Sex Roles, 54*(1–2), 127–137.

Clifford, A., Lang, L., & Chen, R. (2012). Effects of maternal cigarette smoking during pregnancy on cognitive parameters of children and young adults: A literature review. *Neurotoxicology & Teratology, 34*(6), 560–570. doi:10.1016/j.ntt.2012.09.004

Cnattingius, S., Signorello, L. B., et al. (2000). Caffeine intake and the risk of first-trimester spontaneous abortion. *New England Journal of Medicine, 343*(25), 1839–1845.

Cobb, N. K., & Abrams, D. B. (2011). E-cigarette or drug-delivery device? Regulating novel nicotine products. *New England Journal of Medicine, 365*(3), 193–195. doi:10.1056/NEJMp1105249

Cochran, G. M., & Harpending, H. (2009). *The 10,000-year explosion*. New York, NY: Basic Books.

Coelho, V. A., Marchante, M., et al. (2017). Promoting a positive middle school transition: A randomized controlled treatment study examining self-concept and self-esteem. *Journal of Youth & Adolescence, 46*(3), 558–569. doi:10.1007/s10964-016-0510-6

Cohen, H. (2006). Two stories of PTSD. *Psych Central*. Retrieved on July 20, 2020, from psychcentral.com/lib/two-stories-of-ptsd

Cohen, K., & Collens, P. (2013). The impact of trauma work on trauma workers: A metasynthesis on vicarious trauma and vicarious posttraumatic growth. *Psychological Trauma, 5*(6), 570–580. doi:10.1037/a0030388

Cohen, L. J., Forman, H., et al. (2010). Comparison of childhood sexual histories in subjects with pedophilia or opiate addiction and healthy controls: Is childhood sexual abuse a risk factor for addictions? *Journal of Psychiatric Practice, 16*(6), 394–404. doi:10.1097/01.pra.0000390758.27451.79

Cohen, S., Evans, G. W., et al. (1981). Cardiovascular and behavioral effects of community noise. *American Scientist, 69*, 528–535.

Cohen, S., Tyrrell, D. A., & Smith, A. P. (1993). Negative life events, perceived stress, negative affect, and susceptibility to the common cold. *Journal of Personality & Social Psychology, 64*(1), 131–140. doi:10.1037/0022-3514.64.1.131

Cohn, E., Bucolo, D., et al. (2009). Reducing white juror bias: The role of race salience and racial attitudes. *Journal of Applied Social Psychology, 39*(8), 1953–1973. doi:10.1111/j.1559-1816.2009.00511.x

Colangelo, J. J. (2007). Recovered memory debate revisited: Practice implications for mental health counselors. *Journal of Mental Health Counseling, 29*(2), 93–120.

Colby, S. L., & Ortman, J. M. (2016). *Projections of the size and composition of the U.S. Population: 2014 to 2060.* Retrieved July 20, 2020, from https://www.census.gov/library/publications/2015/demo/p25-1143.html

Cole, M. W., Yarkoni, T., et al. (2012). Global connectivity of prefrontal cortex predicts cognitive control and intelligence. *Journal of Neuroscience, 32*(26), 8988–8999. doi:10.1523/JNEUROSCI.0536-12.2012

Cole, T., Barrett, D. J. K., & Griffiths, M. D. (2011). Social facilitation in online and offline gambling: A pilot study. *International Journal of Mental Health & Addiction, 9*(3), 240–247. doi:10.1007/s11469-010-9281-6

Colin, A. K., & Moore, K., & West, A. N. (1996). Creativity, oversensitivity, and rate of habituation. *EDRA: Environmental Design Research Association, 20*(4), 423–427. doi:10.1016/0191-8869(95)00193-X

Collins, A. M., & Quillian, M. R. (1969). Retrieval time from semantic memory. *Journal of Verbal Learning & Verbal Behavior, 8*, 240–247. doi:10.1016/S0022-5371(69)80069-1

Collins, N. L., Cooper, M. L., et al. (2002). Psychosocial vulnerability from adolescence to adulthood: A prospective study of attachment style differences in relationship functioning and partner choice. *Journal of Personality, 70*(6), 965–1008. doi:10.1111/1467-6494.05029

Comas-Diaz, L. (2012). *Multicultural care: A clinician's guide to cultural competence.* Washington, DC: American Psychological Association.

Comer, R. J. (2018). *Abnormal psychology* (10th ed.). New York, NY: Palgrave MacMillan.

Compton, W. C., & Hoffman, E. (2019). *Positive psychology: The science of happiness and flourishing* (3rd ed.). Boston, MA: Cengage Learning.

Concha, A., Mills, D. S., et al. (2014). Using sniffing behavior to differentiate true negative from false negative responses in trained scent-detection dogs. *Chemical Senses, 39*(9), 749–754. doi:10.1093/chemse/bju045

Confer, J. C., Easton, J. A., et al. (2010). Evolutionary psychology: Controversies, questions, prospects, and limitations. *American Psychologist, 65*(2), 110–126. doi:10.1037/a0018413

Conley, K. M., & Lehman, B. J. (2012). Test anxiety and cardiovascular responses to daily academic stressors. *Stress & Health, 28*(1), 41–50. doi:10.1002/smi.1399

Conley, T. D., Moors, A. C., et al. (2011). Women, men, and the bedroom: Methodological and conceptual insights that narrow, reframe, and eliminate gender differences in sexuality. *Current Directions in Psychological Science, 20*(5), 296–300. doi:10.1177/0963721411418467

Conlon, K. E., Ehrlinger, J., et al. (2011). Eyes on the prize: The longitudinal benefits of goal focus on progress toward a weight loss goal. *Journal of Experimental Social Psychology, 47*, 853–855. doi:10.1016/j.jesp.2011.02.005

Connolly, T. M., Boyle, E. A., et al. (2012). A systematic literature review of empirical evidence on computer games and serious games. *Computers & Education, 59*(2), 661–686. doi:10.1016/j.compedu.2012.03.004

Conron, K. J., Mimiaga, M. J., & Landers, S. J. (2010). A population-based study of sexual orientation identity and gender differences in adult health. *American Journal of Public Health, 100*(10), 1953–1960. doi:10.2105/AJPH.2009.174169

Constantino, M. J., Coyne, A. E., et al. (2017, February 9). Therapeutic alliance, subsequent change, and moderators of the alliance—outcome association in Interpersonal Psychotherapy for depression. *Psychotherapy*, n.p. doi:10.1037/pst0000101

Conway, M. A., Cohen, G., & Stanhope, N. (1992). Very long-term memory for knowledge acquired at school and university. *Applied Cognitive Psychology, 6*(6), 467–482. doi:10.1002/acp.2350060603

Cook, R., Bird, G., et al. (2014). Mirror neurons: From origin to function. *Behavioral & Brain Sciences, 37*(2), 177–192. doi:10.1017/S0140525X13000903

Cook, S. G. (2013). Behavioral interviews: Hire for the competencies needed. *Women in Higher Education, 22*(3), 23–24. doi:10.1002/whe.10437

Coolidge, F. L., & Wynn, T. (2009). *The rise of Homo Sapiens: The evolution of modern thinking*. New York, NY: Wiley-Blackwell.

Cooper, H. (2010). *Research synthesis and meta-analysis*. Thousand Oaks, CA: Sage.

Cooper, J. (2007). *Cognitive dissonance: Fifty years of a classic theory*. Thousand Oaks, CA: Sage.

Cooper, J., Bennett, E. A., & Sukel, H. L. (1996). Complex scientific testimony: How do jurors make decisions? *Law & Human Behavior, 20*(4), 379–394.

Cooper, M., & McLeod, J. (2011). Person-centered therapy: A pluralistic perspective. *Person-Centered & Experiential Psychotherapies, 10*(3), 210–223. doi:10.1080/14779757.2011. 599517

Cooper, P. J., & Murray, L. (2001). The treatment and prevention of postpartum depression and associated disturbances in child development. *Archives of Women's Mental Health, 3*(Suppl. 2), 5.

Cooper, R. P., Abraham, J., et al. (1997). The development of infants' preference for motherese. *Infant Behavior & Development, 20*(4), 477–488. doi:10.1016/S0163-6383(97)90037-0

Cooper, S. J. (2008). From Claude Bernard to Walter Cannon: Emergence of the concept of homeostasis. *Appetite, 51*(3), 419–427. doi:10.1016/j.appet.2008.06.005

Corballis, M. C. (2010). Visions of the split brain. *New Zealand Journal of Psychology, 39*(1), 5–7.

Corbin, W. R., & Fromme, K. (2002). Alcohol use and serial monogamy as risks for sexually transmitted diseases in young adults. *Health Psychology, 21*(3), 229–236.

Corcoran, R. (2010). The allusive cognitive deficit in paranoia: The case for mental time travel or cognitive self-projection.

In P. R. Shaver & M. Mikulincer (Eds.), *Human aggression and violence: Causes, manifestations, and consequences* (pp. 15–33). Washington, DC: American Psychological Association. doi:10.1037/12346-001

DeWall, C. N., Lambert, N. M., et al. (2011). So far away from one's partner, yet so close to romantic alternatives: Avoidant attachment, interest in alternatives, and infidelity. *Journal of Personality & Social Psychology, 101*(6), 1302–1316. doi:10.1037/a0025497

Dewar, M., Della Sala, S., et al. (2010). Profound retroactive interference in anterograde amnesia: What interferes? *Neuropsychology, 24*(3), 357–367. doi:10.1037/a0018207

Dewey J. (1910). *How we think.* Lexington, MA: D.C. Heath. Retrieved July 20, 2020, from http://www.gutenberg.org/files/37423/37423-h/37423-h.htm

Dexter, C. A., Wong, K., et al. (2013). Parenting and attachment among low-income African American and Caucasian preschoolers. *Journal of Family Psychology, 27*(4), 629–638. doi:10.1037/a0033341

DeYoung, C. G., Hirsh, J. B., et al. (2010). Testing predictions from personality neuroscience: Brain structure and the Big Five. *Psychological Science, 21*(6), 820–828. doi:10.1177/0956797610370159

Di Lorenzo, P. M., & Youngentob, S. L. (2013). Taste and olfaction. In R. J. Nelson, S. Y. Mizumori, & I. B. Weiner (Eds.), *Handbook of psychology* (Vol. 3): *Behavioral neuroscience* (2nd ed., pp. 272–305). New York, NY: Wiley.

Diamond, M. (2009). Human intersexuality: Difference or disorder? *Archives of Sexual Behavior, 38*(2), 172.

Diano, S., Farr, S. A., et al. (2006). Ghrelin controls hippocampal spine synapse density and memory performance. *Nature Neuroscience, 9*, 381–388. doi:10.1038/nn1656

Dick-Niederhauser, A., & Silverman, W. K. (2006). Separation anxiety disorder. In J. E. Fisher & W. T. O'Donohue (Eds.), *Practitioner's guide to evidence-based psychotherapy* (pp. 627–633). New York, NY: Springer. doi:10.1007/978-0-387-28370-8_62

Dicke-Bohmann, A. K., & Cox, C. B. (2015, December 23). *Predicting successful responses to emergencies: The emergency responsiveness scale. Current Psychology,* n.p. http://dx.doi:10.1007/s12144-015-9402-2

Diehl, A. B., & Dzubinski, L. M. (2016). Making the invisible visible: A cross-sector analysis of gender-based leadership barriers. *Human Resource Development Quarterly, 27*(2), 181– 206. doi:10.1002/hrdq.21248

Diehl, M., Chui, H., et al. (2014). Change in coping and defense mechanisms across adulthood: Longitudinal findings in a European American sample. *Developmental Psychology, 50*(2), 634–648.

Diekelmann, S., & Born, J. (2010). The memory function of sleep. *Nature Reviews Neuroscience, 11*(2), 114–126

Diener, E. (2013). The remarkable changes in the science of subjective well-being. *Perspectives on Psychological Science, 8*(6), 663–666. doi:10.1177/1745691613507583

Diener, E., & Chan, M. Y. (2011). Happy people live longer: Subjective well-being contributes to health and longevity. *Applied Psychology: Health & Well-Being, 3*(1), 1–43. doi:10.1111/j.1758-0854.2010.01045.x

Diener, E., Scollon, C. N., & Lucas, R. E. (2009). The evolving concept of subjective well-being: The multifaceted nature of happiness. *Social Indicators Research* Series, *39*, 67–100. doi: 10.1007/978-90-481-2354-4_4

Dieterich, S. E., Assel, M. A., et al. (2006). The impact of early maternal verbal scaffolding and child language abilities on later decoding and reading comprehension skills. *Journal of School Psychology, 43*(6), 481–494. doi:10.1016/j.jsp.2005.10.003

Dietrich, A., & Stoll, O. (2010). Effortless attention, hypofrontality, and perfectionism. In B. Bruya (Ed.), *Effortless attention: A new perspective in the cognitive science of attention and action* (pp. 159–178). Cambridge, MA: MIT Press.

Dietz, W. H. (2015). The response of the US Centers for Disease Control and Prevention to the obesity epidemic. *Annual Review of Public Health, 36*, 575–596. doi:10.1146/annurev-publhealth-031914-122415

Dijk, D., & Lazar, A. S. (2012). The regulation of human sleep and wakefulness: Sleep homeostasis and circadian rhythmicity. In C. M. Morin & C. A. Espie (Eds.), *The Oxford handbook of sleep and sleep disorders* (pp. 38–60). New York, NY: Oxford University Press. doi:10.1093/oxfordhb/9780195376203.013.0003

Dik, B. J., Byrne, Z. S., & Steger, M. F. (2013). *Purpose and meaning in the workplace.* Washington, DC: American Psychological Association. doi:10.1037/14183-000

Dikotter, F., Laamann, L., & Xun, Z. (2008). *Narcotic culture: A history of drugs in China.* Chicago, IL: University of Chicago Press.

Dillard, A. J., Midboe, A. M., & Klein, W. M. P. (2009). The dark side of optimism: Unrealistic optimism about problems with alcohol predicts subsequent negative event experiences. *Personality & Social Psychology Bulletin, 35*, 1540–1550. doi:10.1177/0146167209343124

Dimberg, U., & Söderkvist, S. (2011). The voluntary facial action technique: A method to test the facial feedback hypothesis. *Journal of Nonverbal Behavior, 35*(1), 17–33. doi:10.1007/s10919-010-0098-6

Dimsdale, J. E. (2011). Medically unexplained symptoms: A treacherous foundation for somatoform disorders? *Psychiatric Clinics of North America, 34*(3), 511–513. doi:10.1016/j.psc.2011.05.003

Dingus, T. A., Klauer, S. G., et al. (2006). The 100-car naturalistic driving study: Phase II. Results of the 100-car field experiment. *National Highway Traffic Safety Administration Report No. DOT HS 810 593.* Retrieved July 20, 2020, from https://www.researchgate.net/publication/329070715_The_100-Car_Naturalistic_Driving_Study_Phase_II_-_Results_of_the_100-Car_Field_Experiment

Distin, K. (2006). *Gifted children: A guide for parents and professionals.* London, UK: Jessica Kingsley Publishers.

Dixon, M. J., Smilek, D., & Merikle, P. M. (2004). Not all synaesthetes are created equal: Projector versus associator synaesthetes. *Cognitive, Affective, & Behavioral Neuroscience, 4*(3), 335–343. doi:10.3758/CABN.4.3.335

Dixon, R. W., Youssef, G. J. et al. (2016). The relationship between gambling attitudes, involvement, and problems in adolescence: Examining the moderating role of coping strategies and parenting styles. *Addictive Behaviors, 58*, 42–46. doi:10.1016/j.addbeh.2016.02.011

Dixon, S. V., Graber, J. A., & Brooks-Gunn, J. (2008). The roles of respect for parental authority and parenting practices in parent-child conflict among African American, Latino, and European American families. *Journal of Family Psychology, 22*(1), 1–10. doi:10.1037/0893-3200.22.1.1

Dobelle, W. H. (2000). Artificial vision for the blind by connecting a television camera to the visual cortex. *American Society of Artificial Internal Organs, 46*, 3–9.

Dobson, K. S., Backs-Dermott, G. J., & Dozois, D. J. A. (2000). Cognitive and cognitive-behavioral therapies. In C. R. Snyder & R. E. Ingram (Eds.), *Handbook of psychological change: Psychotherapy processes and practices for the 21st century* (pp. 409–428). New York, NY: Wiley.

Dobson, P. W., & Gerstner, E. (2010). For a few cents more: Why supersize unhealthy food? *Marketing Science, 29*(4), 770–778. doi:10.1287/mksc.1100.0558

Dodge, T., Williams, K. J., et al. (2012). Judging cheaters: Is substance misuse viewed similarly in the athletic and academic domains? *Psychology of Addictive Behaviors, 26*(3), 678–682. doi:10.1037/a0027872

Dodson, E. R., & Zee, P. C. (2010). Therapeutics for circadian rhythm sleep disorders. *Sleep Medicine Clinics, 5*(4), 701–715. doi:10.1016/j.jsmc.2010.08.001

Doherty, M. J. (2009). *Theory of mind: How children understand others' thoughts and feelings.* New York, NY: Psychology Press.

Doidge, N. (1997). Empirical evidence for the efficacy of psychoanalytic psychotherapies and psychoanalysis. *Psychoanalytic Inquiry, Suppl.*, 102–150. doi:10.1080/07351699709534161

Dollard, J., & Miller, N. E. (1950). *Personality and psychotherapy: An analysis in terms of learning, thinking and culture.* New York, NY: McGraw-Hill.

Domhoff, G. W. (2003). *The scientific study of dreams: Neural networks, cognitive development, and content analysis.* Washington, DC: American Psychological Association.

Domhoff, G. W. (2011). Dreams are embodied simulations that dramatize conceptions and concerns: The continuity hypothesis in empirical, theoretical, and historical context. *International Journal of Dream Research, 4*(2), 50–62.

Domhoff, G. W., & Schneider, A. (2008). Similarities and differences in dream content at the crosscultural, gender, and individual levels. *Consciousness & Cognition, 17*(4), 1257–1265. doi:10.1016/j.concog.2008.08.005

Domingo, R. A., & Goldstein-Alpern, N. (1999). "What dis?" and other toddler-initiated, expressive language-learning strategies. *Infant-Toddler Intervention, 9*(1), 39–60.

Domingos, A. I., Vaynshteyn, J., et al. (2011). Leptin regulates the reward value of nutrient. *Nature Neuroscience, 14*(12), 1562–1568. doi:10.1038/nn.2977

Domjan, M. (2015). *The principles of learning and behavior* (7th ed.). Boston, MA: Cengage Learning.

Dömötör, Z., Ruíz-Barquín, R., & Szabo, A. (2016). Superstitious behavior in sport: A literature review. *Scandinavian Journal of Psychology, 57*(4), 368–382. doi:10.1111/sjop.12301

Donaldson, J. M., Vollmer, T. R., et al. (2013). Effects of a reduced time-out interval on compliance with the time-out instruction. *Journal of Applied Behavior Analysis, 46*(2), 369–378.

Donnellan, M., Kenny, D. A., et al. (2012). Using trait-state models to evaluate the longitudinal consistency of global self-esteem from adolescence to adulthood. *Journal of Research in Personality, 46*(6), 634–645. doi:10.1016/j.jrp.2012.07.005

Dooling, D. J., & Lachman, R. (1971). Effects of comprehension on retention of prose. *Journal of Experimental Psychology, 88*, 216–222. doi:10.1037/h0030904

Doran, S. M., Van Dongen, H. P., & Dinges, D. F. (2001). Sustained attention performance during sleep deprivation. *Archives of Italian Biology, 139*, 253–267.

Doty, R. L. (2012). Has human olfaction evolved primarily to provide flavor to foods? *Trends in Neurosciences, 35*(2), 79–80. doi:10.1016/j.tins.2011.10.001

Douglas, K. S., Guy, L. S., & Hart, S. D. (2009). Psychosis as a risk factor for violence to others: A meta-analysis. *Psychological Bulletin, 135*(5), 679–706. doi:10.1037/a0016311

Doumas, D. M., Miller, R., & Esp, S. (2017). Impulsive sensation seeking, binge drinking, and alcohol-related consequences: Do protective behavioral strategies help high risk adolescents? *Addictive Behaviors, 64*, 6–12. doi:10.1016/j.addbeh.2016.08.003

Dovidio, J. F., & Penner, L. A. (2001). Helping and altruism. In M. Hewstone & M. Brewer (Eds.), *Handbook of social psychology* (pp. 162–195). London, UK: Blackwell.

Dovidio, J. F., Gaertner, S. L., et al. (2002). Why can't we just get along? *Cultural Diversity & Ethnic Minority Psychology, 8*(2), 88–102. doi:10.1037/1099-9809.8.2.88

Dovidio, J. F., Piliavin, J. A., et al. (2006). *The social psychology of prosocial behavior.* Mahwah, NJ: Erlbaum.

Dow-Edwards, D. (2011). Translational issues for prenatal cocaine studies and the role of environment. *Neurotoxicology & Teratology, 33*(1), 9–16. doi:10.1016/j.ntt.2010.06.007

Dowling, K. W. (2005). The effect of lunar phases on domestic violence incident rates. *Forensic Examiner, 14*(4), 13–18.

Doyle, D. M., & Molix, L. (2016). Disparities in social health by sexual orientation and the etiologic role of self-reported discrimination. *Archives of Sexual Behavior, 45*(6), 1317–1327. doi:10.1007/s10508-015-0639-5

Drane, C. F., Modecki, K. L., & Barber, B. L. (2017). Disentangling development of sensation seeking, risky peer affiliation, and binge drinking in adolescent sport. *Addictive Behaviors, 66*, 60–65. doi:10.1016/j.addbeh.2016.11.001

Dresler, M., Wehrle, R., et al. (2012). Neural correlates of dream lucidity obtained from contrasting lucid versus non-lucid REM sleep: A combined EEG/fMRI case study. *Sleep, 35*(7), 1017–1020.

Drews, F. A., Yazdani, H., et al. (2009). Text messaging during simulated driving. *Human Factors, 51*(5), 762–770. doi:10.1177/0018720809353319

Drigotas, S. M. (2002). The Michelangelo phenomenon and personal well-being. *Journal of Personality, 70*(1), 59–77. doi:10.1111/1467-6494.00178

Driver, J. L., & Gottman, J. M. (2004). Daily marital interactions and positive affect during marital conflict among newlywed couples. *Family Process, 43*(3), 301–314.

Drummond, M., Douglas, J., & Olver, J. (2007). Anosmia after traumatic brain injury: A clinical update. *Brain Impairment, 8*(1), 31–40. doi:10.1375/brim.8.1.31

Drury, S., Hutchens, S. A., et al. (2012). Philip G. Zimbardo on his career and the Stanford Prison Experiment's 40th anniversary. *History of Psychology, 15*(2), 161–170. doi:10.1037/a0025884

Dryden, W. (2011). *Understanding psychological health: The REBT perspective.* New York, NY: Routledge/Taylor & Francis.

Dryer, R., Tyson, G. A., & Kiernan, M. J. (2013). Bulimia nervosa: Professional and lay people's beliefs about the causes. *Australian Psychologist, 48*(5), 338–344.

Drymalski, W. M., & Washburn, J. J. (2011). Sudden gains in the treatment of depression in a partial hospitalization program. *Journal of Consulting & Clinical Psychology, 79*(3), 364–368. doi:10.1037/a0022973

Duckitt, J., & Sibley, C. G. (2010). Personality, ideology, prejudice, and politics: A dual-process motivational model. *Journal of Personality, 78*(6), 1861–1893. doi:10.1111/j.1467-6494.2010.00672.x

Duckworth, A. L., Gendler, T. S., & Gross, J. J. (2014). Self-control in school-age children. *Educational Psychologist, 49*(3), 199–217. doi:10.1080/00461520.2014.926225

Duckworth, A. L., Peterson, C., et al. (2007). Grit: Perseverance and passion for long-term goals. *Journal of Personality & Social Psychology, 92*(6), 1087–1101. doi:10.1037/0022-3514.92.6.1087

Duclos, S. E., & Laird, J. D. (2001). The deliberate control of emotional experience through control of expressions. *Cognition and Emotion, 15*, 27–56.

Duffield, C., Baldwin, R., et al. (2014). Job enrichment: Creating meaningful career development opportunities for nurses. *Journal of Nursing Management, 22*(6), 697–706. doi:10.1111/jonm.12049

Duffy, J. F., & Wright, K. P., Jr. (2005). Entrainment of the human circadian system by light. *Journal of Biological Rhythms, 20*(4), 326–338. doi:10.1177/0748730405277983

Duffy, S., & Verges, M. (2009). It matters a hole lot: Perceptual affordances of waste containers influence recycling compliance. *Environment & Behavior, 41*(5), 741–749.

Duncan, B. L., & Reese, R. J. (2013). Empirically supported treatments, evidence-based treatments, and evidence-based practice. In G. Stricker, T. A. Widiger, et al. (Eds.), *Handbook of psychology* (Vol. 8): *Clinical psychology* (2nd ed., pp. 489–513). New York, NY: Wiley.

Duncan, C. C. (2013). The Genain Quadruplets: A 55-year follow-up of two of four monozygous sisters with schizophrenia. *Schizophrenia Research, 48*, 186–187. doi:10.1016/j.schres.2013.06.011

Duncan, J. (2005). Frontal lobe function and general intelligence: Why it matters. *Cortex, 41*(2), 215–217. doi:10.1016/S0010-9452(08)70896-7

Duncker, K. (1945). On problem solving. *Psychological Monographs, 58*(270).

Dunlop, S. M., & Romer, D. (2010). Adolescent and young adult crash risk: Sensation seeking, substance use propensity and substance use behaviors. *Journal of Adolescent Health, 46*(1), 90–92. doi:10.1016/j.jadohealth.2009.06.005

Dunlosky, J., & Rawson, K. A. (2015). Practice tests, spaced practice, and successive relearning: Tips for classroom use and for guiding students' learning. *Scholarship of Teaching & Learning in Psychology, 1*(1), 72–78. doi:10.1037/stl0000024

Dunlosky, J., Rawson, K. A., et al. (2013). Improving students' learning with effective learning techniques: Promising directions from cognitive and educational psychology. *Psychological Science in the Public Interest, 14*, 4–58. doi:10.1177/1529100612453266

Dunning, D., Heath, C., & Suls, J. M. (2004). Flawed self-assessment: Implications for health, education, and the workplace. *Psychological Science in the Public Interest, 5*(3), 69–106. doi:10.1111/j.1529-1006.2004.00018.x

Durán, L. K., Roseth, C. J., Hoffman, P. (2010). An experimental study comparing English-only and Transitional Bilingual Education on Spanish-speaking preschoolers' early literacy development. *Early Childhood Research Quarterly, 25*(2), 207–217. doi:10.1016/j.ecresq.2009.10.002

Durand, V. M., & Barlow, D. H. (2019). *Essentials of abnormal psychology* (8th ed.). Boston, MA: Cengage Learning.

Durham, M. G. (2009). *The Lolita effect.* New York, NY: Overlook Press.

Dutton, D. G., & Aron, A. P. (1974). Some evidence for heightened sexual attraction under conditions of high anxiety. *Journal of Personality & Social Psychology, 30*, 510–517. doi:10.1037/h0037031

DuVernet, A. M., Dierdorff, E. C., et al. (2015). Exploring factors that influence work analysis data: A meta-analysis of design choices, purposes, and organizational context. *Journal of Applied Psychology, 100*(5), 1603–1631. doi:10.1037/a0039084

Dvash, J., Gilam, G., et al. (2010). The envious brain: The neural basis of social comparison. *Human Brain Mapping, 31*(11), 1741–1750. doi:10.1002/hbm.20972

Dyer, J., Gregersen, H., & Christensen, C. (2013). *The innovator's DNA: Mastering the five skills of disruptive innovators.* Boston, MA: Harvard Business Press.

Dyer, K. A. (2001). Dealing with death and dying in medical education and practice. *Journey of Hearts.* Retrieved July 20, 2020, from http://www.journeyofhearts.org/kirstimd/AMSA/outline.htm

Dyukova, G. M., Glozman, Z. M., et al. (2010). Speech disorders in right-hemisphere stroke. *Neuroscience & Behavioral Physiology, 40*(6), 593–602. doi:10.1007/s11055-010-9301-9

Dywan, J., & Bowers, K. S. (1983). The use of hypnosis to enhance recall. *Science, 222*, 184–185. doi:10.1126/science.6623071

Eagly, A. H. (2009). The his and hers of prosocial behavior: An examination of the social psychology of gender. *American Psychologist, 64*(8), 644–658.

Eagly, A. H. (2013). Women as leaders: Paths through the labyrinth. In M. C. Bligh & R. E. Riggio (Eds.), *Exploring distance in leader-follower relationships: When near is far and far is near* (pp. 191–214). New York, NY: Routledge/Taylor & Francis.

Eagly, A. H., & Carli, L. L. (2007). *Through the labyrinth: The truth about how women become leaders.* Watertown, MA: HBS Press Book.

Eagly, A. H., Eaton, A., et al. (2012). Feminism and psychology: Analysis of a half-century of research on women and gender. *American Psychologist, 67*(3), 211–230. doi:10.1037/a0027260

Eardley, A. F., & Pring, L. (2007). Spatial processing, mental imagery, and creativity in individuals with and without sight. *European Journal of Cognitive Psychology, 19*(1), 37–58. doi:10.1080/09541440600591965

Earleywine, M. (2011). *Humor 101.* New York, NY: Springer.

Easterbrooks, M., Bartlett, J., et al. (2013). Social and emotional development in infancy. In R. M. Lerner, M. Easterbrooks, et al. (Eds.), *Handbook of psychology* (Vol. 6): *Developmental psychology* (2nd ed.) (pp. 91–120). New York, NY: Wiley.

Eastman, C. I., Molina, T. A., et al. (2012). Blacks (African Americans) have shorter free-running circadian periods than Whites (Caucasian Americans). *Chronobiology International, 29*(8), 1072–1077. doi:10.3109/07420528.2012.700670

Ebben, M. R., & Spielman, A. J. (2009). Non-pharmacological treatments for insomnia. *Journal of Behavioral Medicine, 32*(3), 244–254. doi:10.1007/s10865-008-9198-8

Ebbinghaus, H. (1885). *Memory: A contribution to experimental psychology.* (H. A. Ruger & C. E. Bussenius, Trans.) New York, NY: New York Teacher's College, Columbia University.

Eckert, M. J., & Racine, R. J. (2006). Long-term depression and associativity in rat primary motor cortex following thalamic stimulation. *European Journal of Neuroscience, 24*(12), 3553–3560. doi:10.1111/j.1460-9568.2006.05220.x

Eddy, K. T., Dutra, L., et al. (2004). A multidimensional meta-analysis of psychotherapy and pharmacotherapy for obsessive-compulsive disorder. *Clinical Psychology Review, 24*(8), 1011–1030. doi:10.1016/j.cpr.2004.08.004

Edenfield, T. M., & Blumenthal, J. A. (2011). Exercise and stress reduction. In R. J. Contrada & A. Baum (Eds.), *The handbook of stress science: Biology, psychology, and health* (pp. 301–319). New York, NY: Springer.

Edgerly, S. (2015). Red media, blue media, and purple media: News repertoires in the colorful media landscape. *Journal of Broadcasting & Electronic Media, 59*(1), 1–21. doi:10.1080/08838151.2014.998220

Edmondson, A. (2012). *Teaming: How organizations learn, innovate, and compete in the knowledge economy.* New York, NY: Wiley.

Edwards, A., & Polman, R. (2012). *Pacing in sport and exercise: A psychophysiological perspective.* Hauppauge, NY: Nova Science Publishers.

Ehret, A. M., Joormann, J., & Berking, M. (2015). Examining risk and resilience factors for depression: The role of self-criticism and self-compassion. *Cognition & Emotion, 29*(8), 1496–1504. doi:10.1080/02699931.2014.992394

Eidelson, R. J., & Eidelson, J. I. (2003). Dangerous ideas. *American Psychologist, 58*(3), 182–192. doi:10.1037/0003-066X.58.3.182

Eifert, G. H., & Lejuez, C. W. (2000). Aversion therapy. In A. E. Kazdin (Ed.), *Encyclopedia of psychology* (Vol. 1, pp. 348–350). Washington, DC: American Psychological Association.

Eigenberg, H., McGuffee, K., et al. (2012). Doing justice: Perceptions of gender neutrality in the jury selection process. *American Journal of Criminal Justice, 37*(2), 258–275. doi:10.1007/s12103-011-9139-x

Einarsen, S., & Hoel, H. (2008). Bullying and mistreatment at work: How managers may prevent and manage such problems. In A. Kinder, R. Hughes, & C. L. Cooper (Eds.), *Employee well-being support: A workplace resource* (pp. 161–173). New York, NY: Wiley.

Eisendrath, S. J., Gillung, E., et al. (2014). A preliminary study: Efficacy of mindfulness-based cognitive therapy versus sertraline as first-line treatments for major depressive disorder. *Mindfulness.* doi:10.1007/s12671-014-0280-8

Eisendrath, S., Chartier, M., & McLane, M. (2011). Adapting mindfulness-based cognitive therapy for treatmentresistant depression. *Cognitive & Behavioral Practice, 18*(3), 362–370. doi:10.1016/j.cbpra.2010.05.004

Eisler, I., Simic, M., et al. (2007). A randomized controlled treatment trial of two forms of family therapy in adolescent anorexia nervosa: A five-year follow-up. *Journal of Child Psychology & Psychiatry, 48*(6), 552–560. doi:10.1111/j.1469-7610.2007.01726.x

Ekman, P. (1993). Facial expression and emotion. *American Psychologist, 48*(4), 384–392. doi:10.1037/0003-066X.48.4.384

Ekman, P., & Cordaro, D. (2011). What is meant by calling emotions basic. *Emotion Review, 3*(4), 364–370. doi:10.1177/1754073911410740

Ekman, P., Levenson, R. W., & Friesen, W. V. (1983). Autonomic nervous system activity distinguishes among emotions. *Science, 221*, 1208–1210. doi:10.1126/science.6612338

Eldridge, M., Saltzman, E., & Lahav, A. (2010). Seeing what you hear: Visual feedback improves pitch recognition. *European Journal of Cognitive Psychology, 22*(7), 1078–1091. doi:10.1080/09541440903316136

Elkington, K. S., Hackler, D., et al. (2012). Perceived mental illness stigma among youth in psychiatric outpatient treatment. *Journal of Adolescent Research, 27*(2), 290–317. doi:10.1177/0743558411409931

Elkins, D. N. (2012). Toward a common focus in psychotherapy research. *Psychotherapy, 49*(4), 450–454. doi:10.1037/a0027797

Elkins, G. R., Barabasz, A. F., et al. (2015). Advancing research and practice: The revised APA Division 30 definition of hypnosis. *American Journal of Clinical Hypnosis, 57*(4), 378–385. doi:10.1080/00029157.2015. 1011465

Elli, K. A., & Nathan, P. J. (2001). The pharmacology of human working memory. *International Journal of Neuropsychopharmacology, 4*(3), 299–313. doi:10.1017/S1461145701002541

Ellickson, P. L., Martino, S. C., & Collins, R. L. (2004). Marijuana use from adolescence to young adulthood. *Health Psychology, 23*(3), 299–307. doi:10.1037/0278-6133.23.3.299

Elliott, M., & Williams, D. (2003). The client experience of counselling and psychotherapy. *Counselling Psychology Review, 18*(1), 34–38.

Elliott, M., Browne, K., & Kilcoyne, J. (1995). Child sexual abuse prevention: What offenders tell us. *Child Abuse & Neglect, 19*(5), 579–594.

Elliott, R., & Farber, B. A. (2010). Carl Rogers: Idealistic pragmatist and psychotherapy research pioneer. In L. G. Castonguay, J. C. Muran, et al. (Eds.), *Bringing psychotherapy research to life: Understanding change through the work of leading clinical researchers* (pp. 17–27). Washington, DC: American Psychological Association.

Ellis, A. (1979). The practice of rational-emotive therapy. In A. Ellis & J. Whiteley (Eds.), *Theoretical and empirical foundations of rational-emotive therapy* (pp. 1–6). Monterey, CA: Brooks/Cole.

Ellis, A. (1995). Changing rational-emotive therapy (RET) to rational emotive behavior therapy (REBT). *Journal of Rational-Emotive & Cognitive Behavior Therapy, 13*(2), 85–89. doi:10.1007/BF02354453

Ellis, A., & Ellis, D. J. (2011). *Rational emotive behavior therapy*. Washington, DC: American Psychological Association.

Ellis, D. (2019). *The essential guide to becoming a master student* (5th ed.). Boston, MA: Cengage Learning.

Ellis, K. A., & Nathan, P. J. (2001). The pharmacology of human working memory. *International Journal of Neuropsychopharmacology, 4*(3), 299–313. doi:10.1017/S1461145701002541

Ellison-Wright, I., & Bullmore, E. (2010). Anatomy of bipolar disorder and schizophrenia: A meta-analysis. *Schizophrenia Research, 117*(1), 1–12. doi:10.1016/j.schres.2009.12.022

Emerson, E. (2009). Relative child poverty, income inequality, wealth, and health. *Journal of the American Medical Association, 301*(4), 425–426. doi:10.1001/jama.2009.8

Engel, G. L. (2012). The need for a new medical model: A challenge for biomedicine. *Psychodynamic Psychiatry, 40*(3), 377–396. doi:10.1521/pdps.2012.40.3.377

Engelen, E., & Röttger-Rössler, B. (2012). Current disciplinary and interdisciplinary debates on empathy. *Emotion Review, 4*(1), 3–8. doi:10.1177/1754073911422287

Engelhard, I. M., van Uijen, S. L., et al. (2015). The effects of safety behavior directed towards a safety cue on perceptions of threat. *Behavior Therapy, 46*(5), 604–610. doi:10.1016/j.beth.2014.12.006

Engler, B. (2014). *Personality theories* (9th ed.). Boston, MA: Cengage Learning.

English, T., John, O. P., et al. (2012). Emotion regulation and peer-rated social functioning: A 4-year longitudinal study. *Journal of Research in Personality, 46*(6), 780–784. doi:10.1016/j.jrp.2012.09.006

Enns, M. W., Cox, B. J., & Clara, I. P. (2005). Perfectionism and neuroticism: A longitudinal study of specific vulnerability and diathesis-stress models. *Cognitive Therapy & Research, 29*(4), 463–478. doi:10.1007/s10608-005-2843-04

Enrici, I., Adenzato, M., et al. (2011). Intention processing in communication: A common brain network for language and gestures. *Journal of Cognitive Neuroscience, 23*(9), 2415–2431. doi:10.1162/jocn.2010.21594

Epstein, S. (2003). Cognitive-experiential self-theory of personality. In T. Millon & M. J. Lerner (Eds.), *Comprehensive handbook of psychology: Personality and social psychology* (Vol. 5, pp. 159–184). New York, NY: Wiley.

Erez, D. L., Levy, J., et al. (2010). Assessment of cognitive and adaptive behaviour among individuals with congenital insensitivity to pain and anhidrosis. *Developmental Medicine & Child Neurology, 52*(6), 559–562. doi:10.1111/j.1469-8749.2009.03567.x

Erickson, C. D., & Al-Timimi, N. R. (2001). Providing mental health services to Arab Americans. *Cultural Diversity & Ethnic Minority Psychology, 7*(4), 308–327. doi:10.1037/1099-9809.7.4.308

Ericsson, K. A., & Charness, N. (1994). Expert performance. *American Psychologist, 49*(8), 725–747. doi:10.1037/0003-066X.49.8.725

Ericsson, K. A., & Chase, W. G. (1982). Exceptional memory. *American Scientist, 70*, 607–615.

Ericsson, K. A., & Pool, R. (2016). *Peak: Secrets from the new science of expertise*. New York: Houghton Mifflin Harcourt.

Erikson, E. H. (1963). *Childhood and society*. New York, NY: Norton.

Erlacher, D., & Schredl, M. (2004). Dreams reflecting waking sport activities: A comparison of sport and psychology students. *International Journal of Sport Psychology, 35*(4), 301–308.

Ertmer, D. J., & Jung, J. (2012). Prelinguistic vocal development in young cochlear implant recipients and typically developing infants: Year 1 of robust hearing experience. *Journal of Deaf Studies & Deaf Education, 17*(1), 116–132. doi:10.1093/deafed/enr021

España, R. A., Oleson, E. B., et al. (2010). The hypocretin orexin system regulates cocaine self-administration via actions on the mesolimbic dopamine system. *European Journal of Neuroscience, 31*(2), 336–348. doi:10.1111/j.1460-9568.2009.07065.x

Essien, E. J., Monjok, E., et al. (2010). Correlates of HIV knowledge and sexual risk behaviors among female military personnel. *AIDS & Behavior, 14*(6), 1401–1414.

Estefan, L. F., Coulter, M. L., & VandeWeerd, C. (2016). Depression in women who have left violent relationships: The unique impact of frequent emotional abuse. *Violence Against Women, 22*(11), 1397–1413. doi:10.1177/1077801215624792

Ethier, K. A., Kershaw, T., et al. (2003). Adolescent women underestimate their susceptibility to sexually transmitted infections. *Sexually Transmitted Infections, 79*, 408–411.

Evans, G. W. (2006). Child development and the physical environment. *Annual Review of Psychology, 57*, 423–451.

Evans, G. W., & Fuller-Rowell, T. E. (2013). Childhood poverty, chronic stress, and young adult working memory: The protective role of self-regulatory capacity. *Developmental Science, 16*(5), 688–696. doi:10.1111/desc.12082

Evans, G. W., Lepore, S. J., & Schroeder, A. (1996). The role of interior design elements in human responses to crowding. *Journal of Personality & Social Psychology, 70*(1), 41–46.

Evans, G. W., Lercher, P., & Kofler, W. W. (2002). Crowding and children's mental health: The role of house type. *Journal of Environmental Psychology, 22*, 221–231.

Evans, G. W., Ricciuti, H. N., et al. (2010). Crowding and cognitive development: The mediating role of maternal responsiveness among 36-month-old children. *Environment & Behavior, 42*(1), 135–148.

Evans, G. W., & Wener, R. E. (2007). Crowding and personal space invasion on the train: Please don't make me sit in the middle. *Journal of Environmental Psychology, 27*(1), 90–94.

Evardone, M., Alexander, G. M., & Morey, L. C. (2007). Hormones and borderline personality features. *Personality & Individual Differences, 44*(1), 278–287. doi:10.1016/j.paid.2007.08.007

Everitt, B. J., & Robbins, T. W. (2016). Drug addiction: Updating actions to habits to compulsions ten years on. *Annual Review of Psychology, 67*, 23–50. doi:10.1146/annurev-psych-122414-033457

Eysenck, H. J. (1994). The outcome problem in psychotherapy: What have we learned? *Behaviour Research & Therapy, 32*(5), 477–495. doi:10.1016/0005-7967(94)90135-X

Eysenck, H. J. (Ed.). (1981). *A model for personality*. New York, NY: Springer-Verlag.

Eysenck, H. J. (1952). The effects of psychotherapy: An evaluation. *Journal of Consulting Psychology, 16*, 319–324.

Fabian, J. (2011). Neuropsychology, neuroscience, volitional impairment and sexually violent predators: A review of the literature and the law and their application to civil commitment proceedings. *Aggression & Violent Behavior*, doi:10.1016/j.avb.2011.07.002

Fabrega, H., Jr. (2004). Culture and the origins of psychopathology. In U. P. Gielen, J. M., Fish, et al. (Eds.), *Handbook of culture, therapy, and healing* (pp. 15–35). Mahwah, NJ: Erlbaum.

Fain, G. L. (2003). *Sensory transduction*. Sunderland, MA: Sinauer.

Fandakova, Y., Shing, Y., & Lindenberger, U. (2012). Differences in binding and monitoring mechanisms contribute to lifespan age differences in false memory. *Developmental Psychology*, doi:10.1037/a0031361

Fang, A., & Wilhelm, S. (2015). Clinical features, cognitive biases, and treatment of body dysmorphic disorder. *Annual Review of Clinical Psychology, 11*, 187–212. doi:10.1146/annurev-clinpsy-032814-112849

Farah, M. J. (2004). *Visual agnosia* (2nd ed.). Cambridge, MA: MIT Press.

Farah, M. J. (2006). Prosopagnosia. In M. J. Farah & T. E. Feinberg (Eds.), *Patient-based approaches to cognitive neuroscience* (2nd ed., pp. 123–125). Cambridge, MA: MIT Press.

Farah, M. J., Haimm, C., et al. (2009). When we enhance cognition with Adderall, do we sacrifice creativity? A preliminary study. *Psychopharmacology, 202*(1–3), 541–547. doi:10.1007/s00213-008-1369-3

Farah, M. J., Illes, J., et al. (2004). Neurocognitive enhancement: What can we do and what should we do? *Nature Reviews Neuroscience, 5*, 421–425. doi:10.1038/nrn1390

Faraut, B., Boudjeltia, K. Z., et al. (2011). Benefits of napping and an extended duration of recovery sleep on alertness and immune cells after acute sleep restriction. *Brain, Behavior, & Immunity, 25*(1), 16–24. doi:10.1016/j.bbi.2010.08.001

Farmer, R. F., & Chapman, A. L. (2016). *Behavioral interventions in cognitive behavior therapy: Practical guidance for putting theory into action* (2nd ed.). Washington, DC: American Psychological Association. doi:10.1037/14691-000>

Farr, R. H. (2017). Does parental sexual orientation matter? A longitudinal follow-up of adoptive families with school-age children. *Developmental Psychology, 53*(2), 252–264. doi:10.1037/dev0000228

Farrand, P., Confue, P., et al. (2009). Guided self-help supported by paraprofessional mental health workers: An uncontrolled before-after cohort study. *Health & Social Care in the Community, 17*(1), 9–17. doi:10.1111/j.1365-2524.2008.00792.x

Farroni, T., Massaccesi, S., et al. (2004). Gaze following in newborns. *Infancy, 5*(1), 39–60. doi:10.1207/s15327078in0501_2

Fava, G. A. (2016). Psychosomatic medicine. In G. Fink (Ed.), *Stress: Concepts, cognition, emotion, and behavior* (pp. 457–463). San Diego, CA: Elsevier.

Fawcett, J. M., Russell, E. J., et al. (2013). Of guns and geese: A meta-analytic review of the "weapon focus" literature. *Psychology, Crime & Law, 19*(1), 35–66. doi:10.1080/1068316X.2011.599325

Federal Bureau of Investigation. (2019). *FBI Releases 2018 Crime Statistics*. Retrieved July 20, 2020, from https://www.fbi.gov/news/pressrel/press-releases/fbi-releases-2018-crime-statistics

Feinberg, T. E., & Mallatt, J. (2016). The nature of primary consciousness. A new synthesis. *Consciousness & Cognition, 43*, 113–127. doi:10.1016/j.concog.2016.05.009

Feldman, R., Gordon, I., et al. (2013). Parental oxytocin and early caregiving jointly shape children's oxytocin response and social reciprocity. *Neuropsychopharmacology, 38*(7), 1154–1162. doi:10.1038/npp.2013.22

Feldman, S. (2003). Enforcing social conformity: A theory of authoritarianism. *Political Psychology, 24*(1), 41–47. doi:10.1111/0162-895X.00316

Fenesi, B., Heisz, J. J., et al. (2014). Combining best-practice and experimental approaches: Redundancy, images, and misperceptions in multimedia learning. *Journal of Experimental Education, 82*(2), 253–263. doi: 10.1080/00220973.2012.745472

Fenton, M. C., Keyes, K., et al. (2012). Psychiatric comorbidity and the persistence of drug use disorders in the United States. *Addiction, 107*(3), 599–609. doi:10.1111/j.1360-0443.2011.03638.x

Ferguson, C. J. (2015). Does media violence predict societal violence? It depends on what you look at and when. *Journal of Communication, 65*, E1–E22. doi:10.1111/jcom.12129

Ferguson, C. J., & Dyck, D. (2012). Paradigm change in aggression research: The time has come to retire the General Aggression Model. *Aggression & Violent Behavior, 17*(3), 220–228. doi:10.1016/j.avb.2012.02.007

Ferguson, C. J., Miguel, C. N., & Hartley, R. D. (2009). A multivariate analysis of youth violence and aggression: The influence of family, peers, depression, and media violence. *Journal of Pediatrics, 155*(6), 904–908. doi:10.1016/j.jpeds.2009.06.021

Ferini-Strambi, L. L., Marelli, S. S., et al. (2013). Effects of continuous positive airway pressure on cognition and neuroimaging data in sleep apnea. *International Journal of Psychophysiology, 89*(2), 203–212. doi:10.1016/j.ijpsycho.2013.03.022

Fernald, A. (1989). Intonation and communicative intent in mothers' speech to infants: Is the melody the message? *Child Development, 60*(6), 1497–1510. doi:10.2307/1130938

Fernald, A., Perfors, A., & Marchman, V. A. (2006). Picking up speed in understanding: Speech processing efficiency and vocabulary growth across the 2nd year. *Developmental Psychology, 42*(1), 98–116. doi:10.1037/0012-1649.42.1.98

Fernandez, J., Grizzell, J., & Wecker, L. (2013). The role of estrogen receptor β and nicotinic cholinergic receptors in postpartum depression. *Progress in Neuro-Psychopharmacology & Biological Psychiatry, 40*, 199–206. doi:10.1016/j.pnpbp.2012.10.002

Ferrara, P., Vitelli, O., et al. (2013). Factitious disorders and Münchausen syndrome: The tip of the iceberg. *Journal of Child Health Care, 17*(4), 366–374. doi:10.1177/1367493512462262

Ferrari, J. R., & Pychyl, T. A. (2012). 'If I wait, my partner will do it:' The role of conscientiousness as a mediator in the relation of academic procrastination and perceived social loafing. *North American Journal of Psychology, 14*(1), 13–24.

Ferraro, P. J., & Price, M. K. (2013). Using non-pecuniary strategies to influence behavior: evidence from a large-scale field experiment. *Review of Economics & Statistics, 95*(1), 64–73. doi:10.3386/w17189

Ferraro, P. J., Miranda, J. J., & Price, M. K. (2011). Persistence of treatment effects with norm-based policy instruments: Evidence from a randomized environmental policy experiment. *American Economic Review, 101*(3), 318–322. doi:10.1257/aer.101.3.318

Festinger, L. (1957). *A theory of cognitive dissonance*. Stanford, CA: Stanford University Press.

Festinger, L., & Carlsmith, J. M. (1959). Cognitive consequences of forced compliance. *Journal of Abnormal & Social Psychology, 58*, 203–210. doi:10.1037/h0041593

Ficca, G., Axelsson, J., et al. (2010). Naps, cognition and performance. *Sleep Medicine Reviews, 14*(4), 249–258. doi:10.1016/j.smrv.2009.09.005

Field, J. E., Kolbert, J. B., et al. (2009). *Understanding girl bullying and what to do about it: Strategies to help heal the divide*. Thousand Oaks, CA: Corwin Press.

Fields, R. D. (2013). Neuroscience: Map the other brain. *Nature, 501*(7465), 25–27.

Fields, R. M., & Margolin, J. (2001). *Coping with trauma*. Washington, DC: American Psychological Association.

Filbey, F. M., Schacht, J. P., et al. (2009). Marijuana craving in the brain. *Proceedings of the National Academy of Sciences, 106*(31), 13016–13021. doi:10.1073/pnas.0903863106

Fine, C. (2010). *Delusions of gender*. New York, NY: Norton.

Fine, L. E. (2011). Minimizing heterosexism and homophobia: Constructing meaning of out campus LGB life. *Journal of Homosexuality, 58*(4), 521–546. doi:10.1080/00918369.2011.555673

Fink, M. (2013). Rediscovering catatonia: The biography of a treatable syndrome. *Acta Psychiatrica Scandinavica, 127*(Suppl. 441), 1–47. doi:10.1111/acps.12038

Finkel, E. J., & Eastwick, P. W. (2015). Interpersonal attraction: In search of a theoretical Rosetta Stone. In M. Mikulincer, P. R. Shaver, et al. (Eds.), *In APA handbook of personality and social psychology, Volume 3: Interpersonal relations* (pp. 179–210). Washington, DC: American Psychological Association. doi:10.1037/14344-007

Fiore, D., Dimaggio, G., et al. (2008). Metacognitive interpersonal therapy in a case of obsessive-compulsive and avoidant personality disorders. *Journal of Clinical Psychology, 64*(2), 168–180. doi:10.1002/jclp.20450

Fiorina, C. (2006). *Tough choices: A memoir*. New York, NY: Penguin.

Fireman, G., Kose, G., & Solomon, M. J. (2003). Self-observation and learning: The effect of watching oneself on problem solving performance. *Cognitive Development, 18*(3), 339–354. doi:10.1016/S0885-2014(03)00038-8

Firestone, P., Kingston, D. A., et al. (2006). Long-term follow-up of exhibitionists: Psychological, phallometric, and offense characteristics. *Journal of the American Academy of Psychiatry & the Law, 34*(3), 349–359.

Fischbach, A., Baudson, T. G., et al. (2013). Do teacher judgments of student intelligence predict life outcomes? *Learning & Individual Differences, 27*, 109–119. doi:10.1016/j.lindif.2013.07.004

Fischer, A. H., Manstead, A. S., et al. (2004). Gender and culture differences in emotion. *Emotion, 4*(1), 87–94. doi:10.1037/1528-3542.4.1.87

Fischer, C., & Kächele, H. (2009). Comparative analysis of patients' dreams in Freudian and Jungian treatment. *International Journal of Psychotherapy, 13*(3), 34–40.

Fischer, P., & Greitemeyer, T. (2013). The positive bystander effect: Passive bystanders increase helping in situations with high expected negative consequences for the helper. *Journal of Social Psychology, 153*(1), 1–5. doi:10.1080/00224545.2012.697931

Fischer, P., Kastenmüller, A., & Greitemeyer, T. (2010). Media violence and the self: The impact of personalized gaming characters in aggressive video games on aggressive behavior. *Journal of Experimental Social Psychology, 46*(1), 192–195. doi:10.1016/j.jesp.2009.06.010

Fischer, P., Krueger, J. I., et al. (2011). The bystander-effect: A meta-analytic review on bystander intervention in dangerous and non-dangerous emergencies. *Psychological Bulletin, 137*(4), 517–537. doi:10.1037/a0023304

Fisher, B. S., Cullen, F. T., & Daigle, L. E. (2005). The discovery of acquaintance rape: The salience of methodological innovation and rigor. *Journal of Interpersonal Violence, 20*(4), 493–500.

Fisher, R. P., & Geiselman, R. E. (1987). Enhancing eyewitness memory with the cognitive interview. In M. M. Gruneberg, P. E. Morris, et al. (Eds.), *Practical aspects of memory: Current research and issues* (pp. 34–39). New York: Wiley.

Fiske, P. (2015). Know your network. *Nature, 524*(7566), 507–508. doi:10.1038/nj7566-507a

Fiske, S. T., Cuddy, A. J., et al. (2002). A model of (often mixed) stereotype content: Competence and warmth respectively follow from perceived status and competition. *Journal of Personality & Social Psychology, 82*(6), 878–902. doi:10.1037/0022-3514.82.6.878

Fite, R. E., Lindeman, M. I. H., et al. (2017). Knowing oneself and long-term goal pursuit: Relations among self-concept clarity, conscientiousness, and grit. *Personality & Individual Differences, 108*, 191–194. doi:10.1016/j.paid.2016.12.008

Flaskerud, J. H. (2009). What do we need to know about the culture-bound syndromes? *Issues in Mental Health Nursing, 30*(6), 406–407. doi:10.1080/01612840902812947

Flegal, K. M., Carroll, M. D., et al. (2010). Prevalence and trends in obesity among U.S. adults, 1999–2008. *Journal of the American Medical Association, 303*(3), 235–241. doi:10.1001/jama.2009.2014

Fleming, J. (2012). The effectiveness of eye movement desensitization and reprocessing in the treatment of traumatized children and youth. *Journal of EMDR Practice and Research, 6*(1), 16–26. doi:10.1891/1933-3196.6.1.16

Fletcher, R., St George, J., & Freeman, E. (2013). Rough and tumble play quality: Theoretical foundations for a new measure of father–child interaction. *Early Child Development & Care, 183*(6), 746–759. doi:10.1080/03004430.2012.723439

Flinker, A., Korzeniewska, A., et al. (2015). Redefining the role of Broca's area in speech. *Proceedings of the National Academy of Sciences, 112*(9), 2871–2875. doi:10.1073/pnas.1414491112

Flora, J., & Segrin, C. (2015). Family conflict and communication. In L. H. Turner & R. West (Eds.), *The SAGE handbook of family communication* (pp. 91–106). Thousand Oaks, CA: Sage.

Florida Medical Examiners Commission. (2018). *Drugs identified in deceased persons by Florida Medical Examiners: 2017 annual report.* Retrieved July 20, 2020, from https://www.fdle.state.fl.us/MEC/Publications-and-Forms/Documents/Drugs-in-Deceased-Persons/2017-Annual-Drug-Report.aspx

Floridi, L., Taddeo, M., & Turilli, M. (2009). Turing's imitation game: Still an impossible challenge for all machines and some judges: An evaluation of the 2008 Loebner contest. *Minds & Machines, 19*(1), 145–150. doi:10.1007/s11023-008-9130-6

Flowe, H. D., & Ebbese, E. B. (2007). The effect of lineup member similarity on recognition accuracy in simultaneous and sequential lineups. *Law & Human Behavior, 31*(1), 33–52. doi:10.1007/s10979-006-9045-9

Flowers, S. (2011). Mindfully shy. In B. Boyce (Ed.), *The mindfulness revolution: Leading psychologists, scientists, artists, and meditation teachers on the power of mindfulness in daily life* (pp. 166–176). Boston, MA: Shambhala Publications.

Flynn, B. S., Worden, J. K., et al. (2011). Evaluation of smoking prevention television messages based on the elaboration likelihood model. *Health Education Research, 26*(6), 976–987. doi:10.1093/her/cyr082

Flynn, J. R. (2012). *Are we getting smarter? Rising IQ in the twenty-first century*. New York, NY: Cambridge University Press. doi:10.1017/CBO9781139235679

Flynn, J. R. (2013). The "Flynn Effect" and Flynn's paradox. *Intelligence, 41*(6), 851–857. doi:10.1016/j.intell.2013.06.014

Fochtmann, L. J. (2016). Evidence for the continuing benefits of electroconvulsive therapy. *American Journal of Psychiatry, 173*(11), 1071–1072. doi:10.1176/appi.ajp. 2016.16080880

Foley, S., & Gambescia, N. (2015). The complex etiology of delayed ejaculation: Assessment and treatment implications. In K. M. Hertlein, G. R. Weeks, et al. (Eds.), *Systemic sex therapy* (2nd ed., pp. 107–124). New York: Routledge/Taylor & Francis.

Folkman, S., & Moskowitz, J. T. (2004). Coping: Pitfalls and promise. *Annual Review of Psychology, 55*, 745–774. doi:10.1146/annurev.psych.55.090902.141456

Fonken, L. K., Aubrecht, T. G., et al. (2013). Dim light at night disrupts molecular circadian rhythms and increases body weight. *Journal of Biological Rhythms, 28*(4), 262–271. doi:10.1177/0748730413493862

Fontaine, K. R., Redden, D. T., et al. (2003). Years of life lost due to obesity. *Journal of the American Medical Association, 289*, 187–193. doi:10.1001/jama.289.2.187

Forbes, G. B., Adams-Curtis, L. E., & White, K. B. (2004). First-and second-generation measures of sexism, rape myths and related beliefs, and hostility toward women: Their interrelationships and association with college students' experiences with dating aggression and sexual coercion. *Violence Against Women, 10*(3), 236–261.

Ford, G. G., Gallagher, S. H., et al. (1999). Repositioning the home plate umpire to provide enhanced perceptual cues and more accurate ball-strike judgments. *Journal of Sport Behavior, 22*(1), 28–44.

Ford, J. D. (2012). Ethnoracial and educational differences in victimization history, trauma-related symptoms, and coping style. *Psychological Trauma: Theory, Research, Practice, & Policy, 4*(2), 177–185. doi:10.1037/a0023670

Forgas, J. P. (2011). She just doesn't look like a philosopher…? Affective influences on the halo effect in impression formation. *European Journal of Social Psychology, 41*(7), 812–817. doi:10.1002/ejsp.842

Forgas, J. P., Cooper, J., & Crano, W. D. (Eds.) (2010). *The psychology of attitudes and attitude change*. New York, NY: Psychology Press.

Forgeard, M. J. C., & Seligman, M. E. P. (2012). Seeing the glass half full: A review of the causes and consequences of optimism. *Pratiques Psychologiques, 18*(2), 107–120. doi:10.1016/j.prps.2012.02.002

Forney, W. S., Forney, J. C., & Crutsinger, C. (2005). Developmental stages of age and moral reasoning as predictors of juvenile delinquents' behavioral intention to steal clothing. *Family & Consumer Sciences Research Journal, 34*(2), 110–126. doi:10.1177/1077727X05280666

Forsyth, D. R. (2014). *Group dynamics* (6th ed.). Boston, MA: Cengage Learning.

Fortunato, L., Young, A. M., et al. (2010). Hook-up sexual experiences and problem behaviors among adolescents. *Journal of Child & Adolescent Substance Abuse, 19*(3), 261–278.

Foster, C. A., Witcher, B. S., et al. (1998). Arousal and attraction: Evidence for automatic and controlled processes. *Journal of Personality & Social Psychology, 74*(1), 86–101. doi:10.1037/0022-3514.74.1.86

Foster, G., & Ysseldyke, J. (1976). Expectancy and halo effects as a result of artificially induced teacher bias. *Contemporary Educational Psychology, 1*, 37–45. doi:10.1016/0361-476X(76)90005-9

Fougnie, D., & Marois, R. (2007). Executive working memory load induces inattentional blindness. *Psychonomic Bulletin & Review, 14*(1), 142–147. doi:10.3758/BF03194041

Fournier, N, M., & Duman, R. S. (2012). Role of vascular endothelial growth factor in adult hippocampal neurogenesis: Implications for the pathophysiology and treatment of depression. *Behavioural Brain Research, 227*(2), 440–449. doi:10.1016/j.bbr.2011.04.022

Fowers, B. J., & Davidov, B. J. (2006). The virtue of multiculturalism: Personal transformation, character, and openness to the other. *American Psychologist, 61*(6), 581–594. doi:10.1037/0003-066X.61.6.581

Fowler, J. H., & Christakis, N. A. (2010). Cooperative behavior cascades in human social networks. *Proceedings of the National Academy of Sciences, 107*(12), 5334–5338. doi:10.1073/pnas.0913149107

Fox, K. C. R., Dixon, M. L., et al. (2016). Functional neuroanatomy of meditation: A review and meta-analysis of 78 functional neuroimaging investigations. *Neuroscience & Biobehavioral Reviews, 65*, 208–228. doi:10.1016/j.neubirev.2016.03.021

Fox, M., Thayer, Z., & et al. (2017). Assessment of acculturation in minority health research. *Social Science & Medicine, 176*, 123–132. doi:10.1016/j.socscimed.2017.01.029

Frajo-Apor, B., Pardeller, S., et al. (2016). Emotional intelligence deficits in schizophrenia: The impact of non-social cognition. *Schizophrenia Research, 172*, 131–136. doi:10.1016/j.schres.2016.02.027

Frances, A. (2012). DSM 5 is guide, not bible—Ignore its ten worst changes. *Psychology Today*. Retrieved July 20, 2020, from http://www.psychologytoday.com/blog/dsm5-in-distress/201212/dsm-5-is-guide-not-bible-ignore-its-ten-worst-changes

Frank, J. D., & Frank, J. (2004). Therapeutic components shared by all psychotherapies. In A. Freeman, M. J. Mahoney, et al. (Eds.), *Cognition and psychotherapy* (2nd ed., pp. 45–78). New York, NY: Springer.

Frank, C., Land, W. M., et al. (2016, January 8). Perceptual-cognitive changes during motor learning: The influence of mental and physical practice on mental representation, gaze behavior, and performance of a complex action. *Frontiers in Psychology, 6*, Article 1981.

Frankl, V. (1955). *The doctor and the soul*. New York, NY: Knopf.

Franz, B. A., Skinner, D., & Murphy, J. W. (2017). Defining "community" in community health evaluation: Perspectives from a sample of nonprofit Appalachian hospitals. *American Journal of Evaluation, 39*, 237–256. doi:10.1177/1098214017722857

Franzoi, S. L. (2002). *Social psychology*. New York, NY: McGraw-Hill.

Frazier, A. (2012). The possible selves of high-ability African males attending a residential high school for highly able youth. *Journal for the Education of the Gifted, 35*(4), 366–390. doi:10.1177/0162353212461565

Freberg, L. A. (2021). *Discovering behavioral neuroscience: An introduction to biological psychology* (4th ed.). Boston, MA: Cengage Learning.

Fréchette, S., Zoratti, M., & Romano, E. (2015). What is the link between corporal punishment and child physical abuse? *Journal of Family Violence, 30*(2), 135–148. doi:10.1007/s10896-014-9663-9

Frederick, D. A., & Fales, M. R. (2016). Upset over sexual versus emotional infidelity among gay, lesbian, bisexual, and heterosexual adults. *Archives of Sexual Behavior, 45*(1), 175–191. doi:10.1007/s10508-014-0409-9

Frederickson, N., Petrides, K. V., & Simmonds, E. (2012). Trait emotional intelligence as a predictor of socioemotional outcomes in early adolescence. *Personality & Individual Differences, 52*(3), 323–328. doi:10.1016/j.paid.2011.10.034

Fredrickson, B. L., & Branigan, C. (2005). Positive emotions broaden the scope of attention and thought-action repertoires. *Cognition & Emotion, 19*(3), 313–332. doi:10.1080/02699930441000238

Freedman, D. H. (2011). How to fix the obesity crisis. *Scientific American, February*, 40–47. doi:10.1038/scientificamerican0211-40

Freeman, D., & Garety, P. A. (2004). *Paranoia: The psychology of persecutory delusions*. New York, NY: Routledge.

Freeman, N. K. (2007). Preschoolers' perceptions of gender appropriate toys and their parents' beliefs about genderized behaviors: Miscommunication, mixed messages, or hidden truths? *Early Childhood Education Journal, 34*(5), 357–366. doi:10.1007/s10643-006-0123-x

French, S. E., Kim, T. E., & Pillado, O. (2006). Ethnic identity, social group membership, and youth violence. In N. G. Guerra & E. P. Smith (Eds.), *Preventing youth violence in a multicultural society*(pp. 47–73). Washington, DC: American Psychological Association.

Freud, S. (1900). *The interpretation of dreams*. London, UK: Hogarth.

Freud, S. (1949). *An outline of psychoanalysis*. New York, NY: Norton.

Freund, A. M., & Ritter, J. O. (2009). Midlife crisis: A debate. *Gerontology, 55*(5), 582–591. doi:10.1159/000227322

Frew, J. (2013). Gestalt therapy. In J. Frew & M. D. Spiegler (Eds.), *Contemporary psychotherapies for a diverse world* (pp. 215–257). New York, NY: Routledge/Taylor & Francis.

Fridriksson, J., Hubbard, H., et al. (2012). Speech entrainment enables patients with Broca's aphasia to produce fluent speech. *Brain: A Journal of Neurology, 135*(12), 3815–3829. doi:10.1093/brain/aws301

Friedman, H. S. (2002). *Health psychology* (2nd ed.). Englewood Cliffs, NJ: Prentice-Hall.

Friedman, M., & Rosenman, R. H. (1983). *Type A behavior and your heart*. New York, NY: Knopf.

Friese, M., Messner, C., & Schaffner, Y. (2012). Mindfulness meditation counteracts self-control depletion. *Consciousness & Cognition, 21*(2), 1016–1022. doi:10.1016/j.concog.2012.01.008.

Fritz, C. O., Morris, P. E., et al. (2007). Comparing and combining retrieval practice and the keyword mnemonic for foreign vocabulary learning. *Applied Cognitive Psychology, 21*(4), 499–526. doi:10.1002/acp.1287

Fritzell, J., Rehnberg, J., et al. (2015). Absolute or relative? A comparative analysis of the relationship between poverty and mortality. *International Journal of Public Health, 60*(1), 101–110. doi:10.1007/s00038-014-0614-2

Fry, R. (2012). *Improve your memory* (6th ed.). Boston, MA: Cengage Learning.

Fryar, C. D., Carroll, M. D., et al. (2014). Prevalence of overweight, obesity and extreme obesity among adults: United States, 1960–62 through 2011–2012. *National Center for Health Statistics NCHS Data Brief No. 360, February*. Retrieved July 20, 2020, from www.cdc.gov/nchs/data/hestat/obesity_adult_11_12/obesity_adult_11_12.htm

Fryar, C. D., Hirsch, R., et al. (2007). Drug use and sexual behaviors reported by adults: United States, 1999–2002. *Advance data from vital and health statistics; no. 384*. Retrieved July 20, 2020, from http://www.cdc.gov/nchs/data/ad/ad384.pdf

Frydman, M. (1999). Television, aggressiveness, and violence. *International Journal of Adolescent Medicine & Health, 11*(3–4), 335–344. doi:10.1515/IJAMH.1999.11.3-4.335

Fu, J. H., Morris, M. W., et al. (2007). Epistemic motives and cultural conformity: Need for closure, culture, and context as determinants of conflict judgments. *Journal of Personality & Social Psychology, 92*(2), 191–207. doi:10.1037/0022-3514.92.2.191

Fukai, S., Akishita, M., et al. (2010). Effects of testosterone in older men with mild-to-moderate cognitive impairment. *Journal of the American Geriatrics Society, 58*(7), 1419–1421.

Fuller, T. E. (2012). *The insanity offense: How America's failure to treat the seriously mentally ill endangers its citizens.* New York, NY: Norton.

Fuller-Rowell, T. E., Evans, G. W., & Ong, A. D. (2012). Poverty and health: The mediating role of perceived discrimination. *Psychological Science, 23*(7), 734–739. doi:10.1177/0956797612439720

Funder, D. C. (2010). *The personality puzzle* (5th ed.). New York, NY: Norton.

Fuqua, D. R., & Newman, J. L. (2002). Creating caring organizations. *Consulting Psychology Journal: Practice & Research, 54*(2), 131–140.

Furnham, A., Chamorro-Premuzic, T., & Callahan, I. (2003). Does graphology predict personality and intelligence? *Individual Differences Research, 1*(2), 78–94.

Furnham, A., Richards, S. C., & Paulhus, D. L. (2013). The dark triad of personality: A 10 year review. *Social & Personality Psychology Compass, 7*(3), 199–216. doi:10.1111/spc3.12018

Gable, S. L., Reis, H. T., et al. (2004). What do you do when things go right? *Journal of Personality & Social Psychology, 87*(2), 228–245. doi:10.1037/0022-3514.87.2.228

Gadzella, B. M. (1995). Differences in processing information among psychology course grade groups. *Psychological Reports, 77,* 1312–1314.

Gaertner, S. L., Dovidio, J. F., et al. (2000). Reducing intergroup conflict: From superordinate goals to decategorization, recategorization, and mutual differentiation. *Group Dynamics, 4*(1), 98–114. doi:10.1037/1089-2699.4.1.98

Gainforth, H. L., West, R., et al. (2015). Assessing connections between behavior change theories using network analysis. *Annals of Behavioral Medicine, 49*(5), 754–761. doi:10.1007/s12160-015-9710-7

Galankin, T., Shekunova, E., & Zvartau, E. (2010). Estradiol lowers intracranial self-stimulation thresholds and enhances cocaine facilitation of intracranial self-stimulation in rats. *Hormones & Behavior, 58*(5), 827–834. doi:10.1016/j.yhbeh.2010.08.006

Galanter, M., Hayden, F., et al. (2005). Group therapy, self-help groups, and network therapy. In R. J. Frances, S. I. Miller, et al. (Eds.), *Clinical textbook of addictive disorders* (3rd ed., pp. 502–527). New York, NY: Guilford.

Galati, D., Scherer, K. R., & Ricci-Bitti, P. E. (1997). Voluntary facial expression of emotion: Comparing congenitally blind with normally sighted encoders. *Journal of Personality & Social Psychology, 73*(6), 1363–1379. doi:10.1037/0022-3514.73.6.1363

Galati, F. (2015). Complexity of judgment: What makes possible the convergence of expert and nonexpert ratings in assessing creativity. *Creativity Research Journal, 27*(1), 24–30. doi:10.1080/10400419.2015.992667

Galatzer-Levy, R. M. (2012). Obscuring desire: A special pattern of male adolescent masturbation, Internet pornography, and the flight from meaning. *Psychoanalytic Inquiry, 32*(5), 480–495. doi:10.1080/07351690.2012.703582

Galea, S., & Resnick, H. (2005). Posttraumatic stress disorder in the general population after mass terrorist incidents: Considerations about the nature of exposure. *CNS Spectrums, 10*(2), 107–115.

Galea, S., Ahern, J., et al. (2002). Psychological sequelae of the September 11 terrorist attacks in New York City. *New England Journal of Medicine, 346*(13), 982–987. doi:10.1056/NEJMsa013404

Gallagher, S. (2004). Nailing the lie: An interview with Jonathan Cole. *Journal of Consciousness Studies, 11*(2), 3–21.

Gallese, V., Rochat, M. J., & Berchio, C. (2013). The mirror mechanism and its potential role in autism spectrum disorder. *Developmental Medicine & Child Neurology, 55*(1), 15–22. doi:10.1111/j.1469-8749.2012.04398.x

Galliher, R. V., Jones, M. D., & Dahl, A. (2011). Concurrent and longitudinal effects of ethnic identity and experiences of discrimination on psychosocial adjustment of Navajo adolescents. *Developmental Psychology, 47*(2), 509–526. doi:10.1037/a0021061

Gallo, M. M. (2015). *"No one helped": Kitty Genovese, New York City, and the myth of urban apathy.* Ithaca, NY: Cornell University Press.

Galsworthy-Francis, L., & Allan, S. (2014). Cognitive behavioural therapy for anorexia nervosa: A systematic review. *Clinical Psychology Review, 34*(1), 54–72. doi:10.1016/j.cpr.2013.11.001

Gambescia, N., & Weeks, G. R. (2015). Systemic treatment of erectile disorder. In K. M. Hertlein, G. R. Weeks, et al. (Eds.), *Systemic sex therapy* (2nd ed., pp. 72–89). New York: Routledge/Taylor & Francis.

Ganis, G. (2013). Visual mental imagery. In S. Lacey & R. Lawson (Eds.), *Multisensory imagery* (pp. 9–28). New York, NY: Springer. doi:10.1007/978-1-4614-5879-1_2

Ganster, D. C., Fox, M. L., & Dwyer, D. J. (2001). Explaining employees' health care costs: A prospective examination of stressful job demands, personal control, and physiological reactivity. *Journal of Applied Psychology, 86,* 954–964. doi:10.1037/0021-9010.86.5.954

Garcia, E. E. (2008). Bilingual education in the United States. In J. Altarriba & R. R. Heredia (Eds.), *An introduction to bilingualism: Principles and processes* (pp. 321–343). Mahwah, NJ: Erlbaum.

Garcia-Barrera, M. A., Direnfeld, E., et al. (2013). Psychological assessment: From interviewing to objective and projective measurement. In C. A. Noggle & R. S. Dean (Eds.), *The neuropsychology of psychopathology* (pp. 473–493). New York, NY: Springer.

García-Rodríguez, O., Secades-Villa, R., et al. (2013). Probability and predictors of relapse to smoking: Results of the National Epidemiologic Survey on Alcohol and Related Conditions (NESARC). *Drug And Alcohol Dependence, 132*(3), 479–485. doi:10.1016/j.drugalcdep.2013.03.008

Garcia-Sierra, A., Rivera-Gaxiola, M., et al. (2011). Bilingual language learning: An ERP study relating early brain responses to speech, language input, and later word production. *Journal of Phonetics, 39*(4), 546–557. doi:10.1016/j.wocn.2011.07.002

Gardner, H. (2008). Birth and the spreading of a "meme." In J. Q. Chen, S. Moran, et al. (Eds.), *Multiple intelligences around the world* (pp. 3–16). San Francisco, CA: Jossey-Bass.

Gardner, H. (2011). The theory of multiple intelligences. In M. A. Gernsbacher, R. W. Pew, et al. (Eds.), *Psychology and the real world: Essays illustrating fundamental contributions to society* (pp. 122–130). New York, NY: Worth.

Gardner, S. E., Betts, L. R., et al. (2017). The role of emotion regulation for coping with school-based peer-victimisation in late childhood. *Personality & Individual Differences, 107,* 108–113. doi:10.1016/j.paid.2016.11.035

Garety, P. A., & Freeman, D. (2013). The past and future of delusions research: From the inexplicable to the treatable. *British Journal of Psychiatry, 203,* 327-333.

Garlow, S. J., Purselle, D. C., & Heninger, M. (2007). Cocaine and alcohol use preceding suicide in African American and white adolescents. *Journal of Psychiatric Research, 41*(6), 530–536. doi:10.1016/j.jpsychires.2005.08.008

Garrosa, E., Moreno-Jiménez, B., et al. (2008). The relationship between socio-demographic variables, job stressors, burnout, and hardy personality in nurses: An exploratory study. *International Journal of Nursing Studies, 45*(3), 418–427. doi:10.1016/j.ijnurstu.2006.09.003

Garza-Villarreal, E. A. (2016). Music-induced analgesia: The neurobiology of the analgesic effects of music in acute and chronic pain. In M. Hashefi (Ed.), *Music therapy in the management of medical conditions* (pp. 9–23). Hauppauge, NY: Nova Science Publishers, viii, 157 pp.

Gass, R. H., & Seiter, J. S. (2014). *Persuasion: Social influence and compliance gaining* (5th ed.). Boston, MA: Allyn & Bacon.

Gastner, M. T., Shalizi, C. R., & Newman, M. E. J. (2005). Maps and cartograms of the 2004 US presidential election results. *Advances in Complex Systems, 8*(1), 117–123. doi:10.1142/S0219525905000397

Gates, A. I. (1917). Recitation as a factor in memorizing. *Archives of Psychology, 40,* 104.

Gaumon, S., Paquette, D., et al. (2016). Anxiety and attachment to the mother in preschoolers receiving psychiatric care: The father–child activation relationship as a protective factor. *Infant Mental Health Journal, 37*(4), 372–387. doi:10.1002/imhj.21571

Gavett, B. E., & Horwitz, J. E. (2012). Immediate list recall as a measure of short-term episodic memory: Insights from the serial position effect and item response theory. *Archives of Clinical Neuropsychology, 27*(2), 125–135. doi:10.1093/arclin/acr104

Gawronski, B. (2012). Back to the future of dissonance theory: Cognitive consistency as a core motive. *Social Cognition, 30*(6), 652–668. doi:10.1521/soco.2012.30.6.652

Gazzaniga, M. S. (2015). *Tales from both sides of the brain: A life in neuroscience.* New York: Ecco/HarperCollins.

Geddes, L. (2008). Could brain scans ever be safe evidence? *New Scientist, Oct 3,* 8–9.

Gegenfurtner, K. R., & Kiper, D. C. (2003). Color vision. *Annual Review of Neuroscience, 26,* 181–206. doi:10.1146/annurev.neuro.26.041002.131116

Geher, G. (2014). *Evolutionary psychology 101.* New York, NY: Springer.

Geiselman, R. E., Fisher, R. P., et al. (1986). Enhancement of eyewitness memory with the cognitive interview. *American Journal of Psychology, 99,* 385–401.

Gejman, P. V., Sanders, A. R., & Duan, J. (2010). The role of genetics in the etiology of schizophrenia. *Psychiatric Clinics of North America, 33*(1), 35–66. doi:10.1016/j.psc.2009.12.003

Gentile, M. (2010). *Giving voice to values: How to speak your mind when you know what's right.* New Haven, CT: Yale University Press.

Genty, E., Breuer, T., et al. (2009). Gestural communication of the gorilla (Gorilla gorilla): Repertoire, intentionality, and possible origins. *Animal Cognition, 12*(3), 527–546. doi:10.1007/s10071-009-0213-4

German, T. P., & Defeyter, M. A. (2000). Immunity to functional fixedness in young children. *Psychonomic Bulletin & Review, 7*(4), 707–712. doi:10.3758/BF03213010

Gershoff, E. T., & Bitensky, S. H. (2007). The case against corporal punishment of children: Converging evidence from social science research and international human rights law and implications for U.S. public policy. *Psychology, Public Policy, & Law, 13*(4), 231–272. doi:10.1037/1076-8971.13.4.231

Gerstein, E. R. (2002). Manatees, bioacoustics, and boats. *American Scientist, 90*(March–April), 154–163. doi:10.1511/2002.2.154

Ghaemi, S. N. (2010). *The rise and fall of the biopsychosocial model: Reconciling art and science in psychiatry.* Baltimore, MD: Johns Hopkins University Press.

Gheitury, A., Sahraee, A., & Hoseini, M. (2012). Language acquisition in late critical period: A case report. *Deafness & Education International, 14*(3), 122–135. doi:10.1179/1557069X12Y.0000000008

Giancola, P. R., Josephs, R. A., et al. (2010). Alcohol myopia revisited: Clarifying aggression and other acts of disinhibition through a distorted lens. *Perspectives on Psychological Science, 5*(3), 265–278. doi:10.1177/1745691610369467

Giarratano, J. C., & Riley, G. (2004). *Expert systems, principles and programming* (4th ed.). Boston, MA: Cengage Learning.

Gibson, E. J., & Walk, R. D. (1960). The "visual cliff." *Scientific American, 202*(4), 67–71. doi:10.1038/scientificamerican0460-64

Gilboa, A., & Tal-Shmotkin, M. (2012). String quartets as self-managed teams: An interdisciplinary perspective.

Psychology of Music, 40(1), 19–41. doi:10.1177/0305735610377593

Gilchrist, A. L., Cowan, N., & Naveh-Benjamin, M. (2009). Investigating the childhood development of working memory using sentences: New evidence for the growth of chunk capacity. *Journal of Experimental Child Psychology, 104*(2), 252–265. doi:10.1016/j.jecp.2009.05.006

Giletta, M., Calhoun, C. D., et al. (2015). Multi-level risk factors for suicidal ideation among at-risk adolescent females: The role of hypothalamic-pituitary-adrenal axis responses to stress. *Journal of Abnormal Child Psychology, 43*(5), 807–820. doi:10.10007/s10802-014-9897-2

Gillan, C. M., & Robbins, T. W. (2014). Goal-directed learning and obsessive-compulsive disorder. *Philosophical Transactions of Royal Society B*. Retrieved July 20, 2020, from http://rstb.royalsocietypublishing.org/content/369/1655/20130475

Gillan, C. M., & Sahakian, B. J. (2015). Which is the driver, the obsessions or the compulsions, in OCD? *Neuropsychopharmacology, 40*(1), 247–248. doi:10.1038/npp.2014.201

Gillespie, C. F., & Nemeroff, C. B. (2007). Corticotropin-releasing factor and the psychobiology of early-life stress. *Current Directions in Psychological Science, 16*(2), 85–89. doi:10.1111/j.1467-8721.2007.00481.x

Gillespie-Lynch, K., Greenfield, P. M., et al. (2011). The role of dialogue in the ontogeny and phylogeny of early symbol combinations: A cross-species comparison of bonobo, chimpanzee, and human learners. *First Language, 31*(4), 442–460. doi:10.1177/0142723711406882

Gillespie-Lynch, K., Greenfield, P. M., et al. (2014). Gestural and symbolic development among apes and humans: Support for a multimodal theory of language evolution. *Frontiers in Psychology, 5*, Article 1228. doi:10.3389/fpsyg.2014.01228

Gilligan, C. (1982). *In a different voice*. Cambridge, MA: Harvard University Press.

Gilroy, K. E., & Pearce, J. M. (2014). The role of local, distal, and global information in latent spatial learning. *Journal of Experimental Psychology: Animal Learning & Cognition, 40*(2), 212–224. doi:10.1037/xan0000017

Gilson, L. L., Maynard, M. T., et al. (2015). Virtual teams research 10 years, 10 themes, and 10 opportunities. *Journal of Management, 41*(5), 1313–1337. doi:10.1177/0149206314559946

Ginet, M., Py, J., & Colomb, C. (2014). The differential effectiveness of the cognitive interview instructions for enhancing witnesses' memory of a familiar event. *Swiss Journal of Psychology, 73*(1), 25–34. doi:10.1024/1421-0185/a000118

Gino, F., & Flynn, F. J. (2011). Give them what they want: The benefits of explicitness in gift exchange. *Journal of Experimental Social Psychology, 47*, 915–922. doi:10.1016/j.jesp.2011.03.015

Giummarra, M. J., Gibson, S. J., et al. (2007). Central mechanisms in phantom limb perception: The past, present and future. *Brain Research Reviews, 54*(1), 219–232. doi:10.1016/j.brainresrev.2007.01.009

Gladwell, M. (2005). *Blink: The power of thinking without thinking*. New York, NY: Little, Brown.

Glass, D., Meyer, A., & Rose, D. H. (2013). Universal design for learning and the arts. *Harvard Educational Review, 83*(1), 98–119.

Glass, J., & Owen, J. (2010). Latino fathers: The relationship among machismo, acculturation, ethnic identity, and paternal involvement. *Psychology of Men & Masculinity, 11*(4), 251–261. doi:10.1037/a0021477

Gleason, J. B., & Ratner, N. B. (2013). *The development of language* (8th ed.). Boston, MA: Allyn & Bacon.

Gleason, O. C., Pierce, A. M., et al. (2013). The two-way relationship between medical illness and late-life depression. *Psychiatric Clinics of North America, 36*(4), 533–544. doi:10.1016/j.psc.2013.08.003

Glenn, E. N. (Ed.). (2009). *Shades of difference: Why skin color matters*. Palo Alto, CA: Stanford University Press.

Glick, P. (2008). When neighbors blame neighbors: Scapegoating and the breakdown of ethnic relations. In V. M. Esses & R. A. Vernon (Eds.), *Explaining the breakdown of ethnic relations: Why neighbors kill: Social issues and interventions* (pp. 123–146). Malden, MA: Blackwell. doi:10.1002/9781444303056.ch6

Global Footprint Network. (2020a). *Ecological footprint*. Retrieved July 20, 2020, from https://www.footprintnetwork.org/our-work/ecological-footprint/

Global Footprint Network. (2020b). *Personal footprint calculator*. Retrieved July 20, 2020, from https://www.footprintcalculator.org

Gloria-Bottini, F., Magrini, A., & Bottini, E. (2009). The effect of genetic and seasonal factors on birth weight. *Early Human Development, 85*(7), 439–441. doi:10.1016/j.earlhumdev.2009.02.004

Glover, R. J. (2001). Discriminators of moral orientation: Gender role or personality? *Journal of Adult Development, 8*(1), 1–7.

Gobet, F. (2005). Chunking models of expertise: Implications for education. *Applied Cognitive Psychology, 19*(2), 183–204. doi:10.1002/acp.1110

Gobet, F., & Simon, H. A. (1996). Recall of random and distorted chess positions: Implications for the theory of expertise. *Memory & Cognition, 24*(4), 493–503. doi:10.3758/BF03200937

Göckeritz, S., Schultz, P. W., et al. (2010). Descriptive normative beliefs and conservation behavior: The moderating roles of personal involvement and injunctive normative beliefs. *European Journal of Social Psychology, 40*(3), 514–523. doi:10.1002/ejsp.643

Godnig, E. C. (2003). Tunnel vision: Its causes & treatment strategies. *Journal of Behavioral Optometry, 14*(4), 95–99.

Godoy, R., Zeinalova, E., Reyes-García, V., et al. (2010). Does civilization cause discontentment among indigenous Amazonians? Test of empirical data from the Tsimane' of Bolivia. *Journal of Economic Psychology, 31*(4), 587–598.

Goel, N. (2012). Genetics of sleep timing, duration, and homeostasis in humans. *Sleep Medicine Clinics, 7*(3), 443–454. doi:10.1016/j.jsmc.2012.06.013

Gogate, L. J., Bahrick, L. E., & Watson, J. D. (2000). A study of multimodal motherese: The role of temporal synchrony between verbal labels and gestures. *Child Development, 71*(4), 878–894. doi:10.1111/1467-8624.00197

Goldberg, C. (2001). Of prophets, true believers, and terrorists. *The Dana Forum on Brain Science, 3*(3), 21–24.

Goldberg, R. (2019). *Drugs across the spectrum* (8th ed.). Boston, MA: Cengage Learning.

Golden, T. D., Veiga, J. F., & Simsek, Z. (2006). Telecommuting's differential impact on work-family conflict: Is there no place like home? *Journal of Applied Psychology, 91*(6), 1340–1350.

Goldenberg, H., & Goldenberg, I. (2013). *Family therapy: An overview* (8th ed.). Pacific Grove, CA: Brooks/Cole.

Goldfried, M. R. (2001). Integrating gay, lesbian, and bisexual issues into mainstream psychology. *American Psychologist, 56*(11), 977–987.

Golding, J. M., Bradshaw, G. S., et al. (2007). The impact of mock jury gender composition on deliberations and conviction rates in a child sexual assault trial. *Child Maltreatment, 12*(2), 182–190.

Goldstein, A., Déry, N., et al. (2016). Stress and binge drinking: A toxic combination for the teenage brain. *Neuropsychologia, 90*, 251–260. doi:10.1016/j.neuropsychologia.2016.07.035

Goldstein, E. B. (2015). *Cognitive psychology: Connecting mind, research, and everyday experience* (4th ed.). Boston, MA: Cengage Learning.

Goldstein, E. B., & Brockmole, J. R. (2017). *Sensation and perception* (10th ed.). Boston, MA: Cengage Learning.

Goldstein, M. H., Schwade, J., et al. (2010). Learning while babbling: Prelinguistic object-directed vocalizations indicate a readiness to learn. *Infancy, 15*(4), 362–391. doi:10.1111/j.1532-7078.2009.00020.x

Goldston, D. B., Molock, S. D., et al. (2008). Cultural considerations in adolescent suicide prevention and psychosocial treatment. *American Psychologist, 63*(1), 14–31. doi:10.1037/0003-066X.63.1.14

Goman, C. K. (2008). *The nonverbal advantage: Secrets and science of body language at work*. San Francisco, CA: Berrett-Koehler.

Gomes, A. R., Faria, S., & Lopes, H. (2016). Stress and psychological health: Testing the mediating role of cognitive appraisal. *Western Journal of Nursing Research, 38*(11), 1448–1468. doi:10.1177/0193945916654666

Gomez, R., & McLaren, S. (2007). The inter-relations of mother and father attachment, self-esteem and aggression during late adolescence. *Aggressive Behavior, 33*(2), 160–169. doi:10.1002/ab.20181

Gonzalez, M., Durrant, J. E., et al. (2008). What predicts injury from physical punishment? A test of the typologies of violence hypothesis. *Child Abuse & Neglect, 32*(8), 752–765. doi:10.1016/j.chiabu.2007.12.005

Gonzalez, V. M., Reynolds, B., & Skewes, M. C. (2011). Role of impulsivity in the relationship between depression and alcohol problems among emerging adult college drinkers. *Experimental & Clinical Psychopharmacology, 19*(4), 303–313. doi:10.1037/a0022720

González-Vallejo, C., Lassiter, G. D., et al. (2008). "Save angels perhaps": A critical examination of unconscious thought theory and the deliberation-without-attention effect. *Review of General Psychology, 12*(3), 282–296. doi:10.1037/a0013134

Goode, E. (1996). Gender and courtship entitlement: Responses to personal ads. *Sex Roles, 34*(3–4), 141–169. doi:10.1007/BF01544293

Goodman, G. S., Quas, J. A., Ogle, C. M. (2010). Child maltreatment and memory. *Annual Review of Psychology, 61*, 325–351. doi:10.1146/annurev.psych.093008.100403

Goodman-Delahunty, J., Greene, E., & Hsiao, W. (1998). Construing motive in videotaped killings: The role of jurors' attitudes toward the death penalty. *Law & Human Behavior, 22*(3), 257–271.

Gopie, N., Craik, F. I. M., & Hasher, L. (2011). A double dissociation of implicit and explicit memory in younger and older adults. *Psychological Science, 22*(5), 634–640. doi:10.1177/0956797611403321

Gopnik, A. (2016). *The gardener and the carpenter: What the new science of child development tells us about the relationship between parents and children*. New York: Farrar, Straus & Giroux.

Gordon, A. K., & Kaplar, M. E. (2002). A new technique for demonstrating the actor-observer bias. *Teaching of Psychology, 29*(4), 301–303. doi:10.1207/S15328023TOP2904_10

Gordon, I., Zagoory-Sharon, O., et al. (2010). Oxytocin and the development of parenting in humans. *Biological Psychiatry, 68*(4), 377–382. doi:10.1016/j.biopsych.2010.02.005

Gordon, J. R., Pruchno, R. A., et al. (2012). Balancing caregiving and work: Role conflict and role strain dynamics. *Journal of Family Issues, 33*(5), 662–689. doi:10.1177/0192513X11425322

Gordon, K. A., Wong, D. D. E., et al. (2011). Use it or lose it? Lessons learned from the developing brains of children who are deaf and use cochlear implants to hear. *Brain Topography, 24*(3–4), 204–219. doi:10.1007/s10548-011-0181-2

Gordon, R. M. (2001). MMPI/MMPI-2 changes in long-term psychoanalytic psychotherapy. *Issues in Psychoanalytic Psychology, 23*(1–2), 59–79.

Gorman, A. D., Abernethy, B., & Farrow, D. (2011). Investigating the anticipatory nature of pattern perception in sport. *Memory & Cognition, 39*(5), 894–901. doi:10.3758/s13421-010-0067-7

Gorman, A. D., Abernethy, B., & Farrow, D. (2013). The expert advantage in dynamic pattern recall persists across both attended and unattended display elements. *Attention, Perception, & Psychophysics, 75*(5), 835–844. doi:10.3758/s13414-013-0423-3

Gosling, S. D., & Mason, W. (2015). Internet research in psychology. *Annual Review of Psychology, 66,* 877–902. doi:10.1146/annurev-psych-010814-015321

Gottman, J. M. (1994). *Why marriages succeed or fail.* New York: Simon & Schuster.

Gottman, J. M., & Krokoff, L. J. (1989). Marital interaction and satisfaction: A longitudinal view. *Journal of Consulting & Clinical Psychology, 57*(1), 47–52.

Gould, D., Voelker, D. K., et al. (2014). Imagery training for peak performance. In J. L. Van Raalte & B. W. Brewer (Eds.), *Exploring sport and exercise psychology* (3rd ed., pp. 55–82). Washington, DC: American Psychological Association. doi:10.1037/14251-004

Gould, E., Schieder, J., & Geier, K. (2016). What is the gender pay gap and is it real? The complete guide to how women are paid less than men and why it can't be explained away. Retrieved July 20, 2020, from https://www.epi.org/publication/what-is-the-gender-pay-gap-and-is-it-real/

Gourville, J. T., & Soman, D. (2005). Overchoice and assortment type: When and why variety backfires. *Marketing Science, 24*(3), 382–395. doi:10.1287/mksc.1040.0109

Gowensmith, W., Murrie, D. C., & Boccaccini, M. T. (2013). How reliable are forensic evaluations of legal sanity? *Law & Human Behavior, 37*(2), 98–106. doi:10.1037/lhb0000001

Grack, C., & Richman, C. L. (1996). Reducing general and specific heterosexism through cooperative contact. *Journal of Psychology & Human Sexuality, 8*(4), 59–68. doi:10.1300/J056v08n04_04

Graham, J., Haidt, J., & Nosek, B. A. (2009). Liberals and conservatives rely on different sets of moral foundations. *Journal of Personality and Social Psychology, 96*(5), 1029–1046. doi:10.1037/a0015141

Graham, J., Nosek, B. A., et al. (2011). Mapping the moral domain. *Journal of Personality and Social Psychology, 101*(2), 366–385. doi:10.1037/a0021847

Grande, T., Rudolf, G., et al. (2003). Progressive changes in patients' lives after psychotherapy. *Psychotherapy Research, 13*(1), 43–58. doi:10.1093/ptr/kpg006

Grandner, M. A., & Kripke, D. F. (2004). Self-reported sleep complaints with long and short sleep: A nationally representative sample. *Psychosomatic Medicine, 66,* 239–241. doi:10.1097/01.PSY.0000107881.53228.4D

Grangeon, M., Guillot, A., & Collet, C. (2011). Postural control during visual and kinesthetic motor imagery. *Applied Psychophysiology & Biofeedback, 36*(1), 47–56. doi:10.1007/s10484-011-9145-2

Granrud, C. E. (2006). Size constancy in infants: 4-month-olds' responses to physical versus retinal image size. *Journal of Experimental Psychology: Human Perception & Performance, 32*(6), 1398–1404. doi:10.1037/0096-1523.32.6.1398

Granrud, C. E. (2009). Development of size constancy in children: A test of the metacognitive theory. *Attention, Perception, & Psychophysics, 71*(3), 644–654. doi:10.3758/APP.71.3.644

Grant-Jacob, J. A. (2016). Love at first sight. *Frontiers in Psychology, 7,* Article 1113. doi:10.3389/fpsyg. 2016.01113

Grant, B. (2010). Getting the point: Empathic understanding in nondirective client-centered therapy. *Person-Centered & Experiential Psychotherapies, 9*(3), 220–235. doi:10.1080/14779757.2010.9689068

Grant, B. F., Hasin, D. S., et al. (2006). The epidemiology of *DSM-IV* panic disorder and agoraphobia in the United States: Results from the National Epidemiologic Survey on Alcohol and Related Conditions. *Journal of Clinical Psychiatry, 67*(3), 363–374. doi:10.4088/JCP.v67n0305

Grant, I., Gonzalez, R., & et al. (2001). Long-term neurocognitive consequences of marijuana. In *National Institute on Drug Abuse Workshop on Clinical Consequences of Marijuana,* August 13, 2001, Rockville, MD.

Grant, T. M., Jack, D. C., et al. (2011). Carrying the burdens of poverty, parenting, and addiction: Depression symptoms and self-silencing among ethnically diverse women. *Community Mental Health Journal, 47*(1), 90–98. doi:10.1007/s10597-009-9255-y

Gravetter, F. J., & Forzano, L.-A. B. (2019). *Research methods for the behavioral sciences* (6th ed.). Boston, MA: Cengage Learning.

Gravetter, F. J., & Wallnau, L. B. (2017). *Statistics for the behavioral sciences* (10th ed.). Boston, MA: Cengage Learning.

Gravetter, F. J., Wallnau, L. B., & et al. (2021). *Essentials of statistics for the behavioral sciences* (10th ed.).

Gray, S. A. O., & Sweeney, K. K., et al. (2016). "Am I doing the right thing?": Pathways to parenting a gender variant child. *Family Process, 55*(1), 123–138. doi:10.1111/famp.12128

Gray, S. J., & Gallo, D. A. (2016). Paranormal psychic believers and skeptics: A large-scale test of the cognitive differences hypothesis. *Memory & Cognition, 44*(2), 242–261. doi:10.3758/s13421-015-0563-x S

Gredler, M. E. (2012). Understanding Vygotsky for the classroom: Is it too late? *Educational Psychology Review, 24*(1), 113–131. doi:10.1007/s10648-011-9183-6

Greene, D. C., & Britton, P. J. (2012). Stage of sexual minority identity formation: The impact of shame, internalized homophobia, ambivalence over emotional expression, and personal mastery. *Journal of Gay & Lesbian Mental Health, 16*(3), 188–214. doi:10.1080/19359705.2012.671126

Greene, D., & Lepper, M. R. (1974). How to turn play into work. *Psychology Today, 8*(4), 49.

Greene, E., & Heilbrun, K. (2014). *Wrightsman's psychology and the legal system* (8th ed.). Boston, MA: Cengage Learning.

Greenfield, P. M. (1997). You can't take it with you: Why abilities assessments don't cross cultures. *American Psychologist, 52,* 1115–1124. doi:10.1037/0003-066X.52.10.1115

Greenspan, J. D., Coghill, R. C., et al. (2008). Quantitative somatic sensory testing and functional imaging of the response to painful stimuli before and after cingulotomy for obsessive-compulsive disorder (OCD). *European Journal of Pain, 12*(8), 990–999. doi:10.1016/j.ejpain.2008.01.007

Greenwood, J. G., Greenwood, J. J., et al. (2006). A survey of sidedness in Northern Irish schoolchildren: The interaction of sex, age, and task. *Laterality: Asymmetries of Body, Brain & Cognition, 12*(1), 1–18. doi:10.1080/13576500600886630

Gregoire, C. (2016). *Why psychology should be a part of the fight against climate change.* Retrieved July 20, 2020, from www.huffingtonpost.com/entry/climate-change-psychology_us_5674272ee4b014efe0d52186

Gregory, B. T., Albritton, M. D., & Osmonbekov, T. (2010). The mediating role of psychological empowerment on the relationships between P–O fit, job satisfaction, and in-role performance. *Journal of Business & Psychology, 25*(4), 639–647.

Gregory, D. (2016). Inner speech, imagined speech, and auditory verbal hallucinations. *Review of Philosophy & Psychology, 7*(3), 653–673. doi:10.1007/s13164-015-0274-z

Gregory, R. L. (1990). *Eye and brain: The psychology of seeing.* Princeton, NJ: Princeton University Press.

Gregory, R. L. (2000). Visual illusions. In A. Kazdin (Ed.), *Encyclopedia of psychology* (Vol. 8, pp. 193–200). Washington, DC: American Psychological Association.

Gregory, R. L. (2003). Seeing after blindness. *Nature Neuroscience, 6*(9), 909–910.

Greifeneder, R., Scheibehenne, B., & Kleber, N. (2010). Less may be more when choosing is difficult: Choice complexity and too much choice. *Acta Psychologica, 133*(1), 45–50. doi:10.1016/j.actpsy.2009.08.005

Greitemeyer, T. (2010). Effects of reciprocity on attraction: The role of a partner's physical attractiveness. *Personal Relationships, 17*(2), 317–330. doi:10.1111/j.1475-6811.2010.01278.x

Greitemeyer, T. (2011). Effects of prosocial media on social behavior: When and why does media exposure affect helping and aggression? *Current Direction in Psychological Science, 20,* 251–255.

Greitemeyer, T. (2012). Acting prosocially reduces retaliation: Effects of prosocial video games on aggressive behavior. *European Journal of Social Psychology, 42,* 235–242.

Grello, C. M., Welsh, D. P., & Harper, M. S. (2006). No strings attached: The nature of casual sex in college students. *Journal of Sex Research, 43*(3), 255–267.

Grenèche, J., Krieger, J., et al. (2011). Short-term memory performances during sustained wakefulness in patients with obstructive sleep apnea-hypopnea syndrome. *Brain & Cognition, 75*(1), 39–50. doi:10.1016/j.bandc.2010.10.003

Grenier, G., & Byers, E. S. (1995). Rapid ejaculation: A review of conceptual, etiological, and treatment issues. *Archives of Sexual Behavior, 24*(4), 447–472.

Griffin, W. A. (2002). Family therapy. In M. Hersen & W. H. Sledge (Eds.), *Encyclopedia of psychotherapy* (pp. 787–791). San Diego, CA: Academic Press.

Griffiths, M. D. (2012). Internet sex addiction: A review of empirical research. *Addiction Research & Theory, 20*(2), 111–124. doi:10.3109/16066359.2011.588351

Griggs, R. A. (2015). The Kitty Genovese story in introductory psychology textbooks: Fifty years later. *Teaching of Psychology, 42*(2), 149–152. doi:10.1177/0098628315573138

Griggs, R. A. (2017). Milgram's obedience study: A contentious classic reinterpreted. *Teaching of Psychology, 44*(1), 32–37. doi:10.1177/0098628316677644

Grigorenko, E. L. (2005). The inherent complexities of gene-environment interactions. *Journals of Gerontology, 60B*(1), 53–64. doi:10.1093/geronb/60.Special_Issue_1.53

Grilly, D. M., & Salamone, J. (2012). *Drugs, brain, and behavior* (6th ed.). Englewood Cliffs, NJ: Prentice Hall.

Grobstein, P., & Chow, K. L. (1975). Perceptive field development and individual experience. *Science, 190,* 352–358.

Grönbladh, A., Nylander, E., & Hallberg, M. (2016). The neurobiology and addiction potential of anabolic androgenic steroids and the effects of growth hormone. *Brain Research Bulletin, 126,* 127–137. doi:10.1016/j. brainresbull.2016.05.003

Gros, D. F., Morland, L. A., et al. (2013). Delivery of evidence-based psychotherapy via video telehealth. *Journal of Psychopathology & Behavioral Assessment, 35*(4), 506–521. doi:10.1007/s10862-013-9363-4

Gross, J. J. (2013). Emotion regulation: Taking stock and moving forward. *Emotion, 13,* 359–365. doi:10.1037/a0032135

Gruberger, M., Levkovitz, Y., et al. (2015). I think therefore I am: Rest-related prefrontal cortex neural activity is involved in generating the sense of self. *Consciousness & Cognition, 33,* 414–421. doi:10.1016/j.concog.2015.02.008

Grubin, D., & Madsen, L. (2005). Lie detection and the polygraph: A historical review. *Journal of Forensic Psychiatry & Psychology, 16*(2), 357–369. doi:10.1080/14789940412331337353

Guastello, D. D., & Guastello, S. J. (2003). Androgyny, gender role behavior, and emotional intelligence among college students and their parents. *Sex Roles, 49*(11–12), 663–673.

Guay, R. P. (2013). The relationship between leader fit and transformational leadership. *Journal of Managerial Psychology, 28*(1), 55–73. doi:10.1108/02683941311298869

Güçlütürk, Y., Jacobs, R., & van Lier, R. (2016). Liking versus complexity: Decomposing the inverted U-curve. *Frontiers in Human Neuroscience, 10,* Article 112.

Guéguen, N., & Lamy, L. (2012). Men's social status and attractiveness: Women's receptivity to men's date requests. *Swiss Journal of Psychology, 71*(3), 157–160. doi:10.1024/1421-0185/a000083

Guéguen, N., & Pascual, A. (2003). Status and people's tolerance towards an ill-mannered person: A field study. *Journal of Mundane Behavior, 4*(1), 29–36.

Guéguen, N., Martin, A., & Meineri, S. (2011). Similarity and social interaction: When similarity fosters implicit behavior toward a stranger. *Journal of Social Psychology, 151*(6), 671–673. doi:10.1080/00224545.2010. 522627

Guéguen, N., Martin, A., et al. (2016). The foot-in-the-door technique, crime, and the responsive bystander: A field experiment. *Crime Prevention & Community Safety, 18*(1), 60–68. doi:10.1057/cpcs.2015.20

Guerin, S. A., Robbins, C. A., et al. (2012). Retrieval failure contributes to gist-based false recognition. *Journal of Memory & Language, 66*(1), 68–78. doi:10.1016/j.jml.2011.07.002

Gugliandolo, M. C., Costa, S., et al. (2015). Trait emotional intelligence and behavioral problems among adolescents: A cross-informant design. *Personality and Individual Differences, 74,* 16–21. doi:10.1016/j.paid.2014.09.032

Guidetti, M., Conner, M., et al. (2012). The transmission of attitudes towards food: Twofold specificity of similarities with parents and friends. *British Journal of Health Psychology, 17*(2), 346–361. doi:10.1111/j.2044-8287.2011.02041.x

Gujar, N., McDonald, S., et al. (2011). A role for REM sleep in recalibrating the sensitivity of the human brain to specific emotions. *Cerebral Cortex, 21*(1), 115–123. doi:10.1093/cercor/bhq064

Gündogan, N. Ü., Durmazlar, N., et al. (2005). Projected color slides as a method for mass screening test for color vision deficiency (a preliminary study). *International Journal of Neuroscience, 115*(8), 1105–1117. doi:10.1080/00207450590914365

Gupta, M. A. (2013). Review of somatic symptoms in post-traumatic stress disorder. *International Review of Psychiatry, 25*(1), 86–99. doi:10.3109/09540261.2012.7 36367

Gurlitt, J., Dummel, S., et al. (2012). Differently structured advance organizers lead to different initial schemata and learning outcomes. *Instructional Science, 40*(2), 351–369. doi:10.1007/s11251-011-9180-7

Gurung, R. (2014). *Health psychology: A cultural approach* (3rd ed.). Boston, MA: Cengage Learning.

Güth, W., Levati, M. V., & von Wangenheim, G. (2010). Mutual interdependence versus repeated interaction: An experiment studying voluntary social exchange. *Rationality & Society, 22*(2), 131–158. doi:10.1177/1043463110366230

Guthrie, R. V. (2004). *Even the rat was white: A historical view of psychology* (2nd ed.). Boston, MA: Allyn & Bacon.

Haaken, J., & Reavey, P. (Eds.). (2010). *Memory matters: Contexts for understanding sexual abuse recollections.* New York, NY: Routledge/Taylor & Francis.

Haas, B. W., Omura, K., et al. (2007). Is automatic emotion regulation associated with agreeableness? A perspective using a social neuroscience approach. *Psychological Science, 18*(2), 130–132.

Haber, R. N. (1970). How we remember what we see. *Scientific American, 222*(5), 104–112. doi:10.1038/scientificamerican0570-104

Haber, R. N., & Haber, L. (2000). Eidetic imagery. In A. E. Kazdin (Ed.), *Encyclopedia of psychology* (Vol. 3, pp. 147–149). Washington, DC: American Psychological Association.

Hackman, R. (2002). *Leading teams: Setting the stage for great performances.* Boston, MA: Harvard Business School Press.

Hafer, C. L., & Sutton, R. (2016). Belief in a just world. In C. Sabbagh & M. Schmitt (Eds.), *Handbook of social justice theory and research* (pp. 145–160). New York, NY: Springer.

Haga, S. M., Kraft, P., & Corby, E.-K. (2010). Emotion regulation: Antecedents and well-being outcomes of cognitive reappraisal and expressive suppression in crosscultural samples. *Journal of Happiness Studies, 10*(3), 271–291. doi:10.1007/s10902-007-9080-3

Haghbin, M., McCaffrey, A., & Pychyl, T. A. (2012). The complexity of the relation between fear of failure and procrastination. *Journal of Rational-Emotive & Cognitive-Behavior Therapy, 30*(4), 249–263. doi:10.1007/s10942-012-0153-9.

Haidt, J. (2007). The new synthesis in moral psychology. *Science, 316*(5827), 998–1002. doi: 10.1126/science.1137651

Haidt, J. (2012). *The righteous mind: Why good people are divided by politics and religion.* New York, NY: Pantheon.

Haidt, J. (2013). Moral psychology for the twenty-first century. *Journal of Moral Education, 42*(3), 281–297. doi:10.1080/0 3057240.2013.817327

Hakun, J. G., Ruparel, K., et al. (2009). Towards clinical trials of lie detection with fMRI. *Social Neuroscience, 4*(6), 518–527. doi:10.1080/17470910802188370

Hald, G. M. (2006). Gender differences in pornography consumption among young heterosexual Danish adults. *Archives of Sexual Behavior, 35*(5), 577–585.

Hald, G. M., Seaman, C., & Linz, D. (2014). Sexuality and pornography. In D. L. Tolman, L. M. Diamond, et al. (Eds.), *APA handbook of sexuality and psychology* (Vol. 2): *Contextual approaches* (pp. 3–35). Washington, DC: American Psychological Association. doi:10.1037/14194-001

Hales, C. M., Carroll, M. D., et al. (2020). Prevalence of obesity and severe obesity among adults: United States, 2017–2018. *National Center for Health Statistics Health E-Stats, September.* Retrieved July 20, 2020, from https://www.cdc.gov/nchs/products/databriefs/db360.htm

Hales, D. (2021). *An invitation to health: Choosing to change* (19th ed.). Boston, MA: Cengage Learning.

Halim, M., Ruble, D. N., & Amodio, D. M. (2011). From pink frilly dresses to 'one of the boys': A social-cognitive analysis of gender identity development and gender bias. *Social & Personality Psychology Compass, 5*(11), 933–949. doi:10.1111/j.1751-9004.2011.00399.x

Hall, D., & Buzwell, S. (2013). The problem of free-riding in group projects: Looking beyond social loafing as reason for non-contribution. *Active Learning in Higher Education, 14*(1), 37–49. doi:10.1177/1469787412467123

Hall, E. T. (1966). *The hidden dimension.* Garden City, NY: Doubleday.

Hall, N. C., Perry, R. P., et al. (2007). Attributional retraining and elaborative learning: Improving academic development through writing-based interventions. *Learning & Individual Differences, 17*(3), 280–290. doi:10.1016/j.lindif.2007.04.002

Hall, S. P. (2009). *Anger, rage, and relationships. An empathic approach to anger management.* New York: Routledge/Taylor & Francis.

Hallahan, D. P., Kauffman, J. M., & Pullen, P. C. (2015). *Exceptional learners* (13th ed.). Boston, MA: Pearson/Allyn & Bacon.

Halliday, G. (2010). Reflections on the meanings of dreams prompted by reading Stekel. *Dreaming, 20*(4), 219–226. doi:10.1037/a0020880

Halmai, Z., Dome, P., et al. (2013). Associations between depression severity and purinergic receptor p2rx7 gene polymorphisms. *Journal of Affective Disorders, 150*(1), 104–109. doi:10.1016/j.jad.2013.02.033

Halonen, J. S., & Santrock, J. W. (2013). *Your guide to college success: Strategies for achieving your goals* (7th ed.). Boston, MA: Cengage Learning.

Halpern, D. F. (2003). *Thought and knowledge: An introduction to critical thinking* (4th ed.). Mahwah, NJ: Erlbaum.

Halpern-Felsher, B. L., Cornell, J., et al. (2005). Oral versus vaginal sex among adolescents: Perceptions, attitudes, and behavior. *Pediatrics, 115,* 845–851.

Hamlin, J. (2013). Moral judgment and action in preverbal infants and toddlers: Evidence for an innate moral core. *Current Directions in Psychological Science, 22*(3), 186–193. doi:10.1177/0963721412470687

Hammond, D. C. (2008). Hypnosis as sole anesthesia for major surgeries: Historical & contemporary perspectives. *American Journal of Clinical Hypnosis, 51*(2), 101–121. doi:10.1080/00029157.2008.10401653

Hammond, D. C. (2013). A review of the history of hypnosis through the late 19th century. *American Journal of Clinical Hypnosis, 56*(2), 174–191.

Hampshire, A., Highfield, R. R., et al. (2012). Fractionating human intelligence. *Neuron, 76*(6), 1225–1237.

Hampson, S. E., Edmonds, G. W., et al. (2013). Childhood conscientiousness relates to objectively measured adult physical health four decades later. *Health Psychology, 32*(8), 925–928. doi:10.1037/a0031655

Hancock, J. (2011). *Brilliant memory training: Stop worrying about your memory and start using it—to the full!* Upper Saddle River, NJ: FT Press.

Haney, C., Banks, C., & Zimbardo, P. (1973). Interpersonal dynamics in a simulated prison. *International Journal of Criminology & Penology, 1,* 69–97. Downloaded April 3, 2017, from http://pdf.prisonexp.org/ijcp1973.pdf

Hans, V. P., Kaye, D. H., et al. (2011). Science in the jury box: Jurors' comprehension of mitochondrial DNA evidence. *Law & Human Behavior, 35*(1), 60–71.

Hansen, C. J., Stevens, L. C., & Coast, J. R. (2001). Exercise duration and mood state: How much is enough to feel better? *Health Psychology, 20*(4), 267–275. doi:10.1037/0278-6133.20.4.267

Hansen, K., Höfling, V., et al. (2013). Efficacy of psychological interventions aiming to reduce chronic nightmares: A meta-analysis. *Clinical Psychology Review, 33*(1), 146–155. doi:10.1016/j.cpr.2012.10.012

Hansen, N. B., Lambert, M. J., & Forman, E. M. (2002). The psychotherapy dose-response effect and its implications for treatment delivery services. *Clinical Psychology: Science & Practice, 9*(3), 329–334. doi:10.1093/clipsy/9.3.329

Hanton, S., Mellalieu, S. D., & Hall, R. (2004). Self-confidence and anxiety interpretation: A qualitative investigation. *Psychology of Sport & Exercise, 5*(4), 477–495. doi:10.1016/S1469-0292(03)00040-2

Hanyu, H., Sato, T., et al. (2010). The progression of cognitive deterioration and regional cerebral blood flow patterns in Alzheimer's disease: A longitudinal SPECT study. *Journal of the Neurological Sciences, 290*(1–2), 96–101. doi:10.1016/j.jns.2009.10.022

Happé, F., Cook, J. L., et al. (2017). The structure of social cognition: In(ter) dependence of sociocognitive processes. *Annual Review of Psychology, 68,* 243–267. doi:10.1146/annurev-psych-010416-044046

Haq, I. U., Foote, K. D., et al. (2010). Smile and laughter induction and intraoperative predictors of response to deep brain stimulation for obsessive-compulsive disorder. *NeuroImage, (Mar. 10),* [np].

Harb, G. C., Brownlow, J. A., et al. (2016). Posttraumatic nightmares and imagery rehearsal: The possible role of lucid dreaming. *Dreaming, 26*(3), 238–249. doi:10.1037/drm0000030

Harb, G. C., Thompson, R., et al. (2012). Combat-related PTSD nightmares and imagery rehearsal: Nightmare characteristics and relation to treatment outcome. *Journal of Traumatic Stress, 25*(5), 511–518. doi:10.1002/jts.21748

Hardaway, C. A., & Gregory, K. B. (2005). Fatigue and sleep debt in an operational navy squadron. *International Journal of Aviation Psychology, 15*(2), 157–171. doi:10.1207/s15327108ijap1502_3

Harden, K. P., Quinn, P. D., & Tucker-Drob, E. M. (2012). Genetically influenced change in sensation seeking drives the rise of delinquent behavior during adolescence. *Developmental Science, 15*(1), 150–163. doi:10.1111/j.1467-7687.2011.01115.x

Hardin, G. (1968). The tragedy of the commons. *Science, 162,* 1243–1248.

Hardin, M., & Greer, J. D. (2009). The influence of gender-role socialization, media use, and sports participation on perceptions of gender-appropriate sports. *Journal of Sport Behavior, 32*(2), 207–226.

Harding, D. J., Fox, C., et al. (2002). Studying rare events through qualitative case studies: Lessons from a study of rampage school shootings. *Sociological Methods & Research, 31*(2), 174–217. doi:10.1177/0049124102031002003

Hare, R. D. (2006). Psychopathy: A clinical and forensic overview. *Psychiatric Clinics of North America, 29*(3), 709–724. doi:10.1016/j.psc.2006.04.007

Harel, A., Gilaie-Dotan, S., et al. (2010). Top-down engagement modulates the neural expressions of visual expertise. *Cerebral Cortex, 20*(10), 2304–2318. doi:10.1093/cercor/bhp316

Harley, T. A. (2014). *The psychology of language: From data to theory* (4th. ed.) Hove, UK: Psychology Press.

Harlow, H. F., & Harlow, M. K. (1962). Social deprivation in monkeys. *Scientific American, 207*, 136–146.

Harlow, J. M. (1868). Recovery from the passage of an iron bar through the head. *Publications of the Massachusetts Medical Society, 2*, 327–347.

Harm Reduction International. (2020). *What is harm reduction?*. Retrieved July 20, 2020, from https://www.hri.global/what-is-harm-reduction

Harmison, R. J. (2011). Peak performance in sport: Identifying ideal performance states and developing athletes' psychological skills. *Sport, Exercise, & Performance Psychology, 1*(S), 3–18. doi:10.1037/2157-3905.1.S.3

Harnett, P., O'Donovan, A., & Lambert, M. J. (2010). The dose response relationship in psychotherapy: Implications for social policy. *Clinical Psychologist, 14*(2), 39–44. doi:10.1080/13284207.2010.500309

Harrell, J. P., & Medford, E. (2012). History, prejudice, and the study of social inequities. *Behavioral & Brain Sciences, 35*(6), 433–434. doi:10.1017/S0140525X12001203

Harrigan, J. A. (2005). Proxemics, kinesics, and gaze. In J. A. Harrigan, R. Rosenthal, et al. (Eds.), *The new handbook of methods in nonverbal behavior research*. New York, NY: Oxford University Press.

Harrington, R. (2013). *Stress, health and well-being: Thriving in the 21st century*. Boston, MA: Cengage Learning.

Harris, C. (2004). The evolution of jealousy. *American Scientist, 92*, 62–71.

Harris, J. C. (2010). *Intellectual disability: A guide for families and professionals*. New York, NY: Oxford University Press.

Harris, J., Hirsh-Pasek, K., & Newcombe, N. S. (2013). Understanding spatial transformations: Similarities and differences between mental rotation and mental folding. *Cognitive Processing, 14*(2), 105–115. doi:10.1007/s10339-013-0544-6

Harris, L. R., & Jenkin, M. R. M. (Eds.) (2011). *Vision in 3D environments*. New York, NY: Cambridge University Press.

Hart, C. L., Ksir, C. J., & Ray, O. S. (2013). *Drugs, society, and human behavior* (15th ed.). New York, NY: McGraw-Hill.

Hart, D., & Carlo, G. (2005). Moral development in adolescence. *Journal of Research on Adolescence, 15*(3), 223–233. doi:10.1111/j.1532-7795.2005.00094.x

Hart, J. E., Mourot, J. E., & Aros, M. (2012). Children of same-sex parents: In and out of the closet. *Educational Studies, 38*(3), 277–281. doi:10.1080/03055698.2011.598677

Hartgens, F., & Kuipers, H. (2004). Effects of androgenic-anabolic steroids in athletes. *Sports Medicine, 34(8)*, 513–54.

Hartlep, K. L., & Forsyth, G. A. (2000). The effect of self-reference on learning and retention. *Teaching of Psychology, 27*(4), 269–271. doi:10.1207/S15328023TOP2704_05

Hartley, S. (2012). *Peak performance every time*. New York, NY: Routledge/Taylor & Francis.

Hartmann, A. S., Greenberg, J. L., & Wilhelm, S. (2013). The relationship between anorexia nervosa and body dysmorphic disorder. *Clinical Psychology Review, 33*, 675–685. doi:10.1016/j.cpr.2013.04.002

Hartmann, E. (2011). *The nature and functions of dreaming*. New York, NY: Oxford University Press.

Hartmann, P., Reuter, M., & Nyborg, H. (2006). The relationship between date of birth and individual differences in personality and general intelligence: A large-scale study. *Personality & Individual Differences, 40*(7), 1349–1362. doi:10.1016/j.paid.2005.11.017

Hartung, C. M., Lefler, E. K., et al. (2010). Halo effects in ratings of ADHD and ODD: Identification of susceptible symptoms. *Journal of Psychopathology & Behavioral Assessment, 32*(1), 128–137. doi:10.1007/s10862-009-9135-3

Hashibe, M., Straif, K., et al. (2005). Epidemiologic review of marijuana use and cancer risk. *Alcohol, 35*(3), 265–275. doi:10.1016/j.alcohol.2005.04.008

Hashimoto, I., Suzuki, A., et al. (2004). Is there training-dependent reorganization of digit representations in area 3b of string players? *Clinical Neurophysiology, 115*(2), 435–447. doi:10.1016/S1388-2457(03)00340-7

Hasin, D. S., Kerridge, B. T., et al. (2016). Prevalence and correlates of DSM-5 cannabis use disorder, 2012–2013: Findings from the National Epidemiologic Survey on Alcohol and Related Conditions–III. *American Journal of Psychiatry, 173*(6), 588–599. doi:10.1176/appi.ajp.2015.15070907

Haslam, S. A., & Reicher, S. D. (2006). Debating the psychology of tyranny: Fundamental issues of theory, perspective and science. *British Journal of Social Psychology, 45*, 55–63.

Haslam, S. A., Reicher, S. D., et al. (2016). Questioning authority: New perspectives on Milgram's 'obedience' research and its implications for intergroup relations. *Current Opinion in Psychology, 11*, 6–9. doi:10.1016/j. copsyc.2016.03.007

Hatch, L. (2011). The American Psychological Association Task Force on the Sexualization of Girls: A review, update and commentary. *Sexual Addiction & Compulsivity, 18*(4), 195–211. doi:10.1080/10720162.2011.613326

Hauck, F. R., Moore, C. M., et al. (2002). The contribution of prone sleeping position to the racial disparity in sudden infant death syndrome. *Pediatrics, 110*, 772–780.

Hauck, P. A. (2011). Assertion strategies. In H. G. Rosenthal (Ed.), *Favorite counseling and therapy techniques* (2nd ed., pp. 155–157). New York, NY: Routledge.

Hausenblas, H. A., Campbell, A., et al. (2013). Media effects of experimental presentation of the ideal physique on eating disorder symptoms: A meta-analysis of laboratory studies. *Clinical Psychology Review, 33*(1), 168–181. doi:10.1016/j.cpr.2012.10.011

Hawe, P. (2015). Lessons from complex interventions to improve health. *Annual Review of Public Health, 36*, 307–323. doi:10.1146/annurev-publhealth-031912-114421

Hawks, J., Wang, E. T., et al. (2007). Recent acceleration of human adaptive evolution. *Proceedings of the National Academy of Sciences, 104*(52), 20753–20758.

Haycraft, E., & Blissett, J. (2010). Eating disorder symptoms and parenting styles. *Appetite, 54*(1), 221–224. doi:10.1016/j.appet.2009.11.009

Hayes, M. R. (2012). Neuronal and intracellular signaling pathways mediating GLP-1 energy balance and glycemic effects. *Physiology & Behavior, 106*(3), 413–416. doi:10.1016/j.physbeh.2012.02.017

Hayes, M. R., De Jonghe, B. C., & Kanoski, S. (2010). Role of the glucagon-like-peptide-1 receptor in the control of energy balance. *Physiology & Behavior, 100*(5), 503–510. doi:10.1016/j.physbeh.2010.02.029

Hayes, R. M., Abbott, R. L., et al. (2016). It's her fault: Student acceptance of rape myths on two college campuses. *Violence Against Women, 22*(13), 1540–1555. doi:10.1177/1077801216 630147

Hayes, S. C., Strosahl, K. D., & Wilson, K. G. (2012). *Acceptance and commitment therapy: The process and practice of mindful change* (2nd ed.). New York, NY: Guilford.

Hayne, H., & Rovee-Collier, C. (1995). The organization of reactivated memory in infancy. *Child Development, 66*(3), 893–906. doi:10.2307/1131957

Hays, N. A. (2013). Fear and loving in social hierarchy: Sex differences in preferences for power versus status. *Journal of Experimental Social Psychology, 49*(6), 1130–1136. doi:10.1016/j.jesp.2013.08.007

Hayward, L. C., & Coles, M. E. (2009). Elucidating the relation of hoarding to obsessive compulsive disorder and impulse control disorders. *Journal of Psychopathology & Behavioral Assessment, 31*(3), 220–227. doi:10.1007/s10862-008-9106-0

Head, L. S., & Gross, A. M. (2009). Systematic desensitization. In W. T. O'Donohue & J. E. Fisher (Eds.), *General principles and empirically supported techniques of cognitive behavior therapy* (pp. 640–647). New York, NY: Wiley.

Healey, C., Morriss, R., et al. (2013). Self-harm in postpartum depression and referrals to a perinatal mental health team: An audit study. *Archives of Women's Mental Health, 16*(3), 237–245. doi:10.1007/s00737-013-0335-1

Hearn, S., Saulnier, G., et al. (2012). Between integrity and despair: Toward construct validation of Erikson's eighth stage. *Journal of Adult Development, 19*(1), 1–20.

Heath, R. G. (1963). Electrical self-stimulation of the brain in man. *American Journal of Psychiatry, 120*, 571–577.

Hebb, D. O. (1949). *The organization of behavior*. New York, NY: Wiley & Sons.

Hebblethwaite, S., & Norris, J. (2011). Expressions of generativity through family leisure: Experiences of grandparents and adult grandchildren. *Family Relations, 60*(1), 121–133. doi:10.1111/j.1741-3729.2010.00637.x

Hebl, M. R., King, E. G., & Lin, J. (2004). The swimsuit becomes us all: Ethnicity, gender, and vulnerability to self-objectification. *Personality & Social Psychology Bulletin, 30*, 1322–1331.

Hecht, J. (2007). *The happiness myth: Why what we think is right is wrong*. New York, NY: HarperCollins.

Hedden, T., Ketay, S., et al. (2008) Cultural influences on neural substrates of attentional control. *Psychological Science, 19*(1), 12–17. doi:10.1111/j.1467-9280.2008.02038.x

Heidemeier, H., & Göritz, A. S. (2016). The instrumental role of personality traits: Using mixture structural equation modeling to investigate individual differences in the relationships between the Big Five traits and life satisfaction. *Journal of Happiness Studies, 17*(6), 2595–2612. doi:10.1007/s10902-015-9708-7

Heiman, G. W. (2014). *Basic statistics for the behavioral sciences* (7th ed.). Boston, MA: Cengage Learning.

Heimann, M., & Meltzoff, A. N. (1996). Deferred imitation in 9- and 14-month-old infants: A longitudinal study of a Swedish sample. *British Journal of Developmental Psychology, 14*(Mar.), 55–64. doi:10.1111/j.2044-835X.1996.tb00693.x

Hein, L. C., & Berger, K. C. (2012). Gender dysphoria in children: Let's think this through. *Journal of Child & Adolescent Psychiatric Nursing, 25*(4), 237–240. doi:10.1111/jcap.12014

Heinrichs, R. W. (2001). *In search of madness: Schizophrenia and neuroscience*. New York, NY: Oxford University Press.

Heisel, M. J., Flett, G. L., & Hewitt, P. L. (2003). Social hopelessness and college student suicide ideation. *Archives of Suicide Research, 7*(3), 221–235. doi:10.1080/13811110301557

Helenius, D., Munk-Jørgensen, P., & Steinhausen, H. (2012). Family load estimates of schizophrenia and associated risk factors in a nationwide population study of former child and adolescent patients up to forty years of age. *Schizophrenia Research, 139*(1–3), 183–188. doi:10.1016/j.schres.2012.05.014

Helgeson, V. S. (2012). *The psychology of gender* (4th ed.). Englewood Cliffs, NJ: Prentice Hall.

Hélie, S., & Sun, R. (2010). Incubation, insight, and creative problem solving: A unified theory and a connectionist model.

Psychological Review, 117(3), 994–1024. doi:10.1037/a0019532

Helle, L., & Säljö, R. (2012). Collaborating with digital tools and peers in medical education: Cases and simulations as interventions in learning. *Instructional Science, 40*(5), 737–744. doi:10.1007/s11251-012-9216-7

Helton, W. S. (2007). Skill in expert dogs. *Journal of Experimental Psychology: Applied, 13*(3), 171–178. doi:10.1037/1076-898X.13.3.171

Helton, W. S. (2009). Exceptional running skill in dogs requires extensive experience. *Journal of General Psychology, 136*(3), 323–332. doi:10.3200/GENP.136.3.323-336

Henderson, T. L., Roberto, K. A., & Kamo, Y. (2010). Older adults' responses to Hurricane Katrina: Daily hassles and coping strategies. *Journal of Applied Gerontology, 29*(1), 48–69. doi:10.1177/0733464809334287

Henley, T. (2019). *Hergenhahn's an introduction to the history of psychology* (8th ed.). Boston, MA: Cengage Learning.

Hennenlotter, A., Dresel, C., et al. (2009). The link between facial feedback and neural activity within central circuitries of emotion: New insights from botulinum toxin-induced denervation of frown muscles. *Cerebral Cortex, 19*(3), 537–542. doi:10.1093/cercor/bhn104

Hennessey, B. A., & Amabile, T. M. (2010). Creativity. *Annual Review of Psychology, 61*, 569–598. doi:10.1146/annurev.psych.093008.100416

Henningsen, D., & Henningsen, M. (2013). Generating ideas about the uses of brainstorming: Reconsidering the losses and gains of brainstorming groups relative to nominal groups. *Southern Communication Journal, 78*(1), 42–55. doi:10.1080/10417 94X.2012.717684

Hennink-Kaminski, H., & Reichert, T. (2011). Using sexual appeals in advertising to sell cosmetic surgery: A content analysis from 1986 to 2007. *Sexuality & Culture, 15*(1), 41–55. doi:10.1007/s12119-010-9081-y

Henrich, J., Heine, S. J., & Norenzayan, A. (2010). The weirdest people in the world? *Behavioral & Brain Sciences, 33*, 61–135. doi:10.1017/S0140525X0999152X

Henry, J. F., & Sherwin, B. B. (2012). Hormones and cognitive functioning during late pregnancy and postpartum: A longitudinal study. *Behavioral Neuroscience, 126*(1), 73–85. doi:10.1037/a0025540

Henry, P. K., Murnane, K. S., et al. (2010). Acute brain metabolic effects of cocaine in rhesus monkeys with a history of cocaine use. *Brain Imaging & Behavior, 4*(3–4), 212–219. doi:10.1007/s11682-010-9100-5

Henry, S. G., Penner, L. A., et al. (2016, December 19). Associations between thin slice ratings of affect and rapport and perceived patient-centeredness in primary care: Comparison of audio and video recordings. *Patient Education & Counseling*, n.p. doi:10.1016/j.pec.2016.12.020

Hensley, B. J. (2016). *An EMDR therapy primer: From practicum to practice* (2nd ed.). New York: Springer.

Hensley, L. C. (2016). The draws and drawbacks of college students' active procrastination. *Journal of College Student Development, 57*(4), 465–471. doi:10.1353/csd.2016.0045

Hepper, P. G., Dornan, J. C., & Lynch, C. (2012). Fetal brain function in response to maternal alcohol consumption: Early evidence of damage. *Alcoholism: Clinical & Experimental Research, 36*(12), 2168–2175. doi:10.1111/j.1530-0277.2012.01832.x

Herbenick, D., Reece, M., et al. (2010a). Sexual behavior in the United States: Results from a national probability sample of men and women ages 14–94. *Journal of Sexual Medicine, 7*(Suppl. 5), 255–265. doi:10.1111/j.1743-6109.2010.02012.x

Herbenick, D., Reece, M., et al. (2010b). An event-level analysis of the sexual characteristics and composition among adults ages 18–59: Results from a national probability sample in the United States. *Journal of Sexual Medicine, 7*(Suppl. 5), 346–361. doi:10.1111/j.1743-6109.2010.02020.x

Herculano-Houzel, S. (2012). The remarkable, yet not extraordinary, human brain as a scaled-up primate brain and its associated cost. *Proceedings of the National Academy of Sciences, 109*(Suppl. 1), 10661-10668. doi:10.1073/pnas.1201895109

Heriot, S. A., & Pritchard, M. (2004). " Reciprocal Inhibition as the main basis of psychotherapeutic effects" by Joseph Wolpe (1954). *Clinical Child Psychology & Psychiatry, 9*(2), 297–307. doi:10.1177/1359104504041928

Herman, J. L., & Tetrick, L. E. (2009). Problem-focused versus emotion-focused coping strategies and repatriation adjustment. *Human Resource Management, 48*(1), 69–88. doi:10.1002/hrm.20267

Hermanto, N., Moreno, S., & Bialystok, E. (2012). Linguistic and metalinguistic outcomes of intense immersion education: How bilingual? *International Journal of Bilingual Education and Bilingualism, 15*(2), 131–145. doi:10.1080/13670050.2 011.652591

Hermes, E. D. A., & Rosenheck, R. A. (2016). Implementing computer-based psychotherapy among veterans in outpatient treatment for substance use disorders. *Psychiatric Services, 67*(2), 176–183. doi:10.1176/appi. ps.201400532

Herold, D. K. (2010). Mediating media studies: Stimulating critical awareness in a virtual environment. *Computers & Education, 54*(3), 791–798. doi:10.1016/j.compedu.2009.10.019

Herren, C., In-Albon, T., & Schneider, S. (2013). Beliefs regarding child anxiety and parenting competence in parents of children with separation anxiety disorder. *Journal of Behavior Therapy & Experimental Psychiatry, 44*(1), 53–60. doi:10.1016/j.jbtep.2012.07.005

Hettich, P. I., & Landrum, R. E. (2014). *Your undergraduate degree in psychology: From college to career.* Thousand Oaks: Sage.

Hewit, J. K., Cronin, J. B., & Hume, P. A. (2012). Understanding change of direction performance: A technical analysis of a 180° ground-based turn and sprint task. *International Journal of Sports Science & Coaching, 7*(3), 493–501.

Hickok, G. (2014). *The myth of mirror neurons: The real science of communication and cognition.* New York: Norton.

Higbee, K. L., Clawson, C., et al. (1990). Using the link mnemonic to remember errands. *Psychological Record, 40*(3), 429–436.

Higham, P. A., & Gerrard, C. (2005). Not all errors are created equal: Metacognition and changing answers on multiple-choice tests. *Canadian Journal of Experimental Psychology, 59*(1), 28–34. doi:10.1037/h0087457

Hilgard, E. R. (1977). *Divided consciousness* (pp. 32–51). New York, NY: Wiley.

Hilgard, E. R. (1994) Neodissociation theory. In S. J. Lynn & J. W. Rhue (Eds.), *Dissociation: Clinical, theoretical and research perspectives* (pp. 32–51). New York, NY: Guilford.

Hill, J., Ford, W. R., & Farreras, I. G. (2015). Real conversations with artificial intelligence: A comparison between human–human online conversations and human–chatbot conversations. *Computers in Human Behavior, 49*, 245–250. doi:10.1016/j.chb.2015.02.026

Hinrichs, K. T. (2007). Follower propensity to commit crimes of obedience: The role of leadership beliefs. *Journal of Leadership & Organizational Studies, 14*(1), 69–76. doi:10.1177/1071791907304225

Hintzman, D. L. (2005). Memory strength and recency judgments. *Psychonomic Bulletin & Review, 12*(5), 858–864. doi:10.3758/BF03196777

Hinzman, L., & Kelly, S. D. (2013). Effects of emotional body language on rapid out-group judgments. *Journal of Experimental Social Psychology, 49*(1), 152–155. doi:10.1016/j.jesp.2012.07.010

Hipp, J. R., Butts, C. T., et al. (2013). Extrapolative simulation of neighborhood networks based on population spatial distribution: Do they predict crime? *Social Networks, 35*(4), 614–625. doi:10.1016/j.socnet.2013.07.002

Hirshbein, L., & Sarvananda, S. (2008). History, power, and electricity: American popular magazine accounts of electroconvulsive therapy, 1940–2005. *Journal of the History of the Behavioral Sciences, 44*(1), 1–18. doi:10.1002/jhbs.20283

Hirstein, W. (2005). *Brain fiction: Self-deception and the riddle of confabulation.* Cambridge, MA: MIT Press.

Hobson, J. A. (2000). Dreams: Physiology. In A. Kazdin (Ed.), *Encyclopedia of psychology* (Vol. 3, pp. 78–81). Washington, DC: American Psychological Association.

Hobson, J. A. (2005). Sleep is of the brain, by the brain and for the brain. *Nature, 437*(7063), 1254–1256. doi:10.1038/nature04283

Hobson, J. A. (2009). The neurobiology of consciousness: Lucid dreaming wakes up. *International Journal of Dream Research, 2*(2), 41–44.

Hobson, J. A., & Schredl, M. (2011). The continuity and discontinuity between waking and dreaming: A dialogue between Michael Schredl and Allan Hobson concerning the adequacy and completeness of these notions. *International Journal of Dream Research, 4*(1), 3–7.

Hodges, N., & Williams, M. (Eds.). (2012). *Skill acquisition in sport: Research, theory and practice.* New York, NY: Psychology Press.

Hodgins, H. S., & Adair, K. C. (2010). Attentional processes and meditation. *Consciousness & Cognition, 19*(4), 872–878. doi:10.1016/j.concog.2010.04.002

Hodson, G., & Hewstone, M. (Eds.). (2013). *Advances in intergroup contact.* New York, NY: Psychology Press.

Hodson, G., MacInnis, C. C., & et al. (2017). Bowing and kicking: Rediscovering the fundamental link between generalized authoritarianism and generalized prejudice. *Personality & Individual Differences, 104*, 243–251. doi:10.1016/j.paid.2016.08.018

Hodson, R., & Sullivan, T. A. (2012). *The social organization of work* (5th ed.). Boston, MA: Cengage Learning.

Hoeft, F., Gabrieli, J. E., et al. (2012). Functional brain basis of hypnotizability. *JAMA Psychiatry, 69*(10), 1064–1072. doi:10.1001/archgenpsychiatry.2011.2190

Hoenig, K., Müller, C., et al. (2011). Neuroplasticity of semantic representations for musical instruments in professional musicians. *Neuroimage, 56*(3), 1714–1725. doi:10.1016/j.neuroimage.2011.02.065

Hoerger, M., Chapman, B. P., et al. (2012). Emotional intelligence: A theoretical framework for individual differences in affective forecasting. *Emotion, 12*(4), 716–725. doi:10.1037/a0026724

Hoff, E. (2014). *Language development* (5th ed.). Boston, MA: Cengage Learning.

Hoff, E., & Tian, C. (2005). Socioeconomic status and cultural influences on language. *Journal of Communication Disorders, 38*(4), 271–278. doi:10.1016/j.jcomdis.2005.02.003

Hoffart, A. (2005). Interpersonal therapy for social phobia: Theoretical model and review of the evidence. In M. E. Abelian (Ed.), *Focus on psychotherapy research* (pp. 121–137). Hauppauge, NY: Nova Science Publishers.

Hoffman, E. (2008). Abraham Maslow: A biographer's reflections. *Journal of Humanistic Psychology, 48*(4), 439–443. doi:10.1177/0022167808320534

Hogan, E. H., Hornick, B. A., & Bouchoux, A. (2002). Focus on communications: Communicating the message: Clarifying the controversies about caffeine. *Nutrition Today, 37*, 28–35.

Hohwy, J., & Fox, E. (2012). Preserved aspects of consciousness in disorders of consciousness: A review and conceptual analysis. *Journal of Consciousness Studies, 19*(3–4), 87–120.

Hohwy, J., & Rosenberg, R. (2005). Unusual experiences, reality testing and delusions of alien control. *Mind & Language, 20*(2), 141–162. doi:10.1111/j.0268-1064.2005.00280.x

Holbrook, T., Moore, C., & Zoss, M. (2010). Equitable intent: Reflections on universal

design in education as an ethic of care. *Reflective Practice, 11*(5), 681–692.
Holden, C. (1980). Twins reunited. *Science, 80*, Nov., 55–59.
Holdsworth, E., Bowen, E., et al. (2014). Client engagement in psychotherapeutic treatment and associations with client characteristics, therapist characteristics, and treatment factors. *Clinical Psychology Review, 34*(5), 428–450. doi:10.1016/j.cpr.2014.06.004
Holland, J. L. (1997). *Making vocational choices.* Odessa, FL: Psychological Assessment Resources.
Holliday, R. E., Humphries, J. E., et al. (2012). Reducing misinformation effects in older adults with cognitive interview mnemonics. *Psychology and Aging, 27*(4), 1191–1203. doi:10.1037/a002203
Hollins, M. (2010). Somesthetic senses. *Annual Review of Psychology, 61*, 243–271. doi:10.1146/annurev.psych.093008.100419
Holloway, T., Moreno, J. L., et al. (2013). Prenatal stress induces schizophrenia-like alterations of serotonin 2A and metabotropic glutamate 2 receptors in the adult offspring: Role of maternal immune system. *Journal of Neuroscience, 33*(3), 1088–1098. doi:10.1523/JNEUROSCI.2331-12.2013
Holly, J. E., & Harmon, S. M. (2012). Sensory conflict compared in microgravity, artificial gravity, motion sickness, and vestibular disorders. *Journal of Vestibular Research: Equilibrium & Orientation, 22*(2–3), 81–94.
Holman, A., & Sillars, A. (2012). Talk about "hooking up": The influence of college student social networks on nonrelationship sex. *Health Communication, 27*(2), 205–216. doi:10.1080/10410236.2011.575540
Holman, E. A., Silver, R. C., et al. (2008). Terrorism, acute stress, and cardiovascular health: A 3-year national study following the September 11th attacks. *Archives of General Psychiatry, 65*(1), 73–80. doi:10.1001/archgenpsychiatry.2007.6
Holmes, E. K., & Huston, A. C. (2010). Understanding positive father–child interaction: Children's, father's, and mother's contributions. *Fathering, 8*(2), 203–225. doi:10.3149/fth.1802.203
Holmes, M. (2002). Rethinking the meaning and management of intersexuality. *Sexualities, 5*(2), 159–180. doi:10.1177/136346070 2005002002
Holmes, T. H., & Rahe, R. H. (1967). The social readjustment rating scale. *Journal of Psychosomatic Research, 11*(2), 213–218. doi:10.1016/0022-3999(67)90010-4
Holz, J., Piosczyk, H., et al. (2012). EEG sigma and slow-wave activity during NREM sleep correlate with overnight declarative and procedural memory consolidation. *Journal of Sleep Research, 21*(6), 612–619. doi:10.1111/j.1365-2869.2012.01017.x
Hölzel, B. K., Lazar, S. W., et al. (2011). How does mindfulness meditation work? Proposing mechanisms of action from a conceptual and neural perspective. *Perspectives on Psychological Science, 6*(6), 537–559. doi:10.1177/1745691611419671
Homan, A. C., Buengeler, C., et al. (2015). The interplay of diversity training and diversity beliefs on team creativity in nationality diverse teams. *Journal of Applied Psychology, 100*(5), 1456–1467. doi:10.1037/apl000001
Hooper, N., Erdogan, A., et al. (2015). Perspective taking reduces the fundamental attribution error. *Journal of Contextual Behavioral Science, 4*(2), 69–72. doi:10.1016/j.jcbs.2015.02.002
Hooyman, N., & Kiyak, H. A. (2011). *Social gerontology: A multidisciplinary perspective* (9th ed.). Boston, MA: Pearson/Allyn & Bacon.
Hopton, A., Thomas, K., & MacPherson, H. (2013). The acceptability of acupuncture for low back pain: A qualitative study of patient's experiences nested within a randomised controlled trial. *PLoS ONE, 8*(2). doi:e56806. doi:10.1371/journal.pone.0056806
Hopwood, C. J., Donnellan, M. B., et al. (2011). Genetic and environmental influences on personality trait stability and growth during the transition to adulthood: A three-wave longitudinal study. *Journal of Personality & Social Psychology, 100*(3), 545–556. doi:10.1037/a0022409
Horgan, J. (2005). The forgotten era of brain chips. *Scientific American, 293*(4), 66–73. doi:10.1038/scientificamerican1005-66
Horn, R. R., Williams, A. M., et al. (2005). Visual search and coordination changes in response to video and point-light demonstrations without KR. *Journal of Motor Behavior, 37*(4), 265–274.
Horne, M. R., Gilroy, K. E., et al. (2012). Latent spatial learning in an environment with a distinctive shape. *Journal of Experimental Psychology: Animal Behavior Processes, 38*(2), 139–147. doi:10.1037/a0027288
Horsley, R. R., Osborne, M., et al. (2012). High-frequency gamblers show increased resistance to extinction following partial reinforcement. *Behavioural Brain Research, 229*(2), 438–442. doi:10.1016/j.bbr.2012.01.024
Hortensius, R., & de Gelder, B. (2014). The neural basis of the bystander effect: The influence of group size on neural activity when witnessing an emergency. *NeuroImage, 93*, 53–58. doi:10.1016/j.neuroimage.2014.02.025
Hosch, H. M., & Cooper, D. S. (1982). Victimization as a determinant of eyewitness accuracy. *Journal of Applied Psychology, 67*, 649–652. doi:10.1037/0021-9010.67.5.649
Hosemans, D. (2015). Meditation: A process of cultivating enhanced well-being. *Mindfulness, 6*(2), 338–347. doi:10.1007/s12671-013-0266-y
Hough, L. M., & Connelly, B. S. (2013). Personality measurement and use in industrial and organizational psychology. In K. F. Geisinger, B. A. Bracken, et al. (Eds.), *APA handbook of testing and assessment in psychology* (Vol. 1): *Test theory and testing and assessment in industrial and organizational psychology* (pp. 501–531). Washington, DC: American Psychological Association. doi:10.1037/14047-028
Houghton, D. P. (2008). Invading and occupying Iraq: Some insights from political psychology. *Peace & Conflict: Journal of Peace Psychology, 14*(2), 169–192. doi:10.1080/10781910802017297
Howard, I. P. (2012). *Perceiving in depth* (Vol. 3): *Other mechanisms of depth perception.* New York, NY: Oxford University Press. doi:10.1093/acprof:oso/9780199764167.001.0001
Howard, K. I., Krause, M. S., et al. (2001). Syzygy, science, and psychotherapy: The Consumer Reports study. *Journal of Clinical Psychology, 57*(7), 865–874. doi:10.1002/jclp.1055
Howe, L. C., & Krosnick, J. A. (2017). Attitude strength. *Annual Review of Psychology, 68*, 327–351. doi:10.1146/annurev-psych-122414-033600
Howes, O., McCutcheon, R., et al. (2015). Glutamate and dopamine in schizophrenia: An update for the 21st century. *Journal of Psychopharmacology, 29*(2), 97–115. doi:10.1177/0269881114563634
Howell, D. C. (2014). *Fundamental statistics for the behavioral sciences* (8th ed.). Boston, MA: Cengage Learning.
Hsieh, P., Colas, J. T., & Kanwisher, N. (2011). Pop-out without awareness: Unseen feature singletons capture attention only when top-down attention is available. *Psychological Science, 22*(9), 1220–1226. doi:10.1177/0956797611419302
Hu, Y., & Ericsson, K. A. (2012). Memorization and recall of very long lists accounted for within the Long-Term Working Memory framework. *Cognitive Psychology, 64*(4), 235–266. doi:10.1016/j.cogpsych.2012.01.001
Hu, Y., Ericsson, K. A., et al. (2009). Superior self-paced memorization of digits in spite of a normal digit span: The structure of a memorist's skill. *Journal of Experimental Psychology: Learning, Memory, & Cognition, 35*(6), 1426–1442. doi:10.1037/a0017395
Huang, M.-H., & Rust, R. T. (2011). Sustainability and consumption. *Journal of the Academy of Marketing Science, 39*(1), 40–54.
Hubble, M.A., Duncan, B. L., & Miller, S. D. (Eds.). (1999). *The heart and soul of change: What works in therapy.* Washington, DC: American Psychological Association.
Hubel, D. H., & Wiesel, W. N. (2005). *Brain & visual perception: The story of a 25-year collaboration.* New York, NY: Oxford University Press.
Hübner, R., & Volberg, G. (2005). The integration of object levels and their content: A theory of global/local processing and related hemispheric differences. *Journal of Experimental Psychology: Human Perception & Performance, 31*(3), 520–541. doi:10.1037/0096-1523.31.3.520
Hudson, C. G. (2016). A model of deinstitutionalization of psychiatric care across 161 nations: 2001–2014. *International Journal of Mental Health, 45*(2), 135–153. doi:10.1080/0 0207411.2016.1167489
Hudson, N. W., & Fraley, R. C. (2015). Volitional personality trait change: Can people choose to change their personality traits? *Journal of Personality & Social Psychology, 109*(3), 490–507. doi:10.1037/pspp0000021
Huebner, R. B., & Kantor, L. (2011). Advances in alcoholism treatment. *Alcohol Research & Health, 33*(4), 295–299.
Hughes, A. (2008). The use of urban legends to improve critical thinking. In L. T. Benjamin, Jr. (Ed.), *Favorite activities for the teaching of psychology.* Washington, DC: American Psychological Association.
Hughes, D. F. (2013). Charles Bonnet syndrome: A literature review into diagnostic criteria, treatment and implications for nursing practice. *Journal of Psychiatric & Mental Health Nursing, 20*(2), 169–175. doi:10.1111/j.1365-2850.2012.01904.x
Hughes, J. R., & Callas, P. W. (2011). Is delaying a quit attempt associated with less success? *Nicotine & Tobacco Research, 13*(12), 1228–1232. doi:10.1093/ntr/ntr207
Hughes, M., Brymer, M., et al. (2011). Posttraumatic stress among students after the shootings at Virginia Tech. *Psychological Trauma, 3*(4), 403–411. doi:10.1037/a0024565
Human Connectome Project. (2013). Retrieved July 20, 2020, from http://www.humanconnectomeproject.org
Human, L. J., Biesanz, J. C., et al. (2014). To thine own self be true: Psychological adjustment promotes judgeability via personality–behavior congruence. *Journal of Personality & Social Psychology, 106*(2), 286–303. doi:10.1037/a0034860
Humes, K. R., Jones, N. A., & Ramirez, R. R. (2011). Overview of race and Hispanic origin: 2010. *U.S. Census Bureau News, 2010 Census Brief C2010BR-02.* Retrieved July 20, 2020, from http://www.census.gov/prod/cen2010/briefs/c2010br-02.pdf
Humphrey, R. H. (2014). Effective leadership: Theory, cases and applications. Thousand Oaks, CA: Sage.
Hunter, J. P., Katz, J., & Davis, K. D. (2003). The effect of tactile and visual sensory inputs on phantom limb awareness. *Brain, 126*(3), 579–589. doi:10.1093/brain/awg054
Hunter, S., Hurley, R. A., & Taber, K. H. (2013). A look inside the mirror neuron system. *Journal of Neuropsychiatry & Clinical Neurosciences, 25*(3), 170–175.
Huntsinger, J. R. (2013). Does emotion directly tune the scope of attention? *Current Directions in Psychological Science, 22*(4), 265–270. doi:10.1177/0963721413480364
Huston, H. C., & Bentley, A. C. (2010). Human development in societal context. *Annual Review of Psychology, 61*, 411–437. doi:10.1146/annurev.psych.093008.100442
Hutchinson, S. R. (2004). Survey research. In K. deMarrais & S. D. Lapan (Eds.), *Foundations for research: Methods of inquiry in education and the social sciences: Inquiry and pedagogy across diverse contexts* (pp. 283–301). Mahwah, NJ: Erlbaum.
Hutchinson, S., Lee, L. H., et al. (2003). Cerebellar volume of musicians. *Cerebral Cortex, 13*(9), 943–949. doi:10.1093/cercor/13.9.943

Hutchison, K. E., McGeary, J., et al. (2002). The DRD4 VNTR polymorphism moderates craving after alcohol consumption. *Health Psychology, 21*(2), 139–146. doi:10.1037/0278-6133.21.2.139

Hyde, J. S., & DeLamater, J. D. (2014). *Understanding human sexuality* (12th ed.). New York, NY: McGraw-Hill.

Hyde, J. S., & Else-Quest, N. (2013). *Half the human experience* (8th ed.). Boston, MA: Cengage Learning.

Hyman, R. (2007). Talking with the dead, communicating with the future and other myths created by cold reading. In S. Della Sala (Ed.), *Tall tales about the mind & brain: Separating fact from fiction* (pp. 218–232). New York, NY: Oxford University Press.

Hysenbegasi, A., Hass, S. L., & Rowland, C. R. (2005). The impact of depression on the academic productivity of university students. *Journal of Mental Health Policy & Economics, 8*(3), 145–151.

Iacono, W. G. (2008). Effective policing: Understanding how polygraph tests work and are used. *Criminal Justice & Behavior, 35*(10), 1295–1308. doi:10.1177/0093854808321529

Iacono, W. G. (2011). Encouraging the use of the Guilty Knowledge Test (GKT): What the GKT has to offer law enforcement. In B. Verschuere, G. Ben-Shakhar, et al. (Eds.), *Memory detection: Theory and application of the Concealed Information Test* (pp. 12–23). New York, NY: Cambridge University Press.

Iannone, M., Bulotta, S., et al. (2006). Electrocortical effects of MDMA are potentiated by acoustic stimulation in rats. *BMC Neuroscience, February 16*, 7–13. doi:10.1186/1471-2202-7-13

Imbimbo, C., Verze, P., et al. (2009). A report from a single institute's 14-year experience in treatment of male-to-female transsexuals. *Journal of Sexual Medicine, 6*(10), 2736–2745.

Immordino-Yang, M. H. (2008). How we can learn from children with half a brain. *New Scientist, 2664*, 44–45.

Impett, E. A., Gordon, A. M., et al. (2010). Moving toward more perfect unions: Daily and long-term consequences of approach and avoidance goals in romantic relationships. *Journal of Personality & Social Psychology, 99*(6), 948–963.

Impett, E. A., Strachman, A., et al. (2008). Maintaining sexual desire in intimate relationships: The importance of approach goals. *Journal of Personality & Social Psychology, 94*(5), 808–823.

Imuta, K., Henry, J. D., et al. (2016). Theory of mind and prosocial behavior in childhood: A meta-analytic review. *Developmental Psychology,* 52(8), 1192–1205. doi:10.1037/dev0000140

Ingalhalikar, M., Smith, A., et al. (2014). Sex differences in the structural connectome of the human brain. *Proceedings of the National Academy of Sciences, 111*(2), 823–828. doi:10.1073/pnas.1316909110

Ingham, A. G., Levinger, G., et al. (1974). The Ringelmann effect: Studies of group size and group performance. *Journal of Personality & Social Psychology, 10*, 371–384. doi:10.1016/0022-1031(74)90033-X

Ingiosi, A. M., Opp, M. R., & Krueger, J. M. (2013). Sleep and immune function: Glial contributions and consequences of aging. *Current Opinion in Neurobiology, 23*(5), 806–811. doi:10.1016/j.conb.2013.02.003

Ingravallo, F., Gnucci, V., et al. (2012). The burden of narcolepsy with cataplexy: How disease history and clinical features influence socio-economic outcomes. *Sleep Medicine, 13*(10), 1293–1300. doi:10.1016/j.sleep.2012.08.002

Innocence Project. (2020). *DNA exonerations in the United States.* Retrieved July 20, 2020, from https://www.innocenceproject.org/dna-exonerations-in-the-united-states/

Insel, T. R. (2010). Rethinking schizophrenia. *Nature, 468*(7321), 187–193. doi:10.1038/nature09552

Inta, D., Meyer-Lindenberg, A., & Gass, P. (2011). Alterations in postnatal neurogenesis and dopamine dysregulation in schizophrenia: A hypothesis. *Schizophrenia Bulletin, 37*(4), 674–680. doi:10.1093/schbul/sbq134

Intaitė, M., Noreika, V., et al. (2013). Interaction of bottom-up and top-down processes in the perception of ambiguous figures. *Vision Research, 89*, 24-31. doi:10.1016/j.visres.2013.06.011

Inzlicht, M., & Schmeichel, B. J. (2012). What is ego depletion? Toward a mechanistic revision of the resource model of self-control. *Perspectives on Psychological Science, 7*(5), 450–463. doi:10.1177/1745691612454134

Inzlicht, M., Gutsell, J. N., & Legault, L. (2012). Mimicry reduces racial prejudice. *Journal of Experimental Social Psychology, 48*(1), 361–365. doi:10.1016/j.jesp.2011.06.007

Iosif, A., & Ballon, B. (2005). Bad moon rising: The persistent belief in lunar connections to madness. *Canadian Medical Association Journal, 173*(12), 1498–1500. doi:10.1503/cmaj.051119

Ipser, J. C., Singh, L., & Stein, D. J. (2013). Meta-analysis of functional brain imaging in specific phobia. *Psychiatry & Clinical Neurosciences, 67*(5), 311–322. doi:10.1111/pcn.12055

Irish, M., Landin-Romero, R., et al. (2018). Evolution of autobiographical memory impairments in Alzheimer's disease and frontotemporal dementia: A longitudinal neuroimaging study. *Neuropsychologia, 110*, 14–25. doi:10.1016/j.neuropsychologia.2017.03.014

Irish, M., & Piguet, O. (2013). The pivotal role of semantic memory in remembering the past and imagining the future. *Frontiers in Behavioral Neuroscience, 7*, 27. doi:10.3389/fnbeh.2013.00027

Irwin, M. R. (2015). Why sleep is important for health: A psychoneuroimmunology perspective. *Annual Review of Psychology, 66*, 143–172. doi:10.1146/annurev-psych-010213-115205

Isaacs, D. (2011). Corporal punishment of children: Changing the culture. *Journal of Paediatrics and Child Health, 47*(8), 491–492. doi:10.1111/j.1440-1754.2011.02143.x

Isbell, E., Stevens, C., et al. (2016). 5-HTTLPR polymorphism is linked to neural mechanisms of selective attention in preschoolers from lower socioeconomic status backgrounds. *Developmental Cognitive Neuroscience, 22*, 36–47. http://dx.doi.:10.1016/j.dcn.2016.10.002

Iskra-Golec, I. (2016). Individual differences in circadian rhythm parameters and work-family spillover in shift workers. In I. Iskra-Golec, J. Barnes-Farrell, & P Bohle (Eds.), *Social and family issues in shift work and non standard working hours* (pp. 181–202). Cham, Switzerland: Springer International Publishing. doi:10.1007/978-3-319-42286-2_9

Ivanco, T. L., & Racine, R. J. (2000). Long-term potentiation in the pathways between the hippocampus and neocortex in the chronically implanted, freely moving rat. *Hippocampus, 10*, 143–152.

Iverson, R. D., & Zatzick, C. D. (2011). The effects of downsizing on labor productivity: The value of showing consideration for employees' morale and welfare in high-performance work systems. *Human Resource Management, 50*(1), 29–44.

Ivtzan, I., Gardner, H. E., et al. (2013). Wellbeing through self-fulfilment: Examining developmental aspects of self-actualization. *The Humanistic Psychologist, 41*(2), 119–132. doi:10.1080/08873267.2012.712076

Iyengar, S. S., & Lepper, M. R. (2000). When choice is demotivating: Can one desire too much of a good thing? *Journal of Personality & Social Psychology, 79*(6), 995–1006. doi:10.1037/0022-3514.79.6.995

Izard, C. E. (1990). Facial expressions and the regulation of emotions. *Journal of Personality & Social Psychology, 58*(3), 487–498. doi:10.1037/0022-3514.58.3.487

Izard, C. E. (2007). Basic emotions, natural kinds, emotion schemas, and a new paradigm. *Perspectives on Psychological Science, 2*, 260–280.

Izard, C. E. (2011). Forms and functions of emotions: Matters of emotion–cognition interactions. *Emotion Review, 3*(4), 371–378. doi:10.1177/1754073911410737

Izard, C. E., Fantauzzo, C. A., et al. (1995). The ontogeny and significance of infants' facial expressions in the first 9 months of life. *Developmental Psychology, 31*(6), 997–1013. doi:10.1037/0012-1649.31.6.997

Izard, C. E., Woodburn, E. M., & Finlon, K. J. (2010). Extending emotion science to the study of discrete emotions in infants. *Emotion Review, 2*(2), 134–136. doi:10.1177/1754073909355003

Izuma, K. (2013). The neural basis of social influence and attitude change. *Current Opinion in Neurobiology, 23*, 456–462. doi:10.1016/j.conb.2013.03.009

Jack, D. C., & Ali, A. (2010). *Silencing the self across cultures: Depression and gender in the social world.* New York, NY: Oxford University Press.

Jackson, D., & Newberry, P. (2016). *Critical thinking: A user's manual* (2nd ed.). Boston, MA: Cengage Learning.

Jackson, L. M. (2011). *The psychology of prejudice: From attitudes to social action.* Washington, DC: American Psychological Association.

Jackson, S. L. (2016). *Research methods and statistics: A critical thinking approach* (5th ed.). Boston, MA: Cengage Learning.

Jackson, S. L. (2017). *Statistics plain and simple* (4th ed.). Boston, MA: Cengage Learning.

Jacob, A., Prasad, S., et al. (2004). Charles Bonnet syndrome: Elderly people and visual hallucinations. *British Medical Journal, 328*(7455), 1552–1554. doi:10.1136/bmj.328.7455.1552

Jacobs, J., Lega, B., & Anderson, C. (2012). Explaining how brain stimulation can evoke memories. *Journal of Cognitive Neuroscience, 24*(3), 553–563. doi:10.1162/jocn_a_00170

Jacobs, N., van Os, J., et al. (2008). Heritability of intelligence. *Twin Research & Human Genetics, 10*(Suppl.), 11–14. doi:10.1375/twin.10.supp.11

Jacobs, S. R., & Dodd, D. K. (2003). Student burnout as a function of personality, social support, and workload. *Journal of College Student Development, 44*(3), 291–303. doi:10.1353/csd.2003.0028

Jacobs-Stewart, T. (2010). *Mindfulness and the 12 steps: Living recovery in the present moment.* Center City, MN: Hazelden Foundation.

Jaeggi, S. M., Buschkuehl, M., et al. (2008). Improving fluid intelligence with training on working memory. *Proceedings of the National Academy of Sciences, 105*(19), 6829–6833. doi:10.1073/pnas.0801268105

Jaehnig, W., & Miller, M. L. (2007). Feedback types in programmed instruction: A systematic review. *Psychological Record, 57*(2), 219–232.

Jaffe, J., Beatrice, B., et al. (2001). Rhythms of dialogue in infancy. *Monographs of the Society for Research in Child Development, 66*(2), i–vi, 1–132.

James, W. (1890). *The principles of psychology.* Retrieved July 20, 2020, from http://psychclassics.yorku.ca/James/Principles/

Jamieson, J. P. (2010). The home field advantage in athletics: A meta-analysis. *Journal of Applied Social Psychology, 40*(7), 1819–1848. doi:10.1111/j.1559-1816.2010.00641.x

Jamieson, J. P., & Mendes, W. B. (2016). Social stress facilitates risk in youths. *Journal of Experimental Psychology: General, 145*(4), 467–485. doi:10.1037/xge0000147

Janis, I. L. (1989). *Crucial decisions.* New York, NY: Free Press.

Janis, I. L. (2007). Groupthink. In R. P. Vecchio (Ed.), *Leadership: Understanding the dynamics of power and influence in organizations* (2nd ed., pp. 163–176). Notre Dame, IN: University of Notre Dame Press.

Janssen, S. A., & Arntz, A. (2001). Real-life stress and opioid-mediated analgesia in novice parachute jumpers. *Journal of Psychophysiology, 15*(2), 106–113. doi:10.1027//0269-8803.15.2.106

Janusek, L., Cooper, D., & Mathews, H. L. (2012). Stress, immunity, and health outcomes. In V. Rice (Ed.), *Handbook of stress, coping, and health: Implications for nursing research, theory, and practice* (2nd ed., pp. 43–70). Thousand Oaks, CA: Sage.

Jarrold, C., & Hall, D. (2013). The development of rehearsal in verbal short-term memory. *Child Development Perspectives, 7*(3), 182–186. doi:10.1111/cdep.12034

Jarvin, L., & Sternberg, R. J. (2003). Alfred Binet's contributions to educational psychology. In B. J. Zimmerman & D. H. Schunk (Eds.), *Educational psychology: A century of contributions* (pp. 65–79). Mahwah, NJ: Erlbaum.

Jaschik, S. (2011). The enduring gender gap in pay. *Inside Higher Ed, April 5*. Retrieved July 20, 2020, from https://www.insidehighered.com/news/2011/04/05/the_enduring_gender_gap_in_faculty_pay

Javitt, D. C., Zukin, S. R., et al. (2012). Has an angel shown the way? Etiological and therapeutic implications of the PCP/NMDA model of schizophrenia. *Schizophrenia Bulletin, 38*(5), 958–966. doi:10.1093/schbul/sbs069

Jeffries, F. W., & Davis, P. (2013). What is the role of eye movements in eye movement desensitization and reprocessing (EMDR) for post-traumatic stress disorder (PTSD)? A review. *Behavioural & Cognitive Psychotherapy, 41*(3), 290–300. doi:10.1017/S1352465812000793

Jegindø, E., Vase, L., et al. (2013). Pain and sacrifice: Experience and modulation of pain in a religious piercing ritual. *International Journal for the Psychology of Religion, 23*(3), 171–187. doi:10.1080/10508619.2012.759065

Jenkins, A. C., & Mitchell, J. P. (2011). Medial prefrontal cortex subserves diverse forms of self-reflection. *Social Neuroscience, 6*(3), 211–218. doi:10.1080/17470919.2010.507948

Jenkins, J. G., & Dallenbach, K. M. (1924). Oblivescence during sleep and waking. *American Journal of Psychology, 35*, 605–612.

Jerabek, I., & Standing, L. (1992). Imagined test situations produce contextual memory enhancement. *Perceptual & Motor Skills, 75*(2), 400.

Jervis, L. L., Boland, M. E., & Fickenscher, A. (2010). American Indian family caregivers' experiences with helping elders. *Journal of Cross-Cultural Gerontology, 25*(4), 355–369. doi:10.1007/s10823-010-9131-9

Jiang, L., Bazarova, N. N., & Hancock, J. T. (2013). From perception to behavior: Disclosure reciprocity and the intensification of intimacy in computer-mediated communication. *Communication Research, 40*(1), 125–143. doi:10.1177/0093650211405313

Joel, S., Gordon, A. M., et al. (2013). The things you do for me: Perceptions of a romantic partner's investments promote gratitude and commitment. *Personality & Social Psychology Bulletin, 39*(10), 1333–1345.

Joffe, R. T. (2006). Is the thyroid still important in major depression? *Journal of Psychiatry & Neuroscience, 31*(6), 367–368.

Johansen, J. P., Wolff, S. E., et al. (2012). Controlling the elements: An optogenetic approach to understanding the neural circuits of fear. *Biological Psychiatry, 71*(12), 1053–1060. doi:10.1016/j.biopsych.2011.10.023

Johansson, V., Garwicz, M., et al. (2013). Beyond blind optimism and unfounded fears: Deep brain stimulation for treatment resistant depression. *Neuroethics, 6*(3), 457–471. doi:10.1007/s12152-011-9112-x

Johnson, B. T., & Boynton, M. H. (2010). Putting attitudes in their place: Behavioral prediction in the face of competing variables. In J. P. Forgas, J. Cooper, et al. (Eds.), *The psychology of attitudes and attitude change* (pp. 19–38). New York, NY: Psychology Press.

Johnson, C. S., & Lammers, J. (2012). The powerful disregard social comparison information. *Journal of Experimental Social Psychology, 48*(1), 329–334. doi:10.1016/j.jesp.2011.10.010

Johnson, C. S., & Stapel, D. A. (2010). It depends on how you look at it: Being versus becoming mindsets determine responses to social comparisons. *British Journal of Social Psychology, 49*(4), 703–723. doi:10.1348/014466609X476827

Johnson, J. J. M., Hrycaiko, D. W., et al. (2004). Self-talk and female youth soccer performance. *Sport Psychologist, 18*(1), 44–59.

Johnson, K. J., & Fredrickson, B. L. (2005). "We all look the same to me": Positive emotions eliminate the own-race bias in face recognition. *Psychological Science, 16*(11), 875–881. doi:10.1111/j.1467-9280.2005.01631.x

Johnson, M. W., & Griffiths, R. R. (2013). Comparative abuse liability of GHB and ethanol in humans. *Experimental & Clinical Psychopharmacology, 21*, 112–123. doi:10.1037/a0031692

Johnson, R., Nessler, D., & Friedman, D. (2013). Temporally specific divided attention tasks in young adults reveal the temporal dynamics of episodic encoding failures in elderly adults. *Psychology & Aging, 28*(2), 443–456. doi:10.1037/a0030967

Johnson, S. J., Batey, M., & Holdsworth, L. (2009). Personality and health: The mediating role of trait emotional intelligence and work locus of control. *Personality & Individual Differences, 47*(5), 470–475. doi:10.1016/j.paid.2009.04.025

Johnson, T. J. (2002). College students' self-reported reasons for why drinking games end. *Addictive Behaviors, 27*(1), 145–153. doi:10.1016/S0306-4603(00)00168-4

Johnson, W., Turkheimer, E., et al. (2009). Beyond heritability: Twin studies in behavioral research. *Current Directions in Psychological Science, 18*(4), 217–220. doi:10.1111/j.1467-8721.2009.01639.x

Johnstone, P. M., Nábelek, A. K., & Robertson, V. S. (2010). Sound localization acuity in children with unilateral hearing loss who wear a hearing aid in the impaired ear. *Journal of the American Academy of Audiology, 21*(8), 522–534. doi:10.3766/jaaa.21.8.4

Joiner, T. E., Jr. (2010). *Myths about suicide*. Cambridge, MA: Harvard University Press.

Joinson, C., Heron, J., et al. (2009). A prospective study of age at initiation of toilet training and subsequent daytime bladder control in school-age children. *Journal of Developmental & Behavioral Pediatrics, 30*(5), 385–393. doi:10.1097/DBP.0b013e3181ba0e77

Jonason, P. K., Koenig, B. L., & Tost, J. (2010). Living a fast life: The Dark Triad and life history theory. *Human Nature, 21*(4), 428–442. doi:10.1007/s12110-010-9102-4

Jonason, P. K., & Lavertu, A. N. (2017). The reproductive costs and benefits associated with the Dark Triad traits in women. *Personality & Individual Differences, 110*, 38–40. doi:10.1016/j. paid.2017.01.024

Jonason, P. K., & Webster, G. D. (2010). The dirty dozen: A concise measure of the dark triad. *Psychological Assessment, 22*(2), 420–432. doi:10.1037/a0019265

Jonason, P. K., Webster, G. D., et al. (2012). The antihero in popular culture: Life history theory and the dark triad personality traits. *Review of General Psychology, 16*(2), 192–199. doi:10.1037/a0027914

Jones, G. (2012). Why chunking should be considered as an explanation for developmental change before short-term memory capacity and processing speed. *Frontiers in Psychology, 3*, 167. doi:10.3389/fpsyg.2012.00167

Jones, K. L., & Streissguth, A. P. (2010). Fetal alcohol syndrome and fetal alcohol spectrum disorders: A brief history. *Journal of Psychiatry & Law, 38*(4), 373–382.

Jones, O. D., Marois, R., et al. (2013). Law and neuroscience. *Journal of Neuroscience, 33*(45), 17624–17630. doi:10.1523/JNEUROSCI.3254-13.2013

Jones, P., Blunda, M., et al. (2013). Can mindfulness-based interventions help adolescents with cancer? *Psycho-Oncology, 22*(9), 2148–2151. doi:10.1002/pon.3251

Jones, S. R., & Fernyhough, C. (2007). A new look at the neural diathesis-stress model of schizophrenia: The primacy of social-evaluative and uncontrollable situations. *Schizophrenia Bulletin, 33*(5), 1171–1177. doi:10.1093/schbul/sbl058

Jones, W. R., & Morgan, J. F. (2010). Eating disorders in men: A review of the literature. *Journal of Public Mental Health, 9*(2), 23–31. doi:10.5042/jpmh.2010.0326

Jonides, J., Lewis, R. L., et al. (2008). The mind and brain of short-term memory. *Annual Review of Psychology, 59*, 193–224. doi:10.1146/annurev.psych.59.103006.093615

Jonkmann, K., Becker, M., et al. (2012). Personality traits moderate the Big-Fish–Little-Pond effect of academic self-concept. *Learning & Individual Differences, 22*(6), 736–746. doi:10.1016/j.lindif.2012.07.020

Joo, E. Y., Tae, W. K., et al. (2010). Reduced brain gray matter concentration in patients with obstructive sleep apnea syndrome. *Sleep: Journal of Sleep & Sleep Disorders Research, 33*(2), 235–241.

Jordan, K. (2010). Vicarious trauma: Proposed factors that impact clinicians. *Journal of Family Psychotherapy, 21*(4), 225–237. doi:10.1080/08975353. 2010.529003

Jordan, M. I., & Mitchell, T. M. (2015). Machine learning: Trends, perspectives, and prospects. *Science, 349*(6245), 255–260. doi:10.1126/science.aaa8415

Jordano, M. L., & Touron, D. R. (2017). Stereotype threat as a trigger of mind-wandering in older adults. *Psychology & Aging*, n.p. doi:10.1037/pag0000167

Jorm, A. F. (2012). Mental health literacy: Empowering the community to take action for better mental health. *American Psychologist, 67*(3), 231–243. doi:10.1037/a0025957

Jorm, A. F., Korten, A. E., Rodgers, B., et al. (2002). Sexual orientation and mental health. *British Journal of Psychiatry, 180*(5), 423–427.

Joseph, D. L., Jin, J., et al. (2015). Why does self-reported emotional intelligence predict job performance? A meta-analytic investigation of mixed EI. *Journal of Applied Psychology, 100*(2), 298–342. doi:10.1037/a0037681

Jou, J., & Flores, S. (2013). How are false memories distinguishable from true memories in the Deese–Roediger–McDermott paradigm? A review of the findings. *Psychological Research, 77*(6), 671–686. doi:10.1007/s00426-012-0472-6

Jowett, G. S. (2006). Brainwashing: The Korean POW controversy and the origins of a myth. In G. S. Jowett & V. O'Donnell (Eds.), *Readings in propaganda and persuasion: New and classic essays*(pp. 201–211). Thousand Oaks, CA: Sage.

Joyce, S. P. (2020). *Guide to personal online reputation management*. Retrieved July 20, 2020, from https://www.job-hunt.org/reputation-management/reputation-management.shtml

Juarez, L., Soto, E., & Pritchard, M. E. (2012). Drive for muscularity and drive for thinness: The impact of pro-anorexia websites. *Eating Disorders: The Journal of Treatment & Prevention, 20*(2), 99–112. doi:10.1080/10640266.2012.653944

Judge, T. A., Weiss, H. M., et al. (2017). Job attitudes, job satisfaction, and job affect: A century of continuity and of change. *Journal of Applied Psychology, 102*(3), 356–374. doi:10.1037/apl0000181

Judson, S. S., Johnson, D. M., & Perez, A. U. (2013). Perceptions of adult sexual coercion as a function of victim gender. *Psychology of Men & Masculinity*, doi:10.1037/a0030448

Juhl, J., Sand, E. C., & Routledge, C. (2012). The effects of nostalgia and avoidant attachment on relationship satisfaction and romantic motives. *Journal of Social & Personal Relationships, 29*(5), 661–670. doi:10.1177/0265407512443433

Juliano, L. M., & Griffiths, R. R. (2004). A critical review of caffeine withdrawal: Empirical validation of symptoms and signs, incidence, severity, and associated features. *Psychopharmacology, 176*(1), 1–29. doi:10.1007/s00213-004-2000-x

Julien, R. M. (2011). *A primer of drug action* (12th ed.). New York, NY: Worth.

Jun, H. (2010). *Social justice, multicultural counseling, and practice: Beyond a conventional approach*. Thousand Oaks, CA: Sage.

Jung, C. G. (1961). *Memories, dreams, reflections*. New York: Pantheon.

Jurd, R. R. (2011). TiNS special issue: Hippocampus and memory. *Trends in Neurosciences, 34*(10), 499–500. doi:10.1016/j.tins.2011.08.008

Jussim, L., & Harber, K. D. (2005). Teacher expectations and self-fulfilling prophecies: Knowns and unknowns, resolved and unresolved controversies. *Personality & Social Psychology*

Review, 9(2), 131–155. doi:10.1207/s15327957pspr0902_3

Jussim, L., Crawford, J. T., & Rubinstein, R. S. (2015). Stereotype (in) accuracy in perceptions of groups and individuals. *Current Directions in Psychological Science, 24*(6), 490–497. doi:10.1177/0963721415605257

Justman, S. (2011). From medicine to psychotherapy: The placebo effect. *History of the Human Sciences, 24*(1), 95–107. doi:10.1177/0952695110386655

Kafka, M. P. (2010). Hypersexual disorder: A proposed diagnosis for *DSM-V*. *Archives of Sexual Behavior, 39*(2), 377–400.

Kahlenberg, S. G., & Hein, M. M. (2010). Progression on Nickelodeon? Gender-role stereotypes in toy commercials. *Sex Roles, 62*(11–12), 830–847. doi:10.1007/s11199-009-9653-1

Kahn, R. E., Ermer, E., et al. (2016). Emotional intelligence and callous-unemotional traits in incarcerated adolescents. *Child Psychiatry & Human Development.* Advance online publication. doi:10.1007/s10578-015-0621-4

Kahneman, D. (2011). *Thinking, fast and slow.* New York, NY: Farrar, Straus & Giroux.

Kahneman, D., Slovic, P., & Tversky, A. (1982). *Judgment under uncertainty: Heuristics and biases.* Cambridge, MA: Cambridge University Press.

Kaida, K., Åkerstedt, T., et al. (2008). Performance prediction by sleepiness-related subjective symptoms during 26-hour sleep deprivation. *Sleep & Biological Rhythms, 6*(4), 234–241. doi:10.1111/j.1479-8425.2008.00367.x

Kail, R. V., & Cavanaugh, J. C. (2019). *Human development: A life-span view* (8th ed.). Boston, MA: Cengage Learning.

Kaiser, R. B., & Wallace, W. T. (2016). Gender bias and substantive differences in ratings of leadership behavior: Toward a new narrative. *Consulting Psychology Journal: Practice & Research, 68*(1), 72–98. doi:10.1037/cpb0000059

Kalat, J. W. (2021). *Biological psychology* (13th ed.). Boston, MA: Cengage Learning.

Kalat, J. W., & Shiota, M. N. (2012). *Emotion* (2nd ed.). Boston, MA: Cengage Learning.

Kallio, S., & Revonsuo, A. (2003). Hypnotic phenomena and altered states of consciousness: A multilevel framework of description and explanation. *Contemporary Hypnosis, 20*(3), 111–164. doi:10.1002/ch.273

Kalmijn, M. (2010). Educational inequality, homogamy, and status exchange in Black-White intermarriage: A comment on Rosenfield. *American Journal of Sociology, 115*(4), 1252–1263.

Kalyuga, S., & Hanham, J. (2011). Instructing in generalized knowledge structures to develop flexible problem solving skills. *Computers in Human Behavior, 27*(1), 63–68. doi:10.1016/j.chb.2010.05.024

Kalyuga, S., Renkl, A., & Paas, F. (2010). Facilitating flexible problem solving: A cognitive load perspective. *Educational Psychology Review, 22*(2), 175–186. doi:10.1007/s10648-010-9132-9

Kamenov, K., Twomey, C., et al. (2017). The efficacy of psychotherapy, pharmacotherapy and their combination on functioning and quality of life in depression: A meta-analysis. *Psychological Medicine, 47*(3), 414–425. doi:10.1017/S0033291716002774

Kamimori, G. H., Johnson, D., et al. (2005). Multiple caffeine doses maintain vigilance during early morning operations. *Aviation, Space, & Environmental Medicine, 76*(11), 1046–1050.

Kamin, L. J. (1981). *The intelligence controversy.* New York, NY: Wiley.

Kammrath, L. K., Mendoza-Denton, R., & Mischel, W. (2005). Incorporating If . . . Then . . . personality signatures in person perception: Beyond the person-situation dichotomy. *Journal of Personality & Social Psychology, 88*(4), 605–618.

Kan, K., Wicherts, J. M., et al. (2013). On the nature and nurture of intelligence and specific cognitive abilities: The more heritable, the more culture dependent. *Psychological Science, 24*(12), 2420–2428. doi:10.1177/0956797613493292

Kanas, N., & Manzey, D. (2008). *Space psychology and psychiatry* (2nd ed.). New York, NY: Springer.

Kanayama, G., Kean, J., et al. (2013). Cognitive deficits in long-term anabolic-androgenic steroid users. *Drug & Alcohol Dependence, 130*(1–3), 208–214. doi:10.1016/j.drugalcdep.2012.11.008

Kandler, C. (2012). Knowing your personality is knowing its nature: The role of information accuracy of peer assessments for heritability estimates of temperamental and personality traits. *Personality & Individual Differences, 53*(4), 387–392. doi:10.1016/j.paid.2012.01.004

Kapinos, K. A., & Yakusheva, O. (2011). Environmental influences on young adult weight gain: Evidence from a natural experiment. *Journal of Adolescent Health, 48*(1), 52–58. doi:10.1016/j.jadohealth.2010.05.021

Kaplan, A. (2008). Clarifying metacognition, self-regulation, and self-regulated learning: What's the purpose? *Educational Psychology Review, 20*(4), 477–484. doi:10.1007/s10648-008-9087-2

Kaplan, J. S. (2012). The effects of shared environment on adult intelligence: A critical review of adoption, twin, and MZA studies. *Developmental Psychology, 48*(5), 1292–1298. doi:10.1037/a0028133

Kaplan, P. S. (1998). *The human odyssey.* Pacific Grove, CA: Brooks/Cole.

Kaplan, R. M., & Saccuzzo, D. P. (2018). *Psychological testing: Principles, applications, and issues* (9th ed.). Boston, MA: Cengage Learning.

Kapleau, P. (1966). *The three pillars of Zen.* New York, NY: Harper & Row.

Kappe, R., & van der Flier, H. (2010). Using multiple and specific criteria to assess the predictive validity of the Big Five personality factors on academic performance. *Journal of Research in Personality, 44*(1), 142–145. doi:10.1016/j.jrp.2009.11.002

Karageorgis, C. I., & Terry, P. C. (2011). *Inside sport psychology.* Champaign, IL: Human Kinetics.

Kardas, E. P. (2014). *History of psychology: The making of a science.* Boston, MA: Cengage Learning.

Kark, R., & Eagly, A. H. (2010). Gender and leadership: Negotiating the labyrinth. In J. C. Chrisler & D. R. McCreary (Eds.), *Handbook of gender research in psychology* (Vol. 2): *Gender research in social and applied psychology* (pp. 443–470). New York, NY: Springer.

Karpicke, J. D., & Blunt, J. R. (2011). Retrieval practice produces more learning than elaborative studying with concept mapping. *Science, 331*(6018), 772–775. doi:10.1126/science.1199327

Karpicke, J. D., & Smith, M. A. (2012). Separate mnemonic effects of retrieval practice and elaborative encoding. *Journal of Memory and Language, 67*(1), 17–29.

Kasser, T. (2016). Materialistic values and goals. *Annual Review of Psychology, 67*, 489–514. doi:10.1146/annurev-psych-122414-033344

Kassin, S. M. (2005). On the psychology of confessions: Does innocence put innocents at risk? *American Psychologist, 60*(3), 215–228. doi:10.1037/0003-066X.60.3.215

Kassin, S. M., Fein, S., & Markus, H. R. (2021). *Social psychology* (11th ed.). Boston, MA: Cengage.

Kastytis, S., Nida, Z., et al. (2015). Type A behavior pattern is not a predictor of premature mortality. *International Journal of Behavioral Medicine, 22*(2), 161–169. doi:10.1007/s12529-014-9435-1

Kataria, S. (2004). A clinical guide to pediatric sleep: Diagnosis and management of sleep problems. *Journal of Developmental & Behavioral Pediatrics, 25*(2), 132–133. doi:10.1097/00004703-200404000-00012

Katz, D. L., & Meller, S. (2014). Can we say what diet is best for health? *Annual Review of Public Health, 35*, 83–103. doi:10.1146/annurev-publhealth-032013-182351

Katz, J. (2013). The Three Block Model of Universal Design for Learning (UDL): Engaging students in inclusive education. *Canadian Journal of Education, 36*(1), 153–194.

Katz, P. A. (2003). Racists or tolerant multiculturalists? *American Psychologist, 58*(11), 897–909.

Kaufman, J. C. (2009). *Creativity 101.* New York, NY: Springer.

Kaufman, J. C., & Sternberg, R. J. (Eds.). (2010). *The Cambridge handbook of creativity.* New York, NY: Cambridge University Press.

Kawada, R., Yoshizumi, M., et al. (2009). Brain volume and dysexecutive behavior in schizophrenia. *Progress in Neuro-Psychopharmacology & Biological Psychiatry, 33*(7), 1255–1260. doi:10.1016/j.pnpbp.2009.07.014

Kaye, W. H., Wierenga, C. E., et al. (2013). Nothing tastes as good as skinny feels: The neurobiology of anorexia nervosa. *Trends in Neurosciences, 36*(2), 110–120. doi:10.1016/j.tins.2013.01.003

Kearney, A. J. (2006). A primer of covert sensitization. *Cognitive & Behavioral Practice, 13*(2), 167–175. doi:10.1016/j.cbpra.2006.02.002

Kearney, C., & Trull, T. (2018). *Abnormal psychology and life: A dimensional approach* (3rd ed.). Boston, MA: Cengage Learning.

Kearney, M. S., & Levine, P. B. (2012). Why is the teen birth rate in the United States so high and why does it matter? *Journal of Economic Perspectives, 26*(2), 141–163.

Keating, C. (2010). Theoretical perspective on anorexia nervosa: The conflict of reward. *Neuroscience & Biobehavioral Reviews, 34*(1), 73–79. doi:10.1016/j.neubiorev.2009.07.004

Keefe, F. J., Huling, D. A., et al. (2012). Virtual reality for persistent pain: A new direction for behavioral pain management. *Pain, 153*(11), 2163–2166.

Keegan, J., Parva, M., et al. (2010). Addiction in pregnancy. *Journal of Addictive Diseases, 29*(2), 175–191. doi:10.1080/10550881003684723

Keel, P. K., & Klump, K. L. (2003). Are eating disorders culture-bound syndromes? Implications for conceptualizing their etiology. *Psychological Bulletin, 129*(5), 747–769. doi:10.1037/0033-2909.129.5.747

Keith, T. Z., & Reynolds, M. R. (2010). Cattell-Horn-Carroll abilities and cognitive tests: What we've learned from 20 years of research. *Psychology in the Schools, 47*(7), 635–650. doi:10.1002/pits.20496

Kell, C. A., Morillon, B., et al. (2011). Lateralization of speech production starts in sensory cortices: A possible sensory origin of cerebral left dominance for speech. *Cerebral Cortex, 21*(4), 932–937. doi:10.1093/cercor/bhq167

Keller, M. C., & Young, R. K. (1996). Mate assortment in dating and married couples. *Personality & Individual Differences, 21*(2), 217–221.

Kelly, E. (2010). *I always knew I was a girl.* Retrieved July 20, 2020, from https://www.salon.com/2010/11/20/how_i_became_a_woman/

Kelly, M. P., Strassberg, D. S., & Turner, C. M. (2006). Behavioral assessment of couples' communication in female orgasmic disorder. *Journal of Sex & Marital Therapy, 32*(2), 81–95. doi:10.1080/00926230500442243

Kendon, A. (2016, July 20). Reflections on the "gesture-first" hypothesis of language origins. *Psychonomic Bulletin & Review,* n.p. doi:10.3758/s13423-016-1117-3

Kennedy, M., Kreppner, J., et al. (2016). Early severe institutional deprivation is associated with a persistent variant of adult attention-deficit/hyperactivity disorder: Clinical presentation, developmental continuities and life circumstances in the English and Romanian adoptees study. *Journal of Child Psychology & Psychiatry, 57*(10), 1113–1125. doi:10.1111/jcpp.12576

Kendall-Tackett, K. (Ed.). (2010). *The psychoneuroimmunology of chronic disease: Exploring the links between inflammation, stress, and illness.* Washington, DC: American Psychological Association.

Kendler, K. S., & Schaffner, K. F. (2011). The dopamine hypothesis of schizophrenia: An historical and philosophical analysis. *Philosophy, Psychiatry, & Psychology, 18*(1), 41–63. doi:10.1353/ppp.2011.0005

Kennedy, S. H., Giacobbe, P., et al. (2011). Deep brain stimulation for treatment-resistant depression: Follow-up after 3 to 6 years. *The American Journal of*

Psychiatry, 168(5), 502–510. doi:10.1176/appi.ajp.2010.10081187

Kenny, P. J., & Markou, A. (2006). Nicotine self-administration acutely activates brain reward systems and induces a long-lasting increase in reward sensitivity. *Neuropsychopharmacology, 31*(6), 1203–1211. doi:10.1038/sj. npp.1300905

Kenrick, D. T., Griskevicius, V., et al. (2010). Renovating the pyramid of needs: Contemporary extensions built upon ancient foundations. *Perspectives on Psychological Science, 5*, 292–314. doi:10.1177/1745691610369469

Keough, M. B., & Yong, V. (2013). Remyelination therapy for multiple sclerosis. *Neurotherapeutics, 10*(1), 44–54. doi:10.1007/s13311-012-0152-7

Keren, E., & Mayseless, O. (2013). The freedom to choose secure attachment relationships in adulthood. *Journal of Genetic Psychology: Research & Theory on Human Development, 174*(3), 271–290. doi:10.1080/00221325.2012.681326

Kern, J. K., Geier, D. A., et al. (2012). Evidence of parallels between mercury intoxication and the brain pathology in autism. *Acta Neurobiologiae Experimentalis, 72*(2), 113–153.

Kernis, M. H., & Goldman, B. M. (2005). Authenticity, social motivation, and psychological adjustment. In J. P. Forgas, K. D. Williams, & S. M. Laham (Eds.), *Social motivation: Conscious and unconscious processes* (pp. 210–227). New York, NY: Cambridge University Press.

Kernis, M. H., & Lakey, C. E. (2010). Fragile versus secure high self-esteem: Implications for defensiveness and insecurity. In R. M. Arkin, K. C. Oleson, et al. (Eds.), *Handbook of the uncertain self* (pp. 360–378). New York, NY: Psychology Press.

Kerns, R. D., Sellinger, J., & Goodin, B. R. (2011). Psychological treatment of chronic pain. *Annual Review of Clinical Psychology, 7*, 411–434. doi:10.1146/annurev-clinpsy-090310-120430

Kessler, D. A. (2009). *The end of overeating: Taking control of the insatiable American appetite.* Emmaus, PA: Rodale Press.

Kessler, R. C. (2010). The prevalence of mental illness. In T. L. Scheid & T. N. Brown (Eds.), *A handbook for the study of mental health: Social contexts, theories, and systems* (2nd ed., pp. 46–63). New York, NY: Cambridge University Press.

Kety, S. S. (1979, Sept.). Disorders of the human brain. *Scientific American, 241*, 202–214. doi:10.1038/scientificamerican0979-202

Keysers, C., Xiao, D.-K., et al. (2005). Out of sight but not out of mind: The neurophysiology of iconic memory in the superior temporal sulcus. *Cognitive Neuropsychology, 22*(3–4), 316–332. doi:10.1080/02643290442000103

Khan, K. M., Thompson, A. M., et al. (2012). Sport and exercise as contributors to the health of nations. *The Lancet, 380*(9836), 59–64. doi:10.1016/S0140-6736(12)60865-4

Kida, T. E. (2006). *Don't believe everything you think.* Buffalo, NY: Prometheus.

Kiddoo, D. A. (2012). Toilet training children: When to start and how to train. *Canadian Medical Association Journal, 184*(5), 511–512. doi:10.1503/cmaj.110830

Kiecolt-Glaser, J. (2010). Stress, food, and inflammation: Psychoneuroimmunology and nutrition at the cutting edge. *Psychosomatic Medicine, 72*(4), 365–369. doi:10.1097/PSY.0b013e3181dbf489

Kiernan, M., Brown, S. D., et al. (2013). Promoting healthy weight with "stability skills first": A randomized trial. *Journal of Consulting & Clinical Psychology, 81*(2), 336–346. doi:10.1037/a0030544

Kievit, R. A., van Rooijen, H., et al. (2012). Intelligence and the brain: A model-based approach. *Cognitive Neuroscience, 3*, 89–97. doi:10.1080/17588928.2011.628383

Kiff, C. J., Lengua, L. J., & Bush, N. R. (2011). Temperament variation in sensitivity to parenting: Predicting changes in depression and anxiety. *Journal of Abnormal Child Psychology, 39*(8), 1199–1212. doi:10.1007/s10802-011-9539-x

Kihlstrom, J. F. (2013). Neuro-hypnotism: Prospects for hypnosis and neuroscience. *Cortex, 49*(2), 365–374. doi:10.1016/j.cortex.2012.05.016

Kim, K. H., Cramond, B., & VanTassel-Baska, J. (2010). The relationship between creativity and intelligence. In J. C. Kaufman & R. J. Sternberg (Eds.), *The Cambridge handbook of creativity* (pp. 395–412). New York, NY: Cambridge University Press.

Kim, S.-K., Lee, Y. M., et al. (2013). The defensible space theory for creating safe urban neighborhoods: Perceptions and design implications in the United States and South Korea. *Journal of Architectural & Planning Research, 30*(3), 181–196.

Kim, S., Oah, S., & Dickinson, A. M. (2005). The impact of public feedback on three recycling-related behaviors in South Korea. *Environment & Behavior, 37*(2), 258–274. doi:10.1177/0013916504267639

Kimhi, Y. (2014). Theory of mind abilities and deficits in autism spectrum disorders. *Topics in Language Disorders, 34*(4), 329–343. doi:10.1097/TLD.0000000000000033

Kimmerer, R. W. (2013). *Braiding sweetgrass: Indigenous wisdom, scientific knowledge, and the teachings of plants.* Minneapolis, MN: Milkweed.

Kimura, R., MacTavish, D., et al. (2012). Beta amyloid-induced depression of hippocampal long-term potentiation is mediated through the amylin receptor. *Journal of Neuroscience, 32*(48), 17401–17406. doi:10.1523/JNEUROSCI.3028-12.2012

King, B. E. (2012). *Human sexuality today* (7th ed.). Englewood Cliffs, NJ: Prentice Hall.

King, N. J., Muris, P., & Ollendick, T. H. (2005). Childhood fears and phobias: Assessment and treatment. *Child & Adolescent Mental Health, 10*(2), 50–56. doi:10.1111/j.1475-3588.2005.00118.x

King, P. M. (2009). Principles of development and developmental change underlying theories of cognitive and moral development. *Journal of College Student Development, 50*(6), 597–620. doi:10.1353/csd.0.0104

Kinnunen, L. H., Moltz, H., et al. (2004). Differential brain activation in exclusively homosexual and heterosexual men produced by the selective serotonin reuptake inhibitor, fluoxetine. *Brain Research, 1024*(1–2), 251–254. doi:10.1016/j.brainres.2004.07.070

Kinsey, A., Pomeroy, W., & Martin, C. (1948). *Sexual behavior in the human male.* Philadelphia, PA: Saunders.

Kinsey, A., Pomeroy, W., & Martin, C. (1953). *Sexual behavior in the human female.* Philadelphia, PA: Saunders.

Kipp, M. (2016). Remyelination strategies in multiple sclerosis: A critical reflection. *Expert Review of Neurotherapeutics, 16*(1), 1–3. doi:10.1586/14737175.2016.1116387

Kirby, D. B. (2008). The impact of abstinence and comprehensive sex and STD/HIV education programs on adolescent sexual behavior. *Sexuality Research & Social Policy, 5*(3), 18–27.

Kirk, S. A., Gallagher, J. J., & Coleman, M. R. (2015). *Educating exceptional children* (14th ed.). Boston, MA: Cengage Learning.

Kirmayer, L. J., & Ryder, A. G. (2016). Culture and psychopathology. *Current Opinion in Psychology, 8*, 143–148. doi:10.1016/j.copsyc.2015.10.020

Kirsch, I., & Lynn, S. J. (1995). The altered state of hypnosis. *American Psychologist, 50*(10), 846–858. doi:10.1037/0003-066X.50.10.846

Kirsch, I., & Sapirstein, G. (1998). Listening to Prozac but hearing placebo: A meta-analysis of antidepressant medication. *Prevention & Treatment, 1*, art. 0002a. doi:10.1037/1522-3736.1.1.12a

Kirsch, I. (2005). The flexible observer and neo-dissociation theory. *Contemporary Hypnosis, 22*(3), 121–122. doi:10.1002/ch.2

Kirsh, S. J. (2010). *Children, adolescents, and media violence: A critical look at the research* (2nd ed.). Thousand Oaks, CA: Sage.

Kiser, L. J., Heston, J. D., & Paavola, M. (2006). Day treatment centers/Partial hospitalization settings. In T. A. Petti & C. Salguero (Eds.), *Community child & adolescent psychiatry: A manual of clinical practice and consultation* (pp. 189–203). Washington, DC: American Psychiatric Publishing.

Kish, A. M., & Newcombe, P. A. (2015). "Smacking never hurt me!": Identifying myths surrounding the use of corporal punishment. *Personality & Individual Differences, 87*, 121–129. doi:10.1016/j.paid.2015.07.035

Kishimoto, N., Yamamuro, K., et al. (2016). Distinctive Rorschach profiles of young adults with schizophrenia and autism spectrum disorder. *Neuropsychiatric Disease & Treatment, 12*, 2403–2410.

Kisilevsky, B. S., & Hains, S. J. (2011). Onset and maturation of fetal heart rate response to the mother's voice over late gestation. *Developmental Science, 14*(2), 214–223.

Kitayama, S., Markus, H. R., & Kurokawa, M. (2000). Culture, emotion, and well-being: Good feelings in Japan and the United States. *Cognition & Emotion, 14*, 93–124. doi:10.1080/026999300379003

Kjellgren, A., Buhrkall, H., & Norlander, T. (2011). Preventing sick-leave for sufferers of high stress-load and burnout syndrome: A pilot study combining psychotherapy and the flotation tank. *International Journal of Psychology & Psychological Therapy, 11*(2), 297–306.

Klahr, D., & Nigam, M. (2004). The equivalence of learning paths in early science instruction: Effects of direct instruction and discovery learning. *Psychological Science, 15*, 661–667.

Kleiman, E. M., Miller, A. B., & Riskind, J. H. (2012). Enhancing attributional style as a protective factor in suicide. *Journal of Affective Disorders, 143*(1–3), 236–240. doi:10.1016/j.jad.2012.05.014

Klein, B., Richards, J. C., & Austin, D. W. (2006). Efficacy of Internet therapy for panic disorder. *Journal of Behavior Therapy & Experimental Psychiatry, 37*(3), 213–238. doi:10.1016/j.jbtep.2005.07.001

Klein, D. W., & Kihlstrom, J. F. (1986). Elaboration, organization, and the self-reference effect in memory. *Journal of Experimental Psychology: General, 115*, 26–38.

Klein, G. (2013). *Seeing what others don't: The remarkable ways we gain insights.* New York, NY: Public Affairs Books.

Klein, K., & Boals, A. (2001). Expressive writing can increase working memory capacity. *Journal of Experimental Psychology: General, 130*(3), 520–533. doi:10.1037/0096-3445.130.3.520

Klein, L. A., & Houlihan, D. (2010). Relationship satisfaction, sexual satisfaction, and sexual problems in sexsomnia. *International Journal of Sexual Health, 22*(2), 84–90. doi:10.1080/19317610903510489

Kleinmann, M., & Klehe, U. (2011). Selling oneself: Construct and criterion-related validity of impression management in structured interviews. *Human Performance, 24*(1), 29–46. doi:10.1080/08959285.2010.530634

Klinger, E. (2013). Goal commitments and the content of thoughts and dreams: Basic principles. *Frontiers in Psychology, 4*, 415.

Klohnen, E. C., & Luo, S. (2003). Interpersonal attraction and personality: What is attractive—self similarity, ideal similarity, complementarity or attachment security? *Journal of Personality & Social Psychology, 85*(4), 709–722. doi:10.1037/0022-3514.85.4.709

Kloos, B., Hill, J., et al. (2021). *Community psychology: Linking individuals and communities* (4th ed.). Boston, MA: Cengage Learning.

Klösch, G., & Holzinger, B. (2014). Dream content analysis: Methodological and theoretical approaches. *Psychotherapie Forum, 19*(3–4), 121–129. doi:10.1007/s00729-014-0023-2

Knafo, D. (2012). Alone together: Solitude and the creative encounter in art and psychoanalysis. *Psychoanalytic Dialogues, 22*(1), 54–71.

Kneer, J., Glock, S., & Rieger, D. (2012). Fast and not furious? Reduction of cognitive dissonance in smokers. *Social Psychology, 43*(2), 81–91. doi:10.1027/1864-9335/a000086

Knickmeyer, R. C., & Baron-Cohen, S. (2006). Fetal testosterone and sex differences. *Early Human Development, 82*(12), 755–760.

Knoops, K. T., de Groot, L. C., et al. (2004). Mediterranean diet, lifestyle factors, and 10-year mortality in elderly European men and women. *Journal of the American Medical Association, 292*(12), 1433–1439. doi:10.1001/jama.292.12.1433

Koch, I., Lawo, V., et al. (2011). Switching in the cocktail party: Exploring intentional control of auditory selective attention. *Journal of Experimental Psychology: Human Perception & Performance, 37*(4), 1140–1147. doi:10.1037/a0022189

Koch, I., Poljac, E., et al. (2018). Cognitive structure, flexibility, and plasticity in human multitasking—An integrative review of dual-task and task-switching research. *Psychological Bulletin, 144*(6), 557–583. doi: 10.1037/bul0000144

Koçkaya, G., & Wertheimer, A. (2011). Can we reduce the cost of illness with more compliant patients? An estimation of the effect of 100% compliance with hypertension treatment. *Journal of Pharmacy Practice, 24*(3), 345–350. doi:10.1177/0897190010389336

Koek, W. (2011). Drug-induced state-dependent learning: Review of an operant procedure in rats. *Behavioural Pharmacology, 22*(5–6), 430–440. doi:10.1097/FBP.0b013e328348ed3b

Kohen, D. P. (2011). Chronic daily headache: Helping adolescents help themselves with self-hypnosis. *American Journal of Clinical Hypnosis, 54*(1), 32–46. doi:10.1080/00029157.2011.566767

Kohlberg, L. (1969). The cognitive-developmental approach to socialization. In A. Goslin (Ed.), *Handbook of socialization theory and research* (pp. 1–134). Chicago, IL: Rand McNally.

Kohlberg, L. (1981). *Essays on moral development* (Vol. I): *The philosophy of moral development*. San Francisco, CA: Harper.

Kohler, P. K., Manhart, L. E., & Lafferty, W. E. (2008). Abstinence-only and comprehensive sex education and the initiation of sexual activity and teen pregnancy. *Journal of Adolescent Health, 42*(4), 344–351.

Köke, A., Schouten, J. S., et al. (2004). Pain reducing effect of three types of transcutaneous electrical nerve stimulation in patients with chronic pain: A randomized crossover trial. *Pain, 108*(1–2), 36–42. doi:10.1016/j.pain.2003.11.013

Kolb, B., Whishaw, I. Q., & Teskey, G. C. (2019). *An introduction to brain and behavior* (6th ed.). New York, NY: Freeman-Worth.

Kolb, B., Gibb, R., & Gorny, G. (2003). Experience-dependent changes in dendritic arbor and spine density in neocortex vary with age and sex. *Neurobiology of Learning & Memory, 79*(1), 1–10. doi:10.1016/S1074-7427(02)00021-7

Kolb, B., Mychasiuk, R., et al. (2011). Brain plasticity and recovery from early cortical injury. *Developmental Medicine & Child Neurology, 53*, 4–8. doi:10.1111/j.1469-8749.2011.04054.x

Kolodny, A., Courtwright, D. T., et al. (2015). The prescription opioid and heroin crisis: A public health approach to an epidemic of addiction. *Annual Review of Public Health, 36*, 559–574. doi:10.1146/annurev-publhealth-031914-122957

Komisaruk, B. R., Beyer-Flores, C., & Whipple, B. (2006). *The science of orgasm*. Baltimore, MD: Johns Hopkins University Press.

Kornhaber, M. L., & Gardner, H. (2006). Multiple intelligences: Developments in implementation and theory. In M. A. Constas & R. J. Sternberg (Eds.), *Translating theory and research into educational practice: Developments in content domains, large-scale reform, and intellectual capacity* (pp. 255–276). Mahwah, NJ: Erlbaum.

Kornilov, S. A., Tan, M., et al. (2012). Gifted identification with aurora: Widening the spotlight. *Journal of Psychoeducational Assessment, 30*(1), 117–133. doi:10.1177/0734282911428199

Koschate, M., & van Dick, R. (2011). A multilevel test of Allport's contact conditions. *Group Processes & Intergroup Relations, 14*(6), 769–787. doi:10.1177/1368430211399602

Kossek, E. E., & Michel, J. S. (2011). Flexible work schedules. In S. Zedeck (Ed.), *APA handbook of industrial and organizational psychology* (Vol. 1): *Building and developing the organization* (pp. 535–572). Washington, DC: American Psychological Association.

Kosslyn, S. M. (1983). *Ghosts in the mind's machine*. New York, NY: Norton.

Kosslyn, S. M. (1985). Stalking the mental image. *Psychology Today, 19*(5), 22–28.

Kosslyn, S. M., Ball, T. M., & Reiser, B. J. (1978). Visual images preserve metric spatial information: Evidence from studies of image scanning. *Journal of Experimental Psychology: Human Perception & Performance, 4*, 47–60. doi:10.1037/0096-1523.4.1.47

Kosson, D. S., Suchy, Y., et al. (2002). Facial affect recognition in criminal psychopaths. *Emotion, 2*(4), 398–411. doi:10.1037/1528-3542.2.4.398

Kost, K., Maddow-Zimet, I., & Arpaia, A. (2017). *Pregnancies, births and abortions among adolescents and young women in the United States, 2013: National and state trends by age, race and ethnicity*. New York: Guttmacher Institute. Retrieved July 20, 2020, from https://www.guttmacher.org/report/us-adolescent-pregnancy-trends-2013

Kosten, T. R., Wu, G., et al. (2013). Pharmacogenetic randomized trial for cocaine abuse: Disulfiram and dopamine β-hydroxylase. *Biological Psychiatry, 73*(3), 219–224. doi:10.1016/j.biopsych.2012.07.011

Kotagal, S. (2012). Hypersomnia in children. *Sleep Medicine Clinics, 7*(2), 379–389. doi:10.1016/j.jsmc.2012.03.010

Kotkin, M., Daviet, C., & Gurin, J. (1996). The *Consumer Reports* mental health survey. *American Psychologist, 51*(10), 1080–1082. doi:10.1037/0003-066X.51.10.1080

Kott, A. A. (2011). Masturbation is associated with partnered sex among adolescent males and females. *Perspectives on Sexual and Reproductive Health, 43*(4), 264. doi:10.1363/4326411_1

Kottler, J. A., & Chen, D. D. (2011). *Stress management and prevention: Applications to daily life* (2nd ed.). New York, NY: Routledge.

Kottler, J. A., & Shepard, D. S. (2015). *Introduction to counseling: Voices from the field* (8th ed.). Boston, MA: Cengage Learning.

Kouzes, J., & Posner, B. (2014). *The student leadership challenge*. San Francisco, CA: Wiley.

Kovera, M., & Cutler, B. L. (2013). *Jury selection*. New York, NY: Oxford University Press.

Kovrov, G. V., Rusakova, I. M., et al. (2012). Specificity of sleep-wakefulness cycle during a 105-day isolation. *Human Physiology, 38*(7), 695–698. doi:10.1134/S0362119712070109

Kowert, P. A. (2002). *Groupthink or deadlock: When do leaders learn from their advisors? SUNY series on the presidency*. Albany, NY: State University of New York Press.

Kozica, S. L., Deeks, A. A., et al. (2012). Health-related behaviors in women with lifestyle-related diseases. *Behavioral Medicine, 38*(3), 65–73. doi:10.1080/08964289.2012.685498

Krahé, B., & Möller, I. (2010). Longitudinal effects of media violence on aggression and empathy among German adolescents. *Journal of Applied Developmental Psychology, 31*(5), 401–409. doi:10.1016/j.appdev.2010.07.003

Krahé, B., Möller, I., et al. (2011). Desensitization to media violence: Links with habitual media violence exposure, aggressive cognitions, and aggressive behavior. *Journal of Personality & Social Psychology, 100*(4), 630–646. doi:10.1037/a0021711

Krakow, B., & Zadra, A. (2006). Clinical management of chronic nightmares: Imagery rehearsal therapy. *Behavioral Sleep Medicine, 4*(1), 45–70. doi:10.1207/s15402010bsm0401_4

Krall, E. A., Garvey, A. J., & Garcia, R. I. (2002). Smoking relapse after 2 years of abstinence: Findings from the VA Normative Aging Study. *Nicotine & Tobacco Research, 4*(1), 95–100. doi:10.1080/14622200110098428

Kramer, U., Despland, J. N., et al. (2010). Change in defense mechanisms and coping over the course of short-term dynamic psychotherapy for adjustment disorder. *Journal of Clinical Psychology, 66*(12), 1232–1241. doi:10.1002/jclp.20719

Krantz, M. J., Sabel, A. L., et al. (2012). Factors influencing QT prolongation in patients hospitalized with severe anorexia nervosa. *General Hospital Psychiatry, 34*(2), 173–177. doi:10.1016/j.genhosppsych.2011.08.003

Kraus, N., & Slater, J. (2016). Beyond words: How humans communicate through sound. *Annual Review of Psychology, 67*, 83–103. doi:10.1146/annurev-psych-122414-033318

Kreager, D. A., & Staff, J. (2009). The sexual double standard and adolescent peer acceptance. *Social Psychology Quarterly, 72*(2), 143–164.

Kreger Silverman, L. (2013). *Giftedness 101*. New York, NY: Springer.

Krentz, H., Miltenberger, R., & Valbuena, D. (2016). Using token reinforcement to increase walking for adults with intellectual disabilities. *Journal of Applied Behavior Analysis, 49*(4), 745–750. doi:10.1002/jaba.326

Krettenauer, T., Colasante, T., et al. (2014). The development of moral emotions and decision-making from adolescence to early adulthood: A 6-year longitudinal study. *Journal of Youth & Adolescence, 43*(4), 583–596. doi:10.1007/s10964-013-9994-5

Krishnan, H. A., & Park, D. (2005). A few good women on top management teams. *Journal of Business Research, 58*, 1712–1720.

Ksir, C. J., Hart, C. L., et al. (2015). *Drugs, behavior, and society* (2nd ed.). New York: McGraw-Hill.

Kteily, N. S., Hodson, G., & Bruneau, E. (2016). They see us as less than human: Meta-dehumanization predicts intergroup conflict via reciprocal dehumanization. *Journal of Personality & Social Psychology, 110*, 343–370. doi:10.1037/pspa0000044

Kteily, N. S., Sidanius, J., & Levin, S. (2011). Social dominance orientation: Cause or "mere effect"? Evidence for SDO as a causal predictor of prejudice and discrimination against ethnic and racial outgroups. *Journal of Experimental Social Psychology, 47*(1), 208–214. doi:10.1016/j.jesp.2010.09.009

Ku, K. Y. L., & Ho, I. T. (2010). Metacognitive strategies that enhance critical thinking. *Metacognition & Learning, 5*(3), 251–267.

Kübler-Ross, E. (1975). *Death: The final stage of growth*. Englewood Cliffs, NJ: Prentice-Hall.

Kudo, F. T., Longhofer, J. L., & Floersch, J. E. (2012). On the origins of early leadership: The role of authoritative parenting practices and mastery orientation. *Leadership, 8*(4), 345–375.

Kuehn, B. M. (2012). Marijuana use starting in youth linked to IQ loss. *Journal of the American Medical Association, 308*(12), doi:10.1001/2012.jama.12205

Kuehner, C. (2017). Why is depression more common among women than among men? *The Lancet Psychiatry, 4*(2), 146–158. doi:10.1016/S2215-0366(16)30263-2

Kugler, T., & Bornstein, G. (2013). Social dilemmas between individuals and groups. *Organizational Behavior & Human Decision Processes, 120*(2), 191–205. doi:10.1016/j.obhdp.2012.07.007

Kuiper, N. A., & McHale, N. (2009). Humor styles as mediators between self-evaluative standards and psychological well-being. *Journal of Psychology: Interdisciplinary & Applied, 143*(4), 359–376. doi:10.3200/JRLP.143.4.359-376

Kumsta, R., & Heinrichs, M. (2013). Oxytocin, stress, and social behavior: Neurogenetics of the human oxytocin system. *Current Opinion in Neurobiology, 23*(1), 11–16. doi:10.1016/j.conb.2012.09.004

Kupfersmid, J. (2012). The Oedipus complex: It made no sense then, it makes no sense now. In M. Holowchak (Ed.), *Radical claims in Freudian psychoanalysis: Point/Counterpoint* (pp. 27–40). Lanham, MD: Jason Aronson.

Kyaga, S., Landén, M., et al. (2013). Mental illness, suicide and creativity: 40-year prospective total population study. *Journal of Psychiatric Research, 47*(1), 83–90. doi:10.1016/j.jpsychires.2012.09.010

La Roche, M., & Lustig, K. (2013). Being mindful about the assessment of culture: A cultural analysis of culturally adapted acceptance-based behavior therapy approaches. *Cognitive & Behavioral Practice, 20*(1), 60–63. doi:10.1016/j.cbpra.2012.04.002

Laasonen, M., Kauppinen, J., et al. (2012). Project DyAdd: Classical eyeblink conditioning in adults with dyslexia and ADHD. *Experimental Brain Research, 223*(1), 19–32. doi:10.1007/s00221-012-3237-y

LaBar, K. S. (2007). Beyond fear: Emotional memory mechanisms in the human brain. *Current Directions in Psychological Science, 16*(4), 173–177. doi:10.1111/j.1467-8721.2007.00498.x

LaBerge, S. (2014). Lucid dreaming: Paradoxes of dreaming consciousness. In E. Cardeña, S. Lynn, et al. (Eds.), *Varieties of anomalous experience: Examining the scientific evidence* (2nd ed., pp. 145–173). Washington, DC: American Psychological Association. doi:10.1037/14258-006

Laborda, M. A., & Miller, R. R. (2011). S-R associations, their extinction, and recovery in an animal model of anxiety: A new associative account of phobias without recall of original trauma. *Behavior Therapy, 42*(2), 153–169. doi:10.1016/j.beth.2010.06.002

Labov, W. (1973). The boundaries of words and their meanings. In C. J. N. Bailey & R. W. Shuy (Eds.), *New ways of analyzing variation in English* (pp. 340–373). Washington, DC: Georgetown University Press.

LaBrie, R. A., & Shaffer, H. J. (2007). Gambling with adolescent health. *Journal of Adolescent Health, 40*(5), 387–389. doi:10.1016/j.jadohealth.2007.02.009

Lachman, M. E., Röcke, C., et al. (2008). Realism and illusion in Americans' temporal views of their life satisfaction: Age differences in reconstructing the past and anticipating the future. *Psychological Science, 19*(9), 889–897. doi:10.1111/j.1467-9280.2008.02173.x

Lackamp, J. M., Osborne, C., & Wise, T. N. (2009). Paraphilic disorders. In R. Balon & R. T. Segraves (Eds.), *Clinical manual of sexual disorders* (pp. 335–370). Arlington, VA: American Psychiatric Publishing.

Lackner, J. R., & DiZio, P. (2005). Vestibular, proprioceptive, and haptic contributions to spatial orientation. *Annual Review of Psychology, 56*, 115–147. doi:10.1146/annurev.psych.55.090902.142023

Ladouceur, R., Lachance, S., & Fournier, P. M. (2009). Is control a viable goal in the treatment of pathological gambling? *Behaviour Research & Therapy, 47*(3), 189–197. doi:10.1016/j.brat.2008.11.004

Laible, D. J., & Thompson, R. A. (2002). Mother-child conflict in the toddler years: Lessons in emotion, morality, and relationships. *Child Development, 73*(4), 1187–1203. doi:10.1111/1467-8624.00466

Lam, R., & Mok, H. (2008). *Depression*. New York, NY: Oxford University Press.

Lamb, R. J., Kirby, K. C., et al. (2010). Shaping smoking cessation in hard-to-treat smokers. *Journal of Consulting & Clinical Psychology, 78*(1), 62–71. doi:10.1037/a0018323

Lamb, T. D. (2011). Evolution of the eye. *Scientific American, July*, 64–69.

Lambert, E. G., Clarke, A., et al. (2009). Multivariate analysis of reasons for death penalty support between male and female college students: Empirical support for Gilligan's "ethic of care." *Criminal Justice Studies: A Critical Journal of Crime, Law, & Society, 22*(3), 239–260. doi:10.1080/14786010903166957

Lambert, M. J., & Ogles, B. M. (2002). The efficacy and effectiveness of psychotherapy. In M. J. Lambert (Ed.), *Handbook of psychotherapy and behavior change* (5th ed., pp. 130–193). New York, NY: Wiley.

Lambert, W. E. (1987). The effects of bilingual and bicultural experiences on children's attitudes and social perspectives. In P. Homel, M. Palij, & D. Aaronson (Eds.), *Childhood bilingualism*. Hillsdale, NJ: Erlbaum.

Lammers, G. J., Bassetti, C., et al. (2010). Sodium oxybate is an effective and safe treatment for narcolepsy. *Sleep Medicine, 11*(1), 105–106. doi:10.1016/j.sleep.2009.08.003

Lammers, J., Stoker, J. I., et al. (2016). To have control over or to be free from others? The desire for power reflects a need for autonomy. *Personality & Social Psychology Bulletin, 42*(4), 498–512. doi:10.1177/0146167216634064

Lamont, K. T., Somers, S., et al. (2011). Is red wine a SAFE sip away from cardioprotection? Mechanisms involved in resveratrol- and melatonin-induced cardioprotection. *Journal of Pineal Research, 50*, 374–380. doi:10.1111/j.1600-079X.2010.00853.x

Lampinen, J. M., Neuschatz, J. S., & Cling, A. D. (2012). The psychology of eyewitness identification. Hove, UK: Psychology Press.

Lamprecht, R., Dracheva, S., et al. (2009). Fear conditioning induces distinct patterns of gene expression in lateral amygdala. *Genes, Brain & Behavior, 8*(8), 735–743. doi:10.1111/j.1601-183X.2009.00515.x

Lamy, L., Fischer-Lokou, J., & Guéguen, N. (2012). Priming emotion concepts and helping behavior: How unlived emotions can influence action. *Social Behavior and Personality, 40*(1), 55–62. doi:10.2224/sbp.2012.40.1.55

Lan Yeung, V. W., & Kashima, Y. (2010). Communicating stereotype-relevant information: How readily can people individuate? *Asian Journal of Social Psychology, 13*(4), 209–220. doi:10.1111/j.1467-839X.2010.01313.x

Lanciano, T., Curci, A., & Semin, G. (2010). The emotional and reconstructive determinants of emotional memories: An experimental approach to flashbulb memory investigation. *Memory, 18*(5), 473–485. doi:10.1080/09658211003762076

Landa, Y., Silverstein, S. M., et al. (2006). Group cognitive behavioral therapy for delusions: Helping patients improve reality testing. *Journal of Contemporary Psychotherapy, 36*(1), 9–17. doi:10.1007/s10879-005-9001-x

Landini, F. (2015). Contributions of community psychology to rural advisory services: An analysis of Latin American rural extensionists' point of view. *American Journal of Community Psychology, 55*, 359–368. doi:10.1007/s10464-015-9712-4

Landy, F. J., & Conte, J. M. (2009). *Work in the 21st century: An introduction to industrial and organizational psychology* (3rd ed.). Malden, MA: Blackwell.

Lane, C. (2009, June 3). A slippery slope: Pathologizing bitterness. *Psychology Today*. Retrieved July 20, 2020, from https://www.psychologytoday.com/ca/blog/side-effects/200906/slippery-slope-pathologizing-bitterness

Lane, R. D. (2014). Is it possible to bridge the biopsychosocial and biomedical models? *Biopsychosocial Medicine, 8*, 3.

Lang, P. J. (2016). Imagery in therapy: An information processing analysis of fear. *Therapy, 47*(5), 688–701. doi:10.1016/j.beth.2016.08.011

Lane, R. D., Ryan, L., et al. (2015). Memory reconsolidation, emotional arousal, and the process of change in psychotherapy: New insights from brain science. *Behavioral & Brain Sciences, 38*, e1. doi:10.1017/S0140525X14000041

Langens, T. A., & Schmalt, H. D. (2002). Emotional consequences of positive daydreaming: The moderating role of fear of failure. *Personality & Social Psychology Bulletin, 28*(12), 1725–1735.

Langleben, D. D. (2008). Detection of deception with fMRI: Are we there yet? *Legal & Criminological Psychology, 13*(1), 1–9. doi:10.1348/135532507X251641

Langleben, D. D., & Moriarty, J. (2013). Using brain imaging for lie detection: Where science, law, and policy collide. *Psychology, Public Policy, & Law, 19*(2), 222–234. doi:10.1037/a0028841

Langleben, D. D., Loughead, J. W., et al. (2005). Telling truth from lie in individual subjects with fast event-related fMRI. *Human Brain Mapping, 26*(4), 262–272. doi:10.1002/hbm.20191

Långsjö, J. W., Alkire, M. T., et al. (2012). Returning from oblivion: Imaging the neural core of consciousness. *Journal of Neuroscience, 32*(14), 4935–4943. doi:10.1523/JNEUROSCI.4962-11.2012

Lanphear, B. P. (2015). The impact of toxins on the developing brain. *Annual Review of Public Health, 36*, 211–230 doi:10.1146/annurev-publhealth-031912-114413

Larimer, M. E., Neighbors, C., et al. (2011). Descriptive drinking norms: For whom does reference group matter? *Journal of Studies on Alcohol & Drugs, 72*(5), 833–843.

Larsen, R. J., & Buss, D. M. (2014). *Personality psychology* (5th ed.). New York, NY: McGraw-Hill.

Larsen, R. J., & Kasimatis, M. (1990). Individual differences in entrainment of mood to the weekly calendar. *Journal of Personality & Social Psychology, 58*(1), 164–171. doi:10.1037/0022-3514.58.1.164

Larson, M. E., Houlihan, D., & Goernert, P. N. (1995). Effects of informational feedback on aluminum can recycling. *Behavioral Interventions, 10*(2), 111–117.

Larsson, B., Carlsson, J., et al. (2005). Relaxation treatment of adolescent headache sufferers: Results from a school-based replication series. *Headache: Journal of Head & Face Pain, 45*(6), 692–704. doi:10.1111/j.1526-4610.2005.05138.x

Larsson, J. O., Larsson, H., & Lichtenstein, P. (2004). Genetic and environmental contributions to stability and change of ADHD symptoms between 8 and 13 years of age: A longitudinal twin study. *Journal of the American Academy of Child & Adolescent Psychiatry, 43*(10), 1267–1275. doi:10.1097/01.chi.0000135622.05219.bf

Lattal, K. A., Reilly, M. P., & Kohn, J. P. (1998). Response persistence under ratio and interval reinforcement schedules. *Journal of the Experimental Analysis of Behavior, 70*(2), 165–183. doi:10.1901/jeab.1998.70-165

Lau, C. Q. (2012). The stability of same-sex cohabitation, different-sex cohabitation, and marriage. *Journal of Marriage & Family, 74*(5), 973–988.

Laub, J. H., & Sampson, R. J. (2003). *Shared beginnings, divergent lives: Delinquent boys to age 70*. Cambridge, MA: Harvard University Press.

Laughlin, P. R. (2011). *Group problem solving*. Princeton, NJ: Princeton University Press.

Laureys, S., & Boly, M. (2007). What is it like to be vegetative or minimally conscious? *Current Opinion in Neurology, 20*, 609–613.

Laureys, S., Antoine, S., et al. (2002). Brain function in the vegetative state. *Acta Neurologica Belgica, 102*(4), 177–185.

Lautsch, B. A., Kossek, E. E., & Eaton, S. C. (2009). Supervisory approaches and paradoxes in managing telecommuting implementation. *Human Relations, 62*(6), 795–827.

Lavigne, F., Dumercy, L., et al. (2012). Dynamics of the semantic priming shift: Behavioral experiments and cortical network model. *Cognitive Neurodynamics, 6*(6), 467–483. doi:10.1007/s11571-012-9206-0

Lavin, M. (2012). On behalf of free association. In M. Holowchak (Ed.), *Radical claims in Freudian psychoanalysis: Point/Counterpoint* (pp. 153–166). Lanham, MD: Jason Aronson.

Lavy, S., & Littman-Ovadia, H. (2017). My better self: Using strengths at work and work productivity, organizational citizenship behavior, and satisfaction. *Journal of Career Development, 44*(2), 95–109. doi:10.1177/0894845316634056

Lavy, S., Mikulincer, M., & Shaver, P. R. (2010). Autonomy–proximity imbalance: An attachment theory perspective on intrusiveness in romantic relationships. *Personality & Individual Differences, 48*(5), 552–556.

Lawson, T. J., Jordan-Fleming, M. K., & Bodle, J. H. (2015). Measuring psychological critical thinking: An update. *Teaching of Psychology, 42,* 248–253. doi:10.1177/0098628315587624

Lawter, L., Kopelman, R. E., & Prottas, D. J. (2015). McGregor's theory X/Y and job performance: A multilevel, multi-source analysis. *Journal of Managerial Issues, 27*(1–4), 84–101.

Lazar, A. S., Santhi, N., et al. (2013). Circadian period and the timing of melatonin onset in men and women: Predictors of sleep during the weekend and in the laboratory. *Journal of Sleep Research, 22*(2), 155–159. doi:10.1111/jsr.12001

Lazarevich, I., Irigoyen, C., et al. (2016). Relationship among obesity, depression, and emotional eating in young adults. *Appetite, 107,* 639–644. doi:10.1016/j.appet.2016.09.011

Lazarus, R. S. (1991a). Cognition and motivation in emotion. *American Psychologist, 46*(4), 352–367. doi:10.1037/0003-066X.46.4.352

Lazarus, R. S. (1991b). Progress on a cognitive–motivational–relational theory of emotion. *American Psychologist, 46*(8), 819–834. doi:10.1037/0003-066X.46.8.819

Lazenka, M. F., Legakis, L. P., et al. (2016). Opposing effects of dopamine D1- and D2-like agonists on intracranial self-stimulation in male rats. *Experimental & Clinical Psychopharmacology, 24*(3), 193–205. doi:10.1037/pha0000067

Le, T. N. (2011). Life satisfaction, openness value, self-transcendence, and wisdom. *Journal of Happiness Studies, 12*(2), 171–182. doi:10.1007/s10902-010-9182-1

Le Berre, A. P., Rauchs, G. G., et al. (2012). Impaired decision-making and brain shrinkage in alcoholism. *European Psychiatry, 29*(3), 125–133. doi:10.1016/j.eurpsy.2012.10.002

Le Pelley, M. E., Reimers, S. J., et al. (2010). Stereotype formation: Biased by association. *Journal of Experimental Psychology: General, 139*(1), 138–161. doi:10.1037/a0018210

Le Texier, T. (2019). Debunking the Stanford Prison Experiment. *American Psychologist, 74*(7), 823–839. doi:10.1037/amp0000401

Leal, M. C., Shin, Y. J., et al. (2003). Music perception in adult cochlear implant recipients. *Acta Oto-Laryngologica, 123*(7), 826–835. doi:10.1177/8755123312437050

Ledgerwood, A., & Trope, Y. (2010). Attitudes as global and local action guides. In J. P. Forgas, J. Cooper, & W. D. Crano (Eds.), *The psychology of attitudes and attitude change* (pp. 39–58). New York, NY: Psychology Press.

LeDoux, J. E. (2000). Emotion circuits in the brain. *Annual Review of Neuroscience, 23,* 155–184. doi:10.1146/annurev.neuro.23.1.155

LeDoux, J. E. (2012). A neuroscientist's perspective on debates about the nature of emotion. *Emotion Review, 4*(4), 375–379. doi:10.1177/1754073912445822

Lee, J., Husman, J., et al. (2016). Development and validation of the persistent academic possible selves scale for adolescents (PAPSS). *Learning & Individual Differences, 52,* 19–28. doi:10.1016/j.lindif.2016.09.005

Lee, S. W., Clemenson, G. D., & Gage, F. H. (2011). New neurons in an aged brain. *Behavioural Brain Research.* doi:10.1016/j.bbr.2011.10.009

Lee, Y.-H., Dunbar, N., et al. (2016). Digital game based learning for undergraduate calculus education: Immersion, calculation, and conceptual understanding. *International Journal of Gaming & Computer-Mediated Simulations, 8*(1), 13–27. doi:10.4018/IJGCMS. 2016010102

Leenaars, A. A., Lester, D., & Wenckstern, S. (2005). Coping with suicide: The art and the research. In R. I. Yufit & D. Lester (Eds.), *Assessment, treatment, and prevention of suicidal behavior* (pp. 347–377). New York, NY: Wiley.

Leeper, R. W. (1935). A study of a neglected portion of the field of learning: The development of sensory organization. *Pedagogical Seminary & Journal of Genetic Psychology, 46,* 41–75.

Lefebvre, C. D., Marchand, Y., et al. (2007). Determining eyewitness identification accuracy using event-related brain potentials (ERPs). *Psychophysiology, 44*(6), 894–904.

Lefkowitz, E. S., & Zeldow, P. B. (2006). Masculinity and femininity predict optimal mental health: A belated test of the androgyny hypothesis. *Journal of Personality Assessment, 87*(1), 95–101.

Lefmann, T., & Combs-Orme, T. (2013). Early brain development for social work practice: Integrating neuroscience with Piaget's theory of cognitive development. *Journal of Human Behavior in the Social Environment, 23*(5), 640–647. doi:10.1080/10911359.2013.775936

Lefrançois, G. R. (2012). *Theories of human learning: What the professors said* (6th ed.). Boston, MA: Cengage Learning.

Leidner, B., Castano, E., et al. (2010). Ingroup glorification, moral disengagement, and justice in the context of collective violence. *Personality & Social Psychology Bulletin, 36*(8), 1115–1129.

Leiter, M. P., & Maslach, C. (2005). *Banishing burnout: Six strategies for improving your relationship with work.* San Francisco, CA: Jossey-Bass.

Leiter, M. P., Gascón, S., & Martínez-Jarreta, B. (2010). Making sense of work life: A structural model of burnout. *Journal of Applied Social Psychology, 40*(1), 57–75. doi:10.1111/j.1559-1816.2009.00563.x

Lejuez, C. W., Eifert, G. H., et al. (2000). Preference between onset predictable and unpredictable administrations of 20 carbon-dioxide-enriched air: Implications for better understanding the etiology and treatment of panic disorder. *Journal of Experimental Psychology: Applied, 6*(4), 349–358. doi:10.1037/1076-898X.6.4.349

Leming, M. R., & Dickinson, G. E. (2021). *Understanding dying, death, and bereavement* (9th ed.). Boston, MA: Cengage Learning.

Lemma, A., Target, M., & Fonagy, P. (2011). The development of a brief psychodynamic intervention (dynamic interpersonal therapy) and its application to depression: A pilot study. *Psychiatry: Interpersonal & Biological Processes, 74*(1), 41–48. doi:10.1521/psyc.2011.74.1.41

Lemogne, C., Nabi, H., et al. (2010). Hostility may explain the association between depressive mood and mortality: Evidence from the French GAZEL cohort study. *Psychotherapy & Psychosomatics, 79*(3), 164–171. doi:10.1159/000286961

Lenze, S. N., & Potts, M. A. (2017). Brief Interpersonal Psychotherapy for depression during pregnancy in a low-income population: A randomized controlled trial. *Journal of Affective Disorders, 210,* 151–157. doi:10.1016/j.jad.2016.12.029

Lenzenweger, M. F., & Gottesman, I. I. (1994). Schizophrenia. In V. S. Ramachandran (Ed.), *Encyclopedia of human behavior* (Vol. 4, pp. 41–59). San Diego, CA: Academic.

León, I., & Hernández, J. A. (1998). Testing the role of attribution and appraisal in predicting own and other's emotions. *Cognition & Emotion, 12*(1), 27–43. doi:10.1080/026999398379763

Leotti, L. A., Iyengar, S. S., & Ochsner, K. N. (2010). Born to choose: The origins and value of the need for control. *Trends in Cognitive Sciences, 14*(10), 457–463. doi:10.1016/j.tics.2010.08.001

Lepage, M. M., Sergerie, K. K., et al. (2011). Emotional face processing and flat affect in schizophrenia: Functional and structural neural correlates. *Psychological Medicine, 41*(9), 1833–1844. doi:10.1017/S0033291711000031

LePort, A. K. R., Mattfeld, A. T., et al. (2012). Behavioral and neuroanatomical investigation of Highly Superior Autobiographical Memory (HSAM). *Neurobiology of Learning & Memory, 98*(1), 78–92. doi:10.1016/j.nlm.2012.05.002

Leppänen, J. M. (2011). Neural and developmental bases of the ability to recognize social signals of emotions. *Emotion Review, 3*(2), 179–188. doi:10.1177/1754073910387942

Lerner, D., & Henke, R. M. (2008). What does research tell us about depression, job performance, and work productivity? *Journal of Occupational & Environmental Medicine, 50*(4), 401–410.

Lerner, J. S., Li, Y., et al. (2015). Emotion and decision making. *Annual Review of Psychology, 66,* 799–823. doi:10.1146/annurev-psych-010213-115043

Lertzman, R. (2015). *Environmental melancholia.* London, UK: Routledge.

Lerum, K., & Dworkin, S. L. (2009). "Bad girls rule": An interdisciplinary feminist commentary on the report of the APA task force on the sexualization of girls. *Journal of Sex Research, 46*(4), 250–263.

Lessow-Hurley, J. (2013). *Foundations of dual language instruction* (6th ed.). Boston, MA: Allyn & Bacon.

Lester, D. (2006). Sexual orientation and suicidal behavior. *Psychological Reports, 99*(3), 923–924.

Lettvin, J. Y. (1961). Two remarks on the visual system of the frog. In W. Rosenblith (Ed.), *Sensory communication* (pp. 757–776). Cambridge, MA: MIT Press.

Leucht, S., Heres, S., et al. (2011). Evidence-based pharmacotherapy of schizophrenia. *International Journal of Neuropsychopharmacology, 14*(2), 269–284. doi:10.1017/S1461145710001380

Leuner, B., & Gould, E. (2010). Structural plasticity and hippocampal function. *Annual Review of Psychology, 61,* 111–140. doi:10.1146/annurev.psych.093008.100359

LeUnes, A. (2008). *Sport psychology* (4th ed.). New York, NY: Psychology Press.

Leung, K., & Wang, J. (2015). Social processes and team creativity in multicultural teams: A socio-technical framework. *Journal of Organizational Behavior, 36*(7), 1008–1025. doi:10.1002/job.2021

Levant, R. F. (2003). Treating male alexithymia. In L. B. Silverstein & T. J. Goodrich (Eds.), *Feminist family therapy: Empowerment in social context* (pp. 177–188). Washington, DC: American Psychological Association.

Levant, R. F. (2011). Research in the psychology of men and masculinity using the gender role strain paradigm as a framework. *American Psychologist, 66*(8), 765–776. doi:10.1037/a0025034

Levant, R. F., Allen, P. A., & Lien, M. (2013). Alexithymia in men: How and when do emotional processing deficiencies occur? *Psychology of Men & Masculinity.* doi:10.1037/a0033860

Levant, R. F., Good, G. E., et al. (2006). The Normative Male Alexithymia Scale: Measurement of a gender-linked syndrome. *Psychology of Men & Masculinity, 7*(4), 212–224. doi:10.1037/1524-9220.7.4.212

Levant, R. F., Hall, R. J., et al. (2009). Gender differences in alexithymia. *Psychology of Men & Masculinity, 10*(3), 190–203.

Levant, R. F., & Powell, W. A. (2017). The gender role strain paradigm. In R. F. Levant & Y. J. Wong (Eds.), *The psychology of men and masculinities* (pp. 15–43). Washington, DC: American Psychological Association. doi:10.1037/0000023-002

Levashina, J., Hartwell, C. J., et al. (2014). The structured employment interview: Narrative and quantitative review of the research literature. *Personnel Psychology, 67*(1), 241–293. doi:10.1111/peps.12052

LeVay, S. (2011). *Gay, straight, and the reason why.* New York, NY: Oxford University Press.

LeVay, S., Baldwin, J., et al. (2015). *Discovering human sexuality* (3rd ed.). Sunderland, MA: Sinauer Associates.

Levenson, E. A. (2012). Psychoanalysis and the rite of refusal. *Psychoanalytic Dialogues, 22*(1), 2–6. doi:10.1080/10481885.2012.646593

Levenston, G. K., Patrick, C. J., et al. (2000). The psychopathic observer. *Journal of Abnormal Psychology, 109,* 373–385. doi:10.1037/0021-843X.109.3.373

Levi, A. M. (1998). Are defendants guilty if they were chosen in a lineup? *Law &*

Human Behavior, 22(4), 389–407. doi:10.1023/A:1025718909499

Levi, D. (2017). *Group dynamics for teams.* Thousand Oaks: Sage.

Levin, J. (2010). Gestalt therapy: Now and for tomorrow. *Gestalt Review, 14*(2), 147–170.

Levin, R., & Fireman, G. (2002). Nightmare prevalence, nightmare distress, and self-reported psychological disturbance. *Sleep: Journal of Sleep & Sleep Disorders Research, 25*(2), 205–212.

Levin, R., & Nielsen, T. (2009). Nightmares, bad dreams, and emotion dysregulation: A review and new neurocognitive model of dreaming. *Current Directions in Psychological Science, 18*(2), 84–88. doi:10.1111/j.1467-8721.2009.01614.x

Levy, D. L., Coleman, M. J., et al. (2010). The genetic basis of thought disorder and language and communication disturbances in schizophrenia. *Journal of Neurolinguistics, 23*(3), 176–192. doi:10.1016/j.jneuroling.2009.08.003

Lewandowski, G. W. Jr., Aron, A., & Gee, J. (2007). Personality goes a long way: The malleability of opposite-sex physical attractiveness. *Personal Relationships, 14*(4), 571–585. doi:10.1111/j.1475-6811.2007.00172.x

Lewis, C., & Lovatt, P. J. (2013). Breaking away from set patterns of thinking: Improvisation and divergent thinking. *Thinking Skills & Creativity, 9*, 46–58. doi:10.1016/j.tsc.2013.03.001

Lewis, M. B. (1995). Self-conscious emotions. *American Scientist, 83* (Jan–Feb), 68–78.

Lewis, M. B. (2012). Exploring the positive and negative implications of facial feedback. *Emotion, 12*(4), 852–859. doi:10.1037/a0029275

Li, C., Ford, E. S., et al. (2009). Associations of health risk factors and chronic illnesses with life dissatisfaction among U.S. adults: The Behavioral Risk Factor Surveillance System, 2006. *Preventive Medicine, 49*(2–3), 253–259. doi:10.1016/j.ypmed.2009.05.012

Li, W., Farkas, G., et al. (2013). Timing of high-quality child care and cognitive, language, and preacademic development. *Developmental Psychology, 49*(8), 1440–1451. doi:10.1037/a0030613

Lichtman, A. H., & Martin, B. R. (2006). Understanding the pharmacology and physiology of cannabis dependence. In R. Roffman & R. S. Stephens (Eds.), *Cannabis dependence. Its nature, consequences and treatment* (pp. 37–57). New York, NY: Cambridge University Press.

Liddell, S. K. (2003). *Grammar, gesture and meaning in American Sign Language.* Cambridge, MA: Cambridge University Press.

Lieberman, J. D. (2011). The utility of scientific jury selection: Still murky after 30 years. *Current Directions in Psychological Science, 20*(1), 48–52. doi:10.1177/0963721410396628

Lieberman, J. D., & Sales, B. D. (2007). *Scientific jury selection.* Washington, DC: American Psychological Association.

Liechti, M. E., Dolder, P. C., et al. (2016, October 7). Alterations of consciousness and mystical-type experiences after acute LSD in humans. *Psychopharmacology*, n.p. doi:10.1007/s00213-016-4453-0

Light, T. P., Chen, H. L., & Ittelson, J. C. (2011). *Documenting learning with e-portfolios.* New York, NY: Jossey-Bass.

Liles, E. E., & Packman, J. (2009). Play therapy for children with fetal alcohol syndrome. *International Journal of Play Therapy, 18*(4), 192–206. doi:10.1037/a0015664

Lilgendahl, J., Helson, R., & John, O. P. (2013). Does ego development increase during midlife? The effects of openness and accommodative processing of difficult events. *Journal of Personality, 81*(4), 403–416. doi:10.1111/jopy.12009

Lilienfeld, S. O. (2007). Psychological treatments that cause harm. *Perspectives on Psychological Science, 2*(1), 53–70. doi: 10.1111/j.1745-6916.2007.00029.x

Lilienfeld, S. O., Ammirati, R., & Landfield, K. (2009). Giving debiasing away: Can psychological research on correcting cognitive errors promote human welfare? *Perspectives on Psychological Science, 4*(4), 390–398. doi:10.1111/j.1745-6924.2009.01144.x

Lilienfeld, S. O., Lynn, S. J., et al. (2010). *50 great myths of popular psychology: Shattering widespread misconceptions about human behavior.* London, UK: Wiley-Blackwell.

Lilienfeld, S. O., Ruscio, J., & Lynn, S. J. (Eds.). (2008). *Navigating the mindfield: A user's guide to distinguishing science from pseudoscience in mental health.* Buffalo, NY: Prometheus Books.

Lin, F. R., Thorpe, R., et al. (2011). Hearing loss prevalence and risk factors among older adults in the United States. *Journals of Gerontology: Series A: Biological Sciences & Medical Sciences, 66A*(5), 582–590. doi:10.1093/gerona/glr002

Lin, T., & Peng, T. K. (2010). From organizational citizenship behaviour to team performance: The mediation of group cohesion and collective efficacy. *Management & Organization Review, 6*(1), 55–75. doi:10.1111/j.1740-8784.2009.00172.x

Lindemann, B. (2001). Receptors and transduction in taste. *Nature, 413*, 219–225. doi:10.1038/35093032

Linderoth, B., & Foreman, R. D. (2006). Mechanisms of spinal cord stimulation in painful syndromes: Role of animal models. *Pain Medicine, 7*(Suppl. 1), S14–S26. doi:10.1111/j.1526-4637.2006.00119.x

Lindsay, R. L., Kalmet, N., et al. (2013). Confidence and accuracy of lineup selections and rejections: Postdicting rejection accuracy with confidence. *Journal of Applied Research in Memory & Cognition, 2*(3), 179–184. doi:10.1016/j.jarmac.2013.06.002

Lindsey, B. J., Fabiano, P., & Stark, C. (2009). The prevalence and correlates of depression among college students. *College Student Journal, 43*(4, PtA), 999–1014.

Lindson-Hawley, N., Banting, M., et al. (2016). Gradual versus abrupt smoking cessation: A randomized, controlled noninferiority trial. *Annals of Internal Medicine*, March 15. doi:10.7326/M14-2805

Linsley, P., Digan, J., & Nugent, S. (2016). Emotional intelligence as part of clinical engagement. *British Journal of Mental Health Nursing, 5*(1), 32–37. doi:10.12968/bjmh.2016.5.1.32

Linting, M., Groeneveld, M. G., et al. (2013). Threshold for noise in daycare: Noise level and noise variability are associated with child wellbeing in home-based childcare. *Early Childhood Research Quarterly, 28*, 960–971. doi:10.1016/j.ecresq.2013.03.005

Lipka, J., Miltner, W. H. R., & Straube, T. (2011). Vigilance for threat interacts with amygdala responses to subliminal threat cues in specific phobia. *Biological Psychiatry, 70*(5), 472–478. doi:10.1016/j.biopsych.2011.04.005

Lippke, S., Nigg, C. R., & Maddock, J. E. (2012). Health-promoting and health-risk behaviors: Theory-driven analyses of multiple health behavior change in three international samples. *International Journal of Behavioral Medicine, 19*(1), 1–13. doi:10.1007/s12529-010-9135-4

Liu, Y., Gao, J., et al. (2000). The temporal response of the brain after eating revealed by functional MRI. *Nature, 405*, 1058–1062. doi:10.1038/35016590

Livingston-Thomas, J., Nelson, P., et al. (2016). Exercise and environmental enrichment as enablers of task-specific neuroplasticity and stroke recovery. *Neurotherapeutics, 13*(2), 395–402. doi:10.1007/s13311-016-0423-9

Llorens, R., & Noé, E. (2016). Through the eyes of neglect patients: A preliminary eye-tracking study of unilateral spatial neglect. *Journal of Neuropsychiatry & Clinical Neurosciences, 28*(1), e8–e9. doi:10.1176/appi.neuropsych.15060156

Lobbestael, J., Cima, M., & Arntz, A. (2013). The relationship between adult reactive and proactive aggression, hostile interpretation bias, and antisocial personality disorder. *Journal of Personality Disorders, 27*(1), 53–66. doi:10.1521/pedi.2013.27.1.53

Loeber, R., & Hay, D. (1997). Key issues in the development of aggression and violence from childhood to early adulthood. *Annual Review of Psychology, 48*, 371–410. doi:10.1146/annurev.psych.48.1.371

Loftus, E. F. (2003). Make-believe memories. *American Psychologist, 58*(11), 867–873. doi:10.1037/0003-066X.58.11.867

Loftus, E. F., & Palmer, J. C. (1974). Reconstruction of automobile destruction: An example of interaction between language and memory. *Journal of Verbal Learning & Verbal Behavior, 13*, 585–589. doi:10.1016/S0022-5371(74)80011-3

Lokuge, S., Frey, B. N., et al. (2011). Depression in women: Windows of vulnerability and new insights into the link between estrogen and serotonin. *Journal of Clinical Psychiatry, 72*(11), 1563–1569. doi:10.4088/JCP.11com07089

LoLordo, V. M. (2001). Learned helplessness and depression. In M. E. Carroll & J. B. Overmier (Eds.), *Animal research and human health: Advancing human welfare through behavioral science* (pp. 63–77). Washington, DC: American Psychological Association.

Long, C. R., Seburn, M., et al. (2003). Solitude experiences: Varieties, settings, and individual differences. *Personality & Social Psychology Bulletin, 29*(5), 578–583.

Longo, M. R., Long, C., & Haggard, P. (2012). Mapping the invisible hand: A body model of a phantom limb. *Psychological Science, 23*(7), 740–742. doi:10.1177/0956797612441219

Lopez, M. A., & Basco, M. A. (2015). Effectiveness of cognitive behavioral therapy in public mental health: Comparison to treatment as usual for treatment-resistant depression. *Administration & Policy in Mental & And Mental Health Services Research, 42*(1), 87–98. doi:10.1007/s10488-014-0546-4

López, S. R., & Guarnaccia, P. J. J. (2000). Cultural psychopathology. *Annual Review of Psychology, 51*, 571–598. doi:10.1146/annurev.psych.51.1.571

Lord, C., & Bishop, S. L. (2015). Recent advances in autism research as reflected in DSM-5 criteria for autism spectrum disorder. *Annual Review of Clinical Psychology, 11*, 53–70. doi:10.1146/annurev-clinpsy-032814-112745

Lorenzo, G. L., Biesanz, J. C., & Human, L. J. (2010). What is beautiful is good and more accurately understood: Physical attractiveness and accuracy in first impressions of personality. *Psychological Science, 21*(12), 1777–1782. doi:10.1177/0956797610388048

Lounsbury, D. W., & Mitchell, S. G. (2009). Introduction to special issue on social ecological approaches to community health research and action. *American Journal of Community Psychology, 44*(3–4), 213–220. doi:10.1007/s10464-009-9266-4

Lovibond, S. H., Mithiran, X., et al. (1979). The effects of three experimental prison environments on the behavior of non-convict volunteer subjects. *Australian Psychologist, 14*, 273–287.

Lowman, R. L. (Ed.). (2013). *Internationalizing multiculturalism: Expanding professional competencies in a globalized world.* Washington: American Psychological Association.

Lu, Z. L., & Dosher, B. (2014). *Visual psychophysics: From laboratory to theory.* Cambridge, MA: MIT Press.

Lucas, C., & Bayley, R. (2011). Variation in sign languages: Recent research on ASL and beyond. *Language & Linguistics Compass, 5*(9), 677–690. doi:10.1111/j.1749-818X.2011.00304.x

Lucy, J. A. (2016). Recent advances in the study of linguistic relativity in historical context: A critical assessment. *Language Learning, 66*(3), 487–515. doi:10.1111/lang.12195

Lum, D. (2011). *Culturally competent practice: A framework for understanding* (4th ed.). Boston, MA: Cengage Learning.

Lum, J. A. G., & Bleses, D. (2012). Declarative and procedural memory in Danish-speaking children with specific language impairment. *Journal of Communication Disorders, 45*(1), 46–58. doi:10.1016/j.jcomdis.2011.09.001

Lumley, M. A. (2004). Alexithymia, emotional disclosure, and health: A program of research. *Journal*

of Personality, 72(6), 1271–1300. doi:10.1111/j.1467-6494.2004.00297.x

Luna, B., Marek, S., et al. (2015). An integrative model of the maturation of cognitive control. *Annual Review of Neuroscience, 38*, 151–170. doi:10.1146/annurev-neuro-071714-034054

Lundholm, L., Haggård, U., et al. (2013). The triggering effect of alcohol and illicit drugs on violent crime in a remand prison population: A case crossover study. *Drug & Alcohol Dependence, 129*(1–2), 110–115. doi:10.1016/j.drugalcdep.2012.09.019

Lupien, S. P., Seery, M. D., & Almonte, J. L. (2010). Discrepant and congruent high self-esteem: Behavioral self-handicapping as a preemptive defensive strategy. *Journal of Experimental Social Psychology, 46*(6), 1105–1108. doi:10.1016/j.jesp.2010.05.022

Luppa, M., Heinrich, S., et al. (2007). Cost-of-illness studies of depression: A systematic review. *Journal of Affective Disorders, 98*(1–2), 29–43. doi:10.1016/j.jad.2006.07.017

Luria, A. R. (1968). *The mind of a mnemonist*. New York, NY: Basic.

Lussier, R., & Achua, C. (2016). *Leadership: Theory, application, & skill development* (6th ed.). Boston, MA: Cengage Learning.

Lutz, J., Brühl, A. B., et al. (2016). Neural correlates of mindful self-awareness in mindfulness meditators and meditation-naïve subjects revisited. *Biological Psychology, 119*, 21–30. doi:10.1016/j.biopsycho.2016.06.010

Luyster, F. S., Strollo, P. R., et al. (2012). Sleep: A health imperative. *Sleep: Journal of Sleep & Sleep Disorders Research, 35*(6), 727–734.

Luyten, P., & Blatt, S. J. (2011). Integrating theory-driven and empirically-derived models of personality development and psychopathology: A proposal for DSM V. *Clinical Psychology Review, 31*(1), 52–68. doi:10.1016/j.cpr.2010.09.003

Lykken, D. T. (1998). *A tremor in the blood: Uses and abuses of the lie detector*. New York, NY: Plenum.

Lykken, D. T. (2001). Lie detection. In W. E. Craighead & C. B. Nemeroff (Eds.), *The Corsini encyclopedia of psychology and behavioral science* (3rd ed., pp. 878–880). New York, NY: Wiley.

Lyn, H., Franks, B., & Savage-Rumbaugh, E. S. (2008). Precursors of morality in the use of the symbols "good" and "bad" in two bonobos (*Pan paniscus*) and a chimpanzee (*Pan troglodytes*). *Language & Communication, 28*(3), 213–224. doi:10.1016/j.langcom.2008.01.006

Lynch, K. B., Geller, S. R., & Schmidt, M. G. (2004). Multi-year evaluation of the effectiveness of a resilience-based prevention program for young children. *Journal of Primary Prevention, 24*(3), 335–353. doi:10.1023/B:JOPP.0000018052.12488.d1

Lynn, S. J., & Kirsch, I. (2006). Introduction: Definitions and early history. In S. J. Lynn & I. Kirsch (Eds.), *Essentials of clinical hypnosis: An evidence-based approach* (pp. 3–15). Washington, DC: American Psychological Association.

Lynn, S. J., & O'Hagen, S. (2009). The sociocognitive and conditioning and inhibition theories of hypnosis. *Contemporary Hypnosis, 26*(2), 121–125. doi:10.1002/ch.378

Lynn, S. J., Green, J. P., et al. (2015). Grounding hypnosis in science: The "new" APA Division 30 definition of hypnosis as a step backward. *American Journal of Clinical Hypnosis, 57*(4), 390–401. doi:10.1080/00029157.2015.1011472

Lynn, S. J., Kirsch, I., & Rhue, J. W. (2010). An introduction to clinical hypnosis. In S. Lynn, J. W. Rhue, & I. Kirsch (Eds.), *Handbook of clinical hypnosis* (2nd ed.) (pp. 3–18). Washington, DC: American Psychological Association.

Lynne-Landsman, S. D., Graber, J. A., et al. (2011). Is sensation seeking a stable trait or does it change over time? *Journal of Youth & Adolescence, 40*(1), 48–58. doi:10.1007/s10964-010-9529-2

Lyons, H., Manning, W., et al. (2013). Predictors of heterosexual casual sex among young adults. *Archives of Sexual Behavior, 42*(4), 585–593. doi:10.1007/s10508-012-0051-3

Lyons, R. (2011). The spread of evidence-poor medicine via flawed social-network analysis. *Statistics, Politics, & Policy, 2*(1). doi:10.2202/2151-7509.1024

Lyubomirsky, S., & Tucker, K. L. (1998). Implications of individual differences in subjective happiness for perceiving, interpreting, and thinking about life events. *Motivation & Emotion, 22*(2), 155–186. doi:10.1023/A:1021396422190

MacDuffie, K., & Mashour, G. A. (2010). Dreams and the temporality of consciousness. *American Journal of Psychology, 123*(2), 189–197. doi:10.5406/amerjpsyc.123.2.0189

Macht, M., & Simons, G. (2011). Emotional eating. In I. Nyklicek, A. Vingerhoets, & M. Zeelenberg (Eds.), *Emotion regulation and well-being* (pp. 281–295). New York, NY: Springer.

MacIver, K., Lloyd, D. M., et al. (2008). Phantom limb pain, cortical reorganization and the therapeutic effect of mental imagery. *Brain: A Journal of Neurology, 131*(8), 2181–2191. doi:10.1093/brain/awn124

MacKay, D. G., & Hadley, C. (2009). Supra-normal age-linked retrograde amnesia: Lessons from an older amnesic (H.M.). *Hippocampus, 19*(5), 424–445. doi:10.1002/hipo.20531

MacKenzie, M. J., Nicklas, E., et al. (2015). Spanking and children's externalizing behavior across the first decade of life: Evidence for transactional processes. *Journal of Youth & Adolescence, 44*(3), 658–669. doi:10.1007/s10964-014-0114-y

Maddi, S. R. (2013). *Hardiness: Turning stressful circumstances into resilient growth*. New York, NY: Springer.

Maddi, S. R., Harvey, R. H., et al. (2009). The personality construct of hardiness, IV: Expressed in positive cognitions and emotions concerning oneself and developmentally relevant activities. *Journal of Humanistic Psychology, 49*(3), 292–305. doi:10.1177/0022167809331860

Maddock, J. E., & Glanz, K. (2005). The relationship of proximal normative beliefs and global subjective norms to college students' alcohol consumption. *Addictive Behaviors, 30*(2), 315–323. doi:10.1016/j.addbeh.2004.05.021

Maddock, J. E., Laforge, R. G., et al. (2001). The College Alcohol Problems Scale. *Addictive Behaviors, 26*, 385–398. doi:10.1016/S0306-4603(00)00116-7

Maddox, K. B. (2004). Perspectives on racial phenotypicality bias. *Personality & Social Psychology Review, 8*(4), 383–401. doi:10.1207/s15327957pspr0804_4

Madon, S., Willard, J., et al. (2011). Self-fulfilling prophecies: Mechanisms, power, and links to social problems. *Social & Personality Psychology Compass, 5*(8), 578–590. doi:10.1111/j.1751-9004.2011.00375.x

Madras, B. K. (2013). History of the discovery of the antipsychotic dopamine D2 receptor: A basis for the dopamine hypothesis of schizophrenia. *Journal of the History of the Neurosciences, 22*(1), 62–78. doi:10.1080/0964704X.2012.678199

Maggin, D. M., Chafouleas, S. M., et al. (2011). A systematic evaluation of token economies as a classroom management tool for students with challenging behavior. *Journal of School Psychology, 49*(5), 529–554. doi:10.1016/j.jsp.2011.05.001

Maguire, E. A., Intraub, H., & Mullally, S. L. (2016). Scenes, spaces, and memory traces: What does the hippocampus do? *Neuroscientist, 22*(5), 432–439. doi:10.1177/1073858415600389

Maguire-Jack, K., Gromoske, A. N., & Berger, L. M. (2012). Spanking and child development during the first 5 years of life. *Child Development, 83*(6), 1960–1977. doi:10.1111/j.1467-8624.2012.01820.x

Mah, K., & Binik, Y. M. (2001). The nature of human orgasm: A critical review of major trends. *Clinical Psychology Review, 21*(6), 823–856.

Mahler, H. I. M., Beckerley, S. E., & Vogel, M. T. (2010). Effects of media images on attitudes toward tanning. *Basic & Applied Social Psychology, 32*(2), 118–127. doi:10.1080/01973531003738296

Mahmoodabadi, S. Z., Ahmadian, A., et al. (2010). A fast expert system for electrocardiogram arrhythmia detection. *Expert Systems, 27*(3), 180–200.

Maier, N. R. F. (1949). *Frustration*. New York, NY: McGraw-Hill.

Maier, S. F., & Seligman, M. E. P. (2016). Learned helplessness at fifty: Insights from neuroscience. *Psychological Review, 123*(4), 349–367. doi:10.1037/rev0000033

Maisto, S. A., Galizio, M., & Connors, G. J. (2018). *Drug use and abuse* (8th ed.). Boston, MA: Cengage Learning.

Malan, L., Hamer, M., et al. (2012). Defensive coping, urbanization, and neuroendocrine function in Black Africans: The THUSA study. *Psychophysiology, 49*(6), 807–814. doi:10.1111/j.1469-8986.2012.01362.x

Malan, L., Malan, N. T., et al. (2008). Coping with urbanization: A cardiometabolic risk? The THUSA study. *Biological Psychology, 79*(3), 323–328.

Malhi, G. S., & Outhred, T. (2016). Therapeutic mechanisms of lithium in bipolar disorder: Recent advances and current understanding. *CNS Drugs, 30*(10), 931–949. doi:10.1007/s40263-016-0380-1

Malmberg, L., & Flouri, E. (2011). The comparison and interdependence of maternal and paternal influences on young children's behavior and resilience. *Journal of Clinical Child & Adolescent Psychology, 40*(3), 434–444. doi:10.1080/15374416.2011.563469

Mamen, M. (2004). *Pampered child syndrome: How to recognize it, how to manage it and how to avoid it*. Carp, ON: Creative Bound.

Manber, R., Kraemer, H. C., et al. (2008). Faster remission of chronic depression with combined psychotherapy and medication than with each therapy alone. *Journal of Consulting & Clinical Psychology, 76*(3), 459–467. doi:10.1037/0022-006X.76.3.459

Mancini, M. A., & Wyrick-Waugh, W. (2013). Consumer and practitioner perceptions of the harm reduction approach in a community mental health setting. *Community Mental Health Journal, 49*(1), 14–24. doi:10.1007/s10597-011-9451-4

Mangos, P. M., & Hulse, N. A. (2017). Advances in machine learning applications for scenario intelligence: Deep learning. *Theoretical Issues in Ergonomics Science, 18*(2), 184–198. doi:10.1080/1463922X.2016.1166406

Manning, R., Levine, M., & Collins, A. (2007). The Kitty Genovese murder and the social psychology of helping: The parable of the 38 witnesses. *American Psychologist, 62*(6), 555–562. doi:10.1037/0003-066X.62.6.555

Manning, R. P. C., Dickson, J. M., et al. (2017). A systematic review of adult attachment and social anxiety. *Journal of Affective Disorders, 211*, 44–59. doi:10.1016/j.jad.2016.12.020

Mantovani, A., Simpson, H. B., et al. (2010). Randomized sham-controlled trial of repetitive transcranial magnetic stimulation in treatment-resistant obsessive-compulsive disorder. *International Journal of Neuropsychopharmacology, 13*(2), 217–227. doi:10.1017/S1461145709990435

Mantyla, T. (1986). Optimizing cue effectiveness: Recall of 600 incidentally learned words. *Journal of Experimental Psychology: Learning, Memory, & Cognition, 12*(1), 66–71. doi:10.1037/0278-7393.12.1.66

Maran, M. (2010). *My lie: A true story of false memory*. San Francisco, CA: Jossey-Bass/Wiley.

Marazziti, D., & Baroni, S. (2012). Romantic love: The mystery of its biological roots. *Clinical Neuropsychiatry, 9*(1), 14–19.

Marcel, M. (2005). *Freud's traumatic memory: Reclaiming seduction theory and revisiting Oedipus*. Pittsburgh, PA: Duquesne University Press.

Marco, E. M., Romero-Zerbo, S. Y., et al. (2012). The role of the endocannabinoid system in eating disorders: Pharmacological implications. *Behavioural Pharmacology,*

23(5–6), 526–538. doi:10.1097/FBP.0b013e328356c3c9

Marecek, J., & Gavey, N. (2013). DSM-5 and beyond: A critical feminist engagement with psychodiagnosis. *Feminism & Psychology, 23*(1), 3–9. doi:10.1177/0959353512467962

Marian, D. E., & Shimamura, A. P. (2012). Emotions in context: Pictorial influences on affective attributions. *Emotion, 12*(2), 371–375. doi:10.1037/a0025517

Mariani, R., Mello, C., et al. (2011). Effect of naloxone and morphine on arcaine-induced state-dependent memory in rats. *Psychopharmacology, 215*(3), 483–491. doi:10.1007/s00213-011-2215-6

Mark, G. P., Shabani, S., et al. (2011). Cholinergic modulation of mesolimbic dopamine function and reward. *Physiology & Behavior, 104*(1), 76–81. doi:10.1016/j.physbeh.2011.04.052

Mark, K., Janssen, E., & Milhausen, R. (2011). Infidelity in heterosexual couples: Demographic, interpersonal, and personality-related predictors of extradyadic sex. *Archives of Sexual Behavior, 40*(5), 971–982. doi:10.1007/s10508-011-9771-z

Mark, T., Tomic, K., et al. (2013). Hospital readmission among Medicaid patients with an index hospitalization for mental and/or substance use disorder. *Journal of Behavioral Health Services & Research, 40*(2), 207–221. doi:10.1007/s11414-013-9323-5

Markoff, J. (2011). *Computer wins on 'Jeopardy!': Trivial, it's not.* Retrieved July 20, 2020, from https://www.nytimes.com/2011/02/17/science/17jeopardy-watson.html

Markova, G., & Perry, J. T. (2014). Cohesion and individual well-being of members in self-managed teams. *Leadership & Organization Development Journal, 35*(5), 429–441. doi:10.1108/LODJ-04-12-0058

Markowitz, F. E. (2011). Mental illness, crime, and violence: Risk, context, and social control. *Aggression & Violent Behavior, 16*, 36–44. doi:10.1016/j.avb.2010.10.003

Markowitz, J. C. (2017). *Interpersonal psychotherapy for posttraumatic stress disorder.* New York: Oxford University Press.

Marks, L. E. (2014). Synesthesia: A teeming multiplicity. In E. Cardeña, S. Lynn, et al. (Eds.), *Varieties of anomalous experience: Examining the scientific evidence* (2nd ed., pp. 79–108). Washington, DC: American Psychological Association. doi:10.1037/14258-004

Markus, H. R., Uchida, Y., et al. (2006). Going for the gold: Models of agency in Japanese and American contexts. *Psychological Science, 17*(2), 103–112. doi:10.1111/j.1467-9280.2006.01672.x

Markus, H., & Nurius, P. (1986). Possible selves. *American Psychologist, 41*, 954–969. doi:10.1037/0003-066X.41.9.954

Marshall, R. D., Bryant, R. A., et al. (2007). The psychology of ongoing threat: Relative risk appraisal, the September 11 attacks, and terrorism-related fears. *American Psychologist, 62*(4), 304–316. doi:10.1037/0003-066X.62.4.304

Marsiglia, F. F., Kulis, S., et al. (2004). Ethnicity and ethnic identity as predictors of drug norms and drug use among preadolescents in the U.S. Southwest. *Substance Use & Misuse, 39*(7), 1061–1094. doi:10.1081/JA-120038030

Martens, R., & Trachet, T. (1998). *Making sense of astrology.* Amherst, MA: Prometheus.

Martin, B. (2011). *Children at play: Learning gender in the early years.* Sterling, VA: Trentham Books.

Martin, C. L., & Ruble, D. N. (2009). Patterns of gender development. *Annual Review of Psychology, 61*, 353–381.

Martin, D., & Yurkovich, E. (2014). "Close-knit" defines a healthy Native American, Indian family. *Journal of Family Nursing, 20*(1), 51–72. doi:10.1177/1074840713508604

Martin, E. K., Taft, C. T., & Resick, P. A. (2007). A review of marital rape. *Aggression & Violent Behavior, 12*(3), 329–347.

Martin, E., & Weiss, K. J. (2010). Knowing moral and legal wrong in an insanity defense. *Journal of the American Academy of Psychiatry & the Law, 38*(2), 286–288.

Martin, G., & Pear, J. (2011). *Behavior modification: What it is and how to do it* (9th ed.). Upper Saddle River, NJ: Prentice-Hall.

Martin, L. R., Friedman, H. S., & Schwartz, J. E. (2007). Personality and mortality risk across the life span: The importance of conscientiousness as a biopsychosocial attribute. *Health Psychology, 26*(4), 428–436. doi:10.1037/0278-6133.26.4.428

Martin, S. (2007). The labyrinth of leadership. *Monitor on Psychology*, July/August, 90–91.

Martínez-Alvarez, R., Mah, Y. H., et al. (2016). A fast pathway for fear in human amygdala. *Nature Neuroscience, 19*(8), 1041–1049. doi:10.1038/nn.4324

Martinez-Gonzalez, M. A., Gual, P., et al. (2003). Parental factors, mass media influences, and the onset of eating disorders in a prospective population-based cohort. *Pediatrics, 111*, 315–320. doi:10.1542/peds.111.2.315

Martinko, M. J., Douglas, S. C., & Harvey, P. (2006). Understanding and managing workplace aggression. *Organizational Dynamics, 35*(2), 117–130.

Martin-Raugh, M. P., Kell, H. J., & Motowidlo, S. J. (2016). Prosocial knowledge mediates effects of agreeableness and emotional intelligence on prosocial behavior. *Personality & Individual Differences, 90*, 41–49. doi:10.1016/j.paid.2015.10.024

Martynhak, B. J., Louzada, F. M., et al. (2010). Does the chronotype classification need to be updated? Preliminary findings. *Chronobiology International, 27*(6), 1329–1334. doi:10.3109/07420528.2010.490314

Marx, B. P., Gross, A. M., & Adams, H. E. (1999). The effect of alcohol on the responses of sexually coercive and noncoercive men to an experimental rape analogue. *Sexual Abuse: Journal of Research & Treatment, 11*(2), 131–145.

Mashour, G. A., Walker, E. E., & Martuza, R. L. (2005). Psychosurgery: Past, present, and future. *Brain Research Reviews, 48*(3), 409–419. doi:10.1016/j.brainresrev.2004.09.002

Maslow, A. H. (1954). *Motivation and personality.* New York, NY: Harper.

Maslow, A. H. (1967). Self-actualization and beyond. In J. F. T. Bugental (Ed.), *Challenges of humanistic psychology* (pp. 279–286). New York, NY: McGraw-Hill.

Maslow, A. H. (1969). *The psychology of science.* Chicago, IL: Henry Regnery.

Maslow, A. H. (1970). *Motivation and personality.* New York, NY: Harper & Row.

Maslow, A. H. (1971). *The farther reaches of human nature.* New York, NY: Viking.

Masse, L. C., & Tremblay, R. E. (1997). Behavior of boys in kindergarten and the onset of substance use during adolescence. *Archives of General Psychiatry, 54*(1), 62–68. doi:10.1001/archpsyc.1997.01830130068014

Masten A. S. (2014). *Ordinary magic: Resilience in development.* New York, NY: Guilford.

Masters, J. L., & Holley, L. M. (2006). A glimpse of life at 67: The modified future-self worksheet. *Educational Gerontology, 32*(4), 261–269. doi:10.1080/03601270500494022

Masters, W. H., & Johnson, V. E. (1966). *Human sexual response.* Boston, MA: Little, Brown.

Masters, W. H., & Johnson, V. E. (1970). *The pleasure bond: A new look at sexuality and commitment.* Boston, MA: Little, Brown.

Mastroianni, G. R. (2015). Obedience in perspective: Psychology and the Holocaust. *Theory & Psychology, 25*(5), 657–669. doi:10.1177/0959354315608963

Masuda, T., Gonzalez, R., et al. (2008). Culture and aesthetic preference: Comparing the attention to context of East Asians and Americans. *Personality & Social Psychology Bulletin, 34*(9), 1260–1275. doi:10.1177/0146167208320555

Mather, G. (2011). *Foundations of sensation and perception* (3rd ed.). Hove, UK: Psychology Press.

Mather, M. (2016). The affective neuroscience of aging. *Annual Review of Psychology, 67*, 213–238. doi:10.1146/annurev-psych-122414-033540

Mathy, F., & Feldman, J. (2012). What's magic about magic numbers? Chunking and data compression in short-term memory. *Cognition, 122*(3), 346–362. doi:10.1016/j.cognition.2011.11.003

Matson, J. L., & Boisjoli, J. A. (2009). The token economy for children with intellectual disability and/or autism: A review. *Research in Developmental Disabilities, 30*(2), 240–248. doi:10.1016/j.ridd.2008.04.001

Matsumoto, D., & Hwang, H. S. C. (2019). Culture, emotion, and expression. In K. D. Keith (Ed.), *Cross-cultural psychology: Contemporary themes and perspectives* (2nd ed., pp. 501–515). West Sussex, UK: Wiley-Blackwell.

Matsumoto, D., Hwang, H. C., et al. (2016). The body: Postures, gait, proxemics, and haptics. In D. Matsumoto, D., H. C. Hwang, & M. G. Frank (Eds.), *APA handbook of nonverbal communication* (pp. 387–400). Washington, DC: American Psychological Association. doi:10.1037/14669-015

Matsumoto, D., & Juang, L. (2017). *Culture and psychology* (6th ed.). Boston, MA: Cengage Learning.

Mattanah, J. F., Lopez, F. G., & Govern, J. M. (2011). The contributions of parental attachment bonds to college student development and adjustment: A meta-analytic review. *Journal of Counseling Psychology, 58*, 565–596. doi:10.1037/a0024635

Matthew, C. T., & Sternberg, R. J. (2009). Developing experience-based (tacit) knowledge through reflection. *Learning & Individual Differences, 19*, 530–540.

Matthews, K. A., & Gallo, L. C. (2011). Psychological perspectives on pathways linking socioeconomic status and physical health. *Annual Review of Psychology, 62*, 501–530. doi:10.1146/annurev.psych.031809.130711

Matthews, P. H., & Matthews, M. S. (2004). Heritage language instruction and giftedness in language minority students: Pathways toward success. *Journal of Secondary Gifted Education, 15*(2), 50–55. doi:10.4219/jsge-2004-448

Matthies, E., Selge, S., & Klöckner, C. A. (2012). The role of parental behaviour for the development of behaviour specific environmental norms: The example of recycling and re-use behaviour. *Journal of Environmental Psychology, 32*(3), 277–284. doi:10.1016/j.jenvp.2012.04.003

Matusitz, J., & Breen, G. (2012). An examination of pack journalism as a form of groupthink: A theoretical and qualitative analysis. *Journal of Human Behavior in the Social Environment, 22*(7), 896–915. doi:10.1080/10911359.2012.707933

Mayer, E. L. (2002). Freud and Jung: The boundaried mind and the radically connected mind. *Journal of Analytical Psychology, 47*, 91–99.

Mayer, J. D. (2005). A tale of two visions: Can a new view of personality help integrate psychology? *American Psychologist, 60*(4), 294–307. doi:10.1037/0003-066X.60.4.294

Mayer, R. E. (2004). Should there be a three-strikes rule against pure discovery learning? *American Psychologist, 59*(1), 14–19. doi:10.1037/0003-066X.59.1.14

Mayer, R. E. (2011). *Applying the science of learning.* Boston, MA: Allyn & Bacon.

Mayer, R. E. (2014). Research-based principles for designing multimedia instruction. In V. A. Benassi, C. E. Overson, & C. M. Hakala (Eds.), *Applying science of learning in education: Infusing psychological science into the curriculum.* Retrieved July 20, 2020, from teachpsych.org/ebooks/asle2014/index.php

Mayes, S. D., Calhoun, S. L., et al. (2009). IQ and neuropsychological predictors of academic achievement. *Learning & Individual Differences, 19*(2), 238–241.

Mazar, N., Amir, O., & Ariely, D. (2008). The dishonesty of honest people: A theory of self-concept maintenance. *Journal of Marketing Research, 45*(6), 633–644.

Mazerolle, M., Régner, I., et al. (2012). Stereotype threat strengthens automatic recall and undermines controlled processes in older adults. *Psychological Science, 23*(7), 723–727. doi:10.1177/0956797612437607

Mazzoni, G., Heap, M., & Scoboria, A. (2010). Hypnosis and memory: Theory, laboratory research, and applications. In S. J.

Lynn, J. W. Rhue, et al. (Eds.), *Handbook of clinical hypnosis* (2nd ed., pp. 709–741). Washington, DC: American Psychological Association.

McAdams, D. P., & McLean, K. C. (2013). Narrative identity. *Current Directions in Psychological Science, 22*(3), 233–238.

McAdams, D. P., & Pals, J. L. (2006). A new Big Five: Fundamental principles for an integrative science of personality. *American Psychologist, 61*(3), 204–217. doi:10.1037/0003-066X.61.3.204

McAlister, A. L., Ama, E., Barroso, C., et al. (2000). Promoting tolerance and moral engagement through peer modeling. *Cultural Diversity & Ethnic Minority Psychology, 6*(4), 363–373.

McAvoy, J. (2012). Exposing the authoritarian personality. In N. Brace & J. Byford (Eds.), *Investigating psychology: Key concepts, key studies, key approaches* (pp. 16–56). New York, NY: Oxford University Press.

McCabe, D. L., Butterfield, K. D., & Trevino, L. K. (2012). *Cheating in college: Why students do it and what educators can do about it.* Baltimore, MD: Johns Hopkins University Press.

McCabe, M. P. (2015). Female orgasmic disorder. In K. M. Hertlein, G. R. Weeks, et al. (Eds.), *Systemic sex therapy* (2nd ed., pp. 171–190). New York: Routledge/Taylor & Francis.

McCaffrey, T. (2012). Innovation relies on the obscure: A key to overcoming the classic problem of functional fixedness. *Psychological Science, 23*(3), 215–218. doi:10.1177/0956797611429580

McCall, W. V., Prudic, J., et al. (2006). Health-related quality of life following ECT in a large community sample. *Journal of Affective Disorders, 90*(2–3), 269–274. doi:10.1016/j.jad.2005.12.002

McCall, W. V., Rosenquist, P. B., et al. (2011). Health-related quality of life in a clinical trial of ECT followed by continuation pharmacotherapy: Effects immediately after ECT and at 24 weeks. *The Journal of ECT, 27*(2), 97–102. doi:10.1097/YCT.0b013e318205c7d7

McCalley, L. T., de Vries, P. W., & Midden, C. J. (2011). Consumer response to product-integrated energy feedback: Behavior, goal level shifts, and energy conservation. *Environment and Behavior, 43*(4), 525–545. doi:10.1177/0013916510371053

McCarthy, B. W. (1995). Bridges to sexual desire. *Journal of Sex Education & Therapy, 21*(2), 132–141.

McCarthy, B. W., & Fucito, L. M. (2005). Integrating medication, realistic expectations, and therapeutic interventions in the treatment of male sexual dysfunction. *Journal of Sex & Marital Therapy, 31*(4), 319–328.

McCarthy, M. M., Arnold, A. P., et al. (2012). Sex differences in the brain: The not so inconvenient truth. *Journal of Neuroscience, 32*(7), 2241–2247. doi:10.1523/JNEUROSCI.5372-11.2012

McCarthy-Jones, S., Barnes, L. J., et al. (2011). When words and pictures come alive: Relating the modality of intrusive thoughts to modalities of hypnagogic/hypnopompic hallucinations. *Personality & Individual Differences, 51*(6), 787–790. doi:10.1016/j.paid.2011.07.003

McClelland, D. C. (1961). *The achieving society.* New York, NY: Van Nostrand.

McClelland, D. C. (1975). *Power: The inner experience.* New York, NY: Irvington.

McClelland, D. C. (1994). The knowledge-testing-educational complex strikes back. *American Psychologist, 49*(1), 66–69. doi:10.1037/0003-066X.49.1.66

McClung, C. A. (2011). Circadian rhythms and mood regulation: Insights from pre-clinical models. *European Neuropsychopharmacology, 21*, S683–S693. doi:10.1016/j.euroneuro.2011.07.008

McCluskey, U. (2002). The dynamics of attachment and systems-centered group psychotherapy. *Group Dynamics, 6*(2), 131–142. doi:10.1037/1089-2699.6.2.131

McCormick, N. B. (2010). Sexual scripts: Social and therapeutic implications. *Sexual & Relationship Therapy, 25*(1), 96–120.

McCrae, R. R., & Costa, P. T. Jr. (2001). A five-factor theory of personality. In L. A. Pervin & O. P. John (Eds.), *Handbook of personality* (pp. 139–153). New York, NY: Guilford.

McCrae, R. R., & Costa, P. T. Jr. (2013). Introduction to the empirical and theoretical status of the five-factor model of personality traits. In T. A. Widiger & P. Jr. Costa (Eds.), *Personality disorders and the five-factor model of personality* (3rd ed., pp. 15–27). Washington, DC: American Psychological Association. doi:10.1037/13939-002

McDaniel, M. A., Maier, S. F., & Einstein, G. O. (2002). "Brain-specific" nutrients: A memory cure? *Psychological Science in the Public Interest, 3*(1), 12–38. doi:10.1111/1529-1006.00007

McFadden, J. R., & Rawson Swan, K. T. (2012). Women during midlife: Is it transition or crisis? *Family and Consumer Sciences Research Journal, 40*(3), 313–325. doi:10.1111/j.1552-3934.2011.02113.x

McGaugh, J. L., & Roozendaal, B. (2009). Drug enhancement of memory consolidation: Historical perspective and neurobiological implications. *Psychopharmacology, 202*(1–3), 3–14. doi:10.1007/s00213-008-1285-6

McGowan, S., & Behar, E. (2013). A preliminary investigation of stimulus control training for worry: Effects on anxiety and insomnia. *Behavior Modification, 37*(1), 90–112. doi:10.1177/0145445512455661

McGrath, R. E., & Carroll, E. J. (2012). The current status of "projective" "tests." In H. Cooper (Ed.), *APA handbook of research methods in psychology: Foundations, planning, measures, and psychometrics* (Vol. 1, pp. 329–348). Washington, DC: American Psychological Association.

McGrath, R. E., & Moore, B. A. (Eds.). (2010). *Pharmacotherapy for psychologists: Prescribing and collaborative roles.* Washington, DC: American Psychological Association.

McGregor, D. (1960). *The human side of enterprise.* New York, NY: McGraw-Hill.

McGregor, I., McAdams, D. P., & Little, B. R. (2006). Personal projects, life stories, and happiness: On being true to traits. *Journal of Research in Personality, 40*(5), 551–572. doi:10.1016/j.jrp.2005.05.002

McGrew, S., et al. (2017). The challenge that's bigger than fake news: Civic reasoning in a social media environment. *American Educator, 41*(3), 4–9.

McGue, M., Bouchard, T. R., et al. (1993). Behavioral genetics of cognitive ability: A life-span perspective. In R. Plomin & G. E. McClearn (Eds.), *Nature, nurture & psychology* (pp. 59–76). Washington, DC: American Psychological Association. doi:10.1037/10131-003

McGuinness, T. M., Dyer, J. G., & Wade, E. H. (2012). Gender differences in adolescent depression. *Journal of Psychosocial Nursing & Mental Health Services, 50*(12), 17–20. doi:10.3928/02793695-20121107-04

McIntosh, W. D., Harlow, T. F., & Martin, L. L. (1995). Linkers and nonlinkers: Goal beliefs as a moderator of the effects of everyday hassles on rumination, depression, and physical complaints. *Journal of Applied Social Psychology, 25*(14), 1231–1244. doi:10.1111/j.1559-1816.1995.tb02616.x

McKay, A. (2005). Sexuality and substance use: The impact of tobacco, alcohol, and selected recreational drugs on sexual function. *Canadian Journal of Human Sexuality, 14*(1–2), 47–56.

McKeever, L. (2006). Online plagiarism detection services: Saviour or scourge? *Assessment & Evaluation in Higher Education, 31*(2), 155–165. doi:10.1080/02602930500262460

McKeganey, N. (2012). Harm reduction at the crossroads and the rediscovery of drug user abstinence. *Drugs: Education, Prevention & Policy, 19*(4), 276–283. doi:10.3109/09687637.2012.671867

McKenna, M. W., & Ossoff, E. P. (1998). Age differences in children's comprehension of a popular television program. *Child Study Journal, 28*(1), 52–68.

McKim, W. A. (2013). *Drugs & behavior: Introduction to behaviorial pharmacology* (7th ed.). Englewood Cliffs, NJ: Prentice Hall.

McLay, R. N. (2012). *At war with PTSD: Battling post traumatic stress disorder with virtual reality.* Baltimore, MD: Johns Hopkins University Press.

McLay, R. N., & Spira, J. L. (2009). Use of a portable biofeedback device to improve insomnia in a combat zone, a case report. *Applied Psychophysiology & Biofeedback, 34*(4), 319–321. doi:10.1007/s10484-009-9104-3

McLean, K. C., & Pasupathi, M. (2012). Processes of identity development: Where I am and how I got there. *Identity: An International Journal of Theory and Research, 12*(1), 8–28. doi:10.1080/15283488.2011.632363

McLewin, L. A., & Muller, R. T. (2006). Childhood trauma, imaginary companions, and the development of pathological dissociation. *Aggression & Violent Behavior, 11*(5), 531–545. doi:10.1016/j.avb.2006.02.001

McMahon, C. G., Jannini, E., et al. (2013). Standard operating procedures in the disorders of orgasm and ejaculation. *Journal of Sexual Medicine, 10*(1), 204–229. doi:10.1111/j.1743-6109.2012.02824.x

McMahon, S., & Koltzenburg, M. (2013). *Wall & Melzack's textbook of pain* (6th ed.). San Diego, CA: Elsevier.

McMahon, S. D. (2018). Schools as vehicles to assess experiences, improve outcomes, and effect social change. *American Journal of Community Psychology, 61*, 267–275. doi:10.1002/ajcp.12253

McMahon, T. (2014). Will quitting porn improve your life? *Macleans Magazine*, January 20. Retrieved July 20, 2020, from http://www.macleans.ca/society/life/can-swearing-off-porn-improve-your-life/

McMahon, T. R., & Kenyon, D. B., & Carter, J. S. (2013). "My culture, my family, my school, me": Identifying strengths and challenges in the lives and communities of American Indian youth. *Journal of Child & Family Studies, 22*(5), 694–706. doi:10.1007/s10826-012-9623-z

McManus, F., Muse, K., et al. (2015). Relating differently to intrusive images: The impact of mindfulness-based cognitive therapy (MBCT) on intrusive images in patients with severe health anxiety (hypochondriasis). *Mindfulness, 6*(4), 788–796. doi:10.1007/s12671-014-0318-y

McManus, I. C., Moore, J., et al. (2010). Science in the making: Right hand, left hand. III: Estimating historical rates of left-handedness. *Laterality: Asymmetries of Body, Brain & Cognition, 15*(1–2), 186–208. doi:10.1080/13576500802565313

McNally, R. J., & Clancy, S. A. (2005). Sleep paralysis, sexual abuse, and space alien abduction. *Transcultural Psychiatry, 42*(1), 113–122. doi:10.1177/1363461505050715

McNamara, D. S., & Scott, J. L. (2001). Working memory capacity and strategy use. *Memory & Cognition, 29*(1), 10–17. doi:10.3758/BF03195736

McNamara, P. (2011). *Spirit possession and exorcism: History, psychology, and neurobiology* (Vols. 1 & 2). Westport, CT: Praeger.

Mcquaid, N. E., Bibok, M. B., & Carpendale, J. I. M. (2009). Relation between maternal contingent responsiveness and infant social expectations. *Infancy, 14*(3), 390–401. doi:10.1080/15250000902839955

McRobbie, H., & Hajek, P. (2007). Effects of rapid smoking on post-cessation urges to smoke. *Addiction, 102*(3), 483–489. doi:10.1111/j.1360-0443.2006.01730.x

McVea, C. S., Gow, K., & Lowe, R. (2011). Corrective interpersonal experience in psychodrama group therapy: A comprehensive process analysis of significant therapeutic events. *Psychotherapy Research, 21*(4), 416–429. doi:10.1080/10503307.2011.577823

Meadow, T. (2011). "Deep down where the music plays": How parents account for childhood gender variance. *Sexualities, 14*(6), 725–747. doi:10.1177/1363460711420463

Mecklinger, A. (2010). The control of long-term memory: Brain systems and cognitive processes. *Neuroscience & Biobehavioral Reviews, 34*(7), 1055–1065. doi:10.1016/j.neubiorev.2009.11.020

Medda, P., Perugi, G., et al. (2009). Response to ECT in bipolar I, bipolar II and unipolar depression. *Journal of Affective Disorders, 118*(1–3), 55–59. doi:10.1016/j.jad.2009.01.014

Meeks, T. W., & Jeste, D. V. (2009). Neurobiology of wisdom: A literature overview. *Archives of General Psychiatry, 66*(4), 355–365. doi:10.1001/archgenpsychiatry.2009.8

Meevissen, Y. M., Peters, M. L., & Alberts, H. J. (2011). Become more optimistic by imagining a best possible self: Effects of a two week intervention. *Journal of Behavior Therapy & Experimental Psychiatry, 42*(3), 371–378. doi:10.1016/j.jbtep.2011.02.012

Mega, C., Ronconi, L., & De Beni, R. (2014). What makes a good student? How emotions, self-regulated learning, and motivation contribute to academic achievement. *Journal of Educational Psychology, 106*(1), 121–131. doi:10.1037/a0033546

Megreya, A. M., White, D., & Burton, A. M. (2011). The other-race effect does not rely on memory: Evidence from a matching task. *The Quarterly Journal of Experimental Psychology, 64*(8), 1473–1483. doi:10.1080/17470218.2011.575228

Meguerditchian, A., Vauclair, J., & Hopkins, W. D. (2013). On the origins of human handedness and language: A comparative review of hand preferences for bimanual coordinated actions and gestural communication in nonhuman primates. *Developmental Psychobiology, 55*(6), 637–650. doi:10.1002/dev.21150

Mehta, P. J., & Beer, J. (2010). Neural mechanisms of the testosterone-aggression relation: The role of orbitofrontal cortex. *Journal of Cognitive Neuroscience, 22*(10), 2357–2368.

Meichenbaum, D. (2009). Stress inoculation training. In W. T. O'Donohue & J. E. Fisher (Eds.), *General principles and empirically supported techniques of cognitive behavior therapy* (pp. 627–630). Hoboken, NJ: Wiley.

Meier, B. P., & Wilkowski, B. M. (2013). Reducing the tendency to aggress: Insights from social and personality psychology. *Social & Personality Psychology Compass, 7*(6), 343–354. doi:10.1111/spc3.12029

Meijer, E. H., & Verschuere, B. (2010). The polygraph and the detection of deception. *Journal of Forensic Psychology Practice, 10*(4), 325–338. doi:10.1080/15228932.2010.481237

Meineri, S., Dupré, M., et al. (2016). Door-in-the-face and but-you-are-free: Testing the effect of combining two no-pressure compliance paradigms. *Psychological Reports, 119*(1), 276–289. doi:10.1177/0033294116657064

Meini, C., & Paternoster, A. (2012). Mirror neurons as a conceptual mechanism? *Mind & Society, 11*(2), 183–201. doi:10.1007/s11299-012-0106-0

Meireles, E., & Primi, R. (2015). Validity and reliability evidence for assessing Holland's career types. *Paidéia, 25*(62), 307–315. doi:10.1590/1982-43272562201504

Melero, E. (2011). Are workplaces with many women in management run differently? *Journal of Business Research, 64*(4), 385–393. doi:10.1016/j.jbusres.2010.01.009

Melrose, S. (2015). Seasonal affective disorder: An overview of assessment and treatment approaches. *Depression Research & Treatment*, Article ID 178564. doi:10.1155/2015/1785

Meltzoff, A. N. (2005). Imitation and other minds: The "Like Me" Hypothesis. In S. Hurley & N. Chater (Eds.), *Perspectives on imitation: From neuroscience to social science* (Vol. 2): *Imitation, human development, and culture* (pp. 55–77). Cambridge, MA: MIT Press.

Melzack, R. (1999). From the gate to the neuromatrix. *Pain, Aug. Suppl. 6*, S121–S126. doi:10.1016/S0304-3959(99)00145-1

Melzack, R., & Katz, J. (2006). Pain in the 21st century: The neuromatrix and beyond. In G. Young, A. W. Kane, et al. (Eds.), *Psychological knowledge in court: PTSD, pain, and TBI* (pp. 129–148). New York, NY: Springer.

Memili, E., Chang, E. P. C., et al. (2015). Role conflicts of family members in family firms. *European Journal of Work & Organizational Psychology, 24*(1), 143–151. doi:10.1080/1359432X.2013.839549

Memon, A., Meissner, C. A., & Fraser, J. (2010). The Cognitive Interview: A meta-analytic review and study space analysis of the past 25 years. *Psychology, Public Policy, & Law, 16*(4), 340–372. doi:10.1037/a0020518

Mendelson, D., & Goes, F. S. (2011). A 34-year-old mother with religious delusions, filicidal thoughts. *Psychiatric Annals, 41*(7), 359–362.

Méndez-Bértolo, C., Moratti, S., et al. (2016). A fast pathway for fear in human amygdala. *Nature Neuroscience, 19*(8), 1041–1049. doi:10.1038/nn.4324

Mercer, T., & McKeown, D. (2010). Interference in short-term auditory memory. *Quarterly Journal of Experimental Psychology, 63*(7), 1256–1265. doi:10.1080/17470211003802467

Meyer, G. J., Finn, S. E., et al. (2001). Psychological testing and psychological assessment: A review of evidence and issues. *American Psychologist, 56*(2) 128–165. doi:10.1037/0003-066X.56.2.128

Meyer, I. H., Ouellette, S. C., et al. (2011). "We'd be free": Narratives of life without homophobia, racism, or sexism. *Sexuality Research & Social Policy, 8*(3), 204–214. doi:10.1007/s13178-011-0063-0

Meyer, T. (2014). Type D personality is unrelated to major adverse cardiovascular events in patients with coronary artery disease treated by intracoronary stenting. *Annals of Behavioral Medicine, 48*(2), 156–162. doi:10.1007/s12160-014-9590-2

Meyerbröker, K., & Emmelkamp, P. M. (2010). Virtual reality exposure therapy in anxiety disorders: A systematic review of process-and-outcome studies. *Depression & Anxiety, 27*(10), 933–944. doi:10.1002/da.20734

Meyers, L. (2006). Behind the scenes of the "Dr. Phil" show. *Monitor on Psychology, 37*(9), 63.

Meyers, L. (2007). The problem with DNA. *Monitor on Psychology, 38*(6), 52–53.

Michaels, J. W., Blommel, J. M., et al. (1982). Social facilitation and inhibition in a natural setting. *Replications in Social Psychology, 2*, 21–24.

Michaliszyn, D., Marchand, A., et al. (2010). A randomized, controlled clinical trial of in virtuo and in vivo exposure for spider phobia. *Cyberpsychology, Behavior, & Social Networking, 13*(6), 689–695. doi:10.1089/cyber.2009.0277

Michalko, M. (2006). *Thinkertoys: A handbook of creative-thinking techniques* (2nd Ed.). Berkeley, CA: Ten Speed Press.

Mickelson, K. D., Kessler, R. C., & Shaver, P. R. (1997). Adult attachment in a nationally representative sample. *Journal of Personality & Social Psychology, 73*(5), 1092–1106.

Mickes, L., Flowe, H. D., & Wixted, J. T. (2012). Receiver operating characteristic analysis of eyewitness memory: Comparing the diagnostic accuracy of simultaneous versus sequential lineups. *Journal of Experimental Psychology: Applied, 18*(4), 361–376. doi:10.1037/a0030609

Middaugh, S. J., & Pawlick, K. (2002). Biofeedback and behavioral treatment of persistent pain in the older adult: A review and a study. *Applied Psychophysiology & Biofeedback, 27*(3), 185–202. doi:10.1023/A:1016208128254

Middlehurst, R. (2015). Investing in leadership development: The UK experience. *International Higher Education*. Retrieved July 2020, from https://ejournals.bc.edu/ojs/index.php/ihe/article/view/8613

Middleton, H. (2015). The medical model: What is it, where did it come from and how long has it got? In D. Loewenthal (Ed.), *Critical psychotherapy, psychoanalysis and counselling: Implications for practice* (pp. 29–40). New York: Palgrave Macmillan, xxxviii, 309. doi:10.1057/9781137460585.0008

Miehls, D. (2017). Hegemonic views of masculinity and bullying: Clinical work with men who were bullied as children. *Clinical Social Work Journal, 45*(1), 56–64. doi:10.1007/s10615-016-0581-6

Mikulincer, M., & Shaver, P. R. (Eds.). (2010). *Prosocial motives, emotions, and behavior: The better angels of our nature.* Washington, DC: American Psychological Association.

Miles, L. K., Karpinska, K., et al. (2010). The meandering mind: Vection and mental time travel. *PLoS ONE, 5*(5): e10825. doi:10.1371/journal.pone.0010825

Milgram, S. (1963). Behavioral study of obedience. *Journal of Abnormal & Social Psychology, 67*, 371–378. doi:10.1037/h0040525

Milgram, S. (1965). Some conditions of obedience and disobedience to authority. *Human Relations, 18*, 57–76. doi:10.1177/001872676501800105

Milgram, S. (1970). The experience of living in the cities: A psychological analysis. *Science, 167*, 1461–1468.

Milgram, S., Bickman, L., & Berkowitz, L. (1969). Note on the drawing power of crowds of different size. *Journal of Personality & Social Psychology, 13*, 79–82. doi:10.1037/h0028070

Miller, A. L., Lambert, A. D., & Neumeister, K. (2012). Parenting style, perfectionism, and creativity in high-ability and high-achieving young adults. *Journal for the Education of the Gifted, 35*(4), 344–365.

Miller, D. T., & Prentice, D. A. (2016). Changing norms to change behavior. *Annual Review of Psychology, 67*, 339–361. doi:10.1146/annurev-psych-010814-015013

Miller, G. A. (1956). The magical number seven, plus or minus two: Some limits on our capacity for processing information. *Psychological Review, 63*, 81–97. doi:10.1037/0033-295X.101.2.343

Miller, G. T., Jr., & Spoolman, S. (2016). *Environmental science* (15th ed.). Boston, MA: Cengage Learning.

Miller, J., & Garran, A. M. (2008). *Racism in the United States: Implications for the helping professions.* Boston, MA: Cengage Learning.

Miller, L. E., Grabell, A., et al. (2012). The associations between community violence, television violence, intimate partner violence, parent–child aggression, and aggression in sibling relationships of a sample of preschoolers. *Psychology of Violence, 2*, 165–178. doi:10.1037/a0027254.

Miller, M. A., & Rahe, R. H. (1997). Life changes scaling for the 1990s. *Journal of Psychosomatic Research, 43*(3), 279–292. doi:10.1016/S0022-3999(97)00118-9

Miller, M., Hemenway, D., & Azraela, D. (2007). State-level homicide victimization rates in the US in relation to survey measures of household firearm ownership, 2001–2003. *Social Science & Medicine, 64*(3), 656–664. doi:10.1016/j.socscimed.2006.09.024

Miller, N. E. (1944). Experimental studies of conflict. In J. McV. Hunt (Ed.), *Personality and the behavior disorders* (Vol. 1, pp. 431–465). New York, NY: Ronald Press.

Miller, N. E., & Bugelski. R. (1948). Minor studies of aggression: II. The influence of frustration imposed by the in-group on attitudes expressed toward out-groups. *Journal of Psychology, 25*, 437–442. doi:10.1080/00223980.1948.9917387

Miller, N., Pedersen, W. C., et al. (2003). A theoretical model of triggered displaced aggression. *Personality & Social Psychology Review, 7*(1), 75–97. doi:10.1207/S15327957PSPR0701_5

Miller, P. H. (2011). Piaget's theory: Past, present, and future. In U. Goswami (Ed.), *Piaget's theory: Past, present, and future* (pp. 649–672). West Sussex, UK: Wiley-Blackwell.

Miller, R. (2012). *Intimate relationships* (6th ed.). New York, NY: McGraw-Hill.

Miller, W. R., & Munoz, R. F. (2005). *Controlling your drinking: Tools to make moderation work for you.* New York, NY: Guilford.

Millings, A., Walsh, J., et al. (2013). Good partner, good parent: Responsiveness mediates the link between romantic attachment and parenting style. *Personality & Social Psychology Bulletin, 39*(2), 170–180. doi:10.1177/0146167212468333

Millman, R. B., & Ross, E. J. (2003). Steroid and nutritional supplement use in professional athletes. *American Journal *on Addictions, 12*(Suppl. 2), S48–S54. doi:10.1080/713830544

Mills, S., White, M., et al. (2017). Health and social determinants and outcomes of home cooking: A systematic review of observational studies. *Appetite, 111,* 116–134. doi:10.1016/j.appet.2016.12.022

Milne, R., & Bull, R. (2002). Back to basics: A componential analysis of the original cognitive interview mnemonics with three age groups. *Applied Cognitive Psychology, 16*(7), 743–753. doi:10.1002/acp.825

Milner, B. (1965). Memory disturbance after bilateral hippocampal lesions. In P. Milner & S. Glickman (Eds.), *Cognitive processes and the brain* (pp. 97–111). Princeton, NJ: Van Nostrand.

Miltenberger, R. G. (2016). *Behavior modification: Principles and procedures* (6th ed.). Boston, MA: Cengage Learning.

Milton, F., Bealing, P., et al. (2017). The neural correlates of similarity- and rule-based generalization. *Journal of Cognitive Neuroscience, 29*(1), 150–166. doi:10.1162/jocn_a_01024

Minda, J. P., & Smith, J. D. (2011). Prototype models of categorization: Basic formulation, predictions, and limitations. In E. M. Pothos & A. J. Wills (Eds.), *Formal approaches in categorization* (pp. 40–64). New York, NY: Cambridge University Press.

Minnes, S., Min, M. O., et al. (2016). Executive function in children with prenatal cocaine exposure (12–15 years). *Neurotoxicology & Teratology, 57,* 79–86. doi:10.1016/j.ntt.2016. 07.002

Minton, H. L. (2000). Psychology and gender at the turn of the century. *American Psychologist, 55*(6), 613–615. doi:10.1037/0003-066X.55.6.613

Mintz, A., DeRouen, K., et al. (2010). *Groupthink versus high-quality decision making in international relations.* New York, NY: Columbia University Press.

Miotto, K., Darakjian, J., et al. (2001). Gamma-hydroxybutyric acid: Patterns of use, effects and withdrawal. *American Journal on Addictions, 10*(3), 232–241. doi:10.1080/105504901750532111

Mirsky, A. F., & Duncan, C. C. (2005). Pathophysiology of mental illness: A view from the fourth ventricle. *International Journal of Psychophysiology, 58*(2–3), 162–178. doi:10.1016/j.ijpsycho.2005.06.004

Mirsky, A. F., Bieliauskas, L. M., et al. (2000). A 39-year follow-up of the Genain quadruplets. *Schizophrenia Bulletin, 3,* 5–18.

Mischel, W. (1974). Processes in the delay of gratification. *Advances in Experimental Social Psychology, 7,* 249–292. doi:10.1016/S0065-2601(08)60039-8

Mischel, W. (2004). Toward an integrative science of the person. *Annual Review of Psychology, 55,* 1–22. doi:10.1146/annurev.psych.55.042902.130709

Mischel, W. (2014). *The marshmallow test: Mastering self-control.* New York, NY: Little, Brown, & Co.

Mischel, W., & Shoda, Y. (2010). The situated person. In B. Mesquita, L. F. Barrett, & E. R. Smith (Eds.), *The mind in context* (pp. 149–173). New York, NY: Guilford.

Mischel, W., Shoda, Y., & Smith, R. E. (2008). *Introduction to personality: Toward an integration* (8th ed.). Hoboken, NJ: Wiley.

Mitchell, D. (1987). Firewalking cults: Nothing but hot air. *Laser, Feb.*, 7–8.

Mitchell, L. A., MacDonald, R. A., et al. (2007). A survey investigation of the effects of music listening on chronic pain. *Psychology of Music, 35*(1), 37–57. doi:10.1177/0305735607068887

Mitchell, M. E., Lebow, J. R., et al. (2011). Internet use, happiness, social support and introversion: A more fine-grained analysis of person variables and Internet activity. *Computers in Human Behavior, 27*(5), 1857–1861. doi:10.1016/j.chb.2011.04.008

Mitchell, N. S., Dickinson, L. M., et al. (2010). Determining the effectiveness of Take Off Pounds Sensibly (TOPS), a nationally available nonprofit weight loss program. *Obesity, 19,* 568–573. doi:10.1038/oby.2010.202

Mitka, M. (2009). College binge drinking still on the rise. *Journal of the American Medical Association, 302*(8), 836–837. doi:10.1001/jama.2009.1154

Mizock, L., & Harkins, D. (2011). Diagnostic bias and conduct disorder: Improving culturally sensitive diagnosis. *Child & Youth Services, 32*(3), 243–253. doi:10.1080/0145935X.2011.605315

Moayedi, M., & Davis, K. D. (2013). Theories of pain: From specificity to gate control. *Journal of Neurophysiology, 109*(1), 5–12. doi:10.1152/jn.00457.2012

Mock, S. E., & Eibach, R. P. (2012). Stability and change in sexual orientation identity over a 10-year period in adulthood. *Archives of Sexual Behavior, 41*(3), 641–648. doi:10.1007/s10508011-9761-1

Moerman, D. E. (2002). The meaning response and the ethics of avoiding placebos. *Evaluation & the Health Professions, 25*(4), 399–409. doi:10.1177/0163278702238053

Moffitt, T. E., Arseneault, L., et al. (2011). A gradient of childhood self-control predicts health, wealth, and public safety. *Proceedings of the National Academy of Sciences, 108*(7), 2693–2698. doi:10.1073/pnas.1010076108

Moghaddam, B. (2002). Stress activation of glutamate neurotransmission in the prefrontal cortex. *Biological Psychiatry, 51*(10), 775–787. doi:10.1016/S0006-3223(01)01362-2

Moghaddam, F. M. (2013). *The psychology of dictatorship.* Washington, DC: American Psychological Association. doi:10.1037/14138-008

Mojtabai, R., Olfson, M., et al. (2011). Barriers to mental health treatment: Results from the national comorbidity survey replication. *Psychological Medicine, 41*(8), 1751–1761. doi:10.1017/S0033291710002291

Mokdad, A. H., Marks, J. S., et al. (2004). Actual causes of death in the United States, 2000. *Journal of the American Medical Association, 291,* 1238–1245. doi:10.1001/jama.291.10.1238

Moksnes, U. K., & Espnes, G. A. (2012). Self-esteem and emotional health in adolescents: Gender and age as potential moderators. *Scandinavian Journal of Psychology, 53*(6), 483–489. doi:10.1111/sjop.12021

Molenberghs, P., Cunnington, R., & Mattingley, J. B. (2012). Brain regions with mirror properties: A meta-analysis of 125 human fMRI studies. *Neuroscience & Biobehavioral Reviews, 36*(1), 341–349. doi:10.1016/j.neubiorev.2011.07.004

Moller, A. C., Merchant, G., et al. (2017). Applying and advancing behavior change theories and techniques in the context of a digital health revolution: Proposals for more effectively realizing untapped potential. *Journal of Behavioral Medicine, 40*(1), 85–98. doi:10.1007/s10865-016-9818-7

Monahan, C. I., Beeber, L. S., & Harden, B. (2012). Finding family strengths in the midst of adversity: Using risk and resilience models to promote mental health. In S. Summers & R. Chazan-Cohen (Eds.), *Understanding early childhood mental health: A practical guide for professionals* (pp. 59–78). Baltimore, MD: Paul H Brookes.

Monahan, J., Steadman, H. J., et al. (2001). *Rethinking risk assessment: The MacArthur Study of Mental Disorder and Violence.* New York, NY: Oxford University Press.

Monde, K., Ketay, S., et al. (2013). Preliminary physiological evidence for impaired emotion regulation in depersonalization disorder. *Psychiatry Research, 209,* 235–238. doi:10.1016/j.psychres.2013.02.020

Moneta, G. B. (2012). Opportunity for creativity in the job as a moderator of the relation between trait intrinsic motivation and flow in work. *Motivation & Emotion, 36*(4), 491–503. doi:10.1007/s11031-012-9278-5

Mongeau, P. A., Knight, K., et al. (2013). Identifying and explicating variation among friends with benefits relationships. *Journal of Sex Research, 50*(1), 37–47. doi:10.1080/00224499.2011.623797

Montenigro, P. H., Corp, D. T. et al. (2015). Chronic traumatic encephalopathy: Historical origins and current perspective. *Annual Review of Clinical Psychology, 11,* 309–330. doi:10.1146/annurev-clinpsy-032814-112814

Montgomery, P., & Dennis, J. (2004). A systematic review of non-pharmacological therapies for sleep problems in later life. *Sleep Medicine Reviews, 8*(1), 47–62. doi:10.1016/S1087-0792(03)00026-1

Monti, M. M. (2012). Cognition in the vegetative state. *Annual Review of Clinical Psychology, 8,* 431–454. doi:10.1146/annurev-clinpsy-032511-143050

Monti, M. M., Vanhaudenhuyse, A., et al. (2010). Willful modulation of brain activity in disorders of consciousness. *New England Journal of Medicine, 362*(7), 579–589. doi:10.1056/NEJMoa0905370

Montoya, E. R., Terburg, D., et al. (2012). Testosterone, cortisol, and serotonin as key regulators of social aggression: A review and theoretical perspective. *Motivation & Emotion, 36*(1), 65–73. doi:10.1007/s11031-011-9264-3

Montoya, R. M., & Horton, R. S. (2012). The reciprocity of liking effect. In M. A. Paludi (Ed.), *The psychology of love* (Vols. 1–4, pp. 39–57). Santa Barbara, CA: Praeger.

Montoya, R. M., & Horton, R. S. (2013). A meta-analytic investigation of the processes underlying the similarity-attraction effect. *Journal of Social & Personal Relationships, 30*(1), 64–94. doi:10.1177/0265407512452989

Montoya, R. M., & Insko, C. A. (2008). Toward a more complete understanding of the reciprocity of liking effect. *European Journal of Social Psychology, 38,* 477–498. doi:10.1002/ejsp.431

Montreal Declaration on Intellectual Disabilities. (2004). Retrieved July 20, 2020, from https://www.researchgate.net/publication/230203845_The_Montreal_Declaration_on_Intellectual_Disabilities_of_2004_An_Important_First_Step

Moore, R. (2009). *Understanding Jonestown and Peoples Temple.* Westport, CT: Praeger.

Moore, S. A., & Zoellner, L. A. (2007). Overgeneral autobiographical memory and traumatic events: An evaluative review. *Psychological Bulletin, 133*(3), 419–437. doi:10.1037/0033-2909.133.3.419

Moore, T. O. (2001). Testosterone and male behavior: Empirical research with hamsters does not support the use of castration to deter human sexual aggression. *North American Journal of Psychology, 3*(3), 503–520.

Moors, A. (2016). Automaticity: Componential, causal, and mechanistic explanations. *Annual Review of Psychology, 67,* 263–287. doi:10.1146/annurev-psych-122414-033550

Moran, E. F. (2010). *Environmental social science: Human–environment interactions and sustainability.* Malden, MA: Wiley-Blackwell.

Moran, F. (2010). *The paradoxical legacy of Sigmund Freud.* London, UK: Karnac Books.

Moran, J. M., Jolly, E., & Mitchell, J. P. (2014). Spontaneous mentalizing predicts the fundamental attribution error. *Journal of Cognitive Neuroscience, 26*(3), 569–576. doi:10.1162/jocn_a_0051

Moreno, J. L. (1953). *Who shall survive?* New York, NY: Beacon.

Moreno, M. M., Linster, C., et al. (2009). Olfactory perceptual learning requires adult neurogenesis. *Proceedings of the National Academy of Sciences, 106*(42), 17980–17985. doi:10.1073/pnas.0907063106

Moreno-Cabrera, J. (2011). Speech and gesture: An integrational approach. *Language Sciences, 33*(4), 615–622. doi:10.1016/j.langsci.2011.04.021

Morgan, J. P. (Ed.). (2005). *Psychology of aggression.* Hauppauge, NY: Nova Science Publishers.

Morin, A. (2006). Levels of consciousness and self-awareness: A comparison and integration of various neurocognitive views. *Consciousness & Cognition, 15*(2), 358–371. doi:10.1016/j.concog.2005.09.006

Morina, N., Ijntema, H., et al. (2015). Can virtual reality exposure therapy gains be generalized to real-life? A meta-analysis of studies applying behavioral assessments. *Behaviour Research & Therapy, 74*, 18–24. doi:10.1016/j.brat.2015.08.010

Morisse, D., Batra, L., et al. (1996). A demonstration of a token economy for the real world. *Applied & Preventive Psychology, 5*(1), 41–46. doi:10.1016/S0962-1849(96)80025-4

Morley, T. E., & Moran, G. (2011). The origins of cognitive vulnerability in early childhood: Mechanisms linking early attachment to later depression. *Clinical Psychology Review, 31*(7), 1071–1082. doi:10.1016/j.cpr.2011.06.006

Morrison, M. (2012). *Using humor to maximize living: Connecting with humor* (2nd ed.). Lanham, MD: Rowman & Littlefield Education.

Morrison, M., DeVaul-Fetters, A., et al. (2016). Stacking the jury: Legal professionals' peremptory challenges reflect jurors' levels of implicit race bias. *Personality & Social Psychology Bulletin, 42*(8), 1129–1141. doi:10.1177/0146167216651853

Morrison, R. G., & Wallace, B. (2001). Imagery vividness, creativity and the visual arts. *Journal of Mental Imagery, 25*(3–4), 135–152.

Moscovitch, M., Cabeza, R., et al. (2016). Episodic memory and beyond: The hippocampus and neocortex in transformation. *Annual Review of Psychology, 67*, 105–134. doi:10.1146/annurev-psych-113011-143733

Moseley, P., Fernyhough, C., & Ellison, A. (2013). Auditory verbal hallucinations as atypical inner speech monitoring, and the potential of neurostimulation as a treatment option. *Neuroscience & Biobehavioral Reviews, 37*, 2794–2805. doi:10.1016/j.neubiorev.2013.10.001

Moser, D., Anderer, P., et al. (2009). Sleep classification according to AASM and Rechtschaffen & Kales: Effects on sleep scoring parameters. *Sleep, 32*(2), 139–149.

Mosher, W. D., Chandra, C., & Jones, J. (2005). *Sexual behavior and selected health measures: Men and women 15–44 years of age, United States, 2002.* Retrieved July 20, 2020, from http://www.cdc.gov/nchs/data/ad/ad362.pdf

Mosley, M. (2011). *Alien Hand Syndrome sees woman attacked by her own hand.* Retrieved July 20, 2020, from https://www.bbc.com/news/uk-12225163

Moskowitz, G. B., & Li, P. (2011). Egalitarian goals trigger stereotype inhibition: A proactive form of stereotype control. *Journal of Experimental Social Psychology, 47*(1), 103–116.

Motivala, S. J., & Irwin, M. R. (2007). Sleep and immunity: Cytokine pathways linking sleep and health outcomes. *Current Directions in Psychological Science, 16*(1), 21–25. doi:10.1111/j.1467-8721.2007.00468.x

Motraghi, T. E., Seim, R. W., et al. (2014). Virtual reality exposure therapy for the treatment of posttraumatic stress disorder: A methodological review using CONSORT guidelines. *Journal of Clinical Psychology, 70*(3), 197–208. doi:10.1002/jclp.22051

Mõttus, R., Johnson, W., & Deary, I. J. (2012). Personality traits in old age: Measurement and rank-order stability and some mean-level change. *Psychology & Aging, 27*(1), 243–249. doi:10.1037/a0023690

Moutsiana, C., Fearon, P., et al. (2014). Making an effort to feel positive: Insecure attachment in infancy predicts the neural underpinnings of emotion regulation in adulthood. *Journal of Child Psychology & Psychiatry, 55*, 999–1008.

Mowbray, T. (2012). Working memory, test anxiety and effective interventions: A review. *Australian Educational & Developmental Psychologist, 29*(2), 141–156. doi:10.1017/edp.2012.16

Mukherjee, A. (2015). Effective use of discovery learning to improve understanding of factors that affect quality. *Journal of Education for Business, 90*(8), 413–419. doi:10.1080/08832323.2015.1081866

Mulavara, A. P., Feiveson, A. H., et al. (2010). Locomotor function after long-duration space flight: Effects and motor learning during recovery. *Experimental Brain Research, 202*(3), 649–659.

Müller, B. C. N., Gerasimova, A., et al. (2016). Concentrative meditation influences creativity by increasing cognitive flexibility. *Psychology of Aesthetics, Creativity, & the Arts, 10*(3), 278–286. doi:10.1037/a0040335

Müller, B. H., Kull, S., et al. (2011). One-session computer-based exposure treatment for spider-fearful individuals: Efficacy of a minimal self-help intervention in a randomised controlled trial. *Journal of Behavior Therapy & Experimental Psychiatry, 42*(2), 179–184. doi:10.1016/j.jbtep.2010.12.001

Müller, V. C. (2012). Introduction: Philosophy and theory of artificial intelligence. *Minds & Machines, 22*(2), 67–69. doi:10.1007/s11023-012-9278-y

Mundy, A. (2004). Divided we stand. *American Demographics, 26*(5), 26–31.

Munroe-Chandler, K., Hall, C., & Fishburne, G. (2008). Playing with confidence: The relationship between imagery use and self-confidence and self-efficacy in youth soccer players. *Journal of Sports Sciences, 26*(14), 1539–1546. doi:10.1080/02640410802315419

Munsey, C. (2006). RxP legislation made historic progress in Hawaii. *APA Monitor, June*, 42.

Murayama, K., Kitagami, S., et al. (2016). People's naiveté about how extrinsic rewards influence intrinsic motivation. *Motivation Science, 2*(3), 138–142. doi:10.1037/mot0000040

Murayama, K., Matsumoto, M., et al. (2015). How self-determined choice facilitates performance: A key role of the ventromedial prefrontal cortex. *Cerebral Cortex, 25*(5), 1241–1251. doi:10.1093/cercor/bht317

Murphy, B. C., & Dillon, C. (2015). *Interviewing in action in a multicultural world* (5th ed.). Boston, MA: Cengage Learning.

Murphy, D., & Joseph, S. (2016). Person-centered therapy: Past, present, and future orientations. In Cain, D. J., Keenan, K., & Rubin, S. (Eds.). *Humanistic psychotherapies: Handbook of research and practice* (2nd ed., pp. 185–218). Washington, DC: American Psychological Association. doi:10.1037/14775-007

Murphy, D., & Page, I. (2008). Exhibitionism: Psychopathology and theory. In D. Laws & W. O'Donohue (Eds.), *Sexual deviance: Theory, assessment, and treatment* (2nd ed.). New York, NY: Guilford.

Murphy, G., & Greene, C. M. (2016). Perceptual load induces inattentional blindness in drivers. *Applied Cognitive Psychology, 30*(3), 479–483. doi:10.1002/acp.3216

Murray, A., McKenzie, K., et al. (2013). Estimating the level of functional ability of children identified as likely to have an intellectual disability. *Research in Developmental Disabilities, 34*(11), 4009–4016. doi:10.1016/j.ridd.2013.08.008

Murray, C. D., Pettifer, S., et al. (2007). The treatment of phantom limb pain using immersive virtual reality: Three case studies. *Disability & Rehabilitation, 29*(18), 1465–1469. doi:10.1080/09638280601107385

Murray, D. A. B. (Ed.). (2009). *Homophobias: Lust and loathing across time and space.* Durham, NC, Duke University Press,

Murrell, A. R., Christoff, K. A., & Henning, K. R. (2007). Characteristics of domestic violence offenders: Associations with childhood exposure to violence. *Journal of Family Violence, 22*(7), 523–532. doi:10.1007/s10896-007-9100-4

Music, G. (2011). *Nurturing natures: Attachment and children's emotional, sociocultural, and brain development.* Hove, UK: Psychology Press.

Mussen, P. H., Conger, J. J., et al. (1979). *Psychological development: A life span approach.* New York, NY: Harper & Row.

Mustafa, F. (2013). Schizophrenia past clozapine: What works? *Journal of Clinical Psychopharmacology, 33*(1), 63–68. doi:10.1097/JCP.0b013e31827a813b

Mustanski, B. S., Chivers, M. L., & Bailey, J. M. (2002). A critical review of recent biological research on human sexual orientation. *Annual Review of Sex Research, 13*, 89–140.

Myers, M. W., & Hodges, S. D. (2013). Empathy: Perspective taking and prosocial behavior: Caring for others like we care for the self. In J. J. Froh & A. C. Parks (Eds.), *Activities for teaching positive psychology: A guide for instructors* (pp. 77–83). Washington, DC: American Psychological Association. doi:10.1037/14042-013

Myers, S. G., & Wells, A. (2015). Early trauma, negative affect, and anxious attachment: The role of metacognition. *Anxiety, Stress, & Coping: An International Journal, 28*, 634–649. doi:10.1080/10615806.2015.1009832

Nadel, L. L., Hupbach, A. A., et al. (2012). Memory formation, consolidation, and transformation. *Neuroscience & Biobehavioral Reviews, 36*(7), 1640–1645. doi:10.1016/j.neubiorev.2012.03.001

Naderi, K., Takatalo, J., et al. (2018). Computer-aided imagery in sport and exercise: A case study of indoor wall climbing. *Graphics Interface Conference 2018.* Retrieved July 19, 2020, from https://graphicsinterface.org/wp-content/uploads/gi2018-13.pdf

Nahari, G. (2012). Elaborations on credibility judgments by professional lie detectors and laypersons: Strategies of judgment and justification. *Psychology, Crime & Law, 18*(6), 567–577. doi:10.1080/1068316X.2010.511222

Naitoh, P., Kelly, T. L., & Englund, C. E. (1989). *Health effects of sleep deprivation.* U.S. Naval Health Research Center Report, No. 89–46.

Najdowski, C. J. (2010). Jurors and social loafing: Factors that reduce participation during jury deliberations. *American Journal of Forensic Psychology, 28*(2), 39–64.

Nakamura, J., & Csikszentmihalyi, M. (2003). The motivational sources of creativity as viewed from the paradigm of positive psychology. In L. G. Aspinwall & U. M. Staudinger (Eds.), *A psychology of human strengths: Fundamental questions and future directions for a positive psychology* (pp. 257–269). Washington, DC: American Psychological Association.

Nakamura, Y., Goto, T. K., et al. (2011). Localization of brain activation by umami taste in humans. *Brain Research, 1406*, 18–29. doi:10.1016/j.brainres.2011.06.029

Nakayama, H. (2010). Development of infant crying behavior: A longitudinal case study. *Infant Behavior & Development, 33*(4), 463–471. doi:10.1016/j.infbeh.2010.05.002

Nance, A. R. (2015). Social media selection: How jury consultants can use social media to build a more favorable jury. *Law & Psychology Review, 39*, 2015, 267–286.

Nandagopal, K., & Ericsson, K. (2011). An expert performance approach to the study of individual differences in self-regulated learning activities in upper-level college students. *Learning & Individual Differences, 22*(5), 597–609. doi:10.1016/j.lindif.2011.11.018

National Academies of Sciences, Engineering, and Medicine. (2017). *The health effects of cannabis and cannabinoids: The current state of evidence and recommendations for research.* Washington, DC: The National Academies Press. doi:10.17226/24625.

National Academy of Sciences. (2003). *The polygraph and lie detection.* Washington, DC: The National Academies Press.

National Alliance on Mental Illness. (2019). *Risk of suicide.* Retrieved July 20, 2020, from www.nami.org/Learn-More/Mental-Health-Conditions/Related-Conditions/Suicide

National Center for PTSD. (2019). *Epidemiology of PTSD.* Retrieved July 20, 2020, from https://www.ptsd.va.gov/professional/treat/essentials/epidemiology.asp

National Committee on Pay Equity. (2015a). *The wage gap over time: In real dollars, women see a continuing gap.* Washington, DC: Author. Retrieved June 12, 2016, from http://www.pay-equity.org/info-time.html

National Committee on Pay Equity. (2015b). *Women of color in the workplace.*

Washington, DC: Author. Retrieved June 12, 2016, from http://www.pay-equity.org/info-race.html

National Down Syndrome Society. (2020). *Down syndrome.* Retrieved July 20, 2020, from https://www.ndss.org/about-down-syndrome/down-syndrome/

National Institute of Child Health and Human Development. (2016). *Phenylketonuria (PKU).* Retrieved February 20, 2020, from https://www.nichd.nih.gov/health/topics/pku/Pages/default.aspx

National Institute of Child Health and Human Development. (2017a). *Link between child care and academic achievement and behavior persists into adolescence.* Retrieved July 13, 2020, from https://www.nichd.nih.gov/newsroom/resources/links/transcript051410

National Institute of Child Health and Human Development. (2017b). *Sudden infant death syndrome (SIDS) overview.* Retrieved July 20, 2020, from www.nichd.nih.gov/health/topics/sids/Pages/default.aspx

National Institute of Mental Health. (2010). *Turning the corner, not the key, in treatment of serious mental illness.* February 23, 2016, from http://www.nimh.nih.gov/about/director/2010/turning-the-corner-not-the-key-in-treatment-of-serious-mental-illness.shtml

National Institute of Mental Health. (2016a). *Depression basics.* Retrieved July 20, 2020, from https://www.nimh.nih.gov/health/publications/depression/index.shtml#pub12

National Institute of Mental Health. (2016b). *Attention deficit hyperactivity disorder (ADHD): The basics.* Retrieved July 20, 2020, from https://www.nimh.nih.gov/health/publications/attention-deficit-hyperactivity-disorder-adhd-the-basics/qf-16-3572_153275.pdf

National Institute of Mental Health. (2018). *Statistics.* Retrieved July 20, 2020, from www.nimh.nih.gov/health/statistics/index.shtml

National Institute of Mental Health. (2020). *Postpartum depression.* Retrieved July 20, 2020, from https://www.nimh.nih.gov/health/publications/postpartum-depression-facts/index.shtml

National Institute of Neurological Disorders and Stroke. (2019). *Brain basics: Understanding sleep.* Retrieved July 20, 2020, from www.ninds.nih.gov/disorders/brain_basics/understanding_sleep.htm

National Institute on Alcohol Abuse and Alcoholism. (2015). *College drinking.* Retrieved July 20, 2020, from http://pubs.niaaa.nih.gov/publications/CollegeFactSheet/CollegeFactSheet.pdf

National Institute on Alcohol Abuse and Alcoholism. (2020). *Tips to try.* Retrieved July 21, 2020, from https://www.rethinkingdrinking.niaaa.nih.gov/Thinking-about-a-change/strategies-for-cutting-down/Tips-To-Try.aspx

National Institute on Deafness and Other Communication Disorders. (2016). *Quick statistics about hearing.* Retrieved July 17, 2020, from www.nidcd.nih.gov/health/statistics/quick-statistics-hearing

National Institute on Deafness and Other Communication Disorders. (2019). *Noise-induced hearing loss.* Retrieved July 17, 2020, from www.nidcd.nih.gov/health/noise-induced-hearing-loss

National Institute on Drug Abuse. (2014). *Drugs, brains, and behavior: The science of addiction.* Retrieved July 21, 2020, from www.drugabuse.gov/publications/drugs-brains-behavior-science-addiction/preface

National Institute on Drug Abuse. (2018). *Tobacco addiction.* Retrieved July 21, 2020, from https://www.drugabuse.gov/publications/principles-drug-addiction-treatment-research-based-guide-third-edition/evidence-based-approaches-to-drug-addiction-treatment/pharmacotherapies/tobacco-addiction

National Institute on Drug Abuse. (2020a). *Fentanyl DrugFacts.* Retrieved July 21, 2020, from www.drugabuse.gov/publications/drugfacts/fentanyl

National Institute on Drug Abuse. (2020b). *Marijuana as medicine DrugFacts.* Retrieved July 21, 2020, from https://www.drugabuse.gov/publications/drugfacts/marijuana-medicine

National Institute on Drug Abuse. (2020c). *Marijuana research report.* Retrieved July 21, 2020, from https://www.drugabuse.gov/publications/research-reports/marijuana/letter-director

National Institute on Drug Abuse. (2020d). *MDMA (Ecstasy/Molly) DrugFacts.* Retrieved July 21, 2020, from www.drugabuse.gov/publications/drugfacts/mdma-ecstasymolly

National Institutes of Health. (2020). *Color vision deficiency.* Retrieved July 19, 2020, from http://ghr.nlm.nih.gov/condition/color-vision-deficiency

Nätti, J., & Häikiö, L. (2012). Flexible work and work–family interaction. *Community, Work & Family, 15*(4), 381–382. doi:10.1080/13668803.2012.725548

Nau, S. D., & Lichstein, K. L. (2005). Insomnia: Causes and treatments. In P. R. Carney, J. D. Geyer, et al. (Eds.), *Clinical sleep disorders* (pp. 157–190). Philadelphia, PA: Lippincott Williams & Wilkins.

Nawrot, E., Mayo, S. L., & Nawrot, M. (2009). The development of depth perception from motion parallax in infancy. *Attention, Perception, & Psychophysics, 71*(1), 194–199.

Nay, W. R. (2014). *The anger management workbook: Use the STOP method to replace destructive responses with constructive behavior.* New York: Guilford.

Neff, L. A., & Geers, A. L. (2013). Optimistic expectations in early marriage: A resource or vulnerability for adaptive relationship functioning? *Journal of Personality & Social Psychology, 105*(1), 38–60. doi:10.1037/a0032600

Negriff, S., & Trickett, P. K. (2010). The relationship between pubertal timing and delinquent behavior in maltreated male and female adolescents. *Journal of Early Adolescence, 30*(4), 518–542. doi:10.1177/0272431609338180

Nehlig, A. (Ed.). (2004). *Coffee, tea, chocolate, and the brain.* Boca Raton, FL: CRC Press.

Neikrug, A. B., & Ancoli-Israel, S. (2012). Diagnostic tools for REM sleep behavior disorder. *Sleep Medicine Reviews, 16*(5), 415–429. doi:10.1016/j.smrv.2011.08.004

Neisser, U. (1967). *Cognitive psychology.* New York, NY: Appleton-Century-Crofts.

Neitz, J., & Neitz, M. (2011). The genetics of normal and defective color vision. *Vision Research, 51*(7), 633–651. doi:10.1016/j.visres.2010.12.002

Nellis, A., & Savage, J. (2012). Does watching the news affect fear of terrorism? The importance of media exposure on terrorism fear. *Crime & Delinquency, 58*(5), 748–768. doi:10.1177/0011128712452961

Nelson, C. A. (1999). How important are the first 3 years of life? *Applied Developmental Science, 3*(4), 235–238. doi:10.1207/s1532480xads0304_8

Nelson, G., Van Andel, A. K., et al. (2012). Exploring outcomes through narrative: The long-term impacts of better beginnings, better futures on the turning point stories of youth at ages 18–19. *American Journal of Community Psychology, 49*(1–2), 294–306. doi:10.1007/s10464-011-9466-6

Nelson, T. D. (2005). Ageism: Prejudice against our feared future self. *Journal of Social Issues, 61*(2), 207–221. doi:10.1111/j.1540-4560.2005.00402.x

Nestor, P. G., Nakamura, M., et al. (2015). Attentional control and intelligence: MRI orbital frontal gray matter and neuropsychological correlates. *Behavioural Neurology*, Article 354186.

Nettle, D. (2005). An evolutionary perspective on the extraversion continuum. *Evolution & Human Behavior, 26*, 363–373. doi:10.1016/j.evolhumbehav.2004.12.004

Nettle, D. (2008). The personality factor: What makes you unique? *New Scientist, February 9*, 36–39.

Neubert, J. C., Mainert, J., et al. (2015). The assessment of 21st century skills in industrial and organizational psychology: Complex and collaborative problem solving. *Industrial & Organizational Psychology, 8*(2), Jun 2015, 238–268. doi:10.1017/iop.2015.14

Neufeind, J., Dritschel, B., et al. (2009). The effects of thought suppression on autobiographical memory recall. *Behaviour Research & Therapy, 47*(4), 275–284. doi:10.1016/j.brat.2008.12.010

Neufeld, R. W. J., Carter, J. R., et al. (2003). Schizophrenia. In P. Firestone & W. L. Marshall (Eds.), *Abnormal psychology: Perspectives* (2nd ed., pp. 343–370). Toronto, ON: Prentice Hall.

Neukrug, E. S. (2014). *A brief orientation to counseling.* Boston, MA: Cengage Learning.

Neukrug, E. S., & Fawcett, R. C. (2020). *Essentials of testing and assessment: A practical guide for counselors, social workers, and psychologists* (Enhanced 3rd ed.). Boston, MA: Cengage Learning.

Neville, H. A., Awad, G. H., et al. (2013). Color-blind racial ideology: Theory, training, and measurement implications in psychology. *American Psychologist, 68*(6), 455–466. doi:10.1037/a0033282

Nevo, E., & Breznitz, Z. (2013). The development of working memory from kindergarten to first grade in children with different decoding skills. *Journal of Experimental Child Psychology, 114*(2), 217–228. doi:10.1016/j.jecp.2012.09.004

Newell, B. R. (2012). Levels of explanation in category learning. *Australian Journal of Psychology, 64*(1), 46–51.

Newman, B. R., & Newman, P. R. (2018). *Development through life: A psychosocial approach* (13th ed.). Boston, MA: Cengage Learning.

Newman, R. S., Rowe, M. L., et al. (2016). Input and uptake at 7 months predicts toddler vocabulary: The role of child-directed speech and infant processing skills in language development. *Journal of Child Language, 43*(5), 1158–1173. doi:10.1017/S0305000915000446

Ng, T. H., & Feldman, D. C. (2010). Human capital and objective indicators of career success: The mediating effects of cognitive ability and conscientiousness. *Journal of Occupational & Organizational Psychology, 83*(1), 207–235. doi:10.1348/096317909X414584

Nguyen, T. Q., Gwynn, R. C., et al. (2008). Population prevalence of reported and unreported HIV and related behaviors among the household adult population in New York City, 2004. *AIDS, 22*(2), 281–287. doi:10.1097/QAD.0b013e3282f2ef58

Nickerson, C., Diener, E., & Schwarz, N. (2011). Positive affect and college success. *Journal of Happiness Studies, 12*(4), 717–746. doi:10.1007/s10902-010-9224-8

Nickerson, R. S., & Adams, M. J. (1979). Long-term memory for a common object. *Cognitive Psychology, 11*, 287–307. doi:10.1016/0010-0285(79)90013-6

Nicoletti, A. (2009). Teens and drug facilitated sexual assault. *Journal of Pediatric & Adolescent Gynecology, 22*(3), 187.

Niedzwienska, A. (2004). Metamemory knowledge and the accuracy of flashbulb memories. *Memory, 12*(5), 603–613. doi:10.1080/09658210344000134

Niehaus, D. J. H., Stein, D. J., et al. (2005). A case of "Ifufunyane": A Xhosa culture-bound syndrome. *Journal of Psychiatric Practice, 11*(6), 411–413. doi:10.1097/00131746-200511000-00009

Niehaus, J. L., Cruz-Bermúdez, N. D., & Kauer, J. A. (2009). Plasticity of addiction: A mesolimbic dopamine short-circuit? *American Journal on Addictions, 18*(4), 259–271. doi:10.1080/10550490902925946

Nielsen, J. A., Zielinski, B. A., et al. (2013). An evaluation of the left-brain vs. right-brain hypothesis with resting state functional connectivity magnetic resonance imaging. *PLoS ONE, 8*(8), e71275. doi:10.1371/journal.pone.0071275

Nielsen, M., & Dissanayake, C. (2004). Pretend play, mirror self-recognition and imitation: A longitudinal investigation through the second year. *Infant Behavior & Development, 27*(3), 342–365. doi:10.1016/j.infbeh.2003.12.006

Niemiec, C. P., Ryan, R. M., & Deci, E. L. (2009). The path taken: Consequences of attaining intrinsic and extrinsic aspirations in post-college life. *Journal of Research in Personality, 43*(3), 291–306. doi:10.1016/j.jrp.2008.09.001

Nieuwoudt, J. E., Zhou, S., et al. (2012). Muscle dysmorphia: Current research and potential classification as a disorder. *Psychology of Sport & Exercise, 13*(5), 569–577. doi:10.1016/j.psychsport.2012.03.006

Nigbur, D., Lyons, E., & Uzzell, D. (2010). Attitudes, norms, identity and environmental behaviour: Using an expanded theory of planned behaviour to predict participation in a kerbside recycling programme. *British Journal of Social Psychology, 49*(2), 259–284.

Nijboer, T. W., & Jellema, T. (2012). Unequal impairment in the recognition of positive and negative emotions after right hemisphere lesions: A left hemisphere bias for happy faces. *Journal of Neuropsychology, 6*(1), 79–93. doi:10.1111/j.1748-6653.2011.02007.x

Nijstad, B. A., De Dreu, C. W., et al. (2010). The dual pathway to creativity model: Creative ideation as a function of flexibility and persistence. *European Review of Social Psychology, 21*(1), 34–77. doi:10.1080/10463281003765323

Nirenberg, S., & Pandarinath, C. (2012). Retinal prosthetic strategy with the capacity to restore normal vision. *Proceedings of the National Academy of Sciences, 109*(37), 15012–15017. doi:10.1073/pnas.1207035109

Nisbett, R. E. (2005). Heredity, environment, and race differences in IQ: A commentary on Rushton and Jensen. *Psychology, Public Policy, & Law, 11*(2), 302–310. doi:10.1037/1076-8971.11.2.302

Nisbett, R. E. (2009). *Intelligence and how to get it: Why schools and cultures count.* New York, NY: Norton.

Nisbett, R. E., & Miyamoto, Y. (2005). The influence of culture: Holistic versus analytic perception. *Trends in Cognitive Sciences, 9*(10), 467–473. doi:10.1016/j.tics.2005.08.004

Nisbett, R. E., & Wilson, T. D. (1977). Telling more than we can know: Verbal reports on mental processes. *Psychological Review, 84*(3), 231–259. doi:10.1037/0033-295X.84.3.231

Nisbett, R. E., Aronson, J., et al. (2012). Intelligence: New findings and theoretical developments. *American Psychologist, 67*(2), 130–159. doi:10.1037/a0026699

Niven, K., Sprigg, C. A., & Armitage, C. J. (2013). Does emotion regulation protect employees from the negative effects of workplace aggression? *European Journal of Work & Organizational Psychology, 22*(1), 88–106. doi:10.1080/13594 32X.2011.626200

Njeri, I. (1991, January 13). Beyond the melting pot. *Los Angeles Times*, E-1, E-8.

Noftle, E. E., & Flegeson, W. (2010). Age differences in Big Five behavior averages and variabilities across the adult life span: Moving beyond retrospective, global summary accounts of personality. *Psychology & Aging, 25*(1), 95–107. doi:10.1037/a0018199

Noland, J. S., Singer, L. T., et al. (2005). Prenatal drug exposure and selective attention in preschoolers. *Neurotoxicology & Teratology, 27*(3), 429–438. doi:10.1016/j.ntt.2005.02.001

Nolen-Hoeksema, S. (2020). *Abnormal psychology* (8th ed.). New York, NY: McGraw-Hill.

Nolet, K., Rouleau, J.-L., et al. (2016). How ego depletion affects sexual self-regulation: Is it more than resource depletion? *Journal of Sex Research, 53*(8), 994–1007. doi:10.1080/002244 99.2015.1096887

Noltemeyer, A., Bush, K., et al. (2012). The relationship among deficiency needs and growth needs: An empirical investigation of Maslow's theory. *Children & Youth Services Review, 34*(9), 1862–1867. doi:10.1016/j.childyouth.2012.05.021

Norenzayan, A., & Nisbett, R. E. (2000). Culture and causal cognition. *Current Directions in Psychological Science, 9*, 132–135. doi:10.1111/1467-8721.00077

Norlander, T., Bergman, H., & Archer, T. (1998). Effects of flotation rest on creative problem solving and originality. *Journal of Environmental Psychology, 18*(4), 399–408. doi:10.1006/jevp.1998.0112

Norlander, T., Bergman, H., & Archer, T. (1999). Primary process in competitive archery performance: Effects of flotation REST. *Journal of Applied Sport Psychology, 11*(2), 194–209. doi:10.1080/10413209908404200

Norman, D. A. (1994). *Things that make us smart.* Menlo Park, CA: Addison-Wesley.

Norman, P., Conner, M. T., & Stride, C. B. (2012). Reasons for binge drinking among undergraduate students: An application of behavioural reasoning theory. *British Journal of Health Psychology, 17*(4), 682–698. doi:10.1111/j.2044-8287.2012.02065.x

Norman, T. R. (2009). Melatonin: Hormone of the night. *Acta Neuropsychiatrica, 21*(5), 263–265. doi:10.1111/acn.2009.21.issue-510.1111/j.1601-5215.2009.00411.x

Northouse, P. G. (2016). *Leadership: Theory and practice* (7th ed.). Thousand Oaks, CA: Sage.

Nosek, B. A., Greenwald, A. G., & Banaji, M. R. (2005). Understanding and using the implicit association test: II. Method variables and construct validity. *Personality & Social Psychology Bulletin, 31*(2), 166–180. doi:10.1177/0146167204271418

Nosko, A., Tieu, T. T., et al. (2011). How do I love thee? Let me count the ways: Parenting during adolescence, attachment styles, and romantic narratives in emerging adulthood. *Developmental Psychology, 47*(3), 645–657.

Novella, E. J. (2010). Mental health care in the aftermath of deinstitutionalization: A retrospective and prospective view. *Health Care Analysis, 18*(3), 222–238. doi:10.1007/s10728-009-0138-8

Novelli, D., Drury, J., & Reicher, S. (2010). Come together: Two studies concerning the impact of group relations on 'personal space.' *British Journal of Social Psychology, 49*(2), 223–236.

Nucci, L. P., & Gingo, M. (2011). The development of moral reasoning. In U. Goswami (Ed.), *The development of moral reasoning* (pp. 420–444). London, UK: Wiley-Blackwell.

Nunes, K. L., Hermann, C. A., et al. (2013). Childhood sexual victimization, pedophilic interest, and sexual recidivism. *Child Abuse & Neglect, 37*(9), 703–711. doi:10.1016/j.chiabu.2013.01.008

O'Conner, T. G., Marvin, R. S., et al. (2003). Child–parent attachment following early institutional deprivation. *Development & Psychopathology, 15*(1), 19–38. doi:10.1017/S0954579403000026

O'Hare, A. E., Bremner, L., et al. (2009). A clinical assessment tool for advanced theory of mind performance in 5 to 12 year olds. *Journal of Autism & Developmental Disorders, 39*(6), 916–928. doi:10.1007/s10803-009-0699-2

O'Neal, C. W., Mallette, J. K., & Mancini, J. A. (2018). The importance of parents' community connections for adolescent well-being: An examination of military families. *American Journal of Community Psychology, 61*, 204–217. doi:10.1002/ajcp.12222

Oakley, D. A., & Halligan, P. W. (2010). Psychophysiological foundations of hypnosis and suggestion. In S. J. Lynn, J. W. Rhue, & I. Kirsch (Eds.), *Handbook of clinical hypnosis* (2nd ed., pp. 79–117). Washington, DC: American Psychological Association.

Oakley, D. A., Whitman, L. G., & Halligan, P. W. (2002). Hypnotic imagery as a treatment for phantom limb pain: Two case reports and a review. *Clinical Rehabilitation, 16*(4), 368–377. doi:10.1191/0269215502cr507oa

Oakley, R. (2004). How the mind hurts and heals the body. *American Psychologist, 59*(1), 29–40. doi:10.1037/0003-066X.59.1.29

Oates, J. M., & Reder, L. M. (2011). Memory for pictures: Sometimes a picture is not worth a single word. In A. S. Benjamin (Ed.), *Successful remembering and successful forgetting: A festschrift in honor of Robert A. Bjork* (pp. 447–461). New York, NY: Psychology Press.

Oberle, E. (2009). The development of Theory of Mind reasoning in Micronesian children. *Journal of Cognition & Culture, 9*(1–2), 39–56. doi:10.1163/156853709X414629

Oberman, L. M., & Ramachandran, V. S. (2015). The role of the mirror neuron system in the pathophysiology of autism spectrum disorder. In P. F. Ferrari & G. Rizzolatti (Eds.), *New frontiers in mirror neurons research* (pp. 380–396). New York: Oxford University Press. doi:10.1093/acprof:oso/9780199686155.003.0021

Odinot, G., Wolters, G., & van Giezen, A. (2013). Accuracy, confidence and consistency in repeated recall of events. *Psychology, Crime & Law, 19*(7), 629–642. doi:10.1080/1068316X.2012.660152

Oestergaard, S., & Møldrup, C. (2011). Optimal duration of combined psychotherapy and pharmacotherapy for patients with moderate and severe depression: A meta-analysis. *Journal of Affective Disorders, 131*(1–3), 24–36. doi:10.1016/j.jad.2010.08.014

Oexle, N., Ajdacic-Gross, V., et al. (2017). Mental illness stigma, secrecy and suicidal ideation. *Epidemiology & Psychiatric Sciences, 26*(1), 53–60. doi:10.1017/S2045796015001018

Ogden, C. L., Carroll, M. D., et al. (2010). Prevalence of high body mass index in U.S. children and adolescents, 2007–2008. *Journal of the American Medical Association, 303*(3), 242–249. doi:10.1001/jama.2009.2012

Ogrodniczuk, J. S., Piper, W. E., & Joyce, A. S. (2011). Effect of alexithymia on the process and outcome of psychotherapy: A programmatic review. *Psychiatry Research, 190*(1), 43–48. doi:10.1016/j.psychres.2010.04.026

Oishi, S., Kesebir, S., & Diener, E. (2011). Income inequality and happiness. *Psychological Science, 22*(9), 1095–1100. doi:10.1177/0956797611417262

Okiishi, J., Lambert, M. J., et al. (2003). Waiting for supershrink: An empirical analysis of therapist effects. *Clinical Psychology & Psychotherapy, 10*(6), 361–373. doi:10.1002/cpp.383

Olafsen, A. H., Halvari, H., et al. (2015). Show them the money? The role of pay, managerial need support, and justice in a self-determination theory model of intrinsic work motivation. *Scandinavian Journal of Psychology, 56*(4), 447–457. doi:10.1111/sjop.12211

Ollendick, T. H., & Muris, P. (2015). The scientific legacy of Little Hans and Little Albert: Future directions for research on specific phobias in youth. *Journal of Clinical Child & Adolescent Psychology, 44*(4), 689–706. doi:10.10 80/15374416.2015.1020543

Olpin, M., & Hesson, M. (2021). *Stress management for life: A research-based experiential approach* (5th ed.). Boston, MA: Cengage Learning.

Olshansky, M. P., Bar, R. J., et al. (2015). Supplementary motor area and primary auditory cortex activation in an expert break-dancer during the kinesthetic motor imagery of dance to music. *Neurocase, 21*(5), 607–617. doi:10.1080/1 3554794.2014.960428

Olson, M., & Hergenhahn, B. (2013). *Introduction to the theories of learning* (9th ed.). Englewood Cliffs, NJ: Prentice Hall.

Olsson, A., Nearing, K., & Phelps, E. A. (2007). Learning fears by observing others: The neural systems of social fear transmission. *Social Cognitive & Affective Neuroscience, 2*(1), 3–11. doi:10.1093/scan/nsm005

Olsson, E. M., El Alaoui, S., et al. (2010). Internet-based biofeedback-assisted relaxation training in the treatment of hypertension: A pilot study. *Applied Psychophysiology & Biofeedback, 35*(2), 163–170. doi:10.1007/s10484-009-9126-x

Ong, A. D., Zautra, A. J., & Reid, M. C. (2010). Psychological resilience predicts decreases in pain catastrophizing through positive emotions. *Psychology & Aging, 25*(3), 516–523. doi:10.1037/a0019384

Opland, D. M., Leinninger, G. M., & Myers, M. G., Jr. (2010). Modulation of the mesolimbic dopamine system by leptin. *Brain Research, 1350*, 65–70. doi:10.1016/j.brainres.2010.04.028

Oppliger, P. A. (2007). Effects of gender stereotyping on socialization. In R. W. Preiss, B. M. Gayle, et al. (Eds.), *Mass media effects research: Advances through meta-analysis* (pp. 199–214). Mahwah, NJ: Erlbaum.

Oral Cancer Foundation. (2019). *Oral cancer facts*. Retrieved April 18, 2020, from https://oralcancerfoundation.org/facts/

Oren, E. E., & Solomon, R. R. (2012). EMDR therapy: An overview of its development and mechanisms of action. *European Review of Applied Psychology, 62*(4), 197–203. doi:10.1016/j.erap.2012.08.005

Orenstein, P. (2011). *Cinderella ate my daughter*. New York, NY: HarperCollins.

Orleans, C. T., Gruman, J., & Hollendonner, J. K. (1999). Rating our progress in population health promotion: Report card on six behaviors. *American Journal of Health Promotion, 14*(2), 75–82. doi:10.4278/0890-1171-14.2.75

Ormrod, J. E. (2014). *Educational psychology: Developing learners* (8th ed.). Boston, MA: Allyn & Bacon.

Orr, A. C., & Hammig, S. B. (2009). Inclusive postsecondary strategies for teaching students with learning disabilities: A review of the literature. *Learning Disability Quarterly, 32*(3), 181–196.

Osgood, C. E. (1952). The nature and measurement of meaning. *Psychological Bulletin, 49*, 197–237. doi:10.1037/h0055737

Oskamp, S., & Schultz, P. W. (2005). *Attitudes and opinions* (3rd ed.). Mahwah, NJ: Erlbaum.

Ossorio, P. N. (2011). Myth and mystification: The science of race and IQ. In S. Krimsky & K. Sloan (Eds.), *Race and the genetic revolution: Science, myth, and culture* (pp. 173–194). New York, NY: Columbia University Press.

Oster, H. (2005). The repertoire of infant facial expressions: An ontogenetic perspective. In J. Nadel & D. Muir (Eds.), *Emotional development: Recent research advances* (pp. 261–292). New York, NY: Oxford University Press.

Otgaar, H., & Smeets, T. (2010). Adaptive memory: Survival processing increases both true and false memory in adults and children. *Journal of Experimental Psychology: Learning, Memory, & Cognition, 36*(4), 1010–1016. doi:10.1037/a0019402

Overmier, J. B., & LoLordo, V. M. (1998). Learned helplessness. In W. T. O'Donohue (Ed.), *Learning and behavior therapy* (pp. 352–373). Boston, MA: Allyn & Bacon.

Overson, C. E. (2014). Applying multimedia principles to slide shows for academic presentation. In V. A. Benassi, C. E. Overson, et al. (Eds.), *Applying science of learning in education: Infusing psychological science into the curriculum* (pp. 252–258). Society for the Teaching of Psychology.

Owens, J., & Massey, D. S. (2011). Stereotype threat and college academic performance: A latent variables approach. *Social Science Research, 40*(1), 150–166. doi:10.1016/j.ssresearch.2010.09.010

Oyserman, D., Bybee, D., et al. (2004). Possible selves as roadmaps. *Journal of Research in Personality, 38*(2), 130–149. doi:10.1016/S0092-6566(03)00057-6

Page, M., Taylor, J., & Blenkin, M. (2012). Context effects and observer bias—Implications for forensic odontology. *Journal of Forensic Sciences, 57*(1), 108–112. doi:10.1111/j.1556-4029.2011.01903.x

Pagel, J. F. (2012). The synchronous electrophysiology of conscious states. *Dreaming, 22*(3), 173–191.

Palmer, S. E., & Beck, D. M. (2007). The repetition discrimination task. An objective method for studying perceptual grouping. *Perception & Psychophysics, 69*(1), 68–78. doi:10.3758/BF03194454

Pan, Y., Storm, D. R., & Xia, Z. (2013). Role of adult neurogenesis in hippocampus-dependent memory, contextual fear extinction and remote contextual memory: New insights from ERK5 MAP kinase. *Neurobiology of Learning & Memory, 105*, 81–92. doi:10.1016/j.nlm.2013.07.011

Panksepp, J., & Pasqualini, M. S. (2005). The search for the fundamental brain/mind sources of affective experience. In J. Nadel & D. Muir (Eds.), *Emotional development: Recent research advances* (pp. 5–30). New York, NY: Oxford University Press.

Panksepp, J., & Watt, D. (2011). What is basic about basic emotions? Lasting lessons from affective neuroscience. *Emotion Review, 3*(4), 387–396. doi:10.1177/1754073911410741

Papanicolaou, A. C. (Ed.). (2006). *The amnesias: A clinical textbook of memory disorders*. New York, NY: Oxford University Press.

Paquette, S., & Heitzman, A. M. (2014). Job analysis. In R. H. Robinson (Ed.), *Foundations of forensic vocational rehabilitation* (pp. 145–166). New York: Springer.

Paradis, C. M., Solomon, L. Z., et al. (2004). Flashbulb memories of personal events of 9/11 and the day after for a sample of New York City residents. *Psychological Reports, 95*(1), 304–310. doi:10.2466/PR0.95.5.304-310

Park, E., Shipp, D. B., et al. (2011). Postlingually deaf adults of all ages derive equal benefits from unilateral multichannel cochlear implant. *Journal of the American Academy of Audiology, 22*(10), 637–643. doi:10.3766/jaaa.22.10.2

Park, H. J., Li, R. X., et al. (2009). Neural correlates of winning and losing while watching soccer matches. *International Journal of Neuroscience, 119*(1), 76–87. doi:10.1080/00207450802480069

Park, H., & Lennon, S. J. (2008). Beyond physical attractiveness: Interpersonal attraction as a function of similarities in personal characteristics. *Clothing & Textiles Research Journal, 26*(4), 275–289. doi:10.1177/0887302X07309714

Park, I., Lee, N., et al. (2012). Volumetric analysis of cerebellum in short-track speed skating players. *Cerebellum, 11*(4), 925–930. doi:10.1007/s12311-012-0366-6

Park, Y. S., Kim, B. K., et al. (2010). Acculturation, enculturation, parental adherence to Asian cultural values, parenting styles, and family conflict among Asian American college students. *Asian American Journal of Psychology, 1*(1), 67–79. doi:10.1037/a0018961

Parke, R. D. (2004). Development in the family. *Annual Review of Psychology, 55*, 365–399. doi:10.1146/annurev.psych.55.090902.141528

Parker, A., Ngu, H., & Cassaday, H. J. (2001). Odour and Proustian memory. *Applied Cognitive Psychology, 15*(2), 159–171.

Parker, E. S., Cahill, L., & McGaugh, J. L. (2006). A case of unusual autobiographical remembering. *Neurocase, 12*(1), 35–49. doi:10.1080/13554790500473680

Parker, P. D., & Salmela-Aro, K. (2011). Developmental processes in school burnout: A comparison of major developmental models. *Learning & Individual Differences, 21*, 244–248. doi:10.1016/j.lindif.2011.01.005

Parlade, M., Messinger, D. S., et al. (2009). Anticipatory smiling: Linking early affective communication and social outcome. *Infant Behavior & Development, 32*(1), 33–43. doi:10.1016/j.infbeh.2008.09.007

Pascual, A., Carpenter, C. J., et al. (2016). A meta-analysis of the effectiveness of the low-ball compliance-gaining procedure. *European Review of Applied Psychology, 66*(5), 261–267. doi:10.1016/j.erap.2016.06.004

Pascual, A., Guéguen, N., et al. (2013). Foot-in-the-door and problematic requests: A field experiment. *Social Influence, 8*(1), 46–53. doi:10.1080/15534510.2012.696038

Pashler, H., McDaniel, M., et al. (2008). Learning styles: Concepts and evidence. *Psychological Science in the Public Interest, 9*(3), 105–119. doi:10.1111/j.1539-6053.2009.01038.x. Epub 2008 Dec 1

Patall, E. A., Cooper, H., & Robinson, J. C. (2008). The effects of choice on intrinsic motivation and related outcomes: A meta-analysis of research findings. *Psychological Bulletin, 134*(2), 270–300. doi:10.1037/0033-2909.134.2.270

Paternoster, R., & Pogarsky, G. (2009). Rational choice, agency, and thoughtfully reflective decision making: The short and long-term consequences of making good choices. *Journal of Quantitative Criminology, 25*(2), 103–127.

Paton, S. (2013). Introducing Taylor to the knowledge economy. *Employee Relations, 35*(1), 20–38. doi:10.1108/01425451311279393

Paulson, G. W. (2012). *Closing the asylums: Causes and consequences of the deinstitutionalization movement*. Jefferson, NC: McFarland.

Paulsson, T., & Parker, A. (2006). The effects of a two-week reflection–intention training program on lucid dream recall. *Dreaming, 16*(1), 22–35. doi:10.1037/1053-0797.16.1.22

Pavlov, I. P. (1927). *Conditioned reflexes*. Translated by G. V. Anrep. New York, NY: Dover.

Payne, B. K., Krosnick, J. A., et al. (2010). Implicit and explicit prejudice in the 2008 American presidential election. *Journal of Experimental Social Psychology, 46*(2), 367–374.

Payne, K. (2009). Winning the battle of ideas: Propaganda, ideology, and terror. *Studies in Conflict & Terrorism, 32*(2), 109–128. doi:10.1080/10576100802627738

Payne, K., & Sheeran, P. (2018). Try to resist misinterpreting the Marshmallow Test. *Behavioral Scientist*. Retrieved July 21, 2020, from https://behavioralscientist.org/try-to-resist-misinterpreting-the-marshmallow-test/

Pearce, C. L., Conger, J. A., & Locke, E. A. (2007). Shared leadership theory. *Leadership Quarterly, 18*(3), 281–288.

Pearce, C. L., Manz, C. C., & Sims, H. P., Jr. (2009). Where do we go from here? Is shared leadership the key to team success? *Organizational Dynamics, 38*(3), 234–238.

Pedersen, A. F., Bovbjerg, D. H., & Zachariae, R. (2011). Stress and susceptibility to infectious disease. In R. J. Contrada & A. Baum (Eds.), *The handbook of stress science: Biology, psychology, and health* (pp. 425–445). New York, NY: Springer.

Pedraza, C., García, F. B., & Navarro, J. F. (2009). Neurotoxic effects induced by gammahydroxybutyric acid (GHB) in male rats. *International Journal of Neuropsychopharmacology, 12*(9), 1165–1177. doi:10.1017/S1461145709000157

Peek, F., & Hanson, L. L. (2007). *The life and message of the real Rain Man: The journey of a mega-savant*. Port Chester, NY: Dude Publishing.

Peira, N., Fredrikson, M., & Pourtois, G. (2014). Controlling the emotional heart: Heart rate biofeedback improves cardiac control during emotional reactions. *International Journal of Psychophysiology, 91*(3), 225–231. doi:10.1016/j.ijpsycho.2013.12.008

Pelletier, L. G., Baxter, D., & Huta, V. (2011). Personal autonomy and environmental sustainability. In V. I. Chirkov, R. N. Ryan, et al. (Eds.), *Human autonomy in cross-cultural context: Perspectives on the psychology of agency, freedom, and well-being* (pp. 257–278). New York, NY: Springer.

Pelton, T. (1983). The shootists. *Science, 83*(4), 84–86.

Pemment, J. (2013). The neurobiology of antisocial personality disorder: The quest for rehabilitation and treatment. *Aggression & Violent Behavior, 18*(1), 79–82. doi:10.1016/j.avb.2012.10.004

Penfield, W. (1957). Brain's record of past a continuous movie film. *Science News Letter, April 27*, 265.

Penfield, W. (1958). *The excitable cortex in conscious man*. Springfield, IL: Charles C Thomas.

Pennebaker, J. W. (2004). *Writing to heal: A guided journal for recovering from trauma and emotional upheaval*. Oakland, CA: New Harbinger Press.

Pennebaker, J. W., & Chung, C. K. (2007). Expressive writing, emotional upheavals, and health. In H. S. Friedman & R. C. Silver (Eds.), *Foundations of health psychology* (pp. 263–284). New York, NY: Oxford University Press.

Peoples, C. D., Sigillo, A. E., et al. (2012). Friendship and conformity in group opinions: Juror verdict change in mock juries. *Sociological Spectrum, 32*(2), 178–193. doi:10.1080/02732173.2012.646163

Peplau, L. A. (2003). Human sexuality: How do men and women differ? *Current Directions in Psychological Science, 12*(2), 37–40.

Pepperberg, I. M. (2017). Animal language studies: What happened? *Psychonomic Bulletin & Review, 24*(1), 181–185. doi:10.3758/s13423-016-1101-y

Pereira, G. M., & Osburn, H. G. (2007). Effects of participation in decision making on performance and employee attitudes: A quality circles meta-analysis. *Journal of Business & Psychology, 22*(2), 145–153. doi:10.1007/s10869-007-9055-8

Pereira, M., Estramiana, J., & Gallo, I. (2010). Essentialism and the expression of social stereotypes: A comparative study of Spain, Brazil and England. *Spanish Journal of Psychology, 13*(2), 808–817.

Perloff, R. M. (2010). *The dynamics of persuasion: Communication and attitudes in the 21st century*. New York, NY: Psychology Press.

Perls, F. (1969). *Gestalt therapy verbatim*. Lafayette, CA: Real People Press.

Perry, G. (2013). *Behind the shock machine: The untold story of the notorious Milgram psychology experiments*. New York, NY: New Press.

Perry, J. L., Joseph, J. E., et al. (2011). Prefrontal cortex and drug abuse vulnerability: Translation to prevention and treatment interventions. *Brain Research Reviews, 65*, 124–149. doi:10.1016/j.brainresrev.2010.09.001

Perry, J., Fowler, J., & Howe, A. (2008). Subject and interviewer determinants of the adequacy of the dynamic interview. *Journal of Nervous & Mental Disease, 196*(8), 612–619. doi:10.1097/NMD.0b013e318181327f

Perry, R. P. (2003). Perceived (academic) control and causal thinking in achievement settings. *Canadian Psychology, 44*(4), 312–331. doi:10.1037/h0086956

Pérusse, F., Boucher, S., & Fernet, M. (2012). Observation of couple interactions: Alexithymia and communication behaviors. *Personality & Individual Differences, 53*(8), 1017–1022. doi:10.1016/j.paid.2012.07.022

Pesant, N., & Zadra, A. (2006). Dream content and psychological well-being: A longitudinal study of the continuity hypothesis. *Journal of Clinical Psychology, 62*(1), 111–121. doi:10.1002/jclp.20212

Pescatello, L. S. (2001). Exercising for health. *Western Journal of Medicine, 174*(2), 114–118.

Peters, M. L., Meevissen, Y. M., & Hanssen, M. M. (2013). Specificity of the best possible self intervention for increasing optimism: Comparison with a gratitude intervention. *Terapia Psicologica, 31*, 93–100.

Peters, W. A. (1971). *A class divided*. Garden City, NY: Doubleday.

Peterson, B. E., Pratt, M. W., et al. (2016). The authoritarian personality in emerging adulthood: Longitudinal analysis using standardized scales, observer ratings, and content coding of the life story. *Journal of Personality, 84*(2), 225–236. doi:10.1111/jopy.12154

Peterson, C., & Chang, E. C. (2003). Optimism and flourishing. In C. Keyes & J. Haidt (Eds.), *Flourishing: Positive psychology and the life well-lived* (pp. 55–79). Washington, DC: American Psychological Association. doi:10.1037/10594-003

Peterson, C., & Park, N. (2010). What happened to self-actualization? Commentary on Kenrick et al. (2010). *Perspectives on Psychological Science, 5*(3), 320–322. doi:10.1177/1745691610369471

Peterson, C., & Seligman, M. E. P. (2004). *Character strengths and virtues*. Washington, DC: American Psychological Association.

Peterson, C., & Vaidya, R. S. (2001). Explanatory style, expectations, and depressive symptoms. *Personality & Individual Differences, 31*(7), 1217–1223. doi:10.1016/S0191-8869(00)00221-X

Peterson, C., Semmel, A., et al. (1982). The attributional style questionnaire. *Cognitive Therapy & Research, 6*, 287–299. doi:10.1007/BF01173577

Peterson, L. R., & Peterson, M. J. (1959). Short-term retention of individual verbal items. *Journal of Experimental Psychology, 58*, 193–198. doi:10.1037/h0049234

Petri, H. L., & Govern, J. M. (2013). *Motivation: Theory, research, and application* (6th ed.). Boston, MA: Cengage Learning.

Petrovsky, N., Ettinger, U., et al. (2014). Sleep deprivation disrupts prepulse inhibition and induces psychosis-like symptoms in healthy humans. *Journal of Neuroscience, 34*(27), 9134–9140. doi:10.1523/JNEUROSCI.0904-14.204

Pett, M. A., & Johnson, M. J. M. (2005). Development and psychometric evaluation of the Revised University Student Hassles Scale. *Educational & Psychological Measurement, 65*(6), 984–1010. doi:10.1177/0013164405275661

Petticrew, M. P., Lee, K., & McKee, M. (2012). Type A behavior pattern and coronary heart disease: Philip Morris's "crown jewel." *American Journal of Public Health, 102*(11), 2018–2025. doi:10.2105/AJPH.2012.300816

Pettigrew, T. F. (2016). In pursuit of three theories: Authoritarianism, relative deprivation, and intergroup contact. *Annual Review of Psychology, 67*, 1–21. doi:10.1146/annurev-psych-122414-033327

Peverly, S. T., Brobst, K. E., et al. (2003). College adults are not good at self-regulation. *Journal of Educational Psychology, 95*(2), 335–346. doi:10.1037/0022-0663.95.2.335

Pezdek, K., Avila-Mora, E., & Sperry, K. (2010). Does trial presentation medium matter in jury simulation research? Evaluating the effectiveness of eyewitness expert testimony. *Applied Cognitive Psychology, 24*(5), 673–690.

Philippe, F. L., Koestner, R., & Lekes, N. (2013). On the directive function of episodic memories in people's lives: A look at romantic relationships. *Journal of Personality & Social Psychology, 104*(1), 164–179. doi:10.1037/a0030384

Phillips, D. A., & Lowenstein, A. E. (2011). Early care, education, and child development. *Annual Review of Psychology, 62*, 483–500. doi:10.1146/annurev.psych.031809.130707

Phillips, J., Sharpe, L., et al. (2010). Subtypes of postnatal depression? A comparison of women with recurrent and de novo postnatal depression. *Journal of Affective Disorders, 120*(1–3), 67–75.

Phillips, K. M., Jim, H. L., et al. (2012). Effects of self-directed stress management training and home-based exercise on stress management skills in cancer patients receiving chemotherapy. *Stress & Health, 28*(5), 368–375. doi:10.1002/smi.2450

Phillips, K. W., Rothbard, N. P., & Dumas, T. L. (2009). To disclose or not to disclose? Status distance and self-disclosure in diverse environments. *Academy of Management Review, 34*(4), 710–732.

Piaget, J. (1951, original French, 1945). *The psychology of intelligence*. New York, NY: Norton.

Piaget, J. (1952). *The origins of intelligence in children*. New York, NY: International University Press.

Pierrehumbert, B., Ramstein, T., et al. (2002). Quality of child care in the preschool years. *International Journal of Behavioral Development, 26*(5), 385–396. doi:10.1080/01650250143000265

Pilgrim, D. (2011). The hegemony of cognitive-behaviour therapy in modern mental health care. *Health Sociology Review, 20*(2), 120–132.

Piliavin, I. M., Rodin, J., & Piliavin, J. A. (1969). Good Samaritanism: An underground phenomenon? *Journal of Personality & Social Psychology, 13*, 289–299. doi:10.1037/h0028433

Piliavin, J. A., & Siegl, E. (2015). Health and well-being consequences of formal volunteering. In D. A. Schroeder & W. G. Graziano (Eds.), *The Oxford handbook of prosocial behavior* (pp. 494–523). New York: Oxford University Press.

Pinel, J. P., Assanand, S., & Lehman, D. R. (2000). Hunger, eating, and ill health. *American Psychologist, 55*(10), 1105–1116. doi:10.1037//0003-066X.55.10.1105

Pinel, P., & Dehaene, S. (2010). Beyond hemispheric dominance: Brain regions underlying the joint lateralization of language and arithmetic to the left hemisphere. *Journal of Cognitive Neuroscience, 22*(1), 48–66. doi:10.1162/jocn.2009.21184

Pinker, S. (2011). *The better angels of our nature: Why violence has declined*. New York, NY: Viking.

Pinker, S., & Jackendoff, R. (2005). The faculty of language: What's special about it? *Cognition, 95*(2), 201–236. doi:10.1016/j.cognition.2004.08.004

Piomelli, D. (2014). More surprises lying ahead: The endocannabinoids keep us guessing. *Neuropharmacology, 76*(Part B), 228–234.

Piper, A., Jr. (2008). Multiple personality disorder: Witchcraft survives in the twentieth century. In S. O. Lilienfeld, J. Ruscio, & S. J. Lynn (Eds.), *Navigating the mindfield: A user's guide to distinguishing science from pseudoscience in mental health* (pp. 249–268). Amherst, NY: Prometheus Books.

Pirson, M., Ie, A., & Langer, E. (2012). Seeing what we know, knowing what we see: Challenging the limits of visual acuity. *Journal of Adult Development, 19*(2), 59–65.

Pivtoraiko, M., Mellinger, D., & Kumar, V. (2013). Quadrotor maneuver generation using motion primitives. *Proceedings of the IEEE International Conference on Robotics and Automation*, Karlsruhe, Germany.

Plakun, E. (2012). Treatment resistance and psychodynamic psychiatry. Concepts psychiatry needs from psychoanalysis. *Psychodynamic Psychiatry, 40*(2), 183–209. doi:10.1521/pdps.2012.40.2.183

Plassmann, H., O'Doherty, J., et al. (2008). Marketing actions can modulate neural representations of experienced pleasantness. *Proceedings of the National Academy of Sciences, 105*(3), 1050–1054. doi:10.1073/pnas.0706929105

Plaze, M., Paillère-Martinot, M., et al. (2011). Where do auditory hallucinations come from? A brain morphometry study of schizophrenia patients with inner or outer space hallucinations. *Schizophrenia Bulletin, 37*(1), 212–221. doi:10.1093/schbul/sbp081

Plazzi, G., Vetrugno, R., et al. (2005). Sleepwalking and other ambulatory behaviours during sleep. *Neurological Sciences, 26*(Suppl. 3), s193–s198. doi:10.1007/s10072-005-0486-6

Pliner, P., & Mann, N. (2004). Influence of social norms and palatability on amount consumed and food choice. *Appetite, 42*(2), 227–237. doi:10.1016/j.appet.2003.12.001

Plomin, R., & Deary, I. J. (2015). Genetics and intelligence differences: Five special findings. *Molecular Psychiatry, 20*(1), 98–108. doi:10.1038/mp.2014.105

Plötner, M., Over, H., et al. (2015). Young children show the bystander effect in helping situations. *Psychological Science, 26*(4), 499–506. doi:10.1177/0956797615569579

Plous, S. (2003). *Understanding prejudice and discrimination*. New York, NY: McGraw-Hill.

Plutchik, R. (2003). *Emotions and life*. Washington, DC: American Psychological Association.

Pokorny, S. B., Jason, L. A., & Schoeny, M. E. (2003). The relation of retail tobacco availability to initiation and continued smoking. *Journal of Clinical Child & Adolescent Psychology, 32*, 193–204. doi:10.1207/S15374424JCCP3202_4

Poland, J., & Caplan, P. J. (2004). The deep structure of bias in psychiatric diagnosis. In P. J. Caplan & L. Cosgrove (Eds.), *Bias in psychiatric diagnosis. A project of the association for women in psychology* (pp. 9–23). Lanham, MD: Jason Aronson.

Polit, D. F., & Beck, C. (2013). Is there still gender bias in nursing research? An update. *Research In Nursing & Health, 36*(1), 75–83. doi:10.1002/nur.21514

Polivy, J., & Herman, C. P. (2002). Causes of eating disorders. *Annual Review of Psychology, 53*, 187–213. doi:10.1146/annurev.psych.53.100901.135103

Pollard, S., & Cooper-Thomas, H. D. (2015). Best practice recommendations for situational judgment tests. *Australasian Journal of Organisational Psychology, 8*, Article e7. doi:10.1017/orp.2015.6

Polusny, M. A., Ries, B. J., et al. (2011). Effects of parents' experiential avoidance and PTSD on adolescent disaster-related posttraumatic stress symptomatology. *Journal of Family Psychology, 25*(2), 220–229. doi:10.1037/a0022945

Pomaki, G., Supeli, A., & Verhoeven, C. (2007). Role conflict and health behaviors: Moderating effects on psychological distress and somatic complaints. *Psychology & Health, 22*(3), 317–335. doi:10.1080/14768320600774561

Popma, A., Vermeiren, R., et al. (2007). Cortisol moderates the relationship between testosterone and aggression in delinquent male adolescents. *Biological Psychiatry, 61*(3), 405–411. doi:10.1016/j.biopsych.2006.06.006

Portugal, E., Cevada, T., et al. (2013). Neuroscience of exercise: From neurobiology mechanisms to mental health. *Neuropsychobiology, 68*(1), 1–14.

Post, J. M. (2011). Crimes of obedience: "Groupthink" at Abu Ghraib. *International Journal of Group Psychotherapy, 61*(1), 49–66. doi:10.1521/ijgp.2011.61.1.48

Post, L. M., Feeny, N. C., et al. (2015). Posttraumatic stress disorder and depression co-occurrence: Structural relations among disorder constructs and trait and symptom dimensions. *Psychology & Psychotherapy: Theory, Research & Practice.* Advance online publication. doi:10.1111/papt.12087

Powell, M. D., & Ladd, L. D. (2010). Bullying: A review of the literature and implications for family therapists. *American Journal of Family Therapy, 38*(3), 189–206. doi:10.1080/01926180902961662

Powell, R. A., Honey, P. L., & Symbaluk, D. G. (2017). *Introduction to learning and behavior* (5th ed.). Boston, MA: Cengage Learning.

Power, M. (2010). *Emotion-focused cognitive therapy.* New York, NY: Wiley/Blackwell.

Prat-Sala, M., & Redford, P. (2012). Writing essays: Does self-efficacy matter? The relationship between self-efficacy in reading and in writing and undergraduate students' performance in essay writing. *Educational Psychology, 32*(1), 9–20. doi:10.1080/01443410.2011.621411

Prause, N. (2012). Theoretical, statistical and construct problems perpetuated in the study of female orgasm. *Sexual & Relationship Therapy, 27*(3), 260–271. doi:10.1080/14681994.2012.732262

Preckel, F., Holling, H., & Wiese, M. (2006). Relationship of intelligence and creativity in gifted and non-gifted students: An investigation of threshold theory. *Personality & Individual Differences, 40*(1), 159–170. doi:10.1016/j.paid.2005.06.022

Price, D. D., Finniss, D. G., & Benedetti. F. (2008). A comprehensive review of the placebo effect: Recent advances and current thought. *Annual Review of Psychology, 59*, 565–590. doi:10.1146/annurev.psych.59.113006.095941

Price, J., & Davis, B. (2009). *The woman who can't forget: The extraordinary story of living with the most remarkable memory known to science—A memoir.* New York, NY: Simon & Schuster.

Prichard, E., Propper, R. E., & Christman, S. D. (2013). Degree of handedness, but not direction, is a systematic predictor of cognitive performance. *Frontiers in Psychology, 4, 9.*

Prime, D. J., & Jolicoeur, P. (2010). Mental rotation requires visual short-term memory: Evidence from human electric cortical activity. *Journal of Cognitive Neuroscience, 22*(11), 2437–2446. doi:10.1162/jocn.2009.21337

Prochaska, J. O., & Norcross, J. C. (2014). *Systems of psychotherapy: A transtheoretical analysis* (8th ed.). Boston, MA: Cengage Learning.

Prochnow, D. D., Höing, B. B., et al. (2013). The neural correlates of affect reading: An fMRI study on faces and gestures. *Behavioural Brain Research, 237*, 270–277. doi:10.1016/j.bbr.2012.08.050.

Prodan, C. I., Orbelo, D. M., & Ross, E. D. (2007). Processing of facial blends of emotion: Support for right hemisphere cognitive aging. *Cortex, 43*(2), 196–206. doi:10.1016/S0010-9452(08)70475-1

Prokhorov, A. V., Kelder, S. H., et al. (2010). Project aspire: An interactive, multimedia smoking prevention and cessation curriculum for culturally diverse high school students. *Substance Use & Misuse, 45*(6), 983–1006. doi:10.3109/10826080903038050

Pruessner, M., Cullen, A. E., et al. (2017). The neural diathesis-stress model of schizophrenia revisited: An update on recent findings considering illness stage and neurobiological and methodological complexities. *Neuroscience & Biobehavioral Reviews, 73*, 191–218. doi:10.1016/j. neubiorev.2016.12.013

Prus, A. (2017). *Drugs and the neuroscience of behavior: An introduction to psychopharmacology* (2nd ed.). Boston, MA: Cengage Learning.

Przybylski, A. K., Weinstein, N., et al. (2012). The ideal self at play: The appeal of video games that let you be all you can be. *Psychological Science, 23*(1), 69–76. doi:10.1177/0956797611418676

Przepiorka, A., Błachnio, A., & Díaz-Morales, J. F. (2016). Problematic Facebook use and procrastination. *Computers in Human Behavior, 65*, 59–64. doi:10.1016/j.chb.2016.08.022

Puente, R., & Anshel, M. H. (2010). Exercisers' perceptions of their fitness instructor's interacting style, perceived competence, and autonomy as a function of self-determined regulation to exercise, enjoyment, affect, and exercise frequency. *Scandinavian Journal of Psychology, 51*(1), 38–45.

Putwain, D. W., & Aveyard, B. (2016, November 10). Is perceived control a critical factor in understanding the negative relationship between cognitive test anxiety and examination performance? *School Psychology Quarterly*, n.p. doi:10.1037/spq0000183

Pychyl, T. A. (2013). *Solving the procrastination puzzle: A concise guide to strategies for change.* New York, NY: Tarcher/Penguin.

Quednow, B. B., Jessen, F., et al. (2006). Memory deficits in abstinent MDMA (ecstasy) users: Neuropsychological evidence of frontal dysfunction. *Journal of Psychopharmacology, 20*(3), 373–384. doi:10.1177/0269881106061200

Quigley, B. M., & Leonard, K. E. (2000). Alcohol, drugs, and violence. In V. B. Van Hasselt & M. Hersen (Eds.), *Aggression and violence: An introductory text.* Boston, MA: Allyn & Bacon.

Quinn, P. C., Bhatt, R. S., & Hayden, A. (2008). Young infants readily use proximity to organize visual pattern information. *Acta Psychologica, 127*(2), 289–298. doi:10.1016/j.actpsy.2007.06.002

Raag, T., & Rackliff, C. L. (1998). Preschoolers' awareness of social expectations of gender: Relationships to toy choices. *Sex Roles, 38*(9–10), 685–700.

Rabinak, C. A., Angstadt, M., et al. (2013). Cannabinoid facilitation of fear extinction memory recall in humans. *Neuropharmacology, 64*, 396–402. doi:10.1016/j.neuropharm.2012.06.063

Rabius, V., Wiatrek, D., & McAlister, A. L. (2012). African American participation and success in telephone counseling for smoking cessation. *Nicotine & Tobacco Research, 14*(2), 240–242. doi:10.1093/ntr/ntr129

Rachman, S. (2013). *Anxiety* (3rd. ed.). New York, NY: Routledge.

Radermacher, A., & Walia, G. (2013, March). Gaps between industry expectations and the abilities of graduates. In *Proceedings of the 44th ACM technical symposium on computer science education* (pp. 525–530). Retrieved July 21, 2020, from http://dl.acm.org/citation.cfm?id=2445351

Radvansky, G. A. (2017). *Human memory* (3rd ed.). Boston, MA: Pearson/Allyn & Bacon.

Raes, E., Decuyper, S., et al. (2013). Facilitating team learning through transformational leadership. *Instructional Science, 41*(2), 287–305. doi:10.1007/s11251-012-9228-3

Raffin, E., Richard, N., et al. (2016). Primary motor cortex changes after amputation correlate with phantom limb pain and the ability to move the phantom limb. *NeuroImage, 130*, 134–144. doi:10.1016/j.neuroimage. 2016.01.063

Ralston, A. (2004). *Between a rock and a hard place.* New York, NY: Atria Books.

Ramachandran, V. S. (1995). 2-D or not 2-D—that is the question. In R. Gregory, J. Harris, P. Heard, & D. Rose (Eds.), *The artful eye* (pp. 249–267). Oxford, UK: Oxford University Press.

Raman, R., & Sarkar, S. (2016). Predictive coding: A possible explanation of filling-in at the blind spot. *PLoS ONE, 11*(3), Article e0151194.

Range, F., Möslinger, H., & Virányi, Z. (2012). Domestication has not affected the understanding of means-end connections in dogs. *Animal Cognition, 15*(4), 597–607. doi:10.1007/s10071-012-0488-8

Rantanen, J., Metsäpelto, R. L., et al. (2007). Long-term stability in the Big Five personality traits in adulthood. *Scandinavian Journal of Psychology, 48*(6), 511–518. doi:10.1111/j.1467-9450.2007.00609.x

Raphael-Leff, J. (2012). "Terrible twos" and "terrible teens": The importance of play. *Journal of Infant, Child & Adolescent Psychotherapy, 11*(4), 299–315. doi:10.1080/15289168.2012.732841

Raposo, A., Han, S., & Dobbins, I. G. (2009). Ventrolateral prefrontal cortex and self-initiated semantic elaboration during memory retrieval. *Neuropsychologia, 47*(11), 2261–2271. doi:10.1016/j.neuropsychologia.2008.10.024

Rasmussen, S. A., Eisen, J. L., & Greenberg, B. D. (2013). Toward a neuroanatomy of obsessive-compulsive disorder revisited. *Biological Psychiatry, 73*(4), 298–299. doi:10.1016/j.biopsych.2012.12.010

Rathus, R., Nevid, J., & Fichner-Rathus, L. (2013). *Human sexuality in a world of diversity* (9th ed.). Boston, MA: Allyn & Bacon.

Rathus, S. A. (2014). *Childhood and adolescence: Voyages in development* (5th ed.). Boston, MA: Cengage Learning.

Ray, S. L., Wong, C., et al. (2013). Compassion satisfaction, compassion fatigue, work life conditions, and burnout among frontline mental health care professionals. *Traumatology, 19*(4), 255–267. doi:10.1177/1534765612471144

Raymo, J. M., Warren, J. R., et al. (2010). Later-life employment preferences and outcomes: The role of midlife work experiences. *Research on Aging, 32*(4), 419–466.

Raymond, D., & Noggle, C. (2013). *Clinical neuropsychology: Biological and cognitive foundations for evaluation and rehabilitation.* New York, NY: Springer.

Raz, M. (2013). *The lobotomy letters: The making of American psychosurgery.* Rochester: University of Rochester Press.

Reason, J. (2000). The Freudian slip revisited. *The Psychologist, 13*(12), 610–611.

Reed, J. D., & Bruce, D. (1982). Longitudinal tracking of difficult memory retrievals. *Cognitive Psychology, 14*, 280–300. doi:10.1016/0010-0285(82)90011-1

Reed, S. K. (2013). *Cognition: Theory and applications* (9th ed.). Boston, MA: Cengage Learning.

Regan, P. C., Levin, L., et al. (2000). Partner preferences: What characteristics do men and women desire in their short-term sexual and long-term romantic partners? *Journal of Psychology & Human Sexuality, 12*(3), 1–21. doi:10.1300/J056v12n03_01

Reger, G. M., Koenen-Woods, P., et al. (2016). Randomized controlled trial of prolonged exposure using imaginal exposure vs. virtual reality exposure in active duty soldiers with deployment-related posttraumatic stress disorder (PTSD). *Journal of Consulting & Clinical Psychology, 84*(11), 946–959. doi:10.1037/ccp0000134

Regev, L. G., Zeiss, A., & Zeiss, R. (2006). Orgasmic disorders. In J. E. Fisher & W. T. O'Donohue (Eds.), *Practitioner's guide to evidence-based psychotherapy* (pp. 469–477). New York, NY: Springer Science.

Regnerus, M., & Uecker, J. (2011). *Premarital sex in America: How young Americans meet, mate, and think about marrying.* New York, NY: Oxford University Press.

Regoeczi, W. C. (2008). Crowding in context: An examination of the differential responses of men and women to high-density living environments. *Journal of*

Health & Social Behavior, 49(3), 254–268. doi:10.1177/002214650804900302

Reid, M. R., Mackinnon, L. T., & Drummond, P. D. (2001). The effects of stress management on symptoms of upper respiratory tract infection, secretory immunoglobulin A, and mood in young adults. *Journal of Psychosomatic Research, 51*(6), 721–728. doi:10.1016/S0022-3999(01)00234-3

Reid, R. C., Carpenter, B. N., et al. (2012). Report of findings in a *DSM-5* field trial for hypersexual disorder. *Journal of Sexual Medicine, 9*(11), 2868–2877. doi:10.1111/j.1743-6109.2012.02936.x

Reiff, S., Katkin, E. S., & Friedman, R. (1999). Classical conditioning of the human blood pressure response. *International Journal of Psychophysiology, 34*(2), 135–145. doi:10.1016/S0167-8760(99)00071-9

Reifman, A. S., Larrick, R. P., & Fein, S. (1991). Temper and temperature on the diamond: The heat-aggression relationship in major league baseball. *Personality & Social Psychology Bulletin, 17*(5), 580–585. doi:10.1177/0146167291175013

Reijntjes, A., Kamphuis, J. H., et al. (2013a). Too calloused to care: An experimental examination of factors influencing youths' displaced aggression against their peers. *Journal of Experimental Psychology: General, 142*(1), 28–33. doi:10.1037/a0028619

Reijntjes, A., Thomaes, S., et al. (2013b). Youths' displaced aggression against in- and out-group peers: An experimental examination. *Journal of Experimental Child Psychology, 115*(1), 180–187. doi:10.1016/j.jecp.2012.11.010

Reinberg, A., & Ashkenazi, I. (2008). Internal desynchronization of circadian rhythms and tolerance to shift work. *Chronobiology International, 25*(4), 625–643. doi:10.1080/07420520802256101

Reis, H. T., Maniaci, M. R., et al. (2011). Familiarity does indeed promote attraction in live interaction. *Journal of Personality & Social Psychology, 101*(3), 557–570. doi:10.1037/a0022885

Reis, S. M. (Ed.). (2016). *Reflections on gifted education: Critical works by Joseph S. Renzulli and colleagues*. Waco, TX: Prufrock Press.

Reis, S. M., & Renzulli, J. S. (2010). Is there still a need for gifted education? An examination of current research. *Learning & Individual Differences, 20*(4), 308–317. doi:10.1016/j.lindif.2009.10.012

Reisner, A. D. (2006). A case of Munchausen syndrome by proxy with subsequent stalking behavior. *International Journal of Offender Therapy & Comparative Criminology, 50*(3), 245–254. doi:10.1177/0306624X05281880

Reiss, S., & Havercamp, S. M. (2005). Motivation in developmental context: A new method for studying self-actualization. *Journal of Humanistic Psychology, 45*(1), 41–53. doi:10.1177/0022167804269133

Reivich, K., Gillham, J. E., et al. (2013). From helplessness to optimism: The role of resilience in treating and preventing depression in youth. In S. Goldstein & R. B. Brooks (Eds.), *Handbook of resilience in children* (2nd ed., pp. 201–214). New York, NY: Springer. doi:10.1007/978-1-4614-3661-4_12

Reker, M., Ohrmann, P., et al. (2010). Individual differences in alexithymia and brain response to masked emotion faces. *Cortex, 46*(5), 658–667. doi:10.1016/j.cortex.2009.05.008

Remland, M. S., Jones, T. S., & Brinkman, H. (1991). Proxemic and haptic behavior in three European countries. *Journal of Nonverbal Behavior, 15*(4), 215–232.

Rescorla, R. A. (1987). A Pavlovian analysis of goal-directed behavior. *American Psychologist, 42*, 119–129. doi:10.1037/0003-066X.42.2.119

Rescorla, R. A. (2004). Spontaneous recovery. *Learning & Memory, 11*(5), 501–509. doi:10.1101/lm.77504

Resnick, B. (2017). Brain activity is too complicated for humans to decipher: Machines can decode it for us. Retrieved February 21, 2020, from www.vox.com/science-and-health/2016/12/29/13967966/machine-learning-neuroscience

Restak, R. M. (2001). *The secret life of the brain*. New York, NY: Dana Press.

Revillo, D. A., Paglini, M. G., et al. (2014). Spontaneous recovery from extinction in the infant rat. *Behavioural Brain Research, 274*, 149– 157. doi:10.1016/j.bbr.2014.08.009

Revonsuo, A., Kallio, S., & Sikka, P. (2009). What is an altered state of consciousness? *Philosophical Psychology, 22*(2), 187–204. doi:10.1080/09515080902802850

Reynald, D. M., & Elffers, H. (2009). The future of Newman's defensible space theory: Linking defensible space and the routine activities of place. *European Journal of Criminology, 6*(1), 25–46. doi:10.1177/1477370808098103

Rhee, S. H., & Waldman, I. D. (2011). Genetic and environmental influences on aggression. In P. R. Shaver & M. Mikulincer (Eds.), *Human aggression and violence: Causes, manifestations, and consequences* (pp. 143–163). Washington, DC: American Psychological Association.

Ribeiro, A. C., LeSauter, J., et al. (2009). Relationship of arousal to circadian anticipatory behavior: Ventromedial hypothalamus: One node in a hunger arousal network. *European Journal of Neuroscience, 30*(9), 1730–1738. doi:10.1111/j.1460-9568.2009.06969.x

Rice, K. G., Richardson, C. E., & Clark, D. (2012). Perfectionism, procrastination, and psychological distress. *Journal of Counseling Psychology, 59*(2), 288–302. doi:10.1037/a0026643

Rice, L., & Markey, P. M. (2009). The role of extraversion and neuroticism in influencing anxiety following computer-mediated interactions. *Personality & Individual Differences, 46*(1), 35–39. doi:10.1016/j.paid.2008.08.022

Richardson, K. (2013). The eclipse of heritability and the foundations of intelligence. *New Ideas in Psychology, 31*(2), 122–129. doi:10.1016/j.newideapsych.2012.08.002

Richeson, J. A., & Sommers, S. R. (2016). Toward a social psychology of race and race relations for the twenty-first century. *Annual Review of Psychology, 67*, 439–463. doi:10.1146/annurev-psych-010213-115115

Ridenour, T. A., Maldonado-Molina, M., et al. (2005). Factors associated with the transition from abuse to dependence among substance abusers: Implications for a measure of addictive liability. *Drug & Alcohol Dependence, 80*(1), 1–14.

Rideout, V. (2015). *The common sense census: Media use by tweens and teens*. Retrieved July 21, 2020, from www.commonsensemedia.org/sites/default/files/uploads/research/census_researchreport.pdf

Riela, S., Rodriguez, G., et al. (2010). Experiences of falling in love: Investigating culture, ethnicity, gender, and speed. *Journal of Social & Personal Relationships, 27*(4), 473–493. doi:10.1177/0265407510363508

Rigakos, G. S., Davis, R. C., et al. (2009). Soft targets? A national survey of the preparedness of large retail malls to prevent and respond to terrorist attack after 9/11. *Security Journal, 22*(4), 286–301. doi:10.1057/palgrave.sj.8350084

Righetti, F., Rusbult, C., & Finkenauer, C. (2010). Regulatory focus and the Michelangelo phenomenon: How close partners promote one another's ideal selves. *Journal of Experimental Social Psychology, 46*(6), 972–985. doi:10.1016/j.jesp.2010.06.001

Riggio, H. R., & Garcia, A. L. (2009). The power of situations: Jonestown and the fundamental attribution error. *Teaching of Psychology, 36*(2), 108–112. doi:10.1080/00986280902739636

Rihmer, Z., Dome, P., et al. (2012). Psychiatry should not become hostage to placebo: An alternative interpretation of antidepressant–placebo differences in the treatment response in depression. *European Neuropsychopharmacology, 22*(11), 782–786. doi:10.1016/j.euroneuro.2012.03.002

Rijken, N. H., Soer, R., et al. (2016). Increasing performance of professional soccer players and elite track and field athletes with peak performance training and biofeedback: A pilot study. *Applied Psychophysiology & Biofeedback, 41*(4), 421–430. doi:10.1007/s10484-016-9344-y

Riley, A., & Riley, E. (2009). Male erectile disorder. In R. Balon & R. T. Segraves (Eds.), *Clinical manual of sexual disorders* (pp. 213–249). Arlington, VA: American Psychiatric Publishing.

Riley, W., Jerome, A., et al. (2002). Feasibility of computerized scheduled gradual reduction for adolescent smoking cessation. *Substance Use & Misuse, 37*(2), 255–263.

Rind, B., Tromovitch, P., & Bauserman, R. (1998). A meta-analytic examination of assumed properties of child sexual abuse using college samples. *Psychological Bulletin, 124*(1), 22–53.

Rindermann, H., Becker, D., et al. (2017). Survey of expert opinion on intelligence: The Flynn effect and the future of intelligence. *Personality & Individual Differences, 106*, 242–247. doi:10.1016/j.paid.2016.10.061

Riquelme, H. (2002). Can people creative in imagery interpret ambiguous figures faster than people less creative in imagery? *Journal of Creative Behavior, 36*(2), 105–116. doi:10.1002/j.2162-6057.2002.tb01059.x

Riser, R. E., & Kosson, D. S. (2013). Criminal behavior and cognitive processing in male offenders with antisocial personality disorder with and without comorbid psychopathy. *Personality Disorders: Theory, Research, & Treatment, 4*(4), 332–340. doi:10.1037/a0033303

Ritchey, M., Dolcos, F., et al. (2011). Neural correlates of emotional processing in depression: Changes with cognitive behavioral therapy and predictors of treatment response. *Journal of Psychiatric Research, 45*(5), 577–587. doi:10.1016/j.jpsychires.2010.09.007

Ritchie, T. D., Sedikides, C., et al. (2011). Self-concept clarity mediates the relation between stress and subjective well-being. *Self & Identity, 10*(4), 493–508. doi:10.1080/15298868.2010. 493066

Ritter, J. (1998). Uniforms changing the culture of the nation's classrooms. *USA Today*, Oct. 15, 1A, 2A.

Ritter, S. M., van Baaren, R. B., & Dijksterhuis, A. (2012). Creativity: The role of unconscious processes in idea generation and idea selection. *Thinking Skills & Creativity, 7*(1), 21–27. doi:10.1016/j.tsc.2011.12.002

Riva, G. (2009). Virtual reality: An experiential tool for clinical psychology. *British Journal of Guidance & Counseling, 37*(3), 337–345. doi:10.1080/03069880902957056

Rivers, S. E., Brackett, M. A., et al. (2012). Measuring emotional intelligence in early adolescence with the MSCEIT-YV psychometric properties and relationship with academic performance and psychosocial functioning. *Journal of Psychoeducational Assessment, 30*(4), 344–366. doi:10.1177/0734282912449443

Rizzo, A., Cukor, J., et al. (2015). Virtual reality exposure for PTSD due to military combat and terrorist attacks. *Journal of Contemporary Psychotherapy, 45*(4), 255–264. doi:10.1007/s10879-015-9306-3

Rizzolatti, G., Fogassi, L., & Gallese V. (2006). Mirrors in the mind. *Scientific American, 295*(5), 54–61.

Roberto, M., & Koob, G. F. (2009). First congress of "Alcoholism and stress: A framework for future treatment strategies": Introduction to the proceeding. *Alcohol, 43*(7), 489–490. doi:10.1016/j.alcohol.2009.10.008

Roberts, B. W., & Mroczek, D. (2008). Personality trait change in adulthood. *Current Directions in Psychological Science, 17*(1), 31–35. doi:10.1111/j.1467-8721.2008.00543.x

Roberts, B. W., Kuncel, N. R., et al. (2007). The power of personality: The comparative validity of personality traits, socioeconomic status, and cognitive ability for predicting important life outcomes. *Perspectives on Psychological Science, 2*(4), 313–345. doi:10.1111/j.1745-6916.2007.00047.x

Roberts, R. D., & Lipnevich, A. A. (2012). From general intelligence to multiple intelligences: Meanings, models, and measures. In K. R. Harris, S. Graham,et al. (Eds.), *APA educational psychology handbook* (Vol. 2): *Individual differences and cultural and contextual factors* (pp. 33–57). Washington, DC: American Psychological Association. doi:10.1037/13274-002

Roberts, T., & Zurbriggen, E. L. (2013). The problem of sexualization: What is it and how does it happen? In E. L. Zurbriggen & T. Roberts (Eds.), *The sexualization of girls and girlhood: Causes, consequences, and resistance* (pp. 3–21). New York, NY: Oxford University Press.

Roberts, W. A. (2002). Are animals stuck in time? *Psychological Bulletin, 128*(3), 473–489. doi:10.1037/0033-2909.128.3.473

Roberts, W. A., & Roberts, S. (2002). Two tests of the stuck-in-time hypothesis. *Journal of General Psychology, 129*(4), 415–429. doi:10.1080/00221300209602105

Robins, R. W., Gosling, S. D., & Craik, K. H. (1998). Psychological science at the crossroads. *American Scientist, 86*, 310–313. doi:10.1511/1998.4.310

Robinson, A. (2010). *Sudden genius? The gradual path to creative breakthroughs*. New York, NY: Oxford University Press.

Robinson, D. N. (2008). *Consciousness and mental life*. New York, NY: Columbia University Press.

Robinson, T. E., & Berridge, K. C. (2003). Addiction. *Annual Review of Psychology, 54*, 25–53. doi:10.1146/annurev.psych.54.101601.145237

Robson, H., Sage, K., & Ralph, M. (2012). Wernicke's aphasia reflects a combination of acoustic-phonological and semantic control deficits: A case-series comparison of Wernicke's aphasia, semantic dementia and semantic aphasia. *Neuropsychologia, 50*(2), 266–275. doi:10.1016/j.neuropsychologia.2011.11.021

Roca, M., Parr, A., et al. (2010). Executive function and fluid intelligence after frontal lobe lesions. *Brain: A Journal of Neurology, 133*(1), 234–247. doi:10.1093/brain/awp269

Rock, A. (2004). *The mind at night: The new science of how and why we dream*. New York, NY: Basic Books.

Rodríguez-Villagra, O., Göthe, K., et al. (2013). Working memory capacity in a go/no-go task: Age differences in interference, processing speed, and attentional control. *Developmental Psychology, 49*(9), 1683–1696. doi:10.1037/a0030883

Roebers, C. M., & Feurer, E. (2015). Linking executive functions and procedural metacognition. *Child Development Perspectives*. doi:10.1111/cdep.12159

Roediger, H. L. III, & McDermott, K. B. (1995). Creating false memories: Remembering words not presented on lists. *Journal of Experimental Psychology: Learning, Memory, and Cognition, 21*(4), 803–814. doi:10.1037/0278-7393.21.4.803

Roese, N. J., Pennington, G. L., et al. (2006). Sex differences in regret: All for love or some for lust? *Personality & Social Psychology Bulletin, 32*(6), 770–780.

Roets, A., & Van Hiel, A. (2011). Allport's prejudiced personality today: Need for closure as the motivated cognitive basis of prejudice. *Current Directions in Psychological Science, 20*(6), 349–354. doi:10.1177/0963721411424894

Roffman, J. L., Brohawn, D. G., et al. (2011). MTHFR 677C>T effects on anterior cingulate structure and function during response monitoring in schizophrenia: A preliminary study. *Brain Imaging & Behavior, 5*(1), 65–75. doi:10.1007/s11682-010-9111-2

Rogers, C. R. (1959). A theory of therapy, personality, and interpersonal relationships, as developed in the client-centered framework. In S. Koch (Ed.), *Psychology: A study of a science* (Vol. 3, pp. 184–256). New York, NY: McGraw-Hill.

Rogers, C. R. (1961). *On becoming a person: A therapist's view of psychotherapy*. Boston, MA: Houghton Mifflin.

Rogers, P., & Soule, J. (2009). Cross-cultural differences in the acceptance of Barnum profiles supposedly derived from Western versus Chinese astrology. *Journal of Cross-Cultural Psychology, 40*(3), 381–399. doi:10.1177/0022022109332843

Rogowsky, B. A., Calhoun, B. M., et al. (2015). Matching learning style to instructional method: Effects on comprehension. *Journal of Educational Psychology, 107*(1), 64–78. doi:10.1037/a0037478

Roid, G. H., & Pomplun, M. (2012). The Stanford-Binet Intelligence Scales, Fifth Edition. In D. P. Flanagan & P. L. Harrison, P. L. (Eds.), *Contemporary intellectual assessment: Theories, tests, and issues* (3rd ed., pp. 249–268). New York: Guilford Press.

Roja, I., & Roja, Z. (2010). Use of cognitive hypnotherapy and couples therapy for female patients with psychogenic vaginismus. *Contemporary Hypnosis, 27*(2), 88–94.

Rollero, C., Gattino, S., & De Piccoli, N. (2013). A gender lens on quality of life: The role of sense of community, perceived social support, self-reported health and income. *Social Indicators Research*, doi:10.1007/s11205-013-0316-9

Rollins, A. L., Bond, G. R., et al. (2010). Coping with positive and negative symptoms of schizophrenia. *American Journal of Psychiatric Rehabilitation, 13*(3), 208–223. doi:10.1080/15487768.2010.501297

Rolls, E. T. (2008). Top-down control of visual perception: Attention in natural vision. *Perception, 37*(3), 333–354. doi:10.1068/p5877

Rolls, E. T. (2014). *Emotion and decision-making explained*. New York: Oxford University Press.

Romero, M., Usart, M., & Ott, M. (2015). Can serious games contribute to developing and sustaining 21st century skills? *Games & Culture, 10*(2), 148–177. doi:10.1177/1555412014548919

Roney, J. R. (2003). Effects of visual exposure to the opposite sex: Cognitive aspects of mate attraction in human males. *Personality & Social Psychology Bulletin, 29*, 393–404.

Roos, P. E., & Cohen, L. H. (1987). Sex roles and social support as moderators of life stress adjustment. *Journal of Personality & Social Psychology, 52*, 576–585.

Rosa, N. M., & Gutchess, A. H. (2011). Source memory for action in young and older adults: Self vs. close or unknown others. *Psychology & Aging, 26*(3), 625–630. doi:10.1037/a0022827

Rosch, E. (1977). Classification of real-world objects: Origins and representations in cognition. In P. N. Johnson-Laird & P. C. Wason (Eds.), *Thinking: Reading in cognitive science* (pp. 212–222). Cambridge, MA: Cambridge University Press.

Rosen, R. C., Marx, B. P., et al. (2012). Project VALOR: Design and methods of a longitudinal registry of post-traumatic stress disorder (PTSD) in combat-exposed veterans in the Afghanistan and Iraqi military theaters of operations. *International Journal of Methods in Psychiatric Research, 21*(1), 5–16. doi:10.1002/mpr.355

Rosenhan, D. L. (1973). On being sane in insane places. *Science, 179*(4070), 250–258. doi:10.1126/science.179.4070.250

Rosenkranz, M. A., Jackson, D. C., et al. (2003). Affective style and in vivo immune response: Neurobehavioral mechanisms. *Proceedings of the National Academy of Sciences, 100*, 11148–11152. doi:10.1073/pnas.1534743100

Rosenthal, M. (2013). *Human sexuality: From cells to society*. Boston, MA: Cengage Learning.

Rosenthal, N. E. (2013). *Winter blues: Everything you need to know to beat seasonal affective disorder* (4th ed.). New York, NY: Guilford.

Rosenthal, R. (1973). The Pygmalion effect lives. *Psychology Today, Sept*, 56–63.

Rosenthal, R. (1994). Science and ethics in conducting, analyzing, and reporting psychological research. *Psychological Science, 5*, 127–134. doi:10.1111/j.1467-9280.1994.tb00644.x

Rosner, R. I. (2012). Aaron T. Beck's drawings and the psychoanalytic origin story of cognitive therapy. *History of Psychology, 15*(1), 1–18. doi:10.1037/a0023892

Ross, C. A., Schroeder, E., & Ness, L. (2013). Dissociation and symptoms of culture-bound syndromes in North America: A preliminary study. *Journal of Trauma & Dissociation, 14*(2), 224–235. doi:10.1080/15299732.2013.724338

Ross, M., & Wang, Q. (2010). Why we remember and what we remember: Culture and autobiographical memory. *Perspectives on Psychological Science, 5*(4), 401–409.

Ross, M., Heine, S. J., et al. (2005). Cross-cultural discrepancies in self-appraisals. *Personality & Social Psychology Bulletin, 31*(9), 1175–1188. doi:10.1177/0146167204274080

Ross, P. E. (2006). The expert mind. *Scientific American, 294*(7), 64–71.

Rossignol, S., & Frigon, A. (2011). Recovery of locomotion after spinal cord injury: Some facts and mechanisms. *Annual Review of Neuroscience, 34*, 413–440. doi:10.1146/annurev-neuro-061010-113746

Rotter, J. B., & Hochreich, D. J. (1975). *Personality*. Glenview, IL: Scott, Foresman.

Rousseau, D. M., & Gunia, B. C. (2016). Evidence-based practice: The psychology of EBP implementation. *Annual Review of Psychology, 67*, 667–692. doi:0.1146/annurev-psych-122414-033336

Rowland, D. L. (2007). Sexual health and problems: Erectile dysfunction, premature ejaculation, and male orgasmic disorder. In J. E. Grant & M. N. Potenza (Eds.), *Textbook of men's mental health* (pp. 171–203). Washington, DC: American Psychiatric Publishing.

Rowley, S. J., Varner, F., et al. (2012). Toward a model of racial identity and parenting in African Americans. In J. M. Sullivan & A. M. Esmail (Eds.), *African American identity: Racial and cultural dimensions of the Black experience* (pp. 273–288). Lanham, MD: Lexington Books.

Royle, N. A., Booth, T., et al. (2013). Estimated maximal and current brain volume predict cognitive ability in old age. *Neurobiology of Aging, 34*(12), 2726–2733. doi:10.1016/j.neurobiolaging.2013.05.015

Rozin, P., Kabnick, K., et al. (2003). The ecology of eating: Smaller portion sizes in France than in the United States help explain the French paradox. *Psychological Science, 14*(5), 450–454. doi:10.1111/1467-9280.02452

Rubenstein, C., & Tavris, C. (1987). Special survey results: 2600 women reveal the secrets of intimacy. *Redbook, 159*, 147–149.

Rucker, D. D., Tormala, Z. L., et al. (2014). Consumer conviction and commitment: An appraisal-based framework for attitude certainty. *Journal of Consumer Psychology, 24*(1), 119–136. doi:10.1016/j.jcps.2013.07.001

Rudolph, C. W., & Baltes, B. B. (2017). Age and health jointly moderate the influence of flexible work arrangements on work engagement: Evidence from two empirical studies. *Journal of Occupational Health Psychology, 22*(1), 40–58. doi:10.1037/a0040147

Ruggiero, V. R. (2015). *Becoming a critical thinker* (8th ed.). Boston, MA: Cengage Learning.

Rummell, C. M., & Levant, R. F. (2014). Masculine gender role discrepancy strain and self-esteem. *Psychology of Men & Masculinity*. doi:10.1037/a0035304

Runco, M. A. (2012). *Creativity: An interdisciplinary perspective*. New York, NY: Routledge.

Runco, M. A. (2015). Meta-creativity: Being creative about creativity. *Creativity Research Journal, 27*(3), 295–298. doi:10.1080/10400419.2015.1065134

Runco, M. A., & Acar, S. (2012). Divergent thinking as an indicator of creative potential. *Creativity Research Journal, 24*(1), 66–75. doi:10.1080/10400419.2012.652929

Rusconi, E., & Mitchener-Nissen, T. (2013). Prospects of functional magnetic resonance imaging as lie detector. *Frontiers in Human Neuroscience, 7*, 594.

Rushton, J. P., & Jensen, A. R. (2005). Thirty years of research on race differences in cognitive ability. *Psychology, Public Policy, & Law, 11*, 235–294. doi:10.1037/1076-8971.11.2.235

Russell, A., Stevenson, R. J., & Rich, A. N. (2015). Chocolate smells pink and stripy: Exploring olfactory-visual synesthesia. *Cognitive Neuroscience, 6*(2–3), 77–88. doi:10.1080/17588928.2015.1035245

Russell, S., & Norvig, P. (2020). *Artificial intelligence: A modern approach* (4th ed.). Retrieved August 1, 2020, from http://aima.cs.berkeley.edu

Russo, M. B., Brooks, F. R., et al. (1998). Conversion disorder presenting as multiple sclerosis. *Military Medicine, 163*(10), 709–710.

Rutter, M., Beckett, C., et al. (2009). Effects of profound early institutional deprivation: An overview of findings from a UK longitudinal study of Romanian adoptees. In G. Wrobel & E. Neil (Eds.), *International advances in adoption research for practice* (pp. 147–167). London, UK: Wiley-Blackwell.

Rutter, V. B., & Singer, T. (Eds.), (2015). *Ancient Greece, modern psyche: Archetypes evolving*. New York: Routledge.

Rutz, C., & St. Clair, J. H. (2012). The evolutionary origins and ecological context of tool use in New Caledonian crows. *Behavioural Processes, 89*(2), 153–165. doi:10.1016/j.beproc.2011.11.005

Ruva, C., McEvoy, C., & Bryant, J. B. (2007). Effects of pre-trial publicity and jury deliberation on juror bias and source memory errors. *Applied Cognitive Psychology, 21*(1), 45–67. doi:10.1002/acp.1254

Ryan, K. M. (2011). The relationship between rape myths and sexual scripts: The social construction of rape. *Sex Roles, 65*(11–12), 774–782. doi:10.1007/s11199-011-0033-2

Ryan, M. P. (2001). Conceptual models of lecture learning: Guiding metaphors and model-appropriate notetaking practices. *Reading Psychology, 22*(4), 289–312. doi:10.1080/02702710127638

Ryan, R. M., & Deci, E. L. (2017). *Self-determination theory: Basic psychological needs in motivation, development, and wellness*. New York: Guilford.

Ryan, R. M., Curren, R. R., & Deci, E. L. (2013). What humans need: Flourishing in Aristotelian philosophy and self-determination theory. In A. S. Waterman (Ed.), *The best within us: Positive psychology perspectives on eudaimonia* (pp. 57–75). Washington, DC: American Psychological Association. doi:10.1037/14092-004

Ryckman, R. M. (2013). *Theories of personality* (10th ed.). Boston, MA: Cengage Learning.

Ryff, C. D., & Singer, B. (2009). Understanding healthy aging: Key components and their integration. In V. L. Bengston, D. Gans, et al. (Eds.), *Handbook of theories of aging* (2nd ed., pp. 117–144). New York, NY: Springer.

Saarimäki, H., Gotsopoulos, A., et al. (2016). Discrete neural signatures of basic emotions. *Cerebral Cortex, 26*(6), 2563–2573. doi:10.1093/cercor/bhv086

Saber, J. L., & Johnson, R. D. (2008). Don't throw out the baby with the bathwater: Verbal repetition, mnemonics, and active learning. *Journal of Marketing Education, 30*(3), 207–216. doi:10.1177/0273475308324630

Sachdev, P. S., & Chen, X. (2009). Neurosurgical treatment of mood disorders: Traditional psychosurgery and the advent of deep brain stimulation. *Current Opinion in Psychiatry, 22*(1), 25–31. doi:10.1097/YCO.0b013e32831c8475

Sack, R. L. (2010). Jet lag. *The New England Journal of Medicine, 362*(5), 440–447. doi:10.1056/NEJMcp0909838

Sackett, P. R., & Lievens, F. (2008). Personnel selection. *Annual Review of Psychology, 59*, 419–450.

Sackett, P. R., Walmsley, P. T., & Laczo, R. M. (2013). Job and work analysis. In N. W. Schmitt, S. Highhouse, et al. (Eds.), *Handbook of psychology* (Vol. 12): *Industrial and organizational psychology* (2nd ed., pp. 61–81). New York, NY: Wiley.

Sacks, O. (2010). *The mind's eye*. New York, NY: Knopf.

Şahin, F., Gürbüz, S., et al. (2017). Leaders' managerial assumptions and transformational leadership: The moderating role of gender. *Leadership & Organization Development Journal, 38*(1), 105–125. doi:10.1108/LODJ-11-2015-0239

Sailor, W. (2015). Advances in schoolwide inclusive school reform. *Remedial & Special Education, 36*(2), 94–99. doi:10.1177/0741932514555021

Sakaluk, J. K., & Milhausen, R. R. (2012). Factors influencing university students' explicit and implicit sexual double standards. *Journal of Sex Research, 49*(5), 464–476. doi:10.1080/00224499.2011.569976

Saksida, L. M., & Wilkie, D. M. (1994). Time-of-day discrimination by pigeons. *Animal Learning & Behavior, 22*, 143–154. doi:10.3758/BF03199914

Salas, E., Shuffler, M. L., et al. (2015). Understanding and improving teamwork in organizations: A scientifically-based practical guide. *Human Resources Management, 54*, 599–622. doi:10.1002/hrm.21628

Sales, B. D., & Hafemeister, T. L. (1985). Law and psychology. In E. M. Altmeir & M. E. Meyer (Eds.), *Applied specialties in psychology* (pp. 331–373). New York, NY: Random House.

Salimpoor, V. N., Benovoy, M. M., et al. (2011). Anatomically distinct dopamine release during anticipation and experience of peak emotion to music. *Nature Neuroscience, 14*(2), 257–262. doi:10.1038/nn.2726

Salisbury, A. G., & Burker, E. J. (2011). Assessment, treatment, and vocational implications of combat related PTSD in veterans. *Journal of Applied Rehabilitation Counseling, 42*(2), 42–49.

Sallinen, M., Holm, A., et al. (2008). Recovery of cognitive performance from sleep debt: Do a short rest pause and a single recovery night help? *Chronobiology International, 25*(2–3), 279–296. doi:10.1080/0742052080210710

Sallinen, M., Sihvola, M., et al. (2017). Sleep, alertness and alertness management among commercial airline pilots on short-haul and long-haul flights. *Accident Analysis & Prevention, 98*, 320–329. doi:10.1016/j.aap.2016.10.029

Salloum, A., & Overstreet, S. (2012). Grief and trauma intervention for children after disaster: Exploring coping skills versus trauma narration. *Behaviour Research & Therapy, 50*(3), 169–179. doi:10.1016/j.brat.2012.01.001

Salomons, T. V., Nusslock, R., et al. (2015). Neural emotion regulation circuitry underlying anxiolytic effects of perceived control over pain. *Journal of Cognitive Neuroscience, 27*(2), 222–233. doi:10.1162/jocn_a_00702

Sam, D. L., & Berry, J. W. (2010). Acculturation: When individuals and groups of different cultural backgrounds meet. *Perspectives on Psychological Science, 5*(4), 472–481. doi:10.1177/1745691610373075

Sample, I. (2014, February 14). Male sexual orientation influenced by genes, study shows. *The Guardian*. Retrieved July 21, 2020, from www.theguardian.com/science/2014/feb/14/genes-influence-male-sexual-orientation-study

Samson, D., & Apperly, I. A. (2010). There is more to mind reading than having theory of mind concepts: New directions in theory of mind research. *Infant & Child Development, 19*(5), 443–454.

Sanchez, J. E., Yoxsimer, A., et al. (2012). Uniforms in the middle school: Student opinions, discipline data, and school police data. *Journal of School Violence, 11*(4), 345–356. doi:10.1080/15388220.2012.706873

Sánchez, P., García-Calvo, T., et al. (2009). An analysis of home advantage in the top two Spanish professional football leagues. *Perceptual & Motor Skills, 108*(3), 789–797.

Sandvik, A. M., Bartone, P. T., et al. (2013). Psychological hardiness predicts neuroimmunological responses to stress. *Psychology, Health & Medicine, 18*(6), 705–713. doi:10.1080/13548506.2013.772304

Sanes, J. R., & Masland, R. H. (2015). The types of retinal ganglion cells: Current status and implications for neuronal classification. *Annual Review of Neuroscience, 38*, 221–246. doi:10.1146/annurev-neuro-071714-034120

Sansone, R. A., & Sansone, L. A. (2010). Road rage: What's driving it? *Psychiatry, 7*(7), 14–18.

Santarcangelo, E. L., & Scattina, E. (2016). Complementing the latest APA definition of hypnosis: Sensory-motor and vascular peculiarities involved in hypnotizability. *International Journal of Clinical & Experimental Hypnosis, 64*(3), 318–330. doi:10.1080/00207144. 2016.1171093

Sansone, R. A., Leung, J. S., & Wiederman, M. W. (2013). Self-reported bullying in childhood: Relationships with employment in adulthood. *International Journal of Psychiatry in Clinical Practice, 17*(1), 64–68. doi:10.3109/13651501.2012.709867

Santelices, M. P., Guzmán G. M., et al. (2011). Promoting secure attachment: Evaluation of the effectiveness of an early intervention pilot programme with mother–infant dyads in Santiago, Chile. *Child: Care, Health & Development, 37*(2), 203–210. doi:10.1111/j.1365-2214.2010.01161.x

Sapolsky, R. (2005). Sick of poverty. *Scientific American, 293*(6), 92–99.

Sarason, I. G., & Sarason, B. R. (2005). *Abnormal psychology* (11th ed.). Mahwah, NJ: Prentice Hall.

Sarkova, M., Bacikova-Sleskova, M., et al. (2013). Associations between assertiveness, psychological well-being, and self-esteem in adolescents. *Journal of Applied Social Psychology, 43*(1), 147–154. doi:10.1111/j.1559-1816.2012.00988.x

Sautter, J. M., Tippett, R. M., & Morgan, S. (2010). The social demography of Internet dating in the United States. *Social Science Quarterly, 91*(2), 554–575. doi:10.1111/j.1540-6237.2010.00707.x

Savin-Williams, R., Joyner, K., et al. (2012). Prevalence and stability of self-reported sexual orientation identity during young adulthood. *Archives of Sexual Behavior, 41*(1), 103–110.

Saxbe, D. E. (2017). Birth of a new perspective? A call for biopsychosocial research on childbirth. *Current Directions in Psychological Science, 26*(1), 81–86. doi:10.1177/096372141 6677096

Saxton, M. (2010). *Child language: Acquisition and development*. Thousand Oaks, CA: Sage.

Saxvig, I. W., Lundervold, A. J., et al. (2008). The effect of a REM sleep deprivation procedure on different aspects of memory function in humans. *Psychophysiology, 45*(2), 309–317. doi:10.1111/j.1469-8986.2007.00623.x

Scannell, S., & Mulvilhill, M. (2012). *Big book of brainstorming games*. New York, NY: McGraw-Hill.

Schachter, S., & Wheeler, L. (1962). Epinephrine, chlorpromazine, and amusement. *Journal of Abnormal and Social Psychology, 65*, 121–128. doi:10.1037/h0040391

Schacter, D. L. (1996). *Searching for memory: The brain, the mind, and the past*. New York, NY: Basic Books.

Schacter, D. L. (2012). Adaptive constructive processes and the future of memory. *American Psychologist, 67*(8), 603–613. doi:10.1037/a0029869

Schafer, M., & Crichlow, S. (2010). *Groupthink versus high-quality decision making in international relations*. New York, NY: Columbia University Press.

Schaie, K. W. (2005). *Developmental influences on adult intelligence: The Seattle longitudinal study*. New York, NY: Oxford University Press.

Schalke, D., Brunner, M., et al. (2013). Stability and change in intelligence from age 12 to age 52: Results from the Luxembourg MAGRIP study. *Developmental Psychology, 49*(8), 1529–1543. doi:10.1037/a0030623

Scharinger, C., Rabl, U., et al. (2010). Imaging genetics of mood disorders. *NeuroImage, 3*(3), 810–821. doi:10.1016/j.neuroimage.2010.02.019

Schechter, E. (2012). Intentions and unified agency: Insights from the split-brain phenomenon. *Mind & Language, 27*(5), 570–594. doi:10.1111/mila.12003

Scheibe, S., Sheppes, G., & Staudinger, U. M. (2015). Distract or reappraise? Age-related differences in emotion-regulation choice. *Emotion, 15*, 677–681. doi:10.1037/a0039246

Scheinkman, M. (2008). The multi-level approach: A road map for couples therapy. *Family Process, 47*(2), 197–213.

Schenck, C. H., & Mahowald, M. W. (2005). Rapid eye movement and non-REM sleep parasomnias. *Primary Psychiatry, 12*(8), 67–74.

Scherbaum, C. A., Sabet, J., et al. (2013). Examining faking on personality inventories using unfolding item response theory models. *Journal of Personality Assessment, 95*(2), 207–216. doi:10.1080/00223891.2012.725439

Schermer, V. L. (2015). Psychodrama in perspective: An interview with Jonathan Moreno on his father, Jacob Moreno, and the lasting impact of his ideas. *Group Analysis, 48*(2), 187–201. doi:10.1177/0533316415580539

Schetter, C. D. (2011). Psychological science on pregnancy: Stress processes, biopsychosocial models, and emerging research issues. *Annual Review of Psychology, 62*, 531–558. doi:10.1146/annurev.psych.031809.130727

Schick, T., & Vaughn, L. (2014). *How to think about weird things: Critical thinking for a new age* (7th ed.). New York, NY: McGraw-Hill.

Schifrin, N. (2013, October 7). How Malala Yousafzai's courage inspired a nation: "We are no longer afraid." *ABC News*. Retrieved July 21, 2020, from http://abcnews.go.com/International/malala-yousafzais-courage-inspired-nation-longer-afraid/story?id=20452967

Schiller, D., Eichenbaum, H., et al. (2015). Memory and space: Towards an understanding of the cognitive map. *Journal of Neuroscience, 35*(41), 13904–13911. doi:10.1523/JNEUROSCI.2618-15.2015

Schiller, P. H., Slocum, W. M., et al. (2011). The integration of disparity, shading and motion parallax cues for depth perception in humans and monkeys. *Brain Research, 1377*, 67–77. doi:10.1016/j.brainres.2011.01.003

Schinazi, V. R., Nardi, D., et al. (2013). Hippocampal size predicts rapid learning of a cognitive map in humans. *Hippocampus, 23*(6), 515–528. doi:10.1002/hipo.22111

Schiraldi, G. R., & Brown, S. L. (2001). Primary prevention for mental health: Results of an exploratory cognitive-behavioral college course. *Journal of Primary Prevention, 22*(1), 55–67. doi:10.1023/A:1011040231249

Schizophrenia Working Group of the Psychiatric Genomics Consortium. (2014). Biological insights from 108 schizophrenia-associated genetic loci. *Nature, 511*(7510), 421–425. doi:10.1038/nature13595

Schlaepfer, T. E., Cohen, M. X., et al. (2008). Deep brain stimulation to reward circuitry alleviates anhedonia in refractory major depression. *Neuropsychopharmacology, 33*(2), 368–377. doi:10.1038/sj.npp.1301408

Schleicher, S. S., & Gilbert, L. A. (2005). Heterosexual dating discourses among college students: Is there still a double standard? *Journal of College Student Psychotherapy, 19*(3), 7–23.

Schlund, M. W., & Cataldo, M. F. (2010). Amygdala involvement in human avoidance, escape and approach behavior. *NeuroImage, 53*(2), 769–776. doi:10.1016/j.neuroimage.2010.06.058

Schmader, T., Croft, A., & Whitehead, J. (2014). Why can't I just be myself? A social cognitive analysis of the working self-concept under stereotype threat. *Social Psychological & Personality Science, 5*(1), 4–11. doi:10.1177/1948550613482988

Schmahmann, J. D. (2010). The role of the cerebellum in cognition and emotion: Personal reflections since 1982 on the dysmetria of thought hypothesis, and its historical evolution from theory to therapy. *Neuropsychology Review, 20*(3), 236–260. doi:10.1007/s11065-010-9142-x

Schmalzl, L., Thomke, E., et al. (2011). "Pulling telescoped phantoms out of the stump": Manipulating the perceived position of phantom limbs using a full-body illusion. *Frontiers in Human Neuroscience, 5*, 121. doi:10.3389/fnhum.2011.00121

Schmelz, M. (2010). Itch and pain. *Neuroscience & Biobehavioral Reviews, 34*(2), 171–176. doi:10.1016/j.neubiorev.2008.12.004

Schmidt, F. L., & Hunter, J. E. (1998). The validity and utility of selection methods in personnel psychology. *Psychological Bulletin, 124*(2), 262–274.

Schmidt, S., Roesler, U., et al. (2014). Uncertainty in the workplace: Examining role ambiguity and role conflict, and their link to depression—A meta-analysis. *European Journal of Work & Organizational Psychology, 23*(1), 91–106. doi:10.1080/1359432X.2012.711523

Schmitt, D. P., & Allik, J. (2005). Simultaneous administration of the Rosenberg Self-Esteem Scale in 53 nations: Exploring the universal and culture-specific features of global self-esteem. *Journal of Personality & Social Psychology, 89*(4), 623–642. doi:10.1037/0022-3514.89.4.623

Schmitt, N., & Golubovich, J. (2013). Biographical information. In K. F. Geisinger, B. A. Bracken, et al. (Eds.), *APA handbook of testing and assessment in psychology* (Vol. 1): *Test theory and testing and assessment in industrial and organizational psychology* (pp. 437–455). Washington, DC: American Psychological Association. doi:10.1037/14047-025

Schmuck, P., & Vlek, C. (2003). Psychologists can do much to support sustainable development. *European Psychologist, 8*(2), 66–76.

Schnakers, C. C., Perrin, F. F., et al. (2009). Detecting consciousness in a total locked-in syndrome: An active event-related paradigm. *Neurocase, 15*(4), 271–277. doi:10.1080/13554790902724904

Schnakers, C., & Laureys, S. (2012). *Coma and disorders of consciousness*. New York, NY: Springer. doi:10.1007/978-1-4471-2440-5

Schneider, K. J., Bugental, J. F. T., & Pierson, J. F. (2001). *The handbook of humanistic psychology*. Thousand Oaks, CA: Sage.

Schneider, K. J., Galvin, J., & Serlin, I. (2009). Rollo May on existential psychotherapy. *Journal of Humanistic Psychology, 49*(4), 419–434. doi:10.1177/0022167809340241

Schneider, R. L., Arch, J. J., & Wolitzky-Taylor, K. B. (2015). The state of personalized treatment for anxiety disorders: A systematic review of treatment moderators. *Clinical Psychology Review, 38*, 39–54. doi:10.1016/j.cpr.2015.02.004

Schneider, T. R., Lyons, J. B., & Khazon, S. (2013). Emotional intelligence and resilience. *Personality & Individual Differences, 55*(8), 909–914. doi:10.1016/j.paid.2013.07.460

Schneiderman, N., Antoni, M. H., et al. (2001). Health psychology: Psychological and biobehavioral aspects of chronic disease management. *Annual Review of Psychology, 52*, 555–580. doi:10.1146/annurev.psych.52.1.555

Schramm, D. G., Marshall, J. P., et al. (2012). Religiosity, homogamy, and marital adjustment: An examination of newlyweds in first marriages and remarriages. *Journal of Family Issues, 33*(2), 246–268. doi:10.1177/0192513X11420370

Schreiber, F. R. (1973). *Sybil*. Chicago, IL: Regency.

Schuck, K., Keijsers, G. P. J., & Rinck, M. (2011). The effects of brief cognitive-behaviour therapy for pathological skin picking: A randomized comparison to wait-list control. *Behaviour Research & Therapy, 49*(1), 11–17. doi:10.1016/j.brat.2010.09.005

Schultz, D. H., & Helmstetter, F. J. (2010). Classical conditioning of autonomic fear responses is independent of contingency awareness. *Journal of Experimental Psychology: Animal Behavior Processes, 36*(4), 495–500. doi:10.1037/a0020263

Schultz, D. P., & Schultz, S. E. (2010). *Psychology and work today* (10th ed.). Englewood Cliffs, NJ: Prentice Hall.

Schultz, D. P., & Schultz, S. E. (2016). *A history of modern psychology* (11th ed.). Boston, MA: Cengage Learning.

Schultz, D. P., & Schultz, S. E. (2017). *Theories of personality* (11th ed.). Boston, MA: Cengage Learning.

Schuster, J., Hoertel, N., & Limosin, F. (2011). The man behind Philippe Pinel: Jean-Baptiste Pussin (1746–1811): Psychiatry in pictures. *British Journal of Psychiatry, 198*(3), 198–241. doi:10.1192/bjp.198.3.241a

Schuster, M. A., Stein, B. D., et al. (2001). A national survey of stress reactions after the September 11, 2001, terrorist attacks. *New England Journal of Medicine, 345*(20), 1507–1512. doi:10.1056/NEJM200111153452024

Schwab, S. G., & Wildenauer, D. B. (2013). Genetics of psychiatric disorders in the GWAS era: An update on schizophrenia. *European Archives of Psychiatry & Clinical Neuroscience, 263*(Suppl. 2), 147–154. doi:10.1007/s00406-013-0450-z

Schweckendiek, J., Klucken, T., et al. (2011). Weaving the (neuronal) web: Fear learning in spider phobia. *NeuroImage, 54*(1), 681–688. doi:10.1016/j.neuroimage.2010.07.049

Schwenzer, M. (2008). Prosocial orientation may sensitize to aggression-related cues. *Social Behavior & Personality, 36*(8), 1009–1010. doi:10.2224/sbp.2008.36.8.1009

Schwitzgebel, E. (2011). *Perplexities of consciousness*. Cambridge, MA: MIT Press.

Sclafani, A., & Springer, D. (1976). Dietary obesity in adult rats: Similarities to hypothalamic and human obesity syndromes. *Psychology & Behavior, 17*, 461–471. doi:10.1016/0031-9384(76)90109-8

Scoboria, A., Mazzoni, G., et al. (2002). Immediate and persisting effects of misleading questions and hypnosis on memory reports. *Journal of Experimental Psychology: Applied, 8*(1), 26–32. doi:10.1037/1076-898X.8.1.26

Scoboria, A., Mazzoni, G., et al. (2012). Personalized and not general suggestion produces false autobiographical memories and suggestion-consistent behavior. *Acta Psychologica, 139*(1), 225–232. doi:10.1016/j.actpsy.2011.10.008

Scollon, C. N., Koh, S., & Au, E. W. M. (2011). Cultural differences in the subjective experience of emotion: When and why they occur. *Social & Personality Psychology Compass, 5*(11), 853–864. doi:10.1111/j.1751-9004.2011.00391.x

Scott, R. (2012). Amphetamine-induced psychosis and defences to murder. *Psychiatry, Psychology & Law, 19*(5), 615–645. doi:10.1080/13218719.2012.738022

Scruggs, T. E., & Mastropieri, M. A. (2007). Science learning in special education: The case for constructed versus instructed learning. *Exceptionality, 15*(2), 57–74.

Sears, S., & Kraus, S. (2009). I think therefore I om: Cognitive distortions and coping style as mediators for the effects of mindfulness meditation on anxiety, positive and negative affect, and hope. *Journal of Clinical Psychology, 65*(6), 561–573. doi:10.1002/jclp.20543

Segal, N. L. (2012). *Born together–reared apart: The landmark Minnesota Twin Study*. Cambridge, MA: Harvard University Press. doi:10.4159/harvard.9780674065154

Segal, Z. V., Williams, J. G., & Teasdale, J. D. (2013). *Mindfulness-based cognitive therapy for depression* (2nd ed.). New York, NY: Guilford.

Segerdahl, P., Fields, W., & Savage-Rumbaugh, S. (2005). *Kanzi's primal language: The cultural initiation of primates into language*. New York, NY: Palgrave MacMillan.

Segerstrom, S., & Miller, G. E. (2004). Psychological stress and the human immune system: A meta-analytic study of 30 years of inquiry. *Psychological Bulletin, 130*(4), 601–630. doi:10.1037/0033-2909.130.4.601

Segraves, R., & Woodard, T. (2006). Female hypoactive sexual desire disorder: History and current status. *Journal of Sexual Medicine, 3*(3), 408–418.

Segraves, T., & Althof, S. (2002). Psychotherapy and pharmacotherapy for sexual dysfunctions. In P. E. Nathan & J. M. Gorman (Eds.), *A guide to treatments that work* (2nd ed., pp. 497–524). London, UK: Oxford University Press.

Seidman, B. F. (2001). Medicine wars. *Skeptical Inquirer*, Jan.–Feb., 28–35.

Seitz, A., & Watanabe, T. (2005). A unified model for perceptual learning. *Trends in Cognitive Sciences, 9*(7), 329–334. doi:10.1016/j.tics.2005.05.010

Sela, L., & Sobel, N. (2010). Human olfaction: A constant state of change-blindness. *Experimental Brain Research, 205*, 13–29. doi:10.1007/s00221-010-2348-6

Seligman, M. E. P. (1972). For helplessness: Can we immunize the weak? In *Readings in Psychology Today* (2nd ed.). Del Mar, CA: CRM.

Seligman, M. E. P. (1989). *Helplessness*. New York, NY: Freeman.

Seligman, M. E. P. (1998). *Learned optimism*. New York, NY: Pocket Books.

Seligman, M. E. P. (2003). Positive psychology: Fundamental assumptions. *Source Psychologist, 16*(3), 126–127.

Selye, H. (1976). *The stress of life*. New York, NY: Knopf.

Senécal, C., Julien, E., & Guay, F. (2003). Role conflict and academic procrastination: A self-determination perspective. *European Journal of Social Psychology, 33*(1), 135–145. doi:10.1002/ejsp.144

Serfass, D. G., & Sherman, R. A. (2013). Personality and perceptions of situations from the Thematic Apperception Test. *Journal of Research in Personality, 47*(6), 708–718. doi:10.1016/j.jrp.2013.06.007

Serra, M. J., & Metcalfe, J. (2009). Effective implementation of metacognition. In D. J. Hacker, J. Dunlosky, et al. (Eds.), *Handbook of metacognition in education* (pp. 278–298). New York, NY: Routledge.

Sessa, V. I., & London, M. (2006). *Continuous learning in organizations: Individual, group, and organizational perspectives*. Mahwah, NJ: Erlbaum.

Seto, M. C. (2008). *Pedophilia and sexual offending against children: Theory, assessment, and intervention*. Washington, DC: American Psychological Association.

Seto, M. C. (2009). Pedophilia. *Annual Review of Clinical Psychology, 5*, 391–407.

Seto, M. C., Cantor, J. M., & Blanchard, R. (2006). Child pornography offenses are a valid diagnostic indicator of pedophilia. *Journal of Abnormal Psychology, 115*(3), 610–615.

Seybolt, D. C., & Wagner, M. K. (1997). Self-reinforcement, gender-role, and sex of participant in prediction of life satisfaction. *Psychological Reports, 81*(2), 519–522. doi:10.2466/PR0.81.6.519-522

Seyle, D. C., & Newman, M. L. (2006). A house divided? The psychology of red and blue America. *American Psychologist, 61*(6), 571–580. doi:10.1037/0003-066X.61.6.571

Shaffer, D. R. (2009). *Social and personality development* (6th ed.). Boston, MA: Cengage Learning/Wadsworth.

Shaffer, D. R., & Kipp, K. (2014). *Developmental psychology: Childhood and adolescence* (9th ed.). Boston, MA: Cengage Learning.

Shafton, A. (1995). *Dream reader*. Albany, NY: SUNY Press.

Shamloul, R. (2010). Natural aphrodisiacs. *Journal of Sexual Medicine, 7*(1, Pt 1), 39–49. doi:10.1111/j.1743-6109.2009.01521.x

Shanks, D. R. (2010). Learning: From association to cognition. *Annual Review of Psychology. 61*, 273–301. doi:10.1146/annurev.psych.093008.100519

Shapiro, D. A., Barkham, M., et al. (2003). Time is of the essence: A selective review of the fall and rise of brief therapy research. *Psychology & Psychotherapy: Theory, Research & Practice, 76*(3), 211–235. doi:10.1348/147608303322362460

Shapiro, F. (2012). EMDR therapy: An overview of current and future research. *European Review of Applied Psychology, 62*(4), 193–195. doi:10.1016/j.erap.2012.09.005

Shapiro, S. L., & Walsh, R. (2006). The meeting of meditative disciplines and Western psychology: A mutually enriching dialogue. *American Psychologist, 61*(3), 227–239. doi:10.1037/0003-066X.61.3.227

Shapiro-Mendoza, C. K., Kimball, M., et al. (2009). US infant mortality trends attributable to accidental suffocation and strangulation in bed from 1984 through 2004: Are rates increasing? *Pediatrics, 123*(2), 533–539. doi:10.1542/peds.2007-3746

Sharf, R. S. (2016). *Theories of psychotherapy & counseling: Concepts and cases* (6th ed.). Boston, MA: Cengage Learning.

Sharma, S., Powers, A., et al. (2016). Gene × environment determinants of stress- and anxiety-related disorders. *Annual Review of Psychology, 67*, 239–261. doi:10.1146/annurev-psych-122414-033408

Shaver, P. R., & Mikulincer, M. (Eds.). (2011). *Human aggression and violence: Causes, manifestations, and consequences*. Washington, DC: American Psychological Association.

Shaw, E., & Delaporte, Y. (2011). New perspectives on the history of American Sign Language. *Sign Language Studies, 11*(2), 158–204. doi:10.1353/sls.2010.0006

Shaywitz, B. A, Shaywitz, S. E., et al. (1995). Sex differences in the functional organization of the brain for language. *Nature, 373*, 607–609. doi:10.1038/373607a0

Shedler, J. (2010). The efficacy of psychodynamic psychotherapy. *American Psychologist, 65*(2), 98–109. doi:10.1037/a0018378

Shepard, R. N. (1975). Form, formation, and transformation of internal representations. In R. L. Solso (Ed.), *Information processing and cognition: The Loyola Symposium* (pp. 87–122). Hillsdale, NJ: Erlbaum.

Sheppes, G., Suri, G., & Gross, J. J. (2015). Emotion regulation and psychopathology. *Annual Review of Clinical Psychology, 11*, 379–405. doi:10.1146/annurev-clinpsy-032814-112739

Sherif, M., Harvey, O. J., et al. (1961). *Intergroup conflict and cooperation: The Robbers Cave experiment*. University of Oklahoma, Institute of Group Relations. Retrieved July 21, 2020, from http://psychclassics.yorku.ca/Sherif/

Shermer, L. O., Rose, K. C., & Hoffman, A. (2011). Perceptions and credibility: Understanding the nuances of eyewitness testimony. *Journal of Contemporary Criminal Justice, 27*(2), 183–203. doi:10.1177/1043986211405886

Shermer, M. (2011). *The believing brain*. New York, NY: Holt.

Shih, J. J., & Krusienski, D. J. (2012). Signals from intraventricular depth electrodes can control a brain–computer interface. *Journal of Neuroscience Methods, 203*(2), 311–314. doi:10.1016/j.jneumeth.2011.10.012

Shillingsburg, M. A., Kelley, M. E., et al. (2009). Evaluation and training of yes-no responding across verbal operants. *Journal of Applied Behavior Analysis, 42*(2), 209–223. doi:10.1901/jaba.2009.42-209

Shimotake, A., Matsumoto, R., et al. (2015). Direct exploration of the role of the ventral anterior temporal lobe in semantic memory: Cortical stimulation and local field potential evidence from subdural grid electrodes. *Cerebral Cortex, 25*(10), 3802–3817. doi:10.1093/cercor/bhu262

Shiner, R. L., Buss, K. A., et al. (2012). What is temperament now? Assessing progress in temperament research on the twenty-fifth anniversary of Goldsmith et al. (1987). *Child Development Perspectives, 6*(4), 436–444. doi:10.1111/j.1750-8606.2012.00254.x

Shins, S. H., Miller, D. P., & Teicher, M. H. (2012). Exposure to childhood neglect and physical abuse and developmental trajectories of heavy episodic drinking from early adolescence into young adulthood. *Drug & Alcohol Dependence, 127*(1–3), 31–38. doi:10.1016/j.drugalcdep.2012.06.005

Shmerling, R. H. (2019, December 10). Can vaping damage your lungs? What we do (and don't) know. *Harvard Health Blog*. Retrieved July 21, 2020, from https://www.health.harvard.edu/blog/can-vaping-damage-your-lungs-what-we-do-and-dont-know-2019090417734

Shook, J. R. (2013). Social cognition and the problem of other minds. In D. D. Franks & J. H. Turner (Eds.), *Handbook of neurosociology* (pp. 33–46). New York, NY: Springer. doi:10.1007/978-94-007-4473-8_4

Shorrock, S. T., & Isaac, A. (2010). Mental imagery in air traffic control. International *Journal of Aviation Psychology, 20*(4), 309–324. doi:10.1080/10508414.2010.487008

Shutter, J. M., & Camras, L. A. (2010). Emotional facial expressions in infancy. *Emotion Review, 2*(2), 120– 129. doi:10.1177/1754073909352529

Short, S. E., Ross-Stewart, L., & Monsma, E. V. (2006). Onwards with the evolution of imagery research in sport psychology. *Athletic Insight: Online Journal of Sport Psychology, 8*(3), 1–15.

Siefert, C. J. (2010). Screening for personality disorders in psychiatric settings: Four recently developed screening measures. In L. Baer & M. A. Blais (Eds.), *Handbook of clinical rating scales and assessment in psychiatry and mental health* (pp. 125–144). Totowa, NJ: Humana Press.

Siegel, M., Ross, C. S., & et al. (2013). The relationship between gun ownership and firearm homicide rates in the United States, 1981–2010. *American Journal of Public Health, 103*(11), 2098–2105. doi:10.2105/AJPH.2013.301409

Siegel, D. J. (2007). *The mindful brain: Reflection and attunement in the cultivation of well-being*. New York, NY: Norton.

Siegel, R. D. (2010). *The mindfulness solution: Everyday practices for everyday problems*. New York, NY: Guilford.

Siegel, R. K. (2005). *Intoxication: The universal drive for mind-altering substances*. Rochester, VT: Park Street Press.

Siegler, R. S. (2005). *Children's thinking* (4th ed.). Mahwah, NJ: Erlbaum.

Siegler, R. S., DeLoache, J. S., & Eisenberg, N. (2013). *How children develop* (4th ed.). New York, NY: Worth.

Siegman, A. W., & Feldstein, S. (2014). *Nonverbal behavior and communication*. Hove, UK: Psychology Press.

Sielski, R., Rief, W., & Glombiewski, J. A. (2017). Efficacy of biofeedback in chronic back pain: A meta-analysis. *International Journal of Behavioral Medicine, 24*(1), 25–41. doi:10.1007/s12529-016-9572-9

Sienaert, P., Vansteelandt, K., et al. (2010). Randomized comparison of ultra-brief bifrontal and unilateral electroconvulsive therapy for major depression: Cognitive side-effects. *Journal of Affective Disorders, 122* (1–2), 60–67. doi:10.1016/j.jad.2009.06.011

Sigelman, C. K., & Rider, E. A. (2018). *Life-span human development* (9th ed.). Boston, MA: Cengage Learning.

Silber, B. Y., & Schmitt, J. A. J. (2010). Effects of tryptophan loading on human cognition, mood, and sleep. *Neuroscience & Biobehavioral Reviews, 34*(3), 387–407. doi:10.1016/j.neubiorev.2009.08.005

Silla, I., & Gamero, N. (2014). Shared time pressure at work and its health-related outcomes: Job satisfaction as a mediator. *European Journal of Work & Organizational Psychology, 23*(3), 405–418. doi:10.1080/1359432X.2012.752898

Silveri, M. C., Ciccarelli, N., & Cappa, A. (2011). Unilateral spatial neglect in degenerative brain pathology. *Neuropsychology, 25*(5), 554–566. doi:10.1037/a0023957

Silverman, W. H. (2013). The future of psychotherapy: One editor's perspective. *Psychotherapy, 50*(4), 484–489. doi:10.1037/a0030573

Silverstein, C. (2009). The implications of removing homosexuality from the DSM as a mental disorder. *Archives of Sexual Behavior, 38*(2), 161–163.

Silvia, P. J. (2015). Intelligence and creativity are pretty similar after all. *Educational Psychology Review, 27*(4), 599–606. doi:10.1007/s10648-015-9299-1

Silvia, P. J., Wigert, B., et al. (2012). Assessing creativity with self-report scales: A review and empirical evaluation. *Psychology of Aesthetics, Creativity, & the Arts, 6*(1), 19–34. doi:10.1037/a0024071

Simister, J., & Cooper, C. (2005). Thermal stress in the U.S.A.: Effects on violence and on employee behaviour. *Stress & Health, 21*, 3–15. doi:10.1002/smi.1029

Simner, M. L., & Goffin, R. D. (2003). A position statement by the International Graphonomics Society on the use of graphology in personnel selection testing. *International Journal of Testing, 3*(4), 353–364. doi:10.1207/S15327574IJT0304_4

Simons, D. A., & Wurtele, S. K. (2010). Relationships between parents' use of corporal punishment and their children's endorsement of spanking and hitting other children. *Child Abuse & Neglect, 34*(9), 639–646. doi:10.1016/j.chiabu.2010.01.012

Simons, D. J., & Chabris, C. F. (1999). Gorillas in our midst: Sustained inattentional blindness for dynamic events. *Perception, 28*, 1059–1074. doi:10.1068/p2952

Simons, D. J., & Levin, D. T. (1998). Failure to detect changes to people during a real-world interaction. *Psychonomic Bulletin & Review, 5*(4), 644–649. doi:10.3758/BF03208840

Simon-Thomas, E. R., et al. (2005). Behavioral and electrophysiological evidence of a right hemisphere bias for the influence of negative emotion on higher cognition. *Journal of Cognitive Neuroscience, 17*(3), 518–529. doi:10.1162/0898929053279504

Simonton, D. K. (2009). Varieties of (scientific) creativity: A hierarchical model of domain-specific disposition, development, and achievement. *Perspectives on Psychological Science, 4*(5), 441–452. doi:10.1111/j.1745-6924.2009.01152.x

Simonton, D. K. (2016). Defining creativity: Don't we also need to define what is not creative? *Journal of Creative Behavior, 52*(1), n.p. doi:10.1002/jocb.137

Simpson, J. A., & Rholes, W. S. (2017). Adult attachment, stress, and romantic relationships. *Current Opinion in Psychology, 13*, 19–24. doi:10.1016/j.copsyc.2016.04.006

Sims, T., Hogan, C. L., & Carstensen, L. L. (2015). Selectivity as an emotion regulation strategy: Lessons from older adults. *Current Opinion in Psychology, 3*, 80–84. doi:10.1016/j.copsyc.2015.02.012

Singer, J. D. (2005). Explaining foreign policy: U.S. decision-making and the Persian Gulf War. *Political Psychology, 26*(5), 831–834.

Singh, B., Murad, M., et al. (2013). Meta-analysis of Glasgow Coma Scale and Simplified Motor Score in predicting traumatic brain injury outcomes. *Brain Injury, 27*(3), 293–300. doi:10.3109/02699052.2012.743182

Singh, K., Dawson, M. E., et al. (2013). Can human autonomic classical conditioning occur without contingency awareness? The critical importance of the trial sequence. *Biological Psychology, 93*(1), 197–205. doi:10.1016/j.biopsycho.2013.02.007

Sinha, R., Garcia, M., et al. (2006). Stress-induced cocaine craving and hypothalamic-pituitary-adrenal responses are predictive of cocaine relapse outcomes. *Archives of General Psychiatry, 63*(3), 324–331. doi:10.1001/archpsyc.63.3.324

Sipos, A., Rasmussen, F., et al. (2004). Paternal age and schizophrenia: A population based cohort study. *British Medical Journal, 329*(7474), 1070. doi:10.1136/bmj.38243.672396.55

Sirin, S. R., Ryce, P., et al. (2013). The role of acculturative stress on mental health symptoms for immigrant adolescents: A longitudinal investigation. *Developmental Psychology, 49*(4), 736–748. doi:10.1037/a0028398

Sirois, F. M., & Tosti, N. (2012). Lost in the moment? An investigation of procrastination, mindfulness, and well-being. *Journal of Rational-Emotive & Cognitive Behavior Therapy, 30*(4), 237–248.

Sjöqvist, F., Garle, M., & Rane, A. (2008). Use of doping agents, particularly anabolic steroids, in sports and society. *Lancet, 371*(9627), 1872–1882. doi:10.1016/S0140-6736(08)60801-6

Skeels, H. M. (1966). Adult status of children with contrasting early life experiences. *Monograph of the Society for Research in Child Development, 31*(3), 1–56.

Skinner, B. F. (1938). *The behavior of organisms.* Englewood Cliffs, NJ: Prentice-Hall.

Slagt, M., Dubas, J. S., et al. (2016). Differences in sensitivity to parenting depending on child temperament: A meta-analysis. *Psychological Bulletin, 142*(10), 1068–1110. doi:10.1037/bul0000061

Slof-Op't Landt, M. C. T., Claes, L., et al. (2016). Classifying eating disorders based on "healthy" and "unhealthy" perfectionism and impulsivity. *International Journal of Eating Disorders, 49*(7), 673–680. doi:10.1002/eat.22557

Sloman, A. (2008). The well-designed young mathematician. *Artificial Intelligence, 172*(18), 2015–2034. doi:10.1016/j.artint.2008.09.004

Smith, A. P., Christopher, G., & Sutherland, D. (2013). Acute effects of caffeine on attention: A comparison of non-consumers and withdrawn consumers. *Journal of Psychopharmacology, 27*(1), 77–83.

Smith, A. P., Clark, R., & Gallagher, J. (1999). Breakfast cereal and caffeinated coffee: Effects on working memory, attention, mood and cardiovascular function. *Physiology & Behavior, 67*(1), 9–17. doi:10.1016/S0031-9384(99)00025-6

Smith, C. (2011). *Lost in transition: The dark side of emerging adulthood.* New York, NY: Oxford University Press.

Smith, C. A., & Kirby, L. D. (2011). The role of appraisal and emotion in coping and adaptation. In R. J. Contrada & A. Baum (Eds.), *The handbook of stress science: Biology, psychology, and health* (pp. 195–208). New York, NY: Springer.

Smith, D. J., Anderson, J., et al. (2015). Childhood IQ and risk of bipolar disorder in adulthood: prospective birth cohort study. *British Journal of Psychiatry Open, 1*, 74–80. doi:10.1192/bjpo.bp.115.000455

Smith, D., & Wakefield, C. (2016). Imagery in sport. In A. M. Lane (Ed.), *Sport and exercise psychology* (2nd ed., pp. 232–249). New York: Routledge/Taylor & Francis.

Smith, J. (2014). Prototypes, exemplars, and the natural history of categorization. *Psychonomic Bulletin & Review, 21*(2), 312–331. doi:10.3758/s13423-013-0506-0

Smith, M. L., Cottrell, G. W., et al. (2005). Transmitting and decoding facial expressions. *Psychological Science, 16*(3), 184–189. doi:10.1111/j.0956-7976.2005.00801.x

Smith, M., Vogler, J., et al. (2009). Electroconvulsive therapy: The struggles in the decision-making process and the aftermath of treatment. *Issues in Mental Health Nursing, 30*(9), 554–559. doi:10.1080/01612840902807947

Smith, S. J., Zanotti, D. C., et al. (2011). Individuals' beliefs about the etiology of same-sex sexual orientation. *Journal of Homosexuality, 58*(8), 1110–1131. doi:10.1080/00918369.2011.598417

Smith, T. W. (2006). *American sexual behavior: Trends, socio-demographic differences, and risk behavior.* University of Chicago National Opinion Research Center GSS Topical Report No. 25. Retrieved July 26, 2020, from https://www.norc.org/PDFs/Publications/AmericanSexualBehavior2006.pdf

Smith, T. W., & Traupman. E. K. (2011). Anger, hostility, and aggressiveness in coronary heart disease: Clinical applications of an interpersonal perspective. In R. Allan & J. Fisher (Eds.), *Heart and mind: The practice of cardiac psychology* (2nd ed., pp. 187–198). Washington, DC: American Psychological Association.

Smith, T. W., Ruiz, J. M., & Uchino, B. N. (2004). Mental activation of supportive ties, hostility, and cardiovascular reactivity to laboratory stress in young men and women. *Health Psychology, 23*(5), 476–485. doi:10.1037/0278-6133.23.5.476

Smyth, J. M., & Pennebaker, J. W. (2008). Exploring the boundary conditions of expressive writing: In search of the right recipe. *British Journal of Health Psychology, 13*(1), 1–7. doi:10.1348/135910707X260117

Smyth, J. M., Pennebaker, J. W., & Arigo, D. (2012). What are the health effects of disclosure? In A. Baum, T. A. Revenson, et al. (Eds.), *Handbook of health psychology* (2nd ed.) (pp. 175–191). New York, NY: Psychology Press.

Snitz, B. E., O'Meara, E. S., et al. (2009). Ginkgo biloba for preventing cognitive decline in older adults: A randomized trial. *Journal of the American Medical Association, 302*(24), 2663–2670. doi:10.1001/jama.2009.1913

Snow, C. P. (1961). Either-or. *Progressive*, Feb, 24.

Snowman, J., & McCown, R. (2015). *Psychology applied to teaching* (14th ed.). Boston, MA: Cengage Learning.

Snyder, A., Bahramali, H., et al. (2006). Savant-like numerosity skills revealed in normal people by magnetic pulses. *Perception, 35*(6), 837–845. doi:10.1068/p5539

Sobczak, J. A. (2009). Alcohol use and sexual function in women: A literature review. *Journal of Addictions Nursing, 20*(2), 71–85. doi:10.1080/10884600902850095

Sobel, E., Shine, D., et al. (1996). Condom use among HIV/infected patients in South Bronx, New York. *AIDS, 10*(2), 235–236.

Sobolewski, J. M., & Amato, P. R. (2005). Economic hardship in the family of origin and children's psychological well-being in adulthood. *Journal of Marriage & Family, 67*(1), 141–156. doi:10.1111/j.0022-2445.2005.00011.x

Soderstrom, M. (2007). Beyond babytalk: Re-evaluating the nature and content of speech input to preverbal infants. *Developmental Review, 27*(4), 501–532. doi:10.1016/j.dr.2007.06.002

Soemer, A., & Schwan, S. (2012). Visual mnemonics for language learning: Static pictures versus animated morphs. *Journal of Educational Psychology, 104*(3), 565–579. doi:10.1037/a0029272

Solari, C. D., & Mare, R. D. (2012). Housing crowding effects on children's well-being. *Social Science Research, 41*(2), 464–476. doi:10.1016/j.ssresearch.2011.09.012

Solomon, E. P., Solomon, R. M., & Heide, K. M. (2009). EMDR: An evidence-based treatment for victims of trauma. *Victims & Offenders, 4*(4), 391–397. doi:10.1080/15564880903227495

Solomon, J. L., Marshall, P., & Gardner, H. (2005). Crossing boundaries to generative wisdom: An analysis of professional work. In R. J. Sternberg & J. Jordan (Eds.), *A handbook of wisdom: Psychological perspectives* (pp. 272–296). New York, NY: Cambridge University Press.

Solowij, N., Stephens, R. S., et al. (2002). Cognitive functioning of long-term heavy cannabis users seeking treatment. *Journal of the American Medical Association, 287*, 1123–1131. doi:10-1001/pubs.JAMA-ISSN-0098-7484-287-9-joc11416

Soman, D. (2010). Option overload: How to deal with choice complexity. *Rotman Magazine, Fall*, pp. 42–47.

Sommer, I. E. (2010). Sex differences in handedness, brain asymmetry, and language lateralization. In K. Hugdahl & R. Westerhausen (Eds.), *The two halves of the brain: Information processing in the cerebral hemispheres* (pp. 287–312). Cambridge, MA: MIT Press.

Sommer, K. L., Parson, C., et al. (2012). Sex and need for power as predictors of reactions to disobedience. *Social Influence, 7*(1), 1–20. doi:10.1080/15534510.2011.640198

Sommerville, J. A., Schmidt, M. H., et al. (2013). The development of fairness expectations and prosocial behavior in the second year of life. *Infancy, 18*(1), 40–66. doi:10.1111/j.1532-7078.2012.00129.x

Sorge, G. B., Toplak, M. E., & Bialystok, E. (2017). Interactions between levels of attention ability and levels of bilingualism in children's executive functioning. *Developmental Science, 20*(1), n. p. doi:10.1111/desc.12408

Sorkhabi, N. (2012). Parent socialization effects in difference cultures: Significance of directive parenting. *Psychological Reports, 110*(3), 854–878. doi:10.2466/10.02.17.21.PR0.110.3.854-878

Sörqvist, P. (2010). Effects of aircraft noise and speech on prose memory: What role for working memory capacity? *Journal of Environmental Psychology, 30*(1), 112–118.

Sousa, K., Orfale, A. G., et al. (2009). Assessment of a biofeedback program to treat chronic low back pain. *Journal of Musculoskeletal Pain, 17*(4), 369–377. doi:10.3109/10582450903284828

Soussignan, R. (2002). Duchenne smile, emotional experience, and autonomic reactivity. *Emotion, 2*(1), 52–74. doi:10.1037/1528-3542.2.1.52

Southgate, V. (2013). Do infants provide evidence that the mirror system is involved in action understanding? *Consciousness*

& Cognition, 22(3), 1114–1121. doi:10.1016/j.concog.2013.04.008

Soyez, V., & Broekaert, E. (2003). How do substance abusers and their significant others experience the re-entry phase of therapeutic community treatment: A qualitative study. *International Journal of Social Welfare, 12*(3), 211–220. doi:10.1111/1468-2397.00454

Spalding, K. L., Arner, E., et al. (2008). Dynamics of fat cell turnover in humans. *Nature, 453*, 783–787. doi:10.1038/nature06902

Sparfeldt, J. R., Rost, D. H., et al. (2013). Test anxiety in written and oral examinations. *Learning & Individual Differences, 24*, 198–203. doi:10.1016/j.lindif.2012.12.010

Special, W. P., & Li-Barber, K. (2012). Self-disclosure and student satisfaction with Facebook. *Computers in Human Behavior, 28*(2), 624–630. doi:10.1016/j.chb.2011.11.008

Spector, P. E. (2012). *Industrial and organizational psychology: Research and practice* (6th ed.). New York, NY: Wiley.

Spence, S. A., Kaylor-Hughes, C., et al. (2009). Toward a cognitive neurobiological account of free association. *Neuropsychoanalysis, 11*(2), 151–163.

Spencer, S. J., Logel, C., & Davies, P. G. (2016). Stereotype threat. *Annual Review of Psychology, 67*, 415–437. doi:10.1146/annurev-psych-073115-103235

Spencer-Thomas, S., & Jahn, D. R. (2012). Tracking a movement: U.S. milestones in suicide prevention. *Suicide & Life-Threatening Behavior, 42*(1), 78–85. doi:10.1111/j.1943-278X.2011.00072.x

Spengler, M., Brunner, M., et al. (2015). Student characteristics and behaviors at age 12 predict occupational success 40 years later over and above childhood IQ and parental socioeconomic status. *Developmental Psychology, 51*(9), 1329–1340. doi:10.1037/dev0000025

Spenhoff, M., Kruger, T. C., et al. (2013). Hypersexual behavior in an online sample of males: Associations with personal distress and functional impairment. *Journal of Sexual Medicine, 10*(12), 2996–3005. doi:10.1111/jsm.12160

Sperry, R. W. (1968). Hemisphere deconnection and unity in conscious awareness. *American Psychologist, 23*, 723–733. doi:10.1037/h0026839

Spiegler, M. D. (2013a). Behavior therapy I: Traditional behavior therapy. In J. Frew & M. D. Spiegler (Eds.), *Contemporary psychotherapies for a diverse world* (pp. 259–300). New York, NY: Routledge/Taylor & Francis.

Spiegler, M. D. (2013b). Behavior therapy II: Cognitive-behavioral therapy. In J. Frew & M. D. Spiegler (Eds.), *Contemporary psychotherapies for a diverse world* (pp. 301–337). New York, NY: Routledge/Taylor & Francis.

Spiegler, M. D., & Guevremont, D. C. (2016). *Contemporary behavior therapy* (6th ed.). Boston, MA: Cengage Learning.

Spiro, W. P., & Spiro, C. S. (2005). *Divided minds: Twin sisters and their journey through schizophrenia*. New York, NY: St. Martin's Press.

Sporer, S. L. (2001). Recognizing faces of other ethnic groups. *Psychology, Public Policy, & Law, 7*(1), 36–97. doi.10.1037/1076-8971.7.1.36

Sporns, O. (2011). *Networks of the brain*. Cambridge, MA: MIT Press.

Sporns, O. (2013). The human connectome: Origins and challenges. *Neuroimage, 80*, 53–61. doi:10.1016/j.neuroimage.2013.03.023

Sporns, O., & Betzel, R. F. (2016). Modular brain networks. *Annual Review of Psychology, 67*, 613–640. doi:10.1146/annurev-psych-122414-033634

Sprecher, S., Treger, S., & Wondra, J. D. (2013). Effects of self-disclosure role on liking, closeness, and other impressions in get-acquainted interactions. *Journal of Social & Personal Relationships, 30*(4), 497–514.

Sprecher, S., & Treger, S. (2015). The benefits of turn-taking reciprocal self-disclosure in get-acquainted interactions. *Personal Relationships, 22*(3), 460–475. doi:10.1111/pere.12090

Squire, L. R. (2004). Memory systems of the brain: A brief history and current perspective. *Neurobiology of Learning & Memory, 82*, 171–177. doi:10.1016/j.nlm.2004.06.005

Squire, L. R., & Wixted, J. T. (2011). The cognitive neuroscience of human memory since H.M. *Annual Review of Neuroscience, 34*(0147–006), 259–288. doi:10.1146/annurev-neuro-061010-113720

Sroufe, L. A., Egeland, B., et al. (2005). Placing early attachment experiences in developmental context: The Minnesota Longitudinal Study. In K. E. Grossmann, K. Grossmann, et al. (Eds.), *Attachment from infancy to adulthood: The major longitudinal studies* (pp. 48–70). New York, NY: Guilford.

Stacks, A. M., Oshio, T., et al. (2009). The moderating effect of parental warmth on the association between spanking and child aggression: A longitudinal approach. *Infant & Child Development, 18*(2), 178–194. doi:10.1002/icd.596

Stallen, M., De Dreu, C. W., et al. (2012). The herding hormone: Oxytocin stimulates in-group conformity. *Psychological Science, 23*(11), 1288–1292. doi:10.1177/0956797612446026

Stall-Meadows, C., & Hebert, P. R. (2011). The sustainable consumer: An in situ study of residential lighting alternatives as influenced by infield education. *International Journal of Consumer Studies, 35*(2), 164–170.

Stangor, C. (2015). *Research methods for the behavioral sciences* (5th ed.). Boston, MA: Cengage Learning.

Stanovich, K. E. (2019). *How to think straight about psychology* (11th ed.). New York, NY: Pearson.

Stapel, D. A., & Marx, D. M. (2007). Distinctiveness is key: How different types of self-other similarity moderate social comparison effects. *Personality & Social Psychology Bulletin, 33*(3), 439–448. doi:10.1177/0146167206296105

Starkman, B. G., Sakharkar, A. J., & Pandey, S. C. (2012). Epigenetics: Beyond the genome in alcoholism. *Alcohol Research: Current Reviews, 34*(3), 293–305.

Statista. (2020). *Number of people in the U.S. who used ecstasy (MDMA) in the past year from 2009 to 2018*. Retrieved July 21, 2020, from https://www.statista.com/statistics/611689/mdma-use-during-past-year-in-the-us/

Stawiski, S., Dykema-Engblade, A., & Tindale, R. (2012). The roles of shared stereotypes and shared processing goals on mock jury decision making. *Basic & Applied Social Psychology, 34*(1), 88–97. doi:10.1080/01973533. 2011.637467

Steblay, N. K. (2013). Lineup instructions. In B. L. Cutler (Ed.), *Reform of eyewitness identification procedures* (pp. 65–86). Washington, DC: American Psychological Association. doi:10.1037/14094-004

Steele, C. M. (1997). A threat in the air: How stereotypes shape intellectual identity and performance. *American Psychologist, 52*(6), 613–629. doi:10.1037/0003-066X.52.6.613

Steele, C. M., & Aronson, J. (1995). Stereotype threat and the intellectual test performance of African Americans. *Journal of Personality & Social Psychology, 69*(5), 797–811. doi:10.1037/0022-3514.69.5.797

Steele, V. R., Rao, V., et al. (2017). Machine learning of structural magnetic resonance imaging predicts psychopathic traits in adolescent offenders. *NeuroImage, 145*(Part B), 265–273. doi:10.1016/j.neuroimage.2015.12.013

Stefurak, T., Taylor, C., & Mehta, S. (2010). Gender-specific models of homosexual prejudice: Religiosity, authoritarianism, and gender roles. *Psychology of Religion & Spirituality, 2*(4), 247–261.

Steiger, A. (2007). Neurochemical regulation of sleep. *Journal of Psychiatric Research, 41*, 537–552. doi:10.1016/j.jpsychires.2006.04.007

Stein, G. L., Cupito, A. M., et al. (2014). Familism through a developmental lens. *Journal of Latina/o Psychology, 2*(4), 224–250. doi:10.1037/lat0000025

Stein, L. M., & Memon, A. (2006). Testing the efficacy of the cognitive interview in a developing country. *Applied Cognitive Psychology, 20*(5), 597–605. doi:10.1002/acp.1211

Stein, M. D., & Friedmann, P. D. (2005). Disturbed sleep and its relationship to alcohol use. *Substance Abuse, 26*(1), 1–13. doi:10.1300/J465v26n01_01

Stein, M. I. (1974). *Stimulating creativity* (Vol. 1). New York, NY: Academic.

Stein, M. T., & Ferber, R. (2001). Recent onset of sleepwalking in early adolescence. *Journal of Development, Behavior, & Pediatrics, 22*, S33–S35.

Stein, R. (2017). "Trumping" conformity: Urges towards conformity to ingroups and nonconformity to morally opposed outgroups. *Journal of Experimental Social Psychology, 70*, 34–40. doi:10.1016/j.jesp.2016.12.007

Steinberg, L. (2001). Adolescent development. *Annual Review of Psychology, 52*, 83–110. doi:10.1146/annurev.psych.52.1.83

Steiner, B., & Wooldredge, J. (2009). Rethinking the link between institutional crowding and inmate misconduct. *The Prison Journal, 89*(2), 205–233.

Steinman, S. A., Smyth, F. L., et al. (2013). Anxiety-linked expectancy bias across the adult lifespan. *Cognition & Emotion, 27*(2), 345–355. doi:10.1080/02699931.2012.711743

Steinmayr, R., & Spinath, B. (2009). The importance of motivation as a predictor of school achievement. *Learning & Individual Differences, 19*(1), 80–90. doi:10.1016/j.lindif.2008.05.004

Steketee, G., Frost, R. O., et al. (2010). Waitlist-controlled trial of cognitive behavior therapy for hoarding disorder. *Depression & Anxiety, 27*(5), 476–484. doi:10.1002/da.20673

Stemler, S. E., & Sternberg, R. J. (2006). Using situational judgment tests to measure practical intelligence. In J. A. Weekley & R. E. Ployhart (Eds.), *Situational judgment tests: Theory, measurement, and application* (pp. 107–131). Mahwah, NJ: Erlbaum.

Stephens, D. P. (2012). The influence of mainstream Hip Hop's female sexual scripts on African American women's dating relationship experiences. In M. A. Paludi (Ed.), *The psychology of love* (Vols. 1–4, pp. 169–183). Santa Barbara, CA: Praeger.

Stephens, K., Kiger, L., et al. (1999). Use of nonverbal measures of intelligence in identification of culturally diverse gifted students in rural areas. *Perceptual & Motor Skills, 88*(3, Pt. 1), 793–796. doi:10.2466/PMS.88.3.793-796

Stern, S. L., Dhanda, R., & Hazuda, H. P. (2001). Hopelessness predicts mortality in older Mexican and European Americans. *Psychosomatic Medicine, 63*(3), 344–351.

Sternberg, R. J. (1988). *The triangle of love*. New York, NY: Basic.

Sternberg, R. J. (2004). Culture and intelligence. *American Psychologist, 59*(5), 325–338. doi:10.1037/0003-066X.59.5.325

Sternberg, R. J. (2007). Race and intelligence: Not a case of black and white. *New Scientist*, Oct. 27, 16.

Sternberg, R. J. (2017). *Cognitive psychology* (7th ed.). Boston, MA: Cengage Learning.

Sternberg, R. J., & Grigorenko, E. L. (2005). Cultural explorations of the nature of intelligence. In A. F. Healy (Ed.), *Experimental cognitive psychology and its applications* (pp. 225–235). Washington, DC: American Psychological Association.

Sternberg, R. J., Grigorenko, E. L., et al. (2011). Intelligence, race, and genetics. In S. Krimsky & K. Sloan (Eds.), *Race and the genetic revolution: Science, myth, and culture* (pp. 195–237). New York, NY: Columbia University Press.

Stetz, T., Button, S. B., & Porr, W. B. (2009). New tricks for an old dog: Visualizing job analysis results. *Public Personnel Management, 38*(1), 91–100.

Stevens, F. L. (2016). The anterior cingulate cortex in psychopathology and psychotherapy: Effects on awareness and repression of affect. *Neuropsychoanalysis, 18*(1), 53–68. doi:10.1080/15294145.2016.1149777

Stevens, R., Bernadini, S., & Jemmott, J. B. (2013). Social environment and sexual risk-taking among gay and transgender African American youth. *Culture, Health & Sexuality, 15*(10), 1148–1161. doi:10.1080/13691058.2013.809608

Stickgold, R. (2013). Parsing the role of sleep in memory processing. *Current Opinion in Neurobiology, 23*(5), 847–853. doi:10.1016/j.conb.2013.04.002

Stickgold, R., & Walker, M. (2004). To sleep, perchance to gain creative insight? *Trends in Cognitive Sciences, 8*(5), 191–192. doi:10.1016/j.tics.2004.03.003

Stinson, F. S., Dawson, D. A., et al. (2007). The epidemiology of DSM-IV specific phobia in the USA: Result from the National Epidemiologic Survey on Alcohol and Related Conditions. *Psychological Medicine, 37*(7), 1047–1059. doi:10.1017/S0033291707000086

Stix, G. (2010). Alzheimer's: Forestalling the darkness. *Scientific American, 302*, 50–57. doi:10.1038/scientificamerican0610-50

Stix, G. (2011). The neuroscience of true grit. *Scientific American, 304*, 28–33. doi:10.1038/scientificamerican0111-29a

Stöber, J. (2004). Dimensions of test anxiety: Relations to ways of coping with pre-exam anxiety and uncertainty. *Anxiety, Stress & Coping, 17*(3), 213–226. doi:10.1080/ 10615800412331292615

Stokes, D., & Lappin, M. (2010, February 2). Neurofeedback and biofeedback with 37 migraineurs: A clinical outcome study. *Behavioral & Brain Functions, 6*, ArtID 9. Retrieved July 21, 2020, from www.ncbi.nlm.nih.gov/pubmed/20205867

Stone, J., Perry, Z. W., & Darley, J. M. (1997). "White men can't jump." *Basic & Applied Social Psychology, 19*(3), 291–306. doi:10.1207/15324839751036977

Stoop, R., Hegoburu, C., & van den Burg, E. (2015). New opportunities in vasopressin and oxytocin research: A perspective from the amygdala. *Annual Review of Neuroscience, 38*, 369–388. doi:10.1146/annurev-neuro-071714-033904

Stoppard, J. M., & McMullen, L. M. (Eds.). (2003). *Situating sadness: Women and depression in social context*. New York, NY: New York University Press.

Storr, A. (1988). *Solitude: A return to the self.* New York, NY: Free Press.

Strack, F., & Förster, J. (Eds.). (2009). *Social cognition: The basis of human interaction.* New York, NY: Psychology Press.

Strack. F., Martin, L. L., & Stepper, S. (1988). Inhibiting and facilitating conditions of facial expressions: A non-obtrusive test of the facial feedback hypothesis. *Journal of Personality & Social Psychology, 54*, 768–777. doi:10.1037/0022-3514.54.5.768

Straub, R. (2012). *Health psychology* (3rd ed.). New York, NY: Worth.

Strayer, D. L., Drews, F. A., & Crouch, D. J. (2006). A comparison of the cell phone driver and the drunk driver. *Human Factors, 48*(2), 381–391. doi:10.1518/001872006777724471

Strenger, C. (2016). *Freud's legacy in the global era.* New York, NY: Routledge/Taylor & Francis.

Stricker, G. (2011). PsyD programs. In J. C. Norcross, G. R. VandenBos, et al. (Eds.), *History of psychotherapy: Continuity and change* (2nd ed., pp. 630–639). Washington, DC: American Psychological Association. doi:10.1037/12353-040

Strickhouser, J. E., & Zell, E. (2015). Self-evaluative effects of dimensional and social comparison. *Journal of Experimental Social Psychology, 59*, 60–66. doi:10.1016/j.jesp.2015.03.001

Strickhouser, J. E., Zell, E., et al. (2017). Does personality predict health and well-being? A metasynthesis. *Health Psychology*, n.p. doi:10.1037/hea0000475

Strickland, S. A. (2015). Pedophilia. In D. L. Dobbert & T. X. Mackey (Eds.), *Deviance: Theories on behaviors that defy social norms* (pp. 171–180). Santa Barbara, CA: Praeger/ABC-CLIO.

Striedter, G. F., Srinivasan, S., & Monuki, E. S. (2015). Cortical folding: When, where, how, and why? *Annual Review of Neuroscience, 38*, 291–307. doi:10.1146/annurev-neuro-071714-034128

Stroebe, W., Papies, E. K., & Aarts, H. (2008). From homeostatic to hedonic theories of eating: Self-regulatory failure in food-rich environments. *Applied Psychology, 57*, 172–193. doi:10.1111/j.1464-0597.2008.00360.x

Strong, B., DeVault, C., & Cohen, T. C. (2014). *The marriage and family experience: Intimate relationships in a changing society* (12th ed.). Boston, MA: Cengage Learning.

Strote, J., Lee, J. E., & Wechsler, H. (2002). Increasing MDMA use among college students: Results of a national survey. *Journal of Adolescent Health, 30*(1), 64–72. doi:10.1016/S1054-139X(01)00315-9

Strubbe, M. J. (2005). What did Triplett really find? A contemporary analysis of the first experiment in social psychology. *American Journal of Psychology, 118*, 271–286.

Stumbrys, T., Erlacher, D., et al. (2012). Induction of lucid dreams: A systematic review of evidence. *Consciousness & Cognition, 21*(3), 1456–1475. doi:10.1016/j.concog.2012.07.003

Stuss, D. T., & Knight, R. T. (2002). *Principles of frontal lobe function*. New York, NY: Oxford University Press.

Suarez, E., & Gadalla, T. M. (2010). Stop blaming the victim: A meta-analysis on rape myths. *Journal of Interpersonal Violence, 25*(11), 2010–2035.

Sue, D., Sue, D. W., et al. (2016). *Understanding abnormal behavior* (11th ed.). Boston, MA: Cengage Learning.

Sue, D., Sue, D. W., et al. (2017). *Essentials of understanding abnormal behavior* (3rd ed.). Boston, MA: Cengage Learning.

Suedfeld, P., & Steel, G. D. (2000). The environmental psychology of capsule habitats. *Annual Review of Psychology, 51*, 227–253.

Suedfeld, P., & Borrie, R. A. (1999). Health and therapeutic applications of chamber and flotation restricted environmental stimulation therapy (REST). *Psychology & Health, 14*(3), 545–566. doi:10.1080/08870449908407346

Suh, H., Rice, K. G., et al. (2016). Measuring acculturative stress with the SAFE: Evidence for longitudinal measurement invariance and associations with life satisfaction. *Personality & Individual Differences, 89*, 217–222. doi:10.1016/j.paid.2015.10.002

Suhay, E. (2015). Explaining group influence: The role of identity and emotion in political conformity and polarization. *Political Behavior, 37*(1), 221–251. doi:10.1007/s11109-014-9269-1

Suinn, R. M. (1975). *Fundamentals of behavior pathology* (2nd ed.). New York, NY: Wiley.

Suls, J. M., Luger, T., & Martin, R. (2010). The biopsychosocial model and the use of theory in health psychology. In J. M. Suls, K. W. Davidson, et al. (Eds.), *Handbook of health psychology and behavioral medicine* (pp. 15–27). New York, NY: Guilford.

Summers, A., Hayward, R. D., & Miller, M. K. (2010). Death qualification as systematic exclusion of jurors with certain religious and other characteristics. *Journal of Applied Social Psychology, 40*(12), 3218–3234.

Sun, Y., & Han, Z. (2018). Climate change risk perception in Taiwan: Correlation with individual and societal factors. *International Journal of Environmental Research & Public Health, 15*, 91–100. doi:10.3390/ijerph15010091

Sunnafrank, M., Ramirez, A., & Metts, S. (2004). At first sight: Persistent relational effects of get-acquainted conversations. *Journal of Social & Personal Relationships, 21*(3), 361–379. doi:10.1177/0265407504042837

Sunnhed, R., & Jansson-Fröjmark, M. (2014). Are changes in worry associated with treatment response in cognitive behavioral therapy for insomnia? *Cognitive Behaviour Therapy, 43*(1), 1–11. doi:10.1080/16506073.2013.846399

Susilo, T., Wright, V., et al. (2015). Acquired prosopagnosia without word recognition deficits. *Cognitive Neuropsychology, 32*(6), 321–339. doi:10.1080/02643294.2015.1081882

Sussman, G. (Ed.). (2011). *The propaganda society: Promotional culture and politics in global context.* New York: Peter Lang.

Sutin, A. R., & Costa, P. T. Jr. (2010). Reciprocal influences of personality and job characteristics across middle adulthood. *Journal of Personality, 78*(1), 257–288. doi:10.1111/j.1467-6494.2009.00615.x

Sutterer, D. W., & Awh, E. (2016). Retrieval practice enhances the accessibility but not the quality of memory. *Psychonomic Bulletin & Review, 23*(3), 831–841. doi:10.3758/s13423-015-0937-x

Suzuki, L., & Aronson, J. (2005). The cultural malleability of intelligence and its impact on the racial/ethnic hierarchy. *Psychology, Public Policy, & Law, 11*, 320–327. doi:10.1037/1076-8971.11.2.320

Swanson, S. A., Crow, S. J., et al. (2011). Prevalence and correlates of eating disorders in adolescents: Results from the national comorbidity survey replication adolescent supplement. *Archives of General Psychiatry, 68*(7), 714–723. doi:10.1001/archgenpsychiatry.2011.22

Swartz, T. B., & Arce, A. (2014). New insights involving the home team advantage. *International Journal of Sports Science & Coaching, 9*(4), 681–692. doi:10.1260/1747-9541.9.4.681

Syed, E. C. J., Grima, L. L., et al. (2016). Action initiation shapes mesolimbic dopamine encoding of future rewards. *Nature Neuroscience, 19*(1), 34–36. doi:10.1038/nn.4187

Synhorst, L. L., Buckley, J. A., et al. (2005). Cross informant agreement of the Behavioral and Emotional Rating Scale: 2nd Edition (BERS-2) parent and youth rating scales. *Child & Family Behavior Therapy, 27*(3), 1–11. doi:10.1300/J019v27n03_01

Szaflarski, J. P., Rajagopal, A., et al. (2011). Left-handedness and language lateralization in children. *Brain Research, 1433*, 85–97. doi:10.1016/j.brainres.2011.11.026

Szollos, A. (2009). Toward a psychology of chronic time pressure: Conceptual and methodological review. *Time & Society, 18*(2–3), 332–350. doi:10.1177/0961463X09337847

Szpak, A., & Allen, D. (2012). A case of acute suicidality following excessive caffeine intake. *Journal of Psychopharmacology, 26*(11), 1502–1510. doi:10.1177/0269881112442788

Tabak, N. T., Green, M. F., et al. (2015). Perceived emotional intelligence is impaired and associated with poor community functioning in schizophrenia and bipolar disorder. *Schizophrenia Research, 162*(1), 189–195. doi:10.1016/j.schres.2014.12.005

Taber, K. H., Black, D. N., et al. (2012). Neuroanatomy of dopamine: Reward and addiction. *Journal of Neuropsychiatry And Clinical Neurosciences, 24*(1), 1–4. doi:10.1176/appi.neuropsych.24.1.1

Tackett, J. L., & Krueger, R. F. (2011). Dispositional influences on human aggression. In P. R. Shaver & M. Mikulincer (Eds.), *Human aggression and violence: Causes, manifestations, and consequences* (pp. 89–104). Washington, DC: American Psychological Association.

Tafarodi, R. W., Shaughnessy, S. C., et al. (2011). The reporting of self-esteem in Japan and Canada. *Journal of Cross-Cultural Psychology, 42*(1), 155–164. doi:10.1177/0022022110386373

Tafrate, R. C., & Kassinove, H. (2009). *Anger management for everyone: Seven proven ways to control anger and live a happier life.* Atascadero, CA: Impact Publishers.

Taitz, I. (2011). Learning lucid dreaming and its effect on depression in undergraduates. *International Journal of Dream Research, 4*(2), 117–126.

Talbot, N. L., & Gamble, S. A. (2008). IPT for women with trauma histories in community mental health care. *Journal of Contemporary Psychotherapy, 38*(1), 35–44. doi:10.1007/s10879-007-9066-9

Tal-Or, N., & Papirman, Y. (2007). The fundamental attribution error in attributing fictional figures' characteristics to the actors. *Media Psychology, 9*(2), 331–345. doi:10.1080/15213260701286049

Tam, H., Jarrold, C., et al. (2010). The development of memory maintenance: Children's use of phonological rehearsal and attentional refreshment in working memory tasks. *Journal of Experimental Child Psychology, 107*(3), 306–324. doi:10.1016/j.jecp.2010.05.006

Tamis-LeMonda, C. S., Shannon, J. D., et al. (2004). Fathers and mothers at play with their 2- and 3-year-olds: Contributions to language and cognitive development. *Child Development, 75*(6), 1806–1820. doi:10.1111/j.1467-8624.2004.00818.x

Tandon, R., Heckers, S., et al. (2013). Catatonia in DSM-5. *Schizophrenia Research, 150*, 26–30. doi:10.1016/j.schres.2013.04.034

Tang, C. Y., Eaves, E. L., et al. (2010). Brain networks for working memory and factors of intelligence assessed in males and females with fMRI and DTI. *Intelligence, 38*(3), 293–303. doi:10.1016/j.intell.2010.03.003

Tannen, D. (1995, September-October). The power of talk: Who gets heard and why. *Harvard Business Review*. Retrieved July 21, 2020, from https://hbr.org/1995/09/the-power-of-talk-who-gets-heard-and-why#

Taraban, R., Rynearson, K., & Kerr, M. (2000). College students' academic performance and self-reports of comprehension strategy use. *Reading Psychology, 21*(4), 283–308. doi:10.1080/027027100750061930

Taris, T. W., Bakker, A. B., et al. (2005). Job control and burnout across occupations. *Psychological Reports, 97*(3), 955–961. doi:10.2466/PR0.97.7.955-961

Tarquinio, C. C., Brennstuhl, M. J., et al. (2012). Eye movement desensitization and reprocessing (EMDR) therapy in the treatment of victims of domestic violence: A pilot study. *European Review of Applied Psychology, 62*(4), 205–212. doi:10.1016/j.erap.2012.08.006

Tatum, J. L., & Foubert, J. D. (2009). Rape myth acceptance, hypermasculinity, and SAT scores as correlates of moral development: Understanding sexually aggressive attitudes in first-year college men. *Journal of College Student Development, 50*(2), 195–209. doi:10.1353/csd.0.0062

Tauber, A. I. (2010). *Freud, the reluctant philosopher*. Princeton, NJ: Princeton University Press.

Tavakoli, S., Lumley, M. A., et al. (2009). Effects of assertiveness training and expressive writing on acculturative stress in international students: A randomized trial. *Journal of Counseling Psychology, 56*(4), 590–596. doi:10.1037/a0016634

Tavris, C., & Aronson, E. (2007). *Mistakes were made (but not by me): Why we justify foolish beliefs, bad decisions, and hurtful acts*. New York, NY: Harcourt.

Tay, L., & Diener, E. (2011). Needs and subjective well-being around the world. *Journal of Personality and Social Psychology, 101*(2), 354–365. doi:10.1037/a0023779

Taylor, C. A., Manganello, J. A., et al. (2010). Mothers' spanking of 3-year-old children and subsequent risk of children's aggressive behavior. *Pediatrics, 125*(5), e1057–e1065. doi:10.1542/peds.2009-2678

Taylor, D. J., & Roane, B. M. (2010). Treatment of insomnia in adults and children: A practice-friendly review of research. *Journal of Clinical Psychology, 66*(11), 1137–1147. doi:10.1002/jclp.20733

Taylor, G. J., & Taylor-Allan, H. L. (2007). Applying emotional intelligence in understanding and treating physical and psychological disorders: What we have learned from alexithymia. In R. Bar-On, M. J. G. Reuven, et al. (Eds.), *Educating people to be emotionally intelligent* (pp. 211–223). Westport, CT: Praeger.

Taylor, K. (2004). *Brainwashing: The science of thought control*. New York, NY: Oxford University Press.

Taylor, L. D., & Ruiz, J. (2013). Empowerment and aggression: Understanding violence in America's girls. *Analyses of Social Issues & Public Policy, 13*(1), 401–403. doi:10.1111/asap.12010

Taylor, R., Thomson, H., et al. (2017). Does working memory have a single capacity limit? *Journal of Memory & Language, 93*, 67–81. doi:10.1016/j.jml.2016.09.004

Taylor, S. E. (2011). The future of social-health psychology: Prospects and predictions. *Social & Personality Psychology Compass, 5*, 275–284. doi:10.1111/j.1751-9004.2011.00360.x

Taylor, S. E. (2021). *Health psychology* (11th ed.). New York, NY: McGraw-Hill.

Taylor, S. E., & Master, S. L. (2011). Social responses to stress: The tend-and-befriend model. In R. J. Contrada & A. Baum (Eds.), *The handbook of stress science: Biology, psychology, and health* (pp. 101–109). New York, NY: Springer.

Teff, K. L., & Silva, C. M. (2015). Waking up to the importance of sleep and circadian rhythms for metabolic health: The need for in-depth phenotyping. *Sleep: Journal of Sleep & Sleep Disorders Research, 38*(12), 1847–1848. doi:10.5665/sleep.5224

Teglasi, H. (2010). *Essentials of TAT and other storytelling assessments* (2nd ed.). Hoboken, NJ: Wiley.

Tennesen, M. (2007). Gone today, hear tomorrow. *New Scientist, March 10*, 42–45.

Tennie, C., Greve, K., et al. (2010). Two-year-old children copy more reliably and more often than nonhuman great apes in multiple observational learning tasks. *Primates, 51*(4), 337–351. doi:10.1007/s10329-010-0208-4

Teo, A. R., & Gaw, A. C. (2010). Hikikomori, a Japanese culture-bound syndrome of social withdrawal? A proposal for DSM-5. *Journal of Nervous & Mental Disease, 198*(6), 444–449. doi:10.1097/NMD.0b013e3181e086b1

Teresi, L., & Haroutunian, H. (2011). *Hijacking the brain: How drug and alcohol addiction hijacks our brains. The science behind Twelve-Step recovery*. Bloomington, IN: AuthorHouse.

Terman, L. M., & Merrill, M. A. (1937/1960). *Stanford-Binet Intelligence Scale*. Boston, MA: Houghton Mifflin.

Terman, L. M., & Oden, M. (1959). *The gifted group in mid-life* (Vol. 5): *Genetic studies of genius*. Stanford, CA: Stanford University Press.

Terry, C. (2006). History of treatment of people with mental illness. In J. R. Matthews, C. E. Walker, et al. (Eds.), *Your practicum in psychology: A guide for maximizing knowledge and competence* (pp. 81–103). Washington, DC: American Psychological Association.

Terry, D. J., & Hogg, M. A. (1996). Group norms and the attitude-behavior relationship. *Personality & Social Psychology Bulletin, 22*(8), 776–793. doi:10.1177/0146167296228002

Teufel-Shone, N. I., Staten, L. K. et al. (2005). Cohesion and conflict in an American Indian community. *American Journal of Health Behavior, 29*(5), 413–422. doi:10.5993/AJHB.29.5.4

Teyber, E., & McClure, F. H. (2017). *Interpersonal process in therapy: An integrative model* (7th ed.). Boston, MA: Cengage Learning.

Thakral, P. P. (2011). The neural substrates associated with inattentional blindness. *Consciousness & Cognition, 20*(4), 1768–1775. doi:10.1016/j.concog.2011.03.013

Thanellou, A., & Green, J. T. (2011). Spontaneous recovery but not reinstatement of the extinguished conditioned eyeblink response in the rat. *Behavioral Neuroscience, 125*(4), 613–625. doi:10.1037/a0023582

Thase, M. E. (2006). Major depressive disorder. In F. Andrasik (Ed.), *Comprehensive handbook of personality and psychopathology: Adult psychopathology* (Vol. 2, pp. 207–230). New York, NY: Wiley.

The Nature Conservancy. (2020). *Carbon footprint calculator*. Retrieved July 21, 2020, from http://www.nature.org/greenliving/carboncalculator/

Thoma, C. A., Bartholomew, C. C., & Scott, L. A. (2009). *Universal design for transition: A roadmap for planning and instruction*. Baltimore, MD: Brookes Publishing.

Thomas, A. K., Bulevich, J. B., & Dubois, S. J. (2011). Context affects feeling-of-knowing accuracy in younger and older adults. *Journal of Experimental Psychology: Learning, Memory, & Cognition, 37*(1), 96–108. doi:10.1037/a0021612

Thomas, E. M. (2004). *Aggressive behaviour outcomes for young children: Change in parenting environment predicts change in behaviour*. Ottawa, ON: Statistics Canada. Retrieved July 21, 2020, from https://www150.statcan.gc.ca/n1/en/pub/89-599-m/89-599-m2004001-eng.pdf?st=7FJqXSDx

Thomas, S. P. (2013). The global phenomenon of urbanization and its effects on mental health. *Issues in Mental Health Nursing, 34*(3), 139–140. doi:10.3109/01612840.2013.762857

Thompson, E. R., & Barnes, K. (2012). Meaning of sexual performance among men with and without erectile dysfunction. *Psychology of Men & Masculinity*, doi:10.1037/a0029104

Thompson, R. J., Payne, S. C., et al. (2015). Applicant attraction to flexible work arrangements: Separating the influence of flextime and flexplace. *Journal of Occupational & Organizational Psychology, 88*(4), 726–749. doi/10.1111/joop.12095/pdf

Thornton, S. N. (2010). Thirst and hydration: Physiology and consequences of dysfunction. *Physiology & Behavior, 100*(1), 15–21. doi:10.1016/j.physbeh.2010.02.026

Thrift, A. G. (2010). Design and methods of population surveys. *Neuroepidemiology, 34*(4), 267–269. doi:10.1159/000297758

Thurson, T. (2008). *Think better: An innovator's guide to productive thinking*. New York, NY: McGraw-Hill.

Thyen, U., Richter-Appelt, H., et al. (2005). Deciding on gender in children with intersex conditions: Considerations and controversies. *Treatments in Endocrinology, 4*(1), 1–8.

Tikotzky, L., Chambers, A. S., et al. (2012). Postpartum maternal sleep and mothers' perceptions of their attachment relationship with the infant among women with a history of depression during pregnancy. *International Journal of Behavioral Development, 36*(6), 440–448.

Till, B. D., & Priluck, R. L. (2000). Stimulus generalization in classical conditioning: An initial investigation and extension. *Psychology & Marketing, 17*(1), 55–72. doi:10.1002/(SICI)1520-6793(200001)17:1<55::AID-MAR4>3.0.CO;2-C

Till, B. D., Stanley, S. M., & Priluck, R. (2008). Classical conditioning and celebrity endorsers: An examination of belongingness and resistance to extinction. *Psychology & Marketing, 25*(2), 179–196. doi:10.1002/mar.20205

Tine, M., & Gotlieb, R. (2013). Gender-, race-, and income-based stereotype threat: The effects of multiple stigmatized aspects of identity on math performance and working memory function. *Social Psychology of Education, 16*, 353–376. doi:10.1007/s11218-013-9224-8

Tinti, C., Schmidt, S., et al. (2014). Distinct processes shape flashbulb and event memories. *Memory & Cognition, 42*(4), 539–551. doi:10.3758/s13421-013-0383-9

Tipples, J., Atkinson, A. P., & Young, A. W. (2002). The eyebrow frown: A salient social signal. *Emotion, 2*(3), 288–296. doi:10.1037/1528-3542.2.3.288

Titov, N. (2011). Internet-delivered psychotherapy for depression in adults. *Current Opinion in Psychiatry, 24*(1), 18–23. doi:10.1097/YCO.0b013e32833ed18f

Toates, F. (2011). *Biological psychology* (3rd ed.). Boston, MA: Pearson/Allyn & Bacon.

Tolin, D. F., McKay, D., et al. (2015). Empirically supported treatment: Recommendations for a new model. *Clinical Psychology: Science & Practice, 22*(4), 317–338. doi:10.1111/cpsp.12122

Tolkacheva, N., van Groenou, M. B., & van Tilburg, T. (2014). Sibling similarities and sharing the care of older parents. *Journal of Family Issues, 35*(3), 312–330. doi:10.1177/0192513X12470619

Tolman, E. C., & Honzik, C. H. (1930). Degrees of hunger, reward and non-reward, and maze performance in rats. *University of California Publications in Psychology, 4*, 241–256.

Tolman, E. C., Ritchie, B. F., & Kalish, D. (1946). Studies in spatial learning: II. Place learning versus response learning. *Journal of Experimental Psychology, 36*, 221–229. doi:10.1037/h0060262

Tom, G., Tong, S., & Hesse, C. (2010). Thick slice and thin slice teaching evaluations. *Social Psychology of Education, 13*(1), 129–136. doi:10.1007/s11218-009-9101-7

Tomasi, D., & Volkow, N. D. (2012). Laterality patterns of brain functional connectivity: Gender effects. *Cerebral Cortex, 22*(6), 1455–1462. doi:10.1093/cercor/bhr230

Toneatto, T. (2002). Cognitive therapy for problem gambling. *Cognitive & Behavioral Practice, 9*(3), 191–199. doi:10.1016/S1077-7229(02)80049-9

Torrente, M. P., Gelenberg, A. J., & Vrana, K. E. (2012). Boosting serotonin in the brain: Is it time to revamp the treatment of depression? *Journal of Psychopharmacology, 26*(5), 629–635. doi:10.1177/0269881111430744

Toyota, H., & Kikuchi, Y. (2005). Encoding richness of self-generated elaboration and spacing effects on incidental memory. *Perceptual & Motor Skills, 101*(2), 621–627.

Trainor, L. J., & Desjardins, R. N. (2002). Pitch characteristics of infant-directed speech affect infants' ability to discriminate vowels. *Psychonomic Bulletin & Review, 9*(2), 335–340. doi:10.3758/BF03196290

Tramontana, J. (2011). *Sports hypnosis in practice: Scripts, strategies, and case examples.* Bethel, CT: Crown House Publishing.

Tran, L., & Rimes, K. A. (2017). Unhealthy perfectionism, negative beliefs about emotions, emotional suppression, and depression in students: A mediational analysis. *Personality & Individual Differences, 110*, 144–147. doi:10.1016/j.paid.2017.01.042

Travis, F., Arenander, A., & DuBois, D. (2004). Psychological and physiological characteristics of a proposed object-referral/self-referral continuum of self-awareness. *Consciousness & Cognition, 13*, 401–420. doi:10.1016/j.concog.2004.03.001

Traxler, M. J. (2011). *Introduction to psycholinguistics: Understanding language science.* New York, NY: Wiley-Blackwell.

Treatment Advocacy Center. (2018). *Fast facts.* Retrieved July 21, 2020, from www.treatmentadvocacycenter.org/evidence-and-research/fast-facts

Treffert, D. A. (2010). *Islands of genius: The bountiful mind of the autistic, acquired, and sudden savant.* London, UK: Jessica Kingsley Publishers.

Treffert, D. A. (2014). Savant syndrome: Realities, myths and misconceptions. *Journal of Autism & Developmental Disorders, 44*(3), 564–571.

Treffert, D. A., & Christensen, C. D. (2005). Inside the mind of a savant. *Scientific American, 293*(6), 108–113. doi:10.1038/scientificamerican1205-108

Tregear, S., Resto, J., et al. (2010). Continuous positive airway pressure reduces risk of motor vehicle crash among drivers with obstructive sleep apnea: Systematic review and meta-analysis. *Sleep: Journal of Sleep & Sleep Disorders Research, 33*(10), 1373–1380.

Trentowska, M., Bender, C., & Tuschen-Caffier, B. (2013). Mirror exposure in women with bulimic symptoms: How do thoughts and emotions change in body image treatment? *Behaviour Research & Therapy, 51*(1), 1–6. doi:10.1016/j.brat.2012.03.012

Treves, T. A., & Korczyn, A. D. (2012). Modeling the dementia epidemic. *CNS Neuroscience & Therapeutics, 18*(2), 175–181. doi:10.1111/j.1755-5949.2011.00242.x

Triandis, H. C., & Suh, E. M. (2002). Cultural influences on personality. *Annual Review of Psychology, 53*, 133–160. doi:10.1146/annurev.psych.53.100901.135200

Tripp, D. A., Stanish, W., et al. (2011). Fear of reinjury, negative affect, and catastrophizing predicting return to sport in recreational athletes with anterior cruciate ligament injuries at 1 year postsurgery. *Sport, Exercise, & Performance Psychology, 1*(S), 38–48. doi:10.1037/2157-3905.1.S.38

Trocmé, N., MacLaurin, B., et al. (2001). *Canadian Incidence Study of Reported Child Abuse and Neglect.* Retrieved July 21, 2020, from https://www.canada.ca/content/dam/phac-aspc/migration/phac-aspc/publicat/cissr-ecirc/pdf/cmic_e.pdf

Troll, L. E., & Skaff, M. M. (1997). Perceived continuity of self in very old age. *Psychology & Aging, 12*(1), 162–169. doi:10.1037/0882-7974.12.1.162

Troup, C., & Rose, J. (2012). Working from home: Do formal or informal telework arrangements provide better work–family outcomes? *Community, Work & Family, 15*(4), 471–486. doi:10.1080/13668803.2012.724220

Trujillo, L. T., Kornguth, S., & Schnyer, D. M. (2009). An ERP examination of the different effects of sleep deprivation on exogenously cued and endogenously cued attention. *Sleep, 32*(10), 1285–1297.

Trull, T., & Prinstein, M. (2013). *Clinical psychology* (8th ed.). Boston, MA: Cengage Learning.

Truscott, D. (2014). Gestalt therapy. In G. R. VandenBos, E. Meidenbauer, et al. (Eds.), *Psychotherapy theories & techniques: A read* (pp. 187–194). Washington, DC: American Psychological Association. doi:10.1037/14295-021

Tsai J., El-Gabalawy R., et al. (2015) Post-traumatic growth among veterans in the USA: Results from the National Health and Resilience in Veterans Study. *Psychological Medicine, 45*(1), 165–179. doi:10.1017/S0033291714001202.

Tsintsadze-Maass, E., & Maass, R. W. (2014). Groupthink and terrorist radicalization. *Terrorism & Political Violence, 26*(5), 735–758. doi:10.1080/09546553.2013.805094

Tulving, E. (1989). Remembering and knowing the past. *American Scientist, 77*(4), 361–367.

Tulving, E. (2002). Episodic memory. *Annual Review of Psychology, 53*, 1–25. doi:10.1146/annurev.psych.53.100901.135114

Tunney, R. J., & Fernie, G. (2012). Episodic and prototype models of category learning. *Cognitive Processing, 13*(1), 41–54.

Turenius, C. I., Htut, M. M., et al. (2009). GABA(A) receptors in the lateral hypothalamus as mediators of satiety and body weight regulation. *Brain Research, 1262*, 16–24. doi:10.1016/j.brainres.2009.01.016

Turgoose, D., Glover, N., et al. (2017, March 2). Empathy, compassion fatigue, and burnout in police officers working with rape victims. *Traumatology*, n.p. doi:10.1037/trm0000118

Turiano, N. A., Mroczek, D. K., et al. (2013). Big 5 personality traits and interleukin-6: Evidence for 'healthy neuroticism' in a U.S. population sample. *Brain, Behavior, & Immunity, 28*, 83–89. doi:10.1016/j.bbi.2012.10.020

Turkheimer, E., Haley, A., et al. (2003). Socioeconomic status modifies heritability of IQ in young children. *Psychological Science, 14*, 623–628. doi:10.1046/j.0956-7976.2003.psci_1475.x

Tversky, A., & Kahneman, D. (1981). The framing of decisions and the psychology of choice. *Science, 211*, 453–458. doi:10.1126/science.7455683

Tversky, A., & Kahneman, D. (1982). Judgments of and by representativeness. In D. Kahneman, P. Slovic, et al. (Eds.), *Judgment under uncertainty: Heuristics and biases* (pp. 84–98). Cambridge, MA: Cambridge University Press.

Twemlow, S. W., & Sacco, F. C. (2012). *Preventing bullying and school violence.* Washington, DC: American Psychiatric Publishing.

U.S. Census Bureau. (2020). *Income and Poverty in the United States: 2018.* Retrieved July 21, 2020, from https://www.census.gov/content/dam/Census/library/publications/2019/demo/p60-266.pdf

U.S. Department of Energy Office of Science. (2019). *All About the Human Genome Project (HGP).* Retrieved July 13, 2020, from www.genome.gov/10001772/#al-2

U.S. Department of Energy. (2020). *What is the smart grid?* Retrieved July 21, 2020, from https://www.smartgrid.gov/the_smart_grid/index.html

Underwood, B. J. (1957). Interference and forgetting. *Psychological Review, 64*, 49–60. doi:10.1037/h0044616

United Nations. (2019). *World population prospects 2019.* Retrieved July 21, 2020, from https://population.un.org/wpp/

United Nations Programme on HIV/AIDS. (2020). *Global AIDS update 2020.* Retrieved July 21, 2020, from https://aids2020.unaids.org/report/

Unsworth, G., & Ward, T. (2001). Video games and aggressive behaviour. *Australian Psychologist, 36*(3), 184–192. doi:10.1080/00050060108259654

Unsworth, N., Brewer, G. A., & Spillers, G. J. (2012). Variation in cognitive failures: An individual differences investigation of everyday attention and memory failures. *Journal of Memory and Language, 67*(1), 1–16. doi:10.1016/j.jml.2011.12.005

Uziel, L. (2007). Individual differences in the social facilitation effect: A review and meta-analysis. *Journal of Research in Personality, 41*(3), 579–601. doi:10.1016/j.jrp.2006.06.008

Vadillo, M. A., & Luque, D. (2013). Dissociations among judgments do not reflect cognitive priority: An associative explanation of memory for frequency information in contingency learning. *Canadian Journal of Experimental Psychology, 67*(1), 60–71. doi:10.1037/a0027617

Vago, D. R., & Nakamura, Y. (2011). Selective attentional bias towards pain-related threat in fibromyalgia: Preliminary evidence for effects of mindfulness meditation training. *Cognitive Therapy & Research, 35*(6), 581–594. doi:10.1007/s10608-011-9391-x

Valadez, J. J., & Ferguson, C. J. (2012). Just a game after all: Violent video game exposure and time spent playing effects on hostile feelings, depression, and visuospatial cognition. *Computers in Human Behavior, 28*, 608–616. doi:10.1016/j.chb.2011.11.006

Valeggia, C. R., & Snodgrass, J. J. (2015). Health of indigenous peoples. *Annual Review of Anthropology, 44*, 117–135. doi:10.1146/annurev-anthro-102214-013831

Valins, S. (1967). Emotionality and information concerning internal reactions. *Journal of Personality & Social Psychology, 6*, 458–463. doi:10.1037/h0024842

Valkenburg, P. M., Peter, J., & Walther, J. B. (2016). Media effects: Theory and research. *Annual Review of Psychology, 67*, 315–338. doi:10.1146/annurev-psych-122414-033608

Vallerand, A. H., Saunders, M. M., & Anthony, M. (2007). Perceptions of control over pain by patients with cancer and their caregivers. *Pain Management Nursing, 8*(2), 55–63. doi:10.1016/j.pmn.2007.02.001

Vallerand, R. J., Paquet, Y., et al. (2010). On the role of passion for work in burnout: A process model. *Journal of Personality, 78*(1), 289–312. doi:10.1111/j.1467-6494.2009.00616.x

Van Blerkom, D. L. (2012). *College study skills: Becoming a strategic learner* (7th ed.). Boston, MA: Cengage Learning.

van Dam, C. (2006). *The socially skilled child molester: Differentiating the guilty from the falsely accused.* Binghamton, NY: Haworth Maltreatment & Trauma Press.

van de Pol, P. C., & Kavussanu, M. (2012). Achievement motivation across training and competition in individual and team sports. *Sport, Exercise, & Performance Psychology, 1*(2), 91–105. doi:10.1037/a0025967

van der Hart, O., Lierens, R., & Goodwin, J. (1996). Jeanne Fery: A sixteenth-century case of dissociative identity disorder. *Journal of Psychohistory, 24*(1), 18–35.

van der Kamp, J., & Cañal-Bruland, R. (2011). Kissing right? On the consistency of the head-turning bias in kissing. *Laterality: Asymmetries of Body, Brain & Cognition, 16*(3), 257–267. doi:10.1080/13576500903530778

van Dierendonck, D., & Te Nijenhuis, J. (2005). Flotation restricted environmental stimulation therapy (REST) as a stress-management tool: A meta-analysis. *Psychology & Health, 20*(3), 405–412. doi:10.1080/08870440412331337093

van Dierendonck, D., Díaz, D., et al. (2008). Ryff's six-factor model of psychological well-being, a Spanish exploration. *Social Indicators Research, 87*(3), 473–479. doi:10.1007/s11205-007-9174-7

van Dijk, E., Parks, C. D., & van Lange, P. M. (2013). Social dilemmas: The challenge of human cooperation. *Organizational Behavior & Human Decision Processes, 120*(2), 123–124. doi:10.1016/j.obhdp.2012.12.005

Van Iddekinge, C. H., Putka, D. J., & Campbell, J. P. (2011). Reconsidering vocational interests for personnel selection: The validity of an interest-based selection test in relation to job knowledge, job performance, and continuance intentions. *Journal of Applied Psychology, 96*(1), 13–33.

Van Lange, P. M., Joireman, J., et al. (2013). The psychology of social dilemmas: A review. *Organizational Behavior & Human Decision Processes, 120*(2), 125–141. doi:10.1016/j.obhdp.2012.11.003

Van Lawick-Goodall, J. (1971). *In the shadow of man*. New York, NY: Houghton Mifflin.

Van Volkom, M. (2009). The effects of childhood tomboyism and family experiences on the self-esteem of college females. *College Student Journal, 43*(3), 736–743.

Van Vugt, M. (2009). Averting the tragedy of the commons: Using social psychological science to protect the environment. *Current Directions in Psychological Science, 18*(3), 169–173.

Vance, A. (2015). *Elon Musk: Tesla, SpaceX, and the quest for a fantastic future*. New York: HarperCollins.

Vance, E. (2016). *Suggestible you: The curious science of your brain's ability to deceive, transform, and heal*. Washington, DC: National Geographic Books.

Vandenbeuch, A., Tizzano, M., et al. (2010). Evidence for a role of glutamate as an efferent transmitter in taste buds. *BMC Neuroscience, 11*. doi:10.1186/1471-2202-11-77

Vandewalle, G., Hébert, M., et al. (2011). Abnormal hypothalamic response to light in seasonal affective disorder. *Biological Psychiatry, 70*(10), 954–961. doi:10.1016/j.biopsych.2011.06.022

Vanheule, S., Vandenbergen, J., et al. (2010). Interpersonal problems in alexithymia: A study in three primary care groups. *Psychology & Psychotherapy: Theory, Research & Practice, 83*(4), 351–362. doi:10.1348/147608309X481829

Vartanian, O., & Suedfeld, P. (2011). The effect of the flotation version of restricted environmental stimulation technique (REST) on jazz improvisation. *Music & Medicine, 3*(4), 234–238. doi:10.1177/1943862111407640

Vasa, R. A., Carlino, A. R., & Pine, D. S. (2006). Pharmacotherapy of depressed children and adolescents: Current issues and potential directions. *Biological Psychiatry, 59*(11), 1021–1028. doi:10.1016/j.biopsych.2005.10.010

Vasquez, E. A., Lickel, B., & Hennigan, K. (2010). Gangs, displaced, and group-based aggression. *Aggression & Violent Behavior, 15*(2), 130–140. doi:10.1016/j.avb.2009.08.001

Vaughn, L. (2016). *The power of critical thinking: Effective reasoning about ordinary and extraordinary claims* (5th ed.). New York, NY: Oxford University Press.

Veale, J. F., Clarke, D. E., & Lomax, T. C. (2010). Biological and psychosocial correlates of adult gender-variant identities: A review. *Personality & Individual Differences, 48*(4), 357–366.

Velakoulis, D., & Pantelis, C. (1996). What have we learned from functional imaging studies in schizophrenia? The role of frontal, striatal and temporal areas. *Australian & New Zealand Journal of Psychiatry, 30*(2), 195–209. doi:10.3109/00048679609076095

Velez, J. A., Greitemeyer, T., et al. (2016). Violent video games and reciprocity: The attenuating effects of cooperative game play on subsequent aggression. *Communication Research, 43*(4), 447–467. doi:10.1177/0093650214552519

Verma, M. M., & Howard, R. J. (2012). Semantic memory and language dysfunction in early Alzheimer's disease: A review. *International Journal of Geriatric Psychiatry, 27*(12), 1209–1217. doi:10.1002/gps.3766

Vernon-Feagans, L., Garrett-Peters, P., et al. (2012). Chaos, poverty, and parenting: Predictors of early language development. *Early Childhood Research Quarterly, 27*(3), 339–351. doi:10.1016/j.ecresq.2011.11.001.

Vincent, N., Lewycky, S., & Finnegan, H. (2008). Barriers to engagement in sleep restriction and stimulus control in chronic insomnia. *Journal of Consulting & Clinical Psychology, 76*(5), 820–828. doi:10.1037/0022-006X.76.5.820

Visser, B. A., Bay, D., et al. (2010). Psychopathic and antisocial, but not emotionally intelligent. *Personality & Individual Differences, 48*(5), 644–648. doi:10.1016/j.paid.2010.01.003

Vlachou, S., & Markou, A. (2011). Intracranial self-stimulation. In M. C. Olmstead (Ed.), *Animal models of drug addiction* (pp. 3–56). Totowa, NJ: Humana Press.

Vogler, R. E., Weissbach, T. A., et al. (1977). Integrated behavior change techniques for problem drinkers in the community. *Journal of Consulting & Clinical Psychology, 45*, 267–279.

Vojdanoska, M., Cranney, J., & Newell, B. R. (2010). The testing effect: The role of feedback and collaboration in a tertiary classroom setting. *Applied Cognitive Psychology, 24*(8), 1183–1195. doi:10.1002/acp.1630

Volberg, R. A. (2012). Still not on the radar: Adolescent risk and gambling, revisited. *Journal of Adolescent Health, 50*(6), 539–540. doi:10.1016/j.jadohealth.2012.03.009

Volk, L., Chiu, S.-L. et al. (2015). Glutamate synapses in human cognitive disorders. *Annual Review of Neuroscience, 38*, 127–149. doi:10.1146/annurev-neuro-071714-033821

Volpicelli, J. R., Ulm, R. R., et al. (1983). Learned mastery in the rat. *Learning & Motivation, 14*, 204–222. doi:10.1016/0023-9690(83)90006-1

Vontress, C. E. (2013). Existential therapy. In J. Frew & M. D. Spiegler (Eds.), *Contemporary psychotherapies for a diverse world* (pp. 131–164). New York, NY: Routledge/Taylor & Francis.

Voss, J. L., Lucas, H. D., & Paller, K. A. (2012). More than a feeling: Pervasive influences of memory processing without awareness of remembering. *Cognitive Neuroscience, 3*, 193–207. doi: org/10.1080/17588928.2012.674935

Vriends, N., Michael, T., et al. (2012). Associative learning in flying phobia. *Journal of Behavior Therapy & Experimental Psychiatry, 43*(2), 838–843. doi:10.1016/j.jbtep.2011.11.003

Vrtička, P., & Vuilleumier, P. (2012). Neuroscience of human social interactions and adult attachment style. *Frontiers in Human Neuroscience*, 6. doi:10.3389/fnhum.2012.00212

Vuillermot, S., Weber, L., et al. (2010). A longitudinal examination of the neurodevelopmental impact of prenatal immune activation in mice reveals primary defects in dopaminergic development relevant to schizophrenia. *Journal of Neuroscience, 30*(4), 1270–1287. doi:10.1523/JNEUROSCI.5408-09.2010

Vygotsky, L. S. (1962). *Thought and language*. Cambridge, MA: MIT Press.

Vygotsky, L. S. (1978). *Mind in society*. Cambridge, MA: Harvard University Press.

Wade, K. A., Green, S. L., & Nash, R. A. (2010). Can fabricated evidence induce false eyewitness testimony? *Applied Cognitive Psychology, 24*(7), 899–908. doi:10.1002/acp.1607

Wagenmakers, E.-J., Beek, T., et al. (2016). Registered replication report: Strack, Martin, & Stepper (1988). *Perspectives on Psychological Science, 11*(6), 917–928. doi:10.1177/1745691616674458

Wager, T. D., Rilling, J. K., et al. (2004). Placebo-induced changes in MRI in the anticipation and experience of pain. *Science, 303*, 1162–1166. doi:10.1126/science.1093065

Wagner, M. (2012). Sensory and cognitive explanations for a century of size constancy research. In G. Hatfield & S. Allred (Eds.), *Visual experience: Sensation, cognition, and constancy* (pp. 63–86). New York, NY: Oxford University Press. doi:10.1093/acprof:oso/9780199597277.003.0004

Wagner, S. H. (2013). Leadership and responses to organizational crisis. *Industrial & Organizational Psychology: Perspectives on Science & Practice, 6*(2), 140–144. doi:10.1111/iops.12024

Wakefield, J. C. (1992). The concept of mental disorder. *American Psychologist, 47*(3), 373–388. doi:10.1037/0003-066X.47.3.373

Waldinger, M. D. (2009). Delayed and premature ejaculation. In R. Balon & R. T. Segraves (Eds.), *Clinical manual of sexual disorders* (pp. 267–292). Arlington, VA: American Psychiatric Publishing.

Walker, E., Kestler, L., et al. (2004). Schizophrenia: Etiology and course. *Annual Review of Psychology, 55*, 401–430. doi:10.1146/annurev.psych.55.090902.141950

Walker, I., & Crogan, M. (1998). Academic performance, prejudice, and the Jigsaw classroom. *Journal of Community & Applied Social Psychology, 8*(6), 381–393. doi:10.1002/(SICI)1099-1298(199811/12)8:6<381::AID-CASP457>3.0.CO;2-6

Walker, M. P., & Stickgold, R. (2006). Sleep, memory, and plasticity. *Annual Review of Psychology, 57*, 139–166. doi:10.1146/annurev.psych.56.091103.070307

Walker, S. P., Wachs, T. D., et al. (2011). Inequality in early childhood: Risk and protective factors for early child development. *The Lancet, 378*(9799), 1325–1338. doi:10.1016/S0140-6736(11)60555-2

Wallach, M. A., & Kogan, N. (1965). *Modes of thinking in young children*. New York, NY: Holt.

Waller, G., Gray, E., et al. (2014). Cognitive-behavioral therapy for bulimia nervosa and atypical bulimic nervosa: Effectiveness in clinical settings. *International Journal of Eating Disorders, 47*(1), 13–17. doi:10.1002/eat.22181

Waller, T., Lampman, C., & Lupfer-Johnson, G. (2012). Assessing bias against overweight individuals among nursing and psychology students: An implicit association test. *Journal of Clinical Nursing, 21*(23–24), 3504–3512. doi:10.1111/j.1365-2702.2012.04226.x

Wallis, J., Lipp, O. V., & Vanman, E. J. (2012). Face age and sex modulate the other-race effect in face recognition. *Attention, Perception, & Psychophysics, 74*(8), 1712–1721. doi:10.3758/s13414-012-0359-z

Walters, G. D. (2011). Criminal thinking as a mediator of the mental illness–prison violence relationship: A path analytic study and causal mediation analysis. *Psychological Services, 8*(3), 189–199. doi:10.1037/a0024684

Wampold, B. E., Minami, T., et al. (2005). The placebo is powerful: Estimating placebo effects in medicine and psychotherapy from randomized clinical trials. *Journal of Clinical Psychology, 61*(7), 835–854. doi:10.1002/jclp.20129

Wandersman, A., & Florin, P. (2003). Community interventions and effective prevention. *American Psychologist, 58*(6/7), 441–448. doi:10.1037/0003-066X

Wang, Q. (2013). *The autobiographical self in time and culture*. New York, NY: Oxford University Press.

Wang, Q., & Conway, M. A. (2004). The stories we keep: Autobiographical memory in American and Chinese middle-aged adults. *Journal of Personality, 72*(5), 911–938.

Wang, S.-H., & Morris, R. G. M. (2010). Hippocampal-neocortical interactions in memory formation, consolidation, and reconsolidation. *Annual Review of Psychology, 61*, 49–79. doi:10.1146/annurev.psych.093008.100523

Wang, S. S., & Brownell, K. D. (2005). Public policy and obesity: The need to marry science with advocacy. *Psychiatric Clinics of North America, 28*(1), 235–252. doi:10.1016/j.psc.2004.09.001

Wang, Z., Han, W., et al. (2014). The neuroprotection of Rattin against amyloid β peptide in spatial memory and synaptic plasticity of rats. *Hippocampus, 24*(1), 44–53. doi:10.1002/hipo.22202

Ward, A. F. (2013). Supernormal: How the Internet is changing our memories and our minds. *Psychological Inquiry, 24*(4), 341–348. doi:10.1080/1047840X.2013.850148

Ward, L. M. (2004). Wading through the stereotypes: Positive and negative associations between media use and Black adolescents' conceptions of self. *Developmental Psychology, 40*, 284–294.

Wark, G. R., & Krebs, D. L. (1996). Gender and dilemma differences in real-life moral judgment. *Developmental Psychology, 32*(2), 220–230.

Warren, D. J., & Normann, R. A. (2005). Functional reorganization of primary visual cortex induced by electrical stimulation in the cat. *Vision Research, 45*, 551–565. doi:10.1016/j.visres.2004.09.021

Washton, A. M., & Zweben, J. E. (2009). *Cocaine and methamphetamine addiction: Treatment, recovery, and relapse prevention*. New York, NY: Norton.

Waters, F., Blom, J. D., et al. (2016). What is the link between hallucinations, dreams, and hypnagogic–hypnopompic experiences? *Schizophrenia Bulletin, 42*(5), 1098–1109. doi:10.1093/schbul/sbw076

Watson, D. L., & Tharp, R. G. (2014). *Self-directed behavior: Self-modification for personal adjustment* (10th ed.). Boston, MA: Cengage Learning.

Watson, J. B. (1913/1994). Psychology as the behaviorist views it. *Psychological Review, 101*(2), 248–253. doi:10.1037/0033-295X.101.2.248

Watson, J. M., & Strayer, D. L. (2010). Supertaskers: Profiles in extraordinary multitasking ability. *Psychonomic Bulletin & Review, 17*(4), 479–485. doi:10.3758/PBR.17.4.479

Watson, R. A., & Yeung, T. M. (2011). What is the potential of oligodendrocyte progenitor cells to successfully treat human spinal cord injury? *BMC Neurology, 11* doi:10.1186/1471-2377-11-113

Watts, T. W., Duncan, G. J., & Quan, H. (2018). Revisiting the Marshmallow Test: A conceptual replication investigating links between early delay of gratification and later outcomes. *Psychological Science, 29*(7), 1159–1177. doi:10.1177/0956797618761661

Waytz, A., Epley, N., & Cacioppo, J. T. (2010). Social cognition unbound: Insights into anthropomorphism and dehumanization. *Current Directions in Psychological Science, 19*(1), 58–62. doi:10.1177/0963721409359302

Weaver, Y. (2009). Mid-life: A time of crisis or new possibilities? *Existential Analysis, 20*(1), 69–78.

Weber, K., Giannakopoulos, P., et al. (2012). Personality traits are associated with acute major depression across the age spectrum. *Aging & Mental Health, 16*(4), 472–480. doi:10.1080/13607863.2011.630375

Wechsler, D. (2008). *Wechsler Adult Intelligence Scale* (4th ed.) *(WAIS-IV)*. San Antonio, TX: Pearson.

Wedding, D., & Corsini, R. J. (2014). *Case studies in psychotherapy* (7th ed.). Boston, MA: Cengage Learning.

Weekley, J. A., & Polyhart, R. E. (Eds.). (2006). *Situational judgment tests: Theory, measurement, and application*. Mahwah, NJ: Erlbaum.

Weeks, G. R., & Gambescia, N. (2009). A systemic approach to sensate focus. In K. M. Hertlein, G. R. Weeks, et al. (Eds.), *Systemic sex therapy* (pp. 341–362). New York, NY: Routledge/Taylor & Francis.

Weigold, A., Weigold, I. K., & Russell, E. J. (2013). Examination of the equivalence of self-report survey-based paper-and-pencil and Internet data collection methods. *Psychological Methods, 18*(1), 53–70. doi:10.1037/a0031607

Weinberg, R. A. (1989). Intelligence and IQ. *American Psychologist, 44*(2), 98–104. doi:10.1037/0003-066X.44.2.98

Weiner, B. A., & Carton, J. S. (2012). Avoidant coping: A mediator of maladaptive perfectionism and test anxiety. *Personality & Individual Differences, 52*(5), 632–636. doi:10.1016/j.paid.2011.12.009

Weingarten, K. (2010). Reasonable hope: Construct, clinical applications, and supports. *Family Process, 49*(1), 5–25. doi:10.1111/j.1545-5300.2010.01305.x

Weinstein, N. D. (1989, December 8). Optimistic biases about personal risks. *Science, 246*, 1232–1233. doi:10.1126/science.2686031

Weinstein, Y., & Shanks, D. R. (2010). Rapid induction of false memory for pictures. *Memory, 18*(5), 533–542. doi:10.1080/09658211.2010.483232

Weintraub, M. I. (1983). *Hysterical conversion reactions*. New York, NY: SP Medical & Scientific Books.

Weir, K. (2013). The health-wealth gap. *Monitor on Psychology, 44*(9), July/August, 36–41.

Weishaar, M. E. (2006). A cognitive-behavioral approach to suicide risk reduction in crisis intervention. In A. R. Roberts & K. R. Yeager (Eds.), *Foundations of evidence-based social work practice* (pp. 181–193). New York, NY: Oxford University Press.

Weiss, M., Allan, B., & Greenaway, M. (2012). Treatment of catatonia with electroconvulsive therapy in adolescents. *Journal of Child & Adolescent Psychopharmacology, 22*(1), 96–100. doi:10.1089/cap.2010.0052

Weissman, A. M., Jogerst, G. J., & Dawson, J. D. (2003). Community characteristics associated with child abuse in Iowa. *Child Abuse & Neglect, 27*(10), 1145–1159. doi:10.1016/j.chiabu.2003.09.002

Weitzenhoffer, A. M., & Hilgard, E. R. (1959). *Stanford Hypnotic Susceptibility Scale. Forms A and B*. Palo Alto, CA: Consulting Psychologists Press.

Welch, R. D., & Houser, M. E. (2010). Extending the four-category model of adult attachment: An interpersonal model of friendship attachment. *Journal of Social & Personal Relationships, 27*(3), 351–366. doi:10.1177/0265407509349632

Wellings, K., Collumbien, M., et al. (2006). Sexual behaviour in context: A global perspective. *Lancet, 368*(9548), 1706–1738.

Wells, G. L., & Olson, E. A. (2003). Eyewitness testimony. *Annual Review of Psychology, 54*, 277–295. doi:10.1146/annurev.psych.54.101601.145028

Welsh, B. C., Mudge, M. E., & Farrington, D. P. (2010). Reconceptualizing public area surveillance and crime prevention: Security guards, place managers and defensible space. *Security Journal, 23*(4), 299–319. doi:10.1057/sj.2008.22

Weltzin, T. E., Weisensel, N., et al. (2005). Eating disorders in men: Update. *Journal of Men's Health & Gender, 2*(2), 186–193. doi:10.1016/j.jmhg.2005.04.008

Wentland, J. J., & Reissing, E. D. (2011). Taking casual sex not too casually: Exploring definitions of casual sexual relationships. *Canadian Journal of Human Sexuality, 20*(3), 75–91.

Wenzel, A. J., & Lucas-Thompson, R. G. (2012). Authenticity in college-aged males and females, how close others are perceived, and mental health outcomes. *Sex Roles, 67*(5–6), 334–350. doi:10.1007/s11199-012-0182-y

Wertheimer, M. (1959). *Productive thinking*. New York, NY: Harper & Row.

Werthmann, J., Roefs, A., et al. (2011). Can(not) take my eyes off it: Attention bias for food in overweight participants. *Health Psychology, 30*(5), 561–569. doi:10.1037/a0024291

Wessel, I., & Wright, D. B. (Eds.). (2004). *Emotional memory failures*. Hove, UK: Psychology Press.

West, D., & Sutton-Spence, R. (2012). Shared thinking processes with four deaf poets: A window on 'the creative' in 'creative sign language.' *Sign Language Studies, 12*(2), 188–210. doi:10.1353/sls.2011.0023

West, M. A. (2012). *Effective teamwork: Practical lessons from organizational research*. Oxford, UK: Blackwell.

Wester, W., & Hammond, D. (2011). Solving crimes with hypnosis. *American Journal of Clinical Hypnosis, 53*(4), 249–263. doi:10.1080/00029157.2011. 10404355

Wethington, E., Kessler, R. C., & Pixley, S. J. E. (2004). Turning points in adulthood. In O. G. Brim, C. D. Ryff, et al. (Eds.), *How healthy are we? A national study of well-being at midlife* (pp. 425–450). Chicago, IL: University of Chicago Press.

Wheeler, G., & Axelsson, L. (2015). *Gestalt therapy*. Washington, DC: American Psychological Association. doi:10.1037/14527-000

Whitbourne, S. K., & Halgin, R. P. (2013). *Abnormal psychology: Clinical perspectives on psychological disorders* (7th ed.). New York, NY: McGraw-Hill.

White, T. L., & McBurney, D. H. (2013). *Research methods* (9th ed.). Boston, MA: Cengage Learning.

White-Ajmani, M., & Bursik, K. (2011). What lies beneath: Dogmatism, intolerance, and political self-identification. *Individual Differences Research, 9*(3), 153–164.

Whitley, B. E., & Kite, M. E. (2010). *The psychology of prejudice and discrimination* (2nd ed.). Boston, MA: Cengage Learning.

Whyte, S., & Torgler, B. (2017). Preference versus choice in online dating. *Cyberpsychology, Behavior, & Social Networking, 20*(3), 150–156. doi:10.1089/cyber.2016.0528

Wickwire, E. M., Whelan, J. P., & Meyers, A. W. (2010). Outcome expectancies and gambling behavior among urban adolescents. *Psychology of Addictive Behaviors, 24*(1), 75–88. doi:10.1037/a0017505

Widen, S. C., & Russell, J. A. (2008). Children acquire emotion categories gradually. *Cognitive Development, 23*, 291–312. doi:10.1016/j. cogdev.2008.01.002

Widner, R. L., Otani, H., & Winkelman, S. E. (2005). Tip-of-the-tongue experiences are not merely strong feeling-of-knowing experiences. *Journal of General Psychology, 132*(4), 392–407. doi:10.3200/GENP.132.4.392-407

Wiebe, S. A., & Johnson, S. M. (2016). A review of the research in emotionally focused therapy for couples. *Family Process, 55*(3), 390–407. doi:10.1111/famp.12229

Wiederman, M. W. (1999). Volunteer bias in sexuality research using college student participants. *Journal of Sex Research, 36*(1), 59–66.

Wiederman, M. W. (2001). Gender differences in sexuality: Perceptions, myths, and realities. *Family Journal—Counseling & Therapy for Couples & Families, 9*(4), 468–471.

Wild, B., Rodden, F. A., et al. (2003). Neural correlates of laughter and humour. *Brain: A Journal of Neurology, 126*(10), 2121–2138. doi:10.1093/brain/awg226

Wilhelm, K., Wedgwood, L., et al. (2010). Predicting mental health and well-being in adulthood. *Journal of Nervous and Mental Disease, 198*(2), 85–90.

Wilke, J., & Saad, L. (2013). Older Americans' moral attitudes changing. Retrieved July 21, 2020, from https://news.gallup.com/poll/162881/older-americans-moral-attitudes-changing.aspx

Wilkinson, D., & Abraham, C. (2004). Constructing an integrated model of the antecedents of adolescent smoking. *British Journal of Health Psychology, 9*(3), 315–333. doi:10.1348/1359107041557075

Wilkinson, M. (2006). The dreaming mind-brain: A Jungian perspective. *Journal of Analytical Psychology, 51*(1), 43–59. doi:10.1111/j.0021-8774.2006.00571.x

Wilkinson, R. G., & Pickett, K. E. (2006). Income inequality and population health: A review and explanation of the evidence. *Social Science & Medicine, 62*(7), 1768–1784. doi:10.1016/j. socscimed.2005.08.036

Wilkinson, R. G., & Pickett, K. E. (2007). The problems of relative deprivation: Why some societies do better than others. *Social Science & Medicine, 65*(9), 1965–1978. doi:10.1016/j. socscimed.2007.05.041

Wilkinson, R. G., & Pickett, K. E. (2009). Income inequality and social dysfunction. *Annual Review of Sociology, 35*, 493–511. doi:10.1146/annurev-soc-070308-115926

Willander, J., & Larsson, M. (2006). Smell your way back to childhood: Autobiographical odor memory. *Psychonomic Bulletin & Review, 13*(2), 240–244. doi:10.3758/BF03193837

Williams, D. G., & Morris, G. (1996). Crying, weeping or tearfulness in British and Israeli adults. *British Journal of Psychology, 87*(3), 479–505. doi:10.1111/j.2044-8295. 1996. tb02603.x

Williams, J. L., Aiyer, S. M., et al. (2014). The protective role of ethnic identity for urban adolescent males facing multiple stressors. *Journal of Youth and Adolescence, 43*(10), 1728–1741. doi:10.1007/s10964-013-0071-x

Williams, J. M. (2010). *Applied sport psychology: Personal growth to peak performance* (6th ed.). New York, NY: McGraw-Hill.

Williams, R. (1989). *The trusting heart: Great news about Type A behavior.* New York, NY: Random House.

Williams, R. L. (2013). Overview of the Flynn effect. *Intelligence, 41*(6), 753–764. doi:10.1016/j.intell.2013.04.010

Williams, R. L., & Eggert, A. (2002). Note-taking predictors of test performance. *Teaching of Psychology, 29*(3), 234–237.

Willingham, D. T., & Riener, C. (2019). *Cognition: The thinking animal* (4th ed). New York: Cambridge University Press.

Wilson, S. B., & Kennedy, J. H. (2006). Helping behavior in a rural and an urban setting: Professional and casual attire. *Psychological Reports, 98*(1), 229–233.

Wilson, S. L. (2003). Post-institutionalization: The effects of early deprivation on development of Romanian adoptees. *Child & Adolescent Social Work Journal, 20*(6), 473–483. doi:10.1023/B:CASW.0000003139.14144.06

Wilson, T. D. (2004). *Strangers to ourselves: Discovering the adaptive unconscious.* Cambridge, MA: Harvard University Press.

Wilson, T. D. (2009). Know thyself. *Perspectives on Psychological Science, 4*(4), 384–389.

Wilson, T. D., & Nisbett, R. E. (1978). The accuracy of verbal reports about the effects of stimuli on evaluations and behavior. *Social Psychology, 41*(2), 118–131. doi:10.2307/3033572

Wiltink, J., Hoyer, J., et al. (2016). Do patient characteristics predict outcome of psychodynamic psychotherapy for social anxiety disorder? *PLoS ONE, 11*(1). doi:10.1371/journal.pone.0147165

Wimpenny, J. H., Weir, A. A., et al. (2009). Cognitive processes associated with sequential tool use in New Caledonian crows. *PLoS ONE, 4*(8): e6471. doi:10.1371/journal.pone.0006471

Winfree, L. T. Jr., & Jiang, S. (2010). Youthful suicide and social support: Exploring the social dynamics of suicide-related behavior and attitudes within a national sample of U.S. adolescents. *Youth Violence & Juvenile Justice, 8*(1), 19–37. doi:10.1177/1541204009338252

Wingood, G. M., DiClemente, R. J., et al. (2003). A prospective study of exposure to rap music videos and African American female adolescents' health. *American Journal of Public Health, 93,* 437–439. doi:10.2105/AJPH.93.3.437

Winkleby, M., Ahn, D., & Cubbin, C. (2006). Effect of cross-level interaction between individual and neighborhood socioeconomic status on adult mortality rates. *American Journal of Public Health, 96*(12), 2145–2153. doi:10.2105/AJPH.2004.060970

Winner, E. (2003). Creativity and talent. In M. H. Bornstein, L. Davidson, et al. (Eds.), *Well-being: Positive development across the life course* (pp. 371–380). Mahwah, NJ: Erlbaum.

Winter, D. D. N., & Koger, S. M. (2010). *The psychology of environmental problems* (3rd ed.). New York, NY: Psychology Press.

Wise, R. A., & Safer, M. A. (2010). A comparison of what U.S. judges and students know and believe about eyewitness testimony. *Journal of Applied Social Psychology, 40*(6), 1400–1422. doi:10.1111/j.1559-1816.2010.00623.x

Wise, R. A., Gong, X., et al. (2010). A comparison of Chinese judges' and US judges' knowledge and beliefs about eyewitness testimony. *Psychology, Crime & Law, 16*(8), 695–713. doi:10.1080/10683160903153893

Wiseman, M., & Davidson, S. (2012). Problems with binary gender discourse: Using context to promote flexibility and connection in gender identity. *Clinical Child Psychology & Psychiatry, 17*(4), 528–537. doi:10.1177/1359104511424991

Wiseman, R., & Watt, C. (2006). Belief in psychic ability and the misattribution hypothesis: A qualitative review. *British Journal of Psychology, 97*(3), 323–338. doi:10.1348/000712605X72523

Witherington, D. C., Campos, J. J., et al. (2005). Avoidance of heights on the visual cliff in newly walking infants. *Infancy, 7*(3), 285–298. doi:10.1207/s15327078in0703_4

Witkiewitz, K., Villarroel, N., et al. (2011). Drinking outcomes following drink refusal skills training: Differential effects for African American and non-Hispanic White clients. *Psychology of Addictive Behaviors, 25*(1), 162–167. doi:10.1037/a0022254

Witt, C. M., Schützler, L., et al. (2011). Patient characteristics and variation in treatment outcomes: Which patients benefit most from acupuncture for chronic pain? *The Clinical Journal of Pain, 27*(6), 550–555. doi:10.1097/AJP.0b013e31820dfbf5

Wixted, J. T. (2004). The psychology and neuroscience of forgetting. *Annual Review of Psychology, 55,* 235–269. doi:10.1146/annurev.psych.55.090902.141555

Wohl, M. J. A., Pychyl, T. A., & Bennett, S. H. (2010). I forgive myself, now I can study: How self-forgiveness for procrastinating can reduce future procrastination. *Personality & Individual Differences, 48*(7), 803–808. doi:10.1016/j.paid.2010.01.029

Wolpe, J. (1974). *The practice of behavior therapy* (2nd ed.). New York, NY: Pergamon.

Wong, P. T. (2011). Positive psychology 2.0: Towards a balanced interactive model of the good life. *Canadian Psychology, 52*(2), 69–81. doi:10.1177/0022167811408729

Wong, W. (2015). *Essential study skills* (8th ed.). Boston, MA: Cengage Learning.

Wood, W., & Rünger, D. (2016). Psychology of habit. *Annual Review of Psychology, 67,* 289–314. doi:10.1146/annurev-psych-122414-033417

Woods, A. M., Racine, S. E., & Klump, K. L. (2010). Examining the relationship between dietary restraint and binge eating: Differential effects of major and minor stressors. *Eating Behaviors, 11*(4), 276–280. doi:10.1016/j.eatbeh.2010.08.001

Woods, J. (2013). Group analytic therapy for compulsive users of internet pornography. *Psychoanalytic Psychotherapy, 27*(4), 306–318. doi:10.1080/02668734.2013.853907

Woods, S., & West, M. (2020). *The psychology of work and organizations, 3rd ed.* Boston, MA: Cengage Learning.

Woods, S. C., & Ramsay, D. S. (2011). Food intake, metabolism and homeostasis. *Physiology & Behavior, 104*(1), 4–7. doi:10.1016/j.physbeh.2011.04.026

Wooldridge, T., & Lytle, P. (2012). An overview of anorexia nervosa in males. *Eating Disorders: Journal of Treatment & Prevention, 20*(5), 368–378. doi:10.1080/10640266.2012.715515

Woollett, K., & Maguire, E. A. (2011). Acquiring "the Knowledge" of London's layout drives structural brain changes. *Current Biology, 21*(24), 2109–2114. doi:10.1016/j.cub.2011.11.018

World Bank. (2018). *Poverty and shared prosperity 2018: Piecing together the poverty puzzle.* Washington, DC: World Bank. Retrieved July 21, 2020, from https://openknowledge.worldbank.org/bitstream/handle/10986/30418/9781464813306.pdf

World Health Organization. (2018). *ICD-11.* Retrieved August 12, 2020, from https://www.who.int/classifications/icd/en/

World Health Organization. (2019). *WHO report on the global tobacco epidemic, 2019.* Retrieved July 21, 2020, from https://apps.who.int/iris/bitstream/handle/10665/326043/9789241516204-eng.pdf?ua=1

World Health Organization. (2020). *Deafness and hearing loss.* Retrieved July 17, 2020, from https://www.who.int/news-room/fact-sheets/detail/deafness-and-hearing-loss

Worthen, J. B., & Hunt, R. R. (2010). *Mnemonology: Mnemonics for the 21st century.* Hove, UK: Psychology Press.

Wortman, J., Lucas, R. E., & Donnellan, M. (2012). Stability and change in the Big Five personality domains: Evidence from a longitudinal study of Australians. *Psychology & Aging, 27*(4), 867–874. doi:10.1037/a0029322

Wouters, S., Germeijs, V., et al. (2011). Academic self-concept in high school: Predictors and effects on adjustment in higher education. *Scandinavian Journal of Psychology, 52*(6), 586–594. doi:10.1111/j.1467-9450.2011.00905.x

Wraga, M. J., Boyle, H. K., & Flynn, C. M. (2010). Role of motor processes in extrinsically encoding mental transformations. *Brain & Cognition, 74*(3), 193–202. doi:10.1016/j.bandc.2010.07.005

Wright, K. R., Bogan, R. K., & Wyatt, J. K. (2013). Shift work and the assessment and management of shift work disorder (SWD). *Sleep Medicine Reviews, 17*(1), 41–54. doi:10.1016/j.smrv.2012.02.002

Wright, P. B., & Erdal, K. J. (2008). Sport superstition as a function of skill level and task difficulty. *Journal of Sport Behavior, 31*(2), 187–199.

Wright, P. J., Tokunaga, R. S., et al. (2017, March 2). Pornography consumption and satisfaction: A meta-analysis. *Human Communication Research,* n.p. doi:10.1111/hcre.12108

Wright, T. A., & Bonett, D. G. (2007). Job satisfaction and psychological well-being as nonadditive predictors of workplace turnover. *Journal of Management, 33*(2), 141–160.

Wrightsman, L. S., & Fulero, S. M. (2009). *Forensic psychology* (3rd ed.). Boston, MA: Cengage Learning.

Wroe, A. L., & Wise, C. (2012). Evaluation of an adapted cognitive behavioural therapy (CBT) group programme for people with obsessive compulsive disorder: A case study. *Cognitive Behaviour Therapist, 5*(4), 112–123.

Wrosch, C., Jobin, J., & Scheier, M. F. (2016, February 22). Do the emotional benefits of optimism vary across older adulthood? A life-span perspective. *Journal of Personality, 85,* 388–397. doi:10.1111/jopy.12247

Wyatt, J. W., Posey, A., et al. (1984). Natural levels of similarities between identical twins and between unrelated people. *The Skeptical Inquirer, 9,* 62–66.

Xerri, C. (2012). Plasticity of cortical maps: Multiple triggers for adaptive reorganization following brain damage and spinal cord injury. *Neuroscientist, 18*(2), 133–148. doi:10.1177/1073858410397894

Xu, T.-X., & Yao, W.-D. (2010). D1 and D2 dopamine receptors in separate circuits cooperate to drive associative long-term potentiation in the prefrontal cortex. *Proceedings of the National Academy of Sciences, 107*(37), 16366–16371. doi:10.1073/pnas.1004108107

Yahnke, B. H., Sheikh, A. A., & Beckman, H. T. (2003). Imagery and the treatment of phobic disorders. In A. A. Sheikh (Ed.), *Healing images: The role of imagination in health* (pp. 312–342). Amityville, NY: Baywood Publishing.

Yamamoto, N., & Philbeck, J. W. (2013). Peripheral vision benefits spatial learning by guiding eye movements. *Memory & Cognition, 41*(1), 109–121. doi:10.3758/s13421-012-0240-2

Yanchar, S. C., Slife, B. D., & Warne, R. (2008). Critical thinking as disciplinary practice. *Review of General Psychology, 12*(3), 265–281. doi:10.1037/1089-2680.12.3.265

Yang, L., & Ornstein, T. J. (2011). The effect of emotion-focused orientation at retrieval on emotional memory in young and older adults. *Memory, 19*(3), 305–313. doi:10.1080/09658211.2011.561803

Yang, S., & Zheng, L. (2011). The paradox of de-coupling: A study of flexible work program and workers' productivity. *Social Science Research, 40*(1), 299–311.

Yapko, M. D. (2011). *Mindfulness and hypnosis: The power of suggestion to transform experience.* New York, NY: Norton.

Yarmey, D. (2010). *Eyewitness testimony.* In J. M. Brown & E. A. Campbell (Eds.), *The Cambridge handbook of forensic psychology* (pp. 177–186). New York, NY: Cambridge University Press.

Yedidia, M. J., & MacGregor, B. (2001). Confronting the prospect of dying. *Journal of Pain & Symptom Management, 22*(4), 807–819. doi:10.1016/S0885-3924(01)00325-6

Yi, H., & Qian, X. (2009). A review on neurocognitive research in superior memory. *Psychological Science (China), 32*(3), 643–645.

Yiend, J. (2010). The effects of emotion on attention: A review of attentional processing of emotional information. *Cognition & Emotion, 24*(1), 3–47. doi:10.1080/02699930903205698

Yim, I. S., Tanner, S., et al. (2015). Biological and psychosocial predictors of postpartum depression: Systematic review and call for integration. *Annual Review of Clinical Psychology, 11*, 99–137. doi:10.1146/annurev-clinpsy-101414-020426

Yip, P. S., & Thorburn, J. (2004). Marital status and the risk of suicide: Experience from England and Wales, 1982–1996. *Psychological Reports, 94*(2), 401–407. doi:10.2466/PR0.94.2.401-407

Yonas, A., Elieff, C. A., & Arterberry, M. E. (2002). Emergence of sensitivity to pictorial depth cues: Charting development in individual infants. *Infant Behavior & Development, 25*(4), 495–514. doi:10.1016/S0163-6383(02)00147-9

Yontef, G. (2007). The power of the immediate moment in gestalt therapy. *Journal of Contemporary Psychotherapy, 37*(1), 17–23. doi:10.1007/s10879-006-9030-0

Yoon, J., & Bruckner, T. A. (2009). Does deinstitutionalization increase suicide? *Health Services Research, 44*(4), 1385–1405. doi:10.1111/j.1475-6773.2009.00986.x

Yoonessi, A., & Baker, C. L. (2011). Contribution of motion parallax to segmentation and depth perception. *Journal of Vision, 11*(9), 1–21. doi:10.1167/11.9.13

Youn, H., Sutton, L., et al. (2016). On the universal structure of human lexical semantics. *Proceedings of the National Academy of Sciences, 113*(7), 1766–1771. doi:10.1073/pnas.1520752113

Young, A. A. (2012). Brainstem sensing of meal-related signals in energy homeostasis. *Neuropharmacology, 63*(1), 31–45. doi:10.1016/j.neuropharm.2012.03.019

Young, J. K. (2012). *Hunger, thirst, sex, and sleep: How the brain controls our passions.* Lanham, MD: Rowman & Littlefield.

Young, L. N., Winner, E., & Cordes, S. (2013). Heightened incidence of depressive symptoms in adolescents involved in the arts. *Psychology of Aesthetics, Creativity, & the Arts, 7*(2), 197–202. doi:10.1037/a0030468

Young, R. (2005). Neurobiology of savant syndrome. In C. Stough (Ed.), *Neurobiology of exceptionality* (pp. 199–215). New York, NY: Kluwer Academic Publishers.

Young, S. M., & Pinsky, D. (2006). Narcissism and celebrity. *Journal of Research in Personality, 40*(5), 463–471. doi:10.1016/j.jrp.2006.05.005

Yuille, J. C., & Daylen, J. (1998). The impact of traumatic events on eyewitness memory. In C. Thompson, D. Herrmann, et al. (Eds.), *Eyewitness memory: Theoretical and applied perspectives* (pp. 155–178). Mahwah, NJ: Erlbaum.

Zachariae, R. (2009). Psychoneuroimmunology: A bio-psycho-social approach to health and disease. *Scandinavian Journal of Psychology, 50*(6), 645–651. doi:10.1111/j.1467-9450.2009.00779.x

Zammit, A. R., Ezzati, A., et al. (2017). Roles of hippocampal subfields in verbal and visual episodic memory. *Behavioural Brain Research, 317*, 157–162. doi:10.1016/j.bbr.2016.09.038

Zampetakis, L. A., & Moustakis, V. (2011). Managers' trait emotional intelligence and group outcomes: The case of group job satisfaction. *Small Group Research, 42*(1), 77–102. doi:10.1177/1046496410373627

Zaraska, N. M. (2016, November–December). Hear the violet, Taste the velvet. *Scientific American Mind*, 64–69.

Zarcadoolas, C., Pleasant, A., & Greer, D. S. (2006). *Advancing health literacy: A framework for understanding and action.* San Francisco, CA: Jossey-Bass.

Zeidan, F., Johnson, S. K., et al. (2010). Effects of brief and sham mindfulness meditation on mood and cardiovascular variables. *Journal of Alternative & Complementary Medicine, 16*(8), 867–873. doi:10.1089/acm.2009.0321

Zeidner, M., Matthews, G., & Roberts, R. D. (2012). The emotional intelligence, health, and well-being nexus: What have we learned and what have we missed? *Applied Psychology: Health & Well-Being, 4*(1), 1–30. doi:10.1111/j.1758-0854.2011.01062.x

Zeigler-Hill, V., Holden, C. J., et al. (2016). The dark sides of high and low self-esteem. In V. Zeigler-Hill & Marcus, David K. (Eds.), *The dark side of personality: Science and practice in social, personality, and clinical psychology* (pp. 325–340). Washington, DC: American Psychological Association. doi:10.1037/14854-017

Zeiler, K., & Wickström, A. (2009). Why do 'we' perform surgery on newborn intersexed children? The phenomenology of the parental experience of having a child with intersex anatomies. *Feminist Theory, 10*(3), 359–377.

Zeisel, J. (2006). *Inquiry by design: Environment/behavior/neuroscience in architecture, interiors, landscape, and planning.* New York, NY: Norton.

Zell, E., & Krizan, Z. (2014). Do people have insight into their abilities? A metasynthesis. *Perspectives on Psychological Science, 9*(2), 111–125. doi:10.1177/1745691613518075

Zellner, D. A., Harner, D. E., & Adler, R. L. (1989). Effects of eating abnormalities and gender on perceptions of desirable body shape. *Journal of Abnormal Psychology, 98*(1), 93–96. doi:10.1037/0021-843X.98.1.93

Zellner, M. (2011). The cognitive unconscious seems related to the dynamic unconscious: But it's not the whole story. *Neuropsychoanalysis, 13*(1), 59–63.

Zemishlany, Z., Aizenberg, D., & Weizman, A. (2001). Subjective effects of MDMA ("Ecstasy") on human sexual function. *European Psychiatry, 16*(2), 127–130. doi:10.1016/S0924-9338(01)00550-8

Zenasni, F., Mourgues, C., et al. (2016). How does creative giftedness differ from academic giftedness? A multidimensional conception. *Learning & Individual Differences, 52*, 216–223. doi:10.1016/j.lindif.2016.09.003

Zentall, T. R. (2002). A cognitive behaviorist approach to the study of animal behavior. *Journal of General Psychology, 129*(4), 328–363.

Zentall, T. R. (2010). Coding of stimuli by animals: Retrospection, prospection, episodic memory and future planning. *Learning & Motivation, 41*(4), 225–240. doi:10.1016/j.lmot.2010.08.001

Zentall, T. R. (2011). Perspectives on observational learning in animals. *Journal of Comparative Psychology, 126*(2), 114–128. doi:10.1037/a0025381

Zepeda, C. D., Richey, J. E., et al. (2015). Direct instruction of metacognition benefits adolescent science learning, transfer, and motivation: An in vivo study. *Journal of Educational Psychology, 107*(4), 954–970. doi:10.1037/edu0000022

Zhang, B., Hao, Y. L., et al. (2010). Fatal familial insomnia: A middle-age-onset Chinese family kindred. *Sleep Medicine, 11*(5), 498–499. doi:10.1016/j.sleep.2009.11.005

Ziegler, M., Dietl, E., et al. (2011). Predicting training success with general mental ability, specific ability tests, and (un)structured interviews: A meta-analysis with unique samples. *International Journal of Selection & Assessment, 19*(2), 170–182. doi:10.1111/j.1468-2389.2011.00544.x

Zietsch, B. P., Miller, G. F., et al. (2011). Female orgasm rates are largely independent of other traits: Implications for "female orgasmic disorder" and evolutionary theories of orgasm. *Journal of Sexual Medicine, 8*(8), 2305–2316. doi:10.1111/j.1743-6109.2011.02300.x

Zimbardo, P. G. (2007). *The Lucifer Effect: Understanding how good people turn evil.* New York, NY: Random House.

Zink, N., & Pietrowsky, R. (2013). Relationship between lucid dreaming, creativity and dream characteristics. *International Journal of Dream Research, 6*(2), 98–103.

Ziv, I., Leiser, D., & Levine, J. (2011). Social cognition in schizophrenia: Cognitive and affective factors. *Cognitive Neuropsychiatry, 16*(1), 71–91. doi:10.1080/13546805.2010.492693

Zoccola, P. M., Green, M. C., et al. (2011). The embarrassed bystander: Embarrassability and the inhibition of helping. *Personality & Individual Differences, 51*(8), 925–929. doi:10.1016/j.paid.2011.07.026

Zvyagintsev, M., Clemens, B., et al. (2013). Brain networks underlying mental imagery of auditory and visual information. *European Journal of Neuroscience, 37*(9), 1421–1434.

Name Index

C

E

F

K

X

Y

Z

Subject Index/Glossary

C

D

E

M

N

O

T

X

Y

Z